FERHENGA BIRÛSKÎ

Kurmanji – English Dictionary

Volume One

A - L

I dedicate this book to my dear friends

Birûsk Tugan and Zoya Nazari and Ramin, Zanyar and Luqman and to all our friends who left us too soon.

Ez vê pirtûkê dikim diyarî bo hevalên xwe

Birûsk Tûẍan û Zoya Nazarî û her wisa bo Ramîn, Zanyar û Luqman yên ku zû xatira xwe ji me xwest.

FERHENGA BIRÛSKÎ

Kurmanji - English
Dictionary
Volume One
A-L

Compiled by

Michael L. CHYET

LANGUAGE SERIES

TRANSNATIONAL PRESS LONDON
2020

FERHENGA BIRÛSKÎ

Kurmanji – English Dictionary

Volume One A-L

Compiled by Michael L. CHYET

[Language Series: 1]

First Published in 2020 by TRANSNATIONAL PRESS LONDON in the United Kingdom, 12 Ridgeway Gardens, London, N6 5XR, UK.

www.tplondon.com

ISBN: 978-1-912997-04-6 (paperback)

ISBN: 978-1-912997-05-3 (hardcover)

Cover Image and Design: Secor & Ahmad and Gizem Çakır

www.tplondon.com

FOREWORD

It is certainly a great honor and privilege to write the foreword for the second edition of this monumental Kurdish-English dictionary. Since its first edition, it has enjoyed an outstanding reputation for its high quality and has been widely used by students of Kurdish. Therefore, the world of Kurdish studies welcomes the second edition of this comprehensive Kurdish-English Dictionary, which is the product of three decades of scholarly endeavor by Dr. Michael L. Chyet, a trained linguist and lexicographer.

I cannot express the joy and excitement I felt when, for first time, I put my hands on my very own signed copy of the first edition 16 years ago. In 2002 when I was asked to teach Kurdish language courses, I desperately started searching for teaching materials for my classes. Particularly back then, it was extremely hard to find textbooks and dictionaries for students of Kurdish, due to the limited body of Kurdish language materials. Eventually, I heard of an American linguist who spoke all Kurdish dialects and was an expert on Kurmanji-Kurdish. That American polyglot was Michael L. Chyet. A few days later Michael and I met at Union Station in Washington D.C. to discuss teaching materials for Kurdish. What was even more remarkable was his astonishingly flawless Kurdish, which throughout our conversation caused me to think that I was conversing with a fellow Kurd. That day marked the beginning not only of a great friendship, but also of a very fruitful scholarly collaboration that enabled me to take my first steps into a new phase of the world of linguistics. Michael let me observe his Kurdish language classes at the Washington Kurdish Institute and lent me a copy of his unpublished textbook for my own classes. Thanks to his textbook, and the first edition of this dictionary, I was able to successfully teach my classes. Over the years, this academic association has contributed immensely to my own publications on Kurdish.

As a product of modern lexicography and an invaluable reference for modern Kurdish, the dictionary subsumes a number of existing dictionaries as well as including vocabulary compiled from Kurdish folklore and modern literature, Kurdish journals, Michael's own field notes and his native informants. This latest edition includes a number of features which will appeal not only to language learners and linguists, but also to ethnologists, historians, anthropologists and folklorists.

First of all, with its expanded vocabulary it will satisfy the student's criteria for core vocabulary in addition to contemporary words and neologisms. Every entry has been packed with an immense amount of information in a lucid and comprehensible form. This dictionary, while displaying the richness of the Kurdish language, contributes greatly to the standardization of Kurmanji Kurdish, by making the most commonly used form the main entry and others as secondary, accommodating regional varieties and preferences. What is more, it endeavors to provide a good sense of the full range of possible meanings of a word, including different nuances of meaning and synonyms.

The dictionary also pioneers the use of corpus linguistics by gathering information about the headwords and how they are used in a cultural context and with idiomatic expressions, a feature crucial to language learners. Citations from authentic Kurdish texts help readers ascertain the contextual use of Kurdish words in everyday situations and written materials.

Another feature that makes this dictionary unique is the lexicographical and grammatical access it provides to some major topics of grammar. For instance, for ease of use and acquiring linguistic knowledge, entries distinguish the gender of nouns, phonological aspects such as gutturals and emphatic consonants, as well as the aspirated/non-aspirated consonant dichotomy. As far as verbs are concerned, each infinitive verb is accompanied by the present tense stem, which is one of the most challenging aspects of verb conjugation in Kurdish. Providing the present stem of all verbs – also used in the subjunctive and future tense inflections – is greatly appreciated by both linguists and language learners. Likewise, the transitivity of each verb is indicated, which is crucial to the syntax and the concept of ergativity in Kurdish. Examples of the past tense, which is easily derived from the infinitive, are often provided in citations.

Another important and beneficial aspect of this dictionary is that the main entries are given in both Latin and Arabic orthographies, making it accessible to Kurds using either script. Equally important is that this second edition expands the English-Kurdish index of the first edition into a full-fledged second volume, offering a good deal of new vocabulary.

Compiling such a colossal dictionary is no small task. It takes a great amount of time, patience and diligence. I had the opportunity to witness Michael's enthusiasm, tenacity, and dedication to further improve the quality of his dictionary with the second edition. With its features and comprehensiveness, Ferhenga Birûskî is setting a new standard for lexicographers of the Kurdish language.

On many occasions, Michael has expressed his wish to train a cadre of Kurdish lexicographers so that the work he has started will be continued and built upon by a new generation of linguists. In a sense, he wishes to pass the torch to future scholars of the Kurdish language. I hope this wish comes true as there aren't many trained lexicographers of Kurdish.

This foreword would be incomplete if I did not mention Michael's famous motto: "Zimanê ku zarok pê nepeyivin bê paşeroj e" or "A language not spoken by children has no future." The audience of this self-explanatory motto are Kurdish parents who, Michael feels, must encourage their children to speak their mother tongue, instead of Turkish, Arabic or Persian, lest Kurdish die out one day: this is an imminent danger hanging like the sword of Damocles over the future of the Kurdish language.

The world of Kurdish studies is eternally indebted to Michael for this significant contribution and his continuous effort to help elevate Kurdish to the level of other well-established national languages.

Deniz Ekici, Ph.D.
U.C. Berkeley

Introduction to Ferhenga Birûskî

The second edition of my Kurmanji-English dictionary, which I would like to call "Ferhenga Birûskî" to honor the memory of my beloved friend and colleague Birûsk Tugan, contains considerably more entries, and in many cases offers fuller information on earlier entries. In addition, I have found and corrected several typographical errors. Moreover, it is to be accompanied by a companion English to Kurdish volume.

It is my goal to accurately reflect the language as it exists today, providing variant spellings, synonyms, and regional usage, as well as etymologies. The late Iranist D.N. MacKenzie advised me early on to avoid filling my dictionary with "ghost words". He suggested that I base all the entries in my dictionary on texts (both written and orally generated), to ensure that I am reflecting the language as it is used by its speakers. The earlier dictionaries include words of unknown provenance, which may have no existence outside those pages.

Nothing need be taken on faith: everything that I present is rigorously sourced. The entries in the dictionary routinely contain one or more sample sentences exemplifying usage (from different writers and periods, when possible); in addition, each word has been searched in the existing dictionaries, and variant forms are cross-referenced. Each entry ends with an apparatus in square brackets, featuring the sources in which the word appears. Ideally, the minimum number of sources is two: in rare cases I have added words with a single source, and marked such entries with an asterisk (*), to encourage future kurdologists to investigate these words more fully.

Another goal is to provide all the words that a reader might need to look up while reading. I have endeavored to supply the necessary vocabulary by using as my source material works of fiction, journalistic essays, folk literature, memoirs, and poetry; television, radio and internet sources have also been used. I have succeeded in tracking down the meanings of several words encountered in texts which do not appear in the other dictionaries. If I had a team of co-workers, many of the limitations that have prevented this work from being more complete would be eliminated. Although I have not been blessed with co-workers, I have enjoyed copious help from a number of Kurds.

Let me begin by offering thanks to trained linguists and native Kurmanji speakers Husein Muhammed, Newzad Hirorî, Ergin Öpengin, Deniz Ekici, Behrooz Shojai and to Mirad Gundikî for their prompt response to my questions regarding Kurdish language, vocabulary, phonology and usage. I am also profoundly grateful to my dear friend Hêmin "Science" for pointing out some of the shortcomings of the map which my beloved father created for the first edition. Another dear friend, Luqman Ahmed, added Hêmin's corrections as well as other important features to update the map. My partner Christopher Secor has also helped with the map and cover design, as well as offering welcome spiritual support.

In general, a close connection with native speakers has enabled me to become aware of errors and to correct them. First and foremost, the aspirated/unaspirated consonant pairs Ç-K-P-T were not adequately dealt with in the first edition. The Soviet scholars actually have reversed the aspirated/unaspirated quality of Ç! Whereas all of the aforementioned scholars agree on this point, until recently, I was unaware of it, and assumed that Professors Kurdoev, Bakaev, Orbeli and the like were accurately distinguishing between these consonant pairs. Working on this dictionary has been a wonderful, if sobering, experience. I feel very humbled; I am painfully aware of how much there still is to learn about this language and its speakers, even after 33 odd years of study.

A special debt of gratitude goes to Husein Muhammed, who took the time to painstakingly go through all the entries in the files for letters Ç, K, P, and T, and identify which words begin with aspirated variants of these letters, as well as emphatic T̲ when necessary. Moreover, I continually showered him with questions about the ± aspiration of these consonants when not in initial position (such as the –**ç**- in *miçiqîn* = 'to stop flowing' or in *nêçîrvan* = 'hunter'), and he patiently and dutifully responded to all my queries. As a result, all the headwords in the dictionary entries systematically show the ± aspirated and emphatic nature of the words – for the first time in a dictionary of this scope, if I am not mistaken. However, since these features are generally not indicated in Kurmanji publications or dictionaries -- with the exception of those from the Soviet scholars (including the glaring shortcoming mentioned above, regarding the letter Ç) – cross-references for printed sources appear as they did in their original source materials. Consequently, the cross-references cannot be relied upon to indicate accurately the aspiration (or emphatic nature of S̲-T̲-Z̲). The cross-reference is intended to direct the reader to the full entry for the word in question, where these features are provided. Words collected from informants, on the other hand, do include the aspiration whenever possible. I have also preserved the forms of the words as they appear in the Soviet Kurdish sources, rather than erasing the record of that erroneous phenomenon. So, for example, one will find:

çep/ç'ep [K/B] چەپ *adj.* left (direction).

Here **çep** represents the actual pronunciation, while **ç'ep** [K/B] represents the way this word is listed in Kurdoev [K] and Bakaev [B] respectively. This information may be useful to future scholars.

My dear friend and colleague Deniz Ekici has done me the honor of writing the foreword to this volume. Words cannot describe my appreciation for his help over the years. He has often provided that second pair of eyes that a piece of research should have before it is submitted for publication.

Another cherished friend, Ernest Tucker, had shown me how to transfer files in the early days of the first edition, and once again has provided welcome assistance facilitating the publication of this volume.

My professor Martin Schwartz, now Professor Emeritus from the University of California, Berkeley, was prompt in sending updates to the etymologies of several words in the *Ferheng*. His constant interest and guidance has been a source of inspiration throughout my career.

Michael Sims, friend, colleague and student, came to my rescue in the last days prior to publication, helping me figure out (via Skype no less!) how to format various aspects of this publication. This is yet another field in which he is a source of pride.

I pride myself on learning from my students, in addition to teaching them. My student Jenny Miller and her husband Jowan have introduced me to many Efrînî dialect words that I have gladly added to this *Ferheng*. Other students have asked thought-provoking questions, and all I can say is: "Keep 'em coming!"

I am also grateful to Îsmaîl Taha Şahîn for sending me the *Ferhenga Sindî* [FS] via e-mail. Îsmaîl is extremely knowledgeable about the Kurmanji of his region, and his familiarity with the names and habits of the birds of Kurdistan is unparalleled. I hope to include more of his information in future publications.

I would like to repeat my debt of gratitude to Geoffrey Haig, now of the University of Bamberg, for making his *Corpus of Kurmanji Kurdish* (CCKNT) available to me. It consists of texts from the Kurdish newspaper *Azadiya Welat* and from *CTV*, which broadcasts news items in Kurdish over the Internet. A typical reference from this resource looks like this: (AW73C2), where AW = Azadiya Welat. I drew a great many sample sentences from this rich corpus for the first edition, before the advent of the internet.

There are no doubt others worthy of mention whose names should have been included. To those fine people I say: Please accept my humblest apologies.

The *Ferhenga Birûskî* was created using the Mellel word processing program on a MacBook Air computer, Mac Operating System (macOS) High Sierra, Version 10.13.6. With the exception of the Syriac font, all other fonts were supplied by the MacBook. For Aramaic and Syriac, the AramaicLS/Dot font used to print this work is available from Linguist's Software, Inc., PO Box 580, Edmonds, WA 98020-0580 USA, tel. (425) 775-1130 www.linguistsoftware.com.

Review of Kurdish Dictionaries

The two earliest dictionaries are Ahmed-i Khani's *Nûbara biçûkan* (1094 A.H. = 1682-83 A.D.) and Garzoni's *Grammatica e vocabolario della lingua kurda* (Roma 1787). The former was a rhyming Arabic-Kurdish lexicon for use in Islamic *kuttābs*, to teach basic Arabic words to Kurdish schoolboys. It is available in a reprint edition through the Philo Press in Amsterdam. The latter was written by an eighteenth century Italian missionary, Maurizio Garzoni, to enable missionaries to converse with Kurmanji speakers. My distinguished colleague Amir Hassanpour has a detailed discussion of Kurdish lexicography in his fine book *Nationalism and Language in Kurdistan, 1918-1985* (1992). He deals largely with Sorani, the central dialect of Kurdish, and with monolingual dictionaries.

In the introduction to the first edition of my dictionary, I discuss in detail the sources I used up to that point. With the notable exception of the inaccuracy of the notation of aspiration for Ç in the dictionaries of the Soviet scholars Kurdoev and Bakaev, most of what I wrote then is still relevant. It is perhaps noteworthy that the importance given to the work of Kurdoev [K] and Îzolî [IFb] in the first edition has been superceded by Farqînî [ZF3], Sindî [FS], Wîkîferheng [Wkt] and Botî [BF] in the second edition. In what follows I will begin with bibliographic resources which have appeared since 2003, followed by the ones I mentioned in the first edition.

•ZF3 = Farqînî, Zana. *Ferhenga Kurdî-Tirkî & Kürtçe-Türkçe Sözlük*, çapa 1. (Stenbol: Enstîtuya Kurdî ya Stenbolê, 2004), 2132 p.

and

•ZF = Farqînî, Zana. *Ferhenga Kurdî/Tirkî & Türkçe/Kürtçe Sözlük,* çapa 6. (Stenbol: Enstîtuya Kurdî ya Stenbolê, 2012), 1504 p.

Zana Farqînî's dictionaries are impressive for the comprehensive nature of the vocabulary in them. The definitions are in Turkish. The gender of nouns and the transitivity of verbs is regularly indicated. The main weakness is in the phonetic representation (or lack thereof). No distinction is made between aspirated/unaspirated consonant pairs (Ç-K-P-T), nor are the guttural sounds ('-Ḧ-Ẍ) or the emphatics (S̱-Ṯ-Ẕ) represented. The lack of representing these sounds is typical for

Kurdish books written by and for the Kurds of Turkey (Bakurîs), who are not familiar with the Arabic alphabet.

•FS = Sindī, Khālid Muḥammad. *Ferhenga Sindî* ([Iraq], 2010), 1 v. [Behdini Kurmanji in Arabic script]

This is arguably the most comprehensive Behdinani dictionary in existence. However, that assertion needs a clarification: the speech of the *Sindî* tribe, together with the *Gullî* and *Silêvanî*, is typical of the Zaxo (Zakho) region, today part of Iraqi Kurdistan, but historically part of Botan to the north, rather than of Behdinan to the south. The creation of Iraq put this region on the same side of the border as the neighboring Behdinan region. This dictionary contains vocabulary for the whole of Kurmanji-speaking Iraqi Kurdistan, from Şingal [Sinjar] in the west to Akrê in the east. The dictionary is in the Arabic alphabet, employing the standard Kurdish orthography; moreover, it regularly supplies the gender of nouns and the conjugated forms of verbs. Sample sentences, as well as variant forms of the words, and synonyms, are regularly provided. The definitions are in Kurmanji. Because the dictionary is in the Arabic script, the gutturals ('-Ḧ-Ẍ) and the emphatics (S̱-Ṯ) are systematically represented (but, curiously, not Ẕ). However, no distinctions between aspirated and unaspirated Ç-K-P-T are provided. Since Kurds who do not know the Arabic alphabet cannot read this, I have included a fair number of sample sentences from this dictionary, indicating the source with the designation (FS).

•BF = Botî, Kamêran Silêman. *Ferhenga Kamêran, Kurdî-Kurdî* (Duhok: Spîrêz, 2006), 775 p.

Although the author's name is Botî, the vocabulary of the dictionary – with entries explained in Kurmanji – is largely that of Behdinan. The dictionary is in the Latin orthography for Kurmanji, *excluding* the indication of ± aspiration, as well as gutturals and emphatics. The gender of nouns and the conjugation of verbs are often provided, as well as useful sample sentences. Unfortunately typographical errors abound, which the author could eliminate through a rigorous proof-reading, if he intends to publish a second edition.

•Wkt = *Kurdish Wiktionary* (http://ku.wiktionary.7val.com/;s=Wpe1BxLyxN4D0-FU9IxVt01/w/)

This online dictionary contains entries of varying quality. Some list alternative forms of a word, which are extremely helpful. Some include a sample sentence from a citation not found elsewhere. Some provide equivalents in a variety of languages, and with translations of varying quality. However, some are borrowed directly from another source, such as BF, and do not add anything new. The definitions are in Kurmanji, making this an important Kurmanji-Kurmanji dictionary.

•FD = Demîrhan, Umîd. *Ferhenga destî: Kurdî bi Kurdî* (Doğubeyazit: Sewad, 2007), 496 p.

This is a small dictionary, with entries explained in Kurmanji. The present tense of common verbs is provided, although the gender of nouns is not. As with ZF3, the Latin orthography does not distinguish aspirated consonants, gutturals or emphatics. Some useful proverbs and idioms are provided.

•G = Gazî, Mustafa. *Ferheng: Kurdî-Tirkî* (Diyarbakir: Enstîtuya Kurdî ya Amedê, 2006), 166 p.

This is another small dictionary, with entries explained in Turkish. The gender of nouns is regularly given (e. = eril, i.e. masculine; d. = dişil, i.e. feminine). Although the aspiration of Ç-K-P-T is not indicated, the guttural sounds ' and Ḧ are indicated with an understroke (e̲ = 'e; h̲ = ḧ); Ẍ is not indicated, nor are the emphatics S̱ or Ṯ. The vocabulary is largely that of the author's native region of Qerejdaẍ (Karacadağ), to the southwest of Diyarbakir. Dictionaries which specialize in the dialect of a particular region are most welcome; I hope that there will be many more like this one.

•BFK = Bozarslan, M. Emîn. *Ferhenga Kurdî* (Istanbul: Weşanên Deng, 2011-), v. 1 (A-D)

Only the first volume of this massive Kurmanji dictionary has appeared so far, by one of the pioneers of written Kurmanji. M.E. Bozarslan's explanations in Kurmanji are extremely useful, although he had created his own grammatical terminology. We await further volumes with bated breath. His *Baxçê zimên* (Diyarbakır : Weşanên Deng, 2008-) [BZ], of which I have only seen volume one, includes helpful comments on Kurmanji usage. For instance, he points out that the word ***tarîx*** has two meanings: 1) 'history,' now usually replaced by the word ***dîrok*** in Kurmanji and ***mêjû*** in Sorani; and 2) 'date' (e.g., April 2, 1931), for which ***tarîx*** is still the correct term.

As noted above, none of those listed above existed when I compiled the first edition. Consulting them has enabled me to glean meanings of neologisms (newly coined terms), as well as to complement and expand on words that appear in the earlier dictionaries. Also, by judicious googling on the internet, I have found sample sentences, from a variety of different sources, and in a variety of contexts. I strive to use only examples that manifest correct grammatical usage. Grammatical inconsistencies have been marked with [sic], for example in cases where logical direct object and past tense transitive verbs do not agree (in ergative past tense constructions).

In the course of my fieldwork, I collected many words for which I could find no independent corroboration. These new dictionaries, particularly FS, BF, Wkt and ZF3, have often provided the second source which is so important in lexicography. This has enabled me to include several terms which I collected from my dear friend Birûsk, such as *ḧut*, *kulecergî* and *p'osîde*. There is still a long list of such words which have not been included in this edition. Perhaps a new generation of Kurdologists will be able to research them for future inclusion.

In what follows, I present (with updates) my comments on the sources of the first edition, most of which I continued to consult in preparing the second edition:

•JJ = Auguste Jaba & Ferdinand Justi. *Dictionnaire Kurde-Français* (St.-Pétersbourg: Eggers et Cie, 1879), xviii, 463 p. This is the first important early Kurdish foreign language dictionary. The entries are in Arabic script with a rather unsystematic Latin transcription. Earlier vocabularies, such as those of Garzoni, Rhea, Lerch, and Prym & Socin, are subsumed into this work.

•HH = Yusuf Ziyaeddin Pasa. *al-Hadīyah al-Ḥamīdīyah* الهدية الحميدية. (Beirut, 1975), 56, 240 p. = Mohammad Mokri. *Recherches de Kurdologie: Dictionnaire Kurde-Arabe de Dia' Ad-Din Pacha al-Khalidi* : introduction et notes linguistiques, notice sur la phonétique et la graphie arabo-persane du dialecte kurmândji, Textes et étude religieux, linguistiques et ethnographiques (Langues et civilisation iraniennes), no. 4 (Beyrouth & Paris, 1975), 56, 240 p.

First published in 1892 (imprint: [Istanbul] : Der Saadet Şirket-i Mürtebiye Matbaası, 319 pages), this is a Kurdish-Arabic dictionary based on the dialect of Bitlis, Turkish Kurdistan. Ziya al-Din Pasha, a Palestinian Arab, was a high-ranking Ottoman official, and he composed the dictionary while he was *kaymakam* (governor) of Motkî in the vilayet of Bitlis. It is in Arabic script, and although it predates the modern orthography, it employs a system that corresponds exactly to the modern orthographies. This book was reissued in Turkey in 1978 in Latin script, with Turkish translations rather than the original Arabic, by M. Emin Bozarslan.

•B = Ch. Kh. Bakaev. *Kurdsko-Russkiĭ Slovar' Курдско-Русский Словарь... = Xebernama Kurmancî-*R̄*ûsî*: okolo 14000 slov s prilozheniem grammaticheskogo ocherka kurdskogo iazyka (Moscow : Gosudarstvennoe Izdatel'stvo Inostrannykh i Natsional'nykh Slovareĭ, 1957), 618 p.

This Kurdish-Russian dictionary was the work of a trained linguist, a native speaker of the language. The entries are in the Cyrillic alphabet, differentiating guttural e'/ḧ/ẍ from e/h/x and distinguishing both aspirated/unaspirated consonant pairs (p/p'; t/t'; k/k'). As mentioned above, I have recently discovered that as a general rule the Soviet scholars have reversed ç and ç': in other words, what is elsewhere heard as an aspirated ç, is marked here as *un*aspirated, and vice versa. The gender of nouns, as well as the ± transitivity and present stem of verbs, are provided. Entries are often illustrated with sample sentences. A survey of grammar is included, with tables for verb conjugations and noun inflections.

None of the three dictionaries mentioned so far include modern technical coinages, although Bakaev does feature some pan-Soviet vocabulary items.

•K = K. K. Kurdoev. *Ferhenga Kurdî-Rûsî = Kurdsko-Russkiĭ Slovar' Курдско-Русский Словарь* (Moscow : Gosudarstvennoe izd-vo inostrannykh i natsional'nykh slovareĭ, 1960), 890 p.

When it first appeared, this large Kurdish-Russian dictionary purported to be the most comprehensive Kurmanji dictionary in existence. The dictionary entries are in the Latin script accompanied by a Cyrillic phonetic script in brackets (presumably for the convenience of Russian speakers), distinguishing aspirated/unaspirated consonant pairs (with the same confusion for Ç as mentioned above for Bakaev) in the bracketed phonetic script only, but differentiating guttural e'/ḧ/ẍ from e/h/x throughout. The vague designation ю-к [iuzhno-kurdskiĭ = Southern Kurdish] sometimes refers to the Behdinani dialects of Kurmanji, while at other times it refers to the Sorani dialect: these are two distinct entities, and should be treated separately. Often words taken from Jaba & Justi's dictionary are given this designation. As with Bakaev, there is a grammatical section at the back that, among other things, briefly outlines the morphology of the Kurdish noun and verb. Kurdoev also wrote a good detailed grammar of Kurmanji Kurdish [K2].

•A = Musa Anter. *Ferhenga Khurdî-Tirkî = Kürdçe-Türkçe Sözlük* (İstanbul : Yeni Matbaa, 1967), 167 p.

This small Kurdish-Turkish dictionary was compiled while the author was in prison in Istanbul. This had been the only dictionary available in Turkey until the 1990's, even though it had long been banned. In the course of reading Kurdish texts I have occasionally come across words that were explained in this dictionary alone, such as ***çerxî***, a silver coin in use during the Ottoman Empire. It also features much of the distinctive vocabulary of the Mardin region, as Musa Anter was from a village near Nusaybin in that province.

•JB3 = Joyce Blau. *Kurdish-French-English Dictionary = Dictionnaire Kurde- Français-Anglais* (Bruxelles : Centre pour l'Étude des Problèmes du Monde Musulman Contemporain, 1965), xvii, 263 p.

This was an early attempt by Kamuran Bedir Khan of the Sorbonne to compile a dictionary of literary Kurmanji, for which his student Joyce Blau has been given credit. The words which appear in it are largely taken from the Kurdish journals of the 1930s and 1940s, which endeavored to create a vocabulary to deal with modern issues.

•JB1 = Joyce Blau. *Le Kurde de 'Amadiya et de Djabal Sindjar : Analyse linguistique, textes folkloriques, glossaires* (Paris : C. Klincksieck, 1975), 252 p.

This important early contribution by the same scholar consists of a linguistic analysis, folkloristic texts with French translation, and accompanying glossaries of Southern Kurmanji material she collected in Amadiya and the Yezidi region of Jabal Sinjar, Iraqi Kurdistan, in 1967 and 1968.

•IF[b] = D. Îzolî. *Ferheng : Kurdî-Tirkî, Türkçe-Kürtçe* [1st ed.] (Den Haag : Komełey Xwêndkaranî Kurd le Ewrupa, [1987]), 413 p.; [2. ed.] (Istanbul: Deng Yayınları, 1992), 913 p.

This is a Kurdish-Turkish and Turkish-Kurdish dictionary, put together by a Kurd from the Dersim/Tunceli region in Turkey. What makes this dictionary unique is the words peculiar to the compiler's native region, some of which appear in print for the first time, e.g. **hîlî** = 'mirror' (< Armenian hayeli), **havlêk** = 'broom' (< Armenian avel). Several of my informants in northern California are from this region, so I have independent confirmation of these latter items. The first edition was published in Europe, and was therefore not readily available in Kurdistan itself. The second edition, published in Istanbul, is a considerable improvement on the first. Many typos have been corrected, and the entries have been more carefully arranged. When it first came out, the editorial staff of the newly founded Kurdish newspapers *Welat, Welatê Me*, and *Azadîya Welat* made broad use of this second edition. It is noteworthy that Sorani vocabulary items are included as well.

•GF = Ali Seydo Ali Gewranî. *Ferhenga Kurdî Nûjen : Kurdî - Erebî = al-Qāmūs al-Kurdī al-Ḥadīth : Kurdī - 'Arabī* [القاموس الكردي الحديث : كردي- عربي] ('Ammān : Sharikat al-Sharq al-Awsaṭ, 1985), 670 p.

This dictionary by a Jordanian Kurd aims to cover the entire vocabulary used in the important Kurdish journals *Hawar* and *Ronahî* and the newspaper *Roja Nû*, all of which appeared in the 1930s and 1940s. Consequently, a good deal of journalistic vocabulary is included.

•TF = Torî. *Ferheng : Kurdî-Tirkî, Türkçe-Kürtçe* (İstanbul : Koral, 1992), 496 p.

A Kurmanji-Turkish and Turkish-Kurmanji dictionary, which includes vocabulary from his native Tur 'Abdin region. Torî gives fairly detailed definitions in Turkish, which often illuminate meanings that are rather sparsely covered elsewhere. Being of fairly recent vintage, this dictionary includes several of the most recent neologisms.

•FJ = Muhemed Cemîl Seyda. *Ferhenga Jîn : Kurdî-Erebî, bi zaravê Kurmancî* = Qāmūs al-Ḥayāh قاموس الحياة (Beyrut : Çapxan Emîral, 1987), 424 p.

This is a Kurmanji-Arabic dictionary, featuring the vocabulary of the Kurds of Lebanon, who are predominantly from the Omeri tribe of Mardin. The vocabulary of that region of Mardin in Kurdistan of Turkey is therefore reflected here. Often the same definition is shared between this Gewranî's dictionary (GF).

•OK = Feryad Fazil Omar. *Kurdisch-Deutsches Wörterbuch = Ferhenga Kurdî-Elmanî* (Berlin : Verlag für Wissenschaft und Bildung, Kurdische Studien, 1992), 721 p.

This is the first Kurmanji dictionary to provide main entries in both Arabic and Latin script, thereby making it accessible to Kurds in Iraq and Iran as well as to those in Turkey. The gender of nouns is regularly provided, as is the ± transitivity and present stem of all verbs.

•Tsab = Ruslan Lazarevich Tsabolov. *Etimologicheskiĭ Slovar' Kurdskogo IAzyka Этимологический Словарь Курдского Языка* (Moskva : "Vostochnaia lit-ra" RAN, 2001-2010), 2 v.

I have only seen volume one of this etymological dictionary. It includes both Kurmanji and Sorani words, written phonologically rather than using the Kurdish orthography. Entries are taken largely from Russian (Soviet) sources, and consequently erroneously present the aspiration of the letter Ç. In addition to etymologies, citations from literary and folkloric sources are often provided.

Other dictionaries that I have occasionally consulted include:

•Hej = Hejar. *Henbane borîne: farhang-i Kurdī-Farsī* (Tihrān: Surūsh, 1369), 1035 p.

•PF = Elî Paksêrêşt. *Ferhenga Kurdiya (Kurmancî)-Farisî* ([Iran], [200-?]), 457 p.

•MJ = Mela Xelîl Mişextî. *Ferhenga merg û jî* (Hewlêr: Aras, 2006), 560 p.

Two important phraseological dictionaries:

•XF = M. U. Khamoian. *Kurdsko-Russkiĭ Frazeologicheskiĭ Slovar′ Курдско-Русский Фразеологический Словарь: soderzhit okolo 8000 frazeologicheskikh stateĭ* (Erevan : Izdatel′stvo AN Armianskoĭ SSR, 1979) 273 p.

This is a Kurdish-Russian phraseological dictionary, in Cyrillic script, preserving both the aspirated/unaspirated dichotomy (including erroneously marked Ç) and the gutturals e'/ḧ/ẍ. This work goes beyond what one can hope to find in standard foreign language dictionaries. It specializes in idioms and expressions, and is essential for the serious student of folk literature. There are frequent illustrative examples, mostly from orally generated texts.

•AId = Sadiq Baha' al-Din Amêdî. *Îdyemêt Kurdî: al-muṣṭalaḥāt wa-al-kināyāt al-lughawīyah fī al-lughah al-Kurdīyah* ئیدیه‌مێت کوردی : المصطلحات والكنايات اللغوية في اللغة الكردية (Baghdad: al-Sha'b, 1973), 160 p.

This dictionary of Kurdish idioms, an invaluable tool in studying the Behdinani dialects of Kurmanji, was written by an important Kurdish scholar from Behdinan in Iraqi Kurdistan. It is in Kurmanji in Arabic script, with explanations in Kurmanji and in Arabic.

These dictionaries from a foreign language to Kurmanji should be mentioned:

•F = I. O. Farizov. *Ferhenga Urisî-Kurmancî = Russko-Kurdskiĭ Slovar′ Русско-Курдский Словарь* (Moscow : Gosudarstvennoe izd-vo inostrannykh i natsional′nykh slovareĭ, 1957), 781 p.

This is a Russian-Kurdish dictionary, whose definitions are of variable accuracy. It has recently been translated into Turkish as: I.O. Farîzov. *Türkçe-Kürtçe Sözlük = Ferhenga Tirkî-Kurdî*, redaksiyon Timuré Xelîl Muradov, Rusça'dan çeviri ve uyarlama Mehmet Demir [2. baskı] (Ankara : Özge, 1994), 344 p.

•SC = S. Siabandov & A. Chachan. *Xebernama Ermeni-K'urdî = Հայ-Քրդերեն Բառարան* (Erevan : HayPetHrat, 1957), 352 p.

This is an Armenian-Kurdish dictionary. The Kurdish is in Cyrillic characters, preserving the aspirated (!) and guttural distinctions.

•RZ = Reşo Zîlan. *Svensk-Kurdiskt Lexikon (Nordkurdiska) = Ferhenga Swêdî-Kurdî (Kurmancî)* (Stockholm : Statens Institut för Läromedel, 1989), 311 p.

A Swedish-Kurmanji dictionary in Latin script, intended to help Kurdish immigrants in Sweden to learn Swedish. There is also a Swedish-Sorani dictionary published by the same institute. Because the dictionary is intended for Kurmanji-speaking Kurds from all parts of Kurdistan, the Kurdish definitions for any given Swedish word often list several different equivalents, which has the added benefit of supplying Kurdish synonyms. The dictionary includes an entire section with pictures, featuring the names of various items--in Swedish only.

•AF = Amîrxan. *Ferhenga Arebî-Kurdî* = المعجم العربي الكردي (Vienna: Verlag Berger, 1997), 982 p.

This is an Arabic-Kurmanji dictionary. The author is a Syrian Kurd.

•AD = Amîrxan. *Kurdisch Deutsch: Kurdî - Almanî* (Ismanning, Germany: Max Hueber Verlag, 1992), 2 vol. [vol. 2: *Deutsch Kurdish: Almanî - Kurdî*]

This two-volume Kurdish-German and German-Kurdish dictionary is by the author of the Arabic-Kurmanji dictionary mentioned above (AF). Several words from the dialect of Efrîn are only found here. As of this writing, almost nothing has been published about the Kurmanji dialect of Efrîn, or of Rojava [Syrian Kurdistan] in general.

•Şamîl Esgerov. *Sê Ferheng = Üç lügat* [=3 dictionaries]: 1) Kurdî-Azerbaycanî; 2) Azerbaycanî-Kurdî; 3) Ferhenga Mişarê Zimanê Kurdî [=Kurdish rhyming dictionary] (Bakû : Elnur-P, 1999), 640 p.

This is an Azeri [Azerbaijani Turkish]-Kurdish and Kurdish-Azeri dictionary. The Kurdish is that of the Serhedan region, i.e., the dialect of Kars, Ağrı, Armenia, Azerbaijan, and the hinterland of Urmia in extreme northwestern Iranian Kurdistan.

Mention should be made of the other existing Kurdish-English dictionaries, and one English-Kurdish dictionary:

•Aziz Amindarov. *Kurdish-English/English-Kurdish Dictionary* (New York : Hippocrene Books, 1994), 313 p.

•RF = Baran Rizgar. *Kurdish-English English-Kurdish Dictionary = Ferheng Kurdî-Îngîlîzî Îngîlîzî-Kurdî* (London : M.F. Onen, 1993), 400 p.

This is an easy-to-use English-Kurmanji dictionary.

•CS = Çelebî, Ferdîdon & Danko Sipka. *Kurmanji Kurdish-English glossary* (Springfield, VA: Dunwoody Press, 2002), 408 p.

"This glossary, containing about 20,000 terms, is intended for native speakers of English. Its principal goal is to help them read Kurmanji texts." (p. vi). It is largely derived from Kurdoev's Kurmanji-Russian dictionary (1960), with some modern vocabulary added. This dictionary was published after the first edition of my dictionary went to press. I have been looking up words in it since then, and about half the time I find the words I am searching for. The gender of nouns and ± transitivity of verbs is regularly indicated.

•SS= Saadalla, Salah. *Saladin's English-Kurdish Dictionary = Qamûsa Selahedîn Îngilîzî-Kurdî* ([Baghdad : Dar al-Ḥurrīyah], 1998), 1183 p. [1st ed.]; (Istanbul : Avesta ; Paris : Institut Kurde de Paris, 2000), 1477 p. [2nd ed.]

The first edition (1998) was published in Baghdad, with Kurdish definitions in the Arabic script. The second edition (2000), was published in Istanbul by the Kurdish Institute of Paris, in the Latin alphabet. One finds in it many obscure and superfluous English words, some of which are quite amusing (e.g., gressorial, invigorately, iodination, sacculation, thrasonical). Often the Sorani equivalent is given, rather than the desired Kurmanji word.

Perhaps surprisingly, Salah Saadalla's English-Kurmanji dictionary reflects a lack of awareness of Kurmanji as used by speakers in Turkey, Syria, or Iran. Even though the Kurds of Iraq use the Arabic alphabet, one would expect the serious lexicographer to be conversant with the dictionary's target language in all the alphabets in which it is written, as Sindî (FS) clearly does. Moreover, the modern Kurmanji vocabulary which has been developing by leaps and bounds over the past 30 years is conspicuously absent from this dictionary. Even more so than the Kurmanji-speaking Kurds of Turkey and Syria, the Behdinani (Southern Kurmanji) speakers of Iraq borrow liberally from neighboring Sorani. If the dictionary had covered both this usage and the usage of Kurmanji speakers beyond the borders of Iraq, it would have met the needs of most Kurmanji speakers, as well as learners of the language. In point of fact, this dictionary is woefully inconsistent, often supplying the Sorani definition while not providing the necessary Kurmanji one. What is needed today is a dictionary which provides access to all Kurmanji usage, in Turkey, Iraq, Iran and Syria. This dictionary fails to provide such access, instead limiting itself to Iraqi Kurdish usage. Nevertheless, I have occasionally found independent confirmation of words here, for example: *k'erx*, a synonym for *kelek*, meaning 'raft'; this word appears in MacKenzie's *Kurdish Dialect Studies* in a text from Zaxo (M-Zx), and until the publication of FS and ZF3, this was the only Kurdish source which included it.

A few last citations and comments:

•CCG = Aykoç, Fêrgîn Melîk. *Çavkaniyên çanda gel* (İstanbul: Weşanên Ar, 2012-), v. 1.

One of the fringe benefits of my job as cataloger of Kurdish books at the Library of Congress is the opportunity to see first hand such treasures as this work by F.M. Aykoç, which includes a great many words and expressions relating to the traditional Kurdish way of life (Kurdewarî). I have endeavored to incorporate a good deal of this vocabulary into the *Ferhenga Birûskî*. Several other works like this have appeared for the dialects of Sorani.

•Bedirhan, Kâmuran. *Dictionnaire Kurde-Francais = Ferhenga Kurdî-Fransizî / Kamuran* A. Bedir Khan, Joséfa Bertolino, Kendal Nezan (İstanbul: Avesta, 2017), 1995 pages.

Although I have not actually held this dictionary in my hands yet, I have read the introduction and seen some of the definitions. It includes the original entries of Kâmuran Bedirhan, plus a great many more words. The additions are due in part to the fact that the dictionary includes Sorani (SOR) and Zaza (ZAZA) entries. The entries are in the Latin orthography, and include the gender of nouns, and the present tense and ± transitivity of verbs. The French introduction does a nice job of explaining the complexities involved in an undertaking such as the one which they and I have embarked upon. The Kurdish Institute of Paris (IKP) is the sponsor of this project.

Lastly, the IKP also hosts a semi-annual (twice yearly) Kurmanji workshop (*Civîna Kurmancî*), which just celebrated its thirtieth anniversary in Stockholm in December 2017. I have attended many of the sessions, and have gathered a considerable amount of material from the knowledgeable Kurmanji native speakers who attend. The *Civîna Kurmancî* has published its findings in several volumes, entitled *Kurmancî: rojnameya taybetî ya Enstîtuya Kurdî ya Parîsê li ser pirsên zaravê kurmancî* [Kmc]. The first volume combined the first twenty sessions, and the second one combined the first forty sessions. A third one is now being prepared, combining the first sixty sessions (30 x 2 = 60). This monumental work represents thirty years of toiling by a group of linguistic experts who are a Kurdish near equivalent to the Alliance Française. The vocabulary items are given in the original Kurmanji, together with Turkish, French and English equivalents. Neither the gender of nouns nor the ± transitivity of verbs has been provided, although I have encouraged them to provide this information for their upcoming compilation.

The dictionary of a living language is never complete. I continue to add words to the dictionary, and will be working on this edition until the day it goes to press. As I toil to meet the mid-September 2018 deadline which I have convinced the publisher to grant me, I am convinced more strongly with every passing day that this project should be carried out by a group of lexicographers, rather than by me alone. There is only so much that a single individual can accomplish in days that consist of a mere 24 hours each. I would be more than happy to train a cadre of Kurdish lexicographers, so that the knowledge I have amassed does not die with me. Likewise, both future editions of the dictionary and I would no doubt benefit from their detailed native intuition regarding the Kurdish language. It has been said that the best linguistic and anthropolical work consists of a team: a trained outsider working together with informed insiders.

It is my fervent hope that future editions of this work will be carried out by a group of Kurdish lexicographers. I have marked with an asterisk (*) words that I know need more information. Should any of you be interested in taking me up on my offer, let me point out that with the advent of Skype and the internet, an ongoing long distance relationship is easily maintained. I have been teaching Kurmanji and Sorani via Skype for the past several years, and have had students from all over the Americas. For Europe and the Middle East, weekend sessions are negotiable as well.

I am painfully aware of how incomplete this new contribution is, although it contains considerably more material than its predecessor did. Although I have only grazed the surface of such domains as the names of plants, birds and insects, and the names of Kurdish foods and dances, I hope that I have established a framework which those who come after me can follow.

How to use the dictionary

Every entry is structured as follows:

The main entry [head word] is in both Latin and Arabic orthography, followed by an abbreviation indicating its part of speech [*adj.* = adjective; *prn.* = pronoun, etc.]. Nouns are designated as masculine (*m.*) or feminine (*f.*) or plural (*pl.*), with the sources for the gender when there is a conflict [*m.*(ZF3)/*f.*(FS) = Farqînî gives the noun as masculine, Sindî gives it as feminine]. Please note the distinction between *m.&f.* if the person can be of either gender; and *m./f.* indicating that some sources give the noun's gender as *m.* while others give it as *f.* The gender abbreviation is followed in brackets by the two inflections: ezafeh first, followed by the oblique case ending, e.g., **(-a;-ê).** For a noun with both genders, the full forms for *m.&f.* and *m./f.* would be **(-ê/-a;-î/-ê)**, with the first in each pair [i.e., *(-ê;-î)*] for *m.*, and the second in each pair [i.e. **(-a;-ê)**] for *f.* Please note that the order is sometimes reversed [i.e., *f./m.*]. Verbs are designated as intransitive (*vi.*) or transitive (*vt.*), followed in brackets by the present stem, and any other irregularities that may pertain. [e.g., **kirin I** کرن *vt.* **(-k-/-ke-** [Bw/M/SK/Hk]**)**. = **kirin I** (to do, etc.) is transitive (*vt.*), and the present indicative is di**k**im, di**k**î, di**k**e, di**k**in, or in Behdinani and Hekkari sources [Bw/M/SK/ Hk]: di**ke**m, di**ke**y, di**ke**t[in], di**ke**yn, di**ke**n; the present subjunctive would replace the prefix di- with bi-, yielding bi**k**im, etc./bi**ke**m, etc.] This information should enable the user to inflect the word fully.

Only main entries are in bold; cross-references are in regular type. If there are two or more words which are identical in alphabetization, each one is assigned a Roman numeral, e.g. **kirin I** = to do; k'irin II = tick. Note that k'irin II (a cross-reference for **qirnî**) has an aspirated k [k'], whereas **kirin I** does not.

Within each entry, if a word has several definitions, they are numbered: 1), 2), 3), etc. For each individual meaning, synonyms {syn: } are supplied, as well as variant forms {also: }, if they pertain only to that particular meaning of the word. If the word has only one definition, the variant forms and synonyms come after the definition and sample sentences. Expressions formed with the word in question are set off by a hyphen -, e.g., **-bawer kirin** = to believe.

A new feature in this edition is the *italicization* of the head word in each sample sentence, and in the accompanying translation whenever possible, e.g.: **•Wî *şimik* kir piyê xwe** (FS) He put *slippers* on his feet, to illustrate the word **şimik** = 'slippers'. Each sample sentence or phrase is set off by a bullet •. The source of the sentence or phrase is given in abbreviated form in parentheses, e.g., (FS; or: Z-2, 68; or: RojevaKurd 29.iii.2011), followed by an English translation. If a citation contains a grammatical error, it is quoted as is and followed by the notation [sic], e.g., **•...sê kuştin, yêk birîndar kirin** [sic] (SK 48:508) ...they killed three and wounded one (where **yêk** clearly requires **birîndar kir**). The key to the abbreviations may be found in the preliminary material at the beginning of this volume.

As mentioned above, after the definitions, variant forms {also: } and synonyms {syn: } are provided. These are followed by an etymology or linguistic comment. If the Pokorny Proto-Indo- European root is known, it is provided [Pok.][1],

1. We are well aware of the shortcomings of Pokorny's monumental work, such as the lack of laryngeals (since the theory of laryngeal reconstruction was developed after the appearance of that work). The paltry listing of Kurdish cognates in Pokorny's dictionary (no more than ten, some of which are erroneous) is also indicative of what was available at the time. Updates to Pokorny of which I am aware are: *LIV, Lexikon der indogermanischen Verben : die Wurzeln und ihre Primärstammbildungen* / Helmut Rix, Martin Kümmel [et al.]. 2. Aufl. (Wiesbaden: Reichert, 2001) and Cheung, Johnny. *Etymological dictionary of the Iranian verb* (Leiden : Brill, 2007).

followed by relevant forms in Early, Middle, and Modern Iranian languages, followed by Sorani [Sor], Southern Kurdish (Kelhori) [SoK], Zaza- Dumili [Za], and Gurani-Hawrami [Hau] forms, where possible. Unless otherwise noted, the Sorani material is taken from Shafiq Qazzaz's *The Sharezoor*[2]. If there are other languages with cognate forms, such as German [Ger], English [Eng], French [Fr], Russian [Rus] or Armenian [Arm], they are added after these. If the word in question is borrowed from another language, such as Arabic [Ar], Turkish [T], or Aramaic [Arc], this is also indicated. When direct transmission is in doubt, material is provided for comparative purposes (cf.).

Please note that the notation **t̲** (underlined t) has two distinct representations: when referring to a Kurdish word, it represents the emphatic T (Arabic ط), e.g. **t̲ov** طۆڤ [FS/HH] = 'seed'; when referring to an Arabic word in the etymological part of an entry, it represents the unvoiced dental fricative th ('th' in English 'thing'; Arabic thā' ث, Greek θ), e.g. Ar ṯawrah ثورة = 'revolt, riot'.

If a noun or an adjective has an abstract noun derived from it, the forms of the abstract noun [which generally ends in -î (including -tî, -anî, -ayî, ahî, etc.)] are provided next, in brackets {}.

Since everything in the dictionary is sourced, the apparatus at the end of each entry shows which dictionaries and other sources (including informants) attest the word. This information--again in abbreviated form--is in square brackets []. Each source appears only once in the brackets, even if a particular source provides more than one form. All the abbreviations are explained in the sections following this introductory essay.

Words marked with an asterisk (*) lack adequate attestation. It is hoped that future editions of this dictionary will provide the missing data.

If there are words related in meaning or category to the main entry, the related words appear in angle brackets <> at the end of the entry. The user is referred to these words in this manner.

A variant form of the main entry which has its own main entry has a reference such as "See also **pişkul**." Such forms also appear in bold type as a variant form, e.g., under **bişkul**: {also: bişqul (Mzg); buşqul (IF-2); **pişkul**}. To find the variant forms of **pişkul**, one should look up that entry.

The English-Kurdish volume is greatly expanded. It purports to include access to all the Kurmanji entries in the first volume. Because I worked from Kurdish to English rather than vice versa, there are no doubt many English words for which no equivalent has been provided. Again, it is hoped that future editions will remedy this shortcoming.

Lastly, I would like to point out that this preliminary section of the dictionary concludes with several charts. One set lists the two different systems for naming the months of the year. The two calendars are included in the hopes that by clarifying that there are indeed two distinct systems, the all too common practice of imposing the names of Iranian Solar months [System Two] on the months of the Gregorian calendar [System One] will be nipped in the bud. Kurdish folklore has provided names for all the "System One" months in Kurmanji, and a cursory glance at the dictionary entries for the Kurmanji month names will show one or more proverbs or sayings involving each month [e.g., **Deynê *Şibatê* li *Adarê* ye** = *February*'s debt is due in *March*]. The final section is a table of the names of the countries of the Middle East, Central Asia, North Africa, Europe, and a few other places. In the English to Kurdish volume, there is a corresponding list of geographical names from English to Kurdish. Adjectives corresponding to these countries can be found among the dictionary entries.

Michael L. Chyet
Washington, DC,
September 2018

2. *Ferhengî Şarezûr* (Erbil, Kurdistan: Aras, 2000), 601 p.

ABBREVIATIONS

also = variant forms
see also = refers reader to a variant form with a full entry
syn = synonym (in denotation, not necessarily in connotation)
< = derived from [another language]
--> = borrowed into [another language]
≠ = antonym/opposite
~ = alternating with [in etymologies]
• = illustrative phrases/sentences
* = of questionable reliability
abbr. = abbreviation
acc. = accusative case
adj. = adjective
adv. = adverb
anat. = anatomy
ans. = answer
astr. = astrology
Avak = special thanks to Anne Avakian
biol. = biology
bk-î = someone else (bê[h]vankesî)
bot. = botany
cf. = compare
clq. = colloquial
conj. = conjunction
dat. constr. = dative construction [i.e., with object following verb]
def. = definite
dem. = demonstrative
dim. = diminutive
dir. obj. = direct object
do. = ditto
E = east
euph. = euphemism, euphemistic
f. = feminine gender (of noun)
fig. = figurative
fk-ê = someone (filankesê)
ft-î = something (filantißtî)
fut. = future tense
gen. = genitive case (for comparative purposes)
geog. = geography
govt. = government
gram. = grammar, grammatical
imp. = imperative
impf. = imperfect
indc. = indicative mood
indef. = indefinite
inf. = infinitive
interj. = interjection
intrg. = interrogative
lit. = literal
m. = masculine gender (of noun)
mil. = military
n. = noun; neuter
neg. = negative
neol. = neologism
nom. = nominative case
num. = number, numeral
obl. = oblique case
pf. = perfect
pl. = plural
poet. = poetic
pp. = past participle
prep. = preposition
pr. mod. = preposed modifier
prn. = pronoun
prv. = proverb
psp. = postposition
qv = which see
rdl. = riddle
rel. prn. = relative pronoun
rev. con. = reverse construction
sing. = singular
s.o. = someone
stg. = something
subj. = subjunctive mood
syn. = synonym
tr. = translation; translated
vi. = intransitive verb
voc. = vocative
vt. = transitive verb (with ergative past tense)
W = west
zool. = zoological

Languages:

Akk[adian]
Alb[anian]
Ar[abic]
Ar[amai]c
Arm[enian]
Av[estan]
Az[erbaijani] T[urkish]
Azer[baijani dialect of Kurdish]
Bulg[arian]
Fr[ench]
Geo[rgian]
Germ[an]
Gr[eek]
Hau[rami] (Gorani)
Heb[rew]
I[ndo-]E[uropean]
Ind[o]-Ir[anian]
Ir[anian]
It[alian]
K[urmanji Kurdish]
Lat[in]
Latv[ian] (=Lettish)
Lith[uanian]
Mid[dle] P[ersian]
Mod[ern] Gr[eek]
N[eo-]A[ramaic]
NENA = Northeastern Neo-Aramaic, term suggested by Robert Hoberman to refer to the largest Neo-Aramaic dialect cluster, spoken by the Jews of Kurdistan and the Assyrians and Chaldeans.
O[ld] C[hurch] S[lavonic]
O[ld] Ir[anian] (=Proto Iranian)
O[ld] P[ersian]
Oss[etic]
Pahl[avi] = Zoroastrian Middle Persian
Parth[ian]
P[ersian]
Rus[sian]
S[ans]k[ri]t
S[erbo]-Cr[oat]
S[o]gd[ian]
Sor[ani]
So[uthern]K[urdish] = Kelhori
Sp[anish]
Syr[iac]
T[urkish]
Za[za]

Abbreviations of Sources Used in Compiling this Dictionary

A = Musa Anter. *Ferhenga Khurdî-Tirkî = Kürdçe-Türkçe Sözlük* (İstanbul: Yeni Matbaa, 1967), 174 p. [Mardin, Turkey]

AA = Aziz R. Akrawy [Akreyî]. *Rêbera Sêzimanî* = الدليل اللغوي الثلاثي = *The Trilingual Guide: Kurdî* - عربي - *English* (Iraq, 1980)

AB = M. Emin Bozarslan. *Alfabe*, 2nd ed. (Borås, Sweden: Invandrarförlaget, 1980), 64 p. [Turkey]

Abbasian = Alikhan Abbasian & Vardan Voskanian. "A Kurdish Philosophy of Death: A Kurdish Tale from Armenia," *Acta Kurdica* 1 (1994), 143-145.

AD = Amîrxan. *Kurdisch Deutsch: Kurdî - Almanî* (Ismanning, Germany: Max Hueber Verlag, 1992), 2 vol. [vol. 2: Deutsch Kurdish: Almanî - Kurdî]

Adak = Abdurrahman Adak. *Destpêka edebiyata Kurdî ya klasîk* (Istanbul: Nûbihar, 2013), 414 p.

AF = Amîrxan. *Ferhenga Arebî-Kurdî* = المعجم العربي الكردي (Vienna: Verlag Berger, 1997), 982 p. [Arabic-Kurmanji dictionary]

Ah - Musa Anter. *Hatıralarım* (İstanbul: Yön Yayıncılık, 1991), 246 p. [Mardin, Turkey]

AI = Abbas Ismaîl. *Em Beranên Ber Kêrê ne* (Qamişlo, 1998), 115 p.

AId = Sadiq Baha' al-Din Amêdî. *Îdyemêt Kurdî: al-muṣṭalaḥāt wa-al-kināyāt al-lughawīyah fī al-lughah al-Kurdīyah* (Baghdad: al-Sha'b, 1973), 160 p.

AKR = Laura Shepherd. *Advanced Kurmanji Reader* (Hyattsville, MD : Dunwoody Press, 2009), 505 p.

A&L = Garnik Asatrian & Vladimir Livshits. "Origine du système consonantique de la langue Kurde," *Acta Kurdica* 1 (1994), 81-108.

Alkan = Abbas Alkan. "Demsala neqişandî," *Nûdem* 20 (1996), 70-77.

AR = Sadiq Baha' al-Din Amêdî. *R̄êzmana Kurdî: Kirmancîya jorî û jêrî ya hevberkirî* (Baghdad: Wezaretî Fêrkirdinî Bała w Lêkołînewey Zanyarî, Zankoy Ṣalāḥ al-Dīn, 1987), 481 p.

Ardû = Hesenê Metê. *Ardû: ji kurteçîrokên gelêrî* (Stockholm: Weşanên Welat, 1990), 173 p. [Literary Kurmanji]

AW = *Azadiya Welat* (Istanbul, 1996-) [Kurmanji newspaper, continuation of Welatê Me; references such as "AW69A1" designates passages taken from Geoffrey Haig's Corpus of Kurmanji Kurdish (CCKNT) consisting of 483 texts, totalling around 214,000 words. It contains texts from two Kurdish publications: *Azadiya Welat*, a weekly Kurdish newspaper, and *CTV*, a company which broadcasted news items in Kurdish on the Internet]

AX = Ahmed Xanî. *Mam i Zin = Mem û Zîn*, tr. M. B. Rudenko (Moscow: Izdatel'stvo Vostochnoi Literatury, 1962), 249, 196 p. [17th-century literary]

AZ = Ahmad 'Abd Allah Zero. *Mamikên Kurdî* (Bex̌da: Komarî 'Îraq, Wezaretî Roşinbîrî w R̄ageyandin, Dezgay R̄oşinbîrî w Biławkirdnewey Kurdî, 1985), 102 p. [Mostly Kurmanji (Behdinani) riddles, in Arabic script]

B = Ch.Kh. Bakaev. *Kurdsko-Russkiĭ Slovar' ... okolo 14000 slov s prilozheniem grammaticheskogo ocherka kurdskogo iazyka* (Moscow: Gosudarstvennoe Uzdatel'stvo Inostrannykh i Natsional'nykh Slovareĭ, 1957), 618 p. [USSR]

Ba = Ch.Kh. Bakaev. *IAzyk Kurdov SSSR* (Moscow: Nauka, 1973), 350 p. [USSR]

Ba2 = Ch.Kh. Bakaev. *Osnovy Kurdskoĭ Orfografii* (Moscow: Nauka, 1983), 272 p. [USSR]

Ba3 = Ch.Kh. Bakaev. *Rol' IAzykovykh Kontaktov v Razvitii IAzyka Kurdov SSSR* (Moscow: Nauka, 1977), 284 p. [USSR]

Ber = *Berbang: Kovara Federasyona Komelên Kurdistanê li Swêd* [journal published in Sweden]

BF = Kamêran Silêman Botî. *Ferhenga Kamêran, Kurdî-Kurdî* (Duhok: Spîrêz, 2006), 775 p.

BFK = M. Emîn Bozarslan. *Ferhenga Kurdî* (Istanbul: Weşanên Deng, 2011-), v. 1 (A-D)

BG = Paul Beidar. *Grammaire Kurde* (Paris: Paul Geuthner, 1926), 77 p. [Zakho, Iraq, & Cizre, Mardin, Turkey]

BH = Behcet Hirorî. *Gotgotk: peyveka kehî û dujmineke kujek* (Dihok: Çapxana Hawar, 1996), 62 p. [Scientific study of the rumor (gotgotk), in Kurmanji in Arabic script]

BK = Kemal Badıllı. *Türkçe İzahlı Kürtçe Grameri (Kürmançça Lehçesi)* (Ankara: Ankara Basım ve Ciltevi, 1965), 160 p. [Kurdish grammar of province of Urfa and city of Cizre, province of Şirnak (formerly part of Mardin)]

Bkp = M. Emîn Bozarslan. *Kemal Paşa Weledê kê ye?: meselokên sîyasî* (Uppsala, Sweden : Weşanxana Deng, 1993)

BM = Gunilla Bergström. *Ma Tu Tirsonek î Alfons Oberg?* (Stockholm: Kurdiska Förlaget/Çapxana Kurd, 1981), 30 p. [Kurmanji translation of Swedish children's book]

BN = Makhmud Baiazidi [Mahmud Bayazidi]. *Nravy i obychai kurdov* = عادات و رسوماتنامه اکرادیه , tr. M. B. Rudenko (Moscow: Izd-vo vostochnoi lit-ry, 1963), 202 p. [Kurmanji ethnographic texts in Arabic script, by the same informant as JR]

BR = Musa Anter. *Birîna Reş = Kara Yara* (İstanbul: Ekin Basımevi, 1965), 80 p. [Mardin]

Brauer = Erich Brauer. *The Jews of Kurdistan*, completed and edited by Raphael Patai (Detroit: Wayne State University Press, 1993), 429 p.

BX = Emir Djeladet Bedir Khan & Roger Lescot. *Grammaire Kurde (Dialecte kurmandji)* (Paris: Librairie d'Amérique et d'Orient, 1970), 371 p. [Bohtan (Siirt), Turkey]

BZ = M. Emîn Bozarslan. *Baxçê zimên* (Diyarbakır : Weşanên Deng, 2008-)

CA = Mûrad Ciwan. *Ahmedê Xanî: Jiyan, Berhem û Bîr û Baweriyên Wî* (Istanbul: Doz ; Stockholm: Kurdiska Kulturstiftelsen, 1997), 336 p.

CB = Cemşid Bender. *Kürt Mutfak Kültürü ve Kürt Yemekleri* (İstanbul: Melsa Yayınları, 1992), 381 p.

CCG = Aykoç, Fêrgîn Melîk. *Çavkaniyên çanda gel* (İstanbul: Weşanên Ar, 2012-), v. 1.

CG = Alessandro Coletti. *Grammatica e Dizionario della Lingua Curda con Esercizi e Letture* (Roma: Edizione A.C., 1985), 2 vols. [Handwritten manuscript: mostly Sorani & Mukri; some Kurmanji (see PS)]

Chn = Perwîz Cîhanî. *Şîroveya Mem û Zîne Ehmedê Xanî* (Istanbul: Nûbihar, 2013), 816 p.

CP = Gabar Çiyan. *Ji dîna dîntir: Pêkenokên me: lêkolîn* (Norsborg, Sweden: Çand - Kultur, [1993?]), 57 p.

CS = Ferdîdon Çelebî & Danko Sipka. *Kurmanji Kurdish-English glossary* (Springfield, VA: Dunwoody Press, 2002), 408 p.

CT = Mûrad Ciwan. *Türkçe açıklamalı Kürtçe dilbilgisi: Kurmanc lehçesi* (Bälinge, Sweden: Jîna Nû, 1992), 224 p.

CTV = [Geoffrey Haig's Corpus of Kurmanji Kurdish (CCKNT) consisting of 483 texts, totalling around 214 000 words, containing texts from two Kurdish publications: *Azadiya Welat*, a weekly Kurdish newspaper, and *CTV*, a company that broadcasted news items in Kurdish on the Internet]

Cxn = Cigerxwîn. *Jînenîgariya min* (Spanga, Sweden: APEC, 1995), 414 p.

Cxn-KE = Cigerxwîn. *Kîne Em?*, 2. baskı (İstanbul: Pelê Sor, 1992), 415 p.

Cxn-1 = Cigerxwîn. *Dîwana Yekan* (İstanbul: Deng, 1992), pp. 16-263.

Cxn-2 = Cigerxwîn. *Sewra Azadî* (İstanbul: Deng, 1992), pp. 265-468.

Cxn-4 = Cigerxwîn. *Ronak: Dîwana 4'a* (Stokholm: Roja Nu, 1980), 208 p.

Cxn-5 = Cigerxwîn. *Zend-Avista: Dîwana 5'a* (Stokholm: Roja Nu, 1981), 176 p.

Cxn-7 = Cigerxwîn. *Hêvi: Dîwana 7'a* (Stokholm: Roja Nu, 1983), 186 p.

DBgb = Diyar Bohtî. *Gul bişkivîn : roman* (Köln: Mezopotamien Verlag, 2006), 496 p.

DE = Ekici, Deniz. *Kurmanji Kurdish reader* (Hyattsville, MD: Dunwoody Press, 2007), 253 p.

DM = [Roger Lescot; Nureddin Zaza] *Destana Memê Alan = Kürtçe-Türkçe Memê Alan Destanı* (İstanbul: Özgürlük Yolu Yayınları, 1978), 389 p. [Mardin, Turkey]

Dqg = Xelîl Duhokî. *Qefteka gulan ji baxçê peyv û dahînana Kurdan* (Hewlêr: Wezaretî Roşinbîrî w Lawan, 2010), 165 p.

Drş = Dêrşewî, Mele Mehmûd. *Miştaxa çiya ji gotinên pêşiya* (Stockholm, 1989), 275 p.

DS = *Türkiye'de Halk Ağzından Derleme Sözlüğü* (Ankara: Türk Tarih Kurumu, 1963-1982), 12 vols. [Turkey: primarily Turkish, but includes several Kurdish words, although failing to identify them as such]

Dz = Ordikhane Dzhalil & Dzhalile Dzhalil. *Mesele û Met'elokê K'urda bi Zimanê K'urdî û Rûsî = Kurdskie Poslovitsy i Pogovorki na Kurdskom i Russkom IAzykakh* (Moscow: Glavnaia redaktsiia vostochnoĭ literatury, 1972), 454 p.

[Kurmanji proverbs; also includes Sorani proverbs from Iraq]

DZK = Baran. *Dersên Zmanê Kurdi = Türkçe izahlı Kürtçe Dil Dersleri,* 2. baskı (İstanbul: Deng, 1991), 167 p.

EH = Emin E'vdal. *Heleqetîêd pizmamtîê nav K'urdada* (Erêvan: Neşireta Akadêmîa RSS Ermenîstanêye Ulma, 1965), pp. 213-[237]

EI² = *Encyclopaedia of Islam.* 2d ed. (Leiden : E. J. Brill, 1960-1997), vols. 1-9

Elîfba Ezdîkî = Ḧesenê Şêx-Me'mûdê & 'Ezîzê 'Emer. *Elîfba Ezdîkî* (Erevan, 2005)

EM = Ernest N. McCarus. *A Kurdish-English Dictionary: Dialect of Sulaimania, Iraq* (Ann Arbor: The University of Michigan Press, 1967), x, 194 p.

EP = *Kurdskie Epicheskie Pesni-Skazy* (Moscow: Izd-vo vostochnoĭ literatury, 1962), 242 p. [USSR]

Epl = Hesenê Metê. *Epîlog: çîrok* (Stockholm: Weşanên Nûdem, 1998), 141 p. [short stories in modern literary Kurmanji]

EŞ = Ereb Şemo. *Şivanê Kurd: Roman* (Istanbul: Weşanên Deng, 1994), 3d ed., 112 p.

EW = Words gathered with the help of a friend.

F = I. O. Farizov. *Ferhenga Ûrisî-Kurmancî = Russko-Kurdskiĭ Slovar'* (Moscow: Gosudarstvennoe izd-vo inostrannykh i natsional'nykh slovareĭ, 1957), 781 p. [USSR]

FB = Facebook (facebook.com)

FD = Umîd Demîrhan. *Ferhenga destî: Kurdî bi Kurdî* (Doğubeyazit: Sewad, 2007), 496 p.

FE = Fexrî Ebdo. *Deng û Rengê Çayê Kurmênc* (http://www.jindires.com/Niviskar/fexri/filklor2013.html)

FH = Fawaz Husên. *Siwarên Êşê* (Huddinge, Sweden: Weşanên Welat, 1994), 111 p.

FJ = Muhemed Cemîl Seyda. *Ferhenga Jîn: Kurdî-Erebî, bi zaravê Kurmancî* = قاموس الحياة (Beyrut: Çapxan Emîral, 1987), 424 p.

FK = *Folklora Kyrmança* (Erevan, 1936), 661 p. [Folkloristic texts in Kurmanji collected in Soviet Armenia. References are listed by subsection and number: subsections are abbreviated as follows: (kk) = Keř u K'ulikê Silêmanê Silîvî; (eb) = Epos û Beyt'; (kb) = K'ilamê Bengîtîyê, Zarotîyê û Govenda; (kg) = K'ilamê Govenda; (ez) = K'ilamêd 'Evdalê Zeynikê; (ph) Poêm û Ḧikyat. E,g,, FK-kk-1 refers to the first (1) text under the subsection 'Keř u K'ulikê Silêmanê Silîvî' (kk)]

FKS = Murād Ḥāmid 'Alī. *Ferhenga Kaniya Sipî* (Duhok: Spîrêz, 2008), 270 p.

FS = Khālid Muḥammad Sindī. *Ferhenga Sindî* ([Iraq], 2010), 1 v. [Behdini Kurmanji in Arabic script]

FŞA = Têmûrê Hesen (Hasanyan). *Ferhenga Şirovekirina Aboriyê* {Dr_Hasanyan_17.11.13.pdf}

FT = Faki Teĭran. *Sheĭkh San'an,* kriticheskiĭ tekst, perevod, primechaniia i predislovie M.B. Rudenko (Moscow: Izd-vo Nauka, 1965), 157 p. [Literary and folk versions of the poem "Şêx Sen'an" by the early Kurdish poet Feqîyê Teyra + Russian translations]

FZT = *Ferhenga Zaravên Teknîkî = Teknik Terimler Sözlüğü = Glossary of Technical Terms* (Ankara: Türkiye Mühendis ve Mimar Odaları Birliği, 2014), 175 p.

G = Mustafa Gazî. *Ferheng: Kurdî-Tirkî* (Diyarbakir: Enstîtuya Kurdî ya Amedê, 2006), 166 p.

GF = Ali Seydo Ali Gewranî. *Ferhenga Kurdî Nûjen: Kurdî - Erebî = al-Qāmūs al-Kurdī al-Ḥadīth: Kurdī - 'Arabī* [كردي -عربي: القاموس الكردي الحديث] ('Ammān: Sharikat al-Sharq al-Awsaṭ, 1985), 670 p. [Kurdish-Arabic dictionary]

GL = Ayhan Geverî. *Leyl-name* (Istanbul: Nûbihar, 2012), 107 p.

GMK = Gîw Mukriyanî. *Ferhengî Kurdistan* ([Iraqi Kurdistan], 1999), 940 p.

GShA = Kreyenbroek, Philip G. & Khalil Jindy Rashow. *God and Sheikh Adi are perfect : sacred poems and religious narratives from the Yezidi tradition* (Wiesbaden: Harrassowitz, 2005), 435 p.

GW = Zeynelabidîn Zinar. *Gotinên Watedar* (Stockholm: Pencînar, 2016), 241 p.

H = *Hawar* (Stockholm: Nûdem, 1998), 2 vols. [complete reprint edition of the newspaper Hawar, originally appeared 1932-1943 in Syria]

Hamelink = Wendelmoet Hamelink. *The Sung Home: Narrative, Morality and the Kurdish Nation* (Leiden: Brill, 2016), 462 p.

HB = Hayri Başbuğ. *Göktürk-Uygur Zaza-Kurmanç Lehçeleri Üzerine bir Araştırma* (Ankara: Türk Kültürünü Araştırma Enstitüsü, 1984), 88 p. [Hani, Diyarbakir, Turkey]

HCK = Hajie Jndi (ed.). *Ḧik'yat'êd cima'eta Kurdîê* (Erevan: Neşîreta AÒ. R'SS Ermenîê, 1961-), v. 1-6.

HD = Haydar Diljen. *Zimanê min I* (Uppsala: Jîna Nû, 1990), 78 p.

Hej = Hejar. *Henbane borîne: farhang-i Kurdī-Farsī* (Tihrān: Surūsh, 1369), 1035 p. [Sorani dictionary by the late poet Hejar; includes Behdinani vocabulary as well]

HG = Hassan Ghazi & Hewa Cardoi. *Svensk-sydkurdiskt lexikon = Ferhengî Swêdî Kurdî* (Stockholm: Statens Institut för Läromedel, 1992), 309, 64 p. [Swedish-Sorani dictionary]

HH = Yusuf Ziyaeddin Pasa. *al-Hadīyah al-Ḥamīdīyah* (Beirut, 1975), 56, 240 p. = Mohammad Mokri. Recherches de Kurdologie: Dictionnaire Kurde-Arabe de Dia' Ad-Din Pacha al-Khalidi: introduction et notes linguistiques, notice sur la phonétique et la graphie arabo-persane du dialecte kurmândji, Textes et étude religieux, linguistiques et ethnographiques (Langues et civilisation iraniennes), no. 4 (Beyrouth & Paris, 1975). [Muş, Turkey]

HM = Hugo Makas. *Kurdische Texte im Kurmanji-Dialekte aus der Gegend von Märdîn, nebst Kurdische Studien* (St, Petersburg, 1897-1926; reprint ed.: Amsterdam: APA - Philo Press, 1979), 2 vol. in 1 [Mardin, Turkey]

HoK = Sadiq Baha' al-Din Amêdî. *Hozanvanêt Kurd* (Bexda: Çapxaney Kor̄î Zanyarî 'Êraq, 1980), 426 p. [Anthology of Kurmanji poets, mostly from Bahdinan and Hekkari, in Arabic script]

HoK2 = Sadiq Behaedîn Amêdî. *Hozanvanêt Kurd* (Stockholm: Pencînar, 1998), 465 p. [same as above, in Latin script]

HR = Hellmut Ritter. "Kurmanci-Texte aus dem Ṭūr'Abdîn," I. Kärboran: *Oriens*, 21-22 (1968-69), 1-135; II. Yeziden: *Oriens*, 25-26 (1976), 1-37. [Villages of Kärboran (I.) and Ṭāqa (II.) of the Ṭūr'Abdîn region of Mardin, Turkey]

Hv = *Hêvî: Kovara Çandîya Giştî = Hîwa: Govarêkî Rûnakbîrîy Giştîye* (Paris: 1983-) [literary: also publishes in Soranî and Zaza]

HYab = Helîm Yûsiv. *Ausländer Beg* (Diyarbakir: Lîs, 2011),

HYma = Helîm Yûsiv. *Mêrê Avis* (Istanbul: Avesta, 1997), 184 p.

IC = Derince, M. Şerif, E. Öpengin & G. Haig. *Introductory Course in Kurmanji Kurdish* (Uppsala : Uppsala University, 2008), 183 p.

IF = D. Îzolî. *Ferheng: Kurdî-Tirkî, Türkçe-Kürtçe* (Den Haag: Komeley Xwêndikaranî Kurd le Ewrupa, [1987]), 413 p. [Turkey]

IFb = D. Îzoli. *Ferheng: Kurdi-Tırki, Türkçe-Kürtçe.* [2d ed.] (Istanbul: Deng Yayınları, 1992), 913 p.

IS = *Iranskiĭ Sbornik ... I.I. Zarubina* (Moscow: Izd-stvo Vostochnoĭ Literatury, 1963), pp. 219-248; 249-255.

J = Hajie Jndi. *Ḧik'yatêd Cima'eta K'urdîê* (Erevan: Haypethrat, 1959), 113 p. [Soviet Armenia, USSR]

JB1 = Joyce Blau. *Le Kurde de ᶜAmadiya et de Djabal Sindjar: Analyse linguistique, textes folkloriques, glossaires* (Paris: C. Klincksieck, 1975), 252 p. [Amadiya & Jabal Sinjar, Northern Iraq]

JB2 = Joyce Blau. *Kurdish Kurmandji Modern Texts* (Wiesbaden: Otto Harrassowitz, 1968), 58 p. [literary]

JB3 = Joyce Blau. *Kurdish-French-English Dictionary = Dictionnaire Kurde- Français-Anglais* (Bruxelles: Centre pour l'Etude des Problèmes du Monde Musulman Contemporain, 1965), 263 p. [literary]

JH = Ḥajī Ja'far. *Hindek Kevnebawerêt Xelkî li Behdînan* (Baghdad, 1993), 67 p. [on folk beliefs and superstitions in Behdinan, in Behdinani Kurmanji in Arabic script]

JJ = Auguste Jaba & Ferdinand Justi. *Dictionnaire Kurde-Français* (St.-Pétersbourg: Eggers et Cie, 1879), 463 p. [?Hakkari]

JR = Alexandre Jaba. *Recueil de Notices et de Récits Kourdes* (St.-Pétersbourg: Eggers et Cie, 1860; repr. Amsterdam: APA - Philo Press, 1979), 111, 128 p. [?Hakkari]

K = K. K. Kurdoev. *Ferhenga Kurdî-Rûsî = Kurdsko-Russkiĭ Slovar'* (Moscow: Gosudarstvennoe izd-vo inostrannykh i natsional'nykh slovareĭ, 1960), 890 p. [primarily USSR]

K2 = K. K. Kurdoev. *Grammatika Kurdskogo IAzyka (Kurmandzhi)*: Fonetika, Morfologiia (Moscow-Leningrad: Izd-vo Akademii Nauk SSSR, 1957), 343 p. [primarily USSR]

K3 = K. K. Kurdoev & Z. A. IUsupova. *Ferhengî Kurdî-R̄ûsî (Soranî) = Kurdsko-Russkiĭ Slovar' (Sorani)* (Moscow:

Russkiĭ IAzyk, 1983), 752 p. [Sorani Kurdish-Russian dictionary]

K-ça = Hamit Kılıcaslan. *Çîrokên Hayqar* (unpublished manuscript: Stockholm, 1998) [translation of M. H. Dolapönü. Haykar'ın Meseleleri (İstanbul, 1963)--tales of Ahikar, translated from Syriac]

K-dş = Qenatê Kurdo [= K.K. Kurdoev]. "Derheqa şovêd Mem û Zîna zargotî û şova Mem û Zîna Ehmedê Xanî," *Govarî Korî Zanyarî Kurd* [=The Journal of the Kurdish Academy], 6 (1978), pp. 78-110.

KH = Karl Hadank. *Untersuchungen zum Westkurdischen: Bōtī und Ezädī*, Arbeiten aus dem Institut für Lautforschung an der Universität Berlin, Nr. 6 (Berlin: Institut für Lautforschung an der Universität Berlin ; Leipzig: Otto Harrassowitz, 1938), 60 p. [texts in Botani and Yezidi dialects, including some Yezidi prayers]

KHT = Mehmet Bayrak. *Kürt Halk Türküleri = Kilam û Stranên Kurd: İnceleme--Antoloji* (Ankara: Öz-Ge, 1991), 300 p.

Kmc = *Kurmancî: rojnameya taybetî ya Enstîtuya Kurdî ya Parîsê li ser pirsên zaravê kurmancî, hejmarên 1-20* (Paris: Institut Kurde de Paris, 1999), 439 p. [issues 1-20 of the newsletter of the Civîna Kurmancî (Kurmanji Language Workshop) of the Kurdish Institute of Paris, with Kurdish, Turkish, French, and English glossaries and indexes]

KO = Khanna Omarkhali. *Kurdish Reader: modern literature and oral texts in Kurmanji* (Wiesbaden: Harrassowitz Verlag, 2011), 282 p.

K'oroxlî = Hajie Jndi [Hacîyê Cindî]. *Şaxêd eposa "K'oroxlî" bi zmanê kurmancî = "K'yoṛōghli" ēposi k'rdakan patmnerě = Kurdskie skazy ėposa "Kër-ogly"*(Erevan: Haykakan SSṚ GA hratarakch'ut'yun, 1953), 237 p.

K[s] = Same as K above, designating a borrowing from Southern dialects (a vague term, sometimes meaning Southern Kurmanji [Behdinani], and sometimes meaning Soranî [& Mukrî])

KS = Firat Cewerî. *Kevoka Spî* (Stockholm: Nûdem, 1996), 60 p.

KSJ = *Kurdish Studies Journal.*

KZ = Geew Mukriyany. *Kolke Zêrîne = Rainbow* (Arbil, Iraq: Arbil Press, 1966), 240 p. [Iraq--mostly Soranî, some Behdinani]

L = Roger Lescot. *Textes Kurdes* (Paris: Paul Geuthner, 1940-42) 2 vols. [tales, proverbs & riddles in vol. 1 from Mardin, Turkey; in vol. 2: Mîşo from Meqtelê, Syria; Sebrî from Mardin, Turkey; Hawar from Serhedan (=Turco-Iranian & Turco-Soviet border region)]

Lab = Hesenê Metê. *Labîrenta Cinan: roman* (Huddinge, Sweden: Weşanên Welat, 1994), 197 p. [short stories in modern literary Kurmanji]

LC = Mahmûd Lewendî. *Computera ber dilê min!: çîrok û nivîsên mîzahî* (Stockholm: APEC, 1996), 160 p. [jokes; the author is from Qerejdax, between Siverek and Diyarbakir]

LM = Mahmûd Lewendî. *Mala xwedê: pêkenîn* (Vällingby, Sweden: Weşanên Hêlîn, 1992), 118 p. [jokes]

Lwj = Philip G. Kreyenbroek. "The Lawîj of Môr Basîliôs Shim'ûn : a Kurdish Christian Text in Syriac Script," *Journal of Kurdish Studies* 1 (1995), 29-53.

Lx = Peter J.A. Lerch. *Forschungen über die Kurden und die Iranischen Nordchaldäer:* I. Kurdische Texte gesammelt und herausgegeben mit deutscher Übersetzung und einer Einleitung, II Kurdische Glossare für die Kurmanji- und Zaza-Mundarten mit einer historischen Einleitung, Anhängen und Zusätzen (St.-Petersburg, 1857-58; repr. Amsterdam: APA - Philo Press, 1979), 2 vols. in 1 (225 p.)

LY = Roger Lescot. *Enquête sur les Yezidis de Syrie et du Djebel Sindjār*, Mêmoires de l'Ènstitut français de Damas, tome 5 (Beyrouth, 1938), 277 p. [includes Yezidi terms and texts from Djebel Sindjār in Iraqi Kurdistan & Djebel Sim'ān in Syrian Kurdistan]

M = D. N. MacKenzie. *Kurdish Dialect Studies* (London: Oxford University Press, 1961-62) 2 vols. [Forms are from Akre (=Ak) unless otherwise marked: Amadiya (=Am); Sheikhan (=Sh); Zakho (=Zx); Surçi tribe (=Sr), Northern Iraq]

M2 = D. N. MacKenzie. "The Origins of Kurdish," *Transactions of the Philological Society* (1961), 68-86.

M5 = D. N. MacKenzie. "Gender in Kurdish," *Bulletin of the School of Oriental and African Studies* 16 (1954), 528-41.

MB = Mehmet Emin Bozarslan. *Meyro: Çîrokin* (İstanbul: Çıra Yayınları, 1979), 143 p. [Short stories in Kurdish with Turkish translations, Turkey]

MC-1 = Cassette tape in the possession of Michael L. Chyet. [Van, Turkey]

MD = Margreet Dorleijn. *The Decay of Ergativity in Kurmanci: Language Internal or Contact Induced?* (Tilburg: Tilburg University Press, 1996), 183 p. [includes texts elicited from informants from Diyarbakir (Dy), Beytûşşebab (Byt), Hazro (Hzr), etc.]

MG = Mirad Gundikî. Author of short stories available on the internet. Native of Gundik near Şirnex [Şırnak].

MJ = Mela Xelîl Mişextî. *Ferhenga merg û jî* (Hewlêr: Aras, 2006), 560 p.

MK = Margaret Kahn. *Borrowing and Variation in a Phonological Description of Kurdish* (Ann Arbor: Phonetics Laboratory, The University of Michigan, 1976), doctoral thesis [Reza'iyeh (Urmiyah), Province of West Azerbaijan, Northwest Iran]

MK2 = Margaret Kahn. *Kurmanji-English, English-Kurmanji Lexicon* (Ann Arbor: The University of Michigan, 1974), typescript [Silvan, Diyarbakir, Turkey]

MK3 = Margaret Kahn. *Children of the Jinn: In Search of the Kurds and Their Country* (New York: Seaview Books, 1980), 302 p.

MUm = Mehmed Uzun. *Mirina Kalekî Rind: roman* (Stockholm: Orfeus, 1987), 135 p.

MUs = Mehmed Uzun. *Siya Evînê: roman* (Stockholm: Orfeus, 1989), 222 p.

MXC = *Meselok û xeberokêd cma'eta K'urda*, bernivîsa, berdagotin û nivîsarnasî ê Ḧecîê Cndî (Erevan, 1985)

Nbh = *Nûbihar*, journal published in Istanbul, 1992-

Noel = Edward Noel. "The Character of the Kurds as Illustrated by Their Proverbs and Popular Sayings." *BSOAS* 1, iv (1920), 79-90.

Nofa = Hecî Nohsan. *Nofa* (İstanbul: Weşanên Do, 2014), 139 p.

OK = Feryad Fazil Omar. *Kurdisch-Deutsches Wörterbuch = Ferhenga Kurdî-Elmanî* (Berlin: Verlag für Wissenschaft und Bildung, Kurdische Studien, 1992), 721 p.

OM = Oskar Mann. *Die Mundart der Mukri-Kurden*, Kurdisch-Persische Forschungen, 4 (Berlin: G. Reimer, 1906-1909), 2 vols. [orally-generated texts in Mukri (Sorani of Iranian Kurdistan) in early phonetic script + German translation]

OrK = Iosif Abgarovich Orbeli. *Kurdsko-russkiĭ slovar'* in: *Izbrannye trudy v dvukh tomakh* (Moskva : "Nauka," 1968-2002), v. 2, pt. 2.

OS = Osman Sebrî [Apo]. *Gotinin xav nepijîn bê tav*, ed. by Hemreş Reşo (Ratingen [?], 1981), vii, 160 p. [poems by one of the foremost modern Kurdish poets]

PB = Peter Pikkert. *A Basic Course in Modern Kurmanji* (Genk, Belgium: Alev Books, 1991), 59 p.

PÇ = Şivan Perwer. *Çîroka Newrozê* (Uppsala: Şivan Production, 1990), 37 p. [Children's book in Kurmanji which tells the story of Kurdish Newroz (New Year's)]

PF = Elî Paksêrêşt. *Ferhenga Kurdiya (Kurmancî)-Farisî* ([Iran], [200-?]), 457 p.

PS = Eugen Prym & Albert Socin. *Kurdische Sammlungen: Erzählungen und Lieder in den Dialekten des Tûr 'Abdîn und von Bohtan* (St. Petersburg et al.: Eggers & Co., [1887-] 1890), 2 vols. in 4 [Tûr 'Abdîn (Mardin), Turkey & Zakho, Bohtan (=Behdinan), Iraq] (PS-I = Tûr 'Abdîn, Mardin, Turkey; PS-II = Zakho, Bohtan, Iraq)

Qazzaz = Shafiq Qazzaz. *The Sharezoor = Ferhengî Şarezûr* (Erbil, Kurdistan: Aras, 2000), 601 p.

R = *Resen*: rojnameyeka giştîye, noke dû ḧeftîya carekê derdikevît (Dihok) [Religious newspaper in Kurmanji in Arabic script, published in Dihok]

RC2 = Rıza Çolpan. [Author of articles available on the internet]. Native of Tunceli/Dêrsim.

RD = Baran Rizgar. *Uygulamalı Kürtçe Dersleri = Dersên Kurdî* (London: M.F. Onen, 1993), 389 p.

RF = Baran Rizgar. *Kurdish-English English-Kurdish Dictionary = Ferheng Kurdî-Îngîlîzî Îngîlîzî-Kurdî* (London: M.F. Onen, 1993), 400 p. [Kurmanji in Latin script]

RJ = R.F. Jardine. *Bahdinan Kurmanji*: a grammar of the Kurmanji of the Kurds of Mosul division and surrounding districts of Kurdistan (Baghdad: Government Press, 1922), 114 p. [Mosul, Iraq]

RK = M.B. Rudenko. *Kurdskie Narodnye Skazki* (Moscow: Nauka, Glavnaia Redaktsiia Vostochnoĭ Literatury, 1970), 247 p. [Kurdish folktales in Russian translation]

RN = *Roja Nû*: Rojnama Siyasî ya hefteyî (1943-1946) (Uppsala: Weşanên Jîna Nû, 1986), [73 issues]

RN2 = *Roja Nû*: kovara hunerî çandî û edebî (Stockholm: Komkar-Swêd, 1979-)

Rnh = Celadet Bedirxan (ed.), *Ronahî*: supplément illustré de la revue Kurde Hawar (1942-1945) (Uppsala: Jîna Nû, 1985), [28 issues]

Ro = *Rojname* (Dec 1991) [Newspaper published simultaneously in Sweden and Turkey, after the 1991 lifting of the ban on Kurdish in Turkey: only 1 issue was published]

Roj = *Roj*: govareke roşenbîrî demdemî bingeha Êzidiya li dervey welat (Hannover, Germany, Aug 1996-) [Yezidi journal published in Arabic and Kurmanji]

RR = Mustafa Aydogan. *Rêbera Rastnivîsînê* (Komxebata Kurmancîyê, 2017)

Rwş = *Rewşen*: Kovara Navenda Çanda Mezopotamya (Istanbul, February 1992-) [Kurmanji journal published by the Upper Mesopotamian Cultural Center, Istanbul]

RT = *R'ya T'eze*: R̄ojnema Mexlûqetîê--Polîtîkîê, Kûltûrîê (Erevan, 1930-) [='The New Way', Kurmanji newspaper published in Erevan, Armenia, in Cyrillic characters]

RZ = Reşo Zîlan. *Svensk-Kurdiskt Lexikon (Nordkurdiska) = Ferhenga Swêdî-Kurdî (Kurmancî)* (Stockholm: Statens Institut för Läromedel, 1989), 311, 64 p. [Swedish-Kurmanji dictionary]

S = E. B. Soane. *Grammar of the Kurmanji or Kurdish Language* (London: Luzac & Co., 1913), 289 p. [Turkey & Iraq: an early work, largely outdated]

SB = Sebrî Botanî. "Topa Sultanî," *Dugir* 5 (1997), 50-52.

SB2 = Sebrî Botanî. *Dilistan* (Bex̌da: Çapxana al-Ḥawādith, 1984)

ŞBS = Şahînê Bekirê Soreklî. "Wekheviya jin û mêran di civatê de" *Nûdem* 26 (1998), 61-65.

ŞBS-W = Şahînê Bekirê Soreklî. *Wendabûn: romana kurdî* (Bonn: Verlag für Kultur und Wissenschaft, Dr. Thomas Schirrmacher, 1987)

SBx = Selahattin Bulut. *Xadim* (Istanbul: Avesta, 2012), 90 p.

SC = S. Siabandov & A. Chachan. Xebernama Ermeni-K'urdî = Հայ-Քրդերեն Բառարան (Erevan: HayPetHrat, 1957), 352 p. [Soviet Armenia]

S&E = I. A. Smirnova & K. R. Eiiubi. *Fonetika Kurdskogo IAzyka (Dialekt Mukri)* (Leningrad: Nauka, 1985), pp. 303-30. [primarily Iran]

SF = Yaşar Kemal. *Siltanê Fîlan: roman*, wergera ji tirkî Mustafa Aydogan (Järfälla, Sweden: Nûdem, 1998), 239 p. [Kurmanji translation of the Turkish novel Fil Sultan]

SH= Sidqî Hirorî. *Evîn û Şewat: roman* (Järfälla, Sweden: Nûdem, 1998), 109 p.

SK = B. Nikitine. *Šamdīnānī Kurdish.* (ed. by D. N. MacKenzie). Unpublished texts. [Şemdinli, Hekkârî, Turkey; comparative notes for Akre appear as SK-Ak]

SS = Salah Saadalla. *Saladin's English-Kurdish Dictionary = Qamûsa Selaĥedîn Îngilîzî-Kurdî* ([Baghdad: Dār al-Ḥurrīyah], 1998), 1183 p. [1st ed.]; (Istanbul: Avesta; Paris: Institut Kurde de Paris, 2000), 1477 p. [2d ed.]

ST = Yousuf Zangana & Jawad Mella. *The Tale of Suto and Tato*, collected and translated into English by E. B. Soane and B. Nikitin [sic], rewritten in Southern and Northern Kurdish by Yousuf Zangana and Jawad Mella, Kurdologia Publications, no. 7 (London: Kurdologia Publications, 1988), 33, 30 p. [Original text in Southern Kurmanji in Arabic alphabet (ST-o); reworked text in Kurmanji in Latin alphabet (ST-l); also includes translations into Sorani in Arabic script and English (also appears in SK)]

SW = Stig Wikander. *Recueil de textes kourmandji* (Uppsala: A.-B. Lundequistska Bokhandeln; Wiesbaden: Otto Harrassowitz, 1959), 108 p. [literary]

SW1 = Stig Wikander. *Antolojîya Tekstên Kurdî* (Stockholm: Orfeus, 1996), 179 p. [reprint edition]

Sweetnam = Denise L. Sweetnam. *Kurdish Culture*: A Cross-Cultural Guide (Bonn: Verlag für Kultur und Wissenschaft, 1994), 335 p.

ŞWWM = Dilawer Zeraq. *Şevên winda wêneyên meçhûl* (Diyarbakır: Lîs, 2016), 92 p.

TaRK = Samî Tan. *Rêzimana Kurmancî* (Stenbol: Enstîtuya Kurdî, 2011), 405 p.

TF = Torî. *Ferheng: Kurdî-Tirkî, Türkçe-Kürtçe* (İstanbul: Koral, 1992), 496 p.

TG = Tuncer Gülensoy. *Kürmanci ve Zaza Türkçeleri Üzerine bir Araştırma: İnceleme ve Sözlük* (Ankara: Türk Kültürünü Araştırma Enstitüsü, 1983), 69 p. [Turkey]

TG2 = Tuncer Gülensoy. *Doğu Anadolu Osmanlıcası* (Ankara: Türk Kültürünü Araştırma Enstitüsü, 1986), 535 p. [Turkey]

Tof = Hesenê Metê. *Tofan* (Stockholm: Nefel, 2000), 85 p.

TS = *Tarama Sözlüğü*. (Ankara: Türk Tarih Kurumu, 1963-77), 8 vols.

Tsab = Ruslan Lazarevich Tsabolov. *Etimologicheskiĭ slovar' kurdskogo iazyka* (Moskva : "Vostochnaia lit-ra" RAN, 2001-2010), 2 v.

Tsb = R. L. Tsabolov. *Ocherk istoricheskoĭ morfologii Kurdskogo iazyka* (Moscow: Nauka, 1978), 90 p. [study of the historical morphology of the Kurdish language]

Tsb2 = R. L. Tsabolov. *Ocherk istoricheskoĭ fonetiki Kurdskogo iazyka* (Moscow: Nauka, 1976), 101 p. [study of the historical phonetics of the Kurdish language]

VoA = Voice of America Kurdish airshow broadcasts (1992-present)

W&E = Taufiq Wahby & C. J. Edmonds. *A Kurdish-English Dictionary* (Oxford: Clarendon Press, 1966), 179 p. [Sorani Kurdish-English dictionary]

Wkp = Wîkîpedîya https://ku.wikipedia.org/wiki/ [Kurdish Wikipedia]

Wkt = http://ku.wiktionary.7val.com/;s=Wpe1BxLyxN4D0-FU9IxVt01/w/

Wlt = *Welat* (Istanbul, 1992-94) [Kurmanji newspaper]

WM = *Welatê Me* (Istanbul, 1994-1996) [Kurmanji newspaper, continuation of Welat]

WT = W.M. Thackston. *Kurmanji Kurdish: a reference grammar with selected readings* ([Cambridge, Mass.]: Harvard University, 2006), 264 p.

XF = M.U. Khamoian. *Kurdsko-Russkiĭ Frazeologicheskiĭ Slovar':* soderzhit okolo 8000 frazeologicheskikh stateĭ (Erevan: Izdatel'stvo AN Armianskoĭ SSR, 1979), 273 p. [primarily USSR & Behdinan, Iraqi Kurdistan]

YK = Muḥammad Ḥasan Binavî. *Yarîyêt Kurdî* (Hewlêr: Çapxana Roşinbîrî û Lawan, 1987), v. 1

YPA = Kadri Yıldırım, Raman Pertev & Mustafa Aslan. *Ji Destpêkê heta niha Folklora Kurdî* (Mardin: Mardin Artuklu Üniversitesi, 2013), 205 p.

YSFL = Yona Sabar. *The Folk Literature of the Kurdistani Jews: An Anthology* (New Haven & London: Yale University Press, 1982), 250 p. [primarily Jews of Zakho, Iraq]

YSZx = Yona Sabar. "Multilingual Proverbs in the Neo-Aramaic Speech of the Jews of Zakho, Iraqi Kurdistan," *International Journal of Middle East Studies* 9 (1978a), 215-35. [primarily Jews of Zakho, Iraq]

YZ = M. B. Rudenko. *Literaturnaia i Fol'klornye Versii Kurdskoĭ Poemy "IUsuf i Zelikha"* (Moscow: Nauka, 1986), 367 p. [USSR]

Z = Ordikhane Dzhalil & Dzhalile Dzhalil. *Zargotina K'urda = Kurdskiĭ Fol'klor* (Moscow: Nauka, 1978), 2 vols. [primarily USSR]

ZF = Zana Farqînî. *Ferhenga Kurdî/Tirkî & Türkçe/Kürtçe Sözlük*, çapa 6. (Stenbol: Enstîtuya Kurdî ya Stenbolê, 2012), 1504 p.

ZF2 = Zana Farqînî. *Ferhenga Kurdî-Tirkî & Kürtçe-Türkçe Sözlük*, çapa 2. (Stenbol: Enstîtuya Kurdî ya Stenbolê, 2005), 2132 p.

ZF3 = Zana Farqînî. *Ferhenga Kurdî-Tirkî & Kürtçe-Türkçe Sözlük*, çapa 1. (Stenbol: Enstîtuya Kurdî ya Stenbolê, 2004), 2132 p.

ZM = Zh.S. Musaelian. *Zambil'frosh:* Kurdskaia poema i eë fol'klornye versii (Moscow: Nauka, 1983), 178 p. [USSR]

ZZ = Zeynelabidîn Zinar. *Xwençe* (Stockholm: Weşanxaneya Çanda Kurdî, 1989-1997), 10 vols. [collection of Kurdish folklore, mostly in Kurmanji of Turkey; each vol. indicated as follows: ZZ-1 = vol. 1; ZZ-2 = vol. 2, etc.]

Sources for Linguistic Comparison

Abaev = V. I. Abaev. *Istoriko-etimologicheskiĭ slovar' osetinskogo iazyka* (Moscow; Leningrad, 1958-1989), 4 vols.

AC-1 = Ahmet Caferoğlu. *Doğu İllerimiz Ağızlarından Toplamalar: I. Kars, Erzurum, Çoruh İlbaylıkları Ağızları* (İstanbul: Bürhaneddin Basımevi, 1942), 294 p. [Texts in & glossaries of the Turkish dialects of Kars, Erzurum, and Artvin]

AC-2 = Ahmet Caferoğlu. *Güney-Doğu İllerimiz Ağızlarından Toplamalar: Malatya, Elâzığ, Tunceli, Gaziantep ve Maraş Vilâyetleri Ağızları* (İstanbul: Bürhaneddin Basımevi, 1945), 304 p. [Texts in & glossaries of the Turkish dialects of Malatya, Elâzığ, Tunceli, Gaziantep, and Maraş]

AC-3 = Ahmet Caferoğlu. *Anadolu İlleri Ağızlarından Derlemeler: Van, Bitlis, Muş, Karaköse, Eskişehir, Bolu ve Zonguldak İlleri Ağızları* (İstanbul: İstanbul Üniversitesi Edebiyat Fakültesi, 1951), 288 p. [Texts in & glossaries of the Turkish dialects of Van, Bitlis, Muş, Karaköse (=Ağrı), Eskişehir, Bolu and Zonguldak]

Achar = Hrach'eay Acharean. *Hayeren Armatakan Bararan* (Erevan: Erevani Hamalsarani Hratarakch'ut'yun, 1971-1979), 4 vols.

Am Her = Calvert Watkins. "Indo-European Roots", in: *The American Heritage Dictionary of the English Language*, ed. William Morris (Boston: Houghton Mifflin, 1976), pp. 1505-50.

Atılcan = İhsan Coşkun Atılcan. *Erzurum Ağzı, Halk Deyimleri ve Folklor Sözlüğü* (Erzurum, 1977), 167 p.

Bartholomae = Christian Bartholomae. *Altiranisches Wörterbuch* (Berlin & New York: Walter De Gruyter, 1961), 1980 p.

Boyce = Mary Boyce. *A Word-list of Manichaean Middle Persian and Parthian* (Leiden: E.J. Brill; Tehran & Liège: Bibliothèque Pahlavi, 1977), 172 p.

Brand = Wilhelm Brandenstein & Manfred Mayrhofer. *Handbuch des Altpersischen* (Wiesbaden: O. Harrassowitz, 1964), 160 p.

Buck = Carl Darling Buck. *A Dictionary of Selected Synonyms in the Principal Indo-European Languages: A Contribution to the History of Ideas* (Chicago & London: The University of Chicago Press, 1949, 1988), 1515 p.

Clauson = Sir Gerard Clauson. *An Etymological Dictionary of Pre-Thirteenth-Century Turkish* (Oxford: The Clarendon Press, 1972), 988 p.

Costaz = Louis Costaz. *Dictionnaire Syriaque-Français = Syriac-English Dictionary* = قاموس سرياني عربي (Beyrouth: Imprimerie Catholique, 1963), xxiii, 421 p.

Delitzsch = Friedrich Delitzsch. *Assyrisches Handwörterbuch* (Leipzig: J. C. Hinrichs; Baltimore: The John Hopkins Press; London: Luzac, 1896), 730 p.

Doerfer = Gerhard Doerfer. *Türkische und Mongolische Elemente im Neupersischen: unter besonderer Berücksichtigung älterer neupersischer Geschichtsquellen vor allem der Mongolen- und Timuridenzeit* (Wiesbaden: Franz Steiner Verlag, 1963-75), 4 vols.

Fat = Ismaïl Kamandâr Fattah. *Les dialectes kurdes méridionaux: étude linguistique et dialect[o]logique,* Acta Iranica 37 (Leuven: Peeters, 2000), 919 p.

Fischer & Jastrow = *Handbuch der arabischen Dialekte,* mit Beitragen von P. Behnstedt ... [et al.] ; bearb. und hrsg. von Wolfdietrich Fischer und Otto Jastrow (Wiesbaden: Harrassowitz, 1980), 312 p.

Fraenkel = Siegmund Fränkel. *Die aramäischen Fremdwörter im Arabischen* (Leiden: E.J. Brill, 1886), 327 p.

Garbell = Irene Garbell. *The Jewish Neo-Aramaic Dialect of Persian Azerbaijan: Linguistic Analysis and Folkloristic Texts* (London: Mouton, 1965), 342 p.

Gemalmaz = Efrasiyap Gemalmaz. *Erzurum İli Ağızları* (Erzurum, 1978), 3 vols.

Gersh = Ilya Gershevitch. *A Grammar of Manichean Sogdian* (Oxford : Basil Blackwell, 1954), 307 p.

Hadank = Karl Hadank. *Mundarten der Zâzâ, hauptsächlich aus Siwerek und Kor* (Berlin: Walter de Gruyter, 1932), xiii, 398 p. + map

Hangin = Gombojab Hangin et al. *A Modern Mongolian-English Dictionary* (Bloomington : Indiana Univ., 1986), 900 p.

Haoma = David Stophlet Flattery and Martin Schwartz. *Haoma and Harmaline: The Botanical Identity of the Indo-*

Iranian Sacred Hallucinogen "Soma" and its Legacy in Religion, Language, and Middle Eastern Folklore, University of California Publications, Near Eastern Studies, vol. 21 (Berkeley: University of California Press, 1989), vii, 211 p.

Henning Verbum = W. B. Henning. "Das Verbum des Mittelpersischen der Turfanfragmente," *Zeitschrift für Indologie und Iranistik* 9 (1933), 158-235.

Hetzron = Robert Hetzron. "The Morphology of the Verb in Modern Syriac (Christian Colloquial of Urmi)," *Journal of the American Oriental Society 89* (1969), 112-127. [Neo-Aramaic dialect of the Christians of Urmi (Reza'iyeh), Kurdistan of Iran]

Hoberman = Robert D. Hoberman. *The Syntax and Semantics of Verb Morphology in Modern Aramaic: A Jewish Dialect of Iraqi Kurdistan* (New Haven: American Oriental Society, 1989), xii, 226 p.

Horn = Paul Horn. *Grundriss der neupersischen Etymologie* (Strassburg: Trübner, 1893), 386 p.

HR2 = Hellmut Ritter. *Ṭūrōyo: die Volkssprache der syrischen Christen des Ṭūr ʿAbdîn: B: Wörterbuch* (Beirut ; Wiesbaden: Franz Steiner Verlag, 1979), 589 p. [Ṭūrōyo, Neo-Aramaic language spoken in Ṭūr ʻAbdîn region of province of Mardin, Kurdistan of Turkey]

Hübsch = H. Hübschmann. *Persische Studien* (Strassburg: Trübner, 1895), 287 p.

Jeffery = Arthur Jeffery. *The Foreign Vocabulary of the Qur'an* (Baroda, India: Oriental Institute, 1938), 311 p.

Kent = Roland G. Kent. *Old Persian: Grammar, Texts, Lexicon,* American Oriental Series, 33 (New Haven, Conn.: American Oriental Society, 1953), 219 p.

Krotkoff = Georg Krotkoff. *A Neo-Aramaic Dialect of Kurdistan: Texts, Grammar, and Vocabulary* (New Haven, Conn.: American Oriental Society, 1982), 172 p. [Neo-Aramaic dialect of the village of Aradhin, 10 miles west of Amadia, Kurdistan of Iraq]

Laufer = Berthold Laufer. *Sino-Iranica: Chinese Contributions to the History of Civilization in Ancient Iran* (Chicago: Field Museum of Natural History, 1919; reprint: Taipei: Ch'eng-Wen Publishing Company, 1967), 185-630 p.

Lopat = Lopatinskii, L. *Evreisko-Arameiskīe teksty*. in: *Sbornik" Materialov" dlia opisaniia miestnosteĭ i plemen" Kavkaza*, Vyp. 20, Otdel" 2, (Tiflis": Kantseliariia Glavnonachal'stvuiushchago Grazhdanskoiu Chastiiu na Kavkaz i Kozlovskago, 1894), pp. 1-32 [second numeration in this volume]

M3 = D. N. MacKenzie. *A Concise Pahlavi Dictionary* (London: Oxford University Press, 1971), 236 p.

M4 = D. N. MacKenzie. *The Dialect of Awroman (Hawrāmān-ī Luhōn): Grammatical Sketch, Texts, and Vocabulary* (København: Det Kongelige Danske Videnskabernes Selskab, 1966), 140 p.

Maclean = Arthur John Maclean. *Dictionary of the Dialects of Vernacular Syriac as Spoken by the Eastern Syrians of Kurdistan, North-West Persia and the Plain of Mosul* (Oxford: Clarendon Press, 1901; reprinted: Amsterdam: Philo Press, 1972), 334 p.

Macuch = Rudolf Macuch. *Handbook of Classical and Modern Mandaic* (Berlin : W. de Gruyter, 1965), 649 p.

Mal = Malmisanij. *Zazaca-Türkçe Sözlük = Ferhengê Dımılki-Tırki* (Uppsala: Jina Nû, 1987), 431 p.

Mayrhofer = Manfred Mayrhofer. *Etymologisches Wörterbuch des Altindoarischen* (Heidelberg: C. Winter, 1986-[1990]), [8] fascicles

M. Jastrow = Marcus Jastrow. *Sefer ha-milim = A Dictionary of the Targumim, the Talmud Babli and Yerushalmi, and the Midrashic Literature* (New York: The Judaica Press, 1985, c1971), 2 vols. in 1.

Morg = Georg Morgenstierne. *Indo-Iranian Frontier Languages* (Oslo: Universitetsforlaget, 1973), 2 vols.

Morg2 = Georg Morgenstierne. *Etymological Vocabulary of the Shughni Group* (Wiesbaden: Dr. Ludwig Reichert, 1974), 119 p.

Morg3 = Georg Morgenstierne. "The Development of Iranian R + Consonant in the Shughni Group," in: *W.B. Henning Memorial Volume* (London: Lund Humphries, 1970), pp. 334-42.

Nadeliaev = V. M. Nadeliaev et al. (ed.) *Древнетюркский словарь* [Drevnetiurkskiĭ slovar' =Old Turkic dictionary] (Leningrad: Nauka, 1969), 988 p.

Oraham = Alexander Joseph Oraham. *Oraham's Dictionary of the Stabilized and Enriched Assyrian Language and*

English (Chicago : Consolidated Press, 1943), 576 p.

PN = Eugen Prym & Albert Socin. *Der Neu-Aramaeische Dialekt des Ṭûr 'Abdîn; a. die Texte; b. Übersetzung.* (Göttingen: Vandenhoeck & Ruprecht, 1881), v. 1, pp. 1-5; v. 2, pp. 1-8, [375] [Neo-Aramaic (Ṭūroyo) text in phonetic transcription (v. 1) + German translation (v. 2)]

Pok = Julius Pokorny. *Indogermanisches etymologisches Wörterbuch* (Bern: Francke, 1959-1969), 2 vols.

Pyn-Sm = J. Payne Smith. *A Compendious Syriac Dictionary Founded Upon the Thesaurus Syriacus of R. Payne Smith* (Oxford: The Clarendon Press, 1990 [1903]), 623 p.

Radloff = W. Radloff. *Versuch eines Wörterbuches der Türk-Dialecte* (St. Petersburg : M. Eggers & Co., 1893-1911), 4 v.

Ras = V. S. Rastorgueva. *Sravnitel'no-istoricheskaia grammatika zapadnoiranskikh iazykov* [= Comparative historical grammar of the western Iranian languages] (Moscow: Nauka, 1990), 253 p.

RC = Redhouse *Çağdaş Türkçe-İngilizce Sözlüğü = Contemporary Turkish-English Dictionary* (İstanbul: Redhouse Yayınevi, 1983), 455 p.

RTI = Redhouse *Yeni Türkçe-İngilizce Sözlük = New Redhouse Turkish- English Dictionary* (İstanbul: Redhouse Yayınevi, 1981), 1292 p.

Sabar: Bereshit = Yonah Sabar. *Sefer Bereshit be-Aramit Ḥadashah* [= The Book of Genesis in Neo-Aramaic in the Dialect of the Jewish Community of Zakho], 'Edah ve-Lashon, 9 (Jerusalem: Hebrew University Language Traditions Project, 1983), 294 p.

Sabar: Dict = Yonah Sabar. *A Jewish Neo-Aramaic Dictionary: Dialects of Zakho and Vicinity (Iraqi Kurdistan)* Including Words from Oldest Manuscripts and Bible Translations, Folk Literature and Everyday Speech. typescript (Los Angeles, 1995).

Sabar: Dict2 = Yonah Sabar. *A Jewish Neo-Aramaic Dictionary: Dialects of Amidya, Dihok, Nerwa and Zakho, northwestern Iraq* (Wiesbaden: Harrassowitz, 2002), 337 p.

Sabar: Shemot = *Yonah Sabar. Sefer Shemot be-Aramit Ḥadashah* [= The Book of Exodus in Neo-Aramaic in the Dialect of the Jewish Community of Zakho], 'Edah ve-Lashon, 12 (Jerusalem: Hebrew University Language Traditions Project, 1988), 181 p.

Todd = Terry Lynn Todd. *A Grammar of Dimili (also known as Zaza)*. Doctoral dissertation. (Ann Arbor: University of Michigan, 1985), xv, 277 p.

TS = *Tarama Sözlüğü* (Ankara: Türk Tarih Kurumu, 1963-77), 8 vols.

Vahman = Fereydun Vahman. *Ardā Wirāz Nāmag: The Iranian 'Divina Commedia'* (London & Malmö: Curzon, 1986), 326 p. [Pahlavi (Middle Persian) text and glossary]

vSoden = W. von Soden. *Akkadisches Handwörterbuch* (Wiesbaden: Harrassowitz, 1965-81), 3 vols.

Yar-Shater = Ehsan Yar-Shater. *A Grammar of Southern Tati Dialects* (The Hague & Paris: Mouton, 1969), 276 p.

Place of Origin of Informants

Abbreviation	*Kurdish name*	*"Official" name*	*Province (country)*
Ad	Mensûr/Şemşûr	Adıyaman	Adıyaman (T)
Ag	Agirî	Ağrı	Ağrı (T)
Ak	Akrê	Akrê ('Aqrah)	Dihok (Iq)
Am	Amêdî	Amêdî (al-'Amādīyah)	Dihok (Iq)
Amd	Amûdê	Amûdê ('Āmūdā)	Ḥasakah (S)
Bar	Barzanî (tribe)		Dihok (Iq)
Bg	Çapaxçûr/Çewlîg	Bingöl	Bingöl (T)
Bşk	Başqale	Başkale	Van (T)
Bt	Bilîs	Bitlis	Bitlis (T)
Btm	Êliĥê	Batman	Batman (T)
Bw	Berwarî (tribe)		Dihok (Iq)
Bzd	Bazîd	Doğubayazit	Ağrı (T)
Czr	Cizîra Bohtan	Cizre	Şırnak (T)
Çnr	Çinar	Çınar	Diyarbakır (T)
Dh	Dihok	Dihok (Dahūk)	Dihok (Iq)
Drk	Dêrîk	Derik	Mardin (T)
Dy	Amed/Dîyarbekir	Diyarbakır	Diyarbakır (T)
Dyd	Dîyadîn	Diyadin	Ağrı (T)
Efr	'Efrîn	'Efrîn ('Afrīn)	Ḥalab/Aleppo (S)
Elb	Elbistan	Elbistan	K.Maraş (T)
Elk	Elkî	Beytüşşebap	Hakkâri (T)
Erg	Erẍanî	Ergani	Diyarbakır (T)
Erh	Dihê	Eruh	Siirt (T)
Frq	Farqîn	Silvan	Diyarbakır (T)
Grc	Kercos	Gercüş	Batman (T)
Gz	Dîlok/'Êntab	Gaziantep	Gaziantep (T)
Haz	Ĥazo	Kozluk	Batman (T)
Hk	Colemêrg	Hakkâri	Hakkâri (T)
Hym		Haymana	Ankara (T)

Ig	Îxdîr	Iğdır	Iğdır (T)
Kg	Gêxî	Kiğı	Bingöl (T)
Kk	Kîkan (tribe)		Ḥasakah (S)
Klk	Kûlik	Kâhta	Adıyaman (T)
Kp	Kop	Bulanık	Muş (T)
Kr	Qers	Kars	Kars (T)
Krb	Kerboran	Dargeçit	Mardin (T)
Krç	Dep	Karakoçan	Elâzığ (T)
Kş		Kırşehir	Kırşehir (T)
Mdt	Midyad	Midyat	Mardin (T)
Ml	Milanî (tribe)		(Iran)
Mlt	Meletîye	Malatya	Malatya (T)
Mrş	Mer'aş	[Kahraman]Maraş	K.Maraş (T)
Msl	Mûsil	Mosul (al-Mawṣil)	Nineveh (Iq)
Msr	Misirc	Kurtalan	Siirt (T)
Mş	Mûş	Muş	Muş (T)
Mtk	Motkî	Motki	Bitlis (T)
Mzg	Mêzgir/Mazgêrd	Mazgirt	Tunceli (T)
Nsb	Nisêbîn	Nusaybin	Mardin (T)
Omr	Omerî (tribe)		Mardin (T)
Plt		Polatlı	Ankara (T)
Prw	Perwarî	Pervari	Siirt (T)
Ptn	Panos	Patnos	Ağrı (T)
Qmş	Qamişlok	al-Qāmishlī	Ḥasakah (S)
Qrj	Qerejdax̄	Karacadağ	Diyarbakır (T)
QtrE	Qotur - Elend	Qaṭūr	W. Azarbāyjān (Ir)
Qzl	Qiziltepe/Qoser	Kızıltepe	Mardin (T)
Rh	R̄iha	Ş. Urfa	Ş. Urfa (T)
Rwn	Rewan	Erevan	Armenia
Slm	Selmas	Salmās	W. Azarbāyjān (Ir)
Slv	Silêvanî (tribe)		Zaxo (Iq)
Snd	Sindî (tribe)		Zaxo (Iq)

Sr	Sêrt	Siirt	Siirt (T)
Srk	Sîwerek/Sêrek	Siverek	Ş. Urfa (T)
Şmd	Şemdînan	Şemdinli	Hakkâri (T)
Şng	Şengal	Sinjār	Nineveh (Iq)
Şnx	Şirnex	Şırnak	Şırnak (T)
Şx	Şêxan	Shaykhān	Dihok (Iq)
Tkm	Tatos	Tekman	Erzurum (T)
Trg	Tergewer/Tirgewer	Targavar	W. A̲zarbāyjān (Ir)
Twn	Tetwan	Tatvan	Bitlis (T)
Urm	Ûrmîye/Wirmê	Urūmīyah	W. A̲zarbāyjān (Ir)
Wn	Wan	Van	Van (T)
Wr	Wêranşehir	Viranşehir	Ş. Urfa (T)
Xp	Xarpût	Elâzığ	Elâzığ (T)
Xrs		Khurāsān	Khurāsān (Ir)
Ẍrz	Ẍarzan	Garzan	Batman (T)
Zeb	Zêbarî (tribe)		Dihok (Iq)
Zx	Zaxo	Zākhū	Dihok (Iq)

STANDARD KURDISH ORTHOGRAPHY TABLE

Roman (Hawar)	Cyrillic	Arabic
A a	А а	ئا \ ا *
B b	Б б	ب
C c	Щ щ	ج
Ç ç	Ч ч	چ
Ç’ ç’	Ч’ ч’	چ
D d	Д д	د
[Ḍ] [ḍ]		ض
E e	ә ә	ئه \ ه *
‘E ‘e (E') (e')	ә’ ә’	عه
Ê ê	Е е	ئێ \ ێ *
F f	Ф ф	ف
G g	Г г	گ
H h	h h	ه
Ḧ ḧ	h’ h’	ح
I i	Ь ь	
Î î	И и	ئی \ ی *
J j	Ж ж	ژ
K k	К к	ك
K’ k’	К’ к’	ك
L l	Л л	ل
Ł ł		ڵ
M m	М м	م
N n	Н н	ن
O o	О о	ئۆ \ ۆ *[3]
P p	П п	پ
P’ p’	П’ п’	پ
Q q	Q q	ق
R r	Р р	ر
R̄ r̄	Р’ р’	ڕ
S s	С с	س
Ş ş	Ш ш	ش

3. * Initial vowels begin with a hamzah kursi (ئـ)

[S̱/Ṣ] [s̱/ṣ]	[C̱] [c̱]	ص
T t	Т т	ت
T' t'	Т' т'	ت
[Ṯ/Ṭ] [ṯ/ṭ]	[Ṯ] [т̱]	ط
U u	Ö ö	*ئو \ و
Û û	У у	*ئوو \ وو
V v	В в	ڤ
W w	W w	و [consonant]
X x	Х х	خ
Ẍ ẍ	Г' г'	غ
Y y	Й й	ی [consonant]
Z z	З з	ز
'	'	ع

CALENDAR SYSTEMS

SYSTEM ONE	***SYSTEM TWO***	
(Gregorian)	(Iranian Solar)	
1 January	(Jan-Feb)	11 Behmen بهمن
2 February	(Feb-Mar)	12 Esfend اسفند
3 March	(Mar-Apr)	1 Ferverdīn فروردين
4 April	(Apr-May)	2 Ordībehešt اردى بهشت
5 May	(May-Jun)	3 Xurdad خرداد
6 June	(Jun-Jul)	4 Tīr تير
7 July	(Jul-Aug)	5 Murdad مرداد
8 August	(Aug-Sept)	6 Šehrīver شهريور
9 September	(Sep-Oct)	7 Mehr مهر
10 October	(Oct-Nov)	8 Aban آبان
11 November	(Nov-Dec)	9 Azer آذر
12 December	(Dec-Jan)	10 Dey دى

Please see the detailed charts on the following pages for System One (the Gregorian calendar) and System Two (the Iranian Solar calendar)

SYSTEM ONE

(Gregorian: Christian - International: New Year on January 1)

English names	*Kurdish names*
1 January	Kanûna Paşîn (Kanûna Duwê) / Çileya Paşîn
2 February	Sibat (Şubat)
3 March	Adar (Avdar)
4 April	Nîsan
5 May	Gulan
6 June	Ḧezîran (Xezîran)
7 July	Tîrmeh / Temûz
8 August	Tebax / Ab
9 September	Îlon
10 October	Çirîya Pêşîn (Çirîya Yekê) / Cotmeh
11 November	Çirîya Paşîn (Çirîya Duwê) / Mijdar
12 December	Kanûna Pêşîn (Kanûna Yekê) / Çileya Pêşîn

SYSTEM TWO

(Iranian Solar: New Year on March 21: seasonally based)

	Persian name	*Sorani Kurdish names*
Spring (Mar-Apr) ARIES	1 Ferverdīn فروردین	Nwêr̄oj نوێرۆژ / Xakelêwe خاکەلێوە
(Apr-May) TAURUS	2 Ordībehešt اردی بهشت	Gułan گوڵان / Banemer̄ بانەمەڕ
(May-Jun) GEMINI	3 Xurdād خرداد	Cozerdan جۆزەردان / Codirew جۆدِرەو / Baranbir̄an بارانبڕان / Bextebaran بەختەباران / Kewbedar کەوبەدار [Hejar]

SYSTEM TWO (continued)
(Iranian Solar: New Year on March 21)

	Persian name	*Sorani Kurdish names*	
Summer			
(Jun-Jul)	4 Tīr تیر / Coxînan جۆخینان	Germaciman گەرماجِمان / Pûşpeř پووشپەڕ	CANCER
(Jul-Aug) LEO	5 Murdād مرداد	Xermanan خەرمانان / Mîwegenan میوەگەنان / Gelawêj گەلاوێژ	
(Aug-Sept) VIRGO	6 Šehrīver شهریور	Berewpayîz بەرەوپاییز / Miştaxan مِشتاخان	
Autumn/Fall			
(Sep-Oct) LIBRA	7 Mehr مهر	Mîran میران / Gełarêzan گەڵاریزان [Hejar] / Řezber ڕەزبەر [Karwan] / Sermawez سەرماوەز [Karwan] / Kewçerîn کەوچەرین [Hejar]	
(Oct-Nov) SCORPIO	8 Aban آبان	Gełarêzan گەڵاریزان [Ş. Qezzaz] / Serpełe سەرپەڵە	
(Nov-Dec) SAGITTARIUS	9 Azer آذر	Agirdan ئاگِردان / Sermawez سەرماوەز [G.Mukriyanî]/ Kewberdar کەوبەردار [G. Mukriyanî]	
Winter			
(Dec-Jan) CAPRICORN	10 Dey دی	Sehołbendan سەهۆڵبەندان / Befranbar بەفرانبار	
(Jan-Feb) AQUARIUS	11 Behmen بهمن	Řêbendan ڕێبەندان	
(Feb-Mar) PISCES	12 Esfend اسفند	Řeşemê ڕەشەمێ / Polan پۆلان	

Geographical names [Kurdish to English]

Albanya ئالبانیا Albania
Asya ئاسیا Asia
Awistralya ئاوستralیا Australia
Awistriya ئاوِستریا Austria
Azerbeycan ئازەربەیجان Azerbaijan
Banglades بانگلادەش. Bangladesh
Behreyn بەهرەین Bahraini
Belûçistan بەلووچِستان Baluchistan [region]
Bengal بەنگال Bengal [region]
Welatê Baskî وەلاتێ باسکی Basque Country [Wkp: also Baskistan]
Belçîka بەلچیکا Belgium.
Bosniya û Herzegovîna بۆسنِیا و هەرزەگۆڤینا Bosnia and Hercegovina
Brîtaniya بریتانِیا Britain
Brîtaniya Mezin بریتانِیا مەزِن Great Britain
Bulgaristan بولگارستان Bulgaria
Cezayîr جەزاییر. Algeria [Wkp: Cezayir]
Komara Çekî کۆمارا چەکی Czech Republic
Ç'în چین China
Danîmarka دانیمارکا Denmark
Efẍanistan ئەفغانِستان Afghanistan
Elmanya ئەلمانیا Germany [Wkp: Almanya]
Efrîqa ئەفریقا Africa
Ermenîstan ئەرمەنیستان Armenia
Etyopya ئەتیۆپیا. Ethiopia [Wkp: Etiyopya]
Ewrûpa ئەورووپا Europe
Filipîn فِلِپین. The Philippines
Filistîn فِلِستین Palestine
Firensa فِرەنسا France [Wkp: Fransa]
Flander فلاندەر Flanders [region of Belgium]
Gurcistan گورجِستان Georgia
Hindistan هِندِستان India
Holenda هۆلەندا Holland, the Netherlands
Îndonezya ئیندۆنەزیا Indonesia
Îslend ئیسلەند Iceland
Îraq ئیراق Iraq
Îran ئیران Iran
Îrlanda ئیرلاندا Ireland [Wkp: Îrlenda]
Îsraîl ئیسرائیل Israel [Wkp: Îsrael]
Îtalya ئیتالیا Italy
Japon ژاپۆن Japan
Hungarya هونگاریا Hungary = Macaristan. [Wkp: Hûngarya]
K'atalonya کاتالۆنیا *adj.* Catalonia
K'eneda کەنەدایی Canada [Wkp: Kanada]
K'irwatiya کِرواتی. Croatia [Wkp: Kroatya]
K'oreya Bakur کۆرەیا باکور North Korea
K'oreya Başûr کۆرەیا باشوور South Korea
K'urdistan کوردِستان Kurdistan
K'uweyt کووەیت Kuwait
Lîbya لیبیا Libya
Lubnan لوبنان Lebanese. [Wkp: Libnan]
Macaristan ماجارِستان Hungary
Makedonya ماکەدۆنیا. (Northern) Macedonia
Malta مالتا Malta
Meẍrîb مەغریب *adj.* Morocco [Wkp: Mexribî/Maroko]
Misir مِسِر Egypt
Meksîk مەکسیك Mexico
Mongolya مۆنگۆلیا Mongolia
Norwec نۆروەج. Norway [Wkp: Norwêc]
P'akistan پاکِستان Pakistan
P'olonya پۆلۆنیا Poland
P'ortugal پۆرتوگال Portugal [Wkp: Portûgal]
Qazaxistan قازاخستان Kazakhstan
Qirgizistan قِرگِزستان Kirghizistan
Qeter قەتەر Qatar
Qibris قِبرِس Cyprus
Qudus قودوس Jerusalem
Řomanya ڕۆمانیا Romania
Řûsya ڕووسیا Russia
Sirbistan سِربِستان Serbia [Wkp: Serbistan]
Skotlenda سکۆتلەندا Scotland
Slovakya سلۆڤاکیا Slovakia
Slovenya سلۆڤەنیا Slovenia
Spanya سپانیا Spain
Sûdan سوودان Sudan
Sûrî سووری Syria
Swêd سوێد Sweden
Swîsre سویسرە Switzerland
T'irkiye تِرکِیە Turkey
T'acîkistan تاجیکِستان Tajikistan
T'irkmanistan تِرکمانِستان Turkmenistan [Wkp: Turkmenistan]
T'îbet تیبەت Tibet
T'ûnis توونِس Tunisia
'Uman عومان Oman
'Urdun ئوردون Jordan
Ûkrayna ئووکراینا Ukraine

Ûzbekistan ئووزبەکِستان Uzbekistan

Walonya والۆنیا Wallonia [region of Belgium]

Welatên Yekgirtî yên Emrîka وەلاتێن یەکگِرتی یێن ئەمریکا U.S.A. America [Wkp: Dewletên Yekbûyî yên Amerîkayê]

Wêlz وێلز Wales [Wkp: Wales]

Yemen یەمەن Yemen

Yewnanistan یەونانِستان Greece

A ئا

abdestxane ئابدەستخانە (SK) = toilet. See **avdestxane**.

abid ئـــابـِــد *m.&f.* **().** devout, pious person; ascetic: •***Abidek* li wê derê heye, ibadet dike û Quranê dixwînit** (Rnh 2:17, 308) There is a *pious man* there, he worships, and reads the Koran. {also: [âbid] عابد (JJ); <‘abid> عابد (HH)} <Ar ‘ābid عابد = worshipper, adorer' [Rnh/K/IFb/JJ/HH/OK]

aborî ئـابـۆری *f.* **(-ya;).** 1) economy (JB3/IF); 2) {also: ebûrî [3] (K)} living, life, existence (K); sustenance, support (TF); 3) *[adj.]* economic(al), financial (A): •**Endamên malbata min ji min hêvî dikirin ku ez zanîngehê biqedînim, bibim xwedî peywir û alîkarîya *aborî* bi wan re bikim** (Wlt 1:35, 16) Members of my family expected me to finish college, get a job, and help them out *financially*. [(neol)A/JB3/IF/(GF)/TF//K]

abring ئابرِنگ = sheep shears. See **hevring**.

abrîng ئابرینگ = sheep shears. See **hevring**.

acer ئاجەر (Wkt) = new. See **‘ecer**.

aciz ئـاجِـز/‘**aciz** عـــاجـِــز *adj.* [+**ji**]. 1) unhappy, upset, despairing, sick [and tired] (of) : •**"Çima tu naxwî"? Go: "Bavo, ez *ji* goşt *aciz* bûme"** (L) "Why don't you eat?" He said, "Dad, I'm *sick of* meat" •**Gelikî bêna min tenge, ez *acizim*** (L) I am troubled and *anxious* •**Seydayê min pirr bi vê nezanîna min êşiya û *aciz* bû** (Wlt 2:66, 2) My teacher was very grieved and *troubled* by this gap in my knowledge [lit. 'by this ignorance of mine'] •**Wellah, ez gelikî *ji* canê xwe *aciz* bûme** (L) By God, I'm *fed up with* my life; -**‘aciz kirin** (SK) to disturb, bother, upset: •**Û neferatêt quşonî ket-ket tê-bigehînin ko ser-bi-xo r̄e‘îyetê *‘aciz neken* we milletî dil-xoş biken** (SK 56:658) And they should give the personnel of the army to understand, one by one, that they should not independently *annoy* the populace, and they should placate the people; 2) tired, exhausted (B); 3) uncomfortable, suffering: •[**Zanî ku mar kûvîyek dabeland lê strûyên** [sterène] **wî neçûne xwarê û mane li gewrîya wî da û *jê aciz* bû**] (BG, 25) He understood that the snake had swallowed a wild animal, but its horns had not gone down and had stayed in his throat and he was *suffering from* this. {also: ‘eciz (Z-2); êciz (B-2); [âdjiz] عــاجــز (JJ); <‘aciz> عـــاجـــز (HH); [ajeze] (BG) = ennuyé, torturé} <Ar ‘ājiz عـــاجــز = 'powerless, unable' {acizayî; acizî; êcizayî} [L/B/JJ/HH/SK//Z-2//BG] <bêk'êf; bihecîn; dilteng; qehirîn; tengav>

aciza•yî ئاجزایی/‘**aciza•yî** عاجِزایی *f.* **(;•yê).** 1) being unhappy, upset, despairing, sick [and tired] of; 2) fatigue, exhaustion (B). {also: acizî (IF); êcizayî (B-2); [âjezaiè] (BG) = ennui, peine, torture} [B/BG//IF] <aciz; diltengî>

acizî ئـــاجِـــزی (IF) = being unhappy; exhaustion. See **acizayî**.

acûr ئـاجـوور (A/IFb/CS/CCG) = type of cucumber. See **‘ecûr**.

aç'ar ئـاچـار/**aç'ar̄** ئـاچـاڕ [K] *m.* **(; aç'êr).** rye: -**nanê aç'ar** (B/K) rye bread. {syn: şilêl} Cf. T çavdar [K/B] <ceh; genim>

ada ئـــادا *f.* **(;-ê).** island. {also: ade II (B); [āda] ادا (JJ)} {syn: cizîr; dûrgeh; girav II} < T ada = 'island' [F/K/JJ//B]

Adar ئـــــادار *f.* **(-a;-ê).** March *(month)*: •***Adar* e, dew li dar e** (AB) It is *March*, **dew** [yoghurt & water] is in the wood [=wooden churner] *[prv.]* •[**Hejde bi *Adarê*, milyakete tête xwarê, gazî dikete bihar e**] (BG) On *March* 18th, the angel comes down, and shouts out, "It's springtime!" *[prv.]* •**Deynê Şibatê li *Adarê* ye** (L-1, #95, 202) February's debt is due in *March*. {also: [adar آدار/hadar هـــــادار/[azer آذر]] (JJ); <adar> آدار (HH); [adâr] (BG); [ādār] (RJ)} Syr ādar ܐܕܪ [Heb adar אדר] --> Ar ādār آذار; *corresponds to last part of* Reşemê ڕەشـەمـێ/Polan پـۆلان (P esfand اسـفـنـد) [Pisces] *& 1st part of* Newroz[mang] [نەورۆز[مانگ/Xakelêwe خاکەلێوە (P farvardīn فـروردیـن) [Aries] [K/A/JB3/IFb/B/JJ/HH/GF/TF/OK/BG/RJ]

ad•e I ئـادە *m.*(Bw)/*f.*(K/OK) **(•ê/ ;).** weed: •**Subahî dê çîn nav zevya pişt gundî, tûtin, bacansorka gelek *ade* yê tê hatî** (Bw) Tomorrow we will go to the fields behind the village, there are many *weeds* there among the tobacco and eggplant: -**ade kirin** (SK) to weed: •**Min bîstanek çandîye. Were, biçîn, *ade bikeyn*** (SK 21:193) I have planted a garden. Come, let us go and *weed* it. {also: ede (K-2); 'ede (K); [ada] ادا (JJ-Rh)} [Bw/IFb/SK/OK//JJ-Rh//K] <aşêf; gîya; xepar>

ade II ئادە (B) = island. See **ada**.

'adet عادەت [JJ/HH/SK]/**adet** ئادەت [A/IFb/GF/OK/AD] *m./f.*(OK/AD) **(-ê/ ;).** 1) {syn: kevneşop; r̄ewişt; tîtal; t'or̄e} custom: **•Çawa *'edetê* miletê Muẍur-Zemînê dixast** (FK-eb-1) As the *custom* of the people of M.Z. demanded; **-t'erka edet dan** (K)/~ **kirin** (SK) to break a habit, abandon a custom: **•Wextê Nadir Şah ew ḧukme kir, li her cîyekî ew *'adet hate terk kirin*** (SK 11:104) When Nadir Shah made this command, the *custom was abandoned* everywhere; 2) habit: **•Ewcar wextê dîsa li-ser *'adetê* xo marî xo li stukira r̄îwî aland û derbaz bûn, marî xo gîro kir, xokêt xo nekirinewe** (SK 2:12) Then, when the snake wound himself round the fox's neck again in the usual way [lit. 'upon his *habit*'] and they crossed over, the snake delayed and did not unwind its coils. {also: adet (A/IFb/GF/AD); 'adet (SK); 'edet (K/B); edet (F); [âdet] عـــادت (JJ); <'adet> عـــادت (HH)} < Ar 'ādah عادة--> T âdet [FK-1/K/B//F//A/IFb/GF/OK/AD//JJ/HH/SK]

adir ئادِر (TF) = epilepsy. See **'edro**.

adodik ئـــادۆدِك (BF/BFK) = stick for uprooting plants. See **adûde**.

adu ئادو (IFb) = enemy; competitor. See **'edû**.

aduda ئـــادودا (OrK) = stick for uprooting plants. See **adûde**.

adûde ئـــادوودە *f.* **().** long wooden stick with sharp tip for uprooting thorny plants, such as *kereng* (qv.) [amûra derhênana kengirê; = T kazgıç]. {also: adodik (BF/BFK); aduda (OrK)} {syn: xilç} [FJ/GF//OrK//BF/BFK] <bist I; misas>

aferandin ئافەراندِن (TF) = to create. See **afirandin**.

Afganî ئافگانی (BF/Wkt) = Afghani. See **Efẍanî**.

afir̄ ئـــافِر/**afir** ئـــافِر [IS] *f./m.*(Bw) **(;-ê).** 1) (wooden) feeding-trough, manger (Msr/Bw); 2) stable: **•Hema wî çaxî Borê Memê k'etibû bîrê, zik lê werimî bû, Memê *afir̄*da ber serê Bor rûniştibû û digirîa** (FK-eb-1) Just at that time Mem's horse Bor had fallen into a well, his belly had swollen up, and Mem sat in the *stable* at Bor's head and wept. {also: hafir̄, m. (Bw); [âfir] افـــــــر (JJ); <afir> افر(HH)} < O Ir *ā-hvar-ana (='that which provides food' agent noun) ; Mid P āxwarr- = 'manger, stable' (M3); Sgd ''xwyr- [āxwaraya- *causative*] = 'to feed'; cf. T afır [Bitlis; Varto, Muş; Kırıkhan, Amik ovası, Gâvurdağı, Hatay; Karaözü, Gemerek-Sivas] = 'feeding trough in a stable' (DS, v. 1, p. 72) [Msr/B/JJ/HH//Bw] <axur>

afirandin ئـــافِـــرانـــدِن *vt.* **(-afirîn-).** 1) {syn: çêkirin; xuliqandin} to create, make; to invent: **•Her berhem divê li gor dem û rewşa ku tê de *hatiye afirandin*, were nirxandin** (Wlt 1:39, 11) Every work of art should be evaluated according to the time and conditions in which it *was created* **•Karên wiha jî divê di bin çavdêriyên Neteweyên Yekbûyî (NY) de *bên afirandin*** (Wlt 1:37, 16) Such things should *be created* under the supervision of the UN **•Xwedê *em afirandin* wê dîsa jî biafirîne** (IFb) God *created us* and he will create again **•Zargotina me pir̄ dewlemend e. Miletê me ew zargotin *afirandiye*, niha jî *diafirîne*. Ew kaniyeke gur̄ e** (Wlt 2:59, 16) Our folklore is very rich. Our people *has created* this folklore, and *is* still *creating* it. It is a gushing source; 2) {syn: berhem} *[f.]* (literary) work, work of art, opus (Ber/K). {also: aferandin (TF); efrandin (Ber/F); 'efirandin (-'efirîn-) (K/B); [afrāndin] افراندن (JJ)} Cf. P āfarīdan آفریدن [Ber/F/JJ/ /Wlt/JB3/IFb/GF//TF//K/B]

afret ئافرەت *f.* **(;-ê).** woman, lady, female person: **•Ew hozana ji layê *afretê*ve dihête vehandin** ('Ebdulla, B.Y. Hozana afretan di edebê Kurdîda, 16) That poetry which is composed by *women* [lit. '*woman*']. {syn: jin; k'ulfet; pîrek} <Ar 'awrah عــــــورة = 'pudendum, genitals, *used as synecdoche for the entire woman*' --> T avrat; Sor afret ئـــافـــرەت = 'woman (used in addressing one's wife)' ['Ebdulla/K/IFb/FJ/ZF/Wkt/CS]

Afrîkayî ئـــافـــريـــكـــايـــی (BF/ZF3/Wkp) = African. See **Efrîqayî**.

Afrîkî ئافریکی (BF/ZF3) = African. See **Efrîqayî**.

Afrîqeyî ئافریقەیی (IFb) = African. See **Efrîqayî**.

afsûn ئافسوون (IFb) = magic. See **efsûnî**.

afû ئافوو (B) = pardon. See **'efû**.

Afxanî ئافخانی (Wkt) = Afghani. See **Efẍanî**.

aga ئاگا (A) = information, knowledge. See **agah**.

agadar ئـــاگـــــادار (K/A/CS) = informed, aware. See **agahdar**.

agadarî ئـــاگـــــاداری (K/A/CS) = information, being informed. See **agahdarî**.

agah ئـــاگـــاه *m.* **().** information, knowledge, awareness: ***-fk-î* agah bûn ji *ft-î*** (SK) to be aware of: **•Eslen min tesdîq nekirîye û min negotîye baş e û min *agahî* ji wê şolê nîye** (SK 54:592) I haven't confirmed it and I haven't said it's okay, and I have no *knowledge* of that affair **•Ez di xewêda me, min**

***agah* ji hingo nîye** (SK 28:256) I'm asleep, I cannot hear you [=I have no *awareness* of you] **•Melaê mêwan *agah* ji tedbîr o ḧekaêta Mam Bapîr o imam nebo** (SK 17:163) The guest mullah was not *aware* of the plan or of the story of Mam Bapir and the imam **•Sebr ken. Ewan xatir-cem in, hîç *agah* ji me nîye** (SK 48:488) Be patient. They are sure of themselves, they are not *aware* of us. {also: aga (A); agahî, f. (SK-2/ZF-2); ageh (CS-2/Tsab-2/JB1-S); <agah> آگـــــاه (HH)} {syn: hay I} Cf. P āgāh آگـاه = 'aware, informed' & āgāhī آگاهی = 'information, notice'; Sor aga ئاگا = 'information, knowledge' [SK/K/IFb/HH/ZF/Tsab/CS//A//JB1-S]

agahdar ئاگاهدار *adj.* informed (about), well-informed, aware (of), knowledgeable (about), versed (in), conversant (with): **-agahdar bûn** (IFb/ZF) to be informed about: **•...Pirr li kerê xwe *agahdar bûm*, hetanî ku vê dawiyê ez ji hinek kirinên wî tirsiyam** (HYma 12) I *paid attention* to my donkey, until recently I was frightened by some of his actions; **-agahdar kirin** (IFb/ZF) to inform, let s.o. know: **•Ez ko nexwaş bûm min bavê xwe *agahdar kir*** (IFb) As soon as I got sick, I *let* my father *know* **•Te çima *ez agahdar nekirim*?** (IFb) Why *didn't* you *let me know*? {also: agadar (K-2/A/CS-2); agehdar (GF/FJ/CS-2)} {syn: haydar; serwext} < agah + -dar; Sor agadar ئـــاگــــادار = 'informed, having knowledge (of stg.)' [HYma/K/IFb/ZF/CS//A//GF/FJ]

agahdarî ئـاگـاهـداری *f.* **().** information, knowledge, being informed about stg.: **•Dixwazim li ser azbata qehremanê vê çîrokê ji xwendevana re hinek *agahdarî* bidim** (ZZ-1, 172) I want to give the readers some *information* about the ancestry of the hero of this story. {also: agadarî (K-2/A/CS-2); agehdarî (GF)} {syn: haydarî} Sor agadarî ئاگاداری = 'watchfulness, vigilance, alertness; care' [ZZ/K/IFb/ZF/CS//A//GF]

agahî ئاگاهی, f. (SK/ZF) = information, knowledge. See **agah**.

ageh ئاگەه (CS/Tsab/JB1-S) = information, knowledge. See **agah**.

agehdar ئـاگـەهـدار (GF/FJ/CS) = informed, aware. See **agahdar**.

agehdarî ئاگەهداری (GF) = information, being informed. See **agahdarî**.

agir ئـــاگِـــر *m.* **(-ê; êgir** [BK/K], **vî agirî).** fire, flame: **•Her kesê peşkekê ji awa tizbîyêt min wexotewe, cendekê wî *agirê* cehennemê nabînît** (SK 12:119) Whoever drinks a drop of the water from my rosary, his body will not see *the fire* of Hell **•Qehwe danî ser *êgir*** (Qzl) She put the coffee on *the fire*; **-agir berdan** (K) to set fire to: ***•Agir berdide* qesir û qûnaxa xo** (Z-3) He *sets fire to* his manor; **-agir k'etin** = to catch fire: **•Çiqas xirabyê bikî, *agir* be'rê *nak'ewe*** (Dz) No matter how much evil you do, the sea *won't catch fire* [lit. 'fire won't fall to the sea'] *[prv.]* **•Ko *agir* li çiyê *ket*, ter û hişk tev de dişewitin** (BX) When the mountain *catches fire*, wet and dry burn together *[prv.]*; **-li ser agir bûn** (ZF) to be in a difficult situation: **•Bûka reben *li ser agir e*** (İ.Tepe. Apê Kal, 19) The poor daughter-in-law *is screwed* (i.e., *in an awkward position*) **•Xelkê Sûrê *li ser agir e*** (Doğruhaber 9.11.15) The people of Sur *are in trouble*. {also: **ar I**; [àghir آگـــر /ār آر] (JJ); <agir> آگـــر (HH); [âguerr] (BG); [āger] (RJ)} {syn: alav I; p'êt I} [Pok. āt(e)r- 69.] 'fire': M. Schwartz: *ādur --> *ā'ur --> āgur & āwur & ār. cf. M Per ādur (<O Ir *ātṛm *acc.*, cf. Av ātrəm *acc.*) --> P āδar [Āẕer] آذر in compounds & as name of month. P ātaš/ātiš آتش < Mid P ātaxš, a learned borrowing from Av ātarš *nom.*; Sor agir ئاگر/ar ئار/awir ئاگر; Za adir *m.* (Todd); Hau ɛr *m.* (M4) [K/A/JB3/IFb/B/JJ/HH/SK/GF/TF/OK/BK/BG/RJ/MK2] See also **ar I**. <berheste; bizot; heste; k'irpît; neftik; řejî; tenî; xwelî>

agirbazî ئـاگِـربـازی *f.* **(;-yê).** fireworks, fire crackers: **•Hinek ciwan diçin li serbanî *agirbazî* (havaî fîşek) diteqînin** (çandname.com: Dawetên Herêma Mûşê-3) Some youths go up onto the roof and set off *fire crackers*. Cf. P ātašbāzī آتـشـبـازی; Sor agirbazî ئـاگِربـازی = 'playing with fire; firewords' [Çandname/K/IFb/GF/ZF3/Wkt/SS/CS]

agirkuj ئـاگِـرکـوژ *m.* **().** fireman, firefighter. [K/A/IFb/GF/RF/RZ]

agirp'arêz ئـاگِـرپـارێـز (B/K/GF) = fire worshipper. See **agirp'erest**.

agirp'arêzî ئـاگِـرپـارێـزی (B/K/GF) = fire worship. See **agirp'erestî**.

agirp'eres ئـاگِـرپـەرەس (K/A/JJ) = fire worshipper. See **agirp'erest**.

agirp'eresî ئـاگِـرپـەرەسی (K/A) = fire worship. See **agirp'erestî**.

agirp'erest ئاگِرپەرەست *m.* **().** fire worshipper: **•Meriv dibêje qeyê *agirperestekî* dema medan e** (Tof)

One could say he was *a fire worshipper* from the time of the Medes. {also: agirp'arêz (B/K-2/GF-2); agirp'eres (K/A); agirperist (AD); [àghir-peres] آگـــرپـــرس (JJ)} Cf. P āẕar'parast آذرپـــرســـت; Sor agirperist ئاگرپەرست [Tof/IFb/GF/TF//AD//K/A/JJ//B]

agirp'erestî ئاگِرپەرستى *f.* **(;-yê).** fire worship. {also: agirp'arêzî (B/K-2/GF-2); agirp'eresî (K/A)} Cf. P āẕar'parastī آذرپرستى [IFb/GF/TF//K/A//B]

agirperist ئـــاگِـــرپـــەرســـت (AD) = fire worshipper. See **agirp'erest**.

ah û zar ئاه و زار *m.* **().** cry(ing), weep(ing), sob(bing): **-ah û zar kirin** (B)/**ahûzarî kirin** (HCK) to sob, cry, weep: **•Keçikê gelek *ahûzarî kir*** (HCK-1, 207) The girl *sobbed* a lot. {also: ahûzarî (HCK); cf. also <ah> آه (HH) = 'sighing, regret'} {syn: girî} Cf. Sor ah û nałe ئاه و نالە = 'groaning, cries of grief/distress' [HCK//K/B/CS]

ahûzarî ئاهووزارى (HCK) = sob(bing). See **ah û zar**.

aîdiyet ئـــائـــيـــدِيـــەت *f.* **(-a;).** (sense of) belonging, connectedness, membership: **•Dema ku mirov keresteyên maddî yên wekî cil û berg, tiştên xeml û xêzê, çêkirina peyker û avahiyan mêze bike hebûna *aîdiyeteke* kolektîf diyar e** (YPA, 13) When one looks at concrete materials such as clothing, ornaments, sculpture and buildings, the existence of a collective sense of *belonging* [identity] is apparent **•Mesela me û *aîdiyeta* me ya dewletê jî weha ye** (Nbh 132:3) The story of us and our sense of *belonging* to the state is like that too. <Ar 'ā'id عـائـد = 'returning; belonging (to)' --> 'ā'idīyah عـائـديـة = 'belonging (n.), being part of, membership' [Nbh/YPA/ZF] <endam>

aj ئـــاژ *f.* **().** sprout, young shoot, sucker, bud [T filiz, sürgün]: **-aj dan** (ZF3) to put forth shoots, sprout, grow: **•Pêmirîşk: ...Hin cureyên wan di nava avê de *aj didin*, heşîn dibin ... ji xeynî cihên pirr sar û pirr germ, li her derê *aj dide*** (Wkp:Çûng) Buttercups: Some types *put forth shoots* in the water [and] grow ... except for very cold and very hot places, it grows everywhere. {also: ajda (Kmc-1086)} {syn: bişkoj; gupik III; terh; zîl} Cf. Sor weç وەچ = 'shoot, sending forth of new growth' [Bêrtî tribe (between Bingöl & Xarput)/IFb/ZF3/FD/Wkt/CS//Kmc-1084]

ajda ئاژدا (Kmc-1086) = sprout, shoot. See **aj**.

ajnaberî ئاژنابەرى, f. (JB3/OK) = swimming. See **ajnê**.

ajne ئاژنە (IFb) = swimming. See **ajnê**.

ajnê ئـاژنـێ *f.* **().** swimming: **•Ew bo *ajnê* zîrek e** (FS) S/he is skilled *at swimming*; **-ajnê kirin** (Rh) to swim. {also: ajnaberî, f. (JB3/OK); ajne (IFb)} {syn: avjenî; melevanî; sobahî} [Pok. snā-/snə-(t-)/ snāu-/sn-eu-/sn-et- 971.] 'to flow, moisture': Skt snáti/snāyate = 'bathes'; Av snayeitē = 'washes, rinses'; P šanā شنا = 'swimming'; =Sor mele مەلە; Za asnaw [Ad/Kg/GF/Rh/FS/G//IFb//JB3/OK]

ajo ئاژۆ (G/GF) = driver. See **ajotvan**.

ajok ئاژۆك (GF) = driver. See **ajotvan**.

ajokar ئاژۆكار (FD/ZF3/Wkt) = driver. See **ajotvan**.

ajotin ئـــاژۆتِـــن *vt.* **([d]ajo-).** 1) to drive, conduct, lead: **•Xort da pey boẍ, dêla boẍ girt...anî hat girêda cotê xwe, *ajot*** (J) The young man ran after the bull, took hold of the bull's tail...He took it, came, [and] tied it to his plough, [and] *drove it on* **•Hat dîna xwe daê, xort wê boẍ girêdaye û *dajo*** (J) He went to have a look, [he saw that] the youth had tied up the bull and *was driving it* **•*Bajon*, emê herin** (L) *Drive* [your horses] onward, let's go; 2) {syn: dirêj kirin[c]; domîn; k'işandin[6]; k'udandin; vek'işîn [2]} to take place, last, continue, go on: **•Ji destpêka dema A. virda heta niha asîmîlasyonek (mêjîşûştin) fireh li vî beşê Kurdistanê *dajo*** (Ber) Since the beginning of the period of A., assimilation (brainwashing) *has gone on* widely in this part of Kurdistan **•...Lê vê demê jî kurt *ajot*** (Ber) ...But this period *lasted* [a] short [time]. {also: hajotin (M/Bw); [ajoutin اژوتـــيـــن/hajoutin هـاژوتـيـن] (JJ); <ajotin آژوتن (tajo) (تـاژو)> (HH); [ajotene (ad'ajome)] (BG) = pousser une bête} Sor ajûtin ئاژووتن (ajû) (W&E)/ajwan ئاژوان (ajo) (M-Mukri)/hajo[ş]tin هاژۆشتن (M-Arbil). *Often linked with* [Pok kseubh- 625.] 'to rock back and forth': Av xšaob- = 'to incite to motion, excite' & P āšoftan آشـفـتـن (-āšūb-) (آشـوب) = 'to disturb, agitate' (see Tsb 40 & 50) [J/BX/K/A/JB3/IF/B/JJ/HH/BG//M/Bw]

ajotkar ئاژۆتكار (ZF3/CS) = driver. See **ajotvan**.

ajotvan ئـــاژۆتـــڤـــان *m.&f.* **(-ê/-a;-î/ê).** driver, chauffeur: **•*Ajotvanê* tirumbêlê canê xwe ji dest da** (kurdistan media.com 16.iii.2016) *The driver of* the car lost his life **•Ew *ajovanê* taksiyê ye** (Wkt) He is a taxi *driver* **•Hêj nasnameya *ajokarê* wê nehatiye diyarkirin** (Wkt:aa.com.tr/kk i.2016) The identity of its *driver* has not been announced. {also: ajo (G/GF); ajok (GF-2); ajokar (FD/ZF3/Wkt-2); ajotkar (ZF3-2/CS); ajovan (ZF3-2/Wkt)} [(neol)IFb/AD//Wkt//FD/ZF3//CS//G/GF]

ajovan ئاژۆڤان (ZF3/Wkt) = driver. See **ajotvan**.

akincî ئـاكِـنـجـى *m.&f.* **(-yê/;).** inhabitant, resident: **•Ew *akincîyê* Zaxo ye** (FS) He is an *inhabitant* of

Zakho He •**Ew li bajarî *akincî* ye** (FS) He is a *resident* in the city. {syn: niştecih} <T akıncı = 'raider' (<akın + cı) [VoA/OK/Bw/FS] <bineci; binelî>

akoşk•e ئاكۆشكە *f.* (;•ê). window: •**Tu nêzîkî min bî ezê xwe xim, ji *akoşkê* bavêm** (HCK-3, #2, 22) If you come near me, I will throw myself out *the window*. {also: akûşke (K/B-2)} {syn: p'encere; şibak} < Rus okoško окошко, *dim. of* okno окно = 'window' [HCK/B//K] <p'ace>

akûşke ئاكووشكە (K/B) = window. See **akoşke**.

al ئال *f.* (-a;). (war) banner, flag: •***Ala* min pêl dide** (AB) My *flag* is waving. {also: ala, m. (-yê;) (Bw/IFb/GF/OK)} {syn: bêraq} Cf. T al = 'red, scarlet': perhaps banners were often red; Sor ała ئاڵا = 'standard, pen' [AB/K/A/JB3/TF//Bw/IFb/GF/OK]

ala ئالا, m. (-yê;) (Bw/IFb/GF/OK) = flag. See **al**.

alan ئالان (IFb/RF) = echo. See **olan**.

alandin ئالاندِن *vt.* (**-alîn-/-alê[n]-**). 1) to wind, twist (a rope) (K): •**Marî jî xo li stukira r̄îwî *aland*** (SK 2:11) And the snake *wound* itself round the fox's neck; 2) {syn: weranîn} to wrap (JB3): •**Memê qap'ûtê hêşîn serê xwe *dalîne*** (EP) M. *wraps* the green overcoat around his head [to protect him from the evil eye]; 3) to interlace (JB3). [Pok. 3. al- 27] 'to wander/roam about aimlessly; also, to be emotionally lost' -- see **alîn**. [Z-1/EP-7/K/JB3/B/SK]

alastin ئالاستِن *vt.* (**-alês-**). to lick: •**Sultan Êzî go ji Qadî şiro re: "Kas ra ke, çîçek danî ser nînoka xa". Go: "*Balêse*!" Weqtê *alist*, li ezmana qapi ve bû** (LY) Sultan Ezi said to the judge, "Pick up the cup, and put a little on your fingernail." [Then] he said, "*Lick* [it]!" When he *licked it,* in the heavens a door opened up. {also: alêstin; alistin (LY); alîstin (-alîs-) (M/FS); [alistin الستين/listin لستين] (JJ); <alîstin آليستن (dalîse) (داليسه)> (HH); [lis kirin] (RJ)} [Pok. leiĝh- 668.] 'to lick': Skt √lih [léḍhi]; O Ir √l/raiz; Av raēz-; Sgd rys-; Khotanese Saka rräys- [rrəz-]; Pamir dialects: Yidgha & Munji nerīz-; Ormuri las-yēk; Parachi līs- [lušt]; Sanglechi lēs-; Wakhi lix̌-; Shughni ∂ak- (Morg); Southern Tati dialects: Takestani u-listan (Yar-Shater); P līsīdan ليسيدن/ lištan لشتن (-lēs-)(ليش)/ listan لستن/ līštan ليشتن; Sor lêsîn[ewe] لێسین[ەوە]/ listin[ewe] لستن[ەوە]; Za lêsenã [listiş] (Srk); Hau lêsay (lês-) vt. (M4); Cf. Arm lizel լիզել; Rus lizat' лизать [L/F/K/JB3/B/SC//JJ/LY//HH//M/FS//RJ]

alav I ئالاڤ *f.* (**-a;-ê**). flame. {also: [alaoû] علو (JJ)} {syn: agir & ar I; p'êt I} Cf. P 'alov علو --> T alev [Z-1/K/B//JJ]

alav II ئالاڤ *m.* (**-ê;**). instrument, tool, utensil. {syn: amîr; p'ergal II[3]} [Qzl/IFb/GF/FJ]

Albanî ئالبانى *adj.* Albanian. {also: Elbanî (Wkt/CS)} {syn: *Arnawidî} Sor Elbanî ئەلبانی [IFb/BF/SS//Wkt/CS]

alek ئالەك *f.* (**-a;**). cheek. {syn: gup; hinarik; lame; r̄û [3]} Cf. T al = 'scarlet' [Snd/IFb/ZF3/FS]

alêstin ئالێستِن = to lick. See **alastin**.

alfabe ئالفابە *f.* (**-ya;**). alphabet: •**Gelê me xerîbê *alfabeya* xwe ye** (Wlt 1:21, p. 2) Our people is a stranger to its own *alphabet* •**Tê xuyakirin ku, nemir du tîp ji *alfabeya* xwe avêtine, ew herdu tîp ev in: Ḧ - Ẍ** (Wlt 1:42, 10) It seems that the dearly departed [=Celadet Bedirxan] removed two letters from his *alphabet*; those two letters are Ḧ and Ẍ. {also: alfavît, f. (B); alifba, m. (K); elfabe (K/JB3); elîfba (Ber); elîfbê (A)} [AB/Wlt//K/JB3//A//Ber//B] <tîp>

alfavît ئالفاڤیت (B) = alphabet. See **alfabe**.

alif ئالِف *m.* (**-ê;**). fodder, forage, feed *(for farm animals)*: •**Wî *alifê* zivis̱tanê bo pezê xo berhev kir** (FS) He gathered winter *fodder* for his sheep; **-alif kirin** (K/B)/**~dan** (K) to feed, give feed to *(animals)*. {also: [alef] علف (JJ); <alif> آلف (HH)} {syn: alîk I; êm} <Ar 'alaf علف = 'fodder, forage, provender'; Sor ałif ئاڵِف = 'fodder grass' [F/K/A/IFb/B/HH/SK/OK/FS/BF/ZF3//JJ//(GF)] <p'ût I>

alifba ئالِفبا, m. (K) = alphabet. See **alfabe**.

alik ئالِك *f.* (). small, thin bird; starling, zool. *Sturnidae* [Fr étourneau]: •**Teyr tîrê [=tirî] dixwin, bextê *alik* bi reş e** (L) All the birds eat grapes, only the *starling* has no luck [lit. 'the *starling's* luck is black'] *[prv.]*. {also: alîk II (IFb/GF/FS)} {syn: garanîk; r̄eşêlek; zerzûr} [HB/L/A//IFb/GF/ZF3/FS]

alistin ئالِستِن (LY/JJ) = to lick. See **alastin**.

alizîn ئالِزین (Bw) = to get entangled. See **alozyan**.

alî ئالى *m.* (**-[y]ê;**). side, direction: •***alîyê* çep[ê]** (K/B/MK2) left *side* •***alîyê* rast[ê]** (K/B/MK2) right *side* •**[li] wî *alî*** = in that *direction*; on that *side*; **-alîyê...** = in the direction of, facing: •***alîê* r̄ohilatê** (Ba2) *facing* east(ward) •**Ser p'êşa Dûmanlûêye *alîê* Zerîbxane** (Ba2) On the slope of [Mount] Dumanlu *facing* Zeribkhaneh; **-[xwe li] alîyê *fk-î* girtin** (K/B) to support s.o., side with, take s.o.'s side (in a dispute); **-alî kirin** (Msr/MK2) to help. See **arîk'arî**; **-xwe ji ber *ft-î* dan alî** (Kk) = to shirk one's responsibility. See under **dan I**; **-ji alîyê**

... **ve** =: a) by *(agent with passive verb)* {syn: bi destê...; ji terefê...}: •**Lê belê, pê hisiyan ku çandiniyên wan *ji alîyê* leşkerên Tirk *ve*, hatine şewitandin** (CTV142) But they found out that their crops had been burned *by* the Turkish soldiers; b) from the point of view of: •**Bûyera revandina Cevat Soysal, îro-jî *ji alîyê* hûqûqî *ve*, hate nîqaş kirin** (CTV184) The incident of the kidnapping of Cevat Soysal has been debated today also *from* a legal *standpoint*; -**ji her alî** (K)/**ji ȟemû alîya[n]** (K/B)/**ji her layekîwe** (SK) from all sides, from every which way, from all around: •**Ewcar *ji her layekîwe* xulamêt paşa xiȓ bûnewe, dest bi şeȓî kirin** [sic] (SK 24:225) Then the pasha's men gathered *from all sides* and began to fight. {also: la (SK/Bw/Zeb); [ali] الى (JJ)} {syn: hêl II; mil [3]; k'êlek; tenişt; teref} *This word exemplifies how O Iranian **-rd-** becomes **-l-** in Kurdish*: O Ir *arda- *m.*: Av arəδa- *m.* = 'side, half'; Skr ardhá- = 'half' & árdha- = 'side'; Oss ārdæg = 'half'; Sor la لا = 'side, direction, part, half' [F/K/A/IFb/B/JJ/JB1-A/GF/TF/OK/MK2//SK/Bw/Zeb]

alîgir ئالیگر *m.&f.* **(-ê/;).** supporter, backer, partisan. {syn: mêldar [1]; piştîvan} {alîgirî} [(neol)IFb/GF/TF/ZF3] <alînegir>

alîgirî ئالیگری *f.* **(-ya;).** support, backing: -**alîgirîya *fk-ê* kirin** (Wlt) to back, support: •**Ji 165 nûnêran ... 60-70 bi destnivîsên îmzeyên xwe *alîgirîya me dikin*** (Wlt 1:37, 16) Out of 165 representatives ... 60-70 *support us* with their signatures. {syn: mêldarî; piştgirî} [(neol)Wlt/TF/ZF3] <alîgir>

alîjiyan bûn ئالیژیان بوون *vi.* **(alîjiyan -b-).** to die, pass away, decease: •**Kawî[s] Axa di sala 1936'an de *alîjiyan dibe*** (Antolojiya Dengbêjan, v. 2, 159) K.A. *passes away* in the year 1936 •**Serokê nemir di 1ê adarê de çavên xwe ji jiyana bêbext re digirt û dest bi jiyaneke bêdawî dikir. Herçî ew *alîjiyan bûbû* jî, wî dilê gelê xwe de ciyekî taybetî girtibû** (PDK-Xoybûn website) The immortal leader closed his eyes on deceitful life on the first of March and began a life without end. Even though he *had passed away*, he had left a special place in the heart of his people •**Tê gotin ku Meyrem Xan di sala 1949'an de li Bexdayê *alîjiyan bûye*** (Antolojiya Dengbêjan, v. 2, 192) It is said that M.X. *passed away* in 1949 in Baghdad. {syn: çûn ber dilovanîya xwedê; mirin; wefat bûn/kirin} [Antolojiya Dengbêjan/PDK-Xoybûn website]

alîk I ئالیك *f.(Bw)/m.(JB1-A/OK/SK)* **(-a/-ê;).** fodder, forage, feed *(for livestock)*: •**Spêdê zû me *alîk da* dewara û da rê** (Bw) Early in the morning we *fed* the cattle and sent them on their way. {also: [alíka] علیق(JJ-G)} {syn: alif; êm} <Ar 'alīq علیق = 'fodder, forage, provender'; Sor alîk ئالیك = 'fodder' [Bw/IFb/JB1-A/SK/OK//JJ-G] <p'ût I>

alîk II ئالیك (IFb/GF/FS) = small bird. See **alik**.

alîkar ئالیكار (Wlt/IFb) = helper. See **arîk'ar**.

alîk'arî ئالیكاری (B/F) = help. See **arîk'arî**.

alîn ئالین *vi.* **([d]al-).** 1) to get caught, hooked, entangled *(e.g., one's foot)*; to twist, twirl, wind around, get wrapped around *(vi.)* (B): •**Şoka wî di sindoqê *aliya*, sindoq kêşa** (GShA 226) His hook *got caught up* in the box, he dragged the box [ashore]; 2) {syn: hilîngiftin; hilpekîn; lik'umîn; şelifîn; teȟisîn} to stumble, trip: -**p'ê alîn** (K) to stumble, trip: •[**Ew Ismaîl pîr û ȟeftê salî bû îcarî *pê* li secadeyekê *dale* û dikeve**] (JR) This Ismail has grown old, seventy years old, then his *foot gets caught* (= he *trips*) on a carpet [in the mosque] and he falls; 3) to confuse, mix up (IF). {also: [aliian] الیان (JJ)} Cf. Sor: Suleimaniyeh alan ئالان (-alê-); Arbil aran ئاران (-arê-); [Pok. 3. al- 27] 'to wander/roam about aimlessly; also, to be emotionally lost': M. Schwartz: Gr alaínō ἀλαίνω/aláomai ἀλάομαι/ ēláskō ἠλάσκω = 'I wander about' & alētēr ἀλητηρ *m.* = 'name of dance in Ithaca & Sicyon' & ēleós ἠλεός = 'bewildered, dumbfounded' & alētēs ἀλήτης = 'vagabond, bum'; Lith ãluôt = 'to roam about' & Latv ãl'a = 'half-crazed person'. *Also Ir words for **madness**, e.g.* Sgd ''r'k [ārē] = 'crazy, mad'; Pahl halag = 'foolish, imprudent' (M3); P hār هار & K har = 'wild, rabid'; Oss ærræ (Abaev). *The Kurdish verbs **alîn** and **alandin** show different variations of the essential notion of movement away from a center or goal.* [JR/JJ//K/IFb/B/GF/TF/ZF] <alandin; [ȓa]şiqitîn>

alînegir ئالینەگر *adj.* neutral, non-aligned, non-partisan: •**M.Ş., wek mirovek* *alînegir* dihate nasîn** (Wlt 1:41, 3) M.Sh. was known as a [politically] *neutral* person. [(neol)Wlt/IFb/OK] <alîgir>

alînok ئالینۆك *m./f.(FS)* **(;/-ê).** chick-peas (garbanzo beans) *soaked in water, split in two, lightly roasted and added to rice*. [Bw/OK/FS] <nok>

alîsor ئالیسۆر (A/IF/ZF3) = type of pear. See **alîsork**.

alîsork ئالیسۆرك *f.* **(-a;).** *type of pear*: one which has one red side (autumn fruit) (Msr); a type of pear which is red in some places (IF). {also: alîsor (A/IF/ZF3); <alîṣor> آلیصور (HH)} < alî = 'side' + sor = 'red' [Msr//A/IF/ZF3//HH] <hermê; ḧezîranî; încas [1]; karçîn; kirosik>

alîstin ئالیستِن (-alîs-) (M/HH/FS) = to lick. See **alastin**.

alîyan ئالییان = to stumble. See **alîn**.

alkan ئالکان (Rwn) = wave (of the sea). See **êlk'an**.

Alkuşta ئالکوشتا = men's folk dance. See **Yarxişte**.

Almanî ئـالـمـانـی (IFb/ZF3/BF/CS) = German. See **Elmanî**.

almas ئـالـمـاس *m./f.(B)* **(; /-ê).** diamond (K/F/JJ): **-aqût û almast** (Z-2)/**alqût û almaz** (Z-2)/**alqut û almas** (Z-2) rubies and diamonds. {also: almast (Z-2/B); almaz (Z-2); [almas] الماس (JJ); [halmās] (RJ)} [Z-2/B//K/F/JJ//RJ] <yaqût>

almast ئالماست (Z-2/B) = diamond. See **almas**.

almaz ئالماز (Z-2) = diamond. See **almas**.

alos ئـالـۆس (GF/OK) = upset; confused; entangled. See **aloz**.

aloz ئـالـۆز *adj.* 1) troubled, upset, disturbed: **•Helbet karê serekî yê vî tabûrî belavkirina gotgotkan û çêkirina řewşeka** ***aloz*** **e di nêv milletî de** (BH, 60) Surely the main job of this [fifth] column is to spread rumors and to create a *troubled* situation among people **•Vê dawiyê rewşa Tirkiyeyê** ***aloz*** **e** (AW78A4) Lately Turkey is in a *troubled* state [lit. 'Turkey's condition is *disturbed*']; 2) confused, muddled (SK/OK); 3) entangled, complex, complicated. {also: alos (GF-2/OK-2); [aloz bouin] الوز بوین (JJ)} <Syr √'-l-ş ܐܠܨ = 'to press close: a) to press, urge, compel; b) to straiten, hem in'; Sor ałoz ئـاڵـۆز = 'unnatural, unpredictable, temperamental' [Zeb/Dh/K/A/SK/GF/OK]

alozî ئـالـۆزی *f.* **(-ya;-yê).** disturbance, trouble, difficulty, problem: **•De ka em ji** ***aloziya*** **hesp xelas bin** (HYma, 45) Come, let's get rid of the *problem of* the horse **•Tu tenê dikarî** ***aloziyên*** **min fêm bikî** (HYma, 51) You alone can understand my *troubles*. {syn: arêşe; pirsgirêk; t'eşqele} Sor ałozî ئـاڵـۆزی = 'entanglement, complication, complexity' [HYma/A/IFb/GF/TF/FJ/CS] <aloz>

alozyan ئـالـۆزیـان *vi.* **(-alozyê-).** to get entangled (strings, wires). {also: alizîn (Bw); [alozin الوزین/aloz bouin الـوز بـویـن] (JJ)} <Syr √'-l-ş ܐܠܨ = 'to press close: a) to press, urge, compel; b) to straiten, hem in'; Sor ałozan ئاڵۆزان/ałoskan ئـاڵۆسکان [Dh/Zeb//JJ//Bw]

alqut ئالقوت (Z-2) = ruby. See **yaqût**.

alqût ئالقوت (Z-2) = ruby. See **yaqût**.

alt' ئـالـت/**alt** [EP-8]: **-alt' bûn** (K/B) to be beaten, defeated; **-alt' kirin** (K) to beat, defeat, subdue {syn: zora dijmin birin}: **•Şah Abas nikar bû xan û kuřê wî** ***alt bike*** (EP-8) Shah Abbas could not *subdue* the khan and his sons. < T alt = 'underside, bottom': cf. T alt etmek = 'to beat, overwhelm' & alt olmak = 'to be beaten, be overcome' [EP-8/K/B] <birin [3]; řa>

altax ئـالـتـاخ *m.* **().** informer, slanderer, stool-pigeon: **•*Altaxek* hat girtin** (FS) *An informer* has been caught. {syn: destkîs; geveze; mixenet; nemam; qumsî; xayîn; xwefiroş} {altaxî} Cf. T alçak = 'low; base, mean' [HB/A/FS] <'ewan II>

altaxî ئـالـتـاخـی *f.* **().** slander, informing on, denouncing. {syn:'ewanî; geveztî; qumsîtî; şeř II[2]; şilt'ax} [A/FS] <altax>

alt'dar ئالتدار *m.* **().** victor, winner: **•Xanê Ç'engzerîn bi k'uřê xweřa wê** ***altdar*** **derk'etana, wekî xayînt'îya Mehmûdê Merekanî ne bûya** (EP-8, #69) Khan Chengzerin and [lit. 'with'] his sons would have come out *victorious* if not for the treachery of Mehmud Merekanî. {also: alt'indar (B); alt'ker (K)} {syn: serdest} [EP-8//B//K] <alt'>

alt'indar ئالتِندار (B) = victor. See **alt'dar**.

alt'indarî ئـالـتِـنـداری *f.* **(;-yê).** victory: **•K'îjan şerê wana berê xwe bidayê, bi** ***altindarî*** **û k'ubar vedigerîyan** (Z-1) Whatever battle they went to, they would return *victory* [lit. 'in victory'] and revered. {syn: serfirazî [1]} [Z-1/K/B] <alt'; alt'dar>

alt'ker ئالتکەر (K) = victor. See **alt'dar.**

alu ئالو (IF) = being on edge (of teeth) . See **alû.**

alû I ئـالـوو *adj.* on edge *of one's teeth as a result of a tickling sensation or of rubbing them against metal* (IF) {T kamaşmak}: **-alû bûn** (IF) to be set on edge (of teeth) {syn: sekihîn}: **•Diranê min** ***ḧalû bûne*** (K) My teeth *were set on edge*; **-diran ḧilû kirin** (F) to set one's teeth on edge: **•Min diranê xwe** ***ḧalû kirine*** (K) I *set* my teeth *on edge* {also: alu (IF-2); ḧalû (K); ḧilû II (F); ḧulî I (B)} {syn: xidok (IF)} [IF//K//F//B] <diran; harsim; kuh; sekihîn>

alû II ئالوو (K/JJ) = plum. See **ḧilû I.**

alûce ئالووجە (A) = plum. See **alûçe.**

alûç•e ئـالـووچـە *f.* **(;•ê).** 1) cherry-plum (kind of small green plum, bot. *Prunus divaricata*): **-dara alûça** (F) plum tree; 2) pear (HH). {also: alûce (A); [e(h)luciak] (JJ-G); <alûçe> آلـوچـه (HH)} Cf. P ālūče آلوچه = 'damson' (type of Asiatic plum) < ālū

آلـو = 'plum'; Sor hełûje هـەڵـووژە [F/K/A/IFb/B/HH//JJ] <dembûl; hêrûg [1]; ȟilû I; încas [2]; şilor>

alûm•e ئـالـوومـە *m.* (**•ê; **). 1) {syn: p'idî[1]} gums (Wn); 2) {syn: p'idî[2]} palate, roof of the mouth (IFb). [Wn/IFb]

amade ئـامـاده *adj.* ready, willing: **•Evdilkerîm li ser doza Kurdîtîyê xwedîyê bawerîyeka temam û zexm û qayim e, *amade* ye ku di rîya wê dozê da her tiştê xwe fîda bike, lê belê ne *amade* ye ku bi qasê mûyek jî ji rîya wê dozê avarê bibe** (Bkp, 32) On the issue of Kurdish nationalism E. is possessed of a faith which is perfect and strong, he is *ready* to sacrifice everything for the sake of that cause, but he is not *ready* to budge even the width of a hair from this issue **•Li gorî hin îdîayan Atîna ji bo xwe ji daxwazên Kohen rizgar bike, wê soz bide Amerîka ku di der barê PKKê de ji bo hevkariyê *amade* ye** (CTV107) According to some claims, in order to free itself of [William] Cohen's demands, Athens will promise America that it is *ready* to cooperate regarding the PKK; **-amade kirin** (GF) to prepare, make ready: **•Nûbihara Biçûkan, berhema Seydayê Xanî ya ku ji bo xwendekarên Medresê *amadekiriye*** (Nbh 124:26) N.B., the work which Ahmadî Khanî *prepared* for madrasah pupils. {also: [amadé] امـاده (JJ)} {syn: ȟazir} Cf. P āmāde آمـاده; Sor amade ئـامـاده [A/JB3/IFb/JJ/GF/RZ/ZF] <r̄azî>

aman ئـامـان *m.(Bw/IFb/JB1-A)/f.(K/JJ/OK)* (**-ê/-a; **). 1) vessel, container, pot: **-amanê avê** (Bw) water container; 2) [*pl.*] {syn: firaq} dishes, plates: **•Here, *amana* bîne** (Bw) Go bring some *plates*. {also: eman (SK-2); [aman] امـــــان (JJ)} {syn: derdan II} <Arm aman աման; Sor aman ئـامـان = 'household utensils' [Bw/A/IFb/JJ/JB1-A/SK/OK] <firaq>

ambar ئامبار (A/IFb) = storehouse. See **'embar**.

ameliyat ئامەلیات (IFb) = operation. See **'emeliyat**.

Amerîkanî ئـامـەریـکـانـی (IFb/ZF3) = American. See **Emrîkî**.

Amerîkayî ئـامـەریـکـایـی (ZF3/BF) = American. See **Emrîkî**.

Amerîkî ئامەریکی (ZF3/BF) = American. See **Emrîkî**.

amêr ئامێر (TF/Hej) = instrument. See **amîr**.

amin ئامِن (K/B) = secure; reliable. See **emîn**.

amîn ئامین (HCK) = secure; reliable. See **emîn**.

amîr ئـامـیـر *m.(Dh)/f.(OK)* (**/-a; **). instrument, tool, implement: **-çek û amîrêt leşkirî** (Zeb) military weapons and instruments. {also: amêr (TF); amûr, f. (OK); amûret (GF/RZ); <amîr ئامیر /amêr ئامێر> (Hej)} {syn: alav II; p'ergal II[3]} cf. Sor amraz ئامراز [Zeb/Dh/Hej//TF//OK//GF/RZ] <k'el û p'el>

amojin ئـامـۆژِن *f.* (**-a;-ê**). wife of paternal uncle, aunt. {also: amojn (K/B); amoş (Krç)} {syn: jinap; jinmam} {Cf. Ar mart-'amm امرأة عمّ; T yenge} [A/Rh//K/B//Krç] <ap; mam; xaloş; xaltî; met>

amojn ئامۆژن (K/B) = aunt. See **amojin**.

amoş ئامۆش (Krç) = aunt. See **amojin**.

Amrîkayî ئامریکایی (Wkt) = American. See **Emrîkî**.

Amrîkî ئامریکی (Wkt) = American. See **Emrîkî**.

amûr ئاموور, f. (OK) = instrument. See **amîr**.

amûret ئامووره‌ت (GF/RZ) = instrument. See **amîr**.

an ئان (Msr) = or. See **yan I**.

ana ئانا (MK2) = now. See **niha**.

anaka ئاناكا = now. See **niha**.

ancax ئانجاخ *adv.* only; hardly, scarcely, barely: **•*Encax* ez kari bim nanekî bixwim** (L) I could *scarcely* eat one [piece/loaf] of bread; **-ancax-ancax** = barely, hardly, scarcely: **•Dewle ze'f girane, ew *ancax-ancax* dik'işîne jorê** (Ba) The bucket is very heavy, he can *barely* pull it up [out of the well]. {also: encax (L); [anjáγ] انـجـغ (JJ)} {syn: hew; t'enê [2]} <T ancak = 'only' [BX/B//L//JJ]

anemetî ئـانـەمـەتـی *f.* (**).**1) entrusting [of an object to someone] for safekeeping: **•Lê *anemetî* webe kale bavê mino** (EP-7) May my old father be *entrusted* to you; 2) deposit, pledge. {also: [anemé] انـمـه (JJ); emanet (-a;) (Z-3); yemanet, m. (-ê;). (L)} ?<Ar amānah امانة-->T emanet [EP-7/K//JJ//Z-3//L]

-anê انـێ *f.: In Behdini dialects, the names of all games end with **-anê**: e.g.,* **per̄kanê** = 'card game', **veşartkanê** = 'hide-and-seek'.

anêka انێكا = now. See **niha**.

angaşt ئـانـگـاشـت *f.* (**;-ê**). claim, assertion, maintaining *(that stg. is true)*: **•Jixwe *angaştên* di vî warî de dûr û dirêj in** (Nbh 125:16) *Claims* in this field [or, matter] are lengthy. {also: angoşt (FJ)} {syn: îdî'a} [Nbh/ZF//FJ]

angoşt ئانگۆشت (FJ) = claim, assertion. See **angaşt**.

ango ئـانـگـۆ It means, that is to say, in other words, namely, i.e. {also: angot (GF-2); anku (Bw)} {syn: dêmek; ye'nî} [(neol)K/IF/GF]

angot ئانگۆت (GF) = i.e. See **ango**.

aniha ئانِها = now. See **niha**.

anika ئانِكا = now. See **niha**.

anîn ئانین *vt.* (**[t]în-;** *neg.subj.* **neyn-**).1) {syn: standin} to bring: **•Memê xezalê digire, *tîne* cem Qeret'aj-**

dîn û didê (FK-eb-2, 298) M. catches the gazelle, *brings* it to Q. and gives it to him •**Yêk** [=**Yên ku**] *ez anîme* **vira, wê min dîsa bibin** (Z-1, 47) Those who *brought me* here, will take me back again; **-anîn serê pozê** ***fk-î*** (Kmc) *see under* **poz**; **-anîn zman** (IFb)/**anîn zimên** (AW) to express: •**Li aliyê din gelek filistînî nerazîbûna xwe li hemberî biryarê** ***tînin zimên*** (AW71A3) On the other hand many Palestinians *are expressing* their dissatisfaction with the decision; **-bi dest ve înan** (VoA)/**dest**[**ê xweva**] **anîn** (K) to get, obtain, acquire, procure; **-ser anîn** = to do [stg.] to [s.o.], cause [stg.] to befall [s.o.]: •**Wana...tiştek** ***serê wî nan[î]ye*** (Ba) They *didn't do* anything *to* him (cf. ser hatin); 2) to complete, accomplish, carry out (şerda=tasks): •**Şerdê go min jê re gotîye nikare** ***bîne*** (L) He can't *complete* the task I told (=gave) him; 3) {also: jin anîn} to marry *(said of the man)*, cf. **mêr kirin** *(said of the woman)*: •**Dîya min qebûl nake go ez te** ***bînim*** (L) My mother won't let me [lit. 'doesn't accept that I'] *marry* you; 4) {syn: welidandin} to bear, bring forth *(offspring)*: •**Sê kara** ***tîne*** (J) She [=a nanny goat] *brings forth* three kids (=baby goats). {also: hanîn (Ba3); înan (M/MK); **înandin**; [anin انين/inan اينان] (JJ); <anîn آنين (tîne) (تينه)> (HH); inaindene (d'ineme) (BG) = apporter, faire venir; īnān (RJ)} [Pok.1. nei- 760.] 'to lead': Skt √nī [nayati]; Av & O P nay- = 'to lead, guide'; Mid P nīdan (nay-) = 'to lead' & ānīdan (ānay-) = 'to bring, lead' (M3); Sor hênan هێنان; Za anã [ardiş] (Todd) [K/A/JB3/B/JJ/HH//M/MK2/RJ//Ba3//BG] See also **înandin**. <birin>

anîşik ئانیشك (MK2) = elbow. See **anîşk**.

anîşk ئانیشك *f.* **(-a;-ê).** elbow: •**Behrem Fêris zadê xû xar û k'ete ser** ***enîşka*** **xû** (M-Am) Bahram Féris ate his food and leaned back on his *elbow*. {also: anîşik (MK2); enişk (JB3); enîşk (M-Am); 'enîşk (K/B); [enichk] انيشك (JJ); [enishk] (RJ)} probably <*arnişk: [Pok. 8. el- 307.] 'elbow, forearm'--> Proto-IE *Eel-n-: Skt aratni- *m.* = 'elbow'; Av araθni- attested as arəθnå m. (dual) = 'elbow' & frārāθni- = 'ell'; OP arašânâišânom [arašni-] = 'ell'; Sgd ''r'ync [āre/inč] = 'cubit'; Pahl ārešn = 'cubit'; Ormuri & Parachi ārunǰ; Pamir dialects: Sanglechi ārinǰ; Wakhi ōrīnǰ; Shughni ārenj/wištyērn = 'elbow' (Morg); Southern Tati dialects (all *f.*): Chali arešni; Takestani aršinia; Ebrahim-abadi aršenia; Eshtehardi areškenji; Sagz-abadi areškenjia = 'elbow' (Yar-Shater); P āranj آرنج/āran آرن = 'elbow' & araš ارش = 'cubit; forearm'; Sor anîşk ئانیشك /anîsk ئانیسك; Za ârâsnä/ârisnä (Hadank); Hau erejno *m.* (M4); also T arşın ='ell, yard, cubit (60-70 c.)' & Rus aršín аршин = 'measure equal to 28 inches or 71 cm.'; Cf. Lat ulna = 'forearm'; Gr ōlenē ὠλένη *f.* = 'elbow'; Germanic *alinō in OEng eln = 'forearm, cubit'. [K/B//MK2//A/M-Am//JB3/JJ/RJ]

anku ئانكو (Bw) = i.e. See **ango**.

ant'êx ئانتێخ (B) = dung thrown onto hot ashes to preserve the fire. See **ant'êẍ**.

ant'êẍ ئانتێغ *f.* **(-a;-ê).** decomposing dung which is thrown onto the hot ashes of a hearth fire *in order to save the fire for the next day*: •**Ewî lê nhêrî, wê biřçîya bimre,** ***ant'êẍa*** **agir xwey kir, ji xweřa nêç'îr dikir** (EH) He looked and saw that she was dying of hunger, [so] he took care to preserve (the *dung* on) the fire, and went out hunting. {also: ant'êx (B-2)} Cf. T antık [Erzurum] = 'fire buried in ashes' (DS, v. 1, p. 281) < Arm ant'eł անթեղ= 'ash for covering fire' (Avak). *For an example of the practice of kindling a fire in this way, although not specifically using this term, see*: Mahmut Makal. *A Village in Anatolia* [translation of *Bizim Köy*] (London : Vallentine, Mitchell, 1954), p. 13, under **Matches**. [EH/B] <agir; helemor; k'erme; qelax; t'epik II; xwelî>

ap ئاپ *m.* **(-ê ; êp** [BK]/**apê** [B], **vî apî).** paternal uncle, father's brother. {also: [âp] عاپ (JJ); <ap> ءاپ (HH)} {syn: mam} [cf. Ar 'amm عَم, P 'amū عمو, T amca] [K/A/JB3/IF/BK/HH/B/Rh/MK2//JJ] <amojin/jinap; met; pismam; qîzap; xal>

apik ئاپك *f.* (). riddle. {syn: mamik (K/JB3); met'el; têderxistinok} [Bg/ZF3]

aprax ئاپراخ (Wkt) = stuffed grape leaves. See **îprax**.

aqar ئاقار *m./f.* **(-ê/-a; /-ê).** 1) {syn: war} (someone's) land, territory, area: •**Ma niha tu nayê ez** ***aqarê*** **xwe nîşanê te bidim?** (ZZ-3, 258) Now won't you come let me show you my *territory*?; 2) area *(in square meters, kilometers, etc.)*: •***Aqara*** **Kurdistanê 520,000 km2 ye** (IFb) The *area of* Kurdistan is 520,000 square kilometers. {also: eqar (GF-2); <aqar اقار/'eqar عقار> (HH)} < Ar 'aqār عقار = 'real estate, immovable property'; Sor aqar ئاقار = 'direction/line/course on which stg. is moving, pointing, or racing' [ZZ/IFb/B/GF/HH]

aqil I ئاقل/**'aqil** عاقل [SK-2] *adj.* smart, intelligent: •**Ûsibê min kuřekî** ***aqile*** (Ba) My Joseph is a *smart* boy; **-aqiltir** = smarter, more intelligent. {also: [ākel] عـاقـل (JJ); [akell] (BG); ['aqil] (RJ)} {syn: aqiljîr; aqilmend; aqiltîj (Bw); bi zihn (Bw); bi fêm; jîr; serwext; zîx I} < Ar 'āqil عـاقـل {aqilî (K/A)} [Ba/K/A/JB3/B/SK/RJ//JJ/BG]

aqil II ئـاقِل *m.* **(-ê; êqil).** intelligence, cleverness, sense, wisdom,"brains"; sense, reason (JB3); "...a complex concept, fundamental in most Muslim cultures, from Morocco to Afghanistan, that can be glossed as reason or social sense... the social sense and self-control of honorable persons" {from: Lila Abu-Lughod. Veiled Sentiments: Honor and Poetry in a Bedouin Society (Berkeley et al.: University of California Press, c1986), pp. 90, 108}: **•*Aqilê* xwe ji dûwê řep hilîna** (Dz) She got her "*brains*" from the protruding tail [folk saying, cf. "the lion's share"] **•"Řovî, te ev *aqil* ji k'u girtye?"** (Dz) "Fox, where did you get your *sense/brains* from?"; **-aqilê *fk-ê* [ne]biřîn** [+ **ji**] (mostly neg.) : = a) [not] to understand, comprehend; b) [not] to want, choose, be interested in; [not] to like, care for: •[Memê went to try out his father's 40 horses. He put his hand on the back of each horse, and each horse's back broke] **Memê *aqilê wî* t'u bora *nebiřî*** (EP) M. *wasn't "excited" about* any of the horses; **-aqilê *fk-ê* [na]girtin** [+ **ji**] *(mostly neg.)* (HR-I) [not] to like, care for: **•Dih jî vî wextî dido weke te hatin, go: *'eqlê mi ji* wa her duwa *negirt*** (HR-I, 3:31) Yesterday at about this time two [fellows] like you came, but *I didn't like* them. {also: aql (SK-2); eqil (JB3); 'eql (SK); [aqil] عـقـل (JJ); <'eql> عـقـل (HH); [akell] (BG); ['aql] (RJ)} {syn: ȟiş; sewda I} <Ar 'aql عـقـل [K/A/B/JJ/MK2//JB3//HH/SK/HR-I//BG//RJ]

aqilbend ئاقِلبەند (B) = clever. See **aqilmend**.

'aqildar عاقِلدار *m.* **().** wise man, sage: **•Dîsa Nemrûd hana xo bire ber jîrik û *'eqldarêt* xo ... Liser gotina 'eqildara ewan çil qîz çil xort anîn û 'ereq danê** (GShA, 230) Again N. took his problems to their wise and *intelligent men* ... As the wise had told them they fetched 40 girls and 40 young men and gave them arak. {also: 'eqildar (GF); 'eqldar (SK)} {syn: aqilmend; maqûl} <Ar 'aql عقل = 'sense, reason' + -dar [GShA/GF//SK//JB1-A]

aqilî ئـاقِـلـی *f.* **(-ya;-yê).** smartness, intelligence. {also: aqiltî (B-2)} [K/A/B/Wkt]

aqiljîr ئـاقِـلژیـر *adj.* clever, smart (EP-7): **•Qeretajdînê *aqiljîr*** (EP-7) *Clever* Qeretajdin. {syn: aqil I; aqilmend; aqiltîj (Bw); bi fêm; bi zihn; jîr; zîx I} [EP-7]

aqilkuřîn ئـاقِـلـكـوڕیـن *adj.* crazy, mad, insane: **•Memê minî devdînî *aqilkuřîne*** (EP) My crazy, *mad* Memê. {syn: devdîn; dîn; şêt} [EP-7]

aqilmend ئـاقِـلـمـەنـد *adj.* 1) {syn: aqil I; aqiljîr; aqiltîj (Bw); bi fêm; bi zihn; jîr; zîx I} clever, smart, intelligent; wise; 2) sensible; 3) *[m.]* {syn: 'aqildar} smart person, wiseman. {also: aqilbend (EP-7/B); aqlmend (SK); <'eqilmend> عـقـلـمـنـد (HH)} [EP-7/B//K/A/IFb/BF/ZF3/Wkt/FS//SK//HH]

aqilsivik ئـاقِـلـسِـڤِـك *adj.* weak-witted, feeble-minded, imbecile, foolish: **•Meryê *aqilsivik* t'ucara lê meke řik'** (Dz-#1083) Never make a *foolish* man angry *[prv.]*. {also: [aqil siwik] عـقـل سـڤـك (JJ)} {syn: bêaqil; eȟmeq; sefîh; xêtik} <aqil II + sivik = 'light(weight)' [Dz/F/K/A/IF/B/JJ/BF/ZF3] <aqil II>

aqiltî ئاقِلتی (B) = intelligence. See **aqilî**.

aqiltîj ئـاقِـلـتـیـژ *adj.* smart, clever, sharp. {syn: aqil I; aqiljîr; aqilmend; bi fêm; bi zihn (Bw); jîr; zîx I} <aqil II + tîj [=tûj] = 'sharp' [Bw]

aqit ئاقِت *m./f.(ZF3)* **(-ê/;).** grape molasses, thick syrup made from boiled grape juice [T pekmez]. {also: aqîd (FS); <aqîd> آقـیـد (HH)} {syn: dims; doşav; mot} T akıt [Malatya; Urfa; *Kilis, *Nizip -Gaziantep; *Afşin, *Elbistan -Maraş; Hisarcık *Yayladağı -Hatay] = 'grape molasses or sugar made into candy through boiling' (DS, v.1, p. 150, 153) & akide = 'sugar candy' <Ar 'aqīd عـقـيـد = 'thick (of grape molasses)' < 'aqada عقد = 'to thicken, congeal (liquid)' [Mzg/IF/Krç/ZF3/G//HH/FS]

aqîd ئاقید (FS/HH) = grape molasses. See **aqit**.

aql ئاقل (SK) = intelligence, sense. See **aqil II**.

aqlmend ئاقلمەند (SK) = clever, smart. See **aqilmend**.

Aqû ئـاقـوو *m.* nickname for Jacob (Yaqûb): **-Aqû p'êxember** (Ba) Jacob the Prophet [Ba]

aqût ئاقووت (Z-2/K) = ruby. See **yaqût**.

ar I ئـار *m.(K/Kg)/f.* **(-ê [Kg]/ ; êr [BK/K]/).** 1) {syn: alav I; p'êt I} fire; 2) ash(es). {also: **agir**; [àghir آگـر /ār آر] (JJ)} <O Ir *āθr- (A&L p.86 [VI,4] + note 14 [p. 101]): Pashto ōr; Baluchi ās; Sor agir ئـاگـر/ar ئـار/awir ئـاور; Za adir *m.* (Todd). *A&L reject Tsabolov's etymology* <*ātar- (Tsb2 p.9) [Rh/Kg/K/A/IF/BK/JJ] See also **agir**.

ar II ئار (K/A/SK/MK2/BF/FS) = flour. See **ard**.

aram ئـارام *adj.* 1) calm, quiet, peaceful, still, serene: **•Fînlandiya welatê herî *aram* ê cîhanê hate destnîşankirin** (Rûdaw 21.iv.2017) Finland has been designated the most *peaceful* country in the world •**Rewşa Kerkûk û derdora wê *aram* e** (Sputnik Kurdistan 15.x.2017) The condition of Kerkuk and surroundings is *calm*; 2) [*f.*] (HB/K/A/JB3) = calmness, tranquility. See **aramî I**. [Pok. 2. erə-, rē- ; rē-u̯ā, rō-u̯ā 338.] 'to rest' ; 'rest(fulness)' : Av airime = 'still, calm (*erə-mo-) , armaē-šad = 'sitting still'; P ārām آرام; Sor aram ئارام [Rûdaw/A/IFb/FJ/ZF3/Wkt/RZ/BF/FD/Kmc] <aramî I>

aramî I ئارامی *f.* **(-ya;-yê).** calm(ness), quiet, tranquility, serenity: •***Aramiya* herêmê têk nebin** (ZF3) Don't upset *the calm of* the region •**Her ku otobês diçû ew çend *aramiya* di dilê wan de kêm dibû** (N.Mîro.Gava mirî biaxife, 35) The more the bus went, the more *the quiet* in their hearts shrank [i.e., the more distraught they became]. {also: aram; aramîtî (Wkt-2/GF-2); aramtî (Wkt-2)}Cf. P ārām آرام [N.Mîro/K(s)/IFb/GF/ZF3/Wkt/BF/FD//HB/K/A/JB3]

Aramî II ئارامی *f.* () *& adj.* Aramaic, Syriac: •**Piştî sedsala 8an û 7an a berî zayînê zimanê *aramî* li Mezopotamyayê belav dibe** (Wkp: Suryanî) After the 8th and 7th centuries BC, the *Aramaic* language spreads in Mesopotamia. [Wkt/SS/Kmc] <Suryanî>

aramîtî ئارامیتی (Wkt/GF) = calmness, tranquility See **aramî I**.

aramtî ئارامتی (Wkt) = calmness, tranquility See **aramî I**.

aran I ئاران *f.* **(;-ê).** *geographic term denoting various types of land forms*: 1) desert, wilderness (GF); place with a hot, dry climate (B/JB2): •**Yêrê wî gundî *aran* bû, zivistana wî gundî qe t'unebû, her carna berf dik'et ew jî zû diȟeliya** (JB2-Şamilov) That village was situated in a *warm plain*, it had no winter at all, [and] every time snow fell it quickly melted; 2) valley (EP-5): •**Leylê diçe ç'îê, Mecrûm dimîne *aranê*** (EP-5, #22) Leyla goes to the mountain, Mejrum remains in the *valley* [or, *desert*?]; 3) meadow; pasture (K). [EP-5/K/B/GF/FS/FD] <ç'ol; gelî II; mêrg; newal>

aran II ئاران (TF/GF) = to ache; to be upset or irritated. See **arîn**.

araq ئاراق (K/B) = arak. See **'ereq**.

arav ئاراڤ *f.* **(-a;-ê).** soapy or sudsy water, particularly after washing clothes in it: •**Wê *arava cilka* rişt** (FS) She poured out *the laundry water*. {also: erav (Haz); [araw] آراڤ (JJ)} Sor araw ئاراو [Haz//K/A/IFb/JJ/GF/TF/OK/RF/FD/G/FS/ZF3] <av>

arbeşk ئاربەشك *m./f.(FS/ZF3)* **(;/-ê).** flint stone: •**Wî agir bi *arpeşê* hil kir** (FS) He lit the fire with a flint stone; -**kevirê arbeşk/berê arbeşk** (Qzl) do. {also: arpeş[k] (FS)} {syn: berheste; heste} [Qzl/Kmc-#1133/ZF3/Wkt//FS]

ard ئارد *m.* **(-ê ; êrd, vî ardî).** flour: •**Wê *ar* kir nan** (FS) She made *the flour* into bread; -**ardê ceh** (BF) barley flour; -**ardê genim** (BF)/**arê genimî** (FS) wheat flour. {also: ar II (K/A/SK/MK2/BF-2/FS); <ar> آر (HH); [ar] (RJ) = flour (in cooking)} {syn: arvan [2]} <O Ir *ārta- (A&L p.84 [IV, 2]): P ārd آرد; Sor ard ئارد; Za ardî *pl.* = 'flour' & arriş *m.* = 'flour (supply)' (Todd); Hau hardî *f.* (M4) [Kg/JB3/ZF3/FD/BF/Wkt//K/A/HH/RJ/MK2/FS] <arvan>

ardû ئاردوو *m.* **(-yê;).** fuel: •**Ji bo *ardûyê* zivistanê, yên ku li çolê sergînan berhev dikin û tînin malê, yên ku li ser sergoyên gund tar û tepikan çêdikin, yên ku li çiyan hejik û êzingan derdixin û dikişînin malên xwe** (Ardû, 72) For winter *fuel*, there are those who gather dung in the wilderness and bring it home, those who make dung patties at the village dung heaps, those who extract firewood from the mountains and haul it home. {also: [ardou] اردو (JJ); <ardu> ئاردو (Hej)} <ar I/agir = 'fire' + dû IV = 'smoke': Sor awirdû ئاوردوو (Hej) = sûtemenî سووتەمەنی [Ardû/K/A/IFb/B/JJ/GF/FS]

arehan ئارەهان (HH/OK) = to ache; to be upset or irritated. See **arîn**.

arezo ئارەزۆ (SK) = desire. See **arzû**.

arezû ئارەزوو (GF) = desire. See **arzû**.

arêşandin ئارێشاندِن (K) = to scratch. See **ȟeȓişandin**.

arêşe ئارێشە *f.* **(-ya;).** problem, issue, question, difficulty, crisis: •***Arêşeya* avê li Duhok hat çare kirin** (BF) The water *problem* in Duhok has been solved •**Ew jî yê *arîşêt* wan bi rêve dibetin** (Çîvaroka Gayê Sor, 2006, 8) And he manages their *problems*. {also: arîşe (Gayê Sor/Wkt); awêşe (Wkt-2); awîşe (MJ/Wkt-2)} {syn: alozî; pirsgirêk; t'eşqele} [Gayê Sor/Wkt//BF/FKS//MJ]

argoşk ئارگوشك (FS) = jaw bone. See **argûşk**[3].

arguşk ئارگوشك (TF) = chin. See **argûşk**.

argûş ئارگووش (Epl) = chin. See **argûşk**.

argûşk ئارگووشك *f.* **(-a;).** 1) {syn: çeng II; erzen} chin: •**Wan destên xwe li hev siwar dike, dide binê *argûşa* xwe, hinekî difikire** (Epl, 13) He brings those hands of his together, puts them under his *chin*, and thinks a little; 2) {syn: behîvok; gelale} tonsils (IFb/GF); 3) jaw bone (FS) [argoşk]. {also: argoşk (FS); arguşk (TF); argûş (Epl)} [Epl/

/IFb/GF/RZ//TF//FS]

arhan ئـــارهـــان (Bw/FJ) = to ache; to be upset or irritated. See **arîn**.

arhane ئارهانه (ZF3) = she-camel. See **arwane**.

arihan ئـارِهـان (GF) = to ache; to be upset or irritated. See **arîn**.

arihîn ئـارِهـيـن (RZ) = to ache; to be upset or irritated. See **arîn**.

ar̄ik' ئارِك (OrK) = ceiling. See **ar̄îk**.

ariyan ئـارِيان (CS/FJ) = to ache; to be upset or irritated. See **arîn**.

arî ئـارى: -arî kirin (Msr/JJ/TF/OK/Rnh 2:17, 307) = to help. See **arîk'arî**.

ar̄îk ئـاريـك [K/B]/**arîk** ئـاريـك [Kmc/IFb/RZ] *f./m. (BFK/QtrE)* **(-a/-ê;-ê).** ceiling: **•Defa Tajdîn di odê da ye, em ê herin *arîkê* biqelêşin, hûn bi pişta min bigirin. Ez ê xwe tê ra dahêlim, ku min xwe daxist, ez ê def û zirnê derxim** (J2, 28) Tajdin's drum is in the room, we'll go break through the *ceiling* [from above], you hold onto me from behind. I'll let myself down [into the room], when I've let myself down, I'll take out the drum and fife. {also: ar̄ik' (OrK); arûk, m. (QtrE)} {syn: asraq; *binban (Kmc); kuşxank (Bw); *qarçik (Kmc/RZ); sapîtke} [J/Kmc-1146/IFb/RZ//K/B//OrK//QtrE]

arîk'ar ئـاريـكـار *m.* **().** 1) helper, aide, assistant: **-alîkar bûn** [+ **ji...re**] (Wlt) to be of help, be of assistance: **•Hûn dikarin ji wan re bibin *alîkar*?** (Wlt 1:49, 16) Can you be of any *help* to them?; 2) [*adj.*] auxiliary, helping (IF/JB3): **-lêkera arîkar** (IF) auxiliary verb. {also: alîkar (Wlt/IFb-2); [ari-kar] ارى كار (JJ)} Cf. P yārīgar يـاريـگر [K/A/JB3/IFb/JJ/GF/TF/OK//Wlt]

arîk'arî ئـاريـكـارى *f.* **(-ya;-yê).** help, assistance: **-arîk'arî kirin** = to help {also: alî kirin (Msr/MK2); arî kirin (Msr-2/TF/OK/Rnh 2:17, 307)}: **•Em *arîk'ariya* wan *dikin*** = We *help* them. {also: alîk'arî (B/F); harîk'arî (JB1-A); yalî (Ag); [ari ارى/ ali الى/ari-kari ارى كارى] (JJ); [hārī kirin] (RJ) = [to] help} Cf. P yārīgarī يـاريـگـرى; = Sor yarmetî يارمەتى [BX/K/A/JB3/IF/JJ/GF/TF/OK//B/F//JB1-A//Ag//RJ]

arîn ئـاريـن *vi.* **(-ar-).** 1) {syn: êşîn; jendin[5]} to ache, hurt, burn: **•Ji jana dil laş *diare*** (O.Basî. Te dil bi xwe re bir, 64) The body *smarts* from heartache **•Ser bi min *arîya*** (CS) I have a headache [lit. 'Head to me *ached*']; 2) to be disturbed, troubled, upset, flustered; to be uncomfortable: **•Her ku ronahiyek vedimirî, dilê wê yî bijokî pê *diariya* û êdî hew dihewiya** (SBx, 21) Every time a light went out, her fluttering heart *was upset* by it and would not calm down; 3) to be sensitive and sore, be extremely irritated *(of gums)* (bo gelek acizbûnê bi kar têt); 4) {syn: aziryan} to be angry, irritated *(of bees)*: **•Ez di ber konzirkêtkekê raborîm ya *arhay* bo (=bû), çendeka rahêla min û êkê bi min veda** (Bw) I passed by a *riled up* hornet's nest, some of them came after me and one of them stung me. {also: aran II (TF-2/GF); arehan (OK); arhan (Bw/FJ); arihan (GF); arihîn (RZ); ariyan (CS-2/FJ-2); aryan (Dh); haran (GF-2); <arehan آرهـــان (diarihe) (دآرهه)> (HH)} [Bw/FJ//Dh//SBx/CS/TF/Wkt//GF//HH/OK//RZ]

arîşe ئـاريـشـه (Gayê Sor/Wkt) = problem, issue. See **arêşe**.

'arîz•e عـاريـزه *f.* **(•a;•ê).** petition, application: **-'arîze dan [bo]** (Bw)/**'erzê dayîn** (B/K) to apply [for]; **-'erza ner̄azîtîyê dayîn** (B) to lodge a complaint; to appeal (a decision); **-'erza şikyat** (B) complaint; appeal. {also: 'erze (K/B); [arizé] عـريـضـه (JJ)} {syn: 'erzih̄al} <Ar 'arīḍah عريضة = 'application, petition' [Bw/JJ//K/B]

Arkuşta ئاركوشتا = men's folk dance. See **Yarxişte**.

armanc ئـارمـانـج *f.* **(-a;-ê).** 1) {syn: mebest; meqsed; merem [1]; nêt [4]} goal, purpose, aim: **•Dijmin ev şexsiyeta li gora *armanca* xwe çêkiribû** (Berxwedan, 10:141, 24) The enemy created this character for [=to serve, lit. 'according to'] its own *purposes*; 2) target; 3) aim *(in shooting)*: **•[Dûmo şeşxaneyê digrite *armancê* û bi kêfa xo diçeqîne]** (JR #27, 80) Dumo takes *aim* with his revolver and pulls the trigger at his leisure. {also: armanç; emanç (A-2); [armadj ارماج/ armandj ارمانج] (JJ); <amanc آمانج/ 'emanc عمانج> (HH)} Cf. P āmāj آماج = 'target'; T amaç; Sor amanc ئامانج [K/A/JB3/IF/JJ/SK//HH]

armanç ئارمانچ = goal. See **armanc**.

armîş ئارميش, f. (SK) = silk. See **hevirmiş**.

armûş ئارمووش = silk. See **hevirmiş**.

aro ئارۆ (AA/AD/BF) = cucumber. See **arû**.

arpeş[k] ئارپەشك (FS) = flint stone. See **arbeşk**.

arsaq ئارساق (R.Jiyan) = ceiling. See **asraq**.

artêş ئارتێش *f.* **(-a;-ê).** army: **•*Artêşa* Tirk tankan dijî Kurdên bakur pêk tîne** (Orient Kurdi 23.xii.2015) The Turkish *army* deploys tanks against the Kurds of the north [=of Turkey]. {syn: esker [2]; leşker; ordî} < P arteš ارتش [(neol)Wlt/TF/ZF]

arû ئـــارووو *m.* **(-yê;).** cucumber. {also: aro (AA/AD/BF)} {syn: xiyar} Sor arû ئـــارووو [Bar/A/IFb/GF/Wkt//AA/AD/BF] <qitik>

arûk ئارووك, m./pl. (QtrE) = ceiling. See **ar̄îk**.

arûng ئاروونگ (Kmc-2) = apricot. See **hêrûg** [2].

arvan ئـارڤـان *m.* **(-ê;).** 1) flour bin; 2) {syn: ard} flour (JJ/HH/MK2): **•T'elîsek *arvan* li ser pişta wîye** (Z-2) There is a sack of *flour* on his back; 3) year's supply of flour or grain (B). {also: [ervan] اروان (JJ); <arvan> آرڤــــان (HH); [avrān] (RJ) = flour (large quantity)} Za ardî *pl.* = 'flour' & arriş *m.* = 'flour (supply)' (Todd) [Z-2/K/A/B/JJ/HH/MK2] <ard>

arvane ئارڤانه (FS/SS) = she-camel. See **arwane**.

arwan ئاروان (ZF3) = she-camel. See **arwane**.

arwan•e ئاروانه *f.* **(•[ey]a;).** she-camel: **•Mecnûn ji bo ku here Leyla xwe bibîne ji xwe *arwaneyek* (deva mê) peyda kir û ket rê, berê xwe da gundê Leylê** (Hindik Rindik 4.xii.2016) Majnun, in order to go see his Leyla, found *a she-camel* and set out, headed for Leyla's village. {also: arhane (ZF3-2); arvane (FS/SS); arwan (ZF3-2)} {syn: dundil; mencî} [Qrj/ZF3//FS/SS] <deve; ĥêştir; lok' II; torim>

arxafk ئـارخـافك (CB) = snack made of flour and water. See **arxavk**.

arxalix ئـــارخـــالِـخ *m.* **(-ê;-î).** man's outer garment or jacket with knee-length flaps: **•Kur̄ k'olosekî kevnî taqî sêrî bû, lingada cote çarixê per̄itî bûn, gorê lingada jî qetîya bûn, *arxalixekî* lê bû, lê *arxalixî* mezin bû, k'ivş bû, ne *arxalixê* wî bû, milê *arxalix* dihat, dik'ete ser destê wî, berstuya wî zefî qetîya bû** (Şamilov. Jîyîna bextewar, 77) The boy had an old felt cap on his head, on his feet were a pair of ragged pigskin shoes, the socks on his feet were also ragged, he had on a *jacket* [*arkhalykh*], but it was too big for him, it was clear that it was not his *arkhalykh*, the sleeves of the *arkhalykh* came down [too far], covering his hands, its collar was extremely torn up **•Usa bîr kir, arxalixekî bûraê xwe, nekirbû xurcêda, nebirbû, şeş ĥev biribû** [sic] **... Heryek arxalix daê** (HCK-2, 85) He remembered that his had not put his brother-in-law's arkhalykh in the saddlebag, had not taken it; he had taken six ... He gave each one [of his brothers] an *arkhalykh*. < Az T arxalıx = 'sleeveless jacket' < arxa = 'back (anat.)' [HCK/K/B/Tsab]

arxavik ئـارخـاڤِك (CB) = snack made of flour and water. See **arxavk**.

arxavk ئـارخـاڤك *f.* **(-a;-ê).** type of snack made of fried flour and water, served with tea: **-arxavka ruhnî** (CB) snack made of flour mixed into butter or oil, then salted [T yağlı miyane/iç]. {also: arxafk (CB-2); arxavik (CB); axavk (Hk)} For recipe, see CB, p. 93 [Hk//IFb/GF/OK/FS//CB] <mirt'oxe; xebûs>

aryan ئاريان (Dh) = to ache; to be upset or irritated. See **arîn**.

arzî ئارزى (MK2) = desire, choice. See **arzû**.

arzu ئارزو (A) = desire. See **arzû**.

arzû ئـــــــــارزوو *f.(K/MK2)/m.(F)* **(-ya/ ;-yê/).** strong desire, wish; choice (MK2): **-arzû kirin** (K/IF/MK2) to desire, wish: **•Ez *arzû dikim* ku sibê hawa xoşbe** (MK2) I *want* the weather to be nice tomorrow. {also: arezo (SK); arezû (GF); arzî (MK2); arzu (A); azuru (K2-Fêrîk)} <P ārezū آرزو --> T arzu; Sor arezû ئارەزوو/ezro ئەزرۆ [K2-Fêrîk//F/K/IFb// MK2//A//SK//GF] <ĥewas; merem; miraz>

asan ئـاسـان *adj.* easy, simple. {also: hesan I (A-2); hêsa [2] (F/K/B/IF); hêsan (IFb-2/GF/TF/OK-2); hêsanî I (JB3); ĥesand (K-2); senayî; [asan] اســـان (JJ); <hêsanî> هـيـسـانـى (HH)} {syn: bi sanahî (Bw); sivik} Cf. P āsān آسـان; Sor asan ئـاسـان; cf. also NENA hasânâ-î/sânâî (Maclean) & hasand (Garbell) {asanî; hêsanî; sanahî; sanayî; [sanáie] سـانـايـه (JJ)} [HB/K/A/IFb/JJ/OK//F//GF/TF/BF/Wkt//JB3/HH] See also **hêsa**.

asanî ئـاسـانـى *f.* **(-ya;-yê).** ease, simplicity: **•*Bi asanî* ez hatim vê derê** (BF) I got/came here *with ease*. {also: hêsanî II (IFb-2/GF-2/TF/OK-2); sanahî (Bw); sanayî (OK); [sanáie] سـانـايـه (JJ)} Sor asanî ئاسانى [A/IFb/GF/OK//TF/BF/Wkt//Bw//OK//JJ]

asayiş ئاسايِش (SK) = security. See **asayîş**.

asayişt ئاسايِشت (IFb) = security. See **asayîş**.

asayîş ئـاسـايـيـش *f.* **(-a;-ê).** 1) {syn: ewlekarî; selametî; tenahî} security, safety; calm, tranquility; 2) security forces (police, etc.): **•Ji xelkên Amûdê şeş kes ... bi guleyên *asayîşan* an yên bi ser YPG'ê ve şehîd ketin** (H. Yûsiv. "Li Amûdê...," Diyarname 5.ii.2016) From the people of Amuda six people ... were killed [lit. 'fell martyrs'] by the bullets of *the security forces* or of the YPG **•Li devera Zaxoyê du endamên *asayîşê* canê xwe ji dest dan** [sic] (KurdistanTV 15.iv.2018) In the Zakho region two members of *the security forces* lost their lives. {also: asayiş (SK); asayişt (IFb); asayîşt (K[s])} < P āsāyiš آســـايـــش = 'tranquility, peace of mind' <āsūdan آســـودن = 'to rest, be quiet'; Sor asayiş ئـاسـايِـش = 'calm, freedom from disturbance, order;

peace' [H.Yûsiv/ZF3/Wkt/FD/SS//SK//IFb//K(s)]

asayîşt ئاسایيشت (K[s]) = security. See **asayîş**.

asê ئاسێ *adj.* 1) caught, stuck *(e.g., in the mud)*; tightly squeezed, pressed: **•Em li wê dirk'ê mayne *'asê*: befr gelek hebû, em mayn di befrê r̄a, em hemî qeremt'în** (M, #713, 330) We got into difficulties (i.e., *stuck*) there: there was a lot of snow and we were stranded in the snow and we were all frozen **•Gule hêta wîda *hasê* bûye** (B) The bullet got *stuck* [or, was *lodged*] in his thigh; 2) inaccessible, difficult of access *(lit. & fig.)* (JJ); well-fortified, impregnable; impassable: **•Berî spêdê 'eskerê Fazil Paşa geheşte serê dola pişta Bab S̱eyfa. Çu rêk[êt] dî nebûn ji laê Barzanê bo Bab S̱eyfa ji x̄eyrî wê dolê. Mulazimê ṯopan got, "Ew dole bo ṯopan *asê* ye..."** (SK 48:487) Before dawn Fazil Pasha's troops reached the head of the combe behind Bab Saifan. There was no other road to Bab Saifan from the Barzan side except by this combe. The lieutenant (in charge) of the guns said, "This combe is *impassable* for the guns" •[**Ḧekaêta şêrekî û gurgekî û r̄îwîekî] Dibêjin carek[ê] her sê bûne hewalêt yêk, çûne çiyayekî *asê*, di şkewtekîda cîê xo girtin** [sic] (SK6:61) [Story of a lion, a wolf, and a fox] They say that all three once became companions. They went to an *inaccessible* mountain and settled down in a cave **•Mus̱tefa Beg mala Osê hinare qesra gundê Kepenkîyan nik Qubad Ax̄aê Zerzan, li wê derê damezirand, çûnkû Osê xudan-dujmin bû û qesra Kepenkîyan jî asê bû** (SK 40:372) Mustafa Beg sent Oso's family to the fort in the village of Kapankian, to Qubad Agha of the Zarzan, and settled it there as Oso had enemies and the fort of Kapankian was *impregnable*; **-asê kirin/hasê kirin**(K): a) to chase into a cul-de-sac, chase, be at s.o.'s heels; b) to squeeze, press up against; c) to make inaccessible or impregnable, to fortify (K/IFb): **-mala cihû hasê kirin** (XF): a) to overpower, to compel s.o. to submit, to make s.o. knuckle under, to show s.o. who's boss: **•Min *tu* mala cihûd *hasê kirî*** (Z-1) I have made you knuckle under/I've shown you who's boss [lit. 'I *have chased you* into the house of the Jews']; b) to non-plus s.o., put s.o. in a difficult situation, pressure s.o. into saying/doing stg.; 3) difficult: **•Nihayet ḧukomet dê wî ḧebs ket, paşî muddetekî gelek pare dê ji wî wergirît û wî berdet. Hingî Suto dê xurttir bît û şola me dê *asêtir* bît** (SK 61:752) At most, Government will imprison him and after a time will take a deal of money from him and release him, when he will become still stronger and our affairs yet more *deranged*; 4) rebellious (IFb/JJ/B). {also: hasê (Z-1/K-2/B); asî (B-2); [äsi] عاصی (JJ); <as̱ê> اصی (HH)} <Ar 'āṣī عاصى ['āṣin عاصِن] = 'rebellious' < √'-ṣ-y عصى = 'to rebel, revolt' [Z-1/B//K/A/JB3/IFb/SK/GF//JJ] <bêgav; daç'ikîn; tengav>

asêgeh ئاسێگەه *f.* **(-a;-ê).** stronghold, fortress, well-fortified area: **•Di hindurê *Asêgeha* Ewripayê de şerine zor û xwîndar destpê kirine** [sic] (RN 1:19, 1) Within *the stronghold of* Europe fierce and bloody battles have begun **•Wer xuya dikir ko evan *asêgeh*a xwe li ser çiyayên Kiswê çêkiri bû** (H2 9:31, 775) It seemed that they had made their *stronghold* in the Kiswah Mountains. < asê + geh [RN/H2/K/A/IFb/GF] <kela>

asên ئاسێن (JB1-A) = iron. See **hesin**.

asik ئاسِك (A/IF/GF) = deer. See **ask**.

asin ئاسِن (A/SK/Bw) = iron. See **hesin**.

asinger ئاسِنگەر (SK) = blacksmith. See **hesinger**.

asî ئاسی (B) = rebellious. See **asê**.

asîman ئاسیمان (IF) = sky. See **'ezman I**.

asîmîlasyon ئاسیمیلاسیۆن *f.* **(-a;-ê).** assimilation. {syn: pişaftin [2]} [(neol)Ber/Wlt/ZF3]

asîmîlekirî ئاسیمیلەکری *adj./pp.* assimilated: **•Ez têgiham ku ez kurdekî *asîmîle kirî* me** (Ber) I realized that I was an *assimilated* Kurd. [Ber/ZF3]

ask ئاسك *f.* **(-a;-ê).** gazelle, deer: **•Ew helbest ku li ser pêstê *askê* hatiye nivîsîn** (Wkp:Hurmizgan) That poem which was written on *deer* skin; **-nêçîra aska** (A) gazelle hunting. {also: asik (A/IF-2/GF); [ask] آسك (JJ)} {syn: gak'ûvî; mambiz; xezal I} [Pok ōkú-s 775.] 'swift': Skt āśú- = 'swift'; Av āsu- = 'swift'; *specifically* **gazelle** [ask]: O Ir *āsuka- = 'rapid, swift' (A&L p. 90 [XIII, 2]): Sgd "s(')wk [āsūk]; Khotanese āskä; Mid P āhūg (M3); P āhū آهو; Sor as[i]k ئاسك; *also borrowed into NENA as āziḵtā in Jewish NENA Bible translation of Nerwa* (Sabar) [K/JB3/IFb/OK/ZF3/BF/FS/Wkt//A/GF] <gak'ûvî; mambiz; pezk'ûvî; şivir; xezal I>

asman ئاسمان (SK) = sky. See **'ezman I**.

aso ئاسۆ *f./m.* **(/-yê;-yê/).** horizon: **•Rengên çiyayên li dawiya asoyê diyar diken** (E.Bamernî. Romana Tavgeyê ... Kulturname 24.i.2015) The colors of the mountains at the end of the horizon are visible. {also: asû (GF-2)}

Sor aso ئاسۆ = 'horizon, sky-line' [Bw/IFb/GF/TF/OK/ZF3]

asoyî ئاسـۆيـى *adj.* horizontal. {syn: çeperast} *Other proposed terms:* *dirêjkanî; *mat (IFb); *ufkî (IFb)} Sor asoyî ئاسۆیی [IFb/GF/ZF3/BF/AD/SS/CS]

aspêj ئاسپێژ (EP-7) = cook. See **aşpêj**.

asraq ئاسراق *f.* **(-a;-ê).** ceiling: **•ber bi beşt û qirşikên *arsaqa* xênî ve** (R.Jiyan. Spîtama, 122) toward the crossbeams and beams of the *ceiling* of the house **•Ez di bin *asraqê* de me yarê min** (Mülemma Dergisi. 3. sayı) I am under the *ceiling* [*roof*?], my beloved **•Silsel li bin *esrexê* xaniyên kevn ên suryanî yên li Mêrdînê dihatin çêkirin; motîfek çargoşe yê tîk bû ku bi rengê turkuaz dihat çêkirin. Li gor vegotinan, suryaniyên ku ji ber çewsandinên nediwêrin derkevin kuçeyan, li bin *esrexên* xwe ev motîf çêdikirin, bi vî awayî daxwaza xwe ya dîtina asîmanê hinek dianîn cih** (diyarname.com 12.v.2012) "Silsel" were made under the *ceilings* of the old Syriac houses of Mardin; It was a square motif, colored turquoise. According to descriptions, Syriac Christians who dared not go out into the streets due to persecutions would paint this motif on their *ceilings*, and in this way they would satisfy somewhat their desire to see the sky. {also: arsaq (R.Jiyan); asrax (ZF3-2/Wkt-2/G); esraq (IFb-2/ZF/Wkt-2); esrax (Wkt-2); esreq (IFb/ZF-2/Wkt); esrex (K/IFb-2/RZ/ZF3-2/CS)} {syn: ar̄îk; kuşxank; sapîtke} Cf. Ar azraq أزرق = 'blue' (see "Silsel" above) [R.Jiyan//ZF3/FD//G//K/RZ/CS//IFb/Wkt]

asrax ئاسراخ (ZF3/Wkt/G) = ceiling. See **asraq**.

ast ئـاسـت *m.(CS)/f.(DE)* **(-ê/-a; /-ê).** level *(of water, learning, etc.)*: **•Kurdiya Nûjen li gorî *asta* kesên ku qet kurdî nizanin** (DE) Modern Kurdish according to *the level of* people who know no Kurdish at all **•Lê hêşta di *astê* pêdivî da nîne** (Bêhnişk, 5) But it still isn't at the necessary *level*. < Sor ast ئاست [(neol)Bêhnişk/CS/DE/DE/FJ/SS]

asteng ئـاسـتـەنـگ/**as̱teng** ئـاسـطـەنـگ [FS] *f.* **(-a;-ê).** obstacle, hindrance, stumbling block; difficulty: **•Rêka wî ket *as̱tengê*** (FS) He encountered an *obstacle* on the way [lit. 'His way fell into an *obstacle*']. [(neol)Wlt/IFb/GF/TF//FS] <şerpeze>

asû ئاسو (GF) = horizon. See **aso**.

Asyayî ئـاسـيـايـى *adj.* Asian, Asiatic. Sor Asyawî ئـاسـيـاوى [IFb/Wkt/ZF3/BF/SS]

aş I ئـــاش *m.* **(-ê; êş, vî aşî).** mill: **•Dixwe dixwe, têr naxwe** [***Aş***] (Ad) It eats and eats and is never full [Riddle; *answer:* A *mill*] **•Ez ji *êş* têm** (BX) I'm coming from *the mill* **•Ez ji *vî aşî* têm** (BX) I'm coming from *this mill* **•Hemî r̄êk diçine *aşî*** (Zeb) All roads lead to Rome [lit. 'to *the mill*']; **-aşê zeferanê ser serê *fk-ê* ger̄andin** (XF): a) to make a scene, cause a scandal: **•Emê beraşê *aşê* ze'frane ser serê te bigerînin** (FK-eb-2) We will cause a scandal [lit. 'We will overturn the millstone of the *mill of* victories on your head']; b) to impose a penalty on, settle accounts with; c) to start a war, cause a massacre; **-ji aş û baş** (ZF3/Wkt) trivial, nonsensical, unimportant, petty, trifling, idle: **•Ji ber ku li Swêdê ji bo pirtûkên bi zimanên cihêreng pere dihat dayin, *ji aş û baş* pirtûk nivîsîne** (tirşik.com:L. Polat 1.ix.2013) Because in Sweden money was given for books in a variety of languages, *frivolous* books were written •... **Muşterî ... dihatin û kafe bi galgalên *ji aş û baş* û xirecir û qerepereyên xwe ên berdayî dikirin wek mala dawetê** (ŞWWM, 12) The customers ... would come and make the cafe [seem] like a wedding house, with their *trivial* chatter and silly quarrels and clamoring; **-ji aş û baş axiftin/peyîvîn/xeber dan** (ZF3) to speak idly, speak nonsense: **•Lê dîsa jî, yekî ku *ji aş û baş napeyive* ji min re dibêje ku sê sed hezar japonî amade ne ku di du mehan de werin peravên me** (Le Monde Diplomatique, Adar 2010, 10) But then again, someone who *doesn't speak idly* tells me that 300,000 Japanese are ready to come to our shores within two months **•Ma tu nizanî Fayze tenê *ji aş û baş diaxêve*** (Wkt) Don't you know that F. only *speaks nonsense*. {also: [àch] آش (JJ); <aş> اش (HH); [âche] (BG); [āsha] (RJ)} Cf. P āsiyā[b] آسيـا[ب]; Sor aş ئـاش = 'mill' & asyaw ئـاسـياو = 'water-mill'; Za ayre *m.* (Todd/Mal) & āriš (Lx); Hau asaw *m.* (M4) [K/A/JB3/B/JJ/HH/JB1-A/GF/TF/OK/BG// RJ/MK2] <destar̄; girik II; keraş>

aş II ئـــــــــاش *m.(ZF3)/f.(K/Wkt)* **().** food (cooked and uncooked); soup, broth, porridge (K/JJ). {also: [àch] آش (JJ)} cf. P āš آش = 'soup, porridge'; Sor aş ئــــــــاش = 'cooked food' [MK2/K/A/IFb/JJ/OK/ZF3] <xwarin>

aşera ئاشەرا (MK2) = obvious. See **aşkere**.

aşewan ئاشەوان (SK) = miller. See **aşvan**.

aşêf ئاشێف *f.* **(-a;-ê).** 1) {syn: ade I} weed; 2) weeding, pulling up weeds: **•Ew çû *aşêva* bîstanî** (FS) S/he went *to weed* the garden; **-aşêf kirin** (IFb/JJ/GF/OK/FS) to weed, pull out weeds: **•Kû bû bihar, dest bi *aşêf* û r̄îşîya dikin** (HR-I, 1:42) When spring comes, they start *weeding* and stacking hay. {also: aşêv (A/GF/BF/FS); 'eşêf (RF); [àchiw] اشيڤ (JJ)} Cf. Ar 'ušb عشب (clq Iraqi 'išib) = 'grass, pasture'; Arc 'aśav עשב/'iśba עשבא & Syr 'sev ܥܣܒ/'esbā ܥܣܒܐ = 'herb, plant, grass' [HR-I/K/IFb/OK//A/GF/BF/FS//JJ//RF] <ade I; xepar>

aşêv ئاشێڤ (A/GF/BF/FS) = weed(ing). See **aşêf**.

aşikar ئاشِكار (JB3/IF) = obvious. See **aşkere**.

aşiq ئاشِق/**'aşiq** عاشِق *m.* **(-ê;).** 1) {syn: dildar; dilk'etî; evîndar} someone in love, lover: •***Aşiqê* te me** (song by Murat Küçükavcı) I'm *in love with* you; 2) {syn: dengbêj} singer; bard, minstrel, troubador, traditional epic reciter (K): •**Ez û tu rahêjin tûrê parsê û herin weke *aşiq* û mitirban ji xwe re li nava eşîr û ebrê bigerrin** (ZZ-10, 136) Let's you and I pick up a beggar's sack and go as *bards* and singers and wander among the tribes and clans; 3) {syn: boşe; dome; lûlî; mirt'ib; qereçî} Roma, Gypsy. {also: <aşiq> اشق (HH)} < Ar 'āšiq عاشق --> T aşık [Z-1/K/JB3/IF/ B/JB1-A&S/JJ/HH/ZF] <evîn; ḧub; kilam; mirt'ib; stiran I>

aşit ئاشِت (OK) = avalanche. See **aşît**.

aşitî ئاشِتی (IFb) = peace. See **aştî**.

aşitîxwaz ئاشِتيخواز (IFb) = peace loving. See **aştîxwaz**.

aşîkar ئاشيكار (A/K) = obvious. See **aşkere**.

aşîrk ئاشيرك (Bw) = goatskin sack. See **'eyarşîrk**.

aşît ئاشيت *f.* **(-a;-ê).** avalanche; landslide: •***Aşût* hat xwar** (FS) The avalanche came [crashing] down. {also: aşit (OK); aşût (OK-2/FS); aşûte (GF); [àchit اشيت (JJ)}/āshūt-a bafrē اشوت (PS)} {syn: ṙenî; şape I; şetele} [K/IFb/JJ/FS//OK//FS//GF] <berf; hezaz; xişîlok>

aşîtî ئاشيتى (K/TF) = peace. See **aştî**.

aşîtîxaz ئاشيتيخاز (OK) = peace loving. See **aştîxwaz**.

aşîtîxwaz ئاشيتيخواز (TF) = peace loving. See **aştîxwaz**.

aşkara ئاشكارا (B) = obvious. See **aşkere**.

aşkela ئاشكەلا (EP-4/EP-7) = obvious. See **aşkere**.

aşkele ئاشكەلە = obvious. See **aşkere**.

aşkera ئاشكەرا (BF) = obvious. See **aşkere**

aşkere ئاشكەرە *adj.* clear, obvious, patent; open, not secret: **-aşkera bûn** (BF)/**aşkira bûn** (FS) to be revealed or exposed: •**Direwa wî *aşkira bû*** (FS) His lie *was exposed* •**Dizî li ser filan kesî *aşkira bû*** (FS) So-and-so's theft *was exposed* [lit. 'The theft *was exposed* on so-and-so']; **-aşkera kirin** (BF)/**aşkira kirin** (FS) to reveal, expose: •**Wî navê xwe yê veşartî *aşkira kir*** (FS) He *revealed* his secret name. {also: [bi] aşera (MK2); aşikar (JB3/IF); aşîkar (A-2/K-2); aşkara (B); aşkela (EP-4/EP-7); aşkele; aşkera (BF); aşkira (FS); eşkere (K-2/A-2/JB3-2); [achikar اشكار/achikara اشكارا] (JJ); <eşkere> اشكره (HH); [ishkera] (RJ)} {syn: berç'av II; diyar; k'ifş; xanê; xuya} Cf. P āšīkār آشيكار; Sor aşkira ئاشكِرا [K/A//IF/JB3/JJ//B//BF//FS//HH//EP-4/EP-7//RJ//MK2]

aşkira ئاشكِرا (FS) = obvious. See **aşkere**.

aşop ئاشۆپ *f.* **(-a;).** imagination: •**Ev kuma çîrokan jî çipkek e ji wî deryayê mezin û berîn ku mirovê Kurd di nav hizir û *aşupa* xu da afirandîn** (X. Dêreşî. Şevbêriyên zarokan, 8) And this collection of stories is a drop from that large and broad ocean which the Kurd has created in his mind and *imagination* •**Keft di nav *aşopan* da** (BF) She took a flight of fancy/got lost in her *imaginings*. {also: aşup (Dêreşî)} {syn: xiyal} [Dêreşî//ZF/SS/BF]

aşopî ئاشۆپی *adj.* imaginary: •**Çîrok li ser çwîçik û teyran, kewalên kehî û kwîvî, mirovan, tiştên *aşupî*** (X. Dêreşî. Şevbêriyên zarokan, 7) stories about birds small and large, herds tame and wild, men, things *imaginary* •**dîtina xewnên *aşupî*** (X. Dêreşî. Şevbêriyên zarokan, 8) having [lit. 'seeing'] *imaginary* dreams. {also: aşupî (Dêreşî)} [Dêreşî//ZF/SS/BF]

aşpez ئاشپەز (K/F) = cook. See **aşpêj**.

aşpêj ئاشپێژ *m.* **(-ê;).** cook, chef: •**Pûtîn: Kalê min *aşpêjê* Lenîn bû** (rojname.com 11.iii.2018) Putin: My grandfather was Lenin's *chef*. {also: aspêj (EP-7); aşpez (K/F); [āzpēsh] آزپيش (JJ-Rh)} {syn: şorbeçî} < aş = 'stew' + pêj- = 'to cook': cf. P āšpaz آشپز; Sor aşpez ئاشپەز [EP-7//A/IF/B/Wkt//K/F//JJ-Rh] <patin>

aşt ئاشت *adj.* reconciled, at peace, on good terms: **-aşt bûn/xwe aşt kirin** (Bw) to be reconciled [with], make up (after being on bad terms): •**Wî *xo aşt kir*** (Bw) He *made up* with me [= **Wî ez axiftim**]; **-aşt kirin** (K)/**aş ~** (JJ/HH): a) to reconcile, make peace [with], bring [two warring parties] together {syn: fesil kirin; li hev anîn}; b) to calm, soothe: •**Erke ku ew Memo *aşt neke*, k'esek ji me nikare wî qayîl bike** (Z-3) If she can't *calm* Memo *down*, none of us will be able to make him agree. {also: [àch kirin] اش كرين (JJ); <aşkirin اشكرن (aşdike) (اشدكه)> (HH)} Cf. P āštī آشتى = 'peace'; Sor aşt ئاشت = 'reconciled' [Z-3/K//JJ/HH]

aştî ئاشتی *f.* **(-ya;-yê).** reconciliation, peace: •**Divê em bi awayekî wisa bixebitin da ku gelê Kurd bikaribe li wan welatên ku tê de dijî, *di aştiyê de***

çand û zimanê xwe biparêze û wan pêş ve bibe (Wlt 1:37, 16) We must struggle so that in the countries where the Kurdish people lives, it may *peacefully* protect its culture and language, and advance them. {also: aşitî (IFb); aşîtî (K/TF)} Cf. Av āxšti- = 'peace'; Pahl āštīh; P āštī آشتی = 'peace' (Horn #31); Sor aştî ئاشتی = 'reconciliation, peace' [Wlt/A/GF/BF/FS//IFb//K/TF] <şeř I>

aştîxaz ئاشتیخاز (OK) = peace loving. See **aştîxwaz**.

aştîxwaz ئاشتیخواز *adj.* peace loving: **•Çendî dewleta Tirk zilm û zora xwe berdewam bike li hemberî miletê Kurd ê *aştîxwaz*** (Wlt 2:59, 7) No matter how long the Turkish state continues its oppression of the *peace-loving* Kurdish nation… {also: aşitîxwaz (IFb); aşîtîxaz (OK-2); aşîtîxwaz (TF); aştîxaz (OK)} Sor aştîxwaz ئاشتیخواز [Wlt/GF//IFb//TF//OK/FS] <aştî>

aşup ئاشوپ (Dêreşî) = imagination. See **aşop**.

aşupî ئاشوپی (Dêreşî) = imaginary. See **aşopî**.

aşût ئاشووت (OK/FS) = avalanche. See **aşît**.

aşûte ئاشووته (GF) = avalanche. See **aşît**.

aşûvan ئاشووڤان (Z-2) = miller. See **aşvan**.

aşvan ئاشڤان *m.* **(-ê; aşvên/aşvîn** [JJ]**).** miller: **•*Aşvanê* aşê mîra bi xulame** (Drş #11, 17) *The miller of* the emir's mill has servants [*prv.*]. {also: aşewan (SK); aşûvan (Z-2); [àchvan] آشوان (JJ); <aşvan> اشڤان (HH); [āshvān] (RJ)} Cf. P āsiyābān آسیابان; Sor aşewan ئاشەوان; Za ārewāň[č]í (Lx)/arwançi (Mal); Hau asawan *m.* (M4) [K/A/B/HH/RJ/MK2/FS//JJ] <aş I>

aşxane ئاشخانه *f.* **(-ya;).** 1) {syn: pêjgeh} kitchen; 2) {syn: xwaringeh [2]; xwarinxane} restaurant: **•Bûrhan li Teksîma Stenbolê di *aşxaneya* xwe de xwarinên kurdî çêdike** (rûdaw.net 16.vi.2017) B. in Istanbul's Taksim makes Kurdish dishes in his *restaurant*; 3) {syn: herem [2]; xwaringeh [1]} dining room (K). {also: [ach-khané] آشخانه (JJ)} < P āš آش = 'stew' + xāne خانه = 'house' [K/IF/Ba2/F/JJ/MK2/ZF3/Wkt] <xwarin>

atûn ئاتوون (A/IFb/GF/HH) = limekiln. See **hêtûn**.

Australî ئائوسترالی (Wkp) = Australian. See **Awistralyayî**.

Austriyayî ئائوستریایی (WKp) = Austrian. See **Awistrî**.

Austrî ئائوستری (Wkp) = Austrian. See **Awistrî**.

aûl ئائوول *f.* **(-a;).** *aul*, mountain settlement in the Caucasus (as a village): **•Cem me *aûl* t'unene, lê gund hene** (K2-Fêrîk) We have no *auls*, but we have villages. <according to Webster's Dictionary, through Russian from Kazan Tatar & Kirghiz [K2-Fêrîk] <gund>

av ئاڤ *f.* **(-a;-ê).** 1) water: **•Herçiqas *av* ji bo hemû jîndaran çavkaniyeke bingehîn be jî, îro di destê mirovên "hemdem" de wek pergaleke ji holê rakirina berhemên dîrokê tê bi kar anîn** (Wlt 1:21, 16) Although *water* is a basic resource for all living things, today it is being used by 'modern' man as an instrument for destroying historical artifacts **•Tu bi *avê* dizanî?** (Qzl) Do you know how to swim?; **-av dan** = to water, irrigate (animals; fields) : **•We bîstanê xwe *av da*** = You *have watered* your garden **•Ku deva *avdin*** (Ba) In order *to water* the camels **•Bir ser kanyê *avde*** (Dz) He took [them] to a spring *to water* [them]; ***-ava* bin kaê** (XF/Dz) insidious, crafty, sly, cunning; untrustworthy, unreliable [lit. '*the water* under the straw']; **-ava çêm** (BK) brook water, stream water; **-ava dev** (F/JJ) saliva, spittle {also: avdev, f. (K/IF); [àw-a dew(i) اڤا دڤ /aw-dew اڤ دڤ (JJ)} {syn: girêz; t'if; t'ûk II}; **-ava jînê** (AB) the water of life; **-ava reş** (Hirço/JJ) coffee; **-ava tirî** (Bw) grape juice; **-ava zelal** (AB/BK) pure, limpid water; 2) {syn: çem; řo II; řûbar; şet} stream, river: **•Digihên ber *avekê*** (L) They reach *a stream*; 3) juice: **-ava p'irteqala** = orange juice; **-ava sêva** = apple juice; **-ava tirî** = grape juice. {also: [àw] اڤ (JJ); <av> اڤ (HH); [âv/âw] (BG); [av] (RJ)} [Pok. 2. ap- 51.] 'water, river' -->*Aop: Skt āp- [āpaḥ *f.pl.*]; Av āp- [āfš (*pl.* āpō) *f.*]; Southern Tati dialects (all *f.*): Chali āva; Takestani [vu(y)a]; Eshtehardi āwa; Xiaraji awa; Sag-abadi owa (Yar-Shater); P āb آب; Sor aw ئاو; Za aw *f.* (Todd); Hau awî *f.* (M4); K av --> T av [Diyadin, Ağrı; Diyarbakır] & ov [Babik-Pötürge, Malatya] = 'water' (DS, v. 1, p. 374; v. 9, p. 3299); Cf. Lith ùpe/Latv upe = 'water'; Lat amnis <*abnis = 'river'; Old Irish abann = 'river'; Welsh afon = 'river' [K/A/JB3/IF/B/JJ/HH/BG/RJ/MK2] <avî I; k'unk>

ava ئاڤا *adj.* 1) {syn: şên} built, built up; prosperous, thriving, flourishing [cf. Ar 'amār عمار]: **-ava bûn** = to be built, constructed: **•Îsal di gundê me da *ava bûye* dibistan** (AB) This year a school *has been built* in our village; **-ava kirin** (BG/RJ/MK2) to build, construct; 2) set, setting *(of the sun)*: **-ava çûn** = to set *(sun)*: **•Roj *çû [ser] ava*** (K/AB) The sun *set*; 3) pregnant *(of mares)* (Bw): **•Mahîna me ya *ava* ye** (Bw) Our mare is *pregnant*. {also: <ava> اڤا (HH); [âvâ(kerene)] (BG); [ava kirin] (RJ)} Cf.

O P *āpāta-; Pahl āpāt & Pāzand āwād; P ābād آباد (Horn #4); Sor awa ئاوا [K/A/JB3/B/HH/BG/RJ/MK2] <[1] avan; [2] řojava; [3] avis>

avahî ئاڤاهی, f. (A/JB3)/m. (FS) = building. See **avayî**.

avan ئاڤان *f.* **(-a;-ê).** settlement, inhabited place: •**Paşê, t'evî çend malê gundîê xwe tê *avana* Artênîêda dibe binelî** (HCK-5, 291) Then, together with some households of fellow villagers he comes to the *settlement of* Arteni and becomes an inhabitant. {also: [āvānī] آڤانی (JJ-S)} {syn: heyşet} [HCK/B//JJ] <ava; şênî>

ava řeş ئاڤا رەش *f.* **().** 1) glaucoma; 2) coffee. See under **av**. Cf. Sor awî řeş da hatin ئاوی رەش دا هاتِن = 'to go blind' [Zeb/A/IFb/GF/OK]

avarê ئاڤارێ (Bkp/BFK) = aside, away. See **averê**.

ava sipî ئاڤا سِپی (GF) = cataracts. See **ava spî**.

ava spî ئاڤا سپی *f.* **().** (eye) cataracts; leucoma/leukoma. {also: ava sipî (GF)} Cf. Sor awî sipî ئاوی سِپی = 'glaucoma' [Zeb/IFb/OK//GF]

avayî ئاڤایی *m.* **(-yê;).** structure, building, house. {also: avahî, f. (A/JB3)/m.(FS); [awahi اڤاهی/awaï اڤای] (JJ)} [Z-922/K/B//A/JB3/JJ/FS] <mal; xanî>

avdel ئاڤدەل (FS) = quail. See **'ebdal**.

avdestxan•e ئاڤدەستخانە *f.* **(•a;•ê).** toilet, water closet, lavatory. {also: abdestxane (SK); 'evdesxane (Rh)} {syn: avřêj I; ç'olik III (Msr); daşir (Dy); destavxane; edebxane [1]; qedemge (Czr)} < P ābdastxāne آبدستخانه [Rh//A/IF/B//SK] See also **destavxane**.

avdev ئاڤدەڤ f. (K/IF/JJ) = saliva. See **ava dev** under **av**.

avdîn ئاڤدین (FS) = revenge. See **'evdîn**.

averê ئاڤەرێ *adv.* aside, away, off the beaten path; departed, deviated (CS): **-averê bûn** (CS)/**avarê bûn** (BFK) to depart, deviate, budge (from): •**Evdilkerîm li ser doza Kurdîtîyê xwedîyê bawerîyeka temam û zexm û qayim e, amade ye ku di rîya wê dozê da her tiştê xwe fîda bike, lê belê ne amade ye ku bi qasê mûyek jî ji rîya wê dozê *avarê bibe*** (Bkp, 32) On the issue of Kurdish nationalism E. is possessed of a faith which is perfect and strong, but he is not ready *to budge* even the width of a hair from this issue •**Leşkerê Tirkîyê, hukumeta sivîl, bi îddîaya ku "ji rîya Kemal Paşa *avarê bûye*", wergerand** (Bkp, 35) The army of Turkey overturned the civil government with the claim that it "*had departed* from the path of Kemal Pasha [=Ataturk]"; **-averê kirin** (JR)/**avarê kirin** (BFK) to divert, turn stg. away (from): •**[Her sê hêstir digel baran *averê kirî*, min xo avête nihalekê]** (JR 4:23) *Having diverted* all 3 mules with their loads, I jumped into a ravine; **-xwe averê kirin** (ZZ) to fly the coop, take to one's heels, make off with: •**Hema ez ê tiştên wî bigirim û *xwe jê averê bikim*** (ZZ-4, 170) I will grab his things and *make off with them.* {also: avarê (Bkp/BFK); <avřê> ئاڤرێ (Hej); [eweri اڤەری/awari اڤاری] (JJ)} <a + ve + řê = 'way'; not the same as P āvāre آواره = 'vagrant, roaming, homeless'; = Sor lader لادەر [JR/JJ//ZZ/CS//Bkp/BFK//Hej] <veder>

avêtin ئاڤێتن *vt.* **([d]avêj-/[d]avê-).** 1) {syn: çeng III kirin} to throw, cast, hurl, toss: •***Davêje* bîrê** (Ba) *He throws* [it] into the well; **-avêtin pişt guh** (GF)/ **bi pişt guh ve havêtin** (Bêhnişk) to neglect, ignore, disregard: •**Rewşenbîr û nivîserêt me qewî xwe lê naken xudan û *bi pişt guh ve dihavên*** (Bêhnişk, 2006, 5) Our intellectuals and writers neglect it and *disregard it*; **-dest avêtin[e]/havêtin** (JB1-A/Bw) [+ *dat. constr.*] = a) to touch: •**Qîzkê *destê xwe avête* Mhemmed Xan** (L) The girl *touched* [lit. 'threw her hand on'] M. Kh.; b) to begin, start (vt.) {syn: dest pê kirin}: •**Em *dest bihavêjînê?*** [pavêjînê] (Bw) Shall we *get started*?; **-xwe avêtin**: a) to jump, pounce {syn: řahiştin}: •**Lawik *xwe avête* ser den** (L) The boy *jumped* (lit. "threw himself") *into* the cauldron •**Wane *xwe avîtne* ser me** (Ba) They *pounced* on us; b) to pretend to be [+ *adj.*]: •**Bêje Memo, bira *xwe* nexweş *bavêje*, neçe nêç'îrê** (Z-1) Tell M. to *malinger/pretend to be sick*, not to go hunting; **-xwe avêtin bextê *yekî*** (IFb)/**xwe avîtin ber bextê *fk-ê*** (XF) to beg, beseech, implore, throw o.s. at s.o.'s feet: •**Min î ku nêhirî nabe, vê carê jî *min xwe havêt bextê wî*** (Lab, 7) When I saw that it wasn't working, then *I threw myself at his feet*; 2) to put, place, insert: •**Hersê kevotk ... morîa xewê *davêne* guhê Memê û Zînê** (FK-eb-2) The three doves ... *insert* slumber pearls into Mem and Zîn's ears; 3) to swing, wield *(a weapon)*: •**Hema zaro şûrê xwe *avêt* ser dûvê marî, dûvê marî peritand** (KH, 34) The child immediately *swung* his sword at the snake's tail, and severed the snake's tail. {also: avitin (Ad/BK); avîtin (B/K/F/Z-1); havêtin (M/Bw); havîtin; [awitin اڤیتن / hawitin هاڤیتن] (JJ); <avêtin اڤیتن (tavêje) (تاڤیژه)> (HH); [avétene (d'avéjeme)] (BG); [avetin] (RJ)} [Pok. 4. u̯eik-/u̯eig- 1130] 'to bend, wind, also denotes quick motions such as hastily ducking a blow' (extension of *u̯ei- 'to bend'): O Ir *ā- (Tsb 72) + *vaig- (Tsb 40): cf. Av vaēg- (*pres.* vaēǰə-) = 'to swing, brandish'; Oss vēɣun = 'to shake'; Baluchi gēǰag = 'to swing, toss'; Mid P [2]wēxtan (wēz) = 'to swing, brandish, throw, pour out' (M3); P āvīxtan آويختن = 'to hang'; Sor hawîştin هـاويـشـتـن (-hawêj-) = 'to throw out' [A/JB3/IFb/HH/GF/BG/RJ/MK2/ZF//Z-1/F/K/B/JJ//Ad/BK//M/Bw]

***avgîr** ئـاڤـگـيـر *f.* **(-a;).** 1) swamp, marsh, bog (Haz); land which retains rain water without drying out (HH); 2) irrigation area (K); 3) (water)well (JB3). {also: avgîz (IF); <avgîr> آڤگير (HH)} [Haz/K/JB3/HH/FJ//IF] <genav>

avgîz ئاڤگيز (IF) = swamp; irrigation area. See **avgîr**.

avḧeyat ئاڤحەيات (XF) = water of life. See **avilḧeyat**.

avik ئـاڤِـك *f.* **(-a;-ê).** 1) {syn: dol I} semen, sperm: **•Germbûna zêde ji bo *avikê* ne baş e** (www.amude.net 28.viii.2008) Excessive heat is not good for *the sperm*; 2) sauce: **-avka goştî** (FS) meat sauce. [Msr/A/IFb/TF/OK/Bw/FS/BF/Wkt] <[1] xira I>

avilḧeyat ئـاڤِلـحـەيـات *f.* **().** water of life, cf. Motif E80, Stith Thompson. *Motif-Index of Folk-Literature* (Bloomington etc.: Indiana Univ. Press, [c1955]), v. 2, p. 412: **•Her kesê peşkekê ji awa tizbîyêt min wexotewe, cendekê wî agirê cehennemê nabînît. Ewe *awa ḧeyatê*ye dideme hingo. Cîyê hingo beḧeşta ebedî ye** (SK 12:119) Whoever drinks a drop of the water from my rosary, his body will not see the fire of Hell. This is the *Water of Life* which I give you and your place will be Paradise eternal **-ava avḧeyat** (XF) My darling *(in speaking to children)*. {also: avḧeyat (XF); avlḧeyat (EH); awa ḧeyatê (SK)} < av = 'water' + Ar al-ḥayā[t] الحياة = 'the life' [EH//XF//SK]

avir̄ ئـاڤِر *m./f.(B)* **(-ê/; /-ê).** 1) scorn, contempt, disdain; 2) look, glance; leer, scornful or contemptuous glance: **•*Awir̄ê* Memê û stîya Zîn k'ete hev û dinê** (Z-2) Mem and Lady Zîn exchanged *glances*; **-avir̄ dan/avir̄ê xwe dan** (K) to leer at, look at s.o. with con-tempt: **•*Avir̄* bi mêranî *dane* mîr** (EP-7) They *looked at* the prince *with contempt* •[be *awyre çāva* le-mü de-näri] (JJ) He looked at me *askance*; 3) frown, sour face (K); 4) wink of the eye (JJ/JB1-A). {also: awir (JB1-A); awir̄ (Z-2); [awyr] عـــور (JJ)} Cf. Sor awir ئــــاوِر = 'stern and authoritarian (facial expression)' [EP-7/K/B//JB1-A/JJ] <me'de; p'irçû>

avis ئـــاڤِـس *adj.* pregnant: *of animals* (K/B/Srk/Kş); *of women* (JB3/OK); *of both* (Ad/Rh/JJ/IF/A): •[By dividing a magic apple in two, and giving half to his mare and half to his wife:] **Hespa teyê *avis* derk'eve, jina teyê ḧemle derk'eve** (Z-921) Your mare will become *pregnant* [avis], and so will your wife [ḧemle] {also: avîs (OK-2); [awis] اڤـيـس (JJ); <avis> اڤـــــس (HH)} {syn: bihemil; bizar; duhala; giran; ḧemle} Av *āpuθra- = 'having recently given birth'; Manichaean Mid P ’bwws = 'with child, pregnant' (Boyce) & Pahl abus = '(woman) having just given birth' (M3); P ābestan آبـــســـتــــن (M. Schwartz: < O Ir *āpuθra- + tanū- = 'body'): Baluchi āpus; Sor awis ئـاوِس/awus ئـــاووس [Ad/K/A/JB3/IFb/B/JJ/HH/ TF/OK/Srk/Krş/Rh] <ava [3]; t'eliqîn; welidîn; zayîn>

avitin ئاڤِتِن (Ad/BK) = to throw. See **avêtin**.

avî I ئاڤی *adj.* 1) liquid, fluid; watery: **•xwarina *avî*** (B) *liquid* food; 2) {≠bejî [1]} aquatic, living in water: **•Masî giyandarekê *avî* ye** (FS) The fish is an *aquatic* creature; 3) irrigated, well-watered (land): **•zevîya *avî*** (BF) *irrigated* field. {also: awî (SK); [awi] اڤـی (JJ); <avî> آڤـی (HH)} [Msr/F/K/A/JB3/IF/B/JJ/HH/SK/FS/BF] <av; bejî>

avî II ئـــاڤـی *f.* **(-ya;-yê).** dew: **•Bi şev *avî* dikevit ser darûbar û gîha û çandî, gul û kulîlk, mîna ku baran li wan barîbe, gişt şil bûn** (FS:MB) At night *the dew* falls on the trees and grass and crops, on the flowers, as if rain has fallen on them, they are all wet; **-gihyaê avî** (B) dew-covered grass. {also: <avî> آڤـی (HH)} {syn: xunav [1]} [F/K/A/IF/B/HH/GF/FS]

avîs ئاڤيس (OK) = pregnant. See **avis**.

avîtin ئاڤيتِن (K/F/Z-1) = to throw. See **avêtin**.

avîvan ئاڤيڤان *f.* **(-a;).** 1) girl who draws water from a well; 2) [*m. or adj.*] man who serves water to guests: **-zelamê avîvan** (FS) water bearer. [Bw/FS/BF]

avjen I ئـــاڤـــژەن *m.* **(-ê;).** swimmer. {syn: melevan; sobek'ar} [IFb/FJ/CS/FS/BF/Wkt/ZF3]

avjen II ئاڤژەن (Ardû/K) = swimming. See **avjenî**.

avjenî ئاڤژەنی *f.* **(-ya;-yê).** swimming: **•Ya xirab, xort bi *avjenê* jî nizane** (Ardû, 68) The bad thing is, the young man doesn't know how *to swim*; **-avjenî kirin** (CS) to swim: **•Mêşan di çavên wî yên sist de *avjenî dikirin*** [sic] (HYma, 33) Flies *were* *swimming* in his weak eyes. {also: avjen II (Ardû/K)} {syn: ajnê; melevanî; sobahî} [HYma/FJ/GF/RZ/CS/FS/ZF3//Ardû/K]

avk'êş ئاڤکێش *m.&f.* **(-ê/;).** water carrier: •**Min jî di jêr de, guhdariya fîxanên nanpêj û** ***avkêşên*** **xwe dikir** (Qzl) And I was listening to the screams of the our baker and *water carriers* from below. Cf. Sor awkêş ئاوکێش [Qzl/K/B/IFb/CS/FJ/TF/AD/GF/OK/BF]

avlêk ئـــاڤـــلـــێـــك *f.* **(-a;).** 1) {syn: cerîvk (Bw); gêzî; k'inoşe; melk'es; sirge (Ad); siqavêl; sivnik; sizik; şicing; şirt I} broom (IF/Krç); 2) broom plant (IF/IFb). {also: havlêk (IF-2/IFb); havlik (Krç)} <Arm awel աւել = 'broom' [cf. also K siqavêl = 'large broom used in sweeping out a stable'] < [Pok. obhel- 772.] 'to sweep, pile up': cf. Gr ophellō ὀφέλλω = 'I sweep' & ophelma ὄφελμα = 'broom' [IF/ZF3//IFb//Krç] <gêzî; maliştin>

avlĥeyat ئاڤلحەیات (EH) = water of life. See **avilĥeyat**.

avr̄abûn ئـاڤرابـوون *f.* **(;-ê).** flooding, rising *(of water), particularly during the spring melt.* [Zeb/IFb/GF/BF] <lehî; lêmişt; sêlav; t[']ofan>

avr̄ej ئاڤرەژ (Msr) = toilet. See **avr̄êj I**.

avr̄ê ئاڤرێ (Hej) = aside, away. See **averê**.

avr̄êj I ئـــاڤـــرێـــژ *f.* **(-a;-ê).** toilet, water closet, lavatory: •**Ew çû** ***avr̄êjê*** (FS) S/he went *to the lavatory*. {also: avr̄ej (Msr); <avrêj> اڤـــريـــژ (HH)} {syn: avdestxane; ç'olik III; daşir; destavxane; edebxane [1]; qedemge} [Msr//IF/HH/ZF3/BF/FS]

avsark ئـاڤـسـارك *f.* **(-a;-ê).** freezer; refrigerator: •**Min pêvajoya çareseriyê neqedandiye lê min ew xistiye** ***avsarkê*** (Sputnik 05.iv.2016) I have not finished the solution process, but I have put it in *the freezer* [=on the back burner?] •**Sê xortên kurd di** ***avsarka*** **kamyonekê de hatibûn dîtin** (Bloga Zinar Ala 2.x.2015) Three Kurdish youths had been found in *the freezer of* a truck •**Xwarinên me ji bo zivistanê amade kiribû** [sic] **ji ber ku ceyran tune di** ***avsarkê*** **de xera bûne** (kelhaamed 02.i.2017) The foods which we had prepared for winter have gone bad in *the freezer* because there is no electricity. < av = 'water' + sar = 'cold' + -k [A/IFb/SS/Wkt] <sarincok>

avxork ئاڤخۆرك *f.* **(-a;-ê).** tumbler, drinking glass: •**Tu jî herdem layê** ***avxorkê*** **yê vala dibînî** (kulturname.com :P. Cihanî 25.vi.2010) And you always see the empty half [lit.'side'] *of the glass*. {also: avxurk (Wkt)} {syn: gilas; p'erdax; p'eyale[2]} [QtrE/Slm/RZ//Wkt] <îstekan>

avxurk ئاڤخورك (Wkt) = drinking glass. See **avxork**.

***av-zar** ئـــاڤ زار: **-av-zar çûn/avzar bûn** (SS) to lose strength, become weak, languish; to be done for. {syn: dest xwe çûn (Z-1); zar-ziman k'etin} [SS]

avzêmk ئاڤزێمك (FS) = buckle. See **avzûn**.

avzon ئاڤزۆن (FS) = buckle. See **avzûn**.

avzûm ئاڤزووم (Wkt/JJ) = buckle. See **avzûn**.

avzûn ئـاڤـزوون *f.* **(-a;).** buckle: •**Wî** ***avzona*** **qayşê** ***girt*** (FS) He *buckled* the belt. {also: avzêmk (FS-2); avzon (FS); avzûm (Wkt); avzûng (IF); avzûnk (Haz); aẍzûm (K); [awzoum اڤـزوم/agzoum اغـزوم] (JJ)} Cf. Ar ibzīm ابـزيـم, Heb avzem אבזם; NENA abzâ ܐܒܙܐ/abzûna ܐܒܙܘܢܐ (Maclean); Sor awzunge ئاوزونگە/awzûne ئاوزوونە [Zx/A//IF//FS//Haz//JJ/Wkt//K]

avzûng ئاڤزوونگ (IF) = buckle. See **avzûn**.

avzûnk ئاڤزوونك (Haz) = buckle. See **avzûn**.

aw ئاو (SK) = water. See **av**.

awa ئـــــــاوا *m.* **(-yê;-yî).** 1) {syn: celeb I; cûr̄e; t'eher} manner, way, style: •**Her pereke wî ji** ***hawakê*** **ye** (L) Every one of his feathers is of *a* [different] *color*; **-bi vî awayî** = thus, in this manner; **–bi çi awayî be jî** (JB3)/**bi her awayî biwa** (SW) (in) any way; 2) {syn: r̄ewş[3]} case *(gram.)*. {also: awayî (K); hawa (L); <awa> آوا (HH)} [SW/A/JB3/HH/K//L]

awa ĥeyatê ئـــاوا حـــەیـــاتـــێ (SK) = water of life. See **avilĥeyat**.

awamte ئـــاوامـــتـــە (Wkt) = useless, worthless. See **hewante**.

awan ئاوان (K/JB1-S) = troublemaker. See **'ewan II**.

awante ئاوانتە (Wkt) = useless, worthless. See **hewante**.

awarte ئـــــــاوارتـــــــە *adj.* 1) exceptional, unusual, extraordinary, out of the ordinary, unexpected; emergency (adj.) {Cf. Ar ṭāri' طـارئ}: **-komcivîna awarte** (Wlt) emergency meeting: •**Di 19'ê Îlona 1992 an de komcivîna** ***awarte*** **ya duyemîn a HEP'ê li Enqerê li dar ket** (Wlt 1:43, 9) On September 19, 1992, the second *emergency* meeting of the People's Labor Party (HEP) took place; **-r̄ewşa awarte** (IFb) state of emergency, exceptional state; 2) excepted to, immune from [+**ji**]: •**Zar̄o** ***ji*** **yasayên sizadanê** ***awarte*** **ne** (FS) Childrfen are *excepted from/immune to* the penal laws. <Hau? [(neol)Wlt/IFb/GF/TF/OK/ZF3/Wkt/FS] <t̲engav>

awayî ئاوایی (K) = manner, way. See **awa**.

awêşe ئاوێشە (Wkt) = problem, issue. See **arêşe**.

awiqandin ئـاوقـانـدِن *vt.* **(-awiqîn-).** to delay, make late, put off, procrastinate: •**Her roja înîyê, em qîzekê dixemilînin û dibin ji vê zihayê mara re, ew wê**

qîzê heyanî dixwe, av tê ... dora qîza hakimê me ye. Destê hakim li qîza xwe nagere, qîza xwe *awiqandîye* (L-I, #4, 114-116) Every Friday, we dress up a girl and bring her to that dragon, and while he eats the girl, there is water [for us to drink] ... it's our ruler's daughter's turn. The ruler can't bear to lose his daughter, he has *delayed* his daughter['s turn]. {also: ewiqandin (A-2/IFb); <'ewiqandin> عـوقـانـدن (HH)} {syn: egle kirin; gîro kirin; taloq kirin} < Ar √'-w-q عـــــــــوق = 'to be delayed, fall behind' [L/A/HH/TF//IFb]

awiqîn ئـــاوِقـــيـن *vi.* **(-awiq-).** to be delayed, be late: •**Wellah, her ro, vê çaxê, Axê Sor dihat, îro çima *awiqî?*** (L-I, 90, l. 33-4) By God, every day at this time the Red Agha used to come, why *is he late* today? {also: ewiqîn (A/IFb/OK); [eviqin] عـوقـيـن (JJ); <'[e]wiqîn> عـوقـيـن (HH)} {syn: egle bûn; gîro bûn} < Ar √'-w-q عوق = 'to be delayed, fall behind' [L/K/TF//A/IFb/OK//JJ/HH] <dereng>

awir ئـــاوِر (JB1-A)/awir̄ ئـــاوِڕ (Z-2) = disdain; frown; wink. See **avir̄**.

Awistiralî ئـــاوِســـتِـــرالـــى (SS) = Australian. See **Awistralyayî**.

Awistiryayî ئاوِستِريايى (Wkt) = Austrian. See **Awistrî**.

Awistralî ئـــاوِســـتـــرالـــى (Wkt/Wkp) = Australian. See **Awistralyayî**.

Awistralyayî ئـــاوِســـتـــرالـــيـــايـــى *adj.* Australian. {also: Australî (Wkp-2); Awistiralî (SS); Awistralî (Wkt-2/Wkp); Ostralî (Wkp-2)} Sor 'Usturalî ئوستورالى [ZF3/Wkt//SS//Wkp]

Awistriyayî ئاوِستِريايى (Wkp) = Austrian. See **Awistrî**.

Awistrî ئـــاوِســـتـــرى *adj.* Austrian. {also: Austriyayî (WKp-2); Austrî (Wkp-2); Awistiryayî (Wkt-2); Awistriyayî (Wkp-2)} {syn: *Nemsawî; *Otrîşî} = Sor Ostriyayî ئۆستِريايى/Nemsawî نەمساوى [Wkt/SS/Wkp]

awî ئاوى (SK) = liquid; irrigated. See **avî I**.

awîşe ئاويشه (MJ/Wkt) = problem, issue. See **arêşe**.

ax ئـــــــــاخ *f.* **(-a;-ê).** 1) dirt, ground, soil, earth: •***Ax* pir bi xêr û bêr e** (AB) *The soil* is very productive •**Wekî** [or **hindî**] ***axê* zor in** [or **mişe ne**] (Zeb) They are a dime a dozen [lit. 'as abundant as *dirt*']; 2) dust (K/JB1-A); 3) matter (JB3/IFb). {also: [àkh] اخ (JJ); <ax> آخ (HH); [âkh] (BG); [akh] (RJ)} *According to Morgenstierne* <*āhaka- {see: **IV. Persian Etymologies** in "Varia," *Norsk Tidsskrift for Sprogvidenskap*, 12 (1942), 266}; P xāk خـاك; Sor ax ئـاخ/xak خـاك; See **Land** in: I. Gershevitch. "Outdoor Terms in Iranian," *A Locust's Leg : Studies in Honour of S.H. Taqizadeh* (London, 1962), pp.76-84; reprinted in his *Philologia Iranica*, ed. by N. Sims-Williams (Wiesbaden : Dr. Ludwig Reichert Verlag, 1985), pp. 170-72. [BK/K/A/JB3/IFb/JJ/HH/JB1-A/GF/BG/RJ/SK] <axlêve>

axa ئاغا (HB/K/A/IFb/TF) = agha. See **ax̌a**.

axaftin ئاخافتِن *vi./vt.* **([d]axêv-/[d]axiv-/[d]axivîn-[B]).** 1) to speak, talk: •**Ez bi hemwelatiyên xwe re li ser vê *axivîm*** (Wlt 1:37, 16) I *spoke* about that to my fellow countrymen •**Hevalê min ligel min *axift*** [=**Hevalê min *ez axiftim***] (Bs) My friend *spoke* to me •**Hêdî baxêve**! = Speak slowly!; 2) [**axiftin** *vt.* **([t-']axêv-)**] to be on speaking terms with s.o., make up with s.o. (Bw): •**Ez hevalê xo *t-'axêvim*** (Bw) I'*m on speaking terms with* my friend [i.e., **Em jêk sil nînin** = We're not mad at each other] •**Ez te *naaxêvim*** (Bw) I'*m not speaking* to you •**Me êk û dû *axift[eve]*** (Bw) We're *back on speaking terms* •**Wî *ez axiftim*** (Bw) He *made up with me* [= **Wî xo aşt kir**]{also: axavtin (A/B); axiftin (M/Bw); axivîn (Wlt); axiwtin (SK); [akhaftin] اخـافـتـيـن (JJ); <axaftin آخافتن (taxêve) (تاخيڤه)> (HH); [akhaftene (d'akheiveme)] (BG); [akheftin] (RJ)} {syn: k'êlimîn; mijûl dan; p'eyivîn; qezî kirin (Kg); qise kirin (Ks); şor kirin; ştex̌ilîn; xeberdan} [BX/Zx/K/JJ/JB3/HH/BG//M/Bw/RJ//A/B//SK]

axatî ئـــاخـــاتـــى (TF) = being an agha, a tribal leader or regional nobleman. See **ax̌atî**.

axavk ئـــاخـــاڤـــك (Hk) = snack made of flour and water. See **arxavk**.

axavtin ئاخاڤتِن (A/B) = to speak. See **axaftin.**

axbandir ئـــاخـــبـــانـــدِر (IFb/Qzl/ZF3) = edible plant. See **ax̌bandir.**

axên ئاخێن (FS) = groan; sigh. See **axîn**.

axiftin ئاخِفتِن (M/Bw) = to speak. See **axaftin.**

axil ئـــــــاخِـــــــل *m.* **(; êxil, vî axilî).** fenced-in area for sheep or cattle, pen, corral. {also: [àghil] اغـل (JJ)} {syn: axur; kotan I; k'ox [1]; mexel} <*ā-hvar-ana; Cf. Pahl **āxwarr-** = 'manger, stable' (M3); Sgd "xwyr- [āxwaraya- *causative*] = 'to feed'; Cf. T ağıl = 'sheepfold' + ağal/ağıla/ağul = 'open pen enclosed with a hedge in which sheep are put at night' (DS, v. 1, p. 81) [HB/F/K/B//JJ] <afir̄; axur; bêrî I; dolge; guhêr̄; gom I; k'ox; k'oz; lêf; mexel>

axir ئـــاخِـــر *interj.* You see, you know; Come on; after all: •*Axir* **bêje, çi dixwezî?** (K) Tell me [*already*], what do you want? •*Axir* **eva sê şev û sê rojê weye, te derê dîwanê dadaye** (EP) *You know*, you've already closed the doors of [your] diwan for three days and nights •*Axir* **ne usane** (K) *You know* it's not like that •*Axir* **xizmet yan bo menafi'ê dunyaê ye yan bo se'adeta axiretê ye** (SK 57:667) *After all*, obedience is either for earthly profit or for happiness in the hereafter •**Deste-birak, ez ji te řazîme, lê naha tu gerekê destûra min bidî, ez berbi mala xwe heřim,** *axir* **ez p'exemberim** (Ba3-3, #6) Brother, I am very happy [here] with you, but now you must let me go home; *after all*, I am a prophet! {also: [akher] (BG) = enfin, n'importe, fin} Cf. P āxar آخر / āxe آخه [EP-7/K/BG/SK]

axiret ئاخِرەت (K/B/SK/GF) = the hereafter. See **axret**.

axirî ئـاخِـرى *f.* **(-[y]a;-yê).** end, ending: •*Axrîya* **wê çawa bû?** (HCK-1, 208) How did it end? What was its *ending* like?; **-axirîyê** (F/Dz) in the end, after all, finally {syn: dawîyê}: •*Axryê* **her ȟeft jî mane t'î** (Dz) *In the end* all seven remained thirsty •**Ûsib gelekî diçerçire, lê** *axirîê* **Zelîxê cîkî digire** (Ba-1, #27) Joseph strives very hard, but *finally* he catches [up with] Zulaikha in a place. {also: axrî (HCK); [akhiri] اخـــرى (JJ)} {syn: dawî; encam; k'utasî} <Ar āxir آخر = 'last, final' [F/K/B/JJ//HCK]

axivîn ئاخڤين (Wlt) = to speak. See **axaftin**.

axiwtin ئاخِوتِن (SK) = to speak. See **axaftin**.

axîn ئـاخـيـن *f.* **(-a;-ê).** 1) {syn: int'în[î]; nalenal; nalîn} groan[ing], moan[ing]: **-axîn k'işandin** (IF) to moan; 2) {syn: ȟezing; k'eser} sigh, deep breath: **-axîna k'ûr dahiştin** (K) to take a deep sigh. {also: axên (FS); axînî (B-2)} [K/IF/B/ZF3/BF//FS]

axînî ئاخينى (B) = groan; sigh. See **axîn**.

axîrk ئاخيرك (GF) = sand fly. See **axûrk**.

axlêv•e ئاخلێڤە *f.* **(;•ê).** 1) early springtime, first days of spring, period of sharp rises in temperature and melting of snow (B); first days of spring, when the winter provisions are almost exhausted and peasants are in straits (Dz): •**Tu řind zanî** *ax̌lêve* **çiye, hema te** *ax̌lêve* **ne dîtye** (Dz) You know well what ***axlêve*** [early spring, a difficult season for peasants] is, but you've never seen it *[prv.]*; 2) flood, high water (at time of spring thaw) (K). {also: axlîfe (Haz); ax̌lêve (Dz); ax̌lêvî; [akhlivé] اخــلــوه (JJ)} *Ascribed erroneously by JJ to* Geo axloba ახლობა = 'newness' [nouveauté] & axlo ახლო = 'close to' [proche de], but cf. Sor xakelêwe خاکەلێوە = 'early spring' *(name of the first month of spring according to one of several local Kurdish calendars [Kurdoev:Soranî])* ; <xak = 'earth'+ lêw = 'lip', hence 'earth cracking open its lips' (explanation courtesy of Shayee Khanaka of Kirkûk). Both xak & ax = 'earth' [Dz//K/B/FS/BF//JJ//Haz] <bihar; lehî>

axlîfe ئاخليفه (Haz) = early spring. See **axlêve**.

axor ئاخۆر (A/L)/axoř ئاخۆڕ (B) = sty, pen. See **axur**.

axpîn ئـاخـپـين *f.* **(-a;-ê).** dung heap; fertilized field: •**Li** *axpîna* **paş malên X'ê, gundiyê bi navê Berzo rastî min hat** (Lab, 10) In the *dung heap* between the houses of X, a villager named Berzo encountered me. {also: [akhpin] اخـپـيـن (JJ)} {syn: poxan; sergo; ting} <Arm ałp աղբ = 'excrement, dung, manure, trash' [Lab/K/IFb/B/JJ/GF] <sergîn>

axret ئـاخـرەت *f.* **(-a;-ê).** the hereafter, the next world, the afterlife: •**Axir xizmet yan bo menafi'ê dunyaê ye yan bo se'adeta** *axiretê* **ye** (SK 57:667) After all, obedience is either for earthly profit or for happiness in *the hereafter* •**Eger meqsoda hingo se'adeta** *axiretê* **ye, elbette hingo mela hene** (SK 57:675) If your goal is happiness in *the hereafter*--well, you have mullahs •**Gulek derk'etîye ji qudretê, / Hin dinê kêrî me tê, / Hin** *axretê* **/ Ew çiye? [pembû]** (Z-1729) A flower has come out from God, / Some of it is of use to us in this world, / Some *in the next* / What is it? *[rdl.; ans.: cotton].* {also: axiret (K-2/B-2/SK/GF)} {syn: piştdawî} < Ar āxirah آخرة = 'the hereafter' [Z/K/IFb/B//SK/GF]

axte ئاختە (MK2) = horse. See **exte** [2].

axur ئـاخــور *m./f.(B/L)* **(-ê/-a; êxur, vî axurî/-ê).** stall, sty, pen *(for animals)*; stable (MK2): •**Sîdar ber bu** *êxur* **dibezî** (MB, 11) Sidar was running toward *the stable*. {also: axor (A); axoř (B); axûr (GF); [akhour] اخــور (JJ); <axor> آخــور (HH); [okhor] (RJ)} {syn: axil; gom I; k'ox [1]} <*ā-hvar- *or* *ā-hvar-ana -- see **afiř**; Cf. Pahl āxwarr- = 'manger, stable' (M3); Sgd ”xwyr- [āxwaraya- *causative*] = 'to feed'; P āxur آخر--> Ar axūr أخــور & T ahır + ahur [Kurdish tribe, Çomar-Çorum; Ardahan-Kars (villages); Erzurum; Kemaliye-Erzincan; Erciş-Van; Hozat-Tunceli; Ağın-Elâzığ (villages); Ağrakos, Suşehri, Gürun-Sivas; Kirkuk] = 'animal stable' (DS, v. 1, pp. 124-25). [K/JB3/IFb/JJ/JB1-A/MK2//GF// B//L/A/HH//RJ] <afiř; axil; bêrî I; dolge; guhêř; gom I; kotan I; lêf;

mexel>

axurk ئاخورك (IFb) = sand fly. See **axûrk**.

axû ئـاخـوو *f.* **(-ya;-yê).** poison, venom. {also: axû (K)} {syn: jehr} < T ağı [HB/K/JB3/ZF3/Wkt] <mergemûş>

axûr ئاخوور (GF) = sty, pen; stable. See **axur**.

axûrik ئاخوورِك (M-Am) = sand fly. See **axûrk**.

axûrk ئـاخـوورك/ئـاخـويـرك *f.* **(;-ê).** sand fly, zool. *Phlebotomus*. {also: axîrk (GF); axurk (IFb); axûrik (M-Am); axwîrk (BF); <axwîrk> ئـاخـويـرك (Hej)} [Zeb/OK/FS//M-Am//Hej/BF//GF//IFb] <mêş; p'êşî II>

axwîrk (BF/Hej) = sand fly. See **axûrk**.

aẍ•a ئـــاغـــا *m.* **(•a[y]ê/•ê;•ê).** agha; tribal leader, or regional nobleman; "Kurdish terminology does not distinguish between leaders of the tribe, clan or lineage: all are simply called *agha*--with a few exceptions ... An *agha* is apparently a leader who rules, but by extension his close relatives may also be given this title. In southern and eastern Kurdistan leaders of the tribe or clan are alternatively called *'reis'* ... [T]he difference between ... titles [*beg* and *agha*] as it existed around Diyarbakir in the 1920s: 'the *agha* is the tribal leader who lives in the mountains among his tribe; the *beg* lives in town, he may be and may not be a tribal chieftain originally. A *beg* is literate, an *agha* illiterate. The *beg* is civilized and he engages in politics, the *agha* fights. *Begs* often possess large land-holdings, the *agha* of the mountains is not the landlord of his tribesmen, who possess their own parcels of land'" [from: Martin van Bruinessen. *Agha, Shaikh and State : The Social and Political Structures of Kurdistan* (London: Zed Books, 1992), p. 80-81; *see entire chapter for full discussion of the* ***agha***]: •**Her şêxek û her *aẍayek* û her begek nabît padşahek bît, û çawa ḧez biket weto digel r̄e'îyeta bêçare biket** (SK 56:654) Every shaikh and *agha* and beg cannot be a king and do as he pleases with the hapless peasantry •**Şêx û beg û *aẍa* zor bo ḧalê xo û menfe'etê zatîyê xo zana û şeytan in, emma r̄e'îyet zor bêçare û nezan û weḧşî ne** (SK 56:655) The shaikhs and begs and *aghas* are very wise and cunning in looking after their own case and their personal profit, but the peasantry are quite hapless and rude and ignorant. {also: axa (HB/K/A/IFb/TF); [aga] اغا (JJ): <aẍa> اغا (HH)} Cf. P āqā آقا, T ağa {axatî; aẍatî; aẍayî} [HB/K/A/IFb/TF//B/HH/SK/JB1-A/GF/FS//JJ] <beg; şêx>

aẍatî ئاغاتى *f.* **(-ya;-yê).** position of agha, a tribal leader or regional nobleman: •**Silêman aẍayê donzdeh ḧezar malê Gêsî. Silêman k'et mir, *aẍatya* êlê k'et destê 'Elîyê Gês[î]** (FK-kk-3) Suleiman was the agha of twelve thousand houses of the Gêsî. [When] Suleiman died, *the title of agha* fell to Ali of the Gêsî. {also: axatî (TF); aẍayî (K-2/GF-2)} [K/B/GF/FS//TF] <aẍa>

aẍayî ئـاغـايـى (K/GF) = being an agha, a tribal leader or regional nobleman. See **aẍatî**.

aẍbandir ئاغباندِر *f.* **().** edible plant which grows in the Siverek Basin of Urfa (Riha) and in Mardin (Mêrdîn): •***Axbandir* ji kîrê k'er dirêjtir / ji goştê berxan xweştir** (Qzl) *Aghbandir* is longer than a donkey's penis / more tasty than lamb's meat [Qzl children's rhyme]. {also: axbandir (IFb/Qzl)} Cf. T ağbaldır [Güney ova villages-Gaziantep] = 'a plant with white, 40-50 cm. long stem, gathered in the springtime and eaten' (DS, v. 1, p. 85) [Haz//Qzl/IFb/ZF3//DS]

aẍlêve ئاغلێڤه (Dz) = early spring. See **axlêve**.

aẍlêvî ئاغلێڤى = early spring. See **axlêve**.

aẍrî ئاغرى (HCK) = end. See **axirî**.

aẍû ئاغوو (K) = poison. See **axû**.

aẍzûm ئاغزووم (K) = buckle. See **avzûn**.

aẍzûtî ئـــاغـــزووتـــى *f.* **(-ya;).** percussion cap, fuse, primer, firepan (of firearm): •[*Agzouti* àghir ne girt = ***Aẍzûtî* agir negirt**] (JR) The *firepan* did not catch fire •[**Êdî Isma'îl Aẍa ji pêşve dibînitin ku *aẍzûtiya* tifingê ji nîva hespan biriqî**] (JR #27, 80) Ismail Agha sees up ahead amid the horses that the *firepan* (Fr bassinet) of the rifle flashed. {also: [agz-outi] اغـــزوتـــى (JJ)} < T ağızotu = 'priming, primer (of gun)' [JR/K/JJ/Tsab] <şor̄e; t'ifing>

ayar ئايار (TF) = goatskin sack. See **'eyar I**.

ayarşîrk ئـــايـــارشـــيـــرك (A/IFb) = goatskin sack. See **'eyarşîrk**.

ayet ئـايـەت *f.* **(-a;-ê).** verse (of the Quran): •***Ayeta* jorîn jî vê pêdivîyê derdixe pêşiya me** (fetwayenkurdi.com 10.ii.2014) The above *[Quranic] verse* presents this necessity to us •**Çend *ayet* dibin sûretek û di Qur'anê de 114 sûret hene** (Wkt) Several *verses* [together] make [lit. 'become'] a surah (=chapter), and in the Quran there are 114 surahs. <Ar āyah آية [fetwayenkurdi/IFb/ZF3/FD/Wkt]

***ayil** ئايِل *adj.* unjust, (in the) wrong, at fault. {also: ayîl (Wkt)} {ayiltî} [HB/A/ZF3//Wkt]

***ayiltî** ئايِلتى *f.* **().** injustice, wrong. [A/ZF3]

ayîl ئاييل (Wkt) = unjust. See **ayil**.

ʻaynik عاینِك (Wn) = mirror. See **ʻeynik**.

Ayslendî ئایسلەندی (SS/Wkt) = Icelandic. See **Îslendî**.

az ئـاز *adj*. 1) {also: aza II (Bw/FS/IFb)/aẕa II (Bw-2)} strong, well, healthy (HB/A/HH); 2) steep *(of hills)* (HB/A); 3) quick; ambitious (JB3). {also: <az> آز (HH)} [HB/A/JB3/HH//Bw/FS/IFb]

aza I ئازا/**aẕa I** ئـاظـا (Bw) *adj*. 1) {syn: r̄izgar; serbest; xelas} free, unrestrained, at large; independent: **-aza bûn/xwe aza kirin** [+ **ji**] (K/B) to be free of, to get rid of {syn: jê rizgar bûn; yaxa xwe xilas kirin}: **•Carekê Ûsib ji mal dir̄eve, ku *ji* Zelîxê *azabe*** (Ba3-1) One day Joseph runs away from home, *to get rid of* Zulaikha; **-aza kirin** (HH/JB1-A/OK/TF) to set free, let go, liberate: **-Min *tu aẕa kirî*** (Bw): a) I *let you go*; b) I *forgave you* [see what follows]; **-ger̄dena *fk-î* aza kirin** (JJ/JB1-A) to forgive s.o. [lit. 'to set s.o.'s neck free']: **•Ji dil u yaqîn *gerdena min aza ke*!** (JB1-A) *Pardon me* sincerely [=I am truly sorry] •[*kardána ta āza kem* (G)] (JJ-G) I *pardon you* [What the judge will say on Judgment Day, according to Garzoni]; **-gerdena xo aza kirin** (XF) to excuse o.s., take one's leave: **•Hakimî gotê: "Mûleta min bide ȟeta subey da ez ruxseta xo eyalê xo bixazim, *ger̄dena xo aza bikem*"** (XF) The ruler said, "Give me until tomorrow to take leave of my family [lit. 'to ask leave of my children, and *free my neck*']; 2) empty, vacant, free; 3) {syn: bizirav; camêr; delîr; zîx I[2]} brave, bold, courageous. {also: azad (A/TF-2) -- (A) proper name; azat (MK2); [azad] ازاد (JJ); <aza-> آزا (HH); [aza] (RJ)} Cf. P āzād آزاد = 'free[d]' ; Sor azad[e] ئازاد[ە]/aza ئازا = 'free' & aza ئـــــــــازا = 'brave, active, efficient, quick, helpful, magnanimous, good (child)' {azadî; azahî; azayî} [F/K/JB3/IFb/B/HH/JB1-A/SK/GF/TF/OK/RZ/RJ/BF/ZF3//JJ/A//MK2]

aza II ئازا (Bw/FS/IFb)/aẕa II ئـاظـا (Bw) = strong. See **az**[1].

azad ئازاد (A/JJ/TF) = free; man's name. See **aza**.

azadî ئـازادی *f.* **(-ya;-yê)**. freedom, liberty: **•Gerek em vê *azadiyê* çawa bi kar bînin?** (jw.org) How should we use this *freedom*? {also: azahî (K/JB3); azayî (K-2/B); [azadi] ازادی (JJ)} {syn: r̄izgarî; serbestî} [AB/JJ/A/ZF3/BF//K/JB3//B]

azadîxah ئـازادیـخـاه (OK) = freedom seeking. See **azadîxwaz**.

azadîxaz ئـازادیـخـاز (OK) = freedom seeking. See **azadîxwaz**.

azadîxwaz ئـازادیـخـواز *adj*. freedom seeking, freedom (or liberty) seeker: **•Ji bo xebata miletê Kurd û xebata nivîskar û rojnamevanê *azadîxwaz*** (Wlt 2:59, 7) For the struggling of the Kurdish nation and the struggling of *freedom-seeking* writers and journalists. {also: azadîxah (OK-2); azadîxaz (OK); azadxwez; azahîxwaz (GF); azaxwez (K)} [Wlt/TF/GF/FS/ZF3//OK//K]

azadxwez ئـــازادیـــخـــوەز = freedom seeking. See **azadîxwaz**.

azahî ئازاهی (K/JB3) = freedom. See **azadî**.

azahîxwaz ئـازاهـیـخـواز (GF) = freedom seeking. See **azadîxwaz**.

azap ئازاپ (EP/B) = bachelor. See **azib**.

azapî ئازاپی (B) = bachelorhood. See **azibî**.

azar ئـــازار *f.* **(-a;-ê).** 1) {syn: çîk; êş; jan} pain, ache, distress, suffering, agony: **•Girtina deriyê Sêmalka êş û *azara* xelkê Rojava zêde kiriye** (Rûdaw 9.vii.2013) Closing the Sêmalik gate has increased the suffering and *distress of* the people of Rojava [Syrian Kurdistan]; 2) reproach, reproof, rebuke: **-azar dan** (IFb/ZF) to rebuke, scold, bawl out: **•Tijda *azarek da* wan: "Dev ji xirecirê berdin!"** (EN) T. *scolded* them, "Quit arguing!" Cf. P āzār آزار = 'injury, trouble, disease'; Sor azar ئـــــازار = 'physical pain/ache; agony, suffering' + azar dan ئـــــــــازار دان = 'to persecute, suppress, torment; to hurt, cause pain (to)' [EN/K/A/IFb/B/FJ/GF/TF/ZF/BF/FS/Wkt]

azat ئازات (MK2) = free. See **aza**.

azaxwez ئـــــازاخـــــوەز (K) = freedom seeking. See **azadîxwaz**.

azayî ئازایی (K/B) = freedom. See **azadî**.

azbat ئـــازبـــات *f.* **(-a;).** lineage, family line, ancestry: **•Dixwazim li ser *azbata* qehremanê vê çîrokê ji xwendevana re hinek agahdarî bidim** (ZZ-1, 172) I want to give the readers some information about *the ancestry of* the hero of this story. {also: azbet (FJ/GF/Kmc-2); ezbet (IFb/FJ-2/Kmc-2/ZF3)} {syn: binemal; îcax} < Ar asbāṭ اسـبـاط, pl. of sibṭ سـبـط = 'tribe; grandson'. [ZZ-1/Kmc//FJ/GF/Wkt//IFb/ZF3] <berek; binemal; îcax; malbat; ocax; ṯayfe>

azbet ئـــازبـــەت (FJ/GF/Kmc) = family line, lineage. See **azbat**.

azeb ئازەب (IFb/GF) = bachelor. See **azib**.

azep ئازەپ (K/GF/ZF3) = bachelor. See **azib**.

azepî ئازەپی (K) = bachelorhood. See **azibî**.

Azerbaycanî ئـازەربـایـجـانـی (BF) = Azerbaijani. See **Azerbeycanî**.

Azerbeycanî ئازەربەیجانی *adj.* Azerbaijani, Azeri. {also: Azerbaycanî (BF)} {syn: Azerî} Sor Azirbayicanî ئازِربایجانی [IFb/Wkt/ZF3//BF]

Azerî ئازەری *adj.* Azeri, Azerbaijani. {syn: Azerbeycanî} [IFb/Wkp/Wkt/ZF3/BF]

azib ئازِب *adj.* 1) unmarried, single; 2) [*m.***(-ê;).**] bachelor: •***Azepê* mala xwe be, paşê xelkê be** (Dz #44, 49) Be *the bachelor of* your own house first, then of others [*prv.*]. {also: azap (EP/B); azeb (IFb/GF); azep (K/GF-2/ZF3); ezeb (ZF); ‘ezep (HCK); [azeb] عزب (JJ); <‘ezeb> عزب (HH)} <Ar ‘azab عزب; Sor ‘azeb عازەب = 'lusty bachelor'; Za ’azeb = 'widower' (Todd) {azapî; azepî; azibî} [EP/B//K/ZF3//A/TF/Wkt//IFb/JJ/GF//HH//ZF//HCK]

azibî ئازِبی *f.* **(;-yê).** bachelorhood. {also: azapî (B); azepî (K); [azebi] عزبی (JJ)} [A/TF//K//B] <azib>

azimandin ئازماندِن (TF) = to invite. See **‘ezimandin**.

azirandin ئازِراندِن *vt.* **(-azirîn-).** to stir up, incite, agitate, provoke *(e.g., bees in a hive)*: •**Welatêt îslamî yêt nermrê weku Pakistanê, ku ewey mêj e têkilî digel Emerîka hene, pitir ziyanê dibînin wextê hest û îĥsasêt bisulmana *têne azirandin*** (VoA[Zeb] 8/26/98) Moderate Islamic countries like Pakistan, which have long-standing ties with the United States, suffer the most when Muslim sensitivities *are stirred up*. {also: <azirandin> ئازاردن (Hej)} cf. P āzordan آزردن = 'to injure, molest, trouble' [VoA/Zeb/GF/Hej] <aziryan; lê sor kirin; nav tê dan; şarandin; xurîn III>

azirîn ئازِرین (Bw/GF) = to be agitated. See **aziryan**.

aziryan ئازِریان *vi.* **(-aziryê-).** to be or get stirred up, be agitated, be upset *(e.g., bees in a hive)*. {also: azirîn (Bw-2/GF)} {syn: arîn [4]} Cf. P āzordan آزردن = 'to injure, molest, trouble' [Bw/Zeb/GF] <azirandin>

azix ئازخ, m. (; êzix) (F/B) = provisions. See **azûẍe** [1].

azman ئازمان (Msr) = sky. See **‘ezman I**.

azmûn ئازموون (IFb/TF/RZ/SS/CS) = test; experience; experiment. See **ezmûn**.

aznîf ئازنیف *f.* **(;-ê).** a game played with dominoes: •**Ew yê *aznîfê* diken** (Bw) They are playing ***aznîf***. Cf. Arm azniw ազնիւ = 'kind-hearted' [Bw/IFb/BF]

azoqe ئازۆقە, m. (BF) = provisions. See **azûẍe**[1].

azuru ئازورو (K2-Fêrîk) = desire. See **arzû**.

azux ئازوخ (K) = provisions. See **azûẍe**[1]; = fat products. See **azûẍe**[2].

azû ئازوو *f.(B)/m.(K)* **(;-yê/).** molar (tooth). {also: [àzou] ازو (JJ)} {syn: [diranên] kursî} [K/B/JJ] <didan>

azûqe ئازووقە (OK) = provisions. See **azûẍe** [1].

azûxe ئازووخە (OK) = provisions. See **azûẍe** [1].

azûẍ•e ئازووغە *f./m.(BF)* **(•a/•eyê;).** 1) {also: azix, m. (; êzix) (F/B); azoqe, m. (BF); azux (K); azûqe (OK-2); azûxe (OK); [azoughé ازوغە/azig ازیغ] (JJ)} provisions, food (for a trip), victuals: •***Azoqeyê* me têra du mehane** (BF) Our *provisions* are enough for 2 months •[**Her yek ji we *azûẍa* şeş rojan digel xo hilkirin** (or **hilgirin**)] (JR #27, 81-2) Each one of you bring six days' worth of *provisions* with him; 2) {also: azux, m. (B/K)} fat products, grease, tallow (K/B). Cf. P āzūγe آزوغە = 'provisions' --> T azık; Sor azûxe ئازووخە = 'victuals, provisions' [JR/JJ//OK//BF//K//F/B] <[1] xwarin; zad; [2] bez I; tewaş>

B ب

ba I بـــــا *m.* **(bayê/bê; bê/bayê** [Z-2], **vî bayî).** wind, breeze: **•*Bakî* tenik t'eşîê dixe** (J) *A* light *wind* drops the spindle **•*Ba* tê** (AB) *The wind* blows [lit. 'comes']; **-ba kirin** (K): a) to blow (wind) ; b) to wave *(vt.)*: **•Nav Cizîrê gurzêd at'aşî *ba kirin*** (EP-7) *They waved* torches [lit. 'clubs of fire'] throughout Jizîr; **-xwe ba kirin** (Ba3/K)/**ba dan** (SK) to shake, reel, stagger, twist (vi.) [see also **badan**]: **•Zelîxe *xwe ba dike*, wekî ji destê wî derk'eve** (Ba3) Z. tries to *shake herself* free of his grasp; ***-bayê* feraşîn** = cool summer *breeze*; ***-bayê* subê** (BK) morning *wind.* {also: [ba] بـا (JJ); <ba> بـــــا (HH)} [Pok. 10. au(e)- 81.] 'to blow' --> *AweE < *Aew-: Skt vāta-[vātaḥ] *m.* & vāyu-[vāyuḥ] *m.* = 'wind; the god of wind'; Av vāta- *m.* (scans as va-a-ta [3 syllables]); Old Indo-Iranian Vāta = 'the wind god', cf. also Vāyu = 'the storm god'; P bād باد; Sor ba با; Za va *m.* (Todd); Hau wa *m.* (M4); Cf. Germ wehen = 'to blow'; Eng wind <*/AweE + nt-/ old participle 'blowing'. See: M. Mokri. "Les Vents du Kurdistan," in: *Recherches de kurdologie : Contribution scientifique aux études iraniennes* (Paris : Librairie Klincksieck, 1970), p. [233]-258. [K/A/JB3/IF/B/JJ/HH/SK/MK2] <p'êl; şemal [7]>

ba II بـا *f.* **(; bê** [B]**).** rheumatism: **-ba girtin/~ k'etin** (B) to suffer from rheumatism: **•*Ba* k'etye wî** (B) He has *rheumatism.* {also: bawî [2]; [ba] بـــا (JJ)} Cf. P bād بـــــاد = 'swelling, inflammation'; Sor badarî باداری [IFb/B/JJ/GF]

ba III با: -ba kirin II (PS-I) = to call. See **bang.**

ba IV با = at the house of. See **bal I.**

bab باب (JB1-A/A/HH/SK) = father. See **bav.**

baba بابا (SK) = father. See **bav.**

babelîsk بابەلیسک *f.* **(-a;-ê).** whirlwind, tornado; strong windstorm; dust devil: **•Kulik bala xwe dayê ku *bobelîskek* ji paş ve rabûye** (ZZ-7, 160) K. saw that *a whirlwind* rose up from behind. {also: babelûs (OK-2); babilîsk (Rnh); babîsok (Wkt-2/Omr); bablîs[e]k (GF); bablîsok (A/IFb-2/TF/OK); bobelîsk (K/B); [babelisk بابلسك (G)/boubelizk بوبلزك/boubelis بوبلس] (JJ); <babelîsk> بابليسك (HH)} [Zeb/IFb/JJ-G/HH//GF//A/TF/OK//K/B] <ba I; firtone>

babelûs بابەلووس (OK) = whirlwind. See **babelîsk.**

babet I بابەت *f./m.* **(/-ê;-ê/-î).** 1) sort, quality, type (JB3/IF); 2) {syn: biyav; dabaş; mijar} subject, topic: **•egerê helbijartina *evî babetî*** ('Ebdulla, B.Y. Hozana afretan di edebê Kurdîda, 5) the reason for choosing *this topic*; 3) connection, relationship (K): **•Di *vê babetê* de, nivîsarên Pehlewî pir li dijî Grêkan diaxifin** (Rwş 3, 23) In *this connection* [or, *manner*], the Pahlavi writers speak out against the Greeks. [Ber/K(s)/JB3/IF]

babet II بابەت *adj.* suitable, fitting, appropriate (A): **•Ancax *babet*e, ko serê herduka bi hevra here ser balgîyekîne** (Z-2, 68) It is only *fitting* that their heads should rest on the same pillow [Cf. T wedding salutation 'Bir yastıkta kocayın' = You should grow old on the same pillow'] **•Ev sûarê hanê *babetê* stiya Zîne** (Z-2, 75) This horseman is *fitting for* Lady Zin **•Ev kar ne[b]abetê te ye** (GF) This job does not suit you **•Pîrê rabû, çû dik'anê, lengerîk t'ijî sêvê *babetî* Xecêra k'irî, anî** (IS-#263) The old woman went to the story and bought a platter full of fine apples for Khej [lit. 'apples *worthy of* Khej']. {syn: hink'ûf; layîq [1]} [Z-2/A/GF]

babetî بابەتی *adj.* objective, unbiased: **•Divêt dîroknivîs berî her tiştî *babetî* (objektîv) be** (nefel.com, xi.2008) Above all else the historian must be *objective* **•Me pêkol kiriye, ku li dwîv şiyanan di şilovekirina hozanên wanda *babetî* bîn** ('Ebdulla, B.Y. Hozana afretan di edebê Kurdîda, 6) We have strived as much as possible to be *objective* in interpreting their poems. ['Ebdulla/Wkt/BF/SS/(GF)]

babilîsk بابلیسك (Rnh) = whirlwind. See **babelîsk.**

babîsok بابیسۆك (Wkt/Omr) = whirlwind. See **babelîsk.**

Bablekan بابلەکان *f./m.(FS)* **(-a/;-ê/).** Bablekan, name of a Kurdish folkdance from the Botan and Behdinan regions: **•*Bablekan* yek ji reqsên heri meş[h]ûrê ... herêma Botanê ye** (Wkp) *B.* is one of the most famous dances ... of the Botan region **•Wan *Bablekanekê* xweş kir** (FS) They danced a nice *Bablekan.* [Wkp/ZF3/BF/FS] <govend>

bablîsek بابلیسەك (GF) = whirlwind. See **babelîsk.**

bablîsk بابلیسك (GF) = whirlwind. See **babelîsk.**

bablîsok بابلیسۆك (A/IFb/TF/OK) = whirlwind. See **babelîsk.**

babolek بابۆلەك (QtrE/Slm) = wart. See **belalûk II.**

bac بـاج *f.* **(-a;-ê).** tax, tribute; duty: **•Eger min *bacek* ba Zînê anî** (FK-eb-1) If I succeed in collecting *a tax* from Zîn; **-bertîl û bac**, [see **bertîl**] {also: [badj بـاج/batch بـاچ] (JJ); <bac> بـاج (HH)} {syn: bêş; olam; xerac [1]; xerc [2]; xûk} [Pok. 1. bhag-107.] 'to share out, apportion; also, to get a share': Skt √bhaj [bhájati] = 'to divide, distribute, allot'; Av √bag *pres. stem* baxša- = 'to distribute, dole out'; O P bāji- *f.* = 'tribute' (Brand); Mid P bāǰ (M3); P bāj باج/bāž باژ/bāz باز --> T baç = 'toll or tax formerly collected from caravans and ships'; Sor bac بـاج; cf. also Arm baž (W: paž) բաժ, a Persian loan word. *The persistence of the O P -j- in P and K is noteworthy: perhaps the legalistic quality of the word has retarded the sound change. **beş I** & **bext** come from the same root.* [Z-1/K/A/B/JJ/HH] <berevker>

bacan بـاجـان *m./f.(Qzl)* **(-ê/;).** 1) *usually* **bacanê r̄eş**: eggplant, aubergine, brinjal, bot. *Solanum melongena*; 2) *usually* **bacanê sor** {also: bacansor (RZ-2)} {syn: firingî; stembolî; şamik} tomato, bot. *Lycopersicum esculentum.* {also: badircan, f. (B); badrîcan (K-2); bahcan (Qzl); balcan (GF-2/Krç/Klk); balican (Kmc-2-2); bancan (GF-2); be'can (Qzl); [badindjane بادنجان/bājān (PS) باجان] (JJ); <bacan> باجان (HH)} Cf. P bādenjān بادنجان = 'eggplant, aubergine' & bādenjān-e ferengī بادنجان فرنگى [=gowje-ye ferengī گوجه فرنگى] = 'tomato'; Sor bayincanî r̄eş بـايـنـجـانـى رەش = 'egg-plant, aubergine' & bayincanî sûr بـايـنـجـانـى سـوور/ şam شـام = 'tomato' [Btm/Grc/Çnr/K/A/IFb/JJ-PS/HH/GF/TF/RZ/Kmc-2/CB//B//Qzl//Krç/Klk//JJ]

bacansor باجانسۆر (RZ) = tomato. See **bacan**.

bacar̄ باجاڕ (FK-eb-1) = city. See **bajar**.

bacenax باجەناخ (ZF3) = brother-in-law. See **bacinax**.

bacik باجِك (IFb) = pepper. See **back**.

bacinax بـاجِـنـاخ *m.* **().** brother-in-law [pl. brothers-in-law], *specifically the relationship between husbands of two sisters*; husband of a man's **baltûz** (qv.) {also: bacenax (ZF3)} {syn: hevbûk; hevling} Cf. P bājināγ بـاجـنـاغ = 'brother-in- law'–> T bacanak = 'brother-in-law', specifically the relationship between husbands of two sisters [Haz//ZF3] <baltûz; cayî>

bacî بـاجـى *f.* **().** 1) {syn: k'ilam; stiran I} song (Msr); dance song (Wkt): **•Li herêma Xerzan - Kurtalan (Misirc), Kozluk (Hezo), Baykan (Xana Hawêl) û herêma Babosiyê ji stran û kilaman re *-bacî-* jî tê gotin** (Wkt: Salihê Kevirbirî di koma "Zimanê Kurdî" ya li ser Rûnameyê de, v.2012) In the region of Garzan - Kurtalan (Misirc), Kozluk (Hazo), Baykan (Khana Hawêl) and the region of Babosî songs are also called '*bacî*'; 2) lament (Msr). {also: <bacî> بـاجـى (HH)} [Msr/Xrz/HH/ZF3/Wkt]

back بـاجـك *m.* **(-ê;).** pepper *(plant, vegetable)*: **-backê sor** (Dy) hot pepper. {also: bacik (IFb)} {syn: bîber; guncik; ḧiçḧar; îsot} [Dy//IFb]

baçarmik باچارمِك (Mrş) = bat *(zool.)*. See **barç'imok.**

baçermok بـاچـەرمـۆك (IF/Mzg/ZF) = bat *(zool.)*. See **barç'imok**.

baçik بـاچِك *f.* **(-a;-ê).** cigarette. {also: <baçîk> بـاچـيـك (HH)} {syn: cigare} [IFb/RF/FD/ZF3/Wkt//HH]

baçimêlk باچمێلك (SBx) = bat *(zool.)*. See **barç'imok.**

badak بـاداك *f.* **().** *type of plant*: ivy, vine. {also: <badak> باداك (HH)} [HB/HH/IFb/ZF3]

ba•dan بـادان *vt.* **(ba-d-).** 1) to twist *(vt.)*:**-xo badan** (Bw) to swagger, walk pompously; 2) to turn *(vt. & vi.)*: **•*Bade* bo rexê rastî** (Bw) *Turn* right!; **-lê badan** (Bkp) to turn one's back on s.o., abandon, forsake **•Vêca *li* wan Kurdên hevalbendên xwe yên wek C. Ç. *badaye*** (Bkp, 29) So *he turned his back on* those Kurdish allies of his, such as J.Ch.; **-r̄ûyê xwe jê badan** (K/JB3) to turn away from s.o.; 3) to wind u *(a clock)* {syn: bar I kirin}: **-saeta xwe badan** (JB3) to wind up one's clock or watch; 4) {syn: şidandin [5]} to screw in. {also: <badan> بادان (badide) (بادده)> (HH)} [HB/K/A/JB3/HH/Bw] <[4]: dernefîs>

badayî بـادايـى *adj. pattern of **bergûz** material*: white with thick black stripes. [Bw] <bergûz>

badem بادەم, f. (K) = almond. See **behîv.**

badilhewa بـادِلـهـەوا (B/GF/QtrE) = in vain. See **badîhewa**.

badircan بادِرجان, f. (B) = eggplant; tomato. See **bacan**.

badîhewa باديهەوا *adv.* in vain: **•*Badîhewa* bû cefê wan** (EP-8) Their labor was *in vain* {also: badilhewa (B-2/GF/QtrE); bedilhewa (B-2); [badi heva] بـادى هوا (JJ); <badî hewa> بـادى هوا (HH)} cf. P bād-i havā بـاد هـوا = 'wind of the air' (Ottoman fiscal term, see EI^{2}, vol. 1, p. 850) [EP-8/K/A/IFb/B/JJ/HH/AId//GF/QtrE] <t'ewş>

badrîcan بادريجان (K) = eggplant; tomato. See **bacan**.

bafon بافۆن (A/IFb) = aluminum. See **fafon**.

bafûn بافوون (GF/TF) = aluminum. See **fafon**.

bagar̄an باگاڕان (Btm) = roof-roller. See **bagirdan**.

bager بـاگـەر/**bager̄** بـاگـەڕ [FS/Wkt] *f.* **(-a;-ê).** 1) {syn:

bahoz; bap'eşk; barove; firtone; hureba; t[']ofan [2]} storm: •**Vê *bagera* hanê her derê di ser hev re derbas kir** (tirsik.net) This *windstorm* threw everything into disarray; 2) {syn: bakuzîrk; bamişt; ħabûr} snowstorm, blizzard (Ag/B); strong wind accompanied by snow (HH). {also: [bagher] بـاگـر (JJ); <bager> بـاگر (HH)} [K/A/JB3/IF/B/JJ/HH/Ag//FS/Wkt] <ba I; baran; berf; 'ewr; şilî; t[']ofan>

bagirdan بـاگِـرداْن *m.* **(-ê;-î).** long stone cylinder for rolling down mud roofs, roof-roller: •**Banek û *bagurdanek* in** (BF) They are like 2 peas in a pod [lit. 'they are a roof and a *roof-roller,* i.e., a perfect match] •**Wî serban bi *bagurdanî* gêřa** (FS) He tamped down the roof with *the roof-roller*. {also: bagařan (Btm); bagurdan (IFb/OK/Zeb/BF/FS); banger (FJ/Kmc/ZF); bangeran (FJ-2/ZF-2); bangêrdan (GF-2); bangor (A/Kmc-2); <banger> بـانـگـر (HH)} {syn: gundor II; lox} Cf. Sor bangirdên بـانـگِـردێن/bagirdan بـاگِـرداْن. *For an illustration, see Atılcan, p. 118.* [A/GF//IFb/Zeb/BF/FS//Btm//FJ/Kmc/ZF/HH//A] <t'apan>

bagurdan بـاگـورداْن (IFb/OK/Zeb/BF/FS) = roof-roller. See **bagirdan**.

baha باها (B) = price; expensive. See **biha**.

bahar باهار (Ba2/A/B) = springtime. See **bihar**.

bahcan باهجان (Qzl) = eggplant; tomato. See **bacan**.

bahîv باهيڤ (OK/AA/FS) = almond. See **behîv**.

bahîvteřk بـاهـيـڤـتـەرك (AA/Elk) = unripe almond. See **behîvteř**.

bahos باهۆس = storm. See **bahoz.**

bahoz بـاهـۆز *f./m.(FS/BF)* **(-a/;-ê/-î)**. storm, hurricane, tornado: •***Bahozê*** [sic] **li coxîna wî da û rakir** (FS) *The storm* struck his threshing floor and lifted it up [i.e., messed it up]. {also: bahos} {syn: bager; bap'eşk; barove; firtone; hureba; t[']ofan [2]} [HB/K/A/ZF3/FS/BF]

bahtof بـاهـطـۆف (FS) = reddish-brown dye for cattle hides. See **batov**.

bahûşk باهووشك (Tsab) = yawn. See **bawişk**.

baîbûn بااييبوون (F) = camomile. See **beybûn**.

baîs بائيس (F)/ba'îs باعيس (SK) = reason. See **bayîs I**.

baîsiz بائيسِز (FK-kk-1) = cause of disaster. See **baysiz**.

bajar بـاژار/**bajař** بـاژار [FS] *m./f.(HM/PS)* **(-ê/-a; bajêr, vî bajarî/). town, city: •Jiyana li *bajêran* ne wek ya gundane** (BF) Life in *cities* is not like that in villages. {also: bacař (FK-eb-1); bajêr (SK/Bw/M/BF); [bajir] بـاژير (JJ)} {syn: beled I; şeher} Cf. P bāzār بـازار = 'market, bazaar'--> T pazar [K/A/JB3/IFb/B/JB1-S/GF/TF//FS//JJ//SK/Bw/M/BF] <heyşet; şênî>

bajarî بـاژاری/**bajařî** بـاژاری [FS/Wkt] *m.* **(-yê;).** city dweller, town dweller, townsman: •**Keçên me têra xortên eşîra me nakin, me keç nîne ku em bidin *bajariyan*** (Lab, 6) We don't have enough girls for our own tribe, we don't have any girls to give [in marriage] to *city folk* •**Muroekî Artûşî koçer digel tacirekî Mûsilî dost bû. Her sal muroê Artûşî diçû Mûsilê ... dibû mêwanê dostê xo. Dostê wî jî gelek qedrê wî digirt ... xarina *bajerîya*, ko şirînî, pilaw, goşt, êprax, şorbawa bi dermanêt bênxoş û tiştê wekî wane bo wî didanane ser sifrê** (SK 31:274) A man of the Artushi nomads was friendly with a merchant of Mosul. Every year the Artushi used to go to Mosul ... and was the guest of his friend. His friend would treat him with great respect ... he would set on the tablecloth *townsmen's* food, which is sweetmeats, pilaf, meat, stuffed vine-leaves, soup with fragrant spices and other such things. {also: bajerî (SK); [bajiri بـاژيـری/bāžārī (PS)] (JJ)} {syn: *bajarvan} [Lab/K/A/IFb/J-PS/GF/TF//FS//SK//JJ]

bajerî باژەری (SK) = city dweller. See **bajarî**.

bajêr باژێر (SK/Bw/M/BF) = town, city. See **bajar**.

bakir باكِر (K) = virgin. See **bik'ur**.

bakire باكِرە (SK) = virgin. See **bik'ur**.

bakur بـاكـور *f.(Ber)/m.(ZF3/Wkt)* **(-a/-ê;).** 1) north; 2) Northern Kurdistan, Kurdistan of Turkey {also: Bakurê Kurdistanê (Wkt)}: •***Bakurê Kurdistanê* ji wê beşa Kurdistanê re tê gotin ku dikevê nav sînorên dewleta Tirkiyê. Gelek caran ji bo *Bakurê Kurdistanê* bêjeya Kurdistana Tirkiyê jî tê bikar anîn** (Wkp) The part of Kurdistan that lies within the borders of the state of Turkey is called *Northern Kurdistan* [Bakur]. Often the term Kurdistan of Turkey is also used for *Northern Kurdistan*. {syn: mifriq; şemal, f. (F)} Sor bakûr بـاكـوور [K/A/JB3/IFb/TF/Ber/Wkt/ZF3] <başûr; cenûb; řo[j]hilat; řo[j]ava>

bakuzîrik باكوزيرِك (BF) = blizzard. See **bakuzîrk**.

bakuzîrk باكوزيرك *f.(Zeb)/m.(OK)* **(/-ê;-ê/).** blizzard, snowstorm with wind: •***Bakuzîrkê* li navçavê wan dida** (FS) *The blizzard* was beating down on their faces. {also: bakuzîrik (BF)} {syn: bager[2]; bamişt; barove; ħabûr} *GF [bakizîrk] and OK define this as "hot wind, simoom"* [Bw/Dh/Zeb/OK/Hej/FS] <hureba>

bal I بـال *prep.* at, at or over s.o.'s house, to or into s.o.'s presence; {cf. Fr. chez, Germ. bei}: •*ba* **min/ li** ***bal*** **min** = *at* my house; *in* my presence [chez moi] •***balê*** (Frq) *at his/her house*; *in his/her presence* [chez lui/elle] •***Ji bal*** **apê xwe dihat** (BX) He was coming *from* his uncle's •**Jinik tê *bal* keç'ikê** (J) The woman comes *to* the girl •**Xwedê ez şandime *bal* te** (Dz) God has sent me *to* you; **-bal ... ve** (BX) in the direction of. {also: ba IV} {syn: ber serê/ber/ser; cem; hinda I; ḧafa [*see* ḧaf]; lalê; li def [*see* def II]; nik I; řex I} < bi alî[yê] = in the direction (of) [BX/F/J/K/A/B]

bal II بـال *f.* **(-a;-ê).** 1) mind, memory, thoughts: **-bala *fk-ê* k'işandin** (Msr) to attract or catch s.o.'s attention, to interest s.o.: •**Ev tişt *bala* min *dik'işîne*** (Msr) This thing *interests* me •**Her wiha ew *balê dikişînin ser* piştevaniya dewletên Ewrûpayê jî** (AW71A3) Likewise they *draw attention to* the support of the European states as well; 2) look, glance: **-bala xwe dan** (K) to look, see {syn: fikirîn II; mêze kirin; nêřîn}: •***Bala xwe danê*, M. razaye bi xewa şîrin** (Z) They *looked and saw* that M. was sound asleep [lit. 'sleeping in sweet sleep']. {syn: bîr I; zên I} <Ar bāl بال [Z/K/A/JB3/B] <balk'êş>

bala بـالا *adv.* up, upward(s), on high. {also: banî I} {syn: jor; ≠xwar} Cf. Av barezah- = 'height'; P bālā بالا (Horn #171); Sor bała باڵا = 'high, height, stature' [K/A/Wkt] <berz; bilind; hevraz>

balafiř بالافِر *f.* **(-a;-ê).** airplane: •**Gelek rêwî li benda *balafirê* bûn** (amidakurd.net 25.vi.2007) Many passengers were waiting for *the airplane.* {also: balefiř (FS)} {syn: fiřoke; teyare} < bala = 'up' + fiř- = 'to fly' [(neol)BX/K/A/JB3/Bw/ZF3//FS]

balafirge بالافرگه (A) = airport. See **balafiřgeh.**

balafiřgeh بـالافِرگـه‌ه *f.* **(-a;-ê).** airport. {also: balafirge (A)} {syn: *firokcih (A); *meṯar (Zx)} [(neol)BX/K/A/JB3/ZF3]

balafiřvan بالافِرڤان *m.* **().** aviator, pilot. {syn: firokevan (K[s])} {balafiřvanî} [(neol)BX/K/A/JB3/ZF3]

balafiřvanî بالافِرڤانى *f.* **().** aviation. [(neol)BX/ZF3]

balagih بالاگِه = pillow. See **balgih.**

balat'îf بالاتيف (F/K/JJ) = butterfly. See **belantîk.**

balav بـالاڤ *f.* **(-a;-ê).** 1) {syn: *kel (Zeb-->Bw)} laundry; washing clothes: •**Ez dê çime *balavê*** (Zeb) I will go do *the laundry*; **-balav kirin** (GF) to wash clothes with running water; 2) bath, bathing: •**Bila bihêt serê min bişot, evřok'e řoja *balava* min e** (JB1-A #29,106) Let her come bathe me [lit. 'wash my head'], today is my *bath* day. {also: balave (K); balaw (JB1-A); berav (IFb-2/B); [balave] بلاوه (JJ-G); <balav> بالاڤ (Hej)} [Zeb/IFb/GF/Hej//JB1-A//K//JJ-G//B] <cilşo>

balave بالاڤه (K) = laundry. See **balav.**

balaxane بالاخانه *f.* **(-ya;-yê).** skyscraper, tall building: •**Li Erebîstana Suudiyê mezintirîn *balaxaneya* cîhanê tê avakirin** (RewanBêj 21.iv.2014) In Saudi Arabia the largest *skyscraper* in the world is being built •**Li Stenbolê di *balaxaneyê* de şewat derket** (RojevaKurd 17.vii.2012) A fire broke out in a *skyscraper* in Istanbul. {also: balexane (FD/CCG)} Sor bałexane باڵخانه [CCG/FD//ZF3/Wkt] <avahî>

balbalok بالبالۆك *f.* **(-a;).** praying mantis, *zool.* Mantis religiosa [Ar faras al-nabī فـرس الـنـبـي, T peygamberdevesi, P āxundak آخـنـدك]. {syn: hespê Fatma nebî; hespê nebî; hespê pêxember} = Sor kule ḧacî كوله حاجى [IFb/FJ/AD/ZF3/BF/Wkt]

balbas بـالـبـاس *m.* **().** man carrying out superior's orders, guard, soldier, policeman: •... **Piştî ku mezinê malmezinan li rîsipiyên dora xwe jî dinêre, tavilê fermanê dide *balbasên* xwe û ji wan re dibêje: ... divê hûn vî xortî bibin û tavilê bi darde bikin ... Bi vê fermanê re *balbas* diçin radihêjin piyê xort, ji wir dûrdixin ku êdî bibin fermana mezinê malmezinan bi cî bînin** (Ardû, 119) After the chief of the aristocrats looks at the elders around him, he immediately gives an order to his *men* and says to them: ... You must take this young man and hang him right away ... At this order *the men* go and grab the young man by his feet, take him away to carry out the order of the chief. [Ardû/GF/FJ] <ersewil>

balcan بـالـجـان (GF/Krç/Klk) = eggplant; tomato. See **bacan.**

balç'emk بالچه‌مك (K) = bat (zool.). See **barç'imok.**

balçermek بالچرمەك (A) = bat (zool.). See **barç'imok.**

balçimk بـالـچـمـك (F)/balç'imk (B) = bat (zool.). See **barç'imok.**

balç'ix بالچخ (K) = hilt of sword. See **balçîq.**

balçîq بـالـچـيـق *f.* **(-a;).** handle, hilt, haft *(of sword)*: •***Balçîqa* şûrê xo dide 'erdê** (Z-3) He points *the hilt of* his sword at the ground. {also: balç'ix (K)} {syn: qebd} Cf. T balçak = 'guard of a sword hilt' [Z-3//K] <şûr>

balefiř بالەفِر (FS) = airplane. See **balafiř.**

balet•e بـالـيـتـه *f.* **(•a;•eyê).** fruit (particularly grapes [AA]) in the early stages of ripening, newly ripening fruit. *Cf.* ***solîn II*** *for a similar concept* *regarding flowers.* [Bw/IFb/OK/AA/FS] <êmîş [1]; fîkî; mêwe>

balexane بـالـەخـانـە (FD/CCG) = skyscraper. See **balaxane**.

balê بالێ (Frq) = at his house. See **bal I**.

balge باڵگە (SK) = pillow. See **balgih**.

balgeh باڵگەه (A)= pillow. See **balgih**.

balgih بـاڵگِە *m. [E] (JB3)/f. [W]* **().** 1) cushion, pillow: **-Du serê çê naçine ser be'lgîkî** (Dz) Two good heads don't rest [lit. 'go'] on one pillow *[prv.]*; 2) support (fig.) (Sor). {also: balagih; balge (SK); balgeh (A); balgî, m. (K); balgîv; be'lgî II, m. (F/Dz/EP/B); **balîf**; balîş (B-2); [balghi بـالـگـى/balíf بـاليف] (JJ); <balgîv بـالـگيف/balge[h] بـالـگه/balgok بـالـگۆك> (HH)} {syn: **balîf**} ?<bal I = 'near' + guh ='ear', cf. Fr oreiller < oreille = 'ear' & Rus poduška подушка <pod под = 'under' + ukho ухо = 'ear' [M. Schwartz: by popular etymology from form like P bāliš?]; O Ir *barziš-; Av barəziš-; Mid P bāliš (M3); P bāliš بـالش = 'cushion, pillow'; Sor balîf بـــالـــيـــف = 'arm rest, cushion'; Za başna *f.* (Todd) & bālišná (Lx) = 'pillow'; see: *Haoma*, §252 ff., pp. 138-40. [BX/K/JB3//F/B//JJ//HH//A//SK] See also **balîf**. <berp'al; zemberîş>

balgî بالگى, m. (K) = pillow. See **balgih**.

balgîv بالگيف = pillow. See **balgih**.

balican بالِجان (Kmc-2) = eggplant; tomato. See **bacan**.

balif بالِف (ZZ-10) = pillow. See **balîf** .

balinç بـالِـنـچ *f.* **().** hole on either side of a man's *bergûz* (traditional Kurdish baggy trousers) at waist level: **-balinçêt peşmê** (Zeb) do. {also: balinçk (Bw)} [Zeb//Bw] <bergûz>

balinçk بـالِـنـچك (Bw) = (pocket) hole of baggy trousers. See **balinç**.

balîf بـاليـف *m./f.(ZF)* **(-ê/-a;).** pillow, cushion: **•Rahişt *wî balîfê* ku xencer tê de çikkirî bû hilda û bir xiste odakê** (ZZ-10, 158) He grabbed *that cushion* in which the dagger was plunged, picked it up and took it to another room. {also: balif (ZZ-10); [balíf] باليف (JJ)} {syn: balgih} Cf. Sor balîf باليف = 'arm rest, cushion' [K/A/JJ/ZF//ZZ] See also **balgih**. <berp'al; zemberîş>

balîlûk باليلوك (Czr) = type of sandwich. See **balolk**.

balîş باليش (B) = pillow. See **balgih**.

balk'êş بـالـكـيـش *adj.* interesting: **•Ev sûlav dîmenekê *balkêş* e** (FS) This waterfall is an *interesting* sight **•Gotinên wî *balkêş* in lê ne bawer im ku rast bin** (Wkt) His words are *interesting* but I don't think they are true/correct. {syn: hewask'ar [3]} < bal II = 'mind, etc.' + k'êş = 'to draw' [(neol)Wlt/IFb/TF/BF/ZF3/Wkt/FS] <bi sebr>

balkon بالكۆن (B/IFb) = balcony. See **palkon**.

balok بالۆك (Wn) = type of sandwich. See **balolk**.

balolk بـالـۆلـك *f.* **(;-ê).** type of sandwich, "wrap" [T dürüm]. {also: balîlûk (Czr); balok (Wn)} {syn: ȟoç} [Elk/Dh/IFb//Wn//Czr]

balt'•e بالتە *m./f.(ZF3)* **(•ê/ ;).** axe, hatchet: **•Despê kir bi *balt'ê* dar biȓîn** (Dz) He began to cut down trees with *an axe*; **-balt'ê avdayî** (Qzl) strong and clever man [lit. 'watered axe']. {syn: bivir; tevir [1]} <T balta -->Ar bālṭah بالطة [F/Dz/K/B/ZF3]

baltuz بالتوز (Haz) = sister-in-law. See **baltûz**.

baltûz/balt'ûz [B] بـالـتـووز *f.* **(-a;-ê).** sister-in-law [pl. sisters-in-law], (a married man's) wife's sister: **•*Baltuzê* min keçekî pir bedewe** (Haz) My *sister-in-law* is a very pretty girl. {also: baltuz (Haz); balt'ûz (B); [baldouz] بالدوز (JJ); <balṯûz> بـالـطـوز (HH)} {syn: diş[1]} < T baldız [Haz/F/K/B/HH//JJ] <cayî; diş; jinbira; jint'î II>

balûk بالووك (Qzl/K/B/JJ/GF) = wart. See **belalûk II**.

balûr بالوور (FJ) = wart. See **belalûk II**.

balyoz بـاليۆز *m.* **(-ê;).** ambassador: **•*Balyozê* Îraqê li Swêdê** (FS) The Iraqi *ambassador* to Sweden. {also: bayloz (K/A/GF-2); [balioz] باليۆز (JJ)} < It bailo/balio; Sor bałyoz بـاڵـيـۆز [VoA/IFb/JJ/GF/TF/BF/FS/ZF3//K/A]

balyozxane بـالـيـۆزخـانـە *f.* **(-ya;).** embassy: **•*Balyoz-xaneya* Amerîkayê li Tehranê** (rudaw.net 15.xii.2014) The American *embassy* in Tehran. {also: baylozxane (K/A/GF)} Sor bałyozxane باڵيۆزخانە [VoA/IFb/GF/TF/ZF3/Wkt//K/A]

bamişt بـامِـشـت *f.* **(;-ê).** snowstorm, blizzard: **•*Bamiştê* dever girt** (FS) *The blizzard* took hold of/closed down the region. {syn: bager[2]; bakuzîrk; ȟabûr} [Haz/IFb/GF/FS/Wkt/ZF3] <bager; bahoz; barove; hureba>

ban I بان (JB1-S/GF) = call; call to prayer. See **bang.**

ban II بـــــــــان *m.* **(-ê; bên, vî banî).** roof: **•*Banek* û bagurdanek in** (BF) They are like 2 peas in a pod [lit. 'they are *a roof* and a roof-roller, i.e., a perfect match] **•Qîza wî li ser *banê* qesrê rûnişt** (L) His daughter sat on *the roof of* the palace. {also: [ban] بـــان (JJ); <ban> بـــان (HH)} {syn: sit'ar [1]} Cf. P bām بـام; Sor ban بـان = 'top sided, rooftop, surface, plateau' [Z/K/A/JB3/B/JJ/HH/GF/TF/Haz]

banandin بـانـانـدِن (A/IFb/FJ/Wkt/G/FD) = to accustom to. See **lê banandin**.

bancan بانجان (GF) = eggplant; tomato. See **bacan**.

bandor باندۆر (IFb/GF) = influence. See **bandûř**.

bandûř باندووڕ/**bandûr** باندوور [K] *f.* **(-a;-ê).** 1) {syn: eger II; t'esîr} influence, effect: •**Ew merîkî** ***bi bandûre*** (K) He is an *influential* person •**Nikarin te ji bin** ***bandûřa*** **min derînin** (FK-eb-2) They won't succeed in removing you from my *influence*; **-avîtin** (B)/**kirin bin bandûra xwe** (K) to bring s.o. under one's influence, to influence s.o.: •**Hema Îskender p'adşatîke baş dikir, çiqas dua' lê dorê hebûn, gişk** ***kire bin bandûřa xwe*** (EH) Iskender ruled well, he was able *to bring under his influence* anyone who had been undecided [?]; **-k'etin bin bandûra** ***fk-ê*** (K/B) to be or fall under s.o.'s influence, to be influenced or affected by s.o.; 2) subordination, submission; 3) person, individual, personage (B); 4) yoke (GF). {also: bandor (IFb-2/GF-2); bendûr (B/F)} [FK-2/EH/K/IFb/GF/TF//B/F//OK]

baneşan بـانـەشـان *f.* **(;-ê).** interjection *(grammatical category)*; exclamation: •**Mirov hestê xwe yên: dilxweşiyê, ecibandinê, kovan û keserê bi alîkariya** ***baneşanan*** **dide der** (M. Aykoç. Rêziman'a destî, 51) One expresses one's feelings of: happiness, admiration, grief and sorrow with the help of *interjections*. {also: bangnîşan (Wkt-2/ZF3-2)} [M.Aykoç/IFb/TF/GF/Kmc/FD/Wkt/ZF3/CS]

bang بـانـگ *m./f.* **(-ê/-a;).** 1) call, shout[ing], yell[ing], cry: **-bang kirin** (RZ) a) to shout, yell, call {syn: gazî kirin}: •**Qundir** ***ban*** **bavê xwe** ***kir*** (L) The gourd *called to* its father; b) to invite; c) to call up on the phone; 2) (Islamic) call to prayer, muezzin's chanting from the minaret of a mosque (SK): -**bang dan** (SK/JJ-G)/~ **kirin** (JJ) to call to prayer: •**Nîmçe melayek li Akrê hebû ... pênc wextê niwêjê** ***bang dida*** (SK 15:145) There was once a rather mediocre mullah in Akre ... he *would give the call to prayer* at the five times of prayer; **-bangê 'eyşa** (JB1-A/OK) evening call to prayer; **-bangê fitarê** (Wkt) call to prayer which brings the daily fast to an end during Ramadan; **-bangê mexrib** (OK) sunset call to prayer: •**Subey zû heta** ***bangê mexreb*** **destê wî betal nedibû li mi'amilê** (M-Ak #652, 294) From morning until the *sunset call to prayer* he used to have no respite from business; **-bangê spêde** (OK) dawn call to prayer; 3) singing, crowing *(of rooster)* (B/JJ-G/GF): •**Bi qelemaçan dilîstin heta** ***banga*** **dîkan** (HYma, 31) They played spades [card game] until *the crow of* the roosters. {also: ba III (PS-I); ban I (L/JB1-S/GF-2); [bank] بـانـك (JJ)} Cf. P bāng بـانـگ = 'cry, clamor'; Sor bang بـــانـــگ = 'call (esp. to 5 ritual prayers), invitation, declaration'; Za veng *m.* = 'voice' (Mal). See **bāng** in: I. Gershevitch. "Iranian Words Containing -ān-," C.E. Bosworth (ed.). *Iran and Islam : In Memory of the Late Vladimir Minorsky* (Edinburgh: Edinburgh University Press, 1971), pp. 279-85; reprinted in his *Philologia Iranica*, ed. N. Sims-Williams (Wiesbaden : Dr. Ludwig Reichert Verlag, 1985), pp. 249-55.[L/JB1-S/K/A/IFb/B/JB1-A/SK/GF/TF/OK//JJ/HH]

Bangalî بانگالی (BF) = Bengali. See **Bengalî**.

banger بانگەر (FJ/Kmc/ZF/HH) = stone roof-roller. See **bagirdan.**

bangeran بـانـگـەران (FJ/ZF) = stone roof-roller. See **bagirdan.**

bangêrdan بانگێردان (GF) = roof-roller. See **bagirdan**.

Bangiladeşî بـانـگِـلادەشـی (BF) = Bangladeshi. See **Bangladeşî.**

Bangladeşî بـانـگـلادەشـی *adj.* Bangladeshi. {also: Bangiladeşî (BF)} [Wkt/Wkp//BF]

bangnîşan بـانـگـنـیـشـان (Wkt/ZF3) = interjection. See **baneşan**.

bangor بـــانـــگـــۆر (A/Kmc) = stone roof-roller. See **bagirdan.**

banî I بانی *adv.* up: **-banî k'etin** = to climb up, ascend: •**Bi derenca re** ***banî ket*** (L) He *climbed up* the stairs. {also: bala} [L/BX/A/JB3/ZF]

banî II بـــانـــی *m./f.(B)* **(; /-yê).** 1) {syn: dîyar II; gir II; kuç'[3]; t'op III; zûr} hill: **-ç'îya û banî** (B) mountains and valleys; **-deşt û banî** (EP-8) hill and dale: •**T'arî k'etibû ser** ***deşt û banîya*** (EP-8) Darkness fell across the plains and mountains ('over *hill and dale*'); 2) plateau on a mountain top (JJ). {also: [bani] بانی (JJ)} [EP-8/K/B/JJ/Tsab] <ç'îya>

banîn بانین (A/IFb) = to grow used to. See **lê banîn**.

banqanot بـانـقـانـۆت (Qmş/Wn) = paper money. See **baqnot**.

banz بـــانـــز *f.* **().** 1) {syn: ç'indik; firqas; lotik} jump, leap: **-banz dan** = to jump, spring. See **bazdan**; 2) running (A). {also: baz II; [banzdan] بـانـزدان (JJ)} [J/K/A/B/JJ] <pengizîn>

bap'eşk بـاپـەشـك *f.* **(;-ê).** storm, windstorm: •***Bapeşkê*** **wa** [sic] **da** (HR 4:45) A *windstorm* pelted them. {syn: bager; bahoz; barove; firtone; hureba; t[']ofan [2]} < ba I = 'wind' + p'eşk I & III [HR/K/AD/GF/A/Tsab] <birûsk>

bapîr باپیر *m.* **(-ê;).** grandfather; old man. {also: bavpîr (B); [bapír/ bab pír/ bā pīr] (JJ); <bapîr> باپیر (HH)} {syn: kalik} [AB/K/A/JB3/IF/JJ/HH/SK/Msr/FS//B] <dapîr>

baq I باق *m.* **(-ê/ ;).** 1) handful: **•Baqê nîskane** (Dz) It's a handful of lentils; 2) bouquet: **•Memo, mi du *baq* gul kiȓîne, yek sor e, yek zeȓ e, ḧeyran, ezê wan ḧerdu gulan ya sor destê min ê ȓastîye, ya zeȓ min ê çepî ye** (MC-1, #153) Memo, I have bought two *bouquets* of flowers, one is red, one is yellow; the red ones are in my right hand, the yellow ones in my left hand. {also: [baq] باق (JJ)} <Ar bāqah باقة = 'bundle; bouquet' [MC-1/Dz/K/A/JB3/IFb/B/JJ/TF]

baq II باق (HB) = frog. See **beq**.

baq III باق (FS) = calf (of leg). See **paq**.

baqnot باقنوت *f.(Ag/Qzl/Drk)/m.(Btm/Qmş/Qtr-E)* **().** (Turkish) lira, paper money, banknote: **•Di her çûyîna bajêr de min li ber dîwarê dibistanê du *panotên* hesinî didayê** [sic] (Epl, 23) Every time I went to town I would give him 2 *liras* in front of the school wall. {also: banqanot (Qmş/Wn); baxnot (Msr-2); p'anglot (Ad); p'anot (Epl); p'anqanot (Qtr-E)} < Eng bank-note [Msr//Qmş/Wn//Qtr-E//Ad//Epl] <p'ere I>

bar I بار *m.* **(-ê; bêr** [BK/K], **vî barî).** load, burden: **-bar kirin** = a) to load up, pack up: **•Mal *bar kirin*, çûn zozanan** (AB) *They packed up* their homes [=tents] and went to the summer pastures; **-bar nebûn**. See **çav**: **çavên fk-î bar nebûn**; b) to wind (a clock) [cf. Ar 'abba'a II عبّأ = 'to load, to wind (clock)'] {syn: badan}. {also: [bar] بار (JJ); <bar> بار (HH)} [Pok.1. bher- 128.] 'to carry, to bear children': P bār بار; Sor bar بار = 'load, child in womb'; Za bar *m.* = 'burden, worry' (Mal); Hau bar *m.* (M4) [K/A/JB3/IFb/B/JJ/HH/SK/GF/OK/BK/ZF]

bar II بار *f.* **(-a;-ê).** river bank. {also: <bar> بار (Hej)} {syn: kevî I[2]} Cf. Mid P bār = 'bank, shore' (M3); = Sor dîw دیو [Bw/Zeb/Hej/FS] <ç'em>

-bar III بار *suffix* -ible/-able:**-bihîzbar** (ZF) audible; **-dîbar** (BX)/**dîtbar** (IFb) visible; **-fêmbar** (ZF) understandable, comprehensible; **-guhêrbar** (BX) variable, changeable; **-qebûlbar** (Bw) acceptable; **-xwarbar** (BX)/**xwarinbar** (ZF) edible. [(neol)BX/Bw/IFb/ZF]

baȓabaȓ باراباڕ (B) = bleating; uproar. See **baȓebaȓ**.

baran باران *f.* **(-a;-ê).** 1) {syn: şilî} rain: **-barana berfê** = snowfall; **-barana guȓ** (B) driving or pouring rain; 2) heavy rainstorm (Ag); 3) precipitation in general, consisting of **şilî** [rain], **berf** [snow], & **şilope** [mixed rain & snow] (Mş). {also: [baran] باران (JJ); <baran> باران (HH)} [Pok 9. au̯(e)-/au̯ed-/au̯er- 78ff.] 'to wet, moisten, flow' --> [c] au̯er- 80.] 'water, rain, river' -->[1. u̯ēr-/u̯er- 80.]: Skt varī *f.pl.* = 'streams, rivers'; Av √vār *pres. stem* vāra-/vāraiia- = 'to rain' & vār- *m.* = 'rain'; Mid P wārān (M3); P bārān باران; Sor baran باران; Za varan *m.* (=yaẍer) (Todd); Hau waran *m.* (M4) [K/A/JB3/IF/B/JJ/HH/SK/Ag/ZF] <barandin; barîn I; berf; bêbaranî; kevlû [1]; şilî>

barandin باراندِن *vt.* **(-barîn-).** to cause to rain; to shower *(with bullets)*, rain down on: **•...û nifir li şeytanê pîs *dibarandin*** (HYma 37) And he *showered* the dirty devil with curses [lit., showered curses on the dirty devil]; **-agir lê barandin** (IFb)/ **gule barandin** (B) to shower with bullets; **-hêsir barandin** (B) to spill tears, weep bitterly: **•*Hêsira mebarîne*** (B) *Don't spill* tears/Don't cry bitterly. Cf. P bārānīdan بارانیدن = 'cause to rain'; Sor barandin باراندِن [K/A/B/IFb/GF/TF/CS/AD/ZF] <baran; barîn I; ȓeşandin>

baraz باراز (HB) = pig. See **beraz**. barbar (GF)/ baȓbar (HR) باربار = bleating; uproar. See **baȓebaȓ**.

barbêr باربێر (F) = barber. See **berber I**.

barç'imok بارچِموٚك *f.* **(-a;).** bat *(flying mouse)*, zool. *Chiroptera*: **•Di navbera herdu baskên derî de Jêhat mîna *baçimêlkekî* xuyabû** (SBx, 11) Between the two wings of the door, J. looked like *a bat*. {also: baçarmik (Mrş); baçermok (IFb/Mzg/ZF); baçimêlk (SBx); balç'emk (K); balçermek (A); balçimk (F); balç'imk (B); berçem (A-2); parçêmk (GF); pelçimok (Qzl); **pîrçemek**; [bārčémik] بارچمك (JJ)} {syn: çekçekîle; çil II; pîrçemek; şevrevînk; şevşevok} [Wn/JJ//IFb/Mzg/ZF//Mrş/ /K//F/B//A//GF//Qzl//SBx] See also **pîrçemek**.

baȓebaȓ/baȓe-baȓ [K] باڕەباڕ *f.* **(-a;-ê).** 1) bleating, sound made by sheep; 2) {syn: biȓbiȓ; *carecar; qareqar; qîȓîn} big fuss, hullaballoo, uproar: **•Ji êvarê ve bela va zarowê te frotye mi, qarqara wa *baȓbara* wa bi serê mi da** (HR 3:289) Since the evening these children of yours have been nothing but trouble, their screaming and *fussing* has given me a headache. {also: baȓabaȓ (B); barbar (GF)/baȓbar (HR)} [HR/GF//K/CD//B] <barîn II>

barger بارگەر (A/CS) = porter, carrier. See **bargir**.

bargir بارگِر *m.* **().** porter, carrier: **•Dibû *bargir* di**

dema werz û mewsim de (HYma, 37) He became a *porter* during the season. {also: barger (A/CS); barhelgir (SS); barhilgir (GF)} {syn: ĥemal} Cf. Sor bargîr بارگیر = 'draft horse' [HYma/K/ZF//A/CS//GF//SS] <kolber>

bargîr باراگیر (Zeb/JJ) = horse. See **bergîr**.

barhelgir بارهەلگِر (SS) = porter, carrier. See **bargir**.

barhilgir بارهِلگِر (GF) = porter, carrier. See **bargir**.

barîn I بارین *vi.* **(-bar-).** to rain, precipitate, fall *(rain, snow)*: •**Baran** ***dibare*** = It'*s raining* •**Berf/befir** ***dibarî*** (Bg) It'*s snowing* •**Şilî** ***dibarî*** (Bg) It'*s raining*. {also: [barin] بارين (JJ)} [Pok 9. au̯(e)-/au̯ed-/au̯er- 78ff.] 'to wet, moisten, flow' --> [c) au̯er- 80.] 'water, rain, river' -->[1. u̯ēr-/u̯er- 80.]: Av √vār *pres. stem* vāra-/vāraiia- = 'to rain'; P bārīdan باريدن; Sor barîn بارین; SoK wâr-/wâri-, vâr-/vâri- (Fata 418); Za vareno [varayiş] (Todd); Hau waray (war-) *vi.* (M4) [K/A/JB3/IF/B/JJ/ZF] <baran; barandin; berf; şilî>

bar̄în II بارین *vi.* **(-bar̄-).** 1) to bleat; to low, moo (M/K/B/A); 2) to roar, howl; to bawl, yell (K/B). [M/K/B/A] <k'alîn; mikîn> See also **bor̄în I**.

barove بارۆڤه *f.* **().** storm of rain and wind. {syn: bager; bahoz; bap'eşk; firtone; hureba; t[']ofan [2]} [Bw/GF/OK] <bakuzîrk; bamişt>

bars بارس *f.* **().** 1) swarm, the swarming of bees (IFb); 2) {syn: zeyî[3] (Haz)} for bees to leave one beehive and enter another one (Mzg). <W Arm bars/E Arm pars պարս = 'hive or swarm of bees' [Mzg/IFb/ZF/Wkt] <hingiv; mêş[a hingiv]; şilxe; zeyî>

barûd بارووود (K/A/ZF) = gunpowder. See **barût**.

barûdpêj بارووودپێژ (ZF) = gunpowder maker. See **barûtpêj**.

barûdpij بارووودپژ (A) = gunpowder maker. See **barûtpêj**.

barût بارووت *f.* **(-a;-ê).** gunpowder: •[**Û dayim gule û** ***barûdê*** **zaf digel xo hildigrin**] (BN 136) And they always take a great deal of bullets and *gunpowder* with them. {also: barûd (K-2/A/ZF); [barout] باروت (JJ); <barût> باروت (HH)} {syn: t'êz} < Mod Gr pyritis πυρῖτις = 'gunpowder' < Gr pyr πῦρ = 'fire': T barut & Ar bārūd بارود & P bārūt باروت; Sor barût بارووت [BN/K/IFb/B/JJ/HH/GF/TF//A/ZF]

barûtpêj بارووتپێژ *m.* **().** gunpowder maker. {also: barûdpêj (ZF); barûdpij (A); barûtpij (K); [barout-pyj] باروت پژ (JJ)} [BN/IFb//K/JJ//A//ZF]

barûtpij بارووتپژ (K) = gunpowder maker. See **barûtpêj**.

barxan•e بارخانه *f.* **(•a;).** 1) load, burden; baggage: •**Ker̄o** ***barxane*** **barkir, t'e[db]îra xulama jî dît, hate ber dîwana 'Emer aẍa. Wê derê** ***barxana*** **xwe danî** (FK-kk-1) Kerro loaded up *the baggage* [or, the animals], took charge of the servants too, [then] came to the divan of Emer Agha. There he set down his *load*; 2) storage place for loads; baggage compartment; pantry, larder; 3) beasts of burden on which baggage is loaded, caravan (HH). {also: <barxane> بارخانه (HH)} Sor bar-u-barxane بار و بارخانه = 'caravan gen[erally] of belongings of a single merchant or traveller, baggage-train (mil.)' [FK-kk-1/K/A/IF/HH/JB1-A/ GF]

basîq باسیق (Krb/GF) = thin sheet of dried apricot. See **bastîq**.

bask باسك *m.* **(-ê;).** 1) {also: bazik (K-2)} {syn: p'er̄ [1 &2]; p'ûrt} feather, plumage; wing: •**Teyrê go li ezmana re difirin, ez** ***baskê*** **wan diqusînim** (L) I pluck out *the feathers of* birds that fly in the skies; **-kesek hildan bin baskê xwe** (B) to take s.o. under one's wing; 2) {syn: mil; pîl} arm *(from fingers to shoulder)*; 3) wrist (Ak/GF). {also: [bask] باسك (JJ); <bask> باسك (HH)} [Pok. bhāghú-s 108.] 'elbow, shoulder'-->*bheAĝu-: Skt bāhu *m.*; Parth bāzūk --> W Arm pazug/E Arm bazuk բազուկ; P bāzū بازو; Sor bask باسك = 'arm, wing, side, low ridge, mountain spur' & bazû بازوو = 'arm' & bahû باهوو = 'upper arm'; Za bazi *m.* = 'forearm; shin' (Todd); Cf. Parth b'zwr [bāzūr] = 'wing'; Mod Gr pēchys πῆχυς = 'forearm; measure of length = 2 ft., or 25-30 in.'; Tokharian pok-->Khotanese Saka pok = 'cubit'; Eng bough. *For verbal root see:* Martin Schwartz. "Hospitalities and Formalities (√WAZ, √BRAZ)," in: *Iranica Varia: Papers in Honor of Professor Ehsan Yarshater* (Leiden : E.J. Brill, 1990), p. 205 [L/K/A/JB3/IFb/B/JJ/HH/GF/TF/OK] <bazin>

Baskî باسکی *adj.* Basque. Sor Baskî باسکی [Wkt/Wkp]

basteq باستێق (K/A/B/ZF) = thin sheet of dried apricot. See **bastîq**.

bastêẍ باستێغ (B) = thin sheet of dried apricot. See **bastîq**.

bastiq باستِق (AD) = thin sheet of dried apricot. See **bastîq**.

bastîq باستیق *f./m.(K/A/AD/ZF)* **(;-ê/).** thin sheet of sun-dried apricot or other dried fruit pulp eaten as a confection, dried and pressed fruit roll {T pestil}. {also: basîq (Krb/GF-2); bastêq (K/A/B/ZF); bastêx̂ (B-2); bastiq (AD)} {syn: ç'îr} Cf. W Arm basdeł պաստեղ; Za bastêx m. (Mal) [Krb//Frq/GF//K/A/B/ZF//AD]

baş باش *adj.* good.{also: <baş> باش (HH)} {syn: ç'ak; ç'ê; qenc; r̄ind; xweş} Cf. Sor baş باش {başî; başîtî} [K/A/JB3/IF/B/HH/SK]

başer باشەر (K). See **başir.**

başewal باشەوال (Frq/K) = not wearing underpants. See **başewala**.

başewala باشەوالا *adj.* not wearing underpants. {also: başewal (Frq/K); başwala (Lab)} Sor bêşewał بێ شەواڵ [Qzl/Ptn//Frq/K] <derpê>

***başikan** باشِکان: **-tilîya başikan** (IF) pinkie, little finger. {syn: qilîç'k/tilîya qilîç'kê; t'ilîya ç'ûk (B); [telīye pečūk] (JJ-PS)} [IF]

başir باشِر: **-başir kirin** (L): a) to comprehend, grasp; b) to be capable of doing something; to succeed in; to find, discover: •**Tiştek li dinyaê *başir nekir*** (L) But she *found nothing* [mais elle ne trouva rien] {also: başer (K/B); [bacher kirin] باشر كرين (JJ)} [L//K/B/JJ]

başî باشی *f.* **().** goodness. {also: başîtî (A)} {syn: ç'akî; qencî} [K/IFb/TF/A]

başîq باشيق (TF) = falcon. See **başok**.

başîtî باشيتی (A) = goodneş. See **başî**.

başok باشۆك *m.(Qzl)/f.(Btm/Ag/Wn)* **().** falcon, predatory bird, zool. *Falco*. {also: başîq (TF); başoke (IFb-2/GF/Qzl); başûke (IFb-2/OK)} {syn: baz I} Sor başoke باشۆکە = 'kind of hawk' [Haz/IFb/Btm/Ag/Wn//TF//GF/Qzl//OK] <elîh; kurt II; sîsalk; xertel>

başoke باشۆکە (IFb/GF/Qzl) = falcon. See **başok**.

başor باشۆر (GF/OK) = south. See **başûr**.

başqe باشقە *adj.* separate; different: •**Aqûb Meyane ot'axeke *başqe*da cî kir** (Ba3-3, #7) Jacob lodged Meyaneh in a *separate* room; **-başqe-başqe** (Ba2) various and sundry: •**Çaxê wana pez ji qir̄bûnê xilaz dikir yanê jî ji destê cerdê derdixist û sax û silamet vedigeȓande gund, serhatîyêd *başqe-başqe* ser wana çê dikirin** (Ba2:1, 204) When they rescued the sheep from destruction or snatched them from the clutches of brigands and returned them safe and sound to the village, they made up *a variety of* stories about them. {also: [bāshqa] باشقه (JJ-PS)} <T başka [Ba3/F/K/A/IFb/B//JJ] <din I>

baştir باشتِر *adj.* better. {syn: çêtir} [IFb/Wkt/ZF3/G] <baş>

başûke باشووکە (IFb/OK) = falcon. See **başok**.

başûr باشوور *f./m.* **(-a/-ê;).** 1) south; 2) Southern Kurdistan, Kurdistan of Iraq {which is actually Central Kurdistan}: •***Başûrê Kurdistanê* ji bo vî perçeyê Kurdistanê te gotin ku di nav sinorên Iraqê de ye. Li *Başûrê Kurdistanê* bajarên Hewlêr, Silêmanî, Mûsil, Kerkûk, Dihok, Xaneqîn û Zaxo hene** (Wkp [corrected]) The part of Kurdistan within the borders of Iraq is called *Başûr* [Southern Kurdistan]. In Başûr there are the cities of Arbil, Sulaimania, Mosul, Kirkuk, Dihok, Khaneqin and Zakho; **-Başûrê biçûk** (Wkt) Syrian Kurdistan [former term proposed by PKK]: •**Fadil Ozçelik li ser rojavayê Kurdistanê dinivisîne: Carna 'Kurdistana rojava', carna 'Başûrê biçûk', carna 'Kurdistana biçûk'** (Avestakurd.net 3.ix.2012) F.O. writes about the west of Kurdistan [Syrian Kurdistan]: Sometimes "Western Kurdistan", sometimes "The little South", sometimes "Little Kurdistan". {also: başor (GF/OK)} {syn: cenûb; jêr [3]; nişîv (Bw)} [K(s)/IFb/TF//GF/OK/Wkt/ZF3] <bakur; r̄o[j]ava; r̄o[j]hilat>

başwala باشوالا (Lab) = not wearing underpants. See **başewala**.

batirsok باتِرسۆك *f.* **(;-ê).** scarecrow: •**Di demên berên de li gundekî *batirsokek* ... dijîya. ... Çaxê çûk bidîtana, zûka milên xwe ji dû alîya vedikirin û bi rewşeke herî tirsî ew ditirsandin û direwandin** (Dilek ağacı/Wish tree/Dara daxwazê, 1) Once upon a time in a village there lived *a scare-crow*... As soon as [he] noticed the birds, [he] would open [his] arms out and look really scary to frighten and chase them away. {syn: reşe[1]} < ba = 'wind, breeze' + tirs- = 'to fear'; = Sor dahoł داهۆڵ [CCG/IFb/ZF/Wkt/BF/FD]

batî باتی *m.* **(-yê;).** testicle(s). {also: batû (IFb); [bàti] باطی (JJ); <batu> باتو (Hej)} {syn: gun; hêlik; *pilik (Wn)} Sor batû باتوو [Qzl/GF//JJ//IFb//Hej] <r̄itil II>

batman I باتمان/**baṭman** باطمان [SK/JB1-A] *f.* **().** unit of weight : varying between 2 and 10 kg; 7.77 kg in Van (SK); 8 kg (MB); 16 kg in Amadiya (JB1-A): •**Ji Stembolê min guhark'ekê kirîye guhî ji *baṭmanekê*, xeleqa wê du min e, nala asênî** (JB1-A, #139) In Istanbul I put in his ear an earring that weighed *a batman*, the hoop of which is two maunds, shaped like a horseshoe. {syn: r̄itil I} Cf. T batman = 'formerly, weight varying between 2 and 8 okas (2.5-10 kg)'; NA batmân ܒܛܡܢ/baṭmân ܒܛܡܢ, *f.* = 'a maund or batman, a weight of various kinds. The usual Urmi batman is about 32 lb. avoirdupois,=8 haptas=3,200 misqals, one-tenth of a load. The grocer's batman, for weighing sugar, medicine, tobacco, etc. is one-fifth of the above, being 640 misqals; the goldsmith's batman is 64 misqals' (Maclean) [MB/K//SK/JB1-A/OK/FS] <min II; r̄itil I>

Batman II باتمان *f.* **().** town [originally called Êlih̄ê] formerly in province of Siirt, but as of May 1990 capital of new province in Kurdistan of Turkey; village of the Beşîrî (tribe), and name of a splendid bridge in its vicinity (HH). {also: <be<u>t</u>man> بطمان (HH)} [IF/A//HH]

batmîş باتميش: **-batmîş bûn** (K/B): a) to be ruined, destroyed *(lit. & fig.)* {syn: hilweşîn}; b) to be disgraced: **•Nevyê te hela zarûnin, serê neh-deh h̄eva şkênandine, sive mezin bivin, lêxin, wê rojê yek-dudu bikujin, ezê lap *batmîş bivim*** (FK-kk-1) Your grandchildren are still children [and] they have smashed in the heads of nine or ten, tomorrow they will grow up, and then they will kill one or two, [and] I *will be completely disgraced*; **-batmîş kirin** (K/B) to destroy, annihilate {syn: hilweşandin}: **•Wana *wê* nava çar-pênc deqada gund t'emam *bat'mîşkirana*** [sic] (Ba2:1, 203) In 4-5 minutes they *would* totally *crush* the village. <T batmış = 'having sunk' [Ba2/K/B]

batof باتۆف (IFb) = reddish-brown dye for cattle hides. See **batov**.

batov باتۆڤ/**ba<u>t</u>ov** باطۆڤ [FS] *f.* **(;-ê).** a plant which yields a reddish-brown powder used in dyeing cattle hides. {also: bah<u>t</u>of (FS-2); batof (IFb-2); botaf (TF); botav (Btm/A/IFb); <ba<u>t</u>of> باطوف (HH); <batuv> باتوڤ (Hej)} [Qzl/GF//HH//FS/Btm/A/IFb//TF] <soring>

batoz باتۆز (Frq) = threshing machine. See **patoz**.

batû باتوو (IFb) = testicle(s). See **batî**.

baûsk بائووسك (IFb) = yawn(ing). See **bawişk**.

bav باڤ *m.* **(-ê;-ê [B]).** father. {also: bab (JB1-A/A-2/SK); baba (SK-2); [bab باب/baw باڤ] (JJ); <bab> باب (HH)} Cf. T baba; Sor bawk باوك {bavî; bavtî; [babi] بابى (JJ)} [K/A/JB3/B/JJ//JB1-A/HH/SK] <dê I; zir̄bav>

baver باڤەر (MK) = belief. See **bawer**.

baverî باڤەرى (B) = belief. See **bawer**.

bavir باڤِر, m. (F) = axe. See **bivir**.

bavî باڤى *f.* **(;-yê).** fatherhood. {also: bavtî (B); [babi] بابى (JJ)} [K//B//JJ]

bavmarî باڤمارى *m.* **().** stepfather. {syn: zir̄bav (K)} [JB3/IFb/Wkt/ZF3] <dêmarî; zir̄dayîk>

bavpîr باڤپير (B) = grandfather. See **bapîr**.

bavtî باڤتى (B) = fatherhood. See **bavî**.

bawar باوار (B) = belief. See **bawer**.

bawarî باوارى (B) = belief. See **bawer**.

bawer باوەر *f.* **().** belief, faith; confidence: **-bawer/bawir kirin** (SK) to believe: **•Eger tu *bawer nakî*, ko...** (Ba) If you *don't believe* that... {also: baver (MK); baverî (B-2); bawar (B-2); bawarî (B-2); bawerî (K-2/B/JB3); bawirî (SK); [baveri] باورى (JJ); <bawar kirin> باواركرن (HH)} {syn: ewle I} Cf. Pahl vāwar (*written* vāpar) & Pāzand vāwar; P bāvar باور (Hübsch #178bis); Sor bawer̄ باوەڕ/bir̄wa بڕوا [K/A/JB3/B//JJ//MK//HH//SK] <bisteyî>

bawerî باوەرى (K/B/JB3/JJ) = belief. See **bawer**.

baweşîn باوەشين (K/A) = fan. See **baweşînk**.

baweşîng باوەشينگ (LM) = fan. See **baweşînk**.

baweşînk باوەشينك *f.* **(-a;-ê).** fan, éventail (manual device made of paper or feathers for creating cool air current): **•Ji bo ku *baweşînga* wî kevn nebe, *baweşîngê* li ba nake** (LM, 22) Lest his *fan* wear out, he doesn't wave *the fan*. {also: baweşîn (K-2/A); baweşîng (LM); [bavechink باوشنك/bavechin باوشين] (JJ)} Sor baweşên باوەشێن [LM//K/IFb/GF/AD//A/JJ] <p'erwane>

baweşk باوەشك (TF) = yawn. See **bawişk**.

baweşkandin باوەشكاندِن (A) = to cause to yawn. See **bawişkandin**.

baweşkîn باوەشكين (A/TF) = to yawn. See **bawişkîn**.

bawirî باوِرى (SK) = belief. See **bawer**.

bawişik باوِشِك (A) = yawn(ing). See **bawişk**.

bawişîn باوِشين (-bawiş-) (M-Am) = to yawn. See **bawişkîn**.

bawişk باوِشك *f.* **(-a;-ê).** yawn, *(fit of)* yawning: **-bawişk anîn** (IFb)/**bawîşk dan** (GF)/**~hatin** (B/RZ)/**~kirin** (K)/**~kişandin** (RZ) to yawn: **•*Bawîşk* têne wî** (B) He *yawns*. {also: bahûşk (Tsab-2); baûsk (IFb-2); baweşk (TF); bawişik (A); bawîşk (B/K/AD/FJ/GF/RZ); [bavychk] باوشك (JJ)} {syn: bîhnişk} Sor bawêşk باوێشك = wenews وەنەوس/wenewz وەنەوز [IFb/JJ//A//B/K/AD/FJ/GF/RZ//TF//Tsab]

bawişkandin باوِشكاندِن *vt.* **(-bawişkîn-).** to cause to yawn. {also: baweşkandin (A-2); bawîşkandin (ZF3)} [A//ZF3]

bawişkîn باوِشكين *vi.* **(-bawişk-).** to yawn: **•Tu nabînî wa ye Jêhat jî *dibawişke*** (SBx, 18) Don't you see? Here J. *is* also *yawning*. {also: baweşkîn (A/TF);

bawişîn (-bawiş-) (M-Am); bawîşkîn (RZ/ZF)} {syn: bêhnijîn [2]; hênijîn [2]} [IFb/FJ/CS//RZ/ZF//A/TF//M-Am]

bawî باوى *m.&f.* **().** 1) person suffering from rheumatism, rheumatic: **•Dîya min nexweş ketîye û *bawî* bûye** (L-1 #3, 68, ll.10-11) My mother has fallen ill and is suffering from *rheumatism* **•Salih Axa got: "Lawê min, tu dikarî herî ber pez?" Mihemed got: "Belê ezê çima nikaribim? Ez ne ker im, ne kor im, ne seqet im û ne ez tawî me, ne ez *bawî* me"** (AW69B4) Salih Agha said, "My son, can you herd sheep?" Mihemed said, "Sure, why not? I'm neither deaf nor blind, nor crippled, I'm neither feverish nor *rheumatic*"; 2) rheumatism. See **ba II**. {also: [bavi] باوى (JJ)} [Qmş/L/K/A/IFb/JJ/GF/OK]

bawîşk باويشك (B/K/AD/FJ/GF/RZ) = yawn. See **bawişk**.

bawîşkandin باويشكاندِن (ZF3) = to cause to yawn. See **bawişkandin**.

bawîşkîn باويشكين (RZ/ZF) = to yawn. See **bawişkîn**.

bax باخ (EP-2) = garden. See **baẍ**.

baxçe باخچه *m.* **(-yê/bexçê; bêxçe** [BK], **vî baxçeyî).** garden: **•Çû nav *baxçe* û rahişt merê şixulî** (ZZ-7) He went into *the garden* and picked up *a* shovel and worked. {also: baẍçe (K/B/GF); bexçe (JB3/TF/ZF3/BF/CS-2); beẍçe (GF-2); [baγché] باغچه (JJ)} {syn: baẍ} Cf. P bāγče باغچه, *dim. of* bāγ باغ --> T bahçe [K/A/IFb/G/FD/SS/CS//JJ/JB3/TF/ZF3/BF]

baxçevan باخچەڤان (A) = gardener. See **baẍvan**.

baxnot باخنۆت (Msr) = lira. See **baqnot**.

baxşandin باخشاندِن (K) = to forgive. See **bexşandin**.

baxşîş باخشيش (K) = tip; bribe. See **bexşîş**.

baxvan باخڤان (FS) = gardener. See **baẍvan**.

baẍ باغ *m.* **(-ê; bêẍ, vî baẍî).** garden; orchard: **-baẍê sêva** (FS) apple orchard. {also: bax (EP-2); [bagh] باغ (JJ)} {syn: baxçe} Cf. P bāγ باغ --> T bağ [EP/K/B/JJ/FS]

baẍçe باغچه (K/B/GF) = garden. See **baxçe**.

baẍçevan باغچەڤان (K) = gardener. See **baẍvan**.

baẍvan باغڤان *m.* **(; baẍvên/bêẍvên, vî baẍvanî).** gardener: **•*Baxvanî* bax avda** (FS) *The gardener* watered the garden. {also: baxçevan (A); baxvan (FS); baẍçevan (K-2); baẍvançî (B-2); bexçevan (JB3); [bákčači باغچەچى/ bagtche-van باغچەوان/ bagvan باغوان] (JJ)} {syn: cenan (AB); rezvan} Cf. P bāγbān باغبان [F/K/B//JJ//FS]

baẍvançî باغڤانچى (B) = gardener. See **baẍvan**.

baybûn بايبوون (B) = camomile. See **beybûn**.

***bayîs I** بايِيس *m.* **().** 1) reason, cause (F/K); 2) author, initiator; culprit (F/K). {also: baîs (F); ba'îs (SK)} < Ar bā'iṯ باعث [EP-7/K//F//SK]

***bayîs II** بايِيس *adj.* 1) miserable, wretched (K); 2) needy (K). < Ar ba'īs بئيس / bā'is بائس [K]

bayloz بايلۆز (K/A/GF) = ambassador. See **balyoz**.

baylozxane بايلۆزخانه (K/A/GF) = embassy. See **balyozxane**.

***baysiz** بايسِز *m.* **(-ê;).** 1) cause of disaster *or* great misfortune; 2) culprit, perpetrator of disaster or great misfortune: **•Ez navime *baîsizê* xûna te** (FK-kk-1) I won't be *guilty of* spilling your blood [lit. 'I won't become the culprit of your blood']. {also: baîsiz (FK-kk-1)} [FK-kk-1//K/B]

baz I باز *m.* **(-ê;).** falcon. {also: bazê (B); be'z II (FK-eb-2); <baz> باز (HH)} {syn: başok} Cf. P/Ar bāz باز [L/K/A/HH//B//FK-eb-2] <elîh; kurt II>

baz II باز = jump. See **banz**.

bazandin بازاندِن (-bazên-) (HR-I) = to cause to run. See **bezandin**.

bazar بازار *f.* **(-a;-ê).** 1) {syn: sûk} market, bazaar, marketplace: **•Xanim, bazirganek hatîye *bazarê*** (Ba3-1) My Lady, a caravan has come to the *marketplace*; 2) haggling, bargaining, trading, deal (HH): **•*Bazara* me ne wilo bû** (JB3) That's not what we agreed on [lit. 'Our *deal* was not thus']; 3) {syn: Le'd; Yekşem} Sunday (SC/Rh): **-Roja bazarê** (F) Sunday. {also: [bazar] بازار (JJ); <bazar> بازار (HH)} Cf. P bāzār بازار --> T pazar [K/A/JB3/B/JJ/HH/SK/Rh] <bajar>

baz•dan بازدان *vt.* **(baz-d-).** 1) {syn: bezîn} to run; 2) {syn: çeng bûn [çeng III]; firqas kirin; hilpekirin; lotik dan xwe; pengizîn; qevz dan [*see* qevz II]} to jump: **•Pîrê *banz dide* ser xwe, dibê...** (J) The old woman *jumps up* and says... ; 3) *[f.]* running, flight (JB3). {also: banz dan; [bāz] باز (JJ); <bazdan بازدان (baz dide) (بازدده)> (HH)} [K/A/JB3/JJ/HH] <banz; bezandin>

bazdeber بازدەبەر (FS) = stepping stone. See **bazeber**.

bazeber بازەبەر *f./m.(SK)* **(-a/ ;-ê/-î).** stepping-stone: **•Dibêjin di nihalekî da řîwîyek hebû. Awek nîw boş bi nîweka nihalê da dihate xar. *Bazeberek* hebû, řîwî lê derbaz dibû her wextê ḧez kiriba** (SK 2:9) They say that there was a fox (living) in a ravine. A fairly full stream came down the middle of the ravine. There were *stepping-stones* (across it) and the fox crossed over whenever he liked.

{also: bazdeber (FS-2); cf. [baz] باز (JJ)} [Zeb/SK/FS] <bihur>

bazê بازێ (B) = falcon. See **baz I**.

bazin بازِن *m.(Frq/Qzl/FS)/f.(B/Mtk)* **(-ê/ ;-a/-ê).** 1) bracelet: **-bazinê zêřî** (FS) golden bracelet; 2) circle. {also: [bazin] بازين (JJ); <bazin> بازن (HH)} Sor bazin بازِن = 'bangle worn on wrist' [K/A/JB3/IFb/B/JJ/HH/GF/OK/Bw] <bask; xirxal; xişir>

bazirgan بازِرگان *m.* **(-ê; bazirgên** [EP/B]/**bazirgîn** [B], **vî bazirganî).** 1) merchant, businessman (K/A/JB3/JJ/SK); 2) {syn: karwan} caravan (Ba/K/B): **•*Bazirganekî* giran** (Ba) A heavy (=loaded) *caravan* **•Tofaneke mezin li *bazirgan* řadive, *bazirgan* t'emam cîda xerq dive xulam-xizmetk'arava** (Ba3-3, #26) A great flood engulfs the *caravan*, and the entire *caravan* drowns on the spot, servants and all. {also: [bazergan] بازرگان (JJ); <bazirgan> بازرگان (HH)} Cf. P bāzirgān بازرگان = 'merchant'; Sor bazirgan بازِرگان = 'draper, merchant' [Ba/K/A/JB3/B/JJ/HH/SK]

bazirganî بازِرگانی *f.* **(-ya;-yê).** commerce, trade, business: **•*Bazirganîya* derve ya Tirkîyê ji sedî 18 zêde bûye** (waarmedia.com 28.ii.2017) Turkey's external *trade* has increased by 18%; **-bazirganiya azad** (FD)/~ **serbest** (FŞA) free trade. {syn: t'icaret} [IFb/ZF3/Wkt/FD]

bazirganbaşî بازِرگانباشی *m.* **().** caravan leader. < bazirgan + T başı = 'its head' [Ba/B] <karwan>

bazîbend بازیبەند *m.* **().** armlet: **•Eve *bazîbendek* lalî te: eker te kiç bû, bo bifiroşe, ȟeta ew kiç mazin tbîtin têra mesrefa wê heye** (M-Ak #645, 292) Here is an *armlet* for you to keep: if you bear a daughter, sell it for her and until the girl grows up there is enough for her expenses **•Wextê řûs kir, zabitî dît *bazîbendek* ya bi milê řastêve. Ȟalen hema xo da paş, destê xo li ser êk da na** (M-Ak #677, 306) When he was stripped, the officer saw an *armlet* on his right shoulder. Immediately they all retreated, placing their hands one upon the other (in homage). {also: bazûbend (K); [bazou-bend] بازوبند (JJ)} Cf. P bāzūband بازوبند; Sor bazûbend بازووبەند [M-Ak//K/JJ] <bazin>

bazûbend بازووبەند (K/JJ) = armlet. See **bazîbend**.

bçrek بچرەك (GF) = bread toasted in butter. See **biçrik**.

be'can بەعجان (Qzl) = eggplant; tomato. See **bacan**.

bed بەد (B) = bustard. See **bet**.

***bedbeşer** بەدبەشەر *adj.* in bad spirits, in a bad mood: **•Îskender, lao, tu çima *bedbeşer* bûyî** (EH) Iskender my boy, why are you *in* such *bad spirits*? < bed = 'bad' + beşer = 'mood' [EH] <beşer I>

bedel بەدەل *f.* **(;-ê).** 1) replacement, substitute, equivalent, exchange: **•Şêx Muȟemmed S̲iddîq got, "Fi-l-ȟeqîqe 'adetê 'eşîretî weto ye, emma 'edaweta hingo do cihet hene. Yêk 'eşîretî ye, bila ew 'eşîretî bît. Yêk şexsî ye, bila ew bi tole bît. Cihetê 'eşîretî we ye, mêrêt Zêbarîyan hatîne kuştin û mêrêt Sûrçîyan jî hatîne kuştin û ji her do 'eşîretan jî talan hatîne birin. Ewane bê ředd û *bedel* bin"** (SK 50:542) Shaikh Muhammad Siddiq said, "Certainly this is the tribal custom, but your enmity has two causes. One is tribal, let that be settled tribally. One is personal and that must be (settled) by a fine. The tribal cause is this, that both Zebari and Surchi men have been killed and plunder has been taken from both tribes. Let these matters go unrequited [lit., 'be without response or *exchange*']"; **-bedel kirin** (Bw) to change, exchange {syn: degîş kirin; guhartin}; 2) *[prep.]* in exchange for: **•Û ji terefê ȟukometê jî emrekî xusosî bo muȟafeza te dê dem e teȟsîl kirin. Û *bedel* wihê mezinêt Rêkanî deh-yêka ȟasilatê xo her sal biden e min** (SK 61:743) And I will have a special order promulgated by the government for your protection. And *in exchange for* that, let the chiefs of the Rekani give me one-tenth of their crops every year. {also: [bedel] بدل (JJ); <bedel> بدل (HH)} < Ar badal بدل = 'substitute, replacement' [Bw/K/IFb/JJ/HH/SK] <bergind>

***bedelnav** بەدەلناڤ *m.* **(-ê;).** pronoun: **-bedelnavê eleqetîyê** (B) relative pronoun (i.e., ko I); **-bedelnavê nîşankirinê** (B) demonstrative pronoun (i.e., ev & ew). {syn: cînav; pronav} <Ar badal بدل = 'exchange, replacement' + nav = 'name, noun' [(neol)B]

bedem بەدەم (B) = almond. See **behîv**.

beden I بەدەن *f.* **(-a;-ê).** city wall, enclosure, rampart: **•Memê delal wexta zengû li Bor xurîya, Bor nola teyra ser *bedenê*řa firîya** (Z-1) When darling Mem spurred Bor [his horse] on, Bor flew over *the wall* like a bird. {also: [beden] بدن (JJ)} {syn: sûr I; şûre I} [Z-1/K/A/JB3/JJ/Dy]

beden II بەدەن *f.(K/B)/m.(JB3/SK)* **(-a/;-ê/).** 1) {syn: can I[2]; gewde; laş} body; 2) torso, trunk (B). {also: <beden> بدن (HH)} <Ar badan بدن --> T beden [K/A/JB3/B/SK] <berat'e [1]; cendek>

bedew بـەدەو *adj.* 1) {syn: cindî; ciwan; gurcî; k'eleş III; spehî; xweşik} pretty, beautiful, handsome; beautiful, magnificent *(of horses)* (JJ): •**Ser wî kulîlkêd ȟemû ȓenga û cûȓa hêşîn dibûn, ç'îya usa *bedew* dibû, mêriv t'irê xalîça Xuȓustanê ser wî ȓaxistine** (Ba2:1, 202) On it [=Mount Dumanlu) flowers of all colors and types would grow, the mountain was so *beautiful*, people thought that Khurasani rugs had been spread out over it; 2) {syn: gurc I[2]; husulcemal} *[m./f.]* a handsome man or beautiful woman. {also: [bedeoŭ بدو/bedevi بـدوى] (JJ)} <Ar badawī بـدوى = 'Bedouin' -->T bedevi at = 'Bedouin horse' *(large, fine breed of horse)* {bedewî; bedewtî; bedewatî; bedewayî} [K/A/JB3/IFb/B/JJ/GF/TF/OK]

bedewatî بەدەواتى (Ba3) = beauty. See **bedewtî.**

bedewayî بەدەوايى (B) = beauty. See **bedewtî.**

bedewî بـەدەوى (K/JB3/B/GF/TF/OK) = beauty. See **bedewtî.**

bedewtî بـەدەوتـى *f.* **(-ya;-yê).** beauty: •**Bi *bedewtîya* Ûsib, bi şewqa dîndara wî ç'evê wî sax dibe** (Ba) From Joseph's *beauty*, from the lustre of his countenance, his (=Jacob's) eyes become whole (or, well). {also: bedewatî (Ba3); bedewayî (B); bedewî (K/JB3/B-2/GF/TF/ OK)} {syn: spehîtî; xweşikî} [Ba/A//K/JB3/GF/TF/OK//B] <bedew>

bedȟal بـەدحـال *adj.* sick, unhealthy, in bad shape. {syn: nexweş} {bedȟalî} [EP/K/B]

bedȟalî بەدحالى *f.* **(;-yê).** being sick, unhealthy, in bad shape; poor health. [K/B] <bedȟal>

bedilç'ek بـەدڵـچـەك *f.(K)/m.(L)* **(/-ê;).** change of clothes: •...**Keçelok şand hemamê, hemamiş kir, *bedlikçekê* minasib lê kir** (L) They sent Bald Boy to the bathhouse, bathed him, and dressed him in a proper *change of clothes.* {also: bedlikçek (L)} {syn: berşo} [L//K]

bedilhewa بەدِلهەوا (B) = in vain. See **badîhewa.**

bedlikçek بـەدلِـكـچـەك (L) = change of clothes. See **bedilç'ek.**

be'ecîn بـەعـەجـيـن (B) = to be exhausted; to sob; to get angry. See **bihecîn.**

befir بەفِر (Bşk/Zx) = snow. See **berf.**

befr بەفر (SK) = snow. See **berf.**

befrî بـەفرى *f.* **(-ya;).** snow shovel. {also: befrîk (IFb/ OK)} {syn: berfmal} Sor befr•mał بـەفـرمـاڵ = 'snow-shovel' [Bw//IFb/OK] <berf>

befrîk بەفريك (IFb/OK) = snow shovel. See **befrî.**

befş بـەفش *m.* **(-ê; bêvş [B]).** reed *(on a loom)*, comb-shaped wooden part of weaving loom which opens the threads to let the shuttle pass through: **-befşê tevnê** (Wn/Elk) do. {also: bevş (IFb-2/B)} Sor bewş بـەوش = 'reed for beating up weft (loom)' [Wn/Elk/K/IFb/GF/FJ//B] <hepik; pîjik; t'evn>

beg بـەگ *m.* **().**1) bey, feudal lord, country gentleman; VIP; prince; "Khan and beg are originally feudal titles bestowed upon paramount chieftains of the tribe. They are usually added to the name, e.g., 'Ali Khan', 'Rasul Beg'. They have gone out of use now, with the feudal roles to which they belonged. ... The term 'beg' was often employed for urbanized Kurds with administrative positions who were at the same time absentee landlords [from: Martin van Bruinessen. *Agha, Shaikh and State : The Social and Political Structures of Kurdistan* (London: Zed Books, 1992), pp. 80-81]; *see also* **aẍa** *for distinctions between* **beg** *and* **aẍa**: •**Şêx û *beg* û aẍa zor bo ȟalê xo û menfe'etê zatîyê xo zana û şeytan in, emma ȓe'îyet zor bêçare û nezan û weȟşî ne** (SK 56:655) The shaikhs and *begs* and aghas are very wise and cunning in looking after their own case and their personal profit, but the peasantry are quite hapless and rude and ignorant; 2) {syn: *as; *bilî (Bw); *yeklî (Wn)} ace *(in card games)* (Qzl). {also: begler (K-2/Ba2); [beg] بك (JJ); <bek> بك (HH)} < T beg -->beğ -->bey (not related to [Pok. 1. bhag- 107.] 'to share out, apportion; also, to get a share') {begayetî; begitî; begî; begîtî; begtî} [HB/K/A/F/JB1-A/JB2/JB3/IFb/B/JJ/SK/GF/Qzl//Ba2//HH] <aẍa; birêz>

begayetî بـەگـايـەتـى *f.* **().** condition of being a bey *or* feudal lord. {also: begitî (HB/IFb); begî (K-2); begîtî (K-2); begtî (K/B); <begîtî> بـگـيـتـى (HH)} [IFb//HB//K/B//HH] <beg>

begem بـەگـەم: **-begem kirin** (MK/B): 1) {syn: k'êf hatin; 'ecibandin} to like; to please: •**Cav dan Al p'aşa, wekî Memê kesek *begem nekir*** (FK-eb-1) They told Al pasha that Mem *didn't like* any of them; 2) to approve of (B/JJ); 3) to acknowledge, admit, recognize (B); 4) {syn: 'ecibandin [2]} to choose. {also: [beghen kirin] بـگن كـريـن (JJ)} < T beğenmek= 'to like' [MK2/Ag/K/B//JJ]

begemî بـەگـەمـى *f.* **(-ya;-yê).** approval: **-begemî dayîn** (B) to approve of, express approval of: •**Ew *begemya* xwe didine cotk'ar û derbaz dibin diçin** (Dz) They express their *approval* to the farmer and continue on their way. [Dz/B] begitî بـــهگِـــتـــی (HB/IFb) = condition of being a bey (feudal lord). See **begayetî**.

begî بـهگـی (K) = condition of being a bey (feudal lord). See **begayetî**.

begîtî بـهگـیـتـی (K) = condition of being a bey (feudal lord). See **begayetî**.

begler بهگلەر (K/Ba2) = Mr.; bey. See **beg**.

begtî بـهگـتـی (K/B) = condition of being a bey (feudal lord). See **begayetî**.

begzade بـــهگـــزاده *m.* **()**. 1) nobleman, son of a lord or beg (JJ); son of a prince, of princely birth (K); 2) {syn: boşe; dome; gewende; mirt'ib; qereçî} nomadic 'Bohemians' who sing and dance (JJ); musician (EP-4); Roma, Gypsy: •**Rokê nihêrî, *bengzade*, mirtiv, wê hema pê k'etine** (EP-4) One day he saw that *musicians*, Gypsies, suddenly appeared; 3) *[adj.]* {also: bengîzade (K)} deeply in love (K). {also: bengzade (EP-4); [bekzadé] بـكـزاده (JJ)} [EP-4//K/JJ] <sazbend>

beh بەه (GF/OK/AA) = quince. See **bih**.

beheşt بەهەشت (A/OK/GF) = paradise. See **bihuşt**.

behê بەهێ (IFb) = quince. See **bih**.

behir بەهِر (IFb) = portion. See **behr I**.

behişt بەهِشت (SB) = paradise. See **bihuşt**.

behitîn بەهِتین *vi.* **(-behit-)**. 1) to blanch, become white *or* pale, lose color, fade (M); 2) to be bewildered or confused (IF). <Ar bahita بـهـت = 'to be bewildered, to fade' [M/IF] <beyîn>

behî بـــهـــی *f.* **(-ya;-yê)**. condolence, comforting *(upon s.o.'s death)*: •**Ez çûme *behîya* filankesî** (Bw) I went to pay a *condolence call* on [the bereaved family of] so and so. {syn: serxweşî [2]; tazîye [1]} [Bw/Zeb/Elk/FS/Wkt] <behîdar; hewarî; şîn I>

behîdar بـــهـــیـــدار *adj.* bereft or bereaved [of], in mourning, having suffered the loss of a loved one. [Bw/Wkt] <behî>

behîf بەهیف (A) = almond. See **behîv**.

behîfterk بەهیفتەرك (A) = unripe almond. See **behîvteř**.

behîv بـــهـــیـــڤ *f.* **(-a;-ê)**. almond. {also: badem (K); bahîv (OK-2/AA/FS); bedem (B); behîf (A); be'îv (Haz); beyv; [beïv] بـأو (JJ); <behîf بـهـیـف/be'îv بـعـیـڤ> (HH)} <O Ir *vātāma- (MacKenzie: personal communication); Southern Tati dialects: Ebrahim-abadi & Sagz-abadi veyma *f.* (Yar-Shater); P bādām بـــادام --> T badem; Sor bayef بایەف = 'bitter-almond tree' (W&E) & bayef بایەف/ bayew بایەو = 'unripe, green almond' (Hej) & bawî بـــاوی = 'almond' (Arbil/Hej); Za vam *f.* (Todd)/ vame (Mal); Hau waham & bayem [F/K/IFb/JB3/TF/OK//AA/FS//A/HH//Haz//JJ] <behîvteř; ç'erez>

behîvok بـهـیـڤـۆك *f.* **()**. tonsil. {syn: gelale} =Sor ałû ئاڵوو [Kmc-3/IFb/OK] <argûşk>

behîvtark بـــهـــیـــڤـــتـــارك (TF) = unripe almond. See **behîvteř**.

behîvteř بەهیڤتەڕ *f.* **()**. unripe, green almond [T çağla]. {also: bahîvteřk (AA/Elk); behîfterk (A); behîvtark (TF); behîvteřk (Xrz/Czr/Qmş/Qzl); <behîfṯer بهیفطر/be'îvṯer بعیڤطر> (HH)} {syn: çil'în (Haz); gêrih (Frq); nîv'în (Mtk)} [Btm/IFb//HH//TF//Xrz/Czr/Qmş/Qzl//A//AA/Elk] <behîv>

behîvteřk بـــهـــیـــڤـــتـــەڕك (Xrz/Czr/Qmş/Qzl) = unripe almond. See **behîvteř**.

behlûk بەهلووك (GF) = wart. See **belalûk II**.

behnişîn بەهنشین (Bw) = to sneeze. See **bêhnijîn**.

behr I بـــهـــر *f.* **(-a;)**. portion, lot, part, share: •**Ev jî *behra* min e** (L) And this is my portion [i.e., this is enough for me] •**[Wellahî *behra* min di wî pîstî da jî heye]** (JR-1) By God, I have a *share* in that goatskin too! {also: behir (IFb-2); behre (IFb); [behr] بـهـر (JJ); <behr> بـهـر (HH)} {syn: beş I[2]; p'ay; pişk} [L/K/A/IFb/JJ/HH/GF/OK]

behr II بەهر (K/JB3/F/IFb) = sea. See **beȟr**.

behre بەهره (IFb) = portion. See **behr I**.

Behreynî بـــهـــرەیـــنـــی *adj.* Bahraini. Sor Beȟreynî بەحرەینی [Wkt/Wkp]

behs بەهس (K/IFb) = discuşion. See **beȟs**.

behvan بـەهڤان *prn.* so-and-so, what's-his-name: •**Filan hat, *behvan* çû** (BX) So-and-so came, *what's-his-name* left •**Filan û *behvan*** (JB3) Mr. so-and-so. {also: bêvan (XF/K/B)} {syn: filan; filankes} [BX/JB3/IFb/GF//XF/K/B]

behw•e بـــهـــوه *f.* **(•a;)**. balcony. {syn: palkon; telar} <Ar bahw بـهـو = 'hall, parlor, drawing room' [Bw] <bersifk>

beȟeşt بەحەشت (SK/M-Ak) = paradise. See **bihuşt**.

beȟr بـــحـــر *f.* **(-a;-ê)**. sea, ocean: •**Ezê heřim *be'rê* bişewtînim** (Dz) I will go set *the sea* on fire •**Gemî li ser řûyê *be'ra* diçe** (Z-2, 67) The ship goes along the surface *of the seas* •**Hildide diçe ber *be'rê*** (Dz) She takes it (picks it up) [and] goes to *the sea* ; -**Beȟra Wanê** (Wn) Lake Van. {also: behr II (K/JB3/F-2/IFb); be'r VI (Dz/F/B); [behr] بـحـر (JJ); <beȟr> بـحـر (HH)} {syn: derya} < Ar baḥr بحر [Wn/K/JB3/IFb//JJ/HH/SK/GF//B/Dz/F]

beȟs بـــهـــحـــس *f.(Qzl)/m.(Bw/Zeb/Hk)* **(-a/-ê;-ê/)**. discussion, talk: •***Beȟsê* me ji mezin û**

mu‘teberan nîye (SK 54:582) We are not talking [lit. 'Our *discussion* is not'] about great and honoured men **•Zemanê berê Ĥekarîyan mîrek hebû, gelek bi-aqil bû, nawê wî Mîr Ĥesen Beg bû. Axiwtinêt wî hemî mesel û işaret û nesîĥet bûn. Rojek[ê] zistan bû, di meclisa wîda bû *beĥsê* çakî û xirabî û wefadarî û bê-wefaîya dostan û xulaman** (SK 29:261) In former times the Hakaris had a Mir who was very wise and whose name was Mir Hasan Beg. His words were all proverbs and hints and advice. One day in winter in his company there was *talk of* the goodness and badness and faithfulness and faithlessness of friends and servants; **-beĥsa** (K/B/Qzl)/**beĥsê *ft-î* kirin** (SK/Hk/Zeb) to discuss, talk about stg {syn: qala *ft-î* kirin [*see* qal I]}: **•Gelek caran babê min Sofî Silêman, ř̄eĥmet li qebrê wî bît, *beĥsê* Xal Eĥmed ř̄eĥmetî *dikir*** (SK 8:81) Many a time my father, Sofi Sulaiman, may mercy be on his grave, *would talk of* the late Uncle Ahmad **•Te zayenda gotina "KALÛME"yê pirsiye. Ez dixwazim raste rast *behsa* wê *bikim*** (Qzl) You have asked about the gender of the word 'kalûme'. I want *to talk* directly *about* that. {also: behs (K/IFb); be‘s II (B-2/K-2); [behs] بحث (JJ); <beĥs kirin بحس كرن (beĥs dike) (بحس دكه)> (HH)} {syn: qal I} < Ar baḥṯ بحث = 'search, examination, study, research' --> T bahs-etmek = 'to discuss'; Sor bas باس [Qzl/K/IFb//B/JJ/HH/SK/JB1-A]

beît بەئیت (F) = verse. See **beyt**.

be‘îv بەعیڤ (Haz) = almond. See **behîv**.

bej بەژ *f.* **(-a;-ê).** dry land, terra firma, land *(as opposed to sea)*: **•Keştiya Nûh li ser çiyayê Cûdî li *bejê* rûnişt** (ZZ-7, 242) Noah's ark rested on *dry land* on Mount Judi. {also: [bej بژ/beji بژى] (JJ); <bej> بژ (HH)} Sor bej بەژ = 'dry land' [K/A/JB3/IF/JJ/HH] <‘erd>

bejî بەژى *adj.* 1) {≠avî I} terrestrial, living on land (Msr); 2) {syn: dêm I} unirrigated, irrigated solely by rainwater *(of land)* (HH). [Msr/K/A/IF/JJ/HH]

bejin بەژن (JB3/IF/F) = stature. See **bejn**.

bejinkurt بەژنكورت (KS/JJ) = short. See **bejnkurt**.

bejinzirav بەژنزراڤ (KS) = shapely. See **bejnzirav**.

bejn بەژن *f.* **(-a;-ê).** 1) {syn: qam[et]; qedqamet} height, stature *(of a person)*: **-bejn û bal**, see under **bejnbal**; 2) {syn: navteng} waist: **-bejna xwe girêdan** (K)/**~girtin** (JR) to gird o.s., put on a *(cartridge)* belt. {also: bejin (JB3/IF/F); [bejin] بژن (JJ); <bejn> بژن (HH)} [Pok. bhereĝh- 140.] 'high' -->*bherĝh- --> proto-IE *bherĝh-nu- --> proto-Ind-Ir *bharźhnu- -->proto-Ir *baržnu-; Av barəšnu-; Mid P bašn = 'top, peak; stature; mane' (M3); P bašn بشن; Za bejn *f.* = 'body (only for height references)' (Todd); cf. Sor bejn-u-bała بەژن و باڵا = 'stature, waist' [K/A/B/HH/Ba2/JB1-A/JB2/ SK//JB3/IF/F/JJ] <bejnbal; bejnzirav>

bejnak بەژناك = someone. See **bejnek**.

bejnbal بەژنبال *f.* **(-a;).** appearance, looks: **•Gava ç'evê wê li Ûsib, li *bejnbala* wî û bedewya wî dik'eve** (Ba) When her eyes fell on Joseph, his *appearance* and beauty. {also: bejn û bal (B)} {syn: dilqe; qelafet; qilix I} Cf. Sor bejn-u-bała بەژن و باڵا = 'stature, waist' [Ba/K/A//B]

bejnbilind بەژنبلند *adj.* tall of stature: **•Memo mêrekî *bejnbilindî* navmilfireyî dêmqemer bû** (Ba2:1, 204) Memo was a man *tall of stature*, broad shouldered, dark complected. [Ba2/K/A/IFb/B] <qîq>

bejnek بەژنەك *prn.* someone, somebody: **•Ji alîyê çîyê ve *bejnak* tê** (L) from the direction of the mountain *someone* is coming. {also: bejnak (L)} [L/K] <hinek [2]>

bejnkurt بەژنكورت *adj.* short *(of stature)*: **•Bavê wî yekî *bejinkurt* bû** (KS, 53) His father was a *short* fellow. {also: bejinkurt (KS); [bejin kourt] بژن كورت (JJ)} <bejn = 'stature' + kurt = 'short' [KS/JJ//K] <kin; kurt I>

bejn û bal بەژن و بال (B) = appearance. See **bejnbal**.

bejnzirav بەژنزراڤ *adj.* shapely, svelte, well-proportioned *(of the human figure)* (K); delicate (BK/IF). {also: bejinzirav (KS); [bejin ziraw] بژن ظراف (JJ)} [BK/K/(A)/IF/B/JJ//KS]

bekirbegî بەكربەگى *adj. pattern of* ***bergûz*** *material:* white with thin black stripes. [Bw] <bergûz>

Bekran بەكران **().** name of a region bounded by Hazo (Kozluk), Batman, and Farqîn (Silvan), in the provinces of Siirt, Batman, and Diyarbakır, inhabited by the Bekrî tribe. [Haz]

Bekrî بەكرى **().** name of a Kurdish tribe inhabiting the region of Bekran (qv.). [Haz]

bel بەل *adj.* erect, bristling, standing on end; pricked up *(of animal's ears)*; prominent; bulging: **-bel bûn** (SK) to bristle, stand up *(of whiskers)*: **•Gurg ř̄abo, got e ř̄îwî, "Simbêlêt min *bel bone*?" Ř̄îwî got, "Wato *bel bone* dê bêjî şaxêt mambizî ne"** (SK 6:68) The wolf got up and said to the fox, "*Have* my whiskers *bristled*?" The fox said,

"They'*ve bristled* so much you'd think they were deer's antlers"; **-guhê xwe bel kirin** (K/B) to prick up one's ears {syn: beliqandin II}. {also: <bel> بـل (HH)} {syn: girj [3]; miç I; qişt; qund; ȓep} Sor bel بەل = 'erect'; Hau bel (M4) [SK/K/IFb/B/HH/GF/OK] <k'ol IV; qer II; taq; xez>

bel•a I بەلا *f.* **(;•ayê/•ê).** misfortune, disaster, catastrophe, calamity: **•Hûnê me li *belakê* biqelibînin** (L) You will drag us into *a disaster*; **-bela xwestin** (L) to bring disaster, look for trouble: **•Carkê B. nerî suwarek ji wê de tê û *belê dixwaze*** (L) Suddenly B. saw a knight heading in his direction, *looking for a fight*. {also: [bela] بلا (JJ); <bela> بلا (HH)} {syn: bêt'ar; boblat; gosirmet; oyîn; qeda; siqûmat; şetele; t'ifaq} <Ar balā' بلاء --> T belâ [L/K/JB3/JJ/B/SK]

bela II بەلا (Z-1/ Z-921/B) = scattered. See **belav**.

bela III بەلا (L) = in order that. See **bila**.

bela-bela بەلا بەلا (B) = scattered. See **belawela**.

belabok بەلابۆک (Wr) = flier, circular. See **belavok**.

belaȟtin بـەلاحتِن vt. (-belêȟ-) (Haz) = to swallow. See **beli'andin**.

belalûk I بەلالووک *f.* **(;-ê).** sour cherry *(fruit and tree)*: **•Qiloç'ê pezk'ûvî dik'eve ȓanê Sîyabend, wî li ser sêrî bi Sîp'anê Xelatê, çil mêtroa bilinde, wî dixîne, / Bi ser kema *belalûkêva* dixîne** (Z-4) The deer's antler goes into Siyabend's thigh, he drops him from the top of [Mount] Sipan of Akhlat, forty meters high, / throws him onto the sharp branches of *the sour cherry tree*. {also: [bälalûk] بلالوك (JJ); <belalûk> بلالوك (HH)} Cf. Sor bełałûk بەڵاڵووک /belalûk بەلالووک = 'morello, small bitter cherry'; P ālū bālū آلو بالو = 'sour cherry' & bālū بالو = 'wart' [Z-4/K/IF/JJ/HH] <gêlaz>

belalûk II بـەلالـووک *f.* **(;-ê).** wart, skin condition. {also: babolek (QtrE/Slm); balûk (Qzl-2/K/B/GF-2); balûr (FJ); behlûk (GF-2); [balouk] /بالوك بالك (JJ)} [QtrE/Slm//Qzl/A/GF/FJ//K/B/JJ]

belantîk بـەلانـتـيـک *f.* **(-a;).** butterfly; moth. {also: balat'îf (F/K); belatînk (GF); belbelîtanik (IFb); belbelîtanîk (A); belîtank (RZ); pelatînk (BF); **p'erîdank**; [balatink بلاتنك/balatif بلاتف (JJ); <belbelîtanik> بلبليتانك (HH)} {syn: fiȓfiȓok; p'iȓp'iȓok; pîrik[4]} [Bw//GF/JJ//F/K//IFb/HH//A//RZ] <bizûz> See also **p'erîdank**.

belaş بەلاش *adj./adv.* free of charge, gratis: **•Derbasbûna mirîşk û kewan *belaş* e** (SW1, 24) Admission is *free* for chickens and partridges [from folktale] **•Şaredariya Qoserê bi hevkariya Şaredariya Îzmîtê li qezaya Qoser a bajarê Mêrdînê şorbeya bêpere û *belaş* belav dike** (Rûdaw 18.iii.2017) The Qoser [Kızıltepe] Municipality, in cooperation with the İzmit Municipality, is distributing *free* soup. {also: [belach] بلاش (JJ); <belaş> بلاش (HH)} {syn: bêp'ere; *herwe; *mift} <Clq Ar balāš بلاش = 'free of charge; in vain' < bilā šay' بلا شيء = 'without a thing' [SW1/K/A/IFb/FJ/GF/TF/JJ/HH/ZF3/Wkt/G/BF/RZ/SS/CS] <hewante>

belatînk بەلاتينك (GF/JJ) = butterfly. See **belantîk**.

belav بەلاڤ *adj.* scattered, dispersed; widespread: **-belav kirin** (K/ZF) to distribute, spread, disperse: **•M. ... ça û qawa dîwanê *bela dikir*** (Z-1) M. *would distribute* (*pass out*) the tea and coffee to the court [members]; **-belav bûn** = to disperse *(vi.)*, (be) adjourn(ed), break up *(vi.)*: **•Sînota p'adşê êvarê *beladibe* diçe** (Z-921) The king's court *adjourns* in the evening **•[Weku şeȓê Rom û Îranê li deşta Aleşkerê bûyî ordûya Romê revî û *belav bûyî*]** (JR #39,120) When the Turco-Iranian war took place on the plain of Eleşkirt, the Turkish army was routed and *dispersed*; **-belav kirin** (ZF/SS) to distribute, pass out. {also: bela II (Z-1/Z-921); belaw (SK); [belaw (kirin)] بلاف (كرين) (JJ); <belav بلاف/bela بلا> (HH)} Sor biław بِڵاو = 'extended, scattered'; Hau weła (M4) [Z-1/B//K/A/JB3/JJ/HH//SK/ZF] <berfireh>

belavela بەلاڤەلا (K/CS) = scattered. See **belawela**.

belavok بەلاڤۆک *f.* **(-a;-ê).** flier/flyer, circular, pamphlet *(intended for maş distribution)*: **•Di 7.10.92an de *belavokek* li Kurdistanê û li Ewrûpa bi sê zimanan hate belavkirin, ew *belavok belavoka* damezirandina Eniya Serxwebûn û Azadiya Kurdistanê bû** (Wlt 1:37, 3) On 7/10/92, a *flyer* was distributed in Kurdistan and in Europe in three languages; that *flyer* was *the flyer* [announcing] the founding of the Front for the Independence and Freeing of Kurdistan. {also: belabok (Wr)} [(neol)Wr//Wlt/IF/TF]

belaw بەلاو (SK) = scattered. See **belav**.

belawela بەلاوەلا *adj.* scattered, disorderly, all over the place: **•Birûyên wî *bela wela* bûbûn û şayîkbûna xwe winda kiribûn** [sic] (SBx, 13) His eyebrows became *disheveled* and lost their smoothness **•Selik ji destên wî ketibû erdê. Kevir *bela wela* bûn** (HYma, 32) The basket fell to the ground from his hands. The stones went *all over the place*. {also:

bela-bela (B); belavela (K/CS-2)} {syn: bê ser û ber; tevlihev} Cf. belav [HYma/A/IFb/TF/GF/Kmc/CS//K//B]

belbelîtanik بـلـبـلـيـتـانِك (IFb/HH) = butterfly. See **belantîk**.

belbelîtanîk بهلبهليتانيك (A) = butterfly. See **belantîk**.

Belcîkayî بهلجيكايى (BF) = Belgian. See **Belçîkî**.

Belcîkî بهلجيكى (BF) = Belgian. See **Belçîkî**.

belç'ik بهلچك (K/B) = leaf. See **belç'im**.

belç'im بـهـلـچـم *m.* **(-ê;).** leaf; large leaf, cabbage leaf (JJ); tree leaves fed to sheep (HH). {also: belç'ik (K-2/B); belç'îm (K); [beltchim] بـلـچـيـم (JJ); <pelçim> پلچم (HH)} {syn: belg; p'el I & p'eř} [IFb/HH/ZF3//K/JJ//B]

Belçîkayî بهلچيكايى (Wkt/Wkp) = Belgian. See **Belçîkî**.

Belçîkî بـهـلـچـيـكـى *adj.* Belgian. {also: Belcîk[ay]î (BF); Belçîkayî (Wkt-2/Wkp-2); Belgî I (Wkp); Beljîk[ay]î (Wkt-2} Sor Belcîkî بهلجيكى [IFb/Wkt/ZF3//BF//Wkp]

belç'îm بهلچيم (K) = leaf. See **belç'im**.

beled I بـهـلـهد *f.* **().** city, town, municipality; palace?: **•Idî mezin bû çawa *beled*** (EP-7) He now grew as big as a *city* (or- *palace*? [W Arm balad պալատ]). {syn: bajar; şeher (Z)} <Ar balad بلد [EP-7/ZF3]

beled II بـهـلـهد *m.* **().** 1) guide, leader, one who knows the territory well; 2) *[adj.]* well acquainted with, familiar with (Ag/Hk): **•Ez wî *beled*im** (Ag) I *know about* that. {also: [beled بلد/beledi بلدى] (JJ)} Cf. P balad بـلـد = 'familiar with' [JR/K/B/JJ/Ag/Hk/ZF3] <şareza>

beledî بـهـلـهدى *f.* **(-ya;).** lightning: **•*Beledî û berq* wê k'evin** (HR 3:61) *Lightning bolts* will strike **•Sê-çar *belediyan* li dû hev vedan** (DBgb, 20) 3 or 4 *bolts of lightening* struck in quick succession [lit. 'after each other']. {syn: berq; birûsk; blêç (IF)} [HR/TF/DBgb/ZF3] <bap'eşk>

belek I بـهـلـهك *adj.* 1) colorful (K/A/IF); bright (of eyes); with very white whites of the eye and very black pupils *(denotes the ideal quality of eyes)* (Wn); 2) {syn: kever} with prominent white blotches *(coloring of animal's coat)* (B); piebald *(of animals and mountains)* (HH) [ablaq ابـلـق]. {also: [belek] بلق (JJ); <belek> بلك (HH)} {Cf. Ar ḥawar حـــــور = "intense blackness of the pupils and whiteness of the surrounding parts of the eyes"; Ar ablaq ابلق = 'piebald'} [Z-1/K/A/IF/Wn/B/HH/ZF3//JJ]

belek II بـهـلـهك *f.* **(-a;).** calf *(of leg)*, shin: **-zeblekêt belek** (Ak) calf muscles. {syn: boqil; ç'îm I; paq} [Ak/IFb/OK/Hej/FS] <ling>

***belelerz** بـهـلـهلـهرز *f.* **().** earthquake. {also: [bile-lerz] بـلـلـرز (JJ)} {syn: bîbelerz; 'erdȟejîn; 'erdlerzîn; zelzele} [F/K//JJ]

belem بـهـلـهم *f.* **(-a;-ê).** (small) boat: **•Penaberên ku di ser behra Egeyê re bi *belemê* derbasî giravên Yewnenîstanê dibûn ketin nav behrê** (basnews 7.iii.2016) Refugees who were crossing the islands of Greece on the Aegean Sea by *boat* fell into the sea. Sor belem بهلهم [Bw/A/IFb/RZ/ZF3] <gemî; keştî>

belendir بـهـلـهنـدِر (TF) = two- or three-year-old sheep. See **berdîr**.

belendîr بـهـلـهنـديـر (FJ) = two- or three-year-old female sheep. See **berdîr**.

belengaz بـهـلـهنـگـاز *adj.* poor, wretched, miserable, unhappy: **•Wextekê jinik dik'eve dimire: qîzik ze'f *belengaz* dibe** (J) The woman falls [ill and] dies: the girl becomes very *unhappy*. {also: [belengaz] بـــلـــنـگـــاز (JJ)} {syn: bikul; dêran II; malxirab; řeben I; şerpeze; xwelîser I} {belengazî} [BX/J/K/A/JB3/B/JJ/ZF3] <kezîkurê>

belengazî بـهـلـهنـگـازى *f.* **(-ya;-yê).** poverty, misery, wretchedness; sorry situation: **•Ȟuk'umeta T'ûrkîaê derheqa ȟalê k'urdayî çetinda, derheqa *belengazîya* wanada nedifikirî** (Ba2-3, 214) The Turkish government did not think about the hard conditions of the Kurds or of their *misery*. {syn: şerpezeyî; xizanî} [B/Ba2/ZF3] <belengaz>

belê بـهـلـــێ *adv.* yes *{more polite than* **erê***}*; yes *in answer to a negative question* [cf. Sor ba بـا; P čerā چرا; clq. Ar mbalā مبلا; Fr si]. {also: [beli] بلى (JJ); <belê> بلى (HH)} {syn: erê} Cf. P bale بله [K/JB3/B/JJ/HH/SK/ZF3/FS]

belg بـهـلـــگ *m.(K/B/ZF3/FS)/f.(JB3)* **().** 1) {syn: belç'im; p'el I & p'eř} leaf; 2) {syn: p'eř [3]; t'ebax II} sheet *(of paper)*: **-belgê k'aẍetê** (FK-eb-1) sheet of paper. {also: [belk] بـلـك (JJ); <belg> بـلـگ (HH)} Cf. Av varekahe; Pahl varg = 'leaf'; P barg بـرگ (Horn #203) [S&E/K/A/JB3/IFb/B/HH/SK/GF/ZF3/FS//JJ] <[2] k'aẍaz; řûp'el>

belge بـهـلـگـه *f.* **(-ya;-yê).** document; proof, evidence: **•Di *belgeyê* de bi awayekî hûrbînî li ser çareseriya Kêşeya Kurd û sedemên wê tê rawestandin** (AW73A1) In *the document*, the solution to the Kurdish Işue is examined in an intricate manner **•Di nav tu *belgeyên* resmî de nehatiye diyarkirin ku Iraqê çekên kîmyewî ji ku derê bi çi awayî bi dest xistine** (AW75C2) It was not stated in any official *documents* how and from where Iraq obtained chemical weapons; -**belge kirin** (AW) to document: •**Ji bo *belgekirin*, arşîvkirin û sazîbûna folklorî û çandî nîqaşên ber fireh pêk tên** (AW70C1) Wide debates take place on *documenting*, archiving, and folkloric and cultural production. < T belge; Sor bełge بەڵگە = 'sign, indication, evidence' [IFb/TF/AD/ZF3/FS]

belgename بەلگەنامە *f.* **().** (written) document, piece of evidence: •**Pêdaçûnek li ser hindek *belgenamên* taybet bi Kurdan ve** (*title of book by* Selaĥ M.S. Hirurî, 2006) A study of some *documents* specific to the Kurds. {syn: 'ehd} <belge + name; Sor bełgename بەڵگەنامە [ZF/CS/ZF3/FS] <belge>

Belgî I بەلگی (Wkp) = Belgian. See **Belçîkî**.

be'lgî II بەعلگی, m. (F/Dz/EP) = pillow. See **balgih**.

beli'andin بەلعاندن *vt.* **(-beli'în-).** to swallow. {also: belaĥtin vt. (-belêĥ-) (Haz); beliĥandin (Haz-2); dabeliandin (da-beliîn-) (IFb); da bellandin (GF); [beleandin] بلعاندین (JJ); <dabelandin دابلاندن (dadibelîne) (دادبلینه)> (HH)} {syn: daqurtandin; daûran; *hişavtin} <Ar bala'a بلع --> P bal'īdan بلعيدن [Haz//ZF3//JJ/SK//IFb//HH//GF]

beliĥandin بەلحاندن (Haz) = to swallow. See **beli'andin**.

bel•im بەلم *f.* **(;•mê).** (discarded) rice chaff [husk]. {also: belm (Zeb-2); [belm] بلم (JJ)} Sor bełm بەڵم = 'rice-straw' [Zeb/IFb/GF/OK/ZF3//JJ] <birinc I; ç'eltûk; 'efare; k'ozer I>

belindir بەلندر (Wlt) = two- or three-year-old sheep. See **berdîr**.

belindîr بەلندیر (IFb/GF) = two- or three-year-old sheep. See **berdîr**.

beliqandin I بەلقاندن *vt.* **(-beliqîn-).** to squirt, spurt *(vt.)*: •**Lawikbûna wî diyar bû, ji ber ko gava pîrikê ew bilind kir wî *beliqand* ser diya xwe** (Nefel 7.ii.2009) It was obvious that he was a boy, because when the midwife picked him up he *squirted* [i.e., pissed] on his mother •**Wek tu dizanî, zebeş jî hemû dibe av. Xwar, mîzê zor dayê û *beliqand* bi ser me de** (Lotikxane 2010?) As you know, watermelons completely turn into water. He ate one, it gave him a lot of urine and he *squirted* it on us *[humorous explanation for God creating rain]*. {also: belqandin (Wkt-2); biliqandin (Kmc-2)} {syn: pijiqandin I} Cf. Syr √b-l-q ܒܠܩ = 'to come or appear unexpectedly' [Nefel/A/IFb/FJ/GF/ZF3/Kmc/Wkt/CS]

beliqandin II بەلقاندن *vt.* **(-beliqîn-).** 1) to stare, open one's eyes wide: •**Gava ya hemberî min rabû ku biçûya tûwaletê, wî çavê xwe li kursiya wê *beliqand* ku were li hemberî min rûne** (E.Karahan. Jinebî 28.iv.2003) When the woman across from me stood up to go to the bathroom, he *stared* at her chair to come sit opposite me •**Kalê devê xwe vekir, çav *beliqandin*, berçavkê xwe řast kirin** (EŞ) The old man opened his mouth, *opened* his eyes *wide*, adjusted his spectacles; 2) to prick up one's ears {syn: guhê xwe bel kirin}: •**Kesekî ew nedît, t'enê jina wîye feqîr guhê xwe *beliqandibû* -- çika nehat** (H.Cindî. Hewarî, 263) No one saw him, only his poor wife *pricked up* her ears [wondering] if he hadn't come yet. Cf. NA bâliq ܒܠܩ = 'to stare' [EŞ/K/Tsab] <beloq>

belîtank بەلیتانك (RZ) = butterfly. See **belantîk** & **p'erîdank**.

Beljîkayî بەلژیکایی (Wkt) = Belgian. See **Belçîkî**.

Beljîkî بەلژیکی (Wkt) = Belgian. See **Belçîkî**.

belkê بەلکێ (B) = perhaps. See **belkî**.

belki بەلك (SK) = perhaps. See **belkî**.

belkî بەلكی *adv.* perhaps, maybe: •***Belkî* çend qorûş bi te de** (L) *Maybe* he'll give you a few coins. {also: belkê (B-2); belki (SK); belko (SK-2); [belkou بلكو/belké بلکه] (JJ); <belkî بلکی/belkû بلکو> (HH)} {syn: çêdibît [see çê]; qemî} Cf. P balke بلکه --> T belki [L/K/B/HH/ZF3/FS//JJ]

belko بەلكۆ (SK) = perhaps. See **belkî**.

belm بەلم (Zeb/JJ) = rice chaff. See **belim**.

Beloçî بەلۆچی (Wkp) = Baluchi. See **Belûçî**.

beloq بەلۆق *adj.* bulging *(of eyes)*; wide-eyed, goggle-eyed, moon-eyed *(in fear or wonder)*; staring: •**Paşê bi carekê ve kenê xwe birî. Çavên wî *beloq* bûbûn. Wî ew çavên xwe yên *beloq* bera ewr dabûn** (KS, 8) Then he suddenly stopped smiling. His eyes bulged out. He looked at the clouds with those goggle eyes of his. {syn: zîq} [KS/IFb/GF/ZF3] <beliqandin II>

belot بەلۆت (ZF3) = acorn. See **p'alûd**.

belqandin بەلقاندن (Wkt) = to squirt. See **beliqandin I**.

belu بەلو (B/IFb) = clear, obvious. See **belû**.

belû بەلوو *adj.* clear, obvious, patent, apparent; well-known. {also: belu (B-2/IFb); beylû (Z-3); bêlu (IFb-2); [bellou] بللو (JJ)} {syn: aşkere; diyar; k'ifş; xanê; xuya} < T belli = 'clear, obvious, known' [Z-3//K/B//IFb//JJ]

Belûcî بەلوجی (IFb) = Baluchi. See **Belûçî**.

Belûçî بەلووچی *adj.* Baluchi. {also: Beloçî (Wkp-2);

Belûcî (IFb)} [Wkt/Wkp//IFb]

belxam بەلخام (ZF3) = phlegm. See **belẍem**.

belxem بەلخەم (B/IF) = phlegm. See **belẍem**.

belẍem بەلغەم *f.* **(-a;-ê).** phlegm, sputum: •***Belxema* min heye** (apertium.org) I am coughing up *sputum* [lit. 'I have phlegm']. {also: belxam (ZF3); belxem (B/IF); bilxem (FS-2); bilẍem (FS-2); [balgam] بلغم (JJ)} Gr phlegma φλέγμα --> Ar /P balγam بلغم--> T balgam; Sor bełẍem بەڵغەم [F/K/JJ/FS//B/IF//ZF3] <çilm; lîk; t'if; t'ûk II>

ben بەن *m.* **(-ê; bên, vî benî).** 1) {syn: werîs} rope, string; 2) belt (A); woman's woolen belt (B): **-benê piştê** (K/YZ-2) = a) belt; b) waist; 3) {syn: şîrox} shoelace(s), shoe string(s) . {also: bend III (OK); [ben] بن (JJ)} Cf. P band بند; Sor ben[d] بەند = 'string, shoe-lace'; Hau ben *m.* = 'woollen string' (M4) [Z-1/K/A/JB3/IFb/B/JJ/GF/TF/Rh//OK] <dav II; qeyt'an; qirnap; werîs>

benaf بەناف (FS) = willow; ash tree; evergreen oak. See **benav**.

benav بەناڤ *f.* **().** *type of tree:* 1) {syn: bî II[1]} willow, bot. *Salix* (K): •**Av zane *benaw* li ku ye** (L) The water knows where *the willow* is *[prv.]*, i.e., a thief knows his accomplice; 2) ash tree, European ash, bot. *Fraxinus excelsior* [T dişbudak] (A/IFb/TF/Kmc-6); 3) evergreen oak, holm oak, bot. *Quercus ilex, from which wooden sticks are made* [Ar sindiyān سنديان] (HH). {also: benaf (FS-2); benaw (L); bênav I (F); binavî II (FS); <benaf> بناف (HH)} [L//K/A/IFb/GF/TF/Kmc-6/ZF3//HH//FS]

benaw بەناو (L) = willow; ash tree; holm oak. See **benav**.

bend I بەند *f.* **(-a;-ê).** 1) {syn: sikir} dam, weir: **-benda avê** = do. {also: [bend-a awi] بندا اڤى (JJ)}; 2) {syn: gotar; nivîs[ar]} *{journalistic)* article; 3) {syn: girê} knot: **-bend kirin** (K/B/A/IFb/GJ/GF) to tie, bind: •**Dîwanê *em* nikarbûn *bend bikirana*, ewê *em bendkirin*** (HCK-3, #2, 28) The government couldn't *tie us up*, [but] she *tied us up*. [Pok. bhendh- 127.] 'to bind'--> O Ir *√band- : Mid P band = 'bond, link' [AB/F/K/A/JB3/B/JJ/FJ/GF]

bend II بەند = slave; human being. See **bende**.

bend III بەند (OK) = string, rope; belt. See **ben**.

benda بەندا (JB3) = waiting. See **bendî**.

bende بەندە *m.* **().** 1) {syn: benî I; 'evd I; k'ole; qûl} slave; 2) {syn: beniadem; 'evdê Xwedê ['evd I]; însan; meriv} human being; creature: •**Gelo *bende* jî ewqa bedew dibin?** (Z-1) Can *human beings* be that beautiful also?; **-t'u bende** (B) nobody, not a soul, no one. {also: bend II; **benî I**; [bendé] بنده (JJ)} <O Ir *bandaka- (A&L pp.82-83 [II] + p.96 [XX]): P bande بنده [Z/K/B/JJ]

bender I بەندەر *f.* **(-a;-ê).** port, seaport, harbor: •***Bendera* San Stefano** (RN) *The port of* San Stefano. {also: [bender] بندر (JJ/G)} < P bandar بندر; Sor bender بەندەر = 'harbor, port' [RN/F/K/A/IFb/JJ-G/GF/TF]

bender II بەندەر (HR-I) = threshing floor. See **bênder**.

bendik I بەندِك *f.* **(-a;-ê).** wild herb used in making cheese, *perhaps* pepper cress, *bot.* Lepidium (B/IFb/HH/G): •**Karê ku bikirina jî nîn bû, lê belkî ji xwe re biçûna pincar, tolik, *bendik* û kirşikan** (Q.Dersilavî. Xezoka Sofî Misto) There was no work for them to do either, but perhaps they would go [pick] *several wild herbs*. {also: <bendik> بندك (HH)} Sor bendik بەندِك = 'aromatic herb used in making cheese' [Dersilavî/IFb/B/G/HH]

bendik II بەندِك *f.* **(-a;-ê).** hyphen (-): •***Bendika* kîtekirinê jî piştî movika hevedudanîyê dihê danîn** (RR 3.1.2.) *The hyphen of* syllabification is placed after the compound segment. Sor bendik بەندِك/xêz خێز/teqeł تەقەڵ = 'hyphen' [RR/IFb/TF/ZF/FS] <xalbendî; xêzik>

bendî بەندى: **-li bendî *fk-ê/ft-î* man/~bûn** (K) to wait for {also: (li) benda... man (JB3/ZF3)}: •**Gelek rêwî *li benda* balafirê *bûn*** (amidakurd.net 25.vi.2007) Many passengers *were waiting for* the airplane. {syn: çav li rê bûn; hêvîyê man; p'an I; sekinîn} [L/K/A//JB3/ZF3]

bendîr بەندیر (Bzd) = two- or three-year-old sheep. See **berdîr**.

bendûr بەندوور (B/F) = influence. See **bandûr̄**.

benefş بەنەفش (K/IFb/GF/JJ) = violet. See **binefş**.

benefşe بەنەفشە (A/F) = violet. See **binefş**.

benefşî بەنەفشی (IFb/GF) = purple. See **binefşî**.

benefşîn بەنەفشین (IFb) = purple. See **binefşî**.

Bengalî بەنگالی *adj.* Bengali. {also: Bangalî (BF)} Sor Bengalî بەنگالی [Wkt/Wkp//BF]

bengîzade بەنگیزادە (K) = in love. See **begzade** [3].

bengzade بەنگزادە (EP-4) = musician. See **begzade** [2].

benişt بەنِشت (Mzg/K/GF) = gum. See **benîşt**.

benî I بەنی *m.* **(-[y]ê;).** slave, servant (K/A/JJ): •**Kur̄o, eva *benîê* mine, min ew ji bîrê derxistye** (Ba3-3, #23) Boys, he's my *slave*, I took him out of the well [or, pit]; **-Ez benî** (M) = I am your servant, at your service; (A) = efendim = Pardon me? *(polite* *way of asking interlocutor to repeat what [s]he said)*. {also: bend II; **bende**; [beni] بـنـی (JJ)} {syn: bende; ‘evd I; k’ole; qûl} <O Ir *bandaka- (A&L p. 82-83 [II] + 96 [XX]) [K/A/JJ/JB1-A] <carî; qerwaş; xizmetk’ar; xulam>

benî II بـهنـی *m.* **()**. 1) {syn: berdilk; gerden[3]; řistik} small gold or silver neckchain, necklace: **-tok û benî** (EP-7) neckchain, woman's adornment made of silver coins; 2) {syn: meşlûr} confection of nuts strung and dipped in boiled grape juice (IFb/A/HH/TF); 3) coat-breast (K). {also: [beni] بـنـی (JJ); <benî> بنی (HH)} [EP-7/K/A/IFb/JJ/HH/GF/TF] <[2] dims; gelwaz; qol II; xarûz>

benîadem بـهنـیـئـادهم *m.* **()**. human being; mankind, humanity: **•Eva çil řoje, wekî min *benîadem* hela nedîtine** (FK-2) It has been 40 days since I’ve seen another *human being* **•Ma to dujminê *benî-ademî* nî?** (SK-I:1) Are you not then the enemy of *mankind*? {also: [beni adem] بـنـی ادم (JJ)} {syn: ‘evdê Xwedê [‘evd I]; meriv} <(clq.) Ar banī ādam بنی آدم = lit. ‘the sons of Adam’, i.e., ‘human beings’; cf. Sor ademîzad ئادەمیزاد [FK-2/SK/K/JJ/OK]

benîş بـهنـیـش *m.* **()**. gown, robe; upper garment with very full sleeves that extend as far as the elbow, made of cloth [Fr. ‘drap‘] for men, and satin for women: **•[Ismaîl Axa tepançeyê di bin *benîşî* dikite]** (JR) Ismail Agha put his pistol under his *garment* (=he hid it there). {also: [benich/beniš] بـنـش (JJ)} Cf. Ar bunuš/binuš بـنـش = ‘cloth upper garment with very full sleeves’ (according to Hava, of T origin); T biniş = ‘parade uniform’ [K/JJ/JR]

benîşt بـهنـیـشـت *m.* **(-ê; bênîşt [B])**. 1) {syn: debûş; şîrêz} gum, resin; 2) {syn: *cûm (Krş)} chewing gum: **-bûn benîştê devê xelkê** (HYma)/~ **xelikî** (BF) to be the subject of gossip, be the talk of the town [lit. ‘to become gum in people’s mouth’]: **•Tu zanî ku kerê te *bûye benîştê devê xelkê*?** (HYma, 46) Do you know that *everyone is talking about* your donkey? {also: benişt (Mzg/K-2/GF); [benoucht] بنوشت (JJ); <benîşt> بنیشت (HH)} Sor binêşt بنێشت [Mzg/GF//K/A/IFb/B/HH/TF/BF/HYma/SS/JJ]

benk بەنك (A/IFb) = terebinth. See **bêmk**.

benok بەنۆك (OK) = terebinth. See **bêmk**.

beok بەئۆك/be‘ok بەعۆك (IFb) = ugly; dirty. See **bi‘ok**.

beq بـهق *f.(F/ZF)/m.(K/B/JB3)* **(-a/-ê; -ê/)**. frog: **•Ma we çîroka *beqê* bihîstîye? *Beqa* ku xwe wek ga didît** (K.Burkay. Aso, 65) Have you heard the story of *the frog*? *The frog* that thought it was a bull [lit. 'that saw itself as a bull']. {also: baq II (HB-2); [baq] بـق (JJ); <beq> بـق (HH)} Cf. T -bağa, cf. kurbağa = ‘frog’, kaplumbağa = ‘turtle’; Sor boq بۆق; NA piqâ ܦܩܐ (Urmia) [F/K/A/JB3/B/HH/ZF//JJ]

beqbeqok بـهقـبـهقـۆك *f.* **(-a;)**. bubble. {also: peqijok (GF-2); peqik I (IFb-2); peqîk (TF); peqîşk (Bw-2/Zx); peqpeqok (GF/Bw-2); peqpeqoşk (Bw); <beqbeqok> بقبقوّك (HH)} =Sor bilq بلّق [Bw//GF//[A]/IFb/HH/ZF3//TF//Zx] <bilqebilq>

beqem بـهقهم *adj.* faded *(of colors)*. {also: <beqem> بقم (HH)} {syn: sîs II} Sor beqem بـهقـهم = ‘dye liable to fade’ [Bw/IFb/HH/RZ/Kmc-16/ZF3] <çilmisîn; řeng>

ber I بـهر *m.* **(-ê;)**. front, face {syn: pêşî I}: **-berê *fk-ê* dan** (L) to take s.o. somewhere: **•*Berê* wê *da* mixara xwe** (L) *He took* her to his cave; **-berê xwe dan** (K): a) to betake o.s., to go, head for: **•Kalê û gundî *berê xwe didine* berb gundekî** (Dz) The old man and the peasant *head* toward a village; b) to look, take a look at (Bw); **-berê xwe [jê] guhastin** (XF) to turn away from; to turn one's back on; to break/discontinue a relationship; to renounce, disavow, give up; to stop paying attention to, to express indifference toward; to stop loving/respecting. [BX/K/A/JB3/B/SK]

ber II بـهر *prep.* 1) before *(time and place)*, in front of; toward: **•*ber* çem** (L) *by or on the banks of* the river **•Bir *ber* tatê** (L) He took her *to or before* the rock **•Xwe da *ber* tûmekî** (L) He hid himself *behind* a bush **•Herwekî here *ber* mirinê** (BX) As if he were *going to* his death; 2) in, under *(weather, conditions, etc.)*: **•Ȟetanî êvarê wana *ber* tavê, suřê û sermê, bin baranê û teyrokê, carna t’î û birçî pez diç’êrand** (Ba2:1, 204) They would graze the sheep until evening *in* sunlight and cold, under rain and hail, sometimes [even] hungry and thirsty; 3) *used in various expressions*: **-ber avîtin** (B) to have a miscarriage *(of animals)*; **-ber çûyîn** (B) to have a miscarriage *(of women or animals)* [also **ji ber çûn** below]; **-ber xwe k’etin** (XF/K/IF/B/F) to lose heart, lose courage; to be depressed, feel dejected; to be upset; to feel embarrassed, ashamed {syn: aciz bûn}: **•Ez pir *ber xwe ketim* ko min arîkariya te nekir bû** (IF) I *felt ashamed* that I hadn’t helped you **•Gevez, çima *ber xwe dik’evî*?** (XF) Gevez, why *are you [so] upset*? **•Zelîxe *ber xwe dik’eve*, ku zêřê wê t’êrê nake** (Ba-1, #16) Zulaikha *is very upset* that her gold is not enough [to buy Joseph]; **-ber xwe kirin** (B) to have an abortion, miscarry, abort *(a foetus)*;

-ber bi = toward(s), in the direction of {also: berb (Dz); berev II (Zeb/Dh/Bw)} **•Kalê û gundî berê xwe didine *berb* gundekî** (Dz) The old man and the peasant head *toward* a village **•*Ber bi* rohelatê çû** (BX) He went *toward* the East **•*Ber bi* êvarê** (BX) *toward* evening **•*Ber bi* xêr e** (BX) He is doing better (lit. "He is *in the direction of* goodness"); **-ber bi ... ve** = toward, in the direction of (approaching); on behalf of: **•*Ber bi* min *ve* dihat** (BX) He was coming *toward* me **•Hinek nivîskar diyar dikin ku MHP xwe ji nû ve saz dike û *ber bi* demokratîkbûnê *ve* diçe** (AW69A1) Some writers declare that the MHP [Nationalist People's Party] is re-making itself and becoming more democratic [lit. 'is going *toward* being democratic']; **-ber hev** = face to face, facing each other [see also **berev**]; **-di ber** = on, at: **•*Di ber* hev didin** (BX) They fight each other [lit. 'They give *at* each other']; **-di ber ... de** = before, in front of *(without motion)*; for: **•*Di ber* mala me *de* darek heye** (BX) *In front of* our house there is a tree **•Di ber hev de** = face to face, side by side; **-di ber ... re** = alongside, in front of *(while in motion)* [par-devant, le long de]: **•*Di ber* qesrê *re* derbas bû** (BX) He passed *alongside (or, in front of)* the palace **•Doktor Sertaç ... *di ber* neynikê *re* çû û hat** (KS, 36) Dr. Sertaç ... went back and forth *in front of* the mirror; **-di ber ... ve** = in front of; because of: **•*Di ber* vê xebata hêja *ve*** (BX) *Because of* this excellent work; **-ji ber** = 1) because of, for: **•*ji ber* çi?** = why? what *for*? **•ji ber ko** = because **•*Ji ber* vê yekê** = *for* this reason **•*Ji ber* vê hindê** = That's why [lit. '*For* this one']; 2) before, from in front of [de devant]: **•*Ji ber* wî rabû** (BX) He fled *from* him, from his presence [Il prit la fuite devant lui] **•*Ji ber* xwe** = *by* oneself; **-ji ber çûn** (Zx/Bw) to have a miscarriage [also **ber çûyîn** above] **•Biçîk *ji ber çû*** (Zx/Bw) She had a miscarriage [lit. 'The little one [=child] *came out in front*']; **-xwe ji ber *ft-î* dan alî** (Kk) = to shirk one's responsibility. See under **dan I**; **-ji ber ... re** = for; **-ji ber ... ve** = a) in front of: **•*Ji ber* mîr *ve* rabû** (BX) He rose *before* the emir *(out of respect)* **•Mêvanê min mêvanekî usane, wekî derê teda be, tê *ji berva* rabî ser xwe** (EP) My guest is such a guest that if he were in your house, [even] you [who are a prince] would rise *before* him *(out of respect)*; b) instead of: **•Min Şemso *ji ber* Tacîn *ve* şand bajêr** (BX) I sent Ş. to town *instead of* T.; c) in the name of, for s.o.'s sake: **•*ji ber* wî *ve*** (BX) *in* his *place*; *in* his *name*, *on* his *behalf*; d) from, away from: **-ji ber şîr ve kirin** (BX) to wean [away from] [lit. 'to remove from milk']; See also **ji ber kirin** alphabetically.

-li ber = a) in front of: **•*Li ber* şêx disekinîn** (BX) They were standing *before* the sheikh; b) near: **•*Li ber* mirinê ye** (BX) He is *near* death, *or,* He is *about to* die; c) with: **•*Li ber* nanê xwe penîr dixwe** (BX) He eats cheese *with* his bread; d) according to: **•Ev gotin *li ber* xelkê eyb e** (BX) This matter is shameful *in the eyes of* the people; e) for: **•*Li ber* Xwedê** = *for* [the love of] God; f) [obl. +] **li ber bûn** (Bw) to intend to, be of a mind to {syn: nêta *yekî* hebûn}: **•Li demên dahatî *te liber e* çi karên edebî encam bidî?** (Helbest 9 [2013], 50) In the future what literary activities *do you intend to* carry out? {also: berî I; [ber] بـر (JJ); <ber>بـر (HH)} {syn: pêş} [BX/K/A/JB3/B/JJ/HH/ZF]

ber III بەر *m.* **(-ê;).** 1) {syn: kevir; kuç'} stone, rock; small stone *{as opposed to **kevir** = large rock}* (Bw): **•Dibêjin bestekî** [sic] ***beran* li-ṯenişt gundê wan heye. Wextê diçin e seferê ji r̄êwe diçin e-naw besta *beran*, çawêt xo dimiçînin, pêş paş diçin, panîa pîê wan geheşt e kîşk *berî* dê înin, bi ṯerazîê kêşin çend der-kewt dê sûndekî mezin o kirêt xot ko, "Ḧetta bi-qeder giranîya *wî berey* pare-y zêr̄ yan zîw neînim nahêmewe"** (SK 12:117) They say that there is a *stony* vale next to their village. When they go on a journey they go first of all to the vale *of stones*, shut their eyes, go back and forth and, whichever *stone* the heel of their foot touches, they will bring it and weigh it in a balance and, however much it turns out, they will swear a mighty and ugly oath that, "I shall not return until I bring the weight *of this stone* in gold or silver"; **-dan ber beran**. See under **dan I**; 2) bullet (A/GF/TF). See **berik II**. {also: bîr III (HB); [ber] بر (JJ); <ber> بر (HH)} Sor berd بەرد [HB/K/A/JB3/IFb/JJ/HH/SK/GF/TF]

ber̄ IV بەڕ/**ber** بەر [A/IFb/JJ/GF] *f.* **(-a;-ê).** kilim, flat-weave pileless rug (IF); striped woolen pileless rug, i.e., p'alas *(used as bedding)* (K/B): **-Berika xwe ji avê derîna** (BF) S/he coped with the problem; S/he managed to accomplish the task [lit. 'S/he took his/her rug out of the water]; **-Lingê xwe**

angorî beřa xwe dirêjke (B) Stretch out your legs according to [the length of] your carpet *[prv.]*. {also: beřik III (SK/BF); [ber] بــــــر (JJ)} {syn: cacim; cil II; gelt; k'ilîm; merş; p'alas; tejik} Sor beře بــــــهڕه [K/B//A/IFb/JJ/GF//SK/BF] <cilik; mehfûr; xalîçe>

ber V بــــهر *f.(K/B)/m.(F/SK)* **(/-ê;-ê/).** 1) {syn: êmîş [1]; fîkî; mêwe} fruit: **•Wan stirî çandin, xiyala wan ew bû dê tirî çinin. Nezanîn** [sic] ***berê*** **stirî stirî ye, tirî nîye** (SK 48:511) They planted thorns, thinking to reap grapes. They did not know that a thornbush bears thorns [lit. 'that *the fruit of* the thornbush is thorns'], not grapes; 2) fruits of one's labor; product; 3) berry (B). {also: berg I (K); [ber] بر (JJ-Rh)} [F/A/JB3/IFb/B/JJ/SK/GF/TF/OK//K]

be'r VI بهعر (Dz/F/B) = sea. See **beĥr**.

beraberî بــــــهرابــــــهری (K/Wkt) = equivalent. See **beranberî**.

***bera•dan** بــــــهرادان *vt.* **(bera-d-).** 1) to banish, expel, exile (K); 2) to leave, abandon (HB/A) [cf. berdan]; 3) to divorce (HB/A). {also: berîdan (K)} [HB/K/A]

beradayî بــــهرادایــــی *adj./pp.* 1) useless, worthless; 2) neglected, abandoned, in bad condition; 3) undisciplined, spoiled, willful (B); 4) on the loose, set free (FS). {also: beredayî (IFb); beředayî (K/B/FS); [beredài] بردهدای (JJ)} [Qzl/A/GF//IFb/JJ//K/B/FS]

berahik بــــهراهِــك *f.* **(;-ê).** 1) vanguard, front *(lit. = troops at head of an army, and fig. = forefront of activity)* (K/F): •[**Mela li** ***berayikê*** **bû**] (JR) The mullah was in *front*; 2) meeting, encounter (JB1-A): **-çon berahîk'ê** (JB1-A) to go out to meet or greet s.o.: **•Wextê** ***çû li berahîya*** **wî, Mîrza Miĥemmedî şîrek li stoê yê kafir da, kuşt** (M-Zx, #754, 350) When he went before him [i.e., *went out to meet* him], Mirza Muhammad struck the monster a blow on the neck with his sword and killed him; (M-Zx); **-hatin berahîyê** (M-Zx) do.: **•Xezalek** ***hat berahîyê,*** **telismê zêřî stoyda** (M-Zx, #753, 348) A gazelle *came before* him, with a gold talisman reound its neck; 3) head of caravan (K). {also: berahî (JB1-A/OK); berahîk (JB1-A-2/OK-2); beraî[k] (SK); [berahik] براهك (JJ)} [K/F/JR/JJ//JB1-A/OK] <pêşwaz; p'êrgîn>

berahî بــــهراهــــی (JB1-A/OK) = front; meeting. See **berahik**.

berahîk بــــهراهــیــك (JB1-A/OK) = front; meeting. See **berahik**.

beraî بهرائی (SK) = front; meeting. See **berahik**.

beraîk بهرائیك (SK) = front; meeting. See **berahik**.

beramberî بــهرامــبــهری (B/bf) = equivalent; across from. See **beranberî**.

berambertî بــــهرامــــبــــهرتــــی (A/B) = equivalent. See **beranberî**.

beran بــــهران *m.* **(-ê; berên, vî beranî).** 1) {syn: pezê nêr} ram, male sheep: **•Serê du** ***b[e]ranan*** **di dîzekê da nakelin** (BF) The heads of two *rams* should not be boiled in one pot [*prv.*]; 2) Aries *(astr.)*. {also: [beran] بــــران (JJ); <beran> بــــران (HH)} [Pok 9. au̯(e)-/au̯ed-/au̯er- 78ff.] 'to wet, moisten, flow' --> [c) au̯er- 80.] 'water, rain, river' -->[2. ūr-/au̯er- 80.] --> *extension* [4. u̯ṛsen-] 'emitting semen = manly': Skt vṛ́ṣṇi- = 'manly; m. ram'; Av varəšni- = 'manly; m. ram'; also OIr *varan-, *acc.* varānam = 'lamb'; Sgd wr'n [w(a)rān] = 'amb'--> Yaghnobi ruōn = 'ram'; Mid P warān = 'ram' (M3); Pamir dialects: Ormuri aurai = 'ram' (Morg); Sor beran بــهران = 'ram (over 4 years old), Aries'; Za beran *m.* = 'ram; hero' (Mal); Hau beran *m.* (M4); Cf. Rus baran баран; Gr arnos ἀρνός <*warnos Ϝαρνός & Mod Gr arní ἀρνί = 'lamb'; K beran--> T baran [Bitlis; Mardin] = 'large, three-year-old ram' & beran [Bitlis] = 'ram' (DS, v. 2, p. 525; v. 2, p. 630) [K/A/JB3/IFb/B/JJ/HH/SK/GF/TF/OK] <berdîr; hogiç; maz I; mî I; qert; şek; xirt>

beranber بــــهرانــبــهر *adj.* 1) in exchange [for -î], equivalent [to -î], : **•Berdêlî: tiştê ku** ***beranberî*** **wî têt dan** (FS) Replacement: something that is given *in exchange for* [or, *as an equivalent to*] it; 2) [*prep.*] **-li beranberî** (FS) opposite, facing, across from: **•Ez** ***li beramberî*** **seydayê xwe rûniştim** (BF) I sat *across from* my teacher **•Mala wan** ***li beranberî*** **rûbarî ye** (FS) Their house is *facing* the river. {also: beraberî (K/Wkt); beramberî (B/BF); berambertî (A/B-2)} Cf. P barābarī بــرابــری --> T beraber = 'together' [F/Ba/ZF3//K/Wkt//A/FS//BF/B] <bergind>

beranek بهرانهك *f.* **(;-ê).** thumb. {also: tilîya beranî (F/K/B); tilîya beranekê (IF-2); [tilouia berani] تــلــویــا بــــرانــــی (JJ)} {syn: girdik; tilîya mezin} =P šašt شــصــت; =Sor kełemust کــهڵــهمــوســت/qamk قــامــك; Za engişta pîle/~pîlli (Mal) [JB3/IF/BF//F/K/B//JJ] <tilî> See also **beranî**.

beranî بــــهرانــــی: **-tilîya beranî** (F/K/B) thumb. {also: beranek, f. (JB3/IF); tilîya beranekê (IF); [tilouia berani] تــلــویــا بــرانــی (JJ)} {syn: girdik; tilîya mezin

(F)} [F/K/B//JJ//JB3/IF] <bêç'î; tilî> See also **beranek**.

beřaq بەراق *adj.* 1) {syn: zelal; ≠şêlo} pure, clear *(e.g., of water)* (Msr); 2) luminous, bright (JJ). {also: [berraq] براق (JJ)} < Ar barrāq برّاق = 'sparkling' [Msr/JJ]

beraş بەراش *m.* **(-ê; berêş, vî beraşî).** millstone: **•Emê *beraşê* aşê ze'frane ser serê te bigeřînin** (FK-eb-2) We will cause a scandal [lit. 'We will overturn *the millstone of* the mill of victories on your head']. {also: [ber-ach] براش (JJ)} < ber = 'stone' + aş = 'mill' [FK-2/K/B/JJ] <aş>

berat' بەرات = news; data. See **berat'e [1]**.

berat'•e بەراتە *f.* **(•a;•ê).** 1) {also: berat'} piece of news, information, data (K); 2) {syn: cendek; cinyaz; k'eleş I; leş; meyt'; term} corpse, dead body (K); animal carcass (B/JJ): **•...Me dî wekî gura ew xwarîye. Ser *berat'a* wî em gelekî girîyan** (Ba3-1, #21) ...We saw that the wolves had eaten him. We cried a great deal over his *corpse*; 3) sign, signal, trace (A/B): **•Xort bê serî û bê *berat'e* unda bû** (B) The youth disappeared without a *trace*. {also: [beraté] براته (JJ)} [Ba3/K/A/B/JJ]

berav بەراڤ *f.* **(-a;-ê).** 1) spot on a river bank where laundry is washed (K/B/JJ): **•Emê herin *beravê* cila bişon** (Haz) We'll go down *to the river* to wash clothes; 2) laundry day (IFb): **•Îro *berava* me ye** (IFb) Today is our *laundry day*; 3) washing of laundry (IFb/B). See **balav**. {also: [ber-aw] براڤ (JJ)} < ber = 'before' + av = 'water, river' [Haz/K/A/IFb/B/JJ/GF] <cilşo> See **balav**.

beravêj بەراڤێژ (F) = inside out; on the contrary. See **berevajî**.

berayik بەرایك (JR) = vanguard. See **berahik**.

beraz بەراز *m.* **(-ê; berêz, vî berazî).** 1) {syn: domiz (Mzg); weĥş (Haz); xinzîr, f. [erudite]} pig; hog; wild boar (IF/JJ/B): **•Tu *berazê* mezin bike hevsar** (FT) Put a harness on *the* largest *hog*; 2) name of a Kurdish tribe inhabiting the region of Surûc in Riha (Urfa) and the Syrian border area; 3) *[adj.]* mean, mean-spirited, unkind (Bw). {also: baraz (HB-2); [beraz] براز (JJ); <beraz> براز (HH)} [Pok. 7. u̯er- 1163.] 'to tear out' --> [extension C. *u̯erĝh-] = 'to root up': Skt varāha- [varāhaḥ]; Proto-IndIr *varāźha- --> O Ir *warāza-; Av varāza-; Mid P warāz --> Arm varaz վարազ; P gorāz گراز = 'hog, boar'; Sor beraz بەراز/weraz وەراز = 'pig'. See also: Alain Christol. "Un Verlan indo-iranien?" in: *LALIES: Actes des sessions de linguistique et de litérature, V, Aussois, 29 août-3 septembre 1983* (Paris : Presses de l'École Normale Supérieure, 1987), pp. 57-64. [K/A/JB3/IF/B/JJ/HH/GF/OK/Haz/Bw] <kûdik; mahû>

berb بەرب (Dz) = toward. See **ber II: ber bi**.

berbang بەربانگ *f.* **(-a;-ê).** 1) {syn: elind; ferec; segur; serê sibê; spêde; şebeq} dawn, early morning: **•Di *berbangê* de, piştî bahozê, du depên kelekê di qûmê de daçikiyan** (Xwende [google] 5.ii.2007) At *dawn*, after the storm, two boards of the raft were stuck in the sand; 2) name of Kurdish magazine published in Sweden. [Ber/F/K/IFb/B/GF/TF/OK] <hingûr>

berban•ik بەربانِك *m.* **(•kê;).** terrace, veranda, porch, patio: **-berbankê xanî** (Zeb/Dh) do. {also: berbank (Zeb)} {syn: bersifk} [Zeb/Dh//IFb/GF/OK]

berbank بەربانك (Zeb) = terrace. See **berbanik**.

berbejin بەربەژِن (A/JJ) = amulet. See **berbejn**.

berbejink بەربەژِنك (BF) = amulet. See **berbejn**.

berbejn بەربەژن *f.* **(-a;-ê).** amulet or charm worn about the waist: **•Here kurê min wê ev *berbejn* te ji mirinê biparêze** (Wlt 2:92, 13) Go, my son, [and] this *amulet* will protect you from death. {also: berbejin (A); berbejink (BF); [berbejiṇ] بربژن (JJ)} <ber = 'in front of, at' + bejn [2] = 'waist'; Sor berbejn بەربەژن = 'pendant (jewellery) (W&E); belt, strap (K2)' [Wlt/K/IFb/GF/TF//A/JJ//BF] <nivişt; t'iberk; t'ilism>

berbend بەربەند: **-berbend kirin** (GF/SS) to ban, prohibit, forbid, prevent {syn: qedexe kirin}: **•Ev hewl ji aliyê polîsan ve *hatiye berbendkirin*** (AW71A6) This attempt *has been banned* by the police. Sor berbend بەربەند/berbest بەربەست = 'obstacle, dam' [AW/GF/SS]

berber I بەربەر *m.* **(-ê;).** barber; hairdresser. {also: barbêr (F); [berber] بربر (JJ); <berber> بربر (HH)} {syn: delak; sertaş} <T berber <It barbiere [EH/K/A/IF/B/JJ/HH/JB1-A//F] <gûzan; kuř IV>

Berberî بەربەری *adj.* Berber: **•Hin gelên Cezayir, Maroko û Tûnis *berberî* ne** (Wkp) Some of the peoples of Algeria, Morocco and Tunisia are *Berbers*. Sor Berberî بەربەری [Wkp/ZF3/BF]

berberoşk بەربەرۆشك *m.(Btm)/f.* **().** 1) place to sunbathe or spread out clothes to dry in the sun (A); 2) shady place to sit in a garden [T gölgelik] (Msr). [Msr/Btm/A] <beřoj; zinar>

berbiçav I بەربِچاڤ *adj.* prominent, eminent, notable,

respected: •**Slo gundda kolxozvanekî gelekî** ***berbiç'e've*** (HCK-2, 195) In the village, Silo is a very *prominent* kolkhoznik. {also: berbiç'e'v (HCK/B)} {syn: navdar} [HCK/B//K/A/FJ/GF] <binav û deng>

berbiçav II بەربِچاڤ (FJ/CS) = obvious, apparent. See **berçav II**.

berbiç'e'v بەربِچەعڤ (HCK/B) = prominent, respected. See **berbiçav I**.

berbijêr بەربِژێر *adv.* down, downward. {also: berjêr (Ba)} < ber + bi = 'toward' + jêr = 'down' [BX/ZF3] <xwar>

berbijor بەربِژۆر *adv.* up, upward. {also: serbijor} {syn: bala; banî I} < ber + bi = 'toward' + jor = 'up' [BX/ZF3] <hevraz>

berbiřî بەربِڕی *adj.* proceeding from the opposite direction, coming out to meet: **-berbiřî bûn** (K/B) to come out to meet, to greet: •**Li bira nihêrî û bi fesal *berbiřî* Ûsib *bû*** (Ba-1, #31) He looked at his brothers and cautiously *went out to greet* Joseph; **-berbiřî çûn** (K/B) do.: **-berbiřî 'eydê çûyîn** (B) to see in the holiday. [Ba-1/K/B] <p'êrgî[n]; pêşwaz>

berbû بەربوو *f.* **(;-yê).** 1) sister of groom *(during wedding),* in charge of the bride during the wedding (Ks); female relative of the groom *(during wedding: there are usually 2-3 berbû's at a wedding)* (Mzg): •**Kî dibe bûk tu xwe dikî *berbûk*!** (BF) Whoever becomes a bride, you make yourself her *escort* [*idiom*], i.e., You stick your nose in everyone else's business/You are nosey; 2) unmarried girl who rides on the horse with the bride as part of the traditional wedding customs (Haz): •***Berbûkên* bûkê li gel wê çûn mala zavayî** (FS) The bride's *escorts* went with her to the house of the groom; 3) {syn: hêwî} one of several wives in a polygynous household (K). {also: berbûk (K/B-2); [ber-bou بربو /ber-bouk بربوك] (JJ)} [Ks/A/B/JJ/Haz/Mzg//K/BF/FS] <bûk I>

berbûk بەربووک (K/B/JJ/BF/FS) = sister of groom, in charge of bride; bride's escort. See **berbû**.

bercêwî بەرجێوی (Btm/Grc) = twin. See **cêwî**.

berçav I بەرچاڤ (JB1-A/JJ) = eyeglasses. See **berçavk**.

berçav II بەرچاڤ *adj.* obvious, apparent, palpable, visible, noticeable: •**Lê tiştê *berçav* ev bû ku hurmet û rûmeta wî zêdetir dibû** (HYma, 52) But the *noticeable* thing was this, that his honor increased. {also: berbiçav II (FJ/CS-2); berç'e'v (B); [beré tchawé] بره چاڤه (JJ)} {syn: aşkere; diyar; k'ifş; xanê; xuya} Cf. Sor berçaw بەرچاو = 'observable, apparent' [HYma/K/A/IFb/GF/JB1-S/TF/CS//B//JJ//FJ]

berçavik بەرچاڤِک, f. (IFb/TF/OK) = eyeglasses. See **berçavk**.

berçavk بەرچاڤک *m./f.(IFb/TF/OK)/pl.(Ag)* **().** glasses, eyeglasses, spectacles: •***Berçavkan* dikete ber çavêt xo** (Dh) He puts on his *glasses* •***Berç'e'vkê* te hene?** (Ag) Do you wear *glasses*? {also: berçav I (JB1-A); berçavik, f. (IFb/OK-2); berçevk (F); berç'e'vk, pl.(Ag)/m. (B); [ber-tchaw] برچاڤ (JJ)} {syn: çavik II} [Ag/B//K/A/GF/OK//F//IFb/TF//JJ/JB1-A]

berçem بەرچەم (A) = bat (zool.). See **barç'imok**.

berç'e'v بەرچەعڤ (B) = obvious, apparent. See **berçav II**.

berçevk بەرچەڤک (F)/berç'e'vk بەرچەعڤک, pl.(Ag)/m. (B) = eyeglasses. See **berçavk**.

berçî بەرچی (HB) = hungry. See **birçî**.

ber•dan بەردان vt. **(ber-d-).** 1) to let go of, leave, abandon [cf. beradan]: •**Mirişkê *berdide*** (Ba) He *lets go of* the chicken •**Îro du ro te *ez* li vê çolê *berdame*** (L) Today [it is] two days since you *left me* in this desert •**Dya xwe jî *berda* çû** (J) As for his mother, *he let her go* [and] she went; **-agir berdan** (K) to set fire to: •***Agir berdide* qesir û qûnaxa xo** (Z-3) He *sets fire to* his manor; **-berdan dû** (L) to set out after, pursue, chase: •**Heya go qenc Teyrê Sêmir biheci, *berda dû* çwîkê beytik** (L) Until the Simurgh got good and mad at the sparrow, and *set out after* her; **-dev ji *f-tî* berdan** (IFb/ZF) to let or leave stg. alone; to renounce, quit: •***Dev jê berde*, bila di cihê xwe de be** (L) *Leave it alone*, let it stay in its place; **-jin berdan** (F) to divorce *(said of man divorcing his wife)*; **-řih/řî/řû berdan** (IFb/K/SS) to grow a beard: •**Rû berdaye** = He has grown a beard; **-serê hespê berdan** (Z-3) to slacken the horse's reins, to ride quickly {≠serê hespê girtin (Z-3)}: •**Ezê bajom, ûn jî *serê hespê xo berdin*, bidine pey min** (Z-3) I'll ride on, and you *let your horses race*, pursue me; 2) {syn: hiştin} to let, allow, permit; 3) to drop, let fall *(e.g., a bomb)*: •**Çekê emerîkanî ê hewayî 30 ton bombe *berdane* hêjagehên Japona** (RN) American aerial forces *dropped* 30 tons of bombs on Japanese targets. {also: [ber-dàin/ber-dan] بردایِن (JJ); <berdan بردان (berdide) (بردده)> (HH)} [K/A/JB3/B/HH//JJ]

berdas بەرداس *f.* **(-a;).** swath, the amount of wheat that a ***p'ale*** (agricultural worker) can grab with one swing of the sickle [**das**]: **•Filankes--*berdasa* wî fireh e** (Qzl) He cuts a wide *swath*, i.e., He is involved in many projects at once/He has his finger in many pies **•Hinek pale--*berdasa* wan fireh e** (Qzl) Some workers cut a wide *swath*. < ber = 'before' + das = 'sickle' [Qzl/IFb/GF/TF/Kmc-1491] <das; destî>

berdeqanî بەردەقانی (BF/FS/SS) = sling, catapult. See **berkanî**.

***berdest I** بەردەست *m./m. & f. (B)* **(-ê;).** 1) servant; 2) assistant; 3) follower, disciple (JB3). {also: berdestî (B)} [Ba3/K/JB3/ZF3//B]

berdest II بەردەست *adj.* 1) available; handy: **•Parên wî yên *berdest* kêm mane** (FS) His *available* money has dwindled; 2) spare, extra [Ar iḥtiyāṭī احتياطي]. [Zeb/K/A/IFb/GF/ZF3/FS] <dûrdest; êrdek>

berdestî بەردەستی (B) = servant; assistant. See **berdest I**.

berdevk I بەردەڤك *m.* **(-ê;).** 1) adviser: **•*Berdevkê* mîr, Bekoyê Ewan e** (Deng - Ahmet Koçer) The emir's *adviser* is Beko Ewan; 2) confidant; 3) {syn: p'eyivdar; qiseker} spokesman: **-*berdevkê* dewletê** (BF) government spokesman. {also: [ber-defk/ berdewk] بردفك (JJ)} JJ: <ber = 'before' + dev = 'mouth', hence 'the one before whom one opens ones mouth, before whom one speaks frankly' [Deng/ K/A/IFb/GF/FS/BF//JJ]

berdewam بەردەوام *adv.* continuously, continually; **-berdewam bûn** (Wlt) to continue (vi.), be continued {syn: dewam bûn; dom bûn; domîn}: **•Serhildan *wê berdewam bibin*** (Wlt 1:32, 2) The revolts *will continue*; **-berdewam kirin** (Wlt) to continue (vt.) {syn: dewam kirin; dom kirin; domandin}: **•Çiqas behsa aştiyê dibe, ew hîn bêtir, behsa şer dikin û her *berdewam dikin*** (Wlt 1:35, 5) No matter how much peace is discussed, they discuss waging war even more, and *continue to do so*. < ber + Ar dawām دوام = 'duration'; Cf. Sor berdewam bûn بەردەوام بوون = 'to persevere, be persistent' (EM) [(neol)Wlt/IFb/GF/OK/Bw] <k'işandin [5]>

berdêlî بەردێلی *f.* **(-ya;-yê).** the practice of marrying a brother and a sister to the sister and brother of another family, forming a double bond: double kinship bond *(the sister of the groom is given in marriage to the brother of the bride)* (K); the exchange of sisters between two brothers [i.e., friends] in order to marry (A); between two families, the marrying of daughters to each other's sons (IF); commutative marriage contracted between first degree relatives (JJ); "Marriage can also be conducted by the exchange of sisters, berdêlî...In this case, the marriage portion is not exacted and only the costs of the wedding remain..." (EI-2) {Cf. Ar badal بدل}: **•Xûşka me--*berdêlîya* me, ĥeft birane** (IS-#156) Our sister is *to be exchanged for* us, [her] seven brothers; 2) groom's sister, designated for marriage to the bride's brother (K). {also: berdêlk; berdîlîk (A); [ber-dili] بردلی (JJ)} [EI-2/K/IF/B//FS//JJ//A] <bûk I; de'wat; zava; zewac>

berdêlk بەردێلك = commutative marriage. See **berdêlî**.

berdil بەردِل (IF/JB3) = lover. See **berdilk** [1].

berdilk بەردِلك *m.&f.* **(; /-ê).** 1) beloved, dear one; lover (K/JJ/IF/JB3) {also: berdil (IF/JB3); [ber-dilik] بردلك (JJ)}; 2) [*f.* **(-a;).**] {syn: benî II; gerden[3]; r̄istik; t'oq} necklace (IF); type of necklace made of silver (A); 3) breastplate (B); 4) {syn: berk'oş; bermalk; bervank; melîtk; mêzer [4]; şalik I} apron; bib. < ber = '[in] front' + dil = 'heart' [K/B/BF/FS/FD/G//JJ//IF/JB3//A]

berdîl بەردیل (IFb/OK) = two- or three-year-old sheep. See **berdîr**.

berdîlîk بەردیلیك (A) = commutative marriage. See **berdêlî**.

berdîlzay بەردیلزای (OK) = two- or three-year-old sheep. See **berdîr**.

berdîr بەردیر *f.* **(-a;-ê).** one-to-two year old ewe, female sheep (Kmc); two year-old female sheep (K/B/Kmc); three year-old ewe (IFb/FJ/GF/JJ). {also: belendir (TF); belendîr (FJ); belindir (Wlt); belindîr (IFb-2/GF-2); bendîr (Bzd); berdîl (IFb/ OK); berdîlzay (OK-2); berindîr (Kmc-2/GF-2); beyindî (GF-2); beyindîr (GF-2); *beyîndi (FJ-2); bêndî (Bsk); [beryndyr/berindīr (PS)] برندیر (JJ)} Sor berdîl بەردیل = '3 year-old sheep' [Bsk//Bzd//F/K/B/ Kmc/GF//TF//Wlt//IFb/OK] <berindir; mî I; tuştîr; xamberdîr>

berebere بەرەبەرە/**bere-bere** [F/K/B] *adv.* gradually, bit by bit, piecemeal: **•Ji lewra, di vê rojnamê de *bere bere* belav dikim** (RN) Therefore, I am publishing [lit. 'spreading'] it *bit by bit* in this newspaper. [RN/JB3/IF//F/K/B]

beredayî بەرەدایی (IFb)/ber̄edayî بەڕەدایی (K/B/FS) = useless; neglected; undisciplined; on the loose. See beradayî.

berek بەرەك *f.* **(-a;-ê).** clan *(tribal subdivision)*: **•Ji qebîla Mehemda ji *bereka* Hewêrîya ... ji êla Sîpka, *bereka* î Sediza** (HCK-2, 195) From the Mehemed tribe from the Hewêrî *clan* ... from the Sîpki tribe, Sediz *clan*. {syn: îcax; ocax} [HCK/K/B] <azbat; 'eşîret; êl; qebîle; tayfe>

berendam بەرەندام *m.* **(-ê;).** candidate: **•Weke ku xuya dibe, îro her kesê ku li Kurdistanê dijî *berendamê* kuştinê ye** (Wlt 1:41, 3) It seems that today everyone who lives in Kurdistan is a *candidate* for being murdered. {syn: *berbijar; *namzet; *navkirî} [(neol)Wlt/IFb] <endam>

berev I بەرەڤ (B/GF/JJ) = together, assembled. See **berhev**.

berev II بەرەڤ (Zeb/Dh/Bw) = toward. See **ber II: ber bi**.

berevaj بەرەڤاژ (K/IFb) = inside out; on the contrary. See **berevajî**.

berevajî بەرەڤاژی *adj.* 1) inside out, backward, reversed; opposite: -**berevajî kirin** (Wlt) to garble, mix up, confuse: **•Rêvebiriya PKG'ê îdia dike ku, me axaftina bi İbrahim İncedursun re, ne wek gotinên wî yên ku ji me re gotine weşandiye û hin tiştan jî *berevajî kiriye*** [sic] (Wlt 1:43, 8) The leadership of PKG claims that we have not published the talk with İbrahim İncedursun the way he said it, and that we *have garbled* some things; 2) disconnected, unrelated; incoherent, nonsensical: -[berevaji goutin] بەرواژی گوتین (JJ) to talk nonsense; -**xeberêd berevaj[î]** (K) nonsense, incoherent speech; 3) [*adv.*] on the contrary: **•Di komcivîna HEP'ê de, bêsekin û rawestin ji bo PKK'ê slogan avêtin, HEP'ê weke ku tune ye hesibandin, rê nade HEP'ê ku bibe xwedî şexsiyet, mezin bibe û geş û zêde bibe, *berevajî*, bi vî awayî rê li ber HEP'ê tê girtin** (Wlt 1:43, 9) In the meeting of HEP (=People's Labor Party), pro-PKK slogans were constantly being chanted, HEP was considered a non-entity: this does not allow HEP to have its own personality, to grow and prosper; *on the contrary*, in this way HEP is being shut off; 4) [*prep.*] {also: berevajiya (Nbh)} as opposed to; in response to: **•Bervajî vê yekê** (IFb) As opposed to *or* in response to that. {also: beravêj (F); berevaj (K-2/IFb); berewaj (TF); bervajî (IFb-2/GF-2); [berevaj(i)] بەرواژ(ی) (JJ)} Sor berewaj بەرەواژ = 'back to front' [Wlt/K/GF/JJ//F//IFb//TF] <dernexûn; dijî; vajî>

berevan بەرەڤان *m.* **(-ê;).** mediator; arbiter, arbitrator; umpire; defender: **•Du kes lê ketin, *berevan* wana jêk vediketin** (Bw) Two people started fighting; *the mediator* separates them (=pulls them apart). {also: berewan (SK)} {syn: navgîn[2]} {berevanî; berewanî} [Bw/IFb/GF/OK//SK]

berevanî بەرەڤانی *f.* **(-ya;-yê).** 1) {syn: bergirî} defense: -**berevanîya *fk-î* kirin** (IFb/RZ) to defend s.o.; 2) mediation (SK/Hej): **•Kerbêt wî dê binewe, dê cûna det, şeřî dê ket. Ehlê serayê jî dê hêne *berewanîyê*, dê wî nehеqq ken, dê qedrê wî şkêt** (SK 52:561) He will lose his temper and become abusive and start fighting. The palace attendants will come between us [=will *mediate* between us], they will put him in the wrong and he will be put to shame. {also: berewanî (SK); <berevanî> بەرەڤانی (Hej)} [IFb/GF/RZ/Hej//SK] <berevan>

berevkar بەرەڤکار (OK) = tax collector. See **berevker**.

berevker بەرەڤکەر *m.* **(-ê;).** 1) collector, gatherer; 2) tax collector (Rnh/OK/GF): **•Bi tenê ez hewceyî mecîdiyekî me, ko ew jî ji *berevkerê* dayina mîr e** (JB2-O.Sebrî/Rnh 14[1943]8-9) All I need is a mejidiye [=coin], and that for the emir's *tax collector*. {also: berevkar (OK-2); berevkir (B); berhevkar (TF/OK)} [JB2/Rnh/GF//B//TF/OK] <bac; xer[a]c>

berevkir بەرەڤکر (B) = tax collector. See **berevker**.

berevok بەرەڤۆك (B/GF/Dz) = collection; brochure. See **berhevok**.

berewaj بەرەواژ (TF) = inside out; on the contrary. See **berevajî**.

berewan بەرەوان (SK) = mediator. See **berevan**.

berewanî بەرەوانی (SK) = mediation. See **berevanî**.

berê بەری (SK) = at first. See **berêda**; berê êvarê بەری ئێڤاری (IFb/ZF) = late afternoon. See **berêvar**.

berêda بەرێدا *adv.* 1) in the beginning, at first; 2) earlier; from time immemorial: **•Lê *berêda* mêr pey jina diçin, jin pey mêra naçin** (EP-7) But *from the earliest times*, men go after women, women don't go after [=pursue] men. {also: berê (SK); [di-beri-da] دبریدا (JJ)} [EP/K/B//JJ]

berêkan•ê بەرێکانێ/بەرئێکانێ *f.* **(•a;).** competition: **•*Berêkana* hozanvanîyê digel kiriye** (HoK, 150) He engaged in a poetry *competition* with him. {also: berîkanî (RZ)} {syn: lec; pêşbazî} =Sor pêşbiřkê پێشبڕکێ [Zeb/HoK//RZ]

berêvar بەریڤار/**ber-êvar** بەرئێڤار *f.* **(-a;-ê).** 1) {syn: 'esir} late afternoon, time before sunset: •***Berêvar* bû, têhna rojê şkestibû** (DBgb, 51) It was *late afternoon*, the heat of the day had broken •**Piştî nimêja xwe ya *berêvarê* kirin** [sic] (DBgb, 52) After they performed their *late afternoon* prayer; 2) light meal eaten at this time: •**Mala wan heřoj *berêvarê* dixun** (FS) Their household eats *an early supper* every day. {also: berêvarê (FJ); berê êvarê (IFb/ZF); [ber eiwari بر ایڤاری/berwari برڤاری] (JJ)} ber + êvar [DBgb/FS//FJ//IFb/ZF//JJ] <êvar; hingûr; moẍrib>

berêvarê بەریڤارێ (FJ) = late afternoon. See **berêvar**.

berêz بەرێز (Ber/K/JB3) = honorable. See **biřêz**.

berf بەرف *f.* **(-a;-ê).** snow: •***Befr* gelek hebû, em mayn di befrê řa, em hemî qeremtîn** (M-Am #713, 330) There was a lot of *snow* and we were stranded in the snow and we all froze •***Berfê* çiya girtin** (FS) *The snow* covered the mountains; **-barîna berfê** (Kg) snowfall. {also: befir; befr (SK); [berf برف/befir بفر] (JJ); <berf برف/befir بفر/berv برڤ> (HH)} [Pok. 2. u̯ep- 1149.] 'to throw, strew': Skt vápra- *m./n.* = 'rampart, embankment'; Av vafra- *m.* = 'snow'; Sgd wfr' [wafra]; Khwarezmian wfyrk (for *wfryk pausal form of *wfrk); Mid P wafr = 'snow' (M3); P barf برف; Pamir dialects: Sanglechi barf; Wakhi warf/barf (Morg); Pashto wāwro; Sor befir بەفر; Za vewr *f.* (Todd); SoK barf/warf/baf(ı)r/waf(ı)r (Fat 232); Hau werue *f.* (M4) [Bg/Kg/K/A/JB3/IFb/B/JJ/HH/GF/TF//SK] <aşît; bamişt; baran; barîn; barove; berfmal; gulîfîtk; kulî II; kurşe; lêlav; řenî; şape I; şilop'e>

Berfanbar بەرفانبار. A Sorani name [Befranbar بەفرانبار] for Persian month of *Dey* دی [Capricorn] (Dec. 22-Jan. 19). See chart of Kurdish months in this volume. <Kanûna Pêşîn; Kanûna Paşîn>

berfeşîr بەرفەشیر *f.* **(-a;-ê).** ice cream: •***Berfeşîra* Zoroyî xoş e** (FS) Z.'s *ice cream* is delicious •**Yê ku *berfeşîr* çêkiriye jinek kurd bûye** (Çandname.com 26.i.2018) The one who made *ice cream* was a Kurdish woman. {syn: qeşaşîr; *bestenî; *dondirme; *qerimok} < berf = 'snow' + şîr = 'milk' [Şnx/FS/Wkt/ZF3]

berfire بەرفِرە (GF/OK) = spacious. See **berfireh**.

berfireh بەرفِرەه *adj.* wide, spacious, roomy; widespread; ample: •***Berfirh* e** (Bw) It is *spacious* [or *ample*] •**Sefewiyan jî ji bo parastina sînorê dewleta xwe li hemberî împaratoriya *berfireh* a Osmaniyan şietî wekî mezhebekî dînî û fermî ... dan** [sic] **xuyakirin** (Zend 2:3[1997], 56) And the Safavids, in order to protect the border of their state against the *expansive* Ottoman Empire, declared Shiism their official religious sect. {*berfireh + -e = **berfirh e** with loss of medial -e- in Bw}. {also: berfire (GF/OK-2)} {syn: berîn; fireh; pehn I} *For etymology see* ***fireh*** [Bw/IFb/OK/RZ//GF] <fireh>

berfmal بەرفمال *f.* **(;-ê).** snow shovel: •**Wî bi *berfmalkê* serban ji berfê paqij kir** (FS) He cleaned the snow off the roof with *the snow shovel*. {also: berfmalik (ZF3); berfmalk (IFb/GF/FS)} {syn: befrî} < berf + mal- = 'to sweep' Sor befr•mał بەفرماڵ = 'snow-shovel' [K/A/RF//IFb/GF/FS//ZF3] <berf>

berfmalik بەرفمالِك (ZF3) = snow shovel. See **berfmal**.

berfmalk بەرفمالك (IFb/GF/FS) = snow shovel. See **berfmal**.

berg I بەرگ (K) = fruit. See **ber V**.

berg II بەرگ *m./f.* **(-ê/-a;).** 1) {syn: cild} volume, tome *(of book)*: •**bergê êkê** = volume one; 2) {syn: cild} cover, binding (of book). Sor berg بەرگ = 'cover, binding (of book), volume, book' [K/A/IFb/TF/GF/Kmc/ZF]

berge بەرگە (FJ/GF/CS) = view, scene. See **bergeh**.

bergeh بەرگەه *f.* **(-a;-ê).** view, panorama; scene, sight: •**Li hêleke axpîna gund mîna ku şerekî mezin daketi be, dengê qêrîn û hewarê bilind dibe; li hêla din jî govend û dîlanek li hev geriyaye. Lawik li hemberî vê *bergehê* mitûmat dimîne** (Ardû, 29) At one side of the village dung heap, it was as if war had broken out, the sound of screaming and calls for help rings out; on the other side, dancing and celebration were going on. The boy was astonished by this *scene*. {also: berge (FJ/GF/CS-2)} {syn: dîmen} [Ardû/K/A/IFb/TF/Kmc/RZ/CS//FJ/GF] <ferc>

bergend بەرگەند (G) = equivalent; exchange. See **bergind**.

bergerî بەرگەری (GF) = defense. See **bergirî**.

bergeş بەرگەش (Msr/GF) = tray. See **berkeş**.

bergind بەرگِند *f.* **(-a;).** 1) {syn: bedel} equivalent: •**Ji ber ku bêjeya kurmancîyê "kar" nêr e, gava ku bêjeya tirkîyê ya *berginda* wê "îş" û bêjeya erebîyê "emel" yan "şixul" di kurmancîyê da dihên bikarînan, zayenda bêjeya kurmancîyê werdigirin** (RR, 19.15) Because the Kurmanji word "kar" is masculine, when the Turkish word *equivalent to* it, "îş", and the Arabic words "emel" or "şixul" are used in Kurmanji, they get the gender of the Kurmanji word; 2) {syn: bedel} exchange: **•Ez ê li *bergendî* solên te sê cot gore bidim te** (G) In *exchange* for your shoes, I will give you three pairs of socks. {also: bergend (G)} [RR/Wkt/ZF/FD//G]

bergirî بـەرگـرى *f.* **(-ya;).** defense; protection. {also: bergerî (GF); bergirtî (GF-2)} {syn: berevanî} Sor bergegirî بەرگەگرى = 'defence, resistance' <berge = 'resistance, ability to bear' [Bw/IFb/OK//GF]

ber•girtin I بـەرگِرتِن *vt.* **(ber-g[i]r-).** to copy, make a copy of, transcribe: **•Me jî ji ser qeyt'anê *bergirt*** (HCK-5, 292) And we *transcribed* it (or: *copied* it down) from the tape. [HCK/K/B]

bergirtî بەرگرتى (GF) = defense. See **bergirî**.

bergîl بەرگيل (A) = horse. See **bergîr**.

bergîr بـەرگـيـر *m./f.(B)* **(; /-ê).** 1) horse, especially hack, used as beast of burden; gelding, castrated horse (K/JJ); 2) sterile nag, unfit for horseback riding (B/Zeb). {also: bargîr (Zeb); bergîl (A); [barghir بارگير/berghir برگير] (JJ)} {syn: bor I[2]; hesp; nijda} Cf. T beygir [Ad/K/B/JJ//A//Zeb] <hesp>

bergîz بـەرگـيـز (FS) = Kurdish homespun jacket. See **bergûz**.

berguh بـەرگـوه (BF) = ear muff; ear phone. See **berguhk**.

berguhk بـەرگـوهـك *f.* **(-a; -ê).** 1) ear muff(s); 2) ear phone(s), ear buds: **•Em ji maxazayê 100 mt dûr ketin û min hew nêrî hevalê min ji berika xwe *berguhka* ku min gava din lê nêrî derxist** (nt [blog] 28.viii.2014) We went 100 m. away from the shop and I happened to notice my friend take out of his pocket *the ear phones* that I had been looking at. {also: berguh (BF)} [nt/K/IFb/ZF3/FD//BF]

bergûsk' بـەرگـووسـك (M-Am) = Kurdish homespun jacket. See **bergûz**.

bergûz بـەرگـويـز/بـەرگـووز [Bw] *m.* **().** traditional Kurdish men's homespun woolen jacket: **•We ḧeçîke xelkê Amêdîêne hemî K'urdin ... Hemî dikene [tkene] ber xo *bergûsk'a*--bêne cilk'êt wa *bergûsk'*. Çê diken [tken] ji hirîê, t şînin, t s̱orin, t kesk'in, t enwa' û eşk'alin** (M-Am #720) As for the people of Amadiye, they are all Kurds ... They all wear *homespun jackets* called '*bergusk*'. They make them of wool and they are blue and red and green and all sorts; **-peşme w bergûz** (M-Ak)/**r̄anî-bergûz** (SK) suit of homespun jacket and trousers {syn: şal û şapik}. {also: bergîz (FS); bergûsk' (M-Am)} [Bw/OK//M-Am//FS] <şal I; şûtik; *material patterns:* badayî; bekirbegî; ker̄anî; keskûyî; kesnedîtî I; piştpez; qehweyî; r̄eşaẍayî; semayî; şekirî; xezalî>

berhem بـەرهـەم *f.* **(-a;-ê).** 1) {syn: afirandin [2]} work *(of art)*, artifact, opus: **•Ev ferheng jî *berhemeke* nû ye** (IFb) This dictionary is also *a* new *work* **•Her *berhem* divê li gor dem û rewşa ku tê de hatiye afirandin, were nirxandin** (Wlt 1:39, 11) Every *work of art* should be evaluated according to the time and conditions in which it was created **•Herçiqas av ji bo hemû jîndaran çavkaniyeke bingehîn be jî, îro di destê mirovên "hemdem" de wek pergaleke ji holê rakirina *berhemên* dîrokê tê bi kar anîn** (Wlt 1:21, 16) Although water is a basic resource for all living things, today it is being used by "modern" man as an instrument for destroying historical *artifacts*; 2) product, result: **•Ev yeka han *berhema* salên wî yên girtîgehê bû** (KS, 7) This was *the result of* his years in prison. Sor berhem بـــەرهـــەم = 'achievement, accomplishment; product, result' [(neol)Wlt/IFb/TF/ZF3/BF]

berheste بەرهەستە *m.* **().** flint[stone] (for striking fire). {also: [ber-hesté] بـرهـسـتـه (JJ)} {syn: arbeşk; heste} Cf. Sor berd•estê بـەردەسـتـێ [F/K/JJ] <agir; çeqandin; k'irpît; qesp II>

berhev بـەرهـەڤ *adv.* together, gathered, aşembled, collected: **-berhev bûn** (K)/**berev ~** (Ba/F) to gather, assemble *(vi.)* {syn: civîn; k'om bûn; t'op bûn [t'op I]; xir̄ ve bûn}: **•Kire gazî, ku ḧemû gurê wan dera *berevî* cem wî *bin*** (Ba) He called all the wolves of those parts *to assemble* before him **•Gur gişk *berev bûn*** (Ba) All the wolves *gathered*; **-berhev dan** (K/GF/OK)/**dan berhev** (Rnh/IFb) to compare: **•Dema em zimanê xwe bi zimanên ko ketine warê nivîsandinê va *bidin ber hev*; divê em sed salî pir ne bînin** (Rnh 3:24, 486) When we *compare* our language with languages that have been written down, we must not see 100 years as a long time; **-berhev kirin** (K)/**berev ~** (B) to collect, gather, assemble *(vt.)* {syn: civandin; k'om kirin; t'op kirin; xir̄ ve kirin}: **•Wana pez ji nava gund berev dikir** (Ba2:1, 204) They would gather the sheep from all over the village. {also: berev I (B/GF-2); [berew برڤ/berhew برهڤ] (JJ)} < ber + hev [Ba/F/B//K/A/JB3/IFb/JJ/GF/(TF)/OK] <civandin; civîn; t'op I>

berhevkar بـهـرهـﭬـكـار (TF/OK) = tax collector. See **berevker**.

berhevok بەرهەڤۆك *f.* **(-a;-ê).** 1) collection, anthology: **•*Berevok* bona zanedar û xwendek'ar û p'iřanya xwendevanên ku bi folklor û zimanê k'urdî va mijûl dibin, bi k'ar tê** (Dz, 40) *The collection* is in use by scholars and students and most readers who are involved in Kurdish folklore and language **•Têkstê wê li sala 1936 da li Êrêvanê li *berhevoka* "Folklora Kurmanca"da çap bûye** (K-dş) The text of it was printed in Erevan in 1936 in *the collection* Folklore of the Kurmandj; 2) brochure, pamphlet (IFb). {also: berevok (B/GF/Dz)} [K-dş/IFb/TF/ZF//B/GF/Dz] <belavok>

berhingar بـهـرهـِنـگـار: **-berhingarî *fk-ê* bûn** = a) to oppose s.o. [Ar ta'arraḍa lahu تـعـرّض لـه/i'tirāḍ اعـتـراض/mu'āraḍah مـعـارضـة]; to attack, bother, pick a fight with [Ar taṣaddá تـصـدّى/taḥarraša تحرّش]: **•Du malêt Kurdane her du *berhingarî* êk *bûn*** (Bw) Two Kurdish families *opposed* one another **•'Eyalêt te *berhingarî* 'eyalêt me *bûn*** (Bw) Your children *ganged up on* our children [dijî wan radibin] **•Ji ber ku miletê Kurd yê ku hertim lêkkevtî û hevrwîşî êk û *berhingarî* serê êkûdu *bûyî* neşiyaye êkatiyeka bîrûra ji bo armancekê xebatê biken di nav xwo da peyda biken** (Hok2, 63) Because the Kurdish nation was always pushing and fighting and *opposing* one another, they could not achieve unity of opinion to strive for a purpose; b) {syn: 'erza *fk-î* şkandin} to scold, reprimand, bawl out: **•Jina wî *berîngar bûê*, gotê "Me cê mêvana nîye, bila bi xo biçine mizgeftê"** (M-Ak, #585, 255) His wife *opposed him* and told him, 'We have no room for guests; let them take themselves off to the mosque"; c) to intercept *(mil.)* (Zeb); d) to encounter, face, grapple with; **-berhingarî *ft-î* kirin** (Sêmêl-Ertûşî) to expose to stg., cause to encounter, face, grapple with: **• Xwedê me ji van hemû êşên we gotîn biparêzit û tu caran me û we *berhingarî* wan *nekit*** (Sêmêl-Ertûşî) May God protect us from all of these illnesses you have mentioned, and may he never *expose* you and us to them. {also: berîngar (M-Ak); <berengar> بـهرهنـگار (Hej)} Sor berengar bûn بـهرهنگار بـوون = 'to encounter (W&E); to grapple with [P gelāvīz گـلاويـز] (Hej)' [Bw/Zeb/HoK2//M-Ak//Hej] <ber sîng girtin>

berik I بەرك (IFb) = pocket. See **berîk**.

ber•ik II بـهـرك *m./f.(K)* **(•kê/ ;).** bullet: **•*Berê* tivingê sînga Baram simtiye** (GF) The rifle *bullet* pierced Baram's chest; **-berk û derman** (Bw) ammunition [lit. 'bullets & gunpowder']. {also: ber III[2] (A/GF-2/TF); [berik] برك (JJ)} {syn: gule} dim. of ber = 'stone' [BW/K/IF/JJ/GF/OK//A/OK] <t'ifing>

beřik III بـهـڕك (SK/BF) = kilim, flat-weave pileless rug. See **beř IV**.

berindir بـهـرِنـدِر *m.* **().** two- or three-year-old male sheep. {syn: şek} [Bsk/Kmc] <berdîr>

berindîr بـهـرِنـديـر (Kmc/GF) = two- or three-year-old female sheep. See **berdîr**.

berî I بـهـرى *prep./conj.* 1) before *(time)*: **•berî nîvro** = before noon **•Di benda *berî* wê da** (BX) In the *preceding* article [lit. 'in the article *before* that'] **•Memi şûrê xwe danî navbera xwe û Zînê, da ko *beriya* mehirê tu tiştê neşerî di navbera wan de neqewimit** (SW) M. put his sword between himself and Z., so that *before* the marriage nothing unlawful might happen between them; **-berî her tiştî** = first of all, first and foremost: **•*Berî her tiştî*, divê em vê pirsa han ji xwe bikin** (Wlt 1:36, 16) *First of all*, we must ask ourselves this question; **-berî ko/berîya ko** + *subj.* = before + -ing; 2) ago: **•Sê sal *berî* niha** (AW69A3) Three years ago [lit. '3 years *before* now']. {also: berîya.../beriya (SW); <berî> بـرى (HH)}} < ber + ji [K/A/JB3/HH/ZF3] See **ber II.**

beřî II بـهـڕى *f.* **(-ya;-yê).** desert, wilderness; plain: *designates desert, plain, or regions that are warm during the winter, such as **Urfa** and **Gaziantep*** (HB): **•Quling ji berîyê hatin** (AB) The cranes came from the wilderness. {also: [beri] بـرى (JJ); <berî> بـرى (HH)} {syn: best; ç'ol; pasar (Haz)} Cf. Ar barrīyah بـرّيـة [AB/K/A/JB3/B/JJ/HH/ZF3] <best; deşt>

berî III بەرى = homesickness. See **bêrî II**.

berî IV بەرى (Ad/B) = pocket. See **berîk**.

berîdan بەريدان (K) = to banish. See **beradan**.

berîk بـهـريك/**berîk'** [JB1-A] *f.* **(-a;-ê).** *(breast)* pocket: **•Ço di ṣindoqê da, derê wê qilf kir û kilîlk kire di *berîka* xo da** (JB1-A #29,106) [He] went into the box, [she] locked its 'door' and put the key in her *(breast) pocket* **•Zêřa ji *berîka* xwe dertîne** (Z-2) He takes gold pieces out of his *breast pocket*. {also: berik I (IFb); berî IV (Ad/B); bêrik (Ad/BX): bêrîk (JB3/LC); [beríka] بـريـكـه (JJ)} {syn: cêb; kûrik I; pizî III} [F/K/SK/Bw/JB1-A//Ad/B//BX//IFb//JB3//JJ] berîkanî بەریکانی (RZ) = competition. See **berêkanê**.

berîn بەرین *adj.* broad, wide, spacious, expansive: **•Ev kuma çîrokan jî çipkek e ji wî deryayê mezin û *berîn* ku mirovê Kurd di nav hizir û aşupa xu da afirandîn** (X. Dêreşî. Şevbêriyên zarokan, 8) And this collection of stories is a drop from that large and *broad* ocean which the Kurd has created in his mind and imagination. {syn: berfireh; fireh; pehn I} Sor berîn بەرین [Derêşî/K(s)/GF/RZ/SS/CS]

berîngar بەرینگار (M-Ak) = opposing. See **berhingar**.

berjen بەرژەن (FJ/FS) = symptom; mark, sign. See **berjeng**.

berjeng بەرژەنگ *f.* **(-a;-ê).** 1) symptom (of a disease): **•*Berjengên* zerkiyê li wî diyar in** (FS) *The symptoms of* hepatitis/jaundice are apparent on him; 2) mark, sign, indication, proof, evidence: **•*Berjengên* baranê hir û ba ne** (BF) *The signs of* a rainstorm are gusts of wind. {also: berjen (FJ/FS-2)} [Bw/GF/BF/Wkt/FS/SS/ZF3//FJ]

berjewend بەرژەوەند (GF/OK) = interest. See **berjewendî**.

berjewendî بەرژەوەندی *f.* **(-ya;-yê).** interest, profit, advantage: **•*Berjewendîyên* hemîyan wekî yek nînin** (Metîn 2[1997]:25) *The interests of* all sides are not alike. {also: berjewend (GF/OK)} {syn: menfa'et} [(neol)Metîn/IFb/TF//BF/GF/OK]

berjêr بەرژێر (Ba) = down. See **berbijêr**.

berkanî بەرکانی *f.* **(;-yê).** sling, catapult; slingshot: **•Wî berek bi *berkanîyê* avêt** (FS) He threw a stone with *the sling* **•Wî destê xwe avêt xw[ê]danka xwe û kevirek jê derxist û bi *berkanî* veweşand, li eniya Golyat xist** (Dawud û Golyat: 1 Samuel 17:49) He reached into his bag, took out a stone and slung it with his *catapult*, striking Goliath on the forehead. {also: berdeqanî (BF/FS/SS); [berekani] برکانی (JJ); <berkanî> برکانی (HH)} {syn: kevirkan} [Dawud û Golyat/A/IFb/ZF/Kmc/HH/Wkt/FD//JJ//BF/FS/SS] <darlastîk; qosk>

berk'eftî بەرکەفتی *adj.* important, significant, noteworthy. {also: berketî (IFb/OK); berkevtî (OK-2)} {syn: giring} [VOA//IFb/OK]

berkeş بەرکەش *f.* **(-a;-ê).** copper tray on which meals are served. {also: bergeş (Msr/GF); <berkeş> برکش (HH)} {syn: mecme'; mersef} [Msr/GF//IFb/HH] <lengerî; sênî; sifre; tiryan>

berketî بەرکەتی (IFb/OK) = significant. See **berk'eftî**.

berkevtî بەرکەڤتی (OK) = significant. See **berk'eftî**.

berkêşan بەرکێشان *f.* **(;-ê).** 1) production (IF): **•pergalên *berkêşanê*** (IF) instruments *of production*; 2) exploitation (JB3). [(neol)IF/JB3]

berk'oş بەرکۆش *f.* **(-a;-ê).** 1) front part of a woman's dress (K/B); 2) {syn: berdilk [4]; bermalk; bervank; melîtk; mêzer [4]; şalik I} apron, garment worn by women about the waist, which hangs down over the lap (IF/HH). {also: <berkoş> برکوش (HH)} [K/B/IFb/HH/GF/OK] <bermalk>

bermaî بەرمائی (F) = remnants. See **bermayî**.

bermal بەرمال *f.* **(-a;-ê).** 1) yard, square or courtyard in front of a house (B/K); 2) vestibule, entry hall (K); 3) salon, parlor (A/IF). [K/A/IF/B/ZF3]

bermalî بەرمالی *f.* **(-ya;-yê).** 1) {syn: kevanî} housewife ; 2) servant girl, maid: **•Diya min bê *bermalî* ye û ez ê wê ji diya xwe re bikim *bermalî*** (ZZ-5, 77) My mother has no *house maid*, and I will make her a *maid* for my mother. [K/A/JB3/B/IFb/FJ/TF/GF/ZF/CS]

bermalk بەرمالك *f./m.(FS)* **(-a/-ê;).** 1) {syn: berdilk [4]; berk'oş; bervank; melîtk; mêzer [4]; şalik I}a) apron; b) bib: **•Wî *bermalk* da ber zařokî û xwarin dayê** (FS) He put *a bib* on the child and gave him food; 2) bath towel; 3) {syn: gêzî} broom (Qzl/Qzl/GF). {also: [bermál] برمال (JJ)} [A/GF/Qzl/Qzl/ZF3/FS//JJ] <berk'oş>

bermay بەرمای (SK) = remnants. See **bermayî**.

berma•yî بەرمایی *f.* **(•yîya;•yê).** 1) remnants, remains, rest, what is left over: **•*Bermayîya* hêrsê hê di dilê wê da [m]abû** (MB-Mayro) *The remnants of* anger had remained in her heart; 2) food left over (F/B/JJ); 3) ruins: **•[Mirov] xwe di nav *bermayên* dîrokeke 5000 sal kevin de dibîne** (Wlt 1:21, 16) One finds oneself amid 5,000-year-old historical *ruins*. {also: bermaî (F); bermay (SK); [bermaï] برمای (JJ)} Cf. Sor bermawe بەرماوە = 'remnants, food left over' [MB/Wlt/K/IFb/B/GF/TF//F//JJ/SK]

bernam•e بەرنامە *f.(IFb/F/K)/m/(OK)* **(•a/;).** program. {also: berneme (K)} < P barnāme برنامه; Sor bername بەرنامە [Ber/F/IFb/GF/TF/OK//K]

bernav بەرناڤ *m.(K/F)/f.(B)* **(-ê/ ; /-ê).** 1) {syn: daçek} preposition: **-bernavê cot bi cot** (K) paired preposition *(e.g., ji ser, li ber; see K2, §386)*; **-bernavê giranbar** (K) compound preposition; **-bernavê hêsa** (K) simple preposition; 2) {syn: pronav} *pronoun (IF/GF). <ber = 'before' + nav = 'name, noun' [(neol)F/K/IF/B/GF/ZF3]

berneme بەرنەمە (K) = program. See **bername**.

beřoj بەڕۆژ/**beroj** بەرۆژ [IFb/HH/ZF3] *f./m.(SK/FS)*

(;/-î). 1) {≠nizar I} sunny side *(of house, mountain, valley, etc.)*; warm place to sit to catch the sun during chilly weather: **•Dibêjin di nihalekêda r̄îwîyek hebû...car diçû *ber̄ojî*, car diçû nizarî** (SK 2:9) They say there was a fox [living] in a ravine…sometimes he would go on *the sunny side*, sometimes on the shady side; 2) *by extension,* [warm] place where sheep are led for grazing during the winter (JJ): **•Pezê şivanî *li ber̄ojî* diçerî** (FS) The shepherd's flock was grazing *on the sunny side*. {also: berroj (A/GF/TF); berr̄oj (K); [berouj] بروژ (JJ); <beroj> بروژ (HH)} < ber = 'before, in front of' + r̄oj = 'sun; day': Sor berr̄oj بەرڕۆژ = 'sunny side of hill, adretto' [SK/FS//IFb/HH/ZF3//A/GF/TF//K//JJ] <berberoşk; zinar>

beroş بەرۆش *f.* **(-a;-ê).** 1) {syn : den I; dişt} cauldron; (copper) cooking pot: **•*Beroş* tijî av e** (AB) *The pot* is full of water **•Min *beroşa* malê girt û anî danî ser kuçik û agir da binî** (LC, 24) I took the household *cauldron* and put it on the hearthstone and lit a fire underneath it **•Te çi danî *beroşê*, tuê wî bixwî** (Dz-#1488) Whatever you put *in the pot*, you will eat it *[prv., cf. Eng 'As you sow, so shall you reap']*; **-binê beroşê** (Qmş) (burnt) rice at bottom of the pot *(considered a delicacy)* {syn: ver̄enk}; 2) pail, bucket: **•Piştî ku diya min dewê xwe dikila, meşka xwe ya reş ji darê dadixist ... bi destê rastê bi lewlebê pêşî û bi yê çepê jî bi lewlebê paşî digirtin û dewê çîl-sipî vala dikir *beroşê*** (Alkan, 71) After my mother churned her buttermilk, she removed her black skin butter churner from the wooden frame … and held the front handle bar with her right hand and the back handle bar with her left, and emptied the snow-white buttermilk into *the pail*; **-beroşa bêr** = milk-pail used in milking sheep. {also: [berouch] بروش (JJ); <beroş> بروش (HH)} [AB/K/JB3/IFb/B/HH/GF/TF/OK//JJ] <mencel; miqilk; qûşxane>

berp'al بەرپال *f./m.(FS)* **(-a/;-ê/-î).** 1) {also: berp'alî (B-2)} cushion one leans on while sitting; bolster *(of a sofa)* (K/B): **•Ew li ser tejê rûnişt û pala xwe da *berpalî*, û di pencerê r̄a li rêhlî nêrî** (FS) S/he sat on the carpet and reclined on *the bolster*, and regarded the woods through the window; 2) slope (K/B): **•Gund li *berpala* çiyayê Rojhilatê bû** (Alkan, 70) The village was on *the slope of* Mount Rojhilat; 3) side (K). [Z-2/K/B/GF/FS]

berp'alî بەرپالی (B) = bolster, cushion. See **berp'al** [1].

berper بەرپەر *m.* **(-ê;).** page *(of a book)*: **•Her wisa govar *berperên* xwe bo hemu kesan vedike** (Roja 1[1996]:4) Likewise, the journal opens its *pages* to everyone. {syn: r̄ûp'el} =Sor lapeṙe لاپەڕە [Roj/Bar/OK]

berpêş بەرپێش *adv.* ahead, forward: **-berpêş kirin** (IFb/GF/FJ/ZF/Wkt): to present, offer; to propose, suggest, recommend: **•Di kilaman da sînor wekî destwerdanên biyaniyan li welatê Kurdan hatine *berpêş kirin*** (econpapers.repec.org: W.Hamelink & H.Barış. Dengbêjs on borderlands) In the songs borders *are presented* as foreign interference in the Kurdish landscape **•Hikûmet *dê* îro bernameya xwe *berpêş bike*** (Wkt) Today the government *will present* its program **•Li pêşangehê gelek wêneyên nirxbilind yên zarrotî û ciwaniya wê *hatin berpêş kirin*** (Wkt) At the exhibition many valuable pictures of her childhood and youth *were presented.* {syn: pêşk'êş kirin} [WT/K/A/IFb/GF/FJ/ZF/Wkt] <qewîtî kirin>

berpirsiyar بەرپرسیار (JB3) = responsible. See **berpirsîyar**.

berpirsiyarî بەرپرسیاری (JB3/Wkt) = responsibility. See **berpirsîyarî**.

berpirsîyar بەرپرسیار *adj.* responsible: **•Lê tol vekirin ne hat bîra wî, li nik wî *berpirsiyar* lawê wî bû** (Dz #22, 390) But revenge did not enter his mind, in his view *the one responsible* was his own son. {also: berpirsiyar (JB3); berpirsyar (ZF3); berpisyar (FS/BF)} {syn: cabdar} {berpirsiyarî; berpirsîyarî} Sor berpirsyar بەرپرسیار [Ber/K//JB3/Dz//ZF3//FS/BF]

berpirsîyarî بەرپرسیاری *f.* **(-ya;-yê).** responsibility: **•Tu bihane û hincet êdî nikare we û me ji vê *berpirs-yarîyê* xelas bike** (kelhaamed.com 1.xii.2016) No excuses can save you or us from this *responsibility*. {also: berpirsiyarî (JB3/Wkt); berpisyarî (BF)} {syn: cabdarî} [K//JB3/Wkt//BF] <berpirsîyar>

berpirsyar بەرپرسیار (ZF3) = responsible. See **berpirsîyar**.

berpisyar بەرپسیار (FS/BF) = responsible. See **berpirsîyar**.

berpisyarî بەرپسیاری (BF) = responsibility. See **berpirsîyarî**.

berq بەرق *f.* **().** lightning bolt: **•Belediya vexa û *berq* k'etin** (HR 3:63) *Lightning bolts* struck. {also: birq (IFb-2} <Ar barq برق = '(flash of) lightning' [HR/K/IFb/CS/TF] <bap'eşk; beledî; birûsk>

berroj بـــەرروژ (A/GF/TF)/berřoj بـــەرڕۆژ (K) = sunny side. See **beřoj**.

bersef بەرسەف (IFb/GF) = porch, balcony. See **bersifk**.

bersifk بـــەرسِـفـك *f.* **(;-ê).** front porch, patio; balcony. {also: bersef (IFb/GF); bersiv II (Dh); <bersivk> بـــەرسـڤـك (Hej)} {syn: berbanik} [Bw//Hej//Dh//IFb/GF] <behwe>

bersing بەرسِنگ. See **bersîng**.

*ber sinîg بەر سِنیگ (XF/AId). See **bersîng**.

bersiv I بـــەرسِـڤ *f.* **(-a;-ê).** answer: •**Ev serê salekê ye ku mamoste Kevanot li bendî *bersivekê* ye, ew *bersiva* ku wî bi dilpekîn dipa, îro nû gîhîştiye destê wî** (Lab, 5) It has been a year that Professor Kevanot has been awaiting *an answer--the answer* he has been awaiting with beating heart has just reached him today; **-bersivdan** (TF)/**bersîv dan** (IFb) to answer, reply {syn: cab dan; vegeřandin}. {also: bersîv (AB/JB3/IFb/GF-2/OK)} {syn: cab [1]} [AB/JB3/IFb/OK//K/A/GF/TF/Bw]

bersiv II بەرسڤ (Dh) = porch, balcony. See **bersifk**.

bersivk بەرسڤك(Hej) = porch, balcony. See **bersifk**.

bersîng بـــەرســیــنــگ: **-bersîng girtin** (Hk) to have a confrontation, confront, attack offensively; to curb, stop: •**Hûn dikarin mîlyoneke mirovan bilez veguhêzine Seulê. Heke me ew mayinên ku ji bo *bersinggirtina* bizaveke wehe … neban, çu kesê ku ez dinasim bawer nedikir ku … me dikarî bizaveke wesa bisekinînin** (VoA[Hk]) You can move a million people into Seoul pretty quickly. And no one I know believes that … we could do anything *to stop* that if we didn't have the strong deterrent of the landmines •**Serekwezîrê Tirkîyê yê parêzyar yê nû Mesût Yilmaz soz daye ku ji bo *bersinggirtina* wan zêdegavîyan pêngavên xurt bihavêjît** (VoA[Hk]) Turkey's new conservative prime minister, Mesut Yilmaz, has promised to take concrete measures *to curb* abuses. {also: bersing; *ber sinîg girtin (XF/AId)} {syn: *berahîya … girtin} [Bw/Hk/GF//XF/AId]

bersîv بـــەرســيــڤ (AB/JB3/IFb/GF/OK) = answer. See **bersiv I**.

bersoj بەرسۆژ (Bw) = heartburn. See **bersojk**.

bersojk بـــەرســۆژك *f.* **(-a;-ê).** heartburn; indigestion: •**Bersoj ya hatî** (or, **ya li**) **min** (Bw) I have indigestion. {also: bersoj (Bw); berşoşk (B); berşoşkî (K/A/Kmc-#1568); [ber-choch] بـــرشـــوش (JJ)} < ber + soj-(sotin) = 'to burn' [Zeb/IFb//Bw//B//K/A/Kmc//B]

berstî بەرستی (B) = collar. See **berstû**.

bersto بەرستۆ (IFb/OK) = collar. See **berstû**.

berstu بەرستو (K/B) = collar. See **berstû**.

berstuk بەرستوك (A) = collar. See **berstû**.

berstû بـــەرســتـــوو *f./m.(OK)* **(-ya/;-yê/).** collar: •**Zelîxe pařa dest davêje *berstûya* wî** (Ba3-3, #29) Zulaikha grabs his *collar* from behind. {also: berstî (B); bersto (IFb/OK); berstu (K/B-2); berstuk (A)} {syn: bestik; girîvan; p'êsîr [2]; pis̲to; yax} [Ba3-1/F/GF//B//IFb/OK//K//A]

berşî بـــەرشـــی *m.&f.* **(-yê/-ya;).** namesake; form of address between namesakes: •**Ew berşiyê min e** (FS) He is my namesake [i.e., He and I have the same name]. [Bw/Dh/FS]

berşo بـــەرشـــۆ *f.* **().** change of clothes, extra set of clothes (K); reserve, spare (JJ): •**[Cilêd <min> dijûn bûyîne, *berşoyêd* <min> bîne, da ez cilêd xwe veguhorim]** (JR) <My> clothes are dirty, bring <my> *spare set* so that I can change •**[Jina Mela Bazîdî înan ew destê cilêd melayî ku *berşo* bûn, daye jaran]** (JR) Mullah Bazîd's wife took the mullah's *spare set of clothes* and donated it to the poor. {also: [ber-chou] بـــرشـــو (JJ)} {syn: bedilç'ek} < ber = 'before, front' + şo- = 'wash' [JR/K/JJ]

berşoşk بەرشۆشك (B) = heartburn. See **bersojk**.

berşoşkî بـــەرشـــۆشـــکـــی (K/A/Kmc-#1568) = heartburn. See **bersojk**.

bert̲eng I بەرطەنگ/**berteng I** بەرتەنگ [GF/OK/Hej] *adj.* narrow, cramped, crowded (e.g., of a dwelling): **-bert̲eng kirin** (Zeb) to oppress, repress, harass {syn: perçiqandin; tepeser kirin} [Zeb/Bw//GF/OK/Hej] <teng I; tengav>

bert̲eng II بەرطەنگ [HR]/**berteng II** بەرتەنگ [K/A/CS] *m.* **(-ê;).** belt, strap, saddle girth, cinch, surcingle: •**… û teng û *bertengê* dewarê xo jdandin** [=şidandin] (HR 4:44) And they tightened the belly straps and *saddle girths* of their steeds. {also: [bertenk] برتنك (JJ)} [HR/K/A/CS//JJ] <teng II>

bertîl بـــەرتـــيـــل *m./f.(B/OK)* **(; /-ê).** bribe; bribery, graft; extortion, embezzlement: •***Bertîl* kevira nerm dike** (L) *The bribe* softens rocks *[prv.]* •**Ezê heřim pêşîya vî bazirganî, jê bistînim *bertîl* û bacêd girane** (Z-1) I'll go after that caravan and get from it (him) great *bribes* and taxes. {also: [bertil] برطيل (JJ); <bertîl> بـــرتـــيـــل (HH)} {syn: bexşîş [3]; řuşet} Cf. Ar bart̲īl برطيل [Z-1/K/IFb/B/JJ/HH/GF/OK]

bertîlxur بـــەرتـــيـــلـــخـــور (K/B/CS) = bribe-taker. See **bertîlxwer**.

bertîlxwer بەرتیلخوەر *m.&f.* **().** bribe-taker: **•Mirovekî** ***bertîlxwer*****, serxweş, dijwar û bêderfe bû** (Cxn, 47) He was *a bribe-taker*, a drunkard, hard and insolent. {also: bertîlxur (K/B/CS)} Sor bertîlxor بەرتیلخۆر = 'susceptible to bribery; person who accepts a bribe' [Cxn/GF//K/B/CS] <bertîl>

berû بەروو/**beřû** بەڕوو [AA] *f.(Kmc-6)/m.(JB3/OK)* **(-ya/-yê;).** acorn: **-berûyê malan** (JB3) mast, edible acorn; **-berûyê pezan** (JB3) [non-edible] acorn. {also: [berú] برو (JJ); <berû> برو (HH)} {syn: p'alûd} Cf. Sor beřû بەڕوو; Za bel[l]î/bellu *f.* (Mal); Hau belû *m.* = 'oak' [K/A/JB3/IFb/JJ/HH/GF/TF/OK/Kmc-6//AA]

***berûk** بەرووك *f.* **(-a;-ê).** 1) chest, breast; front part of body (K); 2) tether, thong, breast-piece *(of harness)* (JJ). {also: [berouk] بروك (JJ)} [K/JJ/ZF3] <hevsar; paşil>

bervajî بەرڤاژی (IFb/GF) = inside out; on the contrary. See **berevajî**.

bervanek بەرڤانەك (B) = apron. See **bervank**.

bervang بەرڤانگ (GF) = apron. See **bervank**.

bervank بەرڤانك *f.* **(-a;-ê).** apron. {also: bervanek (B); bervang (GF); berwank (IFb/OK); [bervanik] بروانك (JJ)} {syn: berdilk [4]; berk'oş; bermalk; melîtk; mêzer [4]; şalik I} Sor berwanke بەروانکە [Elk/F/K//GF//JJ/B/IFb/OK] <berk'oş>

berwal بەروال (GF/HH) = slope. See **berwar**.

berwank بەروانك (IFb/OK) = apron. See **bervank**.

berwar بەروار *m.(K)/f.(IFb/F/B)* **(-ê/-a;/-ê).** 1) {syn: hevraz; jihelî; p'al; pesar; p'êş II[2]; qunt'ar; sîng; teřazin} slope *(of hill)*, incline, descent (K/A/IF/JJ); gradient (JB3): **•Weke hertim pezê xwe berdaye** ***berwarê*** **çiyayê nêzîkî gund** (Ardû, 114) As usual, he led his sheep to a mountain *slope* near the village; 2) bend, twist *(in a road)* (B); 3) {syn: çeperast} across (in crossword puzzles) (Bw); 4) *(calendrical) date (K[s]/JB3/IF): *unacceptable neologism, based on misinterpreting the geographical name* ***Berwarî*** *as a noun meaning 'date'* [see: A.R. Zabihi. *Qamûsî Zimanî Kurdî* (Baghdad : KZK Press, 1977), v.1, pp. 61-2; Amir Hassanpour. *Nationalism and Language in Kurdistan 1918-1985* (San Franciso : Mellen Research University Press, 1992), pp. 401-2} {also: berwal (GF-2); bewrar, f. (F); [ber-var] بروار (JJ); <berwal> بروال (HH)} [EP-7/K/A/JB3/IFb/B/JJ/GF/TF/OK//F//HH]

berx بەرخ *f./m.(OK)* **(-a/-ê;-ê/).** lamb: **-berxa mê** (BK) female lamb; **-berxê nêr** (BK) male lamb. {also: [berkh] برخ (JJ); <berx> برخ (HH)} <*baṛx <*warrak <O Ir *warnaka- (A&L p. 87 [VII, 4] + 94 [XVIII, 1] + 97 [XXI, 6]): Sor berx بەرخ = 'lamb before first shearing'; Za vere[k] *m.* (Mal); Hau were *m.* (M4) [K/A/JB3/IFb/B/JJ/HH/BK/SK/GF/TF/OK] <berdîr; bêçî I; kar I; mî I>

***berxep** بەرخەپ *f.* **().** *on a traditional plow,* the washers which fasten the pins [**xep**] that connect the beam [**mijane**] to the body of the plow [**cot**]. = NENA bôṣâ ܒܘܨܐ/ bôsâ ܒܘܣܐ (<Az T بفصه) = 'wooden ring used in stables; stick bent into a circle fastened to the yoke of a plough and to the beam' (Maclean) [Zeb] <bose II; xep>

berxik بەرخك = dim. of **berx**.

berxvan بەرخڤان *m.* **(-ê; berxvên/berxvîn).** shepherd who tends lambs, lambherd: **•Aĥmê Çolo gelek sala bûye** ***berxvan*****, paşê li gele cîê cudada bûye şivan** (K'oroxlî, 233) A.Ch. *tended lambs* for many years, then in many different places he tended sheep [lit. 'was a shepherd']. {also: [berkh-van] برخوان (JJ)} <berx + -van; Sor berxelewan بەرخەلەوان = 'shepherd of a flock of lambs' {berxvan[t]î} [K'oroxlî/K/B/IFb/FJ/GF/TF/JJ/ZF3/FS] <şivan>

berxvanî بەرخڤانی *f.* **().** lamb tending, profession of shepherding lambs: **-berxvantî kirin** (K) to tend lambs. {also: berxvantî (K-2)} [K/GF/ZF3] <şivantî>

berxvantî بەرخڤانتی (K) = lamb tending. See **berxvanî**.

ber xweda بەرخوەدا (XF)/**berxweda** (K) *adv.* to oneself; quickly; quietly, gently, in a barely audible voice, in a whisper, not saying aloud, not expressing outwardly, mentally: **•Wî çaxî Ûsib** ***ber xweda*** **dibêje Zelîxe** (Ba-1, #16) Then Joseph *quietly* says to Zulaikha ... [Ba-1/K/XF] <ber II>

berxwedan بەرخوەدان *f.* **(-a;-ê).** 1) resistance, endurance; 2) to resist (IFb/GF/Mzg/Krş). See **li ber xwe dan**. [K/IFb/GF/FS] <serhildan>

beryan بەریان (FJ) = lamb dish. See **biryan I**.

berz بەرز *adj.* high. {syn: bilind; quloz} [Pok. bhereĝh- 140.] 'high'-->*bherĝh-; Skt bṛhant- [bṛhat]; O Ir *barza-: Av bərəzant-; Old P *bṛδant-; Sor berz بەرز; Za berz (Todd/JJ); cf. also P burz برز = 'tallness, stature'; Germ Berg = 'mountain'; see: *Haoma* §255, p. 139 [K/A/JB3/IF] See also **bilind**. <bala>

berza بەرزا *adj.* 1) {syn: winda} lost (M/K/Hk): **-berza bûn:** a) to be or get lost (K); b) to be absent (JJ) {also: [berze bouin] برزه بوين (JJ)}; c) to disappear: •"**Sefera te dûr kewt, neko li Dehlewî bibînî, egerne ji destê te ço.“ Digel wê xeberê derwêş ji-pêş çawêt wî *bezir bo*** (SK 44:422) ‘Your journey is longer now. Either you will find (what you seek) in Delhi or not at all.’ With these words the dervish *disappeared* from before his eyes •**Wextê ko ji r̄awê hatinewe ‘Îso cilêt derwêşan di-ber xo kirin, bi şew der-kewt, ço deşta Hewlêrê, bo aşewan. Salek ço, ‘Îso *bezir bo*. Kes nezanî ‘Îso kêwe çoye** (SK 21:191) When they came back from the hunt, Iso put on dervishes' clothes, set off at night and went to the plain of Arbil and became a miller. A year went by and *there was no sign of* Iso. No one knew whither Iso had gone; **-berza kirin** (K/Hk)/**berze kirin** (JB3/Bw): a) to lose, misplace {syn: winda kirin}; b) to destroy, eliminate; to cause to disappear, spirit away: •**Ez r̄azî:me sebeb xo, ji kes ‘aciz nîme, emma ditirsim ko silsila meşaixan ji wî ‘aciz bît, batinî wî bigirin o *bezir ken*** (SK :528) For myself I do not mind, I am not angry with anyone, but I fear that the line of Shaikhs may be angry with him and take him and *spirit* him *away* in secret; 2) absent (K/JJ). {also: berze (K-2/JB3/Bw); bezir (SK); bizir I (K[s]); [berze برزه/bezra بزره] (JJ)} Cf. Sor bizir بزر [M/K/Hk//JJ/JB3/Bw//SK]

berze بەرزە (K/JB3/JJ/Bw) = lost; absent. See **berza**.

berzîn I بەرزین *m.* **().** a colt *or* foal old enough to be ridden, i.e., a three-year old colt. [Trg/A/IFb/GF/FJ/ZF3] <canî; nûzîn>

bes I بەس *adj.* 1) enough, sufficient: ***•Bes* e** = It is *enough* ***•Bese*, min têr xwar** (B) *That's enough*, I've eaten my fill **•Ev *besî* meye** (K) This is *enough for* us; 2) [+ *imperative*] Stop *doing stg.!*, Quit *doing stg.!*: ***•Bes* biçûkêt xelkî bikuje!** (M-Am #730, 336) *Don't* kill people's children *anymore*/ *Stop* killing people's children! ***•Bes* vê gotinê bike!** (IFb) *Quit* saying that!; 3) {syn: lê I; lêbelê} but (Dh): ***•Bes* insan jî lazim e bo xo nesîhetî ji wê hekayetê bigirît** (SK 2:17) *But* man too should draw the moral from this story ***•Bes* xo nekene xesaretê dunya û axiretê** (SK 57:677) *But* do not destroy yourselves in this world and the next. {also: [bes] بس (JJ); <bes> بس (HH)} Cf. P bas بس; Sor bes بەس [M-Am/K/A/IFb/B/SK/JJ/HH/GF/TF/AD] <t'êr I>

be‘s II بەعس (B/K) = discussion. See **beĥs**.

besîre بەسیرە *m.* **().** 1) {syn: cûr I; harsim; şilûr} unripe or sour grapes; 2) sour juice of grapes. {also: bessîre (GF); bêsîre (Bw); [bessíra] بسيره (JJ); <bêsîre> بيسيره (HH)} <Arc besar בסר = ‘to begin to boil, be in the first stage of ripening’ + *participle* besir בסיר (m.)/besira בסירא (f.) = ‘in the early stage of ripening‘: NENA bassi:ra (Krotkoff); cf. Heb boser בסר ‘unripe fruit‘; Sor bersîle بەرسیلە = ‘unripe (of fruits)’ (K3) [A/IFb/JJ/GF//HH/Bw]

beskurk بەسکورك (Kmc-1591/RZ) = collar. See **bestik**.

bessîre بەسسیرە (GF) = unripe grapes. See **besîre**.

best بەست *f.* **(-a;-ê).** 1) {syn: deşt; r̄ast [6]} plain, prairie, steppe; level expanse; lowland: ***•Besteke* xir̄e-xalî k’ete pêşya Memê u Bor** (FK-eb-1) Mem and Bor came upon a barren *plain*; 2) valley, vale: **•Dibêjin *bestekî*** [sic] **beran li-ṯenişt gundê wan heye. Wextê diçin e seferê ji r̄êwe diçin e-naw *besta* beran** (SK 12:117) They say that there is a stony *vale* next to their village. When they go on a journey they go first of all to *the vale of* stones; 3) field, piece of land: **•Li *besta* pêş mala te ew r̄êz bi cêrge bisekine** (Ba3-3, #8) [They] should go line up in a group on *the field* in front of your house. [FK-1/F/K/A/B/SK] <ber̄î II; ç’ol; gelî II>

bestik بەستِك *f.* **(-a;).** collar: **•Ez ê ecêbekê bînime serê gur. Belkî *bestika* xwe ji destê wî xelas kim** (J2, 14) I'll pull a trick on the wolf. Maybe I'll be rid of him [lit. 'free my *collar* from his hand']. {also: beskurk (Kmc-1591/RZ); bestkur (GF)} {syn: berstû; girîvan; p’êsîr [2]; pisto; yax} [J2/ Kmc-1594/ZF3//GF//RZ]

bestin بەستِن *vt.* **(-bend-/-best-[M]/-bestîn-[IF]).** 1) {syn: girêdan} to tie (up), bind; to tie *(animals)* up; 2) to freeze *(vt.)*. {also: [bestin] بستن (JJ)} [Pok. bhendh- 127.] ‘to bind‘--> Skt bandh- [IX badhnāti]; O Ir *band- (Tsb 44): O P & Av basta- <*bazda- (*present stem:* O P bandaya-/Av ba.ndaya- *causative in form*); Sgd βynt- [vend-]; Mid P bastan (band-) = ‘to tie, bind’ & band = ‘bond, link‘; P bastan بستن (band-) (بند); Sor bestin بەستِن (-best-); SoK bas-/basâ-, bast-, basi- (Fat 412); Za bestiş (Mal) [K/IF(s)/M/JJ/SK]

bestkur بەستکور (GF) = collar. See **bestik**.

beş I بەش *f./m.(Ber)* **(-a/-ê;).** 1) {syn: bir̄ [2]; deq [6]} part, section: **•Pirsa hînkirina zimanê kurdî îro li herçar *beşên* Kurdistanê jî qedexeye** (Ber) The question of teaching the Kurdish language today is forbidden in all four *parts of* Kurdistan **•Li vî *beşê* Kurdistanê** (Ber) In this *part of* Kurdistan; 2) {syn: behr I; p'ar II; parî [1]; p'ay; pişk} share. [Pok. 1. bhag- 107.] 'to share out, apportion; also, to get a share': P baxš بخش = 'portion, share, part'; Sor beş بەش; Hau beşe *f.* = 'share, portion' (M4). **bac** & **bext** come from the same root [Ber/K(s)/A/JB3/IF/SK] <beşdar; ker I>

beş II بەش *m.* (). 1) blaze, star, white spot, or mark on the forehead of a horse or cow; 2) *[adj.]* possessing a blaze, star, or white spot on the forehead *(of horses and cattle)* (K/B/IF/HH); 3) outstanding, prominent *(of people)* (K). {also: [bech] بش (JJ); <beş> بش (HH)} [K/IF/B/JJ/HH/ZF3]

beş III بەش: **-beş kirin** (Zeb) to open *(one's mouth)*, bare *(one's teeth)*: **•Gur xwe da ber tehtekê, pez avête alîkî, û diranên xwe li min *beş kirin*** (EŞ, 16) The wolf ran over to a boulder, threw the sheep to one side, and *bared* its teeth to me; **-dev beş kirin** (Zeb) do.: **•Ȓîwî çû, got, "...ȟîleyekî li qelê bikem, belkû tola xo jê wekem" ... Ȓîwî çû bin dara gûzê ... xo li bin gûzê dirêj kir, xo mirand. Çavêt xo ber spî kirin, dewê xo *beş kir*, kêlbêt xo gir kirin, mêş hatine dewê wî** (SK 3:23) The fox went away, saying, "I had better go and play a trick on the crow. Perhaps I can have my revenge on her." ... The fox went beneath a walnut tree ... he stretched himself out at the foot of the walnut tree and made out to be dead. He turned up the whites of his eyes, *hung* his mouth *open* and bared his teeth. Flies came into his mouth [Zeb/EŞ] <qîç kirin; vekirin>

beşavend بەشاڤەند *f.* **(-a;-ê).** rhyme. {syn: paşbend; qafiye; serwa} [Ber/IFb/ZF/CS]

beşdar بەشدار *m.&f.* (). 1) {syn: pişkdar} participant: **-beşdar bûn** (Kmc) to participate, take part (in): **•Hevalên ku di vê civînê de *beşdar bûn* ev bûn** (Kmc) The friends who *took part* in this meeting were the following ...; 2) partner; 3) companion (K[s]); accomplice (K[s]); 4) shareholder (IF); 5) *[adj.]* participating, taking part in. < beş = 'part, share' + -dar = 'one who has'. Sor beşdar بەشدار = 'participant, shareholder' {beşdarî} [Kmc/K(s)/A/JB3/IF/ZF3] <beş I; hevp'ar>

beşdarî بەشدارى *f.* **(-ya;-yê).** participation. [IFb/GF/TF/OK/ZF3] <beşdar>

beşer I بەشەر *f.* **(-a;-ê).** 1) mood, humor, spirits: **•Lê nhêrî *beşera* Îskender xrabe** (EH) She saw that Iskender was in *bad spirits*; **-beşera xweş** (F) good humor, a good mood: ***•Beşera* (wî) *xaş* bû** (XF) (He) was in a *good mood*; 2) external appearance (K); face, countenance (A). [EH/F/K/A/B/XF] <bedbeşer>

beşerxweş بەشەرخوەش *adj.* cheerful, blithe, happy, merry, in good spirits: **•Tê gotin ku merivekî nefspiçûk, destvekirî, nandar, zimanşîrîn û *beşerxweş* bûye** (Nbh 135:75) It is said that he was a humble, generous, hospitable, sweet-talking and *cheerful* person. [Nbh/K/B/A/Wkt] <beşer I>

beşeşîn بەشەشین (TF) = to smile. See **beşişîn**.

beşişîn بەشِشین *vi.* **(-beşiş-).** to smile. {also: beşeşîn (TF)} {syn: bişkurîn; girnijîn; mizicîn} [Qmş/Şnx/A/IFb/ZF3//TF]

beşt بەشت *f.* (). crossbeam, long beam applied to ceiling, transom; beam, girder. {syn: k'êran} [K/A/IFb/GF/TF/AD/ZF3] <garîte; max; mertak; ȓot>

bet بەت *f.* **(-a;-ê).** *various duck-like birds:* 1) bustard, zool. *Otis tarda* (K/IF/JJ): **•Mirîşkê çav li *betê* kir, qûna wê ç'iȓand** (L) When the chicken tried to imitate the *bustard*, she tore her rear end *[prv.]*; 2) duck (B/HH/GF); 3) wild goose (A/JJ); 4) partridge (K). {also: bed (B); [bat] بط (JJ); <be̠t> بط (HH)} Cf. Ar baṭṭ(ah) بط(ة) = 'duck'; P bat[t] بط; Sor bet بەت = 'wild duck'; T bat [Ardahan -Kars] = 'duck' (DS, v.2, p. 568); W Arm pat բադ; cf. also Sp pato & pata; S Cr patka, *both meaning* 'duck', & Alb patë *f.* = 'goose' [L/K/A/IF/GF//JJ/HH//B] <miravî; qaz; sone; werdek>

beta بەتا: **-beta vebûn** (K) to disappear, vanish: **•Kalê li ber p'adşê *betavedibe*** (Z-921) The old man *vanishes* from the king's midst. {syn: ȓoda çûn; (ji ber) winda bûn; ẍeware bûn} [Z-921/K/RZ/Tsab] <berza>

betal بەتاڵ/**be̠tal** بەطاڵ [JJ/HH] *adj.* 1) {syn: vala[3]} free, idle, unoccupied; unemployed; 2) vain, futile, useless; false, sham; worthless, void, abrogated (SK); 3) {syn: boş I; vala} empty, void: **-betal kirin** (K/IFb/ZF/CS): a) to render empty or void: **•Şowq û şemala wîna, herçar lamba *betal kirîye*** [sic] (Z-3) His radiance *cancelled out* the four lamps; b) to cancel, make invalid, invalidate, annul, abolish; c) to stop, cease *doing something*, to quit, drop out of: **•Min zû medrese *be̠tal kir*** (Şx) I *dropped out of* school early; 4) careless, unconcerned; carefree. {also: be̠ttal (SK); [batal] بطال (JJ); <be̠tal> بطال (HH)} <Ar baṭṭāl بطّال = 'idle, unemployed'; Sor betał بەتاڵ = 'empty, unemployed' {betalî; betaltî} [Z-1/K/A/JB3/B/IFb/FJ/GF/

ZF/CS//HH//SK]

betalî بەتالی *f.* **(;-yê).** idleness, inactivity; unemployment: **•Xebata bi nanoziko ji *betaliyê* çêtir e** (ZF3) Working from hand to mouth is better than *being unemployed.* {also: betaltî (B-2); [batalia] بطالی (JJ)} [K/B/ZF3//JJ] <betal>

betaltî بەتالتی (B) = idleness. See **betalî**.

betan بەتان *m.* **(; betên).** 1) {syn: t'emar} vein; sinew, tendon; 2) film, lining *(on meat)* (B/K); lining *(of coat)* (JJ/HH/A/IF). {also: [batán] بطان (JJ); <beṯan> بطان (HH)} Cf. Ar biṭānah بطانة = 'interior; lining (of garment)' [F/K/A/IF/B//JJ/HH]

betilîn بەتِلین/**beṯilîn** بەطِلین [Bw] *vi.* **(-betil-/beṯil-[Bw]).** 1) {syn: qefilîn [2]; r̄e't bûn; westîn} to get or become tired, to tire *(vi.)*: **•Zilamê raketî mîna zilamê mirî ye, em *betilî* ne** (L-5, 140, l. 16) A sleeping man is like a dead man, [and] we are *tired*; 2) to be waterlogged, drink so much that you burst, be bloated (Bw): **•Min hind av ya vexarî, ez ê *beṯilîm*** (Bw) I drank so much water that I *burst*. {also: [batelin] بطلین (JJ)} < Ar √b-ṯ-l بطل = 'to be idle' [Bw/JJ//Qzl/K/IFb/(RZ)]

bet'irpêr بەتِرپێر (K/B/IFb/OK/HH) = three days ago. See **betrapêr**.

bet'irpêrar بەتِرپێرار (K/B/IFb/HH) = three years ago. See **betrapêrar**.

betrapêr بەترapێر *adv.* three days ago. {also: bet'irpêr (K/B/IFb/OK-2); bitirpêr (IFb-2); [pétera per] (JJ-G); <betir pêr> بترپیر (HH)} <Arc bāṯar בָּ[א]תַר = 'after, behind' & Syr bāṯar ܒܬܪ = 'after, following' [cf. NENA bâthar/bâr = 'after, behind' (Maclean) & Turoyo bıṯ[ṯ]ır = do.] + pêr = 'two days ago'; Sor besirpêrê بەسِرپێرێ [Bw/OK//K/IFb/B/HH//JJ-G] <dihî; dusibe; pêr>

betrapêrar بەتراپێرار *adv.* three years ago. {also: bet'irpêrar (K/B/IFb); bitirpêrar (IFb-2/GF); <betir pêrar> بترپیرار (HH)} <Arc bāṯar בָּ[א]תַר = 'after, behind' + pêrar = 'two years ago'; Sor besirpêrar بەسِرپێرار (K2) [OK//K/IFb/B/HH//GF] <par I; pêrar>

beṯṯal بەططال (SK) = idle; worthless. See **betal**.

bevş بەڤش (IFb/B) = comb-shaped loom part. See **befş**.

bewrar بەورار, f. (F) = slope. See **berwar**.

bewse بەوسە (FJ/GF) = washer or hoop attached to plow. See **bose II**.

bexçe بەخچە (JB3/TF/ZF3/BF/CS) = garden. See **baxçe**.

bexçevan بەخچەڤان (JB3) = gardener. See **bax̱van**.

bexdenoz بەخدەنۆز (Wkt/ZF3) = parsley. See **bexdenûs**.

bexdenûs بەخدەنووس *f.* **(-a;-ê).** parsley, bot. *Petroselinum crispum:* **•Me mişara pêşîn kiriye pîvazterk. Me ya duyem kiriye *bexdenûs*** (K.Yildirim.Kurdî 6, 78) We made the first patch for green onions. We made the second one for *parsley*. {also: bexdenoz (Wkt/ZF3-2); bexdûnis (Wkt-2); medenos (AA); mexdenoz (Wkt-2); meydenoz (IFb)} <Ar baqdūnis بقدونس; Sor me'denûs مەعدەنووس [K.Yildirim/ZF3/RZ/CS//Wkt//IFb//AA]

bexdûnis بەخدوونِس (Wkt) = parsley. See **bexdenûs**.

bexêrî بەخێری = fireplace; chimney. See **pixêrîk**.

bexîr•e بەخیرە (•a;•ê) (K/B/F) = fireplace; chimney. See **pixêrîk**.

bexşandin بەخشاندِن *vt.* **(-bexşîn-).** 1) {syn: 'efû kirin; lêborîn; lê xweş bûn} to forgive, pardon: **•Te bi serê mîrê Şeqlawê sûndê, wê carê bê-edebîya me *bibexşe*** (SK 13:127) We conjure you by the head of the Mir of Shaqlawa, *forgive* our rudeness this time; 2) {syn: p'êşk'êş kirin} to present, give *(as a gift)*. {also: bexş- (SK); baxşandin (K); [bekhichandin] بخشاندین (JJ)} Cf. P baxšīdan بخشیدن; Hau bexşay (bexş-) *vt.* = 'to forgive; to distribute' (M4) [K//A/JB3/B//JJ//SK]

bexşîş بەخشیش *f.* **(-a;-ê).**1) tip, monetary gift, gratuity: **-bexşîş û bac** (Z-1) tips and taxes; 2) gift, present; 3) {syn: bertîl; r̄uşet} greasing the palm, kickback, bribe. {also: baxşîş (K); [bekhchich] بخشیش (JJ); <bexşîş> بخشیش (HH)} Cf. P baxšeš بخشش --> Ar baxšīš بخشیش [K//A/JB3/B/JJ/HH] <bertîl>

bext بەخت *m./f.(JJ)* **(-ê/-a;).** 1) {syn: enînivîs; nesîb; qeder II; qismet; yazî} luck, chance, fate, lot, destiny: **-bext û miraz** (XF): a) happiness; b) secret dream; **-[bi] bext ra** (K) luckily, fortunately: ***•bi bextê* gundîar̄a** (Ba2:1, 203) *luckily for* the villagers; **-bextê *fk-ê* anîye/bir̄îye** (B/XF) s.o. got lucky: **•Vê baharê *bextê min bir̄î*** (Ba2-#2, 209) This summer *I got lucky*; **-Ez bextê teme** (K)/**Ez bextê tedame** (B) Please, I beg you: ***•Ez bextê teme*, arîk'arîyê bide min** (K) *Please* help me; **-xwe avêtin bextê *yekî*** (IFb)/**xwe avîtin ber bextê *fk-ê*** (XF) to beg, beseech, implore, throw o.s. at s.o.'s feet: **•Min î ku nêhirî nabe, vê carê jî *min xwe havêt bextê wî*** (Lab, 7) When I saw that it wasn't working, then *I threw myself at his feet*; 2) honor (JB3). {also: [bekht] بخت (JJ); <bext> بخت (HH)} [Pok. 1. bhag- 107.] 'to share out, apportion; also, to get a share': Skt bhaktá- = 'allotted, apportioned‘; Av baxta- = ‘fate, destiny‘; Pahl baxt = ‘fate‘; P baxt بخت (Horn #185)--> T baht; Sor bext بهخت = ‘luck, fortune‘. **bac** & **beş I** come from the same root [Ba2/K/A/JB3/IF/B/HH/JJ/SK] <bêbext>

bextereş بهختهرهش (BK) = unlucky; unhappy. See **bextřeş**.

bextewar بهختهوار *adj.* 1) happy, glad: **•Bekirê Ewan ew merivekî fesad û şeytan bû lema nedihişt Mem û Zîn *bextewar* bin** (K-dş) B.E. was a dişolute and devilish man, therefore he did not let Mem and Zîn be *happy*; 2) lucky, fortunate; 3) loyal, faithful, devoted (K); 4) *[m.]* lucky man (B). {also: bextewer (GF); bextiyar (IFb-2/GF-2); bextîyar (TF); bextyar (OK-2)} Cf. P baxtiyār بختيار --> T bahtiyar; Sor bextyar بهختيار = ‘lucky’ {bextewarî; bextewerî; bext[i]yarî} [K-dS/K/IFb/B//GF/OK//TF]

bextewarî بهختهوارى *f.* **(-ya;-[y]ê).** 1) happiness, felicity; 2) good luck, good fortune: **•Em teřa *bextewarîê* dixwazin** (Ba2:2, 207) We want *good luck* for you [i.e., We are on your side/We have good intentions]; 3) devotion, faithfulness, loyalty (K). {also: bextewerî (GF); bextiyarî (A/GF-2); bextîyarî (TF); bextyarî (OK-2)} [K/IFb/B//GF/OK//A//TF] <bextewar>

bextewer بهختهوهر (GF/OK) = happy; lucky. See **bextewar**.

bextewerî بهختهوهرى (GF/OK) = happineş; luck. See **bextewarî**.

bextiyar بهختِيار (IFb/GF) = happy; lucky. See **bextewar**.

bextiyarî بهختِيارى (A/GF) = happineş; luck. See **bextewarî**.

bextîyar بهختييار (TF) = happy; lucky. See **bextewar**.

bextîyarî بهختييارى (TF) = happineş; luck. See **bextewarî**.

bextřeş بهخترهش *adj.* 1) {syn: bêyom; dêran II; řeben I} unlucky, unfortunate: **•Ezê *bextereş*** (BK) *Unlucky* me (m.) **•Eza *bextereş*** (BK) *Unlucky* me (f.) **•Mîna Zîna *bextřeş*** (Ba) Like *unlucky* Zîn *(from the romance of Mem û Zîn/Memê Alan)*; 2) unhappy (JB3). {also: bextereş (BK)} < bext = ‘luck’ + řeş = ‘black’ {bextřeşî} [K/A/JB3/IF/B/BK]

bextřeşî بهخترهشى *f.* **(-ya;-yê).** 1) unluckiness; misfortune; 2) unhappiness. [IF/B] <bextřeş>

bextyar بهختيار (OK) = happy; lucky. See **bextewar**.

bextyarî بهختيارى (OK) = happiness; luck. See **bextewarî**.

bexçe بهغچه (GF) = garden. See **baxçe**.

bexîre بهغيره (•a;•ê) (B) = fireplace; chimney. See **pixêrîk**.

beyaname بهيانامه (H2/K) = declaration. See **beyanname**.

beyannam•e بهياننامه *f.* **(•a;•ê).** declaration, (written) statement: **•Bi tenê balafirên ingilîzî di ser bajêr re firiyan û hin *beyaname* avêtin ê. Bi van *beyanaman* general Wilson, serfermandarê leşkerên sondxwariyan, ji general Denz dixwest ko bajarê Şamê bajarê berdayî îlan bike û eskerên xwe jê bikişîne** (H2 9:31, 775) English planes only flew over the city and dropped some *statements* [from the air]. In *the statements* General Wilson, commander-in-chief of the allied troops, asked General Denz to declare Damascus a free city and to withdraw his troops from it. {also: beyaname (H2/K)} {syn: daxuyanî; ‘elamet} Cf. P bayān'nāme بياننامه & T beyanname [H2/K//IFb/GF]

beyar بهيار *f.* **(;-ê).** fallow land, stubble field, land not plowed in the autumn after its crops have been harvested: **•‘Erda ku te meȟsûl jêçinî, û dema kêlana wê payîzê neyê kêlan, *beyar* e** (Qzl) Land whose crops you have gathered, and is not plowed in the fall at the time of plowing, is "beyar" **•Ew betek bû, te li *beyarekê* girt** (Qzl) That was a bustard (duck-like bird) you caught in *a fallow field* (i.e., you may not have that opportunity again). {also: [beiar] بيار (JJ)} {syn: xozan} [Qzl/Kmc-8/K/A/IFb/B/JJ/GF/TF] <bor III; gort II; hox; kat II; k’ewşan; k’irêbe; şov; zevî>

beybûn بهيبوون *f.* **(-a;-ê).** 1) camomile (K/IF/F); 2) dandelion (K); 3) jonquil, bot. *Narcissus jonquila* (A).{also: baîbûn (F); baybûn (B-2); bêbûn (Haz); bîbûn; [babuná بابونه /baibūn بيبون] (JJ); <beybûn> بيبون (HH)} Cf. P bābūne بابونه = ‘camomile’ --> Ar bābūnaj بابونج; Sor beybûn بهيبوون/bêbûn بێبوون [K/IF/A/B/JJ/HH/ZF3//F//Haz]

beydar بهيدار (A) = veterinarian. See **beyt’ar**.

beydax بهيداغ (SK) = flag. See **bêraq**.

beyindî بهيندى (GF) = two- or three-year-old female sheep. See **berdîr**.

beyindîr بهيندير (GF) = two- or three-year-old female sheep. See **berdîr**.

beyî بهيى: -beyî bûn (IFb) = to fade; to wither. See **beyîn**.

beyîn بهيين *vi.* **(-bey-).** 1) to fade *(of colors)*; 2) {syn: çilmisîn} to wither, dry up and die *(of plants)*:

•**Giya *beyî bûn*** (IFb) The plants had withered. {also: beyî bûn (IFb); cf. also [behin] بـهـيـن (JJ) = 'to fall off the stalk' [Fr s'égrener]} {syn: sîs [II] bûn} [Bw//IFb] <behitîn; sîs II>

*beyîndi بـهـيـنـدِ (FJ) = two- or three-year-old female sheep. See **berdîr**.

beylû بهيلوو (Z-3) = clear, obvious. See **belû**.

beyraq بهيراق (K/B) = flag. See **bêraq**.

***beyraqbir** بهيراقبِر *m.* **()**. flag-bearer, standard-bearer. {syn: bêraqdar} [K]

beyraqdar بهيراقدار (K/B) = flag-bearer. See **bêraqdar**.

beyt/beyt' [B] بـهـيـت *f.* **(-a;-ê).** 1) verse of poetry; 2) Yezidi religious hymn (K/Z): •**Qewl û beyt'ê êzdîya** (Z-711) Yezidi religious poems and hymns; 3) [primarily Sor & S Kurm] romance, type of story, narrative poem; an orally transmitted story which is either entirely sung or is a combination of sung verse and spoken prose [Amir Hassanpour-Aghdam. "Bayt" in: *Encyclopaedia Iranica*, vol. 4, fasc. 1, pp. 11-12.]. {also: beît (F); [beït] بيت (JJ)} < Ar bayt بـيـت = 'house, verse'; Sor beyt بـهـيـت = 'narrative poem' [K/IF/JJ/SK/ZF3//B/Z-711//F] <destan; **lawij**; qewl>

beyt'ar بـهـيـتـار *m.* **(-ê;).** veterinarian, veterinary surgeon, animal doctor, farrier: •**Beẍdo him *beyt'are*, him nalbende** (FK-kk-13:126) Beghdo is both *a veterinarian* and a blacksmith •[**Illa ji Ekradan barûtpêj û şorecî û *beyṯar* heyn**] (BN 134) [Of professions] there are only gunpowder and saltpeter manufacturers and *veterinarians* from the Kurds. {also: beydar (A); beyt'er (B); [baitar] بـيـطـار (JJ); <beyṯar> بـيـطـار (HH)} < Ar bāyṭār بـيـطـار < Lat veterinae = 'beasts of burden'; Sor beytar بهيتار [FK-kk-13/K/IFb//BN/JJ/HH//B//A]

beyt'er بهيتهر (B) = veterinarian. See **beyt'ar**.

beytik بـهـيـتِـك *m.* **()**. sparrow, zool. *Passer domesticus*: •**Çwîkekî *beytik* hebû, kete qulê** (L-2, 20) There was a *sparrow*, it entered [its] hole. {syn: çûk I; guncêşk} [L/K/IFb/GF/TF/RZ]

beyv بهيڤ = almond. See **behîv**.

bez I بـهـز *m.* **(-ê; bêz, vî bezî)**. fat, grease, lard, suet, tallow: •**R̄ovî r̄abû herçî goştê nerm û *bez* li ber şêr danîn** (Dz) The fox placed all the tender meat and *fat* before the lion. {also: [bez] بـز (JJ); <bez> بـز (HH)} {syn: don} Cf. Skt vedhás = originally: 'one who gives fattening to the deity': <O Ir *wazda- (A&L p.85 [V, 5]): Av vazdah- = 'sturdy' [beständig] *ritual term denoting the strengthening of a divinity by feeding it, offering oblations/ libations of fat, milk, ghee*; Khwarezmian uzda/ā(h) = 'fat, grease'; Pamir dialects: Yidgha wāzd (Morg); Shughni dialects: Yazghulami wūzd; Sarikoli 'wâst'; Wanji waz (Morg2); Pashto wāzda *f.* = 'fat, grease' [Fett]; Gilaki = vaz; Sor bez بـهـز = 'fat'; Za vazd *m.* (Hadank) [Dz/K/A/JB3/B/JJ/HH/SK] <azûxe [2]; çivir; tewaş>

be'z II بهعز (FK-eb-2) = falcon. See **baz I**.

beza بـهـزا *adj.* fleet, swift, speedy, fast running (of horse): -**hespê beza** (BF) speedy horse {syn: *hespê rehwan}. {also: [beza] بـزا (JJ)} {syn: qule[2]} [Qzl/IFb/FJ/GF/JJ/ZF3/BF/FD]

bezandin بهزاندِن *vt.* **(-bezîn-).** to let or make s.o. run, to race *(a horse)* (vt.): •**Hevalekî ji yê me got: Emê li k'erê swar bin, û *bibazênin*** (HR-I, 2:10) One of our friends said, "Let's mount the donkey and *make* her *run*!"; -**hespa xwe bezandin** (IFb) to race one's horse. {also: bazandin (-bazên-) (HR-I); [bezandin] بـزانـديـن (JJ)} for bazandin (HR-I), cf. also bazdan [1] = 'to run' [HR-I//K/IFb/JJ/SK/GF/OK] <bazdan [1]; bezîn>

bezir بهزر (SK) = lost; absent. See **berza**.

beziyan بهزِيان (JB3) = to run. See **bezîn**.

bezîn بـهـزيـن *vi.* **(-bez-).** 1) {syn: bazdan [1]} to run: •**Ji kêfa re *bezîya*, hat malê** (L) Full of joy, he *ran* home; 2) to be defeated (A); 3) [+ *kesekî*] to fight (with) (B). {also: beziyan (JB3); [bezin] بزين (JJ)} [Pok. u̯eĝh- 1118.] 'to move, go, travel': O Ir *vaz- (Tsb 37): Av vaz- (pres. vaza-) = 'to go, travel, fly'; Sor bezîn بهزين = 'to be vanquished; halt to camp'; Za vazdanã [veştiş] = 'to run' (Todd). Also cf. the range of meanings of Ar inhazam انـهـزم VII = 'to be defeated; (Clq Palestinian) to run away' [BX/K/A/JB3/JJ/B/SK/ZF3] <bezandin>

bê I بـێ *prep.* 1) without; -less: •***bê* lez û tirs** (BX) *without* haste or fear, calmly •***bê* min** = *without* me •***bê* tişt** = *without* anything •***bê* xwedê** (Ba) god*less*, *without* God •***bêî* tu dişwariyê** (BX) *without* any difficulty; -**bêî ko** [+ subj.] = without ...-ing: •***Bêî* ko te bigota, min zanî bû** (BX) *Without* your saying, I knew; 2) {syn: ji ... pê ve; ji bilî; pêştir [+*ji*]; xêncî} except for, besides: •***Bê* wan kes ne hat** (BX) No one came *but* them •**Ev erdê han ê gelê kurd e û *bê* wan kes tê de rûnane** (BX) This land belongs to the Kurdish people, and *besides* them nobody lives on it •***Bê* zimanê xwe, gelem-periya xelkên vî bajarî bi tirkî dizanin** (BX)

Besides their own language, most of the people of this city know Turkish; 3) contrary to, against: •***Bê* gotiniya min kir** (BX) He went *against* my advice. {also: bêî (BX-2); bêyî (Z-1); [bi] بـــى (JJ); <bê> بـــــى (HH)} Cf. O P *apaiy (<apa + id) (Hübsch #247); Pahl apē & Pāzand awē; P bī بى; Sor bê بێ; Za bê (Mal & Todd) [BX/K/A/JB3/B/HH/SK//JJ]

bê II بێـــــ *conj.* whether, to see if... *(signals indirect question)*. According to W. Fischer & O. Jastrow [for Arabic as spoken in Mardin]: "bê (Kurdish) introduces general relative sentences" [from: "Text aus Qartmîn (Mardin- Dialekte)", in: *Handbuch der Arabischen Dialekte* (Wiesbaden: Otto Harrassowitz, 1980), pp. 165-69. My translation]: **•Gelî bira, şerîtî bi newqa mi ve girê bidin û min dahêjin bîrê, ezê binerim *bê* ava wê çawa ye** (L) Brothers, tie a rope around my waist and let me down into the well, I will see how its water is **•Emê sualekê lê bikin, *bê* ev çi kesek e, ji ku tê, wê here ku** (L) We'll ask him who he is, where he comes from, where he is going **•Ez wê gavê nizanim *bê* ezê çi ji wan re bêjim** (L) I wouldn't know what to tell them **•Wellah, ezê birê xwe biceribînim, binerim *bê* mêrin, *bê* çewa ne** (L) I'll test my brothers to see if they are men, what they're worth **•Ew çel kepîhatine kuştin. Em nizanin *bê* kî kuştine** (L) These 40 brigands were killed. We don't know who killed them **•Xwedê hebîna, tuê rast ji min re bêje *bê* çima tuê digirî** (L) For the love of God, tell me truly why you are crying! {syn: çika (J/Z); k'a II [2] (EP); qe (Z)} [L/ZF3]

bêaqil بێ ناقِل/**bê'aqil** بێ عاقِل *adj.* stupid. {also: bêaql (SK); bê'eql (SK-2); [bi-aqil] بـى عـقـل (JJ)} {syn: aqilsivik; eĥmeq; sefîh; xêtik} {bêaqilî; bêaqiltî} [K/B/ZF3//JJ//SK] <aqil I; aqil II>

bêaqilî بـێ نـاقِـلـى/**bê'aqilî** بـێ عـاقِـلـى *f.* **(-ya;-yê).** stupidity. {also: bêaqiltî (B-2)} {syn: eĥmeqî} [F/K/B/ZF3] <bêaqil>

bêaqiltî بێ ناقِلتى (B) = stupidity. See **bêaqilî**.

bêaql بێ ناقل (SK) = stupid. See **bêaqil**.

bêavî بـــێ نـــاڤـــى *f.* **(-ya;-yê).** lack of water, drought, waterlessness, aridity: **•Rûyê axê ji *bêavî* biqelişe** (Amîda Kurd: Feratê Dengizî) If the earth's surface should crack from *lack of water*. {also: bêavtî (B-2)} [Amîda Kurd/K/B/IFb/ZF] <bêbaranî>

bêavtî بێ ناڤتى (B) = lack of water. See **bêavî**.

bêbar بێ بار (B) = barren. See **bêber**.

bêbaranî بێ بـارانـى *f.* **(-ya;).** drought, dry spell. {syn: ziwabûn} Cf. Sor bêbaranî بـێ بـارانـى [Dh/K/CS/SS/ZF3] <baran; bêavî>

bêber بێ بەر *adj.* fruitless, barren, sterile *(of trees and plants* [K/B/IFb]; *of people and animals* [IFb/GF]*)*. {also: bêbar (B)} {syn: xirş} [Bw/K/IFb/GF/OK/ZF3//B] <bêweç; bêzuřet; stewir; t'êrber>

bêbext بـــێ بـــەخـــت *adj.* 1) dishonest; dishonorable; unfaithful; 2) miserable, unfortunate; 3) ill-omened (SK); 4) *[m.]* traitor, betrayer. {also: [bi-bekht/bē-bakht] بـى بـخـت (JJ)} < bê = 'without' + bext = 'luck' {bêbextî} [L/K/JB3/B/SK/GF/TF/ZF3//JJ]

bêbextî بـێ بـەخـتـى *f.* **(-ya;-yê).** 1) dishonesty, deceit, perfidy; dishonor; **-bêbextî kirin** (K/B) to act dishonestly, commit an act of deceit: **•Vî wezîrî ev *bêbextîya* digel min kirî û vî melayeş ev *bêbextîya* digel min kirî** (M, #701, 316) This vizier did these *treacherous things* to me, and this mullah also did these *treacherous things* to me; 2) treason, betrayal: **•*Bêbextiya* xwe pêş çavên min kir** (BX) He showed me [lit. 'put before my eyes'] his *dishonesty/betrayal*; 3) misery, misfortune, unhappiness. [BX/K/JB3/B/SK/GF/TF/ZF3] <bêbext>

bêbûn بێبوون (Haz) = camomile. See **beybûn**.

bêcan بـــێ جـــان *adj.* lifeless, dead: **•Şêrê reben wekî rovîkî li ber lingê koçer *bêcan* dikeve erdê** (JB2-O.Sebrî/Rnh 14[1943] 8-9) The poor lion falls *lifeless* to the ground like a fox at the feet of the nomad. [JB2/Rnh/K/IFb/GF/OK/ZF3] <mirin>

bêcar[mîş] [بـێـجـار[مـيـش: -bêcar[mîş] kirin (B) = to cultivate. See **bêcer**.

bêcer** بـێـجـەر: **-bêcer kirin** (EH) = a) to cultivate, till, work (land) (B); b) to succeed (EH): **•Herkê te *bêcerkir*, tê kuřê xwe xlazkî, te *bêcer nekir*, zatî hemîn kuřê te wê heře, wê serê kuřê te lêxe** (EH) If you *succeed*, you will rescue your son; if you *don't succeed*, your son will come anyway, and he will strike off your son's head; c) ?to load up, outfit (IS): **•Ĥeft qent'irme deve t'emam kir, barê wana bi gotina Ĥecî Bek'o *bêcer kir (IS-#189) He completely fitted out seven files of camels, and *loaded them* up as Haji Beko had said to. {also: bêcar[mîş] (B)} Cf. T becermek = 'to succeed'; Az T becärmäk = 'to know how to, be in a position to do stg., prevail' [EH//B]

bêç'ar بێ چار (K/B) = helpless. See **bêçare**.

bêçare بـێ چـارە *adj.* helpless, desperate: **•Her şêxek û her aẍayek û her begek nabît padşahek bît, û**

çawa ĥez biket weto digel r̄e'îyeta *bêçare* biket (SK 56:654) Every shaikh and agha and beg cannot be a king and do as he pleases with the *hapless* peasantry •**Xulase li naw 'Usmanîyan *bêçare* bûn û neşyan bihêne cîyê xo** (SK 48:511) In short, they had no remedy [=were *helpless*] among the Turks and could not return to their own place. {also: bêç'ar (K-2/B-2); [bi-tcharé] بـى چـاره (JJ)} {syn: bêgav} Cf. P bīčāre بـى چاره; Sor bêçare بـى چـــــــاره = 'helpless, beyond remedy' {bêçaretî; bêçareyî; bêç'arî} [K/IFb/B/SK/GF/TF/ZF3//JJ] <belengaz; r̄eben I>

bêçaretî بـــى چـــارەتـــى *f.* **(-ya;-yê).** helplessness, desperation: •**Ji *bêçaretî* û bêgaviyê, min riya herî bi tehlûke ku ji rêwîtiyekê re diviya, hilbijart** (MUm, 12) Out of *desperation* I chose the most dangerous route for a journey. {also: bêçareyî (TF); bêç'arî (K/B)} {syn: bêgavî} [MUm/IFb/ZF3//TF//K/B] <bêçare>

bêçareyî بێ چارەیی (TF) = helplessness. See **bêçaretî**.

bêç'arî بێ چاری (K/B) = helplessness. See **bêçaretî**.

bêçek بـــى چـــەك *adj.* unarmed, disarmed; defenseless: •**Dor li nêzîkî 20 hezar mirovî girtibûn û ew gelên *bêçek* gullebaran dikirin** (Wlt 2:73, 14) Around 20,000 people were captured, and these *unarmed* people were sprayed with bullets. [Wlt/F/K/IFb/B/SK/GF/TF/OK/ZF3] <çek [2&3]; çekdar>

bêçî I بێچی **().** lamb 1-3 weeks old. {also: <bêçî> بێچی (Hej)} [Kmc-8/GF/Hej/ZF3] <berx; mî I>

bêç'î II بێچی *f.* **(-ya;-yê).** 1) {syn: t[']ilî} finger, toe; 2) fingertip (A). {also: bîçî (HB); pêç'î (K/B); pîcî (A); <pîçî> پـيـچـى (HH)} [= Sor emust/[h]engust; kilik; pence; pîlk; qemik] M. Schwartz: Cf. Av. baši-, Pahl bck = 'measurement based on (part of) a finger'. The Pahl form, probably /bač(č)ak/, and the Kurdish form as well, likely represent diminutive formations in -č- to baši-. Against Henning "An Astronomical Chapter of Bundahishn," *Journal of the Royal Asiatic Society*, (1942), p. 235 with footnote #6, Av t̰biši- (glossed by Pahl bck) 'joint (of a finger)' should be a different word, since it cannot be reconciled phonically with the group baši-/bck/bêç'î. The form t̰biši- would be from ProtoIE *du̯is = 'twice, in two' (Av. biž-uuat̰-); the notion of 'joint' being bifurcation. Cf. further [Pok. du̯o(u) 228.] 'two' --> Gothic twis-standan = 'to become separated', Old Norse tvistr = 'bipartite', Middle English twist = 'a branch', Old English twisla = 'tributary of a river', Old High Germ zwisel = 'doubled'. Note also Old Frisian, etc. twist = Germ Zwist = 'quarrel, rift'; Indo-Iranian *dvišta- = 'enemy' (√dviš = 'to be inimical') should also belong here. [Bg/Kg/JB3//HB//K/B//A//HH] <gumik>

bêdeng بـــى دەنـــگ *adj.* 1) silent, quiet: •**Em her du jî niha, piştî xeberdana te, êdî *bêdeng* mabûn** (MUm, 16) Now, after you [finished] talking, both of us remained *silent* •**Tu *bêdeng* be. Ez bi xo dê digel s̱oney axiwim** (SK 4:39) You be *silent*. I shall speak to the drake myself; 2) consonant[al] *(phonetics)* {syn: dengdar}: -**tîpên bêdeng** (RZ) consonants. {also: [bi-denk/be-denk (G)] بـــى دنـــك (JJ)} {syn: mit̰} Sor bêdeng بێ دەنگ {bêdengî} [K/A/IFb/B/SK/GF/TF/OK/AId/ZF3//JJ]

bêdengî بێ دەنگی *f.* **(-ya;-yê).** silence: •**Piştî demekê *bêdengiyeke* mezin çêbû. Ne gêrîk û ne jî Siltanê Fîlan peyivî** (SF 31) After a while *a* great *silence* set in. Neither the ant[s] nor the Elephant Sultan spoke. {syn: mit̰î} [K/A/IFb/GF/TF/OK/ZF3] <bêdeng>

bêder I بێدەر (F/K/B) = threshing floor. See **bênder**.

bêdêr بێدێر (JB1-A) = threshing floor. See **bênder**.

bêdil بـــى دڵ *adj.* 1) heartless; 2) unwilling, against one's will: •**Di her fîrek çayê de jî ez dibînim bê çiqasî *bêdil* e** (Epl, 24) With every sip of tea I see how *displeased* he is •**Şêro *bê dilê xwe* deh dînar dane min** (GF) Shero gave me 10 dinars *against his will*. {also: [be-del] بى دل (JJ)} Sor bêdił بێ دڵ = 'unenthusiastic, disinclined' [Epl/K/A/B/IFb/TF/AD/JJ-G]

bêdilî بـــى دلـــى *f.* **(-ya;-yê).** unwillingness, reluctance; lack of desire (to do stg.): -**bêdilîya *fk-ê* kirin** (Wlt/JB1-A) to go against s.o.'s wishes, disobey, disappoint: •**Bavê min jî nikaribû *bêdiliya* şêxê xwe *bike* û ez neşandim dibistanê** (Wlt 2:66, 2) My father could not *go against the wishes of* his sheikh, so he did not send me to [secular] school. [Wlt/K/A/IFb/JB1-A/OK/AId]

bêdûnda بێ دووندا (K) = childless. See **bê dûnde**.

bêdûndan بێ دووندان (K) = childless. See **bê dûnde**.

bê dûnde بـــى دوونـــده *adj.* childless, without offspring: •**Her tiştê te xwest, min da te, lê belê ez te *bê dûnde* dihêlim** (K-ça) Everything you requested I have given you, but I will leave you *childless*. {also: bêdûnda[n] (K)} {syn: bêzur̄et} [K-ça/A/GF//K] <dûndan; zêdehî>

bê edeb بـــى ئـــەدەب/ **bê 'edeb** بـــى عـــەدەب [K/B] *adj.* rude, impolite, ill-mannered, discourteous: •**Paşî çû**

ħeccê. Derwêşek dît li-naw Ke'be hispîyan dikujît. Mewlana Xalid xo ji wî sil kir, 'To bi çi şer' û bi çi mezheb şola ho *bê-edeb* dikey?' (SK 44:422) Later he went on the pilgrimage [to Mecca]. He saw a dervish inside the Kaaba killing lice. Maulana Khalid lost his temper with him, 'What law and what sect are you following in doing such an *ill-mannered* thing?' •[**Û xwecihî jî dibêjin ku her çî zarokêd ku ji jinêd Ekradan biwelidin *bê edeb* û diz û serkêş dibin**] (BN, 100) And the locals say that whatever children are born of Kurdish women are *rude* and thieving and obstinate. {also: [bi-edeb] بی ادب (JJ)} {syn: bême'rîfet} Cf. P bī adab بی ادب; Sor bê edeb بێ ئەدەب = 'ill-mannered' [BN/SK/GF//JJ//K/B]

bê edebî بێ ئەدەبی/**bê 'edebî** بێ عەدەبی [K/B] *f.*(**-ya; -yê).** rudeness, impoliteness, discourtesy: •**Belê cezaê *bê-edebî* û 'ezman-dirêjîya hingo ewe ye hingo bişelînim, da çu car dî wan terze bê-edebîyane neken** (SK 13:126) But the punishment for your *rudeness* and insolence is that I should strip [=rob] you, so that you aren't ever so rude again •**Te bi serê mîrê Şeqlawê sûndê, wê carê *bê-edebîya* me bibexşe** (SK 13:127) We conjure you by the head of the Mir of Shaqlawa, forgive our *rudeness* this time; -**bê 'edebî kirin** (B) to act rudely: •**Destê min bi demana hingo, min nekujin. Min gelek *bê-edebî kir*** (SK 13:133) I beseech you, don't kill me. I *was* very *rude*. {also: [bi-edebi] بی ادبی (JJ)} Cf. P bī adabī بی ادبی [SK//JJ//K/B]

bê'eql بێ عەقل (SK) = stupid. See **bêaqil**.

bê'esil بێ عەسڵ *adj.* 1) without kith or kin, without pedigree; 2) ignoble, base; ill-mannered; dishonest, dishonorable: •**Binhêrin M. birê me çiqas *bê'esil* derk'et, bihîstîye em tên, k'êleka Zîna xwe dûr nak'eve, wekî pêşîya meda bê** (Z-1) See how *ignoble* our brother M. has turned out to be: he heard that we're coming [and] he won't leave Z.'s side [long enough] to come out and greet us!; 3) ungrateful; 4) unnatural, unusual. {also: [bi-asl] بی اصل (JJ)}< bê = 'without' + 'esil = 'origin' [Z-1/K//JJ]

bê-fayde بێ فایدە (SK) = useless. See **bêfeyde**.

bêfeyda بێ فەیدا (K) = useless. See **bêfeyde**.

bêfeyde بێ فەیدە *adj.* useless, pointless. {also: bê-fayde (SK); bêfeyda (K); [bi-fàidé] بی فایده (JJ)} {syn: bêkêr} < bê = 'without' + feyde = 'use' [Z-1/K/JB3/B//JJ//SK]

bêgav بێ گاڤ *adj.* desperate, in a hopeless situation, in dire straits; forced or stuck, prevented from doing stg.: •**Bi hezaran mirov li derî bajêr *bêgav* mabûn, nikaribûn xwe bigihînin dîlana te** (Wlt 2:73, 14) Thousands of people were *stuck* at the gates to the city, unable to get to your ceremony. {syn: bêçare} <bê = 'without + gav[1] = 'time' {bêgavî} [Wlt/IFb/OK/Hej] <asê; tengav>

bêgavî بێ گاڤی *f.* **(-ya;-[y]ê).** 1) {syn: bêçaretî} desperation; dire straits, hopeless situation; •**Dijmin bêgav mabû û ji ber vê *bêgaviya* xwe meşvanan gullebaran kirin û du xort şehîd ketin** (Wlt 2:73, 14) The enemy became desperate, and because of his *desperation* he shot at the marchers and two young men were made martyrs •**Ji bêçaretî û *bêgaviyê*, min riya herî bi tehlûke ku ji rêwîtiyekê re diviya, hilbijart** (MUm, 12) Out of *desperation* I chose the most dangerous route for a journey; 2) immobility, inability to act: •**Bi *bêgaviya* me ew ketne welatê me** (IFb) Because of our *inability to act*, they entered our country. [Wlt/K/IFb/OK] <bêgav>

bêguman بێ گومان *adj.* 1) hopeless; despairing (K/B); 2) unreliable, untrustworthy (K/B); 3) having lost faith or hope (K/B); 4) {syn: bêşik} doubtless, without a doubt (K/IF). {also: bêgûman (A)} < bê = 'without' + guman = 'doubt' [Z-1/FK-eb-2/K/JB3/IF/B]

bêgunah بێ گوناه (A/SK) = innocent. See **bêguneh**.

bêgune بێ گونە (K/B) = innocent. See **bêguneh**.

bêguneh/bê guneh [RZ] بێ گونەه *adj.* innocent: •**kuştina hindek *bêgunahan*** (SK 56:650) killing some *innocent people*. {also: bêgune (K/B-2); bêgunah (A/SK); [be-ghune] بی گناه (JJ-G)} {syn: bêsûc} P bī gonāh بی گناه; Sor bêgunah بێ گوناه {bêgunehtî} [B/TF/OK/RZ//K/JJ-G//A/SK] <dilsaf>

bêgunehî بێ گونەهی (K/ZF3) = innocence. See **bêgunehtî**.

bêgunehtî بێ گونەهتی *f.* **(-ya;-yê).** innocence. {also: bêgunehî (K/ZF3); bêgunetî (B-2)} {syn: bêsûcî} P bī gonāhī بی گناهی; Sor bêgunahî بێ گوناهی [B//K/ZF3]

bêgunetî بێ گونەتی (B) = innocence. See **bêgunehtî**.

bêgûman بێ گوومان (A) = hopeless; doubtless. See **bêguman**.

bêhal بێ هال (IFb/TF) = exhausted. See **bêħal**.

bêhed بێ هەد (IFb/B) = unlimited. See **bêħed**.

bêhemd بێ هەمد (K) = compulsory. See **bêħemd**.

bêhempa بێ هەمپا *adj.* unique, without peer or equal, peerless, unrivalled, unmatched: **•Pirtûka rojnameger Nadire Mater ya bi navê " Pirtûka Memed..." li ser dîroka "gayrî resmî ya şer" berhemeke *bêhempa* ye** (AW71A2) The book of the journalist Nadire Mater called "Memed's Book" on the 'unofficial history of the war' is a *unique* work. {also: bêhemta (K/SS); bêhevta (K-2/SS-2)} Cf. Sor bêhawta بێ هاوتا = 'unrivalled, unmatched' [AW/IFb]

bêhemta بێ هەمتا (K/SS) = unique, unrivalled. See **bêhempa**.

bêhesab بێ هەساب (B) = countless. See **bêĥesab**.

bêheş بێ هەش (CS) = unconscious. See **bêĥiş**.

bêhetik بێ هەتِك *adj.* shameless; indecent. {also: bêĥetik (K); [bi-hetik] بی هتك (JJ)} {syn: bêşerm} [Dh/Zeb//JJ/K] <hetk>

bêhevta بێ هەڤتا (K/SS) = unique, unrivalled. See **bêhempa**.

bêhêvî بێ هێڤی *adj.* hopeless, despairing, desperate; disappointed: **•Bazirgan te'eccub kir. got. "Subĥanellah, madam ewe kok bît bes noke yêt nekok di çawa ne?" Gelek xemgîr bû, *bê-hîwî* geřyawe** (SK 16:159) The merchant was amazed and said,"Praise be to God, if this one is satisfied, then what will the dissatisfied be like?" He was very depressed and turned back *in despair* **•Mêrik bi awakî *bêhêvî* û dilşikestî ji rîsipî vediqete, berê xwe dide mala xwe û diçe** (Ardû, 19) *Disappointed* and brokenhearted, the fellow takes his leave of the old man and heads for home **•Tu *ji* wê jinkê *bê hîvî boy*** (JB1-A, #136) You *gave up on* that woman. {also: bêhîvî (K/JB1-A/OK-2); bê-hîwî (SK); [be-ivi] بی هڤی (JJ-G)} Sor bê hîwa بێ هیوا [Ardû/IFb/GF/TF/OK//K/JB1-A//JJ-G//SK]

bêhiş بێهِش (IFb/CS/FJ/TF/GF/SS)/bê hiş بێ هش (A) = unconscious. See **bêĥiş**.

bêhîvî بێ هیڤی (K/JB1-A/OK) = hopeless. See **bêhêvî**.

bê-hîwî بێ هیوی (SK) = hopeless. See **bêhêvî**.

bêhn بێهن (A) = smell; breath. See **bîn I**.

bêhnfireh بێهنفرەه (SS/ZF) = patient; tolerant. See **bînfireh**.

bêhnfirehî بێهنفرەهی (RZ/SS/ZF) = patience; tolerance. See **bînfirehî**.

bêhnijandin بێهنژاندِن *vt.* **(-bêhnijîn-).** to cause to sneeze. {also: <bihnijandin بهنژاندن> (HH)} [IF//HH] <bêhnijîn>

bêhnijîn بێهنژین *vi.* **(-bêhnij-/-bênij-[IF]).** 1) {syn: hênijîn [3]; pêkijîn} to sneeze; 2) {syn: bawişkîn; hênijîn [2]} to yawn (IFb/OK). {also: behnişîn (Bw); [behnijin] بهنژین (JJ); <bihnijîn بهنژین (dibihnijî) (دبهنژی)> (HH)} Sor pijmîn پژمین/ pişmîn پشمین = 'to sneeze' [M-Zx/IFb/OK//JJ//HH//Bw] <sebir [2]>

bêhnişk بێهنِشك *f.* **(-a;-ê).** sneeze: **•...û ya gotî çî gava *bêhnişka te hat*, dê zengîn bî** (Bêhnişk, 49) ... and said that when *you sneeze*, you will get rich. {also: bênijik (SS); bênişk (Hej); bihnişt (FJ/GF); bînişk (AD); bîniştek (GF-2); [beenís] بهنیژ (JJ-G)} [Bêhnişk//SS/Hej//FJ/GF//AD//JJ]

bêhnok بێهنۆك *f.* **(-a;-ê).** comma: **•Xalek an *bêhnokeke* di cihê xwe de neyê bikaranîn dikare wateya tevahiya hevokê biguherîne** (H.H.Denîz. Rêkên rastkirin û pêşvebirina nivîsandinê) A period or *comma* which is not used properly can change the entire meaning of the sentence. {also: bîhnok (RZ)} = Sor wêrgul وێرگول (< Fr virgule) [RR/ZF/Wkt//RZ]

bêhntengî بێهنتەنگی *f.* **(-ya;-yê).** 1) shortness of breath; 2) impatience, nervousness: **•Ji bo ku sedema *bêhntengiya* xwe ji bîra bike, carina ji xwe re difîkîne** (Ardû, 63) In order to forget the reason for his *nervousness*, sometimes he whistles to himself. {also: bihntengî (GF); bîhntengî (CS-2); bîntengî (K/GF-2)} [Ardû/IFb/CS/A/AD//GF//K] <hilkehilk>

bêhtir بێهتر (HYma) = more; the most. See **bêtir**.

bêhûde بێ هوودە *adv.* 1) exceptionally, extremely, very much (BK): **•Selaheddînê Eyyûbî *bêhûde* mêrxas bû** (BK) Salah al-Din al-Ayyubi was an *extremely* great hero; 2) useless (JJ). {also: [bi-houdé] بی هوده (JJ)} [BK/ZF3//JJ]

bêĥal بێ حال *adj.* destitute, exhausted, weak: **•Ez *bêĥal* im** (Btm [Ĥatĥatkê]) I am *exhausted.* {also: bêhal (IFb/TF); [be-ahhl] بی حال (JJ)} [Btm [Ĥatĥatkê]/ K/OK/RF//IFb/TF//JJ-G] <bedĥal>

bêĥed بێ حەد *adj.* 1) {syn: bêsînor} unlimited, endless, boundless, infinite; 2) *[adv.]* extremely, tremendously, too (much). {also: bêhed (IFb/B-2); [bi-had] بی حد (JJ)} Cf. P bī ḥadd بی حد = 'boundless, infinite'; Sor bêĥed بێ حەد [Hk/K/B//JJ/ /IFb]

bêĥemd بێ حەمد *adj.* compulsory, forced, obligatory: **-bêĥemdî xwe** (K) involuntarily, willy-nilly, in spite of oneself: **•Wexta Memê derda çû, mîr *bêĥemdî xwe* ji cîyê bilind bû** (Z-1) When Memê entered, the prince *involuntarily* got up from his place. {also: bêhemd (K)} [Z-1/JB3//K]

bêȟesab بى حەساب *adj.* endless, limitless; countless, innumerable: •**Digote xelkî, "Her kesê peşkekê ji awa tizbîyêt min wexotewe, cendekê wî agirê cehennemê nabînît"** ... **Hemîyan bawir dikirin** [sic]. **Mêr û jin û biçûk dihatin, malekî *bêȟisab* bo wî dînan** [sic] (SK 12:119) Whoever drinks a drop of the water from my rosary, his body will not see the fire of Hell... They all believed him. Men, women and children came, bringing him *countless* wealth •**Ez *bêȟesab* bextewar bûm** (Ba2:2, 207) I was *immeasurably* happy [=My joy was boundless]. {also: bêhesab (B-2); bêȟesav (B-2); bê-ȟisab (SK); [bi-hisab بى حساب/bi-hisib بى حسب] (JJ)} Cf. P bī ḥasāb بى حساب = 'countless, innumerable' [Ba2/K/B//SK//JJ]

bêȟesav بى حەساڤ (B) = countless. See **bêȟesab**.

bêȟetik بى هەتِك (K) = shameless. See **bêhetik**.

bê-ȟisab بى حِساب (SK) = countless. See **bêȟesab**.

bêȟiş بى حِش *adj.* unconscious, in a swoon: -**bêȟiş bûn** (K/B)/**bêhiş k'etin** (TF)/~ **man** (IFb) to faint {syn: neȟiş k'etin; xeřiqîn; xewirîn}; -**bêȟiş kirin** (K/B) to cause to faint. {also: bêheş (CS); bêhiş (IFb/CS-2/FJ/TF/GF/SS)/bê hiş (A); [bi-hich] بى هش (JJ)} {syn: neȟiş} [K/B//IFb/CS/FJ/TF/GF/SS/A//JJ] <ȟiş>

bêî بيئى (BX) = without. See **bê I**.

bêîtibar بى ئيتِبار (ZF3) = unreliable; distrustful. See **bêît'bar**.

bêît'bar بى ئيتبار *adj.* 1) unreliable, undependable; 2) distrustful. {also: bêîtibar (ZF3)} < bê = 'without' + îtbar = 'trust' [EP/K/B//ZF3]

bêje بێژە *f./m.(F)* **(-ya/;).** word: •**Bi kurdî *bêjeya* folklorê tê wateya zanista gelêrî an jî lêkolîna li ser gel** (YPA, 11) In Kurdish *the word* 'folklore' means folk science or research about the folk. {syn: lavz; p'eyiv; pirs [2]; xeber} = Sor wuşe ووشە/wişe وشە [(neol)/F/K(s)/JB3/IFb/ZF/RZ] <gilî; gotin; şor; zar I>

bêjin بێژِن *m.&f.* **().** widower *m.*; widow *f.* {also: bîjin (Wkt); [bi-jin/be-žin (PS)/bē-zhin (Rh)] بيژن (JJ); widow = bîjin (RZ/Wkt)} {syn: bî I} Sor bêwe[jin] بێوە[ژِن] = 'widow'. for etymology see **bî I**. [Hk/JJ/GF/OK//RZ/Wkt]

bêjing بێژِنگ *f.* **(-a;-ê).** winnow, fine sieve (for sorting grain) : -**bêjing kirin** (K/B)/**bêjinge xistin** (K) to sift; to sprinkle: •**Xalîyê bi serřa *bêjing dike*** (Z-3) He *sprinkles* dust on top of it. {also: bêjink (A); [bijin بيژن/bijink بيژنك] (JJ); <bêjing> بيژنگ (HH)} {syn: elek, f. (K)} [Pok. 1. u̯eik- 1128.] 'to sort': Skt √vic [VII. vinákti] = 'to sift'; Av √vaēk *in* auua.vaēca- = 'to sort out, pick out'; Pahl wēxtan = 'to sift'; P bīxtan بيختن (-bīz-) (بيز) & bīzīdan بيزيدن; Sor bêjing بێژنگ = 'winnow' & bêjan[ewe] بێژان[ەوە] (-bêjê-)/bêjîn بێژين /(Arbil) bêştin بێشتن = 'to sift'; Hau wêşine *f.* = 'coarse sieve' (M4); Possibly also secondarily associated with √vaēg = 'to swing, brandish' --> K avêtin (-avêj-) = 'to throw' [Krç/K/JB3/B/HH/TF//A//JJ] <mifsik; moxil; seřad>

bêjingfiroş بێژِنگفرۆش *m.* **().** sieve seller. [B/ZF3] <bêjing>

bêjingker بێژِنگکەر *m.* **().** sieve or winnow maker. {also: <bêjingker> بيژنگگر (HH)} [HH/ZF3] <bêjing>

bêjink بێژِنك (A) = winnow, sieve. See **bêjing**.

bê-kar بى كار (SK) = useless. See **bêkêr**.

bêk'êf بى كێف *adj.* sad, depressed; upset: •**Kuřo, hela binhêřin çika Memê min çima îro derengî bûye, diqewime Memeyî *bêk'êf* be?** (Z-1) Boys, go see why my Mem is late today, could he be *upset*? {also: [bi-keïf] بى كيف (JJ)} < bê = 'without' + k'êf = 'pleasure' [EP/K//JJ] <aciz; dilteng>

bêkêr بى كێر *adj.* useless *(also of people)*: •**Werîsê rizî *bêkêr* e** (AB) A worn out rope is *useless*. {also: bê-kar (SK); [bi-kir] بى كير (JJ)} {syn: bêfeyde; p'ûç['] [2]; qels I[3]; t'ewş} < bê = 'without' + kêr = 'useful' [AB/K/A/JB3/B//JJ] <badîhewa; kêr I; kêrhatî>

bêl بێل *m.* **().** part of a herd or flock (BK): •**Hersêk çûn řastî *bêle* pez û bizin hatin** (HCK-5, #8, 56) All three went and came across *part of a flock* of sheep and goats. [BK/FJ/GF] <kerî II; řevo>

bêlu بێلو (IFb) = clear, obvious. See **belû**.

bêmad بى ماد (IFb/FJ/GF) = ill-tempered. See **bême'de**.

bêmahne بى ماهنه (FJ) = nonsensical, senseless. See **bême'na**.

bêmane بى مانە (IFb/Wkt/CS) = nonsensical, senseless. See **bême'na**.

bêma'nî بى ماعنى (K) = nonsensical, senseless. See **bême'na**.

bêma'rîfet بى ماعريفەت (Ba3) = impolite. See **bême'rîfet**.

bêmebest بى مەبەست *adj./adv.* accidental[ly], unintentional[ly]: •**Mamoste xwazt rûpela ku Lîna tiji nivîs kiribû biavêje selika gemarê, lê *bêyî mebest* çavên wî li hevoka "Mamosteyê hêja..." ketin** (Shahînê Soreklî FB 27.xii.2015) The teacher was about to throw into the waste basket the page that L. had filled with writing, but his eyes *accidentally* fell on the sentence "Dear teacher" [Ş.Sorekli/ZF3/Wkt]

bême'd بێ مەعد (GF) = ill-tempered. See **bême'de**.

bême'de بـێ مـەعـدە *adj.* in a bad mood, ill-tempered: •***Bê madî xwe*** **nan dixwe** (IFb) He is eating *without any relish* •**Min ku dît, wekî wezîr *bê me'de* bû, ez pê ḧesyam û min ev yek gotê** (HCK-4, #2, 35) When I saw that the minister was *in a bad mood*, I realized it and told him this •**Tu çiřa *bême'de* dixwî?** (B) Why are you eating *without enthusiasm*? {also: bêmad (IFb/FJ/GF); bême'd (GF-2); [bi-mydé] بی معده (JJ)} Sor bêmad بـێ مـاد = 'sour-faced, forbidding, surly' [HCK/K/B//JJ//IFb/FJ/GF] <me'de; mirûz>

bêmehne بێ مـەهـنـە (ZF) = nonsensical, senseless. See **bême'na**.

bême'na بـێ مـەعـنـا *adj.* meaningless, senseless, nonsensical; stupid (of things or actions): •**Di vê meselê de kî heq û kî neheq e? Nîqaşeke wisa *bême'ne* ye** (ku.rusencakir.com 10.x.2014) Who is right and who is wrong in this matter? Such a question is *meaningless* •**Ev tiştekî pir *bême'ne* ye û nakeve qalibê însaniyetê** (Nerinaazad 8.iii.2017) This is something quite *senseless* and runs counter to the rules of humanity [lit. 'does not enter into the mold of humanity'] {also: bêmahne (FJ); bêmane (IFb/Wkt-2/CS); bêma'nî (K); bêmehne (ZF); bême'ne (B)} [GF/Wkt//B//ZF//IFb/CS//K//FJ] <elet'ewş>

bême'ne بـێ مـەعـنـە (B) = nonsensical, senseless. See **bême'na**.

bême'rifet بێ مەعرِفەت = impolite. See **bême'rîfet**.

bême'rîfet بـێ مـەعـريـفـەت *adj.* 1) {syn: bê edeb} impolite, rude, crude, uncouth; 2) *[m.]* impolite, ill-mannered person. {also: bêma'rîfet (Ba3); bême'rifet; [be-mariféta] بـی مـعـرفـت (JJ)} < bê = 'without' + me'rifet = 'manners' [Z-1/K/B//Ba3//JJ] <me'rîfet>

bêmiraz بێ مِراز *adj.* having failed to attain one's goal or desire; bitter (of people) for having failed to attain one's goal: •**Ewî [bi] cahiltî çi gune kiribû, çima *bêmiraz* ma?** (Abbasian #5:144) What did he do in his youth, why has he remained *without fulfillment of his desires*? [=why did he die young] •**Sofî Mihemed merivekî wisa sik ê *bêmirêz* bû** (ZZ-7, 162) S.M. was an ugly and *bitter* person {also: [bi-meraz] بـی مـراذ (JJ)} < bê = 'without' + Ar murād مـراد = 'desire' (*passive participle of* arāda IV أراد = 'to want' √r-w-d) [Abbasian/K/JJ/OK//ZZ] <canemerg>

bêmirêz بـێ مِـرێـز (ZZ) = bitter for having failed to attain stg. See **bêmiraz**.

bêmk بێمك *f.* (;-ê). terebinth, bot. *Pistacia terebinthus*, the seeds of which are small and with soft shells {as opposed to **kez[w]an**, which are larger and with hard shells} {cf. Ar ḥabb al-xaḍrā' حـــب الـخـضـراء, buṭm بطم}. {also: benk (A/IFb); benok (OK); bêwk (Bw-Kanîya Mezin); binoşk (Zeb); darbenk (IFb-2); <ben بەن/benk بـەنك/bêmk بێمك> (Hej) [bêmk = 'unripe terebinth']; [dār-i beṅk] بـنـك (JJ-Lx)} Sor ben بەن = 'terebinth' [Bw-Tirwaniş & Binavî/Hej//Bw-Kanîya Mezin//A/IFb/JJ//Zeb] <kezan; şengêl>

bên بێن (L/SK) = breath; smell. See **bîn I**.

bêna بـێـنـا *adj.* eternal, everlasting, endless. {syn: bê dawî} Cf. NA be:na = 'time' (Krotkoff) [Ber/JB3]

bênamûs بـێ نـامـووس *adj.* dishonorable, immoral: •**Hey *bênamûs*** (HYma 25) Hey, you *immoral one*! •**Milletê turk *bê-namûs* e, bo çar quroşan dînê xo difiroşin** (SK #482) The Turkish nation is *dishonorable*, they will sell their religion for 4 piasters. {bênamûsî} bê + namûs [HYma/K/B/IFb/FJ/GF/TF/CS/SK//JJ-Rh] <namûs>

bênamûsî بێ نـامـووسی *f.* **(-ya;-yê).** dishonor, lack of honor; immorality; unchasteness: •**Di dawiyê de Temûr Beg îftira li Zarê dike: îftiraya *bênamûsiyê* lê dike** (Nbh 135:93) In the end, T.B. slanders Z.; he claims that he has *acted with dishonor* (or, unchastely). {also: [bē-nāmusī] بـــی ناموسی (JJ) = sans loi (lawless)} [Nbh/K/B/FJ/GF/JJ/Wkt/ZF/CS] <bênamûs>

bê nan û xwe بـێ نـان و خـوێ *adj.* ungrateful. Cf. T nankör = 'ungrateful' < P nān نـان = 'bread' & kūr كور = 'blind' [Zeb/A/IFb/GF] <spasdar>

bênav I بـێـنـاڤ (F) = willow; ash tree; holm oak. See **benav**.

bênder بێندەر *f.* **(-a;-ê).** threshing floor *(in the Middle East [orig.: 'Orient'] wheat is not beaten, but rather crushed with a metal-plated plank which is dragged along by oxen [JJ])* : •**Gufî û zařoka diçine *bêndera* û ji xweřa dileyîzin** (Z-4) Gurî and the children go to *the threshing floor* and play together •[go ōdā̰ke brāhīme meḥō lesā̰r *bēndā̰ra*] (PS-I) He said, "Brahimê Meho's room (=house) is at *the threshing floors* (=removed from the village)". {also: bender II (HR-I); bêder I (F/K/B); bêdêr, (JB1-A); [bēnda̰r] بيندر (PS-I); [bider] بيدر

(JJ); <bênder> بيندر (HH)} {syn: coxîn} Cf. Ar baydar بيدر, Iraqi Ar bēdar, NA bidra (Krotkoff) < *bē(t) + Syr edrā ܐܕܪܐ/Arc idrā אדרא < Akkadian idru (vSoden). See: Georg Krotkoff. "Studies in Neo-Aramaic Lexicology," in: *Biblical and Related Studies Presented to Samuel Iwry* (Winona Lake, Ind.: Eisenbrauns, 1985), p. 130. [Z-4/A/IF/HH/PS-I//F/K/B//JJ//JB1-A//HR-I]

bêndî بێندی, f. (Bsk) = two- or three-year-old female sheep. See **berdîr**.

bênfire بێنفِره (Wkt) = patient; tolerant. See **bînfireh**.

bênfireh بێنفِرەه (FJ) = patient; tolerant. See **bînfireh**.

bênfirehî بێنفِرەهی (Wkt) = patience; tolerance. See **bînfirehî**.

bênijik بێنژك (SS) = sneeze. See **bêhnişk**.

bênişk بێنشك (Hej) = sneeze. See **bêhnişk**.

bênxoş بێنخۆش (SK) = fragrant. See **bînxweş**.

bêol بێ ئۆل *adj.* 1) irreligious, infidel; 2) *general negative term for an untrustworthy or unsavory person* {cf. T dinsiz}. < bê = 'without' + ol = 'religion' [Msr] <k'afir; ol; xwedênenas>

bêoxir بێ ئۆخِر (A) = unlucky. See **bêoẍir**.

bêoẍir بێ ئۆغِر *adj.* unlucky: **•Cî hene, ji merivar̄a *bêoẍirin*** (Z-2) There are places which are *unlucky* for [some] people. {also: bêoxir (A)} {syn: bêyom} [Z-2/K//A] <oẍir>

bêp'ar بێ پار *adj.* **[+ji]** deprived (of), bereft (of), dispossessed (of): **•Di dema xwe ya xortaniya xwe de û li vî welatê pêşk[e]tî, ji xwendin û pêşveçûnê *bêpar* dimênin** (Wlt 5/86, 15) During the period fo their youth and in this progressive country, they are being *deprived* of learning and advancement **•Ew jî weke gelek keçên koçer ji hinek aliyên jiyanê *bêpar* e** (Lab, 8) Like many girls of the nomads, in certain aspects of life she too has been *deprived*; **-bêp'ar bûn** (K) to be deprived (of); **-bêp'ar kirin** (Ber/K/JJ) to deprive (of). {also: [bi-par] بی پار(JJ)} =Sor bêbeş بێ بەش [Ber/F/K/GF//JJ]

bê pare بێ پاره (BF/Wkt) = free of charge; penniless. See **bêp'ere**.

bêp'ere بێپەره/**bê pere** بێ پەره *adj./adv.* 1) free of charge, gratis {syn: belaş}: **•Şaredariya Qoserê bi hevkariya Şaredariya Îzmîtê li qezaya Qoser a bajarê Mêrdînê şorbeya *bêpere* û belaş belav dike** (Rûdaw 18.iii.2017) The Qoser [Kızıltepe] Municipality, in cooperation with the İzmit Municipality, is distributing *free* soup; 2) penniless, broke, moneyless, indigent. {also: bê pare (BF/Wkt-2)} [Rûdaw/K/IFb/RZ/Wkt/ZF3/CS//BF]

bêp'eretî بێ پەرەتی *f.* **(-ya;-yê).** moneylessness, lack of funds, condition of being broke or low on cash: **•Em *ji bêperetiyê* nikarin tu karî bikin** (Wlt 1:49, 16) We cannot do any work *due to lack of capital*. {also: bêpereyî (OK)} [Wlt/K//OK]

bêpereyî بێ پەرەیی (OK) = moneylessness. See **bêp'eretî**.

bêpişt بێ پشت *adj.* defenseless, unprotected, vulnerable; lacking support. [Elk/K/GF]

bêqidoş بێ قِدۆش *adj.* ill-fated, ill-omened, inauspicious, unlucky, unfortunate: **•Ev peyva *bêqidoş* "Nivîskar" bûbû bela serê min** (HYab, 5) This *unlucky* word "Writer" has caused me a lot of trouble. {also: bêqudoş (GF/TF)} {syn: bêyom} bê + Syr qdūš ܩܕܘܫ/qūdšā ܩܘܕܫܐ = 'sanctity, holiness' [HYab/FJ/ZF//GF/TF]

bêqudoş بێ قودۆش (GF/TF) = ill-fated, unlucky. See **bêqidoş**.

bêqûn بێ قوون *adj.* baseless (GF); inappropriate, insolent (Hk): **•pirsyareke *bêqûn*** (Hk) *inappropriate* or *bald* question. [Hk/GF]

bêr بێر *f.* **(-a;-ê).** 1) wooden shovel *(as opposed to* ***mer̄*** *= iron shovel)* (K/F/B/IF/A): **•Ûn r̄ahêjine tevra û *bêra*** (Z-2) You pick up spades and *shovels*; 2) oar, paddle (K/F/B/IF/A/JJ): **-bêr kirin** (K) a) to row; b) to rake; **-dan bêrê** (K) to row. {also: [bir بیر/byr بیر] (JJ); <bêr> بیر (HH)} [Pok. 1. bhedh- 113.] 'to dig': O Ir *badra- [*or* *barθr[y]a- *according to Bailey*]; Av vadar- = 'weapon'; OP vaθra- = 'battle-axe'; MidP byr; Baluchi bard; Southern Tati dialects (all *f.*): Chali & Esfarvini barra; Eshtehardi bāra; Xoznini & Xiaraji bara (Yar-Shater); P bīl بیل & bāl بال = 'spade, oar'; Sor bêł بێڵ = 'spade' & bêrik بێرك = 'large shovel'; cf. E Arm bah բահ <Middle Iranian *bahr; Lat fodere = 'to dig'. See **Spade** in: I. Gershevitch. "Outdoor Terms in Iranian," in: *A Locust's Leg : Studies in Honour of S.H. Taqizadeh* (London, 1962), pp.76-84; reprinted in his *Philologia Iranica*, ed. N. Sims-Williams (Wiesbaden : Dr. Ludwig Reichert Verlag, 1985), pp. 172-73; also: H.W. Bailey. "A Range of Iranica" in: *W. B. Henning Memorial Volume* (London : Lund Humphries, 1970), p. 31 [under **7. tēl**]. [Z-2/F/K/A/IF/B/JJ/HH] <carût; mer̄ II; metirke; tevir>

bêrahm بێ راهم (Ba3-3/B) = merciless. See **bêr̄ehm**.

bêrahmî بی راهمی (B) = mercilessness. See **bêřehmî**.

bêraq بێراق *f.* **(-a;-ê).** flag, banner. {also: beydax̌ (SK); beyraq (K/B); bêreq (HB/A); [baïraq] بيراق (JJ); <bêraq> بيراق (HH)} {syn: al} <P beyrāq بيراق --> T bayrak; Sor beyax بەیاخ/beydaq بەیداق (Mukri-OM) [HH//HB/A//K/B//JJ//SK]

bêraqdar بێراقدار *m.* **().** flag-bearer, standard-bearer. {also: beyraqdar (K/B); <bêraqdar> بيراقدار (HH)} {syn: beyraqbir (K)} [HH//K/B]

bêřehm بێ رەحم *adj.* cruel, pitiless, merciless: **•Birê qelpe *bêřahm* divên: "Mîrê me, birakî wî jî hebû, navê wî Ûsiv bû, ew jî mîna vî xirav bû, lê me řokê ew batmîş kir bê ser-berate"** (Ba3-3, #38) The dishonest, *merciless* brothers say: "Our emir, he had a brother named Joseph who was as bad as him, but one day we did away with him without leaving a trace." {also: bêrahm (Ba3-3/B); bêrem (F); [bi-rehm] بی رحم (JJ)} {bêrahmî; bêřehmî; bêremî} [Ba3/B//K/ZF3]

bêřehmî بێ رەهمی *f.* **(-ya;-yê).** cruelty, mercilessness. {also: bêrahmî (B); bêremî (F)} [K/ZF3//B//F] <bêřehm>

bêrem ب رەم (F) = merciless. See **bêřehm**.

bêremî بێ رەمی (F) = mercilessness. See **bêřehmî**.

bêreq بێرەق (HB/A) = flag. See **bêraq**.

bêrê بێ رێ *adj.* inappropriate, unacceptable, illegal, immoral, irregular: **•Amaca min ne ew e ku ez ji van pênc camêran re gotinên *bêrê* bibêjin** [sic] (Z.Zinar. Fermana 33 Rewşenbîran, 2000, 154) It is not my purpose to say *unacceptable* things to these five gentlemen **•Serokê PKKê ... di Televizyona MEDê de dijûn bi hin kesan kirine û peyvine *bêrê* ji devê xwe fiştiqandine** (Z.Zinar, introd.) The leader of the PKK ... cursed some people on MED TV and *inappropriate* words escaped from his mouth. <bê = 'without' + řê = 'road, way' [Zinar/K/A/IFb/CS/F/GF] <řê: ne li řê dîtin>

bêřêz بێ ڕێز *adj.* 1) disorderly, out of line (IFb/ZF); strange (JJ-G) 2) {syn: neřast; ≠řêzdar I} irregular (IF): **-lêkera bêřêz** (IF) irregular verb; 3) disrespectful (A/IF/SK). {also: [be-resa] بی ریز (JJ-G)} Cf. Sor bêřîz بێ ڕیز = 'insignificant, unworthy of esteem' {bêřêzî} [A/IFb/SK/ZF//JJ-G] <řêz>

bêřêzî بێ ڕێزی *f.* **(-ya;-yê).** 1) disorder(liness); 2) lack of respect, disrespect. [IF/ZF3] <bêřêz>

bêrik بێرِك (Ad/BX) = pocket. See **berîk**.

bêrim بێرِم (K/OK) = small lake. See **bêrm**.

bêrî I بێری *f.* **(-ya;-yê).** 1) sheepfold, hut, or shed for milking sheep: **•Êmo ji *bêrîyê* zivirî** (AB) Emo returned from *the sheepfold* **•Pêz** [sic] **hat *bêrîyê*, bi guhanên tijî** (AB) The sheep came to the *sheepfold*, with full udders; 2) sheepmilking (A); sheepmilking, *performed outside in spring and summer, one hour after dawn* (Haz): **•Dest diavêje elban û dide pêşiya bêrîvanan, hêdî hêdî berê xwe didin cihê *bêriya* sibehê** (AW69B4) She grabs the milk pails and leads the milkmaids, they slowly head for the place for the morning *milking*. {also: [biri] بيرى (JJ); <bêrî> بيرى (HH)} Cf. Sor bêre بێرە/bêrê بێرێ [AB/K/A/IF/B/Haz/HH//JJ] <axil; axur; dolge; gom I; guhêř; hevêz = hevşî; lêf; mexel; şevîn>

bêrî II بێری *f.* **(-ya;).** 1) {syn: hesret; mukuřî} longing, yearning, homesickness: **-bêriya ... kirin** (BX): a) to desire, miss, be impatient for {syn: dîna ... derhatin = to be homesick}: **•Min *bêriya te kir*** (JB3) I *miss you (polite formula)* **•Min bêriya welêt kir** (JB3) I am homesick; b) to feel like: **•Birê wî gelikî *berîya* qehwa *kiribûn*** [sic] (L) His brothers *felt like having* coffee; 2) sad poem *(expressing longing or homesickness)*. {also: bîr I[2] (Ag/Kp); berî III} [BX/L/K/A/JB3//Ag/Kp] <bijîn; bîr I[2]>

bêrîk بێریك (JB3/LC) = pocket. See **berîk**.

bêrîvan بێریڤان *f./m.(B)* **(-a/;-ê/ bêrîvên).** 1) *[f.]* sheep milkmaid, one who milks sheep in a sheepfold [*bêrî I*-q.v.]: **•*Bêrîvanan* jî pez dotin** (AB) As for *the milkmaids*, they milked the sheep; 2) *[m.]* one who drives the sheep into the shed for milking (B); 3) one who holds the sheep's head while it is being milked (B); 4) *woman's name.* {also: [biri-van] بيريوان (JJ); <bêrîvan> بيريڤان (HH)} [AB/K/A/IF/Haz/B//JJ] <bêrî I>

bêrm بێرم *m.(K)/f.(ZF3/Wkt)* **(/-a;/-ê).** small mountain lake, tarn, pond; "The many beautiful small glacier and crater lakes on the mountains [of Hakkari] serve as water resources for the inhabitants and their animals in summer pastures" [from: Lale Yalçın-Heckmann. *Tribe and Kinship among the Kurds* (Frankfurt a.M. et al.: Peter Lang, 1991), p. 75]: **•Mêr çem e jin *bêrm*** (Wkt) Man is a river, woman [is] *a tarn*. {also: bêrim (K/OK); birêm (Zeb-->Ak); [bērmé] بيرمه (JJ)} Mid P warm = 'pool, reservoir' (M3) *This word appears once in PS-I as* **bērmek**, *and some dictionaries (IFb/GF) have interpreted the word as bêrmek rather than* *bêrm, seeing the -ek as part of the word rather than as the indefinite article.* [PS-I/A/IFb/GF/ZF3/Wkt//K/OK//JJ//Ak] <gol; gom II; lîç>

bêr̄ûn بێ ڕوون *adj.* without butter or oil, plain. {also: [bi-roun] بى رون (JJ); <bêr̄on> بێ ڕۆن (Hej)} {syn: r̄ij} [Qzl/JJ//Hej] <kêmr̄ûn; r̄ûn>

bêsebir بێ سەبِر *adj.* impatient. {also: bêsebr (JB3); [bi-sebr] بى صبر (JJ)} < bê = 'without' + sebir = 'patience' {bêsebirî (K/B)} [Z/K/JB3/B//JJ]

bêsebirî بێ سەبِری *f.* **(-ya;-yê).** impatience. {also: [bisebri] بيصبرى (JJ)} [K/B//JJ]

bêsebr بێ سەبر (JB3) = impatient. See **bêsebir**.

bêser بێ سەر (IFb/GF) = headless, leaderless. See **bêserî**.

bêserberat' بێ سەربەرات *adv.* 1) untraceable, leaving no tracks, without a trace: **•Me r̄okê ew batmîş kir *bê ser-berate*** (Ba3-3, #38) One day we did away with him *without leaving a trace*; 2) unbeknownst, unknown. {also: bêserberate; bêser-bêberate (F)} <bê = 'without' + ser = 'head' + berat[e] = 'corpse' [Ba3//K//F]

bêserberate بێ سەربەراتە = without a trace. See **bêserberat'**.

bêser-bêberate بێ سەر بێ بەراتە (F) = without a trace. See **bêserberat'**.

bêserî بێ سەری *adj.* 1) headless; 2) without a leader; 3) silly, foolish: **•Xwe kuştiye yan jî xwe bi saxî veşartiye ji bo ku rizgar bibe ji van teşqele û bûyerên *bêserî*** (HYma 29) He has killed himself or buried himself alive in order to be rid of these *silly* problems and events. {also: bêser (IFb-2/GF)} [HYma/K/A/IFb/CS/AD//GF] <ser I>

bê ser û ber/bêserûber بێ سەر و بەر *adj.* sloppy, messy; disorderly; in bad shape: **-bê-ser-û-ber kirin** (M-Am) to beat, defeat, trounce, make mincemeat out of s.o.: **•Ev mirove dê me dete bir̄andin. Eve ma beyna heyvekêda, mirovekî muhacir û hinde evê dî kirî, ew *dê me bê-ser-û-ber ketin*** (M-Am #738, 340) This man will have us finished off. Within a month, a refugee, and he has done all this! He *will destroy us* [=mess us up] **•Mirovek ê hatî meydana min *dê min bê-ser-û-ber ketin*** (M-Am #743, 342) A man has come into the arena (with) me who *will destroy me* **•Wê rojê şer̄ê xwe kir we her k'afir *bê-ser-û-ber kir*** (M-Am #744, 342) They fought (all) that day and he *beat* the monster all the time. {syn: belawela; *bê r̄êk û pêk; *ne lêkdayî; tevlihev} [Bw/M-Am/IFb/GF] <ser û ber>

bêsînor بێ سینۆر *adj.* limitless, boundless, endless: **•dirêjbûneke *bêsînor*** (HYma 19) a *limitless* extension. {syn: bêḧed} [HYma/A/B/IFb] <sînor>

bêsîre بێسیرە (HH/Bw) = unripe grapes. See **besîre**.

bêsûc بێ سووج *adj.* innocent, guiltless: **•Tuyê evî xelqê *bêsûc* û gune qir̄ nekî** (Z-1) Don't destroy this *guiltless* and innocent people. {also: bêsûç; [bi-soutch] بى سوچ (JJ)} {syn: bêguneh} < bê = 'without' + sûc = 'guilt' {bêsûcî; bêsûctî} [Z-1/K/JB3/IF/B//JJ] <dilsaf; gune [1]>

bêsûcî بێ سووجی *f.* **(-ya;-yê).** innocence: **•Eger *bêsûcîya* kesên hatin dardekirin aşkere bibe** (rupelanu.com 10.viii.2016) If *the innocence of* people who have been hanged is revealed .... {also: bêsûctî (B-2)} {syn: bêgunehtî} [K/B/ZF3/Wkt]

bêsûctî بێ سووجتی (B) = innocence. See **bêsûcî**.

bêsûç بێ سووچ = innocent. See **bêsûc**.

bêş بێش *f.* **(-a;).** 1) {syn: bac; olam[1]; xer[a]c; xûk} tax: **•Ḧeta cûhî qutana xwe naxwit, *bêşa xwe* nadit** (YSZx) A Jew does not pay *his tax* until he is beaten [*prv.*]; 2) {syn: cerîme (K/JB3); cirm (K)} fine, penalty. {also: <bêş> بيش (HH)} Cf. NA mbayo:še = 'to pay (as tax)' [Krotkoff: Aradhin (Christian)] [YSZx/K/A/JB3/HH]

bêşerm بێ شەرم *adj.* shameless; impudent: **•Ji r̄êwe gazî kelekokî kir, gotê, "... Tu bo çî hinde *bêşerm* î? Li pêş çawêt hemî kes li ser mirîşkê sûar dibî û şermê ji şay nakey"** (SK 4:50) First (the fox) summoned the cock and said to it, "... Why are you so *shameless*? You mount a chicken in front of everybody and are not ashamed (even) before the king." {syn: bêhetik} Cf. P bīšarm بى شرم; Sor bêşerm بێ شەرم = 'shameless, undignified' {bêşermî} [Zeb/K/A/IFb/B/SK/GF/TF/ZF3]

bêşermî بێ شەرمی *f.* **(;-yê).** shamelessness; impudence. Cf. P bīšarmī بى شرمى [K/B/GF/ZF3] <bêşerm>

bêşik بێ شِك *adj./adv.* doubtless, without a doubt. {also: [be-sck] بى شك (JJ)} {syn: bêguman [3]} < bê = 'without' + şik = 'doubt' [K/JB3/B/ZF3//JJ]

bêşîk بێشیک *f.* **(-a;-ê).** cradle, crib. {also: [bechik] بيشك (JJ)} {syn: bormotk {?} (EP-7); colang; dar[a dergûşê]; landik} < T beşik; Sor bêşik بێشِك/bêşke بێشکە [F/K/B/ZF3//JJ]

bêşk'ertim بێشکەرتم *m.&f.* **(/-a;).** one betrothed while still an infant (still in the cradle): **•Ew bûka Qeret'ajdîne, / *Bêşk'ertima* Ç'ekîne** (EP-7) She is the sister-in-law to be [lit. 'bride'] of Q., / *betrothed to* Çekan *from birth*. {also: [bechik kertmé] بشيك كرتمه (JJ)} < T beşik kertme = 'making a notch on the crib [to indicate betrothal]' {also: bêşkêrtim (ZF3)} [EP-7//ZF3//JJ] <bûk I; dergistî>

bêşkêrtim بێشکەرتیم (ZF3) = one betrothed as an infant. See **bêşk'ertim**.

bêt'ar بێتار *m.(Kmc-20)/f.(IFb)* **(-ê/-a;).** disaster, catastrophe, accident, misfortune: **•*Betarê* wî di xizna wî de be** (Kmc-20) May his *troublemaking* affect only himself **•Bira, dibêne *bêtarek* hate serê torvanane** (L) Brother, they say that *a disaster* has befallen the fishermen **•Serokên usa nezan û derewîn, pir caran *bêtaran* tînin serê gelan** (K.Burkay. Aso, 67) Foolish and false leaders like these often bring *disaster* on the people. {syn: bela I; boblat; gosirmet; oyîn; qeda; siqûmat; şetele; t'ifaq} [L/K/IFb/GF/Kmc-20/ZF]

bêtêhn بێ تێهن (Zeb) = weak; light. See **bêtên**

bêtên بێ تێن *adj.* 1) lacking in energy or power, weak; 2) {syn: sivik} light, lightweight. {also: bêtêhn (Zeb-2)} [Zeb] <tên>

bêt'ifaq بێ تِفاق *adj.* disunited, at odds; on bad terms: **•Kurd qewmekî nexundî ye, tedbîra paşeroja xo nizanin, *bêtifaq* in** (SK 56:643) The Kurds are an illiterate people, improvident of their future and *disunited*. {also: [bi-tefaq] بی تفاق (JJ) = 'désaccord, mésintelligence'} Cf. P bī ettefāq بی اتفاق = 'without union, discordant'<bê + Ar ittifāq اتّفاق; = 'agreement'; =Sor nakok ناکۆك {bêt'ifaqî} [SK/K/B/JJ]

bêt'ifaqî بێ تِفاقی *f.* **(-ya;-yê).** discord, dissension, disunity, lack of cohesion: **•Paşî 'Îso *bê-tifaqî* li naw xulam û re'îyet û mezinêt Smail Paşa peyda bû** (SK 21:191) After Iso's departure *discord* grew among the servants and the subjects and the great men of Ismail Pasha. {also: [bi-tefaq] بی تفاق (JJ)} {syn: cure; dubendî; k'êşe; mişt û mir} [SK/K/B//JJ] <bêt'ifaq>

bêtir بێتِر *adj.* 1) {syn: p'irtir; p'itir; zêdetir} more: **•Bidû vegera wî da tenêtiyê ew *bêhtir* dorpêç kiribû** (HYma, 30) After his return, loneliness had encircled him [even] *more* **•Ronahiya wê *bitir* e û hukmê wê *bitir* e** (GShA 227) Its light is *greater*, so its power is *greater*; 2) {syn: gelemperî; p'iranî; zorbe} most, the most of: **•bêtirî wan** = most of them. {also: bêhtir (HYma); bitir II (GShA)} Cf. P bīštar بیشتر [K/A/JB3/IFb/GF/OK//HYma//GShA]

bêvan بێڤان (XF/K/B) = so-and-so. See **behvan**.

bêvil بێڤِل *f.* **(-a;-ê).** 1) {syn: difn; firn[ik]; ximximk} nostril; 2) {syn: difn; firn; kepî; poz I} nose (K/A/JB3/HH). {also: bihvil (HR-7); [bivíl/bevel] بیول (JJ); <bêvil> بیڤل (HH)} [EP/K/A/JB3/B/HH//JJ] <difn; kepî; poz I>

bêwa بێوا *adj.* bringing bad luck or misfortune, jinxed, unlucky: **•Devê gurî *bêwane*** (B) Mangy camels *are unlucky* **•Sîabendo, Sîabendo! / Min go, were meçe / Nêç'îra gak'ûvîa, / Nêç'îr mêrê camêrra *bê waye*!** (EP-4, #23) O Siyabend, Siyabend / I said, "Come now, don't go / Hunting deer / Hunting *is bad luck* for honorable men." [EP-4/B]

bêweç بێ وەج *adj.* 1) {syn: bêber; bêzuret; stewir} barren, sterile; childless (Msr/IF); 2) puny, thin, undersized (Msr); weak, exhausted (Msr): **•Mala min şewitî ji tere, çima wer *bêweç* bûyî?** (Msr) May my house burn down for you, why have you gotten so *weak*?; 3) dry, arid, barren (JB3/IFb): **•Çîyaê Mereto çîyakî pir *bêweç* e: tu şînayî tê tinîne** (Msr) Mount Mereto is an extremely *barren* mountain: there is no vegetation on it. < bê = 'without' + Ar wajh وجه = 'face' {cf. [bi-vedjh] بی وجه (JJ) = 'futile, worthless, adverse'} {bêweçî} [Haz--> nomads/JB3/IFb/TF/OK/ZF3] <xirş>

bêweçî بێ وەچی *f.* **().** dryness, aridity, barrenness. [JB3/IF/OK/ZF3] <bêweç>

bêwk بێوك (Bw-Kanîya Mezin) = terebinth. See **bêmk**.

bêxayî بێ خایی (Z-921) = ownerless. See **bêxwedî**.

bêxeber بێ خەبەر *adj.* **[+ ji]** unaware (of), ignorant (of), uninformed (about): **•Ewe salek e *ji halê wî bê-xeber* în, nizanîn mirye yan girtiye yan maye** (SK48:515) It's been a year that we *have no news of him*, we don't know if he's dead or captive or alive **•Lê Kurd *ji* roşinbîrên xwe, *ji* fikrên wan *bêxeber* in** (Nbh 132:11) But the Kurds are *unaware of* their intellectuals, *of* their ideas {also: [bi-khaber] بی خبر (JJ)} Sor bêxeber بێ خەبەر [Nbh/K/ZF/SK/CS//JJ] <xeber[1]>

bêxem بێ خەم *adj.* carefree, untroubled, unworried: **•Min hîwîya te qebûl kir, *bêxem be*** (SK 34:311) I have accepted your request [or, granted your favor], *don't worry*. {also: [bi-ghem] بی غم (JJ)} < bê = 'without' + xem = 'worry, care' {bêxemî} [Z/K/B/SK/TF/OK/ZF3//JJ]

bêxemî بێ خەمی *f.* **(-ya;-yê).** carefreeness, lack of concern, freedom from care. [K/B/TF/OK/ZF3]

<bêxem>

bêxeyal بی خەیال = carefree. See **bêxîyal**.

bêxîret بـــێ خـــیـــرەت *adj.* 1) {syn: xemsar} apathetic, lazy, not diligent, not hard working, not industrious: **•Xortekî çû xweřa qîzeke ze'fe *bêxîret* anî** (Dz-anec#16) A young man went and took himself an extremely *undiligent* wife; 2) lacking initiative; lacking zeal, unenthusiastic, unexcited: **•[Suleyman Aẍayî gote Ḧuseyn Aẍayê Zîlî 'Tu çi dibêjî? Ez ... êdî li welatê Îranê nasekinim' ... lakin Ḧuseyn Aẍa *bêẍîret* bûyî, li Îranê mayî]** (JR #39,120) Sulaiman Agha said to Husain Agha of the Zilan, 'What do you say? I ... am not staying in the country of Iran anymore' ... but Husain Agha was *not so excited*, he stayed in Iran]; 3) not held in high esteem, not respected; 4) cowardly (SK/OK); unwilling or unable to stick up for oneself: **•'Îso *bêẍîret bû*, neşya peya bît, lewa çu gustîr nehelgirtin** (SK 22:201) 'Iso *hadn't the courage to* dismount. That's why he didn't pick up any rings. {also: bêẍîret (SK); [be-ghira بـی غـیـره/ be-ghiréta بـی غـیـرت] (JJ-G)} Cf. P bīγayrat بـی غـیـرت = 'cowardly, without zeal'; Sor bêẍîret بـێ غـــیـــرەت = 'apathetic esp. in matters of honor; conniving cuckold' [Dz/K/B/TF/OK//SK//JJ] <xîret>

bêxîyal بـــێ خـــیـــال *adj.* untroubled, carefree: **•Memê ewqasî bêxem û *bêxîyal* bû** (Z-1) Mem was so *free of* cares and *worries*. {also: bêxeyal} [Z-1] <xiyal>

bêxwedî بـــێ خـــودی *adj.* ownerless, abandoned: **•Sibê ezê bik'evim bimirim, t'ext-t'acê min *bêxayî* dimîne** (Z-921) Soon [lit. 'tomorrow'] I will die, and my throne & crown will remain *ownerless* [=I have no heir]. {also: bêxayî (Z-921); bêxwey (B); bêxweyî (A); [bē-xvadī بـــی خـــودی/bi-khouï بـــی خوی] (JJ)} < bê = 'without' + xwedî = 'owner' [L/K/A/JB3//JJ]

bêxwey بێ خوەی (B) = ownerless. See **bêxwedî**.

bêxweyî بێ خوەیی (A) = ownerless. See **bêxwedî**.

bêẍîret بـــێ غـیـرەت (SK) = apathetic, lacking initiative; cowardly. See **bêxîret**.

bêyî بێیی (Z-1) = without. See **bê I**.

bêyom بـــێ یـــۆم *adj.* unlucky, unfortunate: jinxed, accursèd: **•Gelek ponijiye (fikiriye), ku gelo çima rengê hêkên wê reş in. Gotiye: Herhal ev hêlîna min ne rind e û *bêyom* e** (Wlt 1:37, 13) She thought for a long time [about] why her eggs [lit. 'the color of her eggs'] were black. She said, "Apparently this nest of mine is bad and *jinxed.*" {also: bê-yumn (SK)} {syn: bêoẍir} <bê = 'without' + Ar yumn يـــمـــن = 'good luck, good fortune' {bêyomî} [Wlt/Zeb/ZF3//SK]

bêyomî بێ یۆمی *f.* **(-ya;-yê).** unluckiness, misfortune; being jinxed, accursedness: **•Qebahet yê qûna min e, ne yê cih û ne jî yê hêlînê ye, *bêyomî* ya qûna min e, ne yê tu kesî ye** (Wlt 1:37, 13) The fault lies with my rear end, not with the place or with the nest, the *unluckiness* lies with my rear end, not with anyone else. [Wlt/ZF3] <bêyom>

bê-yumn بێ یومن (SK) = unlucky. See **bêyom**.

bêzuřet بێ زوڕەت/**bêzuret** بێ زورەت [F] *adj.* 1) {syn: bê dûnde} childless, without offspring; 2) {syn: bêber; bêweç; stewir} sterile, barren, infertile. {also: bêzuriyet (ZF3); bêzûryet (B)} {bêzuretî; bêzuřetî; bêzûryetî} < bê + Ar durrīyah ذرّيـــــة = 'progeny, offspring' [K/F//ZF3//B] <xirş; zuřet II>

bêzuřetî بێ زوڕەتی/**bêzuretî** بێ زورەتی [F] *f.* **(;-yê).** 1) childlessness; 2) sterility, barrenness, infertility. {also: bêzûryetî (B)} [K/F//B] <bêzuřet>

bêzuriyet بێ زوریەت (ZF3) = childless. See **bêzuřet**.

bêzûryet بـــێ زوریـــەت (B) = childless; barren. See **bêzuřet**.

bêzûryetî بێ زوریەتی (B) = childlessness; barrenness. See **bêzuřetî**.

bi- ب *verbal prefix for the present and past subjunctive, and conditional tenses*: **•(Bila) ez *bi*bînim** (BX ¶180, 164) So that I *may* see **•(Bila) ez *bi*k'evim** (BX ¶180, 164/K2 ¶289, 207) So that I *may* fall **•(Bila) min *bi*dîta** (BX ¶185, 172) So that I *might have* seen **•(Bila) ez *bi*k'etama** (BX ¶161, 138) So that I *might have* fallen **•Ezê *bi*k'etama** (K2 ¶299, 213) I *would* fall/have fallen **•Minê *bi*bijarta** (K2 ¶306, 221) I *would* choose/have chosen. Sor bi- ب; P bi- ب (only with present tense) [BX/K2]

bi ب *prep.* 1) with, by *(instrumental; also manner, time, agent)*: **•Goşt *bi* kêra xwe birî** (BX) He cut the meat *with* his knife **•Dinya *bi* dor e, ne *bi* zor e** (BX) The world goes *with* patience, not *with* violence *[prv.]* **•Xaniyê xwe *bi* destên xwe ava kir** (BX) He built his house *with* his own hands **•Gundê me *bi* destê Hemo hatiye şewitandin** (BX) Our village was burned *by* Hemo {agent} **•Yek heye *bi* sedî; sed heye, ne *bi* yekî** (BX) One can be worth 100, and 100 cannot even be worth one *[prv.]* **•*Bi* navê Xudayê pak ê dilovan û mihrivan** (BX) *In* the name of God, the pure, clement and merciful **•Piştî rohelatê *bi* du saetan** (BX) Two hours after daybreak [lit. 'after daybreak *by* two hours']; **-bi carekê** = at once, suddenly; at all; **-bi çend?** = for how much? *(asking the price)*; **-bi darê zorê** (BX) by force [lit. 'by the stick of violence']; **-bi gotinê** = as they say [en parole]; **-bi qencî** = with goodness [avec bonté]; **-bi sivikahî** (BX) with ease; **-bi tenê/bi tena xwe** = alone, by oneself; **-bi vî awayî** = in this manner/way; **-bi xwe** = oneself, in person [en soi]: **•Mîr *bi xwe* hat** (BX) The emir came *in person* **•Hûn xwe *bi xwe*** = You *in person*; 2) in, into *(motion toward)*: **•Pere *bi* bêrika xwe xist** (BX) He put the money *in* his pocket ***•Bi* hewa ket** (BX) He flew away [lit. 'fell *into* the air']; 3) according to: ***•bi* min** = *according to* me ***•Bi* a min bike** (BX) Do what or as I tell you; Take my advice [lit. 'Do *according to* that [advice] of mine']; 4) *as the complement of certain verbs*: **•Ez *bi* şivan bûm** (BX) I became a shepherd **•Tu hêj *bi* kurmancî nizanî** (BX) You still don't know any Kurdish **•Mîşo gayê xwe *bi* firotin da** (BX) M. gave his bull *for* sale; 5) *used together with postpositions*:

-bi ... da/de = on, across, through: **•Destmala min *bi* avê *de* çû** (BX) The water carried off my handkerchief [lit. 'My handkerchief went *on* the water'] **•Bi rê de** = on the way, en route ***•Bi rê de*, wezîrê hakim pêrgî keçelok bû** (L) *On the way*, the king's vizier encountered Kechelok **•Ez *bi* dehl û rêlan *[de]* diçûm nêçîra hirça** (BX) *Through* the thickets and forests I went bear hunting.

-bi ... r̄a/re = a) with *(accompaniment)* {syn: digel}: **•Em *pev [=bi hev] re* çûn** (BX) We left *together* **•Gurgîn *bi* min *re* hat** (BX) G. came *with* me **•Lazime lawê te *bi* min *re* bê** (L) Your son must come *with* me **•pê re [=bi wî/wê re]** = with him/her; b) by, through *(movement)*: ***•Bi* derenca *re* banî ket** (L) He climbed *up* the stairs ***•Bi* derencê *re* hilkişiya** (BX) He ascended [climbed *up*] the stairs; c) agreeing with: **-Ez *bi* te *ra* me** = I agree *with* you [lit. 'I am with you'].

-bi ... ve = a) with *(accompaniment, belonging, contiguity)*: **•Axa *bi* deh gundên xwe *ve*, bawer dike Keyxosrow e** (BX) The agha, *with* his 10 villages, thinks he is [the emperor] Keykhosrow *[prv.]* **•Bi ser û berê xwe ve** (BX) entirely ***•Bi* t'omerîya cindîyê Cizîrê*va*** (Z-1) *With* all (=the totality of) the nobles of Jezirah **•Botan *bi* Behdînan *ve* ye** (BX) The province of Bohtan is *adjacent to* Behdînan **•Mîr *bi* sed siwarî *ve* bi rê ket** (BX) The emir set out *with* 100 knights **•Ser Dûmanlûê t'u mêşe t'unebûn, vira dar jî hêşîn nedibûn, lê wexta bahar dihat, ew ji xewa giran ȟişyar dibû û *bi* ȟemû r̄enga*va* dixemilî** (Ba2:1, 202) On [Mount] Dumanlu there were no forests, trees did not even grow here, but when springtime came, it awoke from a great sleep and became colorfully [lit. '*with* all colors'] adorned **•Şemso bi min ve ye** (BX) Sh. is with me (i.e., physically present); b) around: **•Êdîka şerît *bi* newqa wî *ve* girêda** (L) Slowly (or, gently) he tied the rope *around* his waist **•firçe: amûrek bidestik e û *bi* serê wê *ve* dav hene** (Wkt) brush: an instrument with a handle and *around* its head there are bristles. {also: [b ب/bé بــه] (JJ)} [bi + wî/wê = pê/vê] Cf. P bi ب / به; Sor be به [BX/K/IF/B/JJ]

bibiq بِــبِــق *f.* **(-a;).** pupil *(of the eye)*. {also: bîbik (A/ZF3); bîbil (IF); bîbok, m. (K-2); pîpik (IF-2); [bibik-a tchawan] ببكا چاڤان (JJ); [bibi] بيبى (JJ-G); <pîbik> پيبك (HH)} {syn: r̄eşik I} < Ar bu'bu' بؤبؤ -> P būbūk بوبوك; Sor bebele-y çaw بەبەلەی چاو/ bîbîle بـيـبـيـلـه; Za bîbiki *f.* (Mal) {cf. also T gözbebeği} [F/K//JJ//A/ZF3//IF//HH] <çav>

bi-cê بِ جێ (SK) = appropriate. See **bicî**.

bicih بِ جِه (JJ/TF/OK) = appropriate. See **bicî**.

bicî بِ جي/بِجى *adj.* 1) appropriate, proper; pertinent; 2) exactly: **•Zilamê go ev keleş kuşti bin û em zanibin *bi cî* bê kî ne, erbabê wan çiye?** (L) If we can find out *exactly* who the men are who killed these brigands, what is our reward? {also: bi-cê (SK); bicih (TF/OK); bi cîh (IFb); [be-djih] بــجــه (JJ)} {syn: di cihê xwe da} < bi = 'in' + cî = 'place' {Cf. T yerinde = 'proper', lit. 'in its place'} [L/K/A//JJ/TF/OK//IFb]

bi cîh بِ جيه (IFb) = appropriate. See **bicî**.

bicrik بِجرِك (FJ) = bread toasted in butter. See **biçrik**.

biçeng بِچەنگ (F) = armpit. See **binç'eng**.

biçîk بِچيك (Zx) = small. See **piçûk**.

biçrêk بِــچــرێــك (GF) = bread toasted in butter. See **biçrik**.

biçrik بِــچــرِك *f.* **().** dish consisting of bread toasted in butter. {also: bçrek (GF-2); bicrik (FJ); biçrêk (GF); <biçrik> بـچـرك (HH)} {syn: hevrîşk} [IFb/HH/CS//FJ//GF]

biçûcik بِچووجِك (A) = tiny. See **biç'ûçik**.

biçûçik بِـچـووچِـك *adj.* tiny, itsy-bitsy: **•lawikê *biçûçik***

(L) *tiny* boy. {also: biçûcik (A)} <dim. of **biçûk/piçûk**> Sor piçkołe پچکۆڵە/piçkołane پچکۆڵانە [L/A/ZF3] <piçûk>

biçûk بچووک (K/SK) = small. See **piçûk**.

biçûkayî بچووکایی (K) = smallness. See **piçûkayî**.

biçûkî بچووکی (K) = smallness. See **piçûkayî**.

biçûkînî بچووکینی (SK) = childhood. See **piçûkayî** [2].

biçûktî بچووکتی (K) = smallness. See **piçûkayî**.

bi deranîn ب دەرانین (PS-I) = to remove. See **deranîn**.

bidû بدوو (Kş) = gums; palate. See **pidî**.

bi'ecîn بعەجین = to be exhausted; to sob; to get angry. See **bihecîn**.

bi fêm ب فێم *adj.* intelligent, bright: •**Di heşt saliya min de bavê min ez danîm ber xwendina Quranê. Ez gelek *bi fêm* bûn** (Wlt 2:66, 2) When I was eight years old my father had me start studying the Koran. I was very *bright*. {syn: aqil I; aqiljîr; aqilmend; aqiltîj (Bw); bi zihn; jîr; zîx I} [Wlt] <fehm; jîr; serwext>

bih بەه *f.* (;-ê). quince, bot. *Cydonia vulgaris*. {also: beh (GF/OK/AA); behê (IFb-2); bihok II (K/A-2/IFb/GF-2/OK-2); biyok (IFb-2/Kmc-2-2); bîvok (F/K-2); [beh به/bi بی] (JJ); <bih> به (HH)} Cf. P bih به; Sor behê بەهێ/bey بەی; Za beyı *f.* (Mal); Hau bey [A/HH/TF/Kmc-2/FS//K/IFb/ZF3//F//JJ/GF/OK/AA]

biha بها *m.* (). 1) {syn: nerx [1]} price, value, worth; 2) [*adj.*] {syn: giran [2]; giranbiha} expensive, costly, dear: •**Mal ji wan r̄a gelek teng e, lê çi bikin, kirêya malên fireh p'ir̄ *buha* ye** (DZK) The house is too small [lit. 'narrow'] for them, but what can they do? The rent on bigger [lit. 'wide'] houses is very *expensive*. {also: baha (B); buha (A); [beha] بها (JJ); <buha> بها (HH)} <P bahā بها = 'price, value'; T baha/paha; Sor beha بەها/ba با = 'price'; Za vaya *f.* = 'price' (Mal) [DZK/A/HH//F/K/IF//JJ//B] <nerx; qedir I; qîmet>

bihar بهار *f.* (-a;-ê). spring(time): •**şînîtî û geşiya *biharê*** (Alkan, 71) the verdure and brilliance *of springtime*; **-biharê** = in the springtime; **-ḧeta biharê** (J) by or until springtime. {also: bahar (Ba2/A/B); buhar (Wlt/L-I); [behar] بهار (JJ); <buhar> بهار (HH)} [Pok. u̯es-r̥, gen. u̯es-n-es 1174.] 'springtime': Skt vasantá- = 'springtime' & vāsará- = 'bright'; Av vaṅhri = 'in spring'; O P vāhara- in θūra•vāhara- = 'second month, April-May' (Kent); Pahl vahār <*vāhar (Hübsch #501); P bahār بهار (Horn #243) -->T (ilk)bahar; Sor behar بەهار; Za wesar *m.* (Todd); Hau wehar *m.* (M4) [Ba2/A/B//F/J/K/JB3/IFb/SK//JJ//HH/Wlt/L-I] <havîn; payîz; zivistan>

bihartin بهارتن (BX) = to pass. See **bihurtin**.

bihecîn بهەجین *vi.* **(-bihec-).** 1) to be(come) exhausted, grown faint (K/B); 2) to cry one's heart out, sob (K/B); 3) **[+ ji]** to get angry, irritated [at] (L/K): •**Ezê herim xwe li nav çavê wî xînim, heyanî go *ji* min *bibihece*** (L) I will throw myself into his eyes, until *he gets angry at* me •**Heya go qenc Teyrê Sêmir *jê bihecî*** (L) Until the Simurgh *got good and mad at her*. {also: be'ecîn (B); bi'ecîn; <be'icîn بعجین (dibe'ice) (دبعجه)> (HH)} [L/K//B//HH] <aciz>

bihemil ب هەمِل/بِهەمِل *adj.* pregnant, "expecting": •**Pîreka wî *bihemil* bû** (L) His wife was *pregnant*. {also: biḧemle (SK)} {syn: avis; bizar; duhala; giran; ḧemle} [L//SK]

biheşt بهەشت (MG) = paradise. See **bihuşt**.

bihevçûn بهەڤچوون (A) = to argue. See **p'evçûn**.

bihevr̄a بهەڤرا *adv.* together: •**Gelî ferḧîta, ancax babete, ko serê herduka *bi hevr̄a* her̄e ser balgîyekîne** (Z-2, 68) O ifreets! It is only fitting that both their heads should rest *together* on a single pillow [=that they should get married] •**Memê û Zînê vedgerin qesrê, rûdinên û şîrin şîrin *bi hevr̄a* xeber didin** (FK-2, 294) Mem and Zîn return to Mem's room, sit and very sweetly talk *with each other* •**Paşê k'omeke çawîşa *bi hevr̄a* çûne derva** (FK-1, 272) Then a group of servants went out *together*. {also: bihevre (A/GF/TF); p'evr̄a (K); pev re (IFb); [behew بهەڤ/behewra بهەڤرا] (JJ)} {syn: pêkve; t'evde} [Z/FK/AD//JJ//A/GF/TF//IFb//K]

bihevre بهەڤرە (A/GF/TF) = together. See **bihevr̄a**.

bi hezaran ب هەزاران *pr. mod.* [by the] thousands: •***Bi hezaran* mirov li derî bajêr bêgav mabûn, nikaribûn xwe bigihînin dîlana te** (Wlt 2:73, 14) *Thousands of* people were stuck at the gates to the city, unable to get to your ceremony •**Ezê her̄me xazgînî. Qîza p'adşê jî *bi ḧezara* çûne, serê ḧemya lê dane** (HCK-5, #41 225) I'm going to go ask for her hand. *Thousands* have gone to ask for the princess' hand, they were all beheaded. {also: bi ḧezara (HCK)} [HCK//BX] <hezar>

bihêz بهێز [IFb/AD]/**bi hêz** ب هێز [AW-2] *adj.* strong, forceful, mighty: •**Her çend dijwarî û zehmetî wê demê hebin jî, bi vîna xwe ya *bi hêz* wan çareser dike** (AW73B1) No matter how many difficulties there may be then, he solves them with his *strong* will •**Tîrêjên ronahiya neynika krîstal, şoqeke *bihêz* li dil û ruhê mirov dixe** (AW70D1) The rays of crystal mirror light send a *forceful* shock through one's heart and soul. {syn: xurt} Sor be hêz بەهێز [IFb/AD] <hêz>

bihin بِهن = smell, odor; breath. See **bîn I**.

bihinfarah بِـهـنـفـاراه (TF) = patient; tolerant. See **bînfireh**.

bihinfarahî بِـهِـنـفـاراهی (TF) = patience; tolerance. See **bînfirehî**.

bihirîn بِهرین (Z-2) = to pass. See **bihurtin**.

bihişt بِهشت (EP) = paradise. See **bihuşt**.

bihîstin بِهیستِن *vt.* **(-bihis-** [K] **/-bihîz-** [K/IF/JB1-S] **/-bihê-** [K/B/JJ/SK] **/-bihîs-** [BX/M-Zx]**).** to hear: **•Wexta Al-p'aşayê kal û jina xweva eva gilîya derheqa Memêda *bihîstin*, qudum çokê wanda nema** (Z-1) When old Al-pasha and his wife *heard* these words about Mem, they felt weak [lit. 'strength did not remain in their knees']. {also: bihîztin; bîstin (Ad/A/IF/M); [behistin] بهستين(JJ); <bihîstin بهيستن (dibhîze) (دبهيزه)> (HH)} {syn: guh lê bûn (Bw): seh kirin (Msr)} [Pok. bheudh-150.] 'to be aware; to make aware': M. Schwartz: Perhaps originally a passive form in -īh-/-ist, cf. Av √baod- --> būiδiia- = 'to be aware (of)' (passive form), cf. also P dān-**ist**-an دانستن = 'to know' *(also a verb of perception)*; Sor bîstin بـيـسـتـن (-biye-/-bîst-). See **6. bustaǰ** in: G. Morgenstierne "Persian Etymologies" in: *Norsk Tidsskrift for Sprogvidenskap*, 5 (1932), 54, reprinted in: Irano-Dardica (Wiesbaden : Dr. Ludwig Reichert Verlag, 1973), p.165. [Ad/A/IF/M//F/K/JB3/B/JJ/HH/JB1-S/SK] <guh dan/kirin; guhdarî kirin; [pê] ĥesîn>

***bihîstok** بِـهـيـسـتـوك *f.* **(-a;-ê).** *neologism referring to several items related to hearing:* 1) (telephone) receiver or earpiece (GF/ZF/CS); 2) {syn: t'elefon} telephone (IFb/CS); 3) {syn: pêlweş (IF); r̄adyo} radio (Wn). [(neol)Wn/IFb/GF/ZF/CS] <îzgeh>

bihîztin بِهيزتِن = to hear. See **bihîstin**.

bihn بِهن (JB3/IF/JB1-S) = smell; breath. See **bîn I**.

bihnfire بِهنفِره (FJ/GF) = patient; tolerant. See **bînfireh**.

bihnişt بِهنِشت (FJ/GF) = sneeze. See **bêhnişk**.

bihntengî بِـهـنـتـەنـگـى (GF) = shortness of breath; nervousness. See **bêhntengî**.

bihnxweş بِهنخوش (GF) = fragrant. See **bînxweş**.

bihok I بِهۆك (K/ZF/CS) = insect. See **bihuk**.

bihok II بِهۆك (K/A/IFb/GF/OK) = quince. See **bih**.

bihor بِهۆر (GW) = passage, crossing, ford. See **bihur**.

bi hose بِ هۆسە *adj.* noisy. [Bw] <hose>

bihost بِهۆست (K/IFb/OK) = (finger) span. See **bost**.

bihoşt بِهۆشت = paradise. See **bihuşt**.

bihoştin بِـهـۆشـتِـن *vt.* **(-bihoş-).** 1) [*vi.*] {syn: ĥelîn} to melt, dissolve *(vi.)* (M/JJ): **•Mezhebê ku esasê wî li ser wan terze delîlane bît wekî dîwarê ser cemedê ye: her wextê hetawek lê det cemed *dê buhujît*, dîwar dê herifît** (SK 60:713) A religion based on such proofs is like an ice-covered wall: whenever the sun hits it the ice *will melt*, [and] the wall will collapse; 2) [*vt.*] {syn: ĥelandin; p'işaftin} to melt *(vt.)*, smelt; 3) to thaw *(vt.)*. {also: buhujîn vi. (-buhuj-) (M/SK/Dh); buhujtin (GF); buhuştin vi. (-buhuj-) (M); bûstin (GF-2); [bhoshtin] بـهـوشـتـن (JJ)} <*bihujtin <O Ir *wi-tač- (A&L p.84 [IV, 2] + 94 [XVIII]) [S&E/K/JJ//GF//M/SK/Dh] <ĥelîn>

bihuk بِـهـوك *f.* **(-a;-ê).** insect, bug: **•Dayê *bihuk* e, jinê ruhik e** (FD) My mother is an *insect* [i.e., loathsome], but my wife is my soul; **-kêzik û bihuk** (FS) all types of insects {also: bihok I (K/ZF/CS); bu'uk (GF-2/FJ-2); buhik (RZ); buhuk (GF/FJ); buĥuk (B/G); buxik (IFb)} [FD/FS//K/ZF/CS//GF/FJ//RZ//B/G//IFb] <axûrk; bi'ok; cobir; k'êzik; mêş; moz; pêşî II; quzgezk; t'evnpîrk>

bihur بِـهـور *m.(K/B)/f.(B)* **(; /-ê).** passage; crossing; passageway; ford: **•Hêj negihaye *bihor*, dawdelingê xwe hildide** (GW, 17) He hasn't reached *the ford* yet, he's [already] taking off his trousers *[prv.]*. {also: bihor (GW); bor II (Bw/GF-2/TF); buhur (GF); [bor بـور/buhur بـوهـر] (JJ); <bûr [bor?]> بـور (HH)} <O Ir *wi-tar- (A&L p.84 [IV, 2]) [L/K/IFb/B//JJ/GF//TF/Bw//HH//GW] <bazeber>

bihurandin بِـهـورانـدِن *vt.* **(-bihurîn-).** 1) to cause to pass; 2) {syn: derbaz kirin} to pass, spend *(time)* (K/IF): **•Ĥeta ko wextê xwe *biborîne* li bilûra xwe dida** (Dz #22, 389) In order *to pass* the [lit. 'his'] time he would play on the flute. {also: borandin (K-2/GF); buhurandin (BK/IFb/TF); [behürtāndin] بـهـرتـانـديـن (JJ) = 'to run out, elapse *(of time)*; <bûrandin بوراندن (dibû[r]îne) (دبورينه)> (HH)} [BK/IFb/TF//K/B//JJ//GF//HH] <bihurtin>

bihurîn بِهورین (K/B) = to pass. See **bihurtin**.

bihurtin بِـهـورتِـن *vi.* **(-bihur-).** 1) {syn: derbaz bûn} to pass, cross over; to enter: **•Dinya şev bû û ez di vir re *bihurtim*** (L) It was getting dark (=becoming night), and I *passed* by here **•Ezê derî ji te re vekim û *bibihure* nav bajarê Dîyarbekir** (L) I'll open the gate for you, and (you) *pass* into the city of Diyarbekir; 2) to pass *(of time, vi.)*: **•Çi roj *naborin* bi dehan çîrok û çîvanok û peyamên cuda cuda nebihîstîn li mal û li nêv bazarî û li daîrên xwe û li her cihekî** (BH-back cover) No day *passes* when [we] haven't heard tens of stories and anecdotes and tales, at home and in the market and in our offices and everywhere; 3) to have an effect on, to influence, work (PS): **•[Gilî lê kirin** [sic] **cem Mîr Zozan, *neborî*]** (PS-I) They complained of him to Mir Zozan, but *it did not work* [i.e., it was to no avail =their complaint fell on deaf ears]; 4) to forgive (OK). See **lêborîn**. {also: bihartin (BX); bihirîn (Z-2); bihurîn (K-2/B); biwartin; borîn II (-bor-) (JB3); buhartin (-bihur-) (IF); bûrîn (A/Ber); [behartin بهارتين/ buhurtin بهورتين/bourin بورين] (JJ); <bûrîn بورين (dibûrî) (دبورى)> (HH)} Sor burdin بوردن (bur-)/bigirdin بِگِردِن [Sinne] = 'to overpass, go beyond, be overripe'; Hau wîerdey (wîer) *vi.* (M4) [L/K//BX//B//A/HH/Ber//JB3//IF/JJ]

bihust بهوست (K/B) = span *(unit of measure)*. See **bost**.

bihuşt بِهوشت *f.* **(-a;-ê).** 1) {syn: cenet} paradise: **•Bapîrê me sera bapîrê-ngo li *beĥeştê* havête derê** (M-Ak, #546) Our ancestor was thrown out of *Paradise* on account of your ancestor **•Çîrok çû deştê, da û babên me çûn *bihuştê*** (Rnh 2:17, 308) The story went to the prairie, our parents went to *paradise [concluding formula for folktales]* **•Her kesê peşkekê ji awa tizbîyêt min wexotewe, cendekê wî agirê cehennemê nabînît. Ewe awa ĥeyatêye dideme hingo. Cîyê hingo *beĥeşta* ebedî ye** (SK 12:119) Whoever drinks a drop of the water from my rosary, his body will not see the fire of Hell. This is the Water of Life which I give you and your place will be *Paradise* eternal; 2) heaven. {also: beheşt (A-2/OK/GF); behişt (SB); beĥeşt (SK/M-Ak); biheşt (MG); bihişt (EP); bihoşt; bihûşt (TF); buhişt (BX); buhuşt (GF-2); [behicht] بهشت (JJ); <bihuşt> بهشت (HH)} [Pok. u̯esu- 1174.] 'better': Skt vásu- = 'good'/vasīyah- = 'better'/vasiṣṭha- = 'best'; O Ir *u̯ahišta- ax^{v}- (Av vahišta- aŋhu- = 'best life, world') <*u̯ahišta- = 'better' (Ras, p.133): Av vaŋhu-/vohu- = 'good'/ vahyå = 'better'/vahištō = 'best' ; Mid P vahišt; P behešt بهشت; Sor beheşt بەهەشت [EP//BX//K/A/JB3/HH/ /TF//JJ/SB//OK/GF//SK/M-Ak]

bihûşt بهووشت (TF) = paradise; heaven. See **bihuşt**.

bihvil بهڤل (HR-7) = nose. See **bêvil**.

biĥemle بحەملە (SK) = pregnant. See **bihemil**.

bi ĥezara بِ حەزارا (HCK) = [by the] thousands. See **bi hezaran**.

bijang بِژانگ *f.* **(;-ê).** eyelash(es). {also: bijank (A/ GF-2); bijî II (K-2); bijûlang; bijûlank (Bşk); bjang, m. (B-2); mijang (A-2/IFb-2/GF-2); mijank (GF-2); mijî (Srk); mijûlank, m. (OK-2); mîjank (Çnr); [mijank] مژانك (JJ); <mijank> مژانك (HH)} [Pok. meigh-/meik- 712.] 'to glitter, twinkle, dark (twinkling before one's eyes)': 2. meik-: Mid P mij(ag) (M3); P može مژه /možegān مژگان (pl.); Baluchi mičāč; Sor birjang برژانگ/mijol مژۆل (K2); Za mije *m.*/mija *f.* (Mal) [F/K/B/IFb/GF/OK/BK//A/ /Bşk//Srk//Çnr//JJ/HH] <birû; çav>

bijank بژانك (A/GF) = eyelashes. See **bijang**.

bijare بِژاره *adj.* choice, select; chosen, selected: **•genimê *bijare*** (K/B) *choice* wheat **•[Ji êla xwe ĥeft sed suwarêd *bijare* bir** [sic]**]** (JR #39,121) He took 700 *choice* riders from his tribe **•Selîm Beg sê-sed mêrêt *bijare* digel xo řa-kirin** (SK 41:400) Salim Beg took 300 *chosen* men with him. {also: bijarte (GF/TF); [bejaré] بژاره (JJ)} Cf. Sor bijar kirdin بژار کردن = 'to pick out, weed, clean (rice)' & bijare kirdin بِژاره کردن = 'to thin out (seedlings), comment on, review (book)' [JR/K/IFb/B/ JJ/SK//GF/TF]

bijarte بژارته (GF/TF) = choice, select. See **bijare**.

bijartin I بِژارتِن *vt.* **(-bijêr-).** 1) to choose, pick, select: **•Ji nav van pirtûkan bo xwe yekê *bibijêre*** (Wkt) *Choose* one of these books for yourself; 2) to sort: **•Wî genim *bijart*, anku zîwan û tiştên dî yên di nav genimî da înan der û avêtin** (FS) He *sorted* the wheat, i.e., removed the darnel [weed] and other things and threw it away. {also: [bejartin بژارتین / bejarin بژارین] (JJ); <bijartin بژارتن (dibjêre) (دبژیره)> (HH)} {syn: jêgirtin; neqandin I} O Ir *secondary causative* *wicāraya- < wicira-: Av vīcira (*root* či) 'to discriminate between, discern, make judgement; Mid P wizārdan (wizār) = 'to separate; explain, interpret; perform, fulfill, redeem' & wizār = 'separation; explanation' (M3); P guzārdan گزاردن/گذاردن = 'to put, place; perform, etc.'; Sor heł•bijardin هەڵبِژاردِن (heł-bijêr-) = 'to select, elect' [F/K/A/JB3/IFb/B/HH/GF/TF/OK/ M/ZF3//JJ] <vavartin>

bijartin II بِژارتِن (M/A/HB) = to roast, grill. See **biraştin**.

bijaştîr بژاشتیر *f.* **(;-ê).** three-year-old sheep; 2-3 year old she-goat (Kmc). {also: bizaştîr (Wlt/A/Kmc/ZF3)} [Wlt/A/Kmc/ZF3//K/B] <berdîr; mî I>

bijî I بِـژى *m.(K)/f.(F/B/OK)* **(/-ya;/-yê).** (horse's) mane (K/B/JJ): **•Nav du ĥevtyada hûn evî Borî usa xwey kin, wekî av berî *bijya*dim bê saxirîyaf̄a derk'eve** (Z-1) In two weeks, you care for this [horse] Bor in such a way that if I water his *mane*, it will come out his croup **•Nava çil şevada usa bikî, avê saxrîa kî, *bijyaf̄a* bavêje, bijya kî, saxrîara bavêje** (EP-7) In the course of 40 nights act in such a way that, when you water his croup, it comes out his *mane*, and when you water his mane, it comes out his croup (=fatten him up). {also: bijîk (OK); bijû (K-2/B-2); [bejou بـژو/ biji بـژى] (JJ)} {syn: gulî I[2]} <*biržu- <*birzu- <O Ir *bṛzu-ka (A&L p.83 [II]); = Sor yał يـــــال. *Regarding the transition* *-rz->-rž->-ž- *see* A. Christensen & K. Barr. *Iranische Dialektaufzeichnungen aus dem Nachlass von F.C. Andreas: Erster Teil* (Berlin, 1939), p. 395. [Z-1/EP/F/K/IFb/B/JJ/GF//OK]

bijî II بِژى (K) = eyelashes. See **bijang**.

bijî III بِـــژى *m.* **(-yê;).** awn, beard *(on the spikelet of grasses such as wheat)*. {syn: dasî[2]} [Qzl/IFb/ZF3] <bijîreş; genim>

bijîjk بِژيژك (IFb/TF) = doctor. See **bijîşk**.

bijîn I بِـــژيــن *vt.* **(-bijî-).** to desire, long for, have an appetite for (IF): **•Berx hatin nava pêz, dilê tevan dibijî şîr, pir dibijî** (AB) The lambs came in among the sheep, very much in desire of milk **•Dilê min *[filantişt]* dibije** (Qmş) I feel like eating or drinking [stg]. [AB/IFb/GF/Qmş/ZF3]

bijîn II بِژين (IFb) = healthy. See **bijûn**[1].

bijîreş بِـژيـرەش *m.* **().** type of wheat with a black awn, also known as ***îtalî*** [T karakılçık buğdayı]. [Qzl/IFb/ZF3] <genim>

bijîşk بِـژيـشك *m.&f.* **().** doctor, physician. {also: bijîjk (IFb/TF); bjîjk (IFb-2); bjîşk (JB3)} {syn: duxtor; ĥekîm; nojdar} <Arm pžišg (W)/bžišk (E) բժիշկ; cf. P pezešk پزشك [K/GF/OK//IFb/TF/ZF3//JB3]

bijlî بِژلى (Zeb) = except for. See **ji bilî**.

bijon بِژۆن (OK/JB1-S) = pure. See **bijûn**[3].

bijû بِژوو (K/B/JJ) = mane. See **bijî I**.

bijûlang بِژوولانگ = eyelashes. See **bijang**.

bijûlank بِژوولانك (Bşk) = eyelashes. See **bijang**.

bijûn بِـــــژوون *adj.* 1) {also: bijîn II (IFb-2)} healthy, healthful, hale and hearty; 2) {syn: t'êrber} rich, fertile, productive *(of land)*: **•Mîr welatekî mezin û fireh, erdekî *bijûn* û dewlemend hebû** (Rnh 3:23, 5) The emir had a *large* and expansive kingdom, [with] fertile and rich land; 3) {also: bijon (OK-2/JB1-S)} pure, clean (OK/JB1-S/Zeb). [Rnh/K/IFb/GF/OK/Zeb//JB1-S]

bi k'ar بـ كــــار: **-bi k'ar anîn** (IFb/GF/TF/OK/RZ) to use, make use of, utilize {syn: 'emilandin; xebitandin}: **•Heval di axaftina xwe de gelek bêjeyên biyanî *bi kar tîne*** (IFb) [Our] friend *uses* many foreign words in his speech **•Ji pêncî carî bêhtir gotina "mist" di şûna gotina "mizdanê" de, bi çewtî *hatiye bikaranîn*** (AW73C2) More than 50 times the word 'mist' *was* incorrectly *used* instead of the word 'mizdan'; **-bi kar hatin** (TF) to be used, be in use. Cf. P be kār bordan بـــه كـــار بردن; Sor be kar hênan به كار هێنان = 'to use' [Wlt/IFb/GF/TF/OK/RZ] <k'ar II>

bikir بِكِر = virgin. See **bik'ur**.

bik'iřçî بِـكِـرچـى *m.* **(-yê;).** customer, buyer: **•Cime't dibe *bikirçîyê* eşyayêd bazirganbaşî** (Ba) The people (public) become *customers* of the caravan leader's wares (=begin to buy his wares). {also: [bekir] بكر (JJ)} [Ba/K/B//JJ] <k'iřîn>

bikul بـ كـول/بِـكـول *adj.* grieved, in distress; wretched, miserable: **•Dilê wî *biqul* [=*bikul*] e** (L) He is upset [lit. 'his heart is *distressed*']; **-bi dilkî bi[k]ul** = with a grieved heart. {also: biqul (confusing **qul** = 'hole' with **kul** = 'grief', according to L)} {syn: belengaz; dêran II; malxirab; řeben I; şerpeze; xwelîser I} < bi = 'in','with' + kul = 'grief' [L/A] <xemgîn>

bik'ur بِــكـــور *adj.* virgin: **-qîza bik'ur** (EP-7) virgin. {also: bakir (K); bakire (SK); bikir; [bakiré باكره/ bikr/bukr بكر] (JJ)} < Ar bikr بكر [EP-7/K//JJ/SK]

bil بِل = except for. See **ji bilî**.

bila بِــلا *conj.* [+ *subj.*] so that, in order that; let, may...: **•*Bela* hakim serê min jêbike** (L) *May* the king chop off my head! **•Bêje bavê xwe, *bira* min bixweze** (J) Tell your father *to* ask for me [in marriage]; **-bila[nî]** (Bw)/**bila be** = OK, all right! So be it!: **•'To ev şeve mêvanê min î.' Derwêşî gotê, '*bila*'** (M-Ak #662) 'Tonight you are my guest.' The dervish said to him, '*So be it*'. {also: bela III (L); bilanî I (Bw-2); bira II (B/J/Ba/Z-1); bra II (EP-7); [bila بلا/bilani بلانى] (JJ); <bila> بلا (HH)} {syn: bona [2]; da II; deqene; ĥeta ko [4]; wekî [2]} = Sor ba با [L//K/A/JB3/JJ/HH/SK/JB1-A&S/OK/Bw//B/J/Ba/Z-1//EP-7]

bilandin بِلاندِن *vt.* **(-bilîn-).** to keep on saying over and over, keep repeating: **•M. li ȟalê xweda got û biland, mîna mervekî ȟeft** [sic] **sala nexweş, *got û biland*** (EP-7) M. kept on repeating it to himself, like a sickly seven[ty]-year-old man, he *kept on repeating* it.{syn: wek'ilandin} [EP-7/K/ZF3]

bilanî I بلانی (Bw/JJ) = so that; let [it be]. See **bila**.

***bilanî II** بـلانـی *adj.* subjunctive, optative: **-řaweya bilanî** (IF/GF) subjunctive mood. {syn: gerane} <bila = 'so that' + -nî = adjectival ending [(neol)IFb/GF/OK] <bila; řawe>

bilbezik بلبەزك (K) = spring flower. See **bilbiz**.

bilbil I بـلـبـل *f./m.(B/F/JB1-A)* **(-a/ ;-ê/).** nightingale, zool. *Luscinia megarhyncos*. {also: [bulbul] بـلـبـل (JJ); <bilbil> بـلـبـل (HH)} Cf. P/Ar bulbul بلبل; T bülbül; Sor bilbil بلبل; Za bilbil *m.* (Mal) [Dy(EW)/F/K/A/IF/B/HH/JB1-A//JJ]

bilbil II بلبل = prattle. See **bile-bil**.

bilbiz بلبز *f.* **().** iris (Xrs); *type of spring flower* (K/JJ); wild tulip (A) {Cf. Ar/P zanbaq زنـبـق}. {also: bilbezik (K); bilbizêk (ZF3); bilbizêq (A/ZF3-2); [bilbezik] بلبزك (JJ)} [Xrs//K/JJ//ZF3//A]

bilbizêk بلبزێك (ZF3) = wild tulip. See **bilbiz**.

bilbizêq بلبزێق (A) = wild tulip. See **bilbiz**.

***bile-bil/bilebil** [B] بلەبل *f.* **(;-ê).** 1) {syn: 'ewte'ewt; kastekast; kute-kut; řeyîn} barking, howling, yelping (F/K); 2) prattle, chatter (B/K). {also: bilbil II; bilebil (B)} [F/K/ZF3//B]

bilet بلەت (Wkt) = ticket. See **bilêt**.

bilez بـلـەز *adj. & adv.* fast, quick(ly), rapid(ly): **•*Bilez* di ber min re derbas bû** (HYma, 29) He *quickly* passed me by. {also: [beléz] بـلـز (JJ)} {syn: lez I; xweş [4]; zû [2]} bi + lez; =Sor xêra خێرا [Hyma/K/A/IFb/FJ/TF/GF/JJ/SK/AD/CS] <lez I>

bilêç بلێچ (RZ/IFb/ZF3) = lightning. See **blêç**.

bilêt بـلـێـت *f.* **(-a;-ê).** ticket (airplane, bus, theater, train, etc.): **•Civîna me di navbera rojên 10 - 17.12. 2016an de ye. Tu dikarî li gor wê *bilêta* xwe bikirî** (Kr) Our meeting is between Dec. 10th and 17th 2016. You can buy your *ticket* according to that **•Heçî pirsa *bilêta* te ya balafirê ye ...** (Kr) As for the question of your airplane *ticket* ... {also: bilet (Wkt-2); bîlet (Wkt-2); bîlêt (Wkt-2)} {syn: *bihêl} <Fr billet; Sor bilît بـلـیـت [Kr/K/B/IFb/FJ/TF/RZ/ZF/BF/Wkt/CS]

bilind بلند *adj.* 1) {syn: berz; quloz; ≠nizm} high, tall: **•ç'iyayên *bilind*** = the *high* mountains; **-bilind bûn** = to rise, go up **•'Erd weke k'axaza cigarê *bilind bûye*** (Ba) The ground *has risen* like (=by the width of) a cigarette paper **•Dû ji kulekê *bilind dibe*** (AB) Smoke *rises* out of a hole; **-bilind kirin** (IFb/OK) to raise, lift: **•Min şivdara xwe *bilind kir* û ser wî da ȟejand** (Ba2:2, 206) I *raised* my staff and waved it at him; 2) loud; 3) *[m.] man's name*. {also: [bilind] بـلـنـد (JJ); <bilind> بـلـنـد (HH)} *Probably a borrowing from* P boland بـلـنـد [Pok. bhereĝh- 140.] 'high'-->*bherĝh-: Skt bṛhant- [bṛhat]; Av bərəzant-; Old P *bṛδant-; Southern Tati dialects: Xoznini beland (Yar-Shater); P boland بلند = 'high' & burz بـرز = 'tallness, stature'; Sor biłind بڵند & berz بەرز = 'high'; Za berz = 'high' (Todd/JJ); Cf. Germ Berg = 'mountain'; see: Haoma §255, p. 139 {bilindahî; bilindayî; bilindî} [K/A/JB3/IFb/B/JJ/HH/SK/GF/TF/OK] See also **berz**.

bilindahî بـلـنـداهـی (Ber/JB3/IFb/OK/ZF3) = highness, tallness. See **bilindayî**.

bilindayî بـلـنـدایـی *f.* **(-ya;-yê).** height, elevation *(lit. & fig.)*; highness, tallness. {also: bilindahî (Ber/JB3/IFb/OK/ZF3); bilindî (BX/IFb-2); [bilindaï] بلنداى (JJ)} Cf. Sor biłindayî بـڵـنـدایـی = 'height (measurement)' & biłindî بـڵـنـدی = 'height, loftiness' [Ber/JB3/IFb/OK/ZF3//K/A/B/TF//JJ//BX] <bilind>

bilindî بـلـنـدی (BX/IFb) = highness, tallness. See **bilindayî**.

bilindp'aye بـلـنـدپـایـە *adj.* of high rank, high-ranking. {also: bilindpayî} [SW/K/ZF3] See also **p'ayebilind**.

bilindpayî بلندپایی = of high rank. See **bilindp'aye**.

biliqandin بلقاندن (Kmc) = to squirt. See **beliqandin I**.

bilî I بـلـی *adj.* [+ *ezafeh*] busy, occupied with: **•Kewên kûvî ... bi dilsafî tev hatin li dorê civîyan û *bilîyê* xwarina lext bûn** (AB, 52) The wild partridges ... naïvely came together and gathered around and were *busy* eating the birdseed; **-biliya canî xwe bûn** (IFb) to be deeply occupied with. {syn: mijûl} [AB/IFb/FJ/CS]

bilî II بلی: -ji bilî = except for. See **ji bilî**.

bilqebilq/bilqe-bilq (K) بـلـقـەبـلـق *f.* **(-a;-ê).** bubbling, gurgling sound, as of soup or stew boiling on the stove: **•Baz dida midbaxê xwarinên ku *pilqe pilqa* wan bû dikeliyan li hev dixist** [sic] (SBx, 8) She hurried to the kitchen, stirred the foods which, with a *bubbling sound*, were boiling **•Bilqe bilqa avê ye** (CS) The water is boiling. {also: pilqe pilq (SBx)} Sor biłqebiłq بڵقەبڵق = 'continued bubbling' [SBx/K/B/IFb/GF/CS/ZF] <beqbeqok> bilûl بلول (B/Bw/OK) = flute. See **bilûr**.

bilûr بـلـوور *f.* **(-a;-ê).** type of flute, shepherd's flute (K/

JJ); kaval, end-blown flute (A/IFb/TF): •**Bilûra min a şîrîn / tu di sariya sibehê / û hingûra êvarê de / hevalê bêhevalan, / destbirayê şivan û dilketiyan î** (Wkt) My sweet *bilûr* / in the cold of the morning / and the evening twilight / you are friend to the friendless / companion of shepherds and the lovelorn •**Çaxa şevînê jî pif dikim *bilûrê*** (AB) Even at the time of the night feeding [of the animals] I blow on my *flute*. {also: bilûl (B-2/Bw/OK-2); blûr (IFb-2); [bilour] بلور (JJ); <bilûr> بلور (HH)} [Pok. 3. bhel- 120.] 'to blow, swell': Sor bilwêr بلوێر [bilör]/bilûr بلوور; cf. also S-Cr frula; Alb fyell; Mod Gr floghera φλογέρα. [AB/F/K/A/IFb/B/JJ/HH/GF/TF/OK//Bw]

bilûrvan بلوورڤان *m.* **(-ê; bilûrvên, vî bilûrvanî).** one who plays the ***bilûr***, piper, flute player: •**Wana gele serhatî û ç'îr̄okêd başqe-başqe zanibûn, ew gişke dengbêj û *bilûrvan* bûn** (Ba2:1, 204) They knew many stories and adventures, they were all storytellers and *flute players*. {also: <bilûrvan> بلورڤان (HH)} [K/IFb/B/HH/GF/TF/OK] <bilûr>

Bilxarî بلخارى (IFb) = Bulgarian. See **Bulgarî**.

bilxem بلخەم (FS) = phlegm. See **belẍem**.

bilxerî بلخەرى (B) = fireplace; chimney. See **pixêrîk**.

bilẍem بلغەم (FS) = phlegm. See **belẍem**.

bilyan بليان *adj.* knowing, aware, knowledgeable, informed: •**'Emrî ser wezîrê xwe Arvan kir, wê şûnda gazî merivê xwe û *blyan kir*** (EH) He ordered his minister Arvan to summon [lit. 'he would summon'] his men afterward and *inform them*. {also: bîlan (F); bîlyan (B); blyan (EH)} Cf. T bilen, *present active participle of* bilmek = 'to know' [EH//K//F//B]

bimbarek بمبارەك *adj.* blessed: **-bimbarek bûn** = to be blessed: •**Hûn ji hev re *bimbarek* bin!** (L) May you be *blessed* together! (said to a couple about to be wed), i.e, Congratulations! {syn: pîroz} < Ar mubārak مبارك [L/K/B]

bimbarekî بمبارەكى *f.* **(-ya;-yê)**: congratulations; **-bimbarekîya desta** (XF) wrestling {also: deste-bimbarekî (Z-1)} {syn: gulaş; pijan I}: •**Em destebimbarekîyê bêne hev** (Z-1) Let's wrestle with each other. [XF/Z-1/B]

bin I بن *m.* **(-ê ;).** foundation, bottom; base: •**Wexta bira ew avîtne** [sic] ***binê* bîrê** (BX) When the brothers threw him to *the bottom of* the well •***binê* dişta** (L) *the bottom of* the cauldrons; **-binê beroşê** (Qmş) (burnt) rice at bottom of the pot *(considered a delicacy)* {syn: ver̄enk}. {also: [byn] بن (JJ)} [BX/K/A/JB3/JJ/SK]

bin II بن *prep.* below, under, beneath: •**Lawik kete *bin* textekî** (L) The boy slid *under* a bed •**Mele kefe dike û tîne, dixe *bin* erdê** (L) The mollah enshrouds [the corpse] and brings it, buries it [lit. 'puts it *under* ground'];

-di bin ... da/de = under, below *(no motion)*: •**Hespê min *di bin* min *de* hate kuştin** (BX) My horse was killed *from under* me (i.e., while I was riding him) •**Kirsî *di bin* masê *de* ye** (BX) The chair is *under* the table •**Sed gund *di bin* destê wî *de* bûn** (BX) 100 villages were *under* his control [lit. 'hand'];

-di bin ... ra/re = downward, below, under *(motion toward)*: •**Malên xelkê delal danî bûn *di bin* malên me *re*** (BX) They set up the tents of the beloved's tribe *below* our tents •***Di bin* çavan *re* li min dinêre** (BX) He looks at me askance [lit. '*under* the eyes'];

-ji bin = from below, from under: •**Destê xwe *ji bin* kulavê xwe derîne** (BX) Take your hand *out from under* your felt [coat];

-ji bin ... de = do.;

-ji bin ... ve = underneath *(motion through)*: •**Jin *bin* pirê *ve* derbas bû** (BX) He passed *under[neath]* the bridge;

-li bin = under, beneath *(motion toward)*: •**Were *li bin* darê rûne** (BX) Come sit *beneath* the tree. {also: binîya; [byn] بن (JJ); <bin> بن (HH)} [L/BX/K/A/JB3/B/JJ/HH/SK]

binalî بنالى (F) = native. See **binelî**.

binam بنام *m.&f.* **().** cousin of the second, third, fourth, etc. degree *(as opposed to **pismam** & **dotmam**, which denote first cousins)*: •**Em *binamêt* êk în** (Bw) We are [second, etc.] *cousins*. <Ar ibn 'amm ابن عمّ = 'son of the paternal uncle, [paternal first] cousin' [Bw] <dotmam; pismam>

binas بناس *pl.* fault: •***Binasêt* wî bûn** (Bw) It was his *fault*. {also: [benase] بناسه (JJ-G)} {syn: sûc; t'awan I} <[Pok. nek̂- 762.] 'death': Skt nāśa- *m.* = 'loss, disappearance, destruction'; O Ir *nās- = 'to get lost; to be destroyed' --> *wi-nāsa- = 'corruption, ruination': Av vī-nās-; O P vi- + nay- = 'injure, harm' (Kent); P gonāh گناه = 'sin, fault'; also Arm vnas վնաս = 'harm'; Cf. also Lat nex, necis = 'death' & noceo, nocere = 'to harm'; Gr nekros νεκρός/nekys νέκυς = 'corpse'. The P form has entered K as **gune**[**h**] (qv.), with the meaning of 'sin'; M. Schwartz: **binas** is the ideal K form, while **gonāh** is the ideal P form. [Bw/Zeb/Elk//JJ-G] <gune I & II; sûc>

binat'ar بِنـاتـار *f.* **(-a;-ê).** 1) low place, depression; lower part of stg., bottom: •**Bizinek *binat'ara* bizinekêda av ne xar** (Dz) One goat would not drink water *at a lower point* than another goat [lit. 'in a goat's lower point']; 2) {syn: bingeh; binî; esas; ȟîm; şengiste} base, basis, fundament, foundation; 3) foot *(of mountain)*: •**Ji wan cewika hinek *binet'ara* ç'îyê digihîştne hev** (Ba2:1, 202) Some of those brooks merged [lit. 'reached each other'] at *the foot of* the mountain. {also: binet'ar (B); [benatar] بناطار (JJ)} Sor bineřet بِنەڕەت [Dz/F/K//JJ//B] <şengiste>

bin av بِن ئاڤ/**binav** بِناڤ: **-binav bûn** (JB3/IF/BX) to sink, drown *(vi.)*; to dip, plunge, immerse, submerge *(vi.)*; to dive {syn: noq bûn; nuqim bûn}; **-binav kirin** (JB3/IF)/**binavî I** ~ (K) to sink, drown *(vt.)*; to dip, plunge, immerse, submerge *(vt.)*: •**Noqavên me hinde zehf gemiyên Japonî ên bar û banzînkêş *bin av kirine* ko**… (RN) Our submarines *have sunk* so many Japanese freight ships and tankers that… [RN/JB3/IF/BX//K] <noq I; nuqim>

binavî I بِناڤى. See **bin av**.

binavî II بِناڤى (FS) = willow; ash tree; evergreen oak. See **benav**.

binav û deng بِناڤ و دەنگ/**binavûdeng** [A/IFb] بِناڤوودەنگ *adj.* famous, prominent, well known. {syn: berbiçav I; navdar} =Sor be nawbang بەناوبانگ [BX/GF//A/IFb]

bi nav û nîşan بِ ناڤ و نيشان *adj.* with fine markings *(of horse)*: •**K'îja k'iȟêlêd *bi nav û nîşan* wana anîne cem Memê** (Z-1) No matter which *fine* bay horses they brought out for Mem …. [Z-1]

binax بِن ئاخ/بِناخ *adj.* underground: **-binax kirin** (K/Wlt) to bury, inter {syn: veşartin [2]}: •**Cenazê gerîla Abdulselam Kisaer li gundê wî Kullika Tekmanê ku girêdayî Erzeromê ye, bi beşdariya girseyeke gel *hate binaxkirin*** (Wlt 2:66, 3) The body of the guerrilla Abdulselam Kısaer *was interred* in his village Kullik, Tekman, in the province of Erzurum, accompanied by [lit. 'with the participation of'] a crowd of people •**Te çend ji birayên xwe bi destên xwe binax kiribûn?** (Wlt 2:73, 14) How many of your brothers have you buried with your own hands? {syn: bin'erd} <bin = 'under' + ax = 'dirt, earth' [Wlt/K]

bincek بِنجەك (HCK) = armpit. See **binç'eng**.

binçav بِنچاڤ *adv. & adj.* under (house) arrest; in custody: •**Di sala 1981'ê de di sîhê meha Îlonê de dijmin ez xistim *binçav*** (Wlt 2:66, 2) In 1981, on the thirtieth of September, the enemy *arrested* me; **-binçav kirin** (Wlt/TF) to arrest, take into custody, detain: •**Di meha Mijdarê de hinek hevalên min *hatin binçavkirin* û li wan îşkence hatibû kirin** (Wlt 2:66, 2) In November some of my friends *were arrested* and tortured. {Cf. T gözaltı = '(house) arrest' [lit. 'under the eye'} [Wlt/TF]

binç'eng بِنچەنگ *f.* **(-a;-ê).** armpit, axilla: •**Rabû t'akî barê deva xwe danî vê *binceka* xwe, t'aê mayîn jî da *binceka* xwe mayîn** (HCK-2, 84) He put one of his camel loads *under one arm*, and put the other load *under* the other *arm* •**Xort girt mî daêda, dîkê xwe da *biç'enga* xwe** (HCK-4, #1, 31) The young man picked up the sheep and gave it to him, and put his rooster under his arm [lit. '*armpit*']. {also: biçeng (F); bincek (HCK); [byn tchenk] بن چنك (JJ)} {syn: k'efş I} Za binçeng m. (Mal); =Sor binbaxeł بِنباخەڵ/bin[h]engił بِنهەنگِڵ [K/A/JB3/IFb/B/GF/OK//JJ//F/HCK]

bindarûk بِنداروك *f.* **(;-ê).** 1) shade, shady place *(under the trees)* (K); 2) place *(generally in the shade of trees)* where girls gather to stroll and play (B/EP-5); awning under which girls gather to play (K): •**Leylê, em hatine *bindarûkê*** (EP-5, #16) Leyla, we have come to stroll *under the trees*; 3) summer festival celebrated by nomadic girls (B). [EP-5/K/B] <zinar [2]>

bindeq بِندەق *f.* **(;-ê).** hazelnut, filbert, bot. *Corylus avellana*: **-dara bindeqê** (IFb) filbert tree, hazelnut tree. {also: bindiq (K-2); findeq (K-2/IFb-2/B/OK-2/CB-2); findiq (GF/Kmc-2-2); [byndiq بندق/findík فندق] (JJ); <bindeq> بندق (HH)} Mid P pondik (M3) --> Ar bunduq بندق; P fondeq/fandoq فندق & bondoq بندق--> T fındık; Sor findiq فِندِق [Dh/Zeb/AA/Kmc-2/CB/K/A/IFb/HH/TF/OK// JJ//B//GF]

bindest بِندەست *adj.* 1) subordinate, under the command of; subject to, dependent on; 2) submissive, obedient; 3) oppressed; 4) *[m.]* prisoner; slave. {bindestî} < bin = 'under' + dest = 'hand' [K/A/JB3/IFb/ZF3/Wkt/G/BF/FD/FS/Kmc]

bindestî بِندەستى *f.* **(-ya;-yê).** 1) subordination, subjection: •**Li Tirkiyê û Îraqê û Sûriyê û Îranê sitemkarî û *bindestiya* dirêj hîştiye ko takekesê**

kurd ji xwe aciz bibe (nefel 20.viii.2008) In Turkey, Iraq, Syria, and Iran long standing oppression and *subordination* has let the Kurdish individual be dissatisfied with himself; 2) dependence; 3) submission, obedience; 4) bondage, slavery; 5) subordinate; slave (B). [K/JB3/IFb/B/BF/FD/FS] <bindest>

bindiq بندِق (K) = hazelnut. See **bindeq**.

binecih بنەجِه (ZF) = original inhabitant. See **binecî**.

binecî بِنەجی *m.* **(-yê;).** native, original inhabitant: **•*Binecihêd* wî yên berê niha hatine deşta Araratê** (X. Çaçan. Benê min qetiya, 21) Its former *inhabitants* have now come to the plain of Ararat. {also: binecih (ZF)} {syn: binelî; xwecihî} [F/K/GF/ /ZF] <akincî>

binefş بِنەفش *f.* **(-a;-ê).** violet, bot. *Viola odorata.* {also: benefş (K-2/IFb-2/GF-2); benefşe (A-2/F); binevş (B); [benewch] بنفش (JJ); <binefş> بنفش (HH)} Cf. P benefše بنفشه; Sor benewşe بەنەوشە/binewşe بِنەوشە/wenewşe وەنەوشە; Hau wenewşe *m.* (M4); T menekşe + benevşe [Erciş-Van] & benövşe [Iğdır-Kars] & benöyşe [Taşburun, Iğdır-Kars] (DS, v. 2, p. 628); Arm manušag [W]/manušak [E] մանուշակ [K/A/IFb/HH/GF/TF/OK//B//F//JJ]

binefşî بنەفشی *adj.* purple, violet. {also: benefşî (IFb/GF); benefşîn (IFb-2); binevşî (Kmc-2); <binefşî> بنفشی (HH)} {syn: erxewanî; mor I; şîrkî} Sor binewşeyî بنەوشەیی [Kmc-2//HH/OK/RZ//IFb/GF] <xemrî>

binelik' بنەلك (B) = native. See **binelî**.

binelî بِنەلی *m.* **(-yê;).** 1) {syn: binecî; xwecihî} native, aborigine, original inhabitant: **•Kurmancekî *binelîyê* wê gelekî ‘eyane** (K2-Fêrîk) [There is] a Kurd who is *a native of* that place who is very prominent; 2) population (B). {also: binalî (F); binelik' (B-2)} [K2-Fêrîk/B//F] <akincî; niştecih>

binemal بِنەمال *f.* **(-a;-ê).** family, lineage, line, house: **•Di dawiyê de jiyana Çîlê ... bû mijara lêkolîneke *binemalê* û secerê** (Nbh 132:16) In the end the life of Ch. ... became the subject of an investigation of the *lineage* and family tree **•Ez *binemala* Ĥacî Mustefa me** (Bw) I am from *the house of* Hajji Mustafa. {syn: berek; îcax} Sor binemał[e] بنەماڵە = ‘aristocratic stock, house, family, dynasty’ [Bw/K(s)/(IFb)/OK/RZ] <azbat; ‘eşîret; mal; malbat; ocax[4]; qebîle; ṯayfe>

binerdik بِنەردك (IFb/GF/FJ) = turnip; potato. See **bin‘erdk**.

binerdî بِنەردی (OK) = potato. See **bin‘erdk**.

bin‘erd بِنعەرد *adj.* underground, subterranean: **•r̄êke bin‘erd** (Z-1) an underground paşage, tunnel. {syn: binax} < bin = ‘under’ + ‘erd = ‘earth’ [Z-1/K/A/B/BK/HH//JJ] <k’ar̄êz>

bin‘erdk بِنعەردك *f.* **().** 1) {also: binerdik (IFb); <bin‘erd> بنعرد (HH)} {syn: şêlim} turnip, bot. *Brassica rapa* (Frq/Qzl/IFb/HH); 2) {also: binerdik (GF/FJ); binerdî (OK); <bin‘erd> بنعرد (HH)} {syn: k’artol} potato (JJ/GF/FJ). {also: binerdik (IFb/GF); [byn-ard] بنارض (JJ); <bin‘erd> بنعرد (HH)} [Frq/Qzl//IFb/GF/FJ//JJ//OK]

binerx بِنەرخ/**bi nerx** بِ نەرخ *adj.* 1) {syn: bi qîmet; xas} precious, valuable, worth(y): **•Gelek beyt û dastanêd kurdî yêd hêja û *bi nerx* hene** (K-dş) There are many valuable and *precious* Kurdish romances and stories; 2) expensive, costly, dear. [K-dş/A/JB3] <nerx>

binet’ar بِنەتار (B) = lower part, bottom; foundation. See **binat’ar**.

binevş بنەڤش (B) = violet. See **binefş**.

binevşî بنەڤشی (Kmc-2) = purple. See **binefşî**.

binête‘tî بنێتەعتی *m.* **().** yellow, sweet grape, elliptical in shape [Ar banātī بناتی]. {also: binêteĥtî (Msr-2); bintatî (IFb); <bintatî> بنتاتی (HH)} [Msr//IF/HH] <tirî>

binêteĥtî بنەتەحتی (Msr) = type of grape. See **binête‘tî**.

binga بِنگا = foundation. See **bingeh**.

binge بِنگە (F/K/B) = foundation. See **bingeh**.

bingeh بِنگەه *f.* **(-a;-ê).** 1) {syn: binat’ar [2]; binî; esas; ĥîm; şengiste} foundation, basis, base; 2) bottom *(of the sea)* (B); 3) root, stem *(of tree)* (B). {also: binga (HB/A); binge (F/K/B-2); [binghé] بنگه (JJ)} Sor binge بِنگە = ‘base’ [JB3/IFb/B/GF/TF//HB/A//F/K/JJ]

bingehîn بِنگەهین *adj.* basic, fundamental: **•Herçiqas av ji bo hemû jîndaran çavkaniyeke *bingehîn* be jî, îro di destê mirovên “hemdem” de wek pergaleke ji holê rakirina berhemên dîrokê tê bi kar anîn** (Wlt 1:21, 16) Although water is a *basic* resource for all living things, today it is being used by "modern" man as an instrument for destroying historical artifacts. {syn: ĥîmlî} [(neol.)Wlt/K/IFb] <bingeh>

***binhemban** بِنهەمبان *m.&f.* **().** youngest child, last-born child, baby of the family. {syn: paşlandik} [Wn]

binî بِنی *f.* **(-ya;).** 1) bottom, lower part; 2) {syn: binat'ar [2]; bingeh; esas; ĥîm; şengiste} base, basis, foundation, fundament; 3) *stable *(for* *animals)* (JB3). {also: [beni] بنى (JJ)} [Ba2/K/A/JB3/B/ ZF3//JJ]

binîa بنيا = under. See **binîya**.

bin'în بنعين (Twn) = unripe almond. See **nîv'în**.

binîya بنيا *prep.* below, under: **•binîa gund** (Ba2) below the village. {also: binîa} {syn: bin II} <ezafeh of **binî**> [Ba2/K/ZF3]

binmilk بنملك *m.* **(-ê;-î).** crutch: **•*Binmilkê* min bide min** (Elk) Give me my *crutch* **•Ew bi *binmilkî* bi rê diçit** (FS) He walks with *a crutch.* {syn: *golte (Dh)} [Elk/Wkt/FS]

binoşk بنۆشك (Zeb) = terebinth. See **bêmk**.

binp'ê بنپێ (B) = step; sole; foot. See **binp'î**.

***binp'î** بنپى *f.* **(-ya;-yê).** 1) step, footboard; 2) sole *(of foot or boot)*; 3) foot *(of inanimate object, e.g., mountain)*; foot of bed: **•Gund *binp'ia* ç'îakîda** (Ba2) The village [was] *at the foot of* a mountain; 4) *prop, support; 5) *floor (of room). {also: binp'ê (B-2)} [Ba2/K/B]

binrax بنراخ (FJ/ZF/Kmc) = mattress. See **binr̄ex**.

binr̄ex بنرەخ *f.* **(-a;-ê).** small, thin mattress for sitting: **•Berseriya minê kevir e / *binrexa* minê 'erd e** (FS) My pillow is a rock / my *mattress* is the ground [song by Ḧeseno Bişar] **•Liser *binrexê* xwe dirêj kir** (BF) S/he stretched out on *the mattress.* {also: binrax (FJ/ZF/Kmc)} {syn: *bincî; cil III; doşek; mitêl; nehlîk} [BF/IFb/RZ/Wkt/FS/CS//FJ/ZF/Kmc]

bintatî بنتاتى (IFb/HH) = type of grape. See **binête'tî.**

Binxet بنخەت *f.* **(-a;-ê).** Syrian Kurdistan, which lies "below the line" (referring to the railroad which forms the border between Turkey and Syria): **•Piştî 2 salan Cemîl û Xezna hevdu revandin û daketin *binxeta* Surî** (www.Zozan.com) After 2 years Jemil and Khezna eloped and went down to Syria (descended *below the line of* Syria) **•Rojavaya Kurdistanê, Başûrê Rojavaya Kurdistanê, Başûrê Biçûk an jî *Binxetê*, navê perçeya Kurdistanê ye ku dikeve nav sînorên Sûriyê** (Wkp) West Kurdistan, Southwest Kurdistan, The Little South or *Below the Line*, the name of the part of Kurdistan that lies within the borders of Syria **•Şervanên Kurdan ji bo ku xwe ji teqîbata dewleta Tirkan xilas bikin diçin *Binxetê*** (Nbh 132:13) In order to free themselves from being pursued by the Turkish state, Kurdish fighters go *below the line* (=to Syria). [Nbh/Wkp/www.Zozan.com] <Serxet>

bi'ok بعۆك *(HH)*/**biok** بئۆك *(HB/RZ) adj.* 1) {syn: k'irêt; sik I} ugly, disgusting *(person)* (HB); 2) {syn: ç'epel; dijûn II; gemarî; mirdar; p'îs; qilêr; qir̄êj} dirty (IFb/CS). {also: beok (IFb/CS); bok (HB-2); <bi'ok> بعوك (HH)} Cf. T bok = 'excrement' [HB/RZ//HH//IFb/CS//RZ] <bihuk>

bi qîmet ب قيمەت *adj.* valuable, precious: **•Ewî t'irê, tiştekî *bi qîmet* undakirîye** (Z-1) It seemed to him that he had lost something *precious.* {syn: binerx; xas} [Z-1/ZF3]

biqul ب قول = sad. See **bikul**.

bir̄ I بر *m./f.* **(-ê/-a; /-ê).** 1) side *(of record, tape, etc.)*; 2) {syn: beş I; deq [6]} part; 3) {syn: cêrge; grûb; k'om II} group *(of people)*: **•*birek* şivan û gavanan** (Ardû, 28) *a group of* shepherds and cowherds **•Dîsa *birek* jin, keç û bûkên salê li cem Zêrê kom bûbûn** (DBgb, 8) Again *a group of* women, girls and brides of one year had gathered at Z.'s house **•Herçî ez û *birekî* wezîrên min em mêldarên elemanan in. Herçî ez û *birekî* wezîrên min ên din, em mêldariya sondxwariyan dikin** (Ronahî) As for me and *one group of* my ministers, we support the Germans. As for me and *a group of* my other ministers [=another group of my ministers], we are in favor of the Allies [punchline of a joke]; 4) side, team, faction *(in a game, argument)*: **•Du *birr* dilîzin** (Kmc-27, 4) Two *teams* play **•Qederê şeş hewy, belkî zêdetir, weto ma. Paşî milletê kurd di Istembolêda do *bir* bo** (SK 53:571) For 6 months, maybe more, it stayed that way. Afterwards, the Kurdish people in Istanbul became two *sides*; 5) *[m.(FK-kk-2)/f.(Hk) (-ê/-a;).]* {syn: col} part of a flock or herd of sheep (B), *smaller than a **kerî II*** (Hk): **•Kerr rabû syar bû hespê, çû, *bir̄ekî* devayê çûr̄, te'zî qewrand** (FK-kk-2) Kerr mounted his horse, and went and routed *a group of* reddish, bare camels; 6) flock *(of chickens)*: **•Kerê xwe li ber deriyê Hecî Sadûn dît ku di nav *birrek* mirîşkên qelew de ye** (HYma, 45) He saw his donkey in front of Haji Sadun's door, which [donkey] was amid *a flock of* plump chickens. [K/B/A/JB3/B/IFb/GF/SK/Hk]

bir̄ II بر *f.* **(;-ê).** *name of a game:* 1) men's game with two teams: the object is to move from one side to the other (Msr); children's game with two teams, in which the defensive team tries to prevent the members of the offensive team from crossing over a line (K); 2) a children's game similar to tag [Rus piatnaški пятнашки] (B). Cf. Za birr *m.* = 'a game played with two groups who run' *also known as* ***çirr*** (Mal) [Msr/K/B]

bira I بـــــرا *m.* **(birayê/birê; birê, vî birayî).** brother: **•Hûn ... miqatî *birê* xwe bin** (Ba) You take care of your *brother*. {also: bra I (JB3/IF-2); brang (EP); [bera] بـرا (JJ); <bira> بـرا (HH)} {syn: kek} [Pok. bhrāter- 163.] 'brother': Skt bhrātṛ [bhrātā] *m.*; O P brātar- (*nom.* brātā); MidP brād *nom.* (brādar *obl.*); P barādar بـرادر; Sor bira بِـرا; Za bira *nom.* (birar *obl.*) *m.* (Todd); Hau bira *m.* (M4); cf. also Arm ełbayr եղբայր; Lat frater; Rus brat брат {biratî I; bratî I} [F/K/A/IF/B/SK//EP//JB3//JJ] <kek; xûşk>

bira II بِرا = so that, in order that. See **bila**.

biȓa III بِـرا/**bira** بِـرا [A] *adj.* 1) {syn: ȓast} true, real, genuine (Msr); 2) {syn: ȓast} right, correct (A): **•Welle, ez bi mesela Guȓî ne ȟesîyame, eger, *biȓa*, Guȓî ko ha be, welle, Guȓî hew pêva li mala min nan û av nexar** (Z-4) By God, I have not heard about this matter with Guri (=Mangyhead), [but] if [it is] *true* that Guri is like that, then he will never again eat bread and water in my house (=I will kick him out). {also: bȓa II (Msr)} <*shortened form of **bi ȓast*** [Msr//A//Z-4]

birajin بِرازِن *m.* **().** brother-in-law, wife's brother. {syn: bûra; xizm [3]} < bira = 'brother' + jin = 'woman, wife' [K/A/ZF3] <t'î II>

birajtin بِراژتِن (-biraj-) (K/OK) = to roast. See **biraştin**.

birakujî بِـــراكـــوژى *f.* **(-ya;-yê).** fratricide, killing of one's *(lit. & fig.)* brothers: **-şeȓê birakujîyê** (Wlt) fratricidal war, civil war. <bira = 'brother' + kuj- (<kuştin) = 'kill' [Wlt/K/IFb/OK/ZF3]

biraştin بِـراشـتِـن *vt.* **(-biraj-/-birêj-**[JB3/M/SK/OK]**/-brêş-**[IF]**).** to roast, grill, cook. {also: bijartin II (M-2/A/HB); birajtin (K/OK-2); braştin (IFb-2/GF); [berichtin بـرشـتـين/brāzhtin (Rh)] (JJ)} {syn: qelandin [1]} [Pok. 6. bher- 137.] *esp.* I. bhereĝ- 'to roast, bake, cook': O Ir *braig- (Tsb 40): MidP brištan (brēž) = 'to roast' (M3); Baluchi brējag/ brǰag; P bereštan بـرشـتـن = 'to roast'; Sor birjan بـرژان ; SoK bırš(ı)n-/bıršân(d)- (Fat 412) [M/JB3/IFb/SK/TF/OK//K//A/HB//JJ] <patin/pijîn; pijandin>

biratî I بِـــــراتـــــى *f.* **(-ya;-yê).** brotherhood: **•Ew** [**=Theofîlos**] **bû sembola *biratiya* kurd û yewnanan** (WM 1:4, 16) He [=Theophilos] was the symbol of Kurdish and Greek *brotherhood*. {also: bratî I (JB3)} [K/A/IF/B//JB3] <bira I>

***biȓatî II** بِـــراتـــى *f.* **(;-yê).** truth, reality; genuineness, authenticity. {also: bȓatî II (Msr)} [Msr] <biȓa III>

biraz بِراز, m. (; birêz) (B) = nephew. See **brazî**.

biraza بِرازا (K) = nephew or niece. See **brazî**.

birazî بِرازى (A/IF) = nephew or niece. See **brazî**.

biȓbiȓ بِـرِبِـر/**birbir** بـربـر [FJ/CS] *f.* **(-a;-ê).** 1) {syn: baȓebaȓ; *carecar; hengame; hêwirze; hoqeboq; qareqar; qerebalix; qîȓeqîȓ} shouting, screaming; din, clamor, uproar: **•Bi *birebira* dengê eskerê li ber deriyê nîzamiyê** (SBx, 12) With *the shouting of* the soldier's voice at the main gate **•Çi *biȓbiȓa* te ye dîsa?** (Qzl) What are you *shouting* about again? **•Li ser kê dikî *biȓbiȓ*?** (Qzl) Who are you *screaming* about?; 2) *sound of a billy goat desirous of mating* (FJ). {also: birebir (SBx/ZF)} [Qzl/FJ/CS//SBx/ZF]

birc بِــــــرج *f.* **(-a;-ê).** 1) tower; 2) {syn: kela} castle, fortress, bastion: **•Siwarekî birîndar, rimh û şûrê wî şikestî bi ẍar hati bû û li ber deriyê *bircê* sekinî bû** (Rnh 3:23, 5) A wounded horseman, his spear and sword broken, came galloping up and stopped before the gate of *the castle*; **-Birca Belek** (EP-7) The famous castle in Jezira Bohtan in which Zîn lived, in the romance of Mem û Zîn; 3) (any) sign of the zodiac, horoscope (K/A/JJ): **•Li rûpela fala we, *birca* cêwîyan dixwînim** (LC, 8) On the Your Luck page, I read the gemini *horoscope*. {also: birç (A); burc (JB3); [bourdj] بـرج (JJ)} < Ar burj بــرج = 'tower; castle; sign of the zodiac' [EP/F/K/IFb/B/JB1-S/ GF/TF/OK//A//JB3//JJ]

birç بِرچ (A) = tower; zodiac sign. See **birc**.

birçî بِــــرچــــى *adj.* hungry: **•Nan û pîvaz xwarina *birçîyan* e** (AB) Bread and onions are [lit. 'is'] the food *of the hungry*; **-t'î-birçî** (J) hungry and thirsty. {also: berçî (HB); birsî (MK/SK/JB1-A/Bw); [birtchi] بـرچـى (JJ); <birçî بـرچـى/birsî بـرسـى> (HH)} Cf. P gorosne گرسنه/gošne گشنه = 'hungry' & بـرهـنـه barahne = 'naked'; Sor birsî بِـرسـى; Za veyşan (Todd) {birçîtî} [F/K/A/JB3/IFb/B/JJ/HH/GF//HB/ /MK/SK/JB1-A/Bw] <t'î III>

birçîbûn بِرچيبوون (F) = hunger. See **birçîtî**.

birçîna [**ȓa**] بِـرچـيـنـا[را]: [dying] of hunger; out of hunger; **-ji birçînan** (ZF3) do. {syn: ji nêza} [K//ZF3]

birçîtî بِرچيتى *f.* **(-ya;-yê).** hunger. {also: birçîbûn (F); [birtchiti بِرچيتى/ bersiti بِرسيتى] (JJ)} {syn: nêz I; xela} Sor birsîyetî بِرسييەتى/birsêtî بِرسێتى [K/A/JB3/IF/JJ/B/ZF3//F] <birçî; t'în II>

birebir بِرەبِر (SBx/ZF) = shouting, clamor. See **biȓbiȓ**.

biȓek بِـــرەك *f.* **(-a;-ê).** saw *(cutting tool)*. {also: [byrk بـرك/berek بـرك] (JJ); <biȓek> بـرّك (HH)} {syn:

mişar II} [HB/K/A/JB3/IFb/B/HH/GF/Wn/Bt/Erh/FS/BF//JJ]

bireser بِـــــــرەســـەر *f.* **(-a;-ê).** object, direct object *(grammar)*: **•Di kurdî de hevok, li ser sê hêmanên bingehîn, kirde, *bireser* û lêkerê, tên sazkirin** (Amîda Kurd) In Kurdish, sentences are founded on 3 elements, subject, *object*, and verb. Cf. Ar maf'ūl bihi مـفـعـول بـه = 'object of a verb phrase'; cf. Sor birdine ser بـردنـه سـەر = 'to carry out, achieve' [(neol)TaRK/Wkt/ZF3] <kirde>

birêm برێم (Zeb-->Ak) = small lake. See **bêrm**.

birêvabirin بِرێڤابِرن (AD) = to conduct, run. See **bi r̄ê ve birin**.

birêveber برێڤەبەر (Wkt) = director. See **r̄êvebir**.

bi r̄ê ve birin ب ڕێـــڤـــە بِـــرن *vt.* **(bi r̄ê ve -b-).** to conduct, manage, carry out, direct, perform, run *(vt.)*. {also: birêvabirin (AD); rêvebirin (IFb)} {syn: meşandin} Sor be r̄êwe birdin بە ڕێوە بردن = 'to manage' [Zeb/Dh/TF//AD//IFb] <r̄êvebir>

bi r̄ê ve çûn ب ڕێـڤـە چـوون *vi.* **(bi r̄ê ve -ç-).** 1) {syn: meşîn} to walk, go: **•Pîrejinek di kûçeke Londrê de *bi rê ve diçû*** (Ronahî) An old woman *was walking* in a London street; 2) *[f.]* walk, stroll, gait. {also: r̄êveçûn (K); r̄êvaçûyîn (B); [bréhva/rehva cióum] بـريـهـوه (JJ)} Sor be r̄êwe çûn بە ڕێوە چوون = 'to go along, live, get along (with)' [Bw/TF/OK//JJ//K//B]

bir̄êz بـرێـز/ب ڕێـز *adj.* 1) {syn: qedirgiran; r̄êzdar II} honorable, respected; 2) Mr., Mister *(as title)*. {also: berêz (Ber/K/JB3)} Sor ber̄êz بـەڕێـز (K2)/ ber̄îz بەڕیز (W&E) [IFb/GF/TF//Ber/K/JB3] <r̄êz II>

birh I برە (K/HH/Erh) = eyebrow. See **birû**.

birh II برە (IFb/GF/CS/HH) = power, force. See **birî**.

birhan بِـــرهـــان (-birhê-) (M-Zx) = to stop *(vi.)*. See **biryan**.

birih بِرِه = eyebrow. See **birû**.

bi rijd ب رِژد (Rûdaw) = insistent. See **r̄ijd**.

birin بِـــرن *vt.* **(-b-/-be-[M-Ak]/-v- [Dz]).** 1) to carry, bring, take *(away from the speaker)*: **•*Bir* ber tatê** (L) *[He] brought/took* [her] to/before the rock **•R̄okê k'ete pêşya bizinê xwe, *bir* ser kanyê avde** (Dz) One day *he lead* his goats to a spring to water them; **-Birin-anîn** = to deal in, buy and sell: **•Mast li Cizîra Bota *dibir û danî*** (Z-2) *She bought and sold* yoghurt in Jizîra Bota; **-hev birin-anîn** (XF): a) to be entangled, mixed up, confused; to deliberate: **•Al-p'aşa û giregirava gelekî hev *birin-anîn*** (Z-1) Al pasha and his men *deliberated* (or were confused); b) to spread *(vi.)*, carry *(of sounds)*; **-şik birin** = to doubt: **•Jin *şikê dibe ser* wî** (Ba) The woman [his wife] *doubts* him; 2) to carry off, kidnap: **•*Te* karê min *birine*?** (J) *Did you take* my kids [=baby goats]?; 3) [**+ji**] {≠ derdan; dor̄andin} to win *(at a game)*, to beat, defeat s.o. (XF/Z-1): **•Qirara wana sê car bûn, k'ê *ji* k'ê *bibira*, wê gilîyê xwe bikira** (Z-1) They decided to play three games, and whoever *won*, would get his wish **•Memo du cara *ji* mîr *bir*** (Z-1) M. *beat* the prince twice [at chess]. {also: [birin] بـــريـــن (JJ); <birin برن (dibe) (دبه)> (HH)} [Pok.1. bher- 128.] 'to carry, to bear children': Skt √bhṛ [I. bharati/III. bíbharti/II. bhárti]; O Ir *bar- (Tsb 38): Av & O P bar- (pres. bara-) = 'to carry, bring'; MidP burdan (bar-) = 'to carry, bear, take, endure' & appurdan (appar-) = 'to steal' (M3); P bordan بـــردن (-bar-) (بر); Sor birdin بِردِن (-be-: 3rd pers. sing. -ba[t]); SoK ba-/bırd- (Fat 412); Za benã [berdiş] *vt.* (Todd); Hau berdey (ber-) *vt.* (M4) {Cf. T götürmek} cf. also Arm berel (E)/perel (W) բերել = 'to bring (toward the speaker)'; Lat ferō, ferre = 'to carry, bear'; Gr fer(n)ō φέρ(ν)ω; Rus brat' брать (ber-) (бер-) = 'to take' [K/A/JB3/IF/JJ/B/SK/M/XF] <anîn>

birinc I بِـــرنـــج *m.(Kmc-6)/f.(OK/RF)* **(-ê/-a; -î/-ê).** *(cooked)* rice: **•Têr goşt û *birincê* dixwin** (ZZ-10, 157) They eat their fill of meat and *rice* **•*Birinca* Qerejdaxê jî li ser navê Amedê bi fermî hate tomarkirin** (Rûdaw 15.iv.2018) *The rice of* Qerejdax [Karacadağ] has officially also been registered under the name of Diyarbakir. {also: birinç (A); brinc (HCK); [birindj] بـرنـج (JJ); <birinc> بـرنـج (HH)} {syn: p'elaw} Cf. Skt vrīhí- = 'rice'; O Ir *vrinǰi-/*vriži-? (Hübsch #208); Av *verenǰa-; O P *vrinǰi-; Semnani varinǰ; Ossetic brinǰ; Baluchi brinǰ; P berenj بـرنـج/gurinj گـرنـج (Horn #208 & Hübsch); T pirinç; Sor birinc بـــــرنـــج = 'rice (husked)'; Za birinc *m.* (Mal); cf. also Arm brinj բրինձ [L/K/JB3/IFb/B/JJ/HH/JB1-S/SK/GF/TF/OK/RF/Kmc-6/G//HCK//A] <belim; ç'eltûk; dohîn; p'ûşk; tûşk>

birinc II برنج *m.* **(; -î/-ê).** brass, bronze, copper. {also: birinç (A); [birindj] بـرنـج (JJ)} Cf. P berenj برنج; T pirinç; Sor birinc بـرنـج = 'brass'; cf. also Arm płinj պղինձ [K/A/JB3/IFb/JJ/TF/RF] <mefreq; mîs; sifir I; şib>

birinç برنچ (A) = rice; brass. See **birinc I** & **II**.

biriqandin بِرِقاندِن *vt.* **(-biriqîn-).** 1) to enlighten, shed light on; 2) {syn: birûskandin; çirûsandin; teyisandin} to cause to shine; to polish, shine *(vt.)*. {also: [beriqandin] برقانديـن (JJ)} [K/B/A/JB3/IFb/B/OK/

/JJ] <biriqîn>

biriqîn بِـرقـيـن *vi.* **(-biriq-).** 1) {syn: birûs[k]în; çirûsîn; teyisîn} to shine, glitter, sparkle: **•Ser sîngê Dûmanlûê cîcîna xulexula cewikêd avê bû, êd ku mînanî mara jorda dişûlikîn, xwaro-maro dibûn, ber tîrêjnêd tavê *dibiriqîn*** (Ba2:1, 202) On the slope of {Mount} Dumanlu here and there was the babbling of brooks [of water], those which crept from above like snakes, twisted around, and *sparkled* under the rays of the sun **•Wekî gîsnê cot; çiqas bê şixulandin ewqas *wê bibiriqe*** (WM 1:2, 10) Like a plowshare, the more it is used, the more *it will shine*; 2) to be reflected (K). {also: birqîn (Z-2); [bereqin] بـرقـيـن (JJ)} [Z-2/Ba2/K/A/JB3/IFb/B/OK//JJ] <biriqandin>

biriqok بِرقۆك *adj.* bright, shining, shiny, brilliant: **•Ew bê rawestan ji bo xemilandina tilî, zendên dest û pê û guhên xwe li gewherên mezintir û *biriqoktir* digeriyan** (EN) They were constantly looking for larger and *shinier* jewels to adorn their fingers, wrists and ankles, and ears **•Ji ber çavên *biriqokî* ên Graniayê di cihê xwe de şaş û metel ma** (EN) Because of Grania's *shining* eyes, he became flustered on the spot. {also: biriqokî (EN-2); birîqok (FJ); biroqankî (A); birqok (Wkt-2); birqokî (K); Cf. [beriqok] برقوك (JJ) = 'reflection'} {syn: beloq; geş; r̄ewşen; r̄on I/r̄ohnî I} Cf. biriqîn = 'to shine' [EN/ZF/Wkt//FJ//K//A]

biriqokî بِرقۆكى (EN) = bright, shiny. See **biriqok**.

biriw بِرِو = eyebrow. See **birû**.

birî I بِـرى *f.* **(-ya;).** power, strength, force, might: **•Û heta ku *birî* di milên wî de heye, bi qaydê koçerane kevir davêje … Û heta ku *biriya* wî heye, kevir divirvirîne** (ZZ-4, 171) And with all *the strength* in his arms, he throws the stone as nomads would … And with all his *might*, he rolls the stone; **-birha avê** (IFb/CS) water power. {also: birh II (IFb/GF/CS); [bir̄î] برى (JJ-Rh); <birh> بره (HH)} {syn: ḧêl; hêz; qedûm [2]; qewat; t'aqet; zexm [2]; zor I} [ZZ/JJ//IFb/GF/HH/CS]

birî II بِرى (ZF3) = eyebrow. See **birû**.

birîn I بـريـن *f.* **(-a;-ê).** wound, injury; wound resulting from a weapon or external blow; emotional wound: **-birîna reş** = a) "black wound," disease common among the poor of Kurdistan; b) *name of a play by Musa Anter*. {also: brîn II (JB3); [birin] بـريـن (JJ); <birîn> برين (HH)} [K/A/JB3/IF/B/JJ/HH/SK/Msr]

bir̄în II بـڕيـن *vt.* **(-bir̄-).** 1) to cut: **-aqilê *fk-ê* nabir̄în** *(mostly neg.)* = a) (not) to understand, comprehend; b) (not) to want, choose, be interested in, care for: •[Memê went to try out his father's 40 horses. He put his hand on the back of each horse, and each horse's back broke] **Memê *aqilê wî* t'u bora *nebir̄î*** (EP) M. *wasn't "excited" about* any of the horses; **-ç'avêd xwe ji *f-tî* nebir̄în** (Ba2) not to take one's eyes off stg.: **•Şivana *ç'avêd xwe ji* pêz *nedibir̄în*** (Ba2) The shepherds *didn't take their eyes off* the sheep; 2) to cut down, fell *(trees)*: **•Darbir̄ çû mêşe dara *bibir̄e*** (Dz) The woodcutter went to the forest to *cut down* trees; 3) to interrupt, cut short: **•Ez xebera wî şekir *dibir̄im*** (K2-Fêr̄îk) I *interrupt* his sweet words. {also: birrin (A); birrîn (IF); brîn I (-bir-) (JB3); brrîn (IF); [birin] بـريـن (JJ); <bir̄în> بـرّيـن (HH)} M. Schwartz: *brīná- -->*brĭná- --> *brn- --> *burr- [Pok. bhrēi- 166.] 'to cut, break'- ->bhreE(y)-: Skt √bhrī [IX. bhrīṇánti] = 'to consume; to hurt, injure'; O Ir *bṛ-/*bṛn- (Tsb 43): Av √brāy- (brīn-); O P *bṛ-na-tiy = 'he cuts'; MidP brīdan (brīn-) & burrīdan (burr-) ='to cut (off), sever' (cf. M3); P borrīdan بريدن; Sor bir̄în بڕين; SoK bırin: bır-/bıri- (Fat 412, 566); Za birrneno [birrnayiş] (Todd); Hau bir̄ey (bir̄-) *vt.* (M4). See: Heinrich Hübschmann. *Armenische Grammatik* (Leipzig : von Breitkopf & Hartel, 1897), v. 1, p. 427; **49. Aw. Nir. 108.** in: Christian Bartholomae. "Arica X." *Indo-Germanische Forschungen*, 9 (1898), 253, note 2. [K/B/M/HH/SK/Msr//A//JB3//IF//JJ] <birîn I; biryan II>

birîndar بـريـنـدار *adj.* 1) wounded, injured, hurt: **-birîndar kirin** (IFb/TF) to hurt, injure, harm: **•Dar serda k'et *birîndar kir*** (Dz) The tree fell down [and] *injured* [him] **•Lê çiqa jî şivana û seêd wana miqatî li pêz nekirana, diqewimî, wekî gura mîk-dudu *birîndar dikirin*** (Ba2) But no matter how much the shepherds and their dogs cared for the sheep, it happened that the wolves *wounded* a sheep or two; 2) *[m.]* casualty. {also: brîndar (JB3); [birin-dar] بـريـنـدار (JJ); <birîndar> بريندار (HH)} [Dz/K/A/JB3/IFb/B/JJ/HH/SK/GF/TF]

birîqok بريقۆك (FJ) = bright, shiny. See **biriqok**.

birîsk بريسك = lightning. See **birûsk**.

Birîtanî بريتانى (BF) = British. See **Brîtanî**.

bir̄iyal بڕيال (K) = decision. See **biryar**.

birk I بِـركـ *f.* **(-a;).** small pool, puddle; swimming pool: **-birka avê** (M-Zx) do.: **•Ew hat ser *birka avê*** (M-Zx #752, 348) He came to *the pool of water*.

{also: <b[i]rk> برك (HH)} < Ar birkah بركة [HB/A/HH/OK/M-Zx]

birk II بِـــــــرك (A/GF) = bridge-like part of plow. See **p'irik**.

birmît بِرميت (Bw) = snuff. See **birmût**.

birmut بِرموت (OK) = snuff. See **birmût**.

birmût بِـرمـووت *f.* **(-a;-ê).** snuff: **•Mişk rabû boçika xwe kire nava *birnotiyê*, kire pozê wezîr** (J2, 41) The mouse went and stuck its tail in *the snuff*, [and] put it into the vizier's nose. {also: birmît (Bw); birmut (OK-2); bir̄nît (FS); birnotî (RZ-2); birnot'î (F/K); bir̄not'î (B); birnût (GF-2/OK)} {syn: nişûk} <T burun otu = 'snuff [lit. 'nose herb']: Sor bir̄nûtî بڕنووتی [Bw//FS//IFb/GF/RZ//OK//F/K/B]

bir̄nît بڕنیت (FS) = snuff. See **birmût**.

birnotî بِرنۆتی (RZ)/birnot'î (F/K)/bir̄not'î بڕنۆتی (B) = snuff. See **birmût**.

birnût بِرنووت (GF/OK) = snuff. See **birmût**.

biro برۆ (SK) = eyebrow. See **birû**.

bir̄ojî بـڕۆژی *adj.* fasting: **•Dibêjin: "Azad îro *bir̄ojî* ye", lê nabêjin "Azad îro r̄ojîgir e"** (FS) They say, "Azad is *fasting* today," but they don't say "Azad is a faster today" [*rojîgir* is used for statements about fasting in general, e.g. fasting every year, but on a specific day one is "*bir̄ojî*"]. [FS/Wkt] <r̄ojî>

biroqankî بِرۆقانکی (A) = bright, shiny. See **biriqok**.

birow I برۆو = eyebrow. See **birû**.

birow II برۆو (K) = eczema; measles. See **bîrov**.

birq برق (IFb) = lightning bolt. See **berq**.

birqîn برقین (Z-2) = to shine. See **biriqîn**.

birqok برقۆك (Wkt) = bright, shiny. See **biriqok**.

birqokî برقۆکی (K) = bright, shiny. See **biriqok**.

birrin بِررِن (A) = to cut. See **bir̄în II.**

birrîn بِررین (IF) = to cut. See **bir̄în II.**

birsî برسی (MK/SK/JB1-A/Bw) = hungry. See **birçî**.

birû بِـروو *m./f.(B)* **(; /-yê).** eyebrow. {also: birh I (K-2/Erh); birih; biriw; birî II (ZF3); biro (SK); birow; buru (Azer); burî; brû; [bourou بـرو / berou بـرو / buri بـری] (JJ); <birh> بـره (HH); ebro; ebrû (A)} [Pok.1. bhrū- 172./2. bhrū- 173.] 'eyebrow': Skt bhrū *f.*; Shughni group: Shughni virůγ̌; Khufi/Roshani/Bartangi/ Oroshori v(i)raw; Sarikoli virɛw; Yazghulami vraw (Morg2); P abrū ابرو; Sor birû بِـــــــروو; Za birwe/birewi (Mal); Hau biro *m.* (M4); cf. also Gr ofrys ὀφρύς *f.*; Rus brov' бровь *f.*; Eng (eye)brow [F/K/IF/B/JJ//A//HH/Erh//ZF3] <bijang; çav>

birûsîn بِـرووسـيـن *vi.* **(-birûs-).** to sparkle, twinkle: **•Carkê li paşîya mixarê nerî go tiştek *dibirûsîne*** (L) Suddenly he noticed something *twinkling* at the back of the cave **•Ev marek e, çavê wî *dibirûsînin*** (L) It's a snake, its eyes *are sparkling*. {also: birûskîn (K)} {syn: biriqîn; çirûsîn; teyisîn} [L/K]

birûsk بِـرووسـك *f.* **(-a;-ê).** lightning, thunderbolt: **-şîşa birûskê** (Z-4) thunderbolt, bolt of lightning. {also: birîsk; brûsk (JB3/IF-2/Wn); bûrûsk (Azer); [birousk] بـروسـك (JJ); <birûsik> بـروسـك (HH)} {syn: beledî; berq; blêç (IF)} Cf. Sor birîske بریسکه [K/A/JB3/IF/B/JJ/HH/Wn/ZF3] <bap'eşk; t[i]rûsk>

birûskîn بِرووسکین (K) = to sparkle. See **birûsîn**.

birx̄î برغی (FS) = screw. See **burx̄î**.

biryan I بـريـان *m./f.(ZF3)* **().** dish of roasted lamb (T tandır kebap). {also: beryan (FJ); [birian] بـريـان (JJ)} {syn: parîv} [Kurd1/IFb/Kmc/JJ/ZF3//FJ]

***biryan II** بـريـان *vi.* **(-biryê-).** 1) to cease, stop, end (vi.) ; 2) to stop flowing, run dry (river bed) (JJ). {also: birhan (-birhê-) (M-Zx); [biriian] بريان (JJ)} [M/JJ] <bir̄în II>

biryar بـريـار *f.* **(-a;-ê).** 1) {syn: qirar [1]} decision: **•Malbata min li ber *biryara* min rabû** (Wlt 1:36, 16) My family was opposed [or, objected] to my *decision*; **-biryar dan** (IFb/TF) to decide; 2) agreement (treaty, pact) . {also: bir̄iyal (K)} Sor bir̄yar بڕیار = 'decision' [Ber/Wlt/IFb/TF/OK//K] <daraz>

biryardar بـريـاردار *adj.* determined *(to do stg.)*, bound and determined, firm in one's determination, having made up one's mind: **•Lê ez *biryardar* bûm ku bimînim** (Wlt 1:36, 16) But I was *firm in my decision* to stay [or, I was *bound and determined* to stay]. [Wlt/ZF3/Wkt] <biryar>

bi sanahî ب سـانـاهـی *adj.* 1) {syn: asan; sivik} easy: **•Tedbîr *bi-senaî* ye, emma ḧetta noke me ji tembelî nekirîye** (SK 19:177) The remedy is *easy*, but up till now we have not applied it out of laziness; 2) *[adv.]* easily. {also: bi-senaî (SK)} [Bw//SK]

bi sebr ب سـبـر *adj.* 1) patient; 2) enjoyable; interesting: **•Filmê Mem û Zînê yê *bi sebr* e** (Bw) The film "Mem û Zîn" is *enjoyable* [or, interesting]. [Bw] <balkêş; sebr>

biseda بسەدا (AD) = [by the] hundreds. See **bi sedan**.

bi sedan ب سـەدان *pr. mod.* [by the] hundreds: **•*Bi sedan* gotin hatin gotin** (HYma, 29) *Hundreds of* things [lit. 'words, utterings'] were said **•Dibîne ku bi dîwaran ve *bi sedan* postên roviyan hene**

(ZZ-3, 149) He sees *hundreds of* fox pelts on the walls. {also: biseda (AD)} [HYma/BX//AD] <sed>

bi-senaî بـ سهنائى (SK) = easy. See **bi sanahî**.

bi ser k'etin بِ سـهـر كـهـتِـن (OK) = to succeed; to win. See **ser•k'etin**.

Bisilman بِسِلمان (Ah/FS) = Muslim. See **Misilman**.

bisk بِـسـك *f.* **(-a;-ê).** bunch, lock of (woman's) hair (K/Haz); bangs (A/IF): **•Bûka me çî hêjaye, / *Bisk* û kezîya berdaye, / Şêrîna dilê zavaya** (Haz) How precious is our bride, / she has let down (or: grown) *bunches* and braids of hair, / the sweet one of the hearts of grooms **•Ew esera *biska* teye** (FT) It is the effect of your hair (i.e., your beautiful *locks* of hair have affected me). {also: [bisk] بــســك (JJ); <bisk> بـسـك (HH)} [K/A/IF/B/JJ/HH/Haz] <çix̂; gulî I; kezî; p'or̄ III; t'ûncik>

biskewît بِـسـكـهويـت (Qzl/Qmş) = biscuit, cracker. See **bîskuwît**.

biskvêt بِسكڤێت (Qtr-E) = biscuit, cracker. See **bîskuwît**.

bismar بِسمار (A) = nail (for hammering) . See **bizmar**.

bispor بِسپۆر (M) = expert (at herding, etc.). See **pispor**.

bist I بِــســت *f.* **(-a;-ê).** iron poker; skewer, spit *(for grilling meat)*: **-bista nanî** (Zx) metal rod with wooden handle used in baking bread. {also: [byst] بست (JJ); <bist> بست (HH)} {syn: cax̂; şîş} [Zx/F/K/A/IFb/B/JJ/HH/JB1-A/GF/TF/OK] <adûde; tîrok; xilç>

bisṯ II بِست (SK) = (finger) span. See **bost**.

bista بِستا (K/JJ) = familiar; confident. See **biste**.

bistan بِـسـتـان *m.* **(-ê; bistên, vî bistanî).** breast *(of a nursing woman)*: **•Ûsiv *bistanê* dê dike devê xwe, dimêje** (Ba3) Joseph puts his mother's *breast* in his mouth [and] sucks [it]; **-bistan dayîn** (B) to nurse *(an infant)*. {also: [bystan] بستان (JJ)} {syn: çiçik; memik} Av fštāna-; Mid P pestān (M3); P pestān پستان = 'breast, teat, nipple' [Ba3/F/K/B/JJ]

bistaq بِـسـتـاق *adj.* low-quality, *of raisins that fall from the vine onto the ground*: **•Wî mêwîj bijartin û *yên pisteq* avêtin** (FS) He sorted the raisins and threw *the bad ones* out. {also: fistaq (GF); pisteq (CB/FS); <pisteq> پـسـتـق (HH)} {syn: teyk (Klk)} [Msr//HH/CB/FS//GF] <mewîj>

biste بِـسـتـه/**bisṯe** بِـسـطـه [Şnx] *adj.* 1) familiar, close *(friend)*, 'like one of the family' [cf. Ar bidūn taklīf بدون تكليف]: **•Em lêk *bisteh* in** (Elk) We are like family; We feel *comfortable* around each other; We *don't stand on ceremony* with one another **•Ez li te [ne] *bisṯe* me** (Şnx) I feel [un]*comfortable* around you **•Yê *biste* ye li mala filan kesî** (Bw) He is *like a member of* so-and-so's *family*; 2) {syn: misoger I; piştrast} confident, sure, assured [Ar wāṯiq واثـق]: **•Ez *bi* te *biste me*** (GF) I *have confidence in* you **•Êdî rovî û quling *biste* li hev dinêrin û galgalê dirêj dikin** (ZZ-3, 258) The fox and stork gaze *confidently* at one another and have a long chat **•Şêro *biste* çû mala xwe** (GF) Shero *confidently* went home. {also: bista (K); bisteh (Elk/OK/FS); [bista (Rh)] بستا (JJ) = confident} *According to JJ*, cf. P gostāx گـسـتـاخ = 'bold, impudent' <Pahl wistāx = 'confident, bold' < Av śtax; Arm vstah վստահ = 'certain, sure' {bistehî; bisteyî} [Bw//Şnx//K/JJ-Rh//Elk/OK/FS]

bisteh بِـسـتـهه (Elk/OK/FS) = familiar; confident. See **biste**.

bistehî بِستههى (GF/FS) = confidence. See **bisteyî**.

bisteyî بِستهيى *f.* **().** confidence: **•*Bi bisteyî* çû** (Bw) He went *confidently*. {also: bistehî (GF/FS)} {syn: bawerî} [Bw//GF/FS] <biste>

bistek بِستهك (K) = moment. See **bîstek**.

bistî بِـسـتـى *f.* **(-ya;).** midrib, central nerve or vein of a leaf. [Zeb/K/IFb/B/GF]

Bisurman بِسورمان (FT) = Muslim. See **Misilman**.

bişaftin بِشـافـتِن (Zeb) = to melt, dissolve; to assimilate. See **p'işaftin**.

bişavtin بِـشـاڤـتِـن (K/IFb/TF/OK) = to melt, dissolve; to assimilate. See **p'işaftin**.

bişirîn بِشِرين (IFb) = to smile. See **bişkurîn**.

bişkaftin بِشكافتِن (Krş/HH) = to unstitch. See **bişkavtin**.

bişkavtin بِـشـكـاڤـتِـن *vt.* **(-bişkev-[K]/-bişkiv-[IF]).** 1) to unbutton (K/IF); 2) to unstitch, undo *(stitches)*, tear apart at the seams (K/IF/B/Krş); 3) to open *(its flowers or blossoms; said of trees)* (K). {also: bişkaftin (-bişkifê-) (Krş); bişkivandin (-bişkivîn-) (B); [bechikaftin بـشـكـافـتـيـن/chikaftin /شـكـافـتـيـن شـكـاڤـتـيـن] (JJ); <bişkaftin بـشـكـافـتـن (dibişkîve) (دبشكيفه)> (HH)} [K/IF//HH/Krş//JJ] <bişkivîn; bişkoj>

bişkifandin بِـشـكِـفـانـدِن (-bişkifîn-) (Haz) = to become unstitched. See **bişkivîn** [2].

bişkifîn بِشكِفين (-bişkêf-) (IF) = to become unbuttoned. See **bişkivîn** [1].

bişkiftin بِـشـكِـفـتِـن (-bişkiv-) (M) = to blossom. See **bişkivîn** [3].

bişkivandin بِشكِڤاندِن (-bişkivîn-) (B) = to unbutton; to unstitch. See **bişkavtin**.

bişkivîn بِـشـكِـڤـيـن *vi.* **(-bişkiv-).** 1) {also: bişkifîn (-bişkêf-) (IF)} to become unbuttoned, unbutton *(vi.)*; 2) {also: bişkifandin (-bişkifîn-) (Haz)} to become unstitched, to come apart at the seams (K/IF/HH); 3) {also: bişkiftin (-bişkiv-) (M)} to open up *(vi.) (of blossoms, flowers, and the like)*, to blossom (K/A/JB3/IF/Haz): **•Berf, ji ser çiyayên me radibe, ji nav berfê, beybûn *dibişkivin*** (Wlt 1:35, 4) The snow melts from our mountains, [and] amid the snow, the chamomile *blossoms* **•Bişkuyê daran *bişkivî*** (IF) The trees' blossoms *have opened.* {also: [bichkewin/bechikiwin] بشكفين (JJ); <pişkivîn پشكفين (dipişkuvî) (دپشكفى)> (HH)} [K/A/JB3/B//IF//JJ//HH//Haz] <bişkavtin; bişkoj>

bişkof بِشكۆف = button. See **bişkoj**.

bişkoj بِشكۆژ *f.* **(-a;-ê).** 1) {syn: mêvok; qumçe} button; 2) {syn: aj; gupik III; terh; zîl} bud. {also: bişkof; bişkok (B/Msr); bişkoşk; bişkov [1]; pişkoj (K-2); pişkok (Msr-2); [pychkoj پشكوژ/ pychkoch پشكوش] (JJ); <bişkûj> بشكوژ (HH)} [F/K/A/JB3/IF/Bw//HH//JJ//B/Msr] <bişkavtin; bişkivîn; gul; solîn II>

bişkok بِشكۆك (B/Msr) = button. See **bişkoj**.

bişkorî بِشكۆرى (K/B) = child laborer; farmhand. See **pişkûrî**.

bişkoşk بِشكۆشك = button. See **bişkoj**.

bişkov بِشكۆڤ *f.* **().** 1) = button. See **bişkoj**; 2) {syn: xulbok (Msr)} buttonhole. [Srk/Dy/ZF3]

bişkul بِشكول *pl./f.(B)* **(;/-ê).** goat manure *(in the shape of little balls)* (Msr/Mzg); sheep or camel dung (K/A/JJ): **-bişkul kirin** (B) to defecate *(of sheep, goats, camels, or rabbits)*. {also: bişqul (Mzg); buşqul (IF-2); k'uşpil (FS); **pişkul**; [pychkoul] پشكول (JJ); <pişkul> پشكل (HH)} Cf. P piškil پشكل = 'orbicular dung of sheep'; Sor pişkil پشكل/pişqil پشقل; Za pişkul *f.* = 'goat droppings' (Todd) [K/Msr/B//A/IFb/JJ/HH/GF//Mzg//FS] <ç'êrt; dirg; guhûr; k'erme; keşkûr; r̄ix; sergîn; sergo; sêklot; tepik; t'ers; t'ert[ik]; zibil; zirîç> See also **pişkul**.

bişkurîn بِشكورين *vi.* **(-bişkur-).** to smile: **•Stêrkên şevê ji me re *dibişirîn*** (IFb) The stars of the night *were smiling* at us. {also: bişirîn (IFb)} {syn: beşişîn; girnijîn; mizicîn} [Bw/ZF3//IFb] <k'enîn>

bişqul بِشقول (Mzg) = goat manure. See **bişkul** & **pişkul**.

bit̄ir̄ I بطِر/**bitir̄** بِتِر [A/G/Wkt] *adj.* 1) {syn: gewî} spoiled, pampered; ill-behaved; pretentious, ostentatious{T fiyakalı, şımarık}: **•Ew kur̄ekê *bit̄ir̄* e, li xo nagirit ku wî şolî bikit** (FS) He is a *spoiled [or, arrogant]* child, he won't deign to do that job; 2) {syn: gewî; qur̄e} arrogant, haughty; insolent, fresh, smart-aleck {T küstah}: **•Heta do pars dikir, îro zengîn bûye *bitir* bûye** (Wkt) Until yesterday he was begging [in the streets], today he's become rich and *arrogant*. {also: <bit̄ir> بطر (HH)} < bi + t̄ir̄ = 'fart' [Ber/A/G/Wkt//HH/FS] <pivikî; qur̄e>

bitir II بِتِر (GShA) = more; the most. See **bêtir**.

bitirpêr بِترپێر (IFb) = three days ago. See **betrapêr**.

bitirpêrar بِترپێرار (IFb/GF) = three years ago. See **betrapêrar**.

bitişt بِ تِشت *adj.* pregnant, expecting: **•Ew ya bi tişt e** (Bw) She is pregnant. {syn: bihemil; bizar; ducanî; duhala; giran I; ħemle; zar II} [Elk/Bw/Ag/GF]

bive-neve بِڤه نەڤه (B) = willy-nilly. See **bivê-nevê**.

bivêj بِڤێژ (K) = poet. See **biwêj I**.

bivê-nevê بِڤێ نەڤێ willy-nilly, whether one likes it or not, absolutely: **•*Bivê nevê* tu hînî zmanê Kurdî bibî** (IFb) You're going to learn Kurdish *whether you want to or not* **•*Bivê nevê* tu were** (K) You absolutely must come [*whether you want to or not*]. {also: bive-neve (B); [bewi newi] بڤى نڤى (JJ); <bivêneve> بڤينڤى (HH)} [K/A/IFb/HH/GF//JJ//B] <viyan>

bivir بِڤِر *m.(SK/F)/f.(K)* **(-ê/ ;).** axe, hatchet: **•Cindî Aẍa bi destê xo Temer bi *biwirî* temam kir** (SK 40:386) Jindi Agha finished Tamar off with his own hands with an *axe*; **-bivirê avdayî** (Qzl) strong and clever man [lit. 'watered axe']; **-kalûmekî biviran** = old, rusty axe. {also: bavir, m. (F); bivr (GF); biwir (SK); [biwir] بڤر (JJ); <bivir> بڤر (HH)} {syn: balt'e; tevir [1]} Sor bîwur بيوور = 'axe' [BX/K/A/JB3/IFb/JJ/TF/OK//GF//SK//F] <kalûme; k'uling; tevirzîn; t'evşo>

bivr بِڤر (GF) = axe. See **bivir**.

biwartin بِوارتن =to pass. See **bihurtin**.

biwêj I بِوێژ *m.* **().**1) {also: bivêj (K)} {syn: helbestvan; hozanvan; şayîr} poet (K/A); 2) {also: biwîje (JB3)} storyteller (JB3). Sor buwêj بووێژ = 'talkative; (n.) poet' [(neol)A/IF//K//JB3]

biwêj II بوێژ *f.* **(-a;-ê).** 1) idiom, expression; 2) phrase. [IFb/FJ/TF/ZF/CS/Wkt]

biwir بِوِر (SK) = axe. See **bivir**.

biwîje بِوێژه (JB3) = storyteller. See **biwêj I** [2].

bixerî بِخەرى (B) = fireplace; chimney. See **pixêrîk**.

bixêrî بِخێرى (A/JB3/HH/FS) = fireplace; chimney. See **pixêrîk**.

bixur بِخور (IFb/TF) = pebble. See **bixûr**.

bixûr بِغوور *m.* **().** pebble; gravel. {also: bixur (IFb/TF)} {syn: xîç'ik; xîz [2]; zuẍr} [Omr//IFb/TF] <ber

III; kevir; xîz>

biyanî بِیـانـی (Ber/JB3/IF/JJ/SK) = foreign; common. See **bîyanî**.

biyav بِیـاڤ *m.* **(-ê;-î).** subject, topic; field of study: **•Di hemû *biyavan*da ew çêker in, em jî çav lêkerîn** (C.Mustafa. Biyavê xwandinê, 2004, 5) In all *fields/topics* they are creators, and we are copiers/imitators **•Ez şiyam li dor vî *biyavî* pertoka "Le'lîxana Guveyî" ji çend deqa ji zar devên çend stranbêja kum bikem ... û li sala 1980 bideme çapê** (M.N.Bamernî. Le'lîxana Guveyî, 1980, 12) Around this *topic* I was able to collect some texts of "Lalikhana Guveyi" from some singers ... and in 1980 have the book published **•Pertuk komeka gotar û vekolînaye di *biyavê* rexnê da** (E.'Ebdulqadir. Têkist di navbera gotara rexneyî û rêbazên edebî da, 1980, 7-8) The book is a collection of articles and studies on *the subject of* [literary] criticism. {syn: babet I[2]; dabaş; mijar; war [4]} [Wkt/Bamernî.Le'lîxanaGuveyî/'Ebdulqadir.Têkist/Mustafa.BiyavêXwandinê]

biyok بیۆك (IFb/Kmc-2) = quince. See **bih**.

***bizaftin** بِزافتِن *vt.* **(-bizêv-[M/K]/-bizêf-[IF]).** 1) {syn: leqandin; lipitandin; livandin} to (cause to) move *(vt.)* (M/JJ); 2) to send, dispatch; to accompany, escort (IF); 3) {syn: biziftin}[vi.] to move, budge, stir (vi.) (K). {also: bizawtin (SK); [bezaftin] بـزافـتـن (JJ)} Cf. Sor bizawtin بِـزاوتِـن [M/IF//JJ//SK] <biziftin>

bi zar بِ زار/بِـزار *adj.* pregnant: **-bi zar bûn** (ZF3) to be pregnant. {syn: avis; bihemil; duhala; giran; ḧemle} < bi = 'with' + zar = 'child' [Wn/ZF3] <avis>

bizaştîr بِـزاشـتـیـر (A/Wlt/Kmc/ZF3) = three-year-old sheep. See **bijaştîr**.

bizav بِـزاڤ *f.* **(-a;).** 1) motion, movement *(lit. & fig.)*: **•Sînama, di esas de *bizav* (hareket) e** (Ber #7, 10) Cinema is basically *movement*; 2) {syn: k'eft û left; p'êk'ol; xebat} effort, attempt, endeavor (VoA/GF/Bw); striving: **•23 milyon dolar yêt danayn bo *bizavêt* wê yêt harîkarîyê bo kêm kirina hindek ji nexoşî û dijwarêt ku rijîma Sedam Ḧiseynê bo gelê 'Îraqê çêkirîn** (VoA) $23 million has been set aside for its [=America's] assistance *efforts* to lessen some of the disease and difficulties which the regime of Saddam Hussein has created for the Kurdish people; **-bizav kirin** (Zeb) to strive, endeavor: **•Her wesa Ingilîzan *bizav kir* ji bo lawazkirina rolê welatên biyanî li wê deverê** (Metîn 62[1997]:26) Likewise, the English *strove* to weaken the role of foreign countries in that region; 3) *[adj.]* *lively, active, full of movement (IFb/TF/OK). Cf. Sor bizêw بِـزێـو = 'restless, fidgety' & bizav بِـزاڤ = 'motion' *(recent borrowing from Kurm)* [(neol)Ber/VoA/K/IFb/GF/TF/OK/Bw] <bizaftin; biziftin>

bizawtin بِـزاوتِـن (SK) = to move. See **bizaftin** & **biziftin**.

bizdîn بِـزدیـن *vi.* **(-bizd-).** 1) {syn: piçan; qetîn} to break, snap, tear *(vi.)* (K/IF/M); to burst, split, crack *(vi.)* (K); to be broken (JJ); to have a relapse (JJ); 2) [+ **ji**] {syn: tirsîn} to be afraid or scared, to fear; to be scared to death; to tremble with horror: **•*Ji* tîrêja tavê ew *bizdîyaye*** (Z-2) He *was frightened by* a ray of sunlight. {also: [byzdiian] بـزدیـان (JJ); <bizdan بـزدان (dibizde) (دبـزده)> (HH)} [Z-2/K/A/IF/M//JJ//HH] <piçan>

bizdok بِـزدۆك (Elk/Slm/IFb/GF) = coward. See **bizdonek**.

bizdonek بِـزدۆنـەك *m.* **().** coward. {also: bizdok (Elk/Slm/IFb-2/GF-2); [byzdounek] بزدونك (JJ)} {syn: newêrek; tirsonek} [Frq/Qrj/K/IFb/GF//JJ//Elk/Slm]

bi zeḧmet ب زحمه‌ت (SK) = difficult. See **zeḧmet** [2].

bizêz بِزێز (Wkt) = clothes moth. See **bizûz**.

***biziftin** بِـزفـتِـن *vi.* **(-biziv-).** to move, budge, stir *(vi.)*. {also: bizaftin (K) [3]; bizawtin (SK); bizivîn (IF)} {syn: leqîn; lipitîn; livîn I} Sor bizûtin بِـزووتِـن/bizwan بزوان (-bizû-) (Mukri)/biziftin بِزِفتن/bizwîn بِزوین (Arbil) [M//IF] <bizaftin>

bi zihn ب زهـن *adj.* smart, clever, sharp. {syn: aqil I; aqiljîr; aqilmend; aqiltîj (Bw); bi fêm; jîr; zîx I} <bi + Ar d̲ihn ذهن = 'intelligence' [Bw]

bizin بِـزن *f./m.(SK)* **(-a;-ê).** goat, she-goat, "nanny" goat, zool. *Capra hircus*: **•*Bizinek* binat'ara *bizinekê*da av ne xar** (Dz) *One goat* would not drink water at a lower point than *another goat* [lit. 'in a goat's lower point'] **•Rûnê gamêşan ji yê *bizinan* pirtire** (AB) Buffalo butter is more plentiful than *goat* butter; **-şîrê bizinê** (B) goat's milk. {also: [bizin] بـزن (JJ); <bizin> بـزن (HH)} [Pok. bhūgo-s 174.] 'male animal of various kinds: stag, ram, he-goat' + feminine suffix -in: Southern Tati dialects (all f.): Danesfani, Ebrahim-abadi, Takestani, Sagz-abadi beza = 'she-goat' (Yar-Shater); Sivandi bǟzä = 'she-kid' & bäzǟ = 'kid' (Morgenstierne in: *A Locust's Leg : Studies in Honour of S.H. Taqizadeh* (London, 1962), pp. 203-4); P boz بز = 'goat'; Sor bizin بِزِن = '[male or female] goat'; Za biz *f.* = '[she-] goat' & bizêk *f./m.* = 'kid (goat)' (Todd); Hau bize *f.* = 'goat' & bizłe *m.* = 'kid' (M4); K--> T bızın [Babik, Pötürge-Malatya; Türkçayırı, Kötüre, Akçaşar, Afşin-Maraş] = 'goat' (DS, v. 2, p. 675); Cf. OEng bucca = 'he-goat'; Eng buck = 'adult male of certain animals, e.g., deer or rabbit' [F/K/A/JB3/IF/B/JJ/HH/SK] <gîsk, m. = one year-old kid; hevûrî = 1-, 2-, or 3-year-old male goat; kûr I = sayis = 3-year-old male goat; kar[ik], f. = kid; nêrî I = billy goat; pez = (flock of) sheep and goats; r̄uyn = reddish goat; tuştîr = young (1-, 2-, or 3-year-old) female goat>

bizir I بِزِر (K[s]) = lost; absent. See **berza**.

bizirav بِـــــــزِراڤ/بِ زِراڤ *adj.* brave, bold, daring, courageous: **•Zilamekî *bizirav* cegerlî weke Ûsufşa nîne** (HR 3:153) There isn't a man as *bold* and daring as Usufsha. {also: [be-zirawé] بـه زراڤه (JJ)} {syn: aza I[3]; camêr; delîr; zîx I[2]} bi + zirav II [HR/A/GF/TF//JJ] <zirav II>

bizivîn بِزڤين (IF) = to move, budge *(vi.)*. See **biziftin**.

bizî بِـزى *f.* (;-yê). elm tree, bot. *Ulmus* [T karaağaç, P nārvan نـــــاروَن]: **-dara biziyê** (RZ) do. {also: bizû (RF-2); <bizû> بـــــــزو (HH)} [Pok. u̯inĝ-/u̯eiĝ-(u̯iĝ-?) 1177] 'elm': O Ir *u̯izu̯- [*wizu- (A&L p.94 [XVIII, 1])]: Zābulistān γuzbe; eastern P, also Samarkand, Sīstān guzm [for gužm]; Talish & Āstārā vizim; Talishi dialect vizmado; Ṭārom vizm; Sor wuzm ووزم & Mukri bûz بـــــووز (Houtum-Schindler); Gurani & Luri wiz; Za bizmêri = 'type of tree' (Mal); cf. also Eng wych (elm); Rus viaz вяз. See: W.B. Henning. "The Kurdish Elm," *Asia Major,* ser. 2, 10 (1963), 68-72. [IFb/RF/RZ//HH]

bizîz بِزيز (Wkt) = clothes moth. See **bizûz**.

bizm بِزم (IF) = bridle; bit. See **bizmîk**.

bizmal بِـــــزمـــــال (Ba/B) = nail *(for hammering)*. See **bizmar**.

bizmar بِـزمـار *m.* **(-ê; bizmêr, vî bizmarî).** (large) nail *(for hammering)*: **•qoře bizmal** (Ba) a handful of nails. {also: bismar (A-2); bizmal (Ba/B-2); mizmar; [bizmar] بـــزمـــار (JJ); <bizmar> بـــزمـــار (HH)} {syn: mix} < Ar mismār مسمار [Ba//K/A/JB3/B/JJ/HH] <ç'akûç>

bizmik بِزمِك (B) = bridle; bit. See **bizmîk**.

bizmilûg بِزملوگ (IFb) = icicle. See **şembelîlk**.

bizmîk بِـزمـيـك *f.* (;-ê). 1) {syn: celew I; dizgîn; gem; qet'irme II; lix̄ab} rein; bridle (K/IF); 2) bit *(of a bridle)* (K); 3) stick placed in the mouth of a lamb or kid for weaning (B/HH). {also: bizm (IF); bizmik (B); [byzmik] بـزمـك (JJ); <bizmik> بـزمـك (HH)} [IF//K/JJ//B/HH]

bizot بِـزۆت/**bizot** بِـظـۆت [JB1-A] *m.(Bw/JB1-A/OK)/ f.(F/B)* **(-ê/ ; /-ê).** ember(s); firebrand. {also: bizotik (OK-2); bizotik' (JB1-A-2); bizut (IFb-2); bizût (K); [bezót] بـــــــزوت (JJ-G)} {syn: k'ozir; p'el II; p'ereng; tiraf} Sor serebizût سەرەبزووت = 'charred stick, brand, meteor' [Bw/F/A/IFb/B/SK/GF/OK//JJ-G//JB1-A/ /K] <agir; helemor; peşk III[1]; xwelî>

bizotik بِزۆتِك (OK)/bizotik' بِظۆتِك (JB1-A) = embers. See **bizot**.

bizrik بِزرِك (IF) = pimple; boil. See **pizik**.

bizut بِزوت (IFb) = embers. See **bizot**.

bizû بِزوو (RF/HH) = elm. See **bizî**.

bizûsk بِزووسك (FS) = clothes moth. See **bizûz**.

bizût بِزووت (K) = embers. See **bizot**.

bizûz بِـــــــزووز *f.* **(-a;-ê).** clothes moth, *zool.* Tinea pellionella: **•Ba *bizûza* berfê ye, merî bizûza çiyê ye** (Nefel/Tsab) The wind is *the moth of* [i.e., eats into] the snow, man is the moth of the mountain *[prv.]* **•*Bizûzkê* li cilkên wî daye** (FS) *The moth* ate his clothes. {also: bizêz (Wkt-2); bizîz (Wkt-2); bizûsk (FS-2); bizûzk (IFb/FS); buzêz (Wkt-2); buzîz (Wkt-2); buzûz (Wkt-2); gizêz (Wkt-2); gizîz (Wkt-2); gizûz (Wkt-2); guzêz (Wkt-2); guzîz (Wkt-2); guzûz (Wkt-2)} Cf. Arc bazozā בזוזא & Syr bāzūzā ܒܙܘܙܐ = 'robber, plunderer, destroyer'; Arm bzez բզեզ = 'beetle, small insect' [Qzl/Btm/K/B/A/IFb/FJ/GF/Kmc/ZF/Wkt/FS/Tsab] <belantîk; fir̄fir̄ok; p'ir̄p'ir̄ok; p'erwane>

bizûzk بِزووزك (IFb/FS) = clothes moth. See **bizûz**.

bî I بـــى *m.&f.* (; /-yê). widow(er) {syn: bêjin}: **-jina bî** (F/IF/B)/**jinebî** (K/A)/**bîjin** (RZ) widow; **-mêrê bî** (F/IF) widower {syn: jinmirî}. {also: bîh (A); [bi] بـى (JJ); <jinebî> ژنـبـى (HH)} [Pok. u̯eidh- 1127.] 'to divide, separate': Skt vidhávā *f.*; O Ir *vidava-: Av viδauuā- *f.*; Mid P wēwag (M3); Southern Tati dialects: Xiaraji vivia *f.* = 'widow' & Chali/ Xiaraji vivá *m.* = 'widower' (Yar-Shater); P bīve/ bēve بـيـوه; Sor bêwe[jin] [بێوه[ژن = 'widow'; Za vîya *f.* = 'widow' (Todd) [F/K/IF/B/JJ//A//HH]

bî II بى *f.* (;-yê). 1) {syn: benav [1]} willow tree, bot. *Salix*: **•Jinê got, "Here, hindek şokêt *bîyê* bîne, li pêş çawêt xelkî sê car xilêfan çêke"** (SK 35:314) His wife said, "Go and bring some *osiers* [type of willow] and make three or four hive-baskets in the sight of people"; **-dara bî** (B) do.; 2) poplar tree (K). {also: [bi بى/ bid بيد/bihouk بهوك/biouk بيوك]

(JJ); <bî> بى (HH)} <*bēh/bīh <O Ir *waiti- (A&L p. 84 [IV, 2] + 94 [XVIII, 1]): Av *vaētī- *f.* ; Pashto vala; Mid P wēd (M3); P bīd/bēd بيد; Sor bî بى/ bîkoł بيكۆڵ = 'willow'; Hau darbî (M4) [K/A/JB3/IFb/ B/JJ/HH/SK/GF/TF/OK/Kmc-6] <bîşeng; sipindar>

bîbelerz بيبەلەرز *f.* **(-a;).** earthquake. {also: bîbelerze (ş); bîvelerz (Zeb-2/RZ-2/SS-2); bomelerze (K[s]/ A)} {syn: belelerz (F/K); 'erdĥejîn; 'erdlerzîn; zelzele} Cf. P būmahan بومهن/būmahīn بومهين = 'earthquake' <O P & Av būmī- = 'earth' [Pok. bheu-, *etc.*: bhū- 146.ff.] 'to grow, blossom, swell, be' + √manθ- = 'to stir, to move *(vi.)*'; Sor bûmelerze بوومەلەرزە & bûlerze بوولەرزە (Mukri) [Zeb/AA/RZ/FS//SS//K(s)/A]

bîbelerze بيبەلەرزە (SS) = earthquake. See **bîbelerz** .

bîber بيبەر *f.* **(-a;-ê).** pepper: **-bîbera r̄eş** (B) black pepper {syn: dermanê germ (Msr/A/JJ-PS)}; **-bîbera sor** (B) red pepper **-bîbera tûj** (ZZ-7) hot pepper. {also: [biber] ببر (JJ); <pîber> پيبر (HH)} {syn: back; guncik; ĥiçĥar; îsot} Cf. T biber; Sor bîber بيبەر [HB/K/JB3/B//JJ//HH]

bîbik بيبك (A/ZF3) = pupil. See **bibiq**.

bîbil بيبل (IF) = pupil. See **bibiq**.

bîbok بيبۆك, m. (K) = pupil. See **bibiq**.

bîbûn بيبوون = camomile. See **beybûn**.

bîc بيج (K/B/EP-5) = bastard. See **pîç**.

bîçek بيچەك (BK) = a little. See **piçek**.

bîçî بيچى (HB) = finger. See **bêç'î II**.

bîh بيه (A) = widow(er). See **bî I**.

bîhn بيهن (K) = smell; breath. See **bîn I**.

bîhnfireh بيهنفِرەه (IFb) = patient; tolerant. See **bînfireh**.

bîhnişk بيهنِشك *f.* **().** yawn. {syn: bawişk} [IFb/CS]

bîhnok بيهنۆك (RZ) = comma. See **bêhnok**.

bîhntengî بيهنتەنگى (CS) = shortness of breath; nervousness. See **bêhntengî**.

bîhr بيهر (IFb) = memory. See **bîr.**

bîjin بيژِن (RZ/Wkt) = widow. See **bêjin II** & **bî I**.

bîjî بيژى (IF/GF) = bastard. See **pîç**.

bîlan بيلان (F) = knowing. See **bilyan**.

bîlet بيلەت (Wkt) = ticket. See **bilêt**.

bîlêt بيلێت (Wkt) = ticket. See **bilêt**.

bîlyan بيليان (B) = knowing. See **bilyan**.

bîn I بين *f.* **(-a;-ê).** 1) smell, odor, scent: **-bîn jê hatin** = to smell of, give off a smell, reek of: **•Keç'ik gava dinêr̄e serê wê, *bîna* kur̄ederê jê tê** (J) When the girl looked at her head, [she noticed that] that a bad *smell* came from it (or her) **•*Bîna* dya min serê te tê** (J) My mother's *smell* is coming [from] your head [=you smell like my mother]; **-bin pozê *fk-ê* k'etin** (Dz) to catch a whiff of, to smell *stg. (vt.)*: **•Nişkêva *bîna* k'ivava *k'ete pozê wan*** (Dz) Suddenly *they smelled* kebabs; **-bihin kirin** (BX) to smell, breathe in: **•Dinya gulek e, *bihin bike* û wê bide hevalê xwe** (BX) The world is a flower, *smell* it and pass it on to the next person *[prv.]*; **-bîna *ft-î* k'işandin** (B) to breathe in: **•Şivan xwer̄a nava kulîlkada diger̄in, *bîna* hewa ç'îyaye t'emiz *dik'işînin*** (Ba2:1, 203) Shepherds roam among the flowers, *breathing in* pure mountain air; 2) breath *(used in expressions dealing with one's mood)*: **-bîna *fk-ê* derhatin** = to be homesick {syn: see bêrî II}: **•Ez hatime welatê xerîb, *bîna min pê dertêye*** (Z-1) I've come to a strange land, *I'm homesick* [lit. 'my breath is leaving over it']; **-bîna xwe derhatin** (EP-7)/**bîna *fk-ê* derk'etin** (XF) to unburden one's heart; to relax, be relieved, get a load off one's mind; **-bên fireh bûn** (L) to calm down, be calm [lit. 'for one's breath to be broad/wide']: **•Dawîyê *bêna min fireh bibe*, ezê bixwim** (L) When *I calm down*, I'll eat; **-bên teng bûn** (L) to be sad, upset [lit. 'for one's breath to be narrow']: **•Bêna min teng e** (L) I'm sad or upset; **-bêna xwe vedan** (Msr) to rest, relax: **•Ezê bêna xwe vedim** (Msr) I will take a rest. {also: bêhn (A-2/IF-2); bên (L/SK); bihin (BX); bihn (JB3/IF/JB1-S); bîhn (K/IF); [behin] بهن (JJ); <bihn> بهن (HH)} <*bŭhn <*bōδn <O Ir *baud-na- [*baud- = 'to sense, perceive, notice, cf. **bihîstin**] (A&L p. 83 [II]): P būy بوى = 'odor, scent'; Sor bên بێن/bon بۆن = 'smell' & bîn بين = 'breath'; A&L reject Tsabolov's connecting **bîn I** with Av vaēnā- & P bīnī بينى = 'nose' (Tsb2, p. 44) [K//A/B//BX//JB3/IF/HH/JB1-S//JJ//L/SK]

bîn II بين (Rh/M-Zx) = to be; to become. See **bûn**.

bînahî بيناهى *f.* **(-ya;-yê).** vision, faculty of sight: **-bînahîya çava** (Mzr) do. {also: bînayî (K/A/ GF-2)} Sor bînayî بينايى [Mzr/Ak/IFb/GF/TF//K/A]

bînanê بينانێ (Z-2) = like, similar to. See **fena** & **mîna**.

bînayî بينايى (K/A/GF) = vision. See **bînahî**.

bînfire بينفِرە (K/B/GF) = patient; tolerant. See **bînfireh**.

bînfireh بينفِرەه *adj.* patient; tolerant. {also: bêhnfireh (SS/ZF); bênfire (Wkt); bênfireh (FJ-2); bihinfarah (TF); bihnfire (FJ/GF); bîhnfireh (IFb); bînfire (K/ B/GF-2); [behin fereh] بهن فره (JJ)} {syn: bi sebr} =Sor pişûdirêj پشوودرێژ = 'patient' &

singfirawan سِنگ فِراوان = 'tolerant' {bêhnfirehî; bênfirehî; bihinfarahî; bînfirehî; bînfiretî} [FJ//K/B//IFb//SS/ZF/JJ//Wkt//FJ/GF//TF]

bînfirehî بينفِرِههی *f.* **(-ya;-yê).** patience; tolerance. {also: bêhnfirehî (RZ/SS/ZF); bênfirehî (Wkt); bihinfarahî (TF); bînfiretî (B)} {syn: sebr; t'ebatî} [GF//B//Wkt//RZ/SS/ZF//TF] <bînfireh>

bînfiretî بينفِرِهتی (B) = patience; tolerance. See **bînfirehî**.

bînişk بينِشك (AD) = sneeze. See **bêhnişk**.

bîniştek بينِشتهك (GF) = sneeze. See **bêhnişk**.

bîntengî بينتهنگی (K/GF) = shortness of breath; nervousness. See **bêhntengî**.

bînxwaş بينخواش (IFb) = fragrant. See **bînxweş**.

bînxweş بينخوهش *adj.* fragrant, aromatic: **•Xarina bajerîya, ko şirînî, pilaw, goşt, êprax, şorbawa bi dermanêt *bênxoş* û tiştê wekî wane bo wî didanane ser sifrê** (SK 31:274) He would set on the tablecloth townsmen's food, which is sweetmeats, pilaf, meat, stuffed vine leaves, soup with *fragrant* spices and other such things. {also: bênxoş (SK); bihnxweş (GF); bînxwaş (IFb); [behn-a khoch] بهنا خوش (JJ)} Sor bonxoş بۆنخۆش [SK//B//GF//IFb//JJ]

bîr I بير *f.* **(-a;-ê).** 1) {syn: bal II} {also: bîhr (IFb-2)} memory: **-bîr k'etin** = to occur to, remember: **•Lê bi şabûna Memê ... nan û av *nak'evne bîra wan*** (EP) From [so much] rejoicing over M. ... *they forget about* food [lit. 'bread'] and water; **-hatin bîra *fk-ê*** = to remember, come to mind: **•*Tê bîra te*, wexta go em hatin ber wê avê?** (L) *Do you remember*, when we went to that river?; **-[ji] bîra *fk-î* çûn/kirin** = to forget: **•Eva t'emîya min wer̄a, hûn wê *bîr nekin*** (Ba) This is my warning to you, *don't forget* it **•Li bedewî û k'emala M. met'elmayî *bîr kiribûn*, wekî nan û emek M.r̄a bînin** (Z-1) They were [so] amazed at M.'s beauty [that] *they forgot* to bring him bread and food; 2) {also: bêrî II} longing, homesickness (Ag/Kp): **-bîra f*k-ê* kirin** (Kp/Ag) to miss, be homesick for, long for: **•Ez *bîra* mala xwe *dikim*** (Kp) I am homesick [lit. 'I *long for* my home']. {also: [ber بر/ bir بير] (JJ)} Sor bîr بير = 'mind, memory'; Za vîr *m.* (Todd); Hau wîr *m.* (M4) [cf. usage of P yād ياد] [K/A/JB3/IFb/B/JJ/JB1-A&S/SK/GF/TF/OK]

bîr II بير *f.* **(-a;-ê).** well, pit: **•30 sal berê seeta bavê min ketibû vê *bîrê*, min jî îro derxist** (LM, 12) 30 years ago my father's watch fell into this *well*, today I brought it out **•Avîtne** [sic] ***bîreke* k'ûr** (Ba) They threw [him] into a deep *well* **•Davêje *bîrê*** (Ba) He throws it in *the well* **•Wexta bira ew avîtne** [sic] **binê *bîrê*** (Ba) When the brothers threw him into the bottom *of the well*. {also: [bir] بير (JJ); <bîr> بير (HH)} < Ar bi'r (bīr) بئر [Ba/K/A/JB3/IFb/JJ/HH/GF/TF/OK] <çal II;; k'ort>

bîr III بير (HB) = rock. See **ber III**.

bîrov بيرۆڤ *f.* **(-a;).** 1) eczema, psoriasis, ringworm; scurf; **-bîrova çavî** (AA/SS)/**bîrova çava** (BR)/**bîroveya çavî** (IFb) trachoma {syn: qiltîş}; **-bîrova hişk** (AA) psoriasis; 2) measles (K/JJ). {also: birow (K); bîrove (IFb/CS/AA); [birow] بروف (JJ); <bîrov> بيروف (HH)} Sor bîro بيرۆ [BR/FJ/TF/GF/HH/ZF/SS//IFb/CS/AA//JJ//K]

bîrove بيرۆڤه (IFb/CS/AA) = eczema, psoriasis. See **bîrov**.

bîskiwî بيسكِوى (IFb) = biscuit, cracker. See **bîskuwît**.

bîskuwît بيسكوويت *f.* **().** biscuit, cracker. {also: biskewît (Qzl/Qmş); biskvêt (Qtr-E); bîskiwî (IFb)} {syn: *hindok (IF); totik I} < Eng biscuit < Fr bis = 'twice' + cuit = 'cooked' [BK//IFb//Qzl/Qmş//Qtr-E]

bîst I بيست *num.* twenty, 20: **•bîst û yek** = twenty-one, 21; **-qur̄na bîsta** (B) the twentieth century. {also: [bist] بست (JJ); <bîst> بيست (HH)} [Pok. u̯ī-kmt-ī 1177.] 'twenty'-->M. Schwartz: ProtoIE *dwidḱm̥tiH, generally given as *wikm̥ti-: Proto-IndIr *vinśati--> Skt viṁśati; O Ir 1)*vinsati--> Ossetic insædz/insæj & 2)*vīsati- --> Av wīsati-; P bīst بيست; Sor bîst بيست; Za vîst (Todd); Hau wîs (M4); Cf. Lat viginti [F/K/A/JB3/IF/B/JJ/HH] <bîstem; didû; du I>

bîst II بيست (F) = span. See **bost**.

bîstan بيستان *m.* **(-ê; bîstên/-î).** *(fruit)* garden: **•Min *bîstanek* çandîye. Were, biçîn, ade bikeyn** (SK 21:193) I have planted *a garden*. Come, let us go and weed it **•Xezal çû, xwe li bîstanî da berze kir** (M-Zx #751, 348) The gazelle went and lost itself in the garden. {also: bostan (; bostên/bostîn) (K/IFb/B/OK-2); <b[u]stan> بستان (HH)} {syn: baxçe; bax̄} Cf. P/Ar bustān بستان = 'fragrant garden' [M-Zx/A/JB3/SK/GF/TF/OK//K/IFb/B//HH]

bîstek بيستهك *f.* **(;-ê).** moment, while, second *(60th of a minute)*: **-bîstekê** (L) for a little while: **•Bisekine, emê *bîstekê* li vê qehwê peye bin** (L) Wait, we're going to stop at this coffeehouse *for a while*. {also: bistek (K); bîstik (A)} [L/K//A] <xêl I>

bîstem بیستەم *adj.* twentieth, 20th. {also: bîstemîn (IFb/TF/GF/CT-2/ZF-2/Wkt-2)} Cf. P bīstom بیستم; Sor bîstemîn بیستەمین [CT/ZF/Wkt//IFb/TF/GF] <bîst I>

bîstemîn بیستەمین (IFb/TF/GF/CT/ZF/Wkt) = twentieth. See **bîstem**.

bîstik بیستِك (A) = moment. See **bîstek**.

bîstin بیستِن (Ad/A/IF/M) = to hear. See **bihîstin**.

bîstsalî بیستسالی *f.* **(;-yê).** 1) twenty-year period; 2) *[adj.]* twenty-year-old, twenty years old. [K/B]

bîşeng بیشەنگ *f.* **().** weeping willow, bot. *Salix babylonica*: **•Ko ew mir, di bi[n] darên *bîşenganr̄*a t'irbeke spî ava kirin** [sic] **û wan ew têda veşart** (Dz #22, 390) When he died, they built a white grave under *the weeping willows* and buried him in it. {also: şengebî (FJ-2/GF-2/Kmc-2)} {syn: bî II} [Dz/K/IFb/GF/FJ/TF/CS/Kmc]

bît'er بیتەر: **–bît'er bûn** (K/B) 1) {syn: p'eyda bûn} to appear, arise, spring up: **•Du kur̄ *jê bît'er bûn*** (HCK-1, 208) 2 boys *sprang from her* [=She bore 2 sons]; 2) to be obtained, gotten. [HCK/K/B]

bîvelerz بیڤەلەرز (Zeb/RZ/SS) = earthquake. See **bîbelerz** .

bîvok بیڤۆك (F/K) = quince. See **bih**.

bîya بییا (Hk) = brother-in-law. See **bûrî**.

bîyanî بییانی *adj.* foreign, strange. {also: biyanî (Ber/JB3/IF/SK); [biiani] بیانی (JJ)} P bīgāne بیگانه; Sor bêgane بێگانە. See **Outside** in: I. Gershevitch. "Outdoor Terms in Iranian," *A Locust's Leg : Studies in Honour of S.H. Taqizadeh* (London, 1962), pp.76-84; reprinted in his *Philologia Iranica*, ed. N. Sims-Williams (Wiesbaden : Dr. Ludwig Reichert Verlag, 1985), pp. 176-78; also **3. bēgāne** in his "Etymological Notes on Persian mih, naxčīr, bēgāne, and bīmār," in: *Dr. J.M. Unvala Memorial Volume* (Bombay, 1964), pp.89-94; reprinted in his *Philologia Iranica*, pp. 192-93. [Ber/JB3/IF/JJ/SK//K]

bjang بژانگ, m. (B) = eyelashes. See **bijang**.

bjîjk بژیژك (IFb) = doctor, physician. See **bijîşk**.

bjîşk بژیشك (JB3) = doctor, physician. See **bijîşk**.

blêç بلێچ *f.(RF)/m.(OK)* **().** lightning. {also: bilêç (RZ/IFb-2/ZF3)} {syn: beledî; berq; birûsk} [IFb/OK/RF//RZ/ZF3] <bap'eşk>

blûr بلوور (IFb) = flute. See **bilûr**.

blyan بلیان (EH) = knowing. See **bilyan**.

bo I بۆ *m.* Dad(dy)! Pop(pa)! (vocative) : **•Ya bo!** (L) Hey, Dad! {also: bavo!} [L] <bav>

bo II بۆ *prep.* for; to: ***•ji bo* hin ramanên siyasî** (BX) *for* some political thoughts; **-ji bo vê (yekê)** = for this reason; **-ji bo Xwedê** (L) for God's sake. {also: ji bo; [ji] bona; [bou] بو (JJ)} [BX/K/A/B//JJ]

boblat بۆبلات *f.* **(-a;-ê).** disaster, catastrophe, calamity, misfortune, tragedy: **•Li gor tiştê ku min di remla xwe de dît, *boblateke* mezin li pêş navçeyê me ye. Di dawîya payiza paşîn de ba û bahozek ê dest pê bike û ew ê heta sê şev û sê rojan bidome** (Ardû, 32) According to the thing that I saw in my cubes, *a disaster* is headed for our area. At the end of the fall, a powerful windstorm will start, and it will last for 3 nights and 3 days **•Ji bilî pirtûka nemir M. Ehmedê Namî Agirê Sînema Amûdê, ta roja îro hîn ti berhem li ser vê *bobelatê* nehatiye çap kirin** (DE, #18, 158) Except for the book The Fire of Amud Cinema by the immortal M. E. N, until today, no work on this *tragedy* has yet been printed **•Wê ew *bobelata* xwezayî di nêzîk de bigihîje gundan jî** (FS: M.Baksî. Xemgînîya Xerzan) That natural *disaster* will soon reach the villages as well. {also: bobelat (CS-2/FJ/K/Kmc/GF/Tsab); [boubelat] بوبلات (JJ)} {syn: bela I; bêt'ar; gosirmet; oyîn; qeda; siqûmat; şetele; t'ifaq} possibly ba = 'wind, breeze' + bela = 'misfortune'; see also Tsab [Ardû/IFb/CS/Kmc/RZ//K/GF/FJ/JJ/Tsab] <babelîsk>

bobelat بۆبەلات (CS/FJ/K/Kmc/GF/Tsab/JJ) = disaster. See **boblat**.

bobelîsk بۆبلیسك (K/B) = whirlwind. See **babelîsk**.

bocî بۆجی *f./m.(B)* **().** dachshund, short and squat dog [Rus taksa такса]: ***•Bocîke* wî hebû** (Ba) He had *a dachshund* **•Cotek tajî û cotek *bonciyên* min jî hene** (ZZ-5, 80) I have a pair of greyhounds and a pair *of dachshunds* as well. {also: boncî (ZZ-5/GF-2); bonjî (GF); bûcî (IFb)} [Ba/B//ZZ//GF//IFb] <kûçik>

boç' بۆچ *f./m.(Mzg)* **(-a/-ê;-ê/).** tail: **•Bizina xez jî ew bizin e ku dora dev, poz, çav, û--heşa ji cenabê te--dora *boça* wê bi rengekî sorê zer, kej an jî qehweyî be** (Hesenê Metê) "Bizina xez" is a goat who has a reddish-yellow, blonde, or brownish color around its mouth, nose, eyes, and --no offense to you--around its *tail*. {also: boç'ik; [bōč] بوچ (JJ)} {syn: dêl II; dû II; k'ilk; kurî I (Bw); qemç[ik]; ter̄î I[1]} < W Arm boč' պոչ [IFb/B/JJ/GF/Mzg] <dûv>

boçi بۆچ (A/IFb/GF) = why. See **boçî**.

boç'ik بۆچِك *f.* **(-a;-ê).** 1) {syn: dêl II; dû II; k'ilk; qemç[ik]; ter̄î I[1]} tail (B): **•Gemê hespa li devê**

hespa nedidan, li binê *boçka* hespa didan (FK-kk-1) They didn't put the horses' bits in their mouths, they put them under the horses' *tail[s]*; 2) end of the spinal column, formed by the sacrum and the coccyx (A); 3) stem *(of some fruits)* (IF); 4) nervous jumping (IF). {also: poç'ik (Dz-#897)} [B/A/IFb/Mzg/Rh] <dûv I>

boçî بۆچی/**bo çî** بۆ چی *interrog. part.* why?: **•Te *bo çî* we'dê xo şkand?** (SK 2:13) *Why* have you broken your promise? **•Tu *bo çî* ho 'aciz î?** (SK 3:20) *Why* are you so miserable? {also: boçi (A/IFb-2/GF)} {syn: *boy; çima; *ji ber çi} [Bw/IFb/SK/JB1-A//A/GF]

bod بۆد = trough or boat made from a log. See **bot**.

Bohtan بـۆهـتـان *f.()*. a region in the provinces of Siirt and Mardin, inhabited by the Botî tribe, encompassing the area between Hazo (=Kozluk) and Misirc (=Kurtalan), whose center is the city of Cizre [Jizirat Ibn 'Amr] in Şırnak province (formerly part of Mardin). {also: Botan (Haz); <buhtan> بـهـتـان (HH)} [K/A/IF//Haz//HH] <Mezra Bohtan>

Bohtanî بۆهتانی (K). See **Bohtî**.

Bohtî بۆهتی *adj.* 1) Kurdish tribe inhabiting the region of Botan (or Bohtan) (qv.); 2) Kurdish Kurmanji dialect spoken in Bohtan. {also: Bohtanî (K); Botî (Haz); <buhtî بـهـتی/buxtî بـختی> (HH)} [A/IF//Haz//K//HH]

bok بۆك (HB) = ugly; dirty. See **bi'ok**.

boke بـۆكـه *m.*(**-yê; **). 1) hero, protagonist, main character: **•*Bokeyên* vê çîrokê Feqe Emer û Feqe Hesen ... berê xwe dabûn Îranê** (O. Sebrî. Li goristaneke Amedê, 53) *The heroes of* this story F.E. and F.H. ... had gone to Iran **•Tiştên dihên serê *bokeyê* romanê trajîk in** (Mehname #40, gulan 2003) The things that happen to the novel's *protagonist* are tragic; 2) [*adj.*] brave, daring, courageous. [O.Sebrî/ZF3/GF/ZF3/FK/Kmc/AD] <gernas; leheng>

bol بـۆل *adj.* plenty, abundant: **•Nanê meyî *bole*** (Ba, #32, 318) We have plenty of bread [lit., our bread is *abundant*]. {syn: boş II} < T bol; Za bol = 'much, very' [Ba/K/B/IFb]

bomb بـۆمـب *f.* **(-a;-ê).** bomb: **-bomb avîtin** (K/B)/ **~kirin** (B) to bomb, bombard. {also: bombe (IF)} [F/K/B//IF]

bombavêj بـۆمـب ئـاڤـێـژ (K[s]/B) = bomber. See **bombeavêj**.

bombe بۆمبه (IF) = bomb. See **bomb**.

bombeavêj بـۆمـبـه ئـاڤـێـژ *f.* **(;-ê).** bomber *(airplane)*: **•*Bombeavêjên* me ên sivik ... li rêhesinên erdê Kaparanikayê xistine** (RN) Our light *bombers* hit the railroads of Kaparanika. {also: bombavêj (K[s]/B)} [(neol)RN/JB3/IF//K(s)/B] <balafir>

bomelerze بـۆمـهـلـهرزه (K[s]/A) = earthquake. See **bîbelerz**.

bon بۆن (M/SK) = to be; to become. See **bûn**.

bona بـۆنـا *prep.* 1) for: **•Ezê *(ji) bo(na)* zaroyên xwe bixebitim** (BX) I will work *for [the benefit of]* my children **•Gula ko min çinî *ji bo(na)* te ye** (BX) The rose which I picked is *for* you **•Pezê nêr *ji bo* kêrê ye** (BX) The ram is destined *for* the knife *[prv.]* **•*Ji bo* hin ramanên siyasî** (BX) *For* some political thoughts; **-ji bona xatirê/ji bo xatirê** (ZF3) for the sake of, because of: **•*Ji bona xatirê* kevnek jina te xwe xistîye vî halî** (L) *Because of* an old woman you are in this [bad] shape; 2) *[conj.]* {syn: bila; da II; deqene; ḧeta ko [4]; wekî [2]} for, in order to [+ *subj.*]: **•Ê go dihere mala hakim, *ji bona* qîza wî bixwaze** (L) Whoever goes to the king's house *in order to* ask for his daughter; **-ji bona xatirê** = [*with neg.*] lest **•*Ji bona xatirê go* tu li çolê *ne*mînî** (L) *So that* you *don't* [have to] stay in the desert, or, Lest you stay in the desert. {also: [ji] **bo II**; ji bona} {syn: seba} according to BX < ji bûyîna = 'from the existence of' [BX/K/JB3/B/ZF3/Wkt] <seba> See also **bo II**.

boncî بـۆنـجـی (ZZ-5/GF) = dachshund, small dog. See **bocî**.

bonjî بۆنژی (GF) = dachshund, small dog. See **bocî**.

boqil بۆقِل *m.* (). calf of the leg (IFb/HH/RZ); leg (HB/A). {also: buqil (HB-2); <bûqil> بـوقل (HH)} {syn: belek II; ç'îm I; paq} [HB/A/IFb/RZ//HH] <ling>

bor I بـــــۆر *adj.* 1) {syn: boz; cûn I; gewr[1]; kew II; xwelîreng} gray/grey; color between brown and white (IF); 2) *[m.]* {syn: bergîr; hesp; nijda} horse (F/K); saddle-horse; fast-horse, racer (EP-7): **•Min *borekî* xweş-xweş dibê** (FT, 151) I need a very fine *saddle-horse*; 3) *name of Mem's horse in many versions of the story of Mem û Zîn (Memê Alan).* [Z-1/EP-7/F/K/IF]

bor II بۆر (Bw/JJ/GF/TF) = crossing, ford. See **bihur**.

bor III بـۆر *f.* **(-a;).** uncultivated land [='erda neajotî]. {also: bûr (Kmc-8-2)} <Arc bor בור = 'uncultivated' & Syr √b-w-r ܒܘܪ = 'to lie uncultivated, waste, neglected'; NENA bûrâ ܒܘܪܐ = 'uncultivated ground' (Maclean) [Qzl/Kmc-8/IFb/GF] <beyar; kat II; k'irêbe>

borandin بـــۆرانـــدِن (K/GF) = to cause to pass. See **bihurandin**.

borîjen بـــۆريـــژەن (ZF) = trumpet; trumpeter. See **borîzan**.

bořîn I بـــۆڕيـــن *vi.* **(-boř-).** 1) to low, moo; to howl, bellow; 2) to sound *(vi.)*, blast (trumpet) (K/B). {also: burrîn (IF); [borin] بـــريـــن (JJ)} [K/B/A/IFb/M/JJ] See also **bařîn II**.

borîn II بۆرين (-bor-) (JB3) = to pass. See **bihurtin**.

borîzan بۆريزان *m.&f.* **().** 1) trumpet: **•Dengê nefîr û zurna û **burîzane*** (Lwj #1, 34) It is the sound of the flute, the zurna and *the burîzan* [a wind instrument, trumpet]; 2) trumpeter, trumpet player (K/A/GF/CS). {also: borîjen (ZF); burîzan (Lwj)} Cf. P būrū'zan بـــــوروزن = 'trumpet player'; T borazan = 'trumpet[er]' [Lwj//IFb/RZ/SS//ZF] <nefîr; zirne>

bormotik بۆرمۆتِك = ?cradle; ?child. See **bormotk**.

***bormotk** بـــۆرمـــۆتـــك *f.* **(-a;).** 1) {syn: bêşîk; dergûş; landik} ?cradle, crib (EP-7) **•Bra bişewite bormotka zêřîne** (EP-7) Let the golden cradle burn; 2) ?child, infant (EP-7). {also: bormotik} [EP-7]

***borxan•e** بـــۆرخـــانـــە *f.* **(;•ê).** stable *(for horses)*. {syn: naxir; stewl; t'ewle} [EP-7] <afiř; axil; axur; extexane>

borxî بۆرغى (OK) = screw. See **burxî**.

bos•e I بـــۆســـە *f.* **(;•ê).** ambush: **-bose danan** (SK/Zeb)/ ~ **[li ber] vedan** (Zeb) to lay an ambush. <T pusu = 'ambush': Sor bûse بووسە [Zeb/IFb/SK/OK]

bos•e II بـــۆســـە/**boṣe** بـــۆصـــە (FS) *m.* **(;-yî).** round washers *fastening pins connecting the beam to the body of the traditional plow*; hoop *fastened to the yoke of a plough and to the beam, placed over ox's head:* **•Gustîlik: di navenda nîr de, li hin deveran ji dar, li hin deveran jî ji hesin xelekek tê bicih kirin ... Li devera Torê jê re "*bose*" dibêjin** (CCG, 17) *Gustîlik* (ringlet): in the center of the yoke, a hoop is placed, in some regions from wood, in others from iron ... In the Tur'abdin region it is called *bose*. {also: bewse (FJ-2/GF-2); <bûse> بوسە (HH)} = NENA bôsâ ܒܘܣܐ/ bôsâ ܒܘܣܐ = 'wooden ring used in stables; stick bent into a circle fastened to the yoke of a plough and to the beam' (Maclean) [CCG/Kmc/FJ/GF/AA//HH/FS] <berxep; xenîke>

Bosnî بۆسنى *adj.* Bosnian. {also: Boşnaqî (ZF3)} [Wkp/BF//ZF3]

bost بـــۆســـت *f.* **(-a;-ê).** span *(unit of measure)*, the distance from the end of the thumb to the end of the little finger of a spread hand (F/K/A/IF/JJ): **•Zînê bihîst ku Memê hatîye, ew *buhustekê* ji 'erdê bilind bû** (FK-eb-1) When Zîn heard that Mem had come, she rose *a span* off the ground. {also: bihost (K-2/IFb/OK); bihust (K/B); bisṯ II (SK); bîst II (F); buhust (FK-eb-1/GF-2); [bost بوست /buhust بهست] (JJ)} Cf. Skr vitasti- *m.*; Av vītasti- *f.*; Baluchi gidisp (Gersh §470, p. 70); Pashto wlešt (Morg); Ormuri jusp/ǰbasp/zbast; Parachi belīšt (Morg); P bedast بـــدســـت (= vajab وجب) = 'a span'; Sor bost بۆست [cf. Ar šibr شبر, T karış] For Av vītasti- see W. Henning. "An Astronomical Chapter of Bundahishn," *Journal of the Royal Asiatic Society*, (1942), p. 236. [A/JJ/GF/OK//F//K/B//IFb//SK//FK-eb-1] <qulaç>

bostan بـــۆســـتـــان, m. (; bostên/bostîn) (K/IFb/B/OK) = garden. See **bîstan**.

boş I بـــۆش *adj.* 1) {syn: betal; vala} empty, vacant; 2) {syn: bêfeyde; bêkêr} null and void, in vain, of no use: **•Meyane divîne *boşe*** (Ba3-3, #8) Meyaneh sees that it is *of no use* **•Zînê dîna xwe daê, k'ilam *boşin*** (EP-7) Z. saw that the songs *are to no avail*; 3) weak (B). {also: [bosc] بـــــــوش (JJ)} < T boş {boşahî I; boşayî} [Z-1/K/A/JB3/IF/B//JJ]

boş II بـــــۆش *adj.* numerous, plentiful, abundant *(of water, or number)*. {also: [boch] بـــوش (JJ); <boş> بـــوش (HH)} {syn: bol} {boşahî II} [Z-1/K/A/JB3/IF/HH/JJ/Zeb] <mişe>

boş III بـــــــۆش *m.* **(-ê;).** string, file, row, train *(of camels)*: **-boşê deva** (DM) A file of camels. {syn: qent'er} [DM/L/K] <deve; hestir; lok'>

boşahî I بـــۆشـــاهـــى *f.* **().** 1) emptiness; 2) uselessness, pointlessness, being in vain. {also: boşayî (IF)} [K//IF] <boş I>

boşahî II بـــۆشـــاهـــى *f.* **().** abundance, plenty. [K/IF] <boş II>

boşayî بـــۆشـــايـــى (IF) = emptiness; uselessness. See **boşahî I**.

boşe بـــۆشـــە *m.* (). Roma, Gypsy: **-merîyê boşe** (F) do. {syn: aşiq; begzade; dome; gewende; lûlî; mirt'ib; qereçî} Cf. W Arm poša[y] պոշայ {boşetî; boşeyî} [K/F/B]

boşetî بـــۆشـــەتـــى *f.* **().** 1) Roma or Gypsy lifestyle; 2) nomadism, nomadic lifestyle. {also: boşeyî (B-2/K-2)} [K/B] <boşe>

boşeyî بۆشەيى (B/K) = Gypsy or nomadic lifestyle. See

boşetî.

Boşnaqî بۆشناقی (ZF3) = Bosnian. See **Bosnî**.

bot بــۆت *f.* ().1) {syn: şikev} hollowed-out log, used as a trough (HB); 2) boat made out of a log (IF). {also: bod; [botek] بوتك (JJ); <boṯ> بوط (HH)} [HB/IFb//HH//JJ]

botaf بـۆتـاف (TF) = reddish-brown dye for cattle hides. See **batov**.

Botan بۆتان (Haz) = Bohtan (geog.) . See **Bohtan**.

botav بــۆتــاڤ (Btm/A/IFb) = reddish-brown dye for cattle hides. See **batov**.

Botî بۆتی (Haz) = native of Bo[h]tan. See **Bohtî**.

boxçe بۆخچە, m. (K) = cloth for wrapping bundles. See **buxçik**.

boxe بۆخە (JB3/IF) = bull. See **boẍ**.

boẍ بـۆغ *m.* **(-ê;).** bull, ox; fertile bull, uncastrated bull (B); young, uncastrated bull (HH). {also: boxe (JB3/IF); boẍe (; boẍê) (K/B); [boga] بـوغـه (JJ); <boẍe> بوغه (HH)} {syn: ga} Cf. T boğa [J//K/B/HH//JB3/IF//JJ] <ga>

boẍçe بـۆغـچـە, m. (; boẍçê) (B) = cloth for wrapping bundles. See **buxçik**.

boẍe بۆغە (; boẍê) (K/B) = bull. See **boẍ**.

boya بۆیا (JJ/GF) = paint. see **boyax.**

boyax بـۆیـاخ *f.* **(-a;-ê).** 1) paint; dye: **•Ew cesareta ku tu rabî porê xwe *boyax bikî* û bi wê boyaxa reş a ku piştî demekê wê dîsa bibe binsipî, biçî nav hevalan** (LC, 6) The courage *to dye* one's hair, and then to go out in public [lit., 'go among friends'] with that black dye that will become white at the roots again after a while; 2) shoe polish: **-boyax kirin** (K/IF) = a) to paint, dye; b) to shine, polish *(shoes)*. {also: boya (GF); boyaẍ (B/HB-2); [boia] بـویـا (JJ)} Cf. T boya; Sor boyax بـۆیـاخ = 'shoe polish' [HB/K/IFb/TF/OK//B//JJ/GF] <derman; r̄eng; s̲ibẍe; xim; ximdar>

boyaẍ بۆیاغ (B/HB) = paint. see **boyax.**

boz بــــۆز *adj.* 1) {syn: bor I; cûn I; gewr[1]; kew II; xwelîreng} grey/gray; 2) *[m.]* horse or donkey with gray coat (B). {also: [boz] بــــوز (JJ)} Cf. T boz; Sor boz بۆز [K/A/JB3/IF/B/JJ]

bra I برا (JB3/IF) = brother. See **bira I**.

bra II برا (EP-7) = so that, in order that. See **bila**.

br̄a III برا (Msr) = true; right. See **bir̄a III**.

brang برانگ (EP) = brother. See **bira I**.

braştin بــراشــتِــن (-brêş-) (IFb/GF) = to roast. See **biraştin**.

bratî I براتی (JB3) = brotherhood. See **biratî**.

br̄atî II براتی(Msr) = truth. See **bir̄atî II**.

braza برازا (Bw/JJ) = nephew or niece. See **brazî**.

brazî بــرازی *m.&f.* **(-yê/-ya;).** nephew or niece *(child of one's brother)*: **•Li şera xal û xwarzî; li xwarina, mam û *brazî*** (BX) For battles, maternal uncle and nephew; for food, paternal uncle and nephew *[prv. illustrating familial relationships]*. {also: biraz, m. (; birêz) (B); biraza (K); birazî (A/IF-2); braza (Bw); [brá-za (JJ-G)/berā-zi (JJ-Lx)/brāzā (JJ-Rh)]; <birazî> بــرازی (HH)} {syn: êgan (Ad); t'or̄in, m. [2]} Cf. P berāderzādeh بـرادرزاده; Sor biraza بِـرازا = 'brother's child, nephew, niece' [BX/JB3/IF//K//Bw/JJ//A/HH//B] <ap; mam; t'îza; xwarzî>

brinc برنج (HCK) = rice. See **birinc I**.

brîn I برین (-bir-) (JB3) = to cut. See **bir̄în II**.

brîn II برین (JB3) = wound. See **birîn I**.

brîndar بریندار (JB3) = wounded. See **birîndar**.

Brîtanî بــریــتــانــی *adj.* British. {also: Birîtanî (BF); Brîtanyayî (ZF3)} Sor Berîtanî بەریتانی [Wkp/SS//BF//ZF3]

Brîtanyayî بریتانیایی (ZF3) = British. See **Brîtanî**.

brrîn برین (IF) = to cut. See **bir̄în II**.

brû برو و = eyebrow. See **birû**.

brûsk برووسك (JB3/IF/Wn) = lightning. See **birûsk**.

buha بوها (A/HH) = price; expensive. See **biha**.

buhar بوهار (HH/L-I/Wlt) = spring. See **bihar**.

buhartin بوهارتِن (-bihur-) (IF) = to pass. See **bihurtin**.

buhik بوهِك (RZ) = insect. See **bihuk**.

buhişt بوهِشت (BX) = paradise. See **bihuşt**.

buhujîn بـوهـوژیـن vi. (-buhuj-) (M/SK/Dh) = to melt, dissolve *(vi.)*. See **bihoştin**.

buhujtin بــوهــوژتِــن (GF) = to melt, dissolve. See **bihoştin**.

buhuk بـوهـوك/buḧuk بـوحـوك (GF/FJ) = insect. See **bihuk**.

buhur بـوهـور (GF/JJ) = passage, crossing, ford. See **bihur**.

buhurandin بوهوراندِن (BK/IFb/TF) = to cause to pass. See **bihurandin.**

buhust بــوهــوســت (FK-eb-1/GF/JJ) = span *(unit of measure)*. See **bost**.

buhuşt بوهوشت (GF) = paradise. See **bihuşt**.

buhuştin بوهوشتِن vi. (-buhuj-) (M) = to melt, dissolve (vi.). See **bihoştin**.

buḧuk بوحوك (B/G) = insect. See **bihuk**.

Bulgarî بــولــگــاری *adj.* Bulgarian. {also: Bilxarî (IFb)}[Wkt/BF/ZF3/CS//IFb]

buqil بوقِل (HB) = leg. See **boqil**.

burc بورج (JB3) = tower; zodiac sign. See **birc**.

burî بورى = eyebrow. See **birû**.

burîzan بـــوريـــزان (Lwj) = trumpet; trumpeter. See **borîzan**.

burrîn بوررين (IF) = to low, moo. See **bor̄în I.**

buru بورو (Azer) = eyebrow. See **birû**.

burxe بورخه (A) = screw. See **burẍî**.

burxî بورخى (IFb/RZ) = screw. See **burẍî**.

burẍe بورغه (F/K/B) = screw. See **burẍî**.

burẍî بورغى *f.* **(-ya;).** 1) screw: **•Wî *birẍî* şidand** (FS) He tightened in *the screw*; 2) drill, gimlet (K/B). {also: birẍî (FS); borẍî (OK); burxe (A); burxî (IFb/RZ); burẍe (F/K/B)} <T burgu ='screw' --> Ar burγī بـرغـى; Sor burxî بـورخـى = 'screw' (K2) [Bw/GF//OK//A//IFb/RZ//F/K/B//FS] <bizmar; dernefîs; mikare>

buşqul بـــوشـــقـــول (IF) = goat manure. See **bişkul** & **pişkul**.

bu'uk بوعوك (GF/FJ) = insect. See **bihuk**.

buxçik بـــوخـــچـــك *f.* (). square cloth for wrapping a bundle. {also: boxçe, m. (K); boẍçe, m. (; boẍçê) (B); [bokcia] بـوغـچـه (JJ)} Cf. T bohça; Sor buxçe بوخچه = 'parcel' [HB/A//K//JJ] <sifre; şalik II>

buxik بوخِك (IFb) = insect. See **bihuk**.

buzêz بوزێز (Wkt) = clothes moth. See **bizûz**.

buzîz بوزيز (Wkt) = clothes moth. See **bizûz**.

buzûz بوزووز (Wkt) = clothes moth. See **bizûz**.

bûcî بووجى (IFb) = dachshund, small dog. See **bocî**.

bûk I بـــووك *f.* **(-a;-ê).** 1) bride: **•*Bûk* li zavê pîroz be** (AB) May *the bride* be blessed to the groom *[marriage greeting]*; 2) young woman marrying into the family (sister-in-law/daughter-in-law) (IF/JB3/JJ); [by extension] young woman: **•Eva *bûka*, jina wî xortîye** (Dz) This *young woman* is that young man's wife **•Dinhêr̄in wê *bûkeke* cahil şuxulê xwe xilas kirye** (Dz) They see *a young girl* has finished her work **•Ew *bûka* Qeret'ajdîne, / Bêşk'ertima Ç'ekîne** (EP) She is the *sister-in-law to-be* [lit. 'bride'] of Q., betrothed to Çekan from birth; 3) doll (K): **-bûka zaroka** (A) do. {also: [bouk] بـــوك (JJ); <bûk> بـــوك (HH)} [Pok. 2. u̯ed(h)- 1115.] 'to lead; to lead home, marry (said of the man)' : Proto Indo-Ir √vadh = 'to lead (the bride)'; Skt vadhū *f.* = 'bride'; O Ir *wadŭ-ka (A&L pp. 84-85 [V, 4]); Av vaδū- = 'wife' & vadəmna = 'she who is led, i.e., bride'; Sgd wδw/wδ; Mid P bayōk (A&L pp. 84-85 [V, 4]) + wayōdagān = 'nuptials, marriage feast' (M3) (M. Schwartz: with plural of institutions, cf. mihragān مهرگان); Southern Tati dialects: Xoznini vayá (Yar-Shater); Shughni group: Yazghulami wað-:west- = 'to marry a woman' (Morg2); P bayo[g] بـيـو[گ]; Sor bûk بووك; Za vêv/veyv = 'bride' (Srk) & veyve *m.* = 'wedding' (Todd); Hau weywe *f.* (M4)/wawa/wawī; Luri bahī(g)/bihīg; cf. OCS vedù, vèsti & Rus √ved- vesti вести = 'to lead'. See: M. Schwartz. "Proto-Indo-European √ĝem," *Monumentum H.S. Nyberg*, Acta Iranica, Series 2: Hommages et Opera Minora, 5 (Leiden : E.J. Brill, 1975), vol. 2, p. 195 ff. [cf. r*ange of meanings of* Ar 'arūs عـــروس = 'bride; doll'] [F/K/A/JB3/IFb/B/JJ/HH/JB1-S/GF/TF] <berbû; bêşk'ertim; dergistî; de'wat; diş; zava; zeyî>

bûk II بــــــــووك (K/A/IFb/B) = sty *(in the eyelid)*. See **bûkik**.

bûka baranê بـــووكـــا بـــارانـــێ *f.* 1) {syn: k'eskesor; kêrestûn} rainbow; 2) {syn: *lopik (FS)} game played by children when there is a drought: they go from house to house asking for alms (Hk); "a traditional handmade doll with a female face, used by Kurdish children (girls) to ask for rain. Children carrying the doll across the region, sing some folklore poems; other people in turn respond with pouring some water over the doll. This tradition which is performed during seasons when people need raining, has roots in Kurdish mythology and culture" (Wkp). bûka baranê = lit. 'bride of the rain'. [Hk/GF/ZF3/Wkt/FS/Wkp]

bûka mara بووكاماra (GF) = lizard. See **bûkmar**.

bûkanî بووكـانـى *f.* **(;-yê).** 1) bridehood, being a bride: **• ...û çû ber sabata xwe, xeml û xêlê *bûkanîyê* li xwe kir, xwe wilo zeynand** (HR 3:282) She went to her box, put on her *bridal* finery, adorned herself; 2) first three months of marriage, honeymoon (CS/FJ/GF); 3) bridal gift: **•Ez jî nizanim ka ew çiyayê ko di hemî payîzan de ji Axê dixeyidî ... dê di vê biharê de weke hemî biharan *bûkaniyek* ji Axê re bikiriya dîyarî ... an, no** (MG. Tavê ew dît) And I don't know whether that mountain which used to get mad at the Earth in the fall ... will make *a bridal gift* to the Earth this spring as in all springs ... or not. {also: bûkî (B); bûkîtî (TF); bûktî (K)} [HR/IFb/GF/FJ/CS/MG] <bûk I>

bûkemar بووكه‌مار (IFb) = lizard. See **bûkmar**.

bûkik بـووكِـك *f.* **(;-ê).** sty *(in the eyelid)*. {also: bûk II (K/A/IFb-2/B); <bûkik> بوكك (HH)} =Sor pizdûk

پزدووك [Frq/IFb/HH/GF/TF//K/A/B]

bûkî بووکی (B) = bridehood. See **bûkanî**.

bûkîtî بووکیتی (TF) = bridehood. See **bûkanî**.

bûkmar بووکمار *f.* **( ).** type of lizard. {also: bûka mara (GF); bûkemar (IFb)} [Zeb/OK//GF//IFb]

bûkmezav•e بـووکـمـەزاڤـە *f.* **(;•ê).** corn poppy, red poppy, field poppy, bot. Papaver rhoeas, *edible plant*: **•Li Çiyayê Kurmênc, *bûkmezavê* di nav giyayin din da dikelînin, û ji bo sermê wek çay vedixin. Dermanê kuxikê ye** (FE) In Çiyayê Kurmênc (Efrin, Syrian Kurdistan), they boil *the poppy* with other herbs, and they drink it for a cold. It is a remedy for a cough. [Fr coquelicot; T gelincik]. [Efr/FE] <p'incar>

bûktî بووکتی (K) = bridehood. See **bûkanî**.

bûm بـــــــووم *m.* **(-ê;).** owl, zool. order *Strigiformes*: **-bûmê kor** (K) eagle owl. {also: [boum] بـوم (JJ)} {syn: kund} Cf. Ar/P būm بوم [F/K/IF/B/JJ]

bûn بـــــــــــوون *vi.* 1) **(**pres. **-im/-**[a]**me;-î;-e;** pl. **–in/ -**[**a**]**ne** [1st prs. pl. **-în/-**[a]**yne** (M/Bw/Zeb/Dh)]**)** to be: **-dibe** = perhaps, maybe: ***•Dibe ku* te t'emî dane Ûsib** (Ba #4, 313) *Perhaps* you warned Joseph; 2) **(**pres. **-b-/-v-)** {syn: lêhatin[1]} to become, get: **•Çel kevok hatin û libsê xwe danîn, *bûn* çel xortê minasib** (L) 40 doves came and removed their garb, *they became* 40 attractive young men **•Qîzik ze'f belengaz *dibe*** (J) The girl *becomes* very upset/unhappy; 3) to be proper, be appropriate, be allowed: **•Li pêş mezinekî xwe *nabe* ku em titûnê bikêşin** (Epl, 23) In front of an elder *it is not all right* for us to smoke tobacco; 4) {also: ji dayîk bûn} to be born: **•Heciyê Cindî sala 1908an ... *ji dayîk bûye*** (KO, 45) Hajie Jndi *was born* ... in 1908 **•Sala *bûyîna* min** (KO, 40) The year of my *birth*. {also: bîn II (Rh/M-Zx); bon (M/ SK); bûyîn (K/IFb-2/B-2); wîn (Ad-2); [boun بـون/ bouin بـوين] (JJ); <bûn بـون (dibe) (دبـە)> (HH)} [Pok. bheu- 146.] --> *bheuH- = 'to be, exist, grow': Skt √bhū [bhavati]; O Ir *bu- (Tsb 37): Av & O P bav- (pres. bava-); P būdan بـــودن; Sor bûn بـــوون; SoK bü(ı)n: aw(ı)m/mawm etc. (Fat 408, 549); Za benã [byayiş] (Todd/Srk); Hau bîey (b-) *vi.* (M4) [K//A/JB3/IFb/JJ/HH/GF//M/SK//Rh/M-Zx] <hebûn>

bûqelemû بـووقـەلـەمـوو (Wkt) = turkey *(fowl)*. See **bûqelemûn**.

bûqelemûn بووقەلەموون *m.* **(-ê;).** turkey *(fowl)*. {also: bûqelemû (Wkt)}{syn: coqcoq; culûx̂; kûrkûr; mirîşka hindistanê (B); şamî (AB)} <P būqalamūn بوقلمون = 'turkey, chameleon' [F//Wkt]

bûr بوور (Kmc-8) = uncultivated land. See **bor III**.

bûra بـــوورا *m.* **(-ê; bûrê).** brother-in-law [pl. brothers-in-law], *(a married man's)* wife's brother {=T kayınço}: **•Ez û *bûre* ê xwe sîyarin** (Haz) My *brother-in-law* and I are riding [on horseback] **•Mêrê met'a min ez nedîtibûm, her gavanê ji nav Melegana dihatin, salixê min jêr̄a didan, wekî kur̄ê Şemoyê *bûrê* wî dixûne, navê wî 'Ereb e** (Tsab, 213 [Arab, 87]) My uncle [paternal aunt's husband] hadn't ever seen me, but the cowherds of the Melegan used to come and tell him about me, that the son of his *brother-in-law* Shemo is studying, and his name is Arab. {also: bîya (Hk); bûre (Haz); bûrî (Ag/RZ-2/Tsab-2); [boura] بـــورا (JJ)} {syn: birajin; xizm [3]} < bûk-bira (Tsab) [Ag/ /Haz//K/IFb/B/JJ/GF/Kmc/RZ/Tsab//Hk] <t'î II> {v}

bûre بووره (Haz) = brother-in-law. See **bûra**.

bûrî بووری (Ag/RZ/Tsab) = brother-in-law. See **bûra**.

bûrîn بوورین (A/Ber) = to pass. See **bihurtin**.

bûrûsk بووورووسك (Azer) = lightning. See **birûsk**.

bûsat بـووسـات *m./f.(B)* **(; /-ê).** 1) dress, attire, apparel (B): **•k'inc û bûsat** (LC) dress and apparel; 2) {syn: hevsar} *(horse's)* harness (K/IF/B); 3) saddle, bridle, and other accessories for saddling a horse (JJ); 4) pole attached to yoke (HH). {also: bûse (IF); bûset (B-2); [pousat] پوسات (JJ); <bûse> بوسه (HH)} Cf. T pusat = 'armor, equipment' [Z-2/EP-7/K/B/ / IF/HH//JJ] <cil; ç'ek; dizgîn; hesp; zîn>

bûse بـــووســە (IF/HH) = 1) dress, attire; 2) harness; 3) pole attached to yoke. See **bûsat**.

bûset بـــووســەت (B) = 1) dress, attire; 2) harness. See **bûsat**.

bûstin بووستِن (GF) = to melt, dissolve. See **bihoştin**.

bûyer بوویەر *f.* **(-a;-ê).** event, occurrence; incident: **•Li pey agahiyan, *bûyer* roja 4 Gulanê danê êvarê pêk hatiye** (AW71A4a) According to reports, *the incident* took place on the 4th of May in the evening hours **•... Memê Alan, Xec û Siyamend, Koroxlî, Topa Sultanê Îslamê û hwd; ko heryekê ji *bûyerekê* an ji xeyala kesekî peyda bûye** (SB, 50) [Stories like] Memê Alan, Khej and Siyamend, Köroğlu, Topa Sultanê Islamê, etc., each of which was created from *an event* [i.e., is a true story] or from someone's imagination. [(neol)Ber/K/JB3/IFb/GF/TF/ OK]

bûyîn بـوویـین (K/IFb/B) = to be; to become; to be born. See **bûn**.

C 

ca جـا *interj.* well! come on! *(in cheering or urging s.o. on)*: •**Kuřo, *ca* heřin binhêřin k'a çiřa Memê îro derengî k'et?** (EP) Son, go [pl.] see why M. is late today. [EP/K/A/B] <de I>

cab جـــاب *f.* **(-a;-ê).** 1) {syn: bersiv I} answer (HH); **-cihab dan** = to answer: •**Xwedê ez şandime bal te, ku ez *caba* pirsêd te *bidim*** (Dz) God has sent me to you *to answer* your questions; 2) {syn: deng û bas; nûçe; xeber} news: •**Wana *cab* gîhandine dîwana Al-p'aşa** (Z-1) They brought *the news* to the court of A.p. •***Cewab* çû cem hakim** (L) *The news* reached the king; **-cabê dan** = to report: •***Cavê didin* bazirganbaşî** (Ba) *They report to* the head of the caravan. {also: cahab (EP-7); cav (K); cewab (L/IFb-2/JB1-S/SK/OK-2); cihab (F); cuhab (GF-2); cûab (Z-2); [djab جاب/djevab جواب] (JJ); <cuwab> جـواب (HH)} Cf. P javāb جـواب, T cevap < Ar jawāb جـواب = 'answer' [Ba/K//F//JB1-S/SK//B/JJ/IFb/GF/OK//HH]

cabdar جابـدار *adj.* 1) {syn: berpirsîyar} responsible; 2) *[m. ().]* defendant, respondent *(in a court trial)*. {also: cavdar (B-2); cihabdar (F)} {cabdarî; cabdartî; cavdar[t]î; cihabdarî} [K2-Fêrîk/K/B/GF//F]

cabdarî جـــابـــدارى *f.* **(;-yê).** responsibility: •***Cabdarî* dik'eve ser te** (B) *The responsibility* falls on you. {also: cabdartî (B-2); cavdar[t]î (B-2); cihabdarî (F)} {syn: berpirsîyarî} [K/B//F] <cabdar>

cabdartî جابدارتى (B) = responsibility. See **cabdarî**.

cacim جـاجـم *f.* **(;-ê).** 1) {syn: beř IV; cil II; gelt; k'ilîm; merş; mêzer [3]; p'alas; tejik [1]} jajim, a type of kilim, (large) flat-weave pileless carpet; type of striped carpet made of coarse wool (B); 2) thin covering spread over blanket (HH). {also: carcim (K/B); <carcîm> جارجيم (HH)} Cf. P jājīm جاجيم, T cicim [A/IFb/GF//K/B/TF//HH]

ca'd•e جـاعـده (JB1-S)/**cad•e** جـاده (GF/RZ/Tsab) *f.* **(;•ê).** street, road, highway: •**Çû Ĥelebê, geřihe di vê *celdê* ve, çû di ya dî ve derk'et** (HR 3:163) He went to Aleppo, he rode into this *street*, and came out the other one •**Mirovê li ser *cadê*** (RZ) The man on *the street*. {also: calde (JB1-S-2); ce'de (GF-2); cehde (FS); celde (HR); <ce'd> جـعـد (HH)} {syn: kolan II; kûçe; zaboq; zikak} < Ar jāddah جادّة = 'boulevard'; Sor cade جـاده = 'street' [HR//JB1-S//GF/RZ/Tsab//HH]

cahab جاهاب (EP-7) = answer; news. See **cab**.

cahil جاهِل *adj.* 1) {also: caĥêl (SK); ciĥêl (Bw)} {syn: ciwan; naşî; xort} young; immature: •**Ezê darê *cahil* jî bibiřim, yê pîr jî** (Dz) I will cut down both *young* trees and old ones •**Dinhêřin wê bûkeke *cahil* şuxulê xwe xilas kirye** (Dz) They see that a *young* girl has finished her work; 2) {syn: naşî; nestêl; nezan; xam} inexperienced, naïve, 'greenhorn'; 3) {also: cahîl (OK)} {syn: nexwendî} illiterate, ignorant, unlettered: •[**Melayek û dû nefer mirofêd *cahil* nexwendî her sê bûyîne oldaşêd yekûdû**] (JR) A mullah and two *unlettered* men were traveling companions. {also: cahîl (OK); cehêl (IFb-2/GF); cihêl (JB1-A/OK); [djahil] جاهل (JJ)} < Ar jāhil جاهل = 'ignorant'; Sor cahêł جاهێڵ/ cehêł جەهێڵ = 'young, youthful' & cahîl جـاهيل = 'ignorant' {cahilî; cahiltî} [F/Dz/Ba2/K/IFb/B/JJ/SK//JB1-A//GF//Bw]

cahilî جاهِلى *f.* **(-[y]a;-yê).** 1) immaturity, inexperience; 2) youth *(time of life)*: •**Sixir hê *cahiltîa* minda soz dabû** (Ba3) In my *youth* Sikhir had already made a promise to me; 3) ignorance (OK). {also: cahiltî (K-2/B-2/Ba3); cahîlî (OK)} [K/B//Ba3//OK]

cahiltî جـاهِـلـتـى (K/B/Ba3) = immaturity, inexperience. See **cahilî**.

cahîl جاهيل (OK) = ignorant. See **cahil**[3].

cahîlî جاهيلى (OK) = ignorance. See **cahilî**.

cahtrîk جاهتريك (Btl) = thyme. See **cat'irî**.

caĥêl جاحێل (SK) = young. See **cahil**[1].

calde جالده (JB1-S) = street. See **ca'de**.

cam جـام *f.* **(-a;-ê).** 1) {syn: şûşe} glass *(material)*: •**Ev aman hemû *cam* in** (Wkt) These vessels are all *made of glass*; **-cama mezinkirinê** (S.Demir) magnifying glass: •**Stîg *cama mezinkirinê* ji bêrîka xwe derxist** (S.Demir. Li Parka Bajêr, 40) S. took *the magnifying glass* out of his breast pocket; 2) pane, sheet of glass: **-cama pencerê** (Wkt/FS) window pane; **-cama tirimbêlê** (FS) windshield; 3) drinking glass, chalice, goblet: **-cama meyê** (ZF3) wine goblet. {also: [ǰām] جـام (JJ)} Av yāma; Mid P ǰām = 'glass; vessel, goblet'; P jām جام; Sor cam جام = 'sheet/pane of glass; mirror' [S.Demir/K/A/B/IFb/FJ/GF/TF/JJ/BF/FD/ZF3/CS/RZ/SS] <avxork; dîndoq; gilas;

peyale; perdax>

camerdî جـــامـــەردى (K) = generosity; bravery. See **camêrî**.

camêr جـامـێـر *adj.* 1) generous, kind-hearted; courteous (JB3); valorous; 2) {syn: aza I[3]; bizirav; delîr; zîx I[2]} brave; 3) [*m.*] {syn: xweşmêr} gentleman; courageous man (JB3). {also: ciwa(n)mêr; comerd; cuwanmêr; <camêr جامير/cuwamêr جواميز/cûmerd جـومـرد> (HH)} Cf. T cömert {camerdî; camêrî} [K/A/JB3/IF/HH] See also **ciwamêr**.

camêrî جـامـێـرى *f.* **(-ya;-yê).** 1) generosity: **-bi camêrî** = a) generous, noble; b) well-mannered; c) valiant, valorous; 2) valor; 3) {syn: cur̄et} bravery, courage. {also: camerdî (K-2); camêrtî (B-2); [djuvanmiri] جوانمرى (JJ)} [K/JB3/B//JJ]

camêrtî جامێرتى (B) = generosity; bravery. See **camêrî**.

cami‘ جامِع (SK) = mosque. See **camî**.

camî جـــــامـــــى *f.* **(;-yê).** mosque, *particularly main mosque*: **•Nîmçe-melayek li Akrê hebo, nawê wî mela ‘Ebbas bo. mu’ezzinê mizgewta *cami‘a* Akrê bo** (SK 15:145) There was once a rather mediocre mullah in Akre whose name was Mullah Abbas. He was the muezzin of *the main mosque of* Akre. {also: cami‘ (SK); [jāma’] جامع (JJ); <camî> جـامـى (HH)} {syn: mizgeft} <Ar jāmi‘ جـامـع --> T cami [B/IFb/HH/ZF/CS//SK//JJ]

camûs جامووس (IF) = buffalo. See **gamêş**.

can I جــــــان *m.* **(-ê; cên, vî canî).** 1) {syn: nefs} soul, spirit: **•Ha *canê*, lawo!** (J) What, my dear son?; **-can kirin** (Z-1) to refresh, freshen up: **•Xulama av anîn** [sic], **wekî Memê dest û r̄ûyê xwe *can ke*** (Z-1) The servants brought water so that Mem could *freshen up* his hands and face; 2) {syn: beden II; gewde; laş} body: **•Spêde helat. Temaşe-y gyanê xo kir, dît hemî *gyanê* wî ji serî ḧetta neynokêt dest o pîyan temam kesk boy** (SK 4:29) Dawn came. He looked at his body and saw that his whole *body* from his head to the nails of his fore- and hind-feet had become completely green; 3) self: **•Hingî Birahîm Xudêyê xo bi Heq naskir û *giyanê* xo ji kifriyê xilas kir** (GShA, 227) So Ibrahim recognized God as the Truth and freed *himself* from unbelief. {also: giyan (GShA); gyan (SK); [djan] جان (JJ); <can> جـان (HH)} Cf. P jān جـان, T can; Sor giyan گِـيـان; Za gan *m.* (Todd); Hau gîan *m.* (M4) [K/A/JB3/B/JJ/HH//SK//GShA]

can II جان (Bw) = beautiful; young. See **ciwan**.

canderme جاندەرمە (Ak) = gendarme. See **cendirme**.

canemerg جـانـەمـەرگ *f.* **().** 1) person who dies young, one who dies in the prime of youth: **•Sedemê wê jî, çima ku em li *canemergên* xwe xwedî derketin û me xwest em wan bi şanazî û bi serbilindî bi gor bikin** (Wlt 2:59, 13) The reason for it [=the reprisal] was that we took care of our *dead young ones*, and that we wanted to bury them with dignity; 2) {also: canemêrg (IFb); [djanemerk] جـانـمـرك (JJ)} crocus (JJ/OK); *saffron (IFb). Sor cuwanemerg جوانەمەرگ = 'having died young' [Wlt/K(s)/JJ/GF/OK/ZF3//IFb] <[1] bêmiraz; [2] pîvok>

canemêrg جـــانـــەمـــێـــرگ (IFb) = crocus; saffron. See **canemerg**[2].

canewar جـــانـــەوار *m.* **(-ê; canewêr, vî canewarî).** wild animal, beast, creature: **•Rojekê, di nava xortan da bû şorê *cenawerê* behrê û ecebane** (L) One day, there was talk among the young men of *the beast of* the sea and other marvels. {also: canewer (SK/IF); cenawer (L); cenawir (IF-2); cenewar; cinawir (A); [djanever] جـــانـــور (JJ); <cinawir> جـــنـــاور (HH)} {syn: dir̄ende; tabe; terawil} Cf. P jānevar جـانـور--> T canavar; Sor canewer جـانـەوەر = 'noxious animal or insect' [L//K/B//SK/IF/JJ//A/HH] <ḧeywan>

canewer جانەوەر (SK/IF/JJ) = beast. See **canewar**.

cang جـانـگ *m.* **(-ê;).** rough, low-quality cloth: **•*Cangê* me bûye rîs** (Zeb) We have failed to progress [lit. 'our *cloth* has become unspun wool', i.e., has gone backward in development] *[proverbial saying]*; **-cang û col** (SK) cloth: **•Hatîme êre bo tişt firotinê. Barê min ew e, hemî libas e, *cang û col* e. Were, bikir̄e** (SK 16:158) I've come here to sell things. That is my load, all clothes and *cloth*. Come and buy. {also: [giánk] جانك (JJ-G); <cang> جـانـگ (Hej)} [Zeb/IFb/SK/OK//JJ-G] <caw; ç’ox>

cangorî جـــانـــگـۆرى *f./m.* **(-ya/-yê;-yê/).** sacrifice: **•Ez *cangorî te* me Sofî** (HYma, 51) May I be *sacrificed in your stead*, Sofi. {syn: gorî; qurban} [HYma/IFb/TF/ZF3]

canî جـــانـــى *f.* **(-ya;-yê).** colt, foal. {also: canîk (ZF3-2); canû; ce’nî (B); ce’nû (B-2); ciwanî II; conî II (A-2); cuhenî (L); [djanou جـانـو/djahnou جـاهـنـو /djahni جاهنى/ djehni جهنى] (JJ); <canî جانى/ce‘nî جـعـنـى/cuwanî جـوانـى> (HH)} {syn: k’ur̄ik [2]} Sor cuwanû جووانوو [AB/K/A/HH/ZF3//B/JJ] <berzîn I; hesp; nûzîn>

canîk جانيك (ZF3) = colt. See **canî**.

cantrî جانترى (Rwn) = thyme. See **cat’irî**.

cantrîk جانتریك (Wn) = thyme. See **cat'irî**.

canû جانوو = colt. See **canî**.

car جار *f.* **(-a;-ê).** time, instance (e.g., once, twice) [Fr. fois, Ger. Mal, Rus raz раз]: •***Cara* yekê min tu li mala Azadî dîtî** (BF) I saw you the first *time* at A.'s house; **-car kirin** (endazyar.org/IFb/Wkt/ZF3) = to multiply. See **carandin**; **-caran** (ZF3) times (in multiplication): •**Çar *caran* dudo dike heşt** [4 *x* 2 = 8] (ZF3) Four *times* two equals eight; **-[ji] carcaran** = from time to time, sometimes; **-cardi[n]** (L) once again; **-carekê** = suddenly; once: •**bi carekê [ve]** = absolutely, completely, totally [tout à fait]: •**Lê zivistanê, / wexta berf dik'et, mal *bi carekêva* bin berfêda unda dibûn** (Ba2-3, 213-214) But in winter, when it would snow, the houses would *completely* disappear under the snow; **-car[i]na** = sometimes, at times; **-hercar** = every time; all the time, constantly; **-î[n]car/îja** (L) this time; **-t'ucar [a]** = never {syn: tu çax; tu wext}. {also: [djar] جار (JJ)} {syn: neqil [2]}. Cf. Mid P jār = 'time, occasion' (M3); Sor car جار [K/A/JB3/B/JJ/BF/ZF3]

carandin جاراندِن *vt.* **(-carîn-).** 1) {syn: lêkdan[4]} to multiply (math.); 2) *f.* **(-a;-ê).** multiplication *(math.)* [Ar ḍarb ضرب, T çarpma, P zarb ضرب]: **-nîşana carandinê** (Kmc) multiplication sign (x). {also: car kirin (endazyar.org/IFb/Wkt-2/ZF3-2)} = Sor lêkdan لێكدان [Kmc/Wkt/ZF3//endazyar.org/IFb]

carcim جارجِم (K/B/TF) = type of carpet. See **cacim.**

cardi جاردِ (L) = again. See **cardin**.

cardin جاردِن *adv.* 1) {syn: dîsa} again, once more; 2) another time (B). {also: cardi (L); careke din[ê] (B); [djareki dini] جاركى دنى (JJ)} [K/A/IFb//B//JJ]

caris جارس *adj.* 1) vile, foul, base; shameless, disgraceful; shrewish: •***Carisa* qîza *carisan*** (İ.Tepe. Apê Kal, 19) You *vile one*, daughter *of vile ones*; 2) [too] deeply involved in stg., immersed in, stuck doing stg., obsessed with (FS/Zeb): •**Ew *bi* kolana rezî ve *caris* e** (FS) He is *immersed in* digging up the vineyard. {also: cariz (K-2/Tsab-2/CS-2); cariz (Tsab-2); [djaris] جارس (JJ)} < Ar jarrasa II جرّس = 'to disgrace'; Cf. Sor caris جارِس = 'annoyed, exasperated' [Tepe/K/IFb/FJ/GF/JJ/Tsab/CS]

cariye جاریه (IFb) = maidservant; female slave. See **carî**.

cariz جارِز (K/Tsab/CS)/cariz جارِز (Tsab) = vile, foul. See **caris**.

carî جاری *f.* **(-ya;-yê).** 1) {syn: qerwaş; xadim [1]} maidservant, handmaid: •**Farxunisafê bakire *cêrya* xwe** (HR 4:20) Farkhunisaf summoned her *handmaid*; 2) female slave. {also: cariye (IFb); cêrî (ZF/HR); [djari جاری /djariié جاریه] (JJ)} < Ar jāriyah جارية [Z-1/EP/K/B/JJ/IFb//HR/ZF] <xizmetk'ar>

carûd جاروود (Kmc/ZF3) metal shovel. See **carût**.

carût جارووت *f.* **(-a;-ê).** metal shovel or trowel with short handle for cleaning out an oven or a fireplace. {also: carûd (Kmc-2)} [Xrp/Qzl/IFb/Kmc-#1953//ZF3] <bêr; mer̄ II>

catik جاتِك (Elk) = thyme. See **cat'irî**.

catir جاتِر (AA/Bw) = thyme. See **cat'irî**.

cat'irî جاتِری *f.* **(-ya;-yê).** marjoram: *fragrant and aromatic mints (Origanum & Majorana) used in cookery* (Ba2); *as a condiment to meat dishes* (B) ; sweet marjoram (JJ); thyme (HH/Haz/ZF3); "Kurdish tea" *(type of grass with fine leaves, used as tea substitute)* (K). {also: cahtrîk (Btl); cantrî (Rwn); cantrîk (Wn); catik (Elk); catir (AA/Bw); ce'tirî (Ml); ce't'irî (B); [djatiri] جاتری (JJ); <çater> چاتر (HH)} Cf. Ar za'tar زعتر /ṣa'tar صعتر = 'thyme'; Arm zat'rin զաթրին = 'oregano'; Sor catre جاتره = 'marjoram, thyme' [Ba2/K/JJ/Haz/ZF3//B//Ml//Btl//Wn//Rwn//AA/Bw//Elk//HH]

cav جاڤ (K) = answer; news. See **cab**.

cavdar جاڤدار (B) = responsible. See **cabdar**.

cavdarî جاڤداری (B) = responsibility. See **cabdarî**.

cavdartî جاڤدارتی (B) = responsibility. See **cabdarî**.

caw جاو *m.* **(-ê;).** cloth; cotton *(print)* (K); calico *(print)* (B); linen; canvas: hand-sewn cloth (A): cotton fabric (JB3); white cotton fabric (HH): •***Cawê* malê pir zexm e** (AB) *Homemade cloth* is very sturdy. {also: [djaoŭ] جاو (JJ); <caw> جاو (HH)} Cf. Sor caw جاو = 'home-spun cotton textile' [AB/K/A/JB3/B/JJ/HH] <cang; ç'ox>

cawbir̄ جاوبِر *f.(K/JB3)/m.* **(-a/-ê;-ê/).** scissors: •**Ji nişke ve *cawbira* ku li ser maseya wî bû avête keviya qrawetê û birî** (E. Huseynî. "Pencereya Peyvê" Pîne #32 [16-28 Feb. 2001], 13) Suddenly with *the scissors* which was on his table he grabbed the edge of the necktie and cut it. {syn: meqes} < caw = 'cloth' + bir̄- = 'to cut' [BX/K/JB3/ZF3] <hevring>

cawî جاوی (IFb) = sister-in-law. See **cayî**.

cax جاخ (TF) = railing; skewer. See **caẍ**.

caẍ جاغ *m.* **(-ê;).** 1) railing, balustrade; banister; grill: •**Ew ê ... ji refikek jora *caxên* nivînan sandoqeke piçûk daxîne xwarê** (Lab, 76) He will take down a small box from a shelf above the bed *railings*; 2) {syn: bist I; şîş} skewer; 3) {syn: pîj I} knitting needle (Ag); 4) metal poles in a fence (Hek). {also: cax (TF); [djag جاغ/tchag چاغ] (JJ)} [Ag/Hk/K/JJ/GF//TF/Lab] <[1]deřabe>

cayî جـایـی *f.* **(-ya;).** sister-in-law *(the relationship of the wives of two brothers, i.e., a woman's husband's brother's wife is her* ***'cayî')*** [T elti]. {also: cawî (IFb); coy (Kg)} {syn: hêwerjin (K[s]); jinbir; jint'î II} [Pok. i̯énəter- 505-6.] 'husband's brother's wife': Skt yātṛi (yấtar-); O Ir yaθr <*yātā; Pashto yor; Sanglechi yūδ; P jārī جـاری/yārī یـاری/ yērī یـیـری; Za cêrî (Siverek); Cf. also Gr enatēr ἐνάτηρ; Lat. janitrices (*pl.*); S-Cr jetrva [Krç/Ad/Rh//IFb//Kg] <bacinax = hevling; baltûz; diş; jinbira>

cebal جەبال (Zeb) = bone doctor. See **cebar II**.

cebar I جـەبـار *m.* **().** 1) {also: cebbar[ê felek] (K)} the Almighty, *one of God/Allah's epithets (Islamic)* (HH); 2) giant (JJ). {also: [djebar] جـــبـــار (JJ); <cebar> جبار (HH)} < Ar al-jabbār الجبّار [EP/K/A/JJ/HH]

cebar II جەبار *m.* **().** bonesetter, osteopath, bone doctor: "The native healers have different reputations, types of training and areas of specialization. ... A second type is the 'osteopath' (*çıkıkçı* in Turkish and *cebar* in Kurdish) who deals with broken or dislocated bones. ... The 'osteopath' is someone usually trained by a similar type of 'expert' [*i.e., one for whom* the knowledge is passed on usually among first kin, mother to son or daughter, father to son or daughter, but it could also be transmitted from an expert to a novice, if there is a special relationship between them], or by some religious healer who also practices osteopathy." [from: Lale Yalçın-Heckmann. *Tribe and Kinship among the Kurds* (Frankfurt a.M. et al. : Peter Lang, 1991), p. 85]. {also: cebal (Zeb); [djebar] جبار (JJ); <cebar> جبار (HH)} < Ar jabbār جبّار [also jābir جابر] = 'bonesetter' < √j-b-r جـبـر = 'to set (broken bones)' {cebarî} For a story which involves a *cebar* (although not called by that name), see the second text from Karboran in HR (pp. 8-15, esp. #23-26; #30-52) [Yalçın-Heckmann/Bw/A/IFb/JJ/HH/GF/TF//Zeb] <nojdar [2]>

cebarî جەباری *f.* **().** profession of bonesetter, osteopath, bone doctor. [K/TF/ZF3] <cebar II>

cebbar جەببار (K)/cebbarê felek جەبباری فەلەك (K) = the Almighty, God. See **cebar**.

cebeş جەبەش (FS/HH) = watermelon. See **zebeş**.

cebexane جەبەخانە (SK/GF) = arsenal; ammunition. See **cebirxane**.

cebhe جەبهە (IFb) = front line. See **cephe**.

ceb•il جـەبِـل *f.* **(•la;•lê).** mixture of mud and water *for making bricks or blocks*: **-cebla axê** (Zeb) do.; **-cebla bloka** (Zeb) mud for making blocks. {also: ceble (Zeb); cebol (GF-2/FS-2); celb (Kmc/GF-2/FS-2)} <Ar jabala جـبـل = 'to mold, form, shape; to mix clay with water' [Zeb//Dh/Zx/FS] <ḧeřî; quř; řiṯam; teqin>

cebilxane جەبِلخانە (IF/SK/GF) = arsenal; ammunition. See **cebirxane**.

cebirandin جـەبِـرانـدِن *vt.* **(-cebirîn-).** to set *(broken bones)*: **•Lingê rastê werimî bû. Me wê** [sic] **bir cem Elîkê, yê bi nav û deng, ku hestiyên şikestî *dicebirandin*** (HYma 18) The right foot had swollen up. We took her to the famous E., who *set* broken bones. {also: cebir kirin (TF); [djebrandin] جـبـرانـديـن (JJ); <cebirandin جـبـرانـدن (dicebirîne (دجبرينه)> (HH)} < Ar √j-b-r جبر = 'to set (broken bones)' [HYma/K/B/GF/JJ/HH/CS/AD//TF] <cebar II; cebirîn>

cebirîn جـەبِـريـن *vi.* **(-cebir-).** to knit *(broken bones)*: **•Hêta min şkestîye, minê şele bûz daye ser, aha hindik maye, *wê cebirî*** (HCK-2, 91) My hip broke, I have put a piece of ice on it, and *it has* almost *knitted*. {also: <cebirîn جـبـريـن (dicebirî (دجبری)> (HH)} {syn: k'ewîn} < Ar √j-b-r جبر = 'to set (broken bones)' [K/B/HH/GF/CS/TF] <cebar; cebirandin>

cebir kirin جـــەبِـــر كِـرِن (TF) = to set bones. See **cebirandin**.

cebirxan•e جـەبِـرخـانـە *f.* **(•a;•ê).** 1) arsenal, artillery depot; 2) ammunition, weapons: **•Here malê meda *cebirxane* heye, hilde, t'edbîra xulama bibîne** (FK-kk-1) In our house (or, Among our possessions) there is *ammunition*, get it, [and] arm the servants. {also: cebexane (SK-2/GF-2); cebilxane (IF/SK/GF); [djibkhané جـبـخـانـه/jäbäl-xāna جبلخانه (JJ-PS)] (JJ); <cebilxane> جبلخانه (HH)} <P jabexāne جـبـەخـانـە = 'arsenal' --> Ar jab(a)xānah جـبـخـانـة & T cephane; Sor cibexane جِبەخانە = 'ammunition' [FK-kk-1/F/K/B//IF/HH/SK/GF//JJ] <ç'ek [3]; sîleh I>

ceble جـەبـلـە (Zeb) = mud and water for building. See **cebil**.

cebol جەبۆل (GF/FS) = mud and water for building. See **cebil**.

cebt جەبت (IFb/GF) = shell for tanning hides. See **ceft**.

ce'de جەعدە (GF) = street. See **ca'de**.

cedew جـەدەو *f.* **(-a;-ê).** gall, abscess, boil, ulcer, skin sore on the back of horses and donkeys. {also: [djideoŭ] جـدو (JJ); <cedew> جـدو (HH)} Sor cidew جدەو [Elk/A/IFb/HH/GF/ZF3//JJ]

cedewî جـەدەوى *adj.* galled, afflicted with skin sores on its back *(of horses and donkeys)*: **-cedewî bûn** (Elk) to be afflicted with skin ulcers on the back: **•Pişta kerê me *cedewî bûye*** (GF) Our donkey's back *is afflicted with 'cedew' [boils]*. {also: <cedewî> جدوى (HH)} [Elk/IFb/HH/ZF3]

cefa جـەفـا *m.* **(;-ê/cefê).** 1) toiling, effort, exertion; trouble, pains: **•Bi *cefakî* mezin ew qayîl bûn ji nava kevira derk'evin** (Ba2:2, 206) With a great deal of coaxing [lit. '*effort*'] they (finally) agreed to come out from among the rocks; **-cefa k'işandin** (K/B): a) to exert effort; b) to be troubled, worried, concerned; 2) {syn: fikar; k'eder; k'erb; k'eser; kovan; kul I; şayîş; t'alaş; tatêl; xem; xiyal [2]} anxiety, worry, care, concern: **-cefa dan[ê]** (K)/ **~dayîn** (B) to trouble, disturb, cause anguish: **•Min gelek *cefa daye* P'erînazê** (EH) I *have caused* Perinaz much *grief*; 3) torment, pain. {also: [djafā] جفا (JJ-Rh); <cefa> جفا (HH)} < Ar jafā' جفاء = 'harshness' [EH/K/IFb/B/JJ-Rh/HH/OK] <cezaret>

ceft جـەفت *f.* **(;-ê).** dry pomegranate shell for tanning hides: **-bi sar û ceft** (Qzl) temporary, unstable [T geçici]. {also: cebt (IFb/GF); *coft (GF-2); <cebt> جـبـت (HH)} Sor cewt جـەوت = 'acorn cup' [Qzl/TF//IFb/GF/HH]

ceger جـەگـەر *f./m.(EP-7)* **(-a/-ê;-ê/).** 1) {syn: k'ezeb[a r̄eş]; mêlak; p'işa r̄eş/pûş} liver *(anat.)*; "[It is] a common Islamic belief that the liver is the seat of courage and vitality" [tr. from: Basile Nikitine. "Essai de classification de folklore à l'aide d'un inventaire social-économique," in: *XVIe Congrès international d'anthropologie et d'archéologie préhistorique : VIe assemblée générale de l'Institut international d'anthropologie. Bruxelles, 1-8 septembre 1935* (Bruxelles : [Imprimerie médicale et scientifique], 1936), v. 2, p. 1004]: **-cegera r̄eş** (IF) liver [cf. T karaciğer]; **-cegera spî** (IF) lung [cf. T akciğer] {syn: k'ezeb; mêlak); p'işa spî; sîh I; =Sor sêpelak}; 2) heart (K). {also: **cerg**; [djigher] جگر (JJ); <ceger> جگر (HH)} [Pok. i̯ekᵘ̯-r̥t 504.] 'liver': Skt yákrt (*gen.* yaknás) *n.*; Av yākar-*n.* (*prob. for* *yakar-); P jegar جگر --> T ciğer; Sor cerg جـەرگ/ciger جـگـەر; Hau yeher *m.* (M4/M2, p.73); cf. Lat iecur *n.*; Gr hēpar ἧπαρ (*gen.* hēpatos ἥπατος) *n.*; Arm leard (W: leart) լեարդ. [J/F/K/A/IF/B/HH//JJ] See also **cerg.**

Cegerxûn جەگەرخوون. See **Cegerxwîn**.

Cegerxwîn جـەگـەرخـويـن *m.* **().** 1) {also: Cegerxûn} man's name (K); 2) nickname of Kurdish tribe (A); 3) "Cegerxwin is the pseudonym of [S]heikh Mouss Hassan, born in 1903 in Djezireh, in Northern Syria. He is the greatest living poet of the Kurmandji Kurds [as of 1968; died in 1984]." (JB2, p. 1). < ceger = 'liver' + xwîn = 'blood' [JB2/K/A]

ceh جـەه *m.* **(-ê; cêh, vî cehî).** barley: **•*Ceh* zer bûn** (AB) *The barley* has turned yellow **•Di destpêkê de min ew bi *ceh* û kayê xwedî dikir ...vê dawiyê min *cehê* xurrû didayê** (HYma, 11) At first I fed him *barley* and straw ... recently I have been giving him pure *barley*; **-ava ceh** = beer [lit. 'barley water'; Cf. P ābejō آبـجـو & W Arm karejur գարեջուր]. {also: cehî (JB1-S); [djeh جـه/ djeoŭ جو] (JJ); <ceh> جه (HH)} [Pok. i̯eu̯o- 512.] 'grain': Av. yawa- *m.*; Southern Tati dialects: Ebrahim-abadi yew (Yar-Shater); P jō جـو; Sor co جـۆ; Za cew *m.* (Todd); Hau yewe *f.* (M4). For the **-h** in **ceh**, cf. P siyāh سياه = 'black' < *syāwa-. See: M2, p.73; M. Schwartz. "The Old Eastern Iranian World View according to the Avesta," in: *The Cambridge History of Iran* (Cambridge, Eng. : Cambridge Univ. Press, 1985), v. 2, pp. 642, 662-63; C. Watkins, "Let Us Now Praise Famous Grains," *Proceedings of the American Philosophical Society*, 122 (1978), 9-17. [F/K/A/JB3/B/JJ/HH/SK//JB1-S]

cehan جەهان (K) = world. See **cîhan**.

cehde جەهدە (FS) = street. See **ca'de**.

cehemîn جـەهـەمـيـن *vi.* **(-cehem-).** to go to hell, be damned *(to spend eternity in hell)*: **•[K'eftar̄] fêm dike ku şêr bi hîleyên wî hesiyaye ... Şêr bang dike, dibêje: "... Qeşmerê teres, divê ku ez careke din te li hizûra xwe nebînim. *Bicehime here*, hêj ku min tu neperçiqandiye"** (Wlt 2:100, 13) [The hyena] understands that the lion has caught onto his ruses ... The lion shouts "... Worthless bum, I don't want to see you in my presence ever again! Now *get the hell out of here*, before I smash you to a pulp" **•Tu bi ku de *dicehemî biceheme*** (KS, 20) You can *go to hell* for all I care! [lit. 'Wherever you go to hell, go to hell'].

{also: cehimîn (TF); cehmîn (K-2); cehnimîn (K)} <cehnem = 'hell' <Ar jahannam جهنّم <Heb ge' Hinom גיא הינום = 'the valley of Hinnom' [KS//TF//K] <cehnem>

cehenem جەهەنەم (IFb/GF/OK) = hell. See **cehnem**.

cehennem جەهەننەم (SK/HH) = hell. See **cehnem**.

cehimîn جەهمین (TF) = to be damned. See **cehemîn**.

cehêl جەهێل (IFb/GF) = young; immature. See **cahil**.

cehî جەهی (JB1-S) = barley. See **ceh**.

cehmîn جەهمین (K) = to be damned. See **cehemîn**.

cehnem جەهنەم *f.* **(-a;-ê).** hell: **•Daimî xiyala şeytanî ew e, welîyan û s̱ofîyan û tobekaran ji r̄êka beḧeştê û necatê derêxît û bibete ser r̄êka *cehennemê* û helakî** (SK 4:42) The devil's thoughts are always directed toward leading holy and pious and repentant men astray from the road to paradise and salvation and setting them on the road to *hell* and destruction **•Her kesê peşkekê ji awa tizbîyêt min wexotewe, cendekê wî agirê *cehennemê* nabînît** (SK 12:119) Whoever drinks a drop of the water from my rosary, his body will not see the fire *of Hell.* {also: cehenem (IFb/GF/OK); cehennem (SK); cenem (F); ce'nim (Msr); [djehenem جهنم/djehendem جهندم] (JJ); <cehennem جهنّم/ceḧennem جحنّم> (HH)} {syn: dojeh} <Ar jahannam جهنّم < Heb gehinom גיהינום < ge hinom גיא הינום = 'valley of Hinom'; cf. T cehennem; Sor cehenem جەهەنەم; Za cahnim *m.* (Todd) [K//IFb/JJ/GF/OK//SK/HH//F//Msr]

cehnimîn جەهنمین (K) = to be damned. See **cehemîn**.

cehş جەهش *m.* **(-ê;).** 1) {syn: dehş; k'ur̄ik [1]} young of donkey, donkey foal; 2) collaborator, Kurd who cooperates with the government against his own people: "Kurds who supported Saddam grew rich and fat. They were able to strut around the great hotels in Baghdad, in the bazaars of the capital and marry off a daughter with crowds gathering to the beat of the **davul** (bass drum) and **zurna** (flute). They wore little skull-caps of gold or multi-coloured woven cloth under their **camane** (head-scarves), their bellies thrust forward over the belts of their Peshmerga-style blue or khaki **shalvar**. These were the **jash** (collaborators)" [from: Sheri Laizer. "Peace and stability?" in: *Into Kurdistan : Frontiers under Fire* (London : Zed Books, 1991), p. 97: **•Îro jî *cehşê* Kurd, ji bo miletê xwe, di destê neyarê xwe de bûye şûr** (WM 1:2, 15) Even today Kurdish *jahshes* [=collaborators] have become a sword in the hand of the enemy against their own people. {also: ceḧşik (Bw); **dehş**; <ceḧşik> جحشك (HH)} < Ar jaḥš جحش; Sor caş جاش/caşeker جاشەکەر/caşk جاشك/caşûle جاشوولە = 'donkey foal'. See also: Martin van Bruinessen. *Agha, Shaikh and State* (London : Zed Books, 1992), p. 40]. [AB/K/A//HH/Bw] See also **dehş**. <[1] k'er III; [2] destkîs; mixenet; xwefiroş>

ceḧşik جەحشك (Bw/HH) = donkey foal. See **cehş**[1].

ceḧtirî جەحتری (Ml) = thyme. See **cat'irî**.

cej•in جەژن *f.* **(•na;•nê).** celebration, festivities *(e.g., wedding, circumcision, New Years)* {T düğün}; holiday: **•*Cejna* we pîroz be** (AB) Congratulations [lit. 'May your *celebration* be blessed'] **•Cejna Newrozê** (JB3) Kurdish New Year, March 21. {also: cejn (A/JB3/IFb/GF/OK)} {syn: de'wat} [Pok. i̯ag- 501.] 'to worship; reverence': Skt yajña-*m.* = 'sacrifice'; O Ir *yaźna-; Av yasna-; O P *yašna- = 'sacred ceremony with sacrifice; act of worship'; Mid P jašn (M3); P jašn جشن; Sor cejn جەژن = 'festival' [AB/K/TF//A/JB3/IFb/GF/OK]

cejn جەژن (A/JB3/IFb/GF/OK) = celebration. See **cejin**.

celaçî جەلاچی (L) = executioner. See **celaçî.**

celad جەلاد (JB1-S) = executioner. See **celaçî**.

celat جەلات *m.* **(-ê ; celêt, vî celatî).** executioner, hangman. {also: celaçî (L); celad (JB1-S); celatçî (K); [djelad] جلاد (JJ); <celad> جلاد (HH)} {syn: sat'orçî} < Ar jallād جلّاد --> T cellat; Sor celad جەلاد [L//K//B//JJ/HH/JB1-S]

celatçî جەلاتچی (K) = executioner. See **celaçî**.

celb جەلب (Kmc/GF/FS) = mud and water for building. See **cebil**.

celd جلد (F/K/ZF/Tsab) = volume (of book); binding. See **cild**.

celde جەلدە (HR) = street. See **ca'de**.

celeb I جەلەب *m.* **(-ê;).** way, manner, mode, method, fashion: **-bi vî celebî** (B) in this manner or fashion; **-çi celebî?** (B) how? in what manner?; **-wî celebî** (B) thus, in such a way. {also: celew II (K); <celeb> جلب (HH)} {syn: awa; cûr̄e; t'eher} <Ar jalaba جلب = 'to attract' [EH/IFb/B/HH/GF/TF//K]

celeb II جەلەب *m.* **().** drove or flock of sheep *for sale or being led to slaughter*: **•Her sal muroê Ar̠tûşî diçû Mûsilê, xurî, r̄ûn, penîr, *celeb* dibir, li Mûsilê difirot** (SK 31:274) Every year the Artushi used to go to Mosul, taking wool, butter, cheese and *livestock*, which he sold in Mosul. {also:

<ceĥeb> جەڵەب (Hej)} [Zeb/IFb/HH/SK/GF/TF//Hej] <col; kerî II; sûrî I>

celew I جەلەو *f.* **(-a;).** 1) {syn: bizmîk [1]; dizgîn; gem; lix̂ab; qet'irme II} rein(s), bridle: •[***Celew* şor kir**] (PS) He slackened *the reins* •**R̄abû ser xwe û bi *cewala* dewara xo girt, û berê wê da qeṣrê** (HR-1, 3:59) He stood up and grabbed his horse by *the reins*, and led her to the castle; 2) wooden ring or hoop passed over a horse's neck when fastening the feedbag (IF). {also: cewal (HR-I); [ja:lau] (PS); [djilou/djileoŭ] جلو (JJ); <celew> جلو (HH)} Sor ciłew جڵەو. According to GF, this word occurs in Hekkâri & Behdinan [PS/IF/HH/GF//JJ] <cuher; hevsar>

celew II جەلەو (K) = way, manner. See **celeb I**.

cem جەم *prep.* at the house of, at, by {cf. Fr chez, Germ bei, Rus u y}: •***cem* me** = *at* our *house*, *by* us [Fr chez nous/Germ bei uns/Rus u nas {у нас}] •**Ew tê *cem* herdehe kur̄e xwe** (Ba) She comes *to* all 10 of her sons •**Ez dixwazim her̄ime *cem* Xwedê** (Dz) I want to go *to* God; **-ji cem** = from, from by the side of [de chez] •***Ji cem* apê min hatiye** (BX) He came *from* my uncle's; **-li cem** = at [the house of] [Fr. chez] *(with or without motion)*: •**Ez duhî *li cem* te bûm** (BX) yesterday I was *at/over* your *house*. {also: [djem] جم (JJ); <cem> جم (HH)} {syn: bal I; hinda I; ḧafa [*see* ḧaf]; lalê; li def (Bw); nik I; r̄ex I} < Ar janb جنب = 'side' [BX/K/JB3/B/JJ/HH/ZF]

cemaet جەمائەت (IF) = group; society. See **cima'et**.

cemed جەمەد *m./f.(SK/Bw)* **(/-a; /-ê).** ice: •**Mezhebê ku esasê wî li ser wan ṯerze delîlane bît wekî dîwarê ser *cemedê* ye: her wextê hetawek lê det *cemed* dê buhujît, dîwar dê herifît** (SK 60:713) A religion based on such proofs is like an *ice*-covered wall: whenever the sun hits it *the ice* will melt, [and] the wall will collapse •**Te *cemeda* ser dilê xwe hiland** (Qzl) You melted *the ice* in your heart; **-cemedê şkandin** (Zeb) to warm up *(of formerly cold relations)*; to break the ice. {also: [djemed] جمد (JJ); <c[e]med> جمد (HH)} {syn: qeşa} < Ar jamad جمد = 'ice' [Erh/K/IFb/JJ/HH/SK/GF/RZ]

cemedanî جەمەدانی *f.* **(-ya;).** kerchief or kaffiyeh which Kurdish men wrap around their head: •**Kilawê dezî û *cemedanîya* sor bo paşa baş e** (SK 47:461) A cotton cap with a red *kerchief* is good for the Pasha. {also: <cemedanî> جمدانی (HH)} {syn: dersok; kevîng; p'oşî; şemil} cf. Sor camane جامانە = 'cotton turban cloth, material used for women's shirts' [Zx/A/IFb/HH/SK/GF]

cemidîn جەمِدین *vi.* **(-cemid-).** 1) {syn: qefilîn [1]; qerimîn; qerisîn; qeşa girtin; qutifîn} to freeze *(vi.)*; 2) to be cold, suffer from the cold (B/IFb): •***Ez dicemidim*** (B) I'*m cold.* {also: [djemedin] جمدين (JJ); <cemidîn جمدين (dicemide) (دجمده)> (HH)} <Ar √j-m-d جمد = 'to freeze, congeal'; Za cemedıyayiş = 'to freeze' (Mal) [Btm/F/K/IFb/B/JJ/HH/OK] <sar; serma; simirîn; sur̄ I; ṯezî II>

cemse جەمسە *f.* **( ).** SUV [sport utility vehicle], a rugged automobile similar to a station wagon but built on a light-truck chassis; used as a military vehicle (Wkt): •**Ji bo girtina Xalid Beg *cemsekî* leşker ji Bilîsê tê Kopê gundê Melemistefa** (Nbh 133:51) In order to arrest Kh.B., a military *SUV* comes to Kop, the village of Mulla Mustafa, from Bitlis •**Medyaya tirkan ji bo xurtkirina van îdîayên xwe fotoyên *cemse* û TIR-ên eskerî yên kevin ji arşîvan derdixe** (Nefel.com iii.2007) In order to back up its claims, the Turkish media takes out old photos of *SUV's* and military trucks out of its archives •**Rojek leşkerên Îranê bi *cemseyek* giran dor li gund girtin** (Nbh 133:54) One day Iranian soldiers in *an SUV* surrounded the village. < GMC [cî-em-sî], brand of American automobile. {also: cî-em-sî (Dh)} [Nbh/Wkt//Dh] <p'îqab; t'aksî; trimbêl>

cenab جەناب *m.* **(-ê;).** 1) *title of respect:* Mister, your honor, the honorable...: •**Çonko *cenabê* mîr zatekî mezin e, ez o r̄îwî xulam în, dibît pişka zatê wî zêdetir bît. Bes lazim e ga bo cenabê mîr bît** (SK 7:71) Since *his excellency* the chief is a great person, while the fox and I are servants, his personal portion must be greater. The ox must therefore be for his excellency the chief; 2) *respectful way of referring to illustrious personalities*: •**Ew her ji min re bi kêf û bi xweşî çêlî *cenabê* Ehmedê Xanî dike ... Tê gotin ko di navbera hezretê Ehmedê Xanî û Xwedê de tenê du buhust û çar tilî mane lê ko tu ji min bipirsî, di navbera wan herdu cenaban da ew du buhust û çar tilîyên ha jî nînin** (Tof, 11) He keeps describing the honorable Ahmed-i Khani to me with pleasure... It is said that between Ahmed-i Khani and God there are only two spans and four fingers, but if you ask me, between those two honored ones there aren't even two spans and four fingers. < Ar janāb جناب = title of respect; Sor cenab جەناب = form of respectful address [Tof/K/IFb/SK/GF] <tu I>

cenan جهنان *m.* **(-ê; cenên, vî cenanî).** gardener: •***Cenên*** **av bir ser zebeşan** (AB) *The gardener* brought water to [i.e., watered] the watermelons. {syn: baẍvan} < Ar jannān جنّان [AB/TF]

cenawer جهناوەر (L) = beast. See **canewar**.

cenawir جهناوِر (IF) = beast. See **canewar**.

cenaz جهناز (ZZ-10) = corpse. See **cinyaz**.

cencer جهنجهر *f.* **(-a;-ê).** threshing machine, wooden threshing sled with flint blades set in the bottom. {also: cencere (GF-2); cercer (IFb-2/TF); cer̄cer̄ (B); cercere (A/IFb-2/GF); <cercer> جرجر (HH)} {syn: patoz} <Ar jarjar جرجر = 'threshing machine' (Hava) [<√j-r-r جرّ = 'to drag']; T carcar [Iğdır-Kars; Erciş-Van; Kilis-Gaziantep; Urfa] & cercer [Gaziantep; Maraş] & cancar [Kerkük] = 'threshing sled' [döven] (DS, v. 3, p. 860); Sor cencer̄ جهنجهڕ = 'threshing sledge, pulley, water-wheel' [Bw/K(s)/IFb/OK/ / HH/TF//B//A/GF] <bênder; kam I>

cencere جهنجهره (GF) = threshing machine. See **cencer**.

cencilok جهنجِلۆك *m.* **(-ê;).** two year-old camel: **-cencilokê ḧêştirê** (FS) do. {also: cenculuk (IFb/GF); cencûlik (ZF3)} [FS//IFb/GF//ZF3] <arwane; dundil; deve; ḧêştir; lok' II; mencî; torim>

cenculuk جهنجولوك (IFb/GF) = young camel. See **cencilok**.

cencûlik جهنجوولِك (ZF3) = young camel. See **cencilok**.

cendek جهندهك *m.* **(-ê;).** corpse, dead body, cadaver; carrion: •**Her kesê peşkekê ji awa tizbîyêt min wexotewe, *cendekê* wî agirê cehennemê nabînît** (SK 12:119) Whoever drinks a drop of the water from my rosary, his *body* will not see the fire of Hell; **-cendekê mirî** (B) do. {also: [djendek] جندك (JJ); <cendek> جندك (HH)} {syn: berat'e[2]; cinyaz; k'eleş I; leş; meyt'; term} [EP-8/K/A/JB3/B/JJ/HH/SK/GF/TF/OK/ZF3]

cenderm جهندهرم (K) = gendarme. See **cendirme**.

cendik جهندِك *f.* **(-a;-ê).** bag, sack: •**Ewî mirovî çi kir, dest da marî, kire di *cendikê* da** (M-Ak, #544) What did the man do but lay hold of the snake and put it in his *bag*. {syn: tûr I} [M-Ak/OK] <cuher; ç'ewal>

cendirm•e جهندِرمه *m.* **(;•ê).** gendarme, policeman: •***Cendirman*** **jê ra qezîyên xirab digotin û lê dixistin** (DZK, 135) *The policemen* insulted them and beat them •**Jinik, cînarekî me heye, *cendirme* ye** (Z-922, 315) Woman, we have a neighbor [who] is a *gendarme*. {also: canderme (Ak); cenderm (K); jandarm (F); <cendirma> جندرما (HH)} <T jandarma <Fr gendarme (*originally* gens d'armes) [Z-922/A/IFb/SK/OK//HH//K//Ak//F] <milîs>

cenem جهنهم (F) = hell. See **cehnem**.

cenet جهنهت *f.* **(;-ê).** paradise, heaven: •**Min hinek sêvên *cenetê* divên** (Rnh 2:17, 308) I need some *paradise* apples; **-çûn cenetê** (K) to end up in paradise. {also: cennet (GF/K-2); cinet['] (F/B); cinnet; [djouné جنه/jén'et (Lx) جنت] (JJ); <cennet> جنّت (HH)} {syn: bihuşt} <Ar jannah جنّة = 'garden; paradise' [Rnh/K/IFb/OK//HH/GF//F/B//JJ]

cenewar جهنهوار = beast. See **canewar**.

ceng جهنگ *f./m.(OK)* **(-a/;-ê/).** 1) {syn: şer̄ I} war, battle: •**Agirê *cengê* ketibû çavên Hesê** (ZZ-10, 142) The fire *of war* entered H.'s eyes; 2) {syn: de'w II; doz} fight, scuffle. {also: [genk] جنگ (JJ); <ceng> جنگ (HH)} < P jang جنگ; Sor ceng جهنگ [F/K/A/JB3/IFb/B/HH/OK/ZF//JJ]

cengk'eştî جهنگکهشتی *f.* **().** battleship: •**Em nikarin rastî *cengkeştiyên* Japonî ên mezin bên** (RN) We cannot encounter large Japanese *battleships*. [RN/K(s)] <fergêt; gemî; keşt[î]; stol>

ce'nim جهعنم (Msr) = hell. See **cehnem**.

ce'nî جهعنی (B) = colt, foal. See **canî**.

cennet جهننهت (GF/K/HH) = paradise. See **cenet**.

cent•e جهنته *f.* **(•a;•ê).** satchel, bag; purse: •**Kur̄ê min, çend pare vê *centê* dane?** (M-Ak #618) My son, how much money is there in this *satchel*? {also: çante (RZ); çendik' II (JB1-A); çente (K/IFb/GF/OK-2); [cänt] جنت (JJ)} {syn: ç'eltik I} Cf. P čante چنته; T çanta; Ar šanṭah شنطة; Sor canta جانتا [M-Ak/SK/OK//K/IFb/GF//JJ//JB1-A//RZ] <parzûn [2]>

ce'nû جهعنوو = colt, foal. See **canî**.

cenûb جهنووب/**ce'nûb** جهعنووب (B) *f.* **(;-ê).** south. {syn: başûr; jêr [3]; nişîv (Bw)} < Ar janūb جنوب [F/K] <bakur; r̄o[j]ava; r̄o[j]hilat>

ceph•e جهپهه *f.* **(•a;).** front, front line, vanguard, battle front: **-Cepha Kurdistanê** (Wlt) The Kurdistan Front. {also: cebhe (IFb)} {syn: 'enî [2]} <Ar jabhah جبهة = 'forehead; (battle) front' --> T cephe [Wlt//IFb/ZF3]

cer جهر *f.(OK)/m.(B)* **(/-ê;).** clay jar, jug *(used for storing water)*: •**Keçik rabû çû ber şûncerikê, tas ji ser devê *cêr* hilanî û *cêr* xwar kir ku tas dagire. Lê *cêr* tijî avbû û giranbû. Keçik nikarî ew** [sic] **ragire. Çembilê *cêr* ji destê wê filitî û *cêr* gindirî. Bû qule-qula devê wî û av jê rijîya** (MB-Meyro) The girl got up and went over to the water jug, lifted the cup from its mouth, and lowered *the jug* to fill up the cup. But *the jug* was full of water, and was rather heavy. The girl could not hold it steady: *the jug*'s handle slipped from her hand, and *the jug* tipped over. With a glug-glug, the water started spilling out. {also: cêr (A/IFb-2/GF-2/TF); cêr̄ (B/Z-2); [djer] جـر (JJ); <cer>جـر (HH)} {syn: gumgum [1]; kûp} Cf. Ar jarrah جـرّة [AB/IFb/JJ/HH/GF/OK//A/TF//B] <gumgum [1]; hincan; k'edûn; kûp; lîn; sewîl>

cercer جـەرجـەر (IFb/TF/HH)/cer̄cer̄ جـەڕجـەڕ (B) = threshing machine. See **cencer**.

cercere جەرجەرە (A/IFb/GF) = threshing machine. See **cencer**.

cerd I جـەرد *f.* **(-a;-ê).** 1) {also: [djerdé] جـرده (JJ)} {syn: nijde} band, gang: **•Diqewimî usa jî, wekî *cerdê* pez t'alan dikir** (Ba2:1, 203) It would happen also that *bandits* would capture some sheep; **-cerda be'ra** (B) *(band of)* pirates; 2) {syn: t'alan [2]} robbery, brigandage; 3) raid, incursion, foray: **•Çaxê mêriv jêla li ḧeç'ê ç'îyê dinihêr̄î, mêriv t'irê wê derê kela çê kirine, ku ji wê derê Ç'ala Sînekê binihêr̄in û ewê ji *cerdê*, ji duşmin xwey kin** (Ba2:1, 203) When one looked at the mountaintop, one would think they had built a fortress there, so that they could see Chala Sinek from there and protect it from *raids*, from the enemy; 4) {also: [djerd] جـرد (JJ); <cerd> جـرد (HH)} {syn: t'alan [2]} booty, spoils (JJ). <Ar jard جـرد, verbal noun of jarada جـرد = 'to peel, to denude, to strip'; Sor cerde جـەردە = 'brigand, highwayman, pirate' [Ba2/K/A/IFb/B/JJ/HH]

cerd II جـەرد (-ê) (Z-3) = javelin; game of jereed. See **cerîd**.

cereme جەرەمە (IFb) = fine, penalty. See **cerîme**.

cerenix جەرەنخ (K[s]) = fight. See **cerenîx**.

cerenîx جـەرەنـيـخ *f.* **(-a;-ê).** 1) struggle, battle, contest; 2) {syn: bêt'ifaqî; cur̄e; de'w II; doz; dubendî; k'eft û left; k'eşmek'eş; k'êşe; mişt û mir̄; xirecir} fight, argument, brawl, scuffle, tussle (K[s]/JJ): **•[Di nîva derê ot'eyê dibe *cerenixa* Meḧmed Begî û Behram]** (JR) At the door to the room *the fight* [between] Mehmed Beg and Behram took place. {also: cerenix (K[s]); şer̄enîx (Zeb) [djerenikh] جرنخ (JJ)} [JJ/JR/Hk//K(s)//Zeb] <mişt û mir̄; şer̄ I>

cereyan جـەرەيـان (ZF3/IFb) = current; electricity. See **ceryan**.

cerg جـەرگ *m.(K)/f.(JJ)* **(-ê** [K]**/-a** [JJ]**;).** liver: **-cerga sipî** (JJ)/**cergê spî** (K) lung {syn: cegera spî; k'ezeb; p'işik (Ag/IF/K/F)/p'işa spî (JB3/IF); sîh (Hk)} {also: cerge (K); **ceger** (F/K); [djerk جـرك / dhigher جگر (JJ); <cerk جرك/ceger جگر> (HH)} {syn: k'ezeb[a r̄eş]; p'işa r̄eş/pûş} Cf. P jegar جگر; T ciğer; Sor cerg جـەرگ/ciger جـگـەر; *for etymology see **ceger**.* [K/A/JB3//JJ/HH] <dil; fater̄eşk; hinav; zirav II> See also **ceger**.

cerge جەرگە (K) = liver. See **ceger** & **cerg**.

cer̄ibandin جـەڕبـانـدن/**ceribandin** جـەربـانـدن [M] *vt.* **(-cer̄ibîn-).** to try, test, experiment: **•Ez dixazim xirabya xwe mêşer̄a *bicêr̄bînim*** (Dz) I want *to try out* my evil on the forest **•KT'ê li dijî kurdan û PKK'ê her rêbaz *ceriband*** (AW77C2) The Turkish Republic *tried* every method against the Kurds and the PKK. {also: cêr̄ibandin (K/B); cêr̄ivandin; <ceribandin جربandن (diceribîne) (دجربينه)> (HH)} {syn: hêçandin} < Ar jarraba II جـــرّب; Cf. NA mjaro:be (Krotkoff) [K/B//M/HH//JB3/IF]

cerîd جـەريـد *f.* **(;-ê).** 1) javelin, spear; 2) *jereed*, equestrian game involving the throwing of javelins; trick riding (B); horse racing (K/A/HH): **-cirîd kirin/dayîn cirîdê/k'etin cirîdê** (B)/**cirîd leyîstin** (IF) to engage in or play the game of jereed. {also: cerd II (-ê) (Z-3); cirîd (B/A/IF); [djerid] جريد (JJ); <cirîd> جـريـد (HH)} Cf. Ar jarīd جـريـد = 'palm branches stripped of their leaves'; 'jereed, blunt javelin used in equestrian games' --> T cirit = 'game of jereed'; 'blunt stick used as javelin in the game of jereed'; W Arm ǰrint ջրինդ; Sor cirît جـريـت = 'javelin'. See: Parry, V.J. "Djerīd," in: EI[2], vol. 2, pp. 532-33. [Z-3//K/JJ//A/IF/B/HH] <k'aşo>

cerîme جەريمە *f.* **().** fine, penalty, mulct. {also: cereme (IFb-2); cer̄me, f. (; cer̄mê) (B); [gerima] جـريـمـه (JJ)} {syn: bêş [2]; cirm (K)}< Ar jarīmah جريمة = 'crime'; Sor cerîme جـەريـمە = 'fine (penalty)' [K/JB3/IFb/OK//JJ//B] See also **cirm**.

cer̄îfk جەڕيفك, m. (FS) = broom. See **cerîvk**.

cerîvk جـەريـڤك *f./m.(FS)* **(;-î).** broom: **•Şirînê mal bi *cer̄îfkî* malî** (FS) Sh. swept the house with *the broom*; **-giya cerîvk** (Bw) broom plant. {also: cer̄îfk, m. (FS); cêrifk (IFb); cêr̄îfk (FS-2); [giárífk] جارفك (JJ-G)} {syn: avlêk; gêzî; k'inoşe; melk'es; sirge; sivnik; sizik; şirt I} Cf. Ar √j-r-f جرف = 'to sweep away'; cf. also P jārūbe جاروبه = 'broom' [Bw//FS//JJ//IFb] <maliştin>

cer̄me جـەڕمـە, f. (; cer̄mê) (B) = fine, penalty. See

cerîme.

ceryan جەریان *f.* **(-a;-ê).** 1) current, flow: **-ceryana elektrîkê** (ZF3) electric current; 2) {syn: kehreb} electricity: **•Xwarinên me ji bo zivistanê amade kiribû** [sic] **ji ber ku *ceyran* tune di avsarkê de xera bûne** (kelhaamed 02.i.2017) The foods which we had prepared for winter have gone bad in the freezer because there is no *electricity*. {also: cereyan (ZF3/IFb-2); ceyran (G); cêreyan (FD)} <Ar jarayān جریان = 'flow, course, stream' [IFb/CS//ZF3//G//FD]

ces جەس *f.* **().** plaster of Paris, gypsum, whitewash. {also: cexs (Msr); [djes جس/djehs جهس] (JJ)} {syn: gec; k'ils} Cf. Ar jiṣṣ جصّ [Msr//A/IFb/JJ/OK]

cesisandin جەسِساندِن *vt.* **(-cesisîn-).** to spy on, examine, test or try out, investigate: **•[Menzila Meĥmed Begî dîtîye û *cesisandîye*]** (JR) He found and *spied on* Mehmed Beg's house. {also: [djesisandin] جسساندين (JJ)} < Ar/P jāsūs جاسوس, T casus = 'spy' [JR/JJ]

ce't'irî جەعتِری (B) = marjoram. See **cat'irî**.

Cevro جەڤرۆ *m.* **().** *common name for a dog*. [Msr] <cewr[ik]; Devr̄eş; Deqê>

cew جەو *f.* **(-a;-ê).** 1) {syn: ç'a I} brook, stream: **•Ser sîngê Dûmanlûê cîcîna xulexula *cewikêd* avê bû** (Ba2:1, 202) On the slope of {Mount] Dumanlu here and there was the babbling of *brooks* (of water); 2) channel, course, (river)bed; 3) {syn: çal II; goncal; k'olge; k'ort II} ditch, gutter, sewer. {also: [djeoŭ/djou] جو (JJ); <cû> جو (HH)} [Ba2/K/JJ//HH] <cû I>

cewab جەواب (L/IFb/JB1-S/SK/OK) = answer; news. See **cab**.

cewahir جەواهِر *m.(OK)/f.(B)* **(;-ê).** 1) jewel, gem; 2) pearl(s) (HH). {also: cewar, f. (EP); [djevahir] جواهر (JJ); <cewahir> جواهر (HH)} < Ar jawāhir جواهر, pl. of jawhar جوهر < P gōhar گوهر [EP//K/A/JB3/IFb/B/JJ/HH/SK/OK/ZF3]

cewal جەوال (HR-I) = bridle. See **celew I**.

cewar جەوار, f. (EP) = pearls; jewels. See **cewahir**.

cewd جەود (GF) = leather flask. See **cewdik**.

cewdik جەودِك *m.* **(-ê;-î).** 1) {syn: k'unk} leather flask, goatskin for holding water; canteen: **•Wî *cewdikê* avê şilqand ka av têda heye yan ne** (FS) He shook *the flask* to see if there was water in it or not; 2) hot water bottle: **•Wî *cewdikê* ava germ da ber pişta xo** (FS) He put the hot water *bottle* on his back; 3) canvas, coarse material from which tents are made (canvas) (Bw). Cf. clq Iraqi Ar jūd جود = 'small animal skin bag' [Bw/IFb/GF/Wkt/BF/ZF3/FS/FD]

cewik جەوِك = dim. of **cew**.

cewr جەور *m./f.(B)* **(; /-ê).** 1) young of animal *(cub, whelp, etc.)*; 2) small dog (B); puppy (HH/JJ). {also: cewrik (IF/ZK3-2); [djevir جور/djevrik جورك] (JJ); <cewrik> جورك (HH)} {syn: çêjik; kûdik} Cf. Ar jarw جرو [AB/K/A/B/ZF3//IF/JJ/HH] <cûcik>

cewrik جەورِك (IF/HH/ZK3) = dim. of **cewr**.

cexs جەخس (Msr) = plaster. See **ces**.

ceyndik جەيندِك (K) = sideburns. See **ceynik** [2].

ceynik جەينِك *f.* **(-a;-ê).** 1) temple *(anat.)*: **•T'ilîya xwe dide ber *cênîka* xwe** (K2-Fêrîk) He puts his finger to his *temple* [=He scratches his temple]; 2) {also: ceyndik (K)} sideburns (IF); 3) down on cheeks, "peach fuzz" (HH). {also: cênik (IFb-2); cênîk (K/B); [djinik جينيك / djinouk جنوك] (JJ); <ceynik> جينك (HH)} [HB/A/IFb/HH//K/B//JJ]

ceyran جەيران (G) = current; electricity. See **ceryan**.

cez جەز (GF/FJ) = pile, heap. See **cêz I**.

Cezaîrî جەزائیری (SS) = Algerian. See **Cezayîrî**.

cezaret جەزارەت *f.* **(;-ê).** 1) punishment, retribution: **•Min P'erînaza xwe carekê *daye czaret*, nha çi bêje me qebûle** (EH) Once I *punished* my [daughter] Perinaz severely, but now I accept whatever she says; 2) {syn: karkinî} trouble, grief: **•Min gelekî *tu dayî czaretê*** (EH) I *caused you* a lot of *grief*. {also: cizaret; czaret (EH)} Cf. Ar jizārah جزارة = 'butchering' [EH//F/K]

Cezayirî جەزایِری (Wkp/Wkt) = Algerian. See **Cezayîrî**.

Cezayîrî جەزاييری *adj.* Algerian. {also: Cezaîrî (SS); Cezayirî (Wkp/Wkt)} Sor Ceza'îrî جەزائیری [BF/IFb//Wkt/Wkp//SS]

cezîre جەزیرە (F) = island. See **cizîr**.

cêb جێب *f.* **(-a;-ê).** pocket (F/K/JJ). {also: cêv; [djib] جيب (JJ); <ceyb> جيب (HH)} {syn: berîk; kûrik I} < Ar jayb جيب --> T cep [EP-7/L/F/K/B/ZF3//JJ//HH]

cêmî جێمی (Hk) = twin. See **cêwî**.

cênik جێنِك (IFb) = temple; sideburns. See **ceynik**.

cênîk جێنیك (K/B) = temple; sideburns. See **ceynik**.

cêr جێر (A/IFb/GF/TF)/ جێڕ cêr̄ (B/Z-2) = jug. See **cer**.

cêreyan جێرەیان (FD) = current; electricity. See **ceryan**.

cêrg•e جێرگە *f.* **(;•ê).** 1) {syn: bir̄ I; grûb; k'om II} group: **•Li besta pêş mala te ew r̄êz bi *cêrge* bisekine** (Ba3-3, #8) [They] should go line up in *a group* on the field in front of your house; **-cêrge-**

cêrge (EP-8) in groups, group by group **•Şeȓvana hespê xwe derxistin/...** ***Cêrge-cêrge*** **rê k'etin** (EP-8) The warriors got out their horses/ ... *Group by group* they set out; 2) {syn: tîpî} detachment *(mil.)*. {also: [djerghe] جـرگـه (JJ)} Cf. Sor cerge جـەرگـه/çerge چـەرگـه = 'assembly, club, institute' [EP-8/K/B//JJ]

cêȓibandin جـێـرِبـانـدِن (K/B) = to try, test. See **ceȓibandin**.

cêrifk جێرِفك (IFb) = broom. See **cerîvk**.

cêȓivandin جێرِڤاندِن = to try, test. See **ceȓibandin**.

cêrî جێرى (HR/ZF) = maidservant. See **carî**.

cêȓîfk جێريفك (FS) = broom. See **cerîvk**.

cêv جێڤ = pocket. See **cêb**.

cêwik جێوِك (Czr/Haz/Klk) = twin. See **cêwî**.

cêwî جێوى *m.* **().** 1) twin; one of a pair: **-bercêwî** (Btm/Grc)/**felqcêwî** (Erg)/**heval cêwî** (Dyd/Wn)/**hevalcêmk** (Bw) twin; 2) {syn: leyl û mecnûn} Gemini *(astr.)*: **•Li rûpela fala we, birca** ***cêwîyan*** **dixwînim** (LC, 8) On your fortune page, I am reading the *gemini* horoscope. {also: cêmî (Hk); cêwik (Czr/Haz/Klk); cêwîk (Msr/GF-2); cimka (K[s]); cimik (OK-2); [jamik جـمـك /djivi جـيـوى /djivik جـيـوك] (JJ); <cêwik> جـيـوك (HH)} [Pok. i̯em- 505.] 'to pair': Skt yamá- *m.*; O Ir *yama-; Av yə̄ma- = 'twin; pair'; Mid P jmyg [ǰamīg] (Boyce); Sor cimik جِـمِـك; Cf. Lat geminus. See: M. Schwartz. “Proto-Indo-European √ĝem” *Monumentum H.S. Nyberg*, Acta Iranica, Series 2: Hommages et Opera Minora, 5 (Leiden : E.J. Brill, 1975), vol. 2, pp. 200-201. [F/K/A/IFb/B/GF/TF/OK//JJ//HH//Btm/Grc//Erg//Dyd/Wn//Hk]

cêwîk جێويك (Msr/GF) = twin. See **cêwî**.

cêz I جـێـز *f.* **(-a;).** pile, heap, stack (of straw, on threshing floor): **•Wî şeqla xwe li** ***cêza*** **genimî da** (FS) He put his seal on *the stack of* wheat. {also: cez (GF-2/FJ-2); dêz (GF-2); [diz] ديـز (JJ)} [Qzl/A/IFb/GF/ZF3/FS//JJ] <*meleme; şeqil>

cêz II جێز, f. (IFb) = dowry; trousseau. See **cihaz.**

cida جدا = separate. See **cuda**.

cifnî جِـفـنـى *f.* **(;-ê).** large bowl *(made of wood or copper), used as tray for serving food*: **•Piştre fîncanên qehwê pêşkêş bikin û bila** ***cifniyên*** **mala Daman Beg bikişine ber mêvanan** (ZZ-10, 127) Afterwards serve cups of coffee and present *the large bowls* of the house of Daman Beg before the guests. < Ar jafnah جفنة = 'bowl' [ZZ/TF/GF/FS/ZF3] <firaq; qûşxane; zerik I>

cifte جِفته (F) = kick. See **çivt**.

cigar•e جِـگـارە *f.* **(;•ê).** cigarette: **•Te** ***cixarên*** **xwe temam bi jahrê pêçane** (ZZ-10, 138) You have rolled your *cigarettes* with poison **-p'eȓe k'axaza cigarê** (Ba) a sheet of cigarette paper; **-cix̄are k'işandin** (B) to smoke. {also: cixare (IFb/ZF); cix̄are, f. (K/F/B); çixarê (A); sîgarêt, f. (F); <cikare جِکارە/cix̄are جِـغـارە> (HH)} {syn: baçek} Sor cigere جِـگـەرە; Za cix̄are (Todd) [Ba//IFb/ZF//F/K/B/HH//A] <heste; k'irpît; neftik; qelûn; qotmok>

cih جِه (A/JB3/IF/Bw) = place; bed. See **cî**.

cihab جِهاب (F) = answer; news. See **cab**.

cihabdar جِهابدار (F) = responsible. See **cabdar**.

cihabdarî جِهابدارى (F) = responsibility. See **cabdarî**.

cihan جِهان (K/GF) = world. See **cîhan**.

cihaz جِـهـاز *m.* **(-ê;).** dowry (K); dowry given to a girl (JJ); trousseau (K/IF); money given by the bride's father (IF). {also: cêz II, f. (IFb); cihêz (K/B/IFb-2); [djehiz جـهـيـز/ djehaz جـهـاز] (JJ); <cihêz> جـهـيـز (HH)} < Ar jihāz جـهـاز = 'set' --> T çeyiz = 'trousseau'; Sor ciyazî جِـيـازى = 'bride’s trousseau' [L//K/B/HH//IFb//JJ] <dermalî; qelen>

ciher جِهەر (GF-Bot/RF) = feedbag. See **cuher**.

cihetnima جِـهـەتـنِـما *f.* **().** compass: **•Li me bû bû nîvê şevê û** ***cihetnima*** **jî nema dişix̄ulî** (Rnh 1:11, 196) It was already past midnight and *the compass* stopped working [=no longer worked]. {also: cihetnuma (ZF3)} [Rnh/GF//ZF3]

cihetnuma جِهەتنوما (ZF3) = compass. See **cihetnima**.

cihê جِـهـێ *adj.* separate; different: **•Lê her yekê bi zimanekî hatine nivîsandin, alfabeya wan ji hevdu** ***cihê*** **ye** (Wlt 1:41, 2) But each one was written in a [separate] language, and their alphabets are *different* from each other; -[**ji hev**] **cihê kirin** (K) to separate *(from one another)*. {also: **cuda**} <O Ir *yuta- (A&L p. 84 [IV, 2] + 93 [XVI]): Av yūta-; Mid P yuδāk (Tsb2, 9) & Manichean Mid P ǰudī (A&L); P judā جدا; Sor ciya جِيا/cwê [cö] جوێ [Wlt/K/A/IFb/B/GF/(TF)] See also **cuda**.

cihêl جِـهـێـل (JB1-A/OK) = young; immature; inexperienced. See **cahil**.

cihêreng جِـهـێـرەنـگ *adj.* different, various, several, a variety of: **•Gelek tiştên** ***cihêreng*** **hatibûn ceribandin** (S.Tan. Xewn û xeyal, Amidakurd.com, x.2007) Many *different* things had been tried **•pirtûkên bi zimanên** ***cihêreng*** (L. Polat. tirşik.com 1.ix.2013) books in *a variety of* languages. [S.Tan/L. Polat/IFb/Wkt/ZF3/RZ/FD]

cihêrengî جِـهـێـرەنـگـى *f.* **(-ya;-yê).** difference, distinction: •[ji Serokatiya belediya Cizîrê re] **Di nav we û serokên belediyên Tirkiyê de, çi *cihêrengî* hene?** (Wlt 1:49) [to the leadership of the municipality of Jizre/Jizîra] What *differences* are there between you and the heads of the municipalities of Turkey? [(neol)Wlt/TF] <cihê>

cihêz جهێز (K/B/IFb) = dowry; trousseau. See **cihaz.**

cihir̄ جهر (IS) = feedbag. See **cuher**.

cihnav جهناڤ (Wkt/BF) = pronoun. See **cînav**.

cihonî جهۆنی (Bw) = mortar. See **conî I**.

Cihû جـهـوو *m.&f.* **().** Jew: **•Ḧeta *Cûhî* qutana xwe naxwit, bêşa xwe nadit** (YSZx) A *Jew* does not pay his tax until he is beaten *[prv.]*; **-jina cihûd** (K)/**k'ulfeta cihû** (B) Jewess; **-mala Cihû hasê kirin** (XF): a) to compel s.o. to submit, to make s.o. knuckle under, to show s.o. who's boss **•Min *tu mala Cihûd hasê kirî*** (Z-1) I have made you knuckle under/I've shown you who's boss [lit. 'I *have confined you to the house of the Jews*']; b) to non-plus s.o., put s.o. in a difficult situation, pressure s.o. into saying/doing stg. {also: Cihûd (Z-1/K/JB3); Cuhî (JB3); Cuhu; Cû II (A-2/SK); Cûhî (YSZx); [djihou] جهو (JJ); <cihû> جهو (HH)} Cf. P johūd جـهـود --> T çıfıt < Ar/P yahūdī يـهـودى < Heb yehudi יהודי; Sor cû جوو/cûleke جوولەکە [Z-1/K/JB3//A/IFb/B/JJ/HH/GF/TF/OK//SK] <file; mexîn>

Cihûd جهوود (K/JB3) = Jew. See **Cihû**.

ciḧêl جـحـێـل (Bw) = young; immature; inexperienced. See **cahil**.

ci'îdok جـعـيـدۆك *f.* **(;-ê).** a fragrant herb which is put with spun garments to protect them from being eaten by termites. {also: <ci'îdok> جعيدوك (HH)} [HB/A/IFb/HH]

cil I جـل *f./pl.(JB1-A&S)* **().** 1) {syn: ç'ek; k'inc; libs} clothing, clothes: **-destek cillik** (JB1-S) a suit of clothes; 2) [*pl.*] {syn: kiras [3]} a woman's cycle, menses, period (Msr): **•K'etme *cila*** (Msr) I am having my *period* **•*Cila* nabînim** (Msr) I haven't had my *period* (and may be pregnant). {also: cillik (JB1-A&S); [djil] جـل (JJ); <cil> جـل (HH)} Cf. NA julla/jilla (pl. julle/jille) = 'clothing' (Krotkoff/ Nakano); Sor cil جـل [K/A/JB3/IF/B/JJ/HH/SK/Msr/ZF3//JB1-A&S]

cil II جل *f.* **(;-ê).** kilim, pileless carpet, napless carpet, flatweave carpet. {syn: ber̄ IV; cacim; gelt; k'ilîm; merş; p'alas; tejik[1]} [Ad/K/A/IFb/B/ZF3] <cilik>

cil III جـــــل *m.* **(-ê;).** 1) {syn: bin̄rex; doşek; mitêl; nehlîk} mattress (Krş/GF); 2) {syn: cî; mitêl} bedding, bedclothes (Mzg/IFb). [Krş/Mzg/IFb/GF]

cild جـلـد *m.* **(-ê;).** 1) {syn: berg II} volume, tome *(of book)*: **•cildê pêşîn** (BZ) volume one; 2) {syn: berg II} cover, binding *(of book)*. {also: celd (F/K/ZF/ Tsab); [djild] جلد (JJ); <cild> جلد (HH)} < Ar jild جـــلـــد = 'skin, hide, leather' --> P 'skin; volume, cover, binding' [BZ/BF/IFb/JJ/HH/CS//F/K/ZF/Tsab]

cildir جلدِر (Wkt) = tailor. See **cildirû**.

cildirû جـلـدِروو *m.&f.* **().** 1) tailor (m.); seamstress (f.): **•Soldirû pêxwasin, *cildirû* bê kirasin** (kurdipedia.org) The cobblers are barefoot, *the tailors* are shirtless *[prv.]*; 2) [*f.*] sewing machine (BF). {also: cildir (Wkt-2); cildirûvan (BF-2); cildrû (RZ/Wkt-2); cildürü (A)} {syn: k'incdirû; t'erzî; xeyat} <cil- = 'clothing' + dirû- = 'to sew'; Sor cildirû جـلـدِروو = bergdirû بەرگدِروو {cildirûtî} [K(s)/GF/BF/Wkt//RZ//A]

cildirûtî جـلـدِرووتِـی *f.* **().** tailoring, sewing: **•Ew ji me jîrtir bûn ko ji destên wan dihat *cildirûtî*, terzîtî, sefarî, xeratî, koçkarî û nalbendî** (Nefel, 2008) They were more skilled than us, as they were proficient in *sewing*, tailoring, tinsmithery, carpentry, cobblery and shoeing horses. {syn: t'erzîtî} [GF/Wkt]

cildirûvan جلدِرووڤان (BF) = tailor. See **cildirû**.

cildrû جلدروو (RZ/Wkt) = tailor. See **cildirû**.

cildûrû جلدووروو ([A]) = tailor. See **cildirû**.

cilik جـلِـك *f.* **(-a;).** horse cloth: **-*Cilika* wî xwar bûye** (FD) He is in a bad situation/fix/pickle [lit. 'His *horse cloth* has become low/fallen']; **-Cilika xwe ji avê derxistin** (ZF3) to cope with a problem, manage to solve or accomplish stg., get by: **•Nikare *cilika xwe ji avê derxîne*** (ŞWWM, 10) She can't *cope with the problem*. [TF/FD/ZF3] <ber̄ IV; cil II>

cillik جِللِك (JB1-A&S) = clothing; horse cloth. See **cil**.

cilq جلق *adj.* 1) hollow, empty: **-serê cilq** (IFb) empty-headed *(of a person)*; 2) rotten *(egg)*: **•Belê serê Erdal, weke hêka qulingan *cilq* bûye** (Wlt 1:37, 13) But Erdal [İnönü]'s head, is *rotten* like a crane's egg *[This plays on both meanings of **cilq**]*. [Wlt/IFb] <p'ûç'; vala>

cilşo جـــلـــشـــۆ *f.* **(-ya;-yê).** laundrywoman, laundress. {also: [jil-šōye] جلشۆيه (JJ); <cilşo> جلشو (HH)} {syn: ç'ekşo (A)} < cil = 'clothes' + şo- = 'wash'; Sor cilşor جلشۆر [K/A/JB3/HH/ZF3//JJ] <balav>

cilûq جلووق (Rh) = turkey (fowl). See **culûẍ**.

cilûx جلووخ (ZF3) = turkey (fowl). See **culûẍ**.

cima'et جماعەت/**cimaet** جمائەت [F] *f.* **(-a;-ê).** 1) group *(of people)*, people: **•*Cime'ta* Kilḧanîê** (Ba) *The* *people of* Kilhaniye (=Canaan?); 2) society; association; 3) assembly, gathering; "At past weddings there would be a separate place apart from the dancing crowd, where people gathered to listen to the performance of one or more dengbêjs. Such a gathering is called dîwan, and the group of people who gathered is called *cemaat*." [from: W. Hamelink. *The Sung Home* (Leiden & Boston: Brill, 2016), p. 154]: •**Hate hindur, selam da *cemaeta* hazir** (ZZ-7, 148) He came inside, greeted the *assembly* [group of men assembled in the emir's diwan]. {also: cemaet (IF); cim'et (Ba); cimiet; **civat**; [djemaet] جماعت (JJ)} < Ar jamā'ah جماعة -> T cemaat; Sor cemat جــەمـــات; Za cemat = 'congregation, crowd' (Todd) [Ba//EP-7/K/SK//F//IF/B//JJ] See also **civat**. <grûb>

*__cimcim•e I__ جـمـجـمـە *m.* (**•ê; **). kettle, coffee pot: **-cimcimê qehwê** = coffee pot. Cf. Ar qumqum قمقم [K]

*__cimcim•e II__ جـمـجـمـە *f./m.(ZF3)* (**;•ê/**). swamp, bog, marsh. {syn: çirav; genav} [F/K/B/ZF3]

cim'et جمعەت (Ba) = group; society. See **cima'et**.

cimiet جِمِئەت = group; society. See **cima'et**.

cimik جمِك (OK) = twin. See **cêwî**.

cimka جمكا (K[s]) = twin. See **cêwî**.

cin جِـن *m.* **()**. jinn, genie, demon, evil spirit; "Centuries ago, Solomon threw 500 of the magical spirits called jinn out of his kingdom and exiled them to the mountains of the Zagros. These jinn first flew to Europe to select 500 beautiful virgins as their brides and then went to settle in what became known as Kurdistan" (MK3, p. xi) : •**Weke *cin* û pîrebokan li vê rewşa te dinêrin** (Lab, 51) They will look at you [lit. 'at your situation'] as if you were a *jinn* or witch; **-cina k'etin** (K/B): a) to go mad; b) to have a seizure, fit, attack *(of epilepsy)*. {also: ec[i]nî (Z-2); cinn (SK); [djin] جـــــن (JJ); <cin> جن (HH)} {syn: ji me çêtir} <Ar jinn جنّ = 'jinn, demons'; Sor cin جـن; Za cin (Todd) [K/A/IFb/B/JJ/HH/GF//SK//Z-2] <dêw; pîrhevok; şeytan>

cinah جِناه (ZF3) = mace, club. See **ciniḧ**.

cinawir جِناوِر (A/HH) = beast. See **canewar**.

cindî جِندى *adj.* 1) noble, elegant, splendid (K/A); good, fine (IFb); 2) {syn: bedew; ciwan [2]; k'eleş III; spehî; xweşik} beautiful, handsome (K/A/IFb/MK); 3) {syn: 'eyan [3]; giregir} [*m.*] nobleman: •**R̄ojekê wan çend giregir û *cindîyê* şeherê Cizîrê hildan** (Z-1) One day they took some notables and *nobles of* the city of Jizîrah. {also: [djindi] جـــنـدى (JJ); <cindî> جندى (HH)} [MK/Z/K/A/IFb/B/JJ/HH]

cineh جِنەه (Dy/IFb/ZF3) = mace, club. See **ciniḧ**.

cinet['] جِنەت (F/B) = paradise. See **cenet**.

cinḧ جِنح (Qrj) = mace, club. See **ciniḧ**.

ciniḧ جِـنِـح *m.* (**;-î**). mace, club, cudgel *consisting of a long thin stick with a rounded head (Qzl): specific types include **badikî**, **şurkanî**, **şûnikî**, and **şeg (şepikî) çem*** (Qzl). {also: cinah (ZF3); cineh (Dy/IFb/ZF3-2); cinḧ (Qrj); cuniḧ (GF); cunuḧ (Qzl-2)} {syn: çomax̌; metreq} [Qzl//Dy/IFb//Qrj//GF//ZF3] <gurz I; hiwêzî>

cinî جِنى (Tof) = knee. See **ejnû**.

cinîyaz جِنيياز (Z-1/F) = corpse. See **cinyaz**.

cinn جِن (SK) = jinn. See **cin**.

cinnet جِننەت = paradise. See **cenet**.

cins جـنـس *m.* (**-ê; **). 1) {syn: cûre; r̄eng; t'exlît} kind, sort, type (K/IFb/HH); 2) race, species (K/B/JJ); 3) {syn: zarav [3]; zayend} gender *(gram.)*: **-cinsê jin** (K/B) feminine gender; **-cinsê mêr** (K/B) masculine gender; 4) sex (K/IFb/B); 5) origin, descent, provenance; background, extraction (K/B). {also: [djins] جـنـس (JJ); <cisn> جـسـن (HH)} < Ar jins جنس = 'type; species' < Gr genos γένος & Lat genus; Sor cisn جسن/cisnat جسنات/cins جنس = 'family origins' [F/K/IFb/B/JJ/ZF3//HH]

cinyaz جـنـيـاز *m.* (**-ê; cinyêz, vî cinyazî**). corpse, dead body. {also: cenaz (ZZ-10); cinîyaz (Z-1/F); [djenazé] جـنـازه (JJ)} {syn: berat'e [2]; cendek; k'eleş I; leş; meyt'; term} < Ar janāzah جـنـازة = 'funeral procession'--> T cenaze = 'corpse, funeral' [Z-1/F/K/B//JJ/ZF3//ZZ]

cir̄ جڕ/**cir** جر *f.* (**-a; **). temperament, disposition, (one's) nature, behavior: •***Cira* wî ne xweş e** (ZF3) He has a *temper*/He has a foul *disposition* •**Eger tu bixwazî zanibî ka *cira* mêr bi hevjîn û zarokên wî re çawa ye, bibîne *cira* wî bi pirtûkên wî re çawa ye** (Bûyerpress 01.xii.2017) If you want to know a man's *disposition* towards his wife and children, see what his *disposition* is towards his books; **-cira xwe xweş kirin** (ZF3) to alter one's behavior or disposition. [Bûyerpress/A/IFb/TF/FJ/ZF3/G/FD/FS/CS]

cird جـرد *m.* (**-ê; **). rat *(rodent)*, zool. *Mus rattus*. {also: cirt (GF-2); <cird> جـرد (HH)} <Ar jura<u>d</u> جـرذ = large rat; Sor circ جـــرج [Bw/IFb/HH/GF/ZF3] <mişk; sêvle>

cir̄e جڕە (R) = argument. See **cur̄e**.

cire-cir جِرەجر (IFb) = argument. See **cur̄e**.

cirîd جـريـد (B/A/IF/HH) = javelin; game of jereed. See **cerîd**.

cirm جِرم *f.* (-a;-ê). 1) fine, penalty, mulct; 2) monetary compensation, damages. {also: [djurm] جـرم (JJ)} {syn: bêş [2]; cerîme (K/JB3)} < Ar jurm جـرم [K/B/ZF3//JJ] See also **cerîme**.

cirmdar جِرمـدار *adj.* fined, sentenced to paying a fine: **-cirmdar kirin** = to fine s.o. [Z-922/K/ZF3]

cirt جِرت (GF) = rat. See **cird**.

cir̄xweş جِرخوش *adj.* sociable, amicable, friendly, with a pleasant disposition, good-natured: •**Eva keçeke *cirxweş* û nerm bû** (S.Demir. Li Parka Bajêr, 40) E. was a *good-natured* and gentle girl. {syn: dilovan; mihrivan; r̄ih̄sivik; xwînşîrîn} < cir̄ + xweş [S.Demir/ZF3/Wkt/CS] <cir̄>

civak جِـڤـاك *f.* (-a;-ê). society: •**Heta ku partiya me tune bû, rewşa jinên Kurd di *civakê* de çawa bû?** (Wlt 1:36, 16) Before our party existed, what was the situation of Kurdish women in *society*? [(neol)Wlt/K/IFb/TF/ZF3] <civat; omet>

civakî جِـڤـاكـى *adj.* social, public: •**Di pêdaketinên *civakî* de, di warê çandî, leşkerî, siyasî û aborî de divê em ji bo jinan cihekî bi dest xin** (Wlt 1:36, 16) In *social* engagements, in the cultural, military, political, and economic arenas, we must make a place for women. [(neol)Wlt/K/IFb/GF/TF/ZF3]

civan جِڤان (Mdt/A/TF/FS) = rendezvous. See **jivan**.

civandin جِـڤـانـدِن *vt.* (-civîn-). to gather, collect, assemble *(vt.)*: •**Pezê xwe li dora xwe *dicivînim*** (AB) I *gather* my sheep around me •**Tu jî aqilê xwe *bicivîne*** (EP) And you *gather* your wits. {also: civvandin (BK); [djewandin] جـڤـانـديـن (JJ); <cevandin جڤاندن (dicevîne) (دجڤینه)> (HH)} {syn: berhev kirin; k'om kirin; t'op kirin; xir̄ ve kirin} < Ar jama‘a جمع [AB/K/A/JB3/IFb/B//JJ/HH//BK]

civat جِـڤـات *f.* (-a;-ê). 1) society: •***Civat* ne wek mahkemê ye. Heqê xweparastinê nade te, ... Bê taloq û bê ku lêbikole, di celsa pêşî de te mahkum dike** (LC, 15) *Society* is not like a court. It doesn't give you the right to defend yourself ... Without delay and without doing any research, it condemns you at the first session; **-Civata Heyva Sor** (BK) The Red Crescent Association (Muslim equivalent of the Red Cross). 2) group; association; assembly; 3) meeting, gathering. {also: cemaet (IF); **cima‘et** (EP/K/IFb-2); cimiet; [djiwat] جـڤـات (JJ); <cefat> جفات (HH)} < Ar jamā‘ah جماعة --> T cemaat; Sor cemat جـەمـات; Za cemat *m.* = 'congregation, crowd' (Todd) [K/A/JB3/IFb/B/JJ/BK/ZF3] <civak> See also **cima‘et**.

civiyan جِڤِيان (JB3/IFb) = to assemble *(vi.)*. See **civîn**.

civîn جِـڤـيـن *vi.* (-civ-). 1) {syn: berhev bûn; k'om bûn; t'op bûn; xir̄ ve bûn} to meet, gather, assemble *(vi.)*; 2) *[f.]* meeting; concentration. {also: civiyan (JB3/IFb); [djiwin] جـڤـيـن (JJ)} < Ar jama‘a جـمـع [Ber/K/A/B/JJ/ZF3//JB3/IFb] <cima‘et; civandin; civat>

civît جِڤيت (GF) = indigo. See **çivît**.

civvandin جِڤڤاندِن (BK) = to collect. See **civandin**.

ciwamêr جِوامێر *adj.* 1) generous, magnanimous, noble: •**Çemê mezin, çemê tijî av, çemê *ciwamêr*** (AB) Great river, river full of water, *magnanimous* river; 2) courteous (JB3); 3) *[m.]* {syn: xweşmêr} gentleman. {also: **camêr**; ciwanmêr (K); comerd; cuwanmêr; [djuvanmir] جـوانـمـر (JJ); <camêr جامير/cuwamêر جوامير/cûmerd جومرد> (HH)} Cf. Sor cuwamêr جووامێر = 'gallant, brave' [AB/JB3//K//JJ//HH] See also **camêr**.

ciwan جِوان *adj.* 1) {syn: cahil} young [also *m.* = young man]: •**Hevala Semîre tu di nava komê de ya *herî ciwan* î** (AW73A3) Comrade Semira, you are the *youngest* member of the group •**Li Hoskan *ciwanên* gund derketibûn rasta bêndera û ji xwe re bi gogê dilîstin** (AW69B4) In Hoskan [village] *the young men of* the village had gone to the threshing floor and were playing ball; 2) {syn: bedew; cindî; k'eleş III; spehî; xweşik} beautiful *(commonest meaning in Behdini & in Sorani)*: •**Pismam, ... eto yê çûye bajera, bîladêt mazin, ete jinêt *cwan* yêt dîtîn, noke te ez nevêm** (M-Ak #633, 286) Cousin, ... you have been to towns and great countries and seen *beautiful* women, now you do not want me [or, do not love me]. {also: can II (Bw); cîvan (B); cuwan (A-2); cwan (M-Ak); [djuvan] جـوان (JJ); <cuwan> جوان (HH)} {ciwanî I (K/A/JB3); cîvanî (B)} [Pok. 3. i̯eu- 510.] 'young'-->*Ayu-He/on- = 'endowed with vitality', cf. *Ae/oyu- = 'vitality' (Av āyu-): Skt yuvan (gen. yunas); Av yuuan- (acc. yuuānəm) = 'young man'; P javān جـوان = 'young'; Sor cwan جـوان /cuwan جـووان = 'young, beautiful'; Cf. Lat juvenis; Rus iunyĭ юный; Germ jung; Eng young. {ciwanî I; cîvanî} [K(s)/A/JB3/IFb/GF/TF//JJ/HH]

ciwange جوانگه (A) = calf, young ox. See **conega**.

ciwanî I جِـوانـى *f.* (-ya;-yê). 1) youth, young age: •**Di malbata me de, hetta di nav eşîra me de--yên ku bi destê hukmatê hatine kuştin û yên ku bi qotikê mirine ne tê de--kes bi *ciwanî* nemirîye**

(LC, 10) In our family, even in our tribe--except for those who were killed by the [Turkish] government or who died from plague--no one has died in his *youth*; 2) beauty. {also: cîvanî (B); [djuvani] جوانى (JJ)} [K/A/JB3/IFb/GF//JJ//B] <ciwan>

ciwanî II جوانى = colt. See **canî**.

ciwanmêr جوانمێر = generous; gentleman. See **camêr** & **ciwamêr**.

cixare جِخاره (IFb/ZF) = cigarette. See **cigare**.

cix̆are جِغاره, f. (K/F/B) = cigarette. See **cigare**.

cizaret جِزارەت = punishment; trouble. See **cezaret**.

cizîr جِزير *f.* **(-a;-ê).** 1) {syn: ada; dûrgeh; girav} island; 2) {also: Cizîra Bo[h]ta; <cizîr> جـزيـر (HH)} the city of Jizirah (T Cizre), on the Tigris River, in historical Bohtan, now in the province of Şirnak in Kurdistan of Turkey [formerly part of the province of Mardin]; it is here that the main part of the romance of Mem û Zîn is said to have taken place. {also: cezîre (F); [gezíra] جـزيـره (JJ)} < Ar jazīrah جزيرة = 'island' [K/B/HH//F/JJ]

cî جـى *m.* **(-yê;).** 1) {syn: der I; dever I; dews I; êrdim; şûn} place, spot: **•*Cîhê* wî vala ye** (IFb) His absence is felt [lit. 'his *place* is empty'] **•*cîkî* bêxwedê** (Ba) *a* godless *place* **•Heryekî ji me xwe *cîkî* veşart** (Ba) Each one of us hid *somewhere*; **-[bi] cî bûn** (K) to be housed, accomodated; to settle down; **-cî girtin** (K): a) to settle down, install o.s.; to take a place, be seated: **•Kevir dileqe hew *cî digire*** (L) Once a rock starts moving, it cannot *stand still [prv.]*; b) to take up space, occupy space: **•Eva feraqa gelek *cî digire*** (B) This plate *takes up* a lot of room; **-cihê xwe girtin** (Zeb) to become [well] entrenched, become current *(of a saying or expression).*{syn: r̄ûniştin [3]}; **-[bi] cî kirin** (Ba) a) to house, put up, accomodate {syn: hêwirandin; ḧewandin}: **•Zelîxe wî ot'axekêda *cî dike*** (Ba) Zelikha *houses* him in a room; b) to place, position, put: **•Mex̆berê M. vedan û Z. paşla M. wêyî delalda *cî kirin*** [sic] **û vegerîyan** (Z-1) They opened M.'s tomb, and *placed* Z. in his arms, and returned; c) to attain, reach *(a goal)*: **•Te mexseda xwe *bi cih kir*?** (HR 3:160) Have you *reached* your goal?; **-cîbicî** (K) *see separate entry*; **-cîcîna** (Ba2) *see separate entry*; **-cîyê bela sebeb** (K/B) for no reason, in vain: **•Te *cî bela sebab* qîza min da undakirinê** (HCK-4, #2, 36) You got my daughter lost *for no reason*; **-[di] cih de** (BX)/**di cîh de** (IFb) immediately, at once: **•Li ser vê yekê hikûmeta Îtalyayê *di cih de* reaksiyona xwe nîşan da** (AW69A6) The Italian government *immediately* reacted to this; **-di cîh[ê xwe] da** (IFb) appropriate, befitting, suitable, apropos {syn: bicî}: **•Ev gotin gelekî *di cihê xwe de* ye** (AW70D2) This statement is very *appropriate* [lit. 'very much in its place'] **•Ev pirsa we gelekî girîng e û *di cih de* ye** (AW69A3) Your question is very important and *apropos*; **-t'u cîyada** (Ba) nowhere: **•Ûsibî xame, hila *t'u cîyada* neçûye** (Ba) Joseph is inexperienced, he has*n't* gone *anywhere* yet; 2) {syn: nivîn; text} {also: cîh (A); cîyê r̄azanê/hêsabûnê} bed, bedding: **•*Cîyê* wan xweş kir** (L) She made them a *place to sleep*/ made up their *beds* **•Êvarê kur̄ k'etne *nava cîya*** (Ba) In the evening the boys got *in bed* [lit. 'fell *into beds*']; 3) source, cause *(of pain or pleasure)*: **•Werin, tedbîrekî weto bikeyn ku pertala wî muroê** [=mirovê] **Kurd bibeyn û ew bizanît û hîç deng neket û r̄azî bît, û r̄azî nebît bo wî *cîyê* axiwtinê nabît** (SK 28:253) Come, let us devise a plan to take this Kurdish fellow's goods, and when he discovers it he will acquiesce and say nothing, and even if he doesn't acquiesce he won't have anything to say [lit. 'it will not be *a source of* speaking for him']; **-cihê daxê** (Bw) unfortunately {syn: mixabin}; **-Cihê dilxoşbûna min e** (Bw) It is my pleasure; **-cihê şanazîyê** (Bw) source of pride. {also: cih (A/JB3/IF-2/Bw); [djih جـه/dji جـى] (JJ); <cih جـه/cî جـى> (HH)} Cf. P jā جا = 'place'; Sor cê جێ/cêga جێگا; Za ca *m.* = 'bed; place' (Todd); Hau yagê *f.* = 'place; bed' (M4) [F/K/IF/B/JJ/HH/Wn//A/JB3/Bw] <bicî>

cîbicî جـى بِـجـى *adv.* right then and there, on the spot, immediately. {also: cû bi cî (B); cî û cî (B)} [K//B]

cîcîna جـى جـيـنـا *adv.* here and there: **•Ser sîngê Dûmanlûê *cîcîna* xulexula cewikêd avê bû** (Ba2:1, 202) On the slope of {Mount] Dumanlu *here and there* was the babbling of brooks (of water). [Ba2/B/GF]

cî-em-sî جى ئەم سى (Dh) = SUV. See **cemse**.

cîh جيه (A) = bed. See **cî** [2].

cîhan جـيـهـان *f.* **(-a;-ê).** world: **•Her wiha helwesta Tirkiyeyê ya nijadperest derkete ber çavê gelê *cîhanê*** (AW69C1) Likewise, Turkey's racist attitude has been noticed by the peoples *of the world*; **-seranserê cîhanê** = around the world. {also: cehan (K); cihan (K-2/GF)} {syn: dinya} Cf. P jahān جهان; Sor cîhan جيهان/cehan جەهان [IFb/OK/

/K/GF]

cîl جـيـل *f.* **(-a;).** generation: •**Divê nifşa** (*cîla*) **nû xwe pêve mijûl bike!** (Wlt) The new *generation* must concern itself with this! {syn: nifş} <Ar jīl جيل [Wlt/GF/TF]

cînar جـيـنـار *m.&f.* **(-ê/-a; cînêr/).** neighbor: •**Jinik, *cînarekî* me heye, cendirme ye** (Z-922, 315) Woman, we have *a neighbor* [who] is a gendarme. {also: cîran (GF-2/SK-2); cîrank' (JB1-A); [djinar جـيـنـار/djiran جـيـران] (JJ); <cîran> جـيـران (HH)} < Ar jīrān جيران = 'neighbors', *pl. of* jār جار; = Sor hawsê هـاوسـێ & dirawsê دراوسـێ {cînarî; cînartî} [F/K/JB3/IFb/B/JJ/HH/GF/SK//JB1-A]

cînarî جـيـنـارى *f.* **(-ya;-yê).** neighborliness; being a neighbor. {also: cînartî (K-2/B-2)} [K/B/ZF3] <cînar>

cînartî جينارتى (K/B) = neighborliness. See **cînarî**.

cînav جـيـنـاڤ *m.* **(-ê;).** pronoun: **-cînavê çiqasîyê** (B) quantitative pronoun; **-cînavê dêma** (B/K/F)/ **~k'esa** (K) personal pronoun; **-cînavê eleqetîyê** (K/B)/**~helaqetîyê** (F) relative pronoun (i.e., ko); **-cînavê hevdutîyê** (K) reciprocal pronoun (i.e., hev); **-cînavê nîşankirinê** (K/B/F) demonstrative pronoun (i.e., ev & ew); **-cînavê pirsa** (B/F)/~ **pirskirinê** (K) interrogative pronoun (i.e., k'î & çi); **-cînavê ser xwe zivirandî** (B) reflexive pronoun (i.e., xwe). {also: cihnav (Wkt-2/BF); cînavk, f. (ZF/FD)} {syn: bedelnav; pronav} <cî = 'place' + nav = 'name, noun' [F/K/IFb/B/GF/SS/Wkt//ZF//BF]

cînavk جيناڤك, f. (ZF/FD) = pronoun. See **cînav**.

cînciq جـيـنـجِـق (Srk/G/ZF3) = glass: marble, jewelry, shards. See **dîndoq**.

cîncix جـيـنـجِـخ (Kmc) = glass: marble, jewelry, shards. See **dîndoq**.

cîncoq جينجۆق (Kmc) = glass: marble, jewelry, shards. See **dîndoq**.

cîncûq جينجووق (ZF3) = glass: marble, jewelry, shards. See **dîndoq**.

cîran جيران (GF/SK) = neighbor. See **cînar**.

cîrank' جيرانك m.&f. (JB1-A) = neighbor. See **cînar**.

cîvan جيڤان (B) = young. See **ciwan**.

cîvanî جيڤانى (B) = youth. See **ciwanî I**.

co جۆ (IFb/A/GF/OK) = canal. See **cû I**.

cobiř جـۆبِـر/**cobir** جـۆبِـر *m.* **(-ê;).** mole cricket, zool. *Gryllotalpa vulgaris* [T danaburnu, Ar ḥarrāqāt حرّاقات/ḥarrāšah حرّاشة, P ābduzdak آبدزدك].{also: cobirk (GF); cûbir (FJ-2/ZF); cûbirk (GF-2/BF-2); cûbrik (FD); <cûbirk> (HH)} [CCG/IFb/FJ/CS/BF//Wkt/FS//GF//ZF//HH//FD] <quzgezk>

cobirk جۆبِرك (GF) = mole cricket. See **cobiř**.

*coft جۆفت (GF) = shell for tanning hides. See **ceft**.

coht جۆهت (TF) = pair; plow. See **cot**.

cohtk'ar جۆهتكار (JB1-S) = farmer. See **cot'k'ar.**

cohtyar جۆهتيار (JB1-S) = farmer. See **cot'k'ar.**

cok جۆك (GF/TF) = canal. See **cû I.**

col جـــــۆل *m.* **(-ê;).** flock, herd, drove *(of sheep)*: •**Li pala hember *colek* mîhên mor di mexeliyê de bû** (Lab, 11) On the slope opposite, *a flock of* purple sheep was in the open-air pen. {also: [jōl-ê d'miyāna] جـــول (JJ); <col> جـــول (HH)} {syn: biř I[5]; kerî II; sûrî I; xar II} <Ar jawl جـــول = 'troop of horses, herd of camels, flock of sheep' [Lab/K/A/IFb/JJ-PS/HH/GF] <celeb II; pez>

colan جۆلان *f.* **(-a;-ê).** 1) {syn: bêşîk; bormotk (EP-7)?; dara dergûşê/dergûş [2]; landik} cradle, crib (K/F); 2) {syn: deydik; dolîdang I; hêlekan; hêzok} swing (K/A/IFb). {also: colane (A/IF); colang (B/F)} Cf. Sor colanê جۆلانێ = 'swinging cradle' [F/K/ZF3//A/IFb]

colane جۆلانه (A/IFb) = swing. See **colan** [2].

colang جۆلانگ (B/F) = cradle. See **colan** [1].

comerd جـۆمـەرد = generous; gentleman. See **camêr** & **ciwamêr**.

con جۆن (Bw/JJ) = gray/grey. See **cûn I**.

conega جـۆنـەگـا *m.* **().** three-year-old calf (Wn/Bşk); young ox (SK); young bull (F). {also: ciwange (A); conge (Wn); [djuvan-ga/djune-ga] جـوانـەگـا (JJ); <conega> جـونـگـا (HH)} < ciwan = 'young' + ga = 'bull'; Cf. Sor cuwanega جوانەگا = 'bull-calf' [Bşk/F/HH/SK//Wn//A//JJ] <ga; golik; k'endik; mozik; parone>

conge جۆنگه (Wn) = calf, young ox. See **conega**.

conî I جۆنى *m.(F/K/OK)/f.(B)* **(; /-yê).** mortar *(made of stone)*; crucible: •[**Û di ekserêd malan da *cuhnî* û mêkut heye bi xwe dermanî diqutin û çê dikin**] (BN 135) And in most households there is *a mortar* and pestle [which they use to] pound and make medicines. {also: cihonî (Bw); cuhnî (BN); [djohni] جوهنى (JJ); <conî> جونى (HH)} Sor conî جـۆنـى = 'stone mortar' (K2) [Bw//JJ/BN//F/K/IFb/B/HH/GF/OK] <desteconî>

conî II جۆنى (A) = colt. See **canî**.

coqcok ۆقجۆك (ZF3) = turkey (fowl). See **coqcoq**.

coqcoq جـــــۆقـــجـــۆق *m.* **(-ê;).** turkey *(fowl)*, zool. *Meleagris gallopavo*. {also: coqcok (ZF3); çoqçoq (Krç)} {syn: culûx; 'elok; kûřkûř; şamî} [Mzg/IFb//Krç//ZF3] <mirîşk>

cor I جۆر (IFb) = feedbag. See **cuher**.

cor II جۆر (SK) = type, kind. See **cûře**.

corik جۆرِك (IF) = feedbag. See **cuher**.

coş جـــــــۆش *f.* **().** 1) {syn: k'el III} boiling, bubbling, seething (n.): **•Terîqetên dînî wekî ava *bi coş* her pêş diketin** (Hawarnet 8.vii.2011) Religious sects kept appearing, like [=as frequent as] *boiling* water; 2) {syn: k'elecan} enthusiasm, excitement, ardor, exuberance, ebullience: **•8'ê Adarê Roja Jinên Kedkar ên Cîhanê li wargeha Mexmûrê ji aliyê bi hezaran jin û xwendekaran ve *bi coşeke mezin* hate pîrozkirin** (ANF News 8.iii.2018) March 8, International Working Women's Day was celebrated *with great enthusiasm* by thousands of women in Makhmur camp.{also: coşî (ANF-2)} [Pok. i̯es- 506.] 'boil, be agitated (of cooking water)': Av yaēšyeiti = 'it boils (vi.)'; P jūš جـوش = 'boiling, effervescence, ardor' (--> T coş-, coşku); Sor coş جـــۆش = 'heat (of battle, enthusiasm, etc.); boiling point' [ANF/K(s)/IFb/ZF3/Wkt/FD/CS]

coşî جۆشی (ANF) = boiling; enthusiasm. See **coş**.

cot/cot' [JB1-A] جـــۆت *m.(K/B)/f.(JB3)* **(-ê/ ;).** 1) pair, couple; *count word for paired items (e.g., shoes, eyes, hands, etc., cf.* ***fer I, kit, t'ek,*** *for one of a pair)*: **•Jineke pîr hebûye ... *cote* gaê wê hebûye** (J) There was an old woman, she had *a pair of* oxen; **-cot bûn** (K/B/IFb/GF/FJ/Kmc/JJ): a) to mate; to geminate: **•Li milekî wîtwîta şehlûl û bilbilan, li milekî dengê qebqeba kewan bû. Diyar bû ku dema *cotbûna* wan e** (DBgb, 7) On one side was the sound of bee eaters and nightingales, on the other side the cooing of partridges. It was obviously their *mating* season; b) to be plowed; 2) {syn: halet; hevcar̄; k'otan II} plow, plough: **•Bavê min çû *cot*** (AB) My father went to *plough*; **-cot ajotin** (JJ)/**cot kirin** = to plow {syn: kêlan}: **•Cotk'ar ... *cotê xwe dike*** (Dz) The farmer ... *plows*; **-cot vekirin** (JJ) to unyoke [oxen from the plow]. {also: coht (TF); cût (IFb-2); [djot] جوت (JJ); <cot> جوت (HH)} [Pok. 2. i̯eu- 508.] 'to join' & [Pok. 2. i̯u-go-m 508.] 'yoke': Old Ir & Av yuxta-; P joft جفت --> T çift; Sor cût جـووت; Za cit *m.* = 'pair or team of oxen' (Todd); Hau hîte *f.* (M4) [Ba2/F/J/K/A/JB3/IFb/B/JJ/HH/JB1-A/SK/GF/OK] <[1] fer I; kit; t'ek; zo; [2] destedû; gîsin; hincar; kêlan; maç' III; maran; mijane; nîr I; sermijank; şûrik; xenîke; xep>

cote xal جۆته خال (SS) = colon (:). See **xalecot**.

cot'ik'ar جۆتکار (JB1-A) = farmer. See **cot'k'ar.**

cot'iyar جۆتیار (JB1-A) = farmer. See **cot'k'ar.**

cot'k'ar جۆتکار *m.* **(-ê;).** farmer, ploughman; peasant: **•*Cotk'ar* ... cotê xwe dike** (Dz) *The farmer ... plows*. {also: cohtk'ar (JB1-S); cohtyar (JB1-S); cot'ik'ar (JB1-A); cot'iyar (JB1-A); cot'yar (K); [djotkar] جوتکار (JJ); <c[o]tyarî> جوتیاری (HH)} {syn: r̄êncber} Cf. T çiftçi; Sor cûtdar جـــووتـــدار/cûtkar جـــووتـــکـار/cûtyar جـــووتـــیـار; Za citêr m./f. (Todd) {cot'k'arî; cot'yarî} [BX/F/K/A/JB3/IFb/B/JJ/ZF3//JB1-A&S//HH] <cot; p'ale>

cot'k'arî جـــۆتـــکـــاری *f.* **(-ya;-yê).** being a farmer or peasant. {also: cot'yarî (K); [djotkari] جـوتـکـاری (JJ)} [K//IFb/B/JJ/ZF3] <cot'k'ar>

Cotmeh جۆتمه‌ه *f.* **(-a;-ê).** October. [(neol)Wlt/ZF3] <Ç'irî>

cotxal جۆتخال (RZ) = colon (:). See **xalecot**.

cot'yar جۆتیار (K) = farmer. See **cot'k'ar.**

cot'yarî جۆتیاری (K) = being a farmer or peasant. See **cot'k'arî**.

covan جۆڤان (FS) = rendezvous. See **jivan**.

coxîn جۆخین *f.* **(-a;-ê).** threshing floor: **•Birayê mazin tê fikirîye *coxîna* xo, wî bi xo gotev xo, "Ez dê çi li hinde genimey kem?"** (M-Ak #597) The elder brother considered his *threshing-floor* and said to himself, "What shall I do with so much wheat?" {also: cuxîn (OK/AA); [djokhin جـوخـيـن/djoghin جوگن] (JJ); <coxîn> جۆخین (Hej)} {syn: bênder} [M-Ak/IFb/JJ/GF/Hej//OK/AA]

coy جۆی (Kg) = sister-in-law. See **cayî**.

cu جو (ZZ-7) = canal. See **cû I.**

cuda جـودا *adj.* separate. {also: cida; **cihê**; [djuda] جـدا (JJ); <cuda> جـــدا (HH)} <O Ir *yuta- (A&L p. 84 [IV, 2] + 93 [XVI]): Av yūta-; Mid P yuđāk (Tsb2, 9); P judā جدا; Sor ciya جیا/cwê (cö) جوێ {cudatî; cudayî} [JR/F/K/IF/B/JJ/HH/SK/Ba2/JB1-A] See also **cihê**.

cudatî جوداتی (K) = separateness. See **cudayî**.

cudaxwaz جـــوداخـــواز *m.&f.* **().** separatist, irredentist, secessionist: **•*Cudaxwaz*, di ferhenga dijminên azadiyê de, her Kurdekî ku dixwaze û dixebite ji bo Kurdistaneke serbixwe û azad** (Wlt 2:73, 7) *Separatist*, in the lexicon of the enemies of freedom, [is] every Kurd who wants and works for a free and independent Kurdistan. <cuda = 'separate' + xwaz- (<xwestin) = 'want(er)' {cudaxwazî} [(neol)Wlt/ZF3]

cudaxwazî جـــــوداخـــــوازی *f.* **(-ya;-yê).** separatism, irredentism, secessionism: **•Sebeba kuştina te, weke qatilan bi xwe dan zanîn sêparatîzma (*cudaxwaziya*) te bû** (Wlt 2:73, 7) The reason for your murder, as the murderers themselves have announced, was your [support of] *separatism*.

[(neol)Wlt/ZF3] <cudaxwaz>

cudayî جـودايـى *f.* **(-ya;-yê).** separateness. {also: cudatî (K); [djudàï] جداى (JJ)} [K//JJ] <cuda>

cuhab جوهاب (GF) = answer; news. See **cab**.

cuhal جوهال (SK) = sack. See **ç'ewal**.

cuhenî جوهەنى (L) = colt. See **canî**.

cuher جـوهـەر *m.* **(-ê;).** feedbag, nosebag, bag of oats or barley hung over a horse's head: **-ceh û cihir̄** (IS)/[djeh djouhour] جـه جـهـور (JJ) feedbag of barley: **•Xecê hespê wî girê da, *ceh û cihir̄* kir** (IS-#123) Khej tied up his horse [and] gave him a *feedbag of barley*. {also: ciher (GF-Bot/RF); cihir̄ (IS); cor I (IFb); corik (IF-2); cur (Zeb); [djuhour /jehōr (PS)/giόri (G)] جـهـور (JJ); <cuher> جـهـر (HH)} [IS//IF/HH/GF//IFb//RF//JJ//Zeb] <cendik; ç'ewal; tûr I>

Cuhî جوهى (JB3) = Jew. See **Cihû**.

cuhnî جوهنى (JJ/BN) = mortar. See **conî I**.

Cuhu جوهو = Jew. See **Cihû**.

culûẍ جـولـووغ *f.* **(-a;-ê).** turkey *(fowl)*, zool. *Meleagris gallopavo*. {also: cilûq (Rh); cilûx (ZF3); cûlûq (Krş)} {syn: coqcoq; 'elok; kûr̄kûr̄; şamî} [Ag//Rh/ /Krş//ZF3] <mirîşk>

Cuma جوما (K) = Friday; week. See **Cume**.

Cume جـومـە *f.* **().**1) {syn: Înî} Friday; 2) {syn: ḧeftê I; înî} week (JJ); 3) *man's name*. {also: Cuma (K); [djumé] جمعه (JJ)} Cf. P jom'eh جمعه < Ar jum'ah جمعة = 'week, Friday'; Sor cum'e جومعه [F/IF/JJ//K]

cuniḧ جونح (GF) = mace, club. See **ciniḧ**.

cunuḧ جونوح (Qzl) = mace, club. See **ciniḧ**.

cur جور (Zeb) = feedbag. See **cuher**.

cur̄e جورە *f.* **().** argument, disagreement: **•Em bi şanazî û serbilindî dibêjîn di çu *cir̄e* û hevr̄ikîyêt navxoyê da heta kêmtirîn behr jî têda nebûye** (R 15 [4/12/96] 2) We can proudly say that we had not even the slightest part in any internal *arguments* or rivalries. {also: cir̄e (R); cire-cir (IFb); <cir̄e-cir̄> جـرەجـر (Hej)} {syn: bêt'ifaqî; cerenîx; de'w II; doz; dubendî; gelemşe; gelş; k'eşmek'eş; k'êşe; mişt û mir̄} < Ar √j-r-r جرّ = 'to pull' [Zeb//R//Hej//IFb]

cur̄et جــــورەت *f.* **().** courage, bravery, fearlessness. {also: [djurat] جـــرأت (JJ)} {syn: camêrî} Cf. P jur'at جرأت < Ar jur'ah جرأة [JR/K/F/JJ]

cuwan جووان (A/HH) = young. See **ciwan**.

cuwanmêr جـووانـمێر = generous; courteous. See **camêr** & **ciwamêr**.

cuxîn جوخين (OK/AA) = threshing floor. See **coxîn**.

cû I جوو *f.* **(-wa;-yê).** 1) {also: co (IFb/A/GF/OK); cok (GF-2/TF); cu (ZZ-7)} irrigation trench, canal, channel: **•coa begî** (M-Zx) the Beg's channel **•*Cû* tijî av e** (AB) *The canal* is full of water **•Îro zilamekî qenciyeke pir mezin bi me re kiriye. Wî şûrê xwe danî ser ava *cuyê* û em derbasî aliyê din bûn** (ZZ-7, 204) Today a man did us a very big favor. He put down his sword over the *canal* water and we crossed to the other side *(said by ants in a folktale)* **•Wî ava *coyê* zêde kir** (FS) He increased the water in *the irrigation ditch*; 2) ground hole of weaving loom (A/IFb) [cû] [T dokuma tezgâhındaki yer çukuru]. {also: **cew**; [djeoŭ/djou] جـــو (JJ); <cû> جـو (HH)} Sor co جـۆ = 'canal' [AB/JJ/HH//A/IFb/ GF/OK//ZZ//TF] <k'ar̄êz; zaboq[3]> See also **cew**.

Cû II جوو (A/SK) = Jew. See **Cihû**.

cûab جووئاب (Z-2) = answer; news. See **cab**.

cûbir جووبِر (FJ/ZF) = mole cricket. See **cobir̄**.

cûbirk جووبِرك (GF/HH/BF) = mole cricket. See **cobir̄**.

cûbrik جووبرك (FD) = mole cricket. See **cobir̄**.

cûcik جــووجــك *m./f.* **(/-a; /-ê).** chick, young of birds: ***-cûcika dilê *fk-ê* qetîn** (Z-1) ?to be heart-broken; ?to be terribly embarrassed; ?to be frightened: •[Mem was in prison, and he looked a mess; when Zîn saw him like this] **Memê gelekî şerm kir û ber xwe k'et. Teyê bigota, *cûcika dilê* Memê *qetîya*** (Z-1) M. was very much ashamed and upset. You might say, the *young bird of* M.*'s heart split*; **-T'aba [t'apa] *cûcikekê* têda t'une/ nemaye** (XF) He is very weak [lit. 'the strength of *a young bird* is not in him']. {also: [djudjik] جوجك (JJ)} {syn: ç'elîk; çîçik III; ferx; varik} [Z-1/K/IF/B/JJ/ XF/ZF3] <cewr; çêje>

***cûg** جــــووگ *f.* **( ).** "knucklebones" (k'ap II) that are smooth [şayik] on the ends. [Qzl] <k'ap II>

cûhalk' جووهالك (JB1-A) = sack. See **ç'ewal**.

Cûhî جووهى (YSZx) = Jew. See **Cihû**.

cûlûq جوولووق (Krş) = turkey (fowl). See **culûẍ**.

cûn I جوون *adj.* gray/grey. {also: con (Bw); [djun] جن (JJ); <cûn> جـون (HH)} {syn: bor I; boz; gewr[1]; kew II; xwelîreng} [K/(A)/IFb/HH/GF/OK//Bw/JJ]

cûn II جوون (BX/K/IFb/M) = to chew. See **cûtin**.

cûr I جوور *m.* **(-ê;).** unripe grapes [T koruk, Ar ḥişrim حـصـرم, P γūre غـوره]. {also: jûr (Haz/GF); <jûr> ژور (HH)} {syn: besîre; harsim; *şilûr (IF)} Cf. P γūre غوره [Msr/RF//Haz/HH/GF] <tirî>

cûr II جوور (GF/TF) = type, kind. See **cûr̄e**.

cûr̄•e جــووره *m.* **(•ê;•êyî).** 1) {syn: cins; r̄eng; t'exlît} type, sort, kind: **•*Cûr̄ê* avayî başqe bû** (FK-eb-1)

The building was of a different kind [lit. '*the type of* the building was different'] •**Ser wî kulîlkêd ȟemû r̄enga û *cûr̄a* hêşîn dibûn** (Ba2:1, 202) On it [=Mount Dumanlu] flowers of all colors and *types* would grow; 2) {syn: awa; celeb I; t'eher} way, manner: **-vî cûr̄eyî** (K)/**bi wî cûr̄eyî** (Z-1) in this way or manner. {also: cor II (SK); cûr II (GF/TF)} Cf. P jūre جوره; Sor cor جۆر [Z-1/K/JB3/IFb/B/OK//GF/TF//SK]

cût جووت (IFb) = pair; plow. See **cot**.

cûtin جـووتِـن *vt.* **(-cû-).** to chew. {also: cûn II (BX/K-2/IFb-2/M); cûyin (BK); cûyîn (B/IFb-2); [djouin جوين/djoun جون] (JJ); <cûtin جوتن (dicû) (دجو)> (HH)} [Pok. g(i̯)eu- 400.] 'to chew': O Ir *jyav- (Tsb 41): P javīdan جـويـدن; Sor cûn[ewe] جـوون[ەوە] (-cû-) /cawîn[ewe] جـاويـن[ەوە] (-caw-); Za cawenã [cawitiş] (Srk); cf. also Rus ževat' жевать; Germ kauen; O Eng cēowan; Eng chew [A/JB3/IFb/HH//BX/K/M//JJ//B//BK] <k'ayîn>

cûyin جووين (BK) = to chew. See **cûtin**.

cûyîn جوويين (B/IFb) = to chew. See **cûtin**.

cûzan جووزان (Rnh/JJ) = razor. See **gûzan**.

cwan جوان (M-Ak) = beautiful. See **ciwan** [2].

czaret جـزارەت (EH) = punishment; trouble. See **cezaret**.

Ç/Ç' چ

ç'a I چـــا *m.* **().** 1) {syn: cew} brook, stream ; 2) {syn: ç'em} river. Cf. T çay = 'brook' [Haz/IF/A/K]

ç'a II چا (Bw) = tea. See **çay**.

ça III چا (Z-920) = how. See **çawa**.

ç'adir چـــادِر *f.* **(-a;-ê).** 1) {syn: ç'arik[2]; ç'arşev[1]; p'erde; pêçe} veil, chador *(worn by Muslim women)* (F/K); 2) {syn: kon; xêvet} tent: **•Pîrê da ser destê xwe, çû ber *çadira* Xecê** (IS-#265) The old woman took it in her hands and went to Khej's *tent*. {also: [tchadir] چـــادر (JJ); <çadir> چـــادر (HH)} Cf. P čādor چادر = 'veil'--> T çadır = 'tent'; & P čatr چـــتـــر = 'tent' [F/K/A/JB3/IF/B/JJ/HH/ZF3] <[1] hêzar; r̄ûpoş; xêlî I; [2] kon>

çaî چائی (F) = tea. See **çay**.

çaîr چائیر (J) = meadow. See **ç'ayîr**.

ç'ak چـــاك *adj.* good: **•*Çak* ewe em her do xo tecribe bikeyn** (SK 6:66) It would be *good* for us both to try **•Di her tiştekîda ins̱af o 'edalet *çak* e** (SK 1:2) Justice and equity are *good* in everything. {syn: baş; ç'ê; qenc} Sor çak چـاك {ç'akî} [A/IFb/GF/SK/ZF3/BF/FD/FS]

ç'akî چاكى *f.* **(-ya;-yê).** goodness, a favor: **•Ma kengî sultanê Istembolê nanek daye te, kêm yan zor *çakîyek* digel te kirîye?** (SK 17:161) When has the Sultan of Istanbul ever given you a loaf, or done you any *good*, great or small? {also: çakîtî (GF-2)} {syn: başî; qencî; xêr I} Sor çakî چـاكـى [K/A/IFb/SK/GF/TF/AD/ZF3]

çakîtî چاكيتى (GF) = goodness. See **ç'akî**.

ç'akûç/çakûç' [B-2] چاكووچ *m.* **(-ê;).** hammer. {also: [tchakoutch] چـاكـوچ (JJ); <çakûç> چاكـوچ(HH)} Cf. Ar šākūš شـاكـوش; P čakoš چـكش; T çekiç; Sor çekuş چـهكوش; Za çakûç *m.* (Todd) [F/K/A/IF/B/JJ/HH] <bizmar; ger̄an II; k'utik I; mêk'ut; mirc; zomp>

ç'al I چال *adj.* 1) with white star blaze on forehead (of horses, goats, etc.): **-bizina çal** (BF/FS) goat with white star on forehead; 2) with white "socks" (of horse) (ZK3/IFb). [Şnx/K/IFb/ZK3/FD/BF/Wkt]

çal II چال *f.* **(-a;-ê).** ditch, pit, hole; well: **•*Çal* tijî zad e** (AB) *The pit* is full of grain/food **•Yê *çalê* bo êkî bikolit, ew bixwe dê kevitê** (BF) He who digs *a pit* for another, will himself fall into it [*prv.*]; **-devê çalê** (L) the mouth of the pit. {syn: cew; goncal; k'olge; k'ort II} Sor çał چـــاڵ = 'deep depression, hollow, hole, pit, ditch'; Hau çałe *f.* (M4) [AB/K/A/JB3/ZF3] <bîr II>

ç'alak چـــالاك *adj.* active; quick, swift; vivid: **•Zarok zimanê xwe yê zikmakî *bi awayekî çalak* û di qadeka fireh de bikar neynin jî zîrekîyeke pasîf li ba wan peyda dibe** (www.scribd.com:Du Ziman Ya Pirtir) Even if children don't use their mother tongue *actively* and in a wide range [of circumstances], they still exhibit a passive ability. {syn: ç'apik I; ç'eleng; ç'ust} [A/IFb/GF/ZF3/BF/FD]

ç'alakî چـالاكـى *f.* **(-ya;-yê).** 1) {syn: lebat I; livbazî} activity; action; 2) quickness, agility (K/TF). [Wlt/K/A/IFb/GF/TF/ZK3] <ç'apikî; ç'elengî>

çalapk چـــالاپـــك (TF) = crawling on all fours. See **ç'arlepî**[1].

çalep'î[ya] [يـا]چـالـــهپـى (B/F) = on all fours. See **ç'arlepî**[2].

ç'and چـانـد *f.* **(-a;-ê).** culture: **•... Parastin, pêşvaçûn û dewlemendkirina *çand* û lîteratûra Kurdên Sovyetê ...** (Ber) The protection, advancement, and enrichment of *the culture* and literature of the Kurds of the Soviet Union **•Zimanê kurdî de vê demê da dibe zimanekî resmî û bi *çanda* kurdî va hevra destpêdike, pêşta diçe** (Ber) The Kurdish language became an official language at that time, and together with Kurdish *culture* it began to advance. {also: çande (IFb-2)} [(neol)Ber/IFb/OK/ZF3] <t'or̄e[3]>

çandayî چاندایى (IFb) = cultural. See **ç'andî**.

çande چانده (IFb) = culture. See **ç'and**.

çandeyî چاندەیى (IFb) = cultural. See **ç'andî**.

ç'andin چـــانـــدِن *vt.* **(-ç'în-/-çin-[B]).** 1) to sow, plant *(seeds)*: **•Min bîstanek *çandîye*** (SK 21:193) I *have planted* a garden **•Vî dûvê mi bibe di ĥewşa xwe da *biçîne*** (HR-7, #11, 2) Take this tail of mine and *plant* it in your yard **•Wan stirî *çandin*, xiyala wan ew bû dê tirî çinin** (SK 48:511) They *planted* thorns, thinking to reap grapes; 2) to cultivate *(land)*; 3) [*f.* ().] planting: **•Tu bo çî zira'eta xelkî dixoy û xirab dikey? Ma xelkî ew *çandine* bo te kirîye?** (SK 4:52) Why do you eat what people sow and spoil it? Have people done this *planting* for you, then?; 4) agriculture (IFb/RZ). See **ç'andinî**. {also: [tchandin] چـانـديـن (JJ);

<çandin چاندن (diçîne) (دچینە)> (HH)} [Pok. 2. k$^{u̯}$ei- 637.] 'to pile up, to gather, put in order': O Ir *kay- (Tsb 43-4): Av ^{1}kay- (pres. činav-/činv-/čin-) = 'to select, exchange, distinguish'; Sor çandin چاندن (çên) = 'to sow' [K/A/JB3/IFb/B/JJ/HH/SK/GF/TF/BK] <çinîn>

ç'andinî چاندِنی *f.* **(-ya;-yê).** agriculture. {also: çandin[4] (IFb-2/RZ-2); <çandinî> چاندنی (HH)} =Sor kişt u kał کشت و کاڵ [Kmc-16/K/A/IFb/HH/TF/OK/RZ/ZF3]

ç'andî چاندی *adj.* 1) cultural: **•doza mafên kurdan û … mafên wî yên *çandî*** (AW 1:36, 9) the issue of Kurdish rights and … its [=that people's] *cultural* rights; 2) sown, planted (B). {also: çandayî (IFb-2); çandeyî (IFb-2)} [Ber/B/GF//IFb]

çanqil چانقِل (IFb) = hook. See **ç'engel I**.

çante چانتە (RZ) = satchel. See **cente**.

ç'an û rex چان و رەخ (Zeb) = circumference. See **ç'ar rex**.

ç'ap I چاپ *f.* **(-a;-ê).** 1) unit of measure for grain (A/K); grain measure known in Turkish as **şinik** [=quarter bushel, 10 liters, (8 kg.)] (IFb); half an *olçek* (ZF); grain measure used in Van (HH): **•Du kulm, ribek e; çar rib, *ç'apek* e; du *ç'ap*, elbek e** (Frq) 2 handfuls are a rib (dry measure), 4 ribs are 1 *çap*, 2 *çaps* are 1 elb; 2) quantity, amount: **-çap kirin** (B) to measure out. {also: çapik II (TF); <çap> چاپ (HH)} Cf. T çap = 'diameter; caliber; size, scale' [K/A/IFb/B/HH/FJ/ZF//TF] <'elb; ribik>

ç'ap II چاپ *f.* **(-a;-ê).** impression; print(ing); edition; publication: **-ç'apa êkê/yekem** = first edition; **-çap kirin** (A/IF/JJ) to print; to publish. {also: [tchap] چاپ (JJ)} {syn: neşir} Cf. P čāp چاپ (earlier čhāp چهاپ, *possibly from Mongolian* [Wkp]); Sor çap چاپ [F/K/(A)/IFb/GF/JJ/ZF] <weşan II; ç'apxane>

çapamenî چاپامەنی (TF) = press. See **ç'apemenî**.

ç'apemenî چاپەمەنی *f.* **(-ya;-yê).** the Press. {also: çapamenî (TF)} Sor çapemenî چاپەمەنی = 'printed publications; the press' (K3) [(neol)Wlt/IFb/GF//TF] <ç'ap II; kovar; řojname>

ç'apik I چاپِك *adj.* lively, active, full of life and motion; quick. {syn: ç'alak; ç'eleng[5]; ç'ust} {çapikayî; ç'apikî} [K/B/ZK3]

çapik II چاپك = unit of measure for grain. See **ç'ap I**.

çapikayî چاپکایی (B) = liveliness. See **ç'apikî**.

ç'apikî چاپکی *f.* **(-ya;).** liveliness, being active and full of life. {also: çapikayî (B)} [K/ZF3//B] <ç'alakî>

ç'apxan•e چاپخانە *f.* **(•eya/•a;•ê).** printing house, publisher. {also: [tchap-khané] چاپ خانە (JJ)} {syn: neşirxane} Cf. P čāpxāne چاپخانە; Sor çapxane چاپخانە [F/K/JB3/JJ/ZF3] <ç'ap II; weşanxane>

ç'aqar چاقار (Efr) = star thistle. See **ç'aqir**.

ç'aqir چاقِر *f.* **(;-ê).** purple or red star thistle, bot. Centaurea calcitrapa, *edible plant*: **•Li Çiyayê Kurmênc, *çaqirê* dikelînin, û wek dermanê gede (mehde) bi kar tînin û vedixun. Dibêjin ew êşeka gede sivik dike** (FE) In Çiyayê Kurmênc (Efrin), they boil *the star thistle*, and use it as a stomach remedy and drink it. They say that it eases stomach aches. {also: ç'aqar (Efr)} [FE/Wîkîpediya//Efr] <p'incar>

ç'ar I چار *num.* **().** four, 4. {also: [tchar] چار (JJ); <çar> چار (HH)} [Pok. k^{W}etwer- 642.] 'four': Skt catur [catvārah̩ *etc.*]; O Ir *čaθvārah: Av čaθvar-/čatur- [f. čataŋr-] (*in compounds* čaθru-*);* Mid P čahār (M3); Parthian čafār; P čahār چهار; Sor çar چار/çwar چوار; Za çiȟar (Todd); Hau çûar (M4); cf. also Arm č'ors չորս [č'orek' չորեք]; Rus četyre четыре [F/K/A/JB3/IFb/B/JJ/HH/SK/JB1-A&S/GF/TF/ZF3] <ç'arêk>

ç'ar II چار (B) = remedy, cure; means. See **çare**.

ç'ara چارا *adj.* fourth, 4th. {also: çaran (K-2/IF/BX); çaranî (K-2); **ç'arem**; çarê (JB1-A/SK/M-Ak); çariyê (JB1-S); çarî (IF-2); çarûm (K[s]); [čarāṅ چاران/ečárāṅ اچاران/chārē چاری (Rh.)] (JJ)} Cf. P čahārom چهارم; Sor çwarem[în] چوارەم[ین]; Za çiȟarin (Todd) [F/K/B//IF/BX/JJ//JB1-A/SK/M-Ak//JB1-S] <çar I>

ç'aran چاران (K/IF/BX/JJ) = fourth. See **ç'ara**.

ç'aranî چارانی (K) = fourth. See **ç'ara**.

çarçeve چارچەڤە (F/K[s]) = frame. See **ç'arçove**.

ç'arçik چارچِك *f.* **(-a;-ê).** 1) square; 2) *[adj.]* square, quadrilateral: **•Kevirên reş û spî ên *çarniçik* li ser rûyê erdê ji paqijiyê dibiriqîn** (FH 8) The black and white *square* stones on the ground sparkled immaculately [lit. 'with cleanliness']. {also: çarçing (GF-2); çarniçik (FH)} *çarniçik* may be influenced by *çarnikal* [FH//K/A/IFb/GF/TF/RZ/ZF3]

ç'arçing چارچنگ (GF) = square. See **ç'arçik**.

ç'arçive چارچڤە (IFb/TF/OK) = frame. See **ç'arçove**.

ç'arçîve چارچیڤە (OK) = frame. See **ç'arçove**.

ç'arçope چارچۆپە (OK) = frame. See **ç'arçove**.

ç'arçove چارچۆڤە *f.* **(-ya;-yê).** frame, framework: **•Di**

nav *çarçoveya* qanûnên Almanya de wezîfeyên Heyva Sor wiha tên rêzkirin... (Wlt 2:59, 4) Within *the framework of* the German legal system [lit. 'the laws of Germany'] the duties of the Red Crescent can be outlined as follows... {also: çarçeve (F/K[s]); çarçive (IFb/TF/OK-2); çarçîve (OK); çarçope (OK-2)} {syn: p'erwaz} <P čārčūb(eh) چارچوبه; Sor çwarçêwe چوارچێوه [Wlt//F/K(s)//IFb/TF//OK]

ç'arde چارده (K/A/JB3/SK) = fourteen. See **ç'ardeh**.

ç'ardeh چـــــارده *num. f.* **(;-ê).** fourteen, 14: **-heyva çardehê** (BX) the moon on the 14th [of the lunar month] *[proverbial expression of beauty]* {also: çardeşevê (JB3/K)} **•Riwê te ji *heyva çardehê* rewşentir e** (BX) Your face is brighter than the *moon on the 14th* [of the lunar month]. {also: çarde (K/A/JB3); deh û çar (Ad/Krç/Bg); [tchardeh] چارده (JJ); <çarde[h]> چارده(HH)} Cf. P čahārdah چهارده; Sor çwarde چوارده; Za çarrês/desuçeȟar (Todd); Hau çûarde (M4) [F/IF/B/JJ/HH//K/A/JB3/SK//Ad/Krç/Bg]

ç'ardehem چـــــاردهـــهم *adj.* fourteenth, 14th. {also: çardehemîn (CT-2/GF-2/Wkt-2); çardemîn (IFb/TF); çardeyem (Wkt); çardeyemîn (Wkt-2)} Cf. P čahārdahom چهاردهم; Sor çwardehem چواردههم/çwardemîn چواردمین [CT/GF/Wkt//IFb/TF] <ç'ardeh>

ç'ardehemîn چـارده‌هه‌مـیـن (CT/GF/Wkt) = fourteenth. See **ç'ardehem**.

ç'ardehxor چـــــاردهـــــخـــۆر (Wkt) = pistol. See **ç'ardexwar**.

ç'ardehxur چـــــاردهـــــخـــور (Wkt) = pistol. See **ç'ardexwar**.

ç'ardehxwer چـــــاردهـــــخـــوهر (Wkt) = pistol. See **ç'ardexwar**.

ç'ardemîn چـــــاردهمـــیـــن (IFb/TF) = fourteenth. See **ç'ardehem**.

ç'ardeşevê چـــاردهشـــهڤـی **().** the moon on the 14th [of the lunar month] *[proverbial expression of beauty]*. {syn: heyva çardehê (BX)} [K/JB3]

ç'ardexor چاردهخۆر (Wkt) = pistol. See **ç'ardexwar**.

ç'ardexur چـــاردهخـــور (Ardû/Wkt/ZF3) = pistol. See **ç'ardexwar**.

ç'ardexwar چـــاردهخـــوار *f.* **(-a;-ê).** Browning HP, type of pistol *(which holds 14 bullets)*: **•Zûzûka rabû ser xwe, beziya kadînê, *çardexura* bavê xwe î rihmetî ji binê kayê derxist û hanî** (Ardû, 134) He quickly got up and ran to the hayloft, took his belated father's *pistol* out from under the hay and brought it. {also: çardehxor (Wkt); çardehxur (Wkt-2); çardehxwer (Wkt-2); çardexor (Wkt-2); çardexur (Ardû/Wkt-2/ZF3)} [Bw/Dy//Ardû//Wkt//ZF3] <debançe>

ç'ardeyem چـــــاردهیـــــهم (Wkt) = fourteenth. See **ç'ardehem**.

ç'ardeyemîn چـــاردهیـــهمـــیـــن (Wkt) = fourteenth. See **ç'ardehem**.

çar•e چـــــاره *f./m.(SK)* **(•a/•eya[Wlt]/;•ê/).** 1) remedy, cure, help; solution: **•Dibêjin di nihalekîda řîwîyek hebû. ... bazeberek hebû, řîwî lê derbaz dibû her wextê ȟez kiriba. ... Marek jî di wê nihalêda hebû. Nedişya li bazeberî derbaz bibît. Zor ȟez dikir ew jî wekî řîwî hat-u-çonê biket, çu *çare* nedît** (SK 2:9) They say that there was a fox (living) in a ravine. ... There were stepping-stones and the fox crossed over whenever he liked. ... There was also a snake in that ravine. He could not cross over the stepping-stones. He very much wanted to come and go like the fox, but could see no *solution* ; 2) means (K/B/JB3/IF); way out of a difficult situation (K/B): **•Çak ewe em her do xo tecribe bikeyn, qemî *çareyekî bikeyn*, bişkînîn** (SK 6:66) It would be best for us both to try and see if we can't *somehow manage* to rend it; 3) possibility; 4) {syn: guman; hêvî; îman; îtbar; omîd} hope (F/B): **•Ewe k'esîb bûn, *ç'ara* wan bizinek bû, ewê jî gura xwar** (B) They were poor, their only *hope* was a goat, and the wolves ate it **•*ç'ara* min** (B) my hope, my *dear (form of address for children and loved ones)*. {also: ç'ar II (B); [tcharé] چاره (JJ); <çare> چـــــاره (HH)} Cf. Mid P čārag = 'means, remedy' (M3); P čāre چاره = 'remedy'--> T çare [F/K/A/JB3/IF/JJ/HH//B]

çarek چارهك (IFb/JJ/GF) = a fourth. See **ç'arêk**.

ç'arem چـــــارهم *adj.* fourth, 4th. {also: **ç'ara**; çaremîn (GF/TF/RZ/CT-2/ZF-2/IFb-2/Wkt-2)} Cf. P čahārom چهارم; Sor çwarem[în] چوارهم[ین] [A/IFb/CT/ZF/Wkt//GF/TF/RZ] <ç'ar I>

çaremîn چـــــارهمـــیـــن (GF/TF/RZ/CT/ZF/IFb/Wkt) = fourth. See **ç'arem**.

çarep'êlî چارپێلی (B) = on all fours. See **ç'arlepî**[2].

çareser چـــارهســـهر: **-çareser bûn** (IFb) to be solved: **•...û hemû pirsgirêk *çareser bibin*** (Wlt 1:35, 5) ...and all the problems *will be solved*; **-çareser kirin** (IFb/TF) to solve: **•Helbet tukes formuleke vekirî ji bo *çareserkirina* probleman jê**

naxwaze, bes qet nebe tesbîtkirina sebebên wan pêwist e (Wlt 1:39, 11) Obviously no one is asking for a formula for *solving* problems, but at least their causes should be identified. Cf. Sor çareser چـــارهســەر = 'means of escape'; 'remedy, cure (EM)' [(neol)Wlt/IFb/TF] <çare; ĥel>

çareserî چـــارهســـەرى *f.* **(-ya;-yê).** solution *(to a problem)*, solving; cure, remedy: •**Boçî xelk bo *çareserîyê* qesta Şêx û seyîda diken** (waartv:bernameTîroj 23.vii.2018) Why people head for sheikhs and sayyids for *a solution/cure* •***Çareserîya* pirsa Sûrîyê û paşeroja Kurdan** (riataza.com 29.xi.2017) *Solving* the issue of Syrian and the future of the Kurds •**Nojdar mijîlî *çareserîya* nexweşî ye** (BF) The doctor is busy *curing* the disease. < çare + ser + -î [(neol)ZF3/FD/BF]

ç'arê چـــارێ (JB1-A/SK/M-Ak/JJ[Rh]) = fourth. See **ç'ara**.

ç'arêk چـــاریێـــك *f.* **(-a;-ê).** a fourth, one-quarter, 1/4: •***Çarêka* (*çaryeka*) zeviya xo dê deme te** (AR, 288) I will give you *a quarter of* my field. {also: çarek (IFb-2/GF-2); çarîk II (CT); çaryek (K-2/A/IFb/GF/TF/BX/CT-2); [tcharik/chārak (Rh)/ ciáhrék (G)] چارك (JJ); <çar[ye]k> چاريك (HH)} Cf. P čārak چـــارك/čār-yak چـــاريـــك/čahār-yak چهاريك; Sor çarek چارهك (Sulaimania & Kerkuk) /çarêk چـــارێك (Arbil) [Zeb/AR/K/B//CT//A/IFb/HH/GF/ TF/ BX//JJ]

ç'argav چـــارگـــاڤ *f.* **().** gallop: •**Min hespê xwe *da çargavî*** (GF) I *made* my horse *gallop*; **-çargavî kirin** (K) to gallop. {also: çargavî (K-2/IFb-2/GF/ TF); [tchargaw] چارگـاف(JJ)} {syn: xar I} <ç'ar = '4' + gav = 'step, pace': cf. T dörtnal [Zeb/Hk/K/IFb/JJ/ /GF/TF]

ç'argavî چارگاڤى (K/IFb/GF/TF) = gallop. See **çargav**.

ç'argayî** چارگايى *adj.* consisting of four (4) bulls or oxen: •**Cotê me *çargayîye (AB) Our plough is a four-bull plough ("a *four-buller*"). [AB]

ç'arhilqe چارهلقه *adv.* all around, from all sides; from everywhere: •***Çarhilqe* merî hatibûn** (B) People came *from all around* •**Min *çarhilqê* xwe nhêrî** (EH) I looked about *in every direction* •**Vira *çarhilqe* ave** (B) *In every direction* there is water [=We are surrounded by water]. {syn: ç'arnikar} [EH/K/B]

ç'arik چـارِك *f./m.(K)* **(-a/;-ê/).** 1) {syn: laç'ik; meles; terĥî} fine muslin or gauze, used for women's headdress (Haz); women's headdress; headband in the form of a long piece of cloth, wrapped around a headdress: •**Li herêma Serhedê (Bakûrê Bakûrê Kurdistanê) jî bi piranî pêşî *çarik* didin serê xwe û kofiyê jî datîn[in] ser *çarikê*** (Wkp:Kofî) And in the Serhed region (in the north of North Kurdistan), [the women] usually put a *çarik* on their head, and put the kofî over the *çarik*; 2) {also: çarîk I (K)} {syn: ç'adir[1]; ç'arşev[1]; p'erde; pêçe} woman's veil (K/JB3). [Haz-valley/K/JB3/IF] <doxe; hêzar; r̄ûpoş; xêlî I>

çarin چارِن (K) = quatrain. See **ç'arîne**.

çarix چـــــارِخ (Z/K/IFb/B/GF) = peasant shoe. See **ç'arox**.

ç'ariyê چاريێ (JB1-S) = fourth. See **ç'ara**.

ç'arî چارى (IF) = fourth. See **ç'ara**.

çarîk I چاريك (K) = woman's veil. See **ç'arik**[2].

ç'arîk II چاريك (CT) = a fourth. See **ç'arêk**.

ç'arîn چـــاريـــن (IFb/GF/TF/FD/FS/BF/Hej) = quatrain. See **ç'arîne**.

ç'arîne چـــاريـــنـــه *f.* **(;-yê).** quatrain, rubaiyyat: •***Çarînên* Xeyamî** (FS) *The Rubaiyyat of* Omar Khayyam •**Sadinî dibêje di vê *çarîneyê* de behsa tivengê tê kirin** (R.R. Yıldız. "Di Helbestên Melayê Bateyî de Evîn û Hezkirin", Bingöl Üniv. Yaşayan Diller Enst. Dergisi) Sadinî says that this *quatrain* is about a rifle [lit. 'in this quatrain a rifle is discussed']. {also: çarin (K); ç'arîn (IFb/GF/TF/FD/FS/BF); <çarîn> چـــاريـــن (Hej)} <çar = '4' + -îne, to parallel Ar rubāʿī رباعي < √ربع √r-b-ʿ = '4' [R.R.Yıldız/Wkt/ZF3/SS//IFb/GF/ TF/FD/FS/BF/Hej//K]

ç'arlep چـــارلـــهپ (GF) = crawling on all fours. See **ç'arlepî**[1].

ç'arlepî چـــارلـــهپـــى *f.* **().** 1) {also: çalapk (TF); çarlep (GF)} crawling on all fours: **-bi çalepîya** (F)/**[bi çarlepî]** (JR) on all fours; 2) *[adv.]* {also: çalep'î[ya] (B/F); çarep'êlî (B-2); çarlepkî (IFb); [tchar-lepi چارلپى/tchar-lepik چارلپيك] (JJ)} on all fours, on one's hands and knees: •**[Dûmo şeşxaneyê digrite destê xo û *bi çarlepî* devarûyî wekû kelban disûrike]** (JR #27, 80) Dumo takes his revolver into his hand and crawls *on all fours* like a dog [lit. 'like dogs']; **-çarlepkî çûn** (IFb) to crawl on one's hands and knees. [JR/K/JJ//GF//IFb//TF//F/ B] <devar̄û>

ç'arlepkî چـــارلـــهپـــكـــى (IFb) = on all fours. See **ç'arlepî**[2].

ç'armêrgî چـــارمـــێـــرگـــى *adv.* (sitting) cross-legged: **-ç'armêrgî vedan** (Msr)/**çarmirgî r̄ûniştin** (K) to sit crosslegged {also: çarmêrkanî (SK-Ak); çarmêrkî (SK/*A); çarmirgî (K); [tchar-mirghi] چارمرگی (JJ)} Sor çwarmeşqî چوارمەشقی/ çwarmêrdekî چوارمێردەکی; Hau çûarmêrde (M4) [Msr//A//K/JJ] <qelefiskî>

ç'armêrkanî چارمێرکانی (SK-Ak) = (sitting) cross-legged. See **ç'armêrgî**.

ç'armêrkî چارمێرکی (SK/*A) = (sitting) cross-legged. See **ç'armêrgî**.

çarmirgî چارمِرگی (K/JJ) = (sitting) cross-legged. See **ç'armêrgî**.

ç'arniçik چارنِچِك (FH) = square. See **ç'arçik**.

çarnikal چارنِکال (B) = four sides; on all [four] sides. See **ç'arnikar**.

ç'arnikar چارنِکار *[pl.]* 1) {syn: ç'ar rex} all four sides: **•Di bajarekî ava û *çarnikarên* wî bi çiyan dorgirtî de** (SW) In a prosperous city whose *four sides* are surrounded by mountains (=surrounded on all four sides by mountains) **•Řabûn, çûn, teftîşa ȟalê Silêmanî biken. Qederekî li *çarnikarêt* gundî geřyan** (SK 10:100) They got up and went to find what was wrong with Sulaiman. For a while they went *all about* the village; 2) *[adv.]* {syn: ç'arhilqe} all around, on all sides, in every direction [Lat. undique]; 3) [*adv.*] on all four sides. {also: çarnikal (B)} [SW/K/ZF3//B]

ç'arox چاروّخ *f.* **(-a;-ê).** peasant shoe or sandal made of leather: **•Tiştek heye, ko girê didim diçe, ko divekim disekine [*çarox*]** (L-I, #11, 232) There is something, which if I tie it, it goes; if I open it, it stops *[rdl.: ans.: peasant shoe]* = **•Vedikim naçe, girêdidim diçe. Ew çiye? [*çarix*]** (Z-1820) I open it, it doesn't go, I tie it, it goes. What is it? *[rdl.: ans: peasant shoe]*. {also: çarix (Z/K/IFb/B/GF-2); [tcharokh/charukh (Rh)] چاروخ (JJ); <çarûx> چاروخ (HH)} {syn: k'alik II} < T çarık [L/JJ/GF/TF/OK//HH//Z/K/IFb/B] <şîrox>

ç'arp'a چارپا (K) = quadruped. See **ç'arpê**.

ç'arpê چارپێ *adj. & m.(K)/f.(B)* four-legged animal, quadruped. {also: ç'arp'a (K-2); ç'arp'î (K-2); [tchar-peï] چارپی (JJ)} Sor çwarpa چوارپا/çwarpê چوارپێ [HCK/K/B/A/IFb/FJ/GF/JJ]

ç'arp'î چارپی (K) = quadruped. See **ç'arpê**.

ç'ar rex چار رەخ *f./pl.* **(-a/ ;).** circumference, all four sides: **-çar rexî *ft-î* geřan** (PS) to walk around the circumference of, circumambulate *(a bldg. or city)*: **•[Ez çûm, min dît / qesrek, *çarrexî* qesrê gerham]** (PS 333, 93, ll. 13-14) I went, I saw a castle, I walked *all around* the castle; **-çar rexî *ft-î* girtin** (PS) to surround {syn: di rex û çana ft-î ziviřîn (see below); dorgirtin; dorpêç kirin; werandin I; weranîn}: **•[Kîka *çarrexê* Bozo *girtîye*]** (PS 42, 221, l. 222) The Kika (tribe) *surrounded* Bozo; **-di řex û çana *ft-î* ziviřîn** (Zeb)/**li çar rexa zivirîn** (JB1-A) to surround; to walk all around stg.: **•Derê wê ve kir û berê xo dayê û *li çar řexa zivirî*** (JB1-A, #26) She opened its door and took a look at it and *walked all around it.* {also: ç'an û rex (Zeb); řex û çan (Zeb); řex û çar (Hk); [čār räx (JJ-PS)/cā:reḥi (PS)] (JJ)} {syn: ç'arnikar} [Zeb/(OK)//IFb/JJ-PS/JB1-A//Hk]

ç'arsed چارسەد/**ç'arṣed** چارصەد [SK] *num.* four hundred, 400. {also: çarsid (B)} Av čaθwārō sata; P čahār ṣad چهارصد; Sor çwarsed چوارسەد [K/A/JB1-S//SK//B]

ç'arsid چارسِد (B) = four hundred. See **çarsed**.

ç'arşef چارشەف = veil; fabric; sheet; shroud. See **ç'arşev**.

Ç'arşem چارشەم *f./m.(JB1-A)* **(-a/;-ê/).** Wednesday: **•*Çarşema* Sor cejna êzdiyan ya herî naskirî ye** (Wkp: "Kofî") Red *Wednesday* [Charshema Sor] is the best known Yezidi holiday. {also: çarşemb (JB3/IF); çarşembî, m. (JB1-A); [tcharchem] چارشم (JJ); <çarş[e]m> چارشم (HH)} Cf. P čahāršanbe چهارشنبه --> T çarşamba; Sor çwarşem[m]e چوارشەممە/çwarşemû چوارشەموو; Za çarşeme (Todd) [F/K/A/B/JJ/Rh/ZF3//JB3/IF//HH//JB1-A]

Ç'arşemb چارشەمب (JB3/IF) = Wednesday. See **Çarşem**.

Ç'arşembî چارشەمبی, m. (JB1-A) = Wednesday. See **Çarşem**.

ç'arşev چارشەڤ *f.* **(-a;-ê).** 1) {syn: ç'adir[1]; ç'arik[2]; p'erde; pêçe} veil, chador *(worn by Muslim women)*; 2) {syn: p'erçe [3]} fabric, cloth; canvas, sackcloth; 3) {syn: sipîç'al} sheet, bedsheet; 4) {syn: k'efen} shroud, cerement. {also: ç'arşef; ç'arşew; [tcharcheb چارشب/ tcharchaf چارشاف] (JJ); <çarşeb> چارشب (HH)} Cf. Ar šaršaf شرشف, T çarşaf = 'sheet'; Hau ça[r]şûe *f.* = 'bridal dress' (M4) [EP-7/K/IF/B//JJ/HH] <hêzar; xêlî I>

ç'arşew چارشەو = veil; fabric; sheet; shroud. See **ç'arşev**.

ç'arûm چارووم (K[s]) = fourth. See **ç'ara**.

ç'aryek چــاریــەك (K/A/IFb/HH/GF/TF/BX/CT) = a fourth. See **ç'arêk**.

çav چاڤ/**ç'av** چاڤ [JB1-S] *m.* **(-ê; çêv, vî çavî).** eye: **-anîn/xistin ber çava[n]** (K) to be noticed, come to s.o.'s attention; **-çav k'etin** [+**li**] = to notice, see, to lay/set eyes on: **•Eva nêzîkî çil roj û çil şevîye, ez rê têm, hê *ç'e'vê* min *li* 'evd û îsana *nek'etye*** (EP-7) It's been almost 40 days and 40 nights that I've been on the road, I *haven't yet laid eyes on* a human being **•Wezîr, go tê li miclisê, *çav li* teyr *dikeve*** (L) When the vizier comes to the assembly, he *notices* the bird [lit. 'His eye falls on the bird'] ; **-çav li *fk-ê* bûn** = to keep an eye on s.o.: **•*Çavê* te *li* min *be*** (L) *Keep an eye on* me [lit. 'Your eye should be on me']; **-çav li r̄ê bûn** = to wait for [lit. 'to have one's eye on the road'] [Cf. Sor çawr̄ê]: **•*Çavê* wê *li rê ye*** (L) She waits [lit. 'Her *eye is on the road*']; **-çavêd xwe ji *ft-î* nebir̄în** (Ba2) not to take one's eyes off stg.; **-çavên *fk-î* bar nebûn** (WT) to be unable to bear (the sight/idea) of, be unable to brook the notion of: **•Dibe ko ji diltengiya ji hev qetandinê *çavên* wan *bar nebûbû* û nehatibûn** (WT, 86) Perhaps from the grief of being separated, they *had not been able to bear the thought* and had not come; **-çavêt xwe germ kirin** (Bw)/~**nerm kirin** (Qzl) to take a nap; **-ser çavê min** = all right, gladly, with pleasure! [lit. 'on my eye[s]']. {also: çaw (SK); çev I (F-2); ç'e'v II (B/Ba/J/Z/EP); [tchaw] چـاڤ (JJ); <çav چـاڤ/çe'v چـعـڤ> (HH)} [Pok. kʷek̂-s- 638.] 'to appear; to see; to show': Skt cakṣ- = 'see, speak'; O Ir *čašman- (Ras, p. 135 & 211): Av čašman-; O P caša- [*nom.-acc.* cašma] (Kent); Pahl čašm; P čašm چشم; Sor çaw چاو; Za çem *m.* (Mal); Hau çem *m.* (M4); See Ras, p.211 for more. [F/K/A/JB3/IFb/JJ/HH/JB1-A&S/GF/TF/ OK//B/ Ba/J/Z/EP//SK] <bibiq; bijang; birû; damirandin; miçandin; niqandin I; r̄eşik I>

çavbirçî چـاڤـبـرچـی *adj.* greedy, covetous, selfish; envious: **•Zikbirçî têr dibin, belê *çavbirçî* têr nabin** (Kurdipedia.org) The hungry [lit. 'hungry of the belly'] can be satiated, but the *covetous* [lit. 'hungry of the eye'] can't be satiated. {also: çavbirsî (Zx/CS-2/Kmc-2/Wkt-2/BF-2/FS); [tchaw birsi] چاڤ برسی (JJ)} {syn: ç'ikûs; çirûk; devbeş; r̄ijd; evsene; qesîs; tima} {çavbirçîtî; çavbirsîtî} < çav = 'eye' + birçî/birsî = 'hungry' [Kurdipedia/K/A/IFb/FJ/BF/TF/ZF/Kmc/Wkt/BF//Zx/JJ/FS]

çavbirçîtî چاڤبرچیتی *f.* **(-ya;-yê).** greed, covetousness, selfishness; envy: **•*Çavbirçîtîya* rêveberên gelên cînar** (Mezopotamya[FB]) *The greed of* the leaders of the neighboring peoples. {also: [tchaw birsiti] چاڤ برسیتی (JJ)} [Mezopotamya/K/GF/Wkt/BF/ ZF3//JJ]

çavbirsî چـاڤـبـرسـی (Zx/CS/Kmc/Wkt/BF/FS/JJ) = greedy. See **çavbirçî**.

çavder چاڤدەر (ZF) = womanizer. See **çavlider**.

çavdêrî چـاڤـدێـری *f.* **(-ya;-yê).** observation; surveillance; supervision; attention: **•Ez ... tim di bin *çavderîya* (observasyon) polîs de bûm** (Ber #7, 9) I ... was always under *the surveillance of* the police. {syn: dîdevanî; nêr̄evanî; zêrevanî} Cf. Sor çawdêrî چاودێری = 'supervision, attention' [(neol)Ber/ JB3/IF/GF] <dîdevanî>

çaver̄ê چــاڤــەڕێ *adj.* waiting, looking forward to, anticipating, expecting: **-çaver̄ê bûn** (K[s]/FB)/~ **kirin** (FB)/**li çawr̄ê man** (SK): to wait for, await, anticipate, expect, look forward to: **•Ehlê mizgewtê nezanîn mela mirîye, *man li çawr̄ê* wî ko noke dê hêt** (SK 15:151) The people of the mosque did not know that the mullah was dead and *were waiting* for him to come **•Ez *çaverê* kax̄eza te*me*** (Bw) I'm *looking forward to* your letter **•Tu *çaverêy* çi *dikî*, êdî ew nahêt (nema tê)** (FB) What *are* you *waiting for*? He's not coming. {also: çavlirê (A); çavrê (FJ/GS/CS); çawr̄ê (SK)} Sor çawer̄ê چــاوەڕێ & çawer̄wan چــاوەڕوان = 'waiting, expectant' [Bw/K(s)/Wkt/FB//A//FJ/GS/CS//SK] <bendî; hêvî>

çavik I چاڤِك *f.* **(-a;-ê).** 1) compartment; chamber; cell: **•Muze wê ji sê *çavikan* pêk were** (PUKMedia 1.vii.2015) The museum will consist of three *chambers* **•Piştî ku herdu *çavikên* sêyemîn û heştemîn ên bendava Feratê hatin xebitandin** (ANHA 6.xi.2017) After the 3rd and 8th *chambers* of the Euphrates Dam have been put into operation; **•Şaheng hêk berdide *çavikê*** (Yumpu: Mêşhingiv çawa çêdibin) The queen bee deposits an egg in *the cell*; 2) drawer: **•Kevçî di *çavikê* de ne** (KürtKültürü. com) The spoons are in *the drawer* **•Min bi darê zorê *çavikeke* şikestî ya maseya karî ya bavê xwe vekiribû** (tirşik.net: Perxudres: B. Kaya 17.viii.2013) I had forced open *a* broken *drawer* in my father's work table. [ZF3/GF/CS/TF/Wkt]

çavik II چـاڤِـك *f.* **(-a;).** eyeglasses, spectacles. {also: çavînk, m. (K) *obsolescent*; [tchawink] چـاڤـیـنـك

(JJ); <çavik> چـــاڤـــك (HH)} {syn: berçavk}Sor çawîlke چاویلکه [Msr/A/IF/HH/G/BF//K/JJ]

çavinî چاڤِنی (IFb) = evil eye. See **çavîn**.

çavîn چاڤین *f.* (). the evil eye: **-çavîn bûn** (Zeb)/**çavinî bûn** (IFb) to be smitten by the evil eye: **•Da *çavîn* nebît** (Zeb) Touch wood! **•Gaê me *çavinî* bû** (IFb) Our cow was *smitten by the evil eye*; **-çavîn kirin** (A/JJ-G) to smite s.o. with the evil eye, to tempt the evil eye. {also: çavîne (ZF3); çavinî (IFb); [ciávîn kem] چـــاڤـــیـــن (JJ)} {syn: nezer[2]} Sor çawînî چاوینی [Zeb/A/JJ-G/OK//ZF3//IFb]

çavîne چاڤینه (ZF3) = evil eye. See **çavîn**.

çavînk چـاڤـیـنـك, m. (K/JJ) = spectacles <*obsolescent*>. See **çavik**.

çavînok چاڤینۆك *m.&f.* (). s.o. with the evil eye. {also: <çavînok چـــاڤـــیـــنـــوك/çavker چـــاڤـــكـــەر> (HH); <çavînok> چاڤینۆك (Hej)} [A/IFb/HH/Hej] <çavîn>

çavkanî چـــاڤـــكـــانـــی *f.* **(-ya;-yê).** 1) {syn: avzê; kanî; selef} spring, source; permanent springs of water or ones that dry up in the summer ; 2) resource *(e.g., natural resource)*: **•Herçiqas av ji bo hemû jîndaran *çavkaniyeke* bingehîn be jî, îro di destê mirovên "hemdem" de wek pergaleke ji holê rakirina berhemên dîrokê tê bi kar anîn** (Wlt 1:21, 16) Although water is a basic *resource* for all living things, today it is being used by "modern" man as an instrument for destroying historical artifacts; 3) {syn: jêder; kan} origin, source *(fig.)*; bibliography: **•Li gor hin *çavkaniyên* ewlekar** (Wlt 1:49, 3) According to reliable *sources*. {also: ç'e'vkanî (B); [tchaw-i kani] چاڤی كانی (JJ)} [Z-2/K/IFb/ZF/RZ/SS/ZF3//B//JJ] <kanî>

çavk'esper چـــاڤـــكـــەســـپـــەر (Xrz) = blue-eyed. See **k'esper**.

çavlider چاڤلِدەر *adj. & m.* someone with a wandering eye; womanizer: **•Ger melayên me doxînsist û *çavlider* bin, gelo wê xelkê reben çi xwelîyê li serê xwe bikin hêê!** (www.lotikxane.com) If our mullahs are weak-moraled and *have wandering eyes*, how unforunate will the poor folk be! {syn: çavder (ZF)} [Lotikxane/IFb/Wkt/GF/TF/Kmc/FB//ZF] <tolaz; zinêk'ar>

çavlirê چـاڤـلِـرێ (A) = waiting, looking forward to. See **çaveřê**.

çavnas چـــاڤـــنـــاس *adj.* acquainted, familiar (with): **-çavnas li *ft-î* bûn** (Ba3) to become acquainted with (stg.), to familiarize o.s. with: **•Here *li* xezne û hebûna min *bive çavnas*** (Ba3-3, #1) Go *familiarize yourself with* my treasures and belongings. <çav = 'eye' + nas = 'acquainted with' [Ba3/ZF3]

çavnebarî چاڤنەباری *f.* **(-ya;-yê).** envy: **-lê çavnebarî kirin** = to envy: **•Lema jî ewê *ç'e'vnebarî li* wî dikir** (Ba) Therefore she *envied* him. {also: ç'e'vnebaharî (XF); ç'e'vnebarî (Ba/B); ç'e'vnebartî (B-2)} {syn: çavřeşî; ȟevsûdî} Cf. Rus nenavist' ненависть = hatred ['unable to look at'] [F/K/IFb/ZF3//XF//B/Ba] <dexesî; k'umřeşî>

çavnêrî چـــاڤـــنـــێـــری (JB3/IFb/GF/OK) = waiting. See **çavnihêrî**.

çavnihêrî چـــاڤـــنِـــهـــێـــری *f.(K/JB3/IF)/m.(Z-1)* **(-ya/-yê; -yê/).** 1) waiting, anticipation, expectation: **-çavnêrîya *fk-î* bûn** (K)/**~kirin** (K/IFb) to wait for s.o. {syn: li bendî fk-ê man; çav li řê bûn; hêvîyê man; p'an I; sekinîn}: **•Em êp'êce wext *ç'avnihêřîya* wana *bûn*** (Ba2:2, 205) We *waited for* them for quite some time; 2) *[adj.]* [+ *ezafeh*] waiting, in anticipation of: **•*Ç'e'vnihêrîyê* řîya Qeret'ajdîn û bira bûn** (Z-1) They were *waiting for* [the arrival of] Q. and [his] brothers **•Em *ç'e'vnihêrîyê* tene** (B) We're *waiting for* you. {also: çavnêrî (JB3/IFb/GF/OK); ç'e'vnihêrî (B/Z-1)} Sor çaweřuwan چـــــــاوەڕووان/çawenuwar چاوەنووار (Sinne) [Z-1/B//K//JB3/IFb/GF/OK]

çavřeşî چاڤڕەشی *f.* **(-ya;-yê).** 1) envy: **-çavřeşî kirin** = a) to be envious; b) to be jealous; 2) jealousy. {syn: çavnebarî; ȟevsûdî} [Z-1/K/A/IF/ZF3] <dexesî; k'umřeşî>

çavrê چـــاڤـــرێ (FJ/GS/CS) = waiting, looking forward to. See **çaveřê**.

çavrî چـــاڤـــری *f./m.(FS)* (). livestock, cattle, bovines: **•Wê salê derdega li nav *çawrîyêt* wan hebû** (SK 30:270) That year there was a cattle plague among their *livestock*. {also: çawrî (SK); <çavrî> چـاڤـری (Hej)} {syn: gařeş; t'ariş} Sor çarewê چـــــــارەوێ (Hej) = řeşewułax ڕەشـــــــەووڵاخ [Zeb/OK/Hej/FS//SK] <dewar; ga; gařan>

çavřonahî چـــاڤـــڕۆنـــاهـــی (K) = congratulations. See **çavřonayî**.

çavřonayî چاڤڕۆنایی *f.* (). congratulations on attaining one's wish [cf. T gözün aydın, Arm ač̣k't loys աչքդ լոյս]: **-çavřonahî dan** (K) to congratulate: **•*Çavřonayî didane*** [sic] **min û dê û bavê min** (Ba2:2, 208) They *congratulated* me and my parents [on my engagement]. {also: çavřonahî (K); çavronî (IFb/GF/ZF3); [tchaw rouni چـــــــاڤ

روونی/tchaw rounahi چاف روناهی] (JJ)} Cf. P čašmat rōšan چشمت روشن; Sor çawit r̄onî bê چاوت ڕۆنی بێ [Ba2//K//IFb/GF/ZF3//JJ] <pîrozî>

çavronî چاڤرۆنی (IFb/GF/ZF3) = congratulations. See **çavr̄onayî.**

çavsor چاڤسۆر *adj.* ferocious, fierce, vicious; fearless, unafraid: •**Bavo tim digote min ku divê di paîzê da şivan çavvekirîtir bin; gur ji birçîna pir *çavsor* dibin, û hema firseteke piçûk bikeve destê wan, xwe davêjin nav pez û çendek jê dibin** (EŞ, 14) Father always told me that in the fall shepherds must be more attentive; the wolves become *fierce* from hunger, and whenever the slightest opportunity presents itself, they jump into the flock and take a few [victims] from it. cf. Sor çawsûr چاوسوور = 'brave'. *Although seemingly* <çav = 'eye' + sor = 'red', *perhaps originally* <Ar jasūr جسور = 'bold, daring' (*for* -v-/-w-, cf. ḧevsûd <Ar ḥasūd حسود = 'jealous, envious') {çavsorî} [EŞ/K/IFb/GF/TF/OK/ZF3]

çavsorî چاڤسۆری *f.* **(-ya;-yê).** 1) {syn: hovîtî} ferocity, fierceness, cruelty; outburst of rage, fury, viciousness, ill-temperedness: •**Apê Musa ... şehîdê nemir rastiya (dewleta Tirk) zilm û zora wê *çavsoriya* wê li hemberî miletê Kurd bi cîhanê bide dîtin** (Wlt 2:59, 7) May Uncle Musa [Anter] … the immortal martyr cause the world to see the truth of the Turkish state, its oppression, its *viciousness* toward the Kurdish nation; 2) courage, bravery, heroism. {also: çawsorî (SK)} Sor çawsûrî چاوسووری = 'courage' [Wlt/K/IFb/GF/TF/OK/ZF3//SK] <çavsor>

çavşîn چاڤشین *adj.* blue-eyed: **-lawê çavşîn** (FS) blue-eyed boy. {syn: k'esper} [ZF3/FD/BF/FS/SS]

çaw چاو (SK) = eye. See **çav.**

ç'awa چاوا *intrg.* 1) {syn: ç'erê (Bg); ç'ilo I; ç'ito} how? •**Ez dixazim her̄ime cem Xwedê, bizanibim çika r̄astya wî *çewane*?** (Dz) I want to go to God, to know *what* his truth *is like* [lit. '*how* his truth is']; 2) *[prep.]* {syn: mîna; wek} like, similar to: •***Çawa* şemaleke zêr** (EP-7) *Like* a golden shine [or a torch of gold]; 3) *[conj.]* as: •***Çawa* tê zanîn** (Ber) *As* is known. {also: ça III (Z-920); çawan (K/A/JB3/IF); çewa (B/Z-1); [tchavan] چاوان (JJ); <çawa چاوا/çawan چاوان> (HH)} Sor çon چۆن [Z-1/B//HH//K/A/JB3/IF/JJ]

çawal چاوال (K) = sack. See **ç'ewal.**

ç'awan چاوان (K/A/JB3/IF) = how. See **ç'awa.**

ç'awîr چاویر (Efr) = grass. See **ç'ayîr**[2].

ç'awîş چاویش *m.* **(-ê;).** 1) servant, valet; usher (JJ); 2) group-, detachment leader *(mil.)*; 3) sergeant (mil.) . {also: [tchaouch] چاوش (JJ)} Cf. T çavuş = 'sergeant' {ç'awîşî} [Z-1/K/ZF3//JJ]

ç'awîşî چاویشی *f.* **(-ya;-yê).** servitude, being a servant or valet: •**Memê ... rabû k'incêd *çawîşîyê* li xwe kir** (FK-eb-1) Mem ... (got up and) donned the clothes of *servitude* (i.e., became a servant). [FK-1/ZF3]

çawr̄ê چاوڕێ (SK) = waiting, looking forward to. See **çaver̄ê.**

çawrî چاوری (SK) = livestock. See **çavrî.**

çawsorî چاوسۆری (SK) = ferocity; bravery. See **çavsorî.**

ç'ax چاخ *m.(K/B)/f.(JB3/IF)* **(-ê/ ;-î/-ê).** (period of) time: **-ç'axê ...** = when *[conj.]*: •***Çaxê* Menglo derî vedike** (J) *When* Menglo opens the door; **-t'u ç'ax** = never {syn: t'u car; t'u wext}; **-wê çaxê/wî çaxî** (Ba) then, at that time. {also: [tchag] چاغ (JJ); <çax> چاخ (HH)} {syn: dem; gav [1]} < T çağ = 'period' [K/A/JB3/IF/B/HH//JJ] <car; wext>

çax̄ چاغ (JJ) = time. See **ç'ax.**

ç'ay چای *f.* **(-a;-ê).** tea: **-çay [ve]xwarin** (B) to drink tea. {also: ç'a II (Bw); çaî (F); [tchài] چای (JJ)} Cf. P čāy چای (< Chinese chá); T çay; Ar šāy شای; Sor ça چا/çayî چایی; Za çay *f.* (Todd); Hau çay *m.* (M4); cf. also Rus čay чай [Z-3/K/A/IFb/B/JJ/JB1-A/SK/GF/TF/OK/ZF3//F//Bw] <qawe; *dark:* giran I/r̄eş/tarî; *light:* sivik/vebûyî/zer I>

çayir چایر (ZF3) = meadow; grass. See **ç'ayîr.**

ç'ayîr چاییر *f.* **(-a;-ê).** 1) {syn: ç'îmen; mêrg} meadow: •**Ji wan cewika hinek ... hêdîka nava *çayîra* r̄a dik'işyan** (Ba2:1, 202) Some of those brooks ... slowly meandered through *the meadows* •**Min ... *çaîra* biç'êrîne** (J) Let me graze in *the meadows*; 2) {also: çawîr (Efr)} {syn: gîya[1]} grass (ZK-3/Efr): •**...diçine nava bax̄çe. *Çayîra* wînakê li çokêye** (ZK-3) They go into the garden. Its *grass* is knee-deep [lit. 'to the knee']. {also: çaîr (J); çawîr (Efr); çayir (ZF3); çayr (K); <çayîr> چاییر (HH)} < T çayır [J//K//ZF3//B/HH//Efr]

çayr چایر (K) = meadow; grass. See **ç'ayîr.**

ç'ayxan•e چایخانه *f.* **(•eya;•ê).** teahouse, teashop: •**...ji bo xwastina coca-colayê ew şande *çayxaneya* herî nêzîk** (KS, 36) ...he sent him to the nearest *teashop* to ask for a Coca-Cola. [KS/K/A/IFb/B/GF/TF/

OK/ZF3] <qawexane>

çe چه = good. See **ç'ê**.

çek چەك *m./f.(K/B/ZF3)/pl.(JB2/B)* **(-ê/ ;-î/).** 1) {syn: cil I; k'inc; libs} [pl. according to B & JB2] clothing, dress, garb; 2) {syn: řext; zirx} armor; 3) {syn: sîleh I} weapons, arms: •[***Çek* û sîlaȟ alateke ȟarbî li nik wan tune**] (JR) They have with them no *weapons* or arms or tool of war. {also: [tchek] چك (JJ); <çek> چك (HH)} [F/K/A/JB3/IF/B/JJ/HH/Ba2/JB2/ZF3] <cebirxane>

çekband چەکبەند *pl.* 1) Kurdish type of *çepken* (=stout jacket with slit sleeves to leave the arms free) (HB/A); vest, waistcoat (IF); 2) military armor (K). {also: çekbend (K/IF/ZF3); <çekbend> چكبند (HH)} [HB/A//K/IF/HH/ZF3]

çekbend چەکبەند (K/IF/ZF3) = vest; armor. See **çekband**.

çekçekîle چەکچەکیلە *m.* **(-yê;).** bat, zool. *Chiroptera.* {also: çekçekûle (IFb/OK/ZF3/FS-2)} {syn: barç'imok; çil II; pîrçemek; şevrevînk; şevşevok} [Dh/K(s)/RZ/FS//IFb/OK/ZF3]

çekçekûle چەکچەکوولە (IFb/OK/ZF3/FS) = bat (zool.). See **çekçekîle**.

çekdar چەکدار *adj.* armed, provided with weapons: •**TC bi hemû hêzên xwe yên *çekdar* êrîş dibe Kurdistanê û agir bi ser ve dibarîne** (Wlt 2:71, 13) The Republic of Turkey with all its *armed* forces is attacking Kurdistan and raining down fire. <ç'ek [2] & [3] + -dar = 'possessed of' [Wlt/K/IFb/GF/TF/OK/ZF3] <çek [2] & [3]; sîleh I>

Çekistanî چەکستانی (Wkt) = Czech. See **Ç'ekî**.

Ç'ekî چەکی *adj.* Czech. {also: Çekistanî (Wkt-2; Çîkî (BF)} [Wkt/ZF3//BF]

çel I چەل (A/IFb) = forty. See **ç'il I**.

çel II چەل *m.* **(-ê;).** tall, pointy mountain peak; stone outcropping on a mountain: -**çel û çîya** (Bw) high mountain peaks. {also: çele I (A)} [Bw/OK/Hej//A/(GF)/ZF3] <çelexte; çîya>

çelak چەلاك (A/IFb/HH/GF) = thin cudgel. See **çilak**.

çelake چەلاکە (Zeb) = thin cudgel. See **çilak**.

çele I چەلە (A) = pointy mountain peak. See **çel II**.

çele II چەلە (OK) = name for 2 winter months. See **Ç'ile I**.

çelem چەلەم (Wkt) = fortieth. See **ç'ilem**.

çelemîn چەلەمین (IFb/Wkt) = fortieth. See **ç'ilem**.

ç'eleng چەلەنگ *adj.* 1) rapid, fast, quick; 2) clever, sharp *(of mind)* (K); 3) *elegant, gracious, splendid (IF); 4) *pretty, good-looking, beautiful (BK/K/IF); 5) {syn: ç'alak; çapik I; ç'ust} alive, active, full of life. {also: [tchelenk] چلنك (JJ); <çelenk> چلنك (HH)} Cf. Za çeleng = 'handsome'; 'man's name' (Todd) {ç'elengî} [K/A/JB3/IF/B/BK//JJ/HH/ZF3]

ç'elengî چەلەنگی *f.* **(-ya;-yê).** 1) rapidity; 2) cleverness, acuity; 3) *splendor; 4) *beauty; 5) liveliness, being active and full of life. [K/B/ZF3] <ç'alakî>

çelext•e چەلەختە *m.* **(•ê;).** 1) outcrop, sharp rock protrusion on a mountain: -**çelextê kevirî** (Zeb) do.; 2) bone-like tumor on back or shoulder (IFb) [çelixt]. {also: çelixt (IFb/GF); çelixte (OK); çelîxt (ZF3); <çilixt> چلخت (Hej)} [Zeb//OK//IFb/GF//Hej//ZF3] <zinar I>

çelê چەلێ (Kg) = name for 2 winter months. See **Ç'ile I**.

ç'eliqandin چەلِقاندِن *vt.* **(-ç'eliqîn-).** to shake (a liquid); to splash, splatter: •**Mast *meçeliqîne*** (ZF3) *Don't splash* the yoghurt •**Wî cewdikê avê *şilqand* ka av têda heye yan ne** (FS) He *shook* the flask to see whether or not there was water in it. {also: çelqandin (IFb/FD/FS-2/BF-2); çiliqandin (FS-2); şilqandin (FS/BF)} [ZF3//IFb/FD//FS/BF] <ç'eliqîn; pijiqandin I>

ç'eliqîn چەلِقین *vi.* **(-ç'eliq-).** to be shaken up *(liquids)*; to splash, spatter *(vi.)*; to sway to and fro, be rough *(of sea)*: •**Hevalê dinê kodik hiltîne diçe şîr didoşe tê. Řêva lingê wî řaşiqitî, go: "Viȟ." Şivanê dinê go: "Kuřo, çi bû?" Go: "Şîr *çeliqî*"** (Z-884) The other friend picks up the pail and goes and fetches milk [lit. 'milks milk'] and returns. On the way his foot slips, and he goes "whoops!" The other shepherd says, "Hey boy, what happened?" [His friend] said, "The milk *has splashed*" •**Şîr di qazanê da *şilqa* û hindek jê rişt** (FS) The milk *sloshed around* in the kettle and some of it spilled over. {also: çelqîn (K/IFb/GF); şilqan (FS); şilqiyan (FS-2)} cf. T çalkalanmak = 'to sway to and fro, be rough (of sea)' [Z-884/B//K/IFb/GF/ZF3//FS]

çelixt چەلِخت (IFb/GF) = stone outcrop. See **çelexte**.

çelixte چەلِختە (OK) = stone outcrop. See **çelexte**.

çelîk چەلیك *m./f.* **(-ê/-a;).** 1) {syn: cûcik; ferx; varik} chick, young of bird: •**Ezê herim ser *çelîkê* xwe** (L) I will go [back] to my *chicks* •**Kund *çêlika* xwe dixwe û paşê bi ser de digirî** (FD) The owl eats its *young* and then it weeps to boot; 2) {syn:

ç'êjik; têjik} young *of other animals*: •**Mişkek û *çêlikên* xwe li derve digerîyan. Bi carekê de çavê wê li pisîkekê ket** (LM, 28) A mouse and her *babies* were outside roaming around. Suddenly she noticed a cat. {also: **çêl IV**; çêlik (K/IFb/ZF); çêlî (K/A); çêlîk (HR)} [L//K/IFb/ZF//A//HR] <çêjik>

çelîxt چەلیخت (ZF3) = stone outcrop. See **çelexte**.

çelqandin چەلقاندِن (IFb/FD/FS/BF) = to shake; to splash. See **ç'eliqandin**.

çelqîn چەلقین (K/IFb/GF) = to splash *(vi.)*. See **ç'eliqîn**.

çelqemast چەلقەماست (B) = drink made of yoghurt and water. See **ç'eqilmast**.

çelte چەلتە (K/A/B/IFb/CS/H) = handbag. See **ç'eltik I**.

ç'eltik I چەلتِك *m.* **(-ê;).** handbag; sack: •**Çend zelam ên bi gopal, das, bivir û *çelte* bi milve wê li nav kelebestan de ... digerin û tên û diçin** (H 56:5) Some men with clubs, sickles, axes and *satchels* [slung] over their shoulders are roaming, coming and going amid the dry riverbeds •**Ka tu wî *çeltikê* xwe yê nanê golikvaniyê bide min!** (ZZ-4, 245) Give me that *bag* of yours for collecting calfherding food. {also: çelte (K-2/A/B-2/IFb/CS/H); <çeltik> چلتك (HH)} {syn: cente} [ZZ/K/B/FJ/GF/HH/ZF3//A/IFb/CS/H]

ç'eltik II چەلتِك = *[rice in the]* husk. See **ç'eltûk**.

ç'eltûk چەلتووك *f./m.(K)* **(-a/;-ê/).** 1) rice in the husk; husk; 2) rice field, rice paddy. {also: ç'eltik II; <çiltûk> چلتوك (HH)} < T çeltik = 'rice in the husk' [HB/K/A/IF/B/ZF3//HH] <belim; birinc I; p'ûşk; tûşk>

çem/ç'em [K/B] چەم *m.* **(-ê; çêm, vî çemî).** 1) {syn: av [2]; ç'a I[2]; r̄o II; r̄ûbar; şet} stream, river: •**Sosik ava genî xwer bû, nikarbû ji *çêm* derbaz bibûya** (FK-kk-13:129) Sosik [the horse] drank putrid water, [and] couldn't cross *the river*; **-ava çem/ava çêm** (BK) river water; **-ber çem** (L) on the bank of the river/stream •**Ez *ber çem* sekinîm** (L) I stood *by the river bank*; 2) cultivated land by the banks of a river (JB1-S/HH/Bw). {also: [tchem] چم (JJ); <çem> چم (HH)} Cf. Sor çom چۆم = 'river, stream' [L/K/A/JB3/IF/B/JJ/HH/JB1-S/Ag/Haz/BK/ZF3] <[2] çewlîk>

çemandin چەماندِن *vt.* **(-çemîn-[IF]/-çemên-[K(s)]).** 1) to bow, bend *(vt.)*; 2) to break *(vt.)*; 3) to wring (JB3); 4) to direct toward (K); 5) *(fig.)* to force s.o. to submit (K). {also: [tchemāndin] چماندين (JJ)} [K(s)/JB3/IFb/JJ/OK/ZF3] <çemîn>

çembil چەمبِل *m.* **(-ê; çêmil [B], vî çem[b]ilî).** handle, ear *(of a jug, vessel, etc.)*: •***Çembilê* cêr ji destê wê filitî û cêr gindirî** (MB-Meyro) The jug's *handle* slipped from her hand, and the jug tipped over. {also: ç'emil (K/B)/çemil (GF-2/ZF3-2); **ç'epil** [3]; [tchemil چمیل/ciambel چنبل (G)] (JJ); <çembil> چمبل (HH)} [MB/A/IFb/HH/GF/TF/OK//K/B//JJ] See also **ç'epil**[3].

çemçe چەمچە (GF) = ladle. See **çemçik**.

çemçik چەمچِك *f.* **(-a;-ê).** ladle, wooden spoon: spoons made of wood for eating yoghurt or ***dew*** *(a drink made of yoghurt and water)*. {also: çemçe (GF); kemçik (Wn); <çemçik> چمچك (HH)} {syn: hesk; k'efgîr} Sor çemçe چەمچە = 'ladle'; Hau çemçe *m.* = 'spoon' (M4) [HB/A/IFb/HH/TF/Qzl/ZF3//GF//Wn] <çoçik; k'efçî>

çemhan چەمهان (Bw) = to bend *(vi.)*. See **çemîn**.

ç'emil (K/B)/çemil (GF/JJ/ZF3) چەمِل = hand; handle. See **çembil** & **ç'epil**.

çemîn چەمین *vi.* **(-çem-).** 1) to bend, bow *(vi.)* (M/K/JJ); to be broken off *(a piece of stg.)* (HH); 2) to make for, head for, be directed toward (K); 3) (fig.) to submit to, resign o.s. to (K). {also: çemhan (Bw); çemyan (-çemê-) (M/OK); [chemīān چمیان/tchewiian چڤیان] (JJ); <çiman چمان (diçime)(دچمه)> (HH)} [K/ZF3//M/JJ/OK//HH//Bw] <çemandin>

çemyan چەمیان (-çemê-) (M/JJ/OK) = to bend *(vi.)*. See **ç'emîn**.

ç'end چەند *intrg.* 1) how many? {cf. **ç'iqas** = how much *for mass nouns*}: •**Saet *çend* e?** (BX) *What* time is it? •**Saet *bi çend* e?** (BX) *How much* does the clock *cost*?; 2) [*pr. mod.*] some, a few: •**Heger ji te re *çend* qurûş lazim in** (L) If you need *a few* pennies •**Rojekê wan *çend* giregir û cindîye şeherê Cizîrê hildan** (Z-1) One day they took *some* elders and nobles of the city of Jizirah. {also: [tchend] چند (JJ); <çend> چند (HH)} O Ir *čvant (Tsb 30): Av čvant-; OP čiyant-; P čand چند; Sor çend چەند/çen چەن; Za çend (Todd); Hau çin[n]/çinne = 'some' (M4) [F/K/A/JB3/IFb/B/JJ/HH/JB1-A&S/SK/GF/TF/OK/ZF3] <ç'iqas>

ç'endek چەندەك. a little, somewhat: **-*çendekî* şûnda** (Ba) *a little bit* later/*a short while* later. {also: çendik I (A)} {syn: hindik; hinekî; piçek} [K/JB3/IF/Ba/ZF3//A] ç'endik I چەندِك (A) = a little. See **çendek.**

çendik' II چەندِك (JB1-A) = satchel. See **cente**.

ç'endî چەندی *conj.* however much (or many), no matter how much (or many): •***Çendî* dewleta Tirk zilm û zora xwe berdewam bike li hemberî miletê Kurd ê aştîxwaz** (Wlt 2:59, 7) *No matter how long* the Turkish state continues its oppression of the peace-loving Kurdish nation... {also: herçend[2]} [Wlt/SK/ZF3]

ç'en•e چەنە *f.* **(•a;•ê).** 1) chin, jaw (B). See **çeng II**; 2) ledge, projection, protuberance; 3) bend, knee, joint: •**serê *çena* kûçê** (K) at *the corner of* the street. Sor çenage چەناگە/çene چەنە; Hau çenake *m.* = 'chin' (M4) [F/K/B/ZF3] <goşe; karêj I; k'unc; qulç'>

çeng I چەنگ *f.* **().** 1) {syn: ç'epil; pank} handful, palm (K/A/IFb/HH): •**Diya min çend nan, du *çeng* mewîj, bîst-sih lib gwîz dixistin tûrikê Gulîstanê** (Alkan, 71) My mother would put some bread, two *handfuls of* raisins, 20-30 walnuts into Gulistan's bag; 2) {syn: dest} hand (K); 3) {syn: ç'epil} *arm from the shoulder to the elbow* (JJ) *or fingers* (TF) (JJ/TF); 4) wing *(of bird)* (HH). {also: [tchenk] چنك (JJ); <çenk> چنك (HH)} [Z-1/K/A/IFb/TFZF3///JJ/HH] <dest>

çeng II چەنگ *f.* **(;-ê).** 1) {syn: argûşk; erzen} chin; 2) {syn: lame [2]} jaw, jaw-bone. {also: **çene** [1]; çenge (B/ZF3); çengû (K-2/B-2); [tchenghé] چنگە (JJ)} Cf. P čāne چانە --> T çene [S&E/K/GF//B/JJ/ZF3] <karêj I>

ç'eng III چەنگ: **-çeng bûn** (GF/TF)/**xwe çeng kirin** (JB1-S/RZ/CS) to jump, hop, leap {syn: ba[n]zdan; firqas kirin; hilpekirin; lotik dan [xwe]; pengizîn; qevz dan [*see* qevz II]; xwe qevaztin}: •**Siltanê Fîlan ji nişka ve *çeng bû* ser piyan û kir qêrîn** (SF 19) The Elephant Sultan suddenly *jumped up* and started screaming •***Xwe çeng kirin* hewa** (SBx, 12) They *jumped* into the air; **-çeng kirin** (TF/CS) to throw, toss {syn: avêtin}. [SF/JB1-S/GF/TF/RZ/CS/ZF3]

ç'eng IV چەنگ *f.* **(;-ê).** harp, lyre: •**Newaya mutrîb û *çengê* / fiẍan avête xerçengê** (Melayê Cizîrî #1) The tune of the singer and *of the harp* / cast a cry to the heavens (lit. to the Crab [constellation]). P čang چنگ; Sor çeng چەنگ [Melayê Cizîrî/K(s)/IFb/ZF/Wkt/BFK]

ç'engal I چەنگال *f.* **(-a;-ê).** fork. {also: çengel II (B); çingal I (GF); <çengal> چنگال (HH)} {syn: ç'etel} Cf. P čangāl چنگال = 'fork' --> T çengel = 'hook'; Sor çingał چنگاڵ = 'hook, fork, talon'. *Other unverified equivalents are:* çartil (Kmc-2209); neçel (AD); sêtêlk (IFb). [Kmc-2209/K/HH/CS//GF/Wkt//B]

çengal II چەنگال (K/FJ) = hook. See **ç'engel I**.

çenge چەنگە (B/JJ/ZF3) = chin; jaw. See **çeng II.**

ç'engel I چەنگەل *m./f.(K/B)* **(-ê/-a; /-ê).** hook: •**Zêdeyî carekê Dîgol *çengelê* xwe bilind dikir di rûwên bargirên ku ne wekî wî dipeyivîn** (HYma, 36) More than once D. pointed his *hook* at the faces of porters who did not speak like him. {also: çanqil (IFb-2); çengal II (K/FJ); çingal II (TF); [tchengal چنگال /tchenghel چنگل] (JJ)} {syn: ç'iqil[2]; nîk; şewk[2]} Cf. P čangāl چنگال = 'fork' --> T çengel = 'hook'; Sor çingał چنگاڵ = 'hook, fork, talon' [HYma/A/B/IFb/JJ/RZ/CS//K/FJ//TF]

çengel II چەنگەل (B) = fork. See **ç'engal I**.

çengû چەنگوو (K/B) = chin; jaw. See **çeng II.**

çente چەنتە (K/IFb/GF/OK) = satchel. See **cente**.

çep/ç'ep [K/B] چەپ *adj.* left *(direction)*. {also: [tchep] چپ (JJ)} {≠r̄ast[1]} Cf. P čap چپ; Sor çep چەپ; Za çep (Mal); Hau çep (M4) [K/A/JB3/IF/B/JJ/ZF3]

ç'epel چەپەل *adj.* dirty, slovenly, unclean. {also: [tchepil] چپل (JJ); <çepel> چپل (HH)} {syn: bi'ok; dijûn II; gemarî; mir̄dar̄; p'îs; qirêj} Cf. Sor çepeł چەپەڵ = 'filthy' [HB/K(s)/A/JB3/IF/HH/ZF3//JJ]

çeper چەپەر/**çeper̄** چەپەڕ [B] *f.* **(-a;-ê).** 1) {syn: {syn: k'ozik; percan; tan} fence, hedge; 2) {syn: k'ozik I; senger} fortifications; rampart, bulwark, barricade; trench, foxhole, ditch: •[**Û li cihê şer̄î fîl-ĥal *çeperan* çê dikin û dikevine bin *çeperê* de'wa dikin**] (BN 136) And at the site of the battle they immediately set up *trenches* and get down into [lit.'under'] them and fight; **-çeper û k'ozik** (GF/IFb)/**k'ozik û çeper** (Bw) trenches and foxholes; **-çeper vedan** (Bw) to prepare for battle. {also: [tcheper] چپر (JJ); <çeper> چپر (HH)} P čapar چپر = 'wattle; a fence, enclosure'; Sor çeper چەپەر = 'wattle fence, palisade' [Bw/K/A/IFb/JJ/HH/GF/TF/OK/ZF3//B] <k'ozik I>

çeper̄ast چەپەڕاست *adj.* 1) {syn: asoyî} crosswise, transverse, horizontal; 2) {syn: berwar [3]} across *(in crosswords)*. Cf. T çapraz = 'crosswise' <P čaprāst چپراست = 'buckle (orig. 'left-right')' [Wlt/TF/ZF3] <serejêr; stûnî; xaçepirs>

çepgêr چەپگێر (SS) = leftist. See **çepgir**.

çepgir چەپگِر *adj.& m.&f.* **().** leftist, left wing: **•Nivîskarê rojnameya Cumhuriyetê Hikmet Çetinkaya di nivîsa xwe de sernavekî wiha bi kar anîbû: "*Çepgirên* neteweperest û rastgirên neteweperest"** (AW69A1) The writer for the newspaper Cumhuriyet, Hikmet Çetinkaya, used this title in his article: "Nationalist *leftists* and nationalist rightists." {also: çepgêr (SS)} [AW/VoA//ZF3/SS]

ç'epik چەپِك *m.* **().** 1) {syn: dest} hand (K); 2) applause: **-çepik dan** (A) to clap, applaud; **-çepik kutan** (K) do.; **-çepikên xwe kutan** (K) {also: çeple lê dan (JB3); çepilk lê xistin (JB3/IF)} to clap, applaud. {also: çeple (JB3); çepilk (JB3)} {Cf. "Çepikli"--(Turkish) name of a Kurdish dance from Gaziantep, which features a clapping motion} cf. Sor çepok چەپۆك = 'slap from above'; Hau çepoke *f.* = 'downward blow with the open hand' (M4) [K/A/JB3/IF/ZF3] <ç'epil>

ç'epil چەپِل *m.* **(-ê; ç'êpil, vî ç'epilî).** 1) {syn: dest} hand, arm (K/JJ/JB1-S); hand *(neg. connotation)* (B); {syn: çeng I} arm *from the elbow to the shoulder* (IFb): **-ç'epilê hev girtin** (IF) to give each other a bear hug; 2) {syn: çeng I; pank} palm of the hand (K); 3) {syn: çembil} handle, knob *(e.g., doorknob, teacup handle)* . {also: ç'emil (B); [tchepil] چپل (JJ); <çepil> چپل (HH)}} [Z-2/K/IFb/JJ/HH/JB1-S/ZF3//B] See also **çembil**. <ç'epik; dest; mil; pîl I>

çepilk چەپلك (JB3) = hand; applause. See **ç'epik.**

çeple چەپلە (JB3) = hand; applause. See **ç'epik.**

çeqal چەقال (IFb/JJ) = jackal. See **ç'eqel**.

ç'eqandin چەقاندِن *vt.* **(-çeqîn-).** 1) to strike fire *(with flint)*; to loose *(cock of gun)*, pull the trigger: **•[Dûmo şeşxaneyê digrite armancê û bi kêfa xo *diçeqîne*]** (JR #27, 80) Dumo takes aim with his revolver and *pulls the trigger* at his leisure; 2) to stick in, insert (SK): **•Her sênîyekî kilkekî kûrî di nawa serî *biçeqînin* weto ko qund řawestît" ... Wextê wan temaşe kir ko têşta wan s̱ewar-- we li nik wan s̱ewar gelek 'eybekî mezin e bo mêwanêt mu'teber--we ser wê hindê řa jî kilkêt kûran li ser sênîyan *çeqandine*, di yêk-û-do fikirîn, destêt xo kêşane paş.** (SK 24:222,224) On each tray *stick* a kid's tail in the middle of the pile so that it stands erect." ... When they saw that their meal was of crushed wheat--and with them crushed wheat [instead of rice] was a most shameful thing for respectable guests--and that in addition the tails of kids had been *stuck* on top of the trays, they looked at each other and withdrew their hands. {also: [tcheqandin] چقاندين (JJ)} [JR/K/IFb/JJ/SK/GF/ZF3] <berheste; heste>

ç'eqel چەقەل *m.* **(-ê;).** jackal, zool. *Canis aureus*: **•Rovî wê** [sic] **fesadiya *çeqel* xist dilê xwe û têde meyand** (ZZ-4, 180) The fox put *the jackal*'s treachery in his heart and let it fester. {also: çeqal (IFb-2); şeqal (K-2); [tcheqal] چقال (JJ); <çeqel> چقل (HH)} {syn: torî I; wawîk} Cf. P šuγāl شغال --> T çakal; Sor çeqeł چەقەڵ [ZZ/K/IFb/FJ/GF/HH/ZF/CS/ZF3//JJ]

ç'eqilmast چەقِلماست *f./m.(KS)* **(-ê;-ê/ç'eqilmêst).** a drink made of yoghurt and water {cf. T yağlı ayran}: **•Min ew tasa *çeqilmêst* a ku hîn qeşa wê neheliyabû ji destê wê girtibû, çend gulp jê vexwaribû** (KS, 49) I took that cup of *çeqilmast*--in which the ice had not yet melted--from her hands and drank a few gulps of it. {also: çelqemast (B); [tchalka-mast] چلقاماست (JJ); <çeqilmast> چقلماست (HH)} < çeqil + mast = 'yoghurt' [K/A/IFb/HH/ZF3//B/JJ] <dew I>

çer چەر (ZF3) = how? See **ç'er'ê.**

çerandin چەراندِن (FS/BF) = to take to pasture. See **çêrandin.**

çerçirîn چەرچِرین *vi.* **(-çerçir-).** 1) to exert o.s., to strive hard; to exhaust o.s.: **•Ûsib gelekî *diçerçire*, lê axirîê Zelîxê cîkî digire** (Ba-1, #27) Joseph *strives* very hard, but finally he catches [up with] Zulaikha in a place; 2) to toil, labor, work; 3) to suffer, be unhappy, grieve; to eat one's heart out, be consumed with worry. [Ba-1/F/K/B]

ç'erçî چەرچی *m.* **(-yê;).** (itinerant) peddlers/pedlars, *formerly a common occupation among Jews*: "A common group among the poor in the larger towns, such as Zakho, were the peddlers who traveled in companies of two or more, riding donkeys and mules and selling certain groceries [such as tea and sugar] and notions [such as needles, buttons, and thread]." (YSFL, p. xxii): **•*Çercî* hat gundê me** (AB) A *peddler* came to our village. {also: [tchertchi] چرچی (JJ); <çerçî> چرچی (HH)} {syn: 'etar [3]} Cf. T çerçi; Sor çerçî چەرچی = Sor wurde[wałe]firoş وردەواڵەفرۆش; Za çerçî (Todd); [AB/K/IFb/B/JJ/HH/GF/ZF3]

çere چەرە (FS) = pasture. See **çêre.**

çeres چەرەس (Tsab) = fruit & nuts. See **ç'erez.**

ç'erez چـــــەرەز *m.* **(-ê;).** dried fruit and nuts, light snacks *served to guests*: **•Cêva xwe t'ijî** ***çerez*** **dikir, k'şmîş, noqit** (HCK-2, 181) He filled his pockets with *snacks*, raisins, chick peas. {also: çeres (Tsab-2); [tcherez] چرز (JJ); <çerez> چرز (HH)} Cf. T çerez < Lat cerezia = 'sour cherry'; Sor çere چـــەرە & çeres چـــەرەس = 'small snacks prepared for social gatherings' [HCK/K/B/IFb/FJ/GF/JJ/HH/Tsab/CS] <behîv; gûz; mewîj; nok>

ç'erê چـــــەرێ *intrg.* how?: **-Çerêye?** (Kg) *How* is it? {also: çer (ZF3)} {syn: ç'awa; ç'ilo I; ç'ito} [Bg//ZF3]

ç'erixandin چەرِخـانـدِن /**çeřixandin** چەڕِخـانـدِن [K] *vt.* **(-çerixîn-).** 1) {syn: zivirandin} to cause to turn or rotate; 2) to cause to turn back, dissuade: **•Her rîsipiyek tiştekî dibêje û axayê serhişk ji ser riya şewutandina gund** ***diçerixînin*** (Ardû, 23) Each village elder says something, and they *dissuade* the stubborn agha from burning down the village. {also: [čarxandin] چرخاندین (JJ)} Cf. P čarxāndan چـــرخــــانـــدن = 'to whirl, spin, rotate (stg.)'; Sor çerixandin چـەرِخـانـدِن = 'to cause to revolve, rotate, turn' [Ardû/K/B/IFb/GF/TF//JJ] <ç'erx>

çerî چەری (FS) = pasture. See **çêre**.

çerîn چەرین (FS/BF) = to graze. See **çêrîn**.

ç'erm چـــــەرم *m.* **(-ê; ç'êrm, vî ç'ermî).** skin, hide: **•Sofî Şêx, zû řabe. Gaê me wê di bi řoĥê da. Eger zû nagiheyê dê mirar bît. Mixabin e. Wekuje, her nebît** ***çermê*** **wî xesar nabît** (SK 30:271) Sofi Shaikh! Our ox is at the point of death. If you do not reach it soon it will (die of itself and) become carrion. It is a pity. Slaughter it, at least do not let *the hide* be wasted. {also: [tcherm] چرم (JJ); <çerm> چرم (HH)} {syn: pîst} [Pok. (s)ker-/(s)kerə-/(s)krē- 938.] 'to cut' (I.A.): Skt cárman- = 'skin, hide'; Av čarᵊman-; OP čarman- n.; Mid P čarm = 'skin, hide, leather' (M3); P čarm چرم = 'leather, hide'; Sor çerm چەرم = 'leather'; Za çerm *m.* [K/A/JB3/IFb/B/JJ/HH/SK/GF/TF/OK] <gurandin>

çerqîn چەرقین (L) = noise. See **şerqîn**.

çerwan چەروان *m.* **(-ê;).** pastureland with green, lush grass *{as opposed to* ***k'oz****, which has brown, dry grass}* (Bw): **•*Çerwanê* pezî li deştê zor e** (FS) *Pastureland* for sheep is plentiful (or difficult) on the plains; **-k'oz û çerwan** (Bw) [all manner of] pastureland *(both dry and lush)*. {also: çerwang (FS-2); [cherewan] چــــروان (JJ-Rh)} [Bw/FS//JJ-Rh] <çêre[geh]; çêrîn; k'oz [2]>

çerwang چـــەروانـــگ (FS) = green pastureland. See **çerwan**.

ç'erx چـــــەرخ *f./m.(Metîn)* **(/-ê;-ê/).** 1) {syn: t'eker} wheel: **-çerx bûn** (IFb) to turn, rotate, spin {syn: zivirîn; zîz bûn [see zîz III]}: **•Dunya li dora xwe** ***çerx nedibû*** (Epl, 7) The world *would not spin* around itself; 2) {syn: sedsal} century: **•Dîroka dagirtina vê deverê jî ya kevn e, dizivirîte** ***çerxê*** **şazdê zayînî** (Metîn 62[1997]:26) The history of the occupation of this region is old--it goes back to the sixteenth *century* A.D. {also: [tcherkh] چـــرخ (JJ)} [Pok. 1.kᵘel-/kᵘelə- 639.] 'to turn' --> kᵘekᵘlo-/kᵘokᵘlo- = 'wheel': Skt cakrá- = 'wheel, circle, sphere'; Av čaxra- *m.* = 'wheel'; P čarx چرخ = 'wheel, sphere'; Sor çerx چـــــــەرخ = 'circle, wheel'; cf. also Gr kyklos κύκλος; Eng wheel < hwēol < *hweg(w)ulá- [Zeb/Metîn/K/A/IFb/B/JJ/GF/TF/OK] <ç'erixandin>

ç'erxî چـــــەرخـی *m.* **().** *(formerly)* coin worth five piasters: **•Ev zêřê hana ji miřa hûr bike, t'emam bike mecidîne, quruş û** ***çerxîne*** (Z-2) Make change for these gold coins, make silver coins, coins of twenty piastres and of *five piastres*. {also: <çerxî> چرخی (HH)} Cf. Sor çerxî چەرخی = 'old silver coin'. In his *Turkish and English Lexicon* (Constantinople : A.H. Boyajian, 1890; repr. Beirut : Librairie du Liban, 1987), p. 718, Sir James W. Redhouse gives the following as one definition of the word [cherkhi] چـرخـی: '(provincial, perhaps Kurdish) a five piastre piece' [Z-2/A/HH/PS]

ç'etel چەتەل *f.(K)/m.(AD/ZF3)* **( ).** fork. {syn: ç'engal I} Cf. T çatal [K/IFb/AD/Kmc-2209/ZF3]

ç'etin چـەتِن *adj.* hard, difficult: **•K'ê ku p'akî haj ji şivantîyê t'unebû, hew zanibû, ku ew tiştekî** ***çetin*** **nîne** (Ba2:1, 203) Those who were not well acquainted with shepherding thought that it was something not very *difficult* **•Memê û Zînêva ĥalekî** ***çetin*****danin** (Z-1) M. and Z. are in a *difficult* position. {also: çetîn (JB3/OK-2/ZF3); [tchetin] چتین (JJ); <çetin> چتن (HH)} {syn: [bi] zeĥmet; dijwar} Cf. T çetin; Az T çətin [Z-1/K/IFb/B/HH/GF/OK//JB3/JJ]

ç'etina•yî چەتِنـایـی *f.* **(•yîya ;•yê).** hardness, difficulty, harshness; quality of being difficult or hard: **•Aqû p'êxember şa dibe, bi** ***çetinayîkê*** **ji cîê xwe řadibe** (Ba #35, 319) The prophet Jacob rejoices, with great *difficulty* he gets up from his place •**Ḧal Memêda nemaye, du-sê r̄oja şûnda Memê wê *çetinayêda* nadebire** (Z-1) M. is in bad shape; in 2 or 3 days he will no [longer] be alive from the hardship of it [=He won't survive this *hardship* more than 2 or 3 days]. {also: ç'etinî (K-2/IFb); çetînayî (ZF3); çetînî (JB3/OK-2)} {syn: dijwarî} [B/K/OK/ZF//IFb//JB3//ZF3] <ç'etin>

ç'etinî چەتِنی (K/IFb) = difficulty. See **ç'etinayî.**

çetîn چەتین (JB3/ZF3) = difficult. See **ç'etin.**

çetînayî چەتینایی (ZF3) = difficulty. See **ç'etinayî.**

çetînî چەتینی (JB3) = difficulty. See **ç'etinayî.**

çev چەڤ (F)/ç'e‘v چـەعـڤ (B/Ba/J/Z/EP) = eye. See **çav.**

ç'e‘vkanî چەعڤکانی (B) = spring, source. See **çavkanî.**

ç'e‘vnebaharî چـەعـڤـنـەبـاهـاری (XF) = envy. See **çavnebarî.**

ç'e‘vnebarî چـەعـڤـنـەبـاری (Ba/B) = envy. See **çavnebarî.**

ç'e‘vnebartî چەعڤنەبارتی (B) = envy. See **çavnebarî.**

ç'e‘vnihêrî چـەعـڤـنِـهـێـری (B/Z-1) = waiting. See **çavnihêrî.**

çevt چەڤت (GF) = wrong. See **ç'ewt.**

ç'ewa چەوا (B/Z-1) = how. See **ç'awa.**

ç'ewal چـەوال *m.* **(-ê; ç'ewêl/çuwêl** [BK], **vî ç'ewalî).** sack, bag: •***çewalê* ard** (IF) *sack of* flour •**Çar *çewal* birinc anîn** (L) They brought four *bags* of rice. {also: cuhal (SK); cûhalk' (JB1-A); çawal (K); çowal; çuwal (BK); [tchuval] چـوال (JJ); <çal چـال/cuwal جـوال> (HH)} {syn: ferde; gûnîk; t'elîs} Cf. P javāl جوال, Ar š[i]wāl شوال, T çuval [L/F/A/IF/B/ZF3//K//BK/JJ//HH] <cendik; cuher; t'êr̄ III; tûr I>

çewlik چەولِك (ZF3) = alluvial soil. See **çewlîk.**

çewlîk چەولیك *f./m.(FS)* **(-a/;-ê/-î).** 1) soil enriched by alluvial deposits, fertile land on a river's bank that becomes inundated when the river overflows; 2) capital city of Bingöl, also known as Çapaxçûr. {also çewlik (ZF3)} [Qzl/Kmc-#2235/FS//ZF3] <çem [2]>

ç'ews چەوس *f.* **(-a;-ê).** pressure; oppression: •**Çima ku ez Kurd im min pirr *çews* (pest) û îşkence ji destê Dewleta Tirk kişandiye** (Wlt 1:36, 16) Because I am a Kurd, I have suffered much *oppression* and torture at the hands of the Turkish state. {syn: fişar; p'est; pêk'utî; zext I} Possibly çesp --> çeps --> çews (H.Muhammed); Cf. Sor çewsawe چـەوسـاوە = 'oppressed, maltreated' [(neol)Wlt/Wkt]

ç'ewt چـەوت *adj.* 1) {syn: şaş I[2]; xelet[2]} wrong, incorrect, false; untrue; 2) {syn: kêr̄ II; xwaro-maro} crooked, bent. {also: çevt (GF-2)} Sor çewt چـەوت = 'crooked, wrong, error, misprint' {ç'ewtî} [K/A/IFb/GF/TF/ZF]

ç'ewtî چـەوتـی *f.* **(-ya;-yê).** 1) {syn: xelet[1]} error, mistake: •**Dost rexne jî li hev digrin, *çewtiyên* hev jî ji hevûdin re dibêjin** (Wlt 1:20, 3) Friends both criticize one another, and tell each other about their [=the other's] *mistakes*; 2) crookedness. [Wlt/A/IFb/TF/ZF] <ç'ewt>

ç'ê چێ *adj.* good: **-ç'ê bûn** = a) to be made, produced: •***Ç'êbû!*** (Bw) There! It's *done*!; b) {syn: p'eyda bûn} to be born: •**Gotin** [sic]**: "K'erê, mizgînya min li te, kur̄ek ji ter̄a *çêbû*." Go: "Barê min zêde bû û êmê min kêm bû"** (Dz #588) They said , "Donkey, I have good news for you, a son *has been born* to you." He said, "My burden has increased and my food has been decreased"; c) to take place, happen; be held *(celebration)*; break out *(war)*: •**Carkê nerî go xatûnek anîye û du cêrî ji pê re ne, gelikî kêfa wî hat. Şaê û dawet di nav bajêr de *çê bû*** (L-1, 34, l. 20-22) [The prince] saw that [Kurê pîrê] brought a young lady with two maidservants, [and] he was very pleased. A wedding celebration *took place* in the city •**Gava ez zaro bûm, şerek *çêbû*** (BX, ¶309, 340) When I was a child, a war *broke out*; d) to be possible: •**Eydî di navbera meda hevaltî *çênabe*** (Dz-anecdote #22, 390) Friendship between us *is not possible*; **-ç'êdibît** (Bw/Zeb) perhaps, maybe {syn: belkî; qemî}; **-ç'ê kirin** = a) to make, produce, put together [Cf. P dorost kardan درست کردن]: •**Solek hesinî ji xwe re *çêkir*** (L) [She] had shoes of iron *made* [for herself]; b) to fix, repair, heal, cure {syn: derman kirin}: •**Nav û dengê wê bihîstiye go çavê hafiza *çêdike*** (L-1 #3, 74, ll.25-26) He had heard of her fame, that she *cures* the eyes of the blind. {also: çe; [tchi] چـی (JJ); <çê> چـێ (HH)} {syn: baş; ç'ak; qenc; r̄ind; xweş} Cf. Sor çak چاك [K/A/JB3/IFb/B/HH//JJ] <bît'er; pê ç'êbûn>

ç'êje چێژە (K) = cub, whelp. See **ç'êjik.**

ç'êjik چـێـژك *m.&f.* **(/-a; /-ê).** cub, whelp, young of animal; the young of carnivorous animals. {also: ç'êje (K); **têjik**; [tchijik] چـیـژك (JJ)} {syn: cewr(ik)} [F/K/IFb/OK/ZF3//JJ] <çelîk; ç'êl IV>

çêl I چێل (JB1-S) = forty. See **ç'il I.**

ç'êl II چـێـل *f.* **(-a;).** mention; description: •**Di tu**

kitêban da *çêla* firîna Mehdî tine (Rnh 2:17, 340) In no book is there a *mention* [or, *description*] of Mehdi's flying; **-çêla *ft-î* kirin** (Rnh)/**çêlî *ft-î* kirin** (Ardû) to mention; to describe {syn: kat I kirin; nitirandin I}: **•Bi şertê ku rîsipî ê heta dawiya bîst û yek mehên din jî jê re *çêlî* wan aqilan *neke*, herdu didine pey hev û derdikevin zozanê warê rîsipî** (Ardû, 18) On condition [=with the understanding] that the old man would *not mention* [or, *describe*] that advice until twenty-one months had passed, the two followed one another out to the summer pasture, the old man's field **•Dûre jî bi zarekî xweş dûrûdirêj ji min re *çêlî* jiyana koçeriyê *kir*** (Lab, 11) Afterward he articulately *described* the nomadic way of life to me in detail **•Şêx, rojêkê ji rojan di nava van şîretan da, *çêla* rabûna cenabê Mehdî *dike*** (Rnh 2:17, 340) One day among those sermons, the sheikh *describes* [or, *mentions*] the rise of the prophet Mehdi. *See etymological note under **ç'êr̄**.* [Rnh/Ardû/Lab/IFb/GF/ZF3] <nitirandin I>

çêl III چێل (K/Hk/Zx/Bw) = cow. See **çêlek.**

çêl IV چێل *m.* **().** young (of animal), cub, whelp, chick, *used as prefix*: **-çêlkê beraz** (AD) piglet; **-çêlkevok** (GF) young of dove; **-çêlkew** (GF)/**çêlîyê kewî** (FS) young of partridge; **-çêlordek** (GF) duckling; **-çêlpisik** (Nofa) kitten: **•Dîlberê xwe ji nav çepilên wî rakişand û wekî *çêl-pisikekê* kir qijinî** (Nofa, 91) D. detached herself from between his arms and mewled like a *kitten*; **-çêlqaz** (GF) gosling; **-çêlîyê rûvî** (FS) fox cub. {also: çelîk; çêle II (G/FS-2); çêlî (A/FS-2)} [Nofa/IFb/GF/FJ/CS/ZF3/FS/AD//G//A] <çêjik>

çêle I چێله (A) = dead of winter. See **Ç'ile I.**

çêle II چێله (G/FS) = young of animal. See **çelîk & çêl IV.**

çêlek/ç'êlek [K/B] چـێـلـهك *f.* **(-a;-ê).** cow: **•*Ç'êlekeke* wan hebûye** (J) They had *a cow.* {also: çêl III (K-2/Hk/Zx/Bw); [tchil چـيـل/tchilek چـيـلـك] (JJ); <çêlek> چيلك (HH)} {syn: mange} [BX/K/A/JB3/IF/B/HH/ZF3//JJ] <ga>

çêlekel چـێـلـهكـهل *f.* **(;-ê).** cow in heat: ***-ç'êlekeleke* gak'ûvîya** (IS-363) *female* deer (doe) *in heat.* <ç'êl[ek] = 'cow' + kel = 'in heat' [IS/FS] <kel I[3]>

çêlik چێلك (K/IFb/ZF) = chick. See **çelîk & çêl IV.**

çêlî II چێلی = chick (A); cub, pup (K). See **çelîk & çêl IV.**

çêlîk چێليك (HR) = chick. See **çelîk & çêl IV.**

ç'êr̄ چێڕ/**çêr** چـێـر [IFb/HH/OK] *m./f.(B/ZF3)* **(; /-ê).** verbal abuse, cursing, cussing, swearing {T küfür, Ar šatīmah شتيمة]: **-ç'êr̄ [lê] kirin** (K) to cuss s.o. out, swear at s.o.; to insult, offend: **•[Herçend min lavahî Memedî kir ku ensaf bike ji hinde malî tiştekî bide min Memedî *çêrî* min *kirî* ez qewrandim]** (JR) No matter how much I begged Memed to be fair and give me something from all those goods, he *cursed* me and chased me away **•...Ji devê wî t'u xebereke *ç'êr̄a* dernediket, ewî qet car *ç'êr̄î* hespa û p'îrê wan nekir** (EP-8) No word *of cursing* left his mouth, he never *cursed* horses or their god-protectors. {also: çêrî (A); [tchir چـيـر] (JJ); <çêr> چـيـر (HH)} {syn: dijûn I; ne'let; nifir̄; qise[3]; sixêf; xeber[3]} *According to Celîlê Celîl, **ç'êr̄** originally means 'talking, speech, words' (cf. **xeber** = 'words, speech; verbal abuse'), and is related to **çîr̄ok** = 'story', qv. Likewise, **ç'êl II** = 'mention' may be cognate.*= Sor cinêw جنێو/cwên [cön] جوێن [EP-8/K/A/B//IFb/HH/GF/TF/OK//JJ/JR] <nifir̄>

çêran چێران (A/JB3/GF) = to graze. See **çêrîn.**

çêrandin/ç'êrandin [K/B] چـێـرانـدِن *vt.* **(-çêrîn-).** to take *(grazing animals)* out to pasture: **•Ĥetanî êvarê wana ber tavê, sur̄ê û sermê, bin baranê û teyrokê, carna t'î û birçî pez *diç'êrand*** (Ba2:1, 204) They would *graze* the sheep until evening in sunlight and cold, under rain and hail, sometimes [even] hungry and thirsty. {also: çerandin (FS/BF); [čairandin چـايـرانـدين/čerãndin چـيـرانـديـن] (JJ); <çêrandin چـيـرانـدن (diçêrîne) (دچـيـريـنـه)> (HH)} Cf. P čarāndan چـرانـدن; Za çiranenã [çiranayiş] (Srk); = Sor lewer̄andin لـەوەڕانـدن [K/B//A/JB3/IF/JJ/HH/M/ZF3//FS/BF] <çêre; çêrîn>

çêrangeh چێرانگەه (A) = pasture. See **çêre & çêregeh.**

çêr•e/ç'êre [K/B] چـێـره *m.(K)/f.(B/JB3)* **(/•a; /•ê).** pasture, pasturage, grazing ground: **•Ew ç'îya cîyê *ç'êra* pez û dewarê gundîya bû** (Ba2:1, 202) That mountain was the place for *the pasturage of* the villagers' sheep and cattle **•Niha ezê herim *ç'êre*** (J) Now I will go *to pasture* **•Vê mîyê bibe *çêrê*** (AB) Take this sheep *to pasture.* {also: çere (FS); çerî (FS-2); [tcheré] چره (JJ); <çêre> چيره (HH)} {syn: çêregeh; mêrg [2]} Cf. Mid P čarag = 'pasture, grazing; flock' (M3); P čerā چـرا; = Sor lewer̄[ge] لـەوەڕ[گـە] [K/B//JB3/IFb/HH/GF/TF/OK/ZF3//JJ/

FS] <çerwan; k'oz [2]> See also **çêregeh.**

ç'êregah چـێـرەگـاه m. (K) = pasture. See **çêre** & **çêregeh.**

çêregeh چێرەگەه *f./m.(K)* **(-a/;-ê/).** pasture, pasturage, grazing ground. {also: çêrangeh (A); ç'êregah m. (K); [tcheregah] چـرەگـاه (JJ)} {syn: çêre; mêrg [2]} Cf. P čerāgāh چـراگـاه; = Sor lewer̄[ge] لەوەڕ[گە] [JB3/IF/ZF3//K/JJ//A] See also **çêre.**

çêriyan چێرِیان (JB3) = to graze. See **çêrîn.**

çêrî چێری (A) = swearing, verbal abuse. See **ç'êr̄.**

çêrîn/ç'êrîn [K/B] چـێـریـن *vi.* **(-ç'êr-).** to graze *(vi., of sheep and cattle)*: •**Li mêrgan pez** ***diçêriya*** (DZK, 135) In the meadows the sheep *were grazing*. {also: çerîn (FS/BF); çêran (A/JB3-2/GF--2); çêriyan (JB3-2); çêryan (-çêryê-) (M/OK-2); [tcheriian چـریـان/tcherin چـریـن] (JJ); <ç[ê]rîn چـیـریـن (diçêre) (دچـیـره)> (HH)} [Pok. I. ku̯el-/ku̯elə- 639.] 'to turn, move about, cautiously look for': O Ir *kar- (Tsb 47): Av & OP kar- (pres. čara-/čaraya-) = 'to be engaged in (a matter)' & Av čarāna- = 'field'; P čarīdan چـریـدن; Za çerenã [çerayiş] (Srk); = Sor lewer̄în لەوەڕین [K/B//IFb/JJ/HH/GF/TF/OK/ZF3//A/JB3/M//FS/BF] <çerwan; çêrandin; çêre; k'oz [2]; palîn I; şevîn>

çêrok چێرۆك (M) = tale. See **çîr̄ok.**

ç'êrt چێرت *f.* **(-a;).** bird droppings: •**Her wiha ji** ***çêrta*** **mirîşkan jî biyogaz tê çêkirin** (parzemin.com) Likewise biogas is made from *the droppings of* chickens. {also: ç'îrt (K/B); [tchirt] چـرت (JJ); <çêrt> چـیـرت (HH)} {syn: zirîç I} Cf. Arm cirt (W: jird) ծիրտ [IF/HH/ZF3//K/B/JJ] <gû; r̄îtin; sergîn; teyr>

çêryan چـێـریـان (-çêryê-) (M/OK) = to graze. See **çêrîn.**

ç'êt چێت *m.* **().** cockerel, young rooster, *less than one year old* (HH). {also: çît II (IFb); <çêt̲> چـيـط (HH)} {syn: şelûf} [Kmc-9/K/ZF3/Wkt//HH//IFb] <dîk>

ç'êtir چـێـتِـر *adj.* better: •**Cîhan bêyî Sedam Hisên** ***çêtir*** **e** (orient-news.com 7.vii.2016) The world is *better* without Saddam Hussein; **-ji me ç'êtir** = jinns, demons. See under **ji me ç'êtir**; **-ç'êtirîn** (ZF3/Wkt) the best: •**Pêşbirka** ***çêtirîn*** **nivîsa rojname-vanî** (scm.bz) The contest of the *best* journalistic article. {syn: baştir; xweştir} ç'ê = 'good' + -tir [K/A/JB3/IF/ZF3/Wkt] <çê>

ç'i چ *intrg. prn.* 1) {also: ç'î; [tché چـه/tchi چـی] (JJ); <çî> چـی (HH)} what: •**Ev** ***çi*** **ye?** = *What* is this? •**Navê te** ***çiye?*** = *What* is your name?; **-çi ... çi** (SK) whether ... or: •**Bo me mirin xoştir e ji jîna ho. Ez bi tewfîqa xudê pence-y xo dê dem e-ber pence-y Suto,** ***çi*** **mirim,** ***çi*** **mam** (SK 61:731) Death is pleasanter than life thus; with God's help I shall terminate Suto's power [lit. 'strike Suto's arm with mine'] *whether* I die *or* live; 2) nothing [+ neg.], anything {cf. **çu** & **t'u II**]: •**Ez çi nabêjim** (Hk/Bw) I won't say anything. Cf. P čī چـی; Sor çî چـی; Za çiçî/çi (Todd); Hau çêş (M4) [K/A/JB3/IFb/B/SK/GF/TF/OK//JJ/HH] <k'î>

ç'i bigre چ بگره (Frq) = almost. See under **girtin.**

çiçax چچاخ (K/F) = when. See **ç'iç'axî.**

ç'iç'axî چـچـاخـی *intrg.* when? {also: çiçax (K/F); çiçaẍ} {syn: ç'iwext (Bg); k'engî} [B//K/F]

ç'içaẍ چچاغ = when. See **ç'iç'axî.**

çiçik/ç'iç'ik [K/B] چـچـك *m./f.(IFb)* **(-ê/-a;/-ê).** 1) {syn: bistan; memik} (woman's) breast: •**Pîrek e,** ***çîçikê*** **xwe avêtîye ser milê xwe** (L) It's an old woman, she has thrown her *breasts* over her shoulders; **-ç'iç'ik dan zaruê** (K) to nurse, suckle, breastfeed an infant; **-ç'ic'ik xwerin/~ mêtin** (K) to suck, nurse *(infant or animal cub/whelp)*; **-zarua ber ç'iç'ik** (K) suckling infant {syn: pitik II}; 2) nipple:**-serê çiçik** (AF) do.; 3) {syn: guhan; guhandîr} udder. {also: çîçik I (L/JB3); [tchitchik] چیچك (JJ); <çiçik> چچك (HH)} Cf. P čučū چچو = 'nipple' [L/JB3/JJ//K/A/IFb/B/HH/GF/AF/ZF3]

çift چفت (XF) = kick. See **çivt.**

çik I چـك *adj.* dried up, desiccated: **-kanîya çik** (FS) dry well; **-rûbarê çik** (FS) dry river bed; **-çik bûn** (Wkt) to dry up, stop flowing (vi.) {syn: çikîn; miçiqîn}: •**Paşî mirina Şêx Saliḧ serkanîya Nehrî** ***çik bû*** (SK 46:449) After the death of Sheikh Salih the spring of Nehri *went dry* •**Robar** ***çik bûye*** (Zx) The river *has dried up*. [SK/Wkt/ZF3/FS/BF] <ḧişk>

***çik II** چـك **( ).** side of knucklebone (k'ap II) that has a crater in it. {syn: diz (Wn); ≠pik (Qzl)} [Qzl] <k'ap II>

ç'ika چـكـا *conj.* to see whether, whether *(signals indirect questions)* "[čka] leitet indirekte Fragen ein" (O. Jastrow. *Daragözü*, p. 103, note 21): •**Em herin, go** ***çika*** **ḧalê xort bû çi?** (J) Let's go see what's happened to the young man •**Ewê qîzê gelekî da ḧişê xwe,** ***çika*** **çawa bike** (EP-7) That girl gave a lot of thought to (or, spent much time thinking about) what she should do •**Ez dixazim her̄ime cem xwedê bizanibim** ***çika*** **r̄astya wî**

çewane? (Dz) I want to go to God, to know what his truth is like •**Kuȓo, hela binhêrin** ***çika*** **Memê min çima îro derengî bûye** (Z-1) Boys, go see why my Mem is late today •**Sivê bira qîz û bûkê şeher t'emam bêne baẍê Tûrkirî,** ***çika*** **Memê min k'îjan qîzê xweȓa diḧebîne** (Z-1) Let all the girls and brides of the city come to the garden of Turkiri tomorrow, to see which girl Mem will fall in love with •**Wezîr, em heȓin,** ***çika*** **ev çitevaye?** (J) Vizier, let's go see what this is all about. {syn: bê II; k'a II[2] (EP); qe (Z)} [J/Z-1/B/ZF3]

çikandin I/ç'ikandin [K/B] چِکاندِن *vt.* **(-çikîn-).** 1) {syn: ḧeşikandin (HM)} to stick, thrust, insert, plunge (into): •**Li dora Memu Alan xencera biçikînin** (HM) "*Stechet* eure Dolche ringsum in Mamu!" (=*Thrust* your daggers into M. A.!); 2) to dig, dig up (K); 3) {syn: çikilandin} to plant *(trees)*: •**Ferzende çû şaqek ji vê darê anî, li hewşê** ***d[a] çikandin*** (RN #61, 3) F. went and brought a branch of this tree, *had* it *planted* in the yard; 4) to hoist, erect (K/IF). {also: [tchikandin] چکاندين (JJ); <çikandin چکاندن (diçikîne) (دچکينه)> (HH)} [HM/A/IFb/JJ/HH/GF/TF/BK/ZF3//K/B] See also **çikilandin.** <daçikandin>

çikandin II/ç'ikandin [K/B] چِکاندِن *vt.* **(-çikîn-).** to stop or staunch the flow of *(water)*; to dry up *(a well)*. {also: [tchikandin] چکاندين (JJ)} {syn: miç'iqandin} [K/B//JJ/GF/TF/BK/ZF3] <biryan [2]; çikîn; pengandin>

ç'ikil چِکِل (K) = branch; variant. See **ç'iqil.**

çikilandin چِکِلاندِن *vt.* **(-çikilîn-).** 1) to plant *(trees)*; 2) to stick in, insert, thrust. {also: [čikelāndin] چکلاندين (JJ)} {syn: çikandin I[3]; dabinartin (JB3); daçikandin (F/K/JJ)} = Sor naştin ناشتن (-nêj-) [JB3/IFb/JJ/OK/ZF3] See also **çikandin I.**

çikiyan چِکِيان (IFb/JJ) = to dry up. See **çikîn.**

çikîn/ç'ikîn [K/B] چِکين *vi.* **(-ç'ik-).** 1) {syn: miç'iqîn} to stop flowing *(of water)*: -**bîna** ***fk-ê*** **diç'ike** (K/B) to pant, gasp for air, choke: •**Xûşk nikare bê,** ***bîna wê diç'ike.*** **Xeber nade; hêsra dibarîne** (K2-Fêrîk) Sister cannot come, *she is panting*. She doesn't speak, she [only] sheds tears; 2) {syn: miç'iqîn} to dry up *(of water source)*: •**Cew** ***ç'ikyaye*** (B) The canal *has dried up* •**Kanî** ***ç'ikîya*** (K) The well *dried up*; 3) {syn: nuqutîn} to drip, trickle (K). {also: çikiyan (IFb); [tchikiian] چکيان (JJ); <çikan چکان (diçike) (دچکه)> (HH)} P čakīdan چکيدن = 'to drip'; Sor çikîn چکين = 'to drip, to dry up (of a well)' (Hej) [K2-Fêrîk/K/A/B/GF/TF//IFb/JJ/OK/ZF3//HH] <çikandin II; herikîn; miç'iqîn>

çikkos چِککۆس (BK) = greedy. See **ç'ikûs.**

çiko چِکۆ (OK/ZF3) = because. See **ç'iku ko.**

çikos چِکۆس (GF) = greedy. See **ç'ikûs.**

çikosî چِکۆسی (GF) = greediness. See **ç'ikûsî.**

çikot چِکۆت (IFb) = greedy. See **ç'ikûs.**

çiksayî چِك سايی (IFb) = clear (of sky). See **ç'îk-sayî.**

ç'iku ko چِکو کۆ *conj.* because, since. {also: çiko (OK/ZF3); <çikû> چکو (HH)} {syn: bona wê yekê ko; **ç'imkî**} [Ad//HH//OK/ZF3] See also **ç'imkî.**

ç'ikûs/çikûs [K] چِکووس *adj.* greedy, stingy, selfish, miserly: •**nanê** ***çikkosan*** (BK) the bread *of the stingy*. {also: çikkos (BK); çikos (GF); çikot (IFb)} {syn: çavbirçî; çirûk[2]; devbeş; qesîs & xesîs; ȓijd} {ç'ikûsî} [BK//K/TF/ZF//GF//IFb]

ç'ikûsî/çikûsî [K] چِکووسی *f.* **(-ya;-yê).** greediness, stinginess, selfishness, miserliness. {also: çikosî (GF)} [K/TF/ZF//GF] <ç'ikûs>

ç'il I/çil [K/B] چِل *num.* **().** forty, 40. {also: çel I (A-2/IFb-2); çêl I (JB1-S); [tchil] چل (JJ); <çil> چل (HH)} O Ir *čaθrusat-: Av čaθwarᵊsatəm; OP *čaθurθat- ~ *čaθursat-; Mid P čehel (M3); P čihil چهل; Sor çil چل; Za çewres (Todd); Hau çil (M4) [L/A/JB3/IFb/JJ/HH/SK/GF/TF/OK//K/B//JB1-S] <ç'ar I; çelê; ç'ilem>

çil II چِل *f.* **().** bat *(flying mouse)*, zool. *Chiroptera*. {also: çilêçilê (GF); çilçilî (A); çîlîçîlî (IFb)} {syn: barç'imok; çekçekîle; dûvmesas; pîrçemek; şevrevînk; şevşevok} *The final -l is emphatic, almost like central Kurdish ł* ڵ [Mdt/TF/AD/ZF3//GF//A//IFb]

çil III چِل *adj.* glutton(ous), gourmand, fond of eating, overeater, greedy (in devouring food), self-indulgent: •**Ew** ***mirovekê çil*** **e** (FS) He is a *glutton*. {syn: xure} [A/ZF3/FS/Wkt]

çilag چِلاگ (IFb/Wkt) = weaver. See **ç'olag.**

çilak چِلاك *m.* **(-ê;-î).** long, thin cudgel, *usually made of mahaleb cherry wood [kinêr]* (Qzl); two-pronged long stick for picking **mazî** [oak galls], **kezan** [terebinth seeds], etc. (Zeb). {also: çelak (A/IFb/GF); çelake (Zeb); <çelak> چلاك (HH)} {syn: ȓot} Sor çełak چەڵاك = 'pole for shaking down fruit, esp. walnuts, from tree' [Qzl//A/IFb/HH/GF//Zeb]

çilçilî چِلچِلی (A) = bat *(flying mouse)*. See **çil II.**

Ç'ile I/Çile [K/B] چِلە *m./f.* **().** 1) forty (40) day period *(after births, weddings, deaths, etc.)* [cf. Ar arba'īnīyah اربعينية]; 2) dead of winter; 40 coldest winter days, starting from December 11 (HH); *names of two winter months*: 3) December: **-Çileya pêşîn** (RZ)/**çeleya pêşîn** (OK)/~**berê** (OK)/**çillê evel** (K) December {syn: K'anûna pêşin, et al.}; *corresponds to last part of* Agirdan ئاگردان/Sermawez سەرماوەز (P azer آذر) [Sagittarius] & 1st part of Sehołbendan سەهۆڵبەندان/Befranbar بەفرانبار (P dey دی) [Capricorn]; 4) January: **-Çileya paşîn** (RZ) January {syn: K'anûna paşin}; corresponds to last part of Sehołbendan سەهۆڵبەندان/Befranbar بەفرانبار (P dey دی) [Capricorn] & 1st part of Nawzistan ناوزستان/Rêbendan ڕێبەندان (P bahman بهمن) [Aquarius]. {also: çele II (OK-2); çelê (Kg); çêle I (A-2); Çille I, m. (K/A)/f.(B-2/GF); [čelé-] چلی (JJ-Lx); <çille> چله (HH)} [Kg/JJ-Lx//IFb/B/OK//K/A/HH/GF] <ç'il I; Ç'irî; zivistan>

çile II چله (B) = forty-day-old. See **ç'ilî**.

ç'ilem چلەم *adj.* fortieth, 40th. {also: çelem (Wkt-2); çelemîn (IFb/Wkt-2); çilemîn (IFb-2)} Cf. čehelom چهلم; Sor çilem[în] چلەم[ین] [GF/Wkt//IFb/ZF3] <çil I>

çilemîn چلەمین (IFb) = fortieth. See **ç'ilem**.

çilêçilê چلێچلێ (GF) = bat *(flying mouse)*. See **çil II**.

çiliq چلق (GF) = branch. See **ç'iqil**.

çiliqandin چلقاندن (FS) = to shake; to splash. See **ç'eliqandin**.

çilixt چلخت (Hej) = outcrop. See **çelexte**.

ç'ilî چلی *adj.* forty-day-old: **-zara çil[l]e** (B) = a) forty-day-old infant; b) babe in arms: **•Bişîne *zareke çilî* bîne, ewê tera bêje, k'a ew gilî rastin yanê derewin** (Ba3-3, #30) Send for a *babe in arms*, he will tell you whether these words are true or false. {also: çile II (B); çille II (B)} <ç'il I = 'forty' [Ba3//B/ZF3]

***çil'în** چلعین (). unripe, green almond [T çağla]. {syn: behîvter; gêrih (Frq); nîv'în (Mtk)} Cf. Sor çwale[badem] چواله[بادەم] [Haz] <behîv>

çilk/ç'ilk [K/B] چلك *f.* **(-a;-ê).** drop *(of a liquid)*: **•*Ç'ilke* xûna Bek'o dik'eve ort'a Memê u Zînê** (FK-eb-2) A *drop of* Beko's blood falls between M. and Z.; **-ç'ilka poz** (K) snot, mucus {syn: çilm; fiş; k'ilmîş; lîk}; **-çilke-çilk** (IF) drop by drop; **-ç'ilke hingiv** (B) drop of honey; **-ç'ilkêd baranê** (B) raindrops. {syn: çipik; dilop; niqitk; p'eşk I} Sor çiłk چڵك = 'body excretions such as ear wax, sweat, pus' [FK-2/K/IFb/B/ZF]

çille I چلله, m. (K/A)/f.(B/GF) = dead of winter; name for two winter months. See **Ç'ile I**.

çille II چلله (B) = forty-day-old. See **ç'ilî**.

çilm چلم *f./m.(FS/BF)* **(/-ê;).** mucus, snot: **•Çilmê wî hat xwar** (FS) His nose ran [lit. 'His mucus came down']. {also: [tchilim] چلم (JJ); <çilm> چلم (HH)} {syn: çilka poz; fiş; k'ilmîş; lîk} Sor çiłm چڵم; Za çilm *m.* (Mal) [F/K(s)/IF/JJ/HH/Bşk/ZF3/Wkt/FS] <belẍem>

ç'ilmêr چلمێر (Bw/Zeb) = door bolt. See **ç'ilmêre**.

ç'ilmêr•e چلمێره *m.(FS)/f.(Wn/Bw/ZF3)* **(; /•ê).** 1) {syn: *dorik (Bw); *qulqulk (Bw)} door bolt, thick wooden bolt on the back of a door which prevents it from being opened: **•Wî *çilmêre da* pişt derîkî** (FS) He *bolted* the door; **-darê ç'ilmêrê** (Zeb) do.; 2) {syn: zomp} large hammer, mallet (Qzl). {also: ç'ilmêr (Bw-2/Zeb); çilmîre (GF/FJ); <çilmêre> چلميره (HH)} < ç'il I = '40' + mêr = 'man' perhaps because the bolted door is so strong that 40 men could not break it down [Bw/Qzl/IFb/HH/Hej/AA/FS/ZF3//GF/FJ//Zeb]

çilmisandin/ç'ilmisandin [K/B] چلمساندن *vt.* **(-çilmisîn-).** to cause to fade, droop, wilt, wither: **•Têhna agirî gul *çilmisand*** (FS) The fire's heat *wilted* the rose. [K/B/ZF3/FS] <çilmisîn>

çilmisîn/ç'ilmisîn [K/B] چلمسين *vi.* **(-çilmis-).** 1) to fade, droop, wilt, wither; to shed its flowers (JB3); 2) to be extinguished, go out, die down (fig.) (K). {also: [chirmisīān] چرمسيان (JJ)} cf. Arc √k-m-š כמש = 'to wrinkle, wither' & NENA kamish/châmich = 'to fade, wither' (Maclean) [L/K/JB3/IFb/B/GF/TF/OK/ZF3/FS//JJ] <beqem; çilmisandin>

çilmîre چلميره (GF/FJ) = door bolt. See **ç'ilmêre**.

ç'ilo I چلۆ *adv.* How? What sort of?: **•Keçeke *çilo* ye?** (ZF3) *What kind of* girl is she?; **-çilo ... wilo** (FD) as...as, as...so: **•Kor *çilo* li Xwedê dinêre, Xwedê jî *wilo* lê dinêre** (FD) *As* the blindman looks at God, *so* does God look at him. {syn: çawa; çerê; çito} [A/IFb/ZF3/FD]

çilo II/ç'ilo [K] چلۆ *m.* **(-yê;).** dried oak branches and leaves, fed to domestic animals during the winter; leafy branches used for sheep fodder: **•Dema ku dibînin ... das û werîs li ser pişta kerê şidandiye û ew ê biçe *çilo*** (Lab, 76) When they see ... a sickle and rope tied to the donkey's back so that [the man] can go to the *çilo* **•Wekê malxweyê malê Silo be, wê xwarina kiflet sor**

çilo **be** (L-I, #55, 197) As the master of the house is Silo, the family's food will be *çilo* **•Xelkê wê dirkê hemî dijîn di kepra ve. [Di]çine çiyay, tiştekî tînin--dibênê *çulî*--dihavêne ser kepra, dibîte sîber û gelek xoş dibin** (M-Am #721, 332) The people there all live in bough shelters. They go to the mountains and bring something called '*chuli*' [young, leafy branches of oak] and put them on top of the shelters and it makes a shade and they are very pleasant; **-dîya çolî** (Zeb) do.; **-malîya çolî** (Zeb) bunches of branches tied together. {also: çilû (FS); çolî II (Zeb/Hej); çulî (M-Am); [tchilou/ciullú] چلو (JJ); <çilo> چلو (HH); <çolî> چۆلی (Hej)} Cf. Sor çił چڵ = 'branch (tree)' [Haz/Bw/A/IFb/HH/GF//K//M-Am//JJ/FS//Zeb/Hej] <dî II; malî I>

çilspî چلسپی (M.Dicle) = snow white. See **çîl-sipî.**

çilû چلوو (FS) = leafy branches used for sheep fodder. See **çilo II.**

ç'im I چم *f./m.(CS)* **(-a/;).** hoof of even-toed (split-hoofed) ruminants, such as that of sheep and cows: **-çîma devê** (Z-4) camel's hoof. {also: çîm II (Z-4)} [IFb/CS//Z-4] <sim>

ç'im II چم *m.* **(;).** heel *(of shoe)*: **•*Çim*: binê pêlavê yê ko dikevit bin panîya pêyê mirovî** (BF) *Heel*: the bottom of the shoe, which lies beneath the heel of a man's foot. {syn: panî I} [Şnx/MG/BF]

ç'ima چما *intrg.* why?: **•Te *çira* ez xapandim** (Dz) *Why* did you trick me? {also: ç'iman (K); ç'ira II (Dz); [tchira چرا/tchirani چرانی/tchi-man چی مان] (JJ); <çima چما/çira چرا> (HH)} {syn: bo çî?} Cf. Mid P çim = reason; çim rāy? = why? (M3) [K//A/JB3/IFb/B/HH/GF/TF/OK//Dz/JJ]

ç'imakî چماکی = because. See **ç'imkî.**

ç'iman چمان (K) = why. See **ç'ima.**

çimk' چمك (K) = because. See **ç'imkî.**

ç'imkî/çimkî [B]/**çimk'î** [K] چمکی *conj.* because. {also: ç'imakî; çimk' (K-2); çimku (B-2); ç'inkî} {syn: bona wê yekê ko; ç'iku ko; lema} Cf. P čūnke چونکه--> T çünkü/çünki; Sor çunke چونکه/çunku چونکو; NA čukun [Z-1/EP/JB3/IFb/OK//B//K] See also **ç'iku ko.**

çimku چمکو (B) = because. See **ç'imkî.**

çinar چنار/**ç'inar** [Z-4] *f.* **(-a;-ê).** 1) plane tree, oriental plane tree, bot. *Platanus orientalis*: **-dara çinarê** (F) do. **•Çû *dareke çinarê*ye mezin birî** (Dz) He went [and] cut down *a* large *plane tree*; 2) name of a town south of Diyarbakir. {also: çînar (K); çîner (B); [tchinar] چینار (JJ); <çinar> چنار (HH)} Cf. T çınar--> Rus činara чинара [Dz/IFb/HH/SK/GF/OK//F//K/JJ//B]

ç'indik/çindik [K] چندك *f.* **(-a;-ê).** hop(ping), skip(ping), jump(ing), leap(ing): **•Çirvîtk: Bazdana zaroka ya bi *çindik* û bi lotik** (SBx, 89) Çirvîtk: Jumping of children with *hopping* and leaping; **-çindik-çindik** (B) hopping and leaping; **-çindik dan** (ZF)/**çindika dan** (GF)/**çindik dan xwe** (IFb)/ **çindik-çindik kirin** (B) to hop, leap. {syn: banz; firqas; lotik; qevz II} [SBx/IFb/GF/ZF/CS/BF/BFK//K/B]

çingal I چنگال (GF) = fork. See **ç'engal I.**

çingal II چنگال (TF) = hook. See **ç'engel I.**

çingçing چنگچنك (IFb/FJ/GF) = tinkling of bells. See **çingeçing.**

çingeçing چنگەچنگ/**ç'inge-ç'ing** [K] *f.* **(-a;-ê).** tinkling of bells, rattling, clinking: **•Di nav *çinge çinga* dengê zengilkan re** (SBx, 12) Amid *the tinkling of* the bells [lit. 'of the sound of bells]. {also: çingçing (IFb/FJ/GF)} Sor ciringe-ciring جرنگەجرنگ = 'sustained tinkling (sound of dropped coin)' & ziringe-ziring زرنگەزرنگ = 'continued tinkling/ringing' [SBx/K/B/ZF//IFb/FJ/GF]

çinîn چنین *vt.* **(-çin-).** 1) {syn: quraftin} to pluck, pick, pull out *(flowers, fruit)*: **•Gula ko min *çinî* ji bo[na] te ye** (BX) The rose which I *picked* is for you; 2) to reap, harvest *(crops)* (A/IFb): **•Wan stirî çandin, xiyala wan ew bû dê tirî *çinin*** (SK 48:511) They planted thorns, thinking to *harvest* grapes; 3) {syn: dirûtin [2]} to mow, cut down (K): **•Merî wusa ji şûrê wan dik'etin, çawa qamîşê birî dik'eve, çaxê wana pê k'êlendîyê tûj *diçinin*** (EP-8) [The enemies'] men fell at their [=the Khan's warriors'] swords, as cut reeds fall, when they *mow* them *down* with sharp scythes; 4) to weave, sew (K/IFb); to knit (M). {also: [tchinin] چنین (JJ); <çinîn چنین (diçine) (دچنه)> (HH)} [Pok. 2. k^{u}ei- 637.] 'to pile up, to gather, put in order': O Ir *kay- (Tsb 43-4): Av [1]kay- (pres. činav-/činv-/čin-) = 'to select, exchange, distinguish'; P čīdan چیدن (-čīn-) (چین) = 'to pick, to arrange'; Sor çinîn[ewe] چنین[ەوە] (-çin-) = 'gather, glean'; Za çînenã [çînayiş] (Srk); Hau çinîey (çin-) *vt.* = 'to pluck' (M4) [BX/K/A/JB3/IFb/B/JJ/HH/SK/GF/TF/OK/M] <ç'andin>

ç'inkî چنکی = because. See **ç'imkî.**

çipik/ç'ipik [Z-2] چپك *f.* **().** drop *(of blood or water)*:

•**Du** ***ç'ipik*** **xûna r̄eş** (Z-2) Two *drops* of black blood. {also: çipk (GF)} {syn: çilk; dilop; niqitk; p'eşk I} [Z-2/OK/Zeb//GF]

çipilandin چِپِلاندِن *vt.* **(-çipilîn-).** to prune, trim, clip *(branches)*; to cut off, lop off: •**Ezê serê memikê xwe** ***biçipilînim*** (SW1) I *will cut off* the tip of my breast. {also: çiplandin (FJ); pejilandin (GF/BF/SS); pejlandin (FJ)}{syn: k'ezaxtin; pejikandin; t'er̄işandin}[CCG/Sw1/IFb/GF/ZF//FJ//GF/BF/SS] <piçandin>

çipk چِپک (GF) = drop. See **çipik**.

çiplandin چِپلاندِن (FJ) = to prune, clip. See **çipilandin**.

ç'iq چِق *m.* **(-ê;).** branch, twig (K/JB3); tip of the branch (IFb): •**Te çima dewsa kevezanê destê xwe ew** ***çiqê*** **t'eze şînbûyî bir̄î?** (Abbasian #6:144) Why have you cut that *green branch* in place of [=to replace] the stick [you carry in] your hand? {also: çuq (HB-2); <çiq> چق (HH)} {syn: çirpî; gulî II; şax [1]; ta VI} According to Abbasian, <Arm dial. čəł ճըղ, (W Arm jyuł ճիւղ); Cf. Sor çil چل [HB/K/JB3/IFb/B/HH/GF] See also **ç'iqil** [1].

ç'iqa چقا (B/Ba2) = how much. See **ç'iqas.**

ç'iqas چِقاس *intrg.* 1) how much {*cf.* **çend** = how many *for count nouns*}: •**Te** ***çiqwas*** **da?** (Qzl) *How much* did you pay?; **-ç'iqas ... ewqas** {or, ... **usa jî**} = as ... as; the ... the: •**Memê** ***çiqas*** **bêxem bû, Al-p'aşa** ***ewqas*** **bêsebir dibû** (Z-1) M. was *as* carefree *as* A. was impatient •***Çiqas*** **Memê zîndanêda dih̄elîya** ***usa jî*** **Zîna delal diha ze'f bona Memê xwe dih̄elîya û dip'er̄itî** (Z-1) *The more* M. "melted" in prison, *the more* darling Z. melted and pined for him; 2) how ...!: •***Çiqas*** **xweş e ev xwendin!** (AB) *How* good this studying or reading is! •**Dibînî Ûsibî** ***çiqas*** **aqile?** (Ba) Do you see *how* smart Joseph is? ;3) [+ *subj.*] how ever much, no matter how much: •***Çiqas*** **xirabyê bikî...** (Dz) *No matter how much* evil you do... •**Lê** ***çiqa*** **jî şivana û seêd wana miqatî li pêz nekirana, diqewimî, wekî gura mîk-dudu birîndar dikirin** (Ba2:1, 203) But *no matter how much* the shepherds and their dogs cared for the sheep, it happened that the wolves wounded a sheep or two. {also: çiqa (B-2/Ba2); çiqasî (Ba); çiqwas (Qzl); [čikás چقاس/tchiqa چقا] (JJ); <çiqas> چقاص (HH)} [K/A/JB3/IFb/B/JJ/TF/OK//HH//Ba//Ba2] <ç'end>

ç'iqasî چقاسی (Ba) = how much. See **ç'iqas.**

ç'iqeys چقەیس (K) = each, every. See **ç'iqeyse.**

ç'iqeyse چقەیسە. [+*pl.*] each, every: •**Çiqeyse rêwîyê go derbas bibin** (L) Every traveler who passes by. {also: çiqeys (K)} {syn: gişk; hemû; her} [L/K] See **ç'iqas.**

ç'iqil چقِل *m.(K)/f.(OK)* **().** 1) {syn: çirpî; gulî II; şax [1]; şewk[4]; t̲a VI} branch: •**Bi 'ezmînva** ***ç'iqlê*** **dara hebûn, eskerê wî gişka sîlih̄ê xwe êxstin û ç'ilqava darda kirin** (EH) Throughout the sky there were tree *branches*, all of his soldiers took off their weapons and hung them up [on the trees]; 2) {syn: ç'engel I; nîk; şewk[2]}{=Sor singulke سنگولکه} hook, projection used for hanging (Zeb/Dh) [çuqum (Zeb)]; 3) variant (K). {also: ç'ikil (K/Dh); çiliq (GF-2); çiqilk (IFb-2); çiqul (TF); çuqulk (IFb-2); çuqum (Zeb); [tchikil] چکل (JJ)} [F/JB3/IFb/B/GF/OK//TF//K/JJ/Dh] <dar I> See also **ç'iq.**

çiqilk چقلك (IFb) = branch. See **ç'iqil.**

çiqir چِقِر *pl.* **().** wrinkles, lines *(in one's face or forehead)*: •***Çiqrên*** **ku şêst û heft salan hûrik hûrik, carinan jî bilez ... li rûyê wê nexşandibûn** (M.Dicle. Nara, 15) *Lines* which had etched themselves very gently, and sometimes in an instant ... into her face •**Hevalê wî baş bala xwe dide pê û li nav çavên wî nihêre, ji bal û** ***çiqrên*** **enîya wî baş derdixist, ku ew niha çi difikire** (A.Tîgrîs. Ken û girîn, 97) His friend takes a good look at him and stares into his eyes, and from *the lines* in his forehead he could surmise what he was thinking right then •**Kare li ser hev di enî de** ***çiqiran*** **çêke, wan çiqran berjor û berjêr bibe bîne** (X.Mîrzengî. hawargotar.blogspot. com) He can make *lines* in his forehead, and cause those lines to move up and down. Cf. T çukur = 'hole, depression, dimple'. [M.Dicle/A.Tîgrîs/X.Mîrzengî]

çiqul چقول (TF) = branch. See **ç'iqil.**

ç'iqwas چقواس (Qzl) = how much. See **ç'iqas.**

ç'ir̄ I چِڕ: **-çir̄ kirin**: 1) to rinse under running water *(dishes)* (EP-7): •**Bona bi destî carîa** ***bide çir̄kirnê*** (FK-eb-2) *To have* them *rinsed* by the maidservants •**Ewê rabû sifrê xweyî kevn t'opkir ... bi caryava bir ser kanîê bişo û** ***çir̄ke*** (EP-7) She gathered up her old food utensils ... and took them with her maidservants to the spring to wash and *rinse* [them]; 2) to cascade, flow down *(of waterfalls)* (IFb). [EP-7/IFb]

çir̄ II چِڕ/**çir II** چِر [IFb] *adj.* stretchable, elastic; sticky, gluey, ropy, viscous, rubbery; sinewy, wiry, stringy; tough *(of meat)* (K); lean, skinny *(of person)* (K): •**axa çir̄** (Zeb/GF) sticky or clay-like earth •**benîştê çiř** (Zeb) stretchy [chewing]gum •**hevîrê çiř** (Zeb) stringy dough •**nanê çiř** (Bw/ Zeb) rubbery bread, which is not easy to chew •**şiva çir** (IFb) resilient stick *(hard to bend because it is young and green and strong)*. {also: <çir> چر (HH); <çiř> چڕ (Hej)} Sor çiř چڕ [Bw/ Zeb/K/IFb/B/HH/GF/Hej]

çir•a I چرا *f.* **(•aya;•ê).** lamp, light: •***Çira* vê ket** (AB) *The lamp* flared up. {also: çiraẍ; [tchira] چرا (JJ); <çira> چرا (HH)} Cf. P čarāγ چراغ, T çırağ; Sor çira چرا; Hau çirawî *f.* (M4) [AB/K/A/JB3/IF/B/JJ/HH] <şemal [3]>

ç'ira II چرا (Dz) = why. See **ç'ima.**

çirahûrk•a چراهوورکا *f.* **(•a;).** Hanukah, Jewish holiday in early winter (December): •**[*Çirahûrka* Cuhiyana serê zivistan e]** (Brauer, 336) *Little lights of t*he Jews, [means] beginning of winter. "'Īdat Chera Hurka" = 'Feast of the small lights' (Hanukah) [Brauer, p.336]; < çira = 'lamp, light' + hûr = 'tiny' [Brauer]

ç'iřandin چڕاندن *vt.* **(-ç'iřîn-).** 1) {syn: diřandin; p'eřitandin; qelişandin [1]/qelaştin} to tear, rip (vt.); 2) to fib, tell lies (Qzl). {also: ç'îrandin (M)} [BK/K/A/JB3/IFb/GF/TF/OK/Qzl//M] <ç'iřîn>

çiranek چرانەک (Kmc) = jet of water; drainpipe. See **şiřik.**

çirav چراڤ *f.* **(;-ê).** 1) {syn: cimcime II; genav} marsh, swamp, bog; muck: •**Li dora bîrê teqan [=teqin] û *çirav*** (Cigerxwîn. Halê gundiya) Around the well [is] mud and *muck* •**Pêşî ji pingav û *çiravan* têne pê** (IFb) Mosquitoes come into existence from *stagnant water*; 2) {also: çireav (RZ-2); şirav (Haz)} waterfall, cascade (ZF3/RZ). [JB2/A/ FJ/GF/CS/ZF3/Wkt/BF]

çiraẍ چراغ = lamp. See **çira I.**

çirçîrok چرچیرۆک = tale. See **çîřok.**

çireav چرەئاڤ (RZ) = waterfall. See **çirav** [2].

çire-çir چرەچر (F)/ç'iřeç'iř چڕەچڕ (B) = creak, squeak, crash. See **ç'irke-ç'irk.**

çir•ik I چرک *f.* **(•ka;).** second, 60th of a minute: •**Ḧeta çend çirkêt dî** (Zeb) In another couple of seconds. {also: çirk (IFb/GF/OK/ZF3)} {syn: kêlî} [Zeb//IFb/GF/OK]

çiř•ik II چڕک *f.* **(•ka;).** boiled *doşav* [grape molasses] mixed with pepper, *believed to be good for the throat.* {also: <çiřik> چڕک (Hej)} [Zeb/Hej] <doşav>

çirik III چرک (IFb/FJ/RZ) = jet of water; drainpipe. See **şiřik.**

ç'irisandin چرساندن (Z-2) = to shine. See **çirûsandin.**

Ç'irî چری *f.* **(-ya;-yê).** *name of two autumn months*: 1) October {syn: Cotmeh (Wlt)} **-Çirîya pêşîn** (GF/OK/RZ)/**Çiriya pêşin** (IFb/B)/**Çirîya berî** (OK-2)/**Çirîya ewil** (JB3)/[tchiriia evel] چریا اول (JJ)/[tjeria awell] (BG) October: •**[Çirîyê û Çirîyê, mal t'êr û t'ijî ye, mirov dibine xweşîyê]** (BG) In October and November, the cattle are sated and full, mankind lives pleasantly *[prv.]*; *corresponds to last part of* Mîran میران/Řezber ڕەزبەر (P mehr مهر) [Libra] & 1st part of Gełarêzan گەڵارێزان (P ābān آبان) [Scorpio]; 2) November {syn: Mijdar (Wlt)} **-Çirîya paşîn** (GF/RZ)/**Çiriya paşin** (IFb/B)/[tchiriia pachi] چریا پاشی (JJ)/[tjeria pâchy] (BG) November; *Some dictionaries (K/JB3/OK) list **Çirîya navîn** as November, and **Çiriya paşîn/paşin** as December, but this is not followed in practice; corresponds to last part of* Gełarêzan گەڵارێزان (P ābān آبان) [Scorpio] & 1st part of Agirdan ئاگردان/ Sermawez سەرماوەز (P azer آذر) [Sagittarius]. {also: <çiřî> چڕی (HH)} Syr tešrī[n] ܬܫܪܝܢ, *name of 2 months*: tešrī qaḏīm ܬܫܪܝ ܩܕܝܡ ('1st t.') = October & tešrī 'ḥrāyā ܬܫܪܝ ܐܚܪܝܐ ('last t.') = November; NENA tširī ܬܫܪܝ/čirī ܟܪܝ; Ar tišrīn تشرين [F/K/JB3/IFb/B/JJ/OK/RZ//HH//BG] <Ç'ile I>

çirîk چریک (Kmc) = jet of water; drainpipe. See **şiřik.**

ç'iřîn چڕین *vi.* **(-ç'iř-).** 1) {syn: diřîn; qelişîn [2]} to be torn, ripped; to tear, rip (vi.); 2) to squeak, creak (B). {also: ç'îryan (-ç'îryê-) (M)} [BK/K/A/IFb/ B/TF/OK//M] <ç'iřandin>

çirîsk چریسک (IFb/CS) = shine, spark. See **çirûsk.**

çirk چرک (IFb/GF/OK/ZF3) = second, 60th of a minute. See **çirik I.**

çirke-çirk چرکەچرک [F/IFb]/**çirkeçirk** [A]/**ç'irke-ç'irk** [K]/**ç'irkeç'irk** [B] *f./m.(L)* **(/-ê; -ê;).** 1) {syn: qirç'e-qirç'} creak(ing), squeak(ing); crackling, crash: •**Bû ... *çîrkeçîrkê* ben û şirîtane** (L) There was *a squeaking of* ropes and lines; 2) {syn: qirç'e-qirç'} gnashing, gritting *(of teeth)* (F/ K/B); 3) {also: çire-çir (F); ç'iřeç'iř (B); ç'îřeç'îř (B-2)} chirring *(of crickets)*. {also: çire-çir (F); ç'iřeç'iř (B); ç'îřeç'îř (B-2); çîrkeçîrk (L)} Cf. Sor çirkeçirk چرکەچرک = 'ticking, clicking, crackle' [L//K//F/IFb//A/B]

çironek چرۆنەک (IFb) = jet of water; drainpipe. See **şiřik.**

ç'irpe چرپە *m.* **().** siege tower (SK); protective shed for besiegers, ***vinea***, a moving fence or shelter for the attacking side (ST[English translation-note, p. 6]); wooden four-legged pavilion-like structure, for attacking fortresses and high-walled structures of the enemy (ST[Sorani-note, p.4 (2nd group)]): **•[Sûto got: Ho nabêt, lazime bi *çirpe* biçîne bin qesrê]** (ST-o, 16 (2nd group)) & **Sûto got: ho nabêt gerek bi *çirpe* bi çine bin avahiyê** (ST-l, 21) Suto said, "This will not do, we must approach the fort with a '*chirpa*'." {also: <çirpe> چرپە (ST-o)} Cf. P čahār pā چهارپا = 'four-legged, quadruped' [ST/SK]

çirpî چرپی *m./f.* **(; /-ê).** branch: **•Destê xwe avîte *çrpîê*, destê xwe avîte cîl û derk'ete r̄eşaê** (HCK-2, 180) He grabbed *the branch*, he grabbed the reed and came out on dry land. {also: çrpî (HCK); [tchirpi] چرپی (JJ); <çirpî> چرپی (HH)} {syn: ç'iq[il]; gulî II; şax; şirtik; şiv; ta VI} Cf. T çırpı = 'dry twig'; Sor çirpî چرپی = 'Y-shaped branch/tree stem used as support (for grape vines)' [HCK/K/B/FJ/GF/JJ/HH/CS] <şewk [4]>

çirs چرس *f.* **().** spark; sparkle. {also: **çirûsk**} {syn: peşk III[1]; p'êt; p'irîsk} [FJ/GF/TF/ZF3/Wkt/SS]

çirsavêj چرساڤێژ *adj.* sparkling, flickering, glittering: **•Gulleyên sor û *çirsavêj* li hewa dilîstin** (Nofa, 94) Red and *sparkling* bullets danced in the air. < çirs + -avêj = 'throwing' [Nofa/ZF3/Wkt]

çirtik چرتِك (RZ) = jet of water; drainpipe. See **şir̄ik**.

çirûk چرووك *adj.* 1) corrupt, dishonest, scandalous; 2) {syn: çavbirçî; ç'ikûs; devbeş; qesîs & xesîs; r̄ijd} stingy, greedy, selfish, miserly, parsimonious (Bw/GF); 3) defective *(of a weapon that fails to go off)* (Bw). {also: [cirúk] چروك (JJ); <çirûk> چروك (HH)} Sor çirûk چرووك = 'parsimonious, stingy, unsound' [Bw/K/JJ/HH/GF/OK]

çirûnek چروونەك (FS) = jet of water; drainpipe. See **şir̄ik**.

çirûsandin/ç'irûsandin [K/B] چرووساندن *vt.* **(-çirûsîn-).** to cause to shine; to polish, shine *(vt.)*. {also: ç'irisandin (Z-2)} {syn: biriqandin; birûskandin; teyisandin} [Z-2/K/B//ZF3]

çirûsîn/ç'irûsîn [K/B] چرووسین *vi.* **(-çirûs-).** 1) to shine *(vi.)*; 2) to give off sparks; 3) to be blinded, dazzled *(by bright light)* (HH). {also: çirûskîn (IFb); çûrisîn (F); [tchiroustin] چیروستین (JJ); <çirisîn چرسین (diçir[i]se) (دچرسە)> (HH)} {syn: biriqîn; birûs[k]în; teyisîn} [K/B//ZF3//IFb//F//JJ//HH]

çirûsk/ç'irûsk [K/B] چرووسك *f.* **(-a;-ê).** 1) shine, sparkle, glisten; 2) {syn: peşk III[1]; p'êt; p'irîsk} spark: **•Di dilê wî da ew qitîska/*çirûska* hêviyê a mayî jî di nav fehma xeman de vemirî** (MG. Jiyaneka Pêguhork) In his heart, even that remaining *spark* of hope was extinguished amid the ashes of anguish. {also: çirîsk (IFb-2/CS-2); **çirs**; çrûsk (GF-2); [cirísk] چرسك (JJ)} Cf. P sirišk سرشك = 'tears, sparks'; Sor çirîske چریسکە/tirîske تریسکە = 'gleam, glitter' [K/B//A/JB3/IFb/FJ/GF/CS//JJ]

çirûskîn چرووسکین (IFb) = to shine. See **çirûsîn**.

çist (K/Tsab)/ç'ist (IFb-2/TF) چست = nimble. See **ç'ust**.

***çit** چت **( ).** in playing with knucklebones [k'ap II], a double win [qezenç], e.g., ***du mîr** (qv.) or **du ker** (qv.)*. {syn: ≠zirt} [Qzl] <k'ap II>

ç'ito چتۆ *intrg.* how?: **•Em *çito* bikin** (L) What [lit. '*how*'] should we do? How should we act? {also: çitow; çituv (M-Ak)} {syn: ç'awa; çerê (Kg); ç'ilo I} [L/K/IFb/SK/GF/OK]

ç'itow چتۆو = how. See **ç'ito**.

ç'ituv چتوڤ (M-Ak) = how. See **ç'ito**.

ç'ivan چڤان (B) = bend, twist. See **çivane**.

çivan•e/ç'ivane [K/B] چڤانە *f./m.(K)* **(;•ê/).** bend, twist, turn(ing) *(e.g., in a road)*: **•Hema wî çaxî me dît çewa gurekî ter̄ikî, tiştekî dêvda nava kevirada *ç'ivana* dide, ḧevraz dir̄eve** (Ba2:2, 205) At that very moment we saw a huge wolf with something in its mouth winding its way [lit. 'it gives *twists*'] through the rocks, running upward **•r̄îya ç'ivan[e]** (B) a winding, serpentine road. {also: ç'ivan (B-2)} [Ba2/F/K/IFb/B/GF]

çivanok چڤانۆك (Wlt-56/RF) = anecdote. See **çîvanok**.

çivir چڤر *adj.* very greasy, oily, rich, fatty *(of food)*. {also: çivr (IFb/GF)} {syn: *bi r̄ûn} P čarb چرب; Sor çewr چەور [Qzl//IFb/GF] <bez I; r̄ij; tewaş>

ç'ivîk چڤیك (Ba2/K/HH) = sparrow. See **çûk I**.

çivît چڤیت *f.* **(-a;-ê).** indigo, bot. *Indigofera ticntoria*. {also: civît (GF); çiwît (IFb/AA); [tchivid] چوید (JJ); <çiwît> چویت (Hej)} {syn: heş} T çivit [Wn/Btm/Xrz//GF//IFb/AA/Hej//JJ]

çivr چڤر (IFb/GF) = greasy. See **çivir**.

çivt چڤت *f.* **(-a;-ê).** 1) {syn: lotik; p'eḧîn; r̄efes; tîzik} kick(ing), strike with the foot: **•...û mîna kareke xezala *çivt dide*, dir̄eve** (Ba-1, #27) ...and she *kicks* like a fawn [and] runs off; **-çivt avîtin** (B)/ **~kirin** (K)/**~lê dan** (K) to kick; 2) butt(ing), strike with the horns. {also: cifte (F); çift (XF)} Cf. Sor cûte جووتە = 'kick with both hind legs' [Ba-1/K/B//XF/

/F]

ç'ivte-ç'ivt چڤتەچڤت *f.* **(-a;-e).** chirping, tweeting *(of birds)*: **•*ç'ivteç'ivta* ç'ivîka** (Ba2) *the chirping of* birds/sparrows. {also: [tchiwe-tchiw چیڤەچیڤ /tchiwte-tchiwt چیڤتەچیڤت] (JJ)} {syn: wîtewît} [Ba2/K/IFb/B/JJ/GF]

ç'i waxt چ واخت (Ag) = when? See **ç'iwext.**

ç'iwext چوەخت *intrg.* when? {also: ç'i waxt (Ag)} {syn: çiçaxî (B); k'engî} < çi = 'what' + wext = 'time' [Bg//Ag]

çiwît چویت (IFb/AA) = indigo. See **çivît**.

çixarê چخارێ (A) = cigarette. See **cigare.**

çix̃ چغ *f.* **(-a;).** bangs *(of hair)*: -*çix̃* **û biskêt xo berdan** (Zeb) to let one's *bangs* grow. {also: <çix̃> چغ (Hej)} [Zeb/Hej] <bisk>

çiya چیا (JB3/IFb/GF/OK/JB1-A) = mountain. See **çîya.**

çiyayî چیایی (Lab/IFb/GF/ZF3) = mountain dweller. See **çîyayî.**

çizirik چزرك (Qrj) = crackling, bits of sheep fat. See **kizik**.

ç'î چی = what. See **çi.**

ç'îa چیئا (B) = mountain. See **çîya**.

çîçek/ç'îç'ek [K/B] چیچەك *f.* **(-a;-ê).** 1) {syn: gul; kulîlk; mom I} flower; 2) *woman's name*. {also: [tchitchek] چچك (JJ)} < T çiçek = 'flower' [HB/JB3/IF/JJ/ZF3//K/B]

çîçelok چیچەلۆك (FJ/GF) = chick. See **çîçik III**.

çîçik I چیچك (L/JB3) = breast; udder. See **çiçik.**

çîçik II/ç'îç'ik [K/B] چیچك *m.* **().** small amount, little bit: **•*Ç'îç'ike* nan bide min** (B) Give me *a little bit of* bread **•Ezê *ç'îç'ikekî* r̄azêm** (B) I am going to sleep *for a little bit*. {also: ç'îç'ike[k] (B); çîçkek (GF); ç'îqek (JB1-S)} {syn: hindik; kêm I; piçek} [EP-5/K/B//ZF3/GF//JB1-S]

çîçik III چیچك *f.* **(-a;).** 1) {syn: cûcik; çelîk; ferx; var̄ik} chick, baby chicken: **•Zarok mîna *çîçikên* birçî bidû de baz didin** (HYma 30) The children run after her like hungry *chicks*; 2) small bird, sparrow. See **çûk I**. {also: çîçelok (FJ-2/GF-2); [ciúciék] ججك (JJ); <çîçik> چیچك (HH)} Sor cûçik جووچك /cûçeɫe جووجەڵە [HYma/A/IFb/FJ/GF/TF/HH/Kmc/CS/ZF3//JB1-A/JJ]

ç'îç'ike[k] [چیچکە[ك] (B) = little bit. See **çîçik II**.

çîçkek چیچکەك (GF) = little bit. See **çîçik II**.

çîdar چیدار *f.* **(;-ê).** legirons, footshackles: **-qeyd û çîdar/qeyd û çîtale** (EP-7) fetters and footshackles. {also: çîtal (EP-7); [tchidar] چیدار (JJ)} Cf. P čadār چدار = 'cord or silk fetters for horses' [Z-1/K/B/JJ] <qeyd; zincîr>

ç'îg چیگ (B) = pain. See **ç'îk.**

çîk/ç'îk [B] چیك *f.* **(-a;-ê).** pain *(labor pains, etc.)*: **•Her *çîkeka* ji ber zayinê dihat ji bo Xezalê gaveka ber bi mirinê ve bû** (MGJiyaneka Pêguhork) Every *pang of* labor pain was another step towards death for Khezal. {also: ç'îg (B-2)} {syn: azar; derd; êş; jan} [MG/CS/ZF3//B]

Çîkî چیکی (BF) = Czech. See **Ç'ekî.**

ç'îk-saî چیك سائی (XF) = clear (of sky). See **ç'îk-sayî.**

ç'îk-sayî چیك سایی *adj.* clear, perfectly clear; sky-blue: **•sibeke *ç'îk-sayî*** (Ba-1, #7) one *bright* morning. {also: çiksayî (IFb); ç'îk-saî (XF)} [Ba-1//XF] <sayî I>

çîlîçîlî چیلیچیلی (IFb) = bat *(flying mouse)*. See **çil II**.

çîl-sipî چیل سپی *adj.* pure white, snow-white: **•dewê *çîl-sipî*** (Alkan, 71) *snow-white* buttermilk **•Têjika piçûk. *Çilspî.* Gilofîtika berfê, wekî ku bikeve nav tasa dimsê** (M.Dicle. Nara, 82) A little kitten. *Snow white*. A snowball, as if it had fallen into a bowl of *dims* [grape molasses] **•weke sê hêkên *çîl-sipî*** (Alkan, 71) like three *snow white* eggs. {also: çilspî (M.Dicle); çîl-spî (IFb/ZF)} {syn: qerqaş; spî I} [Alkan//IFb/ZF//M.Dicle]

çîl-spî چیل سپی (IFb/ZF) = snow white. See **çîl-sipî.**

ç'îm I چیم *m.* **(-ê;).** calf of the leg: **•Lê bi rakirin a lingê wê ra "şirpîn" ji *çîmê* wê hat ... Pê ra jî çizek tûj, ku heta wê gavê nedîtibû, ket *çîmê* wê** (MB, 64) But upon lifting her leg, a crunching sound came from her *calf* ... with it a dull ache, the likes of which she had never before experienced, beset the *calf of her leg*. {syn: belek II; boqil; paq} [MB/A/ZF3] <ling>

çîm II چیم (Z-4} = hoof of even-toed ruminants. See **ç'im I**.

çîman I چیمان (Z-1/K/B) = meadow. See **ç'îmen.**

ç'îman II چیمان *f.* **().** train (rail transport). {syn: trên} <Fr chemin de fer [Efr/AD]

ç'îmen چیمەن *m./f.(ZF3)* **(-ê/-a; çîmên** [K/B], **vî ç'îmenî/-ê).** 1) {syn: ç'ayîr[1]; mêrg} meadow; 2) lawn. {also: çîman I (Z-1/K/B); [tchimen] چمن (JJ); <çîmen چیمن/çîm چیم> (HH)} Cf. P čaman چمن, T çimen [Z-1/K/B//A/JB3/IF/JJ/HH/ZF3]

ç'în/çîn [K] چین *f./m.(K)* **(-a/-ê;).** 1) layer, stratum; 2) {syn: sinif [2]} social class: **•Rizgarîya pîreka Kurd, bi ya netewa wê ve û bi taybetî jî bi ya *çîna* wê ve girêdayî ye** (Ber #7,10) The liberation of the Kurdish woman is tied to the liberation of her nation, and especially to the liberation of her *class*. Rus čin чин = 'rank'; Sor çîn چین = 'stratum, layer, fold, class' [Ber/IF/GF/ZF3//K]

çînar چینار (K) = plane tree. See **çinar.**

çîner چینەر (B) = plane tree. See **çinar.**

Ç'înî چینی *adj.* Chinese. Sor Çînî چینی [IFb/ZF3/BF/SS/Wkt/CS]

çîp چیپ *f.(K/B)/m.(ZF3)* **(-a/;-ê/).** 1) {syn: t'eşk} shin, anat. *tibia* (K); calf *(of leg)* (JB3/IFb); 2) bird's leg (Ad). [Ad/K/JB3/IFb/B/GF/TF/OK/ZF3] <ling>

çîpxar چیپخار *adj.* bow-legged, bandy-legged: **•Lênihêřî, ce'nûê 'Elî anîne – *çîpxar*in, qořin** (K'oroẍlî, 142) He saw that the colts that Ali brought were *bow-legged* and scrawny. [K'oroẍlî/K]

ç'îqek چیقەك (JB1-S) = little bit. See **ç'îç'ik**.

ç'îr چیر *m.* **(-ê;).** thin sheet of sun-dried apricot or other dried fruit pulp *eaten as a confection*; dried pressed fruit roll [T pestil; Ar qamar al-dīn قمر الدين] (IF/A/Mzg); plum (JJ); plum skin (BK). {also: çîrik (A/IF-2); [tchirik] چیرك (JJ)} {syn: bastîq} Arm č'ir չիր = 'dried fruit' [BK/IFb/Mzg/Srk/Kş//A/JJ] <alûçe; hêrûg; încas; kaçkaçk; kitik I; mişmiş>

ç'îrandin چیراندِن (M) = to tear, rip (vt.) . See **ç'iřandin**.

çîranok چیرانۆك = tale. See **çîřok.**

ç'îreç'îr چیرەچیر (B) = creak, squeak, crash. See **ç'irke-ç'irk**.

çîrik چیرِك (A/IF) = pressed fruit roll. See **çîr.**

çîrkeçîrk چیرکەچیرك (L) = creak, squeak, crash. See **ç'irke-ç'irk**.

çîřok چیڕۆك *f.* **(-a;-ê).** story, tale, folktale: **•*Çîrok*, şevên zivistanê xweş derbaz dikin** (AB) *Tales* make winter evenings pass nicely **•Dapîra min ji min ra *çîrokan* dibêje** (AB) My grandmother tells me *stories*; **-çîřok gotin** = to tell a story: **•Hûnê ji mi re *çîrokekê bêjin*** (L) You (will) *tell* me *a story*. {also: çêrok (M); çirçîrok; çîranok; çîrong (MK); [tchi-rouk] چیروك (JJ); <çêrok> چیروك (HH)} {syn: ĥekyat; mesel; qise [1]} *See etymological note under ç'êř*. Sor çîrok چیرۆك [L/F/K/A/JB3/IFb/B/JJ/GF/TF/OK//M/HH//MK] <dîrok I; kurteçîřok>

çîřokbêj چیرۆکبێژ *m.&f.* **(-ê/-a;).** storyteller. {also: çîřokvan (K-2/IFb-2/GF-2/TF); ç'îřokzan (K-2); <çêrokvan> چیرۆکڤان (HH)} {syn: biwêj I[2]; ĥekyatçî; ĥik'îyatdar} < çîřok = 'story' + bêj- = 'to tell' [Ba2/K/IFb/GF/ZF3//TF//HH] <dengbêj>

çîřoknivîs چیرۆکنڤیس *m.&f.* **(-ê/-a;).** short story writer, fiction writer: **•Ĥesenê Metê yek ji *çîroknivîsên* serketî ye** (Dqg, 129) H.M. is one of the successful *short story writer*s. < çîřok + nivîs-; Sor çîroknûs چیرۆکنووس [Dqg/K/AA//IFb/GF/SS] <nivîsk'ar; romannivîs>

çîřokvan چیرۆکڤان (K/IFb/GF/TF) = storyteller. See **çîřokbêj.**

ç'îřokzan چیرۆکزان (K) = storyteller. See **çîřokbêj.**

çîrong چیرۆنگ (MK) = tale. See **çîřok.**

ç'îrt چیرت (K/B) = bird droppings. See **ç'êrt.**

ç'îryan چیریان (-ç'îryê-) (M) = to be torn, ripped. See **ç'iřîn**.

çît I چیت *m.* **(-ê;).** 1) {syn: perde} curtain, drape (K); cloth used as curtain and room divider in tents (A/HH): **•Qîza te jî, di nabên *çît* û perda de ye** (L) As for your daughter, she is in the women's quarters [lit. 'among the *drapes* and curtains']; 2) [*f.*(B)] partition (B); partition made of basket weave used in animal pens (IFb); 3) {syn: fûtik (IFb)} woman's white headdress (IFb/Mzg); 4) calico cloth (K/B). {also: [tchit] چیت (JJ); <çît> چیت (HH)} [L/K/A/JB3/IFb/B/JJ/HH/Mzg]

çît II چیت (IFb) = cockerel. See **ç'êt**.

çîtal چیتال (EP-7) = legirons, footshackles. See **çîdar**.

çîv چیڤ *m.* **(-ê;).** cane, stick, staff, rod; stake, pole: **•*Çîvê* stûre, tixûb dûre, *çîvê* zirave tixûb ave** (BF) [If] *the stick* is thick, the border is far, [if] *the stick* is thin, the border is water [i.e., river or sea]. {syn: cinih̃; ço; çogan; çomaẍ; gopal; kevezan; metreq; şiv} [Bw/OK/BF/Wkt]

çîvanok چیڤانۆك *f.* **(-a;-ê).** 1) anecdote, short tale: **•Çi roj naborin bi dehan çîrok û *çîvanok* û peyamên cuda cuda nebihîstîn li mal û li nêv bazarî û li daîrên xwe û li her cihekî, ku filan berpirsî ho got û filan tiştê bûy ... lê piştî lidûvçûneka biçûk dê derkevit *çîvanokeka* vehandî û mezinkirî û dûr ji rastîyan ... ev *çîvanoke* "gotgotk" in** (BH-back cover) No day passes when [we] haven't heard tens of stories and *anecdotes* and tales, at home and in the market and in our offices and everywhere, that so-and-so said such-and-such, or such-and-such happened ... but after a small investigation it turns out to be a made-up and exaggerated *anecdote*, far from the truth ... these *anecdotes* are "rumors"; 2) formula found in folktales (RF) [T tekerleme]. {also:

çivanok (Wlt-56/RF)} [Bw/A/BH/ZF3//Wlt/RF] <qelîbotk; qirwelk>

çîxin چیخِن *m.* **(-ê;-î).** (tent) stake, post; sharp tool for digging up turnips, radishes, etc.: **•Wî *çîxinek* li hêstirê da ku xweş biçit** (FS) He poked the mule with a *stake* so that it would go fast. {syn: sing I} [Bw/FS]

çîya/ç'îya چـیـیـا [F/K/B] *m.* **(çîyayê/çîyê; çîyê, vî çîyayî).** mountain. {also: çiya (JB3/IFb/GF/OK-2/JB1-A); ç'îa (B-2); [tchiia] چیا (JJ); <çiya> چیا (HH)} {syn: banî II; dîyar II; goh} Cf. P čakād چکاد = 'mountain peak/top/crest'; Sor çiya چِیا = kêw کێو & şax شاخ [AB/TF/OK//F/K/B//JJ//JB3/IFb/HH/GF/JB1-A] <çel II; gir II; qunt'ar>

çîyayî/ç'îyayî [K] چـیـیـایـی *m.&f.* **(-yê/;).** mountain dweller, highlander, mountaineer: **•Ez ne *çiyayî* û ne jî deştî me** (Lab, 7) I am neither a *mountain dweller* nor a plains dweller. {also: çiyayî (Lab/IFb/GF/ZF3)} [Lab/IFb/GF/ZF3//K//A/TF]

ço چـــۆ *m./f.(OK)* **(-yê/-wê** [BK-2]**;).** 1) {syn: çîv; çogan; çomaẍ; gopal; metreq; şiv} stick, staff, rod; shepherd's staff; 2) blow or hit with a stick: **•De ka ez binêrim bê te çend *ço* xwarine, tu mêrekî çawa ye!** (Ardû, 117) Let me see how many times you've been hit with their *stick*, let me see what kind of man you are! {also: çop (A-2); çov (HB); [tcho] چو (JJ)} [HB//K/A/JB3/IFb/GF/OK/BK]

çoçik چۆچك *f.* **(-a;-ê).** ladle *(smaller than* **hesk***)*. {also: çûçik III (IFb); <çûçik> چوچك (HH/Hej)} [K/B/FJ/ZF3//IFb/HH/Hej] <çemçik; hesk>

çog چۆگ (L) = knee. See **çok.**

çogan چۆگان *m.* **(-ê;).** 1) {syn: çîv; ço; çomaẍ; gopal; metreq; şivik} stick, staff, rod; 2) sceptre (HH/GF); 3) hockey stick, cross, golf club, etc. {also: çoẍan [çoğan] (A); [tchougan] چـــوگـــان (JJ); <çûgan> چوگان (HH)} [K/A/JB3/IFb/GF/ZF3//JJ/HH]

çok چـــۆك *f./m.(Bw)* **(-a/-ê;-ê/-î).** knee; kneecap (IF): **•Qudûm hat ber *çokêd* min** (K) I felt strong [lit. 'Strength came to my *knees*'] **•Qudûm *çokê* wanda nema** (Z-1) They felt weak; **-çok dan** (K) to genuflect, kneel. {also: çog; çong (BX/EP-4); koç I (Dh); [tchok] چوك (JJ)} {syn: ejnû; k'abok} Sor çok چـۆك [= ejno ئـەژنـۆ]; Hau çoke *f.* (M4) [Z-1/F/K/JB3/IFb/B/JJ/SK/OK/Bw//BX/EP-4//Dh] <sêvsêvok>

ç'ol/çol چـــۆل [K/B] *f.* **(-a;-ê).** desert, wilderness; prairie, steppe: **•Gavan ji *çolê* hat** (L) The cowherd came [back] from *the prairie* **•We ez berdame vê *çolê* da gur min bixwin** (ZZ-6, 127) You have released me into this *wilderness* so that the wolves may eat me; **-çol û çolistan** (B) do. {also: [tchol چول/tcholi چولی] (JJ); <çol چول/ çolistan چـولـسـتـان> (HH)} {syn: aran I; berî II; pasar I (Haz)} < T çöl = 'desert'; Sor çoł چـــۆڵ = 'unoccupied, deserted, open country, desert'; Hau çoł *m.* (M4) [K/B//A/JB3/IFb/JJ/HH/GF/TF/OK/ZF]

ç'olag چۆلاگ *m.&f.* **().** weaver: **•*çolag*: ji kesên caw û qumaş çêdikin, ên ku berê qumaşên şalên rîs dihivastin. An jî kesê wê dezgehê cawçêkirinê bikartînin re tê gotin** (CCG, 273) "*çolag*": so are called people who make fabric and cloth, those who formerly wove the yarn for trouser cloth. Or the people who use looms for making cloth. {also: çilag (IFb/Wkt); çolang (ZF); çolxe (FS); cf. <çolax چولاخ/ çolûxcî چولوخجی> (HH) = group of Kurds who make baskets)} Sor çoła چۆڵا; cf. T çulha = 'weaver' [CCG//ZF//HH//FS//IFb/Wkt]

çolang چۆلانگ (ZF) = weaver. See **ç'olag.**

ç'olik I چۆلِك = dim. of **ç'ol.**

ç'olik II چۆلِك *m./f.(ZF3)* **(-ê/-a;/-ê).** a cheese made of dried yoghurt or strained ***dew*** [*qv.*] [T çökelek]: **•Diya min a rehmetî ... mehên bihar û havînê de *çolika* me çêdikir û dikir nava post** (M. Memdoğlu 3.v.2016) My late mother ... would make our *cholik cheese* in the spring and summer months and would put it in an animal skin. [IFb/Qzl/ZF3] <ç'ortan; lorik; toraq>

ç'olik III چۆلِك *f.* **(-a;).** toilet, restroom, "head," "loo," "can," *slang term.* {also: <çolik> چـولـك (HH)} {syn: avdestxane; avřêj I; daşir (Dyr); destavxane; edebxane [1]; qedemge (Czr)} Sor çolk چۆلك [Msr/HH/GF]

ç'olî/çolî I [K] چـۆلـی *adj.* 1) having to do with the wilderness; native or resident of the wilderness; 2) {syn: hov; k'ûvî; t'oř II; weĥş [3]} wild. [HB/A/ZF3//K]

çolî II چۆلی (Zeb/Hej) = leafy branches used for sheep fodder. See **çilo II.**

çolxe چۆلخە (FS) = weaver. See **ç'olag.**

çomaq چۆماق (F/JJ) = club; staff; rod. See **çomaẍ.**

çomax چـۆمـاخ (K/Ba2/Ag/ZF3) = club; staff; rod. See **çomaẍ.**

çomaẍ چـۆمـاغ *m.* **(-ê; çomêẍ, vî çomaẍî).** 1) {syn: ciniĥ; çîv; ço; çogan; gopal; kevezan; metreq; şiv[dar]}club, cudgel; staff, crook; rod, staff; stick, cane: **•[Pêxember ... melekekî mezin dît ku deholeke zêde cesîm di esto da ye û**

çomax̄ekî **mezin di destî da ye**] (JR-2) The prophet saw a large angel with a very wide drum [strapped] around his neck and a large *stick* in his hand; 2) a blow with a club: •[**Eger mirofek ji tayifa xwendîyan îh̄san û sedeqeyekê weyaxû te'am û zadekî bidine feqîrekî ez dê *çomax̄ekî* li vê deholê bidim**] (JR-2) If someone from the class of the learnèd should give charity or food to a poor person, I will strike a *blow* on this drum. {also: çomaq (F); çomax (K/Ba2-2/Ag); [tchoumaq] چـومـاق (JJ)} Cf. Az T çomaq [JR/Ba2/B//K/Ag/ZF3//F/JJ]

ç'on چۆن (M) = to go. See **ç'ûn**.

çong چۆنگ (BX/EP-4) = knee. See **çok**.

çop چۆپ (A) = stick. See **ço**.

çoqçoq چۆقچۆق (Krç) = turkey *(fowl)*. See **coqcoq**.

çorîn چـــۆریـــن *f.* **().** wild herb that grows in the mountains, used to season rice (similar to ***lûş*** [lîş]): -**birinca bi lûş û çorîn** (Bar) rice seasoned with these herbs. Cf. Sor çinûr چـنـوور = 'aromatic herb resembling dill' [Bar/Zeb/ZF3/FS]

ç'ortan/çortan [K] چـــۆرتـــان *pl./m.(Krç)* **(-ê; ç'ortîn** [Krç], **vî ç'ortanî)** dried cheese made of curds or skimmed milk, rolled into balls (K/IFb); soft Kurdish cheese, curds (JJ): -**dewê ç'ortan** (Krç) yoghurt drink made with dried curds. {also: [tchortan] چورتـان (JJ); <çortan> چـورتـان (HH)} {syn: keşk} <Arm č'or = 'dry' + t'an = 'yoghurt drink [*dew*, T ayran]' [HB/IFb/JJ/HH/GF/TF/Krç/ZF3//K/Tsab] <ç'olik II; giv; toraq>

çov چۆڤ (HB) = stick. See **ço**.

çowal چۆوال = sack. See **ç'ewal**.

ç'ox چـۆخ *m.* **(-ê;).** 1) broadcloth, thick woolen fabric; heavy, coarse cloth: •**Leylê rabû dawa dêrê xwe, *çuxê* xwe bir̄î** (EP-5, #15) Leyla cut off the lap of her dress, of her *coarse coat*; 2) man's long cloth garment (K/B). {also: çoxe (K[s]/GF); çux (K/B); çux̄ (B-2); [tchoukh] چوخ (JJ); <çox> چوخ (HH)} Cf. T çuha = 'broadcloth'; Hau çoxe *f.*= 'homespun chogha jacket' (M4) [HB/K(s)/A/HH/ZF3//K/B/JJ] <cang; caw>

çoxe چۆخه (K[s]/GF) = broadcloth. See **ç'ox**.

ç'oxik چۆخِك = dim. of **ç'ox**.

çox̄an چۆغان (A) = stick. See **çogan**.

çrpî چرپی (HCK) = branch. See **çirpî**.

çrûsk چرووسك (GF) = shine, spark. See **çirûsk**.

ç'u چـــو (Zx/JJ/JB1-A&S/SK/OK-2) = none, not any. See **t'u II**.

ç'ucar چوجار = never. See **t'u car** under **t'u II**.

ç'ukes چوکەس = no one. . See **t'ukes** under **t'u II**.

çulî چـــولـــی (M-Am) = leafy branches used for sheep fodder. See **çilo II**.

ç'une چونه = there is not.. See **t'une** under **t'u II**.

çuq چوق (HB) = branch. See **ç'iq**.

çuqulk چوقولك (IFb) = branch. See **ç'iqil**.

çuqum چوقوم (Zeb) = hook. See **ç'iqil**[2].

ç'ust چـوسـت *adj.* quick, nimble, agile: •**Wezîfa bende ewe bît, biçim, bigerÿêm, li nêzîkêt gundan nêçîrekî we-bînimewe. Wextê ko min dîtewe bihêm, xeber bidem e gurgî, da ew jî bihêt, harî min bihajot, çonko ew ji min *çusttir* o bi-qowettir:e** (SK 6:63) Let it be my duty to go and wander about and discover some prey near the villages. When I have found it let me come and inform the wolf so that he too may come and help me drive it, for he is *more nimble* and stronger than me. {also: çist (K/Tsab)/ç'ist (IFb-2/TF); çûst (IFb-2); <çiste> چصته (HH)} {syn: ç'alak; ç'apik I; ç'eleng[5]} cf. Sor çust-u-çalak چوست و چالاك = 'energetic, lively' [SK/IFb/OK//K/Tsab//TF//HH]

ç'utişt چوتِشت = nothing. See **t'u tişt** under **t'u II**.

çuwal چووال (BK) = sack. See **ç'ewal.**

çux چـــوخ (K/B) = coarse cloth; man's garment. See **ç'ox**.

çux̄ چوغ (B) = coarse cloth; man's garment. See **ç'ox**.

çûçik I/ç'ûç'ik [K/B] چـــووچِـــك *adj.* 1) {syn: çûk II; piçûk; qicik (Bg)} small, little; 2) *[m.]* child (K); 3) {also: <çûç> چـــووچ (HH)} {syn: hêlik[2], m.; kîr; ter̄ik[2]; xir} baby boy's penis (Msr). {çûçiktî} [Ad/Msr/ZF3/G//K/B///HH]

çûçik II چووچِك (IFb) = sparrow. See **çûk I.**

çûçik III چووچِك (IFb/HH) = ladle. See **çoçik**.

çûçiktî/ç'ûç'iktî [K] چـووچِـكـتـی *f.* **().** 1) {syn: zarotî} childhood; 2) childishness. [K]

çûîk چووئیك (IFb) = sparrow. See **çûk I.**

çûîn چووئین (F/K) = to go. See **ç'ûn.**

çûk I/ç'ûk [K] چـــــــــووك *m.(OK)/f.(K)* **(-ê/-a;-î/).** sparrow, zool. *Passer domesticus* (K/IF/JJ); small bird (A/JB3): -**çwîkê beytik** (L) do. {also: ç'ivîk (Ba2/K-2); çîçik III[2] (IFb-2); çûçik II (IFb-2); çûîk (IFb-2); çwîk (L); [tchouk چـــــوك /tchevik چـوك/čučik (Lx) چـچـك] (JJ); <çûk چـوك/çivîk چڤیك> (HH)} {syn: beytik; guncêşk} [L//A/JB3/IFb/JJ/HH/GF/OK//K]

çûk II/ç'ûk [K/B] چووك *adj.* small; young: •**Kevotka *ç'ûk* gote ya mezin** (FK-eb-1) The *youngest* dove said to the oldest one; **-t'ilîya ç'ûk** (B) pinkie, little finger {syn: qilîç'k/tilîya qilîç'kê; *tilîya başikan (IF); [telīye pečūk] (JJ-PS)}. {syn: çûçik I; piçûk; qicik (Bg)} [K/B/Tsab//ZF3]

ç'ûn/çûn [F/K/B] چـــــوون vi. **(-ç'-/[di]her̄-;** *subj.* **biç'im/her̄im;** *imp.* **her̄e!).** 1) to go: **-bi hev ç'ûn** = to come to blows [en venir aux mains]; **-çûyîn-hatin** (Z-1) comings and goings: **•*Çûyîn-hatina* ewqayê bedew û k'ubara qet dilê Memê ne dih̄ejand** (Z-1) *The comings and goings of* such beautiful and noble [creatures] did not move Mem's heart; 2) to fit; **-Du serê çê *naçine* ser be'lgîkî** (Dz) Two good heads *don't fit* on one pillow *[prv.]*. {also: ç'on (M); *ç'ûndin (Diyarbakir-BX); çûîn (F/K); ç'ûyin (BK/Ag); çûyîn (K/B/IF-2); [tchoun چـون /tchouin چـوين] (JJ); <çûn چـون (diçe) (دچـه)> (HH)} **ç'ûn**: see M2, p.71: [Pok. 2. tu̯ei- 1099.] 'to agitate, shake, toss'--reconstructed by Kent as *qi̯eu- (§104): Skt √cyu [cyavati] = 'to move, shake'; O Ir *čyava- (Schwartz) & *šav-/*šyav- (Tsb 37): Av šav-/šyav-; OP šiyav- (pres. šyav-/šav-/š[u]v-) (Kent); Pamir dialects: Ormuri caw-; Parachi čh-/č(h)īm-; Yidgha šūi-; Sanglechi š-; Wakhi Cāw-; Shughni sāw- = 'to go' (Morg); P šodan شـــدن (-šav-) (شـو) = 'to go (Early New P & Afghani) & to become'; Sor çûn چـوون (-ç-); SoK čığın: č-/či-/čė-/čü-/čıg-/čığ- (Fat 367-368, 555); Za şenã [şyayiş] (Todd/Srk); Hau şiey [past only] *vi.* (M4); **her̄-**: [Pok. 1. ser- 909] 'to flow': Skt √sar [sarati] = 'to flow.' Sgd displays a suppletion from the same root: šw-, with past tense xrt- [A/JB3/IFb/JJ/HH/OK//F/K/B//BK/Ag]

*ç'ûndin چوونڍِن (Diyarbakir-BX) = to go. See **ç'ûn.**

ç'ûr I چـوور *m.* **(-ê;).** angora goat, *variety of domestic goat with long, silky hair (mohair) known as **merez** (qv.).* {also: [tchour] چـور (JJ); <çûr> چـور (HH)} {syn: h̄îtik} Sor kûr كـــوور = 'angora kid' [Bw/Elk/IFb/JJ/HH/GF/TF] <kej II; liva; merez; r̄îs>

ç'ûr̄ II/çûr̄ [K/B] چـــــوور *adj. denoting various pigments for hair:* 1) blonde; 2) red-haired, redhead. {also: [tchour] چــور (JJ); <çûr> چــور (HH)} [K/B//IFb/JJ/HH/GF/RZ/ZF3] <kej I>

çûrisîn چوورسين (F) = to shine. See **çirûsîn**.

çûst چووست (IFb) = nimble. See **ç'ust**.

ç'ûyin چووين (BK/Ag) = to go. See **ç'ûn.**

çûyîn چوويين (K/B/IF) = to go. See **ç'ûn.**

çûyîn-hatin چوويين هاتِن (Z-1) = comings and goings. See under **ç'ûn.**

çwîk چـويـك (L) = sparrow: -çwîkê beytik (L) do. See **çûk I.**

D د

-da دا *psp. postpositional suffix indicating position (place where), used in conjunction with prepositions, or alone in certain dialects*: 1) in, at [=**di ...-da**]: •*di* **nav van salên dawî** *de* (ZF3) *in* these last years •**Em Al-p'aşa, pîrejina wî û Memê delalva bihêlin şeherê Muxurzemînê***da* (Z-1, 45) Let us leave Al-pasha, his old wife, and Memê delal *in* the city of Mukhurzemîn •**Min kesek** ***di*** **dinîyayê***da*, ***di nava*** **ecinîya***da* **û** ***di nava*** **'însana***da*, **weke Memê Alan** ***di*** **xorta***da* **delal ne dîtîye** (Z-2, 68) *In* the whole world, *among* jinns and mortals, I haven't seen any young man as beautiful as Memê Alan; **-têda** = in it, inside it [=di wî/wê da]; 2) from, starting from [=**ji...-da**]: •**Roja xweş** ***ji*** **sibehê** ***de*** **xweş e** (BX) A good day is good *from* the morning *on* [*prv.*]; **-jorda** (K/B) from above; **-zûda** (K/B) since a long time ago. {also: -de III (GF/TF/ZF3); [da] دا (JJ)} Sor -da دا [BX/IFb/B/JJ//GF/TF] <di; ji I>

da I دا (IF/A/JJ) = mother. See **dê I**.

da II دا *conj.* 1) {syn: bila; bona [2]; deqene; ȟeta ko [4]; wekî [2]} [+ *subj.*] in order that, in order to, so that *particularly in southern dialects; sometimes best translated with* ***should*** *or* ***let***: •***Da*** **biçîne mal** (M-Ak, 626) *Let us* go home •...***da*** **bizanît nemaye** (M-Ak) He *should* know that there is none left •***Da ne*****mirîtin sermada** (M-Ak, 544) It *ought not to* (be left to) die in the cold •[**Here gazî gundîyan bike,** ***da*** **perêd wan bidim**] (JJ) Go call the villagers, *so that* I can give [them] their money •**Ȟîleyekê bike** ***da*** **... xilas bibîn** (M-Ak, 556) Make some ruse *so that* we may be saved; **-da ko** (BX/K) do.; 2) until. {also: [da] دا (JJ)} [BX/M/K/JJ/JB1-A&S/SK/GF]

da III دا *In Behdini dialects, modal particle + present stem, forms imperfect and conditional (equivalent in meaning to imperfect)*: e.g., **Ez da çim** = **Ez diçûm** = I would go, I used to go. *Only exists in affirmative: for negative*, **Ez nediçûm** = I would not go: •**Eger min serê xo şûştba, ez** ***da*** **baştir** ***bim*** (Bw) If I were to take a shower (lit. 'wash my head'), I *would feel better* •**Mirovek hebo, hemo r̄ojê bi xo** ***da çite*** **çyay,** ***da*** **bi xo piştîyekê dara** ***înite*** **bajerî, bi xo** ***da firoşît, da det*** **bi nan,** ***da beteve*** **bo xo û dayka xo** (M 242:531) Once there was a man who *used to go* every day to the mountains by himself and *bring* a load of wood to town on his back, (when) he *would* himself *sell* it, *spend* (the proceeds) on food and *take it back* (home) for himself and his mother. [M/Şîrin.Exercises in Kurmanji Grammar] <di->

dabaş داباش *f.* **(-a;-ê).** subject, topic: **-dabaş kirin** (IFb) to investigate, look into, research: •**Anku bes e ku bibêjin Kurd** ***dabaşa*** **(bahsa) biskan, çavan û xiyala guliyan û tuncikên xweşik** ***bikin*****, divê ku êdî bahsa Kurdistanê,** ***dabaşa*** **war, zozan, av, çem, kanî, bax, bostan, gul û gulistanên wê** ***bikin*** (Rwş #2,15) In other words, enough of saying that Kurds *investigate* [only] curls of hair, eyes, and imaginings of beautiful bangs and locks; it is time to study Kurdistan, *to investigate* its encampments, pastures, water, rivers, springs, gardens, and flowers. {also: <dabaş> داباش (HH)} {syn: babet I[2]; biyav; mijar} [Rwş/(K)/A/IFb/HH/ZF3]

dabeliandin دابەلئاندن (da-beliîn-) (IFb) = to swallow. See **beli'andin**.

da bellandin دا بەلاندن (GF) = to swallow. See **beli'andin**.

dabeş دابەش *f.* **(-a;-ê).** division, part: **-dabeş[î ...] bûn** (TF/BF) to be divided (into), be distributed: •**Kurtkirinên bi herfa destpêkê, ji alîyê bilêvkirinê va** ***dabeşî*** **du grûpan** ***dibin*** (RR, 21) Abbreviations with the first letter *are divided into* two groups in regard to pronunciation; **-dabeş kirin** (IFb/FJ/GF/RZ/SS/ZF/BF/FD) to distribute; to divide *(also math.)*: •**Mamosta defter û qelem li ser xwendekaran** ***dabeş kirin*** (BF) The teacher *distributed* the notebooks and pens to the students. Sor dabeş kirdin دابەش كردن = 'to distribute, divide' [RR/IFb/FJ/GF/TF/RZ/SS/ZF/BF/FD]

dabeşkirin دابەشكرن *f.* **(-a;-ê).** division *(math.)* [Ar taqsīm تقسيم, T bölme, P taqsīm تقسيم]. {syn: p'arve-kirin} = Sor dabeş kirdin دابەش كردن [Wkt/ZF3/SS]

da•binartin دابنارتن *vt.* **(da-dinêr-).** to plant *(trees)*; to hoist, raise *(flags)*: •**Em ala rengîn** ***dabinêrin*** **bilindciyan** (IFb) Let's *hoist* the colorful flag high. {syn: çikandin I[3]; çikilandin; daçikandin (F/K/JJ)} = Sor naştin نـاشـتـن (-nêj-) [JB3/IFb/OK/ZF3] <ç'andin>

daçek داچـەك *f.* **(-a;-ê).** preposition: -**daçeka duta** (K) paired preposition (e.g., ji ser, li ber; see K2, §386); -**daçeka hêsa/~asan** (K) simple preposition. {syn: bernav} [(neol)K/IFb/GF/TF/OK/ZK3]

daçikan داچـِكـان (TF/FS) = to be stuck; to stand. See **daçikîn**.

da•çikandin داچِكاندن *vt.* **(da-çikîn-).** to plant *(trees, flowers, etc.)*; to insert, stick, thrust, plunge (into stg.). {also: [da-tchikandin] داچِكاندين (JJ)} {syn: çikandin I[3]; çikilandin; dabinartin (JB3/IF); niç'ikandin [3]} = Sor naştin ناشتن (-nêj-) [F/K/IFb/B/JJ/GF/TF/OK] <ç'andin; çikandin I>

daçikiyan داچـِكـِيـان (FJ) = to be stuck; to stand. See **daçikîn**.

da•çikîn داچـِكـيـن *vi.* **(da-çik-).** 1) to be stuck, thrust into, rooted, planted or fixed [T dikilmek, saplanmak, Ar rasaxa رسـخ]; to get stuck (trapped) in: •**Di berbangê de, piştî bahozê, du depên kelekê di qûmê de *daçikiyan*** (Xwende 5.ii.2007) At dawn, after the storm, two boards of the raft *were stuck* in the sand •**Gilç di qadê r̄a *daçika*** (FS) The sharp stick *got rooted* in the field •**Piyê wî di teqnê r̄a *daçika*** (FS) His foot *got stuck* in the mud; 2) to stand up: •**Bi qijîna Dîlberê re hemû malî li ber Neco *daçikiyan*** (Nofa, 91) When D. screamed, the whole house *stood up* [defiantly] •**Dîlberê çû kirasekî reng-xemrî ku dişibê rengê şevê li xwe kir û dîsa hat li ber Neco *daçikiya*** (Nofa, 93) D. went and put on a wine colored gown that resembled the color of night, then came back and *stood* by N. {also: daçikan (TF-2/FS); daçikiyan (FJ); daçikyan (GF)} [Nofa/TF/ZF3//FJ//GF//FS] <asê>

daçikyan داچـِكـيـان (GF) = to be stuck; to stand. See **daçikîn**.

dad داد *f.* **(-a;-ê).** justice, equity, fairness: •**Pêşketina hizra *dadê* li Kurdistanê** (Wkp) The advancement of the concept of *justice* in Kurdistan. {syn: dadmendî; îsaf} Mid P dād [d't/d'd] = 'law, justice'; P dād داد; Sor dad داد [Wkp/K/A/IFb/ZF3/FS/Wkt/BF/FD]

da•dan دادان *vt.* **(da-d-).** 1) {syn: daxistin [4]; hilkirin[2]; pêxistin; vêxistin; ≠temirandin; ≠vemirandin; ≠vêsandin} to light, kindle, ignite *(stove)*: •**Jinikê r̄abû tendûr *dada*** (Dz) The woman got up and *lit* the stove •**Êzingan bîne, em agir *dadin*** (AB) Bring firewood, so that we can *light* the fire; 2) to lock, shut up: •**Dergêd kelêye pola *dadin*** (Z-1) *Lock* the steel gates of the fortress; 3) {syn: danîn [5]; veniştin} to alight, land, perch, descend from on high (Hk/IFb): •**Hind dît' teyrekî go 'miş', *dada* ser termê wî** (M-Zx, #766, 354) He saw a bird which made a whizzing sound and *alighted* on his [uncle's] body; 4) to grab, descend upon, swoop down upon [+ *dat. constr.*]: •**Gur *dada* bizinê** (IFb) The wolf *grabbed* the goat •**Hulî *dada* mirîşkê û bir** (IFb) The eagle *swooped down on* the chicken and bore it away •**Ji wan yeke ... çend lingan di bîrê da diçe xwarê, *dadide* tûlika xort û dikişîne derve** (Ardû, 68) One of them ... goes down a few feet into the well, *grabs* the young man's curls and pulls him out •**Kûçik *dada* hestî** (CS) The dog *grabbed* the bone. {also: [dadan] دادان (JJ); <dadan دادان (dadide) (دادده)> (HH)} [F/Dz/K/A/JB3/IFb/B/JJ/HH/CS/ZF/Ardû] <[1] serçavk>

dadga دادگا (OK) = court. See **dadgeh**.

dadgah دادگاه (A) = court. See **dadgeh**.

dadge دادگه (K) = court. See **dadgeh**.

dadgeh دادگـەه *f.* **(-a;-ê).** court *(of law)*, law court: •**DED (=Dadgeha Ewlekariya Dewletê)'a Stenbolê** (Wlt 2:103, 8) The State Security Court of Istanbul. {also: dadga (OK); dadgah (A); dadge (K); dadigeh (IFb/OK-2)} Sor dadga دادگا = 'law-court' [(neol)VoA/Wlt/GF/TF//OK//A//K//IFb] <dadpirs>

dadger دادگـەر *m.&f.* **(-ê/;).** judge: •**Wî derdixin pêşberê *dadger*** (H.Akyol. Zava ker in, 9) They bring him before *the judge*. {also: dadgêr̄ (Wkt)} {syn: dadpirs; ħakim; qazî} Sor dadger دادگـەر [(neol)H.Akyol/K/IFb/FJ/GF/TF/ZF3/BF/FD/RZ/SS/CS//Wkt]

dadgêr̄ دادگێر (Wkt) = judge. See **dadger**.

dadigeh دادِگەه (IFb/OK) = court. See **dadgeh**.

dadmend دادمەند *adj.* just, fair, equitable. {dadmendî} [(neol)K(s)/IFb/TF/OK/ZF]

dadmendî دادمـەنـدی *f.* **(-ya;-yê).** justice, fairness, equity: •**Komara Tirkiyê ne weke berê ye. Îro pêşketin, wekhevî heye, *dadmendî* (edalet) heye** (Wlt 2:59, 13) The Turkish Republic is not like before. Nowadays there is progress [and] equality, there is *justice*. {syn: dad; îsaf} [(neol)Wlt/IFb/TF/OK/ZF] <dadmend>

dadpirs دادپِـرس *m.* **(-ê;).** judge *(in a court of law)*, examining magistrate. {syn: dadger; ħakim; qazî} [(neol)A/GF/OK/ZF] <dadgeh>

daêxistin داﺋـێـخـسـتـن (Zeb) = to lower; to close. See **daxistin**.

daf داف (IFb) = trap. See **dav I**.

dafik دافك (Msr/A) = trap. See **dav I**.

da•gerandin داگەراندن *vt.* **(da-gerîn-).** 1) to cause s.o. to turn off *(the road)*; to mislead, lead astray: **•Gelek rêwîngê mîna te ji rê *dadigerîne*** (EP-7) She *leads* many travelers like you off the road; 2) to take or bring down again *(from a high place)*, to lower again (Mzg/IFb) 3) to bring back (JB3/GF); to bring or take back, to return *(vt.)* (Haz); 4) to send away (JB3); to send back (IF). [EP-7/K/JB3/IFb/B/GF/TF/OK/Haz/Mzg/ZF] <dagerîn>

dageriyan داگـەرِيـان (JB3/OK) = to come back. See **dagerîn**.

da•gerîn داگەرين *vi.* **(da-ger-).** 1) to turn, shift, move (K): **•Wexteke kuçer *dadigerin*** (J) Once, the nomads were moving... [lit. '*are moving*']; 2) to return, come back (IFb/TF/GF). {also: dageriyan (JB3/OK); dageryan (GF)} [K/IFb/B/ZF//JB3/OK//GF] <dagerandin>

dageryan داگەريان (GF) = to come back. See **dagerîn**.

dagir داگِر (K/ZF) = occupying. See **dagîr**.

dagirker داگِركەر (Wlt) = occupier. See **dagîrker**.

da•girtin داگـِرتـن *vt.* **(da-gir-).** 1) {syn: t'ijî kirin} to fill up: **•Ji mi re tasekê dahêjin bîrê, *ezê* pê ji we re avê *dagirim*** (L) Lower a bowl into the well for me, I *will fill* it with water for you **•Ji dêl xweşiyê, te dilê min ji xema û kesera *dagirtiye*** (BX) Instead of joy, you *have filled* my heart with pain and concern; **-tifing dagirtin** (IFb) to load a rifle; 2) {syn: bar kirin} to load up (IFb); **-bar dagirtin** (IFb) to pack up a load; 3) to seize from all sides (JJ). {also: [da-ghirtin] داگـرتـيـن (JJ); <dagirtin داگرتن (dadigre) (دادگره)> (HH)} [L/K/A/JB3/IFb/B/JJ/HH/SK/GF/TF/OK/ZF]

dagîr داگـيـر: **-dagîr kirin** (IFb/OK) to occupy, annex, conquer. {also: dagir (K/ZF)} Sor dagîr kirdin داگير كردن = 'to seize, occupy militarily' [IFb/OK//K/ZF]

dagîrk'ar داگـــيــــركــــار (K[s]/OK) = occupier. See **dagîrker**.

dagîrker داگــيــركــەر *m.* **(-ê;).** occupier, invader; conquerer, member of an occupation force; colonizer: ***•Dagirkeran* li her parçeyên Kurdistanê ev jenosîd ceribandine, lê tu car serfiraz nebûne** (Wlt 1:35, 2) *Occupiers* in all parts of Kurdistan have attempted genocide, but they have never succeeded [in wiping out the Kurds] ***•Dagîrkerên* xwînmij, gelek derd û kul dagirtine serê me** (Wlt 1:35, 4) Bloodthirsty *invaders* have filled our heads with much pain and grief. {also: dagirker (Wlt-2); dagîrk'ar (K[s]/OK)} Cf. Sor dagîrker داگـيـركـەر = 'occupying force' [(neol)Wlt/IFb//K(s)/OK]

daha داها (B) = still; already. See **diha**.

da•hatin داهـاتِـن *vi.* **(da[t]ê-).** 1) {syn: dak'etin; peya bûn} to descend, go or get down: **•Berf *datê*** (IF) Snow *is coming down*; 2) to land (GF/OK). [K/JB3/IFb/GF/OK] <dahiştin; dakirin; daxistin [1]>

dahelandin داهـەلانـدن (da-helîn-) (IFb/OK) = to lower. See **dahiştin**.

dahelanîn داهەلانين (OK) = to lower. See **dahiştin**.

dahêlan داهـێــلان (B/JB1-A/SK/OK) = to lower. See **dahiştin**.

dahêlandin داهـێـلانـدن (B/A/GF) = to lower. See **dahiştin**.

dahilandin داهِلاندِن (OK) = to lower. See **dahiştin**.

dahilanîn داهِلانين (K) = to lower. See **dahiştin**.

da•hiştin داهِـشـتِـن *vt.* **(da-hêl-[K]/da-hêj- [L]).** to lower, let down *(e.g., into a pit)*: **•Gelî bira, şerîtî bi newqa mi ve girê bidin û min *dahêjin* bîrê** (L) Brothers, tie a cord around my waist and *let* me *down into* the well **•B. bi şerîtî girêdan û *dahiştin* [sic] hindurê bîrê** (L) They tied a cord to B. and *let* him *down into* the well **•Ji mi re tasekê *dahêjin* bîrê, ezê pê ji we re avê dagirim** (L) *Lower* a bowl into the well for me, I will fill it with water for you. {also: dahelandin (da-helîn-) (IFb/OK); dahelanîn (OK-2); dahêlan (B/JB1-A/SK/OK-2); dahêlandin (B-2/A/GF); dahilandin (OK-2); dahilanîn (da-hilîn-) (K-2); dehlendin (Wlt 2:59, 15); [dà-hichtin] داهشـتـيـن (JJ)} {syn: dakirin; daxistin [1]} Sor dahêştin داهـێـشـتـن/dahêłan داهێلان = 'to let down' [L/K/JJ//IFb/OK//B/JB1-A/SK//A/GF//Wlt]

daholqut داهۆلقوت (FS) = drummer. See **diholkut**.

daholvan داهۆلڤان *m.&f.* **(-ê/;).** drummer: **•Di govendê de tevgera *daholvanan* jî pirr girîng e** (Nbh 135:60) In folk dancing, the behavior *of the drummers* is very important. {syn: defçî; deholjen; diholkut} [Nbh/TF/ZF/Wkt] <mirt'ib; zirnabêj>

dahş داهش (CS) = donkey foal. See **dehş**.

da•k'etin داكـەتِـن *vi.* **(da-k'ev-).** 1) to descend, go down: **•Gavan û jina xwe *daketin* nav gund** (L)

The cowherd and his wife *went down* to the village •**Kurê pîrê *daket* sûkê** (L) The old woman's son *went (down)* to the market; 2) to come out and fight: •**Ezê *dakevim* şerê te** (L) I will take you on [in hand-to-hand combat] [lit. 'I *will descend* to your battle'] •**[Osman beg got "herdu bira *dakevin* hev." Herdu *daketin* hev, ji subehî ĥetta êvarî]** (PS-I 13:30, 1.16-17) Osman beg said, "Let the two of them *fight* each other." The two of them *fought* each other, from morning until evening •**Ya xortê delal, *dakeve* meydanê** (L) O dandy youth, *come out* to the [battle] ground! {also: [da-ketin] داكـتـيـن (JJ); <daketin داكـتـن (dadikeve) (دادكڤه)> (HH)} {syn: dahatin} [K/A/JB3/IFb/B/JJ/HH/GF/TF/OK] <daxistin [1]>

da•kirin داكِـرِن *vt.* **(da-k-).** 1) {syn: dahiştin} to lower, let down; to throw, bring down (K); to unload: •**Ezê îro tasa mewtê li devê te *dakim*!** (L) Today I'*ll ram* the cup of death into your mouth [i.e., down your throat]!; 2) to take in *(an animal)*: •**Kerê wî ji derwe dê mînit, kes *nadaket*** (SK 25:231) His donkey will stay outside, nobody *will take* it *in* (to its stall); 3) *to press (K); {syn: palandin; parzinandin} to strain, filter (IFb); 4) to dip (A/JB3/TF); 5) *to exchange, switch, trade (IFb); 6) *to imprison (HH). {also: <dakirin داكرن (dadike) دادكه> (HH)} [L/K/A/JB3/IFb/HH/SK/GF/TF/OK]

dal دال (IFb) = valley; forest. See **dehl**.

dalebaşî دالـەباشى (K/Tsab) = food carrier at weddings. See **dolebaşî**.

daleh دالـه (FS) = gentle rebuke. See **dalehî**.

dalehî دالـەهـى *f.* (). gentle rebuke, reproach, or chiding: •**Wî gelek *dalehî* ji Zoroyî kirin ku şeřî nekit** (FS) He begged Zoro (lit. 'made many *friendly rebukes* to Z.') not to go to war. {also: daleh (FS-2); dalihî (Wkt-2)} [Dh/Wkt/ZF3/BF/FD/FS]

daleqandin دالـەقـانـدِن (IFb/HH/TF) = to hang. See **daliqandin**.

daleqîn دالـەقين (TF) = to hang *(vi.)*. See **daliqîn**.

daleřeş دالـەڕەش *m.* **(-ê;).** lammergeier, bearded vulture, ossifrage, zool. *Gypaetus barbatus*. {also: delaş (AA)} Sor dałaş دالاش /daraş داراش (Arbil) [Zeb//AA]

dalihî دالِهى (Wkt) = gentle rebuke. See **dalehî**.

da•liqandin دالِـقـانـدِن *vt.* **(da-liqîn-).** to hang (past: hung) *(vt.)*; to hang up *(e.g., coat on a hook)* (Msr): •**Çel keleş ... îslehê xwe timam *daliqandine*** (L) 40 brigands ... *hung up* their weapons •**Min şerma serê xwe *daliqand*, caba wî neda** (Ba2:2, 207) I *hung* my head in shame, did not answer him; -**xwe daleqandin** (IFb) to hang o.s. (past: hanged). {also: daleqandin (IFb); dalqandin (A/GF); [dālaqāndin] دالـقـانـديـن (JJ); <daleqandin دالەقاندن (dadileqîne) (دادلەقينه)> (HH)} {syn: darda kirin; hilawîstin; řaxistin} Cf. Ar ʻallaqa علّق = 'to hang' [L/K/JB3/B/OK/Msr//A/GF//IFb/HH/TF//JJ] <daliqîn>

da•liqîn دالِـقـيـن *vi.* **(da-liq-).** to hang *(vi.)*, to be hanging. {also: daleqîn (TF); dalqîn (GF); [daliqin] داليقين (JJ)} {syn: darda bûn (F/IFb)} [F/K/IFb/B/JJ/OK//TF//GF] <daliqandin>

dalqandin دالقاندِن (A/GF) = to hang. See **daliqandin**.

dalqîn دالقين (GF) = to hang *(vi.)*. See **daliqîn**.

daman دامـان (IFb/OK) = flap, panel *(of a dress)*. See **damen**.

damar دامار (K/IFb/JB3) = vein. See **t'emar**.

damarî دامـارى (Ba/IFb/B/JJ) = stepmother. See **dêmařî**.

dam•e دامه *f.* **(;•ê).** checker(s), draughts: -**kevirê temê** (F) checker piece; -**lîstina temê** (F) game of checkers. {also: teme I (F); [tama طاما /tamé طامه/ dama دامه/ ضامه] (JJ); <dame> دامه (HH)} {syn: k'işik [2]} [Z-2/K/IFb/HH/JB1-S/GF/OK//JJ/F] <kevir [2]; k'işik>

damen دامـەن *m./f.(FS/BF)* **(-ê/damnê** [EP-7]**/-a;).** 1) {syn: dang; daw I[2]} skirt, flap, lower panel, hem *(of a coat, dress)* (K[s]/IFb/JJ); 2) {syn: k'oş} lap; loins (EP-7): •**ji *damnê* dê** (EP-7) from [his] mother's *lap/loins*; 3) foot, skirt *(of a mountain, etc.)* (K[s]). {also: daman (IFb/OK); damil (FS-2); dehmen (FS/BF); [damen] دامـن (JJ)} Cf. P dāman دامـن; Sor dawên داوێـن = 'skirt, lower end, hem; foot of mountain' [EP-7/K(s)/JJ//IFb/OK//FS/BF] <[3]: p'al [2]; qûndax̌>

da•mezirandin دامـەزِرانـدِن *vt.* **(da-mezirîn-).** to found, establish, set up: •**Di salên 1843-1846-an de Mîr Bedir-Xan ji bo *damezrandina* Kurdistanek serbixwe li dijî Împaratoriya Osmanî rabû** (Rnh - intro) In the years 1843-1846, the emir Bedir-Khan rose up against the Ottoman Empire for *the establishment of* an independent Kurdistan •**Partiya Demo[k]rat ya Kurdistanê kengî *hatiye damezrandin*?** (Wkt) When *was* the KDP *founded*? {also: damezrandin (A/Wkt/FS); damizrandin (IFb)} {syn: saz kirin} Sor damezrandin دامەزراندِن [K(s)/ZF3//A/Wkt/FS//IFb] <li dar xistin>

da•mezirîn دامەزِرین *vi.* **(da-mezir-).** 1) to be set up, founded, established; 2) to settle down, set o.s. up, install o.s.: **•Mala Baramî li bajarî *damezra*** (FS) B.'s household settled down in the town; 3) *[f.]* establishment (IF). {also: damezran (FS); damizrîn (IFb)} Cf. Sor damezran دامەزران = 'to be established, get settled' [S&E/K/A//IFb]

dameziriner دامەزِرینەر (ZF) = founder. See **damezrîner**.

damezran دامەزران (FS) = to be established; to settle down. See **damezirîn**.

damezrandin دامەزراندِن (A/Wkt/FS) = to establish. See **damezirandin.**

damezrêner دامەزرێنەر (CS/SS) = founder. See **damezrîner**.

damezrîner دامەزرینەر *m.&f.* **(-ê/;).** founder, establisher: **•*Damezrînerê* Koma Palyaçoyên Kurd Keremo** (VoA, 30.ix.2013) Keremo, *the founder of* the Society of Kurdish Clowns. {also: dameziriner (ZF); damezrêner (CS/SS)} Sor damezrêner دامەزرێنەر [(neol.)VOA//ZF//CS/SS]

damil دامِل (FS) = hem (of dress). See **damen**.

damilandin دامِلاندِن (IFb) = to close *(one's eyes)*. See **damirandin**.

da•mirandin دامِراندِن *vt.* **(da-mirîn-).** to close, shut *(one's eyes)*: **•Çavê xwe yê çepê *dadimirand*, nîşandikir** ... (Cankurd:RN2:56[1998]10) He *would close* his left eye, and make a sign ... **•Min bi lez û bez, xwe tev cilên xwe xiste bin nivînê û çavên xwe *damirandin*** (Cankurd:RN2:56 [1998]12) I quickly jumped into bed with my clothes on and *closed* my eyes. {also: damilandin (IFb)} {syn: miçandin} [RN2//IFb]

damizrandin دامِزراندِن (IFb) = to establish. See **damezirandin.**

damizrîn دامِزرین (IFb) = establishment. See **damezirîn**.

dan I دان vt. **(-d-/-de- [Bw/M]).** 1) to give: **•Ez *didim* ê** = I *give* him/her **•Min *da* ê** = I *gave* him/her **•...ku bive *bidê*** (Dz) ... to take [it and] *give* [it] *to him* **•Hakim qîza xwe *na de* bi pera, *dide* bi şerda** (L) The king *doesn't give* his daughter [in exchange] for money, he *gives* [her] for tasks; **-dan dest** (IFb) to hand over, deliver, surrender stg., give away**; -xwe dan dest** (Qzl/CS) to give o.s. away, surrender o.s., capitulate: **•Di vê jêgirtinê de ji bo edebiyatê du pêwîstî *xwe didin dest*** (R. Alan. Bendname, 109) In this quotation 2 requirements for literature *give themselves away*; **-dan dû/pey** = to follow, pursue. See **dû III** and **pey I**; **-dan ser** (FK-eb-1) to chase, pursue, bear down on, gain on: **•Carekê zilamek li çolê roviyekî dibîne. Ew *dide ser* û rovî jî direve** (ZZ-3, 149) Once a man sees a fox in the wilderness. He *gives chase* and the fox runs away **•Sîarekî wê *daye ser* xezalê** (FK-eb-1) A horseman *was gaining on* the gazelle; 2) {syn: danîn; kirin [2]} to put: **•Ê ko keska pêxember *dide* serê xwe, nahêle tu carî bilewite, ê te, tu ê herî keska pêxember, di nav heriyê *bidî* û tu qîmeta wê nizanî** (RN 3:52, 2) He who *puts* the green [turban?] of the prophet on his head, never lets it get dirty, and you, you will go *put* the prophets green [turban?] in the mud, you don't know its worth **•Kewaniya xwe ya ciwan *dide* kêleka xwe û ji bajarê D'ê hêdî hêdî ber bi bakur dajo** (Lab, 6) He *puts* his pretty wife at his side and slowly drives north from the city D **•Paşê bazirganbaşî Ûsib *dide* ser devekê** (Ba) Then the caravan leader *puts* Joseph on [the back of] a camel; **-dan ber** (Wkt/ZF3) to expose s.o. to, force stg. on s.o., *as in the following examples*: **-dan ber beran** (Hk)/~ **ber keviran** (IFb) to stone to death, pelt with stones {syn: kevir kirin; zebandin}: **•Em te ne ji ber karekî qenc *didin ber keviran*, lê em te ji ber çêran *didin ber keviran*!** (Încîl: John 10:33) For a good work we *stone* thee not; but for blasphemy *do* we *stone* thee **•Polîsan gaza rondikrêj li xelkê reşand. Xelkê jî ew *dan ber beran*** (Hk) The police sprayed tear gas at the people. The people *pelted them with stones*; **-dan ber lingan** (K)/~**bin lingan** (RZ/CS) to trample, stomp on, crush; to disregard, make light of {syn: 'eciqandin; p'elaxtin; pêpes kirin; t'episandin}: **•Ezê sonda xwe *bidime ber lingan* û bêbextiyê li xatûna xwe ya rihmetî bikim** (Ardû, 172) I *will trample on* [or, disregard] my oath and dishonor my late wife; **-dan der** (ZF3) to reveal, show, express (one's feelings): **•Her çend veqetîna ji Gulê ji bo wî zehmet bû jî mêr bû û li xwe danetanî *bide der*** (R.Sorgul. Gurxenêq, 60) No matter how difficult it was for him to be parted from G., he was a man and he did not let himself *show* it;**-xwe dane ber**: a) to hide *(vi.)*: **•*Xwe da ber* tûmekî** (L) He placed himself (i.e., *hid*) behind a bush; b) to expose o.s. to, be exposed to:

•**Li demê havînê bi mîlyona xelk** ***xwe didene ber*** **tava rojê da ku esmer bin** (Ak) During the summer millions of people lie in (i.e., *expose themselves to*) the sun to get a tan; -**xwe dan ber (ziyanê,** *etc.*) (Wkt): to take or run a risk; to take or assume responsibility for: •**Tu çima** ***xwe nadî ber*** **vî karî?** (Kk) Why *don't you shoulder* your responsibility?; -**xwe dane paş** = to retreat. See **paş**; -**xwe ji ber** ***ft-î*** **dan alî** (Kk) to shirk one's responsibility: •**Çima tu** ***xwe ji ber*** **kar** ***didî alî?*** (Kk) Why are *you shirking* your responsibility? [lit. 'Why are you *stepping aside from* the job?']; 3) to pay: -**p'ere dan** (K)/**pare dan** (IFb) to pay: •**Babê min, ko ewe dikir,** ***pare*** **bi kîsê wî dima yan** ***dida?*** **... madam dûmaê dan bît, şeř û kêşekêş çi fayde ye?** (SK 14:144) When my father did this did the money stay in his purse or *did he pay*? ... since one has to pay in the end, what is the point of fighting and struggling? •***Perên*** **ku** ***didane*** **me ne pir bin jî, dîsa jî ji meaşên hemû karmend û karkerên wan zêdetir bûn** (AW72B3) Even if they didn't *pay* us much, it was still more than the salaries of all the other employees and workers; 4) [+ *inf.*] to make, let, cause stg. to happen: •**Wî jêre** ***da*** **zanîn ko...** = He *let* him know that... •**Ew bazirgan** ***dide*** **sekinandinê** (Ba) He *had* the caravan halt •**Kevotka M.** ***dane*** [sic] **razandinê** (EP-7) The doves *put* M. to bed •**Tu dikarî bi kurtayî** ***xwe bidî naskirin*****?** (Ber) Can you briefly *introduce yourself*? {also: dayin I (BK); dayîn I (K/B/Ag); [dàin داين /dan دان] (JJ); <dan دان (dide) (دده)> (HH)} [Pok. dō- 223.] 'to give': O Ir *dā- (Tsb 43): Av dā- (pres dā-/dadā-/daθā-); OP [1]dā- (Kent); P dādan دادن; Sor dan دان (-de-: *3rd pers. sing.* -da[t]); SoK dâyın: da-/dė-/d- & dâ- (Fat 421, 557); Za danã [dayiş] (Todd); Hau day (de-) *vt.* (M4); cf. also Lat dare; Gr didōmi δίδωμι; Rus da(va)t′ да(ва)ть; Arm tal (W dal) տալ [A/JB3/IF/JJ/HH/M//K/B/Ag//BK]

dan II دان *m.(B/OK)/pl.(K)* **(-ê; dên** [B]**).** seed, kernel; grain, *particularly threshed and crushed grain, used in making soups and the like*; cooked grains of wheat (Haz). {also: dehn (K-2); de'n III (B/K-2); [dan دان/dayn/dahen داهن] (JJ)} Cf. P dāne دانه = 'grain, seed, stone (of fruit)'--> T tane; Sor dan دان = 'grain' & denik دەنك = 'single grain' [AB/K/A/IFb/JJ/SK/GF/OK/Haz/Qzl/Wn] <danhêrk; danqut; danû; ħeb; lib>

dan III دان *m.* **(-ê;).** 1) eight-hour period, one-third (1/3) of a day: -**de'nê êvarê** (K) eventide, evening; -**de'nê nîvro** (K) noontime, noon; -**de'nê sibê** (K) morning time, morning: •**Memê mirîye** ***danê sibê*****, ez negihîjime** ***danê nîvřoja*** (Z-1) Mem died in *the morning*, I won't live to see *the noon*; 2) noontime feeding *(of animals)*; lunchtime, lunch: •**Dayka we hate** ***de'na*** (J) Your mother has come for *lunch* •**Hûn paşê derî vekin, werne** ***de'na*** (J) Then you open the door, come to *lunch* •**Wexta** ***de'na*** **nîne, dengê dya me zirave** (J) It's not *lunchtime*, [and] our mother's voice is soft [unlike the voice at the door]; 3) {syn: nîvro} noon. {also: de'n II (K/B/J)} [J/K//Z-1/JB3/IFb/GF/TF/OK] <şevîn>

danan دانان (da-nê-) (SK) = to put down, settle. See **danîn**.

danaqut داناقوت, f. (JB1-A/OK) = crushed wheat. See **danqut**.

danequt دانەقوت, m. (OK) = crushed wheat. See **danqut**.

dang دانگ *f.* **(-a;-ê).** 1) {syn: damen; daw I} hem, lower part of woman's dress: •***Dang*** **di binyata xwe de lêva jêrî ya kirasê jinê ye** (Sêmêl-Ertoşî) *The hem* [dang] is basically the lower 'lip' of a woman's dress; -**danga kirasî** (FS) do.; 2) {syn: damen; k'oş} lap: •**Li devera me Sêmêlê her kesê mirov zaroyê xwe di** ***danga*** **wî de sunet bikit dibite kirîvê mala wî zarokî û viyan di navbera wan de peyda dibit** (Sêmêl-Ertoşî) In our region of Sêmêl, anyone in whose *lap* a [male] child is circumcised becomes the 'kirîv' [± godfather] of that child's household, and good will reigns between them •**Şerma jinê di koşa/*****danga*** **wê de ye** (Sêmêl-Ertoşî) A woman's private parts are [lit. 'shame is'] in her *lap*; •**Zařok rûnişt di** ***danga*** **dayikê de** (Wkt) The child sat in the mother's *lap*; 3) bottom part, foot (of mountain), base, foundation (of house): •***Danga*** **malê jî heye ku wateya binê malê didit** (Sêmêl-Ertoşî) There is also the *dang* of the house, which means the foundation of the house •**Gundê me li** ***danga*** **çiyaye** (BF) Our village is at *the bottom/base of* the mountain. [Sêmêl-Ertoşî/FS/BF/Wkt/ZF3]

danhêrk دانهێرك *f./m.* **(-a/-ê;).** type of crushed wheat *(more finely ground than **savar**, less finely ground than **simîd**)*. {FS: *m.* when uncooked; *f.* when cooked} {also: danhûrik (CB); danhûrk, m. (OK/JB1-A)} <dan II + hêr- = 'to grind'/hûr = 'tiny' [Bw/GF/ZK3/FS//CB//JB1-A/OK] <dan II>

danhûrik دانـــــهـــــوورِك (CB) = crushed wheat. See **danhêrk**.

danhûrk دانـهـوورك, m. (OK/JB1-A) = crushed wheat. See **danhêrk**.

Danimarkî دانِـمـارکـی (BF/SS) = Danish; Dane. See **Danîmarkî**.

danî I دانی *pp./adj.* placed, located, situated: **•Çel text di hindurê wê de *danî* ne** (L) 40 beds were *placed/located* in it. pp. of **danîn** [L] <danîn>

danî II دانی (CB/JJ) = boiled wheat. See **danû**.

danîk دانیك (FS) = boiled wheat. See **danû**.

Danîmarkayî دانـیـمـارکـایـی (ZF3) = Danish; Dane. See **Danîmarkî**.

Danîmarkî دانـیـمـارکـی *adj.* 1) Danish; 2) [*m.&f.* ().] Dane. {also: Danimarkî (BF/SS); Danîmarkayî (ZF3-2); Danmarkî (Wkt-2); Denîmarkî (IFb)} Sor Danîmarkî دانیمارکی [Wkt/CS/ZF3//BF/SS//IFb]

danîn دانین *vt.* **(da[t]în-; imp. dayne/deyne/ dêne; fut. ezê dênim/daynim).** 1) to put, place: **•Azad jî pirtûka xwe ... *datîne* ser maseyê** (AW69B8) Azad *puts* his book on the table **•Ew zêrê gerdena xwe û guharê xwejî *datîne* der t'aê mêzînê** (Ba) She *puts* the gold of her necklace and her earrings ont the pan of the scales **•Nanê xwe *danî* ber xwe nan xwar** (Dz) He *put* his bread before himself (=he took it out) and ate **•Tembûra xwe *danî* ser çoga xwe** (L) He *put* his tambour (a stringed instrument) on his knee; **-serê xwe danîn** = to lie down [lit. 'to put one's head down'] {syn: r̄amedîn}: **•B. *serê xwe danî* û raket** (L) B. *lay down* and went to sleep; **-şer̄ danîn** = to combat, fight: **•*Emê vira şer̄ekî daynin*** (Z-1) We *will battle* each other here; -**xwe cîyê** [or **dewsa**] ***fk-ê/ft-î* danîn** (XF) to pose as, pretend (to be), feign: **•Lê Ûsiv *xwe dewsa* ker̄a *datîne* û naxwaze Zelîxêr̄a xeberde** (BA3-3, #28) But Joseph *pretends to be* deaf [lit. '*puts himself in the place of* the deaf'] and refuses to speak [lit. 'does not want to speak'] to Zulaikha; 2) {syn: şiqitandin} to remove, take off *(clothing)*: **•Çel kevok hatin û libsê xwe *danîn*** (L) 40 pigeons came and *took off* their garb; 3) to name: **•*Navê* yekê *datîne* Şenglo** (J) She *names* one of them "Shenglo"; 4) to subside, abate: **•Ko usa dibêjin, hêrsa Qeret'aj-dîn *datîne*** (Z-3) When they say this, Q.'s anger *subsides*; 5) {syn: dadan [3]; veniştin} to land, alight, perch *(of birds)*; to land *(of airplanes)*; to settle: **•Teyrekî ser serê darê *danî bû*** (EH) A bird *had alighted* on the top of the tree. {also: danan (da-nê-) (SK); [danin] دانـیـن (JJ); <danîn دانـیـن (datîne) (داتینه)> (HH)} although seems to be da- + anîn, may actually come from [Pok. 2. dhē- 235.] 'to set, put': Skt. dhā-; Av dā-; OP ²dā- = 'put, make, create' (Kent); but cf. Mid P nihādan (nih-) = 'put, place, establish' (M3); Sor da-nan دانـان (da-nê-); SoK nâyın: na-, nė-, n-/n[y]â- (Fat 357, 558) [F/K/A/JB3/IFb/B/JJ/HH/ZF//SK]

dankut دانـــــکـــــوت (IFb/GF) = crushed wheat. See **danqut**.

Danmarkî دانـــمـــارکـــی (Wkt) = Danish; Dane. See **Danîmarkî**.

dano دانۆ (Qzl) = boiled wheat. See **danû**.

danqut دانـقـوت *f.(JB1-A/FS)/m.(FS)* **(-a/; /-î).** type of crushed wheat, for use in cooking. {FS: *m.* when uncooked; *f.* when cooked} {also: danaqut, f. (JB1-A/OK); danequt, m. (OK-2); dankut (IFb/GF)} <dan II + qut-/kut- = 'to beat' [Dh/FS//JB1-A/OK/./IFb/GF] <dan II>

danustandin دانـوسـتـانـدِن (JB1-S) = commerce; relations. See **dan û standin**.

danû دانــــوو *m.(B)/f/(FS)/pl.(K)* **(/-ya; /-[y]ê).** boiled whole wheat [T hedik]. {also: danî II (CB-2); danîk (FS-2); dano (Qzl); de'nû (B); [dani دانـــی/ dahni دهـنـی] (JJ); <danû> دانـو (HH)} Sor danû دانـوو = 'grain, cereal' & danûle دانـوولـه 'boiled wheat, porridge of boiled wheat & chick-peas' [Qzl//K/A/IFb/HH/CB/Kmc-2421/FS//B//JJ/CB] <dan II; qeynok>

danûsitandin دانـووسِـتـانـدِن (TF) = commerce; relations. See **dan û standin**.

dan û standin دان و سـتـانـدِن [GF]/**danûstandin** دانـووسـتـانـدِن [Wlt/IFb/OK] *vt.* **(-d- û -stîn-).** 1) to deal, transact business; to negotiate; 2) [*f.* **(-a;-ê).**] transaction, deal, bargain; business, commerce: **•*Dayîn-stendina* (we) ser çîye?** (XF) What are (you) *talking* or *arguing* about?; 3) negotiations, talks; relations, connections: ***-danûstandin* di navbera dewletan** (IFb) international *relations* (IFb/OK); 4) amusements, entertainment (XF). {also: danustandin (JB1-S); danûsitandin (TF); dayîn-stendin (XF); dayîn û standin (K); [dané sitandin] دانـه سـتـانـدیـن (JJ)} <dan = 'to give' + standin = 'to take'; Cf. T alış-veriş = 'shopping, business, dealings' (lit. 'taking-giving'); Clq Ar

xud wa-i'ṭi خـذ واعـطِ (lit. 'take and give'); Arm aṛewtur [W Arm aṛewdur] առեւտուր (lit. 'take and give') = 'business, commerce'; Heb maśa u-matan משא ומתן (lit. 'leading and giving') = 'negotations' [Wlt/IFb/OK/GF//JB1-S//TF//XF//K//JJ] <girtin û berdan>

danzde دانزده (M-Am & Bar/Rh)/danẕde دانظده (JB1-A) = twelve. See **donzdeh**.

dapîr داپـیـر *f.* **(-a;-ê).** grandmother; grandmother on father's side (F/JJ); old woman: **•*Dapîra* min ji min ra çîrokan dibêje** (AB) My *grandmother* tells me stories. {also: daypîr (JB1-S); [da-pir داپیر/da pīr (PS)/día pīr (PS)] (JJ)} {syn: ecî (HB); pîredê; pîrik} <dê I = 'mother' + pîr = 'old (woman)'; Sor dayegewre دایـهگـهوره = 'grandmother' & dapîr داپـیـر = 'old woman, crone'; Za dapîr *f.* = 'grandmother' (Todd) [F/K/JB3/IFb/B/JJ/GF/TF/OK//JB1-S] <bapîr; kalik>

dapîroşk داپـیـرۆشـك *f.* **(-a;-ê).** spider: **-tewnê dapîroşkê** (SK) cobweb. {also: <dapîroşk> داپـیـروشـك (Hej)} {syn: pêrtevînk; p'indepîr; pîr [4]; pîrhevok; pîrik [3]; t'evnpîrk [1]} Sor dapîroçke داپیرۆچکه/dapîroke داپیرۆکه =całcałoke جالْجالْوکه [Zeb/SK/OK/RZ/Hej] <t'evn>

daqul داقول (L) = leaning over. See **daqûl**.

daqulandin داقـولانـدِن (da-qulîn-) (IFb) = to swallow. See **daqurtandin**.

daqultandin داقولتاندِن = to swallow. See **daqurtandin**.

daqurçandin داقـورچـانـدِن = to swallow. See **daqurtandin**.

da•qurtandin داقورتاندِن *vt.* **(da-qurtîn-).** to swallow: **•Gur wê çaxê Şenglo, Menglo, Qalîç'englo *dadiqurtîne*** (J) Then the wolf *swallows up* Sh., M. and Q. [three kids (goats)]. {also: daqulandin (da-qulîn-) (IFb-2); daqultandin; daqurçandin} {syn: beli'andin; daûran (JB3/IF); *hişavtin (IF)} [J/F/K/JB3/IFb/B/GF/OK] <fiř I; qurtandin>

daqûl داقـوول**: -daqûl bûn** (IFb) to bend down, kneel, lean over, bow down: **•Carkê nerî deng ji wan dera nay[ê]; *daqul bû*, nerî go devê mixarakê xwîya ye; ew dixan ji mixarê dikişe** (L-1 #3, ll.14-15, 46) He saw that no sound was coming from there; *he bent down*, and saw that the cave's mouth was visible; the smoke was coming from the cave; **-xwe daqûl kirin** (Qzl) to bend down, kneel {syn: xwe xûz kirin}: **•Ji kerema xwe, *xwe daqûl bike* û li wan binihêre** (SF 24) Please *bend down* and look at them; **-xwe daqûlî 'erdê kirin/daqûlî 'erdê bûn** (Qzl) to kneel on the ground. {also: daqul (L)} [SF/Qzl/IFb//L-1]

dar I دار *f.* **(-a;-ê).** tree: **•Darbiř çû mêşe *dara* bibiře** (Dz) The woodcutter went to the forest to cut down *trees* **•*Dar* sî dide ser me** (AB) *The tree* gives us shade [lit. 'gives shade on us']; **-dara dergûşê** (Dz) cradle, crib {syn: bêşîk; bormotk (EP-7); colang; landik}. {also: [dar] دار (JJ)} <O Ir *dāru- (A&L p. 84 [V]): P dār دار = 'wood, gallows'; Sor dar دار = 'tree, wood, pole, staff, stick, gallows'; Za dar *f.* = 'tree'; for more etymological information see **dar II** below [BX/K/A/JB3/IFb/B/JJ/GF/TF/OK] <daristan; dehl; mêşe>

dar II دار *m.* **(-ê; dêr** [BK/B], **vî darî).** 1) wood; 2) wooden stick: **-bi darê zorê** (BX) by force [lit. 'By the stick of violence']; **-bi darê kotekê, bi darê zorê** (L) by hook or by crook. {also: [dar] دار (JJ); <dar> دار (HH)} Skt dāru-; O Ir *dāru- (A&L p. 84 [V]): Av dāuru-; OP dāru- = 'wood' (Kent); P dār دار = 'wood, gallows'; Sor dar دار = 'tree, wood, pole, staff, stick, gallows'; cf. also Gr dóry δόρυ = 'spear' [BX/K/A/JB3/IFb/B/HH/BK/GF/TF/OK] <êzing; mêşe>

daralînk دارالینك**/dar-alînk** دارئـالـیـنـك [FS] *f.* **(-a;-ê).** dodder, twining leafless parasitic herb, bot. *Cuscuta*. [Zeb/IFb/AA/ZF3/FS] <lavlav>

dar-axac دارئاخاج (Ba3) = gallows. See **daraxaç**.

daraxaç دارئـاخـاچ *f.* **(-a;-ê).** gallows, gibbet: **•Bavê wê lê hatye xezevê, *dar-axac* çêkirye, wê îro Meyanê dardakin** (Ba3-3, #12) Her father was furious, he built a *gallows*, [and] they will hang Meyaneh today. {also: dar-axac (Ba3); daraẍac (K)} {syn: sêdare; sêp'î [2]} <T darağacı = 'gallows' < P dār دار = '(wooden) gallows' + T ağaç = 'tree' [Ba3//B//K]

daraẍac دارغاج (K) = gallows. See **daraxaç**.

daraz داراز *f.* **(-a;-ê).** (legal) sentence, verdict: **-daraz dan** (IFb/OK) to sentence, pass judgement. [(neol)IFb/TF/OK/ZF3] <biryar; qirar>

darbenk داربهنك (IFb) = terebinth. See **bêmk**.

darbest داربـهسـت *f.* **(-a;-ê).** 1) {syn: me'f} stretcher, litter; 2) bier, stretcher on which a corpse is carried: **•Silêman dîtin** [sic]**, mirî ... Jin û biçûk û xizmêt Silêmanî hemî hatin, kirine qorî û girîn û tejî ser serê xo kuř û xolî kirin** [sic]**. Meytê Silêmanî danane** [sic] **ser *darbestê*, înane** [sic] **gundî** (SK 10:100) Then they saw Sulaiman, dead ... Sulaiman's wife and children and relatives all came and began wailing and crying and throwing earth and ashes all over their heads. They placed Sulaiman's corpse on a *stretcher* and brought it to the village **•Xizm û muroêt ‘Ebdî jî ji gundî hatin, řakirin** [sic], ***darbesta*** **wî gehandine** [sic] **gundî. Nîw-sa‘et may bo řojawa bûnê, ew jî temam bû** (SK 18:174) Abdi's relatives and friends came from the village, lifted him and brought his *stretcher* to the village. He too died half an hour before sunset. {also: [dar-best] داربست (JJ)} Cf. P dārbast داربست = 'trellis, scaffolding'; =Sor darebaze دارەبازە/daremeyt دارەمەیت/dareterm دارەتەرم [Dh/Zeb/K/A/IFb/JJ/JB1-A/SK/GF/OK] <sindirîk>

darbiř داربڕ *m.* **(-ê;).** 1) woodcutter, lumberjack: **•*Darbiř* çû mêşe dara bibiře** (Dz) The *woodcutter* went to the forest to cut down trees; 2) {syn: kûçikê avê (F)} beaver (IFb/JJ) ; 3) {syn: darnekol; kutkut} woodpecker (B); 4) *lioncub (A/HH). {also: [dar-byr] داربر (JJ); <darbir> داربر (HH)} < dar = 'wood' (m.)/'tree' (f.) + biř- = 'to cut' [F/Dz/K/A/JB3/IFb/B/JJ/HH/GF/OK/ZF3]

darçîn دارچین *f.* **(-a;-ê).** cinnamon, bot. *Laurus cinnamomum*: **•Bêhna *darçînê* ya xoş e** (Dh) *Cinnamon* has a nice smell. {also: darçînî (GF); [dartchin] دارچین (JJ); <darçîn> دارچین (HH)} Cf. P dārčīn[ī] دارچین[ی] ; Sor darçîn[î] دارچین[ی] [K/A/IFb/B/JJ/HH/TF/OK/CB/ZF3//GF]

darçînî دارچینی (GF) = cinnamon. See **darçîn**.

darda داردا *adj.* hanging: **-darda bûn** (K) {syn: daliqîn} to be hanging, hang *(vi.)*: **•Boẍ da lodka, gur pêva *darda bû*** (J) The bull gave a leap, [and] the wolf *was* completely *[left] hanging*; **-darda kirin** (K/IF/B) {syn: daliqandin; hilawîstin} to hang *(vt.)*: **•Bi ‘ezmînva ç’iqlê dara hebûn, eskerê wî gişka sîliĥê xwe êxstin û ç’ilqava *darda kirin*** (EH) Throughout the sky there were tree branches, all of his soldiers took off their weapons and *hung* them *up* [on the trees]. [F/K/JB3/IF/B] <şor II>

dařêjtin دارێژتن (Zeb/IFb/GF) = to mold; to formulate, compose. See **dariştin**.

darêştin دارێشتن (Wkt) = to mold; to formulate, compose. See **dariştin**.

dařêtin دارێتن (K) = to mold; to formulate, compose. See **dariştin**.

daristan دارستان *f.* **(-a;-ê).** forest, wood(s); grove, copse: **•Aliyê bakur ê vî welatî hemû *daristan* e. *Daristaneke* weha ye ku piling têkevê nema dikare ji nav derkeve** (SF 19) The northern end of this country is all *forest*: it is such a [dense] *forest* that if a tiger enters it, he can't get back out. {syn: dehl [2]; gorange; mêşe; řêl} [K/IFb/GF/OK/ZF3] <dar I & II>

da•riştin دارشتن *vt.* **(da-rêj-).** 1) to cast, mold, form; 2) to formulate, articulate, word, compose, draw up *(plans)*, coin *(words)*: **•Kongire, lêkolînê li ser kar û xebatên civakê di navbera 2 Kongireyan de dike, û program û sîyasetên nû *dadirêje*** (Civaka Aştî û Pêşveçûna Kurdistanê, 2008) Between the 2 congresses, the congress does research on the workings of society, and *formulates* new programs and policies **•NY ji bo vegera penaberên Îraqî planekê *dadirêje*** (Rûdaw 25.i.2011) The NY *is drawing up* a plan for the return of Iraqi refugees. {also: dařêjtin (Zeb/IFb/GF); darêştin (Wkt-2); dařêtin (K)} Sor dařiştin داڕشتن = ‘to cast, found; mold, shape; word, formulate’ [Zeb/IFb/GF//K//SS/Wkt/ZF3]

darî داری (HR-I) = wooden. See **darîn**.

darîn دارین/**dařîn** دارین *adj.* wooden, made of wood: **•Ew jî dibê kevç’îyê hesinî, di nav girara germ da disincirê; ji wê yekê kevç’îyê *darî* qîmetlitir e** (HR-I, 1:40) They also say that iron spoons [lit. 'the iron spoon'] melt [or, heat up] in hot porridge; for this reason *wooden* spoons are [lit. 'the *wooden* spoon is'] more valuable. {also: darî (HR-I)} [Z-1/K/B/GF/ TF/OK//HR-I] <dar I; dar II>

dark’ol دارکۆل (B/F/ZF3) = woodpecker. See **darnekol**.

dark’olk دارکۆلك, m. (K/GF) = woodpecker. See **darnekol**.

darlastîk دارلاستیك *f.* **(;-ê).** slingshot. {syn: qosk} [GF/BF/Wkt/ZF3]

darnekol دارنەکۆل *f.* **(-a;-ê).** woodpecker, zool. *Picus*. {also: dark’ol (B/F/ZF3); dark’olk, m. (K/GF); darqul (F-2)} {syn: darbiř; kutkut} [Dy(EW)//F/B/ZF3//K/GF]

***da•řotin** داڕۆتن *vt.* **(da-řoj-).** to trim, shave, plane. [K]

darqul دارقول (F) = woodpecker. See **darnekol**.

darûk داروك *f.* **(-a;-ê).** spruce or fir tree. {syn: kac [2]} [F/ZF3/FS/Wkt]

das داس *f.* **(-a;-ê).** sickle: **•Îcar wek palîya genimê sor ku çawa meriv dide ber *dasan*, wele ez jî bi mûçingê ketim nav porê xwe** (LC, 5) Like harvesting red wheat, the way one strikes it with *a* *sickle*, that's how I went after my hair with a tweezers; **-das kirin** (JJ) to harvest, reap, cut down, mow; **-das û çakûç** (F) hammer and sickle **•kalûmeke *dasan*** = old, rusty *sickle*. {also: de's II (B); dasû (Haz); [das] داس (JJ); <das داس/dasok داسوك> (HH)} {syn: kasox (IF)} O Ir *dāθra-; Skt dā́tra- *n.*; Southern Tati dialects: Chali, Takestani, Eshtehardi, & Sagz-abadi dāra *f.* = 'sickle' (Yar-Shater); P dās داس; Sor das داس; Za dahrî *f.* = 'tool for splitting wood (all iron, slight sickle shape)' (Todd). See: Georg Morgenstierne. "Das Wort für 'Sichel' in neuindischen und neuiranischen Sprachen," *Göteborgs högskolas årsskrift,* 36, iii (1931), 63-69, reprinted in: *Irano-Dardica* (Wiesbaden : Dr. Ludwig Reichert Verlag, 1973), pp.9-16. [F/K/A/JB3/IFb/JJ/HH/GF/TF/ OK//B//Haz] <berdas; diryas; kalûme; k'êlendî; qalûnç; şalok>

dasik داسِك (A) = dim. of **das**.

Dasinî داسِنى *m.* **(-yê;).** Yezidi: **•*Dasinî* mezhebek e, Êzedî jî dibêjinê** (SK 39:344) *The Dasinis* are a sect, also called Yezidis. {syn: Êzîdî} [Zeb/SK/Hej] <k'irîv [2]>

dasî داسى *m.* **(-yê;).** 1) {syn: stirî I[3]} fishbone: **-de'sîyê me'sî** (Frq) do.; 2) {syn: bijî III} awn, beard *(bot., of grasses)* (K/B/TF). {also: de'sî (Frq/K-2/B)} Sor dask داسك = 'awn, beard of wheat or barley' [Haz/K/IF2/TF/ZF3//Frq/B] <hestî; masî>

dastan داستان (K) = epic poem. See **destan**.

dasû داسو (Haz) = sickle. See **das**.

daşik داشِك (FJ/GF) = donkey foal. See **dehş**.

daş•ir داشِر *f.* **(•ra;•irê).** bathroom, toilet, restroom, lavatory: **•Dûvre--li *daşirê*--tiştek dibe** (BM, p.28) Later--in *the bathroom*--something happens. {syn: avdestxane; avrêj I; ç'olik III; destavxane; edebxane [1]; qedemge (Czr)} [Dy/BM/KS/Kmc-12/ZF3/ BF/G]

daşîr داشير *f.* **(-a;-ê).** wet nurse: **•Min xwarziyê xwe Nadan wek kurê xwe pêsikand, ji ber zarok bû, min ew da 8 *daşîran*** (Qzl) I adopted my nephew Nadan as my son, [and] because he was little, I gave him to 8 *wet nurses*. {also: dêşîr (Kmc); [diia chiri] ديا شيرى (JJ)} {syn: dayîn III} Cf. P dāyah دايه; =Sor dayen دايەن [Qzl/CS//JJ/Kmc] <dê I; mêjandin>

da•ûran دائووران *vt.* **(da-ûr-).** to swallow. {also: [dāwurān (Rh)] داوران (JJ)} {syn: beli'andin; daqurtandin; *hişavtin (IF)} Cf. P ōbārīdan اوباريدن/ōbāštan اوباشتن (-ōbār-) (اوبار) = 'to swallow, devour' [JB3/IFb/JJ-Rh/M/Bw]

dav I داڤ *f.* **(-a;-ê).** trap, snare (K/JB3); trap with a noose, made of horsehair (A/IFb) or goathair (GF); type of trap for catching partridges, *after which the birds are kept in cages (rather than being killed)* (Msr): **•Hon ketin *dava* min** (SW1, 24) You have fallen into my *trap*. {also: daf (IFb); dafik (Msr/A); davik, m. (K/TF-2); daw II (SK); [daw] داڤ (JJ)} <O Ir *dāmA- [*dā- = 'to tie'] (A&L p. 84 [V] + 95 [XIX, 2]): P dām دام; Sor daw داو; Za damı *f.* (Mal) {syn: *muxur (IFb)} [K/JB3/JJ/GF/TF/OK/AA//IFb//Msr/A//SK] <sîte; telhe; tepik I; xefik>

dav II داڤ *f.* **(-a;).** thread, string, fiber: **•'Aqlê muroekî yek *dawa* mû e, ze'îf e, belê wextê gelek mû geheştine yêk-u-do dibîte werîs, kelan pê girê diden** (SK 41:393) A man's mind is but a single thread of hair, and weak, but when many hairs come together it becomes a rope fit to tie buffaloes; 2) bristle, hair, filament: **•firçe: amûrek bidestik e û bi serê wê ve *dav* hene** (Wkt) brush: an instrument with a handle and on its head there are *bristles* **•firçe: alaveke ji *davan* hatî çêkirin destikdare, jibo paqijkirina didanan** (BF) brush: an instrument which is made of *bristles* with a handle, for cleaning the teeth. {also: daw III (SK); [daw] داڤ (JJ)} <O Ir *dā- = 'to tie' [Bw/JJ/OK/FS/BF/Wkt//SK] <ben; dezî; werîs>

davançe داڤانچه (HM) = pistol. See **debançe**.

davik داڤِك, m. (K/TF) = trap. See **dav I**.

daw I داو *f.* **(-a;-ê).** 1) fattail; 2) {syn: damen[1]; dang} hem; skirt, lap: **•Didî *dawa* xeftanê Zînê** (HM) He saw *the hem of* Zîn's caftan **•Leylê rabû *dawa* dêrê xwe, çuxê xwe biřî** (EP-5, #15) Leyla cut off *the lap of* her dress, of her coarse coat. {also: dû II; dûm; dûv I, f. (B)/m.; dûw; [daoŭ] داو (JJ); <daw> داو (HH)} [HM/K/A/IFb/B/ JJ/HH/GF/TF/ OK] See **dû II** & **dûv I**.

daw II داو (SK) = trap. See **dav I**.

daw III داو (SK) = string. See **dav II**.

da'w IV داعو (IS) = argument. See **de'w II**.

dawat داوات, f. (IFb/Bw) = wedding; dance. See **de'wat**.

da•weşandin داوشاندِن *vt.* **(da-weşîn-).** to shake up, stir up: **•Ewî hûtî rahişte kevirekî mezin û dawişande Beyrim** (L) This ogre picked up a large rock and waved it at Beyrim. {also: dawişandin (L); dawşandin (F/K)} {syn: ba kirin

I} [J/JB3/IFb/B/GF/TF/OK//F/K//L]

dawet داوەت, f. (IS/TF/OK/ZF) = wedding; dance. See **de'wat.**

dawişandin داوشـــــانـــــدِن (L) = to shake up. See **daweşandin**.

dawî داوی *f.* **(-ya;-yê).** end, outcome, result: **•*Dawiya* vî mirovî** (JB3/IF) *The fate/end of* this man; **-anîn dawîyê** (K/JB3/IF) to finish, end; **-dawî**[**yê**] = afterward, in the end, finally: **•*Dawîyê* bêna min fireh bibe ezê bixwim** (L) *After* I calm down, I will eat **•Ezê *dawîyê* bixwim** (L) I'll eat *later*; **-vê dawîyê** = recently: **•*Vê dawiyê* min cehê xurrû didayê** (HYma, 11) *Recently* I have been giving him pure barley. {syn: axirî; dûmahî; encam; k'uta[sî]; talî II} [K/JB3/IFb/GF/OK/ZF3]

dawîn داویـــن *adj.* last, final: **•Bi dû payiza jiyanê re koça *dawîn*** (MUs, 7) The *final* migration after the autumn of life. {syn: paşîn} [MUs/K/IFb/GF/ZF3]

dawşandin داوشـــــانـــــدِن (F/K) = to shake up. See **daweşandin**.

dawul داوول (K) = drum. See **dehol**.

dax داخ (IFb/TF/OK) = cattle brand. See **dax̆**.

daxil داخِـــــل *f.* **().** interior, inside: **-daxilî** (JB1-A)/ **daxili** (SK) in, inside of: **•Gundek heye li-naw 'eşîreta Berwarîyan, *daxili* qeza Amedîyê, Spîndar dibêjin ê** (SK 28:252) There is a village among the Barwari tribe, *in* the district of Amadiya, called Spindar; **-daxil bûn** (SK/JJ/ZF): a) to enter {syn: derbaz bûn; [tê]k'etin}: **•Bûk bû k'eçelok *dax̆lî* nava şeher *bû*** (HCK-1, 206) The bride turned into a baldboy [and] *entered* the city **•*Ezê daxil bibim* nav bajêr** (L-5, 146, l. 14-15) I *will enter* the city **•K'esekê dî *dax̆ilî* mala wî *nabît*** (JB1-A, 104, #20) No one else *will enter* his house; b) to join *(a group)*: **•Ez ħez nakem to *daxili* terîqetê *bibî*** (SK 46:445) I don't want you *to join* the tariqah [Sufi order]; **-daxil kirin** (JJ/ZF) to insert, put stg. into {syn: [tê]xistin}. {also: dax̆il (JB1-A); [dakhil] داخل (JJ)} {syn: hindur̄; nav II; zik} < Ar dāxil داخل = 'entering; inside' [L/K/IFb/JB1-S/SK/JJ/ZF//HCK/JB1-A]

da•xistin داخِـــســـتِـــن *vt.* **(da-x-/da-xîn-).** 1) {syn: dahiştin; dakirin} to lower, cause to descend; to take or put down; to remove (JJ): **•Dewlê *dadixe*, wekî avê derxe** (Ba) He *lowers* the bucket [into the well], in order to take out (i.e., get) water **•Ji hespê *daxistin* [sic] qîza Mîrê Bajarê Sêrê** (L) They *helped* the daughter of the Prince of the City of Magic *down off* her horse **•Dizgînê ser qerp'ûzêda *dadixîne*** (EP-7) He *lowers* the bridle onto the pommel [of the horse's saddle]; 2) {syn: girtin [3]} to close, block up; to close, shut, lock (K) *[This is the standard word for 'to close' in Soranî]*; to insert, stick in (K); 3) *to bend, fold over (IF/JB3); 4) {syn: dadan [1]} *to set fire to, light, kindle *(stove)*; to start, turn on *(source of heat or power)* (K); 5) {syn: daliqandin; hilawîstin; r̄axistin} *to hang (K). {also: daêxistin (Zeb); [da-khystin] داخستين (JJ)} [K/A/JB3/IFb/B/JJ/GF/TF/OK/BK] <dahatin; dak'etin>

daxuyanî داخويانى *f.* **(-ya;-yê).** declaration, announcement; manifesto, written statement: **•Di civînê de *daxuyaniyek* ji bo raya giştî bi navê "Leşkerên Tirk derkeve ji Kurdistanê!" hate belav kirin** (Wlt 1:37, 2) At the meeting *a manifesto* of public opinion, entitled "Turkish troops get out of Kurdistan," was circulated. {also: daxûyanî (GF)} {syn: beyanname; 'elamet} [(neol)Wlt/IFb//GF] <belavok>

daxûyanî داخوويانى (GF) = declaration. See **daxuyanî.**

da•xwarin داخـــــوارِن *vt.* **(da-xw-/da-xu-**[EP-8]**/da-xwu-**[K]**).** 1) to yield, give in, cede; 2) to be inferior to: **•Kur̄ *ji* bavê *danaxun*** (EP-8) The sons *are not inferior to* [their] father. {also: daxwerin (K)} [EP-8/B/ZF3//K]

daxwaz داخواز *f.* **(-a;-ê).** 1) {syn: arzû; merem; miraz} wish, desire; need, want, necessity (K): **•Her *daxwazên* wî anîn cih** (JB3) [They] made all his *wishes* come true; **-daxwaz [lê] kirin** (K): a) to demand, require of s.o.; b) to sue, persecute, demand legal action against; c) to show one's desire for (Haz): •[In closing a letter] **Her tim rojên bi dilxweşî *daxwaz dikim*** (Haz) I *hope for* happy days always [for you]; 2) demand, request (K); supplication, entreaty (JJ): **•Lê belê Xumeynî wê *daxwazê* qebûl nake** (Bkp, 8) But Khumeyni doesn't accept that *demand* **•Li gorî hin îdîayan Atîna ji bo xwe ji *daxwazên* Kohen rizgar bike, wê soz bide Amerîka ku di der barê PKKê de ji bo hevkariyê amade ye** (CTV107) According to some claims, in order to free itself of [William] Cohen's *demands*, Athens will promise America that it is ready to cooperate regarding the PKK. {also: daxwez (K); [da-khaz] داخـــواز (JJ)} [BK/JB3/IFb/JJ/GF/OK/ZF//K] <xwestin>

daxwerin داخوەرِن (K) = to yield to. See **daxwarin**.

daxwez داخـــــــــوەز (K) = wish; need; demand. See **daxwaz**.

daẍ داغ *f.* **(-a;-ê).** cattle brand; mark of a cattle brand; **-daẍ bûn** = to be branded: **•Dilê wî bi kesera welêt *dax bûye*** (Wlt 2:104, 11) His heart *was branded* with worry for his country; **-daẍ kirin** (F/Dz) to brand *(cattle)* {syn: k'ewandin}: •[**Şivan**] **... bi şîşêd sorkirî k'erê xwe *daẍ dikin*** (Dz) The shepherds *are branding* their donkeys with red hot skewers. {also: dax (IFb/TF/OK-2); dexdexan (BX); [dag] داغ (JJ); <daẍ> داغ (HH)} Cf. P dāγ داغ = 'hot; mark of a brand' [Dz/K/B/JJ/HH/GF/OK//IFb/TF//BX]

daẍil داغِل (JB1-A) = inside. See **daxil**.

dayan دایان (K[s]) = wet-nurse. See **dayîn III**.

dayê دایێ = mom, mommy. See **dê I**.

dayik دایك (A/JB3/IF/B) = mother. See **dê I**.

dayin I دایِن (BK) = to give. See **dan I**.

dayin II دایِن (A) = wet-nurse. See **dayîn III**.

dayîn I دایین (K/B/Ag) = to give. See **dan I**.

dayîn II دایـیـن *f.* **(-a;).** 1) {syn: diyarî; pêşk'êş; xelat [2]} gift, present; 2) taxes, tribute: **•Gelek wext çû û xelqê bêş û *dayîn* nedane paşayê Romê** (FS) Much time passed and the people did not pay *taxes* to the king [emperor] of Rome. {also: dayînî (K-2)} [EP-7/K/GF/ZF3/FS]

dayîn III دایـــیـــن *f.* **(-a;-ê).** wet-nurse. {also: dayan (K[s]); dayin II (A); dayînge (K); [dàin] دایـن (JJ); <dayîn> دایـیـن (HH)} {syn: daşîr} [Pok. dhē(i)- 241.] 'to suck': P dāyah دایـــه = 'wet nurse'; Sor dayk دایـك = 'mother' & dayen دایـەن/daye دایـە = 'wet-nurse'; Hau dayane *f.* (M4); cf. Gr thēlys θῆλυς = 'female' (adj.) & thēlē θηλή = 'nipple' [JB3/IFb/JJ/HH/GF/TF/OK/Rnh//K//A] <dê I; mêjandin; sawa; şîrmêj>

dayînge دایینگە (K) = wet-nurse. See **dayîn III**.

dayînî داییـنی (K) = gift. See **dayîn II**.

dayîn-stendin دایـیـن سـتـەنـدِن (XF) = commerce; relations. See **dan û standin**.

dayîn û standin دایـیـن و سـتـانـدِن (K) = commerce; relations. See **dan û standin**.

dayk دایك (SK) = mother. See **dê I**.

daypîr دایـپـیـر (JB1-S) = old woman; grandmother. See **dapîr**.

dazdehem دازدەهەم (Wkt) = twelfth. See **dozdehem**.

de I دە *interj.* well, come on; *interjection of urging or encouragement*: **•*De*, qîza hakim gelikî espehî ye** (L) *Indeed*, the king's daughter is very pretty **•*De*, gava qundir wilo ji bavê xwe re got, bavê wî gelikî tirsîya** (L) *Indeed*, when the gourd spoke to its father in that way, its father was very much afraid •[Three riders come to a girl, tell her to come with them. She asks who they are. They say they are the harbingers of happiness. She says:] ***De* wekî usane, ... ezê bêm t'evî we** (EP-7) *Well*, in that case, I'll come with you **•Xûşkê, *de* avê bixwe** (EP-7) Sister, *come* drink [some] water. {also: [da] دە (JJ)} [F/K/B/JJ/GF/TF/OK] <ca>

de II دە = ten. See **deh**.

-de III دە- (GF/TF). See **-da**.

de'at دەعات (Ks) = wedding; dance. See **de'wat**.

deban دەبـــان *m.* **(-ê;).** 1) steel *used in making swords and daggers*; 2) sharp dagger: **•Min paşê bihîst, ku ew bi *debanekî* tûj hatibû kuştin** (Cankurd: RN2 56[1998], 11) I later heard that he had been killed with a sharp *dagger*; 3) *[adj.]* damascened *(steel)* (SK): **•'Ezîz jî *xencera deban* helkêşa, hate pêşîya 'Ebdî** (SK 18:170) Aziz, for his part, drew a *damask dagger* and confronted Abdi. {also: <deban> دبـــــــــان (HH)} Sor xencerêkî deban خـەنـجـەرێـکـی دەبـان = 'extremely sharp dagger' [Cankurd/A/IFb/HH/GF/SK] <p'ola; xencer>

debance دەبانجە (JB3/IFb/OK) = pistol. See **debançe**.

debançe دەبـانـچـە *f.* **(•[ey]a;•ê).** pistol, gun: **•Wextê der-kewt, pîyê xo da-na ser paytûnî, her çaran *t̲epançeyêt* xo li wî xalî kirin** (SK 52:567) When he went out, [and] set his foot on the carriage, the 4 of them emptied their *pistols* into him.{also: davançe (HM); debance (JB3/IFb); demançe (A/B); dep'ançe (K); t̲epançe (SK); [debantché] دبانچە (JJ)} {syn: çardexwar; şeşar; şeşxane} Cf. T tabanca; Sor demançe دەمـانـچـە/debançe دەبـانـچـە/dewançe دەوانـــچـــە [HM//JJ/GF//JB3/IFb/OK//A/B//K//SK] <çardexwar; t'ifing>

debar دەبـــار *f.* **(-a;-ê).** living, livelihood, sustenance; subsistence: **•Xwedê *debarê* bideyê!** (Lab, 41) May God provide him *sustenance*; **-debara xwe kirin** (K/IFb) to get by, support o.s. *(financially)*, earn a livelihood, live on *(stg.)*. {also: debir (B-2); [debar] دبـــار (JJ)} {syn: 'ebûr} < Ar dabbara II دبّر = 'to arrange' [Lab/K/IFb/B/JJ/GF/ZF3] <debirandin>

debaẍ دەبــــــاغ (K/B) = hoof and mouth disease. See **tebeq I**.

debir دەبِر (B) = living, sustenance. See **debar**.

debirandin دەبِـرانـدِن/**debiřandin** دەبِـڕانـدِن (JB1-S) *vt.* **(-debirîn-).** 1) {syn: 'ebûr kirin} to feed, support, sustain (K); 2) to subsist, live, manage to get by, support o.s. (JB3/JB1-S/JJ). {also: debiřandin (JB1-S); [debrandin] دبراندين (JJ); debirîn (Z-1/K)} Cf. NENA dba:ra = 'to live, flourish' & mdabo:re = 'to raise, educate' (Krotkoff); Ar dabbara II دَبّر = 'to arrange' [K/JB3/IFb/B/JB1-S/JJ/TF/OK] <‘ebûr>

debirîn دەبِرین *vi.* **(-debir-).** to live, exist, be alive; to survive: **•Ĥal Memêda nemaye, du-sê řoja şûnda Memê wê çetinayêda *nadebire*** (Z-1) M. is in bad shape; in 2 or 3 days he will no [longer] *be able to manage* (=be alive) from the hardship of it all. {also: debirandin [2]} {syn: jîn} Cf. NA dba:ra = 'to live, flourish'; Ar dabbara II دبّر = 'to arrange' [Z-1/K/TF] <debirandin>

debistan دەبِستان (BK) = school; college. See **dibistan**.

debo دەبۆ (Frq) = a unit of weight. See **devo**.

debûş دەبووش *f.* **(-a;-ê).** gum, natural resin: **-debûşa mewîjan** (Xrz) grape (raisin) resin. {also: demûş (Btm/Qmş); <debûş> دبوش (HH)} {syn: benîşt; şîrêz [2]} Cf. NA dabûshâ ܕܒܘܫܐ = 'sticky' (Maclean) <Arc √d-b-š דבש = 'to cleave to, adhere, touch' [Haz/Xrz/IFb/HH/GF//Btm/Qmş] <şîrêz>

def I دەف *f.* **(-a;-ê).** 1) {syn: dehol} drum: **•*Def* û dewatê wana kir** (J) He threw them a nice wedding party [lit. 'He made them a *drum* and a wedding']; **-def û zirne** = drum and zurna *(oboe-like folk instrument, the most common musical accompaniment to dances at Kurdish celebrations)*; **-defa ç'îyê** (K) mountain slope; **-defka *fk-ê* tête kutan** (Zeb) to be subjected to verbal abuse, to be severely scolded [lit. 's.o.'s drum is being struck']: **•*Defka* Tirkîyê *tête kutan*** (Zeb) Turkey *is taking a verbal beating*; **-defa hewarê** (FK-eb-1) alarm; 2) *tambourine (JB3). {also: dehf I; [dew] دڤ (JJ); <def> دف (HH)} Cf. Ar daff دفّ [F/J/K/JB3/IFb/B/HH/GF/TF/OK//JJ] <çomax; defçî; ‘erebane; t’epliq; zirne>

def II دەف**: -li def** (Bw) at (someone's house), over at {cf. Germ bei, Fr chez, Rus u y}: **•*li def* min** (Bw) *at/over* my house/*by* me. {also: dev II (FS)} {syn: bal I; cem; hinda I; ĥafa [*see* ĥaf]; lalê; nik I; řex I} Cf. Ar daff دفّ = 'side, edge' [Bw/AId//FS]

def III دەف: -defa sîngê (K/Qzl/Qrj) = chest. See **depa sîng** under **dep**.

def‘ IV دەفع (SK/OK)/de‘f V دەعف (B) = jolt, push. See **dehf III**.

de‘f VI دەعف (Xrz) = ponytail. See **dehf II**.

defçî دەفچی *m.* **(-yê;).** drummer, player of a **def** or **dehol**: **•Navê *defçîyê* komê Memo bûye** (WapBaba.com) The name of the group's *drummer* was Memo. {syn: daholvan; deholjen; diholkut; mirt’ib [2]} [EP-4/K/B] <begzade [2]; def I; dehol; zirne>

de‘fik دەعفِك (Btm) = ponytail. See **dehf II**.

defîne دەفینە *f.* **(-ya;-yê).** treasure: **-xizne-defîne** (Z-1) do. {also: [definé] دفينه (JJ); <defîne> دفينه (HH)} {syn: gencîne; xizne} < Ar dafīnah دفينة <√d-f-n دفن = 'to bury, hide' [Z-1/K/IFb/JJ/HH/GF/ZF3]

deft’er دەفتەر *f.* **(-a;-ê).** 1) notebook: **-K’era *deft’era* min ya xwarî** (Zeb) I always have bad luck, I am jinxed [lit. 'Donkeys have eaten my *notebook*']; 2) $10,000 (Dh/Iraqi slang). {also: devt’er (FK-eb-1/B); [defter] دفتر (JJ); <defter> دفتر (HH)} {syn: peřawî} Cf. O P dipī- = 'inscription', Elamite tup-pi, & Akkadian ṭuppu *all three* <Sumerian dup- (Kent); Ar/P daftar دفتر = 'notebook, ledger'; ***dîwan*** *is from the same root* [AB/K/JB3/IFb/JJ/HH/GF/OK//FK-eb-1/B]

degîş دەگیش: **-degîş kirin** (Ks) to change, exchange. {syn: bedel kirin; guhartin} < T değiş- = 'to change' [Ks]

deh دەه *num.* ten, 10: **•Ew tê cem her*deh*e kuřê xwe** (Ba) She comes to her *ten* sons. {also: de II; dehe (B-2); [deh] ده (JJ); <deh> ده (HH)} [Pok. dek̑m̥ 191.] 'ten': Skt daśa; O Ir *dasa: Av dasā; OP daθa; Mid P dah; Parthian das; P dah ده; Sor de ده; Za des (Todd); Hau de (M4); cf. also Lat decem; Gr deka δέκα; Arm tasn տասն (W dasə տասը); Rus desiat' десять. [Ba/K/A/JB3/IFb/B/JJ/HH/GF/TF/OK] <dehêk>

deha دەها *adj.* tenth, 10th. {also: dehan (K-2/IFb/OK); **dehem**; dehê (JB1-A); dehî (IF-2); dehyê (JB1-S); [dehi] دهی (JJ)} Cf. P dehom دهم; Sor dehem دەهەم/deyem[în] دەیەم[ین]; Za desin (Todd) [F/K//IFb/OK//JB1-A//JB1-S//JJ] <deh>

dehan دەهان (K/IFb/OK) = tenth. See **deha**.

dehandin دەهاندِن *vt.* **(-dehîn-).** 1) to digest: **•Xwarina ku dixot, bi zorî *didehînit*** (FS) He scarcely *digests* the food that he eats; 2) [*f.* **(-a;-ê).**] digestion: **-sîstema dehandinê ya mirovî** (Wkp) the human digestive system. {syn: givêrandin} [IFb/ZF3/FD/FS/CS/AD/Wkt]

dehbe دەهبە (IFb/GF/TF/OK) = wild animal, beast. See **tabe**.

dehe دەهە (B) = ten. See **deh**.

dehek دەهەك (GF) = a tenth. See **dehêk**.

dehem دەهەم *adj.* tenth, 10th. {also: **deha**; dehemîn (TF/RZ/IFb-2/OK-2/GF-2/CT-2/ZF-2/Wkt-2); deyem (Wkt-2); deyemîn (Wkt-2)} Cf. P dehom دهم; Sor dehem دەهەم/deyem[în] دەیەم[ین] [A/IFb/GF/CT/ZF/Wkt/OK//TF/RZ]

dehemîn دەهەمین (TF/RZ/IFb/GF/CT/ZF/Wkt/OK) = tenth. See **dehem**.

dehê دەهێ (JB1-A) = tenth. See **deha**.

dehêk دەهێك *f.* **(-a;).** a tenth, a tithe, 1/10: **•Ez ... ji terefê ḧukûmetê jî emrekî xusûsî bo muḧafeza te dê deme teḧsîl kirin, û bedel wihê mezinêt R̄êkanî *deh-yêka* ḧasilatê xo her sal bidene min** (SK 61:743) I ... will also procure a special order from Government for your protection, and in exchange for this the elders of the Rekani shall give me *one-tenth* of their harvests each year. {also: dehek (GF); dehyek (A/GF-2/BK/CT); deh-yêk (SK); dehyîk (K); [dah iek] (JJ); <dehyek> دهیك (HH)} Cf. P dah-yak ده یك; Sor deyek دەیەك (Sulaimania & Kerkuk) /deyêk دەیێك (Arbil) [Zeb/AR//SK//A/JJ/HH/BK/CT//GF]

dehf I دەهف = drum; tambourine. See **def**.

dehf II دەهف *f.* **(-a;-ê).** ponytail, braided horse's tail: **-dehfên hespan** (KS) do.: **•Kirasekî tenik li xweha wî bû, guliyek ji *dehfên hespan* li eniya xwe girêdabû** (KS, 8) His sister was wearing a thin dress, she had tied a braided *ponytail* on her forehead. {also: de‘f VI (Xrz); de‘fik (Btm); dehv (GF-2)} [KS/IFb/GF/ZF3//Xrz//Btm]

dehf III دەهف *f.* **(;-ê).** jolt, push, shove: **-dehf dan** (KS)/**de‘f da[yî]n** (B) to push, shove {syn: deldan [*under* del]}: **•Paşê heta jê hatibû ew ber bi dîwêr ve *dehf dabû*** (KS, p.12) Then he *pushed* [it] to the wall with all his might; **-def‘ kirin** (SK) to repulse, push back. {also: def‘ IV (SK/OK); de‘f V (B); <deḧf> دحف (HH)} <Ar √d-f-‘ دفع = 'to push' [KS/K/TF//SK/OK//B//HH]

dehil دەهل (B) = forest. See **dehl**[2].

dehî دەهی (IF/JJ) = tenth. See **deha**.

dehl دەهل *f./m.(B)* **(-a/;-ê/).** 1) valley (K/OK); wadi (IFb); {syn: newal} gorge, ravine; 2) {syn: daristan; gorange; mêşe; r̄êl} woods, forest (JJ/BX/AB/B/Haz) [dehl]; thicket (K/GF): **•Êzingvan çûn *dehlê* jibo êzingan** (AB) The woodgatherers went to the *forest* for firewood; **-bi dehl û rêlan** (BX) through the woods; 3) fruit orchard (JB3/HH/JJ/PS) [dáhel]; 4) *hothouse, greenhouse (K). {also: dal (IFb-2); dehil, m. (B); deḧl (GF); [dehl [2] / dáhel [3]] دهل (JJ); <deḧl> دحل (HH)} Cf. Ar daγal دغل = 'thicket' [AB/BX/K/JB3/IFb/JJ/TF/OK//B//HH] <dar I; mesîl>

dehlendin دەهلەندن (Wlt 2:59, p.15) = to lower. See **dahiştin**.

dehmen دەهمەن (FS/BF) = hem (of dress). See **damen**.

dehn دەهن (K) = seed. See **dan II**.

dehol دەهۆل *f.* **(;-ê).** drum *(musical instrument)*: "A rhythmic instrument made of a large and rather wide wooden hoop covered on both sides with donkey hide. It is beaten with a stick on one side and on the other (the right side) with a mallet. It is a national instrument usually played with a zurna" ["Davul," in *New Redhouse Turkish English Dictionary*, p. 275]: **•[Te qet çend caran li vê *dehol*ê daye?]** (JR) How many times have you beaten this *drum*? {also: dawul (K); dehul; dewl II; dihol (IFb-2/JB1-S/OK); dohl (JB1-S/OK-2); duhl (PS); [dehoul] دهول (JJ); <dihol> دهول (HH)} {syn: def} Cf. P dohol دهل, T davul; Sor dehoł دەهۆڵ; Za dawulı/dawılı *f.* (Mal) [JB3/IFb/JJ/GF//JB1-S/HH/OK//PS//K] <begzade [2]; çomax̄; def; defçî; govend; mirt'ib [2]; t'epliq; zirne>

deholjen دەهۆلژەن *m.* **(-ê;).** drummer. {also: diholjen (GF)} {syn: daholvan; defçî; diholkut} [IFb/OK//GF] <mirt'ib; zirnabêj>

dehş دەهش *m.&f.* **().** young of donkey or ass, donkey foal. {also: **cehş**; dahş (CS); daşik (FJ-2/GF-2); dehşik (IFb/GF/OK); <deḧşik> دحشك (HH)} {syn: kur̄ik} <Ar jaḥš جحش [K/JB3//IFb/GF/OK//HH//CS] See also **cehş**. <k'er III>

dehşik دەهشك (IFb/GF/OK) = dim. of **dehş.**

dehul دەهول = drum. See **dehol**.

deh û çar دەه و چار (Ad/Krç/Bg) = fourteen. See **çardeh**.

deh û didû دەه و دِدوو (Ad/Krç/Bg) = twelve. See **donzdeh**.

deh û yek دەه و یەك (Ad/Kg/Krç) = eleven. See **yanzdeh**.

dehv دەهڤ (GF) = ponytail. See **dehf II**.

dehw دەهو (L) = fight; request. See **de'w II**.

dehwa دەهوا (GF) = fight; request. See **de'w II**.

dehyek دەهیەك (A/GF/BK/CT) = a tenth. See **dehêk**.

dehyê دەهیێ (JB1-S) = tenth. See **deha**.

deh-yêk دەهیێك (SK) = a tenth. See **dehêk**.

dehyîk دەهییك (K) = a tenth. See **dehêk**.

deḧl دحل (GF) = forest, thicket. See **dehl**[2].

dek' دەك (K/A/IFb/GF) = cunning; trick. See **delk'**.

dek'baz دەكـبـاز *m.* **( ).** trickster, cheat: **•Tu rûvîyê *dekbaz* î, te dek anî serê min, te ez dame kuştinê** (J2, 17) You are a *tricky* fox, you have tricked me, you have [tried to] have me killed; **-řûvîyê dekbaz** (J2, 72) cunning or wily fox. {also: dekvan (ZZ-2); delk'baz (K-2/B-2)} {syn: ȟîlebaz} [J2/K/B/ZF3//ZZ-2] <delk'>

dekvan دەكڤان (ZZ-2) = trickster. See **dek'baz**.

del دەل: **del•dan** دەلـدان *vt.* **(del-d-).** to push, shove: **•Eskerê li pişt wî bi serê jopê di destê xwe de ... pehînek li derê qûnê xist û *delda* derve** (SBx, 11) The soldier behind him, with a billy club in his hand ... kicked him in his rear and *pushed* him outside. {syn: dehf dan} [SBx/CS]

delak/delak' [K] دەلاك *m.* **(-ê; delêk, vî delakî).** 1) {syn: berber I; sertaş} barber; hairdresser; 2) male bath attendant *[cf.* ***serşo*** *= female bath attendant]* (B). {also: dellak (Tsab-2); [delak دلاك/telak تلاك] (JJ); <dellak> دلاك (HH)} < Ar dallāk دلّاك < √d-l-k دلك = 'to rub with the hand, massage' [EH/F/K/B/JJ/OK/Tsab//HH] <gûzan; ȟemamçî; kuř IV; serşo>

delal I دەلال *adj.* beloved, dear one; charming (B); pretty, beautiful; dandy: **•*Delala* min** (BX) My *beloved [said to a woman: ma bien-aimée]* **•*Delalê* min** (BX) My *beloved [said to a man: mon bien-aimé]* **•Ya hakimê *delal*!** (L) My *dear* king! **•Ya qîza min a *delal*** (L) My *dear* daughter. {also: [delāl] دلال (JJ); <delal> دلال (HH)} {delalî} [BX/K/A/JB3/IFb/B/JJ/HH/JB1-S/GF/TF/OK]

delal II دەلال *m.* **(; delêl, vî delalî).** town crier, public crier; herald. {also: dellal (IFb); [delal] دلال (JJ)} < Ar dallāl دلّال [PS-II/K/JJ/JB1-A/OK/ZF3//IFb]

delalî دەلالـى *f.* **(-ya;-yê).** 1) fondness, affection; 2) charm, enchanting quality. [K/JB3/IFb/B/GF/TF/OK/ZF3] <delal I>

delandin دەلاندِن *vt.* **(-delîn-).** to dazzle *(eyes)*: **•Şewqa nênik çavê min *didelîne*** (Frq) The shine of the mirror *is dazzling* my eyes. [Frq/(K)/ZF3] <delîyan>

delaş دەلاش (AA) = lammergeier (type of bird). See **daleřeş**.

deling دەلِنگ *m.(Elk/Bw)/f.(K/B)* **(-ê/ ; /-ê).** lower part of a trouser leg: **•Berîya bighêy avê, *delingê* xwe hilnede** (Z-1339) Before you reach the river, don't roll up *the hem of* your trousers *[prv.]*. {also: delink (IFb); [delink] دلنك (JJ); <delink> دلنك (HH)} [Elk/Bw/K/B/GF/TF/FJ//IFb/JJ/HH] <şalvar>

delink دەلِنك (IFb/JJ/HH) = lower part of trouser leg. See **deling**.

deliqîn دەلِقين (IFb/OK) = to give birth (of dogs). See **t'eliqîn**.

delîn دەلـيـن (K/B) = to be dazzled; to starve. See **delîyan**.

delîr دەلـيـر *adj.* brave, courageous. {also: dilêr (ZF3/FS/BF)} {syn: aza I[3]; bizirav; camêr; zîx I[2]} Cf. P dalīr دلير; Sor dilêr دلێر = 'brave, spirited' {delîrî} [K/OK//ZF3/FS/BF]

delîrane دەلـيـرانـە *adv.* bravely, courageously. {also: dilêrane (ZF3)} [?BX//ZF3]

delîrî دەلـيـرى *f.* **(-ya;).** bravery, courage. {also: dilêrî (ZF3/FS)} {syn: camêrî; cuřet} [K/OK//ZF3/FS] <delîr>

delîv دەليڤ (Wlt) = opportunity. See **delîve**.

delîv•e دەلـيـڤـە *f.* **(•[ey]a;•eyê).** opportunity, chance: **•Heger ew *delîv* (firset) li navbera 1900-1992 ji destên bav û bapîrên me çûn, bila ji destê me neçin** (Wlt) If our forefathers missed this *opportunity* between 1900 and 1992, let us not miss it. {also: delîv (Wlt)} {syn: derfet; fesal [1]; firset; kevlû [2]; k'ês} [Wlt//IFb/GF/TF/ZF3/FS] <mecal>

delîyan دەلـيـيـان *vi.* **(-del-).** 1) {also: delîn (K); dilhan (GF); dilihîn (GF-2); dilyan (GF-2)} to be dazzled *(of eyes)*: **•Ç'avê min *delîn*** (K) My eyes *are tired*; 2) {also: delîn (K/B); diliyan (EŞ); [deliian] دليان (JJ)} to starve, be very hungry, be famished: **•Ji goştê bizina dirandî min perçeyek da Çavreş, lê min bi xwe jê tam nekir û êvarê ji nêza *diliyayî*, ez vegeriyam gund** (EŞ, 16) I gave Chavresh [a dog] a piece of the torn-up goat meat, but I myself did not taste it, and in the evening I returned to the village, *famished*. Cf. T deli = 'crazy' [Frq/JJ//K/B//GF//EŞ] <delandin>

delk' دەلـك *f.* **(;-ê).** cunning, craftiness, guile; ruse, dirty trick, intrigue, scheme; trap *(lit. & fig.)*: **•Ew *bi dek' û dolave*** (K) He is a *schemer*; He is not to be trusted **•Kuř *bi delk'* řokê ji bavê îznê dixwazin** (Ba3-3, #19) One day the boys *slyly* ask their father's leave [to do stg.]; **-delk' kirin** (B) to scheme, plot: **•Ew *delk'a dike*** (B) He's *up to something*. {also: dek' (K/A/IFb/GF)} {syn: fen; fêl I; ȟîle; lêp} [Ba3/B/TF/ZF3//K/A/IFb/GF] <dav I; xapandin>

delk'baz دەلكباز (K/B) = trickster. See **dek'baz**.

dellak دەللاك (Tsab) = barber. See **delak**.

dellal دەللال (IFb) = town crier. See **delal II**.

delme دەلـمـە *m.* **().** *type of garment*: 1) woman's garment, pleated from behind and open in front (GF/DS): •*Delme*-'ent'erî bejnê bûn (Ba-1, #17) *Dresses* fit her well [according to Rus tr.]; 2) type of woman's jacket (DS); 3) embroidered vest (DS); 4) mulla's robe (Hej). {also: <delme> دلـمـه (HH)} Cf. T delme = 'vest, waistcoat' (RTI) & 'embroidered vest' [*Pütürge -Malatya; Gaziantep; Sivas (+ Central & Western Anatolia)] & 'woman's garment open in front' [Bitlis (+ Eskişehir)] & 'type of woman's jacket' [Üstürken -Ağrı; Urfa; (+Amasya, Kayseri)] (DS, v. 4, p. 1414) [Ba-1/HH/GF/DS/Hej] <dêre; 'ent'erî>

delûl دهلوول (GShA) = she-camel. See **dundil**.

delûn دهلوون (FS) = she-camel. See **dundil**.

delûv دهلووڤ (JB3/IFb/OK) = bucket. See **dewl I**.

dem I دهم *f./m.* **(-a/-ê;-ê/-î).** time, period: •**Bi ya we çi ferq di navbera wê *demê* û ya niha de heye?** (WM 1:4, 16) In your opinion, what difference is there between that *time* and now; -**dema ku** (Wlt) when *(conj.)* {syn: gava ku; wexta ku}: •***Dema ku* hêk dike, bala xwe didê ku rengê hêken wê dîsa jî reş in** (Wlt 1:37, 13) *When* she lays eggs, she notices that her eggs [lit. 'the color of her eggs'] are still black. {also: [dem] دم (JJ); <d[e]m> دم (HH)} {syn: çax; gav; wext} Cf. P dam دم = 'time, season, hour, moment'; T dem [K/A/JB3/IFb/B/JJ/HH/GF/TF/OK] <car; gav; serdem; wext>

de'm II دهعم *f.* **(-a;).** (automobile) accident, collision. <clq Iraqi Ar di'am دعـم = 'to run into, collide' & da'ma دعمة = 'accident, collision' (cf. also iṣṭidām اصطدام) [Bw/Zeb]

demançe دهمانچه (A/B) = pistol. See **debançe**.

demar دهمار (FS) = vein. See **t'emar**.

dembûl دهمـبـوول *f.* **(-a;).** plum: -**dara dembûla** (F) plum tree. [F/ZF3] <alûçe; hêrûg [1]; încas [2]; şilor>

demhijmêr دهمـهـژمـێـر (BF) = clock; hour. See **demjimêr**.

demjimêr دهمژمێر *f.* **(-a;-ê).** 1) {syn: saet[2]} clock, watch, timepiece; chronometer: •**Google îsal sê *demjimêrên* jîr bi şêweyekî fermî pêşkêş kirin û ji aliyekî din ve Motorêla jî *demjimêra* xwe a jîr pêşkêş kir û gelek bal kişand bi ser *demjimêra* xwe ya gilover** (PUKmedia 27.viii.2014) This year Google has officially presented three smart *watches* and on the other hand Motorola presented its smart *watch* and drew attention to its round *watch*; 2) {syn: saet[1]} hour, time: •**Gotûbêjên bi salan ji yek *demjimêra* şer baştir e** (KDP.info 15.vii.2015) Negotiations that last years are better than one *hour* of war •**Îro *demjimêr* 12:30 bo heyama yek *demjimêrê* balafirên şer yên Tirkiya gundê Cemşirtê û Cîrgîra ... bi tundî topbaran kirin** (PUKmedia 29.viii.2016) Today at 12:30 for one *hour* Turkish war planes bombed the villages of Jemshirte and Jirgira. {also: demhijmêr (BF); demjmêr (IFb)} [(neol)KDP.info/PUKmedia/Wkt/ZF3/FD/Kmc//IFb//BF]

demjmêr دهمژمێر (IFb) = clock; hour. See **demjimêr**.

demokrasî دهمۆکراسی *f.* **(-ya;-yê).** democracy. {also: demuqratî [1] (K)} [IFb/TF/OK//K]

demokrat دهمـۆکـرات (IFb) = democratic. See **demokratîk**.

demokratîk دهمـۆکـراتـیـك *adj.* democratic: •**Hinek nivîskar diyar dikin ku MHP xwe ji nû ve saz dike û ber bi *demokratîk*bûnê ve diçe** (AW69A1) Some writers declare that the MHP [Nationalist People's Party] is re-making itself and becoming more *democratic*. {also: demokrat (IFb); demuqratî [2] (K)} [Ber//IFb//K]

demsal دهمسال *f.* **(-a;-ê).** season *(of the year)*: •**Roj, ji rojên buharê ne. Lê belê hewaya demê ji me re tê xuyan ku ne ew rojên *demsala* xweşik in** (Wlt 2:59, 13) It is a spring day. But the weather makes it seems as if it is not a day of that lovely *season*. {syn: nîr II; werz[2]} [(neol)Wlt/IFb/TF/OK] <bihar; havîn; payîz; zivistan>

demudest دهمودهست (OK) = immediately. See **dem û dest**.

demuqratî دهموقراتی f. (K) = 1) democracy; 2) *[adj.]* democratic. See **demokrasî** & **demokratîk**.

dem û dest دهم و دهست *adv.* immediately. {also: demudest (OK); <dem u des[t]> دهم ئـوو دهس[ت] (Hej)} {syn: destxweda} Sor dem-u-des دهم و دهس [Zeb//OK/Hej]

demûş دهمووش (Btm/Qmş) = gum, resin. See **debûş**.

den I دهن *m./f.(ZF3)* **(-ê/-a;).** large clay water jar. {also: [den] دن (JJ); <d[e]n> دن (HH)} {syn: cer; dişt; sewîl} [L/A/JB3/IFb/JJ/HH/GF/TF/OK/ZF3] <mencel; sîtil [2]>

de'n II دهعن (K/B/J) = eight-hour period, one-third (1/3) of a day. See **dan III**.

de'n III دهعن (B/K) = seed; grain. See **dan II**.

dendik دهندِك *f.* **(-a;-ê).** stone *(of fruit)*, pit, pip: •**Bawerî bi *dendika* xoxê bîne, bi qeweta xwe ewle be** (Ber 5/86, 20) Believe that the peach has *a pit*, and you'll believe in your own strength. {also: denik; [dendik] دندك (JJ); <d[e]ndik> دندك (HH)} {syn: sîsik I} Sor denik دەنك [K/A/JB3/IFb/B/JJ/HH/GF/TF/OK/ZF3] <t̲ovik>

deng I دەنگ *m.* **(-ê;).** 1) {syn: sewt} voice: **•çiqa *dengê* me hebû** (Ba2:2, 205) at the top of our lungs, in a very loud *voice*; **-deng çûn** [+ *dat. constr.*] = to speak *(of animals & inanimate objects, in folktales)* {syn: k'êlimîn; şteẍilîn}: ***•Deng çû* qundir** (L) The gourd *spoke*; **-deng dan** = a) to vote for (B/OK/XF); b) to sound (like) (Wlt): **•Tîpa (V) *deng dide* weke tîpa (W) ya Kurdî** (Wlt 1:42, 10) The letter 'V' *sounds* like the Kurdish letter 'W'; **-deng[ê xwe] kirin** = to speak: **•Gur *dengê xwe nake*** (J) The wolf *doesn't speak* (=remains silent); **-deng lê kirin** = to call s.o., summon {syn: bang kirin; gazî kirin} ***•Deng li* min *ke*** (J) *Call* me!; **-deng vedan** (Wlt/Bw) to echo, reverberate, resound {syn: olan dan}; 2) sound, noise: **•Bi *dengê* sazî şîrin ... M. ji xewê ç'e'vê xwe vekir** (Z-1) From the sweet *sound* of the saz (=tembûr), Mem awoke and opened his eyes ***•Dengê* tifing û mitralyozan ewçend nîzing bû bûn ko mirov digot qey şer gihaştiye kûçe û kolanên bajêr** (H2 9:31, 775) The *sound* of rifles and machine guns was so close that people were saying that the war had reached the streets of the city; 3) {syn: gotgotk} rumor: **•*Deng* bela dibe** (Z-2) There's a *rumor* afoot/afloat; 4) vote. {also: [denk] دنك (JJ); <d[e]ng> دنگ (HH)} P dang دنگ = 'noise made by the collision of 2 stones, clang, clank, or tingle'; Sor deng دەنگ = 'sound, voice, song, news, rumour, vote'; = Za veng *m.* = 'voice' (Mal); Hau deng *m.* = 'noise, fame' (M4) [K/A/JB3/IFb/B/HH/ GF/TF/OK//JJ] <bilind [2] = 'loud'; ȟişk [3] = 'shrill'>

deng II دەنگ *m.* **(-ê;).** millstone, *primitive village instrument for husking grain, consisting of a vertical stone wheel which turns around a pole in a large, flat stone mortar*: **-dengê savarê** (Haz/Zêrî = Kesme Köprü 2 [Btm]) do. {also: ding f. (-a;-ê) (Frq/IFb/GF/ZF3); dink (GF-2); dîng (GF-2); [dink] دینك (JJ)} P dang دنگ = 'pestle or flail (used in separating rice from its husk), a threshing instrument'; T dink/diñk/denk (DS, v. 4, p. 1507-8) & ding (Gemalmaz) & dink (Atılcan); Sor ding دنگ = 'tub used for husking rice'; Za dengı *f.* = 'large stone used for husking rice or bulgur' (Mal) [Haz/Zêrî = Kesme Köprü 2 (Btm)/TF//Frq/IFb/GF/ZF3//JJ]

dengbêj دەنگبێژ *m.&f.* **(-ê/-a; /-ê).** bard, minstrel, traditional singer; reciter of romances and epics (such as Mem û Zîn, Dimdim, etc.). {also: <d[e]ngbêj> دنگبیژ (HH)} {syn: aşiq} < deng I = 'voice' + bêj- = 'to say, tell' {dengbêjî} [K/A/JB3/IFb/B/HH/GF/TF/OK/ZF3]

dengbêjî دەنگبێژی *f.* **(-ya;-yê).** the art of being a **dengbêj** *(qv.)*; minstrelsy, singing. [K/A/IFb/B/TF/ZF3] <dengbêj>

dengdar دەنگدار *f.* **(-a;-ê)** & *adj.* 1) {syn: bêdeng [2]} consonant *(n. & adj.)*: **•Hingê ew dengê i ji bo berîgirtina kome-*dengdaran* (wek ql, kr, ml) li dawiya peyvê dikeve navbera her du *dengdaran*** (E.Öpengin. "Pirsên Rênivîsa Kurmancî", Derwaze 1, 189) So that sound *i* appears between two *consonants*, in order to prevent *consonant clusters* (like *ql*, *kr*, *ml*) at the end of a word; 2) {syn: dengdêr} vowel (Kmc/RZ/FS). Other proposed terms for *consonant*: tîpên bêdeng (K/RZ/Kmc/FS); nedengdêr (RR); = Sor tîpî nebizwên تیپی نەبزوێن/tîpedengî تیپەدەنگی [(neol)Öpengin/IFb/FJ/TF/ZF3/BF/FD/Wkt/SS/CS] <dengdêr>

dengder دەنگدەر *m.&f.* **(-ê/-a;).** voter, elector: **•Tomar-kirina *dengderên* li derveyî welat dest pê dike** (Rûdaw 31.viii.2017) Registering *voters* abroad is beginning. < deng dan = 'to vote, give one's voice'; Sor dengder دەنگدەر [Rûdaw/ZF3/SS/Wkt]

dengdêr دەنگدێر *f.* **(-a;-ê)** & *adj.* vowel *(n. & adj.)*: **•Dengê [e] *dengdêr* e û bi V (îng. Vowel) tê nimandin** (N.Hirorî. Nihêniyên Befrê/Berfê, Kulturname 18.i.2013) The sound [e] is *a vowel* and is represented by V **•Pîtên *dengdêr* di abeya kurdî da heşt in: a, e, ê, i, î, o, u, û** (BF) In the Kurdish alphabet there are 8 *vowels*: a, e, ê, i, î, o, u, û. = Sor tîpî bizwên تیپی بزوێن cf. Ar ḥarakah حركة = 'vowel; movement' [(neol)RR/K/IFb/FJ/TF/ZF3/BF/FD/Wkt/SS/CS] <dengdar>

dengubas دەنگوباس (OK) = news. See **deng û bas**.

deng û bas دەنگ و باس/**dengûbas** دەنگوباس [A/IFb] *m./f.* **().** 1) news, (new) information: ***•Deng û basên* Kurdistanê çi ne?** (IFb) What's *the news* from Kurdistan?; 2) a sound, a peep, '(neither) hide nor hair': **•Xeberdana me gele wext k'işand, lê t'u *deng û bas* ji lawika nedihat** (Ba2-#2, 205) Our conversation lasted a long time, but there was not *a sound* to be heard from the boys. {also: dengubas (OK); deng û be's (XF)} <deng = 'voice, sound' + û = 'and' + Ar baḥt̲ بحث = 'search,

study'; Sor deng-u-bas دهنگ و باس = 'news' [Ba2/K(s)/A/IFb//OK//XF] <cab [2]; nûçe (neol); xeber>

deng û be's دهنگ و بهعس (XF) = news. See **deng û bas**.

denik دهنك = fruitpit. See **dendik**.

Denîmarkî دهنیمارکی (IFb) = Danish; Dane. See **Danîmarkî**.

de'nû دهعنو (B) = boiled wheat. See **danû**.

dep دهپ *m.(Zeb/FS)/f.(ZF)* **(-ê/-a;).** wooden board or plank: **•Neqebek ya di nîveka mezela wî da ... ewî *depek* danabû ser devê neqebê, nivînêt xo ser çêkirbû** (M-Ak #659, 298) There was a hole in the middle of his room ... he had put *a plank* over the mouth of the hole and had made his bed on it; **-depa sîng** (Wn/ZF)/**depê sîngî** (Bw/Elk)/**defa sing** (K)/**defa sîngê** (Qzl/Qrj)/**derfa sing** (IS) thorax, chest, area between the neck and the diaphragm: **•Eliyê Daman Beg ... rimê** [sic] **avête Hesê, li nêv reha qolincê xist bi derbekê di *defa singê* re avête der** (ZZ-10, 143) Ali D.B. ... threw a lance at H., struck him in the shoulder blades with a single blow and brought it out his *chest* [i.e., out the other side] **•Li ber *defa sîngê* xwe erbaneyekê bi eşq û hunereke welê diricifîne** (Tof, 7) He shakes a tambourine in front of his *chest* with such passion and skill. {also: def III (K/Qzl/Qrj); derf (IS); [dep] دپ (JJ); <dep> دپ (HH)} {syn: keval; t'exte} Arc daf דף/dapā דפא & Syr dafā ܕܦܐ = 'board, plank' [Zeb/Dh/A/IFb/JJ/HH/TF/OK/ZF/FS]

dep'ançe دهپانچه (K) = pistol. See **debançe**.

depȓeş دهپڕهش *f./m.(BF)* **(-a/;-ê/).** blackboard. [Kmc-2532/K(s)/IFb/GF/OK/AD/SS/BF]

deq I دهق *f.* **(-a;-ê).** 1) {syn: kekmek (F); xal II} spot, blotch; point, dot; freckle; beauty mark; 2) anklebone, talus (IFb/GF); knucklebone (HH); 3) tattoo: **-deq kirin** (JJ) to tattoo; 4) pinecone (IFb); 5) callus *(on the hand)*, swelling (IFb); 6) {syn: beş; biȓ I[2]} *part, section (IFb); 7) [m.(OK)] text (OK). {also: [deq] دق (JJ); <deq> دق (HH)} < Ar daqq دقّ = 'beating; tattoo' [EP-7/F/K/A/IFb/B/JJ/HH/GF/TF/OK/ZF3] <nîşan [5]>

deq II دهق *m.* **(-ê;).** largest knucklebone in a set: **-wek *deq* hazir bûn** (Qzl) to be ready and willing. [Qzl/A] <k'ap II>

deqandin دهقاندِن *vt.* **(-deqîn-).** 1) to tattoo; 2) to mark, leave a mark on; 3) *to inlay. {also: [deqandin] دقاندین (JJ)} [MC-1/K/IFb/JJ/GF/TF/OK] <deq [1&2]; tamandin>

deq•e دهقه *f.* **(•eya;•ê).** minute, moment: **•çend *deqe*** (Z-1) [for] a few *minutes*. {also: deqîqe (IFb/JB1-S/SK/OK-2)} {syn: hûrdem (IFb)} < Ar daqīqah دقيقة--> T dakika/dakka [Z-1/K/B/OK//IFb/JB1-S/SK/ZK3]

deqena دهقهنا (GF) = so that. See **deqene**.

deqene دهقهنه *conj.* [+ *subj.*] 1) {syn: bila; bona [2]; da II; ȟeta ko [4]; wekî [2]} so that, in order that: **•Steyfo Ȟaydarî ba kire çend keşa û zlamê wê derê, *deqene* arî wî bikin** (HR-I 2:76) Steyfo Haydari called some of the priests and men of that place, *so that* they might help him; 2) [+ *neg. subj.*] lest, so as not to: **•U ȟeç'iyê xwarina rehne, bi kevç'îyê darî dixun, *deqene* devê wa *neşewitê*** (HR-I 1:38) And as for liquid foods [=soup], they eat them with wooden spoons, *lest* they burn their mouths. {also: deqena (GF)} [HR-I//GF]

Deqê دهقێ *f.* **().** common name for female dogs. [Msr] <Cevro; Devȓeş>

deqîqe دهقیقه (IFb/JB1-S/SK/OK) = minute. See **deqe**.

der I دهر *f.* **(-a;-ê).** place, spot: **•her *dera* jî** (Ba) everywhere **•li filan *derê*** (L) in such and such *a place*; -[**li**] **wê derê** = there, at/in that *place*; **-li wan dera** (L) there, in that *place*, in those *parts*: **•Ew çûn derk'etne cîkî wisa, ku t'u merî *li wan dera* t'unebûn** (Ba) They went [until they] reached a place where there were no people [lit. 'which there were no people *there*']. {also: dere; [der] در (JJ)} {syn: cî I; dever I; dews I; êrdim; şûn} [Ba/K/A/JB3/IFb/B/JJ/SK/GF/TF/OK]

der II دهر *adv./prep.* outside; beyond: **•*Der(ê)* malê baran dibare** (K) In the courtyard [lit. '*outside* the house'] it is raining **•*Der* heqê wan** (BX) About them {See **derheqa**} **•*Ji der* vê avê** (BX) *On the other side of* this river, *beyond* this river **•Xwiya ye ko nivîsevan lîwa Rihayê *derî* Kurdistanê dihesibîne** (BX) It is obvious that the writer considers the district of Urfa *outside of* Kurdistan; **-ji ... der** (K): a) outside of *(physical location)*: **•Ew *ji* şeher *der* dijî** (K) He lives *outside of* the city; b) besides, except for: **•jê der** (K) except for him **•*Ji* koma me *der* kesekî xebat nekirîye** (K) *Except for* our group, nobody did any work; **-jê der bûn** (JB3) to be beyond one's reach, to be impossible (for s.o. to do stg.), unobtainable **•Ev kar *ji* min *der e*** (K) This matter *is beyond* me;

-**der ... da/de** = outside, across from, opposite: •**Kanî jî *der* xan-manê Qeret'ajdîn*da* bû** (EP-7) The spring was *outside/across from/ opposite* Q.'s residence;

-**der ... ve/va** = to the outside of, to: •**Borî bimbareke k'ûçe-k'ûçe Memê digeřîne, / *Der* xan-manê Qeret'ajdîn*va* dertîne** (EP-7) Blessed Bor smoothly transports Mem, / Brings him to [*outside*] the residence of Qeretajdin. {also: [der] ca (JJ); derî II} [BX/K/ JB3/IFb/B/JJ/ JB1-S/SK/GF/TF/OK] <derve>

der III دەر (IFb/F/JB1-A) = door. See **derî I.**

deřabe دەڕابە [Zeb/Hej]/**derabe** دەرابە *m.(Zeb)/f.(B/ ZF3)* (; /**derabê** [B]). *denotes wooden objects such as shutters, railing, wall-partitions*: 1) roll-down shutters (A/IFb); 2) railing, grating (IFb); 3) wooden fence boards (HH); 4) juniper trees [hevris] used for hanging things on (Zeb). {also: cf. [darába dem] دراب (JJ) = 'I divide a room with wooden boards'; <derabe> درابە (HH)} cf. NENA dârâbâ ܕܪܵܒܵܐ = 'railing, balustrade' (Maclean); Geo daraba დარაბა = 'shop shutter'; W Arm daṛaba տառապայ = 'partition (of boards)'; Az T daraba = 'fence made of boards'; T daraba & derebe [Bitlis] = 'wooden partition; shop shutter; railing; grain storage container, etc.' (DS, v. 4, p. 1365) & [Malatya] (AC-2, p. 271) = 'shutter' & [Düzce] (AC-3, p. 231) = 'wooden fence around a garden' & [Erzurum] (Atılcan, p.40; Gemalmaz, v. 3) = 'wall made of wood[en panels]' [Zeb/ Hej//A/IFb/B/HH/GF/ZF3]

deramet I دەرامەت *m.* (**-ê;**). 1) {syn: dikak; êmîş [2]; heşînatî; p'incar} vegetable(s) (Şnx/AZ): •***Deramet* û fêqî û dan û xwarin** (AZ) *Vegetables* and fruits and grains and foods; 2) {syn: dexl û dan; hasil} crops, produce (Zeb/Hej): •**Bi taybet demê mirovî *deramet* çandî** (R 15) Especially when one has planted *crops*. {also: <deramet> دەرامەت (Hej/AZ)} < P dar'āmad درآمد = 'income, profit'; Sor deramed دەرامەد/deramet دەرامەت = 'income, profit' [Şnx/Zeb/AZ/Hej]

derandin دەراندِن (-der-) (IFb) = to scatter. See **dêrandin**.

der•anîn دەرانین/دەرئانین *vt.* (**der[t]în-**). 1) to take out, remove, extract, derive (K/A/JB3/IFb): •**Nezera zařê wane berê maka, / Usanin, be'rêda ç'e'vê masî *dertîne*** (EP-7) The looks of their nursing children are such [that] they *make* the eyes of fish in the sea *pop out* •**Borî bimbareke k'ûçe-k'ûçe Memê digeřîne, / Der xan-manê Qeret'ajdînva *dertîne*** (EP-7) Blessed Bor smoothly transports Mem, / *Brings* him to the residence of Qeretajdin •**Ez tiştekî ji gotina te *dernayînim*** (K) *I can't understand* what you're saying [I'm not getting anything from your words]; 2) to assume, deduce, guess (JB3/IFb). {also: bi deranîn (PS-I); derînan (SK/OK-2); [der-anin درانین/der-inān درینان (Rh)] (JJ); <deranîn درانین (dertîne) (درتینە)> (HH)} [K/A/JB3/IFb/B/JJ/ HH/ GF/TF/OK//SK//PS-I]

derb دەرب *f./m.* (**-a/;-ê/**). 1) blow, stroke, hit (K/B/JJ): •**Ez *derbekî/derbekê* di xewê de li wan *xim*, bêbextî ye** (L) If I *strike* them while they're asleep, it's dishonest; 2) {syn: şêlik} volley, salvo (B); 3) stress, emphasis, accent *(phonological)* (B); 4) power, might (K). {also: zerb (K/B); zerp (FK-eb-2); [zerb/derb] ضرب (JJ) = '[derb] is the Arabic, and [zerb] the Turkish pronunciation'; <derb> درب (HH)} < Ar ḍarb ضرب [L/A/JB3/IFb/ HH/ GF/OK//K/B/JJ//FK-eb-2]

derbare دەربارە *prep.* [+ **da/de**] about, concerning, regarding: •***Der bareyê* wate û naveroka folklorê *de* dîtin û ramanên curbicur hene** (YPA, 11) *Regarding* the meaning and content of folklore there are varied views and opinions •***derbareyî* vê ferhengê *de*** (IFb) *about* this dictionary; -**di derbareya ... de** (RZ) do. {also: derbarê (CS); der barê ... de (ZF); derbarî (CS-2)}{syn: derheqa; li ser [ser II]} < P darbārah-i دربارە; Sor derbare[y ی]ە دەربارە [YPA/IFb/FJ/GF/RZ//ZF/CS]

derbarê دەرباری (CS)/der barê ... de دەر بـاری... دە (ZF) = about. See **derbare**.

derbarî دەرباری (CS) = about. See **derbare**.

derbas دەرباس (A/L/JB1-S/GF/TF/OK). See **derbaz**.

derbaz دەرباز: -**derbaz bûn** = a) to cross, pass, enter (vi.) {syn: bihurtin}: •**Dibêjin di nihalekîda řîwîek hebû. ... bazeberek hebû, řîwî lê *derbaz dibû* her wextê ȟez kiriba. ... Marek jî di wê nihalêda hebû. Nedişya li bazeberî derbaz bibît** (SK 2:9) They say that there was a fox (living) in a ravine. ... There were stepping-stones and the fox *crossed over* whenever he liked. ... There was also a snake in that ravine. He could not cross over the stepping-stones •**Du rêwî řex gomekê *derbaz dibûn*** (Dz) Two travelers *were passing by* an animal pen; b) To enter: •**Ȟeyanî ko Mem îzna wînakê nede, Bengîn nikare *derbazî* dîwana mîr**

bive (Z-3) Until Mem gives him permission, Bengin cannot *enter* the emir's diwan; **-derbaz kirin** = to carry across, transport, cause to cross/ pass *(also fig.)* {syn: buhurandin}: **•Bavê xwe li pişta xwe kir û bi avê re *derbas kir*** (L) He put his father on his back, and *carried* him *across* the stream **•Çîrok, şevên zivistanê xweş *derbaz dikin*** (AB) Stories *make* winter nights *pass* nicely. {also: derbas (A/L/JB1-S/GF/TF/OK-2); [derbaz] دربار (JJ); <derbaz-> دربار (HH)} Sor derbaz bûn دەرباز بوون = 'to escape' & derbaz kirdin دەرباز کردن = 'to rescue' [F/K/JB3/IFb/B/JJ/HH/SK/OK//A/L/JB1-S/GF/TF]

derbazbûyî دەربازبوویی *adj./pp.* 1) passed/past, over, finished, done, through: **-derbazbûyî be** (Wr[Gulistan Perwer]) May it be over soon! Speedy recovery [Formula for wishing s.o. well: Cf. T geçmiş olsun, W Arm anc'aj əlla[y] անցած ըլլայ, Alb qoftë e shkuar]; 2) {syn: gerandî; gerguhêz; = Sor têper تێپەڕ} transitive (K/B): **-fêlê/-a [ne]derbazbûyî** (B/K)/**fêla derbaz [ne]bûînê** (F) [in]transitive verb. [Wr/K/B]

derbeder دەربەدەر *adj.* 1) homeless, (a)stray, itinerant, wandering, roaming, roving; displaced: **•Xuya dibît Sebrî Botanî her ji zarokînîya xo jiyaneka *derbeder* û awareyî borandîye** (H.Ĥ.Miĥemed. Layê hunerî û naveroka hozana Sebrî Botanî, 13) It is apparent that from childhood on S.B. led an *itinerant* and stray lifestyle; 2) *m.&f.* **().** hobo, vagrant, vagabond; fugitive; exile. {also: derbider (FJ/GF/ZF3-2/ Wkt-2)} Sor derbeder دەربەدەر = 'wandering, vagrant, astray; fugitive' [H.Ĥ.Miĥemed/K(s)/A/IFb/TF/ZF/ CS/Wkt//FJ/GF] <derodero; k'oçber; mişext>

derbederî دەربەدەری *f.* **(-ya;-yê).** homelessness, wandering (n.), roaming (n.), roving (n.); displacement: **•Ji bo bîranîna Alan Kurdî û hemû zarokên penaber ên ku di rêwîtiya *derbederiyê* de mirine** (E.A.Nolan. Hêstirên Graniayê) In memory of Alan Kurdi and all child refugees who have died on the journey of *homelessness*. {also: der bi derî (GF)} [E.A.Nolan/K(s)/IFb/TF//GF]

derbider دەربِدەر (FJ/ZF3/Wkt) = homeless. See **derbeder**.

der bi derî دەربِدەری (GF) = homelessness. See **derbederî**.

derç'ik دەرچِك *f.* **(-a;-ê).** threshold, door frame: **•*derç'ika* devê dêrî** (Z-3) the doorway **•Li *derçikê* rawestiya û bihna xwe veda** (murad ciwan.com) She stood at *the threshold* and rested. {also: <derçik> درچك (HH)} {syn: şêmîk; şîpane} [IFb/HH/GF/Z-3/ ZK3] <r̄exderî>

der•çûn دەرچوون *vi.* **(der-ç-).** [+ **ji**] 1) to go out, exit, leave: **•Ew *ji* mal *derçû*** (FS) S/he *went out of* the house; 2) to appear, be visible: **•Xwîn *ji* destê min *der çû*** (IF) There was blood on my hand (=I noticed that my hand was bleeding) [lit. 'blood *came out of* my hand']; 3) to appear, come out, be published or issued *(a publication)*: **•Li Şamê *der diçû*** (Rnh - intro) It [=the journal] *came out* in Damascus; 4) to graduate (from): **•Ew *ji* pola çarê *derneçû* (Ew ma li sinifa çarem)** (Wkt) He *did not graduate from* the 4th grade (He stayed back in the 4th grade) **•Ez îsal *ji* zanîngehê *derçûme*** (Wkt) I *have graduated from* college this year **•Rêjeya xwendekarên *ji* pola xwe *derdiçin* 80% e** (Wkt) The percentage of students who *graduate from* their class is 80 %. Cf. Ar √x-r-j خرج = 'to go out, exit': taxarraja V تخرّج = 'to graduate'; Sor der•çûn دەرچوون = 'to escape, be saved; to go off (fire arm); to pass (exam); to graduate; to be mentioned' [Rnh-intro/K/JB3/IFb/GF/TF/OK/ZF3/BF/Wkt] <kovar>

derd دەرد *m.* **(-ê;).** pain *(lit. & fig.)*, sorrow; trouble, problem, woe: **•Kesekî *derdê* Memê delal nizanbû** (Z-1) Nobody knew dandy Mem's *sorrow* **•De xwedê hebînî yanê ne ez bim kî kane vî *derdî* bikşîne?** (LC, 12) For God's sake, if not for me, who can endure this *trouble*? **Li vî welatê gawiran cilşuştin jî bi serê xwe *derdekî* giran e** (LC, 12) In this country of infidels, doing laundry is a big *headache*. {also: [derd] درد (JJ); <derd> درد (HH)} {syn: azar; çîk; êş; jan} Cf. P dard درد --> T dert [Z-1/K/A/JB3/IFb/B/JJ/HH/SK/GF/TF/ OK] <hesret; xemgînî>

der•dan I دەردان *vt.* **(der-d-).** 1) {syn: berza kirin; winda kirin} to lose (K); 2) {syn: dor̄andin (M/ K[s]); ≠birin [3]} {also: daîn der (F)} to lose, be defeated *(at a game)* (K); 3) to let go (K); to abandon, leave, forego (JB3); 4) to produce (K). [Z-1/EP-7/K/JB3/B/ZF3//F]

derdan II دەردان *f.* **(;-ê).** vessel, utensil, dish; receptacle: **•Kur̄o, t'êr̄ û *derdangê* xwe bînin werne imbarê, xwer̄a nan dagirin** (Ba3-3, #36) Boys, bring your sacks and *receptacles* and go to the storehouse and fill them [=sacks, etc.] with bread [i.e., food]. {also: derdang (Ba3-3/YZ-2,

#278); derdank (IFb)} {syn: aman} [Ba3-3/YZ-2//K/B/F//IFb]

derdang دەردانگ (Ba3-3/YZ-2) = vessel, receptacle. See **derdan II**.

derdank دەردانك (IFb) = vessel, receptacle. See **derdan II**.

dere دەرە = place. See **der I**.

derece دەرەجە (GF) = stairs. See **derenc**.

dereft دەرەفت (TF) = possibility. See **derfet**.

dereke دەرەکە *adj.* 1) local; 2) strange[r], outsider: •**merîyê *dereke*** (B/Z-922) stranger, outsider. [Z-922/K/B/ZK3]

derenc دەرەنج *f./pl.(L)* **(-a;-ê).** stairs, staircase, steps: •**Bi *derenca* re banî ket** (L) He climbed up *the stairs*. {also: derece (GF); derence (TF); derince (K/JB3/IFb/OK); tirancek; <tirince ترنجه/derênce درينجه> (HH)} {syn: nerdewan; pêpelîng; pêstirk} < Ar darajah درجة [BX/L/ZF3//K/JB3/IFb/OK//HH//TF//GF]

derence دەرەنجە (TF) = stairs. See **derenc**.

dereng دەرەنگ *adj.* late, tardy: **-dereng man** (IFb) to be late: •**Mamoste, gava ku ez dihatim mektebê lawikek li pey min bû, hema bela xwe di min dida, ji ber wê ez hinekî *dereng mam*** (LM, 16) Teacher, when I was coming to school a boy was behind me, he was bothering me, that's why *I am* a little bit *late*; **-dereng kirin** = to make s.o. late. {also: [direnk] درنك (JJ); <dereng> درنگ (HH)} {≠zû} [Pok. 5. del- 196.] 'long': Old Ir *darga- = 'long' & *dargant- --> *dagrant- --> *daγrand --> *dērand --> dērang (for -nd --> -ng, cf. P ōrand اورند & ōrang اورنگ = 'throne; glory') & *dranga-; P derang درنگ = 'delay, hesitation, pause' & dīr (older dēr) دير = 'late'; Sor direng درەنگ = 'late'; cf. also Lat longus <*dlong- {derengî} [F/K/A/JB3/IFb/B/HH/SK/GF/TF/OK/SC//JJ] <awiqîn; dirêj; egle; gîro>

derengî دەرەنگی *f.* **(-ya;-yê).** tardiness, lateness: •**Lawik jî *derengîya şevê* çû** (ZZ-10, 160) And the boy went *late at night*. [K/A/JB3/IFb/GF/OK/ZF] <dereng>

derew دەرەو *f.* **(-a;-ê).** lie, fib, falsehood, untruth: •**Eger xebera te *derew* be, ezê şûrekî li stuyê te dim, / Serê te ji gewdê te biqetînim** (Z-2, 68) If what you say is *a lie*, I will take a sword to your neck, / I will sever your head from your body; **-derew kirin** = to tell a lie. {also: direw, f. (JB1-A); [direoû] درو (JJ); <derew> درو (HH)} {syn: vir̄ II} [Pok. 2. dhreugh- 276.] 'to deceive' (verbal stem *dhrugh- & nominal stem *dhrougho- [Kent]) : Skt √druh in drógha- /droha- = '(malicious) injury' & drúhyati = 'deceives'; O Ir *drauga- (A&L p. 84 [V]): Av Druǰ = 'the evil force opposed to Ahuramazda' & draoga- (pres. druž-) = 'to lie, tell a lie'; OP duruj- = 'to lie, deceive' & draujana- = 'deceitful' (Kent); P dorūγ دروغ; Sor diro درۆ; = Za zurı/zûrı *f.* (Mal); Hau dirûê *f.* (M4); cf. also Germ Trug = 'deceit' & [be]trügen = 'to deceive' [K/A/JB3/IFb/B/HH/GF/OK//JJ/JB1-A]

derewçî دەرەوچی (K) = liar. See **derewîn**.

derewçîn دەروەچین (BK) = liar. See **derewîn**.

derewgo دەرەوگۆ (K) = liar. See **derewîn**.

derewîn دەرەوین *m.&f.* **(-ê/;).** 1) {syn: vir̄ek} liar: •**Agir li mala *derewîna* ket, kesî jê bawer nekir** (Wkt:Pêvek) Fire broke out in *the liars'* house, no one believed them *[prv.]*; 2) *[adj.]* untrue, false, fake. {also: derewçî (K); derewçîn (BK); derewgo (K); **derewker** (BX/K/JB3/IF); [direvin] دروين (JJ) *(mistakenly glossed as 'lie')* } [BX//F/K/A/IFb/B/JJ/OK/ZF3] See also **derewker**.

derewker دەرەوکەر *m.&f.* **(-ê/-a;).** liar. {also: derewçî (K); derewçîn (BK); derewgo (K); **derewîn** (F/K/A/IFb/JJ); <derewker> دروكر (HH)} {syn: vir̄ek} [BX/K/JB3/IFb/HH/GF/OK/ZF3] See also **derewîn**.

derêxistin دەرئێخستن/دەرێخستن (der-êx-) (Ba) = to remove. See **derxistin.**

derf دەرف: -derfa sing (IS) = chest. See **depa sîng** under **dep**.

derfet دەرفەت *f.* **(-a;-ê).** chance, possibility, opportunity: •[**Ewî daîm ... her guhdar bû da rojekê *derfetê* bîne û ewê tolê ji Zeman Xanî biderîne**] (JR #39, 120) He was always listening ... so that one day he would have *the chance* to take revenge on Zeman Khan •**Sîstema Sovyetê çi *derfet* û astengî derxistin pêşiya we** (Wlt 2:59, 16) What *opportunities* and obstacles did the Soviet system place before you? {also: dereft (TF-2); [derfet] درفت (JJ)} {syn: delîve; fesal [1]; firset; kevlû [2]; k'ês} ?<Ar ẓurūf ظروف = 'conditions, circumstances'; =Sor hel هەل [Wlt/JJ/TF/OK/AId]

derge دەرگە (K/GF/Z-1/EP-7) = door. See **dergeh**.

dergeh دەرگەه *f.(A/JB3)/m.(B/SK/JB1-A)* **(/dergê** [FK-2]**; /dergê[h]** [B]**).** gate, door; entrance door

(IFb); wide or large door or gate (IF/HH): •**Rojekê dema mexribê çû ber *dergehê* Diyarbekirê** (Rnh 2:17, 306-7) One day at sunset he reached *the gates of* Diyarbekir; -**derge û dîwan** (EP-7) do. {also: derge (K/GF/Z-1/EP-7); [dergheh] درگه (JJ); <derge[h]> درگه (HH)} {syn: derî I; qêpe} Cf. P dar در; Sor der دەر/derga دەرگا/ derge دەرگە. -- *See etymology at derî I*. [Z-1/K/GF//A/ JB3/IFb/B/JJ/HH/JB1-A/SK/TF/OK] See also **derî I**.

dergehvan دەرگەهڤان (IFb/TF/OK/Rnh/FS/BF) = gatekeeper. See **dergevan**.

dergehvanî دەرگەهڤانی (IFb/TF) = profession of gatekeeper. See **dergevanî**.

dergelî دەرگەلی *m.* **(-yê;).** gorge, ravine, canyon. {syn: derteng [1]; geboz; gelî II; zang; zer II} [Zeb]

dergevan دەرگەڤان *m.&f.* **(-ê/;).** gatekeeper, doorman: •***Dergehvana* derî girti bûn** (Rnh 2:17, 307) *The gatekeepers* had closed the gates •***Dergivan*, derî ji me re veke, emê derbas bibin** (L-5, 138, l. 25-26) *Gatekeeper*, open the gate for us, so that we can come in. {also: dergehvan (IFb/TF/ OK-2/Rnh/FS/BF); dergewan (SK); dergivan (L); derk'evan (K[s]); [derghevan] درگوان (JJ)} Sor dergawan دەرگاوان {dergevanî} [L//K/A/JB3/JJ/GF/OK/ /IFb/TF/Rnh/FS/BF//SK]

dergevanî دەرگەڤانی *f.* **(-ya;-yê).** profession of gatekeeper or doorman: •**Diçe şeherê T'bîlîsîê – li Gurcstanê. Li wêderê wextekî xebata *dergevanîê* dike** (HCK-5, 291) He goes to the city of Tbilisi – in Georgia. There he works for a time as a gatekeeper. {also: dergehvanî (IFb/TF)} [HCK/ K/A/FJ/GF//IFb/TF] <dergevan>

dergewan دەرگەوان (SK) = gatekeeper. See **dergevan**.

dergistî دەرگِستی *m.&f.* **(-yê/-ya; /-yê).** fiancé(e), betrothed, engaged; *f.* *approximates Eng* girlfriend: •**Memê bira, tu jî řabe heře ser kanîyê *dergistîya* xwe bi ç'e'vê xwe bibîne / Hege ne bi dilê teye, ezê vêga nîşanîyê vegeřînim** (Z-2, 79) Mem my brother, get up and go to the well, see your *betrothed* with your own eyes / If she is not to your liking, I will annul the engagement •**Qîza hakim ket bin textê *dergistîyê* xwe** (L) The princess got under her *fiancé's* bed. {also: dergîs (IFb-2); dergîst (A/B); dergîstî (EP-4/EP-7); desgirtî (IFb/OK); destgirtî (EP-7/ K-2/IFb-2); dezgirtî (JB1-S); dizgirtî (JB3); [dez-ghirti دزگرتی/dest-ghirti دست گرتی /deste-ghirti دسته گرتی] (JJ); <destgirtî> دستگرتی (HH)} < dest = 'hand' + girtî = 'taken': for another example of such a metathesis involving -r-, see **dersok** below. Sor dezgîran دەزگیران/destgîran دەستگیران; Hau desgiran/dezgiran *m.* & desgirane/ dezgirane *f.* (M4) [L/K/TF//JB3//IFb/OK// A/B//JB1-S//EP-7/JJ/ HH] <bêşk'ertim; bûk I; şîranî; zava>

dergivan دەرگِڤان (L) = gatekeeper. See **dergevan**.

dergîs دەرگیس (IFb) = fiancé(e). See **dergistî**.

dergîst دەرگیست (A/B) = fiancé(e). See **dergistî**.

dergîstî دەرگیستی (EP-4/EP-7) = fiancé(e). See **dergistî**.

dergûş دەرگووش *f.* **(-a;-ê).** 1) {syn: bêşîk; bormotk (EP-7); colan; landik} cradle, crib: •**Stîya 'Ereb, de řabe *dergûşa* kuřî li ber p'êsîra xwe bişidîne, / Ji ber min biřeve û bilezîne** (Z-2, 85) Lady Ereb, get up and fasten the infant['s *cradle*] to your garment [like a papoose], / Then quickly flee before me; -**dara dergûşê** (Dz) do.; 2) infant, baby; newborn infant. {also: derguş (TF); [dergouch] درگوش (JJ); <derkûş> درکوش (HH)} [Dz/K/A/JB3/IFb/B/JJ/GF/OK/ZF3//HH//TF]

der•hatin دەرهاتِن *vi.* **(der[t]ê-).** 1) {syn: derk'etin} to leave, quit: •**Ez nahêlim mêvanê min mal *derê*** (Z-1) I won't let my guest *leave* the house; -**bîna *fk-ê* derhatin** = to be homesick {syn: bêrîya II fk-ê kirin}: •**Ez hatime welatê xerîb, *bîna min* pê *dertêye*** (Z-1) I've come to a strange land, [and] *I'm homesick* [lit. 'My breath is leaving over it']; 2) to turn out to be, to end up: -**avis/ĥemle derhatin** = to become pregnant; 3) *to arrive. {also: [der-hatin] در هاتن (JJ)} [Z-921/K/ JJ/GF/OK]

derheq دەرهەق (TF/OK) = about. See **derheqa**.

derheqa دەرهەقا *prep.* [+ -**da**] about, regarding, concerning (or **di derĥeqa ... da**): •***der heqê* wan** (BX) *about* them •**Tiştê xirab *derheqa* Ûsib*da* got** (Ba) She said bad things *about* Joseph •**Wexta Al-p'aşayê kal û jina xweva eva gilîya *derheqa* Memê*da* bihîstin** (Z-1) When old A.p. and his wife heard these words *about* Mem •**Zelîxe Xatûn jî pê dihese *derheqa* hatina Ûsib*da*** (Ba) Zelikha also hears *about* Joseph's arrival. {also: derheq (TF/OK); der heqê; der-ĥeqq (SK)} {syn: derbare; li ser [ser II]} Cf. T hakkında = 'about' [Ba/K/B//TF/ OK//SK]

der heqê دەر هەقێ = about. See **derheqa**.

derhêner دەرهێنەر *m.* **(-ê;).** producer: •**Kiarostamî wekî yek ji baştirîn *derhênerên* cîhanê tê binavkirin** (AW70B4) Kiarostami is being called [or, is known as] one of the world's best *producers*. {also: derîner (Wkt)} Sor derhêner دەرهێنەر [(neol)AW/ZF3/FD//Wkt]

der-ḧeqq دەر حەقق (SK) = about. See **derheqa**.

derik دەرك (SK) = door. See **derî I**.

derince دەرنجە (K/JB3/IFb) = stairs. See **derenc**.

deristin دەرسِتِن (M) = to split *(vi.)*. See **derizîn**.

deriz دەرِز (GF) = crack. See **derz**.

derizandin دەرِزاندِن *vt.* **(-derizîn-).** 1) to split, crack *(vt.)*; 2) to scratch (K). {also: [derizandin] درزاندين (JJ)} [K/JB3/IFb/JJ/GF/TF/OK/M] <derizîn; derz>

derizîn دەرِزين *vi.* **(-deriz-).** 1) to split, crack *(vi.)*; 2) to get scratched (K). {also: deristin (M); derzîn (GF); [derizin] درزين (JJ); <dirizîn درزين (diderize) (ددرزه)> (HH)} [M//K/JB3/IFb/JJ/TF/OK//HH/ /GF] <derizandin; derz>

der•î I دەری *m.* **(•ê/•îyê; dêrî).** 1) {syn: dergeh; qêpe} door: ***•Dêrî* vekin** = Open *the door*! **•Serdarê çil qerwaşa Gul'eîşê, / Fanosê ji xatûna xweȓa bîne *derîyê* ḧewşê** (Z-2, 69) Gul-aisha, commander of my forty servants, / Bring a lamp for your lady to *the gate* [or, *door*] *of* the yard; 2) point *(in backgammon)* [Cf. T kapı]. {also: der III (IFb-2/ F-2/JB1-A); derik (SK); [deri] دری (JJ); <derî> دری (HH)} [Pok. dhu̯ĕ̄r-, *etc.* 278.] 'door, doorway': Skt dvár-; Av duuara-; Old P du̯vara- *n.*; Mid P dar; Parthian bar (<*dwar-); P dar در; Sor der دەر; Za ber *m.* = 'door; outside' (Mal); Hau bere *m.* = 'door' & ber = 'outside' (M4); cf. also Gr thyra θύρα; Arm duṙ (W: tuṙ) դուռ; Rus dver′ дверь; Germ Tür. [F/K/A/JB3/IFb/B/JJ/HH/ JB1-S/GF/TF/OK/ BK//JB1-A//SK] <ȓexderî; serder; sîvande> See also **dergeh**.

derî II دەری = outside of. See **der II**.

derînan دەرئینان (JJ-Rh/SK/OK) = to remove. See **deranîn**.

derîner دەرینەر (Wkt) = producer. See **derhêner**.

der•k'etin دەرکەتِن *vi.* **(der-k'ev-).** 1) {syn: derhatin} to leave, go or come out of, exit: **•Ew ji bajarê xwe *dernakevin*** = They *don't leave* their town **•Nerî go qundir teqî[y]a, xortek jê *derket*** (L) Suddenly the gourd split open, [and] a young man *came out* of it **•Ew çûn *derk'etne* cîkî wisa, ku t'u merî li wan dera t'unebûn** (Ba) They went [until they] *reached* a place in which there were no people **•P'adşa wezîrê xweva pêva *derk'et*** (J) The king *set out* with his vizier **•P'elte 'ewrê ȓeş *derk'et* û baranê destpê dir** (Z-1) Black storm clouds *came out* and it began to rain; **-ji xebera ... derk'etin** (XF): a) to refuse to comply with *(s.o.'s wishes)*; b) to disobey; 2) {syn: banî k'etin} to ascend, go up, climb: **•B. *derket* ser qesrê** (L) B. *went up* onto [the roof of] the castle; 3) to become: **-avis/ḧemle derk'etin** = to become pregnant {syn: avis/ḧemle derhatin}. {also: derkewtin (SK); [derketin درکتین /derkewtin درکفتين] (JJ); <derketin درکتن (derdikeve) (دردکڤه)> (HH)} *{for the same verb meaning both **to go up** & **to go out**,* cf. Clq Ar ṭili' طلع, T çıkmak, Arm ellel ելնել & Italian salire} [K/A/JB3/ IFb/B/JJ/HH/GF/TF/OK//SK]

derk'evan دەرکەڤان (K[s]) = gatekeeper. See **dergevan**.

derkewtin دەرکەوتِن (SK) = to go out or up. See **derk'etin**.

der•kirin دەرکِرِن *vt.* **(der-k-).** to lance *(a boil)*: **•Heker qunêrê janda, divêt *bihê derkirin*** (N.Shaheen. Dict. of Kurdish Verbs) If the boil hurts, it must *be lanced* **•Ê lingê te *derkir* ezim** (HCK-3, #16, 182) I am the one who *lanced* your foot. {syn: 'eciqandin[2]} Sor der kirdin دەرکردن = 'to lance, open by squeezing (a boil, etc.)' [HCK/K/FJ/TF/ ZF3] <diȓandin>

dermalî دەرمالی *f.* **(-ya;-yê).** bride's dowry, trousseau *(usually in the form of livestock, which remains her property in her husband's house)*: **•Noginek *dermalîya wê* ye. Cî-nivîn cihêzê wê ye** (RiaTaza: Memê û Eyşe) A heifer is *her trousseau*, her dowry is bedding. [K/B/BF/Wkt] <cihaz; qelen>

derman دەرمان *m.* **(-ê ; dermên, vî dermanî).** 1) cure, remedy, medicine; drug: **•Derxwînê beroşê, *dermanê* girarê [Dûv]** (L[1937]) Cover of the pot, *remedy of* the soup *[rdl.; ans.: sheep's fattail (whose grease is used in seasoning food)]*; **-dermanê nehişyarîyê** (JB1-A) soporific; 2) treatment (K): **-derman kirin** (SK) to treat, cure: **•Eger sa'etekê pêştir hung nexoşîya xo bi ḧakîmêt ḧaziq û xêrxaz *derman neken*, mikrobê cehaletê û s̱efrayê sefahetê ... pîçek maye hingo bikujît** (SK 57:660) If you do not have skilled and well-meaning physicians *treat* your disease within the hour, then the microbe of ignorance and the bile of stupidity ... will kill you within a short while; 3) ointment, grease (K); 4) {syn: boyax; ȓeng; xim} paint (K/B); dye (SK): **•"Çawêt min**

sor bûne?" Rîwî got, "Helbet. Dibêjî *dermanê* qirmizî hatîye tê-kirin" (SK 6:68) "Have my eyes become red?' The fox said, "Certainly, you'd think red *dye* had been poured into them"; 5) spice (SK): **•Xarina bajerîya, ko şirînî, pilaw, goşt, êprax, şorbawa bi *dermanêt* bênxoş û tiştê wekî wane bo wî didanane ser sifrê** (SK 31:274) He would set on the tablecloth townsmen's food, which is sweetmeats, pilaf, meat, stuffed vine-leaves, soup with fragrant *spices* and other such things; **-dermanê germ** (Msr/A/JJ-PS) pepper *(spice)*: **•Ne sîr û ne pîvaz, qede li *dermanê germ* bik'eve** (Msr) May disaster befall neither garlic nor onions, but rather *[red] peppers* (=All three are equally bad) *[prv.]*. {also: [derman] درمـــــان (JJ); <derman> درمان (HH)} Cf. P darmān درمان -> T derman; Sor derman دەرمـــان; Za derman *m.* (Mal) [K/A/JB3/IFb/B/JJ/HH/SK/GF/TF/OK] <ç'are; [5]: bîber; ḧiçḧar; îsot>

dermanfiroş دەرمـانـفِـرۆش *m.&f.* **(-ê/-a;).** pharmacist, druggist, chemist *(British usage)*: **•Ev zilam *dermanfi[r]oş* bû û mala wî jî li nêzîk bû** (Nbh 129:7) This man was a *pharmacist* and his home was nearby. {also: dermanfroş (CS)} Sor dermansaz دەرمـانـسـاز /dermanger دەرمـانـگـەر /dermanfiroş دەرمانفِرۆش [Nbh/K/A/IFb/FJ/GF/ZF//CS]

dermanxan•e دەرمـانـخـانـە *f.* **(•eya;•ê).** pharmacy, drugstore: **•*Dermanxane* zêde bûne lê buhayê dermanan wek hev e** (Radio Sweden 9.ii.2011) *Pharmacies* have become more numerous but the price of medicines is the same. Sor dermanxane دەرمانخانە/dermange دەرمانگە [RadioSweden/K/A/B/IFb/GF/RZ/ZF/CS]

dernefîs دەرنەفیس *m.* **(-ê;).** screwdriver. <Fr tournevis [Bw/OK/BF] <badan [4]; burẍî; sist kirin (sist [2]); şidandin [3]; vekirin [3]>

derneqot دەرنـەقـۆت (GF/Wkt) = upside down. See **dernexûn**.

dernexûn دەرنـەخـوون *adj./adv.* upside down: **•...û qelûnê di ser xwelîdankê de *derxûm* ditepîne** (Epl, 24) and he taps the pipe *upside down* over the ashtray. {also: derneqot (GF/Wkt-2); derneẍûn (GF-2); dernixûn (Kmc); derxûm (Epl/Wkt-2)} {syn: vajî} Cf. P nigūn نـگـون = 'inverted, turned upside down'; Sor serew-nixûn سـەرەونـخـوون = 'upside-down, overturned, topsy-turvy' [Epl//A/IFb/GF/FJ/Wkt//Kmc] <berevajî>

derneẍûn دەرنـــەغـــوون (GF) = upside down. See **dernexûn**.

dernixûn دەرنِـــخـــوون (Kmc) = upside down. See **dernexûn**.

derobero دەرۆبەرۆ = stray, roving. See **derodero**.

derodero دەرۆدەرۆ *adj.* homeless, stray, wandering, roving, vagrant: **•Xan êt'îme *derodero*** (EP-8) The Khan is a *homeless* orphan. {also: derobero} [EP-8/K/GF] <derbeder; mişext>

deroze دەرۆزە *f.* **().** begging; alms collecting. {syn: geşt; p'ars; xwazok} Sor deroze دەرۆزە [A/IFb/OK]

derp•ê دەرپـێ *m.* **(•îyê;).** underpants, drawers: **•Kiras û *derpîyan* jî danêm, yan ne?** (SK 37:328) Should I take off my shirt and *drawers* also [or not?]. {also: [derpi] درپــی (JJ); <derpê> درپــی (HH)} Sor derpê دەرپــێ [SK/K/A/IFb/B/HH/GF/TF//JJ] <başewala>

ders دەرس *f.* **(-a;-ê).** lesson: **•Kuřê xo teslîmi mela 'Ebbas kir ko *dersêt* Qur'anê *nîşa* wî *bidet*** (SK 14:145) She entrusted her son to Mullah Abbas, for him *to teach* him the Quran **•Noke sa'et yazde ye, wextê *dersa* qunsolî ye, dibît biçim** (SK 54:625) It is now eleven o'clock, time for the Consul's *lesson*. I must go; **-ders gotin** (SK)/~**dan** (IFb) to teach; **-ders xundin** (SK) to study. {also: [ders] درس (JJ); <ders> درس (HH)} < Ar dars درس [K/JB3/IFb/B/JJ/HH/SK/GF/OK]

dersdar دەرسدار *m.&f.* **(-ê/-a; /-ê).** teacher, instructor: **•*Ders-darê* zimanê kurdî** (RiaTaza) Kurdish language *teacher*. {syn: mamosta} [Ber/K/JB3/IFb/B/GF/OK/ZF3] <seyda>

dersok دەرســــــــۆك *f./m.* **(-a/-ê;).** Kurdish man's headdress; kerchief: **•Dît sindoq-emînî *desroka* xo îna derê, tejî zêř kir, dav şexsekî** (M-Ak, #567, 258) He saw the cashier take out his *kerchief*, fill it with gold and give it to somebody. {also: desrok (M-Ak); [dastruk] دســتــرك (JJ-Rh); [desrók] (JJ-G)} {syn: cemedanî; kevîng; p'oşî; şemil} <dest = 'hand' + řok = (suffix): for another example of such a metathesis involving -r-, see **dergistî** above. Sor desroke دەسرۆکە = 'kerchief' [Hk/Bw//JJ-Rh//M-Ak/JJ-G] <k'ofî; t'emezî>

dersxan•e دەرسـخـانـە *f.* **(•[ey]a ;•ê).** 1) {syn: p'ol III; sinif} class; grade: **•Zozan *dersxana* çarada dixûne** (B) Zozan is in the fourth *grade*; 2) classroom: **•Di *dersxanê* da çend mase hene?** (DZK) How many tables (=desks) are there in the *class(room)*? [DZK/K/IFb/B/GF/OK] <dibistan>

derteng دەرتەنگ/**derṯeng** دەرطەنگ [Zeb] *f.* **(-a-ê).**

narrow passageway: 1) {syn: dergelî; geboz; gelî II; zang; zer II} gorge, ravine, canyon: **•Pez li *derṯengê* diçerit** (FS) The sheep graze in *the ravine*; 2) strait *(geog.)* (Zeb); 3) channel, canal, course (K/JJ). {also: [der-tenk] درتنك (JJ)} Sor derteng دەرتەنگ = 'defile, gorge' [Zeb/Bar/K/ZF3/FS//JJ]

derûnî دەروونی *adj.* internal, inner; spiritual; psychological, mental, emotional: **-nexweşiyên derûnî** (BF) mental illnesses: **•Her ku diçe *nexweşiyên* wan yên *derûnî* girantir dibin** (M. Ozçelik. "Asoyê Dînan", Diyarname 28.x.2014) Their *mental illnesses* are gradually becoming more severe. [M.Ozçelik/IFb/ZF3/Wkt/BF/FD/SS/Kmc]

derva دەرڤا (AB/K/B) = outside. See **derve**.

derve دەرڤە *adv.* outside: **•Kerê me îşev *li derva* maye** (AB) Our donkey stayed *outside* tonight **•Birê wî ê mezin rabû ... go here *derve* ber derîyê miẍarê mîz bike** (L) His eldest brother got up ... to go urinate *outside* the door of the cave; **-ji derveyî ...** = outside of, apart from. {also: derva (AB/K); der ve (IF); [derwé] درڤه (JJ); <derve> درڤه (HH)} Cf. Sor derê دەرێ/derewe دەرەوە; Za teber (Mal)/ tever (Todd/Mal); Hau ber (M4). Cf. **derî** = door. [AB/L/K/B//A/JB3/IF/JJ/HH] <der II>

?dervêş دەرڤێش (A) = dervish. See **dewrêş**.

derwêş دەروێش (IFb/GF/TF/OK) = dervish. See **dewrêş**.

der•xistin دەرخستن *vt.* **(der-x/der-xîn-/-derx-[JJ]).** 1) to take out, remove, extract [faire sortir, expulser]: **•Bihare, xelq gaê xwe *derdixe*!** (J) It's springtime, people *are taking out* their oxen **•Dewlê dadixe, wekî avê *derxe*** (Ba) He lowers the bucket [into the well], in order *to take out* (i.e., get) water **•30 sal berê seeta bavê min ketibû vê bîrê, min jî îro *derxist*** (LM, 12) 30 years ago my father's watch fell into this well, today I *brought* it *out* **•Zikê wî diqelêşe, Şenglo, Menglo, Qalîçenglo *derdixe*** (J) She rips open his stomach [and] *takes out* Sh., M. and Q.; 2) to derive: **•Em li serê sukur ava dikin, jê *derdixin* elektrîka rohnî, a wek zêr** (AB) We build a dam at the top, from which we get *derive* electric light, which [is] like gold; 3) to render, make, cause to be: **•Tu min rûreş *dernexî*!** (L) You're not going to disgrace me!; 4) to produce, compose, make: **•Keçika û jina jî k'ilamêd mêranîyê ser wana *derdixistin*** (Ba2:1, 204) Girls and women *composed* songs of bravery about them; 5) {syn: vegirtin [5]} to break out with/in, come down with *(a disease)*: **•Şivana k'erê xweî ku "yeman" *derxistibûn* danîne 'erdê** (Dz) The shepherds had laid on the ground their donkeys who *had broken out with* "yeman" (an animal disease); 6) *idioms*: **-[ji] ber xwe derxistin** (K/B) to make up, create (out of thin air): **•Ĥetanî naha jî ez ȓastî nizanim, gelo k'îjan salê ji dîa xwe bûme. Salêd ku pasportêd meda hatine nivîsarê me *ber xwe derxistine*** (Ba2, 220) Until now I don't really know what year I was born. The years written in our passports we *made up*; **-jê derxistin** (ZF3/Kmc) to subtract *(math.)*; ***-ft-î* jê [ji *ft-î*] derxistin** (HYma) to tell (stg.) apart from (stg. else), distinguish between 2 things: **•Ker e navên rojan *ji hevdû dernaxîne* wek min e** (HYma, 46) He's dumb, he *can't tell* the days [of the week] *apart*, he's like me **•-Ma te xwe hînî xwendina Kurdî kiriye, keko? –Na, ez hinek tîpan *ji hev dernaxim*** (Epl, 17) Have you taught yourself to read Kurdish, brother? No, I *can't tell* some of the letters *apart*; **-pê re serî dernexistin** (Wkt) not to be able to cope with: **•Kurê wê jî vê rewşê dibîne, lê dike nake *serî bi* diya xwe *re* nikare *derêxe*** (İ.Tepe. Apê Kal, 19) Her son also sees the situation, but no matter how he tries he cannot *cope with* his mother; **-ȓê jê dernexistin** (XF) to be unable to find a way out of a situation, not to know which way to turn: **•M. gelekî şaş û ȟeyrî ma, t'u *ȓê jê dernexist*** (EP-7) M. was perplexed and bewildered, he *didn't know what to do next*; **-tê derxistin** (K/B/ZF) to guess: **•K'î ji wana *tê derdixe*** (Ba) Whichever one of them *guesses* **•Lê kuȓê dinê qet *tê dernexistin*** (Ba) But the other boys *couldn't guess* at all. {also: derêxistin (der-êx-); [der-khystin] درخستين (JJ)} [K/A/JB3/IFb/B/JJ/GF/TF/OK] <derk'etin>

derxûm دەرخووم (Epl/Wkt) = upside down. See **dernexûn**.

derxûn دەرخوون (B/F/IFb/HH/GF/ZF3) = lid. See **derxwîn**.

derxwîn دەرخوین *m.(L)/f.(B/ZF3)* **(-ê/-a; /-ê).** lid, cover *(of pot)*: **•*Derxwînê* beroşê, dermanê girarê [Dûv]** (L) *Cover of* the pot, seasoning of the soup *[rdl.; ans.: sheep's fattail]*. {also: derxûn (B/F/IFb-2/GF-2/ZF3-2); [derkhoum درخم/ derkhoun درخن] (JJ); <derxûn> درخون (HH)} [L/K/A/IFb/GF/TF/OK/ZF3//F/B/JJ/HH]

derya دەریا *f./m.[Derêşî]* **(-ya/-yê;).** sea, ocean: **•Ev kuma çîrokan jî çipkek e ji wî *deryayê* mezin û berîn ku mirovê Kurd di nav hizir û aşupa xu da afirandîn** (X.Dêreşî. Şevbêriyên zarokan, 8) And this collection of stories is a drop from that large and broad *ocean* which the Kurd has created in his mind and imagination **•Hêj qet nebû *derya* û beř, baxoy nivîsî xeyr û şeř** (FT, 174) Neither *sea* nor land existed yet, God had already designated [lit. 'wrote'] good and bad. {also: [терїа/derya (Lx)] دریا (JJ)} {syn: beĥr} Cf. P daryā دریا; Sor derya دەریا/delya دەلیا/zerya زەریا/zirê زرێ [Derêşî/K(s)/A/IFb/FJ/GF/TF/JJ/Kmc/RZ/ZF/Tsab/CS]

derz دەرز *f.* **(-a;-ê).** crack, cleft, split, fissure, slit *(in a glass, plate, etc.)*: **•Çênabê rê bi tu kes û aliyek bê dayîn *derzê* bixe nav birayetiya pêkhatên Iraqê** (basnews.com 25.iii.2014) No one and no group should be allowed to introduce *cracks* between the constituent groups of Iraq **•*Derz* ket şîşa pencerê** (FS) A *crack* formed in the window pane. {also: deriz (GF); [derz/ deriz] درز (JJ); <derz> درز (HH)} {syn: kelş; qelîştek; terk; tîş I} Cf. P darz درز = 'seam, suture'. See **derzî** for etymology. [K/A/JB3/IFb/JJ/HH/TF/OK/ZF3/FS//GF]

derzen دەرزەن *f.* **().** vertebra: **•Řimekê lêdixe li *derzeneka* piştêye** (Z-4) With a spear, he strikes him in his *spinal column*. {syn: movika piştê} [Z-4/Wkt/ZF3] <mezmezk>

derzin دەرزِن *f.* **().** dozen. {also: derzîn (RZ)} [Bw/Dh/FS/Wkt//RZ] <donzdeh; nîvderzin; nûrî>

derzî دەرزی *f.* **(-ya;-yê).** 1) needle: **-dezî û dirêzî** (Slv)/**ta û derzîk** (Am) needle and thread; 2) syringe, shot: **-derzî lêdan** (ZF) to give s.o. a shot, to inoculate; 3) {syn: dirêşûşk; jene} sting(er) *(of insect, scorpion)*. {also: dirêzî (Slv); [derzi درزی/derzik درزك] (JJ); <derzî> درزی (HH)} Cf. P darzī(gar) (درزی(گر = 'tailor'--> T terzi = 'tailor'; [Pok. dhereĝh- 254.] 'firm, to fasten': Pok. specifically mentions P darz درز = 'seam, suture' and similar Iranian words for 'to sew with thread': Skt dṝhyati/dṝm̐hati = 'he fastens' & dṛḍhá- = 'firm'; Av darəzayeiti = 'he ties fast, fetters' & darəza- m. = 'tying, binding, fastening' & dərəz- *f.* = 'fetter'; Southern Tati dialects: Chali, Takestani, Eshtehardi, Xiaraji, & Sagz-abadi darzena *f.* = 'needle' (Yar-Shater); Sor derzî دەرزی = 'needle, tailor'; Za derzinî *f.* = 'needle' & derzenã [deştiş] (Todd) = 'to sew' [Ad/Msr/K/A/JB3/IFb/B/JJ/HH/GF/OK/ZF//Slv] <derzîdank; dezî; dirûtin; şûjin>

derzîdan دەرزیدان (K/B/GF/FJ) = pin cushion. See **derzîdank**.

derzîdang دەرزیدانگ (K) = pin cushion. See **derzîdank**.

derzîdank دەرزیدانك *f.* **(-a;-ê).** pin cushion. {also: derzîdan (K/B/GF/FJ); derzîdang (K-2)} [Qrj/A/IFb//K/B/GF/FJ] <derzî>

derzîn دەرزین (RZ) = dozen. See **derzin**.

des I دەس (BK) = hand. See **dest**.

de's II دەعس (B) = sickle. See **das**.

desgirtî دەسگِرتی (IFb/OK) = fiancé(e). See **dergistî**.

de'sî دەعسی (Frq/K/B) = fishbone; awn (of wheat). See **dasî**.

deslimêj دەسلِمێژ (ZK-3) = Islamic ritual ablutions. See **destnimêj**.

desmal دەسمال (A/B/IFb/JJ/GF) = handkerchief. See **destmal**.

desmê دەسمێ (GF) = Islamic ritual ablutions. See **destnimêj**.

desmêj دەسمێژ (HH/ZZ-3) = Islamic ritual ablutions. See **destnimêj**.

despê دەسپێ. See dest pê [bûn/kirin] under **dest**.

desrok دەسڕۆك (M-Ak/JJ-G) = kerchief. See **dersok**.

dest/dest' [JB1-A] دەست *m.* **(-ê; dêst, vî destî).** 1) hand: **-dest avêtin[e]** [+ *dat. constr.*] = a) to touch: **•Qîzkê *destê xwe avête* Mhemmed Xan** (L) The girl *touched* [lit. 'threw her hand on'] M. Kh.; b) to begin, start *(vt.)* {syn: dest pê kirin}: **•Em *dest bihavêjînê*?** [pavêjînê] (Bw) Shall we *get started*?; **-dest-dest** (K) immediately, suddenly, momentarily: **•Bor *dest-dest* nêzîkî xezalê dibe** (FK-eb-2) *In a second*, Bor nears the gazelle; **-dest ji *ft-î* k'işandin** (Z-1) to give up on, renounce {syn: dev ji *ft-î* berdan; qeran; hiştin; t'erkandin}: **•Ewî û giregirê sînota xweva şîret li Memê dikirin, wekî Memê *destê xwe ji* vê yekê *bik'şîne*** (Z-1) He and the nobles of his côterie advised Mem *to give up on* that; **-dest k'etin** (J) to be obtained, acquired, gotten, gotten hold of: **•Lawo, ĥeta biharê, wekî ga *dest* te *nek'et*, min girêde!** (J) Son, by springtime, if you *haven't obtained* an ox, tie me up [to the plough]!; **-dest pê bûn** = to begin, start *(vi.)* {also: despê; destpê}; **-dest pê kirin** = to begin, start *(vt.)* {syn: dest avêtin[e]}: **•*Despê kir* bi balt'e dar biřîn** (Dz) He *began* to cut down trees with an axe

•Aşiq ***dest bi*** **lêxistina sazê xwe** ***kir*** (Z-1) The singer *began to* play his saz (tembûr); **-destê** ***fk-ê*** **sar bûn** (XF) to lose interest in; to be confused; to lose one's head: ***•Destê*** **P'erî-xatûnê ji mal û ĥala** ***sar bûbû*** (Z-1) Peri-khatun *had lost interest in* her house and chores [lit. 'Peri-khatun's hands had gotten cold from her house and condition']; **-dest xistin** (F) to obtain, acquire, procure, get, get hold of, round up: **•Hine nan yane hine goşt** ***dest dixe*** (Ba) He *gets* a little bread or meat; **-dest xwe çûn** (Z-1): a) to lose strength, become weak, languish; to be done for {syn: av-zar çûn; zar-ziman k'etin}: **•M. jî zîndanêda ĥal t'une, îdî** ***dest xwe çûye*** (Z-1) M. was in bad shape in prison, he *was almost done for*; b) to suffer *(from grief, illness)*; c) to be disabled, to break down, go out of service; **-bi destê** ***fk-ê*** = by (passive agent) {syn: ji alîyê ...-ve; ji terefê...}: **•Gundê me** ***bi destê*** **Hemo hatiye şewitandin** (BX) Our village was burned *by* Hemo; **-ji destê ...** = from, at the hands of: **•Çi zirar hatye serê Ûsib** ***ji destê*** **biraye** (Ba) Any harm that has befallen Joseph is *due to* [lit. 'from the hands of'] [his] brothers; 2) {syn: qat [3]} counting word for suits of clothing (JB1-A&S): **-dest'ek** (JB1-A)/**destek cillik** (JB1-S) a suit of clothing: **•Diçe ser t'erzî,** ***destek*** **cilê efendîya ji xweȓa difesilîne** (Z-2) He goes to a tailor, orders for himself *a suit of* clothes fit for a gentleman; **-destên elbîsa** (JB1-S) sets of clothes, suits; 3) {also: destek, f. (K)} game; set; move *(in a game)* (EP-7/K): **•Bek'ir dîna xwe daê, ma du** ***dest*** **Memê ji mîr bive** (EP-7) B. saw that M. was two *moves* away from beating the prince (at chess). {also: des I (BK-2); [dest] دست (JJ); <dest> دست (HH)} [Pok. 1. ĝhesor- 447.]: 'hand' & *ĝhosto- (Kent): Proto IndIr *źhasta- (Schwartz): Skt hasta- *m.*; O Ir *zasta-: Av zasta-; O P dasta- (Kent); Sgd ∂ast; Pamir dialects: Yidgha last; Ormuri dest/dis; Parachi dôst; Sanglechi dōst; Wakhi dast/lâst; Shughni ∂ust (Morg); Pashto lās; P dast دست; Sor des[t] دەس[ت]; Za dest *m.* (Todd); Hau des *m.* (M4); cf. also Gr agostos ἀγοστός = 'flat of the hand, arm' [F/K/A/JB3/IFb/B/JJ/HH/JB1-A&S/GF/OK/BK] <ç'epil; mil; pîl I; t'ilî I>

destan دەستان *f.* **(-a;-ê).** 1) epic, epic poem; 2) story. {also: dastan (K); [destan دستان/dastan داستان] (JJ)} O Ir *dātastāna- < dāta- = 'law' + -stāna- = 'place, institution': Mid P dāistān/dādestān = 'judgement, verdict, trial, legal case; affair'; P dastān دستان/dāstān داستان = 'story, account'--> T destan; Sor dastan داستان; cf. also Za istanik *f.* = 'story' (Todd). See: M. Schwartz. "Irano-Tocharica," in: *Mémorial Jean de Menasce*, ed. Ph. Gignoux & A. Tafazzoli (Louvain: Imprimerie Orientaliste: Fondation Culturelle Iranienne, 1974), pp. 402-3, 405. [DM/Kdş/A/IFb/JJ/GF//K] <beyt [3]; çîrok; qewl>

destaȓ دەستاڕ *m.* **(-ê; destêȓ, vî destaȓî).** hand mill, grinder, quern. {also: distar (SK/Bw); [destar] دستار (JJ); <destar> دستار (HH)} {syn: girik II} [AB/F/K/A/JB3/IFb/B/JJ/HH/GF/TF/OK//SK/Bw] <aş I>

destav دەستاڤ *f.* **(-a;-ê).** 1) "potty", *euphemistic term for going to the bathroom and for feces and urine* (HH/IFb): **-destava stûr** (Zeb) "number two," *euphemistic term for defecation*; **-destava zirav** (Ak/Zeb) "number one," *euphemistic term for urination*; 2) bathroom, toilet, water closet, lavatory (K/F/B): **•Li van heywanan miqayet be, heta ku ez herim** ***destavê*** (WM 1:2, 6) Look after these animals while I go *to the bathroom*. {also: <destav> دستاڤ (HH)} [F/K/A/IFb/B/HH/GF/TF/OK] See also **destavxane**.

destavxan•e دەستاڤخانە *f.* **(•eya;•ê).** toilet, water closet, lavatory. {syn: avdestxane; avȓêj I; ç'olik III (Msr); daşir (Dy); edebxane [1]; qedemge (Czr)} [F/A/IF/B/ZF3] See also **avdestxane** & **destav**.

destbira دەستبرا *m.* **(-yê; destêbira[k]/destebirê[k] [B]).** 1) adoptive brother/sister; bosom buddy, sworn brother, blood brother; one with whom [fictive] brotherhood has been effected through a handshake (HH): **•[Dayim ez diçûm ji etrafan min dizî dikirin û ĥeywan û mal bi şev tîna Selmasê mala** ***destebirakê*** **xweyê Memed]** (JR) I would always go steal from my surroundings and bring animals and goods by night to Selmas, to the house of my *bosom buddy* Memed; 2) {syn: şoşman} best man *(at a wedding)* (IF). {also: destbirak (A); destbra (IF); destebira (B); destebirak (K/JR/B); destebra (PS); <destbira> دستبرا (HH)} {destbiraktî; destbiratî; destbratî; destebirakî; destebiraktî; destebirayî} [K/HH//A//IF//PS//JR//B] <destxwîşk>

destbirak دەستبراك (A) = adoptive brother; blood brother. See **destbira**.

destbiraktî دەستبراكتی (A) = blood brotherhood. See

destbiratî.

destbiratî دەستبِراتی *f.* **(-ya;-yê).** blood brotherhood, relationship between two adoptive brothers or sworn brothers: •**[Wiha bi vî terzî şeş ḧeft salekan me *destebirayî* digel yekûdû kirin û qewî dost û aşena bûyîn]** (JR) And so it was that we had a *close friendship* for six [or] seven years, and were very dear friends and acquaintances. {also: destbiraktî (A); destbratî (IF); destebirakî (K/B); destebiraktî (B); destebiratî (ZZ); destebirayî (JR)} [K/A/JR/B]

destbiser دەست بِسەر (FJ/GF) = seized; arrested. See **desteser**.

destbra دەستبرا (IF) = adoptive brother; blood brother. See **destbira**.

destbratî دەستبراتی (IF) = blood brotherhood. See **destbiratî**.

destcihonî دەستجِهۆنی (Bw) = pestle. See **desteconî**.

destconî دەستجۆنی (Bw) = pestle. See **desteconî**.

destdirêj دەستدِرێژ *m.&f.* **().** aggressor; offender. {also: destdrêj (IFb/OK); [dest-dirij] دست دريژ (JJ)} Cf. T eli uzun = 'thievish'; Sor desdirêj دەسدرێژ = 'dishonest, corrupt' {destdirêjî} [K/A/GF/TF//IFb/OK//JJ]

destdirêjî دەستدِرێژی *f.* **(-ya;-yê).** aggression, belligerence; offense: -**destdirêjî kirin** (K/IFb) to be aggressive; to do violence to: •**Çawa bi navê zanahiyê *destdirêjiyê* li zanahiyê dike** (Arif Zêrevan.Nûdem 22:11) How he does *violence* to science in the name of science. {also: destdrêjî (IFb/OK)} Sor desdirêjî دەسدرێژی = 'dishonesty, aggression' [Zeb/K/A/GF/TF//IFb/OK] <destdirêj; te'darî; zêdegavî>

destdrêj دەستدرێژ (IFb/OK) = aggressor. See **destdirêj**.

destdrêjî دەستدرێژی (IFb/OK) = aggressor. See **destdirêjî**.

destebimbarekî دەستەبِمبارەکی (Z-1) = wrestling. See **bimbarekî**.

destebira دەستەبِرا (B) = adoptive brother; blood brother. See **destbira**.

destebirak دەستەبِراك (K/JR/B) = adoptive brother; blood brother. See **destbira**.

destebirakî دەستەبِراکی (K/B) = blood brotherhood. See **destbiratî**.

destebiraktî دەستەبِراکتی (B) = blood brotherhood. See **destbiratî**.

destebiratî دەستەبِراتی (ZZ) = blood brotherhood. See **destbiratî**.

destebirayî دەستەبرایی (JR) = blood brotherhood. See **destbiratî**.

destebra دەستەبرا (PS) = adoptive brother; blood brother. See **destbira**.

desteconî دەستەجۆنی *m.* **(-yê;).** pestle. {also: destc[ih]onî (Bw); destecuhnî (FS); [dest-i djohni] دستی جوهنی (JJ)} {syn: mêk'ut} [Bw//OK/ZF3/BF//FS//JJ] <conî I>

destecuhnî دەستەجوهنی (FS) = pestle. See **desteconî**.

destedîvk دەستەدیڤك (BF) = plow handle. See **destedû**.

destedû دەستەدوو *f.* **().** *on a traditional plow,* the handle which the plowman holds. {also: destedîvk (BF); destedûvk, m. (IFb/OK/AA); <destedu> دەستەدو (Hej)} {syn: maç' III} Sor desedû دەسەدوو [Zeb//Hej//IFb/OK/AA//BF] <cot; halet; hincar>

destedûvk, m. دەستەدووڤك (IFb/OK/AA) = plow handle. See **destedû**.

destek دەستەك, f. (K) = game; set; move (in a game) . See **dest** [3].

destemal دەستەمال = handkerchief. See **destmal**.

desteser دەستەسەر *adj.* 1) confiscated, seized: -**desteser kirin** (FS/Wkt/Kmc/ZF): a) to confiscate, seize, impound, sequester (property, etc.); b) to arrest, detain: •**Li wir *hatim* binçavkirin/*desteserkirin*. 28 saet şûnda serbest hatim berdan** (FB, xi.2016) I *was arrested* there. 28 hours later I was released •**Polîsan rojnamevanek *desteser kir*** (Wkt) The police *arrested* a journalist; 2) arrested, confined, detained; under house arrest: •**Zoro *li malê desteser* e** (FS) Z. is *under house arrest*. {also: destbiser (FJ/GF)} Sor dest beser دەست بەسەر = 'detained' [FS/Wkt/ZF/Kmc]

destexîşk دەستەخیشك (SK) = blood sister. See **destxwîşk**.

destexuşk دەستەخوشك (Hej) = blood sister. See **destxwîşk**.

destgeh دەستگەه (OK) = workshop; loom; organization. See **dezgeh**.

destgiran دەستگِران *adj.* 1) sluggish, slow moving; 2) clumsy, inept, awkward, unskilled. [Hk/Zeb/K/A/IFb/GF/OK] <xemsar>

destgirtî دەستگِرتی (EP-7/K/IFb) = fiancé(e). See **dergistî**.

destgork دەستگۆرك *f./m.(FS)* **(-a/-ê;).** glove: •**Jinên Wanî şagerdan, kum û *destgork* ji eskeran re çêkirin** (şehrivangazetesi.com 24.ii.2018) Women students of Van made hats and *gloves* for the soldiers. {syn: lepik [1]} [Bw/FS/BF]

desthel دەستهەل *adj.* handy, agile, good with one's hands: •**Mirovekî *desthel* e** (Zeb) He's a *handyman* •**Hozanvanê jêhatî û şehreza di vehandina hozan û helbestan da, *desthel* û pisporê lêkînana peyivan, evîndarê ciwanîya siruştê Kurdistanê bi çiya û gelî û dol û rûbarên xo ve** (Nisret Hacî. "Feqê Teyran û Çîrokên Binavkirina Wî," Peyam 5-6 [1996], 2) The poet skilled and expert at composing poems and verses, *handy* and clever at putting words together, enamored of the Kurdistan's natural beauty with its mountains, valleys, ravines, and rivers. [Zeb/AId/N.Hacî]

desthelat دەستهەلات (IFb/OK) = power, authority. See **desthilat**.

desthilat دەستهلات *f.* **(-a;-ê).** power, authority: •**Barzanî îddîa kir ku planên Emerîka ji bo hilweşandina *desthilatiya* Saddam Huseyin hene** (CTV57) Barzani claimed that America has plans to destroy Saddam Hussein's *authority* •**Divêt *desthilata* siyasî jî balansê bixe navbera takekes û civakê de** (nefel 20.viii.2008) The political *authorities* should strike a balance between the individual and society. {also: desthelat (IFb/OK); desthilatî (TF)} {syn: ĥuk'um; ȓaye I} Sor desełat دەسەڵات < dest + heł + hat [GF/BF/ZF3//IFb/OK//TF] <emir I>

desthilatdar دەستهلاتدار *adj.* 1) in power, possessed of authority: •**Heke tevgera kurd jî xwe bide ber vê yekê, ku hikûmeteke neteweperest jî *desthilatdar* be, wê guherînên demokratîk pêk werin** (AW75A2) If the Kurdish movement will support that idea, then even if a nationalistic government is *in power*, democratic changes will come about; 2) *[m.&f.]* person in charge or in power: •**Li Tirkiyeyê rejîm divê bi destê *desthilatdaran*, bê guhartin** (AW69A2) In Turkey the regime must be changed by *those in power*. {also: desthelatdar (OK)} [GF/ZF3//OK] <k'arbidest; ȓayedar>

desthilatî دەستهلاتی (TF) = power, authority. See **desthilat**.

desthûçik دەستهووچك (IFb) = sleeve. See **huçik**.

destî دەستی *m.* **().** an armful or bunch--while harvesting, the amount of wheat that a ***p'ale*** (agricultural worker) can grab hold of in his arm at one time. [Qzl/IFb/GF] <berdas; gidîş; qefil>

destk'êş دەستكێش *adj.* being led about by the reins *(of a horse)* (GF): **-destk'êş kirin** (K/B)/**~birin** (B) to walk a horse, to lead (a horse) by the reins; **-ĥespa destk'êş** (B) a horse led by the reins. {destk'êşî} [K/B/GF]

destk'êşî دەستكێشی *f.* **().** act of leading a horse about by the reins: •**Ûsib ji hespê peya dibe û *bi destk'êşî* tê cem pîrê** (Ba-1, #26) Joseph dismounts and, *leading* his horse *by the reins*, comes to the old lady['s house]. [Ba-1] <destk'êş>

destkîs دەستكیس *m.&f.* **(-ê/;).** traitor, informer; collaborator; quisling; spy. {also: deskîs (IFb/OK); [dest-kis] دست كيس (JJ); <deskîs> دەسكیس (Hej)} {syn: altax; mixenet; xayîn; xwefiroş} <dest = 'hand' + kîs = 'purse', i.e., s.o. with his hand in s.o. else's purse <destkîsî> [Dh/JJ//IFb/OK/Hej] <cehş; 'ewan II; geveze; nemam; sîxur>

destkîsî دەستكیسی *f.* **(-ya;).** treason, betrayal, informing (on s.o.); spying, espionage. {also: <deskîsî> دسكيسی (HH); <deskîsî> دەسكیسی (Hej)} [HH/Hej/Wkt] <destkîs>

destkuj I دەستكوژ *m.* **(-ê;-î).** animal not killed according to religious principles (e.g., killed by Christian [bê nivêj], which pious Muslims cannot eat), tref: **-xarina destkuj** (Bw) food which Muslims should not eat [because it was not ritually slaughtered] •**Ev xarine wek ya *destkujî* ye** (Bw) This food tastes like it was *made by infidels* (= ya nexoş e, i.e., it is bad). {also: [dest-kouji] دست كوژی (JJ) = 'meat which is not licit'} [Bw/ZF3/FS//JJ] <mirar>

destlimêj دەستلِمێژ (ZK-3/TF) = Islamic ritual ablutions. See **destnimêj**.

destmal دەستمال *f.* **(-a;-ê).** handkerchief, hanky: •**Doktor Sertaç rabû ser xwe, dîsan bi *destmala* xwe ya kaxizî xwêdana ser çavê xwe û ya eniya xwe ya rût pakij kir, paşê *destmala* xwe xist bêrîka xwe ya hundir** (KS, 37) Dr. Sertaç got up, again wiped the sweat from his naked face and forehead with his paper *handkerchief*, then put his *handkerchief* in his inside pocket. {also: desmal (A-2/B/IFb-2/GF); destemal; dezmal (Z-1); dismal (IFb-2); [desmal دسمال/dest-mal دست مال] (JJ); <desmal> دسمال (HH)} {syn: k'efî; kevnik [1]} <dest = 'hand' + mal- = 'to wipe': Sor desmał دەسماڵ; Za dismal *f.* (Todd) [Z-1//K/A/JB3/IFb/JJ/GF/OK/ /B/HH] <laç'ik>

destmêj دەستمێژ (A/BK) = Islamic ritual ablutions. See **destnimêj**.

destnimêj دەستنِمێژ *f.* **(-a;-ê).** Islamic ritual ablutions *(before prayer)*: •**Eger pîr *bi desmêj* be, çarşem pir in** (ZZ-3, 8) If the old lady is *ritually pure*, there are many Wednesdays *[prv.]*. {also: deslimêj (ZK-3); desmê (GF-2); desmêj (ZZ-3); destlimêj (ZK-3-2/TF); destmêj (A/BK); destnivêj (K-2/M-Zx/OK); dest'nivêj (JB1-A); dest-niwêj (SK); deznevêj (JB1-A); [dest nimij دست نميژ/ destmij دستميژ /desmij دسميژ/ desmi دسمی] (JJ); <desmêj> دسميژ (HH)} Cf. P dast namāz دست نماز; Sor desnwêj [desnöj] دەسنوێژ; Za [desmāǰ] (JJ)/desmaj *m.* (Mal) [K/JB3/IFb/GF/OK//A/BK/JJ//HH/ZZ-3//SK//TF/ZK-3]

destnivêj دەستنڤێژ (K/M-Zx/OK)/dest'nivêj (JB1-A) = Islamic ritual ablutions. See **destnimêj**.

destnivîs دەستنِڤیس *f.* **(-a;-ê).** manuscript. {also: [dest-nivis] دست نویس (JJ)} {syn: destxet [3]} Sor desnûs دەسنووس [Rwş/K/IFb/JJ/GF/OK]

dest-niwêj دەست نِوێژ (SK) = Islamic ritual ablutions. See **destnimêj**.

destnîşan kirin دەستنیشان کِرِن *vt.* **(destnîşan -k-)** to designate, point to, indicate, determine: •**Ji ber ku Alexandre Jaba di sala 1857an de *destnîşan kiriye* ku Mela 60 sal[î] bûye, sala 1797an wek ya rojbûna wî tê pejirandin** (Nbh 129:5) Because A. Jaba *indicated* that Mela [Mahmûd Bayazîdî] was 60 years old in 1857, 1797 has been accepted as his birth year •**Xuya ye ew ji bo bidestxistina wê pirtûka bi Kurdî jî hewl dide, lêbelê nikare peyda bike. Wekî sedem jî ew reva alim û zanayên Kurd ji ber dagirkirina herêmê ji aliyê Rûsan ve *destnîşan dike*** (Nbh 129:8) It is clear that he makes an effort to obtain that book in Kurdish, but he cannot find it. As a reason, he *points to* the flight of Kurdish scholars due to the occupation of the region by the Russians. Cf. Sor destnîşan دەستنیشان = 'picked, marked, nominated; nominee' [Nbh/ZF/TF]

destpê دەستپێ. See dest pê [bûn/kirin] under **dest**.

destpêk دەستپێك *f.* **(-a;-ê).** beginning, start, onset: **-di destpêkê de** [or **da**] = at first, in the beginning: •***Di destpêkê de* min ew bi ceh û kayê xwedî dikir** (HYma, 11) *At first* I fed him barley and straw. [K/JB3/IFb/GF/TF/OK] <dest pê bûn/kirin>

destşo دەستشۆ (K/IFb/B/TF/ZF3) = bathroom sink. See **destşok**.

destşok دەستشۆك *f.* **(-a;-ê).** bathroom sink [Fr lavabo]. {also: destşo (K/IFb/B/TF/ZF3-2)} [Kmc/GF/ZF3//K/IFb/B/TF]

dest û dar دەست و دار *m.* **(-ê;).** situation; condition, state; circumstances, conditions: •**Kurdên Êzidî ... gehiştine welatên din bi daxwaza tenahî û aştîyê û ... heta van salên dumahîyê saloxên wan zor kêm ji me ra dihatin û me kêm ji *dest û darê* wan dizanî** (Metîn 6:3[1992], 49) Yezidi Kurds ... have reached other countries in search of peace and security ... these last few years we have heard little news of them and have found out little about their *situation*. {syn: ḧal; ḧewal; kawdan; r̄ewş[3]} [Zeb/Bw/FS]

destûr دەستوور *f.* **(-a;-ê).** 1) *rule; *order; 2) {syn: heq; ḧed [2]; maf} right *(to do stg.)*: **-destûr dan** = a) to give s.o. the right to; b) to permit, allow, let: •**Naha tu gerekê *destûra* min *bidî*, ez berbi mala xwe her̄im** (Ba3-3, #6) Now you must *let* me head for home; c) to give a break/holiday leave; **-destûra peyvê** (KS) "the floor," the right to speak: •**Di civîna di derheqa jinan de Mamosta Çetîn *destûra peyvê* xwestibû û bi germî dipeyivî** (KS, 44) At the meeting about women, Professor Çetîn was given *the floor* and spoke warmly; 3) {syn: îzin} permission; permit (HH); 4) regulations, statutes; 5) style *(e.g., of clothes)* (Zeb): •**destûra cilka** (Zeb) style of clothes. {also: [destour] دستور (JJ); <destûr> دستور (HH)} Cf. P dastūr دستور [EP-7/K/A/JB3/IFb/B/JJ/HH/GF/TF/OK]

destvala دەستڤالا/**dest vala** دەست ڤالا (A/GF) *adj.* 1) empty-handed: •**Lê çewa bikim, min çi lê bar kir ne anî, ez wa *destvala* têm mala k'irîvê xwe** (Dz-anecdote #15) But what should I do? He didn't bring what I loaded on his back, and so I am coming *empty-handed* to my godfather's house; 2) destitute, impoverished (JJ/HH). {also: [dest-wala] دست ڤالا (JJ); <destvale> دستڤاله (HH)} <dest = 'hand' + vala = 'empty' [Dz/A/IFb/JJ/GF/OK//HH]

destxet دەستخەت *f.* **(-a;-ê).** 1) handwriting; 2) handicraft *(needlework, etc.)* (K/Kmc); 3) {syn: destnivîs} manuscript (K): •**Di serî de *destxeta* bingehîn, ji aliyê medhiyeyê ve ew hemû destxet kêm in** (Nbh 125:51) Regarding the encomium, all the *manuscripts* lack something, first and foremost the manuscript taken as base. Cf. P dast'xaṭṭ دستخط = 'handwriting; autograph; manuscript; written decree'; Sor destxet دەستخەت = 'handwriting' [Nbh/K/IFb/FJ/GF/Kmc/ZF/CS]

destxwe دەستخوە (TF) = immediately. See **destxweda**.

destxweda دهستخوهدا/**dest xweda** دهست خوهدا *adv.* immediately: **•Aqû p'êxember wî kirasî nêzîkî ç'avê xwe dike, wî çaxî herdu ç'avê wî *dest xweda* sax dibin** (Ba-1, #37) Jacob the prophet brings this shirt close to his eyes, and both his eyes are *immediately* cured [of blindness] **•*Destxweda* gilîyê kalê dinîyadîtî hate qedandin** (Z-1) *Immediately* the words of the experienced old man were carried out **•Zînê *destxweda* gilîyê Memî dife'mîne** (Z-1) Zîn *immediately* understands Mem's words. {also: destxwe (TF)} cf. Heb mi-yad מיד = 'immediately' (lit. 'from hand') [Z-1/K/OK//TF]

destxwîşk دهستخويشك *f.* **(-a;).** blood sister, close friend *(between girls or women)*: **•Çak e demekî bigeřyêm, biçim-e lalî *destexîşka* xo, qelê, belko pîçek dilê min řaĥet bibît** (SK 3:20) It would be best for me to go off for a while, to go and see my *dear friend* the crow, then perhaps my heart may find a little solace. {also: destexîşk (SK); <destexuşk> دهستهخوسك (Hej)} Sor destexuşk دعستهخوشك = 'group of friends (girls)' [SK//Hej/ /IFb/GF] <destbira; xûşk>

deş دهش (HB) = sister-in-law. See **diş.**

deşt دهشت *f.* **(-a;-ê).** plain, prairie, steppe: **•Binecihêd wî yên berê niha hatine *deşta* Araratê** (X.Çaçan. Benê min qetiya, 21) Its former inhabitants have now come to *the plain of* Ararat; **-deşt û banî** (EP-8) hill and dale. {also: [decht] دشت (JJ); <deşt> دشت (HH)} {syn: best; řast [6]} Cf. P dašt دشت; Sor deşt دهشت; Hau deşt[e] *f.* (M4) [Ba2/EP-8/K/A/JB3/IFb/B/JJ/HH/JB1-A/SK/GF/TF/OK/JR] <beřî II; çol; gelî II>

deştî دهشتى *m.&f.* **().** plains dweller, one who lives on the flatlands: **•Ez ne çiyayî û ne jî *deştî* me** (Lab, 7) I am neither a mountain dweller nor *a plains dweller.* {also: [dechti] دشتى (JJ)} Cf. P daštī دشتى; Sor deştî دهشتى [Lab/IFb/JJ/GF/TF]

dev I دهڤ *m.* **(-ê; dêv, vî devî).** 1) mouth *(lit. & fig.)*: **•Tiştekî min heye, / Ez destê xwe didime dêlê, / *Devê* xwe vedike. / Ew çiye? [meqes]** (Z-1815) I have something / If I put my hand on its tail / It opens its *mouth.* / What is it? *[rdl.; ans.: scissors]*; **-dev-diran** (XF): a) mouth; b) talk, rumors, gossip; **-dev ji *ft-î/fk-ê* berdan** = a) to leave/let stg. or s.o. alone: **•*Dev jê berde*, bila di cihê xwe de be** (L) *Leave it alone*, so that it stays in its place; b) to give up on, renounce, stop doing stg. {syn: dest ji *ft-î* k'işandin; hiştin; qeran; t'erkandin}; **-dev û çav** (K) face [lit. 'mouth and eyes'] {syn: řû I}; **-dev û lêv** (Z-1/K) mouth and lips; **-devê *fk-ê* nek'etin** [+ *subj.*] (K/XF) not to dare to: **•*Devê te nek'etîyê* tu pêşberî min xeberdî** (K) *You didn't dare* speak against me **•*Devê* bavê kesekî *nek'etye* nav cî û be'lgîê min bivîne** (EP-7) No one['s father] *would dare* to look at my bed and pillow {syn: ĥedê bavê kesekî t'une; wêrîn [+ neg.]}; 2) opening, gate: **•Herin, *devê* xizna min vekin** (L) Go, open the *gate* of my treasury!; **-devê bîrê** (Z-3) mouth or top of a well; **-devê derî** (Haz) [part of a room] closest to the door (where the poorest, lowest class people must sit); 3) edge, rim: •[...**Her sê mirof hatine *devê* çemekî**] (JR-1) All three fellows came to *the edge of* a river; 4) {syn: şilf; tî I} cutting edge, blade: **-devê şûr** = blade of a sword. {also: [dew] دڤ (JJ); <dev> دڤ (HH)} O Ir *zafan/zafar: Av zafar/n- *n.*; Mid P dahān & (daevic) zafar (M3); Pamir dialects: Ormuri dân (Morg); P dahan دهن /dahān دهان = 'mouth', also dam دم = 'breath'; Sor dem دهم; Hau dem *m.* = 'mouth, blade' (M4) [F/K/A/ JB3/IFb/B/JJ/HH/GF/TF/OK] <didan; lêv; ziman>

dev II دهڤ (FS) = at, by. See **def.**

devbeş دهڤبهش *adj.* 1) {syn: çavbirçî; ç'ikûs; çirûk [2]} greedy, miserly; 2) {syn: bêaqil} stupid (Dh). {also: <devbeş> دهڤبهش (Hej)} [Zeb/Dh/Hej/FS]

dev beş kirin دهڤ بهش كرن (Zeb) = to open one's mouth. See **beş III.**

devdîn دهڤدين *adj.* crazy. {syn: dîn II; şêt} [EP-7]

dev•e I دهڤه *f.(K/B)/m.(Ba/F)* **(•a/ ;•ê/).** camel: **•L[a]wik çû ber *devehan*, ji sibehê heya êvarê *devehan* li çolê diçêrîne, n[î]vro wan tîne ser avê û mexel dike** (ZZ-10, 157) The boy tended *the camels*, from morning until evening he lets them graze in the wilderness, at noon he brings them to water and has them sit down **•Serwanekî şêxê Ereba ê *deva* jî heye** (L) The Arab Sheikh also has a camelherd; **-deva mê** = female camel. {also: deveh (ZZ-10); devih (TF); [devé] دوه (JJ); <deve> دڤه (HH)} {syn: ĥêştir} < T deve [Ba/F/K/A/ IFb/B/JJ/HH/GF//ZZ//TF] <arwane = dundil; cencilok; lok' II; qent'er; torim; nixandin; xiya bûn & kirin>

dev•e II دهڤه *f.* **(•a;).** dung or manure, *mixed with straw in animal's stable [kol], heaped up in chunks as hard as rock or cement* (Zeb). {also: devedeştî (BF/ZF3); [dewé] دڤه (JJ); <deve دهڤه/

dewe دەوە> (Hej)} Sor dewe دەوە (Mukri) [Zeb/JJ/Hej//BF/ZF3] <dirg; k'erme; qelax; r̄îx; sergîn; t'epik II; t'ert[ik]>

devedeştî دەڤەدەشتی (BF/ZF3) = dung. See **deve II**.

deveh دەڤەه (ZZ-10) = camel. See **deve I**.

dever I دەڤەر *f.* **(-a;-ê).** 1) {syn: cî [1]; der I; dews I; êrdim; şûn} place, spot; 2) region, area. [Msr/A/JB3/IFb/GF/OK] <herêm>

dever̄û دەڤەڕوو *adv.* face down, prone, prostrate: **-dever̄û k'etin** (B) to sink to one's knees, fall face down: •[**Lakin pawan jî pê naḧesin, *devarû* dikevite nîva hespan**] (JR #27, 80) But even the watchmen are not aware of him, [as] he sneaks *face down* into the midst of the horses. {also: [devarû] دڤارو (JR)} Cf. P damar[ū] (دمر(و) = 'prostrate, flat, prone' [JR//K/IFb/B/(JJ)/GF/OK] <çarlepî>

devgû دەڤگوو *adj.* foul-mouthed. < dev = 'mouth' + gû = 'feces' [Msr/Wkt]

devih دەڤِه (TF) = camel. See **deve**.

devilken دەڤِلکەن (IFb) = smiling, cheerful. See **devlik'en**.

devî دەڤی *m./f.(K/IFb/OK)* **(/-ya; /-yê).** 1) {syn: kem; k'ol III; t'er̄aş II; t'ûm} bush(es), shrub(s); thicket: •**Îcar ez ha wisan tazî ji xwe ra ketibûm nava *deviyekê*, li pawuka kincên xwe mabûm heta ku ziwa bibûna** (ZZ-7, 241) So, naked, I went into *a bush*, waiting for my clothes to dry; 2) bramble; *sapling (JJ). {also: [dewi] دڤی (JJ); <devî> دڤی (HH)} [K/A/JB3/IFb/JJ/HH/GF/TF/OK]

devîn دەڤین (M.Top) = dish of yoghurt and crushed wheat. See **dewîn**.

dev jev دەڤ ژەڤ (HYma) = agape; insatiable. See **devjihev**.

devjihev دەڤژِهەڤ *adj.* 1) agape, with one's mouth open: •**Mêrik ji xweşikiya jinikê hîna wusa *devjihev* û mitûmat e** (Ardû, 171) The man is *agape* and astounded by the woman's beauty •**Sola baweşkiyayî û *dev jev* digot** ... (HYma, 130) The yawning and *gaping* shoe said ...; **-dev ji hev çûn** (IFb/CS) to gape *(with astonishment)*; 2) {syn: evsene} insatiable [T doyumsuz, doymak bilmeyen] (Qzl); 3) {syn: zimandirêj} talkative, loquacious, blabbing, indiscreet (K/JJ). {also: dev jev (HYma)} [Ardû/Qzl/IFb/CS//HYma] <beş II>

devk'en دەڤکەن (K/B/IFb/FJ/RZ) = smiling, cheerful. See **devlik'en**.

devkî دەڤکی *adj.* oral, spoken: •**Lê berhemên edebiyata *devkî*, berhemên hevbeş in** (Ş.Cizîrî. Edebiyata Devkî û Sosyalîzasyon, 166) But works of *oral* literature are shared works. < dev = 'mouth' [Ş.Cizîrî/IFb/TF/RZ/Kmc/ZF/SS/CS] <nivîskî; zar I>

devlik'en دەڤلِکەن/**dev li k'en** دەڤ لِ کەن *adj.* smiling, cheerful, merry: •**Keçikek *dev li ken*, zarxweş û xwînşêrîn e** (SBx, 16) She is a *merry*, well-spoken and likable girl. {also: devilken (IFb); devk'en (K-2/B/IFb-2/FJ-2/RZ)} <dev + li + k'en- [SBx/K/FJ/TF/ZF/CS//IFb//B/RZ] <k'enîn>

devmûç دەڤمووچ (Elk) = puckered up; shut. See **mûç II**.

devo دەڤۆ **().** unit of weight, dry measure: •**Du kulm, ribek e; çar rib, çapek e; du çap, elbek e; *Devo* (an debo) ji elbê biçûktir û [ji] çapê mezintir e** (Frq) 2 handfuls are a rib (dry measure), 4 ribs are 1 çap, 2 çaps are 1 elb; A *devo* is smaller than an elb and larger than a çap •**Ji bîst kîlo genim re, yan jî ji *devoyek* genim re 'kod' tê gotin** (CCG, 72) 20 kgs of wheat, or a *devo* of wheat is called a *kod*. {also: debo (Frq-2)} [CCG/K/Frq] <kod[2]>

devok دەڤۆك *f.* **(-a;-ê).** local dialect, local accent: •**Farqînî an farqînkî an jî silîvî *devoka* kurmancî ya ku li derdora Farqînê tê axavtin e** (Wkp) Farqînî, or Farqînkî or Silîvî is the Kurmanji *dialect* spoken around Farqîn (Silvan). < dev = 'mouth' + -ok; cf. T ağız = 'mouth; local dialect' [Wkp/IFb/ZF/AD/Wkt] <zarava>

Devr̄eş دەڤڕەش *m.* **().** common name for a dog. [Msr] <Cevro; Deqê>

devt'er دەڤتەر (FK-eb-1/B) = notebook. See **deft'er**.

dev û çav دەڤ و چاڤ. See under **dev**.

dew I دەو *m.* **(-ê; dêw, vî dewî).** drink made of yoghurt and water, similar to buttermilk [cf. T ayran]: •**Adar e, *dew* li dar e** (AB) It's March (=springtime), "*dew*" is in the wood [wooden churner] {also: [deoŭ] دو (JJ); <d[e]w> دو (HH)} <O Ir *dauga- (A&L p. 84 [V]): P dūγ دوغ; Sor do دۆ; Za do/dû *m.* (Mal) [K/A/JB3/IFb/B/JJ/HH/GF/BK] <ç'eqilmast; dohîn; doẍeba; mast; şîrêj>

de'w II دەعو *f.* **(-a;-ê).** 1) {syn: ceng [2]; cerenîx; cur̄e; doz; gelemşe; gelş; k'eşmek'eş; k'êşe; nakokî; p'evçûn} fight, argument, dispute: •**Wê derê ort'a wanda gelek *de'w* çû** (Z-1) A great *fight* broke out between them; **-de'w û doz** (Z-1/B)/**de'w-doz** (XF) fight, argument; battle, war: •**Em li dinê diger̄in *de'w û dozin*** (Z-1) We roam the world in search of *fights*; 2) demand, request (B): •**Law, hele here binhêre çi *dehwa* van**

xelkan e (L) Son, go see what those people's *demand* is (=what they want). {also: da‘w IV (IS); dehw (L); dehwa (GF); de‘wa (SK/OK); [dava] دعـــوا (JJ); <de‘wa> دعـــوى (HH)} < Ar da‘wá دعوى--> P da‘vā دعوى -->T dâvâ [Z-1/K/XF/B//JJ/HH/SK/OK//L//GF]

de‘wa دەعوا (SK/OK/JJ/HH) = argument; demand. See **de‘w II**.

dewam دەوام *f.* **(-a;-ê).** durability, sturdiness, solidity (JJ/SK): **-dewam kirin** (Wlt/K[s]) to continue {syn: berdewam bûn & kirin; dom [bûn &] kirin; domîn & domandin}: **•Ev kirinên hovane û tehdît hê jî *dewam dikin*** (Wlt 1:41, 5) These savage deeds and threats *are* still *continuing*. {also: [dewam دوام/doum دوم] (JJ)} <Ar dawām دوام ='duration, permanence'; Sor dewam دەوام = 'continuation, term' & dewam kirdin دوام كـردن = 'to last, continue, attend (school, course, etc.), to persist' (EM) [Wlt/K(s)/SK//JJ] <k’işandin [5]>

dewar دەوار *m.* **(-ê; dêwêr, vî dewarî).** 1) *a collective term for horses, donkeys, and mules [equines]* (Zeb): **•*Dewara* sûwarîya wî jî ker e. Hîç ȟeywan qebûl naket deccal li ser pişta wî sûwar bît ji bil kerî** (SK 25:228) His *mount* will be a donkey. No animal will allow Antichrist to mount on its back except the donkey **•Dibêjin carekê sê kes çûne karwanî, yêkî hebû hesp, yêkî hêstir, yêkî ker. Geheştine řezekî dûr ji gundî, *dewarêt* wan birsî bûbûn, ew jî mandî bûbûn** (SK 8:78) They say that 3 men once went on a caravan, one having a horse, one a mule, and one a donkey. They arrived at a garden far from a village. Their *beasts* had become hungry, and they themselves were tired; 2) {syn: çavrî; gařeş, t’ariş} cattle, livestock [bovines and equines]: **•Ew çîya cîyê ç’êra pez û *dewarê* gundîya bû** (Ba2, 202) That mountain was the place for grazing the sheep and *cattle of* the villagers **•Keçikê dişîne ber *dêwêr*** (J) She sends the girl to [tend] *the cattle*. {also: [davar] دوار (JJ); <d[e]war> دوار (HH)} Cf. T davar = 'goats and sheep'; Za dewar *m.* (Todd) [K/JB3/IFb/B/JJ/HH/SK/GF/OK] <gařan; naxir; pez; sewal I>

de‘wat دەعـــوات/**dewat** دەوات *m./f.(K/B)* **(-ê/-a; /-ê).** 1) {syn: cejin; dîlan [2]} wedding celebration: **-dawet kirin** (ZF): a) to marry s.o. off: **•Zûtir gerekê em *de‘wata* wî *bikin*** (Abbasian #3:143) We should promptly *arrange* his *wedding*; b) to invite {syn: ‘ezimandin; gazî kirin; vexwendin}; **-def û de‘wat** = do.: **•*Def û dewatê* wana kir** (J) He threw them a big *wedding celebration* [lit. 'He made them a drum and a wedding']; 2) {syn: govend; sema} dance, particularly folk dances performed at wedding celebrations and the like (Bw). {also: dawat, f. (IFb/Bw); dawet, f. (IS/TF/OK/ZF); de‘at (Ks); dewet, f. (F); de‘wet (B); [dàvet] داوت/دعـوت (JJ); <de‘wet> دعـوت (HH)} < Ar da‘wah دعـــوة = 'invitation' [Ks//J/K//F//B/HH//IFb/Bw//JJ//IS/TF/OK/ZF] <bûk I; mehir; nikha; zava; zewac>

dewet دەوەت, f. (F) = wedding; dance. See **de‘wat.**

de‘wet دەعوەت (B) = wedding; dance. See **de‘wat.**

dewijn دەوِژن (Qzl/ZF3) = foam on butter. See **dewjin.**

dewik دەوِك (IFb) = foam on butter. See **dewjin.**

dewil دەوِل (A) = bucket. See **dewl I.**

dewisandin دەوســـــانـــدِن vt. **(-dewisîn-).** 1) {syn: ‘eciqandin; heřişandin; p’ekandin; p’elaxtin; p’erçiqandin; pêpes kirin; t’episandin} to press, squeeze, crush, mash; 2) to press down, tread down, trample, tamp, ram *(tobacco in pipe, etc.)* (IFb/K); 3) {syn: çikandin I; ȟeşikandin} to stuff, cram, pack, fill (K); 4) *to take by force, do violence to (JJ). {also: dewsandin (K); [deoŭsandin] دوساندين (JJ); <duwisandin دوساندن (didewisîne) (ددوسينه)> (HH)} <Ar daws دوس < √d-w-s دوس = 'to trample' [M-Zx/IFb/B/JJ/GF/TF/OK//K//HH]

dewîn دەويـــن *f.* **(;-ê).** dish made of *dew* (yoghurt and water) and *danqut* crushed wheat: **•Hindî ku *dewîn* e, / ew derewîn e, / bo min neîne, / çu naqetîne** (Wkt - from Beyta zadî, folk poem from Colemêrg [Hk]) As for *dewîn* / it is a lie (i.e., a fake) / don't bring me any / it doesn't cut it. {also: devîn (M.Top. Hakkari, 169)} Cf. Sor dokułîw دۆكوڵيو/doxewa دۆخـــەوا = 'dish of yoghurt or *do* with rice or cracked wheat [*sawer*] and flavored with mint' [FS/BF/Wkt/ZF3//M.Top]

dewjin دەوژِن *f.* **().** foam on the top of butter. {also: dewijn (Qzl/ZF3); dewik (IFb-2); dewnik (GF); <dewjin> دەوژن (Hej)} cf. Sor dowuk دۆووك = 'sediment of melted butter' [Wn/Kmc-#2661/IFb/Hej//Qzl/ZF3//GF] <k’ef>

dewl I دەوڵ *f.* **(;-ê).** bucket, pail: **•Vira dewlçî *dewlê* hildide** (Ba) Here the bucket carrier picks up *the bucket*. {also: delûv (JB3/IFb-2/OK); dewil (A); dewlik (IFb/JB3-2); dol III (IFb-2); [delou دلو/dōl دول] (JJ); <dûl> دول (HH)} {syn: ‘elb; helgîn

(Krş); satil; sîtil} < Arc dewal דוול/dawlā דוולא & Syr dawlā ܕܘܠܐ ; NENA dôlâ & dôlchâ (Maclean); Sor dołçe دۆڵچە & dołke دۆڵکە. Cf. Ar dalw دلو, Heb deli דלי; P dalv دلو & dūl دول & dim. dūlče دولچە. *It is unclear whether the Krm forms come directly from Arc, or indirectly via* P dūl دول. [Ba/K/IFb/B/GF/TF//JB3/OK//A//JJ//HH] <gadoş; mencelok; zerik [2]>

dewl II دەول = drum. See **dehol.**

dewlçî دەولچی *m.* **().** bucket carrier, water bearer, aquarius. < dewl = 'bucket' + T -çi = '-er' (doer: indicates profession) [Ba] <dewl; sîtil>

dewlemend دەولەمەند *adj.* rich, wealthy *(lit. & fig.)*: **•Zargotina me piȓ *dewlemend* e. Miletê me ew zargotin afirandiye, niha jî diafirîne. Ew kaniyeke guȓ e** (Wlt 2:59, 16) Our folklore is very *rich*. Our people has created this folklore, and is still creating it. It is a gushing source; **-dewlemend kirin** (ZF3) to enrich. {also: dewletmend (SK); [devlemend] دولمند (JJ); <dewlemend> دولمند (HH)} {syn: dewletî; heyî; maldar; xurt [4]} Cf. P dawlatmand دولتمند; Sor dewłemend دەوڵەمەند {dewle[t]mendî} [F/K/JB3/IFb/B/JJ/HH/GF/OK/ZF3] <p'î II>

dewlemendî دەولەمەندی *f.* **(-ya;-yê).** wealth, riches; being rich. {also: dewletmendî (SK)} {syn: dewlet [4]} [JB3/IFb/GF/OK//SK] <dewlemend>

dewlet دەوڵەت *f.* **(-a;-ê).** 1) country, nation, state, land: **•Sefewiyan jî ji bo parastina sînorê *dewleta* xwe li hemberî împaratoriya berfireh a Osmaniyan şîetî wekî mezhebekî dînî û fermî ... dan** [sic] **xuyakirin** (Zend 2:3[1997], 56) And the Safavids, in order to protect the border of their *state* against the expansive Ottoman Empire, declared Shiism their official religious sect; 2) government (K/B): **•Ew *dewleta* ku 'eskerê wê cendirmêt wekî hingo di ling-diȓyay û ji-birsa-mirî bin çawa dişên pilingêt wekî 'Alî bê şeȓ û zeḧmet bigirin û xirab biken?** (SK 14:139) How can a *government*, whose army consists of ragged-trousered, starving zaptiehs like you, catch and destroy leopards like Ali without fighting and trouble? **•Hûn gerekê Ûsib bikujin, wekî *dewlet* û p'atşatî weȓa bimîne** (Ba3-1) You must kill Joseph, so that the *government* and kingship go [lit. 'remain'] to you; 3) strength, power (K): **•Ȓabû ser zînê *dewletê*** (FK-eb-1) He got up onto the saddle *of power (poetic license)*: **-dewlet serê *fk-î*** دەوڵەت سەری (Dh/Bar/Zeb/SK) thanks to s.o., because of s.o. {syn: bi xêra; pêxemet; sexmerat}: **•*dewlet serê* te** = *thanks to* you **•*Dewlet serê* Mam Gurd, min çi minnet bi walîyê te heye?** (SK 36:324) *Thanks to* Mam Gurd, what obligation have I toward your Governor? {syn: bi xêra...}; 4) {syn: dewlemendî} wealth (K/JJ/HH/GF). {also: [daúléta] دولت (JJ); <dewlet> دولت (HH)} < Ar dawlah دولة = 'country; dynasty; change' --> P dawlat دولت & T devlet; Sor dewłet دەوڵەت = 'state, government, riches' [FK-1/K/A/IFb/B/HH/GF/TF/OK//JJ]

dewletî دەولەتی *adj.* 1) {syn: dewlemend; maldar; xurt [4]} rich, wealthy: **•Şikir tu *dewletîî*** (HCK-1, 206) Thank God you are *wealthy*; 2) *[m.&f.]* **().** rich person, rich man: **•Wextekê *dewletîk* hebû. *Dewletî* kuȓê xwe, jina xwe çû ḧec** (HCK-1, 201) Once there was a *rich man*. *The rich man* went on the pilgrimage with his son and his wife. {also: cf. [dauletlü (Lx)] دولتلو (JJ)} Cf. Sor dewłet دەوڵەت = 'state; wealth, riches' [HCK/K/B/FJ/RZ//JJ] <dewlet[4]>

dewletmend دەولەتمەند (SK) = rich. See **dewlemend.**

dewletmendî دەولەتمەندی (SK) = wealth. See **dewlemendî.**

dewlik دەولك (IFb/JB3) = bucket. See **dewl I.**

dewnik دەونك (GF) = foam on butter. See **dewjin.**

dewrêş دەورێش *m.&f.* **().** dervish; beggar; wandering mendicant (HH): **-li xwe kirin dilẍê dewrêşa[n]** (K) to take on the appearance of dervishes, to dress up/disguise o.s. as a dervish. {also: *dervêş (A); derwêş (IFb/GF/TF/OK); [devrich] درویش (JJ); <dirwêş> درویش (HH)} Cf. P/Ar darwīš درويش; Sor derwêş دەروێش; Za dewrêş *m.* (Mal) [Z-922/K/B/JJ//IFb/GF/TF/OK//HH//A] <geşt; p'ars; xwazok>

dewrî دەوری *f.* **(-ya;).** plate, dish. {syn: firaq; teyfik} [Urm/Slm/K(s)/ZF3] <aman>

dews دەوس *f.* **(-a;-ê).** 1) {syn: cî [1]; der I; dever I; êrdim; şûn} place, stead: **•Boẍekî jar *dewsa* wara dimîne** (J) A thin ox stays *in the place/vicinity of* the encampment; **-dewsa** (Z-922/K) *[prep.]* instead of, in place of {syn: dêl III; li şûna}: **•Tu şilfa şûr derxe, darekî çê ke bavêje *dewsa* şilfê** (Z-922) You take off the sword's blade, make one of wood [and] put [lit. 'throw'] [it] *in place of* the blade **•Ḧeft doşeka *dewsa* yekê datîne** (EP-7)

She put down seven mattresses *instead of* one; 2) {syn: r̄êç' II; şop} trace *(of an encampment)*; trail *(of an animal's path)*, footprint (HH): **•Ewê nêzîkaya k'ûpê r̄ûn k'ulme dudu ar ser 'erdê r̄eşand, ku ji *dewsa* linga diz nas bike** (Dz-anec #32) Near the butter jug she sprinkled on the ground a handful or two of flour, so that from *the footprints* she could recognize the thief [i.e., know who the thief was]. {also: [deoŭs] دوس (JJ); <dews> دوس (HH)} <Ar daws دوس = 'tread[ing], trampling, step' [J/K/A/JB3/IFb/B/JJ/HH/JB1-S/GF/TF/OK] <war>

dewsandin دهوسساندِن (K) = to press; to stuff. See **dewisandin**.

dexalet دهخالهت *f.* **(-a;-ê).** refuge, asylum, submission: **-dexaleta *fk-î* kirin** (SK) to submit, surrender, defect to, seek asylum or refuge from: **•Ḧetta par do-hizar mal zêdetir ji Şemdînan û Girdîyan û Biradostan hatin e *dexaletê* û Cenral Lewendoskî hemî qebûl kirin û kax̄ez û beydax̄êt emnîyetê dan ê** (SK 56:649) Up till last year more than two thousand families from Shamdinan and the Girdi and Biradost defected [or, sought *asylum*] and General Levandovski accepted them all and gave them letters and flags of safe-conduct **•Paşî ko mamê Seyyid Ṯaha ji Istembolê hat e Kurdistanê, ma-beyna wî û mamî nexoş bû û Seyyid Ṯaha bû dujminê 'Usmanîyan. Hat e girtin, birin e Istembolê. ji wê-derê firar kir, hat e-naw Urosî, *dexalet kir*** (SK 48:497) After Sayyid Taha's uncle came to Kurdistan from Istanbul, relations between him and his uncle broke down and Sayyid Taha became an enemy of the Turks. He was seized and taken to Istanbul. He fled from there and came among the Russians and *sought refuge*. < Ar √d-x-l دخل = 'to enter' [Bw/SK/ZF3]

dexdexan دهخدهخان (BX) = cattle brand. See **dax̄**.

dexes دهخهس *adj.* 1) {syn: ḧevsûd; k'umr̄eş} jealous; 2) *[m.]* *miser (HH); 3) *slanderer (K). {also: dexis (IFb-2); <dexes> دخس (HH)} {dex[e]sî} [K/IFb/B/HH/OK]

dexesî دهخهسى *f.* **(-ya;-yê).** 1) {syn: ḧevsûdî; k'umr̄eşî} jealousy: **-dexesî kirin** (K/B) to be jealous of; to envy: **•Dîya dehe kur̄a ji boy Ûsib *dexesî dikir*** (Ba3-1) The mother of the ten boys *was jealous* of (or, envied) Joseph; 2) *slander (K). {also: dexsî (TF); [dikhesi] دخسى (JJ)} [B/K/OK//TF//JJ] <çavnebarî; çavr̄eşî>

dexil دهخِل (A/TF) = grains, cereals. See **dexl**.

dexis دهخِس (IFb) = jealous. See **dexes**.

dexl دهخل *m.* **(-ê;-î).** grains, cereals: **•Genimî tçînin û *dexlî* tçînin, cehî tçînin û t'ût'inê jî tkin** (M-Zx #777) They plant wheat and *cereals*, they plant barley and they also grow tobacco; **-dexl û dan** (SK) crops, produce {syn: deramet I; hasil}: **•Dûr̄a keşkele hat e pêş, got, "Zerera min ewe ye. Ez genimê wan dixom, cehê wan, genimeşamîyê wan, ṯale û herzinêt wan, xiro û nîsk û maş û nokêt wan, xulase hemî *dexl-û-danê* wan teqsîr nakem, dixom"** (SK 1:4) Afterward the magpie came forward and said, "This is the damage I do. I eat their wheat, their barley, their maize, their millet, their durra and lentils and grams and chickpeas---in short, I do not stint eating all their *crops*." {also: dexil (A/TF); dex̄il (JB1-A); dex̄l (K[s]); [dekhel] دخل (JJ); <dexl> دخل (HH)} {syn: tene I; zad} Cf. Ar daxl دخل = 'income, revenue'; T tahıl = 'grains, cereals'; NENA dakhlâ ܕܟܠܐ = 'grain, corn, meal' (Maclean); Sor dex̄l دهغڵ = 'wheat, barley' [M-Zx/IFb/HH/SK/GF/AD//A/TF//JJ//JB1-A//K(s)]

dexsî دهخسى (TF) = jealousy. See **dexesî**.

dex̄il دهغِل (JB1-A) = grains, cereals. See **dexl**.

dex̄l دهغل (K[s]) = grains, cereals. See **dexl**.

dey I دهى **().** answer, response: **-dey kirin** = 1) to utter, speak, make a sound: **•Kesî *dey* ne *kir*** (L) No one *answered*/no one *made a sound* **•Wexta qewaza *deyn* Memê *kirin*** (Z-1) When the couriers *spoke to* Mem; 2) to object to, respond to, answer (with anger) (TF). {also: deyn I (L)} [L/K/A/IFb/GF/TF] <deng I>

dey II دهى (JB1-A) = mother. See **dê I.**

deybab دهيباب (JB1-A) = parents. See **dêûbav.**

deydik دهيدِك *f.* **(-a;-ê).** 1) {syn: colan; dolîdang I; hêlekan; hêzok} swing; 2) rocking cradle. {also: deyik (TF)} [A/IFb/GF/OK/ZF3//TF] <landik>

deyem دهيهم (Wkt) = tenth. See **dehem**.

deyemîn دهيهمين (Wkt) = tenth. See **dehem**.

deyin دهيِن, f. (OK) = debt. See **deyn II**.

deyindar دهيِندار (OK) = debtor; in debt. See **deyndar**.

deyk' دهيك (JB1-A/Bw) = mother. See **dê I.**

deyn I دهين: -deyn kirin (L) = to speak. See **dey I**.

deyn II دهين *m.(F/K/B)/f.(OK)* **(-ê/ ;).** debt, money (or property) owed to another: ***•Deynê* min lê ye/li ser e** = He owes me stg. ***•Deynê* Şibatê li Adarê ye** (L-1, #95, 202) February's *debt* is due in

March; **deyn dayîn** (B/JJ) to lend, loan; **-deyn kirin** (B)/[deĭn sitandin] دين ستانديـن (JJ) to borrow; **-ji bin deynê *ft-î* derketin** (J2) to be absolved of a debt, to pay off a debt: **•Em *ji bin deynê* bizinên te *derketin*** (J2, 41) We *have paid off* our *debt* to you for the goats. {also: deyin, f. (OK); [deĭn] ديـن (JJ); <deyn> ديـن (HH)} {syn: qer I} <Ar dayn دَين = 'debt' [F/K/IFb/B/JJ/HH/GF//OK]

deyndar I دەيـنـدار *m.&f.* **(-ê/;).** 1) debtor, person in debt; 2) [*adj.*] indebted, in debt, owing: **•Ew *deyndarê* te ye** = He owes you stg./He is *indebted* to you. {also: deyindar (OK); [deindar] ديندار (JJ); <deyndar> ديندار (HH)} {syn: qerdar} <P daydār ديندار [Bw/F/K/IFb/B/JJ/HH/JB1-A/GF//OK] <deyn II>

deyndar II دەيـنـدار (MG/IFb/GF) = Lebanon oak. See **dîndar II**.

dezgah دەزگـاه (OK/IFb) = workshop; loom; organization. See **dezgeh**.

dezge دەزگـە (K/B/GF/OK) = workshop; loom; organization. See **dezgeh**.

dezgeh دەزگـەه *f.* **(-a;).** 1) joiner's bench (B); workshop; 2) {syn: t'evn} weaving loom; 3) organization, institution, apparatus: **•Berî serhildana 91'an hemû *dezgehên* çandî di bin destê rejîma Baas de bûn** (Wlt 2:101, 16) Before the [19]91 revolt, all the cultural *institutions* were under the control of the Baathist regime; **-dezgehên r̄agihandinê** (VoA) the media. {also: destgeh (OK-2); dezgah (OK/IFb-2); dezge (K-2/B-2/GF/OK-2); [dezghiah] دزگـاه (JJ); <dizgeh> دزگـه (HH)} P dastgāh دستـگـاه = 'apparatus, machine, workshop, etc.' --> T tezgâh = 'counter, loom, workbench'; Sor dezga دەزگـا = 'anvil, workshop, place of business' [Wlt/K/IFb/B/TF//OK//GF//JJ//HH]

dezgirtî دەزگِرتی (JB1-S) = fiancé(e). See **dergistî.**

dezgîn دەزگین (K/Z-2) = rein; bridle. See **dizgîn.**

dezî دەزی *f./m.(FS/Kş)* **(/-yê;).** thread; cotton thread (JJ/SK): **-dezî û dirêzî** (Slv) needle and thread. {also: dezû (M-Ak); [dezi] دزی (JJ); <dezî> دزی (HH)} {syn: ta I; t'êl [2]} Sor dezû دەزوو [Ad/A/IFb/JJ/HH/SK/GF/TF/OK/Kş/FS/ZF3//M-Ak] <dav II; derzî; gulok; masûr>

dezmal دەزمال (Z-1) = handkerchief. See **destmal.**

deznevêj دەزنـەڤـێـژ (JB1-A) = Islamic ritual ablutions. See **destnimêj**.

dezû دەزوو (M-Ak) = thread. See **dezî.**

dê I دێ *f.* **(deya/ diya/ dîya/ dya** [J]/ **cîya** [Dyd]; indef. **deyek/ dêk/ diyek;** voc. **dayê** [Ab/Ag]). mother: **•dayê** = mommy, mom **•*Dîya* wan şîva wan anî** (L) Their *mother* brought their dinner **•Ûsib û Bênams ji *dêkê* bûn** (Ba) Joseph and Benjamin were from *one mother*; **-dê û bav** (B)/ **dêûbav** (JB3)/**dêbav** (K)/**deybab**, pl. (JB1-A) parents; **-ji dayk bûn** = to be born. {also: da I (IF-2/A-2); dayik (A-2/JB3-2/IF-2/B-2); dayk (SK);dey II (JB1-A); deyk' (JB1-A/Bw); [da دا /di دى /diia ديا/daik دايك] (JJ); <dê دى/da دا> (HH)} {syn: in[ik]; mak} [Pok. dhē(i)- 241.] 'to suck': P dāyah دايـه = 'wet nurse'; Sor dayk دايك; Hau eda f. (M4); cf. Gr thēlys θῆλυς = 'female' (adj.) & thēlē θηλή = 'nipple'; cf. also Geo deda დედა = 'mother' {dêtî} [BX/F/K/A/JB3/IFb/HH/GF/TF/OK//JJ//SK] <bav; dayîn III>

dê II دێ [+ *subj.*]. *future tense marker, particularly in the Behdînî sub-dialects (Zakho, Mosul, Jabal Sinjar, Amadiyah & Shamdinan + non-prefixed subj.); corresponds to* **wê** *+ subj. in central and northern Kurmanji sub-dialects; common +subj. in modern standard language instead of* **wê**: **•Ez *dê* bînim** = **Ez wê [Ezê] bibînim** = I will see. {also: wê II} [Zx/M/Bw/Wlt]

dêbav دێباڤ (K) = parents. See **dêûbav.**

dêdar دێدار (IFb/Kmc-40) = Lebanon oak. See **dîndar II**.

dêdik دێدِك *f.* **().** spleen. {also: <dêdik> ديدك (Hej)} {syn: fater̄eşk; teĥêl; xalxalk} [Zeb/OK/Hej/ZF3/FS]

dêhtir دێهتر (TF) = the next day. See **dotir**.

dêjnik دێژنـك *f.* **(-a;-ê).** garden cress, garden peppergrass, bot. *Lepidum sativa*. {also: dêjnk (FJ)} {syn: r̄eşad} [Qzl/IFb//FJ] <t'ûzik>

dêjnk دێژنك (FJ) = garden cress. See **dêjnik**.

dêl I دێـل *f.* **(-a;-ê).** female of any canine species: **•dêlegur** (BX) she-wolf **•dêle se** (JB3) bitch, female dog **•dêlik** (A) bitch, female dog. {also: [deĭl] ديـل (JJ); <dêl> ديـل (HH)} {syn: mak; mê} [Pok. dhē(i)- 241.] 'to suck': Sor deł دەڵ/dêł دێڵ; Hau dełe *f.* (M4); cf. Gr thēlys θῆλυς = 'female' (adj.) & thēlē θηλή = 'nipple' [BX/K/A/JB3/IFb/B/JJ/HH/SK/GF/TF/OK]

dêl II دێـل *f.* **(-a;-ê).** tail: **•*Dêla* boẍ girt** (J) He took hold of the ox's *tail* **•Keftarê genî, em te nas dikin, me *dêla* te di binê postê weşeqê de dîtiye** (Wlt 2:100, 13) Stinking hyena, we know who you are [or, we recognize you], we have seen your *tail* [sticking out] from under the lynx's pelt **•Tiştekî min heye, / Ez destê xwe didime *dêlê*, / Devê

xwe vedike. / Ew çiye? [meqes] (Z-1815) I have something / If I put my hand on its *tail* / It opens its mouth. / What is it? *[rdl.; ans.: scissors]*; **-dêl û dûv**, f. (K) do. {syn: boç'[ik]; dû II; k'ilk; kurî I (Bw); qemç[ik]; teřî I[1]} Cf. Ar d̲ayl ذيل = 'tail' [J/F/K/B/GF/Rh] <dûv I>

dêl III دێل *prep.* instead of: -**ji dêl** (BX)/**ji dêla ... ve** (L) do.: •***Ji dêl*** **xweşiyê, te dilê me ji xema û kesera dagirtiye** (BX) *Instead of* joy, you have filled our heart with pain and concern •***ji dêla*** **zaroka** ***ve*** (L) *instead of* sons/children. {syn: dewsa} Cf. Ar badal بدل [BX/L/IFb/GF/TF/OK]

dêlegur دێلەگور *f.* **(-a;-ê).** female wolf, she-wolf. {also: dêlegurg (OK); [deil-e gour] دیلەگور (JJ)} {syn: dêlik [2]} Za delverg (Todd)--for etymology see **dêl I.** [BX/K/JB3/IFb/B/JJ/GF/TF//OK] <dêl I; gur; mê>

dêlegurg دێلەگورگ (OK) = she-wolf. See **dêlegur**.

dêlese دێلەسە/**dêle se** [JB3] *f.* **().** bitch, female dog. {also: dêleseg} {syn: dêlik} -- for etymology see **dêl I.** [K/IF//JB3]

dêleseg دێلەسەگ = bitch. See **dêlese.**

dêleşêr دێلەشێر *f.* **().** lioness. {also: [dēl-i šīr] (JJ/PS)} {syn: şêra mê (F)} [K/JJ/GF/OK]

dêlik دێلِك *f.* **(-a;-ê).** bitch *(fig. & lit.)*, female dog. {also: [deïlik] دیلك (JJ)} -- for etymology see **dêl I.** [Msr/F/A/IFb/B/JJ/GF/TF/OK] <dêl I>

dêm I دێم *f.* **().** *f.* 1) {also: [dēm] دیم (JJ); <dêm> دیم (HH)} dry farming {cf. bejî [2]}, land irrigated solely by rainwater; 'Dem' "Kind of cultivation carried on by means of rain ... All cultivation in Koordistan is watered solely by the rains, there being no artificial irrigation" {C.J. Rich. *Narrative of a Residence in Koordistan* (London: James Duncan, 1836), vol. 1, p. 56}; (Rich's assertion is contradicted by the following:) "There are nonirrigated [de:m] and irrigated ['a:vi] lands in the [neighborhood of the] village. The irrigated orchards are around the village *[of Aradhin, c. 10 miles west of Amadia, in northern Iraqi Kurdistan]*, while the nonirrigated [fields] are somewhat farther away from it and occupy the entire lower part of the village [property]" {G. Krotkoff. A *Neo-Aramaic Dialect of Kurdistan* (New Haven: American Oriental Society, 1982), pp. 68-69, sentence #4}; 2) {also: [dim] دیم (JJ)} {syn: ȟişk [1]} arid, dry, rainless (IF/JJ). Cf. Ar daym دیم = 'raining gently & incessantly', P dēm دیم = '(crop) produced by dry farming' & P dēmzār دیمزار = 'field watered by rain only' & P dēmī دیمی = 'nurtured by rain only (sown fields)'; Sor dêm دێم [Rich/Krotkoff/K(s)/A/IFb/JJ/HH/GF/OK/CG/Rwn] <bejî [2]>

dêm II دێم *f.(K)/m.(B/FS)/pl.(Qzl)* **(/-ê;).** cheeks and fleshy part of face; area of face bounded by ear, eye, nose, and mouth (wider area of face than ***hinarik*** = cheek): •**dêmên sor** (Qzl) red cheeks (=hinarkên sor) •**Zerîya** ***dêmê*** **wî ne ji nexweşîyê ye** (BF) The pallor of his *cheeks* is not from illness. {also: [dim] دیم (JJ)} [Qzl/K/B/GF/FS//JJ] <hinarik; lame; řû I; sûret I>

dêmarî دێماری *f.* **(-ya;-yê).** stepmother; mother of the children one's husband has by a previous marriage (JJ). {also: damarî (Ba-2/IFb-2/B); [damari] داماری (JJ); <dêmarî> دیماری (HH)} {syn: jinbav; zirdayîk} <dê + marî <O Ir *maθrya- (A&L p. 86 [VI, 4]); cf. Pashto ma(i)ra = 'stepmother'; Za damarî/domarî *f.* (Mal) [Ba/K/JB3/IFb/HH/GF/OK//B/JJ] <bavmarî; hêwî; -ȟilî I; nevisî; zirbav>

dêmek دێمەك. that means, in other words, that is to say, i.e. [C'est à dire]: •***Dêmek*** **te Şenglo, Menglo, Qalîçenglo birîye** [sic] (J) *That means* that [=so] you took Sh., M., and Q. {syn: ango; ye'nî} < T demek = '[that is] to say' [J/K/B/FS]

dêmqemer دێمقەمەر *adj.* dark-complected, dark-complexioned: •**Memo mêrekî bejnbilindî navmilfireyî** ***dêmqemer*** **bû** (Ba2:1, 204) Memo was a man tall of stature, broad shouldered, *dark complected.* {syn: qemer} [Ba2/K]

dên دێن (IS) = sight. See **dîn I.**

dêr دێر *f.* **(-a;-ê).** 1) church: •**Gundekî kevne;** ***dêra*** **wê jî gelekî kevne** (K2-Fêrîk) It is an old village; its *church* is old too; 2) monastery. {also: [deïr] دیر (JJ); <dêr> دیر (HH)} <Syr dayrā ܕܝܪܐ = 'dwelling, habitation; monastery'; cf. Ar dayr دير = 'monastery', also of Arc/Syr origin (Fraenkel, p. 275); Sor dêr دێر = 'monastery' [K2-Fêrîk/F/K/A/ IFb/B/JJ/HH/SK/GF/TF/OK] <qeşe>

dêran I دێران (-dêr-) (JB3/HH/OK) = to winnow; to scatter. See **dêrandin.**

dêran II دێران *adj.* unlucky, unfortunate, having experienced a tragedy or disaster. {syn: belengaz; bikul; malxirab; řeben I; şerpeze; xwelîser I} [Slm/K/A/IFb/B/GF] <bextreş>

dêrandin دێراندِن *vt.* **(-dêrîn-).** 1) {also: dêran (-dêr-) (JB3)} {syn: hilavêtin[3]} to winnow (M-Zx/A/

IFb/JB3); 2) {also: derandin (IFb); dêran I (-dêr-) (JB3/OK); <dêran ديران (didîre) (دديره)> (HH)} to scatter, sprinkle, strew (JB3/IFb/HH); 3) {syn: xûdan} to sweat *vt. (e.g., tears, blood)* (M-Zx). Cf. Ar d̲ará ذرى/d̲arrá II ذرّى/ad̲rá IV أذرى = 'to winnow' [M-Zx/A/IFb/GF/ TF//JB3/HH/OK] <bê[n]der>

dêr•e دێره *m./f.(ZF3)* **(•ê/;).** 'dera,' type of woman's dress; *with long sleeves, open in front, tied at the waist with a drawstring* (Kmc-11): **•Ûsib dide pey wê, dest davêje par̄a *dêrê* wê** (Ba3) Joseph follows her, grabs hold of her *dress* from behind **•Leylê rabû dawa *dêrê* xwe, çuxê xwe bir̄î** (EP-5, #15) Leyla cut off the lap of her *dress*, of her coarse coat. {syn: fîstan} *for illustration, see Kmc-11, page 1; this word is used by nomads [koçer] in the Serhedan region (=Turco-Iranian border) (Kmc-11)* [Ba3/K/B/Kmc-11/ZF3]

dêşîr دێشیر (Kmc) = wet nurse. See **daşîr**.

dêtî دێتى *f.* (;**-yê).** motherhood. [K/B/IFb/GF/ZF3] <dê I; kur̄tî II>

dê û bav دێ و باڤ *pl.* parents. {also: deybab, pl. (JB1-A); dêbav (K); dêwbav (OK)} [JB3/IFb/B//K//OK//JB1-A]

dêv دێڤ (MK/IFb/OK) = demon; ogre. See **dêw.**

dêw دێو *m.* **(-ê;).** demon; ogre. {also: dêv (MK/IFb-2/OK-2); dib; [dev] ديو (JJ); <dêw> ديو (HH)} Cf. P dīv ديو --> T dev; Sor dêw دێو; Hau dêw *m.* (M4) [K/IFb/B/HH/GF/OK//MK/JJ] <cin; ji me çêtir; ferh̄ît; şeytan>

dêwbav دێوباڤ (OK) = parents. See **dê û bav**.

dêxon دێخۆن (FS) = drawstring. See **doxîn**.

dêz دێز (GF) = pile, heap. See **cêz I**.

di- دِ *verbal prefix for the present indicative and imperfect tenses*: **•Ez *di*bînim** (BX ¶180, 161) I see **•Ez *di*k'evim** (BX ¶180, 161/K2 ¶289, 207) I fall **•Min *di*dît** (BX ¶185, 172) I was seeing/used to see/would see **•Ez *di*k'etim** (BX ¶160, 137/K2 ¶296, 211) I was falling/used to fall/ would fall. *Realized as* t- *in* *t*êm = 'I come' & *t*înim = 'I bring'; Sor de- ده/e- ئه; P mī- مى [BX/K2/M/CT/IC] <da III; na->

di دِ *prep.* 1) in; to; within; of *(gives the idea of belonging, location, etc.)*: **•Vî kefçî *di* şorbê meke, pîs e** (BX) Don't put this spoon *in* the soup, it's dirty **•Ez *di* xwe fekirîm** (BX) I was thinking *to* myself **•Rojekê, *di* xwe fekirî** (L) One day she thought *to* herself ... **•Halan *di* hev dan** (BX) They encouraged each other **•Merhem *di* xwe da** (BX) He rubbed/annointed himself with balm **•Zanîna min *di* vî warî** (BX) My knowledge *of* this subject/field; **-digel** *[prep.]* = with [< di + gel = 'group']; 2) *[In combination with postpositions (i.e., ambipositions)]*:

-di ... de/da = in *(location)*, inside: *(the preposition 'di' of 'di ... de' is sometimes elided, particularly in the northern sub-dialects)*: **•*di* mix̄arekê *de*** (L) *in* a cave **•Ez zanim *di* bêrîka te *de* çi heye** (BX) I know what's *in* your pocket **•*Di* bajarê me *de*, sûkeke mezin heye** (BX) *In* our city there is a large market **•*di* van rojan *de*** (BX) *in* (during) these days **•*di* wê wextê *de*** (BX) *at* that time **•*di* gavê *de*** (BX) at once [à l'instant, sur le champ] **•Min hîn *di* spehîtiya te *de* tukes ne dîtiye** (BX) I haven't yet seen anyone as beautiful as you [lit. '*in* your beauty'] **•tê de/têda** = in(side) him/her/it;

-di ... re/r̄a = through, by: **•*di* ku *re*** = *through* where **•Em *di* newalekê *re* derbas bûn** (BX) We passed *through* a gorge **•Ew** [sic] **... *di* pencerê *r̄a* li rêhlî nêrî** (FS) S/he... regarded the woods *through* the window **•Hirçê li ser xênî, *di* rojinê (kulek) *ra* li wan guhdarî dikir** (hindik-rindik: Qisirkeno 18.vii.2011) On the roof, the bear was listening to them *through* the skylight **•Rûbarê Xabîrî *di* Zaxo *ra* diborit** (FS) The Khabur River passes *through* Zakho **•Şivanî çaydankê xwe kir *di nav* felemorê *r̄a* ku çaya wî germ bibit** (FS) The shepherd put his tea kettle *into* the glowing ashes so that his tea would warm up **•Tu *di* ku *re* hatîye?** (L) How (=*by* what route) did you come?;

-di ... ve = in *(motion)*, across, through: **•Ez *di* deştê *ve* hatim** (BX) I came *through/across* the plain **•Min mizmar *di* dîwêr *ve* kir** (BX) I planted the nail *in* the wall **•Şivanî pez bi şevê bir *di* zivingê *ve*** (FS) The shepherd took the sheep *into* the cave at night. [di + wî/wê = tê; di + hev = tev] {also: [di] ده/د (JJ)} [BX/K/JB3/IFb/JJ/B/SK/GF/OK]

dib دِب = demon; ogre. See **dêw.**

dibistan دِبِستان *f.* **(-a;-ê).** 1) {syn: mek't'eb} (elementary) school, grade school: **•*Dibistan* kana zanînê ye** (AB) *School* is the source of knowledge **•*dibistana* seretayî (5 yan 6 salên pêşîn yên xwendina li dibistanan)** (Wkt) elementary *school* (the first 5 or 6 years of study in grade school); 2) *college *(in a university)*, educational institution

(K/BK): •**Piştî kutakirina *dibistana* ewil, li Erzinganê *Dibistana* Ruştiye ya eskerî, li Stenbolê jî *Dibistana* Şer xwendiye** (WM 1:2, 16) After finishing *elementary school*, he studies at Rushdiyeh Military *College* in Erzincan and the *College* of War in Istanbul; **-Debistana Dîrok û Zimanan** (BK) College of History and Languages [T Dil ve Tarih Fakültesi]. {also: debistan (BK)} Cf. P dabestān دبستان = 'elementary school' [AB/K/IFb/OK/BK] <dersdar; mamoste; xwendegeh; zanîngeh>

dibûr دِبوور, f. (B) = shady side. See **dubur**.

Dicl•e دِجلە *f.* (;•ê). Tigris River, *which together with the Euphrates forms Mesopotamia.* {also: Dîcle (A/IF); [didjlé] دجلە (JJ)} Sumerian idigina < id = 'river' + igina = 'lapis lazuli' (W. Heimpel, Univ. Cal. at Berkeley) --> Ar dijlah دجلة, Arc diglaṯ דיגלת [SW/JJ//A/IFb] <Ferat>

didan دِدان *m.* **(-ê; didên, vî didanî).** tooth [pl. teeth]; fang: •[**Mela li berayîkê bû giha pîstekî û pîst bi *dranêd* xo girt**] (JR-1) The mullah was the first one to reach a goatskin [floating in the water] and he grabbed the goatskin with his *teeth* •**Paşî mar hate pêş, got "Zerera min mezintir e ... şûna *didanê* min der-ĥal diperçiwît û dibîte birînekî kirêt"** (SK 1:6) Then the snake came forward and said, "The harm I inflict is greater ... the place where my *fangs* strike swells immediately and becomes an ugly wound." {also: diran (A/B/IFb-2/GF-2/OK-2); dran (JB3/IFb-2/OK-2); [didan ددان/diran دران] (JJ); <didan> ددان (HH)} [Pok. ed- 287.] 'to eat'--> *Eed- > participle *edont-/dont-/dṇt- --> *Ede/ont-: Skt dánta *m.*; <O Ir *dantān (A&L p. 84 [IV, 4]): Av dantan-; Mid P dād/dandān (M3); Pamir dialects: Yidgha lad; Parachi danân; Sanglechi dānd; Wakhi dendik/lând; Shughni ðindūn (Morg); P dandān دندان; Sor dan دان/digan دِگان [Kerkuk]; Za dildar/dindan *m.* (Todd); Hau didan m. (M4); cf. Lat dēns, dentis *m.*; Gr odous ὀδούς, *gen.* odontos ὀδόντος *m.*; Germ Zahn [Bg/Kg/K/IFb/JJ/HH/SK/GF/OK//A/B/JB3/TF] <alû; azû; dev I; lêv; qîl; sekihîn; ziman>

didanfiř دِدانفِڕ (FS/Kmc) = gap-toothed. See **diranfîq**.

didanfîq دِدانفیق (Wkt) = gap-toothed. See **diranfîq**.

didiwan دِدِوان (BX) = second. See **dudua**.

didiyê دِدِیێ (JB1-S) = second. See **dudua**.

dido دِدۆ (BX/IFb/GF/TF/OK) = two. See **didû**.

didu دِدو (BX/K/JJ) = two. See **didû**.

diduyan دِدویان (IF) = second. See **dudua**.

diduyî دِدویی (IF) = second. See **dudua**.

didû دِدوو *num.* two, 2: "didû" is used independently (free form), while "du" is immediately followed by a noun (bound form). Cf. **sisê** vs. **sê**. {also: dido (BX-2/IFb/GF/TF/OK-2); didu (BX/K/JJ); dudu (K/IF); [dedū] ددو (JJ); <diddo ددّو /dû دو> (HH)} [Pok. duō(u)- 228.] 'two': O Ir *duwā/*(n.)* duwai: Av d[u]va/*(n.)* *duue (younger Av duye); P dō دو; Sor dû دوو/duwan دووان; Za didi/di; Hau dûê (M4) [A//BX/K/JJ/OK//IFb/GF/TF//JB3//HH] <bîst; donzdeh; du I; sê; sisê>

difin دِفِن (A/JB1-A/TF/OK) = nose. See **difn.**

difinbilind دِفِنبِلِند (ZF3) = arrogant. See **difnbilind.**

difn دِفن *m.(K)/f.(SK)/pl.(SK)* **(/-a;).** 1) {syn: kepî[1]; poz I} nose: •**Şewek[ê] we qewimî ř̂îwîek hat e serbanê oda ximî, serê xo di kulekêda şor kir, bêna mirîşkan li *difna* wî da** (SK 4:28) One night it so happened that a fox came onto the roof of the dye-house and hung his head down through the skylight, when the smell of chickens assailed his *nose*; 2) {syn: bêvil[1]; firn[ik]; kepî[2]; kulfik I (Wn); ximximk} {also: [difink] دفنك (JJ)} nostril(s); nostrils of a horse (JJ). {also: difin (A/JB1-A/TF/OK); [defn] دفن (JJ); <defin دفن/difnik دفنك> (HH)} [K/JB3/IFb/GF/SK//JJ//HH/Bw//A/JB1-A/TF/OK] <bêvil>

difnbilind دفنبِلِند *adj.* arrogant, haughty, stuck-up, conceited. {also: difinbilind (ZF3)} {syn: nefsmezin; pozbilind} [Bw/GF//ZF3]

difs دِفس (IFb) = grape molasses. See **dims.**

digel دِگەل *prep.* 1) {syn: bi ... re} with *(accompaniment)*: •**digel hev** = together •***Digel* min bû** = He was *with* me; 2) {syn: dijî [2]; gir III; ř̂exme} in spite of, despite: **-digel vê hindê** = a) nevertheless, despite the fact that (BX); b) at the same time, simultaneously (K); **-digel vê yekê** (K) at the same time; **-digel vî çendî** (BX) however; 3) agreeing with: **-Ez *digel* vê çendê nînim** (Zeb) I don't *agree* with this. {also: ligel (Bw); [dighel] دگل (JJ); <digel> دگل (HH)} < di = 'in' + gel = 'group'; Sor legeł لەگەڵ [BX/K/JB3/IFb/JJ/HH/GF/TF/OK/MK//Bw] See also under **di**.

digulî دِگولی (TF) = crotch. See **dugulî**.

dih دِه (Bw) = pile of branches. See **dî II**.

diha دِها *adv.* 1) still, even more: •**Zîna delal *diha ze'f* bona Memê xwe diĥelîya û dip'eritî** (Z-1) Darling Zîn pined *even more* for her Mem; 2) already; 3) {syn: êdî [2]} [+ *neg.*] no more, no longer: •***Diha naçim* ber golika** (EP-5, #11) I won't be a cowherd *any more* [lit. 'No more will I go before the calves']. {also: daha (B)} < T daha = 'more' [J/K]

dihi دهِه = yesterday. See **dihî.**

dihî دِهی *adv.* yesterday; **-doh êvarê** (Frq) last night, yesterday evening. {also: dihi; do II (BX/Wn/Erg/GF/OK-2); doh (A/TF/OK-2); du II (IFb-2); duh (BX-2/F/K/B/IFb); duhê (Wn); duhî (BX-2/JB3/IFb-2/SK/GF-2); duhu (Ad); duhû (M-Zx); dûhû (JB1-A); [dí] دی (JJ); <doh دوه/duhî دهی> (HH)} <O Ir *dauša- (A&L p. 84 [V]): P dūš دوش = 'last night' & dīrūz دیروز = 'yesterday'; cf. also [Pok. ĝhđi̯és etc. 416.] 'yesterday': Av zyō; Sor dwênê [dönê] دوێنێ /dwêke [döke] دوێکه; =Za vizêr (Todd); cf. also Baluchi zī. See I. Gershevitch. "Iranian Chronological Adverbs," *Indo-Iranica: Mélanges présentés à Georg Morgenstierne* (Wiesbaden, 1964), pp.78-88; reprinted in his *Philologia Iranica*, ed. by N. Sims-Williams (Wiesbaden : Dr. Ludwig Reichert Verlag, 1985), pp. 179-89. [BX/Wn/Erg/GF//OK//A/HH/TF//F/K/B/IFb//JB3/SK//M-Zx//Ad//JJ//JB1-A] <betrapêr; îro; pêr; sibeh>

dihn I دِهن (HM) = crazy. See **dîn II.**

dihn II دِهن (IFb) = fat, grease. See **don.**

dihol دِهۆل (IFb/JB1-S/OK/HH) = drum. See **dehol.**

diholjen دِهۆلژه‌ن (GF) = drummer. See **deholjen.**

diholkut دِهۆلکوت *m.* (). drummer. {also: daholqut (FS)} {syn: daholvan; defçî; deholjen} [Bw//GF//IFb/OK] <mirt'ib; zirnabêj>

dij دِژ (JB3/IFb/GF/TF/OK) = in spite of. See **dijî.**

dijar دِژار (B) = difficult. See **dijwar.**

dijarî دِژاری (B) = difficulty. See **dijwarî.**

dijber دِژبەر *adj.* opposing; opposite, facing: •**HEP'a ku nikare bibe xwediyê şexsiyeteke xweser, nikare li hemberî partiyên *dijber* û saziyên dewletê jî, bibe xwedî rûmet û rêz** (Wlt 1:43, 9) [If] the People's Labor Party cannot have an independent identity, it cannot be respected by the *opposition* parties and the instruments of the state. {syn: miqabil; pêşber} [(neol)Wlt/IFb/GF]

dijî دِژی *prep.* 1) against: •**Di salên 1843-1846-an de Mîr Bedir-Xan ji bo damezrandina Kurdistanek serbixwe li *dijî* Împaratoriya Osmanî rabû** (Ronahî - intro) In the years 1843-1846, the emir Bedir-Khan rose up *against* the Ottoman Empire for the establishment of an independent Kurdistan; 2) {syn: digel [2]; gir III; r̄ex̄me} in spite of, despite: •**Lê, gelê me *dijî* wan zordestîyên hovîtî stuyê xwe xwar nekiriye** (Ronak - cover) But *in spite of* these displays of brute violence, our people has not knuckled under. {also: dij (JB3/IFb/GF/TF/OK)} Cf.Sor dij دِژ = 'bad, evil' [Ronak//JB3/IFb/GF/TF/OK]

dijmin دِژمِن *m.&f.* **(-ê/-a;).** enemy, foe: •***Dijmin*...zindanên xwe yên genî, ji keç û xortên me yên ciwan tijî kirin** (Wlt 2:59, 7) *The enemy*...has filled its stinking prisons with our young people [lit. 'young/beautiful girls and youths']. {also: djmin (SC); dujmin (A); duşmin (B/Ba2); [dijmin دژمن/douchmin دشمن] (JJ); <dijmin> دژمن (HH)} {syn: neyar} [Pok. dus- 227.] 'bad, evil; mis-' + [Pok. 3. men- 726.] 'to think; with derivatives referring to various qualitites and states of mind and thought': Av duš.ma(i)niiu- = 'bad spirit --> enemy'; Mid P dwšmyn [dušmen]; P došman دشمن --> T düşman; Sor dijmin دِژمِن/dujmin دوژمِن; Za dişmin *m./f.* (Todd); Hau dijmen *m.* (M4) {dijminahî; dijminayî; dijminî; dijminîtî; djmintî; dujminatî; dujminayî; duşminayî; duşminî; duşmintî} [BX/K/JB3/IFb/JJ/HH/GF/TF//OK//A//Ba2//SC]

dijminahî دِژمِناهی *f.* **(-ya;-yê).** enmity: •**Dasinî mezhebek e, Êzedî jî dibêjinê ... Ew dibêjine 'ulemaêt xo koçek û dibêjine musulmanan Ḧuseynî. Daimî mabeyna Dasinî û Ḧuseynîyan *dujminatî* ye** (SK 39:344) The Dasinis are a sect, also called Yezidis ... They call their own religious authorities 'kochak' and Muslims they call 'Husaini'. There is always *enmity* between the Dasinis and the 'Husainis'. {also: dijminayî (K-2/TF); dijminî (K-2/GF); dijminatî (OK-2); dijminîtî (K-2); djmintî (SC); dujminatî (SK); dujminayî (A); duşminayî (B); duşminî (B-2); duşmintî (B-2)} {syn: neyarî} [K/A/JB3/IFb/OK//TF//GF//B//SC//SK] <dijmin>

dijminatî دِژمِناتی (OK) = enmity. See **dijminahî.**

dijminayî دِژمِنایی (K/TF) = enmity. See **dijminahî.**

dijminî دِژمِنی (K/GF) = enmity. See **dijminahî.**

dijminîtî دِژمِنیتی (K) = enmity. See **dijminahî.**

dijmîn دِژمین (OK/HH) = insult. See **dijûn I.**

dijon دِژۆن (K) = dirty. See **dijûn II.**

dijûn I دِژوون *m./pl (Hk)* **().** insult, abuse, curse: •**Wî *dijûn dane* min** (Hk) He *insulted* me/He called me names. {also: dijmîn (OK); [dijoun] دژون

(JJ); <dijmîn دژمـيـن/dijwîn دژويـن> (HH)} {syn: ç'êr̄; ne'let; nifir̄; qise[3]; sixêf; xeber[3]} Cf. P dušnām دشـنـام = 'reproach'; Sor cwên جـويّـن/ cinêw جـنـيّـو = 'abuse, curse' [Hk/K/JJ/IFb/GF//HH] <nifir̄>

dijûn II دِژوون *adj.* 1) soiled *(clothing)*, flea or lice infested *(clothing)* (IFb); dirty (JJ); dirty, overdue for washing (A); lice infested (K): **•[Cilêd <min> *dijûn* bûyîne, berşoyêd <min> bîne, da ez cilêd xwe veguhorim]** (JR) These clothes are *worn out*, bring my spare set so that I can change. {also: dijon (K); dujîn (A/IFb); [dijoun] دژون (JJ); <dijûn> دژون (HH)} {syn: bi'ok; ç'epelf; gemarî; p'îs; qirêj} [JR/JJ/HH//K//A/IFb]

dijvar دِژڤار = difficult. See **dijwar.**

dijvarî دِژڤارى = difficulty. See **dijwarî.**

dijwar دِژوار *adj.* 1) {syn: [bi] zeh̄met; ç'etin} hard, difficult; 2) tough, fierce, hard, vehement (Bw): **•Baraneka *dijwar* ya dibarît** (Bw) It's raining *hard* **•Şer̄ekî zor *dijwar* e** (Bw) It is a very *tough* war; 3) {syn: tûj [2]} hot, spicy *(peppers, tobacco, karî II* [qv.]: *cf.* ***tûj****, of onions, jajî on its way to going bad, etc.)* (Bw); 4) a man's name. {also: dijar (B); dijvar; dişwar; [dijvar دژوار /dichvar دشـوار] (JJ); <dijwar> دژوار (HH)} Cf. P došvār دشـوار; Sor dijwar دِژوار = 'difficult'; also W Arm tžuar դժուար {dijvarî; dijwarî; dişwarî} [Ber/K/A/JB3/IFb/JJ/HH/ SK/GF/TF/OK/Bw//B]

dijwarî دِژوارى *f.* **(-ya;-yê).** difficulty, hardship: **•bêî tu *dişwariyê*** (BX) without any *difficulty*. {also: dijarî (B); dijvarî; dişwarî} {syn: ç'etinayî} [BX/K/A/JB3/IFb/GF/TF/OK//B] <dijwar>

dikak دِكـاك *pl.* **().** vegetables. {also: dikark (Hk-2)} {syn: deramet I; êmîş [2]; heşînatî; p'incar} cf. NENA dikâké ܕܟܟܐ (Maclean) [Hk/IFb]

dik'an دِكـان *f.* **(-a;-ê).** shop, store: **•Tu alî min li vê *dikanê* bike; em ê bikirrin û bifiroşin** (ZZ-10 151-2) Help me in this *shop*; we will buy and sell. {also: duk'an (B); dûkan (IFb-2); [doukan] دكـان (JJ); <dikan> دكان (HH)} Cf. Ar dukkān/P dokkān دكّـان--> T dükkân [Z-2/Ag/K/A/JB3/IFb/HH/JB1-A&S/GF/TF/OK/ZF//JJ//B]

dik'ançî دِكـانـچـى (Z-2/OK) = shopkeeper. See **dik'andar.**

dik'andar دِكـانـدار *m.&f.* **(-ê/ ; dikandêr/).** shopkeeper, storeowner: **•Ji xwe tiştên ku *dikandarê* me difiroşe jî ne ewqas gelek in** (Lab, 75) However the things which our *shopkeeper* sells are not so great in number. {also: dik'ançî (Z-2/OK-2); duk'ançî (F/B-2); duk'andar (B); [doukan-dar] دكـان دار (JJ); <dikandar> دكـانـدار (HH)} {syn: etar [2]} [Z-2//F//B/JJ//K/IFb/HH/TF/OK/Bw]

dikark دِكارك (Hk) = vegetables. See **dikak**.

dil دِل *m.* **(-ê;).** heart: **•*Dilê* wî biqul [=bikul] e** (L) He is distressed [lit. 'His *heart* is distressed']; **-ber dilê *fk-ê* hatin** (XF) to console, soothe, calm; to dry s.o.'s tears **•P'erî-xatûnê t'u gilî nedidît, wekî *ber dilê* xûşka xwe 'ezîzda *bihata*** (Z-1) Peri-khatun could find no words with which *to console* her dear sister; **-bi dilê *fk-ê*** (Z-1) to s.o.'s liking, as much as one likes, to one's heart's desire: **•Ezê heqê we *bi dilê* we bidim** (Z-1) I will give you a reward *to* your *liking*; **-dilê *fk-ê* danîn** (XF) to feel relieved, calm down: **•H̄evekî p'erç'a *dilê* wana *datîne*** (FK-eb-2) They *calm down* considerably; **-dil k'etin** = to fall in love: **•Qîzik ne bi dilkî *dilketîye*, bi heft dila *dilketîye*** (L) The girl *fell* not one heart['s worth] *in love*, [but rather] seven hearts[' worth]; **-dil kirin** = a) to want, wish, desire (K); to decide, resolve: **•Ez fkirîm, paşê min *dilkir*, wekî wî teyrî ji xwer̄a bigirim** (EH) I thought, then *resolved* to take that bird for myself; b) to dare (Ba2): **•H̄er kerîkî pêz r̄a sê-çar seêd gurêx derdik'etne çolê, ewe usa dir̄ bûn, ku *kesekî dil nedikir* nêzîkî pêz be** (Ba2:1, 203) With every flock of sheep, 3-4 sheepdogs would go out to the wilderness: they were so fierce that *no one dared* approach the sheep; **-dil jê man** = a) to be or get angry at or with, be dissatisfied with: **•*Dilê* wî *ji* min *ma*** (K) He *got angry at* me **•Bira *dilê* te *ji* min *nemîne*** (Z-1) ...So you *won't be dissatisfied with* me; b) to be disappointed with or in: **•*Dilê* wî *ji* min *ma*** (K) He *was disappointed with/in* me; **-dil pêve bûn** (Zeb) mercy. See **dil pêve bûn**; **-dil xwestin** = to wish, desire: **•Tiştê go *dilê wî dixwest* ji xwe re kirî** (L) He bought for himself whatever *his heart desired*; **-hildan dilê xwe**. See under **hildan.** {also: [dil] دل (JJ); <dil> دل (HH)} Probably a borrowing from P del دل: [Pok. k̑ered- 579.] 'heart' + *ĝhrd- for Proto-IndIr *ǰhṛd-: Skt hṛdaya- *n.*; O Ir *zṛdā- (Morg3, p.337): Av zərəd- *(n.)*/zərəδaiia- *(n.)*; Mid P dil; P del دل; Sor dił دِلّ; Za zerrî *f.* (Todd); Hau dił *m.* (M4); cf. also Arm sirt (W: sird) սիրտ; Lat cor, cordis *n.*; Gr kardia καρδία; Rus serdtse сердце; Germ Herz *n.* [K/A/JB3/IFb/B/JJ/

HH/SK/GF/TF/OK] <jidil>

dilç'akî دِلچاكى *f.* (). goodheartedness: **•Ji dilpaqijiya xelkê wî pêva, *dilçakî* û rûnermiya şêx jî ev hezkirina han roj bi roj zêde dikirin** [sic] (Rnh 2:17, 326) In addition to the honesty of his people, the *goodheartedness* and gentleness of the sheikh made this love [for him] increase day by day. [Rnh]

dildar دِلدار *adj.* 1) {syn: aşiq; dilk'etî; evîndar} in love with [+ *ezafeh*]: **•Kê bêhna bêçiya xwe dikir ku Kevanot ê bibe *dildarê* Nêrgisa koçer!** (Lab, 9) Who would have suspected [lit. 'smelled his finger'] that Kevanot would *fall in love with* Nergis the nomad; 2) [*m&f. & adj.*] amateur; volunteer: **•Ji ber ku tenê komên *dildar* mudaxileyî şewatê dikin, şewat natefe** (mezopotamyaajansi.com 23.viii.2018) Because on *volunteer/ amateur* groups are interfering with the conflagration, the fire is not being extinguished. Sor diłdar دِڵدار = 'lover' {dildarî} [Lab/K/A/IFb/GF] <ḧewask'ar; xêrxwaz>

dildarî دِلدارى *f.* **(-ya;-yê).** love, being in love: **•Lê *dildarî* serê xwe bixwe** (Lab, 9) But *love* be damned! [lit. 'let love eat its head']. {also: [dil-dari] دلدارى (JJ)} {syn: eşq; evîndarî; ḧub} Sor diłdarî دِڵدارى = 'love' [Lab/K/A/JJ/GF] <dildar>

dilêr دلێر (ZF3/FS/BF) = brave. See **delîr**.

dilêrane دلێرانه (ZF3) = bravely. See **delîrane**.

dilêrî دلێرى (ZF3/FS) = bravery. See **delîrî**.

dilhan دِلهان (GF) = to be dazzled. See **delîyan** [1].

dilihîn دِلهين (GF) = to be dazzled. See **delîyan** [1].

dilik دِلك *m.* (). hearts *(suit of playing cards)*. {syn: kupe} [MI]

diliyan دِليان (EŞ) = to starve. See **delîyan** [2].

dilk'etî دِلكەتى *adj.* 1) beloved: **•Wekî *dilk'etîya* Memê min layîqî wî nînbe, ezê şeherê Cizîrê xirab kim** (Z-1) If Mem's *beloved* is not worthy of him, I'll lay waste to the city of Jezira; 2) {syn: aşiq; dildar; evîndar} in love. [Z-1/K/A/JB3/IFb/B/GF/OK]

dilmayî دِلمايى *adj.* offended, hurt; angry: **-dilmayî man** = to be offended: **•Memê sê qat heqê wan dayê, wekî ew *dilmayî* nemînin** (Z-1) Mem gave them three times what they deserved, so that they would not be *offended*. [Z-1/K/ZF3]

dilme دِلمە *adj.* soft-boiled *(egg)*: **-hêka dilme** (Czr) do. {also: dilmeyî (Rwn); dilmê (Dh/Elk); dilmo (Xrz); [ek delma] هيك دلمه (JJ-G)} [Czr/A/IFb/TF//Rwn//Dh/Elk//Xrz//JJ-G]

dilmeyî دِلمەيى (Rwn) = soft boiled. See **dilme**.

dilmê دِلمێ (Dh/Elk) = soft boiled. See **dilme**.

dilmînî دِلمينى *f.* **(-ya;).** comfort, solace, consolation: **-dilmînî dan (yekî)** (ZF3) to comfort s.o. {syn: ber dilê fk-ê hatin; t'eselî kirin}; **-dilmînî dan xwe** (ZF3) to console o.s.: **•Min *dilmînî dida xwe*** (ŞWWM, 10) I *consoled myself*. {syn: ḧewî; t'eselî} [ŞWWM/ZF3/Wkt]

dilmo دِلمۆ (Xrz) = soft boiled. See **dilme**.

dilnizm دِلنِزم *adj.* humble, modest, unpretentious. {also: [dil-nizim] دل نزم (JJ)} {syn: nefspiç'ûk} [K/A/IFb/GF/JJ/Wkt]

dilnizmahî دِلنِزماهى (Wkt) = humility, modesty. See **dilnizmî**.

dilnizmî دِلنِزمى *f.* **(-ya;-yê).** humility, modesty, unpretentiousness: **•Vê carê Graniayê ne bi hêrs lê *bi dilnizmî* silav da wî** (EN) then G. greeted him not with anger, but *with humility*. {also: dilnizmahî (Wkt-2); [dil-nizmi] دل نزمى (JJ)} [EN/K/A/GF/JJ/Wkt]

dilob دِلۆب = drop *(of a liquid)*. See **dilop**.

dilop دِلۆپ *f.* **(-a;-ê).** drop *(of a liquid)*: **•Jê tê bîhna pîs tev *av û dûlop* / Tev mêş û kelmêş pêşî û dûpişk** (Cxn-2:412) A bad smell comes from it, with *dripping water* / With flies and gadflies, mosquitoes and scorpions; **-dilop-dilop** (B) drop by drop; **-dilop kirin** (K/IF/JJ/HH) to drip. {also: dilob; dûlop (Cxn); [diloup] دلوپ (JJ); <dilop> دلوپ (HH)} {syn: çilk; çipik; niqitk; p'eşk I} <Arc dlaf דלף = 'to drip': NENA dilpa = 'leak' (Oraham), dâlip ܕܠܦ = 'to drip, to leak' (Maclean); Sor diłop دڵۆپ = 'drop (liquid)' [F/K/A/IFb/B/JJ/HH/GF/TF/OK//Cxn]

dilovan دِلۆڤان *adj.* 1) {syn: mihrivan} tender, affectionate, gentle: **•Bi rastî jî jineke dilpak û *dilovan* e** (Lab, 7) She is truly a *gentle* and pure-hearted woman; 2) {syn: dilreḧm; dilşewat; mihrivan; r̄iḧsivik; xwînşîrîn} benevolent, kind[-hearted] (JJ); merciful, compassionate (IFb/BK/JJ) **•bavekî *dilovan*** (BK) a *merciful* father. {also: [dil-ou-wan] دلوڤان (JJ); <dilûvan> دلوڤان (HH)} {dilovanî} [K/A/JB3/IFb/GF/TF/OK//JJ/HH]

dilovanî دِلۆڤانى *f.* **(-ya;-yê).** 1) tenderness, affection; 2) {syn: dilpêvebûn; dilreḧmî; r̄eḧmet} mercy, compassion: **-çûn ber dilovanîya xwedê** (Zeb/Dh) to die, pass away {syn: alîjiyan bûn; mirin; wefat bûn/kirin}: **•Dema babê wî *çûye ber dilovanîya xwedê*, maye bitinê** (Metîn 77[1998], 51) When his father *passed away*, he was left alone;

3) humility. [IFb/GF/TF/OK]

dilp'ak دِلپـــــاك *adj.* pure of heart; frank, sincere: **•Bi rastî jî jineke *dilpak* û dilovan e** (Lab, 7) She is truly a gentle and *pure-hearted* woman. Sor diłpak دڵـــپــاك = 'innocent (as child), sincere' {dilp'akî} [Lab/K/IFb/GF/TF]

dilp'akî دِلپاكى *f.* **(-ya;-yê).** purity of heart; frankness, sincerity. {also: [dil-paki] دلپاكى (JJ)} [K/IFb/JJ/GF/TF] <dilp'ak>

dilp'aqijî دِلپـاقـژى *f.* **(-ya;-yê).** 1) honesty, integrity, purity of purpose: **•Ji *dilpaqijiya* xelkê wî pêva, dilçakî û rûnermiya şêx jî ev hezkirina han roj bi roj zêde dikirin** [sic] (Rnh 2:17, 326) In addition to the *honesty* of his people, the goodheartedness and gentleness of the sheikh made this love [for him] increase day by day; 2) frankness, sincerity, candor (K/JJ). {also: [dil-pakiji] دل پاكيژى (JJ)} {syn: dilp'ak} [Rnh/K/GF//JJ]

dil pêve bûn دل پێڤه بوون *vi.* **(dilê *fk-î* bi *bk-î* ve -b-).** 1) to take pity on s.o.; to be merciful to or lenient on s.o.: ***•Dilê* min *pêve ma*** (K) I *took pity on* him; 2) [**dilpêvebûn** *f.* **(-a;-ê).**] mercy, leniency {syn: dilovanî; dilr̄eḧmî; r̄eḧmet}: **•Filankes li ber *dilpêvebûnê* nakevît** (Zeb) So-and-so will not be accorded *leniency or mercy*. [Zeb/K/GF] <'efû>

dilq دِلق (IFb) = 1) form; 2) disguise. See **dilqe.**

dilq•e دِلـقـه *m.* **(•ê;).** 1) shape, form, appearance; 2) {syn: qilix I [2]} disguise, costume; dervish's frock (JJ): **-k'etin/li xwe kirin dilẍê dewrêşa[n]** (K) to take on the appearance of dervishes, to dress up or disguise o.s. as a dervish *[common motif in folktales]*: **•Were emê şevekê *bik'evine dilqê dewrêşa*** (Z-921) Come let us *dress up as dervishes* one night. {also: dilq (IFb); dilẍe (K); [delq] دلق (JJ)} [Ks/Z-922//K//IFb/JJ]

dilr̄ahm دِلراهم (B) = kind-hearted. See **dilr̄eḧm.**

dilr̄ahmî دِلراهمى (B) = kindness. See **dilr̄eḧmî.**

dilr̄aḧm دِلراحم (Ba2) = kind-hearted. See **dilr̄eḧm.**

dilrehm دِلرەهم (K/IFb) = kind-hearted. See **dilr̄eḧm.**

dilr̄eḧm دِلـرەحـم *adj.* good-natured, kind-hearted; merciful, compassionate, charitable; magnanimous: **•Şivan gişke mêrxas bûn û wêr̄a t'evayî *dilr̄aḧm* bûn** (Ba2:1, 204) The shepherds were all brave and nevertheless they were *merciful*. {also: dilr̄ahm (B); dilr̄aḧm (Ba2); dilrehm (K/IFb)} {syn: dilovan; dilşewat} {dilr̄ahmî; dilr̄eḧmî} [Ba2//GF/OK//K/IFb//B]

dilr̄eḧmî دِلـرەحـمـى *f.* **(-ya;-yê).** compassion, pity; mercy; kindness, goodness; magnanimity. {also: dilr̄ahmî (B)} {syn: dilovanî; dilpêvebûn; r̄eḧmet} [OK//ZF3//B] <dilr̄eḧm>

dils̱af دِلـصـاف/**dilsaf** دِلـسـاف *adj.* innocent, naïve, simple; honorable: **•Kurd milletekî *dil-s̱af* û weḧsî ye, malê xo nîwekê zêdetir dê kene s̱edeqe bo tekyaêt xulefeyêt mewlana w gelek dê dewletmend bin** (SK 44:428) The Kurds are a *simple* and credulous people; they will give more than half of their property as pious gifts for the convents of Maulana's successors and these will become very rich **•Sebebekî dî ji esbabêt xo-dan-e-paşa Kurdan ji dexaleta dewleta behîye ya urosî eweye, dibêjin dewleta urosî *dil-s̱af* e** (SK 56:651) Another of the reasons for the Kurds' reluctance to submit to the august Russian government is this: it is said that the Russian government is [too] *naïve*. {also: dilsafî (K); [del-sáfi (G)/safi-dil صافى دل] (JJ)} Sor diłsaf دڵساف = 'innocent (as child), sincere' [SK//IFb/OK//K/JJ-G] <bêguneh; bêsûc>

dilsafî دِلسافى (K/JJ-G) = naïve. See **dils̱af.**

dilsoj دِلـــــســـــۆژ *adj.* sad, heart-rending, causing melancholy or sadness, touching: **•Şehîd Sekîn ji bo dayika xwe klameke *dilsoj* distrê** (TRT Nûçe) The martyr Sekin sings a *heart-rending* song for his mother. <dil = 'heart' + soj- = 'burning'; Cf. Sor diłsûtan (pê) (پـێ) دڵـسـووتـان = 'to pity, feel sorry (for)' [ZF/CS/Wkt] <dilsoz>

dilsoz دِلـسـۆز *adj.* loyal, trustworthy, faithful, reliable, devoted: **•Bizavkarên Sûrî dibêjin, hêzên *dilsozî* Serok Beşar Esed hewil didin ku kontrola devereke stratejîk ya bajarê Humsê jinûve bigirin destê xwe** (VoA) Syrian activists say that forces *loyal to* President Bashar al-Asad are trying to retake control of a strategic area of the city of Homs **•Têkiliyên Rûsyayê yên taybet û *dilsoz* bi kurdan re heye** (Rûpela Nû) Russia has special and *trustworthy* relations with the Kurds. <dil = 'heart' + soz = 'burning' (P); Sor diłsoz دڵـسـۆز = 'sincere, true, concerned' {dilsozî} [IFb/FJ/GF/TF/CS/ZF/SS/BF/Wkt] <dilsoj>

dilsozî دِلـسـۆزى *f.* **(-ya;-yê).** loyalty, trustworthiness, faithfulness, fidelity, reliability, devotion: **•Baştirîn *dilsozî* bo şehîdan, bidestanîna serxwebûn û azadiyê ye** (Kurdistan 24) The best [way of showing] *loyalty* to the martyrs is to achieve independence and freedom **•Geşkirina Duhokê**

nîşana *dilsozî* û karkirina hikûmetê û îdareya deverê ye (Hikûmeta Herêma Kurdistanê) The prosperity of Dihok is a sign of the *devotion* and effectivenss of the government and of the regional administration. [IFb/TF/ZF/CS/BF/Wkt]

dilşawat دِلشاوات (TF) = gentle. See **dilşewat**.

dilşewat دِلشەوات *adj.* 1) {syn: dilovan; dilřeĥm} sympathetic, compassionate, merciful, gentle: **•Ewî** [sic] **gelekî *dilşewat* bû û t'u cara merîya řa xirabî nedikir** (Ba2:1, 204) He was very *gentle* and never harmed anyone; 2) *distressed; touching, pathetic; troubling, worrisome. {also: dilşawat (TF); dilşewatî (A)} [Ba2/K/B/IFb/GF/OK//A//TF]

dilşewatî دِلشەواتی (A) = gentle. See **dilşewat**.

dilşikestî دِلشِکەستی (Ardû/A/GF) = brokenhearted. See **dilşkestî**.

dilşkestî دِلشکەستی *adj.* brokenhearted, greatly disappointed: **•Mêrik bi awakî bêhêvî û *dilşikestî* ji rîsipî vediqete, berê xwe dide mala xwe û diçe** (Ardû, 19) Disappointed and *brokenhearted*, the fellow takes his leave of the old man and heads for home. {also: dilşikestî (Ardû/A/GF)} Sor diłşikaw دڵشکاو = 'vexed' [Ardû/A/GF//K/B]

dilt̲eng دِلطەنگ [SK/TF] /**dilteng** دِلتەنگ [K/IFb/B/GF/OK] *adj.* distressed, sad, upset, depressed, troubled, vexed: **•Carekê me'mûrê mêş-hejmarî ji t̲erefê ĥukometê hate Şagulûrdê. Kemo gelek *dil-t̲eng* bû, neko şola wî aşkera bibît** (SK 35:320) Once the bee-counting official came to Shagulurde from the government. Kemo was very *distressed* lest his business should become known **•Şêx Muĥemmed S̲iddîq ... bi tereqqîya Şêx 'Ebdusselami Sanî gelek 'aciz û *dil-t̲eng* bû** (SK 48:471) Shaikh Muhammad Siddiq ... was very annoyed and *vexed* at the progress made by Shaikh Abdussalam II. {also: diltang (TF) = dilt̲eng; [dil tenk] دل تنك (JJ)} Cf. P del'tang دل تنگ = 'sad, annoyed'; Sor diłteng دڵتەنگ = 'sad, vexed' {dilteng[ah]î; dilt̲engî} [SK/TF//K/IFb/B/GF/OK//JJ] <aciz; bêk'êf; bên teng bûn [See **bîn I**]>

diltengahî دِلتەنگاهی (IFb) = distress. See **dilt̲engî**.

dilt̲engî دِلطەنگی/**diltengî** دِلتەنگی *f.* **(-ya;-yê).** distress, sadness, [being] upset, depression, being troubled, vexation: **•Yek, du heval xuya ne bûn; Xwedê zane ne ji bêbextî, dibe ko ji *diltengiya* ji hev qetandinê** (WT, 86) One or two friends did not appear; I doubt it was out of betrayal, perhaps from *the grief of* being separated. {also: diltangî (TF) = dilt̲engî; diltengahî (IFb-2)} Cf. P del'tangī دل تنگی [K/IFb/B/GF/OK/ZF//TF] <acizayî; dilt̲eng>

dilxoş دِلخۆش (SK/OK) = happy. See **dilxweş**.

dilxweş دِلخوەش *adj.* happy, pleased; satisfied: **•Ĥemamçî gelek *dilxweş* bû biçê mala Çelebî bibîne** (Rnh 2:17, 307) The bathhouse owner was very *happy* to go see Chelebi's house. {also: dilxoş (SK/OK-2)} {syn: k'êfxweş} Sor diłxoş دڵخۆش = 'happy' {dilxweşî} [Rnh/K/A/IFb/B/GF/TF/OK//SK]

dilxweşî دِلخوەشی *f.* **(-ya;-yê).** happiness, pleasure, satisfaction; **-bi dilxweşî** (K/IFb/CS): a) *[adj.]* happy: •[In closing a letter] **Her tim rojên *bi dilxweşî* daxwaz dikim** (Haz) I hope for *happy* days always [for you]; b) [*adv.*] happily, with pleasure: **•Her du hatin, di qesra xwe de man *bi dilxweşî*** (SW1, 57) They both came, and stayed *happily* in their castle **•Mela hemî xelat kirin, gelek řazî w memnon bon, bi *dil-xoşî* çon** (SK 39:353) He gave a present to each mullah and they were very pleased and grateful and went away *happy*. {also: dilxoşî (SK); [dil-khochi] دل خوشی (JJ)} {syn: k'êfxweşî} Sor diłxoşî دڵخۆشی = 'happiness, joy, gladness' [SW1/K/A/B/IFb/GF/TF/ZF/RZ/CS//JJ/SK] <dilxweş>

dilẍe دِلغە (K) = 1) form; 2) disguise. See **dilqe.**

dilyan دِلیان (GF) = to be dazzled. See **delîyan** [1].

dilzîz دِلزیز *adj.* tender-hearted, gentle, easily hurt, fragile, delicate. {also: [dil-zizé] دل ضیزه (JJ)} [Ag/GF//JJ] <zîz I & II>

dim دِم *m.* **(-ê;).** beak, bill (of bird): **-dimê mirîşkê** (BF) chicken's beak. {also: dimik (SK/FS)} {syn: nikil [1]} [Bw/BF//SK/FS] <dev>

Dimdim دِمدِم *f.* **().** *name of a fortress in Iranian Kurdistan* (EP-8): **-Kela Dimdim** (EP-8) the fortress of Dimdim, south of Urmiyah/Reza'iyeh in Kurdistan of Iran; *a Kurdish rebellion against Shah Abbas which took place there in 1608-1610 is the subject of a famous Kurdish legend by the same name.* For a study of the legend, see: Ordikhane Dzhalilov. *Kurdskiĭ geroicheskiĭ epos "Zlatorukiĭ khan" (Dymdym)* [= The Kurdish heroic epic "Zlatorukiĭ khan," i.e., The ruler with the golden hand, (Dimdim)] (Moscow: Glavnaia Redaktsiia Vostochnoĭ Literatury, 1967), 206 p. [EP-8/K] <kela>

dimik دِمِك (SK/FS) = beak. See **dim**.

Dimilî دِملی *adj.* 1) 'Zaza', an Iranian language related to Kurdish and Persian spoken in Turkish Kurdistan, particularly in Siverek (Urfa), Çermîk (Dîyarbakir), Gerger (Malatya), Sivrice (Elâzığ/ Xarpût), and Tunceli/Dêrsim: its speakers are ethnically Kurds; "Dimili is an Iranian language, part of the Indo-Iranian subgroup of Indo-European. It is spoken in central eastern Turkey by perhaps as many as one million people. The Turks and Kirmanji speakers around them call the language Zaza which has pejorative connotations" (Mann-Hadank, 1932:1) ... Mann concluded (Mann-Hadank, 1932:19) that Dimili is not a Kurdish dialect and Hadank concluded (1932:4) that the name Dimili is most likely a metathesis of "Daylemî," i.e., the language reflects that of the Daylamites who came from an area called Daylam on the south coast of the Caspian and who were often distinguished from the Kurds in medieval references. Dimili speakers today consider themselves to be Kurds and resent scholarly conclusions which indicate that their language is not Kurdish. Speakers of Dimili are Kurds psychologically, socially, culturally, economically, and politically. It is quite possible, especially since the term Kurd has always been ill-defined (D.N. MacKenzie. "The Origins of Kurdish." *Transactions of the Philological Society*. 1961:69), that speakers of Dimili should be identified as Kurds today. The language, however, is distinct from Kurdish dialects ..." [from: Terry Lynn Todd. *A Grammar of Dimili (also known as Zaza)*. Doctoral dissertation (Ann Arbor : University of Michigan, 1985), pp. iii, v-vi]; 2) *[m./adj.]* The 'Zazas', speakers of the 'Zaza' language. {also: Dumilî; Dumilkî} [Ber/IFb]

dims دِمس *m.(K/B)/f.(Çnr/OK)* **(-ê/-a; /-ê).** grape molasses, thick syrup made from boiled grape juice [T pekmez]: •**Mîna mêşa ku bikeve kûpê** ***dimsê*** **û pêve bimîne** (Lab, 74) Like the fly that falls into a jug *of grape molasses* and gets stuck. {also: difs (IFb-2); [dimiz دمز/dims دمس] (JJ); <dims> دمس (HH)} {syn: aqit; doşav; mot} <Ar dibs دبس = '(grape) molasses, treacle'; cf. Heb devaš דבש = 'honey' [Çnr/K/A/IFb/B/JJ/HH/GF/TF/OK] <ḧelîl; ḧewdel; qawît>

din I دِن *adj.* other; next: •**Lê her dehê** ***dinê*** **jî ji dêkê bûn** (Ba) But as for the *other* ten, they were from one mother •**Ne ew û ne keskî** ***din*** (L) Neither he nor anyone *else*. {also: dinê I (B-2); dî I (Zx/Dh/ Bw/Zeb); dîtir (Hk/Alkan)} Cf. Sor tir تر/dîke دیکه/ke که [K/JB3/IFb/B/GF/TF/OK//Zx/Dh/Bw/Zeb]

din II دِن = world. See **dinya.**

dinê I دِنی (B) = other; next. See **din I.**

dinê II دِنێ (IFb/JB3/GF/OK) = world. See **dinya.**

dinêzan دِنێزان *adj.* worldly, acquainted with the ways of the world, i.e., sophisticated: •**Tu çawa** ***merîkî dinêzan*****, aqlê te ji evê yekê çi dibiře** (K2-Fêrîk) As *a man of the world*, what do you make of this? <dinê/dinya = 'world' + zan- = 'to know' [K2-Fêrîk/ Wkt] <dinya>

ding دِنگ f./m.(Frq/IFb/GF/ZF3) = instrument for husking grain. See **deng II**.

dinîya دِنییا = world. See **dinya.**

dinîyadîtî دِنییادیتی (Z-1) = experienced. See **dinyadîtî.**

dinîyalik دِنییالِك (Z-3) = all of humanity. See **dinyalik.**

dink دِنك (GF) = instrument for husking grain. See **deng II**.

dinya دِنیا *f.* **(-ya; dinyaê** [L]**/dinê).** 1) world: •**Ez li** ***dinyaê*** **li te digerim** (L) I am roaming *the world* in search of you; **-hatin dinyaê** (K) to be born; 2) it (in time and weather expressions, a usage found also in colloquial Arabic) : •***Dinya*** **bû moẍrib** (L) *It* was sunset time [lit. 'The world was sunset'] •***Dinya*** **esr e** (L) *It* is afternoon. {also: din II; dinê II (IFb-2/JB3-2/GF-2/OK-2); dinîya; dunîya (F/K/ B); [douni دنی/dounia دنیا] (JJ); <d[i]nya> دنیا (HH)} < Ar dunyā دنیا = '[lower] world', f. of adná ادنی = 'lower' <√d-n-y دنی & √d-n-w دنو = 'be near' --> T dünya [JB3/IFb/HH/GF/TF/OK//F/K/JJ/B]

dinyadîtî دِنیادیتی *adj.* experienced, 'having seen the world': •**Şeherê Muxurzemînêde kalekî zemanî,** ***dinîyadîtî*** **hebû** (Z-1) In the city of Mukhurzemin there was an *experienced* old man {zemanî =? [lasted through] time}. {also: dinîyadîtî (Z-1); dunîyadîtî} {syn: xam; ≠nestêl} < dinya = 'world' + dîtî = 'having seen' [Z-1/K/JB3/IFb/TF/OK]

dinyalik دِنیالِك *f.* **(;-ê).** the whole world, all of humanity: •**Bi her t'ibî'etê** ***dinîyalikê*****, t'i qisûr nayê serî** (Z-3) Of all of *human* nature, he has no faults [=he has none of the faults common to the rest of humanity]. {also: dinîyalik (Z-3); dunîyalik (B)} <dinya + -lik = Turkish suffix meaning, inter alia, 'intended for': dünyalık = 'intended for the world, hence worldly goods, money' [Z-3//ZF3//B]

diř I دِڕ *adj.* 1) sharp, harsh, abrupt; 2) severe, stern, bleak, cold; 3) wild, impetuous, violent, stormy; 4) fierce, ferocious, savage, cruel *(of animals)*: **•Ḧer kerîkî pêz r̄a sê-çar seêd gurêẍ derdik'et-ne çolê, ewe usa *dir̄* bûn, ku kesekî dil nedikir nêzîkî pêz be** (Ba2:1, 203) With every flock of sheep, 3-4 sheepdogs would go out to the wilderness: they were so *fierce* that no one dared approach the sheep. [Ba2/K/A/IFb/B/GF/OK] <t'und; xurt>

dir̄ II دِڕ (HR-7) = pearl. See **dur̄**.

diraf دِراف (MK2/IF) = dirhem. See **dirav.**

diram دِرام, f. (K) = dirhem. See **dirav.**

diran دِران (A/B/IFb/JJ/GF/TF/OK) = tooth. See **didan.**

dir̄andin دِڕانــــدن *vt.* **(-dir̄în-).** to tear, rip (with the teeth) *(vt.)*: **•Paşî mişk hate pêş, got "... cuhal û hemban û kuwaran jî *didir̄înim* û bi kun dikem"** (SK 1:7) Then the mouse came forward and said, "... I *tear* and make holes in sacks and bags and corn-bins." {also: drandin (JB3); [dirandin] دراندين (JJ); <dirandin دراندن (didirîne) (ددرينه)> (HH)} {syn: ç'ir̄andin; qelişandin [1]/ qelaştin} Cf. P darān[ī]dan درانيدن; Sor dir̄andin (-dir̄ên-) دِڕاندن; Za dirrnenã [dirrnayiş] (Srk) [K/A/ JB3/IFb/B /JJ/HH/SK/GF/ TF/OK/M] <dir̄în I>

diranfîq دِرانــفـيـق *adj.* gap-toothed, with teeth widely spaced: **•Diya min û pîra min her tim digotin yên *diranfîq* nesîbê wan fireh in** (tirşik.net) My mother and grandmother always said that *gap-toothed* people have good luck. {*also*: didanfir̄ (FS/Kmc-2); didanfîq (Wkt-2); dranfîq (Wkt)} [Kmc/G/ZF3//Wkt//FS] <firk III; fîq>

dirav دِراڤ *f.(K)/m.(B/ZK3)* **(/-ê ; /dirêv** [B], **vî diravî).** dirhem, drachma; small coin; money. {also: diraf (MK2/IFb); diram, f. (K); dirhav (TF); draf (IFb-2); drav (IFb-2); [diraw] دراڤ (JJ); <dirav دراڤ /direhv درهـف> (HH)} < Ar dirham درهـم, Gr drachmē δραχμή; Sor diraw دِراو [A/B/JJ/ HH/GF/OK//IFb/MK2/ZF3//TF//K]

diravguhêr دِراڤگوهێر *m.* **(-ê;).** money changer [Ar ṣarrāf صـرّاف]: **•Gule li *diravguhêrekî* hat barandin li bajarê Sermînê** (diyaruna.com 6.vi.2018) In the city of Sermin, *a money changer* was showered with bullets. {also: diravguhur (Zeb); diravvegor (Bar)} [Zeb//GF/Wkt//Bar]

diravguhur دِراڤگوهور (Zeb) = money changer. See **diravguhêr**.

diravî دِراڤـی *adj.* financial, monetary: **•Komeleya Hêvî ya xêrxwaziyê li Serê Kaniyê di heyva Tîrmehê ya bûrî de alîkariya *diravî* pêşkêşî 244 cotkaran li devera Serê Kaniyê kir** (orient-news.net 4.viii.2016) Last July, the benevolent society of Hope [Komeleya Hêvî] in Serê Kanî offered *financial* assistance to 244 farmers in the Serê Kanî region; **-mijara diravî** (BF) financial matter; **-raporta diravî** (BF) financial report. {also: dirhavî (TF); drafî (IFb)} [FJ/GF/Wkt/ZF3/BF/SS//TF//IFb]

diravvegor دِراڤـڤـەگـۆر (Bar) = money changer. See **diravguhêr**.

dirb I دِرب *f.* **(;-ê).** passage, pass, way; path, narrow passage. {also: [dirb] درب (JJ); <dirb> درب (HH)} < Ar darb درب = 'road' [Z-2/K/JJ/HH/ZF3/Wkt] <bihur; 'ewc; kûçe; pêgeh; r̄ê>

dirb II دِرب (Frq) = looks. See **dirûv**.

dir̄dir̄k دِڕدِڕك /**dirdirk** دِردِرك *f.* **(;-ê).** thorn; thornbush. {syn: dir̄î} [B/Wkt] See also **dir̄î**.

dir̄ende دِڕەنــــده *m.* **(-yê;).** wild beast, beast of prey: **•Dema digihe êrdima ko şêr lê, di nişka va *direndeyekî* xurt li pêş xwe dibîne** (JB2-O.Sebrî/Rnh 14[1943] 8-9) When he reaches the spot where the lion is, suddenly he sees a powerful *wild beast* before him. {also: dirinde (IFb/OK); dir̄inde (Bw); dirrende (GF/TF); [dourendé] درنــــده (JJ)} {syn: canewar; tabe; terawil} < P darande درنــــــــده = 'fierce, rapacious, ravenous'; Sor dir̄inde دِڕنــــده = 'fierce, wild beast' [JB2/Rnh/GF/TF//IFb/OK//Bw//JJ] <hov; ḧeywan; k'ûvî>

direw دِرەو, f. (JB1-A) = lie, falsehood. See **derew**.

dirêj دِرێـــژ *adj.* 1) long: **-dirêj kirin** (IFb/ZF): a) to spread out, stretch *(vt.)*; b) to pass or hand stg. to s.o.: **•Dikandar çû ser kursiyê, ew qatê kincan ji jor daxist, hêdîka ew toza ku lê girtibû dawşand û *dirêjî* Doktor Sertaç *kir*** (KS, 36) The shopkeeper got up on a chair and took down the suit of clothes, gently brushed the dust off of it and *handed* it *to* Dr. Sertaç; c) to last, take *(time)* {syn: ajotin[2]; domîn[2]; k'işandin[6]; k'udandin; vek'işîn[2]}: **•Dibe jî lîstik hetanî nîvro *dirêj bike*** (HYma, 31) The game could *last* until noon; **-xwe dirêj kirin** (IFb) to stretch out *(vi.)*, lie down at full length; 2) in the habit of stealing, in expressions like: **-Destê wî *dirêj* e** (Hk) He has *sticky* fingers = He is given to [or, is in the habit of] stealing. {also: drêj (JB3); [dirij] دريـــژ (JJ); <dirêj> دريـــژ (HH)} {≠kin; ≠kort} [Pok. 5. del- 196.] 'long': <O Ir *drājya- (A&L p.

84 [V]) [cf. also *darga- = 'long' & *drājah- = 'length' & *drājiyah- = 'longer']; P derāz دراز; Sor dirêj دِرێژ; Za derg (Todd/Lx)/därg (Hadank); Hau dirêj (M4); cf. also Lat longus <*dlong-; Rus dolgiĭ долгий = 'long (of time)' & dlinnyĭ длинный = 'long (physical length)' {d[i]rêjahî; dirêjayî; dirêj[t]î} [F/K/A/JB3/IFb/B/JJ/HH/JB1-A/SK/GF/TF/OK/ZF] <dereng>

dirêjahî دِرێژاهی *f.* **(-ya;-yê).** length. {also: dirêjatî (SK); dirêjayî (K/A/GF-2/TF/OK-2); dirêjî (K/GF-2/OK-2); dirêjtî (A); drêjahî (JB3); [dirijàï] دریژای (JJ)} [JB3/IFb/GF/OK//K/A/B//JJ] <dirêj>

dirêjatî دِرێژاتی (SK) = length. See **dirêjahî.**

dirêjayî دِرێژایی (K/A/GF/TF/OK) = length. See **dirêjahî.**

dirêjik دِرێژِك (TF) = awl. See **dirêş**.

dirêjî دِرێژی (K/GF/OK) = length. See **dirêjahî.**

dirêjtî دِرێژتی (A) = length. See **dirêjahî.**

dirêş دِرێش *f.* **(-a;-ê).** awl, tool for poking holes in leather, etc.: •**Gurgî got, "Mûêt min girj bûne?" R̄îwî got, "Hey, beh̄s neke! Hemî wekî *dirêşan* qişt r̄a-westane"** (SK 6:69) The wolf said, "Have my hairs stood up?" The fox said, "Oh, don't mention it! They are all standing up as straight as *bradawls*." {also: dirêjik (TF); dirêşe (A/K-2); dirêşik (IFb-2/GF-2/OK) [*often diminutive]; dirêşt (A-2); <dirêşik> دریشك (HH)} <O Ir *drafša(na)- (Morg3, p.337): P derafš درفش; Sor direwş دِرەوش [SK/F/K/IFb/B/GF//A//HH/OK//TF]

dirêşe دِرێشه (A/K) = awl. See **dirêş**.

dirêşik دِرێشِك (IFb/HH/GF/OK) = awl. See **dirêş**.

dirêşk دِرێشك (Wn) = stinger (of bees). See **dirêşûşk**.

dirêşoşk دِرێشۆشك (FS) = stinger (of bees). See **dirêşûşk**.

dirêşûşk دِرێشووشك *f.* **(-a;-ê).** stinger (of bees, scorpions, etc.). {also: dirêşk (Wn); dirêşoşk (FS)} {syn: jene} = Sor pêweder پێوەدەر [Şnx//FS//Wn] <derzî; dirêş>

dirêşt دِرێشت (A) = awl. See **dirêş**.

dirêzî دِرێزی (Slv) = needle. See **derzî**.

dirf دِرف (GF) = looks. See **dirûv**.

dirg دِرگ *m.* **(-ê;).** dung or manure *dried in stables*: •**Ewê *dirgekî* pez jî, ji dêla derxwûn ve danî ser devê beroşê de!** (ZZ-1) She put a piece of sheep *manure* on the open cooking pot, instead of a lid •**Jinik hê nû li xwe varqilî, ku *dirgê rêxê* danîbû ser devê beroşê!** (ZZ-1, 127) The woman just realized that she had put *the dung patty* on the open cooking pot. {also: dirk II (A/IFb)} [ZZ-1/Kmc-2760/FS//A/IFb] <bişkul/pişkul; ç'êrt; deve II; guhûr; k'erme; keşkûr; pesarî; peyîn; qelax; r̄îx; sergîn; sergo; sêklot; t'epik II; t'ers; t'ert[ik]; zibil; zirîç>

dirhav دِرهاڤ (TF) = dirhem. See **dirav**.

dirhavî دِرهاڤی (TF) = financial. See **diravî**.

dirik دِرِك *m.* **().** 1) {syn: stirî I[2]; tûr̄eşk} bramble, blackberry, bot. Rubus fruticosus; 2) thorn (OK). See **dir̄î**. {also: dirîmok (Haz); dirk I (OK)} [Mzg/Srk/IF/ZF3/Wkt//OK//Haz] <dir̄dir̄k; dir̄î>

dirinde دِرِنده (IFb/OK)/dir̄inde دِڕِنده (Bw) = wild beast. See **dir̄ende**.

dirist دِرِست (IFb/GF/OK) = correct, true. See **dirust**.

dir̄î دِڕی *f.(B/Z-1/EP-7)/m.(ZF3)* **(;-yê/).** thorn; thornbush: •**Niqitkeke xûna wî dîsa pekîya ort'a Memê û Zînê, h̄eta naka jî bûye *dir̄ike* xirab** (Z-1) A drop of his blood fell between Mem and Zîn, and it became a bad *thornbush.* •**Al p'aşa serê Bek'o difir̄îne, ç'ilke xûna Bek'o dik'eve ort'a Memê u Zînê, navda digihîje, dibe *dir̄yan*** (FK-eb-2) Al pasha sends Beko's head flying, [and] a drop of Beko's blood falls between Mem and Zîn; it grows in the middle [and] becomes a *thornbush* •**Nav herdada ew niqitka xûnê bû *dir̄ike* uncûz, şîn bû** (EP-7) Between the two of them this drop of blood turned into a *thornbush* and grew. {also: **dirdirk**; **dir̄dir̄k**; dirk I (OK); drî (IF); [diri] دری (JJ); <dirî> دری (HH)} {syn: k[']elem II; stirî I; şewk[3]} Cf. T dırı [Eşke, Divriği--Sivas] = 'thorny bush resembling a rosebush' (DS, v. 4, p. 1469); NA (Turoyo) dırrıh(e) = 'thorn' (HR) [Z-1/EP-7/K/A/JJ/HH/ZF3//B//IF] See also **dir̄dir̄k**.

dirîmok دِریمۆك (Haz) = blackberry, bramble. See **dirik**.

dir̄în دِڕین *vi.* **(-dir̄-).** to tear, rip *(vi.)*, be torn, be ripped (K/IF/JJ): •**Şal û şapikê bavê min *dir̄îyan*** (AB) My father's [Kurdish] suit *tore*. {also: dirrîn (IFb/GF); dir̄yan (-dir̄yê-) (M/SK/OK); [deriian] دریان (JJ); <diran دران (didire) (ددره)> (HH)} {syn: ç'ir̄în; qelişîn [1]} [Pok. 4. der- 206.] 'to split, peel, flay; with derivatives referring to skin & leather': O Ir *dṛ- (Tsb 44): Av dar- & darədar- (*pres.* dərəna-) = 'to split'; OP *dṛ-nā-tiy = 'he splits'; P dar[r]īdan دریدن; Sor dir̄în دِڕین = 'to tear' & dadir̄an دادِڕان = 'to be torn' & dadir̄în دادِڕین = 'to tear off, strip off'; SoK dır(i)-, dır(ı)n-/dırân- (Fat 431); Za dırıyayiş (Mal); Hau dir̄ey (dir̄-) *vt.* = 'to tear' (M4) [AB/K/ZF3//IFb/GF//M/SK/OK/JJ//HH] <dir̄andin>

dirk I دِرك (OK) = thorn. See **dirik & dir̄î**.

dirk II دِرك (A/IFb) = dung. See **dirg**.

dirnax̄ دِرناغ *m.* **(-ê;).** fingernail. {also: [tyrnag] طرنغ (JJ)} {syn: neynûk} <T tırnak [Rh//JJ]

dirrende دِررەندە (GF/TF) = wild beast. See **dir̄ende**.

dirrîn دِررین/دِرین (IFb/GF) = to rip. See **dir̄în**.

dirust دِرووسـت *adj.* 1) {syn: r̄ast} right, proper, correct: **•*Dirust* weto ye weku tu dibêjî** (SK 43:417) It is *true* what you say **•Xiyala me *dirust* derkewt** (SK 32:286) Our idea turned out to be *right*; 2) {syn: r̄ast} true: **•R̄efîqê *dirust* ewe ye li xoşî û ṯengawîyê r̄efîq bit, ne li xoşîyê bi-tinê** (SK 29:269) A *true* [or, *proper*] companion is one who is a companion in pleasant times and in difficulty, not just in pleasant times; **-dirust** (SK)/ **dirûst kirin** (JB1-A) to prepare, make: **•'Elî beg qiyasê neh-deh ser ḧeywanêt qelew ji beranan û şekan înan, dane kuştinewe, birincekî zor jî îna, ziyafetekî mezin *da dirust kirin*** (SK 39:346) Ali Beg brought about nine or ten head of fat young rams and had them slaughtered; he also brought a lot of rice and *had* a big feast *prepared*. {also: dirist (IFb-2/GF-2/OK-2); dirûst (JB1-A/OK-2); durist (K-2/B/ZF3); durust (IFb-2/B-2); [douroust] درست (JJ); <durist> درست (HH)} O Ir *dṛvišta- superlative degree of *dṛva- = 'strong, impregnable' [Pok. deru̯o-/dreu̯o- 214.] 'tree, wood; to be firm, solid, steadfast' (Ras, p.136): Mid P druyist/drust = 'whole, sturdy'; P dorost درست; Sor dirust دِرووسـت = 'right, true, correct, straight, lawful, sound' {dirustî; duristî; durustî} [Bw/K/IFb/SK/GF/OK//JB1-A//B/HH/ZF3//JJ]

dirustî دِرووسـتى *f.* **(-ya;-yê).** rightness, propriety, correctness, truth: **-bi dirustî** (SK) correctly, properly: **•Naw bajêrî qelebalix̄ e ... muro neşêt *bi dirustî* zikrê xudê biket** (SK 38:339) In the city there are crowds and commotion ... and one cannot *properly* worship God. {also: duristî (B/ZF3); durustî (B-2); [drustī] درستى (JJ-Rh)} {syn: r̄astî} Sor dirustî دِرووسـتى = 'correctness, soundness' [K/SK//JJ-Rh//B/ZF3] <dirust>

diruşme دِروشمە (CS) = slogan. See **dirûşm**.

dirûb دِرووب (Frq) = looks. See **dirûv**.

dirûn دِروون (K/B/IFb/M/JJ/TF/OK) = to sew; to mow. See **dirûtin.**

dirûst دِرووسـت (JB1-A/OK) = correct, true. See **dirust**.

dirûşim دِرووشِم (IFb/GF/FJ) = slogan. See **dirûşm**.

dirûşm دِرووشـم *f.* **(-a;-ê).** slogan, motto: **•HRRK bi *dirûşma* 'Em hemû Efrînî ne' festîvala xwe ya 5emîn li Kobaniyê li dar dixe** (krd.sputnik.com 23.iv.2018) With the *slogan* 'We are all Afrinis' the HRRK holds its 5th festival in Kobani **•Ez nabêjim bila di bernameyan de *dirûşman* berz bike ... Qubadî qet dirûşm berz nedikir** (DE, #31, 189) I am not saying he should shout *slogans* on TV programs ... Q. was not shouting *slogans* at all. {also: diruşme (CS); dirûşim (IFb-2/GF/FJ); dirûşme (DE-2); drûşm (Wkt-2); durûşm (Wkt-2)} Cf. P dirafš درفـش/dirōš دروش = 'banner, standard; awl'; Sor diruşm دِروشـم /dirûşm دِرووشـم = 'mark, outward sign; emblem, coat of arms; slogan; rite, ceremony' [DE/IFb/Kmc/SS/ZF3/Wkt//FG/FJ//CS]

dirûşme دِرووشمە (DE) = slogan. See **dirûşm**.

dirûtin دِرووتِـن *vt.* **(-dirû-/-dûr-**[IFb]**/-dirût-**[IF]**).** 1) to sew, stitch: **•Ewî xwe bi k'incdrûr̄a gihîand, k'incê xas ji xwer̄a *da drûtinê*** (FK-eb-1) He betook himself to the tailor, *had* a special garb *made* for himself; 2) {syn: çinîn [2]} to mow, cut down, reap, harvest (JJ/K). {also: dirûn (K/B/IFb-2/TF/OK); drûn (JB3/IF-2); drûtin (JB3-2/IF-2); durûn (BK); [diroun درون /douroun درون] (JJ); <dirûn درون/dirûtin درو تـن (didrû) (ددرو)> (HH)} [Pok. 4. der- 206.] 'to split, peel, flay; with derivatives referring to skin & leather' (p. 208: with u-formation of light (der-eu-) and heavy (derə-u-, dṛ-u-) stems: 'to tear apart, break (ground), reap'): O Ir *dṛ- (Bartholomae *drau̯-) (Tsb 45): MidP drūdan (drūn) = 'to reap, mow' (M3); P dorūdan درودن (derav) (درو) = 'to mow'; Sor dirûn دِروون (-dirû-) = 'to sew'; SoK dür[ı]n-, dir[ı]n-/dürân-, dirân[d]- (Fat 431); Za derzenã [deştiş] (Todd) = 'to sew' [F/A/JB3/IFb/HH//K/B/JJ/TF/OK/M//BK] <derzî; dirwar; kêl II; k'incdirû>

dirûv دِرووڤ *m.* **(-ê;).** facial features, markings; outward appearance, looks: **•*Durûvê* te fena *durûvê* birê teyî** (Srk) You look like your brother [lit. 'your *features* are like the *features* of your brother'] **•Qey *dirbê* (*dirûbê*) 'Ereba *bi* wan *dikeve*?** (Frq) Do they *look like* Arabs? {also: dirb II (Frq-2); dirf (GF-2); dirûb (Frq); drûv (IFb-2); duruv (A); durû II (Mzg); durûv (Srk/GF-2); [dourouw] دروڤ (JJ)} <Ar ḍurūb ضـروب, pl. of

ḍarb ضــــرب = 'kind, sort, specimen, species' [Frq//IFb/GF/OK//A//Mzg//Srk/JJ]

dirwar دِروار *f.* **(-a;-ê).** stitch; seam: **•*Dirwara* vî kirasî can e** (FS) The *stitching* of this shirt is lovely; -**dirwara fiř** (Zeb) wide or loose stitch; -**dirwara hembiz/~a hûr** (Zeb) tight stitch. {also: diryar (FS-2); [druára] دروار (JJ-G)} [Zeb/FS//JJ-G] <dirûtin; kêl II>

diřyan دِريـــان (-diřyê-) (M/SK/OK) = to tear, rip (vi.). See **dirîn**.

diryar دِريار (FS) = stitch; seam. See **dirwar**.

diryas دِريـــاس *f.* **(-a;-ê).** scythe-like implement for cutting down grass (Bw) or for picking fruit (OK): **•Wî giya bi *diryasê* dirû** (FS) He mowed the grass with *the scythe*. {also: diryask (OK-2)} {syn: şalok} [Bw/OK/ZF3/FS] <das>

diryask دِريـــاسك (OK) = scythe-like implement. See **diryas**.

dismal دِسمال (IFb) = handkerchief. See **destmal.**

dist دِست (ZK3/Wkt/FS) = cauldron. See **dişt**.

distan دِستان (GF) = trivet, tripod. See **dûstan**.

distar دِستار (SK/Bw) = hand mill. See **destař**.

diş دِش *f.* **(-a;).** sister-in-law: a) husband's or wife's sister (K/Bw): b) {syn: baltûz} wife's sister (A/IF/HB/HH/TF) {T baldız}; c) {syn: zeyî (IF/Mzg/Srk)} husband's sister (JJ/GF/OK/Haz) {T görümce}; d) {syn: xaltî}*aunt, mother's sister (JJ). {also: deş (HB-2); duşk (K[s]); [dich] ديـــش (JJ); <diş> دش (HH)} Cf. Sor diş دِش = 'husband's sister' [K/A/JB3/IFb/JJ/GF/TF/OK/Haz/HB/Bw/FS] <baltûz; bûk I; bûrî; cayî; jinbir[a]; jint'î II; t'î II; zeyî>

dişliq دِشـــلِـق *f.* **(-a;).** repose, quiet, tranquility, calm; peace of mind, freedom from anxiety: **•Bê te *dîşlîxa* minê nê** (Wkt:aleviforum.com) I am restless [lit. 'My *peace of mind* doesn't come'] without you. {also: dîşlix (Wkt); [dišliq] (LC)} Cf. T dışlık [Elâzığ, Urfa, Kilis-Gaziantep] (DS, v. 4, p.1473-74) [LC/DS//Wkt] <t'enahî>

dişt دِشـــت *f.(K)/m.(L)* **(-a/;-ê/).** ca[u]ldron, large pot: **•Sînemê s̲avar di *distê* da kelandin** (FS) S. cooked the bulgur in the *large pot*. {also: dist (ZK3/Wkt); <deşt> دشـــت (HH)} {syn: beroş; den I} Cf. Ar ṭišt طشت = 'tub, wash basin' [L/K//HH//ZK3/Wkt/FS] <şikev>

dişwar دِشوار = difficult. See **dijwar.**

dişwarî دِشوارى = difficulty. See **dijwarî.**

diwanzde دِوانزده (JB1-S) = twelve. See **donzdeh**.

diwanzdehem دِوانـــزدهـــــهم (Wkt) = twelfth. See **dozdehem**.

diwanzdehemîn دِوانزدههمين (IFb/Wkt) = twelfth. See **dozdehem**.

diwazdeh دِوازدهه (IFb) = twelve. See **donzdeh**.

diwazdehem دِوازدهـــــــــهم (Wkt) = twelfth. See **dozdehem**.

diwazdehemîn دِوازدهـــهمـــين (Wkt) = twelfth. See **dozdehem**.

diwazdemîn دِوازدهمين (IFb) = twelfth. See **dozdehem**.

diyar دِيـــــار *adj.* evident, visible, obvious, apparent: **•*Diyar* e ku hemû kes guhertinê dixwaze** (RN2 14:80 [#37], 8) It is *obvious* that everyone wants change; -**diyar bûn** (JB3/IFb)/**dîhar bûn** (B)/ **dîharmîş bûn** (Z-921) to appear, appear on the scene, come into view; to be disclosed: **•Kalek lê *dîharmîş dibe*** (Z-921) An old man *appears* to him **•Suřa wê *dîhar bû*** (Z-1) Her secret *was exposed*; -**diyar kirin** (JB3/IFb)/**dîhar kirin** (B) to disclose; to state, express, declare: **•Di nav tu belgeyên resmî de *nehatiye diyarkirin* ku Iraqê çekên kîmyewî ji ku derê bi çi awayî bi dest xistine** (AW75C2) It *was not stated* in any official documents how and from where Iraq obtained chemical weapons **•Hinek nivîskar *diyar dikin* ku MHP xwe ji nû ve saz dike û ber bi demokratîkbûnê ve diçe** (AW69A1) Some writers *declare* that the MHP [Nationalist People's Party] is re-making itself and becoming more democratic. {also: dîhar (Z-1/K-2/B); dîharmîş (Z-921); dîyar I; [diiar] ديـــار (JJ)} {syn: aşkere; berçav II; k'ifş; xanê; xuya} Cf. P dīdar ديـــدار = 'sight, vision'; Sor diyar ديار = 'apparent, manifest, obvious, prominent (person), visible, vision'; Hau dîar (M4) [M-Ak//Z-921//K/JB3/IFb/JJ/GF/TF//B]

diyarde دِيـــارده *f.* **(-ya;-yê).** phenomenon [Ar ẓāhirah ظـــاهرة, T görüngü]: **•Li başûr *diyardeya* zewaca keçên temen piçûk zêde bûye** (K24) In Iraqi Kurdistan [lit. 'the south'] *the phenomenon of* marrying teenage girls [lit.'girls of small age'] has increased. <Sor diyarde دِيـــارده = 'phenomenon, observable fact' <diyar دِيـــــــــار = 'apparent', cf. phenomen <Gr phainomenon φαινομενον <phainetai φαινεται = 'it appears' [K24/ZF/CS/Wkt/SS]

diyarî دِيارى *f.* **(-ya;-yê).** gift, present: **•Ez xwe şanaz û bextewer dibînim ku vê *diyarîyê* pêşkêşî ewan bikem** (Ş.Şêx Yezdîn. Yobîla Zêrîna Pêşmêrgeyî, 10) I consider myself proud and lucky to present this *gift* to them **•Wextê ko Smail Paşa zanî *dîharîya* maqûlêt**

Mizûrîyan kûr in, pîçek di dilê xo da sil bû (SK 24:222,224) When Ismail Pasha learnt that *the present of* the Mizuri elders was kids [=young goats], he became a little annoyed in his heart. {also: dîharî (SK); dîyarî (TF); [diiari] ديــــــارى (JJ); <diyarî> ديــــــارى (HH)} {syn: dayîn II; pêşk'êş; xelat [2]} Sor diyarî دِيارى [SK//K/A/IFb/JJ/HH/GF/OK/RZ//TF]

diz I دِز *m.&f.* **().** thief, robber: **•Welleh polîs efendî, ez bi xwe ne *diz* im. Bavê min nexweş e, ez di dewsa wî de kar dikim!** (LM, 14) Mr. policeman, I'm not *a thief.* My father is sick, and I'm filling in for him. {also: dizek (B-2); [diz] دز (JJ); <diz> دز (HH)} O Ir *duždā- = 'having bad intention' (Ras, p.137) [***duž-**: [Pok. dus- 227.] 'bad, evil': Skt duṣ-; Av duš-/duž-]: Mid P duz(d); P dozd دزد; Sor diz دِز; Za dizd (Lx/Mal)/duzd (Mal) *m.* {dizî; dizîtî} [K/A/JB3/IFb/B/JJ/HH/JB1-A/SK/GF/TF/OK] <kose I[2]>

***diz II** دِز **( ).** side of knucklebone (k'ap II) that has a crater in it. {syn: çik II (Qzl); ≠pik (Qzl)} [Wn] <k'ap II>

dizanî دِزانى (IFb) = thievery. See **dizî**.

dizek دِزەك (B) = thief. See **diz.**

dizgirtî دِزگِرتى (JB3) = fiancé(e). See **dergistî.**

dizgîn دِزگين *f.* **(-a;-ê).** 1) {syn: bizmîk; celew I; gem; lix̄ab; qet'irme II} rein, bridle; 2) {syn: bizmîk} (mouth)bit (K); 3) halter (GF). {also: dezgîn (K-2/ Z-2); [dizghin] دزگين (JJ); <dizgîn> دزگين (HH)} < T dizgin [Z-1/F/K/IFb/JJ/HH/GF/OK] <hesp; hevsar>

dizî دزى *f.* **(-ya;-yê).** 1) thievery; 2) theft; **-dizî kirin** (A/B) to steal from, rob: **•Deh salî yî û tu *dizîyê dikî* ha?** (LM, 14) You're ten years old and you're [already] *stealing*? **•Ewî *dizya* min *kirye*, zêřê min dizye** (Ba3-3, #37) He *robbed* me, he stole my gold. {also: dizanî (IFb-2); dizîtî (K-2)} [F/K/A/IFb/B/SK/TF/OK] <diz I; dizîn>

dizîka دِزيــــكــــا *adv.* stealthily, secretly, sneakily: **-bi dizîka** = do.: **•Emê *bi dizîka* birevin** (L) We will *quietly* run away. {also: dizîkava (B-2); dizîva} [L/K/B]

dizîkava دِزيكاڤا (B) = secretly. See **dizîka.**

dizîn دزيــــــــن *vt.* **(-diz-).** to steal, pilfer: **•Qijik penîr *didize*** (AB) The rook (bird) *steals* cheese. {also: [dizin] دزيــــن (JJ); <dizîn دزيــــن (didize) (ددزه)> (HH)} Cf. P dozdīdan دزديدن; Sor dizîn دِزين; Za [diznayîş] (Mal); SoK doz(i)-, dız(i)- (Fat 431); Hau dizîey (diz-) *vt.* (M4) [K/JB3/IFb/B/JJ/HH/SK/TF/OK/ M] <diz I; dizî [kirin]>

dizîtî دِزيتى (K) = thievery. See **dizî.**

dizîva دِزيڤا = secretly. See **dizîka.**

dî I دى (Zx/Dh/Bw/Zeb) = other; next. See **din I.**

dî II دى *f.* **(-ya;).** spiral pile of tree branches with leaves on them *used as fodder for animals in the winter*: **-dîya çolî** (Zeb) do.: **•Tiryanka nanî ji biçûkan ra, *dîha çilî* ji gîskan ra** (BF) A wicker bread tray for the children, *a pile of tree branches* for the goats {also: dih (Bw); dîh (FS/BF); <dî> دى (Hej)} [Zeb/Hej//FS/BF//Bw] <çolî II>

Dîarbek'ir ديـئـاربـەكـر (K) = city of Diyarbakir. See **Dîyarbekr.**

Dîcle ديجله (A/IF) = Tigris River. See **Dicle.**

dîdevan ديـــــدەڤـــان *m.* **(-ê;).** 1) watchman; 2) {syn: nêřevan; zêrevan} observer, scout; monitor; witness: **•*Dîdevanê* qirkirina gundê Koço behsa êrîşên DAÎŞ dike** (VoA 29.viii.2014) *An observer (or witness)* of the destruction of Kocho village speaks about the attacks of ISIS **•Ew dê bîte *dîdevan* bo min dema ez dizewcim** (Wkt) He will be a *witness* for me when I get married. Sor dîdewan ديدەوان = 'watchman' {dîdevanî} [(neol)RN/ K(s)/IF/ZF3/Wkt]

dîdevanî ديدەڤانى *f.* **(-ya;-yê).** observation; witnessing: **•Refên me bi ser qada şerî re firiyane û karê xwe ê *dîdevanî* û nobetdariyê pêk anîne** (RN) Our air squadrons have flown over the battlefield and accomplished their tasks of *observing* and keep watch **•Romî dibêje ku *dîdevanîya* çîrokên mirovên ku ji destê DAIŞ'ê digehijin azadîya xwe ...karê rojnamevanî watedar dike** (rojname.com 24.vii.2017) R. says that *witnessing* the stories of people who attain their freedom from the hands of ISIS … give meaning to the work of journalism. {syn: çavdêrî; nêřevanî; şadetî; zêrevanî} [(neol)RN/K(s)/IF/ZF3/Wkt] <çavdêrî; dîdevan>

dîh ديه (FS/BF) = pile of tree branches. See **dî II**.

dîhar ديهار (Z-1/K-2/B) = evident, apparent. See **diyar.**

dîharî ديهارى (SK) = gift. See **diyarî.**

dîharmîş ديـهـارمـيـش (Z-921) = evident, apparent. See **dîyar I.**

dîk ديــك *m.* **(-ê;).** 1) rooster, cock (F/K/A/JB3/IF/JJ); 2) trigger, cocking-piece (K): **-dîkê t'ivingê** (B) firing pin. {also: [dik] ديك (JJ); <dîk> ديك (HH)} <Ar dīk ديك; Sor dîkil ديكل (=kełeşêr كەڵەشێر); Za dîk *m.* (Todd) [Ks/F/K/A/JB3/IF/B/JJ/HH/ZF3] <ç'êt = şelûf; mirîşk>

dîl ديـــــــــل *m.* **().** prisoner, captive; one arrested or detained, detainee: -**dîl kirin** (K/IF)/~ **girtin** (K/IF) to take prisoner; to arrest: •**Gilya neke t'exsîle / We çewa Ûsiv *girt dîle*?** (Ba3-3, #21) Don't try to hide behind words / How could you *take* Joseph *prisoner*? {syn: girtî [2]; hêsîr I} Sor dîl دیل {dîlî; dîlîtî} [Ba3/F/K/IF/B/ZK3]

dîlan دیلان *f.* **(-a;).** 1) dance song, a dance accompanied by the singing of the dancers (K/JB3); circle of dancers (JJ) [Cf. Ar ṣahjeh صهجة/ saḥjeh سحجة]; 2) {syn: cejin; de'wat} (wedding) celebration; picnic: •**Dîlane e dîlan ... *Dîlana* Xezalê û Lezgîn e** (AB) It is the *wedding celebration* of Kh. and L.; 3) love song. See **dîlok**; 4) *woman's name*. {also: dîlane; [dīlān] دیلان (JJ); <dîlok> دیلوك (HH)} [AB/K/A/JB3/IF/JJ/ JB1-S/Haz//HH] <de'wat; dîlokvan; govend; k'ilam; sema; stiran I>

dîlane دیلانه = dance song; celebration. See **dîlan.**

dîlî دیلی *f.* **(-ya;-yê).** captivity, imprisonment; lack of freedom: •**Bi taybetî xelkekî wek xelkê Kurd ... vê *dîlîtîyê* tu carî qebûl nake** (Ber #7, 10) Especially a people like the Kurdish people ... will never accept this *captivity*. {also: dîlîtî (Ber/ZK3-2)} [Ber//F/K/IF/ZF3] <dîl>

dîlîtî دیلیتی (Ber/ZK3) = captivity. See **dîlî.**

dîlok دیلۆك *f.* **(-a;-ê).** 1) love song (Msr); lyrical songs (K); 2) dance song. See **dîlan** [1]; 3) Kurdish name for [Gazi]antep. {also: dîlan [3]; dîrok II (K); <dîlok> دیلوك (HH)} [Mzg/A/IF/HH//K] <dîlokvan; k'ilam>

dîlokbêj دیلۆکبێژ (K/ZF3) = singer. See **dîlokvan**.

dîlokvan دیلۆکڤان *m.* **(-ê;).** leader of dance songs (at a wedding), singer. {also: dîlokbêj (K/ZF3)} [IF/HH//K/ZF3] <dîlan; dîlok>

dîmen دیمەن *f./m.* **(-a/-ê;).** scene(ry), view, panorama; sight, spectacle: •**Ava ku ji sûlavê dihat xwar, *dîmenekê* can bû** (FS) The water which was falling from the waterfall was a beautiful *sight* •**YPG`ê *dîmenê* balafira keşfê ya artêşa Tirk weşand** (ANHA 12.ii.2018) The YPG published *a view of* the [crashed] helicopter of the Turkish army. {syn: bergeh} <Sor dîmen دیمەن n. = 1) view, scenery, sight; 2) guise, appearance < dî[tin] = 'to see' [Nofa/ANHA/A/IFb/FJ/TF/ZF3/Wkt/FS/FD/CS] <wêne>

dîn I دین *f.* **(-a;-ê).** 1) seeing, sight: -**dîna xwe dan** (F/J/B) to have a look, examine, view, see {syn: {syn: fikirîn II; mêze kirin; nêrîn}: •**Hat *dîna xwe daê*** (J) He came *to have a look at it* •**Padşê *dîna xwe daê* xort hat** (J) The king *saw* that the youth had come [back]; 2) to see. See **dîtin**. {also: dên (IS)} [J/F/B] See also **dîtin.**

dîn II دین *adj.* crazy, mad, insane: -**har û dîn** (HM) totally mad, raving mad [lit. 'rabid and crazy']. {also: dihn I (HM); [din] دین (JJ); <dîn> دین (HH)} {syn: devdîn; neĥiş; şêt} <O Ir *daiwāna-(ka-) (A&L p.84 [V]): P dēvāne [dīvāne] دیوانه = 'crazy: originally '*in the manner of the demons* [dēv دیو]', cf. Ar majnūn مجنون <jinn جنّ; Sor dêwane دێوانه = 'mad' {dînanî; dînayî; dînetî; dînî; dîn[î]tî} [M/HM/K/A/JB3/IF/B/JJ/HH] <gêj>

dîn III دین *m.* **(-ê;-î).** religion, faith: -**dîn û mesheb** (K) creed; denomination; -**ji dîn[ê xwe] derk'etin** (B) to lose one's faith, become an apostate. {also: [din] دین (JJ); <dîn> دین (HH)} {syn: ol} <Ar dīn دين = 'religion' [BX/K/IF/B/JJ/HH] <dîndar III>

dînanî دینانی (K) = insanity. See **dînayî.**

dînar دینار *f.* **(;-ê).** diamonds *(suit of playing cards)*: •**şeşa dînar** (Elk) six of diamonds. {also: <dînar> دینار (Hej)} {syn: karo} [Bw/Elk/Hej]

dînayî دینایی *f.* **().** craziness, madness, insanity. {also: dînanî (K); dînetî (A); dînî (JJ); dînîtî (K/IF); dîntî (K-2); [dini] دینی (JJ)} {syn: neĥişî; şêtî} [K//A//IF//JJ//B/ZF3] <dîn II>

dîndar I دیندار *f.* **(-a;-ê).** (beautiful) face, appearance, countenance: •**bi şewqa *dîndara* wî** (Ba) from the lustre of his *countenance* •**Ew jî dihate meydanê, wekî tek *dîndara* Ûsib bibîne** (Ba) He came to the square just to see Joseph's *countenance*. {syn: dev û çav; r̄û I; serçav; sifet [3]; sûret I[1]} [Ba/K/B/ZF3]

dîndar II دیندار *f.* **().** Lebanon oak, bot. *Quercus Libani*: •... **û dê navê hinekan bikiriyan dar (mazînî, berûnî, *deyndar*, fisteq, xox, hwd.)** (MG. Tavê ew dît) ... and would have called some of them 'trees' (oak [2 kinds], *Lebanon oak*, pistachio, peach, etc.). {also: deyndar II (MG/IFb/GF); dêdar (IFb-2/Kmc-40-2); <dîndar> دیندار (HH/Hej)} [Zeb/HH/AA/Hej/CS/ZF3//MG/IFb/GF//Kmc-40]

dîndar III دیندار *adj.* religious, pious, observant, devout: •**Herwekî ew *dîndar* bû, r̄ojekê gote xwe, "Ez bûm dewlemend, min divê, ez her̄im û mala xwedê t'ewaf bikim"** (Dz #22, 389) As he was *religious*, one day he said to himself, "I've become rich, I want to go and circumambulate the house of God [i.e., make the pilgrimage to Mecca and go around the Kaaba 7 times]". Cf. P dīndār

دیندار ; Sor dîndar دیندار [Dz/K/IFb/FJ/GF/CS] <dîn III; ol; xwedênas>

dîndoq دیندۆق *f.* **(;-ê).** 1) glass marble {syn: mat I; t'ebel; x̄ar III}: •**Zaro bi *dîndoqê* leyst** (FS) The child played with *the marble*; 2) glass jewelry; 3) shattered shards of glass: •**Wî pirta *dîndoqê* avêt** (FS) He threw a shard *of glass*. {also: cînciq (Srk/G/ZF3); cîncix (Kmc-2); cîncoq (Kmc-2); cîncûq (ZF3-2); dîndox (AD/ZF3-2)} [Qzl/Kmc/Wkt/FS//AD//ZF3//Srk/G] <cam; şûşe>

dîndox دیندۆخ (AD/ZF3) = glass: marble, jewelry, shards. See **dîndoq**.

dînetî دینەتی (A) = insanity. See **dînayî.**

dîng دینگ (GF) = instrument for husking grain. See **deng II**.

dînî دینی (JJ) = insanity. See **dînayî.**

dînîtî دینیتی (K/IF) = insanity. See **dînayî.**

dîntî دینتی (K) = insanity. See **dînayî.**

dîrok I دیرۆك *f.* **(-a;-ê).** history: •***Dîroka* dinê ji mere dide zanîn ko heta niho, gelek zimanên dinê hatine kuştin** (BX [Hawar]) World *history* shows (informs) us that up to now, many of the world's languages have been killed off. {syn: t'arîx[2]} cf. Sor dêrîk دێریك = mêjû مێژوو = 'history' [(neol)K/JB3/IF/ZF3/Wkt] <çîr̄ok; ḧekyat>

dîrok II دیرۆك (K) = lyrical songs. See **dîlok**[1].

dîroknas دیرۆکناس *m.&f.* **().** historian: •**Belku gelek *dîroknas* û edebdostên biyanî jî, ev rastiye ya aşkerakirî** (X.Duhokî. Qefteka gulan, 5) But even many foreign *historians* and literature buffs [recognize] this clear fact. {also: dîroknivîs (FJ/CS-2); dîrokvan (IFb-2/GF/SS-2); dîrokzan (IFb-2/TF/SS/CS)} = Sor mêjûnas مێژوناس [X.Duhokî/IFb/ZF//FJ//GF//TF/SS/CS] <dîrok>

dîroknivîs دیرۆکنڤیس (FJ/CS) = historian. See **dîroknas**.

dîrokvan دیرۆکڤان (IFb/GF/SS) = historian. See **dîroknas**.

dîrokzan دیرۆکزان (IFb/TF/SS/CS) = historian. See **dîroknas**.

dîsa دیسا *adv.* 1) again: •**Ewcar wextê *dîsa* li-ser 'adetê xo marî xo li stukira r̄iwî aland û derbaz bûn, marî xo gîro kir, xokêt xo nekirinewe** (SK 2:12) Then, when the snake wound himself round the fox's neck *again* in the usual way and they crossed over, the snake delayed and did not unwind its coils •**Memê *dîsa* li a p'êşî di'îşîne** (Z-2, 79) Memê *once again* noticed the one in front •**Memê, 'ezîzê min, yêk ez anîme vira, wê min *dîsa* bibin** (Z-1, 47) Mem, my dear, those who brought me here will take me away *again*; 2) still, nevertheless: •**Perên ku didane me ne pir bin jî, *dîsa* jî ji meaşên hemû karmend û karkerên wan zêdetir bûn** (AW72B3) Even if the money they gave us was not a lot, *still* it was more than the wages of all their workers. {also: dîsan (A/IFb-2/SK-2/GF-2); [disan دیسان/disani دیسانی] (JJ); <dîsa> دیسا (HH)} Hau dîsan (M4) [BX/Ad/K/JB3/IFb/B/HH/SK/GF//A/JJ] <cardin; ji nû ve>

dîsan دیسان (A/IFb/JJ/SK/GF) = again. See **dîsa.**

dîstan دیستان (IFb) = trivet, tripod. See **dûstan**.

dîşlix دیشلِخ (Wkt) = calm, tranquility. See **dişliq**.

dîtin دیتن *vt.* **(-bîn-/vîn-/-wîn-**[Ag]**/-bîhn-**[JB1-S]**).** 1) to see: •**Min *dît*** = I saw •**We *dît*** = You (pl.) saw •***Dîtinya* ku *dîtin*** (Dz) What do you think they *saw*? [Cf. T 'Bir ne görsünler']; **-di *fk-î* r̄a nedîtin** (Dh/Zeb/AId) to be hesitant to do stg., not to have the heart to do stg., not to bother to do stg.: •**Ez *di xo r̄a nabînim* bêjmê** (Dh) I *am hesitant to* tell him/I *don't have the heart to* tell him •**Ez *têr̄a nabînim ku* vî karî biket** (Dh) I *don't think* he will do it/I *can't see or imagine* him doing it •**Sê r̄oja wekî bima t'î ew** [sic] ***xwer̄a nedidît* biçûa av vexwara, birçî bima *xw[e]r̄a nedidît* nan bixwara** (Dz #16, 382) If she were thirsty for three days, she *wouldn't bother to* drink water, if she were hungry, she *wouldn't bother to* eat bread; 2) {syn: p'eyda kirin; vedîtin} to find: •**Lazime em yarekê jêr̄a *bibînin*** (FK-eb-1) We must *find* him a mate; 3) {syn: seh kirin} to hear, perceive, sense: •**Min *dî* şirqîn ji tatê hat** (L) I *heard* a noise coming [lit. 'came'] from the rock; 4) [*f.* **(-a;).**] {syn: r̄ay} opinion, view: •**bi *dîtina* min** = in my *opinion* •**Lê berî HEP'ê ez *di wê dîtinê de* me *ku* pêşî PKK bê rexnekirin** (Wlt 1:43, 9) But before HEP, I am *of the opinion that* first the PKK should be criticized. {also: dîn I[2]; [ditin] دیتن (JJ); <dîtin دیتن (dibîne) (دبینه)> (HH)} **dîtin:** [Pok. dhei̯ə-: dhi̯ā-: dhī- 243.] 'to see, look': Av ^{2}dā(y)-; OP ^{1}dī- (Kent); **-bîn-:** [Pok. 2. u̯(e)di- 1125.] 'to see, catch sight of; to know': O IndIr *u̯aid-na- (Kent): Skt véda = 'knows' & venati = 'waits' & vindáti = 'finds'; O Ir *u̯aina- (Kent): Av vaēna-; OP vaina- (Kent); P dīdan دیدن (-bīn-) (بین); Sor dîtin دیتن (-bîn-)/bînîn بینین; Za vînenã [dyayiş] (Todd/Srk); SoK (d)ün-, (d)in-, (d)ėn-, di-

/(d)üni-, (d)ini- etc. (Fat 369, 424); Hau dîey/wînay (wîn-) *vt.* = 'to see' & dîay (dîe-) *vt.* = 'to look' (M4) [F/K/A/JB3/IFb/B/JJ/ HH/M/SK/JB1-A&S/GF/TF/OK] <nêrîn; vedîtin>

dîtir دیتِر (Hk/Alkan) = other; next. See **din I.**

dîwan دیــوان *f.* **(-a;-ê).** 1) {syn: dîwanxane [1]} court *(of a prominent person, e.g., a king)*, divan; drawing room, reception hall, audience chamber; "Most aghas have a special room or separate building where travellers can rest, are entertained, given tea and a good meal, and a bed for the night. ... The guest-house has a number of other functions too, as already implied by the names it is given in Kurdish: sometimes mevankhane (guest-house), but usually diwan or diwankhane (court), sometimes odaye gund (village room). In their heyday all male villagers came and sat here in the evenings, and discussed daily matters. Minor disputes were brought here before the agha, decisions regarding the village (or lineage, or tribe) were taken here, the young were taught traditions and etiquette; and entertainment was also centralized here" [from: M. van Bruinessen. *Agha, Shaikh and State* (London: Zed Books, 1992), pp. 81-82): **•'Elî beg qiyasê neh deh ser ḧeywanêt qelew ji beranan o şekan înan, dan e kuştinewe. Birincekî zor jî îna, ziyafetekî mezin da dirust kirin. Paşî mela w baş-koçek digel tabi'êt wan hemî ḧazir kirin, kirin e do r̄êz beramberî yêk-u-do w bi xo li serê jêrî *dîwanê* r̄û-nişt** (SK 39:346) Ali Beg brought about nine or ten head of fat young rams and had them slaughtered. He also brought a lot of rice and had a big feast prepared. Then he summoned the mullah and the head kochak and all their followers and set them in two rows facing each other, and himself sat at the lower end of *the audience chamber* **•Hatine *dîwana* mîr Sêvdîn** (Z-1) They came to Prince Sevdin's *court* **•Ḧeyanî ko Mem îzna wînakê nede, Bengîn nikare derbazî *dîwana* mîr bive** (Z-3) Until Mem gives him permission, Bengin cannot enter the emir's *diwan*; 2) anthology of poems (IF/B). {also: [divan] دیــوان (JJ); <dîwan> دیــوان (HH)} <O Ir *dipi-pāna (Brand); P dīvān دیــوان --> Ar dīwān دیــوان: ***dipi**-: Sumerian dup- --> Elamite tup-pi, tippi = 'inscription' --> OP dipi- *n.* = 'writing, script' &'inscription' --> OP dipi- *n.* = 'writing, script' & dipI- *f.* = 'inscription'. ***Deft'er** is from the same root* [Z-1/K/A/JB3/IF/B/JJ/HH/SK/ZF] See also **dîwanxane.**

dîwanxan•e دیــوانـخـانـه *f.* **(•a;•ê).** 1) {syn: dîwan [1]} drawing room, reception hall; (king's) court; room, hall, audience chamber: **•Kesên ku bêhtir di *dîwanxaneyên* mîran de pêkenok digotin û carna weke şanogerekî bi rola xwe ve radibûn, ew "qeşmer" bûn** (CP, 6) People who told jokes and sometimes acted out their stories in *the courts of* emirs, were "jesters" **•Mam Tal hat, li-naw derê *dîwanxanê* r̄a-westa, destêt xo, muwafiqî 'adetê wî zemanî, li-ser-yêk da-nan, serê xo çemand, got e mîr, 'Mizgînî li cenabê mîr, keşkele hat'** (SK 29:267) Mam Tal came and stood in the doorway of *the audience chamber*, placed his hands one upon the other, as was the custom in those times, bowed his head and said to the Mir, 'Good news for his excellency the Mir, the magpie has come'; 2) government institution (B/K). [K/A/JB3/IF/B/SK/ZF] See also **dîwan.**

dîwar دیــــــوار *m.* **(-ê; dîwêr, vî dîwarî).** wall *(of a house; **beden I** and **sûr** refer to a city wall)*: **•Lawê pîrê li *dîwêr* de hilkişîya** (L) The old woman's boy climbed up *the wall.* {also: [divar] دیوار (JJ); <dîwar> دیوار (HH)} Cf. P dīvār دیوار, T duvar/dıvar; Sor dîwar دیــــــوار; = Za dês *m.* (Todd); Hau dîwar *m.* (M4) [K/A/JB3/IFb/B/JJ/HH/ZF]

dîya mara دیـیـا مـارا *f.* **().** large lizard (Msr); medium-sized lizard (Haz) [lit. 'mother of snakes']. {also: dîyê marê (Haz)} [Msr//Haz]

dîyar I دییار () = evident, apparent. See **diyar.**

dîyar II دیــیــار *m.* **(-ê;).** hill, mound, knoll (K); hill with sparse vegetation, treeless at the top (HM); mountain summit (JJ): **•Ez çûme serê *dîyarekî*, min dî heft beran li pey beranek[î] [Pinê zebeş]** (L) I went to the top *of a hill*, I saw seven rams after [i.e., chasing] another ram *[rdl.; ans.: watermelon plant]* {also: [diâr] دیار (HM); [diiar] دیــار (JJ)} {syn: banî II; gir II; kuç'[3]; t'op III; zûr} [HM/K/A/JJ/L/ZK3] <ç'îya>

Dîyarbakir دیــیــاربــاکِــر = city of Diyarbakir. See **Dîyarbekr.**

Dîyarbekr دییاربـهکر *f.* **(-a;-ê).** city of Diyarbakir (in 1988 pop. c. 600,000[?]), unofficial capital of Kurdistan of Turkey; often called now by former name *Amed*: **-Dîyarbekra r̄eş** (BK) Black Diyarbakir. {also: Dîarbek'ir (K); Dîyarbakir; Dîyarîbakir} [K/BK] dîyarî دییاری (TF) = gift. See **diyarî.**

Dîyarîbakir دیـیـاریـبـاکِـر = city of Diyarbakir. See **Dîyarbekr.**

dîyê marê دییێ مارێ (Haz) = lizard. See **dîya mara.**

dîz دیـــــز *f.* **(-a;-ê).** clay pot, earthenware pot: **•Dîya qîza - p'irûda *dîza, dîz* çê kirin, xelqê birin** (Z-1004) The mother of girls [is] a fashioner of *clay pots*, [after] she made *the pots*, others took them away *[prv.]*. {also: dîze (K-2/GF-2); dîzik (IFb); [diz] دیـــز (JJ); <dîz> دیـــز (HH)} {syn: hincan} Cf. P dīz دیز; Sor dîze دیزه = 'casserole' [Z-1004/K/B/JJ/HH/GF/ZF3//IFb]

dîze دیزه (K/GF) = clay pot. See **dîz.**

dîzik دیزِك (IFb) = clay pot. See **dîz.**

djmin دژمِن (SC) = enemy. See **dijmin.**

djmintî دژمِنتی (SC) = enmity. See **dijminahî.**

do I دۆ (BX/A) = two. See **du I.**

do II دۆ (BX/Wn/Erg/GF/OK) = yesterday. See **Dihî.**

doç'ik دۆچك *f.* **(-a;-ê).** 1) two-pronged beard; 2) {syn: boç'ik; dûv I} tail; 3) corner of eye (JJ): **-doçika çavan** (JJ) stern look, angry look, evil eye [regard dur, regard rude, regarder qqn. de mauvais oeil]; 4) {syn: boç'ik (IF)} stem of a fruit (IF). {also: dûçik (IF-2); [doutchik] دوچـــك (JJ)} ?< dû(v) = 'tail' + T dim. -çik [JR/JJ/K/IF/ZF3]

dodmam دۆدمام (K) = female cousin. See **dotmam.**

doê دۆئـــــــێ (M-Am&Bar&Zx&Gul) = second. See **dudua.**

doh دۆه (A/HH/TF/OK) = yesterday. See **dihî.**

dohin دۆهِن (TF) = grease. See **don.**

dohîn دۆهـــیـــن *f.(Zeb)/m.(SK)* **(-a/ ;-ê/-î).** curds, dish made of ***dew*** [qv.] and rice [birinc]: **•Şirînê pûng kiribû nav *dûhînê* da** (FS) Sh. had put mint into the *dohîn*. {also: duhîn (SK); dûhîn (FS)} [Zeb//SK//FS] <birinc; dew>

dohl دۆهل (JB1-S/OK) = drum. See **dehol.**

dohn دۆهن (A) = fat, grease. See **don.**

doje دۆژه (Tsab) = hell. See **dojeh.**

dojeh دۆژهه *f.* **(-a;-ê).** hell: **•Ḧemû ji x̱emê mirinê û zeyde ji 'ezaba *dojehê* ko dayim teḧlîne** (Lwj #18, 36) All because of the sorrow of dying and even more of the torment *of hell*, which are continually bitter **•T'a ku *dojeh* nebînî, bihişt bi te xweş nabe** (MXC, 727) Until you have seen *hell*, you can't appreciate heaven [lit., heaven won't be delightful for you]. {also: doje (Tsab-2); dojî (K/Tsab-2/CS-2); dûje (Tsab-2); dûjeh (Rnh); [doujé] دوژه (JJ); <dojeh> دوژه (HH)} {syn: cehnem} Cf. P dūzax دوزخ; Sor doje دۆژه [Lwj/IFb/FJ/GF/TF/HH/RZ/Kmc/ZF/Tsab/CS//FK-1/K//JJ//Rnh]

dojî دۆژی (K/Tsab/CS) = hell. See **dojeh.**

dol I دۆل *f.* **(-a;-ê).** 1) {syn: avik} seed, sperm: **•Ne ji *dola* bavê xwe ye** (Qzl) He is a bastard [lit. 'he is not of is father's *seed*']; 2) {syn: nijad} race, breed, species, strain; 3) {syn: dûndan; zêdehî; zuȓet II} descendants, offspring, progeny: **•Tu ne ji *dola* Silmanî** (FK-kk-1) You are not of Silman's *descendants*. {also: [dol] دول (JJ)} <T döl = 'sperm, seed' [FK-kk-1/K/A/IFb/B/JJ/GF/Qzl] <tov; t'oxim>

dol II دۆل *f.* **(-a;-ê).** deep narrow valley, canyon, combe: **•'Eskerê Fazil Paşa li naw *dolê* şaş bûn, nezanîn kêwe biḧelên. Leşkirê 'eşîretan ku digel 'eskerê Fazil Paşa hatibûn hindek şareza bûn, ser kewtine çiyan, xo xilas kirin** (SK 48:488) Fazil Pasha's troops went astray in the middle of *the canyon*, not knowing whither to flee. Some of the tribal force which had come with Fazil Pasha's troops knew the country and climbed up into the hills and so saved themselves. {also: duwêl II (GF-2)} Sor doł دۆڵ [SK/K(s)/IFb/GF/TF/OK/RZ/Zeb/ZF3] <newal>

dol III دۆل (IFb) = bucket. See **dewl I.**

dolab I دۆلاب *f.* **(-a;-ê).** cupboard, closet, cabinet. {also: dolap (K/A); dolav (IFb-2/GF-2); [dolab] دولاب (JJ); <dolab> دولاب (HH)} Cf. Ar dūlāb دولاب = 'wheel; tire; cabinet, cupboard'; T dolap; Sor dołab دۆڵاب [LC/IFb/B/JJ/HH/GF/ZF3]

dolap دۆلاپ (K/A) = cupboard. See **dolab I.**

dolav دۆلاڤ (IFb/GF) = cupboard. See **dolab I.**

doldang دۆلـــــدانـــــگ (FS) = (children's) swing. See **dolîdang I** .

dolebaşî دۆلەباشی *m.* **().** boy who carries food during wedding festivities: **•Evê ȓabû k'ulfet şîret kir, go, ezê bibim *dolebaşî*, ezê eşqî wan yeko-yeko bixum** (HCK-3, #2, 24) She up and advised the woman, saying, "I will be *a food carrier at the wedding*, I'll drink to their health one by one". {also: dalebaşî (K-2/Tsab)} [HCK/K//Tsab] <pêşkese; ȓovî I[2]>

dolg•e دۆلـگه *f.* **(;•ê).** pen or enclosure in which ewes lamb. {also: dolgeh (GF/Wkt-2)} {syn: lêf} < T döl = 'sperm' + -ge[h] = 'place' (<P gāh گاه) [Nikitine//K/B/Wkt//GF] <axil; gom I; k'oz; mexel>

dolgeh دۆلـگەه (GF/WKt) = pen where ewes lamb. See **dolge.**

dolîdang I دۆلیدانگ *f.* **(;-ê).** (child's) swing: **•Zaȓo li**

***doldangê* siyar bûn** (FS) The children climbed on *the swing*. {also: doldang (FS)} {syn: colan; deydik; hêlekan; hêzok} Sor dîlane دیـــــلانـــه/ dêlekane دێلەکانە [Sinneh]; Hau dîlane *f.* (M4) [K/F/ZF3/Wkt//FS]

dolîdang II دۆلیدانگ *f.* **(-a;-ê).** 1) gifts *(distributed to children during Yezidi religious holidays)*; 2) a custom on religious holidays: **•Di vê cejnê da berê adetekî wisa jî hebû ku şeva berê cejnê, zarokên gund li Ermenîstanê gorên ji hiriyê vehûnandî û rengîn nexişday hildidan û navê wê gorê *Dolîdang* (yan Holîdang) bû, bi têleke dirêj ve girêdidan û diçûne ser banê mala cînara û di kolekê ra ew *dolîdang* berdidane xwarê û pê ra jî stiranek digotin: *Dolîdangê, dolîdangê*, Xwẹdê xweyî ke xortê malê. Pîre malê bike qurbangê: Tiştekî bavêje *dolîdangê*** (newroz.com: Cejna Xidir Nebî 19.ii.2010) In this holiday there was a custom that the eve of the holiday, the village children in Armenia would take colorfully adorned woolen knitted socks called "*Dolîdang*" or "Holîdang" and would tie them to a long string and would go to the roof of the neighbor's house and let the *Dolîdang* down through the skylight, while singing a song: "*Dolîdang*, *dolîdang*, may God take care of the young man of the house. May he make the lady of the house a sacrifice, throw something into the *dolîdang* [*stocking*]." {also: dolîdank (B)} [K//B]

dolîdank دۆلـیـدانـك (B) = 1) gifts; 2) custom in which young people go from roof to roof, and let down a stocking through the skylight while asking for gifts. See **dolîdang II.**

dolme دۆلـمـه/**d̲olme** ضـۆلـمـه [Bw] *pl.* stuffed grape leaves. {also: [dolma دولـمـه/tolma طـولـمـه] (JJ); <t̲olme> طـولـمـه (HH)} {syn: îprax} <T dolma = 'being filled up; vegetable stuffed with a mixture of meat and rice' [Bw/K/GF//JJ//HH]

dom I دۆم *f.* **(-a;).** perseverence, persistence (OK); continuance (GF): **-dom kirin** (Wlt/K[s]/IFb/HH/TF/OK) to continue {syn: berdewam bûn & kirin; dewam kirin; domîn & domandin}: **•Alfons paşda vedigere...diçe necaretxanê û *dom dike* malokan çêdike** (BM, 25-26) Then Alfons goes back to the carpentry workshop and *continues* building [or, to build] little houses **•Ger ji îro pê ve jî, êrîşên li ser wan *dom bikin*, dê rewşa wan dijwartir bibe** (Wlt 1:43, 9) If from today on they *continue* their attacks on them, they will be in a more difficult situation. {also: [doum دوم/dewam دوام] (JJ); <dom kirin دوم کـــرن (dom dike) (دوم دکـــــــــــــه)> (HH)} <Ar dawm دوم ='duration, continuance' [Wlt/K(s)/IFb/HH/GF/TF/OK/ZF3/Wkt] <k'işandin [5]>

dom II دۆم (A) = Gypsy. See **dome.**

domam دۆمام (B/JJ) = female cousin. See **dotmam.**

domandin دۆمـــانـــدِن *vt.* **(-domîn-).** to continue *(vt.)*, cause to continue, carry on: **•Na em hêjî negihîştine armanca xwe. Lê em ji bo vê, xebata xwe *didomînin*** (Wlt 1:37, 16) No, we have not yet achieved our goal. But for this reason we *are continuing* our struggle **•Tiştekê ew dixirikand, lê ew ne di haya vê yekê de bû. Wî ji xwe re xewnên xwe *didomandin*** (Wlt 1:45, 16) Something tugged at him, but he was not aware of it. He *carried on with* his dreams. {syn: berdewam kirin; dewam kirin; dom kirin} [(neol)Wlt/IFb/TF/ZF3] <domîn; k'işandin [5]>

dome دۆمـــه *m.* **().** Roma, Gypsy. {also: dom II (A)} {syn: aşiq; begzade; boşe; gewende; mirt'ib; qereçî} Sor dom دۆم = 'villager of Şarî Hewraman (generally skilled in crafts associated with Roma (Gipsies) but especially the making of ***kelaş***, shoes with rag sole)' [Wn/A]

domiz دۆمـــز *m.* **().** pig. {also: [domouz] دومـــز (JJ)} {syn: beraz; weḧş (Haz); xinzîr, f. (F) [erudite]} < T domuz [Mzg//JJ]

domîn دۆمـیـن *vi.* **(-dom-).** 1) {syn: berdewam bûn} to continue *(vi.)*, be continued: **•Ger bi vî awayî *bidomiya*, dê bibûna layiqê gel** (Wlt 1:43, 8) If it *had continued* in this manner, they would have been worthy of the people **•Hê jî girtin û pesta dewleta li Siwêrekê *didome*** (Wlt 1:45, 3) The capture and oppression by the state in Siverek *continues*; 2) {syn: ajotin[2]; dirêj kirin[c]; k'işandin[6]; k'udandin; vek'işîn[2]} to last, take *(time)*. [(neol)Wlt/ZF3/FD] <berdewam; dewam; dom>

don دۆن *m.* **(-ê;).** *(melted)* fat, grease: **•Bîne nanê genimî, *duhn* bide, bêxe leşê min, ezê sax bim** (M-Zx #757) Bring wheat bread, spread it with *fat*, put it on my body and I shall be cured [i.e., come to life again]. {also: dihn II (IFb-2); dohin (TF); dohn (A); duhn (GF-2/M-Zx); dwîn (IFb-2); [don دون/douhen دوهـن] (JJ); <duhn> دهـن (HH)} {syn: bez I} <Ar duhn دهن [F/K/JB3/IFb/B/JJ/GF/ZF3//A/TF//HH/M-Zx] <avdonk; tewaş>

donzdah دۆنزداه (Ba) = twelve. See **donzdeh.**

donzde دۆنزده (K/JB3/IF/B) = twelve. See **donzdeh.**

donzdeh دۆنـزده *num.* twelve, 12. {also: danzde (M-Am & Bar/Rh); danzde (JB1-A); deh û didû (Ad/Krç/Bg); diwanzde (JB1-S); diwazdeh (IFb-2); donzdah (Ba); donzde (K/JB3/IF/B); dozde (Msr); dûwazde (Msr-2); dwanzde (JB1-S/M-Ak & Shn); dwanzde (JB1-A); dwanzdey (JB1-A); dwazde (Msr/SK/M-Sur); dwazde (M-Zx & Gul); [devazdeh دوازده/dounzdeh دونـزده/deh ou dou ده و دو] (JJ); <dwazde[h]> دوازده (HH)} Skt dvā́daśa; Av dvadasa- = twelfth; Mid P dwāzdah (M3); P davāzdah دوازده; Sor dwazde دوازده/dwanze دوانـزه; Za duwês/desudi[di] (Todd); Hau dûanze (M4) [F/Ba/SC//K/JB3/IFb/B//HH/SK//M-Am&Bar/Rh//JJ//JB1-A//JB1-S//Ad/Krç/Bg//Msr] <derzin; didû; dozdehem>

donzdehem دۆنـــزدهـــــم (Wkt) = twelfth. See **dozdehem.**

donzdehemîn دۆنـزدهـهـمـيـن (Wkt) = twelfth. See **dozdehem.**

***doq** دۆق *adj.* standing on end (of knucklebone [k'ap II]). [Qzl] <k'ap II>

dor دۆر *f.* **(-a;-ê).** (one's) turn *(in line)*, circuit: **-di dora ... de/[li] dora...** = around {syn: dorhêla}: **•Cime'ta Misrê *dora* bazirgan berev dibe** (Ba) The people of Egypt gather *around* the caravan **•Pezê xwe *li dora* xwe dicivînim** (AB) I gather my sheep *around* me. {also: [dor] دور (JJ); <dor> دور (HH)} {syn: geř II[2]; nobet; sirê} < Ar dawr دور [BX/K/JB3/IF/B/JJ/HH]

dořandin دۆڕاندِن**/dorandin** دۆراندِن [K(s)/IF/JB3] *vt.* **(-dořîn-/-dořên** [K(s)]**).** 1) {syn: derdan; ≠birin [3]} to lose (a game) (M/K[s]); to give up, forfeit (IF); 2) to spread, diffuse (IF/JB3); 3) to ruin, weaken (IF). Sor dořandin دۆڕاندن (-dořên-) = 'to win (a game), to lose (a game) ' [M//K(s)/JB3/IF/ZF3]

dorbîn دۆربين (L) = binoculars. See **dûrbîn.**

dorçî دۆرچـى *m.* **().** one who stands in line, awaiting his turn, customer: **•Mhemmed Xan xwe kirîye keraş û jina xwe jî kirîye *dorçî*** (L) M. Khan turned himself into a miller, and his wife into a *customer* (one standing in line, waiting to grind grain). {also: dordar (K)} < dor = 'one's turn' + T -ci/-çi = '-er' (e.g., doer) [L/B//K]

dordar دۆردار (K) = one who stands in line. See **dorçî.**

dor•girtin دۆرگِـرتـن *vt.* **(dora ... -gr-).** to surround, encircle: **•Çend sûxteyên min ên wefakar *dora* timobîla me *girtibûn*** [sic] (WT, 86) Some of my loyal students *surrounded* our car. {also: [dor ghirtin] دورگرتن (JJ)} {syn: çar rexî *ft-î* girtin; di rex û çana *ft-î* zivirîn; dorpêç kirin; werandin I; weranîn} [SW/K/A/JB3/IFb/JJ/ZF]

dorhêl دۆرهێل *f.* **(-a;-ê).** surroundings: **-dorhêla** (BX) *[prep.]* around, surrounding {syn: di dora ... de; [li] dora...}. [BX/K/JB3/IF/ZF3]

dorpêç دۆرپـێـچ *f.* **(-a;-ê).** siege, blockade; act of surrounding: **-dorpêç bûn** (ZF) to be surrounded: **•...sînor di navbera Kepez û Toroz de hate danîn û Toroz ji wî alî de bi têlên sitirî û bimbeyan *dorpêç bû*** (X.Remo. Kepez ê xewna, 75) ... the border between [Mt.] Kepez & [Mt.] Taurus was fixed and [Mt.] Taurus *was surrounded* by barbed wire and bombs on that side; **-dorpêç kirin** (ZF/CS) to surround, encircle: **•Bidû vegera wî da tenêtiyê ew bêhtir *dorpêç kiribû*** (HYma, 30) After his return, loneliness had *encircled* him [even] more **•Hêrs kete nava min ji şaqşaqa jinapa min û qîrînên xelkên gund yên ku hawîrdora min *dorpêç kiribû*** (HYma, 21) I was enraged by the carping of my aunt and by the shrieks of the village people, which *had surrounded* me. {syn: çar rexî *ft-î* girtin; di rex û çana *ft-î* zivirîn; dorgirtin; werandin I; weranîn}. < dor = 'turn, circuit' + pêç- = 'to wrap' [HYma/FJ/CS/ZF] <dorhêl; hawirdor>

dost دۆسـت *m.&f.* **(-ê/-a; /-ê).** 1) {syn: heval; hogir; yar [1]; ≠dijmin; ≠neyar} friend: **•Babê min û Xal Eħmed qewî *dost* bûn, wekî biraêt daybabî bûn, malek ħisab bûn** (SK 8:81) My father and Uncle Ahmad were *great friends*, they were like blood brothers, they were (almost) counted as one family **•Eger kesek zerera dujminê muro biket, muro wî kesî nakete *dostê* xo?** (SK 1:2) If someone injures a man's enemy, doesn't the man make that person his *friend*?; 2) *[m.]* male lover (IFb). {also: [dost] دوسـت (JJ); <dost> دوسـت (HH)} [Pok. ĝeus- 399.] 'to taste, enjoy', *in Indo-Iranian & Alb* 'to love': Skt joṣṭár-/jóṣṭar- = 'caring for, loving'; O Ir *źauštar- (Ras, p.135): Av zaoš- = 'to delight in'; O P dauštar- = 'fond of, loving, friend'; Mid P dōst = 'friend' (M3); P dūst دوسـت --> T dost; Sor dost دۆسـت = 'friend'; cf. also Lat gustus = 'taste'; Gr geuomai γεύομαι = 'I taste'; Eng choose {dostanî; dostay[et]î; dostî; dostînî; dostîtî} [K/A/JB3/IFb/B/JJ/HH/SK/GF/TF/OK] dostan دۆستان (GF/Hej) = trivet, tripod. See **dûstan**.

dostanî دۆستانی (IFb/OK) = friendship. See **dostî.**

dostayetî دۆستایەتی (K[s]) = friendship. See **dostî.**

dostayî دۆستایی (A/B) = friendship. See **dostî.**

dostî دۆستی *f.* **(-ya;-yê).** friendship: **•Dijmin kengî bûye dost, heta ku tu li *dostaniya* mar digerî?** (CP, 15) Since when have enemies become friends, that you are seeking *the friendship of* the snake? **•Ma-beyna Şêx 'Ebdusselami Sanî û Seyyid Tahaê Sanî gelek xoş bû, *dostî* hebû** (SK 48:497) Between Shaikh Abdussalam II and Sayyid Taha II there were very pleasant relations and *friendship* **•Paşî dîsa hêdî hêdî bi mexfî dest bi terîqetê kir û *digel* qaimmeqamê Zêbarê, Şewqî Efendî, *dostînî peyda kir*** (SK 47:466) Then (the Shaikh) slowly began to preach the path again in secret and *made friends with* Shevqi Effendi, the district governor of Zebar. {also: dostanî (IFb-2/OK-2); dostayetî (K[s]); dostayî (A/B); dostînî (SK-2); dostîtî (K)} {syn: hevaltî; yarî I[1]} [K/A/IFb/JJ/SK/GF/TF/OK//B] <dost>

dostînî دۆستینی (SK) = friendship. See **dostî.**

dostîtî دۆستیتی (K) = friendship. See **dostî.**

doşab دۆشاب (K/B/JJ/HH) = grape molasses. See **doşav**.

doşak دۆشاك (EP-7) = mattress. See **doşek.**

doşanî دۆشانی *f.* **(;-yê).** milch *(cow, ewe, goat, etc.)*, lactiferous animal. {also: <doşanî> دوشانی (HH)} [Qzl/K/IFb/B/HH/GF/FJ/Hej/ZF] <dotin>

doşav دۆشاڤ *f.* **(-a;-ê).** syrup *(esp. of grapes)*, grape molasses {T pekmez, Arm ṙup ռուպ}. {also: doşab (K-2/B-2); doşaw (SK); [douchab/duscaf (G)/ doshāv (Rh)] دوشاب (JJ); <doşab> دوشاب (HH)} {syn: aqit; dims; mot} According to JJ, this is derived from Mandaic duvšā דובשא, although the Classical Arc form is identical. The Iranian word for water (P āb آب, Krm av, Sor aw) may have played a part in the metathesis from the original Arc form. I.e., because of the viscous nature of grape molasses, **doşav**, etc. may have been perceived as being some sort of water (**av**, etc.). **Dims** is derived from Arab dibs دبس, and is therefore ultimately cognate to **doşav**. <Arc duvšā דובשא = 'honey, glutinous substance': NENA dôshâb ܕܘܫܐܒ/ܕܘܫܒ = 'syrup, treacle, from grapes or honey' esp. in Salmas (Maclean) & dyûshâ ܕܝܘܫܐ (Maclean)/duyša (Christian Urmia) = 'honey'; cf. Heb devaš דבש = 'honey', Ar dibs دبس = 'grape molasses'; P dūšāb دوشاب = 'syrup made of raisins mixed with butter and cream'; Sor doşaw دۆشاو [Bw/K/IFb/B/GF/OK//JJ/HH//SK] <çiřik II>

doşaw دۆشاو (SK) = grape molasses. See **doşav**.

doşek دۆشەك *f.* **(-a;-ê).** mattress; bedding, sleeping mat (JJ): **•Bavê min weke hertim bêdeng li ser *doşeka* xwe rûniştî bû** (Alkan, 73) As always, my father was seated silently on his *mattress* **•bin *doşeka* Ûsib** (Ba) under Joseph's *mattress.* {also: doşak (EP-7); [douchek] دوشك (JJ); <doşek> دوشك (HH)} {syn: *bincî; binřex; cil III; mitêl; nehlîk} < T döşek; Sor doşek دۆشەك; Za doşeg *m.* (Todd) [Ba/A/JB3/IFb/B/JJ/HH/SK/JB1-S/GF/TF]

doşîn دۆشین (IFb/M) = to milk. See **dotin.**

dot دۆت *f.* **(-a;-ê).** girl; daughter *(polite form, used mostly in such compounds as **dotmam** & **dotmîr**).* {also: [doukht دخت/dot دوت] (JJ)} {syn: keç; qîz} [Pok. dhug(h)əter 277.] 'daughter' --> *dhugHter-: Skt duhitṛ; O Ir *duxta- (A&L p. 84 [V]): Av dugədar-/duxtar-; Mid P duxt(ar) (M3); P doxtar دختر; Sor dot دۆت/dwêt [döt] دوێت; cf. also Arm dustr (W: tusdr) դուստր; Gr thygatēr θυγάτηρ; Rus doč′ дочь (*gen.* dočeri дочери); Germ Tochter [K/A/JB3/IF/JJ/B]

dotin دۆتِن *vt.* **(-doş-).** to milk *(a cow or sheep)*: **•Bêrîvanan jî pez *dotin*** (AB) The milkmaids *milked* the sheep **•Elbê bîne, ez çêlekê *bidoşim*** (AB) Bring the bucket, *so that* I *may milk* the cow. {also: doşîn (IFb-2/M); duhotin (Azer); [dotin] دوتین (JJ); <dotin دوتن (didoşe) (ددوشه)> (HH)} [Pok. dheugh- 271.] 'to press, dispense generously, milk': Proto IndIr *dhaugh- = 'to milk'; Skt duh- (orig. dugh-); O Ir *daug-/*dauxš- (Tsb 40): P dūxtan دوختن (-dūš-) (دوش); Sor doşîn دۆشین (-doş-); Za doşenā [ditiş] (Todd/Srk) {for a description of the entire milking cycle among Kurdish nomads, see: B. Nikitine. *Les Kurdes: étude sociologique et historique* (Paris : Imprimerie nationale: Librairie C. Klincksieck, 1956), p. 50, note 1} [BX/K/JB3/IFb/B/JJ/HH//M//Azer] <bêrî I; bêrîvan; doşanî; şevîn; şîr>

dotir: dotira rojê دۆتِرا رۆژێ *adv.* the next day, the following day, the day after: ***•Dotiřa roja* çûna min** (Dz #22, 389) *The day after* I leave. {also: dêhtir (TF); dûtir (GF); [doutira rouji] دوترا روژی (JJ)} {syn: řoja paştir; řojtir} Cf. Sor dwatir دواتر = 'later, after' [Dz/K(s)/IFb/FJ//GF/JJ//TF]

dotmam دۆتمام *f.* **(-a;-ê).** female (first) cousin,

paternal uncle's daughter: A Kurd has the right of refusal of the hand of his **amoza** [=dotmam] (M, note #149, 370); any female relative: **•"Eto vê jinê tbînî, ya xizmeta me tket?" gotê "Belê." Gotê, "Eve *dotmama* min e"** (M #630) "Do you see this woman who is waiting on us?" he replied, "Yes." He told him, "She is my *cousin*." {also: domam (B); dodmam (K); duxtmam; [doumam دومام/doutmam دوتمام/doukhtmam دختمام/dutmān دوتمان] (JJ); <dûtmam> دوتمام (HH)} {syn: qîzap} < dot = 'daughter' + mam = 'paternal uncle'. [K//A/JB3/IFb/GF/TF//B//JJ/HH] <ap; binam (Bw); mam; pismam; qîzmet'>

dotmîr دۆتمیر *f.* **(-a;-ê).** princess, daughter of an emir: **•*Dotmîra* Botanê, Sînemxan Alî Bedr-Xanê** (Kurdîgeh 8.v.2012) *Princess of* Botan, Sinemkhan Ali Bedr-Khan **•Li dawiya şahiyê perî nêzîkî *dotmîrê* bûn û diyariyên delal danê** (nefel.com:H.Muhammed.Sorgula di xewê de 12.xi.2010) At the end of the party the fairies approached *the princess* and gave her lovely gifts. [Kurdîgeh/K/A/IFb/ZF3/FS/Wkt/FD/Kmc] <jinmîr; mîr I; pismîr>

dox دۆخ *f.* **(-a;-ê).** handle *(of a spoon)*; shaft; spindle: **-doxa t'eşîyê** (B) spindle. {also: [doukh] دوخ (JJ)} Sor dûx دووخ = 'spindle of spinning wheel' [Qzl/K/A/IFb/B/GF/FJ//JJ]

doxîn دۆخین *f.* **(-a;-ê).** drawstring, pyjama-cord. {also: dêxon (FS-2); doxwin (TF); doxwîn (L); [doukhin] دوخین (JJ); <doxîn> دۆخین (HH)} {syn: oxçir (Dy)} Sor bendexwên [bendexön] بەندەخوێن [K/A/IFb/B/HH/SK/GF/FS//JJ//L//TF] <maldoxîn = pizî; piçan; şalvar; xilf>

doxînsist دۆخینسِست *adj. & m.* woman-chasing, addicted to sex, sexually promiscuous, lit. someone whose drawstring is loose: **•Ger melayên me *doxînsist* û çavlider bin, gelo wê xelkê reben çi xwelîyê li serê xwe bikin hêê!** (www.lotikxane.com) If our mullahs are *weak-moraled* and have wandering eyes, what will the poor folk do with themselves! [Lotikxane/A/IFb/ZF/FB/Wkt/CS]

doxtir دۆختر (K/B) = doctor. See **duxtor**.

doxwin دۆخوِن (TF) = drawstring. See **doxîn**.

doxwîn دۆخوین (L) = drawstring. See **doxîn**.

***doẍ•e** دۆغە *f.* **(•a;).** bride's white headdress: **-doẍa bûkê** (Bw) do. [Bw] <ç'arik; r̄ûpoş>

doẍeba دۆغەبا *f.* **(-ya;).** stuffed dumplings [kotilk] in boiled yoghurt. {also: doẍeva (Bw[Bêduh]); <doxawe دۆخاوە/doxewa دۆخەوا/doxwa دۆخوا/doẍewa دۆغەوا> (Hej)} P dūγebā دوغبا; Sor doxewa دۆخەوا = dokułîw دۆکوڵیو = 'dish of curds with rice or *sawer* flavored with mint' [Bw//Hej/FS] <dew I; k'utilk; mast>

doẍeva دۆغەڤا (Bw[Bêduh]) = dumplings in yoghurt. See **doẍeba**.

doz دۆز *f.* **(-a;-ê).** 1) {syn: ceng [2]; cerenîx; cur̄e; de'w II; gelemşe; gelş; k'êşe; k'eşmek'eş} fight, quarrel, disagreement, argument: **•Çi *doza* we ketiye nava hevdu?** (ZZ-6, 127) What *argument* has occurred between you two?; **-de'w û doz** (Z-1) do. ; 2) lawsuit, legal action, (law) trial, (court) case: **-doz vebûn** (Wlt) for a court case to be opened, for proceedings to be initiated: **•*Doz* bi hinceta ku bi riya çapemenîyê propagandeya parvekarîyê li dijî Tirkiyeyê hatiye kirin vebûye** (Wlt 2:103, 8) *The trial* was opened on the pretext that separatist propaganda against Turkey was being made through the press; **-doz vekirin** (Wlt) to open a case, initiate proceedings. {also: [douz] دوز (JJ)} [Z-1/K/A/IFb/GF/TF/OK//JJ] <dozger>

dozde دۆزدە (Msr) = twelve. See **donzdeh.**

dozdehem دۆزدەهەم *adj.* twelfth, 12th. {also: dazdehem (Wkt); diwanzdehem (Wkt-2); diwanzdehemîn (IFb/Wkt-2); diwazdehem (Wkt-2); diwazdehemîn (Wkt-2); diwazdemîn (IFb-2); donzdehem (Wkt-2); donzdehemîn (Wkt-2); duwanzdehem (GF/Wkt-2); duwanzdehemîn (Wkt-2); duwazdehem (CT); duwazdehemîn (CT-2); dwanzdehemîn (GF-2)} Cf. P davāzdahom دوازدهم; Sor dûwanzem[în] دووانزەم[ین] [ZF//Wkt//IFb//GF//CT] <donzdeh>

dozger دۆزگەر *m.* **(-ê;).** public prosecutor: **•*Dozgerê* DED (=Dadgeha Ewlekariya Dewletê)'a Stenbolê Mehmet Demircî** (Wlt 2:103, 8) *The public prosecutor* of the State Security Court of Istanbul, Mehmet Demirci **•*Dozkarê* wê dadgehê jê ra cezayê idamê daxwaz dike** (Bkp, 8) *The prosecutor of* that court is requesting the death penalty for him. {also: dozkar (Bkp)} [(neol)Wlt/ZF//Bkp] <doz; ebûqat>

dozkar دۆزکار (Bkp) = public prosecutor. See **dozger**.

draf دراف (IFb) = dirhem. See **dirav.**

drafî درافی (IFb) = financial. See **diravî**.

dran دران (JB3/IFb/OK) = tooth. See **didan.**

drandin درانِدن (JB3) = to tear, rip. See **dir̄andin.**

dranfîq درانفیق (Wkt) = gap-toothed. See **diranfîq**.

drav دراڤ (IFb) = dirhem. See **dirav.**
drêj دریژ (JB3) = long. See **dirêj.**
drêjahî دریژاهی (JB3) = length. See **dirêjahî.**
drî دری (IF) = thorn. See **dirî.**
drûn دروون (JB3/IF) = to sew. See **dirûtin.**
drûşm درووشم (Wkt) = slogan. See **dirûşm.**
drûtin درووتِن (JB3/IF) = to sew. See **dirûtin.**
drûv درووڤ (IFb) = looks. See **dirûv.**

du I دو *num.* two, 2: "didû" is used independently (free form), while "du" is immediately followed by a noun (bound form). Cf. **sisê** vs. **sê**. {also: do (BX/A); dû I; [dou] دو (JJ); <diddo دڎو /dû دو> (HH)} Cf. P dō دو; Sor dû دوو/duwan دووان; Za didi/di--for etymology see **didû**. [BX/K/A/JB3/IF/JJ/B] <didû; sisê; sê>

du II دو (IF) = yesterday. See **dihî.**

du'a دوعـا *m./f.(B)* **(-yê/ ; /-ê).** 1) prayer; incantation: **•Mem sê qat heqê wana dayê, wekî ew dilmayî nemînin û *du'ayê* oxira wî *bikin*** (Z-1) Mem gave them three times what they deserved, so that they wouldn't be offended, and [so that] they *would pray* for his good fortune; 2) blessing; benediction. {also: [doua] دعـا (JJ); <du'a> دعـا (HH)} < Ar du'ā' دعاء [Z-1/K/IF/B/JJ/HH] <t'iberk>

dualî دوئـالـی *adj.* bilateral, two-sided; mutual: **•Şerefedîn Elçî banga PKK û Hikûmeta Tirkiyê kir ku agirbesta *dualî* ragihînin** (Avestakurd) Ş.E. called on the PKK and the Turkish government to declare and *bilateral* cease-fire. {also: dulayî (SS)} [K/IFb/ZF/Wkt//SS]

duanî دوئانی (K) = second. See **dudua.**

du'a-qebûl دوعـا قـەبـوول *m.* () & *adj.* one whose prayers are answered: **•Dê çim e gundê Elenya li-r̄ex qeseba Başqel'e. Dibêjin munasibekî çak li wê-derê heye, qewî *du'a-qebûl* e** (SK 34: 307) I am going to the village of Alanya beside the town of Bashqala. They say there is the shrine of a good man there *whose prayers are accepted* **•*Du'a qebûl* r̄abû sekinî. ... Qeretûyê k'ulfetekê wê pêşberî wî sekinîye ... Welle ezê jî gazî Xwedê kim, du'a bikim, belkî dive benî adem** (HCK-5, #41, 235) *The one whose prayers are answered* stopped ... The figure of a woman [mannequin] was standing before him ... "By Jove, I will call God, I'll pray, maybe it will become human". Cf. P du'ā qabūl دعا قبول [HCK/SK]

dubare دوبـاره: **-dubare kirin** (K/B/OK) to repeat, reiterate, do or say again {syn: ducar kirin; wek'ilandin}: **•Min pêwîst nedît ku li vir careke din ez wê *dubare bikim*** (E.Narozî. Çira 9:38) I saw no need *to repeat* it here another time. {also: dubar (B-2)} Cf. P dūbāre دوبـاره = 'again'; Sor dûbare دووبـاره = 'repitition; again' & dûbare kirdn•ewe دووبـاره کِـردنـەوە = dûpat kirdn•ewe دووپـات کِردنەوە = 'to repeat' [Çira-9/K/IFb/B/OK/RZ] <bilandin>

dubar kirin دوبار کِرِن (B) = to repeat. See **dubare.**

dubendî دوبـەنـدی *f.* **(-ya;-yê).** discord, disagreement, dissension, argument; conflict; split, schism: **•Ew zilam bû semedê** [sic] ***dubendîya* gundîyan** (BZ, v. 1:567) That man caused [or, was the reason for] *the disagreement of* the villagers **•Wî *dubendî* kire nîva hevalan** (IFb) He caused *a split* between the friends; **-dubendî xistin nav** (K) to sow dissension. {syn: bêt'ifaqî; cur̄e; k'êşe; mişt û mir̄; nakokî} = Sor dûberekî دووبـەرەکـی [BZ/K/IFb/FJ/TF/GF/ZF/CS]

dubur دوبـور *m.* **(-ê;).** shady side of mountain. {also: dibûr, f. (B); [debour] دبــــور (JJ)} {syn: nizar I; zimank} {≠ber̄oj} [Slm/Wkt//B/JJ]

ducan دوجان (A/IFb/FJ) = pregnant. See **ducanî.**

ducanî دوجانی *adj.* pregnant. {also: ducan (A/IFb/FJ)} {syn: bih̄emil; bitişt; bizar; duhala; giran I} Sor dûgyan دووگیان [Slm/Qrj/Qzl/ZF3//A/IFb/FJ]

ducar دوجـــار *adv.* again, twice: **-ducar bûn** (K/B/IFb/CS) to be repeated; **-ducar kirin** (K/B/IFb/TF/CS) to repeat {syn: dubare kirin; wek'ilandin}: **•Dûre ez wan gotinên xwe *ducar dikim* û dîsa dibêjim**... (Epl, 17) Afterwards I *repeat* my words and say again .... < du I = 'two' + car = 'time' [Epl/K/A/B/IFb/FJ/TF/GF/CS]

duda دودا (F/B) = second. See **dudua.**

dudil دودِل *adj.* hesitant, wavering, indecisive, irresolute: **-dudil bûn** (K/B/GF/AId) to hesitate, waver. {also: [dou-dil] دودل (JJ)} Cf. P dō del دودل; Sor dûdił دوودِڵ [AId/K/IFb/B/JJ/GF/ZF3]

dudilî دودِلـی *f.* **(-ya;-yê).** hesitation, indecisiveness, irresoluteness: **•Ji ber *dudilîya* xwe ew herdem ya aloze** (Glosbe) Because of her *indecisiveness* she is always upset. Cf. P dō delī دودلی [IFb/GF/ZF3/Wkt]

dudu دودو (K/IF) = two. See **didû.**

dudua دودوئا *adj.* second (ordinal of **two**), 2nd. {also: didiwan (BX); didiyê (JB1-S); diduyan (IF); diduyî (IF-2); doê (M-Am&Bar&Zx&Gul); duanî (K-2); duda (F/B-2); duwûm (K); **duyem**; dûê (M-Shn); dûwê (JB1-A); dwê (M-Sur&Ak); [douvi دووی/douian دویـــان] (JJ)} Cf. P dovvom

دوّم; Sor dûhem[în] [دووهەم[ین; Za didin (Todd) [K/B//BX//JB1-S//IF//M-Am&Bar&Zx&Gul//F//M-Shn//JB1-A//M-Sur&Ak//JJ] <didû; du I>

duem دوئەم (A) = second. See **duyem**.

dugulî دوگولی *f.(Qzl)/m.(ZZ)* **(/-yê;).** crotch; fork (of tree, etc.): **•Kilîta Kumşê di binê guhikê min de honaye û bi *duguliyê* min ve girêdayî ye** (ZZ-10, 163) Kumshe's *[name of horse]* key is woven under my ear and tied to my *crotch.* {also: digulî (TF)} {syn: navřan; şeq[4]} [Qzl/ZZ/ZF3//TF]

duh دوه (BX/F/K/B/IFb) = yesterday. See **dihî.**

duhala دوهـالـی *adj.* pregnant. {also: duhalî (ZF3); duȟalî (F)} {syn: avis; biȟemil; bitişt; bizar; giran I[3]; ȟemle} [K//ZF3//F]

duhalî دوهالا (ZF3) = pregnant. See **duhala**.

duhem دوهەم (IFb) = second. See **duyem**.

duhemîn دوهەمین (IFb/RZ) = second. See **duyem**.

duhê دوهێ (Wn) = yesterday. See **dihî.**

duhêl دوهـێـل *f.* **(;-ê).** thread made of animal skin: **•Şêr go: ez bi werîs nayêm girêdan, lê ez bi *duhêlan* tême girtin ... here iyarekî nû bîne, û bike duhêl û li laşê min bigerîne** (RN 16/7/45, 3) The lion said, "I can't be tied with rope, but I can be caught with *thread made of animal skin* ... go bring a new goatskin bag, and make threads out of it [=cut it into thin strips] and run them around my body. {also: duwêl I (GF); [deval دوال/devil دول] (JJ); <duwêl> دویـــــل (HH)} P dovāl دوال; Sor duwał دووال & duwêł دووێڵ (Hej) = 'thong' [RN/K/IFb/B//HH/GF/ZF3//JJ]

duhî دوهی (BX/JB3/IFb/SK/GF) = yesterday. See **dihî.**

duhîn دوهین (SK) = curds. See **dohîn**.

duhl دوهل (PS) = drum. See **dehol.**

duhn دوهن (GF/HH/M-Zx) = grease. See **don**.

duhotin دوهۆتِن (Azer) = to milk. See **dotin.**

duhu دوهو (Ad) = yesterday. See **dihî.**

duhû دوهوو (M-Zx) = yesterday. See **dihî**.

duȟalî دوحالی (F) = pregnant. See **duhala**.

dujîn دوژین (A/IFb) = dirty. See **dijûn II.**

dujmin دوژمِن (A) = enemy. See **dijmin.**

dujminatî دوژمِناتی (SK) = enmity. See **dijminahî.**

dujminayî دوژمِنایی (A) = enmity. See **dijminahî.**

duk'an دوکان (B) = shop. See **dik'an.**

duk'ançî دوکانچی (F/B) = shopkeeper. See **dik'andar.**

duk'andar دوکـــانـــدار (B/JJ) = shopkeeper. See **dik'andar.**

duk'êl دوکێل (JB1-A/OK) = smoke. See **dûk'el.**

duk'îteyî دوکـیـتـەیـی *adj.* disyllabic, bisyllabic, consisting of two syllables: **•Hemû navên merivan yên vê alfabeyê *dukîteyî* ne** (RR 2.) All men's names [used] in this alphabet are *bisyllabic.* [RR/Wkt] <k'îte>

duktor دوکتۆر (SK) = doctor. See **duxtor**.

dulayî دولایی (SS) = bilateral. See **dualî.**

Dumilî دومِلی = Zaza. See **Dimilî.**

Dumilkî دومِلکی = Zaza. See **Dimilî.**

dundan دوندان (TF) = offspring. See **dûndan.**

dundil دوندِل *f.* **(-a;-ê).** she-camel: **•Rast ço pêşiya wê hermetê û bi serê *delûla* wê girt û tixand** (GShA, 132) She went directly to that woman, made her *[she-]camel* stop and kneel. {also: delûl (GShA); delûn (FS-2); dundul (FJ/GF-2)} {syn: arwane; mencî} cf. Duldul, name of Prophet Muhammad's mule [IFb/GF/SS/FS//FJ//GShA] <deve; ȟêştir; lok' II; torim>

dundul دوندول (FJ/GF) = she-camel. See **dundil.**

dunîya دونییا (F/K/B) = world. See **dinya.**

dunîyadîtî دونییادیتی = experienced. See **dinyadîtî.**

dunîyalik دونییالِك (B) = all of humanity. See **dinyalik.**

dupişk دوپشك (F) = scorpion. See **dûp'işk.**

duř دوڕ/**dur** دور *(ZF) f.* **(;-ê).** pearl (K/IF); jewel (JJ): **-lal [û] dur** (Z-1) rubies and pearls: **•Zînekî usa hespê minřa çê ke, wekî t'emam *lal û duř* be** (Z-1) Make a saddle for my horse that is full of *rubies and pearls*. {also: diř II (HR-7); [dourr] در (JJ); <dur> در (HH)} {syn: mircan [2]} < Ar durr دُرّ [Z-1/K/IFb/B/JJ/HH//ZF] <lal II; xişir>

durbîn دوربین (IF) = binoculars. See **dûrbîn.**

durêyan دورێیان (OK) = crossroads. See **duřiyan.**

durist دورســـــت (K/B/HH/ZF3) = correct, true. See **dirust.**

duristî دورِســـتـــی (B/ZF3) = correctness, truth. See **dirustî.**

duřiyan دوڕِیـان *f.* **(-a;-ê).** crossroads, fork in the road, junction: **•Heta gihîşt serê *duriyanê*, şeş-heft caran ket** (DBgb, 36) By the time he reached *the crossroads*, he fell 6 or 7 times. {also: durêyan (OK); <duř[i]yan> دوڕیـــان (Hej)} {syn: *çarrê} Cf. P dūrāhī دوراهـی; Sor dûrêyan دووڕێـیـان = 'road fork'; Hau dûeřa *m.* (M4) [Zeb/Hej/ZF3//OK]

durust دوروست (IFb/B) = correct, true. See **dirust**.

durustî دوروستی (B) = correctness, truth. See **dirustî.**

duruv دوروڤ (A) = looks. See **dirûv**.

duřû I دوڕوو *adj.* two-faced, hypocritical. {also: [dou-rouï] دوروی (JJ)} {syn: salûs} Cf. P dūrū دورو [cf. clq Palestinian Ar muwajhan مـوجـهـن

< wajhēn وجهين = 'two faces' (dual); T ikiyüzlü] {dur̄ûtî; durûyî} [K/JB3/IFb/JJ/B/ZF3]

durû II دورووو (Mzg) = looks. See **dirûv**.

durûn دوروون (BK) = to sew. See **dirûtin.**

durûşm دوروووشم (Wkt) = slogan. See **dirûşm**.

dur̄ûtî دوڕووتى *f.* **(-ya;-yê).** hypocrisy, two-facedness: **•Dewleta tirk bi nijadperestiyê, bi binpêkirina mafên mirovan û bi *dur̄ûtiya* xwe êdî li cîhanê deng daye** (AW69C2) The Turkish state has made a name for itself in the world for its racism, its suppression of human rights and its *hypocrisy*. {also: durûyî (JB3/GF)} [K/IFb/JJ/B//JB3/GF/ZF3] <dur̄û I>

durûv دورووڤ (Srk/GF) = looks. See **dirûv**.

durûyî دوروويى (JB3/GF) = hypocrisy. See **dur̄ûtî.**

dusbe دوسبه (K) = the day after tomorrow. See **dusibe**.

du sed دوسەد (IF)/dused (K) = two hundred, 200. See **dusid**.

dusibe دوسِبه *adv.* the day after tomorrow: **-siba na duspa** (B) do. {also: dusbe (K-2); dusibê (F); duspa (B)} {syn: sibetir} [K/IF/JB1-S//F//B] <betrapêr; r̄ojtir>

dusibê دوسِبێ (F) = the day after tomorrow. See **dusibe**.

dusid دوسِد *num.* two hundred, 200. {also: du sed (IF); dused (K); dusud (F)} Skt dvé śaté; Av duye sa[i]te [B//K//IF//F] <sed>

duspa دوسپا (B) = the day after tomorrow. See **dusibe**.

dustan دوستان (A/IFb/GF) = trivet, tripod. See **dûstan**.

dusud دوسود (F) = two hundred, 200. See **Dusid**.

Duşem دوشەم *f.* **(-a;-ê).** Monday: **-Dûşemê** (Msr) on Monday; **-Duşemba ko bê** (JB3/IF) next Monday; **-Roja duşembê** (JB3/IF) Monday. {also: Duşemb (JB3/IF); Duşembe (K); Dûşem (Msr); [douchem دوشم /douchenbé دوشنبه] (JJ)} Cf. P dūšanbe دوشنبه; Sor dûşem[m]e دووشەممە/dûşembe دووشەمبە/dûşemû دووشەموو; Za dişeme (Todd/Lx) [F/A/B/Rh//JB3/IF//K//Msr/JJ]

Duşemb دوشەمب (JB3/IF) = Monday. See **Duşem.**

Duşembe دوشەمبه (K) = Monday. See **Duşem.**

duşirmiş دوشِرمِش (F). See **duşurmîş.**

duşirmîş دوشِرميش: **-duşirmîş bûn** (K/B) to think: **•Mêvan *duşurmîş dibe*: "Wextê hatim çir̄a ewî mir̄a go, ezrahîlê min"** (Dz, anecdote #26) The guest *thinks*, "When I came, why did he call me 'my Ezrail'?" {also: duşirmiş (F); duşurmîş (Dz); [dušürmíš دشرمش/dušümíš دشومش] (JJ)} {syn: fikirîn I; hizir kirin; p'onijîn [2]; r̄aman I} < T düşünmüş = 'having thought' [K/B//F//JJ]

duşivan دوشِڤان *m.* **().** shepherd's assistant: **•Keriyê me bi nîzam li dû şivan diçû û *duşivan* û zaro li herdu alî, vir da wê da, bazdidan, ne dihiştin ku nîzam xirab be û bi kopalên xwe an bi fîkandineke xas di nav kerî de ji her pezî re ciyê wî nîşan didan** (SW:Erebê Şemo. Şivanê Kurd, 42) Our flock would follow the shepherd in an orderly way, and *the assistants* and boys on both sides, here and there, would run, not letting the order be lost, and with their staffs or by whistling a signal they would show each sheep its place. [SW/GF/Wkt] <şivan>

duşk دوشك (K[s]) = sister-in-law. See **diş**.

duşmin دوشمِن (Ba2) = enemy. See **dijmin.**

duşminayî دوشمِنايى (B) = enmity. See **dijminahî.**

duşminî دوشمِنى (B) = enmity. See **dijminahî.**

duşmintî دوشمِنتى (B) = enmity. See **dijminahî.**

duşurmîş دوشورميش (Dz). See **duşirmîş.**

duwanzdehem دووانزدەهەم (GF/Wkt) = twelfth. See **dozdehem**.

duwanzdehemîn دووانزدەهەمين (Wkt) = twelfth. See **dozdehem**.

duwazdehem دووازدەهەم (CT) = twelfth. See **dozdehem**.

duwazdehemîn دووازدەهەمين (CT) = twelfth. See **dozdehem**.

duwêl I دووێل (GF/HH) = thread made of animal skin. See **duhêl**.

duwêl II دووێل (GF) = valley. See **dol II**.

duwem دووەم (CT/IFb) = second. See **duyem**.

duwemîn دووەمين (CT) = second. See **duyem**.

duwûm دوووم (K) = second. See **dudua**.

duxtmam دوختمام (JJ) = female cousin. See **dotmam.**

duxtor دوختۆر *m.&f.* **().** medical doctor, physician: **•Çare ewe biçime lalî *duxtorekî*, xo seqet bikem** (M-Ak, #632) The remedy was for me to go to *a doctor* and emasculate myself. {also: doxtir (K/B); duktor (SK)} {syn: bijîşk; ĥekîm; nojdar} <Lat doctor = 'teacher' < docēre = 'to teach' [M-Ak/OK//K/B//SK]

duyem دويەم *adj.* second (ordinal of **two**), 2nd. {also: **dudua**; duem (A); duhem (IFb-2); duhemîn (IFb-2/RZ); duwem (CT/IFb); duwemîn (CT-2); duyemîn (ZF-2/TF/Wkt-2)} Cf. P dovvom دوّم; Sor dûhem[în] دووهەم[ين]/duwem[în] دووەم[ين] [ZF/Wkt//TF//A//CT/IFb//RZ] <didû; du I>

duyemîn دويەمين (ZF/TF/Wkt) = second. See **duyem**.

dû I دوو = two. See **du I.**

dû II دوو *m.* **(-vê/-wê;).** 1) {syn: boç'[ik]; dêl II; doç'ik; k'ilk; kurî I (Bw); qemç[ik]; teřî I[1]} tail: •**Aqilê xwe ji *dûwê* rep hilîna** (Dz) She got her brains/cleverness from the protruding *tail* {Cf. expression "The lion's share"}; 2) back part (JJ); 3) fattail. {also: **daw I**; dûm; **dûv I**, f. (B)/m.; dûw; [dou دو /douï دوى] (JJ); <dûv> دوڤ (HH)} <O Ir *duma- (A&L p.84 [V]): Av duma-; Southern Tati dialects: Chali döma *f.*; Takestani & Eshtehardi döm(b) *m.*; Xiaraji & Sagz-abadi dömb *m.* = 'tail' (Yar-Shater); P dom دم/donb دنب; Sor dûg دووگ [Dz/A/IF/JJ//B/HH] See **daw I** & **dûv I.**

dû III دوو *prep.* after, behind: •***Bi dû* payiza jiyanê *re* koça dawîn** (MUs, 7) The final migration *after* the autumn of life •**Teyrê Sêmir *bi dû* mi *de* hat** (L) The Simurgh came *after* me [in pursuit]; -**[bi] dû k'etin** (JB1-A): a) to pursue, set out after: •***Bi dû* wan *ket*** (L) [She] *set out after* them; b) to strive for stg., be bent on stg.: •**Cahil *dû* xwendinê dik'evin** (B) The young people are *bent on* studying; -**dan dû/dû çûn/dû hatin/dû k'etin** = to follow, pursue: •**Ew *dû* birê xwe *k'et*** [=**Ewî *da dû* birê xwe**], **lê pêřa negihîşt** (B) He *set out after* his brother, but he could not catch up with him •**Min *da dû* bznê** (EH) I *followed* the goat; -**dû mayîn** (IF) to stay behind; -**dû xistin** (B) to send out after or in pursuit of, to sic: •**Me tank *dû* duşmin *xistin*** (B) We *sent* tanks *out after* the enemy; -**ji dû neqetîn** (ZF3) to stalk s.o. {also: dûv II (Bw); [dou دو/douï دوى] (JJ)} {syn: pey I} Sor dway دواى; Za dima (Todd); Hau dima = 'afterward' (M4) [K/IFb/B/JB1-A/SK/GF/ZF3//Bw] <dûřa>

dû IV دوو *m./f.(OK)* **(-[y]ê/;).** 1) {syn: dûk'el; dûman; kadû} smoke: •***Dû* ji kulekê bilind dibe** (AB) *Smoke* rises from the smokehole (in the roof) •**Ji *dûê* tendûra k'êranêd xanîya řeş bûbûn** (Ba2-3, 213) From *the smoke of* the ovens, the beams of the houses had turned black; -**dûyê çixarê** (Xrz) cigarette smoke; 2) {syn: dûk'el; tenî} soot (K). {also: [dou] دو (JJ); <dû> دو (HH)} [Pok. 4. dheu- 261.] base of a wide variety of derivatives meaning "to rise in a cloud" as dust, vapor, or smoke, and related to semantic notions of breath, etc.: O Ir *dūta- (A&L p.84 [IV, 2]): P dūd دود; Sor dû[d] دوو[د] = 'smoke'; Za dû *m.* (Mal) [K/A/JB3/IFb/B/JJ/HH/GF/TF/OK/ZF3] <dûk'el; tenî>

dûbişk دووبِشك (Msr) = scorpion. See **dûp'işk.**

dûçik دووچك (IF) = beard; tail. See **doç'ik.**

dûê دووئى (M-Shn) = second. See **dudua.**

dûhîn دووهين (FS) = curds. See **dohîn.**

dûhû دووهوو (JB1-A) = yesterday. See **dihî.**

dûje دووژه (Tsab) = hell. See **dojeh.**

dûjeh دووژه‌ه (Rnh) = hell. See **dojeh.**

dûkan دووكان (IFb) = shop. See **dik'an.**

dûk'el دووكه‌ل *f.(K/JB1-A/Dh)/m.(JB3)* **(-a/;-ê/).** 1) {syn: kadû} chimney smoke; thick, dark smoke; 2) {syn: hilm} steam, vapor; 3) soot *(thin layer [T is], as opposed to **tenî**, thick layer [T kurum])* (Elk/OK). {also: duk'êl (JB1-A/OK-2); dûkêl (JB3/IFb/OK)} Sor dûkeł دووكه‌ڵ; Hau dûkeł *m.* (M4) [K/A/TF/Elk//JB3/IFb/OK/ZF3//JB1-A] <dû IV>

dûkêl دووكێل (JB3/IFb/OK) = smoke. See **dûk'el.**

dûlop دوولۆپ (Cxn) = drop *(of a liquid).* See **dilop.**

dûm دووم = tail; fattail. See **daw I** & **dû II.**

dûmahî دووماهى *f.* **(-ya;-yê).** end, result: •**Eger xudê řizqek da min zor şukr, û eger neda dîsa řazî me bi irada wî. Bila bimirim, elbette *dûmaîya* hemîyan mirin e** (SK 4:31) If God should grant me my sustenance I shall be most thankful, and even if He should not I shall still be happy to obey His will. Let me die, for certainly death is *the end of* all; -**ê/-a dûmahîkê** (Bw) last, final. {also: dûmahîk (Bw-2/IFb/GF); dûmaî (SK); dûmayî (K); [doumahi] دوماهى (JJ)} {syn: dawî; talî II} [Bw/OK/SS//SK//K//IFb/GF]

dûmahîk دووماهيك (Bw/IFb/GF) = end. See **dûmahî.**

dûmaî دوومائى (SK) = end. See **dûmahî.**

dûman دوومان *f.* **(-a;-ê).** 1) {syn: mij; moran; xumam, f. (JB3)} mist, fog: •[When they learned of Mem and Zîn's deaths] **Ber ç'e'vê Qeret'ajdîn û birava bû *dûman*** (Z-1) It became *foggy* before the eyes of Q. and his brothers; -**mij û dûman** (Ba2) do.: •**nava *mij û dûmanê*da** (Ba2) amid *dense fog*; 2) {syn: dû IV; kadû} smoke (IFb/GF): •**Dema ku wî qelûna pêşîn ji titûnê dagirt, dema ku agir berdayê û *dûman* bi ser xist** (Epl, 7) When he filled the first pipe with tobacco, when he lit it and *smoke* rose from it; 3) dust (HH). {also: [douman] دومان (JJ); <dûman> دومان (HH)} < T duman = 'smoke' --> Rus tuman туман = 'fog' [Z-1/K/JB3/IFb/B/JJ/HH/GF/OK/ZF] <dûk'el>

dûmaqesk دووماقه‌سك (A) = swallow (bird) . See **dûmeqesk.**

dûmayî دوومايى (K) = end. See **dûmahî.**

dûmeqesk دوومەقەسك *f.* **(-a;-ê).** swallow *(bird)*, zool. *Hirundo*: •***Dûmeqeskê* danî ser darê** (B) *The swallow* alighted on the tree. {also: dûmaqesk (A)} {syn: ḧacḧacik; meqesork (F); qerneqûçik (IF)} [F/K/B/IF/ZF3/Wkt//A]

dûn دوون (OK) = to smear. See **dûtin.**

dûndan دووندان *f.* **(-a;-ê).** offspring, descendants, progeny: •**Beybûn *dûndana* Nêçîrvanî û Xezalê bû** (MG. Jiyaneka pêguhork) B. was *the offspring of* N. and Kh. •**Dibêjin du birayêt êk bûn, êk yê dewlemend û kedxuda bû ... lê y[ê] *bê dûndeh û zêdehî* bû** (Bêhnişk, 47) They say there were 2 brothers, one was rich and a village chief ... but he was *childless*. {also: dundan (TF); dûndeh (AA/Bêhnişk)} {syn: dol I; zêdehî; zuřet II} Cf. Sor dûdman دوودمان = 'hearth, family' [IFb/GF/OK//TF//AA/Bêhnişk] <bê dûnde>

dûndeh دوینده‌ه/دووندەه (AA/Bêhnişk) = offspring. See **dûndan.**

dûp'işk دووپشك *f./m.(B/SK)* **(-a/ ;-ê/).** 1) scorpion, zool. Scorpionida: •**Paşî *dûpişk* hat e pêş, got, "Zerera min ewe ye. Ez her wextê bigem e wan bi wan we-didem. Şûna duroşûşika min bi laê kêmîwe deh sa'etan diêşît û hindek jî pê dimirin. Û hemban û meşk û qazan û amanêt sifr jî bi-kun dikem"** (SK 1:5) Then *the scorpion* came forward and said, "This is my injury. Whenever I (can) reach them I sting them. The place of my sting hurts for at least ten hours and some even die from it. And I puncture grain sacks and leather churns and cooking-pots and even copper vessels"; 2) Scorpio (astr.). {also: dupişk (F); dûbişk (Msr); [douw-pichk] دوف پشك (JJ); <dûpişk> دوپشك (HH)} Sor dûpişk دووپشك [K/A/JB3/IFb/HH/SK/GF/OK//F//JJ//Msr]

dûr دویر/دوور [Bw] *adj.* 1) {≠nêzîk} [+ **ji** or -î] far, distant, remote *(from)*: •***dûrî* gund** (L) *far from* the village •**Gundda mal *dûrî* hev hatibûne ava kirinê** (Ba2) In the village the houses had been built *far from* each other •**K'êleka Zîna *xwe dûr nak'eve*** (Z-1) He doesn't *go far* from his Zîn's side; **-dûrva** (K/B)/**ji dûrve** (BX/GF) in the distance, from afar: •**Memê gelekî ji cotk'arî *dûr k'etibû*, dîna xwe da, dûrva sîyarekî wê daye pey kareke xezala** (Z-1, 52) When Mem *had gotten* very *far* from the farmer, he looked and saw in the distance someone mounted on a horse pursuing a fawn; **-dûr kirin** (K/ZF)/~ [ê]**xistin** (K/B) to remove, move or take way, alienate, dismiss, exile: •**Bi vê fermanê re balbas diçin radihêjin piyê xort, ji wir *dûrdixin* ku êdî bibin fermana mezinê malmezinan bi cî bînin** (Ardû, 119) At this order the men go and grab the young man by his feet, *take* him *away* to carry out the order of the chief •**Hin ji wan kuştine û hin jî girtine ji Kurdistanê *dûr xistine*** (Bkp, 7) They killed some of them and they captured some and *exiled them* from Kurdistan; **-dûr û dirêj** (GF/ZF/RZ) detailed, lengthy, drawn out, prolonged {also: dûvdirêj (TF/ZF-2)}: •**Jixwe angaştên di vî warî de *dûr û dirêj* in** (Nbh 125:16) Claims in this field [or, matter] are *lengthy*; 2) unlikely, improbable: •**Hingê eger xulaman destê koçer ne girtî bûna, *ne dûr bû* ko di navçava mîr da jî danîna** (JB2-O.Sebrî/Rnh 14 [1943] 8-9) Then, if the servants had not caught hold of the nomad's hands, *it was not unlikely* that he would have hit into the emir's forehead. {also: [dour] دور (JJ); <dûr> دور (HH)} [Pok. 3. deu- 219.] 'long'--> *dewH- > duH (dū) + ra: Skt dūra-; O Ir *dūra-: P dūr دور; Sor dûr دوور; Za dûrî (Todd)/dûr (Hadank); Hau dûr (M4); cf. Av dav- = 'to make far' [entfernen] {dûrahî; dûrakî; dûranî; dûrayî; dûrî} [K/A/JB3/IFb/B/JJ/HH/GF/TF/OK/ZF]

dûřa دووڕا [K]/**dûra** دوورا [A/IFb] *adv.* afterward, later, then: •**Gelekî li ser difikire û *dûre* biryar dide ku dikare li ser biyografyaya A. Ö. binivîse** (AW75B6) He thinks about it a lot and *later* decides that he can right about the life [lit. 'biography'] of A. O. •**Leşkeran *dûre* 38 kesên li gund dan ber lêdanê û ew birin qereqola jandirme ya navçeyê** (CTV 190) *After that* the soldiers subjected 38 people in the village to beatings and took them to the regional police station •**Soysal 12 roj berê ji aliyê dewleta Moldova ve hate girtin û *dûre*-jî teslimê Tirkiyê hate kirin** (CTV 182) Soysal was arrested 12 days earlier by the state of Moldova and *later* was handed over to Turkey. {also: dû re (IFb-2)} {syn: paşê; şûnda} dû III + -řa [K/A/IFb] <dû III>

dûrahî دوورایی (IFb/GF) = distance. See **dûrî.**

dûrakî دووراکی (JB3) = distance. See **dûrî.**

dûranî دوورانی (K) = distance. See **dûrî.**

dûrayî دوورایی (K/A/B/GF/TF) = distance. See **dûrî.**

dûrbên دووربێن = binoculars. See **dûrbîn.**

dûrbîn دووربین *f.* **(;-ê).** binoculars; spy-glass,

telescope: •*Dorbîn* **da ber çavê xwe** (L) [She] looked into *the telescope* [lit. 'put/gave a telescope before her eyes'] •**Mamê Rezgo çû serê girî, *bi dûrbînê* temaşay deştê kir, dît lawekî taze li serê deştê der-kewt** (SK 37:327) Mam Razgo went to the top of a hillock and scanned the plain *with his binoculars*. He saw a likely lad appear across the plain. {also: dorbîn (L); durbîn (IF-2); dûrbên; dûrebîn (EP-7/TF); [dour-bin] دوربين (JJ); <dûrbîn> دوربين (HH)} Cf. P dūrbīn دوربين = '(orig.) that which sees far' --> T dürbün [F/K/A/IFb/B/JJ/HH/GF//L//EP-7/TF]

dûrdest دووردهست *adj.* unattainable, unreachable, unavailable: •...**Û heger îro ev yeke *dûrdest* be** (F.'Umar: "Pêkolek bo vavartina zimanê nivîsînê," *Peyv* 1 [1993], 17) And if today this is *unattainable*. {also: <dûrd[e]st> دوردست (HH)} [Peyv/IFb/HH/GF] <berdest II>

dû re دوو ره (IFb) = afterward. See **dûr̄a**.

dûrebîn دووره‌بين (EP-7/TF) = binoculars. See **dûrbîn.**

dûrge دوورگه (K[s]/JB3/ZF3/Wkt) = (small) island. See **dûrgeh.**

dûrgeh دوورگه‌ه *f.* **(-a;-ê).** island. {also: dûrge (K[s]/JB3/ZF3/Wkt-2)} {syn: ada; cizîr; girav II} Sor dûrge دوورگه [IF/Wkt//K(s)/JB3/ZF3]

dûrik دوورك *f.* **(-a;-ê).** short song, tune, (sung) couplet; melody (A/IF); little song, couplet, dance song (HM): •**Emê her-yek *dûrekekî* bavînin li-ser Mamu Alan** (HM) Each one of us will sing M.A. *a short song* [lit. 'throw a song on M.A.']; **-dûrika miriya** (IFb) dirge, lament, funeral song. {also: [dūréka] دورك (HM)} Cf. Za dêr *f.* = 'song' (Todd) [HM/K/A/IFb/ZF3] <dîlan; k'ilam; stiran I>

dûrî دووری *f.* **(-ya;).** distance; farness, remoteness. {also: dûrahî (IFb-2/GF-2); dûrakî (JB3); dûranî (K-2); dûrayî (K-2/A/B/GF-2/TF)} [K/JB3/IFb/GF/ZF3//A/B/TF]

dûrkuj دووركوژ *adj.* beautiful from afar, but ugly up close. {also: <dûrkuj> دووركوژ (Hej)} [Dh/Zeb/Hej]

dûstan دووستان *f.* **(;-ê).** trivet, tripod, each of three stones supporting a cooking pot over the fire [Ar uṯfīyah اثفية; T üçayak]: •**Sê bra ne: hersê bra zikreş [*dûstan*]** (L #13, 232) Three brothers, all three with black bellies *[rdl.: ans.: tripod]*. {also: distan (GF-2); dîstan (IFb-2); dostan (GF-2); dustan (A/IFb/GF); <dostan> دۆستان (Hej)} {syn: kuçik II[2]; sêp'î [1]} [L/K/ZF3//A/IFb/GF]

Dûşem دووشهم (Msr) = Monday. See **Duşem.**

dûtin دووتن *vt.* **(-dû-).** to coat, daub, plaster, smear *(with plaster, clay, mud, etc.)*: •**Qesir p'aqij kirin** [sic] **u hinik ĥer̄î têdan, *dûtin*** ... (JB1-S, #197) They tidied up the castle and spread some mud and *coated* [the floor with it]. {also: dûn (OK-2); <dûtin> دووتن (Hej)} {syn: seyandin} Cf. P andūdan اندودن (-andā-) (اندا) = 'to plaster, [be]smear' [JB1-S/GF/OK/Hej] <sewax; têdan>

dûtir دووتر (GF) = the next day. See **dotir**.

dûv I دووڤ *m.(AB)/f.(K)* **(-ê/ ; /-ê).** 1) *(fatty-)*tail, fattail: •***Dûvê* beranê me gir e** (AB) Our ram's *fattail* is big •**Derxwînê beroşê, dermanê girarê [*Dûv*]** (L[1937]) Cover of the pot, seasoning of the soup *[rdl.; ans.: sheep's fattail]*; 2) tail: •**Hema zaro şûrê xwe avêt ser *dûvê* marî, *dûvê* marî peritand** (KH, 34) The child immediately swung his sword at the snake's *tail*, and severed the snake's *tail*. {also: **daw I**; **dû II**; dûm; dûw; [douw] دوف (JJ); <dûv> دوف (HH)} {syn: ter̄î I[2]} <O Ir *duma- (A&L p. 84 [V]): Av duma-; P dom دم/donb دنب; Sor dûg دووگ [AB/K/JB3/IF/B/JJ/HH] <boç'[ik]; dêl II; doç'ik> See **daw I** & **dû II**.

dûv II دووڤ/ دويڤ (Bw) = after, behind. See **dû III**.

dûvdirêj دووڤدرێژ (TF/ZF) = detailed, lengthy. See **dûr: -dûr û dirêj**.

dûw دووو = tail. See **daw I**, **dû II** & **dûv I.**

dûwazde دوووازده (Msr) = twelve. See **donzdeh.**

dûwê دوووێ (JB1-A) = second. See **dudua**.

dûz دووز *adj.* 1) flat, even, level, straight (K/IF/HH): •**Hîvya kesî nes[e]kinî, hema devê xwe ajot *dûz* hat ser warê xwe** (EP-5, #18) She waited for nobody, but rode her camel [and] came *straight* to her camp; 2) [*f.* ().] plain; flat, level land (JJ/B). {also: [douz] دوز (JJ); <dûz> دوز (HH)} < T düz = 'flat, straight' [Z-1/K/IF/B/JJ/HH]

dûzan دووزان, m. (-ê; dûzîn) (K/B/FJ) = razor. See **gûzan**.

dwanzde دوانزده (JB1-S/M-Ak & Shn)/dwanẕde دوانظده (JB1-A) = twelve. See **donzdeh.**

dwanzdehemîn دوانزدهه‌مين (GF) = twelfth. See **dozdehem**.

dwanẕdey دوانزده‌ى (JB1-A) = twelve. See **donzdeh.**

dwazde دوازده (Msr/SK/HH/M-Sur)/dwaẕde دواظده (M-Zx & Gul) = twelve. See **donzdeh.**

dwê دوێ (M-Sur&Ak) = second. See **dudua**.

dwîn دوين (IFb) = fat, grease. See **don.**

E ئه & 'E عه

-e ه *prep.* to: *only occurs in conjunction with a verb and is realized as an enclitic [written •e in the sample sentences below]*: **•Em êvarê p'ere k'axaza cigarê bikn•*e* bin doşeka Ûsib** (Ba) This evening we will place a sheet of cigarette paper under Joseph's mattress **•Hakim B. anî, xist•*e* odakê mezin** (L) The king took B. [and] put him *in* a large room **•Hatin•*e* dîwana mîr Sevdîn** (Z-1) They came *to* prince Sevdin's court **•Hespê brangê min bivn•*e* extexanê** (EP-7) Bring my brother's horse *to* the stable **•Lê bi şabûna Memê ... nan û av nak'evn•*e* bîra wan** (EP-7) From [so much] rejoicing over Mem ... they forgot about food [lit. 'bread'] and water [lit. 'bread and water don't fall *into* their memory'] **•Paşê tên•*e* meydanê** (J) Then they come *to* the square / battlefield **•Vegeryan•*e* mal** (Ba) They returned home; **-e ... da** (HR) into: **•Emê wî kine ç'al•*ê da*** (HR 3:186) We will put him *into* the ditch. O Ir *abi > Mid P etc. ō (M3), Kurdish -e? [M/SK]

e ئه (Ad) = I, me. See **ez**.

'eba عەبا *f./m.(ZF3)* **(-ya/-yê;).** aba, cloak-like woolen wrap; wide, straight-cut cloak of coarse wool (B): **•Bila peşk neyên min û bila *ebayê* min nelewite** (A.Bingöl [FB] 4.v.2012) No drops should come [=splash] on me and my *aba* should not be soiled. {also: eb•e (•a/•eya; •ê) (BK); 'ebe (B); [âba] عبا (JJ)} < Ar 'abā'(ah) عباء(ة) [K/IF/JJ/ZF3//BK//B]

'ebabet عەبابەت (EP-7) = worship. See **ebabetî**.

ebabetî عـەبـابـەتـی *f.* **(-ya;).** worship; religious devotion: **•Ya dara miraza ... me hîvî heye wekî tu *ebabetîya* me bîrnekî** (JB2-Şamilov) O tree of wishes ... we hope that you will not forget our *devotion*. {also: 'ebabet (EP-7)} ?< Ar 'ibādah عبادة = 'worship' [EP-7//K/JB2]

ebadile ئەبادِلە/**'ebadile** عەبادِلە [K] *f.* **(;-ê).** people, folk: **•Tu jî dinerî go *ebadilê* hev du xwarin hengî digirîn û hengî li xwe dixin** (L-I, #4, 116, l. 17-18) You too can see how *the people* have gone mad [lit. 'have eaten each other up'] from so much weeping and beating themselves. {syn: xelq} < Ar 'ibād Allāh عباد الله = 'slaves of Allah, human beings' [L/K] <gel; net'ewe>

'ebd عەبد (K) = slave. See **'evd I**.

'ebdal عەبدال/**ebdal** ئەبدال [IFb/OK] *m.(Bw)* **().** quail, zool. *Coturnix coturnix*; male francolin quail (FS). {also: avdel (FS)} {syn: k'êrasû; kutefir} Sor 'ewdał عـەوداڵ = 'cock-partridge' [Bw/RF//IFb/OK//FS] <kew I; lorî I; p'or I>

ebe ئـەبـە (BK)/'ebe عـەبـە (B) = aba, type of woolen cloak. See **'eba**.

'eborî عەبۆری (Xrz) = girl's headscarf. See **ĥibrî**.

ebreşûm ئەبرەشووم (F) = silk. See **hevirmiş**.

***'ebrik** عەبرِك *f.* **().** raft. {syn: kelek I; k'erx}< Ar √'-b-r عبر = 'to pass, cross' [Haz]

ebrî ئەبری (GF) = girl's headscarf. See **ĥibrî**.

ebro ئەبرۆ = eyebrow. See **birû**.

ebrû ئەبروو (A) = eyebrow. See **birû**.

ebûkat ئەبووكات (OK) = lawyer. See **ebûqat**.

ebûqat ئـەبـووقـات *m.&f.* **(-ê/-a; /-ê).** lawyer, attorney: **•"Ezê bibim rojnamevan. Na! Na! Ezê bibim *ebûqat*, an hakim an jî doktor"** (Wlt 2:103, 16) I'll become a journalist [when I grow up]. No, wait! I'll be a *lawyer*, or a judge or a doctor. {also: ebûkat (OK)} <T avukat <Fr avocat <Lat advocatus = 'lawyer, counselor [lit. 'one who has been called up']' [(neol)Wlt/IFb/ZF3/BF//OK] <dadgeh; dozger>

'ebûr عـەبـوور *m./f.* **(-ê/-a;).** subsistence, sustenance, livelihood, living, getting by; means of supporting o.s.: **•...Ew şorbe difroşe, *'ebûra* wî ew şorbeye** (HCK-5, #41, 230) He sells soup, that soup is his *livelihood*; **-'ebûr kirin** = a) to support (one's family) {syn: debirandin}: **•Ji mêşe dar danî dihatin pê roj bi roj *'ebûrê* zarê xwe *dikir*** (Z-922) He brought wood from the forest and *supported* his children with (=by means of) it; b) to live, subsist (on stg.); **-'ebûrê xwe kirin** = to keep o.s. alive, make ends meet: **•Bi vî t'eherî Ûsib *'ebûrê xwe dike*, namire** (Ba) In this way Joseph *keeps himself alive*, he doesn't die. {also: [abour/oubour] عـبـور (JJ)} {syn: debar} < Ar 'ubūr عبور = 'crossing, traversing' [Ba/Z-1/K/JB3/B/JJ] <aborî; debirandin>

ebûrî ئـەبـووری (K)/'ebûrî عـەبـووری (K) = living, life, existence. See **aborî** [3].

ecac ئەجاج (GF/ZF) = cloud of dust. See **hecac**.

ecayîb ئـەجـايـيـب (IFb) = miracle; wonder; strange. See

'ecêb.

'ecem عەجەم /**ecem** ئەجەم [IFb/JB3] *m.* (). Persian, Iranian (person): •**Çû ba şahê *'ecemo*** (EP-8) He went to the *Persian* king; -**jina 'ecem** (K) Persian woman; -**zimanê 'ecema[n]** (K) Persian language, language of the Persians. {also: [âdjem] عجم (JJ)} {syn: Far[i]s} < Ar 'ajam عجم = 'non-Arabs, Persians' [EP-8/K/B/JJ//IFb/JB3]

'ecer عەجەر/**ecer** ئەجەر *adj.* new, fresh: •**Makîna te *ecer* lê kevn e?** (Efr) Is your car used [lit. '*new* but old']? {also: acer (Wkt-2); ecere (AD-2); hecer (Wkt-2)} {syn: nû; t'aze} <Clq Ar 'ajer عجر = 'unripe, sour (fruit)' --> T acar/acer = 'new; fresh' (DS, v. 1, p. 38) [Efr/AD/ZF3/RZ/Wkt]

ecere ئەجەرە (AD) = new. See **'ecer**.

'ecêb عەجێب/**ecêb** ئەجێب [IFb/JB3] *f.* **(-a;-ê)**. 1) {syn: gosirmet; k'eramet} marvel, wonder, wondrous thing (K/B/JJ); miracle (JJ): •**Kuro, ev ne *ecêb* e. *Ecêb* ev go zilamek heye, jê re dibêjin B., di şevekê de, hûtek kuştîye û çel keleş jî** (L) Boy, this is no *wonder*. *The wonder* is that there's a man called B. who killed a monster and 40 brigands, all in one night; 2) {syn: qezîya} misfortune, bad luck (K): •**Te *'ecêb* anî serê min** (K) You brought/visited *misfortune* on me •**Boẍ *'ecêbeke* wa anî serê min** (J) The bull brought a *misfortune* such as this on me [lit. 'on my head'] •**Mala we t'imê *'ecêbê* giran dest mala me dîne** (Z-1) Your family always brings great *misfortune* on my family; 3) [*adj.*] {syn: seyr} strange (IFb/JB1-S); 4) amazing (K/JB3/IFb); 5) amazed, astonished, surprised, speechless: -**'ecêb man** (K/HH)/**mayîn** (B/IFb) [+ **ser**] to be amazed (at): •**Ew ḧişyar dibe û *ser* xewna xwe *'ecêv dimîne*** (Ba-1, #21) He wakes up and *is amazed at* (=troubled by) his dream •**Mîr *ser* aqilbendîya Ûsib *'ecêb dimîne*** (Ba-1, #22) The emir *is amazed at* (=admires) Joseph's intelligence; 6) terrible (B). {also: 'acaib (JB1-S); ecayîb (IFb-2); ecêv; 'ecêv; [adjib عجيب / agiaib عجايب] (JJ); <'ecêb> عجيب (HH)} < Ar 'ajīb عجيب [K/B/JJ/JB1-S//JB3/IFb]

'ecêbmayî عەجێبمایی/**ecêbmayî** ئەجێبمایی [JB3/IFb] *adj.* amazed, astonished, astounded, surprised: -**'ecêbmayî man** = to be amazed at {syn: guhişîn; ḧeyrîn; met'elmayî bûn}: •**Bedewîya qîzikê *'ecêbmayî dimîne*** (J) She *is amazed at* the girl's beauty. {syn: hicmetî; ḧeyrî; ḧêbetî; mendehoş; met'elmayî; şaşmayî} [J/K//JB3/IFb] <'ecêb; guhişîn>

ecêv ئەجێڤ/'ecêv عەجێڤ = miracle; wonder; strange. See **'ecêb**.

'ecibandin عەجباندِن/**ecibandin** ئەجباندِن [JB3/IFb] *vt.* **(-'ecibîn-)**. 1) {syn: begem kirin; k'êf hatin} to like, appreciate (K/JB3/IFb): •**Ya qîza hakim, te *ez ecibandim*?** (L) O princess, *do* [lit. 'did'] you *like me*?; 2) {syn: begem kirin [4]} to choose, pick; 3) to consider strange (IFb). {also: [adjibandin] عجيباندين (JJ); <'ecibandin عجباندن (di'ecibîne) (دعجبينه)> (HH)} < Ar a'jaba IV أعجب = 'to please, find favor with' [Frq/L/K/JJ/HH//JB3/IFb]

ecinî ئەجِنی (Z-2) = jinn, genie. See **cin**.

'eciqandin عەجِقاندِن/**eciqandin** ئەجِقاندِن [IFb/ZF3/Wkt/CS] *vt.* **(-'eciqîn-)**. 1) {syn: dan ber lingan; dewisandin; her̄işandin; p'ekandin; p'elaxtin; p'erçiqandin; pêpes kirin; t'episandin} to trample, crush, squash (underfoot): •**Şer û pevçûnên li Sûriyê, herî zêde xelkê sivîl *dieciqîne* û perîşan û şerpeze dike** (Çınarın Sesi 29.x.2013) The war and battles in Syria *crush* the civilian population and make them miserable •**Wesayîta zirxî perçeyên aîdî bedena mirovan *dieciqîne*** (mezopotamyaajansi.com 15.ix.2017) A tank *crushes* human body parts; 2){syn: derkirin} to lance (a boil), pop (a zit): •**Wî kulka piyê xwe *'eciqand*** (FS) He *lanced* the boil on his foot. <Ar 'ajjaqa II عجّق = 'to perplex, inconvenience, hinder' [FS/GF//IFb/ZF3/Wkt/CS] <'eciqîn>

'eciqîn عەجِقین/**eciqîn** ئەجِقین [ZF3/Wkt/CS] *vi.* **(-'eciq-)**. 1) to be trampled, crushed, squashed; to be oppressed, suffer: •**Bi salan e jin di bin serdestiya mêr de *dieciqe*** (RewanBêj 8.iii.2016) For years women *have been suffering* under the domination of men; 2) to pop, ripen (of boil): •**Kulka piyê wî *'eciqî*** (FS) The boil on his foot *popped*. [FS/GF//ZF3/Wkt/CS] <'eciqandin>

'eciz عەجِز (Z-2) = unhappy; tired of. See **aciz**.

***ecî** ئەجی *f.* (). grandmother, grandma, grannie. {syn: dapîr; pîrik} [HB]

ecnî ئەجنی (Z-2) = jinn, genie. See **cin**.

'ecûr عەجوور/**ecûr** ئەجوور *m.(FS/CS)/f.(ZF)* **(-ê/;)**. type of cucumber; gherkin, bot. *Cucumis anguria*: -**'Ecûrê tehl e** (Kmc) It is compulsory/You have no choice in it [lit. 'It is a bitter gherkin']/It's a hard pill to swallow. {*also*: acûr (A/IFb/CS/CCG); 'encûr (G/Wkt); incûr (ZF3)} {*syn*: qitik} <Ar

‘ajjūr عــجّــور = 'type of green melon'; T acur = 'gherkin'; = Sor tirozî تِــــرۆزی [Qzl/GF/FS//FJ/ZF/Wkt/ /CCG/A/IFb/CS//G//ZF3]

eçî ئەچی (Srk) = ring, hook. See **heçî I**.

‘edab عــەداب/**edab** ئــەداب [IFb/ZF3] *f.* **(-a;-ê).** pus, matter. {also: edap (TF); edav (Hk); ‘edeb (K); [ādāp (G/Rh)] اداپ (JJ); <‘edab> عـــــداب (HH); <‘edab> عـــەداب (Hej)} {syn: k’êm II; nêm} [Hk/ /HH/GF/Hej//IFb/OK/ZF3//TF//JJ//K]

edap ئەداپ (TF) = pus. See **‘edab**.

edav ئەداڤ (Hk) = pus. See **‘edab**.

‘edeb I عــەدەب/**edeb** ئــەدەب [IFb/JB3] *f.* **(-a;-ê).** 1) {also: ‘edebî II (B)} (good) manners, good breeding (K/B/IF); politeness, courtesy (JJ/JB3): **•*‘Edeba* şeherê wan usa bû** (EP-4) Such was *the custom* of their city [*or* Such were *the manners*...] **•Hûn *edeba* xweda bisekinin** (HCK-3, #2, 23) Mind your *manners*!; **-di cihê edebê da sekinîn** (HR) to stand in the place appropriate to one’s position (of servants): ***•Di cihê edebê da bisekne!*** (HR 4:25) *Stay in your proper place*; 2) *[adj.]* polite, well-mannered, well brought up (B). {also: [edeb] ادب (JJ); <edeb> ادب (HH)} < Ar adab أدب = 'good manners'; Sor edeb ئــەدەب = ‘manners, decorum; literature, culture’ [EP-4/K/B//IFb/JB3/JJ/HH/ZF]

‘edeb II عەدەب (K) = pus. See **‘edab**.

edebiyat ئــەدەبِــيــات *f.* **(-a;-ê).** literature: **•Beşa *edebiyata* klasîk a înstîtuyê li ser wan dixebite** (AW71D5) The Classical *Literature* Department of the institute is working on them **•Haşîm Ehmedzade ji rojhilatê welêt e. Li bajarê Upsala rûdine û yek ji çend kesan e ku li ser dabaşên *edebiyatê* şareza û bi kapasîte ye** (AW69D3) Hashim Ahmadzadeh is from the eastern part of the country [=Iranian Kurdistan]. He lives in the city of Uppsala and is one of several experts on matters *of literature*. {also: ‘edebîyet (K/B); ‘edebyet (B-2)} {syn: t’oȓe[2]; wêje} < Ar adabīyāt أدبيات = ' literature, belles-lettres'; [IFb/ZF/ RZ//K/B]

edebiyatnas ئەدەبِياتناس *m.* **(-ê;).** literary scholar: **•Di vî warî de *edebiyatnasê* kurd Mehmed Uzun wiha nivîsiye** (YPA, 12) In this field the Kurdish *scholar* M. Uzun has written as follows. [YPA/Wkt] <t’oȓevan>

edebî I ئــەدەبــی/**‘edebî** عــەدەبــی [K] *adj.* literary: **•Kovara hunerî, *edebî* û çandî Nûdem bi hejmara xwe ya 29'an derkete pêşberî xwendevanên xwe** (AW72B5) Nûdem, the artistic, *literary*, and cultural journal, has presented its readers with its 29th issue. {also: ‘edebî (K)} {syn: wêjeyî} [IFb/GF/ZF3//K]

‘edebî II عەدەبی (B) = good manners. See **‘edeb** [1].

‘edebîyet عەدەبییەت (K/B) = literature. See **edebiyat**.

edebxan•e ئەدەبخانە *f.* **(•eya;•ê).** 1) {syn: avdestxane; avȓêj I; ç’olik III (Msr); daşir (Dy); destavxane; qedemge (Czr)} toilet, water closet, lavatory; 2) school (SK); 3) brothel (K). {also: ‘edebxane (K[s]); <edebxane> ادبــخـانـه (HH)} [IFb/HH/SK/ZF3// K(s)]

‘edebyet عەدەبیەت (B) = literature. See **edebiyat**.

‘edet عـــەدەت (K/B) /edet ئـــەدەت (F) = custom; habit. See **‘adet**.

‘edil عــــەدِل/**edil** ئـــەدِل [IFb/HB/ZF3] *f.* (). 1) {syn: kelik; sebet; zembîl} large basket (HB); 2) {syn: sewî [1]} basket used in gathering grapes (IFb/ HH). {also: <‘idl> عــــــدل (HH)} [HB/IFb/ZF3//HH] <mekev>

‘edilandin عـەدِلانـدن/**edilandin** ئـەدِلانـدن [IFb/TF] *vt.* **(-‘edilîn-).** 1) to arrange, dispose, fix up (K); to organize, bring into order (K/B): **•Saz û sazbendê xwe *bi‘edlînin*** (Z-2) *Set up* [*Tune*?] your sazes [musical instruments] and your saz players; 2) to calm, pacify, soothe (K/B); 3) {syn: serȓast kirin} to correct (Mdt/IFb/TF). < Ar ‘addala II عـدّل = 'to set in order' [Z-2/K/B/Mdt//IFb/JB3/TF]

‘edilîn عـەدِلـيـن/**edilîn** ئـەدِلـيـن [IFb/TF/ZF/CS] *vt.* **(-‘edil-).** 1) to be orderly, be put in order; 2) to stop, stand still, sit still: **•Eskerê ku ‘ecele dihat, nişkêva *cîyê xweda ‘edilî*, kesî turiş nekir pêşda bê** (H.Cindî. Hewarî, 151) The army that was quickly advancing, suddenly *stopped in its tracks*, no one dared to advance **•Serê wî li ser stuyê wî yê zehîfoçkî *nediedilî*** (SBx, 13) His head *did not sit still* on his weak neck; 3) to calm down; to die down *(wind)*: **•Ba *‘edilîye*** (B) The wind *has died down*. {also: <‘edilîn عـدلـيـن (di‘edilî) (دعـدلـی)> (HH)} < Ar ‘adala (i) عـدل = ‘to be equal’ [SBx/ IFb/ TF/ZF/CS//K/B/HH/Tsab]

‘edr I عەدر (Zx) = land. See **‘erd**.

‘edr II عــەدر (GF/FS)/ edr ئــەدر (IFb) = epilepsy. See **‘edro**.

‘edro عـــەدرۆ *f.* **(;-ê).** epilepsy: **•*‘Edrê* ew girt** (FS) S/he had an epileptic fit [lit. '*Epilepsy* took hold of him/her']. {also: adir (TF); edr (IFb); ‘edr II (GF)} {syn: tep I} = Sor fê فێ [Ag//GF/FS//IFb//TF] 'edu عەدو (HCK) = enemy; competitor. See **'edû**.

'edû عـەدوو/**edû** ئـەدوو [Tsab-2/CS] *m.* **(-[y]ê;).** 1) {syn: dijmin; neyar} enemy, foe: **•*'edûyê* serî** (K) arch *enemy*, sworn *enemy* **•Xwedê zane *'eduê* vî şeherî heye, tiştek hatîye serê vî şeherî** (HCK-2, 181) God knows this city has *an enemy*, something has happened to this city; 2) {syn: hevrik; neyar} competitor, rival. {also: adu (IFb); 'edu (HCK); [adouv] عـــدو (JJ)} < Ar 'adūw عـــدو = 'enemy' [HCK//K/Tsab//CS//JJ//IFb]

'efad عەفاد (FS) = hero. See **'efat**.

'efare عـەفـارە/**efare** ئـەفارە [A/IFb/TF/CCG] *f.* **().** 1) {syn: k'ozer I; *xiz} coarse chaff, waste product from threshing floor; dirt picked up together with wheat while being harvested; remnants of grain after threshing and winnowing; 2) unpicked fruit left on trees after harvest (HH/FS): **•Wan sêvên *'efare* bi dara ve hêlan** (FS) They left those *unpicked* apples on the trees. {also: hifare (GF); 'ifare (GF-2)/ifare (Kmc); 'ufare (Qzl); <'efare> عـفـاره (HH)} <Ar 'afārah عـفـارة = 'gleaning' [Qzl//HH/FS//A/IFb/TF/ZF/CCG//GF] <belim>

'efat عـــەفـــات *m.* **().** hero, brave man (EP-7/B/K); warrior (K): **-'erfat û 'egît** (EP-7) do.: **•*'Erfat û 'egîtê* wê [=Cizîrê] 'Erfan, Ç'ekan û Qeret'ajdîne** (EP-7) Its [=Jezirah's] *heroes* are Erfan, Chekan, and Qeretajdin. {also: 'efad (FS-2); 'erfad (EP-7); 'erfat (EP-7)} {syn: 'egît; fêris; gernas; leheng; mêrxas; p'elewan} [EP-7/FS//B/K]

'efo عەفۆ (JB1-A) = pardon. See **'efû**.

'efrandin عەفراندِن (K/B)/efrandin ئەفراندِن (Ber/F) = to create. See **afirandin**.

Efrîqayî ئـەفريقايـى *adj.* African. {also: Afrîkayî (BF/ZF3/Wkp); Afrîkî (BF-2/ZF3-2); Afrîqeyî (IFb); Efrîqî (Wkt-2)} Sor Eferîq[ay]î ئـەفەريقايـى [Wkt/SS//IFb//BF/ZF3/Wkp]

Efrîqî ئەفريقى (Wkt) = African. See **Efrîqayî**.

efsane I ئەفسانە = greedy; stupid. See **evsene**.

efsene ئەفسەنە (K) = greedy; stupid. See **evsene**.

efsûn ئەفسوون (IFb/JJ/ZF3) = magic. See **efsûnî**.

efsûnî ئـەفـســوونـــى *f.* **(-ya;).** 1) {syn: sêr I} magic, sorcery: **•Em li ser banê mala wî rûniştine û ew ji min re çêlî xweşî û *efsûniya* van deveran dike** (Tof, 10) We have sat down on the roof of his house and he is describing to me the delights and *magic* of those places; 2) [*adj.*] magical, enchanted: **•Xalîçeyên xwe yên *efsûnî* şuştin** (EN) They washed their *magic* carpets. {also: afsûn (IFb-2); efsûn (IFb/ZF3); [efsoun] افـســون (JJ)} Cf. P afsūn افـــســـون = 'incantation?'; Sor efsûn ئەفسوون = 'incantation, sorcery' [Tof//K(s)/IFb/JJ/ZF3]

'efû عـەفـوو/**efû** ئـەفـوو [IFb/RZ] *m.(K)/f.(B/SK/OK)* **(; /-yê, afyê [B]).** forgiveness, pardon: **-afû kirin** (B)/**'efo ~** (JB1-A)/**'efû ~** (K/HH/OK)/**'efw ~** (SK) to forgive, pardon {syn: bexşandin; lêborîn; lê xweş bûn}: **•Lê roja ku mêvana min bû, min jê rica kiribû, ku kekê min *efû bike*. Wê jî soz dabû min ku ewê te *efû bike*** (KS, 9) But on the day that she was my guest, I asked her *to forgive* my (older) brother. And she promised me that she *would forgive* you **•Ya xudê, to li me xoş bî, qusûra me *'efw key*** (SK 9:90) O God, forgive us and *pardon* our fault. {also: afû (B); 'efo (JB1-A); 'efw (SK); [afou] عفو (JJ); <'efû> عفو (HH)} <Ar 'afw عفو = 'pardon' [KS/IFb/RZ//K/JJ/HH/OK//B//JB1-A//SK]

'efw عەفوْ (SK) = pardon. See **'efû**.

Efxanî ئەفخانى (IFb/Wkp) = Afghani. See **Efẍanî**.

Efẍanî ئـەفغانـى *adj.* Afghani. {also: Afganî (BF/Wkt); Afxanî (Wkt-2); Efxanî (IFb/Wkp)} Sor Efẍanî ئەفغانى [Waarmedia//IFb/Wkp//BF/Wkt]

eg ئەگ (GF) = if. See **eger I**.

egal ئــــەگــال *f.* **().** large head kerchief worn while traveling (IFb): •[After Mem and Zîn's death, P'erî-Xatûn lost interest in her household duties] **Sibê ḧeta êvarê, *egaleke* řeş xwe p'êça bû, ser meẍber dûr nedik'et** (Z-1) From morning until evening, she wrapped herself in a black *kerchief*, didn't go far from the graveside. {also: <'egal> عـگـال (HH)} < Ar 'aqāl/'agāl عـقـال = 'string tied around the kaffiyeh (headdress) to keep it in place' [Z-1/IFb/ZF3//HH]

eger I ئەگەر/**'eger** عەگەر [K] *conj.* if: *[+ pres. indc.]*: **•*Eger* ji te re çend qurûş lazim in, here ser kursîya zîv rûne, ezê çend qurûşa bidim te** (L) *If* you need a few cents, come sit on the silver chair [and] I'll give you a few cents **•*Heke* birçî ne, bila bixwin** (BX) *If* they are hungry, let them eat; *[+ past indc.]* **•*Eger* cilkêt baş min dîtin dê bo te kirim** (M-Ak) *If* I see any good clothes I shall buy them for you **•*Heke* îşê wî çû serî, dibêjin ko siûda wî a baş bû** (BX) *If* his affair goes over well, they say that he had good luck; *[+ pres. subj.]* **•*Eker* me bigirin** (M-Ak #562) *If* they should catch us •*Heke* **pirsa wan hebe, bila vê gavê bêjin** (BX) *If* they have a question, let them ask it now; *[+ past subj.]* •"***Eger*** **te hind musa'ede kiriba, pîçek stukira xo kêşaba pêş çawêt min û carekî dî di pêş mirina xo da min çawêt te dîtibana, paşî bila ez miribam, da di dilê min da nebîte keser"** (SK 2:15) "*If* you would be so kind as to stretch your neck a little in front of my eyes so that I could see your eyes once again before my death, then let me die, there would be no regret in my heart" •**Kalê rind, ez dizanim, *eger* tu niha li vê derê, li nik masa min bûyayî, tu dê bi van qisên min bikeniyayî** (MUm, 11) Kind old man, I know, *if* you were here now, at my table, you would laugh at my words. {also: eg (GF-2); eke (Z-3); erge (Z-3); erke (Z-3); ger (GF-2); heger (JB1-S-2); hek; heke (OK-2); hek'e (JB1-A&S-2); hek'er (JB1-S-2); hek'o (JB1-A-2); hergê (F); herke (Z-3); herkê (EP-1); [egher] اگر (JJ); <heke> هكه (HH)} {syn: wekî [3]} Cf. P agar اگــــــــر --> T eğer; Sor eger ئەگەر [K//A/JB3/IFb/B/JJ/JB1-A&S/SK/GF/TF/OK//HH//F]

eger II ئـەگـەر *f./m.* **(-a/-ê;).** 1) {syn: sebeb; sedem I; ûşt} reason, cause: •***egerê* helbijartina evî babetî** (B.Y.'Ebdulla. Hozana afretan di edebê Kurdîda, 5) *the reason for* choosing this topic •**Hebûna mezheb û terîqetan bi *egeran* tên îzahkirin. Di ola êzîdî de *egerên* hebûna van terîqetan, van veqetand-inan çi nin?** (Wlt 2:73, 16) There are *reasons* to explain the existence of the sects and denomina-tions. What are *the reasons for* the existence of these denominations, these distinctions in the Yezidi religion? •**ji ber *egerên* diravî** (VoA) for financial or monetary *reasons*; 2) {syn: bandûr̄; t'esîr} effect, influence. [(neol)Wlt/VoA/(GF)]

'egîd عەگید (FS)/egîd ئەگید (JB3) = hero. See **'egît.**

'egît عـەگـیـت/**egît** ئـەگـیـت [A/IFb/F] *m.* **().** hero, brave person: -**'erfat û 'egît** (EP-7) do.: •**'Erfat û 'egîtê wê [=Cizîrê] 'Erfan, Ç'ekan û Qeret'ajdîne** (EP-7) Its [=Jezirah's] heroes are Erfan, Chekan, and Qeretajdin. {also: egîd (JB3); 'egîd (FS); egît (A/IF/F); [aghit اگت/aghid اگید] (JJ); <'egîd> عگید (HH)} {syn: 'efat; fêris; gernas; leheng; mêrxas; p'elewan} < T yiğit = 'brave young man'; cf. also Ar 'aqīd عـقـیـد = 'military leader' [K/B//L/A/F/IFb/JJ//FS//JB3//HH]

egle ئـەگلە/**'egle** عـەگلە (B). *adj.* 1) late, delayed: -**egle bûn** (K/B/IFb): a) to be late, be delayed; to tarry {syn: awiqîn; gîro bûn}: •**Ez hinekî li deştê *'egle bûm*** (B) I *tarried* for a while in the field; b) to stop *(vi.)*, come to a stop; -**egle kirin** (F/K/B)/ ~**xistin** (K)/~**êxistin** (B): a) to detain, delay {syn: awiqandin; gîro kirin; taloq kirin}: •**Bibaxşîne ... wekî *min tu dayî eglekirinê*** (K2-Fêrîk) Forgive me ... *for having delayed you*; b) to stop *(vt.)*, bring to a stop; 2) [*f.* **(; 'eglê** [B]).] delay; stopping. {also: 'egle (B); [eglé] اگلـه (JJ)} {syn: gîro} <T eğlemek [Trabzon; Kars; Cenciğe -Erzincan; *Ağın -Elâzığ] = 'to cause to stop' (DS, v. 5, p. 1680) + eglemek [*Nizip - Gaziantep] = 'to wait' (DS, v. 5, p. 1673) [K2-Fêrîk/F/K/IFb/ JJ/ZF3//B] <dereng; xurcilîn>

'ehd عـەهد/**ehd** ئـەهد [K/IFb] *m./f.(JB1-A&S/ZF3)* **().** 1) agreement, treaty, pact; 2) promise; 3) {syn: sond} vow, oath: -**ehd xwerin** (K)/~ **kirin** (K) to vow, swear; 4) legal document. {also: [ahd] عـهـد (JJ)} < Ar 'ahd عـهـد = 'promise, pact' [JR/JB1-A&S/JJ/ /K/IFb]

ehl ئـەهـل *m.* **(-ê;).** inhabitant, resident: •**Ez zanim tu ne *ehlê* vî cî ye** (L) I know you're not *a resident of* this place (=You're not from around here). {also: [ehl/ahl] اهــــل (JJ)} {syn: akincî; binelî; niştecih} < Ar ahl أهـل = 'folks, people' [L/Z/K/IFb/JJ] <xelq>

ehmaq ئەهماق (K) = stupid. See **eħmeq.**

ehmaqî ئەهماقی (K) = stupidity. See **eħmeqî.**

ehmeq ئەهمەق (K/IFb) = stupid. See **eħmeq.**

ehmeqî ئەهمەقی (K/IFb) = stupidity. See **eħmeqî.**

ehmeqtî ئەهمەقتی (ZZ-7) = stupidity. See **eħmeqî.**

eħmeq ئـــەحـــمـــەق *adj.* 1) stupid, foolish *(person)*: •**Bavo, merivên *ehmeq* çawa ne? Çima meriv ji hinek kesan re dibêjin, *ehmeq*?** (Ardû, 26) Daddy, what are *stupid* people like? Why do people call some individuals *stupid*?; 2) [*m.&f.* **().**] fool: •***Ehmeqtirînê ehmeqan*** (Ardû, 26) The *most foolish fool*. {also: ehmaq (K-2); ehmeq (K/IFb); [ahhmák (G)] احـمـق (JJ); <eħmeq> احـمـق (HH)} {syn: aqilsivik; bêaqil; sefîh; xêtik} < Ar aḥmaq أحــمــق = 'stupid' --> T ahmak {ehmaqî; ehmeqî; eħmeqî} [Ardû/K/IFb//JJ/HH/SK]

eħmeqî ئـەحـمـەقـی *f.* **(-ya;-yê).** stupidity, foolishness: •**Ji bo ku *ehmeqiya* wî bipîve** (Ardû, 28) In order to measure his *stupidity* •**Wê çaxê ji *ehmeqiya* min bû** (Ardû, 27) That time it was out of [lit. 'from my'] *stupidity* [that I did such & such]. {also: ehmaqî (K-2); ehmeqî (K/IFb); ehmeqtî (ZZ-7); [ehmaqi/ahhmakía (G)] احمقی (JJ)} {syn:

bêaqilî} [Ardû/JJ//K/IFb//ZZ] <eĥmeq>

eîne ئەئینە (F) = mirror. See **‘eyne**.

eînî ئەئینی (F) = same. See **‘eynî**.

ejnu ئەژنو (A/GF) = knee. See **ejnû**.

ejnû ئەژنوو *f.* ( ). knee: **•Ji bo ko ez bi tevger û nezaniyeke xwe vî cîyê miqedes neyêşînim hêdîka li ser herdu *ciniyan* rûdinim** (Tof, 16) In order not to disturb this holy place by my movements or by ignorance, I sit on my *knees*. {also: cinî (Tof); ejnu (A/GF); jenu (GF-2); jinû I (K); junî (IFb-2); [ejnou ئژنو/hejnou هژنو/jinou ژنو] (JJ)} {syn: çok; kabok} [Pok. ĝenu-, ĝneu- 380-381.] 'knee, angle': O Ir jānu *n.*: Av *acc. sing.* žnūm; Mid P zānūg (M3); P zānū زانو; Sor ejno ئەژنۆ [Tof//IFb/JJ/ZF3//A/GF//K]

eke ئەکە (Z-3) = if. See **eger I**.

Ek’rad ئەکراد *m.* (). 1) Kurd; 2) Kurds (coll.): **•[di nîv(a) *Ekradan*]** (JR) among *the Kurds*. {also: K’urd; [ekrad] اکراد (JJ)} < Ar akrād أکراد, pl. of kurdī کردي (also Kūrdī کوردي) = 'Kurd' [JR/K/IFb/JJ] See also **K’urd**.

Ela ئەلا (EP-7) = God. See **Elah**.

‘elac عەلاج (HR) = cure, remedy. See **îlac**.

Elah ئەلاه *m.* **(-ê;).** God, Allah: **•Tu *elaê* xwe** (EP-7) *God* be with you. {also: Ela (EP-7); Ele (B); Eleh (B); Ella (F); Elle (B); Elleh (B)} {syn: Xwedê} < Ar Allāh الله < al- ال = 'the' + ilāh إله = 'god' [EP-7/K/B/F]

‘elam عەلام *m.(K)/f.(B)* **(; /-ê).** notification, informing (K/HH); report (B): **-‘elam kirin** (K/JJ) to notify, inform; **-‘elem dan *fk-ê*** (Z-3) to inform s.o., report stg. to s.o.: **•Hinekî xweyî-xêr hene, diçin *‘elem didine* mîr** (Z-3) There are some good people, they go and *inform* the emir. {also: ‘elem (Z-3); [êlam kirin] اعلام کرین (JJ); <‘elam> اعلام (HH)} < Ar i‘lām إعلام = 'informing' [Z-3//K/B/HH//JJ]

‘elamet عەلامەت/**elamet** ئەلامەت [IFb] *f.* (). 1) {syn: cab} report, news, notification (K/B); 2) {syn: beyanname; daxuyanî} declaration, announcement: **•Al-p’aşa *‘elametî da* şeherê Mxurzemînê** (EP-7) A.p. *had it announced* in the city of Mukhurzemin ...; 3) signal (K/IF); sign, omen (JJ); 4) Koranic verse (JJ). {also: ‘elametî (EP-7/B); [elamet] علامت (JJ)} < Ar ‘alāmah علامة--> T alamet [EP-7/B//K/JJ//IFb]

‘elametî عەلامەتی (EP-7/B) = report; declaration; signal. See **‘elamet**.

‘elaqe عەلاقە *f.* (). interest, concern: **•Ez Mela Se‘îd bê dexl o *‘elaqe* dizanim** (SK 54:620) I consider M.S. [to be] without connection or *interest* [in this matter]; **-‘elaqey ... kirin** (SK) to be interested in: **•Çonko Kerbela li-nik Şî‘e gelek muqeddes o muĥterem e Nadir Şah got, “ez *‘elaqe-y* Kerbelaê *nakem*. Bila wê-derê bi keyfa xo bin”** (SK 11:104) Since Kerbela is very holy and sacred to the Shiah, Nadir Shah said, “I *have no interest in* Kerbela. Let them do what they like there” **•Eger ew ẍewsekî řast e hîç *‘elaqe-y* min *naket*, çonko bi-sebeb malê wî min dest ji dizî kêşa** (SK 38:343) If he is a true Help he *will have no interest in* me, for thanks to his wealth I have given up stealing. {also: eleqe (ZF); [elaqé] علاقه (JJ)} {syn: ĥewas; meraq; pûte} < Ar ‘alāqah علاقة = ‘relation, bond, connection’ [SK/JJ//ZF] <eleqedar>

elaqeder ئەلاقەدەر (IFb) = interested; connected. See **eleqedar**.

‘elb عەلب/**elb** ئەلب [AB/IFb/TF] *f.* **(-a;-ê).** 1) {syn: dewl I; helgîn (Krş); satil; sîtil} wooden bucket, pail : **•*Elbê* bîne, ez çêlekê bidoşim** (AB) Bring *the bucket*, so that I can milk the cow; 2) {also: ‘elbik (Erh/Frq-2)} {syn: fitre} unit of measure for grain, dry measure, c. 12-13 kg. (IFb/HH/Msr): **•Du kulm, ribek e; çar rib, ç’apek e; du ç’ap, *elbek* e** (Frq) 2 handfuls are a 'rib' (dry measure), 4 ribs are 1 'çap', 2 çaps are 1 *elb* **•Teyr got "Tê *‘elbek* garis bidî min, ezê bêm." Go, "Bi qirar ezê du *‘elb* bidim te"** (PS-I:13, 32, l.23-24) The bird said, "If you give me *a measure of* millet, I will come." [The other one] said, "I'll even give you two *measures*." {also: ‘elbik (Erh/Frq-2); [alb] علب (JJ); <‘elb> علب (HH)} cf. Ar ‘ulbah علبة = 'box, can' [AB/IFb/TF//K/JJ/HH/GF/Msr/Frq//Erh] <ç’ap I; fitre I; mencelok; ribik; zerik [2]>

elbane ئەلبانە (IFb) = tambourine. See **‘erebane**.

Elbanî ئەلبانی (Wkt/CS) = Albanian. See **Albanî**.

elbet ئەلبەت (K/IFb) = of course; absolutely. See **helbet**.

‘elbik عەلبِك (Erh/Frq) = unit of measure for grain. See **‘elb**[2].

Ele ئەلە (B) = God. See **Elah**.

Eleh ئەلەه (B) = God. See **Elah**.

‘elem عەلەم (Z-3) = notification, report. See **‘elam**.

elend ئەلەند (ZF3) = dawn. See **elind**.

elep’arçe ئەلەپارچە *adj.* into pieces, limb from limb: **-elep’arçe kirin** (EP-7) to tear limb from limb:

•**Ezê te li ‘erdê xim,** ***elep’arçe bikim*** (EP-7) I'll throw you on the ground and *tear you limb from limb*. [EP-7]

eleqe ئەلەقە (ZF) = interest, concern. See **‘elaqe**.

eleqedar ئـەلـەقـەدار *adj.* 1) [**bi** … **ra**] interested (in): •**Şamîl Esgerov … hê di ciwaniya xwe de** ***bi*** **dîrok û edebiyata Kurdistanê** ***re … eleqedar bûye*** (Wkp) S.E. … already in his youth *was interested in* the history and literature of Kurdistan •**Wê ji bo zimanzan û kesên** ***bi*** **folklorê** ***re eleqeder bibe*** **derfet û delîl** (C.Roj. Hurcahil) It will be an opportunity and proof for linguists and people *interested in* folklore; 2) [**bi** … **ra**] related (to), connected (to): •**Kuştina bavê min** ***bi*** **pirsa Kurd** ***re eleqedar*** **e** (AvestaKurd) The murder of my father is *related to* the Kurdish issue. {also: elaqeder (IFb); eleqeder (C.Roj)} {syn: ĥewask'ar} < ‘elaqe + -dar; cf. T alâkadar [Wkp/ZF/Wkt//C.Roj//IFb] <‘elaqe>

eleqeder ئـەلـەقـەدەر (C.Roj) = interested; connected. See **eleqedar**.

elet’ewş ئـەلـەتـەوش/**‘elet’ewş** عـەلـەتـەوش *adj.* useless, worthless; nonesensical, absurd, ridiculous: •**Bes e, bi van gotinên** ***eletewş*** **pesnê min nede!** (EN) That's enough, don't flatter me with these *useless* words! •**Ku serboriya xwe dinhêrim min gelek tiştinên** ***eletewş*** **xwendine heqqet** (Ç.Zedo: Qisedanek bi Mehmed Şarman re) If I look at my past, I really read many *worthless* things. {also: <‘eletewş> علتوش (HH)} [EN/IFb/FJ/ZF/FS/Wkt//HH] <bême‘na>

elfabe ئەلفابە (K/JB3/IF) = alphabet. See **alfabe**.

‘elimandin عـەلـمـانـدِن/**elimandin** ئـەلـمـانـدِن (IFb) *vt.* (**-‘elimîn-**). 1) {syn: fêr kirin; hel dan/kirin; hîn kirin} to teach, instruct; to educate: •**Wî** ***ez ‘elimandim[e]*** **Înglîzî** (Bw) He *taught me* English [=**Wî Înglîzî nîşa min da**]; 2) {syn: hîn kirin; lê banandin} to accustom (JJ); 3) to correct (JJ). {also: ‘elim dan (JB1-S); [alemāndin] عـلـمـانـديـن (JJ); <‘elimandin علماندن (di‘elimîne) (دعلمينه)> (HH)} [K(s)/JJ/HH/Rh/Bw//IFb//JB1-S]

‘elim dan عەلِم دان (JB1-S) = to teach. See **‘elimandin**.

‘elimîn عەلِمين/**elimîn** ئەلِمين [IFb] *vi.* (**-‘elim-**). [+ *dat. constr.*] 1) {syn: fêr bûn; hîn bûn [hîn I]; hû kirin (Kg)} to learn; 2) {syn: hîn bûn [hîn I]; r̄ahatin} to get used to, grow accustomed to. {also: <‘elimîn علمين (di‘elimî) (دعلمى)> (HH)} [Srk/K(s)/HH/Rh/Bw//IFb]

elind ئـەلِـنـد *f.* (**-a;-ê**). dawn, sunrise, daybreak: •**Ew** ***li elindê*** **ji xwe rabû û çû nav bîstanî** (FS) S/he got up *at dawn* and went into the garden; **-gel elindê** (Bw) at dawn. {also: elend (ZF3)} {syn: berbang; ferec; hingûr [1]; segur; serê sibê; siĥar; spêde; şebeq} [Bw/IFb/FS/BF//ZF3] <hingûr>

elîfba ئـەلـيـفـبـا (Ber)/‘elîfba عـەلـيـفـبـا (B) = alphabet. See **alfabe**.

elîfbe ئەليفبە (IF) = alphabet. See **alfabe**.

elîfbê ئەليفبێ (A) = alphabet. See **alfabe**.

elîh ئـــەلـيـه *m.* (). 1) {syn: teyrê bazî (K)} eagle (K/A/JB3/JJ/Mzg) ; 2) {syn: başok; baz I} falcon, zool. *Falco* (IFb/HH). {also: elo (OK); eloh (IF/OK-2); eluh (GF-2); elûh (K); eylo (JB3/GF); hûlî (Mzg); ilho (Bw); [elouh] الـــوه (JJ); <eloh> الـــوه (HH)} probably a borrowing from P āloh آلـــه; Proto-IE *(H)r̥ĝi-p(t?)-yo-; [Pok. I. reĝ- 855.] 'direct': Skt r̥ji-pyá- = 'immediately soaring high' *epithet of* śyenā- = 'eagle, falcon'; O Ir *r̥zifya-; Av ərəzi-fya- *m.* = 'eagle' (< ərəzu- = 'straight, direct'); Old P *ardufya-; Mid P āluf/āluh (M3); P āloh آله; Sor heło هــەڵــۆ; Hau hełû *m.* (M4); cf. also Arm arcui արծուի/arciw արծիւ. See: **III. Arcui "aigle"** in: Charles de Lamberterie. "Armeniaca I-VIII : Études lexicales," *Bulletin de la Société de Linguistique de Paris*, 73 (1978), 251-62; R. Schmitt. "Der "Adler" im Alten Iran," *Sprache*, 16 (1970), 63-77. [K/JJ//A//OK//JB3/ GF//IFb/HH//Mzg//Bw] <kurt II; sîsalk; xertel>

elk’an ئەلكان = wave. See **êlk’an**.

Ella ئەللا (F) = God. See **Elah**.

Elle ئەللە (B) = God. See **Elah**.

Elleh ئەللەه (B) = God. See **Elah**.

Elmanî ئـەلـمـانـی *adj.* German. {also: Almanî (IFb/ZF3/BF-2/CS)} Sor Ełmanî ئەڵمانی [Wkt/BF/SS//IFb/ZF3/CS]

elo ئەلۆ (OK) = eagle; falcon. See **elîh**.

eloh ئەلۆه (IFb/OK/HH) = eagle; falcon. See **elîh**.

‘elok عـەلـۆك/**elok** ئـەلـۆك [IFb] *f.* (). turkey (fowl). {syn: bûqelemûn (F); coqcoq; culûx̂; kûr̄kûr̄; şamî} [Msr/Bw/FS//IFb/ZF3]

elûh ئەلووه (K/JJ) = eagle; falcon. See **elîh**.

em ئــەم *prn.* (**me**). we; us; our. {also: [em] ام (JJ)} Cf. P mā ما; Sor ême ئێمە; Za ma [BX/K/A/IFb/JJ/B]

‘emal عـــەمـــال *m./f.(Z-1)* (**-ê/-a;**). 1) work, business, occupation; livelihood: •**Vê carê şolê wî we** ***‘emelê*** **wî bî nêçîr** (M-Zx #756, 350) Then his work and *livelihood* became hunting; 2) concern, preoccupation, trouble, worry: **-‘emalê serê … bûn** = to be a cause of concern: •**Ez xwexa zanim, îroda tu** ***‘emela serê minî*** (Z-1) I know (for myself), today you *are trouble to me* •**Hûn *emalê serê wî ne*** (L/K) You are a thorn in his side/ You bring him nothing but trouble/You cause him nothing but grief. {also: ‘emel (K/B/Z-1/M-Zx)} < Ar ‘amal عمل = 'work' [L//K/B/Z-1/M-Zx]

eman ئەمان (SK) = container; dish. See **aman**.

emanet ئەمانەت (-a;) (Z-3) = entrusting [of an object] for safekeeping. See **anemetî**.

‘embar عەمبار/**embar** ئەمبار [IFb/F] *f.* **(;-ê).** storehouse, depository, depot, warehouse; storeroom; granary: •**Kur̄o, t’êr̄ û derdangê xwe bînin werne *imbarê*, xwer̄a nan dagirin** (Ba3-3, #36) Boys, bring your sacks and receptacles and go to *the storehouse* and fill them [=sacks, etc.] with bread [i.e., food]; -**‘embar kirin** (Zeb) to store. {also: ambar (A/IFb-2); enbar (IFb-2); imbar (Ba3-3); <‘embar> عمبار (HH)} <Gr amphoreus ἀμφορεύς & Lat amphora = 'ancient Greek vessel with two handles for storing wine, oil, honey, or grain': Ar/P anbār انبار = 'storehouse'; Hau hemar *m.* (M4); T ambar; Rus ambar амбар [Ba3//K/B/HH/GF//A//F/IFb]

emeg ئەمەگ = food; work. See **emek**.

emek ئەمەك *m.* **(-ê ;).** 1) {syn: xwarin} food (K/B) < T yemek: -***Emekê* min li te helal be** (K): a) Bon appêtit!; b) May my *labor* bring you benefit; 2) {syn: xebat} labor, toil, work (K/IF/JJ) < T emek: -***êmegê* cotane** (L) grain, e.g., barley [lit. 'the [fruit of] *labor of* plows']. {also: emeg; êmeg (L); êmek (K-2); [emek] امك (JJ)} Cf. T yemek = 'food; to eat' [Z-1/K/IFb/JJ/B//L] <alif; êm>

emekħeram ئەمەكحەرام *m.* **().** good-for-nothing, scoundrel (EP-7): •**Gelî *emekħerama*, zû rabin, /Memê ji minr̄a brîndarkin** (EP-7) O *scoundrels*, quickly get up, /Wound M. for me. {syn: qeşmer; sakol; t’ewt’ewe} < emek = 'food' + ħeram = 'forbidden' [EP-7]

‘emel عەمەل (K/B/M-Zx) = work; worry. See **‘emal**.

‘emeliyat عەمەلِیات/**emeliyat** ئەمەلِیات [ZF/RZ/Wkt] *f.* **().** surgical operation, surgery: -**‘emeliyat bûn** (Hk/Wkt) to be operated on, undergo an operation: •**Ez *‘emeliyat* bûm** (Hk) I *had (or, underwent) an operation*; -**‘emeliyat kirin** (Hk/Wkt) to operate (on), perform surgery on: •**Gulçîska min *‘emeliyat kir*, berek jê derêxist** (Hk) I had a kidney operation [lit. 'they *operated on* my kidney'], a stone was removed from it. {also: ameliyat (IFb)} < Ar ‘amalīyāt عمليات, *pl. of* ‘amalīyah عملية = 'operation' [Hk//ZF/RZ/Wkt//IFb]

Emerîkanî ئەمەریکانی (IFb/SS) = American. See **Emrîkî**.

Emerîkî ئەمەریکی (Wkt) = American. See **Emrîkî**.

‘emilandin عەمِلاندن/**emilandin** ئەمِلاندن [IFb] *vt.* **(-‘emilîn-).** to use, employ, utilize. {also: [amilandin] عملاندين (JJ); <‘emilandin عملاندن (di‘emilîne) (دعملينه)> (HH)} {syn: bi kar anîn; xebitandin [1]} < Ar ‘amila عمل = 'to do', cf. also ista‘mala X استعمل ='to use' [Msr/K/B/JJ/HH//IFb]

emin ئەمِن (K) = secure; reliable. See **emîn**.

emir I ئەمِر/**‘emir I** عەمِر [K/B] *m.* **(-ê;).** 1) {syn: ferman; ferwar II; ħukum [2]} command, order: -**emir kirin** (K) to order, command •***Emrî* ser celaçîya kirîye** (L) He issued *a command* to the executioners; 2) permission, leave: •[**Lê *‘emrê* kuştinê nîne**] (PS-I) But [you] don’t have *permission* to kill [him]. {also: [emir] امر (JJ); <emr> امر (HH)} < Ar amr أمر [F/JB3/IFb/JJ//HH//K/B] <desthilat>

‘em•ir II عەمِر/**emir II** ئەمِر [B] *m.* **(•rê;).** age, life: •***‘Emrê* te çend e?** (Bw) How old are you? [lit. 'Your *age* is how much?'] •***Emrê* wî heft sal in** (L) He is seven years old; -**‘emir kirin** (B) to live, thrive, live [long enough] to see: •**Bira *‘emir bike* ...!** (B) *Long live* ...! •**Te ħevtê sal *‘emr kirye*, tu pîreke her̄fî** (EH) You *have lived* seventy years, you are a doddering old woman. {also: ‘emr (RZ); [oumr] عمر (JJ); <‘emr> عمر (HH)} {syn: jî III; t’emen} < Ar ‘umr عمر [L/K/JB3/IFb//JJ//B//HH/RZ] <salî>

‘emirdirêj عەمِردرێژ *adj.* longlasting, long-lived: -**‘emirdirêj bûn** (Kemal Burkay) to be long-lived, last a long time: •***‘Emirdirêj bî*!** (K) I wish you a long life! •**Piştî wê jî, dîsa tevger me ava kir, çend salan berê, heşt rêxistinên Kurd bûn, me hevra gelek wext kar jî kir, lê ew jî *‘emirdirêj* nebû** (Kemal Burkay) After that, again we formed movements, a few years earlier there had been eight Kurdish organizations, and we worked together for a long time, but that too was not *long-lived* [i.e., did not last forever]. {also: cf. [oumr-i dirij] عمرى دريژ (JJ) = longevity} [Kemal Burkay/K] <‘emir II>

Emirkanî ئەمِرکانی (CS) = American. See **Emrîkî**.

emîn ئەمین *adj.* 1) {syn: selamet; t’ena} feeling secure or safe with, trusting of s.o. [+ **bi** (HCK)/**ji** (SK)]: •**Bes ji noke paş hemî teyr o ħeywanatê**

hûrde dê *ji* min *emîn* bin, dê hêne lalî min, ji-ber min naĥelên (SK 4:29) From now on all the birds and small animals will feel *secure with* me, they will come to me and not flee from me **•Ew [=Qanatê Nadir] merivekî ĥelal e, em *pê amin* dibin, bira wî bînin** (H.Cindî. Hewarî, 299) He [Q.N.] is an honest person, we trust him [or, feel *safe with* him], let them bring him **•Ewe Oso mir. Selaĥ ew e, em kur̂êt wî dil-xoş keyn, bînînewe. Paşî ko çak *emîn* bon hemîyan dê kujîn** (SK 40:382) Oso is dead. It is advisable that we placate his sons and bring them back. After they feel good and *safe*, we will kill them all **•Wezîr *pê amîn nebû*, go: "Ezê şirîtekê bavêm nava te, girêdim"** (HCK-1, 209) The wezir *did not trust him*, he said, "I will throw a rope around your waist, and tie it"; 2) {syn: ewlekar; ît'bar; merd; saxlem; xudanbext} reliable, trustworthy, dependable : **•Hung her do dizanin ko li-nik min kesek nîye wekî hingo mu'teber o *emîn*** (SK 52:564) Both of you know that for me there is no one as respected and *reliable* as you **•To qewî muroekî çak o *emîn* î** (SK 50:523) You are a very good and *trustworthy* person. {also: amin (K/B); amîn (HCK); emin (K-2); êmin (GW); [emin/amín (G/Lx)] امين (JJ)} < Ar amīn أمين = 'reliable, honest, faithful'--> T emin = 'sure, certain'; Sor emîn ئەمین = 'trustworthy, reliable' [SK/IFb/JJ/SK/RZ/ZF/Tsab//K/B//HCK//GW] <bawer; biste [2]; misoger; piştrast>

'emr عەمر (HH/RZ) = age. See **'emir II**.

Emrîkî ئەمریكی *adj.* American. {also: Amerîkanî (IFb/ZF3); Amerîkayî (ZF3-2/BF); Amerîkî (ZF3-2/BF-2); Amrîkayî (Wkt-2); Amrîkî (Wkt-2); Emerîkanî (IFb-2/SS); Emerîkî (Wkt-2); Emirkanî (CS)} Sor Emerîkî ئەمەریكی [Wkt/BF//SS//CS//IFb/ZF3//BF]

enbar ئەنبار (IFb) = storehouse. See **'embar**.

encam ئەنجام *f.* **(-a;-ê).** 1) {syn: axirî; dawî; k'uta[sî]} end, conclusion: **-di encamê de** (Wlt) finally, in the end: **•*Di encamê de* ji bo hilgirtina van peywiran (wezîfeyan) ev endam hatin hilbijartin** (Wlt 1:36, 5) *In the end*, these members were elected to carry out these duties; 2) result, outcome. <P anjām انجام; Sor encam ئەنجام [(neol)Wlt/K/IFb/GF/TF] <k'uta>

'encûr عەنجوور (G/Wkt) = type of cucumber. See **'ecûr**.

endam ئەندام *m.* **(-ê;).** 1) {syn: lebat II} limb, organ *(of the body))*: **•Ji banan *endamên* cinsî, qalind, qehwe, tarî û jêkirî dibarin** (HYma 32) From the roofs thick, brown, dark and severed sexual *organs* are raining; 2) {syn: hevalbend [2]} member *(of an organization, etc.)*: **•Di encamê de ji bo hilgirtina van peywiran (wezîfeyan) ev *endam* hatin hilbijartin** (Wlt 1:36, 5) In the end, these *members* were elected to carry out these duties **•*Endamên* malbata min ji min hêvî dikirin ku ez zanîngehê biqedînim, bibim xwedî peywir û alîkarîya aborî bi wan re bikim** (Wlt 1:35, 16) *Members of* my family expected me to finish college, get a job, and help them out financially. {also: [endam] اندام (JJ)} P andām اندام = 'stature; body; limb, organ'; Sor endam ئەندام = 'limb, member (lit. & fig.)' [Wlt/K(s)/A/IFb/JJ/GF/TF] <berendam>

'endeko عەندەكۆ/**endeko** ئەندەكۆ [A/IFb/TF/AD] *f.* **(;-ê).** clover, sweet trefoil: **•Û wilo *'indekoê* dixwê dewara wî** (HR 3:116) And thus his mount eats *clover*. {also: endekû (GF-2); hendeko (FJ); hendekû (GF); hendeqû (GF-2); 'indeko (HR); <ĥendeko> حندكو (HH)} Cf. Ar ḥandaqūq حندقوق = 'sweet trefoil, (yellow) sweet clover; Turoyo (Arc) 'indakko = 'fragrant clover' [HR//A/IFb/TF/AD//FJ//HH//GF]

endekû ئەندەكوو (GF) = clover. See **'endeko**.

'en'ene I عەنعەنە *m.* **().** 1) ego[t]ism; 2) haughtiness, arrogance: **-'en'ene kirin** (K) to be haughty, behave in an arrogant manner: **•Beşera wê xweş dibe û *bi teherekî 'enenekirinê* dîsa li min dinihêre** (K2-Fêrîk) Her mood improves and she looks at me *in an arrogant manner*. <Ar anānī أنانى = 'egotistical' <anā أنا = 'I' [K2-Fêrîk/K]

'engirîn عەنگرین (K/FS) = to be angry. See **erinîn**.

enirîn ئەنرین (A/IFb/BF/ZF/CS/TF/Wkt/SS)/'enirîn عەنرین (K/B/Tsab) = to be angry. See **erinîn**.

'enî عەنی/**enî** ئەنی [F/A/JB3/IFb] *f.* **(-ya;-yê).** 1) {syn: navç'av; ne'tik} forehead, brow: **•*Ênîya* hespê maçî kir** (L) He kissed the horse's *forehead*; 2) {syn: cephe} front *(mil.)*, front line, battle front: **•Qerargeha Hevalbendan a mezin li *Eniya* Behra Spî** (RN) The main Allied headquarters on the Mediterranean *front*. {also: ênî (L); henî (Krç); [ani/ eni] انى (JJ); <enî> انى (HH)} <*anīčaka-, cf. Av ainika- = 'face'; Mid P anīg = 'front, forehead' (M3); P pīšānī (pēš-ānī) پیشانی (M. Schwartz: <*patīčya- + anīka-); Baluchi anīšaγ = 'brow, front, fate'. See: G. Morgenstierne. “Notes on Balochi Etymology,” *Norsk Tidsskrift for Sprogvidenskap*, 5 (1932), 40, reprinted in: *Irano-Dardica* (Wiesbaden : Dr. Ludwig Reichert Verlag, 1973), p.151 [K/B/Rh//F/A/JB3/IFb/JJ/HH//L//Krç] <ç’êre>

enînivîs ئـەنـیـنـڤـیـس *f.* (). destiny, fate. {syn: bext; *çarenivîs; nesîb; qeder II; qismet; yazî} < ‘enî = 'forehead' + nivîs- = 'to write' = that which is written on one's forehead, i.e., one's fate, cf. P sarneveŝt سرنوشت, T alın yazısı, Arm čakatagir ճակատագիր [Haz/ZF3]

enişk ئەنِشك (JB3) = elbow. See **anîşk**.

enîşk ئەنیشك (M-Am)/‘enîşk عەنیشك (K/B) = elbow. See **anîşk**.

‘ent’erî عـەنـتـەری *m.* (). traditional woman’s outer garment, short in front and long in back, with full length sleeves: **•*Delme-‘ent’erî* bejnê bûn** (Ba-1, #17) *The dresses* fit her well [according to Rus tr.]. {also: [enteri] عنتری (JJ); <‘enterî> عنتری (HH)} <Ar ‘antarī عـنـتـري = 'brassière; bodice, corsage' [<‘Antar عـنـتـر name of the hero of an early Arabic epic]; T entari = '(lady’s) dress; Arab’s loose garb' [Ba-1/B/JJ/HH] <delme; dêre>

‘enzêl عەنزێل (HR-I) = raised platform. See **herzal**.

ep’êce ئـەپـێـجـە *adv.* quite, rather: **•*ep’êce* řastî-dûz** (Ba2) *quite* level [of ground] **•Ewî gele ‘erd digirt û *ep’êceyî* dûrî gund bû** (Ba2:1, 203) It occupied a lot of space and was *quite* far from the village. {also: êp’êce (B)} < T epeyce [ep = (intensifying particle) + eyi/iyi = 'good' + -ce = (adverbial suffix) [Ba2//B]

eprî ئەپری (Nsb) = girl's headscarf. See **ĥibrî**.

eqar ئەقار (GF) = territory, area. See **aqar**.

‘eqildar عەقِلدار (GF) = wise man. See **‘aqildar**.

‘eql عەقل (HH/SK) = intelligence, sense. See **aqil II**.

‘eqldar عەقلدار (SK) = wise man. See **‘aqildar**.

erak ئەراك (A) = arak. See **‘ereq**.

eraq ئەراق (TF) = arak. See **‘ereq**.

erav ئەراڤ (Haz) = soapy water. See **arav**.

***erbab** ئەرباب/**‘erbab** عەرباب [K] *m.* **(-ê;).** 1) {syn: armanc; mebest; merem [1]; nêt [4]} goal, aim; desire, wish (K); 2) reward, recompense (L): **•*Erbabê* wan çiye?** (L) What is their *reward*?; 3) expert, one skilled in a matter (IFb). [L/K/IFb]

erbane ئـەربـانـە (A/Tof)/‘erbane عـەربـانـە (GF) = tambourine. See **‘erebane**.

‘erd عـەرد/**erd** ئـەرد [A/JB3/IFb] *m.(K/J/Ba/B/Bw)/f.(J/Dz/Z-1)* **(-ê/-a;-î/ê).** earth, land, ground: (JB3: *m.* = earth [soil]; f. = earth, land, world, territory): **•‘*Erd* weke k’axaza cigarê bilind bûye** (Ba) *The ground* has risen like (=by the width of) a cigarette paper **•*Vî ‘erdî,* vî ezmanî, min nebirîye!** (J) *By this earth*, by this sky, I haven't taken [them] *[an oath]* **•Gaê xwe anî, danî *erdê*** (J) He took his bull and placed him *on the ground* **•T’aê Ûsib ser *li ‘erdê* dimîne** (Ba) The scalepan with Joseph [in it] remains *on the ground* **•Serê gur k’ete *‘erdê*** (Dz) The wolf's head fell *to the ground*; **-bin erdê** (L) underground; **-li ‘erdê dan** (Msr) to knock over (on purpose), drop *(vt.)* {syn: tera kirin}: **•Min ew hilda û *li ‘erdê da*** (Msr) I picked him up and *knocked him on the ground* [cf. Ar aqāma wa-aq‘ada أقام و أقعد]; **-li hemî ‘erda** (Bw) everywhere. {also: ‘edr I (Zx); [ard] ارض (عرد) (JJ)} < Ar arḍ أرض = 'land, earth' [J/Ba/K/B/JJ/Bw//A/JB3/IFb//Zx]

Erdenî ئەردەنی (BF/Wkp) = Jordanian. See **’Urdunî**.

erdhejan ئـەردهـەژان (ZF3) = earthquake. See **‘erdĥejîn**.

‘erdĥejandin عـەردحـەژانـدِن (B) = earthquake. See **‘erdĥejîn**.

erdĥejî ئەردحەژی (F) = earthquake. See **‘erd˙ejîn**.

‘erdĥejîn عەردحەژین/**erdhejîn** ئەردهەژین [IFb] *f.* **(-a;-ê).** earthquake. {also: erdhejan (ZF3); erdĥejî (F); ‘erdĥejandin (B)} {syn: belelerz (F/K); bîbelerz; ‘erdlerzîn; zelzele} [IFb//F//B//ZF3]

***‘erdlerzîn** عـەردلـەرزیـن *f.* (). earthquake. {syn: belelerz (F/K); bîbelerz; ‘erdĥejîn; zelzele} [K]

‘erdnigarî عەردنِگاری [K/GF]/**erdnigarî** ئەردنِگاری *f.* **(-ya;-yê).** geography: **•Şingal bi cografya (*erdnîgarî*)ya Kurdistanê re girêdayîbûye ta ku di 1928an de ku ji aliyê dagirkeran ve hatiye veqetandin** (Rûdaw 23.xii.2014) Shingal [Sinjar] was attached to *the geography of* Kurdistan until in 1928 it was separated by invaders. {also: erdnîgarî (SS/Rûdaw)} [Rûdaw/SS//K/GF//IFb/Kmc/CS]

erdnîgarî ئـەردنـیـگـاری (SS/Rûdaw) = geography. See **‘erdnigarî**.

‘Ereb عـەرەب/**Ereb** ئـەرەب [A/JB3/IFb] *m.&f.* **(; /-ê).** Arab; 2) Negro, Black. {also: [areb] عـرب (JJ)} < Ar ‘arab عـرب, pl. of ‘arabī عـربـی [Z-1/K/JJ/B//A/JB3/IFb]

‘ereban•e عەرەبانە/**erebane** ئەرەبانە [OK] *f.* **(•a;•ê).** tambourine: **•Carê rabû pê û li dora xwe zîz bû. Bi zîzbûnê re, him le *erebana* xwe dixist, ji alîkî**

de jî qesîde digot (LM, 6) So he got up and spun around. While spinning around, he beat on his *tambourine*, and likewise he recited a poem •**Li ber defa sîngê xwe *erbaneyekê* bi eşq û hunereke welê diricifîne** (Tof, 7) He shakes *a tambourine* in front of his chest with such passion and skill. {also: elbane (IFb); erbane (A/Tof); 'erbane (GF); <'erebane> عربانه (HH)} [Ah/A/Tof//HH/FS//IFb//OK//GF] <def>

'ereb•e عەرەبە/**ereb•e** ئەرەبە [IFb/ZF/Kmc/RZ] *f.* **(•a/•eya;•ê).** 1) cart, wagon: **-erebeya agirkujiyê/ îtfaiyeyê** (ZF) fire engine; **-ereba ga** (Kmc/CS)/ **erebeya ga** (Nbh 124:31/ZF) oxcart {syn: gerdûm}; **-erebeya hespan** (ZF) horse-drawn wagon; **-erebeya seqetan** (ZF) wheelchair; 2) car, automobile. See **trimbêl**. {also: [arabané عربانه/ arabé عربه] (JJ); <'erebe> عربه (HH)} < Ar 'arabah عربة = 'carriage, vehicle, wagon'; Sor 'erebane عەرەبانە = 'phaeton; carriage' [Nbh/IFb/ZF/Kmc/RZ//K/B/Tsab/JJ/HH] <fayton; firxûn>

'Erebî عەرەبی *adj.* Arabic. [K/IF/B]

'ereq عەرەق/**ereq** ئەرەق *f.* (;-ê). arak, *rakı*, alcoholic beverage similar to Pernod: •**Divê hûn rabin çil qîz û çil xorta bînin û *'ereqê* bidenê** (GShA, 230) You must bring 40 girls and 40 young men, and give them *arak* [to drink]. {also: araq (K/B); erak (A); eraq (TF); [araq] عرق (JJ); <'ereq> عرق (HH)} < Ar 'araq عرق = 'sweat; arak'; Sor areq ئارەق/'areq عارەق [GShA/JJ /HH//IFb/GF/FJ//K/B//TF//A]

erê ئەرێ *adv.* yes. {also: [eri ارى/ heri هرى] (JJ)} {syn: belê} Cf. P āre آره; Sor erê ئەرێ = 'yes' [F/K/A/JB3/IFb/JJ/B]

erênî ئەرێنی *adj.* affirmative; positive [Ar ījābī ايجابي; P muṣbat مثبت; T olumlu, müsbet]: •**Di civînê da karên *erênî* û nerênî hatin xuyakirin** (BF) At the meeting *positive* and negative deeds were shown •**Min gotê: Tu jî dixwazî? Bersiva wê *erênî* bû (Wê got: belê)** (Wkt) I said to her: "Do you want some too?" Her answer was *affirmative* (She said: yes). {also: erînî (TF)} [K/IFb/GF/ZF3/Wkt/SS/BF//TF] <neyînî>

'erfad عەرفاد (EP-7) = hero. See **'efat**.

'erfat عەرفات (EP-7) = hero. See **'efat**.

'erfît عەرفیت (Z-3) = jinn. See **ferĥît**.

erge ئەرگە (Z-3) = if. See **eger I**.

erguwanî ئەرگووانی (Qzl) = purple. See **erẍewanî**.

erimûş ئەرمووش (IS) = silk. See **hevirmiş**.

erinî ئەرِنی adj. disobedient, rebellious: •**Ev piçûke yê *erinî*** (Zeb) This child is *rebellious*. [Zeb/OK]

erinîn ئەرِنین/**'erinîn** عەرنین [FS] *vi.* **(-erin-).** 1) {syn: k'eribîn; kerbêt fk-î bûnewe = vebûn; simbêlê fk-î melûl bûn; xeyidîn; ẍezibîn} to be or become angry or annoyed, get mad, fly into a rage: •**Lê paşê pir bi kurê xwe ve *erinî* û got ...** (ZZ-4, 212) But afterwards he *became angry* with his son and said ... •**Mele *dierine* û dibêje ...** (ZZ-3, 14) The mulla *becomes annoyed* and says ... ; 2) to refuse to obey *(of children)*; to refuse to give up *(a fight)*. {also: enirîn (A-2/IFb-2/BF-2/ZF/CS/TF/Wkt-2/SS); 'engirîn (K-2/FS-2); 'enirîn (K-2/B/Tsab); 'ernîn (GF); 'eřnîn (K); 'ingirîn (FS-2); 'iniřîn (FS); [arenin] عرنين (JJ); <'erinîn عرنين (di'erinî) (دعرنى)> (HH)} [Zeb/ZZ/IFb/Wkt//JJ/HH//GF//K//B/Tsab//A/BF/ZF/TF/CS//FS] <2: cene girtin; xezirîn>

erîn ئەرین *f.* **(-a;-ê).** unit of length: 66.666 cm. [1 ½ erîn = 1 meter]: •**bi fireya 3 *erîna* û bi dirêjaya 5 *erîna*** (Qzl) 3 *erîns* wide and 5 *erîns* long •**Hayqar bibe bikuje. Serê wî sed *erînî* ji cendekê wî bi dûrxîne** (Qzl) Take Ahiqar and kill him. Remove his head 100 *erîns* from his body. Cf. T arşın = 'ell, cubit, yard' [Qzl/FJ/ZF3] <gez I>

erînî ئەرینی (TF) = affirmative; positive. See **erênî**.

erke ئەرکە (Z-3) = if. See **eger I**.

Ermen ئەرمەن (K) = Armenian. See **Ermenî**.

Ermenêstan ئەرمەنێستان (Ba2) = Armenia. See **Ermenîstan**.

Ermenî ئەرمەنی *m.* (). Armenian *(person)*: **-jina ermenî** = Armenian woman; **-zimanê ermenîya[n]** = Armenian language. {also: Ermen (K-2); Êrmenî (K-2)} {syn: File [2]} [K/JB3/IFb/B] <Ermenîstan; kirûng; Misilmênî>

Ermenîstan ئەرمەنیستان *f.* **(-a;-ê).** Armenia: **-Ȓespûblîka Sovêtîêye Sosîalîstîêye Ermenêstanê [ȒSSE]** (Ba2) the Soviet Socialist Republic of Armenia. {also: Ermenêstan (Ba2)} [Ber/K/JB3//Ba2]

ermûş ئەرمووش = silk. See **hevirmiş**.

'ern عەرن/**ern** ئەرن [A/JB3/IFb] *m./f.(JB3)* **(-ê/-a;).** anger, indignation; irritation; fury, anger, rage: •***Erna* wî danî** (JB3) He calmed down/His *anger* abated; **-'ernê *fk-ê* řabûn/'ernê *fk-ê* pê girtin** (XF) to fly into a rage: •**Bila hinek *irnên min* rabin** (J2, 15) Let *me get* good and *angry*; Let me fly into a rage. {also: iřin, f. (K-2); irn (J2)/iřn (K-2); [ârin] عارين (JJ)} {syn: hêrs} [EP-7/K/B//A/

JB3/IFb//JJ]

'ernîn عەرنین (GF)/'eřnîn عەڕنین (K) = to be angry. See **erinîn**.

ersawil ئەرساوِل (K/B) = guard, soldier. See **ersewil**.

ersewal ئەرسەوال (Tsab) = guard, soldier. See **ersewil**.

ersewil ئـــەرســـەوِل *m.* **(-ê;).** guard, soldier: **•P'adşa *ersewilê* xwe şand** (HCK-5, #41, 225) The king sent his *guard.* {also: ersawil (K-2/B/Tsab-2); ersewal (Tsab-2); hesawil (Tsab-2)} < Rus esaul есаул = 'Cossack captain' < Turkic yasaul = 'head, chief'; Sor yasawuł یـــاســاوول = 'marshal, court officer' [HCK/K/Tsab//B] <balbas>

erûk ئەرووك (GF/JJ-Lx) = plum. See **hêrûg**.

ervaz ئەرڤاز (HH) = uphill slope. See **hevraz**.

erxewanî ئـەرخـەوانـی (FJ/ZF/Kmc/Wkt) = purple. See **erẍewanî**.

erẍewanî ئـــەرغـــەوانـــی *adj.* purple, violet: **•Ji lêvên *erxewanî* min du sed cam / Şeraba hingivînî nû, vexwarî** (Cxn-4: Diyariya yarê) From *purple* lips I have drunk 200 goblets of new honey wine. {also: erguwanî (Qzl); erxewanî (FJ/ZF/Kmc/Wkt)} {syn: binefşî; mor I; şîrkî} Arc argevān ארגוון & argāmān ארגמן & Syr argwān ܐܪܓܘܢ = purple (dye), purple garment (Arc gavān גוון & Syr gwān ܓܘܢ = 'color, hue'); Ar urjuwān أرجـــوان = 'purple'; Sor erxewanî ئـەرخـەوانـی [Qzl//K/GF/CS//Cxn-4/FJ/ZF/Kmc/Wkt]

'erz I عـــەرز/**erz** ئـــەرز [IFb] *f.* **(-a;).** honor, esteem: -**'erza *fk-î* şkandin** (HR-I)/~ **şkênandin** (K) to reprimand severely, scold, bawl out {syn: berhingarî *fk-ê* bûn}; to dishonor: **•Řabû *'erza* min *şkand* û got: "Ê kuřê•m, çima ȟetta řoj bû, ti nehtî, te nego? Vê şevê ezê çi kime şte [=ji te]?"** (HR-I 2:33-34) He *scolded* me and said: "My boy, why didn't you come tell me this while it was still daytime? What can I do for you now that it's nighttime [lit. 'this evening']?"; -**'erz û hila** (XF) one's honor, one's wife and children. {also: [irz] عرض (JJ)} <Ar 'irḍ عرض = 'honor, good repute' [HR-I/K/GF/XF//IFb//JJ] <hurmet [3]; me'rîfet; namûs; qedir I; řêz II; řûmet; şeref>

erz II ئەرز (F/GF/FS) = cedar. See **wurz**.

erzan ئـــەرزان *adj.* cheap, inexpensive. {also: arzan (K-2/B); herzan (K[s]); [erzan] ارزان (JJ); <erzan> ارزان (HH)} Cf. P arzān ارزان; Sor herzan هەرزان = 'cheap' {arzanî; erzanî} [F/K/A/JB3/IFb/JJ/HH/ZF3//B]

erzanî ئـــەرزانـــی *f.* **(-ya;-yê).** cheapness; low price. {also: arzanî (K-2/B); <erzanî> ارزانـــی (HH)} [K/A/IFb/HH/ZF3//B] <biha; erzan; giran>

'erze عەرزە (K/B) = petition. See **'arîze**.

erzehal ئەرزەهال (K[s]) = petition. See **'erziȟal**.

erzen ئـــەرزەن *f.* **(-a;).** chin. {also: erzên (IFb); erzink (IFb-2); erzîn (BX/GF); erzîng (GF-2); erzînik (BX-2); erzînk (Bw); [arzenk] ارزنـــــك (JJ-G); <erzen> ارزن (HH)} {syn: argûşk; çene; çeng II[1]} [BX/GF//A/HH//IFb//JJ-G//Bw]

erzêl ئـــەرزێـــل (RF/IFb)/'erzêl عـــەرزێـــل (GF/HH) = raised platform. See **herzal**.

erzên ئەرزێن (IFb) = chin. See **erzen**.

'erziȟal عـەرزِحـال *f.* **(-a;-ê).** petition, formal request: **•Gelek muro ji her doyan hatin e kuştin, belê mala Şêxê Bicîlê digotin nîw milyon lîre zerer hat ê. Şêxê Bicîlê *'erzi-ȟal* dan e walîyê Mûsilê. Telẍraf kêşan e meqamêt 'aliye** (SK 50:535) Many men were killed on both sides but it was said that the Shaikh of Bijil's family suffered a loss of half a million lire. The Shaikh of Bijil sent *petitions* to the Governor of Mosul. Telegrams were sent to higher authorities **•Jinekê *'erziȟalek* da ȟakimî, gotê, "Mêrê wê jinê yê çê bîyeve, berde"** (M-Ak #615, 280) The woman gave *a petition* to the judge, saying, "My husband has recovered, (so) release him" **•Ya herî rind ev e, ku em *erzûhalekê* binivîsin û bidin hevalekî, bila bibe Stenbolê û bide Siltanê Osmaniyan!** (ZZ-4, 184) The best is that we write *a petition* and give it to a friend, so that he can take it to Istanbul and give it to the Ottoman Sultan. {syn: *daxwazname} {also: erzehal (K[s]); erzuhal (OK); erzûhal (ZZ); [arzhal] عـــرضـــحـــال (JJ)} {syn: 'arîze} < Ar 'arḍ ḥāl عرض حال *or* 'arḍḥāl عرضحال --> Ottoman T arzuhal عـرضـحـال; Sor 'erzeȟal عـەرزەحـال (K3)/'erzuȟal عـەرزوحـال (Sharezoor) = 'petition, presentation (normally written, of a case, grievance, etc.)' [M-Ak/SK//OK//JJ// ZZ//K(s)]

erzink ئەرزنك (IFb) = chin. See **erzen**.

erzîn ئەرزین (BX/GF) = chin. See **erzen**.

erzîng ئەرزینگ (GF) = chin. See **erzen**.

erzînik ئەرزینِك (BX) = chin. See **erzen**.

erzînk ئەرزینك (Bw) = chin. See **erzen**.

erzuhal ئەرزوهال (OK) = petition. See **'erziȟal**.

erzûhal ئەرزووهال (ZZ) = petition. See **'erziȟal**.

esas ئـەسـاس/**'esas** عـەسـاس [K] *m./f.(SK-2)* **(-ê/ ; /-ê).** basis, foundation: **•Lazim e êkê em bikujîn û deynîne bin *esasê* p'irê da da p'ir xo bigiritin**

(M-Zx #774) We must kill someone and put her under *the foundations of* the bridge so that the bridge may hold itself **•Mezhebê ko *esasê* wî li-ser wan terze delîlane *bît* wekî dîwarê ser cemedê ye** (SK 60:713) A religion which *is based on* this type of proof is like a wall [built] on ice. {syn: binat'ar [2]; bingeh; binî; ḧîm; şengiste} < Ar asās أساس [SK/IFb/OK//K]

esbab ئـەسـبـاب (SK) = clothes; reasons; means. See espab.

'ese عەسە/**ese** ئەسە [F] *adv.* 1) {syn: helbet [2]; mitleq; t'eqez} absolutely, without fail, undoubtedly (K/A): **•Ezê *ese* bêm** (F) I will *absolutely* come **•Gere tu *'eseî* meřa bey, yanê na, ezê serê te lêxim** (EP-7) You *absolutely* must come with us, or else I'll chop your head off; 2) really (K); seriously (A/IFb); 3) constantly, always (K). {also: eseh (A/IFb); 'eseî (EP-7); 'esse (K); esseh (IFb-2)} <Ar aṣaḥḥ أصـحّ = 'more correct', elative (comparative) of ṣaḥīḥ صحيح [EP-7/B//F//K//A/IFb]

eseh ئـەسـەھ (A/IFb) = absolutely; really; constantly. See **'ese**.

'eseî عـەسـەئـی (EP-7) = absolutely; really; constantly. See **'ese**.

'esil عـەسِـل/**esil** ئـەسِـل [IFb/ZF3] *m.* **(-ê;).** 1) origin: **-esl û nesl** (IF) essence, true form; 2) family; tribe; 3) nature, character; 4) basis, foundation; 5) original (as opposed to a copy). {also: esl (IFb-2); [asil] اصـل (JJ)} < Ar aṣl أصـل = 'root, origin' [Z-1/K/B//IFb/JJ/F/ZF3]

'esir عـەسِـر/**esir** ئـەسِـر [L/ZF3] *f.* **(-a;-ê).** 1) late afternoon; sunset, dusk: **•Dinya *esr* e** (L) It is *afternoon* **•heya *hukmê esir*** = until *the afternoon* **•ji *esir* û pê ve** (L) from *the late afternoon* on; 2) afternoon prayer time (Islam); 3) epoch, era, period. {also: esr (L-2/IFb); [asr] عصر (JJ)} < Ar 'aṣr عصر [L/ZF3//K/B/JJ//IFb] <serdem>

esker ئـەسـكـەر/**'esker** عـەسـكـەر [B/SK] *m.* **(-ê;).** 1) {syn: serbaz} soldier; 2) {syn: artêş; leşker; ordî} army. {also: 'esker (B); [esker] عسكر (JJ); <'esker> عسكر (HH)} < Ar 'askar عسكر [?<P lašgar لشگر] --> T asker [Z-1/K/JB3/IFb/GF//B/JJ/HH/SK]

esl ئەسل (IFb) = origin. See **'esil**.

esl û nesl ئەسل و نەسل (IFb). See **'esil**.

esman ئەسمان/'esman عەسمان (K/SK/HH) = sky. See **'ezman I**.

espab ئـەسـپـاب *pl.* 1) arms, weapons; armor; equipment, outfit: **•k'inc û *espabê* xwe** (FK-eb-1) his clothing and *equipment*; 2) causes; reasons; means. {also: esbab (SK)} < T espap or esvap = 'clothes' < Ar aṯwāb أثـواب, pl. of ṯawb ثـوب = 'garment' and/or < Ar asbāb أسـبـاب, pl. of sabab سبب = 'reason' [FK-1/K]

espanax ئەسپاناخ (IFb) = spinach. See **spînax**.

Espanî ئەسپانی (Wkt) = Spanish. See **Spanî**.

Espanyayî ئەسپانیایی (Wkt) = Spanish. See **Spanî**.

espehî ئەسپەهی (L) = pretty, beautiful. See **spehî**.

espenaq ئەسپەناق (A) = spinach. See **spînax**.

esr ئەسر (L/IFb) = late afternoon. See **'esir**.

esraq ئەسراق (IFb/ZF/Wkt) = ceiling. See **asraq**.

esrax ئەسراخ (Wkt) = ceiling. See **asraq**.

esreq ئەسرەق (IFb/ZF/Wkt) = ceiling. See **asraq**.

esrex ئـەسـرەخ (K/IFb/RZ/ZF3/CS) = ceiling. See **asraq**.

'esse عـەسـسـە (K) = absolutely; really; constantly. See **'ese**.

esseh ئـەسـسـەھ (IFb) = absolutely; really; constantly. See **'ese**.

estere ئەستەرە = star. See **stêr I**.

estêr ئەستێر (A) = star. See **stêr I**.

estîr[e] ئەستیر[ە] = star. See **stêr I**.

estûrî ئـەسـتـووری (A) = thickness; coarseness. See **stûrî**.

'eşêf عەشێف (RF) = weed(ing). See **aşêf**.

'eşîr عـەشـیـر (K/HH/OK)/eşîr ئـەشـیـر (IFb/TF) = tribe. See **'eşîret**.

'eşîret عـەشـیـرەت/**eşîret** ئـەشـیـرەت [IFb/ZF3] *f.* **(-a;-ê).** tribe; large tribe ... composed of *qabilés* [qebîle] and *thàifés* [tayfe] (from JR, p. 1, note 1a): **•Xwe berde nava *'eşîra* giran** (Z-2) Betake o.s. to the large *tribe*. {also: eşîr (IFb-2/TF); 'eşîr (Z-2/K/OK); [achiret] عشيرت (JJ); [achiré] عشيره (JR); <'eşîr> عـشـيـر (HH)} < Ar 'ašīrah عـشـيـرة. For a detailed discussion of the Kurdish tribal system, see: Martin van Bruinessen. *Agha, Shaikh and State : The Social and Political Structures of Kurdistan* (London: Zed Books, 1992), esp. chapter 2: "Tribes, Chieftains and Non-tribal Groups," pp. 50-132. [Z-2/K/HH//JJ/SK/GF/OK//IFb/ZF3//JR] <berek; binemal; hoz; îcax; obe; qebîle; tayfe>

eşîya ئەشييا (K/EP-8)/'eşîya عەشييا (B) = thing; goods. See **eşya**.

eşken•e ئەشكەنە *f.* **(•a;).** chicken legs in broth, *a local dish in region of Diyarbakir*: **•Çend loqme li *eşkena* ku ji şevê din mabû xist** (M.Dicle. Nara, 5) She took a few pieces from the *eshkena* which was left over from the previous evening. {also: işkene (lezzetler.com-2)} [M.Dicle/FJ/lezzetler.com/nefisyemektarifleri.com]

eşkevt ئەشکەڤت (A) = cave. See **şkeft**.

eşq ئەشق/**'eşq** عەشق [IS] *f.* **(-a;-ê).** 1) {syn: dildarî; evîn[darî]; ḧub} love, passion: •**'Emirê xwedê *eşqa* Mecrûm ser saz *bû*** (EP-5, #10) By God's decree, Mejrum *loved* [to play] the saz [a stringed instrument] •**Li ber defa sîngê xwe erbaneyekê bi *eşq* û hunereke welê diricifîne** (Tof, 7) He shakes a tambourine in front of his chest with such *passion* and skill; -**eşq û mecal** (EP-7) propitious and joyful [time]; -**eşq û muḧbet** (Z-1)/**'eşq-miḧbet** (IS) love, passion: •**ji *eşq û muḧbeta* Zînê** (Z-1) out of *love* for Zîn; 2) happiness (B): •**Wextê kû wilo got, gelekî *'eşqa* wa *hat*** (HR 3:179) When he said that, they *were overjoyed*; -**bi eşqî kesekî şerab xwerin** (K) to drink to s.o.'s health: •**Ezê bibim dolebaşî, go, *ezê eşqî wan* yeko-yeko *bixum*** (HCK-3, #2, 25) I will become [or bring] a boy carrying drinks, I *will drink to their health* one by one. {also: [ascka] عشق (JJ-G); <'işq> عشق (HH)} < Ar 'išq عشق --> T aşk; Sor 'eşq عەشق = 'passion, ardor of love' [Z-1/F/K/IFb/B/ZF//GF//HH//JJ]

eşya ئەشیا/**'eşya** عەشیا [B] *m.* **(-yê;).** 1) {syn: tişt} thing, object; 2) {syn: mal II} merchandise, wares, goods: •**bikirçîyê *eşyayêd* bazirganbaşî** (Ba) customers of the caravan leader's *wares*. {also: eşîya (K/EP-8); 'eşîya (B-2); heşîya (IS); ḧeşîya (F)} < Ar ašyā' أشياء = 'things', *pl. of* شيء šay'--> T eşya = 'belongings, goods' [Ba/IFb/ZF3//EP-8/K//B//F//IS]

et ئەت (GF/B) = older sister. See **etik**.

'etar عەتار/**etar** ئەتار [Wlt/IFb/TF] *m.* **(-ê ; etêr, vî etarî).** 1) perfume seller; 2) {syn: dik'andar} shop keeper, keeper of a general store; 3) {syn: ç'erçî} peddler [or pedlar], hawker, itinerant salesman (TF): •**Ev rewşa han Kurdistan anî bîra me ku *etar[e]k* dihate gund, inca jinên gund li ser serê etar kom dibûn** (Wlt 2:103, 16) This situation made us remember how, back in Kurdistan, when *an itinerant seller* came to the village, the village women would gather around him. {also: [atar] عطار (JJ); <'etar> عطار (HH)} <Ar 'aṭṭār عطّار = 'seller of 'iṭr عطر (perfume), perfume vendor'; Sor 'etar عەتار = 'keeper of general store' [Wlt/IFb/TF/ZF3//JJ/HH/OK/Bw]

'etb عەتب (EH) = shame. See **'et'ib**.

etba ئەتبا/**'etba** عەتبا [K] *m.&f.* **().** 1) *(archaic according to K)* posterity, descendants; 2) followers (JR): •**[Meḧmed beg bi xwe jî neh-deh x̧ulam û *etba* bûye]** (JR) Mehmed beg himself had nine or ten servants and *followers*. {also: [etba] اتباع (JJ)} < Ar atbā' أتباع *(pl.)* = 'followers' [JR/K/JJ]

etê ئەتێ (GF/FD) = older sister. See **etik**.

'et'ib عەتِب *f.* **(;-ê).** shame, disgrace: -**dayîn 'et'ibê** (B) to shame, put to shame; to reproach; -**'et'ibe** (B) It is shameful or disgraceful; -**Pir̄sa 'et'ib tê t'une!** (XF)/**Pirsa 'etb[ê] t'unebe** (EH) = a) Excuse me! Pardon me!: •**Qîza min, *pir̄sa 'et'ib te t'unebe*, tu kîyî?** (XF) My maiden, *pardon me*, [but] who are you?; b) without an ulterior motive, in a straightforward manner. {also: 'etb (EH); <'etib> عتب (HH)} {syn: 'eyb; fedî; fehêt; r̄ûr̄eşî; sosret [2]; şerm; şermezarî; xax} <Ar 'atb عتب = 'censure, blame, rebuke' [EH//B/HH/XF]

etik ئەتِك *f.* **(-a;).** older sister; woman shown the respect due an older sister: •**Wê pir bêriya *etika* xwe kiribû** (Nofa, 93) She missed her *older sister* very much. {also: et (GF-2/B); etê (GF/FD)} [Nofa/ZF3/CS//GF/FD//B] <kek; xûşk>

Etiyopî ئەتیۆپی (SS) = Ethiopian. See **Etyopî**.

etîmxane ئەتیمخانە (Ba2) = orphanage. See **êt'îmxane**.

eto ئەتۆ (M-Ak/SK) = you (sing.), thou. See **tu I**.

etûn ئەتوون (IFb/GF) = limekiln. See **hêtûn**.

Etyopî ئەتیۆپی *adj.* Ethiopian. {also: Etiyopî (SS); Etopyayî (Wkt-2)} [Wkt/BF/SS//Wkp]

Etopyayî ئەتیۆپیایی (Wkt) = Ethiopian. See **Etyopî**.

ev ئەڤ *dem. adj.* **(*oblique:* vî [*m.*]; vê [*f.*]; (e)van [*pl.*]).** this, (pl.) these: •***Ev* çi ye?** = What is *this*? •***Ev* du roj in** (JB3) Two days ago [lit. 'These are two days']. {also: va II (Ad); [ew] اڤ (JJ); <ev> اڤ (HH)} <O Ir ima- (M, v.1, p.220): O P ima- = 'this' (Brand); Sor em ئەم *[adj.]* & eme ئەمە *[prn.]* (Sulaimania & Kerkûk) [BX/F/K/A/JB3/IFb/B/JJ/HH] <ew; han>

evandin ئەڤاندِن *vt.* **(-evîn-).** to love, like: •**Wahş pîvazan *dievîne*** (AB) The pig *loves* onions. {also: 'ecibandin; ḧebandin} Cf. vîyan = 'to want, to like' [AB/IFb/ZF3] <evîn>

'evd I عەڤد/**evd** ئەڤد [JB3/IFb] *m.* **(-ê;).** 1) {syn: bende; benî I; k'ole; qûl} slave; servant; 2) {syn: bende; benîadem; însan; meriv} human being: -**'evdê Xwedê** (Dz) do.; -**'evd û îsan** (EP-7) do.:

•**Eva nêzîkî çil roj û çil şevîye, ez rê têm, hê ç'e'vê min li *'evd û îsana* nek'etye** (EP-7) It's nearly 40 days and 40 nights that I've been on the road, I haven't set eyes on a *human being*. {also: 'ebd (K); [abid] عبد (JJ); <'evd> عه‌فد (HH)} < Ar 'abd عبد = 'slave' [B/HH//K//JB3/IFb//JJ] <carî; xulam>

evd II ئه‌فد (RZ) = revenge. See **'evdîn**.

evde ئه‌فده (FS) = revenge. See **'evdîn**.

'evdesxane عه‌فدەسخانه (Rh) = toilet. See **avdestxane**.

'evdîn عه‌فدین[FS]/**evdîn** ئه‌فدین [H/GF/FS/RZ] *f.* **(-a;).** revenge, vengeance: **-evdîn hilanîn** (RZ)/~ **hildan** (RZ)/~ **vekirin** (H)/**ewd hilanîn** (CS) to take revenge, avenge o.s.: •**Ma Bengî axa ne wesandibû ku bila Gefo bixwîne, mezin bibe, *evdîna* bav û welatiyên xwe *veke*?** (H v. 1, 83 [1932, 1:4]) Didn't Bengi Agha stipulate in his will that Gefo should study, and when he grows up, [that he should] *avenge* his father and compatriots? {also: avdîn (FS-2); evd II (RZ-2); evde (FS-2); ewd (IFb/CS); ewdîn (GF-2); cf. [ouvez] عــوض (JJ) = échange, contrevaleur; <'ewd> عـود (HH) from Ar 'iwaḍ عــــوض} {syn: ĥeyf[1]; t'ol II} < Ar 'iwaḍ عـوض = 'compensation, indemnity' [H/GF/RZ//FS//IFb/CS//HH]

-eve ـــــــــــــفه‌ـ *psp.* re-, again, back: *verbal suffix indicating repetition, limited to southern (Behdinani) dialects*: •**Here û nehêy*eve*!** (Bw) Go and don't come *back*!; **-çûneve** (Bw) to go back inside, get stuck inside the threading canal (said of a drawstring [doxîn]); **-guh lê bûn*eve*** (Bw) to hear again, to hear an echo: •**Min dengê xo guh lê bû*ve*** (Bw) I heard an echo (My voice came back to me); **-vekirin*eve*** (Bw) to reopen, open again; **-vexwarin*eve*** (Bw) to drink again. Sor -ewe ەوه‌ـ [IFb/M/Bw/Dh/Zeb] <ji nû ve>

evin ئه‌ڤن (K) = love. See **evîn**.

evindar ئه‌ڤندار (K) = in love. See **evîndar**.

evindarî ئه‌ڤنداری (K) = love. See **evîndarî**.

evinî ئه‌ڤنی = love. See **evîn**.

evîn ئـه‌ڤـیـن *f.* **(-a;-ê).** 1) {syn: dildarî; eşq; ĥub} love: •**Wan herda bi *evîneke* şîrin hevdu ĥiz kirin** (Z-1) The two of them fell in love [lit. 'liked each other with *a* sweet *love*'] •**Bi van xeberêd *evînîyê*va** (Z-1) With these words *of love*; 2) woman's name. {also: evin (K); evinî; evînî (Z-1); evîntî (Ba3-3); hevîn; [ewin افین/ hewin هڤین] (JJ); <evînî> افـیـنـی (HH)} Cf. vîyan = 'to want, to like' [AB/A/IFb/B/JJ/ZF3//K//HH] <evandin; vîyan>

evîndar ئـه‌ڤـیـنـدار *adj.* in love with [+ *ezafeh*]: •**Eywax gul bû *evîndara* bilbil / ... Delala *evîndara* pismamê / Zerîyê *evîndara* pismamê** (KHT, 201) The rose has fallen *in love with* the nightingale / ... The beauty is *in love with* her [male] cousin / The girl is *in love with* her [male] cousin *[song]*. {also: evindar (K)} {syn: aşiq [1]; dilk'etî} {evindarî; evîndarî} [KHT/IFb/B/GF/TF/OK/ZF3]

evîndarî ئـه‌ڤـیـنـداری *f.* **(;-yê).** love, being in love: •**Ji alî *evîndarîyê* de tu bi talih î** (LC, 88) As far as *love* goes, you are lucky. {also: evindarî (K)} {syn: dildarî; eşq; ĥub} [LC/IFb/B/GF/TF/ZF3//K] <evîndar>

evînî ئه‌ڤینی (Z-1) = love. See **evîn**.

evîntî ئه‌ڤینتی (Ba3-3) = love. See **evîn**.

evor ئه‌ڤۆر (GF) = young male goat. See **hevûrî**.

evran ئـــه‌ڤـــران *m.* **().** poplar tree, bot. *Populus*. {also: hevran (IFb-2); hewr II (ZF/Kmc); hewran II (IFb-2)} {syn: qewax; sipindar} [IFb/SS//ZF/Kmc] <pelk>

evraz ئــــه‌ڤــــراز (Bw/IFb/GF/OK) = uphill slope. See **hevraz**.

evrist ئه‌ڤرست (IFb/JJ) = juniper tree. See **hevris**.

evrî ئـــه‌ڤـــری (GF/OK)/'evrî عـــه‌ڤـــری (Zeb) = girl's headscarf. See **ĥibrî**.

evro ئه‌ڤرۆ (Zx)/evřo ئه‌ڤرۆ (JB1-A) = today. See **îro**.

Evropa ئه‌ڤرۆپا (Ba2) = Europe. See **Ewrûpa**.

evsale ئه‌ڤساله (Zeb) = this year. See **îsal**.

evsene ئـــه‌ڤــســـه‌نــه *adj.* greedy, selfish; insatiable: •**Bênemên jî mîna Ûsivê birê xwe yekî *evsene* bû, ewî zêřê Mîrê Misrê dizî** (Ba3-3, #39) Benjamin was *a greedy one* like his brother, he stole the gold of the emir of Egypt. {also: efsane I; efsene (K)} {syn: çavbirçî; ç'ikûs; çirûk; devbeş; qesîs} {evsenetî} [Ba3/B//K] <ç'ikûs; çirûk; devjihev>

evsenetî ئـــه‌ڤــســـه‌نــه‌تــی *f.* **(-ya;-yê).** greed, selfishness; insatiability. [B] <evsene>

evşeve ئه‌ڤشه‌فه (Zeb) = tonight. See **îşev**.

ew ئـــه‌و *prn./dem. adj.* (*oblique*: **[e]wî** [*m.*]; **[e]wê** [*f.*]; **[e]wan** [*pl.*]). 1) *[prn.]*:

a) he, she, it; they *[in direct case, as subject of vi. or non-past tense vt.; in oblique case, as subject of past tense vt.]*: *[He]*: •***Ew* gelek memnûn bû ji mîr û mîr jî gelek řazî bû ji wî** (SK 7:76) *He* was very grateful to the chief and the chief was very pleased with him •***Wî* jî di bedena xwe de ew hîs dikir** (AW69B1) *He* could feel it in his body; *[She]*:

•**Ewa, dilê min diḧebîne, / *Ew* li vir nîne, / Li Cizîra Bota dimîne, / *Ew* qîza mîr Sêvdîne** (Z-1, 49) The one my heart loves, / *She* is not here, / *She* lives in Jizîra Bota, / *She*'s the daughter of mîr Sêvdîn •***Ewê* zanibû, wekî Memêyî xerîbe, k'esekî wî t'une** (Z-1, 60) *She* knew that Mem was a foreigner, that he had no one; *[It]*: •***Ew* çend seḧet bûn, wekî Memê hatibû** (Z-1, 54) *It* was several hours since Mem had come; *[They]*: •**Çima *ew* kurdî naxwazin?** (AW69A3) Why don't *they* want [to study] Kurdish? •***Ew* sê ne, ez bitinê, ez newêrim e wan** (SK 8:79) *They* are three and I am alone, so I'm no match for them;

b) him, her, it; them *[in direct case, as direct object of past tense vt.; in oblique case, as direct object of non-past tense vt. or as object of prep.]*: *[Him]*: •**Di nûçeyê de li ser kesayetiya Serokê INC'ê yê berê A. Ç. hatiye rawestandin. Tiştê ku ji nûçeyê derdikeve ev e ku CIA'yê *ew* wekî serokê hêzên dijber ên Iraqê berpirsiyar kiriye, lê di rastiya xwe de li ser gelê Iraqê tu bandora *wî nîn e*** (AW69A6) In the news, the personality of the former INC leader A. Ch. was discussed. What comes out in the news is that the CIA made *him* responsible for the Iraqi opposition forces, but in truth *he has no* influence over the Iraqi people •**Rezewan geheşt e *wî*, bê suwal-û-cewab da ber bêrikan, weto kuta hemî gyanê wî r̄eş-û-şîn kir, *ew* jî li wê-derê nîw-mirî hêla** (SK 8:84) The gardener came up *to him* and without further ado set about him with the shovel, beat him until his whole body was black and blue, and left *him* there half-dead; *[Her]*: •**Wekî ew Zîna Sêvdîn bibe, *ewê* jî bike carîya wê** (FK-eb-2, 299) He should make *her* [=Beko's daughter] the maidservant of Sêvdîn's Zîn when he marries her; *[It]*: •**Wî jî di bedena xwe de *ew* hîs dikir** (AW69B1) He could feel *it* in his body; *[Them]*: •**Zînê cahil bû, usa jî Memê, evînî usa *ew* biribûn, wekî gilîyê Bek'oyê qomsî t'exsîr nekirin** (Z-1, 57) Zîn was young and naive, so was Mem, and love had brought *them* to the point where they could find no fault with the words of Beko the slanderer;

c) his, her, its; their *[oblique case, immediately following ezafeh]*: *[His]*: •**pişta *wî*** = *his* back; *[Her]*: •**dilê *wê*** = *her* heart •**Keçeke wî heye navê *wê* Fatimê ye** (AW69B4) He has a daughter, *her* name is Fatima; *[Their]*: •**ji destên *wan*** = from *their* hands;

2) *[dem. adj.]* that, those: [**Eger *ew* mirî mêr e**] (BN, 285) If *that* dead person is a man ... •**Paşê Memê îtqat bû, wekî *ew* Cizîr e, ya ko ew dixaze** (Z-1, 52) Then Mem was sure that *that* Jizira was the one he wanted •**Wî jî *ew* agirê ku li welatê wî pêketibû, giş bi çavên serê xwe didît û dijiya** (AW69B1) He saw with his own eyes and experienced *that* fire which broke out in his country. {also: ewna (Ad/Ag) = 'they, them'; [eoŭ] او (JJ); <ew> او (HH)} <O Ir awa- (M, v.1, p.220); O P ava- = 'that' (Brand); Sor ew ئەو = 'he/she/it; that' & ewan ئەوان = 'they' & ewe ئەوە = 'that one' & ewane ئەوانە = 'those (ones)' [BX/F/K/A/JB3/IFb/B/JJ/HH] <ev; han>

ewan I ئەوان = they; them; their. See **ew**[1] & **wan I**.

'ewan II عەوان/**ewan II** ئەوان [A] *adj.* troublemaker, scheming: -**Bek'irê 'ewana** (XF): a) *name of the villain of the tragic story of Mem û Zîn, who has become a proverbial symbol for treachery and troublemaking; known in Soranî as **Bekirî Mergewer*** {also: Beko 'ewan (JB1-S)}; b) troublemaker; c) two-faced person, hypocrite; schemer; one who is cunning, treacherous, deceitful. {also: awan (K/JB1-S); [avan] عوان (JJ); <'ewan> عوان (HH)} <Ar 'awānī عواني ='traducer, spy' (Hava) {'ewanî} [HH//JJ//K/JB1-S/FS//A] <altax; destkîs; gelac; qumsî; t'ewt'ewe; xwefiroş>

ewana ئەوانا (B) = they; them; their. See **ew** [1] & **wan I**.

'ewanî عەوانی/**ewanî** ئەوانی [ZF3/Wkt] *f.* **(-ya;-yê).** troublemaking, slander: •**Hege tu fesadîyê û li bêbextîyê û li *'ewanîyê* digerî, tê bêyî mala min** (Z-2) If you are looking for corruption, disloyalty, and *slander*, come to my house. {syn: altaxî; geveztî; qumsîtî; şer̄ II[2]; şilt'ax} [Z-2//ZF3/Wkt] <'ewan II>

ewante ئەوانتە (Wkt) = useless, worthless. See **hewante**.

'ewc** عەوج *f.* **().** lane, alley: •**Li zikaka û li *ewcane (L-v. 2, Sebrî) In the streets and *alleys*. [L/Dh] <dirb I; kolan II; kûçe>

ewd ئەود (IFb/CS) = revenge. See **'evdîn**.

ewdîn ئەودین (GF) = revenge. See **'evdîn**.

ewey ئەوەی *conj. & prep.* since, ever since: •**Tu vê so̲ḧbetê tbêjî, *ewey* r̄oja Xodê kirime r̄izqê te û ḧeta nuhu te çu cara ev tiştêt ho̲sa nekirine û**

negotine (JB1-A #14,102) These things [lit. 'this talk'] you are saying, *ever since* the day God gave me to you, you have never acted or spoken like this. {syn: jêlî I; ji ... û vir de; jîrkî} [Zeb/Dh/Bw/JB1-A]

ewê ئەوى = she; her. See **ew** [1].

'ewil عـــەوِل *adj.* first; primary, initial. {also: ewle II (Z-3/K-2); 'ewilî; 'ewilîn; 'ewlin (B); 'ewlîn (B-2); [avil] اول (JJ)} {syn: pêşîn; sift (Ad); yekem} < Ar awwal أوّل = 'first' [Z-3//K//B//JJ]

'ewilî عەوِلى = first. See **'ewil**.

'ewilîn عەوِلين = first. See **'ewil**.

ewiqandin ئەوِقاندن (A/IFb) = to delay. See **awiqandin**.

ewiqîn ئـــەوِقـــيـن (A/IFb/OK) = to be delayed. See **awiqîn**.

ewir ئەوِر (F) = cloud. See **'ewr**.

ewî ئەوى = he; him. See **ew**[1].

'ewîc عـــەويـــج *m.* **(-ê;).** 1) penis: •**Ava wî veřest, anku Ava wî ji *'ewîcê* wî hat xwar** (FS) He took a piss, i.e., His water came down from his *penis*; 2) scrotum, testicles (AA). {also: hewîc (AA)}.{syn: çûçik I[3]; kîr; teřik II; xir I} Cf. Sor ȟewêncî حەوێنجى = 'testicles, balls' (Hej) [FS//AA//Hej]

ewk ئـــــــــــــــــەوك *prn.* thingamajig, thingamabob, whatchamacallit, what's-his-name, fills in the place in the sentence of a word that one has forgotten for the moment, which forgotten word one often remembers by the end of the sentence [Cf. T şey, P čīz چيز, Sor hîn هين]: •**Wî *ewk* a min dît, qelema min dît** = He found my *whatchamacallit*, my pen. {also: ewkê (A); <ewkê اوكـــى/ewk اوك> (HH)} [Msr/IFb/HH//A] <behvan; filan[kes]>

ewkê ئەوكێ (A/HH) = whatchamacallit. See **ewk**.

ewl•e I ئـــەولـــه *f.* **(•a;).** trust, reliance, confidence: •**Ew *bê ewle ye*** (Msr) He *cannot be trusted* •***Ewla* min li te *naê*** (Msr) I *don't trust* you. {also: ewlehî (Wlt-2); <'ewlehî> عولهى (HH)} {syn: bawer[î]} [Msr/IFb/GF/TF/OK//HH] <bawer; îtîqad>

ewle II ئەوله (Z-3/K) = first. See **'ewil**.

ewled ئـــــەولـــــەد *m.* **(-ê;).** child; offspring: –**ewled û tewled** (K)/**ewled-t'ewled** (Z-1) do.: •***Ewled-t'ewledê* wan M. t'enê bû** (Z-1) *Their only child* was M. alone •**Ne *ewledê* p'adşê hebû, ne *t'ewledê* p'adşê hebû** (Z-921) The king had *no children* at all. {also: [evlad] اولاد (JJ)} {syn: kuř II; law; mindal; zaro} < Ar awlād أولاد, pl. of walad ولد = 'boy'--> T evlât = 'child' [EP-7/Z-921/K/IFb/B/JJ]

ewledar ئەولەدار (IFb/GF) = reliable. See **ewlekar**.

ewlehî ئەولەهى (Wlt) = trust, confidence. See **ewle I**.

ewlekar ئـــــەولـــــەكـــار *adj.* reliable, dependable, trustworthy: •**Li gor hin çavkaniyên *ewlekar*** (Wlt 1:49, 3) According to reliable sources. {also: ewledar (IFb/GF)} {syn: emîn [2]; ît'bar [3]; saxlem [2]} [(neol)Wlt//IFb/GF/ZF3] <ewle I>

ewlekarî ئـەولـەكـارى *f.* **(-ya;-yê).** security; reliability, dependability, trustworthiness: •**Hêzên *ewlekariya* dewletê** (Wlt 1:49, 5) State *security* forces. {syn: asayîş; selametî; t'enahî} [(neol)Wlt/IFb/ZF3] <asayîş; ewlekar; t'enahî>

'ewlin عەولِن (B) = first. See **'ewil**.

'ewlîn عەولين (B) = first. See **'ewil**.

ewna ئەونا (Ad/Ag) = they; them. See **ew** [1].

ewqa ئەوقا (B) = so (much). See **ewqas**.

ewqas ئـــەوقـــاس *adv.* so, so much, as much: •***ewqas* bedew** (Z-1) *so* beautiful (that...); -**çiqas...ewqas** {or-...**usa jî**} as...as; the...the: •**Memê *çiqas* bêxem bû, Al-p'aşa *ewqas* bêsebir dibû** (Z-1) M. was *as* carefree *as* A.p. was impatient; -**ewqas jî** [+ *neg.*] = not so very... , not all that...: •**Sîyarê nêç'îrê hela ji şeher *aqas jî* dûr nek'etibûn** (Z-1) The hunting party had not yet gone *all that* far from the city. {also: aqas; ewqa (B-2); ewqeys(e); **haqas**; hewqas} {syn: hind & hinde; ewqedr} [Z-1/K/A/IFb/B]

ewqedr ئەوقەدر *adv.* so, so much, as much. {syn: hind & hinde; ewqas} [JB3/OK]

ewqeys[e] ئەوقەيس[ە] = so (much). See **ewqas**.

'ewr عـــەور/**ewr** ئـــەور [A/JB3/IFb] *f.(F)/m.(K/B/JB3)* **(;-ê/).** cloud. {also: ewir (F); hewr I (K[s]); [aoũr] اور (JJ); <'ewr> عـــور (HH)} {syn: hecac; p'elte} [Pok. m̥bh-ro- 316.] 'cloud': Skt abhrá- *n.* = '(thunder)cloud'; O Ir *abra-: Av aβra- = '(thunder) cloud'; Mid P abr; P abr ابـــر; Sor hewr هـــەور; Za [h]ewr *m.* (Mal); Hau hewr *m.* (M4); cf. also Gr ombros ὄμβρος & Lat imber, *m.* = 'thunderstorm, heavy rain' [F/K/B/HH//A/JB3/IFb/JJ]

ewrazî ئەورازى (SK) = uphill slope. See **hevraz**.

ewřo ئەوڕۆ (SK) = today. See **îro**.

Ewropa ئەورووپا (BF) = Europe. See **Ewrûpa**.

Ewropayî ئەورۆپايى (BF) = European. See **Ewrûpayî**.

Ewropî ئەورۆپى (SS) = European. See **Ewrûpayî**.

Ewrûpa ئـــەورۆپـــا *f.* **(;-yê).** Europe. {also: Evropa (Ba2); Ewropa (BF)} Cf. Ar ūrūb(b)ā اوروبـــا, T Avrupa [Ber/Ba2/JB3/IFb/BK//BF]

Ewrûpayî ئـەورووپـايـى *adj.* European. {also: Ewropayî (BF); Ewropî (SS); Ewrûpî (ZF3-2)} Sor

Ewrupayî ئەوروپایی [IFb/ZF3//BF//SS]

Ewrûpî ئەورووپی (ZF3) = European. See **Ewrûpayî.**

'ewte'ewt/'ewte-'ewt عەوتەعەوت [K]/**ewte-ewt** ئەوتەئەوت [F] *f.* **(-a;-ê).** barking, howling, yelping: ***hewthewta* kûçikan** (DBgb, 20) *the barking of* dogs. {also: hewtehewt (CS); hewthewt (DBgb)} {syn: bile-bil; kastekast; kute-kut; r̄eyîn I} [F//K//B//CS//DBgb] <kûzkûz>

'ewtîn عەوتین/**ewtîn** ئەوتین [IFb/JJ/GF/TF] *vi.* **(-'ewt-/-ewt-** [IFb/JJ/GF/TF]**).** to bark, howl, bay *(of dogs)*: **•Dema ew pisîk wekî kûçikan *bihewte*, ew pisîkên din wê birevin û wê her yek bi cihekî ve bibezin û belav bibin** (AW69B8) When that cat *barks* like a dog, those other cats will scamper and run every which way **•Se *di'ewte*, k'erwan diçe** (B) [Although] the dog *barks*, the caravan goes on *[prv. cf. T 'İt ürür kervan yürür']*. {also: hewtîn (AW); [aúti<n>] اوتین (JJ)} {syn: kastekast kirin; r̄eyîn I} Cf. Ar 'awwá II عوّى = 'to bark' [AW//K/B/GF//IFb/JJ/TF]

exlaq ئەخلاق *m.* **().** 1) character; 2) {syn: r̄ewişt; sinçî} morals, ethics. {also: [ekhlaq] اخلاق (JJ)} <Ar axlāq أخلاق = 'character; morals', *pl. of* xulq خلق = 'innate character'; cf. also T ahlâk; Sor exlaq ئەخلاق = 'personal character' [K/IFb/JJ]

exsîr ئەخسیر (JB1-S) = prisoner. See **hêsîr I.**

exte ئەختە *m./m.&f.(B)* **().** 1) {syn: hêstir II; qa[n]tir} mule (K); 2) castrated horse, gelding (A/IFb/JJ); horse (MK2). {also: axte (MK2); êxte (IFb-2); [ekhté] اخته (JJ)} Cf. P astar استر; Sor êstir ئێستِر [K/A/IFb/B/JJ//MK2] <hesp; k'er III>

externe ئەخترمە (A/IFb) = horse-stealing; booty. See **extirme.**

extexan•e ئەختەخانە *f.* **(•a;•ê).** stable *(for mules)*. {also: [akhtakhānē] اختەخانە (JJ)} {syn: borxane (EP-7); t̠ewle} [EP-7/K/JJ/ZF3]

extirm•e ئەخترمە *f.* **(;•ê).** 1) horse-stealing, horse-thievery (K); 2) plunder, booty, spoils of war *(especially in stolen horses)* (A): **•Pêncî *extirme* înandibû** (EP-8) He brought in (=captured) 50 *horses* **•[Suleyman Ax̄a ... serê Z̲eman Xanî jê kirîye û bi x̄êr ji wî jî s̲ed serî ji 'eceman jê kirî û qederekî jê esîr kirîne û ordûya wan jî yex̄ma kirî û ji sê s̲edî jortirî esp *extirme* istandî]** (JR #39,121) Sulaiman Agha ... beheaded Zeman Khan and besides him he beheaded 100 Persians and took as many prisoners, and despoiled their army and took more than 300 *horses*. {also: exterme (A/IFb); [akhtarma] اخترمه (JJ); <extirme> اخترمه (HH)} < T aktarma = 'transferring' & ah̯darmah̯/ah̯darmak (2.) [Kars; Ortaköy *Sarkışla - Sivas; Diyarbakır; *Hozat -Tunceli; + Central Anatolia & Black Sea coast] = 'to mix up, overturn, upset' [karıştırmak, altüst etmek, çevirmek] (DS, v. 1, p. 128) [EP-8/K/B/HH//A/IFb/JJ]

extûbar ئەختووبار (Bw) = reliable. See **ît'bar** [3].

'eyal عەیال/**eyal** ئەیال [IFb] *m.(K/SK)/f.(OK/JB1-S)/pl.(JB1-A)* **().** dependent(s), family members depending on one for support, i.e., wife and children: **•Jin û biçûk û *'eyalê* kur̄êt Osê hemî çûne tekya Şêx 'Ubeydullah. Ew jî qewî xurt bû: kur̄êt Cindî Ax̄a gazî kirin, çar-sed lîraê 'usmanî ji wan stand, da *'eyalê* kur̄êt Osê** (SK 40:387) The wives and children and *families* of Oso's sons all went to Shaikh Ubeidullah's convent. He was very powerful: he summoned the sons of Jindi Agha and took 400 Ottoman pounds from them and gave them to *the families of* Oso's sons. {also: 'êyal (JB1-S); <'eyal> عیال (HH)} {syn: k'ulfet [2]; zar û zêç; zaro-maro; zav-zêç} <Ar 'iyāl عیال (pl.) = 'dependents, family (depending on s.o.'s support)' [Bw/Snd/K/HH/JB1-A/SK/OK//IFb//JB1-S] <k'ulfet; malbat>

'eyan عەیان/**eyan** ئەیان [IFb] *adj.* 1) {< Ar 'iyān عیان} evident, apparent, obvious, clear; 2) well known; 3) {< Ar a'yān أعیان, *pl. of* 'ayn عین = 'eminent man' } {syn: cindî [3]; giregir} *[m.]* nobleman, aristocrat. {also: <'eyan> عیان (HH)} [K/B/HH//IFb]

'eyar I عەیار/**eyar** ئەیار [A/IFb/OK/AD] *m.* **(-ê; 'eyêr, vî 'eyarî).** goatskin sack *for storing milk, cheese, etc.*: **•Here *iyarekî* nû bîne** (RN) Go bring a new *goatskin sack*. {also: ayar (TF); iyar (RN); [âiar] عیار (JJ); <'eyar> عیار (HH)} {syn: 'eyarşîrk; meşk} <Ar 'iyār عیار = 'standard measure, standard, gauge' [RN//K/B/JJ/HH/GF//TF// A/IFb/OK/AD] <'eyarşîrk>

'eyar II عەیار: **-'eyar kirin** (A) to adjust, tune, set up. < Ar 'iyār عیار = 'gauge, standard measurement' [Wr/A]

'eyarşînk عەیارشینک, m. (FS) = goatskin sack. See **'eyarşîrk.**

'eyarşîrk عەیارشیرک *f./m.(FS)* **(-a/; /-î).** goatskin sack for storing milk, cheese, etc.: **-aşîrka şîrî** (Bw) do. {also: aşîrk (Bw); ayarşîrk (A/IFb); 'eyarşînk, m. (FS); 'eyşîrk (B); <'eyarşîrk> عیارشیرک (HH)} {syn: 'eyar I; meşk} [Bw//K/HH/(GF)//A/IFb//B] <'eyar>

'eyb عەیب/**eyb** ئەیب [IFb/CS] *f.* **(-a;-ê).** 1) {syn: 'et'ib; fedî; fehêt; r̄ûr̄eşî; sosret [2]; şerm; şermezarî; xax} shame, disgrace: **•Eger çak bû qebûl biken, eger xirab bû ez hingî r̄azî me bi *'eyba* xo** (SK 22:202) If it is good then accept it, if it is bad then I am prepared to accept *the shame* **•Li-nik wan sewar gelek *'eybekî* [sic] mezin e bo mêwanêt mu'teber** (SK 24:224) With them crushed wheat [instead of rice] was a most *shameful thing* for respectable guests; **-'Eyb e** (B/JJ) It is a shame/disgrace: **•*'Eyb* e û fihêt e ji te r̄a, kû ti diberdê[yî] x̄ulamê xwe** (HR 4:31) It is *a shame* and a disgrace for you that you are dismissing your servant **•Min çu xirabî digel te nekiriye, min çakî kiriye. ... Te bo çî we'dê xo şkand? Bo te şerm e, *'eyb* e, we neke** (SK 2:13) I have done you no harm, rather have I done well by you. ... Why have you broken your promise? It is *a shame* for you, so do not do this; 2) private parts, genitalia: **•--Tu jinî? Go: --Na! Go:--Wekî usane, *'eyba* xwe nîşanî me de, go, em vira gişk mêrin** (HCK-3, #2, 21) "Are you a woman?" "No!" "In that case, show us your *private parts*, we're all men here". {also: [aïb] عيب (JJ); <'eyb> عيب(HH)} < Ar 'ayb عيب --> T ayıp; Sor 'eyb عەیب = 'shame; defect, flaw' [HR/K/B/GF/JJ/HH/SK//IFb/CS]

'eyd عەید/**eyd** ئەید [A] *f.* **(-a;-ê).** (Muslim) holiday: **-'eyda Qurbane** (DM) the Feast of Immolation, Greater Bayram, 'Īd al-Aḍḥá. {also: [eïd] عيد (JJ)} < Ar 'Īd عيد [DM/K/A/B/JJ]

eydî ئەیدی (IF) = more; still. See **êdî.**

eylo ئەیلۆ (JB3) = eagle; falcon. See **elîh.**

'eyn عەین *adj.* balanced, equal; exact: **•T̲irazî *'eyn* e** (Bw) The scales are *balanced or equal.* < Ar 'ayn عين = 'eye; essence' [Bw/OK] <mêzîn; t'erazî>

'eynat عەینات *f.* **(-a;-ê).** 1) obstinacy, stubbornness, resistance: **-'eynat kirin/kirin 'eynat** (K)/**inta (yekî) pê girtin** (ZF) to be stubborn; to oppose, resist: **•Dêmarîê qîzikê *kir 'eynat*** (HCK-3, #2, 17) The stepmother *opposed* the girl; **-'eynatî kesekîr̄a kirin** (B) to act in spite of, or in defiance of s.o.; 2) hatred; **-'eynat pêra kirin** (K) to act against s.o. {also: int (ZF); înad (IFb); [ynad/ainát (G)] عناد (JJ); <'int> عنت (HH)} < Ar 'inād عناد = 'resistance, opposition; obstinacy'; Sor 'înad عیناد = 'stubborn, pig-headed' [HCK/K/B//IFb/JJ//HH//ZF]

'eyn•e عەینە/**eyne** ئەینە [IFb] *f.* **(•a;•ê).** large mirror: **•Wî serê xwe li ber *'eynê* şe kir** (FS) He combed his hair [lit. 'his head'] before *the mirror.* {also: eîne (F); **'eynik** (Dy/Rh/Klk); cf. also ['ainík] عينك (JJ-PS) = 'pane of glass'} {syn: hêlî; mirêk; nênik I; qotî I (Bşk)} <P ā'īne آئينه--> T ayna [K/B/FS//IFb//F//Dy] See also **'eynik.**

eynekirî ئەینەکری *adj./pp.* covered with mirrors: **•Ew ot'axe çarnikal *eynekirî* bûye** (Ba-1, #17) That room was *covered with mirrors* on all four sides. [Ba/ZF3]

'eynik عەینِك/**eynik** ئەینِك [LC] *f.* **(-a;-ê).** 1) mirror; 2) pocket mirror (Çnr/Msr); 3) large mirror *{as opposed to **nênik** = 'small mirror'}* (Czr/Wn). {also: 'aynik (Wn); cf. also ['ainík] عينك (JJ-PS) = 'pane of glass'} [Czr/Çnr/Dy/Klk/Msr/Rh//Wn//LC] See also **'eyne.**

'eynî I عەینی/**eynî I** ئەینی [Wlt] *adj.* 1) {syn: heman I} same, identical, one and the same: **•Bexçê wî jî *'eynî weke* bexçê wa e, û qesra wî jî *'eynî weke* qesra wa e** (HR 3:115) His garden is *just like* their garden, and his castle is *just like* their castle **•Ew rya tu li ser ya Cizîr *bi 'eynîye*** (EP-8) The road [which] you are on is *the same/very* road to Jezirah (=the road you seek) **•Îro tiştek li kudera dinyayê bibe bila bibe, mirov di *eynî* rojê, heta eynî saetê di kêliyekê de pê dihise** (Wlt 1:37-38, 2) Today wherever in the world a thing may happen, one finds out about it on *the same* day, even in the same hour, in an instant; 2) genuine, authentic, real; 3) exactly: **-'eynî weto** (SK) exactly, just so. {also: eînî (F); [âini] عينى (JJ)} < Ar 'ayn عين = 'eye; essence' --> P --> T aynı [EP-8/K/B/JJ/JB1-A/SK//F//Wlt/ZF/RZ]

Eynî II ئەینی (SK) = Friday. See **Înî.**

'eyşîrk عەیشیرك (B) = goatskin sack. See **'eyarşîrk.**

eywan ئەیوان (IFb) = reception hall; foyer. See **heywan I.**

ez ئەز *prn.* **(min/mi [L/Ad]).** I, me: **•Ez bernedam zik** (Ad) I was not let in (or, They did not let me in); **-ez benî/ez xulam** (M) I am your servant, at your service. {also: e (Ad); [ez/ ezi] از (JJ); <ez> از (HH)} {ezîtî (A)} **ez**: [Pok. eĝ- 291.] 'I (pronoun)' --> Proto IE *Eeĝ-oH(m) ~ Proto IndIr *EeĝH-om: O Ir *azam: Skt aham; Av azəm; O P adam; Sgd (a)zū; Mid P an; Za ez (Todd); cf. also Arm es ես; OCS azŭ; Lat egō; Gr egō ἐγώ; Old Eng ic; **min**: [Pok. 1. me- 702.] 'oblique form of first person singular personal pronoun'-->*E(e)m-: In P and Sor, derivatives of this form have replaced the forms derived from *azam: P man مـن; Sor min مِن [BX/F/K/A/JB3/IFb/B/JJ/HH/JB1-A&S/SK] <min I>

ezbet ئەزبەت (IFb/FJ/Kmc/ZF3) = family line, lineage. See **azbat**.

ezeb ئەزەب (ZF) = bachelor. See **azib**.

'ezep عەزەپ (HCK) = bachelor. See **azib**.

'ezet عـەزەت *f.* **(;-ê).** honor, respect; hospitality: -**'ezet kirin** (B) to be hospitable, to receive (guests); -**'ezet-îk'ram** (XF) do.; -**'ezet-qulix** (XF)/**ezet-qulix** (F)/**qulix û 'ezet** (K): a) honor, respect, deferential treatment; b) care, attention, looking after: •**Ûsib ... wana tîne mala xwe, wanřa *ezet û qulixê dike*** (Ba-1, #29) Joseph ... brings them home [and] *looks after* them. {also: [izet (kirin)] عزت (JJ); <'izzet> عزت (HH)} <Ar 'izzah عزّة = 'power, strength; honor, glory'--> T izzet [Ba-1/K/B//XF//F//JJ//HH]

'ezet-îk'ram عەزەت ئیکرام (XF) = honor. See **'ezet**.

'ezet-qulix عەزەت قولِخ(XF)/ezet-qulix ئەزەت قولِخ (F) = honor. See **'ezet**.

'ezil عـەزِل: -**'ezil kirin** = a) to put aside, remove; b) to depose (a monarch) , remove from office, topple: •**[Dîsanî ji Mehmed begî ditirsa ku Welî Paşa *'ezil bikin* û Mehmed beg bibite mîrê Xinisê]** (JR) But he was still afraid that Mehmed beg *would depose* Welî Pasha and that M.b. would become the emir of Hinis. {also: ezl kirin (IFb)} < Ar 'azl عزل = 'removal' [JR/K//IFb]

'ezimandin عـەزِمـانـدِن/**ezimandin** ئـەزِمـانـدِن [IFb/ZF/Wkt] *vt.* **(-'ezimîn-).** to invite, summon: •**Gava weşaneke bi zimanê kurdî min *diezimîne*, ez ji wan re nabêjim na, ez diçim, fikra xwe dibêjim. Gava weşaneke tirkî jî min *diezimîne*, ez dîsa diçim** (Pirtûkgeh, Firat Ceweri) When a Kurdish language media outlet *invites* me, I don't tell them no, I go, and tell them what I think. And when a Turkish media outlet *invites* me, again I go •**Wê *ez ezimandime* mala xwe. (Wê gotiye min: "Were mala min")** (Wkt) She *has invited me* to her home (She has said to me: "Come to my home") {also: azimandin (TF)} {syn: dawet kirin; gazî kirin; vexwendin} < Clq Ar 'azam عـــــــزم = 'he invited' [K/GF//IFb/ZF/CS/Wkt//TF]

ezîtî ئـەزيـتـی *f.* **(-ya;-yê).** egoism, egocentrism. [A/ZF3/Wkt]

'ezîz عـەزيـز/**ezîz** ئـەزيـز [IFb] *adj.* dear, beloved: •***'ezîzê* min** (Z-1) my *dear* (m.) •**Gazî jina xo kir, "Zû be, doşek û balgan da-nê û zadekî xoş ĥazir ke, ko mêwanekî zor *'ezîz* bo me hatîye"** (SK 8:82) He called to his wife, "Hurry, set out mattresses and cushions and prepare some good food, for a very *dear* guest has come to us." {also: [aziz] عـزيـز (JJ)} {syn: hêja I[3]; xweşdivî} < Ar 'azīz عزيز [EP/K/B/JJ/JB1-A/SK//IFb]

ezl ئەزل (IFb). See **'ezil**.

'ezman I عـەزمـان/**ezman I** ئـەزمـان [F/A/JB3/IFb/Msr] *m./pl.(Msr)* **(-ê; 'ezmên/'ezmîn, vî 'ezmanî).** sky, heaven(s): •**Vî 'erdî, *vî ezmanî*, min nebirîye!** (J) By this earth, *by this sky*, I haven't taken them! *[an oath]*. {also: asîman (IF); asman (SK); azman (Msr-2); esman; 'esman (K/SK-2); [asman] اسمان (JJ); <'esman> عسمان (HH)} {syn: şargeh} [Pok. 2. ak- 18.] 'sharp; stone': Skt áśman- *m.* = 'rock, cliff; heaven'; Av asman- = 'stone; heaven'; O P asman- *m.* = 'sky, heaven'; Mid P asmān (M3) & Manichaean āsmān (Boyce); P āsemān آسمان; Sor asman ئـاسـمـان; Za azmî *f.* (Todd); cf. also Gr akmōn ἄκμων = 'anvil'. See: M. Schwartz. "The Old Eastern Iranian World View according to the Avesta," in: *The Cambridge History of Iran* (Cambridge, Eng. : Cambridge Univ. Press, 1985), v. 2, p. 642; J. Peter Maher. "*H$_a$eḱmon: '(Stone) Axe and 'Sky' in I-E/Battle-Axe Culture," *Journal of Indo-European Studies*, 1, iv (1973), 441-62; reprinted in his *Papers on Language Theory and History*, I (Amsterdam : John Benjamins, 1977), pp.85-106. [B/SC//IF//SK//K/HH//F/A/JB3/IFb] <'ewr; kevir>

ezman II ئـەزمـان (Bw)/'ezman II عـەزمـان (SK) = tongue; language. See **ziman**.

'ezman-dirêj عەزمان دِرێژ (SK) = talkative; impudent. See **zimandirêj**.

'ezman-dirêjî عـەزمـان دِرێـژی(SK) = talkativeness; impudence. See **zimandirêjî**.

ezmûn ئـەزمـوون *f.* **(-a;-ê).** 1) {syn: îmt'îhan} test, examination: •**Pirsên *Ezmûna* Kurdî ya Zanîngeha Mardîn Artukluyê** (HDP) Questions of the Kurdish *Exam of* Mardin Artuklu University; 2) experience: •**Gelek *ezmûn* hene ku em bi hev re parve bikin** (AjansaKurdî) There are many *experiences* for us to share with each other; 3) experiment: •**Bi taybetî *ezmûna* Rêveberiya Xweser û *ezmûnên* din ên ji bo çareseriya pirsgirêkê bêne gotûbêjkirin** (Rûdaw.net) Especially *the experiment of* independent leadership [=self government] and other *experiments* for solving the problem will be discussed. {also: azmûn (IFb-2/ TF/RZ/SS/CS)} cf. P āzmūdan آزمودن = 'to test' & āzmāyiš آزمایش = 'test, experiment'; Sor ezmûn ئەزموون = 'test, trial, experiment' & azmayişt ئازمایشت = 'examination' [AjansaKurdî/IFb/FJ/GF/ZF/// TF/RZ/SS/CS]

êcac ئێجاج (GF) = cloud of dust. See **hecac**.

êciz ئێجِز (B) = unhappy; tired of. See **aciz**.

êcizayî ئێجِزایی (B) = being unhappy; exhaustion. See **acizayî**.

êdî ئێدی *adv.* 1) more; still; already; then; finally: **•Bangê fitarê: gaziya ku ji mizgeftan tê kirin ku *êdî* rojîgir dikarin bixwin û vexwin** (Wkt) The call to break the fast: the call made from mosques [saying] that those fasting can *finally [or, already, or now]* eat and drink **•Dengê şirîna avê dibihîst *êdî*** (MB-Meyro) She could *already* hear the splashing of the water **•*Êdî* bese** (youtube.com: Fermana 74-a Shingal 3.viii.2014) Enough *already*!; 2) {syn: diha [3]} [+ *neg.*] no longer, not anymore; not yet: **•Me bi çavên xwe dît, em *êdî* ji nûçeyên neyînî bawer nakin** (krd.sputniknews.com 19.vi.2018) We saw it with our own eyes, we don't believe negative news *anymore*; 3) now. See **îdî**. {also: eydî (IF-2); idî (EP-7); îda (K/B); îdî; [eĭdi] ایدی (JJ)} *See AKR (p. 57-59) for detailed discussion of **êdî**.* [BX/AB/A/JB3/IF/JJ/AKR//K/B] See also **îdî**. <nema>

êdîka ئێدیکا (L) = slow(ly); quiet(ly). See **hêdî**.

êgan ئێگان *m.&f.* (). nephew or niece. {syn: brazî; t'îza; xwarzî} < T yeğen [Ad/Srk(Za)]

êg•e ئێگە *f.* (;•ê). file (tool), rasp: **-êge kirin** (K/B/JJ) to file down. {also: [éghé] ایگه (JJ)} {syn: k'artik; *qewre (A/IF)} < T eğe; = Sor biřbend بڕبەند & swan سوان (K3) [F/K/B/JJ/ZF3] <hesûn; řenîn; sûtin>

êk I ئێك *prn.* those who... . {also: yê(d) [ko]} [BX] <jêk; lêk; pêk/vêk; têk>

êk II ئێك (JB1-A&S/Bw) = one. See **yek**.

êkdi ئێکدِ = each other. See **êkûdin**.

êkdû ئێکدوو (ZF3) = each other. See **êkûdin**.

êketî ئێکەتی (SS) = unity; union. See **yekîtî**.

êkeyê ئێکەیێ (JB1-S) = first. See **yekem**.

êkê ئێکێ (JB1-A/Bw) = first. See **yekem**.

êkser ئێکسەر (JB1-S) = completely; at once. See **yekser**.

Êkşem ئێکشەم = Sunday. See **Yekşem**.

êkûdi ئێکودِ = each other. See **êkûdin**.

êkûdin ئێکودِن *prn.* each other, one another. (Eastern dialects-BX) . {also: êkdi; êkdû (ZF3); êkûdi; êkûdu(dû)} {syn: hev; yek [3]} [BX//ZF3] See also **yek** [3].

êkûdu ئێکودو = each other. See **êkûdin**.

êkûdudû ئێکودودوو = each other. See **êkûdin**.

êl ئێل *f.* **(-a;-ê).** 1) (nomadic) tribe; the people belonging to one family or tribe (JJ): **•*Êl* çû zozanan** (AB) *The tribe* went to the summer pastures **•[Hûn digel *êlatêd* xwe bar bikin û biçine sînora Romê]** (JR #39,120) Pack up and go with your *people* to the frontier of Turkey **•Nava *êla* bigerînin** (EP-8) Wander among *the tribes*. {also: [el ایل, *pl.* elat ایلات] (JJ)} < T el/il = 'people, tribe'; Sor êl ئێل/'êl عێل = 'tribe' [AB/K/A/IFb/B/JJ/GF/TF] <berek; gel; îcax; t'ayfe>

êlk'an ئێلکان *m.* **(-ê;).** wave(s) of the sea : **•*Êlk'anê* dila ji *êlk'anê* be'ra guřtire** (Dz-#453) *The waves of* the heart are mightier than *the waves of* the sea *[prv.]* **•Xort berjêr nhêřî, *êlk'anê* be'rê řabûne, xuşe-xuşe avêye** (EH) The young man looked down [and saw] *the waves of* the sea rising, [and heard] the rushing of the water. {also: alkan (Rwn); elk'an} {syn: mewc; p'êl} Cf. T yelken = 'sail'--> [ielken] یلکن (JJ) + êlk'en (B). *If this etymology is valid, then perhaps the meaning was changed from **sails** to **waves** due to the lack of familiarity of most Kurds with the sea.* [EH/Dz//Rwn] <beȟr; k'ef>

Êlûn ئێلوون (GF/TF) = September. See **Îlon**.

êm ئێم *m./f.(ZF3)* **( ).** feed, fodder; food *(for animals)*: **-êm dan** (IFb/HH)/~ **kirin** (K) to feed (animals): **•*Êm* û alîkê dewara xo *daneda*** (HR 3:60) He *gave* his horse *feed* and fodder. {also: <êm> ایم (HH)} {syn: alif; alîk I} < T yem [HR/K/A/IFb/FJ/TF/GF/HH/Tsab/CS/ZF3] <emek; p'ût I>

êmanê ئێمانێ (K/B) = approximately. See **êmê**.

êmeg ئێمەگ (L) = food; work. See **emek**.

êmek ئێمەك (K) = food; work. See **emek**.

êmê ئێمێ *prep.* about, approximately, around: **•Em *êmanê* pênc kilomêtran çûn** (K) We went for *approximately* five kilometers **•*Êmanê* seheteke ez hîvîya te bûm** (K) I waited for you *for about* an hour **•*Êmê* du seȟeta k'afirařa tême şeř** (Z-821, 132) I fight the infidels *for about* two hours. {also: êmanê (K/B-2)} [Z-821/B//K]

êmin ئێمِن (GW) = secure; reliable. See **emîn**.

êmîş ئـێـمـیـش *m.* **(-ê;).** 1) {syn: ber V; fîkî; mêwe} fruit(s) (Ag/K/JJ/B): **•Antep t'ijî *êmîş* e** (Ag) [Gazi]antep is full of *fruit* **•Wî ȟeyamî *êmîşî* bol bû, em dizîva dik'etne baẍa, me *êmîş* didizya, carna jî xweyêd hine baẍa gunê xwe li me danîn, îzna me didan, wekî em *êmîşêd* ji dara k'etî: zerdela, sêva, ȟulîya û êd dinê xweřa berevkin** (Ba2-4, 224) At that time [of year] *fruit* was abundant, we would sneak into orchards and steal *fruit*, and sometimes the owners of some orchards would take pity on us and allow us to pick *fruit* which had fallen from the tree: apricots, apples, plums, etc.; 2) {syn: deramet I; dikak; heşînatî; p'incar} vegetable(s) (K); 3) melon (B). {also: [eimich] ايمش (JJ)} < T yemiş = 'food' [Ag/F/K/B/JJ] <balete>

Êmo ئێمۆ *m.* **().** *Man's name.*

ênî ئێنی (L) = forehead. See **'enî**.

êp'erî ئـێـپـەری *m.* **(-yê;).** tramp, vagabond, vagrant, hobo; ragged fellow: **•Eva *êp'erîyê* han ji k'u hat?** (IS-315) Where did this *tramp* come from? [IS/K(s)/SS]

êp'êce ئێپێچە (B) = rather. See **ep'êce**.

êprax ئێپراخ (SK) = stuffed grape leaves. See **îprax**.

êqîn ئـێـقـیـن *adj.* sure, certain, doubtless: **-êqîn kirin** (JB1-S) to convince, persuade {syn: îqna' kirin; qani' kirin}. {also: yeqîn (K); yêqîm (B)} < Ar yaqīn يقين [EP-7/JB1-S//K//B] See also **yeqîn**.

êrat'î ئێراتی (K) = women's headscarf. See **hêratî**.

êrdek ئـێـردەك *f.* **(-a;).** spare horse *(brought on journey to relieve other horses)*: **•Bira řabû hespekê syar bû, hespek avîte *êrdeka* xwe şûnda vegeřya** (HCK-1, 202) The brother got up and mounted his horse, keeping another horse in reserve/along with *a spare horse*, [and] turned back. {also: yedek (GF); <êrdek> ايردك (HH)} < T yedek = 'spare, extra'; Sor yedek یەدەك/ yedeg یەدەگ = 'replacement, stand-by, reserve' [HCK/K/IFb/HH/ZF3//GF] <hesp>

êrdim ئـێـردِم f. **(-a;-ê).** place, spot: **•Berî bîstekê ji wê *êrdimê* bi dûr dikeve û diçe Cizîrê** (JB2-O.Sebrî/Rnh 14[1943] 8-9) In a moment he goes far away from that *place* and goes to Jezira **•Dema digihe *êrdima* ko şêr lê** (JB2-O.Sebrî/Rnh 14[1943] 8-9) When he reaches the *spot* where the lion is. {syn: cî; der I; dever I; dews I; şûn} [JB2/Rnh/GF/OK]

Êrêvan ئێرێڤان (Ba2) = Erevan. See **Řewan**.

êris ئـێـرِس *m.* **().** monk, priest: **•[Meger li wê navê *êrîsan* ji derve ȟesa me kirîne]** (JR #22, 66) But just then *the monks* outside became aware of us **•[Miqdarê deh file û *êrîsan* bi çek westane]** (JR #22, 67) Ten Armenians and *monks* stood armed. {also: êrîs (Tsab-2); [eïris ايريس/hiris هريس] (JJ); <êrês> ايريس (HH)} {syn: k'eşîş; řeben II} < Arm erēc երէց = 'elder, pastor, priest' < Gr 'iereus ἱερεύς?; Sor êrês ئـێـریـس = 'head of Christian community' (Gîw Mukriyanî) [JR/JJ//K/IFb/Tsab/CS/ZF3//HH]

êriş ئێرِش (IFb/OK) = attack. See **êrîş**.

êrîs ئێریس (Tsab) = monk, priest. See **êris**.

êrîş ئـێـریـش *f.* **(-a;-ê).** attack, assault: **•*Êrîşa* gur pez ditirsîne** (AB) The wolf's *attack* scares the sheep; **-êrîş birin [ser]** (K/IFb)/**~dan** (A/IFb)/~ **kirin** (K/IFb) to attack. {also: êriş (IFb/OK-2); hêriş (Bw); [eïrouch] ايـــروش (JJ)} {syn: ȟucûm[kirin]} Sor hêriş هێرش = pelamar پەلامار [AB/K/A/JB3/GF/TF/OK//IFb//JJ//Bw] <şebeyxûn>

Êrmenî ئێرمەنی (K) = Armenian. See **Ermenî**.

êrwe ئێروە (SK) = on this side. See **hêrve**.

êrxat ئێرخات *m.* **(-ê;).** agricultural worker, farmhand. {syn: mişag (IF); p'ale [2]; pişkûrî (IF)} Cf. T ırgat = 'unskilled worker' < Mod Gr erghatis ἐργάτης = 'worker' [IFb/Wkt] <k'arker; xebatkar>

êsir ئێسِر (L) = tears. See **hêstir I**.

êspenax ئێسپەناخ (Wkt) = spinach. See **spînax**.

êsturayî ئـێـسـتـورایـی (A) = thickness; coarseness. See **stûrî**.

êş ئـێـش *f.* **(-a;-ê).** 1) {syn: azar; çîk; derd; jan} ache, pain *(lit. & fig.)*: **•*Êşa* çavan zor e** (AB) An *eyeache* is difficult **•Girtina deriyê Sêmalka *êş* û azara xelkê Rojava zêde kiriye** (Rûdaw) Closing the Sêmalik gate has increased *the suffering* and distress of the people of Rojava [Syrian Kurdistan]; 2) {syn: jan; nesaxî; nexweşî; pejî} epidemic; disease: **-êşa řeş** (K) cholera epidemic, plague; **-êşa zirav** (BR) tuberculosis, TB. {also: [eich] ايش (JJ); <êş> ايش (HH)} Cf. Skt yákṣma- *m.* = 'sickness, disease'; Av yaska- *m.* = 'illness'? or aošah- (M5, p.537); Mid P yask = 'illness, sickness' (M3); *perhaps also* P jask جـــســك = 'trouble'; Sor êş ئـێـش = 'pain, ache'; = Za dej *m.* & veş *m.* (Mal) = 'pain'. See **266. jīš** in: D. Monchi-Zadeh. *Wörter aus Xurāsān und ihre Herkunft* (Leiden : E.J. Brill, 1990), pp. 89-90. [F/K/A/JB3/IFb/B/JJ/HH/SK/GF/TF/OK] <nexweşî>

êşan ئـێـشـان (JB3/IF/HH/SK/OK) = to hurt (vi.) . See

êşîn.

êşandin ئێشاندِن *vt.* **(-êşîn-).** to hurt *(vt.)*, injure, cause pain or damage to; to bother, torment: **•Birakê min heta îro gêrikek *neêşandiye*** (KS, 10) Until today my brother *has not hurt* an ant **•Birîna hêta min *ez diêşandim*** (WT, 87) The wound on my hip *was causing me pain*. {also: [eichandin/ēshāndin (Rh)] ایشانندین (JJ)} [Wlt/K/A/IFb/B/JJ/JB1-S/GF/TF/OK/ZF] <êş; êşîn; îşkence>

êşîn ئێشین *vi.* **([d]êş-).** 1) {syn: arîn; jendin[5]} to hurt, ache, pain *(vi.)*: **•Çavê min *dêşe*** (AB) My eye *hurts* **•Destê min *dêşe*** = My hand *hurts* **•Kêdera te *dêşe*?** (Ba) What *hurts* you?/What part of you *hurts*? [lit. 'What place of you *hurts*?'] **•Tirsa min dawîyê serê me *biêşe*** (L) I'm afraid that later we'll have problems [lit. 'that later our head *may hurt*']; 2) to be upset, be grieved (by) [+ **bi**]: **•Seydayê min pirr *bi* vê nezanîna min *êşiya* û aciz bû** (Wlt 2:66, 2) My teacher *was very grieved* and troubled *by* this ignorance of mine. {also: êşan (JB3/IF/SK/OK); [eichiian] ایشیان (JJ); <êşan ایشان (dêşe) (دیشه)> (HH)} See etymology at **êş**. Sor êşan ئێشان (-êşê-); Hau êşay (êş-) *vi.* (M4) [F/K/IFb/B/GF/TF//JB3/IF/HH/SK/OK//JJ] <êş; êşandin>

êt'îm ئێتیم *m.&f.* **(-ê/-a; /-ê).** orphan; child whose father is dead, but whose mother is still alive (Bw/TF): **•Hung neşêne *hêtîmekî*?** (M-Ak #537) Are you (pl.) unable to defeat *an orphan*? **•Xan *êt'îme* derodero** (EP-8) The Khan *is a* homeless *orphan*; **-êt'îm û sêwî** (Bw) child orphaned of both parents. {also: êyt'îm (JB1-S); hêtîm (M-Ak); [eïtim] ایتیم (JJ)} {syn: sêwî} < Ar yatīm یتیم --> Sor hetîw ھەتیو {êt'îmî; êt'îmtî} [J/F/K/B/JJ/JB1-A/TF/OK/Bw/ZF3//JB1-S//M-Ak] <bî I>

êt'îmî ئێتیمی *f.* **(-ya;-yê).** orphanhood, particularly the loss of one's father. {also: êt'îmtî (K-2/B-2)} {syn: sêwîtî} [K/B/TF/ZF3] <êt'îm>

êt'îmtî ئێتیمتی (K/B) = orphanhood. See **êt'îmî**.

êt'îmxan•e ئێتیمخانه *f.* **(•a;•ê/•eyê).** orphanage: **•Destpêkirina sala 1923-a gundîyêd me pê dihesin, wekî ... li Ermenîstanê ... bona zared biç'ûk, êd ku dê û bavêd wana t'unene, *êt'îmxane* (malêd zara) hatine t'eşkîlkirinê** (Ba2-4, 220) At the beginning of 1923 our villagers find out that ... in Armenia ... *orphanages* (children's houses) have been established for small children who have no parents. {also: etîmxane (Ba2-2)} {syn: sêwîxane} Cf. P yatīmxāne یتیمخانه; Sor hetîwxane ھەتیوخانە (K3) [Ba2/K/B/TF] <êt'îm>

êtûn ئێتوون (Bw/IFb/TF/OK) = limekiln. See **hêtûn**.

êvar ئێڤار *f./m.(JB1-A&S)* **(-a/ ;-ê/).** evening: **-de'nê êvarê** (K) eventide, evening [third of three 8-hour periods which constitute a day]: **•Li pey agahiyan, bûyer roja 4 Gulanê *danê êvarê* pêk hatiye** (AW71A4a) According to reports, the incident took place on the 4th of May *in the evening hours*; **-êvarê** = in the evening; **-her êvar** = every evening: **•Du girtiyên tirk *her êvar* [m]ifteyên girtîgehê didizin, derî vedikin, û bi şev diçin ji xwe re digerin** (AW74B7) Two Turkish prisoners steal the prison keys *every night*, open the door, and go out at night and wander around. {also: êvarî (Dh/Zeb); êwarî (SK); hêvarî (M-Ak); [eiwar] ایڤار (JJ); <êvar ایڤار/hêvar ھیڤار> (HH)} Morg2: O Ir *upa-ayāra- (supercedes Benveniste *upa-yār(a)-), cf. Av ayar/n- *n.* = 'day': Shughni, Khufsi, Roshani, & Bartangi biyōr, Sarikoli biyur, Yazghulami biyer = 'yesterday'; Sgd 'py'rh *f.* = 'last night' [& βy'ryy/βy'r'k = 'evening'], Sarikoli biurn = 'last night,' possibly from *upa-ayārana, but Yazghulami biyan = 'evening' (biyari biyan = 'yestereve'), Yaghnobi piyon = 'yesterday' (prob. from *upa-ayan-) & viyōra = 'evening' (<*abi-ayāra-); M. Schwartz: Khwarezmian by'r; Mid P ēbārag (M3); (early) P ēvār ایوار; Sor êware ئێواره; Za êre *m.* = 'midafternoon [T ikindi]' (Mal); Hau wêrega *m.* (M4). For the Khwarezmian see: M. Schwartz. "On the Vocabulary of the Khwarezmian *Muqaddimatu l-Adab*, as Edited by J. Benzing," *ZDMG*, 120 (1970), 293; R.E. Emmerick "Some Chorasmian and Khotanese Etymologies" *Journal of the Royal Asiatic Society*, i (1970), 69. [F/K/A/JB3/IF/B/JJ/HH//Dh/Zeb//SK//M-Ak] <berêvar; hingûr; şev>

êvarî ئێڤاری (Dh/Zeb) = evening. See **êvar**.

êvist ئێڤست (MG) = juniper tree. See **hevris**.

êvitandin ئێڤِتاندِن *vt.* **(-êvitîn-).** to cause to swell up, turn (a wounded limb) black and blue: **•Zirkêtkê bi destê wî veda û destê wî *êvitand*** (FS) The hornet stung his hand and *caused it to swell up*. {also: êvtandin (ZF3)} {syn: nep'ixandin; p'erçifandin; werimandin} [FS//ZF3] <êvitîn>

êvitî ئێڤِتی *pp.* swollen, black and blue: **•cihê *êvitî*** (BF) *swollen* region, *black and blue* region on the body. {also: êvtî (ZF3)} [BF//ZF3]

êvitîn ئێڤِتین *vi.* **(-êvit-).** to swell up, turn black and blue *(of a wound)*: **•Destê wî *êvitî*** (FS) His hand *is black and blue.* {also: êvtîn (ZF3)} {syn: nep'ixîn; p'erçifîn; werimîn} [Wkt/BF/FS/FD//ZF3] <êvitandin>

êvtandin ئێڤتاندِن (ZF3) = to cause to swell. See **êvitandin**.

êvtî ئێڤتی (ZF3) = swollen, black and blue. See **êvitî**.

êvtîn ئێڤتین (ZF3) = to swell up. See **êvitîn**.

êwarî ئێواری (SK) = evening. See **êvar**.

êwirge ئێوِرگه = abode. See **hêwirge**.

êxbal ئێخبال = good luck; fate. See **îqbal**.

êxistin ئێخِستِن (-êx-) (SK) = to drop; to insert; to strike. See **xistin**.

êxnî ئێخنی (ZF3) = stew. See **êx̄nî**.

êxsîr ئێخسیر (SK) = prisoner. See **hêsîr I**.

êxte ئێخته (IF) = mule. See **exte**.

êx̄bal ئێغبال (K) = good luck; fate. See **îqbal**.

êx̄nî ئێغنی *f.* **(-ya;).** type of stew: 1) stew made with onions and tomatoes [T yahni] (IF); 2) dish made with meat (K); 3) dish made with bulgur [=cracked wheat germ], onions, oil, and spices, rolled into balls (HH); 4) 'bouillonnement' (JJ-G); 5) purée [T ezme] (Msr): **-êx̄nîya kartola** (Msr) potato purée, mashed potatoes. {also: yahnî (IF); êxnî (ZF3); [iakni] یخنی (JJ-G); <êx̄nî> ایغنی (HH)} P yaxnī یخنی = 'kind of gravy; cooked fowl or meat (often served cold)'; Ar yaxnī يخني = 'a kind of ragout'; T yahni = 'stew made with onions and tomatoes'; Sor yêx̄nî یێغنی = 'kind of stew made of meat and onions' [Msr/K/HH//IF//JJ-G//ZF3]

'êyal عێیال (JB1-S) = family. See **'eyal**.

êyt'îm ئێیتیم (JB1-S) = orphan. See **êt'îm**.

Êzdî ئێزدی (K/B) = Yezidi. See **Êzîdî**.

Êzedî ئێزەدی (SK) = Yezidi. See **Êzîdî**.

Êzidî ئێزِدی (IFb) = Yezidi. See **Êzîdî**.

êzing ئێزنگ *m.* **(-ê;).** firewood, kindling wood *(as opposed to **qoçik** (Haz), firewood which is cut and ready to be burned)*: **•*Êzingan* bîne, em agir dadin** (AB) Bring *firewood*, so that we can light the fire. {also: hêzing I; [hej هژ/hezink هزنك] (JJ)} [Pok. aidh-/idh- 12.] 'to burn, fire': Skt idhmá- *m.* = 'fuel'; Av aèsma- = 'firewood' (Horn #1117); Pahl ēsm/[h]ēzam & Mid P ēzm/ēsm (M3); P hīzom هیزم; Sor hêzim هێزِم; Za eizími (Lx)/îzim-i *f.* (Mal); Hau hêzimê *pl.* (M4) [AB/K/A/JB3/IFb/JJ/ZF3] <dar I & II; ȟejik; teȓik [1]; xişt II>

êzingker ئەزنگکەر (K) = woodgatherer. See **êzingvan**.

êzingvan ئێزنگڤان *m.* **(-ê;).**woodgatherer: **•*Êzingvan* çûn dehlê jibo êzingan** (AB) *The woodgatherers* went to the forest (or thicket) for firewood. {also: ezingker (K-2)} [AB/K/IF/ZF3] <darbiȓ>

Êzîdî ئێزیدی *m./adj.* **().** Yezidi: **•Kurê min tu ji Nusêbînî yî înşalah tu ne *Êzidî* yî lê bila bibê. *Êzidî* gelek ji Bisilmanan çêtir in** (Ah) My son, you are from Nusaybin, I hope you are not a *Yezidi*, but then again, so be it. *The Yezidis* are much better than the Muslims **•Min kitêbek li ser *Êzîdiyan* nivîsand** (BX) I wrote a book about *the Yezidis*. {also: Êzdî (K/B); Êzedî (SK); Êzidî (IFb); Yezîdî (A-2); [iezidi] یزیدی (JJ)} {syn: Dasinî} [BX//K/B//A/JJ//IFb//SK] <k'irîv [2]>

êzya ئێزیا (M-Ak) = dragon, serpent. See **zîha**.

F ف

fafon فافۆن *f./m.(FS)* **(;/-î).** aluminum (British: aluminium). {also: bafon (A/IFb-2); bafûn (GF/TF)} Sor fafon فافۆن [Bw/K(s)/IFb/OK/ZF3/Wkt/FS//A//GF/TF]

fal فال *f.* **(-a;-ê).** fortune telling, divination; one's fortune: **-fal avîtin** (K)/**kirin** (K)/**vekirin** (B/ZF)/ **~a xwe vekirin** (K) to tell fortunes: **•Ev *fala* ku herkesî ji min re vedikir, wusan derneket** (WT, 88) The *fortune* which everyone was predicting for me, did not turn out that way. {also: fe'l (B); felik (F); [fal] فال (JJ); <fal> فال (HH)} <Ar fa'l فأل = 'good omen'; Sor fał فاڵ = 'fortune telling'; Za fal m. (Mal) [K/A/IFb/JJ/HH/GF/TF/OK/ZF//B//F] <řemil>

falavêj فالاڤێژ (IFb) = fortune teller. See **falçî**.

falçî فالچى *m.&f.* **().** fortune teller, diviner. {also: falavêj (IFb); faldar (K/ZF3); falikçî (K-2); fe'ldar (B); felikçî (F); [faltchi] فالچى (JJ); <falçî> فالچى (HH)} {syn: pîldar; řemildar}<T falcı <Ar fa'l فأل + -cı = 'doer of an action'; Sor fałçî فاڵچى; Za falçi {falçîtî} [JJ/HH/GF//IFb//K//B//F] <fal>

falçîtî فالچيتى *f.* **().** profession of fortune telling, divination. {also: [faltchiti] فالچيتى (JJ)} Za falçiyey [JJ/GF] <fal; falçî>

faldar فالدار (K/ZF3) = fortune teller. See **falçî**.

falikçî فالِكچى (K) = fortune teller. See **falçî**.

fam فام, f. (JB3/SK/GF/OK) = understanding. See **fehm I**.

fanos فانۆس *f.* **(-a;-ê).** lamp, lantern, light: **•*Fanosê* ji xatûna xweřa bîne derîyê Ħewşê** (Z-2, 69) Bring *a lamp* for your lady to the gate of the yard. {also: fanûs (JB3/IFb/GF); [fanous] فانوس (JJ); <fanûs> فانوس (HH)} {syn: çira I; şemal[3]} < Ar fānūs فانوس [Z-2/K(s)/TF//JB3/IFb/JJ/HH/GF]

fanûs فانووس (JB3/IFb/JJ/HH/GF) = lamp. See **fanos.**

Faris فارِس *m.* **().** a Persian, Iranian. {also: Fars (K/B)} {syn: 'ecem} [A/IF/ZF3//K/B]

Farisî فارِسى (ZF3) = Persian (adj.). See **Farsî**.

Fars فارس (K/B) = Persian (n.). See **Faris**.

Farsî فارسى *adj.* Persian. {also: Farisî (ZF3); [farsi] فارسى (JJ)} [K/JB3/IF/B/JJ//ZF3]

Fat فات (BK). See **Fatê**.

fatareşk فاتارەشك (IF/JB3) = spleen. See **fateřeşk**.

fateřeşk فاتەڕەشك *f.* **(-a;-ê).** spleen. {also: fatareşk (IF/JB3); [fate-rech] فاطه رش (JJ)} {syn: dêdik; pîl, f. (IF); p'işik/piş (A); teħêl; xalxalk} =Sor sipił سِپڵ [Ag/K/B//IF/JB3/ZF3//JJ] <hinav; k'ezeb; p'işik; zirav II>

Fatê فاتێ *f.* **().** *Woman's name (short for Fatima).* {also: Fat (BK); Fato (A)} [AB//A//BK]

Fato فاتۆ (A). See **Fatê**.

fayde فايده (BK/JJ/SK/GF/JB1-A) = use; advantage. See **feyde**.

fayîde فاييده (K/BK) = use; advantage. See **feyde**.

fayton فايتۆن *f.* **(;-ê).** horse-drawn carriage, phaeton: **•Keç'ik têda ma, ewî jî *fayton* hilda çû mala xwe** (HCK-3, #2, 22) The girl stayed there, [but] he took *the carriage* and went home **•Wextê derkewt, pîyê xo da-na ser *paytûnî*, her çaran tepançeyêt xo li wî xalî kirin** (SK 52:567) When he went out, [and] set his foot on *the carriage*, the 4 of them emptied their pistols into him. {also: faytûn (GF-2); p'aytûn, m. (SK)} {syn: kařêt} < Rus faeton < Gr Phaethōn (Shiner), son of Helios/Apollo, *famous for his unlucky driving of the sun-chariot*; Sor fayton فايتۆن [HCK/K/A/IFb/FJ/GF//SK] <'erebe; firxûn; gerdûm>

faytûn فايتوون (GF) = carriage. See **fayton**.

fecer فەجەر, f. (K-poet.) = dawn. See **ferec**.

fecir فەجِر (GF) = dawn. See **ferec**.

fedî فەدى *f.* **(-ya;-yê).** shame, shyness: **-fedî kirin** = to be shy, ashamed: **•Beyrim *fêdî kir* go bêje ...** (L) Beyrim *was ashamed* to say... **•*Fedî meke*!** (Ad) *Don't be shy*! {also: fêdî (L); [fedi] فادى (JJ)} {syn: 'et'ib; 'eyb; fehêt; řûřeşî; sosret [2]; şerm; şermezarî; xax} <Ar faḍīḥah فضيحة = 'shame, disgrace' [Ad/L/K/A/JB3/IF/JJ/ZF3]

fedîkar فەديكار *adj.* ashamed: **•Ji ber ku li ber bavê xwe *fedîkar* bû digirîya** (MB-Meyro) She cried because she felt *ashamed* in her father's presence [lit. 'before her father']. {also: fedîker (IFb)} {syn: şermezar} [MB/GF/TF/ZF3//IFb] <fedî>

fedîkarî فەديكارى *f.* **(-ya;-yê).** shame, disgrace: **•Ya Rebî, li vê *fedîkariyê*, li vê rûreşiyê!** (ZZ-10, 164) My God, such *shame*, such disgrace! {syn: 'et'ib; 'eyb; fedî; fehêt; řûřeşî; sosret [2]; şerm; şermezarî; xax} [ZZ/TF/ZF]

fedîker فەديكەر (IFb) = ashamed. See **fedîkar**.

fedkirîn فەدکِرین (ZF) = to look at. See **fikirîn II**.

fehêt فەهێت *f.* **(-a;-ê).** shame, disgrace; baseness (JJ): •[**Ev poşmanî şerm e û *fihêt* e**] (JR) This [feeling of] regret is a shame and a *disgrace* •**'Eyb e û *fihêt* e ji te r̄a, kû ti diberdê[yî] x̱ulamê xwe** (HR 4:31) It is a shame and *a disgrace* for you to fire your servant •***Ji 'eyb û fêhtîa* em nevegeřihane memlek'etê bavê xwe** (HR 3:178) *Out of shame* we did not return to our father's kingdom. {also: fehît (JB3/OK/ZF3); fêhtî (HR); fihêt (K/A/GF-2/TF); [fehité] فهيته (JJ); <fihêt> فهيت (HH)} {syn: 'et'ib; 'eyb; fedî; gosirmet; r̄ûr̄eşî; sosret [2]; şerm; şermezarî; xax} <Syr √p-h-y = 'to wander, err': pahyūtā ܦܗܝܘܬܐ = 'error' [JR/IFb/GF//K/A/HH/TF//JB3/OK/ZF3//JJ//HR]

fehêtkar فەهێتکار *adj.* 1) {syn: fedîkar; fehêtok; şermezar; şermoke} bashful, shy; 2) shamed, disgraced (GF): •**Xwedê wan *fihêtkar neke*** (GF) May God *not disgrace* them. {also: fehîtkar (JB3/OK); fihêtkar (GF)} [IFb//JB3/OK//GF] <fedî; fehêt>

fehêtok فەهێتۆک *adj.* bashful, shy. {also: fehîto (JB3/OK); fehîtok (ZF3)} {syn: fehêtkar; şermoke} [IFb//JB3/OK//ZF3] <fedî; fehêt>

fehim فەهِم (GF) = understanding. See **fehm I**.

fehimbar فەهمبار (GF) = understandable. See **fêmbar**.

fehît فەهیت (JB3/OK/ZF3) = shame. See **fehêt**.

fehîtkar فەهیتکار (JB3/OK) = shy; shameful; shamed. See **fehêtkar**.

fehîto فەهیتۆ (JB3/OK) = shy. See **fehêtok**.

fehîtok فەهیتۆک (ZF3) = shy. See **fehêtok**.

fehm I فەهم *m.* **(-ê;).** understanding, comprehension; intelligence, sense: -**fehm kirin** (IFb)/**fem kirin** (F)/**fam kirin** (OK) [often + ji] to understand {syn: seh kirin [2]; têgihan [2]; =Sor têgeyştin تێگەیشتِن}: •**Apê Kotê nêta min *fam kir*** (Ba2:2, 205) Uncle Kotey *understood* my thought [or, hesitation] •**Ku *ji* yekê *fe'm neke*, *ji* sedî jî *fe'm nake*** (Z-1497) If he didn't *understand* one, he *won't understand* 100 either *[prv.]* •**Min ji gotina te tiştek *fehm nekir*** (IFb) I *didn't understand* anything you said. {also: fam, f. (JB3/SK/GF-2/OK); fehim (GF); fem (F/OK-2); fe'm (B); fêm (Wlt); fihm; [fehm] فهم (JJ); <fihm> فهم (HH)} < Ar fahm فهم [K/IFb/JJ//JB3/SK/OK//F//GF//B//Wlt] <bi fêm>

fehm II فەهم *f.* **(-a;-ê).** 1) {syn: helemor} white ashes with embers in them (MG): •**Di dilê wî da ew qitîska/çirûska hêviyê a mayî jî di nav *fehma* xeman de vemirî** (MGJiyaneka Pêguhork) In his heart, even that remaining spark of hope was extinguished amid *the ashes of* anguish •***Fehma* kevin ji kuçika agirî pakij kir** (MGJiyaneka Pêguhork) He cleaned *the* old *ashes* from the fireplace; 2) {syn: r̄ejî} charcoal (JB1-S/HH). {also: <feḧm> فحم (HH)} < Ar faḥm فحم = 'charcoal' [MG/JB1-S//HH]

fehmbar فەهمبار (GF) = understandable. See **fêmbar**.

fekar فەکار (GF) = thought; worry. See **fikar**.

fekirin فەکِرِن (GF/CS/RZ) = to think; to look at. See **fikirîn I & II**.

fekirîn فەکِرین (BX/IFb/ZF) = to think; to look at. See **fikirîn I & II**.

fekî فەکی = fruit. See **fîkî**.

fe'l فەعل (B) = fortune telling. See **fal**.

felat فەلات *f.* **(-a;-ê).** liberation, being freed from stg., deliverance: •**Ma Bengî axa ne wesandibû ku bila Gefo bixwîne, mezin bibe, evdîna bav û welatiyên xwe veke û di rêya *felata* welatê xwe de bixebite?** (H v. 1, 83 [1932, 1:4]) Didn't Bengi Agha stipulate in his will that Gefo should study, and when he grows up, [that he should] take revenge for his father and compatriots, and work for the *deliverance/liberation* of his country? •**Roja *felata* bindestan ji destê zordestan nêzîk e** (FS) The day *of liberation of* the subjugated from the hands of tyrants is near. {syn: r̄izgarî; xelasî} [H/K/IFb/FJ/GF/TF/ZF/CS/FS] <felitîn>

fe'ldar فەعلدار (B) = fortune teller. See **falçî**.

Fele فەلە (SK) = Christian; Armenian. See **File**.

felek/felek' [B-2] فەلەک *f.* **(-a;-ê).** 1) {syn: 'ezman} the heavens: •**Berê xwe dane oxirê û pişta xwe dane *felekê*** (HR 3:9) They turned their faces towards good luck and turned their backs on *the heavens [folktale formula]*; 2) luck; fate, destiny (IF/B): -**felek û dewran** = fate, destiny •***Felek û dewran* li serê lawê bava û qîzê bava digere!** (L) *Fate* [lit. '*the heavens* and centuries'] turns on the heads of the sons and daughters of fathers. {also: [felek] فلك (JJ); <felek> فلك (HH)} < Ar falak فلك = 'celestial body or sphere' [L/K/A/IF/B/JJ/HH]

felemor فەلەمۆر (MG/FS) = glowing ashes. See **helemor**.

Felestînî فەلەستینی (BF) = Palestinian. See **Filistînî**.

felik فەلِك (F) = fortune telling. See **fal**.

felikçî فەلِکچی (F) = fortune teller. See **falçî**.

Felistînî فەلِستینی (Wkt) = Palestinian. See **Filistînî**.

felişandin فەلىشاندن *vt.* **(-felişîn-).** 1) to smash to pieces; to destroy; 2) {syn: r̄epandin} to beat s.o. up, beat s.o. black and blue *(so that the victim can barely walk)* (Bw). Cf. also [felesc kem] فلش (JJ-G) = 'je disloque' [=I dislocate, dismember] [Bw/IFb/GF/TF/OK/ZF3] <qir̄ kirin>

felitîn فەلتين *vi.* **(-felit-).** 1) to be rescued, saved, delivered; to get away, escape, run away: **•Ez ancax ji destê wan *filitîm*** (B) I just barely *escaped* from their hands **•Ji bin destê dijmin *filitî*** (IF) He *was delivered* from the enemies' hands; 2) {syn: fetilîn [3]} to become untied or undone, to unravel (B): **•Qayîş *filitî*** (B) The strap *came undone*; 3) to pounce on [+ *dat. constr.*] (L): **•Brayê wî *felitî* wê xwarinê** (L) His friend [lit. 'brother'] *pounced on* the food [Son ami se jeta sur les victuelles]. {also: filitîn (K/B/JJ/Tsab/ZF/BF/CS-2); fitilîn (Tsab-2); [filitin] فلتين (JJ); <felitîn فلتين (difelitî) (دفلتى)> (HH)} < Arc pelaṭ פלט = 'to discharge, vomit; to escape; to detach, take off' & Syr √p-l-ṭ ܦܠܛ = 'to escape, slip out or away; to bring forth (young)'; NENA pḷa:ṭa = 'to come out, escape; to become, result' (Krotkoff) & pâliṭ = 'to go/come out, leave; to result, ensue, become; to escape; to be heard (of a sound)' (Maclean); Turoyo fālit = 'to run'; cf. Ar falata فلت = 'to escape, to be set free'. Note that the Ar form has final **t** rather than emphatic **ṭ** in Turoyo and Arc. Although the initial f- rather than p- suggests Ar rather than Arc derivation, it should be remembered that whereas NENA has no /f/ excepting in certain loan words (e.g., fha:ma = 'to understand', Jewish NENA of Zx)--a feature which it shares with such languages of the Caucasus as Arm and Geo--in Turoyo, the /f/ is preserved, as in the verbs √f-t-l (fótəl) = 'to spin (vi.), revolve' and √f-l-t (fālit) = 'to run'. It is not impossible, however, that both Turoyo and K have borrowed these words from Ar, which in turn borrowed them from Arc [L/JB3/IFb/TF/HH/JB1-S/FS/CS//K/B/JJ/Tsab/ZF/BF] <felat> See also **fetilîn**.

felq فەلق *f.* **(-a;-ê).** 1) leaf, fold *(of door)*; shutter *(of window)*: **•T'ê mêzênê derî di derî ne î di *felq* e, derî *felqkî* vekirye û yekî girtîye** (HR 3:140) You'll see that there are 2 doors with 2 *leaves*, *one leaf* is open and one is closed; 2) lock *(of hair)*: **•Ezê her̄im yekî usa bistînim, *felqa* simêla wî narincî** (Tsab, 1:345) I will go get someone, the *locks of* whose whiskers are orange colored; 3) {syn: ker I; gepek} piece, part, morcel, fragment: ***•felqek* nan** (IFb) *a piece of* bread. Cf. Ar √f-l-q فلق = 'to crack, split, cleave' [HR/Tsab/B/IFb/GF/TF] <der̄abe>

fem فەم (F/OK)/fe'm فەعم (B) = understanding. See **fehm I**.

fe'mkor فەعمكۆر (Mzg/Haz) = stupid. See **korfe'm**.

fen فەن *m.(K)/f.(JB3/B/ZF3)* **(; /-ê).** 1) {syn: delk'} craftiness, slyness, cunning: **•Eva gişk *fenê* tene** (Z-1) These are all your *tricks*/This is all your doing; **-fen û fêl** (Z-1)/**fen û fesal** (JB3) do.; 2) {syn: hiner} skill, dexterity. {also: fend (B-2/IF-2); [fen] فن (JJ)} < Ar fann فَنّ = 'art, skill' [Z-1/K/JB3/IF/B/JJ/ZF3] <fer̄eset>

fena فەنا *prep.* 1) {syn: mîna; nola; wek} like, as, similar to: **•Zanî ku ez jî *fena* wî penabir kirime** (hawargotar.blogspot.com 13.vii.2011) He knew that I had been made a refugee *like* him; 2) *[adv.]* as. {also: fenanî (K); [féni] فنى (JJ)} [BX/JB3/IF/ZF3//K//JJ]

***fenan** فەنان *conj.* as soon as: **•Wexta M. êvarê çû dîwana mîr Sêvdîn, Zînê *fenan* ew dît, go...** (Z-1) When M. went in the evening to prince Sevdin's court, *as soon as* Zin saw him, she said... [Z-1]

fenanî فەنانى (K) = like, as. See **fena**.

fend فەند (EP-7) = candle. See **find**.

feqe فەقە (GF) = theologian; student of religion. See **feqî**.

feqeh فەقەه (K/HH) = theologian; student of religion. See **feqî**.

feqehîtî فەقەهيتى (K) = theology. See **feqîtî**.

feqetî فەقەتى (Wlt/GF) = theology. See **feqîtî**.

feqê فەقێ (OK) = theologian; student of religion. See **feqî**.

feqî فەقى *m.* **(-yê;).** 1) theologian, Islamic jurisprudent (K) [feqîh (OK)]; 2) student of religion, theology student (IFb/JJ) [feqê (OK)]. {also: feqe (GF-2); feqeh (K); feqê (OK); feqîh (SK-2/OK-2); [feqi] فقى (JJ); <feqeh> فقه (HH)} < Ar faqīh فقيه = 'Islamic jurisprudent; elementary school teacher, reciter of the Koran'; Sor feqê فەقێ = 'theological student' {feqehîtî; feqetî; feqîtî} [IFb/JJ/SK/GF/ZF3//K/HH//OK] <mamosta; seyda; suxte; xwendek'ar>

feqîh فەقيه (SK) = theologian; student of religion. See **feqî**.

feqîr فەقير *adj.* 1) {syn: dijgûn; sêfîl [2]; xizan} poor; 2) quiet and inoffensive, innocuous, meek. {also:

[feqir] فقير (JJ)} < Ar faqīr فقير {feqîrî} [F/K/IF/JJ/B/JB1-A/ZF3]

feqîrî فەقیری *f.* **(-ya;-yê).** poverty: **•Lawê min, ez ê tişkî ji te re bêjim, heya emrê kal-kalikê te, tu *feqîriyê* nabînî** (ZZ-10, 145) My boy, I will tell you something, until [you reach] the age of your grandfather, you won't see *poverty* **•Xwediyê me hewqas bi vê *feqîrtiya* xwe me xwedî dike** (ZZ-7, 243) Our owner takes care of us in spite of his *poverty*. {also: feqîrtî (ZZ-7)} {syn: dijgûnî; sêfîlî; xizanî; zivarî} [K/IFb/ZF//ZZ] <belengaz; feqîr; r̄eben>

feqîrtî فەقیرتی (ZZ-7) = poverty. See **feqîrî**.

feqîtî فەقیتی *f.* **(-ya;-yê).** 1) theology, jurisprudence; 2) (Islamic) religious education: **•Bavê min jî nikaribû bêdiliya şêxê xwe bike û ez neşandim dibistanê. Ez şandim gundekî din ji bo *feqetiyê*** (Wlt 2:66, 2) My father could not go against the wishes of his sheikh, so he did not send me to [secular] school. He sent me to another village for my *religious education*; 3) being a theology student. {also: feqehîtî (K-2); feqetî (Wlt/GF)} Sor feqêyetî فەقێیەتی = 'state of being a theological student' [K/ZF3//Wlt/GF] <feqî>

fer I فەر *f.* **(-a;-ê).** one *(of a pair, such as socks, shoes, etc.)*: **•Rabûm mi ew keç'e li ber zêr̄a kire *fera* mêzînê û mi li ber zêr̄a kşand** (HR 3:274) I put that girl in *one pan of* the scales and I weighed her with gold pieces. {also: [fer] فر (JJ)} {syn: kit; t'ek[1]} ?< Ar fard فرد = 'a single one, a single thing, one (of a pair)' [K/A/IF/B/JJ/HR/ZF3] <cot; zo>

fer II فەر *adj.* necessary; essential, vital, critical: **•Deverên Rojhelata Navîn hatîne xweya kirin bi deverên stratîcîyên *fer* ... Her çende welatên mezin pûte û bihayekê *fer* didene wê deverê ji demekê mêje, belê ta noke neşiyayne tenahîyeka berdewam li deverê peyda biken** (Metîn 62[1997]:25) The Middle Eastern regions have been designated as *essential* strategic regions ... Although the major powers have long given attention and *critical* importance to that region, until now thay have not been able to bring permanent stability to it **•Go: kuştina vî weledî li me *fere*** (GShA, 229) It is our *duty* to kill this boy **•Roj êke ji fakterên here *fer* bo berdewamiya jiyanê li vê dinyayê** (Roj 1[1996]:4) The sun is one of the most *essential* factors for the continuation of life in this world. Cf. Ar farḍ فرض = 'duty, requirement' [Roj/Metîn/GShA/K(s)/IFb/OK] <ferz; giring; pêdivî>

fera فەرا (K/BK) = bowl. See **firaq**.

feraq فەراق (B) = bowl. See **firaq**.

ferasat فەراسات = shrewdness; talent. See **fer̄eset**.

feraset فەراسەت (K/IF) = shrewdness; talent. See **fer̄eset**.

feraşîn فەراشین *or* **bayê feraşîn** بایێ فەراشین cool summer breeze. {also: <fer̄aşîn> فەڕاشین (Hej)} [Zeb/GF/ZF3//Hej] <ba I>

Ferat فەرات *m./f.* **(;-î/-ê).** Euphrates River, *which together with the Tigris forms Mesopotamia*: **•*Ferat* çemekî mezin e** (AB) *The Euphrates* is a large river. {also: Firat (OK); [frat] فرات (JJ)} < Sumerian buranuna [bur-a-nuna = 'vessel of - water - of the prince'?] --> Akkadian purattu (Wolfgang Heimpel & Anne Kilmer, Univ. Cal. at Berkeley); Ar furāt فرات, T Fırat [AB//OK//JJ] <Dicle; R̄o II>

ferc فەرج *f.* **(-a;-ê).** 1) {syn: bergeh; t'emaşe} sight, spectacle (K/A): **•[sûretê tajî û ẍezalê] *Ferca* wan xweş e, sebra miro pê tê** (L-I, #4, 108, l. 8-9) [the picture of the hound and the gazelle] *The sight of* them is pleasant, people enjoy it; 2) {syn: qerebalix; sixlet; t'op I} crowd, mob (K): **•Herzem jî ... ji mala pîrê derket û ji xwe re kete nav *fercê*** (L-I, #4, 116, l. 10-11) And Herzem ... left the old lady's house and joined *the crowd*. < Ar tafarraja تفرّج = 'to observe, watch' [L/K/A/ZF3] <bergeh; fer̄icîn>

ferd فەرد (A/TF/ZF3) = sack. See **ferde**.

ferd•e فەردە *m.* **(•ê;).** (factory-made) sack, large sack. {also: ferd (A/TF/ZF3)} {syn: ç'ewal; gûnîk; t'elîs} [Bw/RZ//A/TF/ZF3] <t'êr̄ III>

fere فەرە (IFb) = bowl. See **firaq**.

ferec فەرەج *f.* **(-a;-ê).** 1) {syn: berbang; elind; hingûr [1]; segur; serê sibê; sih̄ar; spêde; şebeq} dawn, daybreak: **-berî fereçê** = before dawn; 2) salvation, deliverance from misfortune: **-fereca xêrê lê vebûn** (Wkt) to be saved or delivered (from misfortune): **•Inşelah vê carê *fereca xêrê li* keçika min *vebe* û muhtaci kesî nebe** (Wkt) Hopefully this time my daughter *will be saved* and won't be beholden to anyone. {also: fecer, f. (K-poet.); fecir (GF); [fedjir] فجر (JJ); <fecar فجار/fecr فجر> (HH)} < Ar fajr فجر [L/IFb/ZF3/Wky//K//JJ/GF/HH]

ferengî فەرەنگی (FJ) = syphilis. See **firengî I**.

Ferensî فەرەنسی (CS) = French. See **Firensî**.

feresat فــەرەســات (HCK) = cleverness; talent. See **fer̄eset**.

fer̄eset فەرەسەت *f.* **(-a;-ê).** 1) cleverness, perspicacity, acumen, shrewdness, resourcefulness; 2) {syn: hiner [2]} talent, ability: **•Jin şikê dibe ser wî û ser *fereseta* kurê wî** (Ba) The woman [=his wife] doubts him and his son's *talent.* {also: ferasat; feraset (K/IF); feresat (HCK); firaset} < Ar firāsah فـراسـة = 'acumen, keen eye, intuitive knowledge' [Ba/B//K/IF//HCK] <fen>

ferezîn فەرزین (FJ) = queen (in chess). See **ferzîn**.

ferfurî فــەرفــوری, m. (JB1-A) = porcelain, china. See **ferfûr**.

ferfûr فــەرفـــوور *m./f.(B/ZF3)* **(/-a;/-ê).** porcelain, china(ware), faïence (K/IF/JJ). {also: ferfurî, m. (JB1-A); [ferfúr فـرفـور/ fagfouri فـغـفـوری] (JJ)} {syn: çînî (F)} Cf. P faγfūr فــغــفــور = 'Chinese emperor; porcelain from China' [K/A/IF/B/JJ/TF/ZF3//JB1-A]

ferfûrî فــەرفـــووری *adj.* (made of) porcelain, china, faïence. [Z-2/K/A/IF/ZF3]

fergêt فــەرگـێـت *f.* **(;-ê).** frigate, warship: **•Wê gavê, Keçelok ket hindurê *fergêtê* û çwîk li ser fergêtê danî** (L) Then the Bald Boy boarded the *frigate*, and the sparrow alit on it. Cf. T fırkata = 'light galley (three-masted warship with 10 or 15 pairs of oars)' (RC) < It fregata [L/K] <cengkeştî>

ferheng فــەرهــەنــگ *f.* **(-a;-ê).** 1) {syn: xebername} dictionary; 2) {syn: çand} culture. {also: ferĥeng (F)} Cf. P farhang فـرهـنـگ = 'culture; dictionary' [K/A/JB3/IF/ZF3/ZF3//F]

ferĥeng فەرحەنگ (F) = dictionary. See **ferheng**.

ferĥît فــەرحــیــت *m.* **(-ê;-î).** jinn: **•*Ferĥîtekî* cina kale, extîyare** (Z-2) An aged and old *jinn* **•Xebera vî *ferĥîtî* r̄aste** (Z-2) This *jinn* is right. {also: 'erfît (Z-3); îfrît (IF); ['afrīt] عفریت (JJ/PS)} {syn: cin; ji me çêtir} < Ar 'ifrīt عفریت, possibly < P āfarīd آفـریـد = 'creature; something blessed' [Z-2//Z-3//IF//JJ/PS] <dêw; ji me çêtir>

fer̄icîn فــەڕجــیــن vi. **(-fer̄ic-).** [+ **li**] to look at, watch, observe: **•Dev ji kar û xebata xwe berdide û tê *lê diferice*** (SW1, 52) He leaves off his work and goes *to look at it* **•Emê herin ji xwe re hindurê wê *lê bifericin*** (L) We will go *look at* the inside of it [=the ship]. {also: [farejin] فــرجــیــن (JJ-PS)} {syn: temaşe kirin} <Clq Ar tafarraj تــفــرّج = 'to watch' [L/PS/JJ/Wkt]

feriĥ فەرِح (HR) = wide. See **fireh**.

ferişt فەرِشت (K) = angel. See **firîşte**.

ferişte فەرِشتە (TF/CS) = angel. See **firîşte**.

ferîk فەریك (GF) = unripe plant. See **firîk**.

ferma فەرما (Ber/CS) = official, formal. See **fermî**.

ferman فــەرمــان *f.* **(-a;-ê).** 1) {syn: emir I; ferwar II; ĥuk'um [2]} order, command, edict, ukase: **•Li gora vê *fermana* hukumetê, divê hun gule bernedin wan, lê belê wan bidin ber singûyan!** (Bkp, 5) According to this government *edict*, you must not shoot bullets at them, but rather stab them with bayonets; **-fermanê fila** (Haz) edict regarding the Armenians (at the beginning of the 20th century); **-ferman dan** (ZF) to order, command s.o. to do stg.; 2) law (A/IF/JB3). {also: **ferwar** II; [ferman] فرمان (JJ); <ferman> فرمان (HH)} O P framānā- *f.* (Brand) <fra- = 'before' + mā- = 'to measure' + na- *(nominal suffix)* (Kent); Mid P framān = 'order, command' (M3) --> Arm hraman հրաման; P farmān فـرمـان --> T ferman; Sor ferman فــەرمــان = 'order, command'; Za ferman *m.* [Haz/K/A/JB3/IF/B/JJ/HH/ZF] <r̄aye I> See also **ferwar II**.

fermandar فــەرمــانــدار *m.* **(-ê;).** 1) superior, commander, person in charge: **•Rayedar û *fermandarên* TC'ê li hev dicivin û biryar û raporekê amade dikin** (Wlt 2:71, 16) The powers that be [lit. 'people in charge and *rulers*'] in the Republic of Turkey convene and prepare a policy decision [lit. 'a decision and a report']; 2) governor, ruler. Sor fermander فەرماندەر [K/A/IFb/B/GF/TF/OK/ZF3] <ferman; qumandar; r̄ayedar>

fermandarî فــەرمــانــداری *f.* **(-ya;-yê).** management, administration, direction, leadership; rulership, government: **•*Fermandarîyê* îlan kir ku 3,000 malbat vegeriyane malên xwe li rojavayê Bexdayê** (diyaruna.com 3.xi.2017) *The administration* announced that 3,000 families have returned to their homes in the west of Baghdad. Sor fermanderî فــەرمــانــدەری [VoA/K/A/IFb/GF/TF/OK/ZF3] <ĥuk'umet>

fermangeh فەرمانگەه *f.* **(-a;-ê).** main office, central office, headquarters: **•Hevalê hemî *fermangeha* ye, tevî *fermangeha* fransizan jî ya ku demekê li vir bû** (HYma, 37) He is a friend *of* all *the offices*, even with the French *headquarters* which was here for a time. {syn: qerargeh} Sor fermanga فەرمانگا/fermange فەرمانگە = 'office, place of employment' [HYma/IFb/FJ/GF/ZF3]

fermanî فەرمانى *adj.* imperative *(gram.)*: **-r̄aweya fermanî** (K/IF/GF) imperative mood. [(neol)K/IF/GF] <r̄awe>

fermî فەرمى *adj.* official, formal: •**Em li gor îdeolojîya netewî û *ferma* (resmî) dihatin perwerde (talîm) kirdin** [sic] (Ber #7, 9) We were educated according to the nationalist and *official* ideology •**Sefewiyan jî ... şîetî wekî mezhebekî dînî û *fermî* ... dan** [sic] **xuyakirin** (Zend 2:3[1997], 56) And the Safavids ... declared Shiism an *official* religious sect. {also: ferma (Ber/CS-2)} [(neol)Ber//TF/ZF/SS/CS/ZF3]

ferq فەرق *f.* **(-a;-ê).** difference, distinction: •**Bes eger dewleta behîye musa'ede bifermot em ehlê Qefqas û Azerbeycan û Kurdistan û Ermenistanê bê tefawuta mezheb û bê *ferq* û cudaîya millet li naw xo ittifaqekî girê deyn** (SK 54:589) So, if the august government approves, we people of the Caucasus and Azerbaijan and Kurdistan and Armenia, regardless of our *differences* of religion and race, shall unite amongst ourselves; **-ferq kirin** (K/JJ/SK/OK): a) to distinguish, discern, tell apart: •**Ewe bo xudan-'eqlan we ye, emma bo emsalêt Tahir Ax̄a, ku *ferqê naken* di ma beyna dew û doşawê da, zor muşkil e** (SK 42:406) It is so for the wise, but for the likes of Tahir Agha, who *cannot discern* buttermilk from grape syrup, it is very difficult; b) to change (vi.), be altered: •**Ew ḧale der-ḧeqq kerî noke jî maye. Kêmek *ferq kirîye*, emma ne çendan** (SK 25:231) This state, with regard to donkeys, still remains now. Things *have changed* a little, but not so much; **-Ferq nîne** (JB1-S) There is no difference; It does not matter: •***Ferqa* wî û kirmancekî nîye li nik xulamêt şêxî** (SK 61:768) To the Shaikh's servants there is no *difference* between him and a [common] Kurmanj. {also: [ferq] فرق (JJ); <ferq> فرق (HH)} {syn: cihêrengî} < Ar farq فرق = 'difference'; Sor ferq فەرق = ciyawazî جياوازى [K/IFb/JJ/HH/SK/JB1-A&S/GF/OK/ZF3]

ferş فەرش *f.* **(-a;).** 1) {syn: lat} flat, level crag; flat rock, slab: •**Çend zelam ... wê li nav kelebestan de, giya, kuç û *ferşan* de digerin û tên û diçin** (H 56:5) Some men ... are roaming, coming and going amid the dry riverbeds, grass, rocks and *crags*; 2) furniture; bed; carpet (JJ). {also: [ferch] فرش (JJ)} < Ar farš فرش = 'furniture' & P farš فرش = 'carpet' [BX/JB3/IFb/JJ/TF/ZF3] <ḧelan; lat>

***ferwar I** فەروار *adj.* 1) splendid, magnificent (K); 2) noisy, stormy (K/B); 3) *[f.]* splendor (K); 4) [f.] storm (B). [K/B]

ferwar II فەروار *f.* **(-a;-ê).** command, order: •**Ya rebî, bikî *ferware*** (EP-7) O Lord, give a *command* •**Du syar 'ecele hatin rêda, / *Ferwara* seferîê nav destada** (EP-7) Two horsemen came swiftly down the road, /With battle *orders* in their hands. {also: ferware (Z-1/EP-7)} {syn: emir I; ferman; ḧukum [2]} [Z-1/EP-7//B/ZF3] See also **ferman**.

ferware فەرواره (Z-1/EP-7) = command. See **ferwar II**.

ferx فەرخ *m.&f.* **(-ê/;).** young of birds, chick. {also: [ferkh] فرخ (JJ); <ferx> فرخ (HH)} {syn: cûcik; ç'elîk; çîçik; var̄ik} [K/IFb/GF/TF/JJ/HH/ZF3/FD]

ferxeşêr فەرخەشێر *m.* **().** lion cub: •**Dengê *ferxeşêran* nema ji kozikan tê** (Nefel 1.v.2010) The sound of *the lion cubs* isn't coming from the enclosure anymore •**Sê *ferxeşêr* bo xwe kedî kirin** (Ş. Epözdemir. Destana Mihemed Axayê Kelhokî) He tamed three *lion cubs*. {syn: têjka şêrî} <ferx + şêr [Kmc/Nefel/Epözdemir]

ferz فەرز *f.* **(-a;-ê).** 1) religious duty required of all Muslims (Cf. Jewish mitsvah): •**Rave derva *ferzek* duda nimêj bike were r̄azê ḧeta sivê** (HCK-1, 201) Go out and do your prayers [lit. do 1 or 2 *duties of* prayer], [then] come sleep until the morning; 2) duty, obligation: •**Li ser min *ferz* e** (IFb) It is my *duty*; 3) supposition, assumption (JJ/SK). {also: [ferz] فرض (JJ)} < Ar farḍ فرض = 'religious duty; assumption'--> T farz [Z-1/IFb/JJ/SK/OK/ZF] <fer II>

ferzîn فەرزين *m.* **(-ê;).** queen (in chess). {also: ferezîn (FJ); [färäs] فرز (JJ-PS); <ferzîn> فرزين (HH)} Cf. Ar firzān فرزان, pl. farāzīn فرازين [K/IFb/FG/HH/ZF/Wkt/Kmc//FJ//JJ] <fêris[2]; fîl[2]; k'erkedan; k'işik; şetrenc>

fesal فەسال *f.* **(;-ê).** 1) {syn: delîve; derfet; firset; kevlû [2]; k'ês} opportunity, occasion, chance; •**Çewa ku *fesal* bik'eve min, ezê bêm** (B) As soon as *the opportunity* presents itself [lit. 'falls to me'], I will come •[**Wekû *fesalê* dibînin yekûdû dikujin**] (JJ) As soon as they see *a chance*, they kill one another; 2) initiative; trick (OK): **-fesal jê stendin** (XF) to steal s.o.'s thunder, nip s.o. else's (a rival's) initiative in the bud; 3) {syn : semt} comfortable position or stance: •**Nêç'îrvan *fesal* ji**

gur hilda û agir kir (B) The hunter took up *a comfortable position* vis-à-vis the wolf, and fired his gun]; 4) *[adj.]* careful, cautious: •**Ew merîkî *fesal*e** (B) He is a *cautious* man; 5) *[adv.]* {also: bi fesal} carefully, cautiously: •**Ewî *fesal* zar̄o hilbir̄î** (B) He *carefully* picked up the child •**Gundê me da kesekî dil nedikir wîr̄a gulaş bigirta, lê wekî nişkêva yekî dil bikira, ewî ew hildibir̄î jorê û, wekî zirarê nedê, *fesal* dadanî ser piştê** (Ba2:1, 204) In our village no one would dare to wrestle with him, but if suddenly someone were to dare, he would pick that person up and, so as not to harm him, *carefully* put him on his back •**Li bira nihêr̄î û *bi fesal* berbir̄î Ûsib bû** (Ba-1, #31) He looked at his brothers and *cautiously* went out to greet Joseph. {also: [fesal] فصال (JJ); <fesal> فصال (HH)} <Ar fiṣāl فصال = 'weaning; separation'; Sor fesał فەساڵ = 'form, shape, figure, appearance' [Ba-1/K/IFb/B/JJ/GF/TF/OK/ZF3//HH]

fesidîn فەسِدین *vi.* **(-fesid-).** to go bad, turn sour *(of milk)*: •**Şîr fesidî** (Bw) The milk went bad. {syn: ḧer̄imîn [2]} [Bw] <r̄izîn; xirab>

fes•il فەسِل *f.* **(•la;).** settlement *(of a feud or dispute)*, reconciliation: -**fesla *fk-î* kirin** (Mdt) to settle or resolve *(a feud between two parties)*, to reconcile, make peace between: •**Dê û bavê xort jî hatine, peyre wan şiyandiye dûv melakî, wî jî *fesla wan kiriye* û ew li hev anîne** (Mdt) The parents of the young man came, then they sent for a mullah, and he *settled the feud between them* [=the two families] and reconciled them. < Ar faṣl فصل = 'parting, detachment, etc.'; Sor fesł فەسڵ = 'settlement of feud' [Mdt/ZF3] <aşt kirin; li hev anîn>

fesilandin فەسِلاندِن *vt.* **(-fesilîn-).** to commission, order *(merchandise, e.g., clothing from a tailor)*; to make to measure, cut out *(a garment)*: •**Diçe ser t'erzî, destek cilê efendîya ji xwer̄a *difesilîne*** (Z-2) He goes to a tailor, orders for himself a suit of clothes fit for a gentleman. < Ar faṣṣala II فصّل [Z-2/ZF3/Wkt] <pîvan>

fetil فەتِل (ZF3) = turn(ing). See **fitil**.

fetilîn فەتِلین *vi.* **(-fetil-).** 1) {syn: veger̄în; zivir̄în} to turn around, return, go or come back (vi.) (K/L): •**Gava ko usa Stîyêr̄a dibêje Memo, Stîyê bi paşva *difitile*** (Z-3) When Memo says that to Stîyê, she *turns* right *around* [and goes back]; 2) to rip, tear *(vi.)*; to split (K); 3) to come untwisted, come undone (B). {also: fitilîn (K/B)} < Arc petal פתל = 'to twist' & pattel פתל = 'to pervert'; NENA pta:la = 'to throw, discard, twist' (Krotkoff) & pâtil ܦܬܠ = 'to make crooked, twist (Old Syr); to turn (vi.), turn the face; to wind a clock' (Maclean); Turoyo fótəl = 'to spin (vi.), revolve'; cf. Ar fatala فتل = 'to twist together, to twine' [L/IF//K/B] See also **felitîn**.

fetisandin فەتِساندن *vt.* **(-fetisîn-).** to strangle, smother, suffocate, choke (vt.): •**Ew zurbe hazirin me bikujin, *bifetisînin*** (Ba2-#2, 210) Those bullies are ready to kill us, *to strangle* us. {also: <fetisandin فطساندن (difetisîne) (دفطصينه)> (HH)} {syn: xeniqandin [1]} <Ar faṭṭas II فطّس = 'to suffocate, strangle, kill' [Ba2/F/K/IF/B/GF/ZF3//HH] <kuştin>

fetkirin فەتکِرِن (CS) = to look at. See **fikirîn II**.

fetkirîn فەتکِرین (BX) = to look at. See **fikirîn II**.

feyd•e فەیدە *f.* **(•a;•ê).** use; advantage, benefit, profit: •**Gotina bê kirin *fayde* nîye** (SK 2:17) There is no *profit* in words without action •**Heker tu bibî şivan tê pezê ciwamêra xodan key, *feyda* te tê nîne, û heker tu bûy cûhtarî jî tê milkê ciwamêra filhan û 'emaret bikî. Dîsa *feyda* me tê nîne** (JB1-S, #206) If you become a shepherd, you will look after the sheep of the notables, which is of no *benefit* to you. If you become a farmer, you will cultivate and work the land of the notables. Once again, there is no *benefit* for us in it •**Hirç kuştin** [sic], **emma çi *fayde* hebo?** (SK 10:101) They killed the bear, but what was the *use*? •**Wextê r̄iwî yeqîn kir ko êdî dirêj kirin *fayde* nîye hinde got e kotirê, "Ewe aqlê te nîye, emma xozî min zanîba ew aqle kê nîşa te daye"** (SK 3:22) When the fox realized that there was no *point* in carrying on he said this much to the pigeon, "This wasn't your idea, but I wish I knew who has given you this sense." {also: fayde (BK/SK/GF/JB1-A); fayîde (K/BK-2); fêde (BK-2/GF-2); [fàidé] فايده (JJ)} {syn: havil; menfa'et & mifa} < Ar fā'idah فائدة [Z-1/IFb/JB3/B/JB1-S//K/BK//JJ/SK/GF/JB1-A]

***feyzil** فەیزل: •**nava feyzil 'eînêr̄a** (EP-7) in the twinkling of an eye. [EP-7]

fêde فێدە (BK/GF) = use; advantage. See **feyde**.

fêdî فێدی (L) = shame. See **fedî**.

fêhtî فێهتی (HR) = shame. See **fehêt**.

fêkî فێکی (K/JB3/B/HH/SC) = fruit. See **fîkî**.

fêl I فـێـل *m./f.(K[4]/B)* **(-ê/ ; /-ê).** 1) {syn: delk'; ȟîle; lêp} *[m.]* trick, prank, ruse; swindling, cheating: **•Sim -- simê k'erêne, *fêl-- fêlê* P'erêne** (Dz #32, 401) The hooves may be donkey's hooves, but *the trick* is Para's *trick* [i.e., I know who did this, but I can't prove it] *[prv.]*; **-fen û fêl** (Z-1) do. {syn: fen û fesal (JB3)}; **-fêl û finaz** (EP-7) do.; 2) *[m.]* plot, intrigue (K/A/B); 3) purpose, intention (IF). {also: [fél] فيل (JJ)} ?< Ar fi'l فعل = 'deed; verb' [Z-1/Dz/K/A/IF/JJ/B/ZF3]

fêl II فـــێـــل *f.(K/F)/m.(B)* **(-a/-ê;-ê/).** 1) {syn: lêker (neol); *pêşing (IF); *pîşk (IF)} verb: **-fêlê/-a (ne)derbazbûyî** (B/K) (in)transitive verb; **-fêlê (ne)r̄ast** (B) (ir)regular verb; 2) action, activity, feat, deed (K). {also: fi'l (SK)} < Ar fi'l فـعـل = 'deed, verb' [F/K/B//SK]

fêm فێم (Wlt) = understanding. See **fehm I**.

fêmbar فـێـمـبـار *adj.* understandable, comprehensible: **•Hêvîya me ew e ku ...tiştên ku hûn binivîsin jî dê ji bo xwendevanan zelaltir û *fêmbartir* bin** (RR) It is our hope that ... the things you write will be clearer and *more comprehensible* for the readers. {also: fehimbar (GF); fehmbar (GF-2)} [RR/ZF//GF]

fêqî فێقی (JB1-A/SK/Bw/Zx) = fruit. See **fîkî**.

fêr فـێـر: **-fêrî *ftî* bûn** (K/IFb/SK/GF/TF) to learn, become acquainted with {syn: 'elimîn; hîn I bûn}: **•Ez nizanim hevalên me çima ... *fêrî* Kurdî *nabin*** (IFb) I don't know why our friends *don't learn* Kurdish **•Kotirekê hêlîna xo di çiyayekî bilind da çêkiribû. Wextê ku kêjik dîînane derê, pîçek firaje dibûn, hêşta temam nedişyan bifir̄in, r̄îwîyek *fêr bûbû* her sal di wî wextî da dihat, kilka xo dihelpisare çiyay, gazî dikire kotirê** (SK 3:18) A pigeon had made her nest on a high mountain. When she hatched out her young and they had grown a little, but could not yet fly properly--every year at that time a fox *had learnt* to come along, to prop its tail up against the mountain and call to the pigeon; **-*fkî* fêrî *ftî* kirin** (IFb/SK/GF/TF) to teach s.o. stg., to acquaint s.o. with stg. {syn: 'elimandin; hîn I kirin}: **•Min noke bi wê ȟîlê *ewane fêre* dîn *kirîne*** (SK 32:289) By this trick I have now *taught them* religion. Sor fêr bûn فـێـربـوون = 'to learn' & pê fêr bûn پێ فێربوون = 'to become accustomed to' & fêr kirdin فێرکِردِن = 'to teach' [K/IFb/SK/GF/TF]

fêris فـــێـــرس *m.* **(-ê;).** 1) {syn: 'efat; 'egît; gernas; leheng; mêrxas; p'elewan} hero; 2) knight *(in chess)* (Z-1). {also: fêriz (B); fêrz (Z-1); <feres> فرس (HH)} < Ar fāris فارس = 'knight' [L/K/A/IFb/GF/TF/ZF3//B//JJ//HH] <ferzîn; fîl [2]; k'erkedan; k'işik; şetrenc>

fêriz فێرز (B) = hero. See **fêris** [1].

fêrz فێرز (Z-1) = (chess) knight. See **fêris** [2].

fêz فـێـز *f.* **(-a;-ê).** top, upper side or part of stg.: **•Emê *fêza* şikevtê kevirekî mezin daynin** (EH) We will place a large rock *on top of* the cave **•Herdu bra jî xwe *di fêza* şkevtê*da* veşartbûn** (EH) Both the brothers hid *on top of* the cave; **-fêza ç'em** (K) upstream; **-fêza gund** (B) upper side of the village: **•Wê *li fêza gundê me* danîye** (EP-5, #12) She [or, it (f. referent)] has set up camp *above our village*; **-xwe dan fêzê** (K) to ascend to the top. {syn: hindav [3]} *Possible etymology:* [Pok. păk- 787.] 'to fasten': Av pāzah- = 'surface'; Khotanese pāysa-; Sgd p'z [*pāza-]; Oss făză [Digoron] & făz [Iron] = 'plain, open space' from: H.W. Bailey. "A Range of Iranica" in: *W. B. Henning Memorial Volume* (London : Lund Humphries, 1970), p. 35 [under **9. ŭărăn făz**]. [EH/K/B] <bala; firêze [2]; hevraz; jor>

fihêt فهێت (K/A/HH/GF/TF) = shame. See **fehêt**.

fihêtkar فـهـێـتـکـار (GF) = shy; shameful; shamed. See **fehêtkar**.

fihm فهم (HH) = understanding. See **fehm I**.

fikar فکار *f.* **(;-ê).** 1) {syn: fikir; hizir; mitale; r̄aman I} thinking, thought: **-fikar kirin** (K/B/IFb): a) to think, ponder: **•Berê *fikar kir*, paşê banzda çû** (HCK-5, #41, 235) First he *pondered* [the matter], then he hopped up and left; b) to worry; 2) {syn: cefa; k'eder; k'erb; k'eser; kovan; kul I; şayîş; t'alaş; tatêl; xem; xiyal [2]} worry, care, concern. {also: fekar (GF-2); <fikar فکار /fikir فکر> (HH)} < Ar fakkara II فكّر = 'to think' [HCK/K/B/IFb/GF/HH]

fik•ir فِـکـر *f.* **(•[i]ra;•irê).** 1) {syn: fikar; hizir; mitale; r̄aman I; xiyal} thought, idea; sense: **•*Fikir* ji serê Memê delal fir̄î** (Z-1) All *sense* flew out of dandy Mem's head **•*Fikra* min heye ku ez xirabiyekê bigehînimê** (ZZ-10, 157) I have *the idea* to do something bad to him; 2) {syn: dîtin; r̄ay} opinion. {also: fikr (JB3); [fikir] فـکـر (JJ)} < Ar fikr فكر [Z-1/K/JB3/IF/B/JJ/ZF3]

fikirin فِکرِن (JB1-A) = to look at. See **fikirîn II**.

fikirîn I فِـکـریـن *vi.* **(-fikir-).** 1) {syn: duşirmîş bûn; hizir kirin; p'onijîn [2]; r̄aman I} to think: **-di xwe**

fekirîn (L) to think to oneself: **•Rojekê, *di xwe fekirî*** (L) One day, she *thought to herself ...* **•Ez *di xwe fekirîm*** (BX) I *was thinking to myself*; 2) to worry, be concerned: **•*Nefikirin*, nanê meyî bole** (Ba-1, #32) *Don't worry*, we have plenty of bread. {also: fekirin; fekirîn (BX); fikirin (JB1-A); fikirmîş bûn (B-2); [fykirin/foukourin] فكرين (JJ)} < Ar fakkara II فكّر = 'to think' [BX//K/IFb/B/ZK3]

fikirîn II فِكِرين *vi.* **(-fikir-).** [+ **li** or *dat. constr.*] to look at, behold: **•Ez *li* bejna te a zirav *difekirîm*** (BX) I *was looking at* your svelte stature **•E(z) *vedikim* ezmana** (Czr) I *look at* the sky **•*Fikirîme* neqşê bêzewal** (Tsab/FT, 2) I *beheld* the immortal image **•[Ĥesen Beg li sa'etê *divekire* û dibêje ku mubarekî, qewî sa'eteke qenc e]** (JR 11, 39) H.B. *looks at* the clock and says, "Bless you, it is an extremely good clock" **•Te *li* diya xwe *fedikir*** (CS) You *were looking at* your mother; **-tê fikirin** (JB1-A)/**di ... fikirîn** (SK) to look at, watch: **•*Di* yêk-u-do *fikirîn*, destêt xo kêşane paş** (SK 24:224) They *looked at* each other and withdrew their hands **•Oso r̄a-bo, hûr *tê fikirî*** (SK 40:358) Oso got up and *took a good look at him*. {also: fedkirîn (ZF-2); fekirin (GF/CS/RZ); fekirîn II (BX/IFb-2/ZF); fetkirin (CS-2); fetkirîn (BX-2); fikirin (JB1-A); vekirin II (Czr); [fykirin/foukourin] فكرين (JJ); <fekirîn فكرين (difekire) (دفكره)> (HH)} {syn: bala xwe dan; dîna xwe dan; mêze kirin; nêr̄în; zên dan (MZ)} < Ar fakkara II فكّر = 'to think'; Sor tê fikrîn تێ فكرين = 'to ponder, observe, note, see, sense' [K/IFb/SK/JJ/Tsab//BX/HH/ZF//GF/CS/RZ//JB1-A//Czr]

fikirmîş bûn فِكِرميش بوون (B) = to think; to look at. See **fikirîn**.

fikr فِكر (JB3) = thought; opinion. See **fikir**.

fi'l فِعل (SK) = action, deed. See **fêl II**.

filan فلان *pr. mod.* so-and-so, such-and-such, what's-his-name: **•Ewe qafilê *fulan* muro ye, ji *fulan* derê têt, dê çît e *fulan* derê, meta'ê wan ewe ye, bi hindî kir̄îne, dê bi hindî firoşin, hinde bar in, hinde dewar in, hinde muro ne, *fulan* millet in, nawê wan ewe ne, mezinê wan ewe ye** (SK 22:205) It is the caravan of *such-and-such* a man, it comes from *such-and-such* a place, it is going to *such-and-such* a place, their merchandise is this, they brought it for so much and will sell it for so much, there are so many loads, so many animals, so many men, they are *such-and-such* people, their names are these, and their leader is So-and-so **•*filan* k'itêb** (B) *such-and-such a* book **•*filan* şagirt** (B) *some* student *or other*; **-filan û behvan** (IFb)/**filan û bêvan** (B)/**filanbêvan** (K)/**filan û fistan** (B) so-and-so and such-and-such. {also: fulan (SK); [fylan] فلان (JJ)} {syn: behvan} < Ar fulān فلان = 'so-and-so'; Sor fiłan فڵان [K/IFb/B/JJ/JB1-A&S/GF/ZF3//SK] <ewk>

filankes فِلانكەس *prn.* so-and-so, such-and-such (a person): **•Sala ku *Filankes* ji Hecê hati bû, fena sala îsalîn dîsa rewşa me xweş bû** (Ardû, 116) The year that *So-and-so* came back from the pilgrimage to Mecca, we were doing well, like we are this year. {also: [fylan kes] فلان كس (JJ); <fulankes> فلانكس (HH)} {syn: behvan} Sor fiłanekes فڵانەکەس [K/A/IFb/B/JJ/JB1-A/ZF3//HH]

Fil•e فِله *m.&f.* (). 1) {syn: Dîyan (A)} Christian *(Armenian or Assyrian)*: **•Û di nefsê Zaxo bi xo da jî *fileh* êt heyn û bisirman jî yêt heyn û Dihî jî yêt heyn** (M-Zx #771) And in Zakho (town) itself there are ('Assyrian') *Christians* and there are Muslims and there are Dihis too; 2) {syn: Ermenî} Armenian: **-fermanê Fila** (Haz) edict regarding the Armenians *(at the beginning of the 20th century)*; 3) {syn: Mexîn} Assyrian or Chaldean (Bw). {also: Fele (SK); Fileh (HB/ZF3); Fillah (A/TF); Fille (SK-2/GF); [felé] فله (JJ); <fille> فله (HH)} ?< Ar fallāḥ فلّاح = 'peasant, farmer'; Sor feƚe فەڵە = 'Christian villager' [HB/ZF3//SK//K/JB3/IFb/B/JJ/Haz//GF/HH//A/TF] <Cihû; Mexîn; Misilmênî; Suryanî>

Fileh فلەه (HB/ZF3) = Christian; Armenian. See **File**.

filehtî فلەهتی (ZF3) = Christianity. See **filetî**.

filetî فِلەتی *f.* **(-ya;-yê).** Christianity; being a Christian (or a *File*, i.e. Assyrian or Armenian): **•Voltaire niviskarê fransiz ku li dijî *filetiyê* derketibû, hêviyên xwe danibûne ser Avista** (Rwş #3, 23) Voltaire, a French writer who came out against *Christianity*, put his hopes on the Avesta. {also: filehtî (ZF3); fillahî (TF); filleyîtî (GF); [feleti] فلتی (JJ) = 'qualité d'Arménien'} [Rwş//ZF3//TF//GF//JJ] <File; Mexîn>

Filipînî فِلِپینی *adj.* Filipino. Sor Fîlîpînî فیلیپینی [IFb/BF/SS//Wkt/CS]

Filistînî فِلِستینی *adj.* Palestinian. {also: Felestînî (BF); Felistînî (Wkt-2)} Sor Fełestînî فەڵەستینی [Wkt/IFb/ZF3/CS//BF]

filitîn فِلِتین (K/B/JJ/Tsab/ZF/BF/CS) = to be rescued,

to escape; to come undone. See **filitîn** and **fetilîn**.
Fillah فِلاّه (A/TF) = Christian; Armenian. See **File**.
fillahî فِلاّهى (TF) = Christianity. See **filetî**.
Fille فِلّه (SK/GF/HH) = Christian; Armenian. See **File**.
filleyîtî فِلّهييتى (GF) = Christianity. See **filetî**.
finas فِناس (ZF3) = cunning, trickery. See **finaz**.
finaz فِـنـاز *m.(K)/f.(B)* **()**. 1) cleverness, cunning, trickery; evil deeds: -**fêl û finaz** (EP-7) trick, prank, ruse, monkey business; 2) mockery, ridicule (B). {also: finas (ZF3); finyaz (K); <finaz̲> فناظ (HH)} [EP-7/B//HH//ZF3//K] <fen; fer̄eset>
fincan فِنجان (A/JB3/IF) = cup. See **fîncan**.
find فِـنـد *m./f.(ZF3)* **(; /-ê)**. candle: •***Find*** **vê ket** (AB) *The candle* flared up •**Vê *findê* hil ke** (FS) Light this *candle*. {also: fend (EP-7); findik (A); [fynd] فـنـد (JJ); <find> فـنـد (HH)} {syn: şema [2]; şemal[k]} [AB/K/JB3/IFb/JJ/HH/ZF3//A] <çira I; findank; fitîl; mûm>
findank فِـنـدانـك *f.* **(-a;-ê)**. 1) {syn: şemdan} candlestick: •**Navekî taybetî yê vê *findankê* heye?** (Wkp:Gotûbêj:Cihûtî) Does this *candlestick* have a special name?; 3) wax candle (JB3/OK). {also: finddang (TF); finddank (IFb)} [JB3/OK/ZF3//IFb//TF] <find>
finddang فِنددانگ (TF) = candlestick. See **findank**.
finddank فِنددانك (IFb) = candlestick. See **findank**.
findeq فِـنـدەق (K/IFb/B/OK/CB) = hazelnut. See **bindeq**.
findik فِندِك (A) = dim. of **find**.
findiq فِندِق (GF/Kmc-2) = hazelnut. See **bindeq**.
findiqî فِـنـدِقـى **()**. Turkish coin: •**Xurcek t'ijî zêrê *findiqî* kir** (EP-7) He filled a saddlebag with gold *findiqs*. [EP-7]
finyaz فِنياز (K) = cleverness; ridicule. See **finaz**.
fir̄ I فِر *f.* **(-a;-ê)**. gulp, sip, swallow, swig: -**fir̄e av** (B) a drink of water: •**Hê qe *fir̄e av* jî venexwarîye** (IS-298) He hasn't even had so much as *a sip of water*; -**fir̄ kirin** (K/IF/B) to slurp while drinking (tea, soup, etc.); -**fir̄ lê dan** (Bw) to sip. {also: firik (A); firk II (K); [fyr فـر/fyrek] فـرك (JJ); <firek> فـرك (HH)} {syn: qurt} [IS/K/IF/B/JJ//HH] <daqurtandin; daûran; gep III; qurtandin>
fir̄ II فِر *adj.* 1) wide, loose *(of stitches)*: -**dirwara *fir̄*** (Zeb) *wide* or *loose* stitch; 2) widely spaced *(of teeth)*. See **firk III**.{also: <fir̄> فـر (Hej)} [Zeb/Hej/FS] <dirwar>
fir̄andin فِرانـدِن *vt.* **(-fir̄în-)**. to cause to fly (off), send flying (K/A/JB3/IF/BK): •**Serê wî *fir̄and*** (JJ) He had his head cut off [lit. 'He caused his head to fly off']. {also: firrandin (BK); frandin (A); [ferandin] فراندين (JJ); <firandin فراندن (difirîne) (دفرينه)> (HH)} [K/JB3/IFb/B/HH/GF/TF//A//BK//JJ] <fir̄în>
firaq فِـراق *f./m.(JB1-S)* **(;-ê/)**. crock, vessel, large bowl; dishes, plates (Msr): •***Firaq* tijî savar e** (AB) *The bowl* is full of [bulgur] groats. {also: fera (K/BK); feraq (B/JB1-S); fere (IFb-2); firax (JB3/IF-2); [fyraq] فراق (JJ); <firax̆> فراغ (HH)} {syn: aman; dewrî; teyfik} [AB/IFb/JJ/Msr//JB3//K/BK//B/JB1-S//HH] <aman; cifnî; lalî II; sênîk>
firaqşo فِـراقـشـۆ *f.* **(-ya;-yê)**. dishwasher *(person)*. {also: firaxşo (Wkt)} < firaq = 'dish(es)' + şo-[şûştin] = 'to wash' [Msr/ZF3//Wkt]
firar فِـرار *m.* **(-ê;)**. fugitive, runaway; deserter. {also: [ferari] فـرارى (JJ)} {syn: qaçax (F); r̄evî (F)} < Ar farrār فـرّار = 'runaway, fugitive' [K/IF/Ba2/JR/ZF3//JJ]
firaset فِراسەت = shrewdness; talent. See **fer̄eset**.
Firat فِرات (OK) = Euphrates. See **Ferat**.
firavîn فِـراڤـيـن *f.* **(-a;-ê)**. 1) {syn: nanê nîvro (B)} lunch, midday meal: •***Firavîna* we çi bû?** (FS) What did you have for *lunch*?; 2) a meal taken between lunch and dinner (HH). {also: firawîn (IF/SK); [ferawin] فراڤين (JJ); <firavîn> فراڤين (HH))} According to JJ < P farāvān فـراوان = 'abundant,' because lunch is the heaviest meal of the day. Another etymology: < O Ir *fra-pīθwa-na- [pīθwa- = 'meat, lunch'] (A&L p. 83 [III, 4] + M. Schwartz): Av ra-piθβīn- = 'noontime' [Zx/K/JB3/IFb/JJ/HH/Msr/Bw//IF/SK/TF] <şîv; taştê>
firawîn فِراوين (IF/SK) = lunch. See **firavîn**.
firax فِراخ (JB3/IF) = bowl. See **firaq**.
firaxşo فِراخشۆ (Wkt) = dishwasher. See **firaqşo**.
firça فِرچا (TF) = brush. See **firçe**.
firç•e فِرچە *f./m.(BF)* **(•[ey|a/•[ey|ê;)**. brush: •***firçe*: amûrek bidestik e û bi serê wê ve dav hene** (Wkt) *brush*: an instrument with a handle and on its head there are bristles •***firçe*: alaveke ji davan hatî çêkirin destikdare, jibo paqijkirina didanan** (BF) *brush*: an instrument which is made of bristles with a handle, for cleaning the teeth; -**firçe kirin** (IFb/BF/CS)/~ **lê xistin** (CS) to brush; -**firça didana** (FS) toothbrush; -**firça riha** (FS)/ **firçeya riyan**/~ **traşê** (ZF3) shaving brush; -**firça reng kirinê** (FS) paint brush. {also: firça (TF)} [IFb/GF/BF/ZF3/FS/Wkt/RZ/AD/SS/CS//TF]
firdik فِـردِك (A/IFb/GF/TF) = dish consisting of

yoghurt, water, and bread. See **firdoqî**.

firdoqî فِـــــردۆقـــــی *f.* **(-ya;-yê).** dish consisting of yoghurt and water [=*dew*] to which pieces of bread have been added. {also: firdik (A/IFb/GF/TF)} [Qzl//A/IFb/GF/TF/ZF3]

fire فِره (K/B) = wide. See **fireh**.

fireh فِرەھ *adj.* wide, broad; spacious: **-bêna** ***fk-ê*** **fireh bûn** (L) to calm down: •**Dawîyê** ***bêna min fireh bibe*****, ezê bixwim** (L) When I *calm down* [lit. 'when my breath will become broad'], I will eat •**Ḧetta wilo belkî** ***bêhna wî feriḧ bibê*** (HR 4:39) By then maybe *he will calm down.* {also: feriḧ (HR); fire (K/B); [fereh] فـره (JJ)} {syn: berfireh; berîn; pehn I; ≠ teng} [Pok. plăt-(plăd-)/plĕt/plŏt-/plət- 833.] 'broad, to spread': Skt práthas- = Av frayah- = 'breadth' & Skt pṛthú- = Av pərəyu- = 'broad, wide'; Mid P frāx = 'large, wide, spacious, ample, prosperous' (M3); P ferāx فراخ --> T ferah; Sor firawan فِـراوان {firehî; firetî; fireyî} [L/A/JB3/IF/JJ/JB1-S//K/B//HR]

firehî فِـــــرەھـــــی *f.* **(-ya;-yê).** 1) width, breadth; 2) spaciousness. {also: firetî (K); fireyî (K-2/B); [ferehi/ ferahi] فـــرهـــی (JJ)} [K//A/IF/JJ/JB1-S/ZF3//B] <fireh>

fireng فِرەنگ, m. (Krş) = tomato. See **firingî**.

firengî I فِـرەنـگـی *f.* **(;-yê).** syphilis, venereal disease: •**Cewrikê din kirmî bû, mîna bi nexweşiya** ***firengiyê*** **lê be** (Wt, 87) The other puppy had worms [lit. 'was wormy'], as if it was afflicted with *syphilis*. {also: ferengî (FJ-2); [frenghi] فرنـگـی (JJ); <firink zeḧmetî> فرنك زحمتی (HH)} < Firenk = Frank, i.e. European [WT/GF/FJ//JJ//HH]

firengî II فِرەنگی (Rh/Frq/Erg/Klk/Bw) = tomato. See **firingî**.

Firensayî فِرەنسایی (BF) = French. See **Firensî**.

Firensî فِـــرەنـــســی *adj.* French. {also: Ferensî (CS); Firensayî (BF-2); Fransî (IFb/BF-2); Frengsawî (ZF3); Frensî (Wkt/SS)} Sor Ferensî فەرەنسی [BF//CS//Wkt/SS//IFb//ZF3]

firetî فِرەتی (K) = width; spaciousness. See **firehî**.

fireyî فِرەیی (K/B) = width; spaciousness. See **firehî**.

firêd فِرێد (Nbh) = warp (of fabric). See **firêt**.

firêqet فِرێقەت *adj.* 1) {syn: tena} calm, serene: •**Bavo tu** ***firîqet*** **be** (Nbh 128:36) Dad, be *calm* [=don't worry] •**Ewî îcar hacetê xwe** ***frêqet*** **derxist serê Îskender kuř kir** (EH) Then he *calmly* took out his equipment and shaved Iskender's head; 2) free. {also: firîqet (Nbh); frêqet (EH); [feriqet] فریقت (JJ)} < P farāγat فراغت = 'leisure, freedom from care' < Ar farāγah فراغة [EH//K/B//JJ//Nbh]

firêt فِـرێـت *f.* **(-a;-ê).** warp *(of a fabric)* [=T çözgü; Ar sadāh سـداة; P tār تـار]: •**Bi bendên hêşîn dihûne** ***firêtên*** **zembîla xwe ye** (Ezra Pound: A Ballad of the Mulberry Road) With green strings she makes *the warp of* her basket. {also: firêd (Nbh 124:32)} = Sor tan تـان/tewn تـەون/řayeł ڕایـەڵ [CCG/Hej//Nbh] <gurd; hevo>

firêz I فِرێز (K) = elevation. See **firêze.**

firêz II فِرێز (IFb/GF/ZF3) = couch grass. See **firîzî**.

firêz•e فِـرێـزە *f.* **(•eya;•ê).** 1) field of stubble: •**Şixrevanî ceh ji** ***firêzê*** **kêşa coxînê** (FS) The grain transporter dragged the barley from *the field of stubble* to the threshing floor; **-mêrge û firêze** (Z-2) meadows and stubble fields; 2) height, elevation, upgrade slope (K). {also: firêz I (K); frêze (IFb); **p'irêz;** <firêz فرێز/firêze فرێزه/perêz پەرێز> (Hej)} [Z-2/A/JB3/Hej/ZF3/FS//IFb//K] <[2] fêz>

fiřfiřok فِـرفِـرۆك *f.* **(-a;-ê).** 1) kite; 2) {syn: belantîk; p'erîdank; p'iřp'iřok; pîrik [4]} moth, butterfly (AB): •***Firfirokê*** **xwe avêt êgir** (AB) *The moth* leapt [lit. 'threw itself'] into the flame. [AB/A/IFb/GF/OK/ZF/FS]

firgûn فِرگوون (GF) = horse-drawn cart. See **firẍûn**.

firik فِرِك (A) = gulp. See **fiř I**.

firikandin فِـــرِكـــانـــدِن *vt.* **(-firikîn-).** 1) {syn: gemirandin; miz I: miz dan} to rub: **-bêvila** ***fkî*** **firikandin/gemirandin/mizdan** (Kmc) to put s.o. in his place, to teach s.o. a lesson; 2) to rub ears of corn so that the kernels of corn fall out (B); 3) {syn: ; miz I: miz dan; p'erixandin} to massage. {also: firkandin (A/FJ/TF/CS/GF-2); [firikandin] فـركـانـديـن (JJ); <firikandin فـركـانـدن (difirikîne) (دفـركـيـنـه)> (HH)} < Ar √f-r-k فـرك = 'to rub', *cognate with* Syr √p-r-k ܦܪܟ = 'to rub, bruise' (> p'erixandin) [Kmc/K/IFb/B/GF/JJ/HH//A/FJ/TF/CS]

firingî فِـرِنـگـی *f.* **(-ya;-yê).** tomato. {also: fireng, m. (Krş); firengî II (Rh/Frq/Erg/Klk/Bw); freng, f. (Rh)} {syn: bacanê sor; stembolî; şamik} Cf. P bādenjān-e ferengī بـادنـجـان فـرنـگـی [=gowje-ye ferengī گوجه فرنگی] = 'tomato' <ferengī فـرنـگـی (Ar ifranj إفرنج) = 'Frank, European' [Rh/Frq/Erg/Klk/Bw/Wkt//IFb/RZ/Kmc-2//Krş//Rh]

firişt فِرِشت (GF) = angel. See **firîşte**.

firişte فِرِشته (CS/JJ) = angel. See **firîşte**.

firîg فِریگ (Antep/IFb) = unripe plant. See **firîk**.

firîk فِـــریـــك *f.* **(-a;-ê).** unripe, green grains or nuts *(pistachioes, wheat, etc.)*: •**Ḧeta genim *firîke*, melle şirîke** (Z-1460) As long as the wheat is *green* the mullah is a partner *[prv.]*. {also: ferîk (GF); firîg (Antep-2/IFb-2); [firik] فـريـك (JJ); <firîk> فـريـك (HH)} Cf. Ar farīk فـريـك = 'dried green wheat grains (used in cooking)'; Sor ferîk فەریك = 'unripe' *gen. prefixed to names of certain fruits, esp. nuts, which may be so eaten, e.g., ferîkebadem = 'unripe almonds' & ferîkenok = 'chick-peas sold on stalk'* [Antep/K/A/IFb/B/JJ/HH/TF/OK/AA/ZF3//GF] <xam>

fir̄în فـڕیـن *vi.* **(-fir̄-).** to fly: •***Fir̄îyan*** (L) *They flew* •**Teyrê go li ezmana re *difirin*** (L) Birds which *fly* in the skies. {also: [fyrin] فـريـن (JJ); <firîn فـريـن (difire) (دفره)> (HH)} [Pok. 2. (s)p(h)er- 993.] 'to jerk, start; to strew': Proto IndIr *√sphar --> *√phar --> O Ir *√far; P parrīdan پـريـدن; Sor fir̄în فڕین = 'to fly; twitch (of eye)'; Za firrenã [firrayiş] (Mal/Srk) & perrenã [perrayiş] (Mal/Todd/Srk) = 'to fly'; Hau pir̄ay/pir̄ey (pir̄-) *vi.* (M4) [L/F/K/A/JB3/IF/B/ZF3//JJ/HH] <fir̄andin; hilfir̄în; p'er̄>

firîqet فریقەت (Nbh) = calm. See **firêqet**.

firîşte فریشته *m.* **(-yê;).** angel: •**Kurro me go qey tu *firîşte* yî** (HYma 50) Son, we thought maybe you were *an angel*. {also: ferişt (K-2); ferişte (TF/CS); firişt (GF); firişte (CS-2); [firichté] فـرشـتـه (JJ)} {syn: melek} Cf. Mid P frēstag = 'apostle, angel' (M3); P firišteh فرشته; Sor firîşte فریشته [HYma/K/IFb/FJ/ZF3//JJ//TF/CS//GF]

firîz فریز (IFb/GF) = couch grass. See **firîzî**.

firîzî فـریـزی *f.* **().** couch grass, quitch grass, bot. *Agropyron repens*. {also: firêz II (IFb/GF-2/ZF3); firîz (IFb-2/GF); firûzî (OK/AA/Zeb); <firêz فریز/ firs فرس/firûzî فـرووزی/firûzû فـرووزوو> (Hej)} {syn: zîwan [2]} Cf. P farēz فـريـز = 'type of grass'; Sor firîz فـریـز = 'bermuda grass; lawn (Kerkûk)' [Bw//IFb/GF/ZF3//OK/AA/Zeb]

firk I فِـرك *f.* **(-a;-ê).** 1) cramp, spasm; charley horse: **-firk k'etin** (ZF) to get or have a cramp: •***Firk ketibû*** **piştê û nigên wî tevizîbûn** (SBx, 13) *A cramp seized* his back and his legs went numb; 2) {syn: girîzok} shudder, quiver (B): **-firk bûn** (GF) to throw *(a foal)*, give birth *(of horses)*: •**Wexta jina te r̄abizê, hespa te *firk dibe*** (Z-921) When your wife gives birth, your mare *will throw a colt*. {also: [firik] فـرك (JJ); <firk> فـرك (HH)} [AB/Z-921/B/IFb/FJ/HH/ZF/CS//JJ]

firk II فِرك (K) = gulp. See **fir̄ I**.

firk III فِـرك *adj.* widely spaced *(of teeth)*: •**Didanên wî jê *fir̄* in** (FS) His teeth are *wide apart*. {*also*: fir̄ II[2] (FS); **fîq**} [A/IFb/TF/ZF3/CS] <diranfîq; qîç>

firkandin فِركاندِن (A/FJ/TF/CS/GF) = to rub, massage. See **firikandin**.

firn فِـرن/**fir̄n** فِـڕن [B] *f./m.(ZF3)* **(-a/;-ê/).** nostril(s); *animal's nostrils; for human beings, **firnik** is used* (IF). {also: fir̄n (B); firnik (K-2/JB3/IF); fir̄nik (Z-2/B-2/Wkt); firnî (ZF3-2)} {syn: bêvil [1]; difn [2]; ximximk} Za pirniki/pirnike/firnik *f.* = 'nose' (Mal) [Z-2//K/ZF3//B//JB3/IF//Wkt] <poz I>

fir̄naq فِڕناق (FS) = proud. See **fir̄nax**.

fir̄nax فِـڕنـاخ *adj.* proud: •**Lê nanga ez gelekî *fir̄nax* bûm. Ez gelekî ji bavê xwe r̄azîme** (HCK-1, 20) But now I'm very *proud*. I'm very pleased with my father •**Mala apê gelek pêr̄a *frnax* bû, gelek pêr̄a şa bû** (HCK-2, 85) The uncle's house was very *proud*, very pleased with him. {also: fir̄naq (FS-2); frnax (HCK-2)} {syn: difnbilind; k'ubar; pozbilind; qube I; qur̄e; serbilind; serfiraz} [HCK/ZF3/FS]

fir̄n•e فِـڕنـه *f.* **(;•ê).** 1) bakery, bake-house (K/B): •**Nanê vê *firnê* timamî tu dixwî** (L) You eat all the bread of this *bakery/oven*; 2) {syn: ten[d]ûr} oven (JB3/B). {also: [fyroun فـرون/ fyrin فـريـن] (JJ)} Cf. Ar furn فـرن = 'oven' < Lat furnus = 'oven, furnace' [L/K/JB3/B//JJ] <kuçik II; t̲endûr; t'ifik>

firnik فِـرنِـك (K/JB3/IF)/fir̄nik فِـڕنِـك (Z-2/B/Wkt) = nostril(s). See **firn**.

firnî فِرنی (ZF3) = nostril(s). See **firn**.

firo فِـرۆ *m.* **(-yê;).** beestings, colostrum, high-protein milk secreted [by cows] for a few days after giving birth, which has been boiled: •**Şirînê şîrê zak kir *firo*** (FS) Sh. made the beestings into *firo* [i.e., she boiled it]. {also: [ferou] فـرو (JJ); <firo> فـرو (HH)} {syn: firşik II; xelendor I; xîç' I; zak} O Ir <*fraša-; Mid P frušag (M3); P furše فـرشـه; Sor fro فرۆ/firîşk فِریشك. See: G. Morgenstierne. "Persian Etymologies," *Norsk Tidsskrift for Sprogviden-skap*, 5 (1932), 55, reprinted in: *Irano-Dardica* (Wiesbaden : Dr. Ludwig Reichert Verlag, 1973), p.166. [K/IF/B/JJ/HH/ZK3/FS] <firşik I & II>

firok فِرۆك (ZF3) = airplane. See **firoke**.

fir̄ok•e فِـڕۆكـه *f.* **(•[ey]a;•ê).** airplane: •**Ew li *fir̄okê* siyar bû** (FS) He boarded *the plane*. {also: firok (ZF3)} {syn: balafir̄; teyare II} Sor fir̄oke فِڕۆکه =

'aircraft' [(neol)AB/K(s)/A/JB3/FS//ZF3/Wkt]

firoşin فِرۆشِن (JB1-A) = to sell. See **firotin**.

firoştin فِرۆشتِن (A/IFb/JB1-A) = to sell. See **firotin**.

firotan فِرۆتان = to sell. See **firotin**.

firotin فِـرۆتِـن *vt.* **(-firoş-).** to sell: **•Tu dê tirimpêla xwe bi çendê *bifiroşî* min?** (Wkt) For how much *will* you *sell* your car to me? **•Wî genim *firot*** (FS) He *sold* the wheat. {also: firoşin (JB1-A); firoştin (A/IFb-2/JB1-A); firotan; frotin; [fyroutin] فـروتـن (JJ); <firotin فـروتـن (difroşe) (دفـروشـه)> (HH)} {≠k'ir̄în} <*fra-waxš- (M2, p.79): P forūxtan فـروختـن (-forūš-) (فروش); Sor firoştin فِرۆشـتِـن; SoK f(ı)ruš- (Fat 352); Za roşenã [rotiş] (Todd); Hau wuretey (wureş-) *vt.* (M4) [K/JB3/IFb/B/HH/SK/GF/TF/OK/FS/Wkt/ZF3/M//JJ//A/JB1-A]

firqas فِـرقـاس *f.* **().** jump, leap, bound, spring: **-firqas kirin** (K/B)/**firqas dan xwe** (K) to jump over. {also: firqaz (ZF3-)}{syn: banz; ç'indik; lotik; qevz II} [EP-7/K/B/ZF3] <çeng bûn [çeng III]; hilpekirin; pengizîn>

firqaz فِرقاز (ZF3) = jump, leap. See **firqas**.

firrandin فِرراندِن (BK) = to cause to fly. See **fir̄andin**.

firsend فِرسەند (IFb/GF/ZF3) = opportunity. See **firset**.

firset فِرسەت *f.* **(-a;).** opportunity, chance: **•Heger ew delîv (*firset*) li navbera 1900-1992 ji destên bav û bapîrên me çûn, bila ji destê me neçin** (Wlt) If our forefathers missed this *opportunity* between 1900 and 1992, let us not miss it **•Heye ku kurd vê *firseta* ku niha ketiye dest, dîsa weke gelek *firsetên* din ji dest bidin** (nerinaazad.com 14.x.2016) Perhaps the Kurds will miss this *chance* which has now fallen into their hands, like many other *opportunities*. {also: firsend (IFb/GF); [furset] فـرصـت (JJ); <furset> فـرسـت (HH)} {syn: delîve; derfet; fesal [1]; kevlû [2]; k'ês} <Ar furṣah فـــرصـــة -->T fırsat [Wlt/K//IFb/GF/ZF3//JJ/HH] <mecal>

firşik I فِـرشِـك *f.(ZF3)/m.(Wkt)* **(/-ê;).**1) lamb or kid's stomach (Ag/Kmc); 2) rennet *(made from milk in lamb's stomach)*; 3) courage, bravery, nerve: **•Wê tu car *firşikê* xwe kêm nekir** (S. Sîsî: *Senîha Xanim û 49an*, Amidakurd.com, 12/2007) She never lost her *nerve*. {also: <firşik> فـــرشـــك (HH)} [Ag/A/IFb/HH/GF/TF/Kmc-3035/ZF3/Wkt] <firo; şîlav>

firşik II فِـرشـك *m.* **(-ê;).** colostrum, beestings, first milk fed to newborn infant or animal: **-firşik kirin** (IFb)/**fişk kirin** (MG) to nurse a newborn for the first time: **•Xwest bi şîrê xwe zaroka xwe *fişk bike*** (MGJiyaneka pêguhork) She wanted [or asked] to *nurse* her child *for the first time* with her own milk. {also: fişk (MG)} {syns: firo; xelendor I; xîç' I; zak} Cf. P furše فـرشـه; Sor fro فـرۆ/firîşk فـريـشـك = 'colostrum, mother's milk secreted for the first time after childbirth' [MG//A/IFb] <firo>

firtine فِرتِنە (IFb) = storm. See **firtone**.

firton•e فِـرتـۆنـە/**firt̲on•e** فِـرطـۆنـە [FS] *f.* **(•eya;•ê).** storm, tempest *(especially at sea)*: **•Wextekê ser r̄ûê be'rê bû *frtone* ... Frtone ze'f bû, qeyk şkest** (HCK-2, 180) Once *a storm* occurred at sea ... The storm was strong, the boat was wrecked. {also: firtine (IFb); firtûne (GF); frtone (HCK-2); [fyrthouné/furtúna (G)] فـرتـونـه (JJ); <firtûnek> فرتونك (HH)} {syn: bager̄; bahoz; barove; hureba; t'ofan} Cf. T fırtına & Gr furtúna φουρτούνα = 'storm' < It fortuna = 'fortune, luck, chance; (poet.) storm, tempest'; Sor fertene فەرتەنە/firtene فِرتەنە = 'stormy weather' [HCK/K/B/FJ/RZ/Tsab/CS/ZF//FS]

firtûne فِرتوونە (GF) = storm. See **firtone.**

firûzî فِروززی (OK/AA/Zeb) = couch grass. See **firîzî**.

firxûn فِـــرخــــوون (IFb/Kmc/ZF3) = horse-drawn cart. See **fir̄xûn**.

fir̄xûn فِرغوون *f.* **(;-ê).** horse-drawn cart; van, estate car; wagon with iron wheels (Nbh 124:32): **•Girt p'erê wî daê, gazî *fr̄xûnê* kir, anî lêkir, anî hat mala xwe** (HCK-3, #2, 18) He took money and gave him it, [then] he summoned *a cart* and brought it and loaded it up, brought it and came home. {also: firgûn (GF); firxûn (IFb/Kmc/ZF3); fr̄xûn (HCK); virxûn (Nbh 124:32)} < Rus furgon фургон < Fr fourgon [HCK//K/B//IFb/Kmc/ZF3//GF//Nbh] <'erebe; fayton; gerdûm>

fis فِــــــس/**fis̠** فِــــص [FS/HH] *f.* **(-a;-ê).** silent fart, noiseless flatulence, "SBD" (=silent but deadly), *as opposed to tir̄* = *audible fart*: **-fis(a kesekî/ê) hatin** (Wkt) to fart silently. {also: [fs] فــــس (JJ); <fis̠> فص (HH)}{syn: k'uş II} Cf. Ar √f-s-w فسو & NENA pâshî ܦܣܐ (Maclean) = 'to break wind noiselessly'; Sor fis فِــس = 'hissing noise' [A/IFb/JJ/GF/TF/OK/ZF3//HH/FS] <tir̄>

fisegur فِـسـەگـور *f.* **(;-ê).** *name given to a variety of different plants*: 1) type of poisonous mushroom, toadstool (A/B/IFb/FD/Wkt); 2) sundew, bot. *Drosera* (AA/IFb[4]/BF); 3) baby's breath, T dikenli çöğen, bot. *Gypsophila* (ZF3); 4) bladder senna, bot. *Colutea arborescens* (Kmc); 5) honeysuckle, bot. *Lonicera* (Kmc). {also: fisegurg

(AA); fisgur (IFb-2/BF); fisgurk (Kmc-2); fisk gurî (GF); <fiska gurî> فصكا گرى (HH)} [A/B/IFb/FD/ZF3/Wkt/Kmc//BF///AA//GF//HH]

fisegurg فِسەگورگ (AA) = *name of several plants*. See **fisegur**.

fisfisok** فِسفِسۆك *adj*. hollow, *quality of a rock or stone: if its interior is full of holes like a sponge (i.e., if the wind blows through it), it is called* ***fisfisok. {syn: kuş} [Wn]

fisgur فِسگور (IFb/BF) = *name of several plants*. See **fisegur**.

fisgurk فِسگورك (Kmc) = *name of several plants*. See **fisegur**.

fisk gurî فِسك گورى (GF) = *name of several plants*. See **fisegur**.

fistan فِستان (RZ) = woman's dress. See **fîstan**.

fistaq فِستاق (GF) = low-quality raisins. See **bistaq**.

fisteq فِستەق (TF/OK/AA/FS/Wkt) = pistachio. See **fistiq**.

fistiq فِستِق *f*. **(-a;-ê).** pistachio, bot. *Pistacia vera*: •***Fisteqa* Entabê wek fêqiyek tê dîtin** (waarmedia.com 2.ii.2017) Antep *pistachioes* are considered a fruit. {also: fisteq (TF/OK-2/AA/FS/Wkt); fistîq (IFb); [fystiq] فستق (JJ)} {syn: p'iste} < Ar fustuq/fustaq فستق < P peste پسته < Mid P *pistak; Sor fistiq فِستِق/fistoq فِستۆق (K3) [Kmc-2/CB/JJ/GF/OK/ZF3//IFb//TF/AA/FS/Wkt]

fistîq فِستيق (IFb) = pistachio. See **fistiq**.

fiş فِش *m./f.(ZF3)* **(-ê/;).** mucus, snot. {also: <fiş> فش (HH)} {syn: çilka poz; çilm; k'ilmîş; lîk} [Msr/IF/HH/ZF3]

fişar فِشار *f*. **(-a;-ê).** pressure: •**Li Almanya jî, Merkel di bin *wê fişarê* de ye** (Nûçeyên rojane 2.ii.2017) In Germany as well, Merkel is under that *pressure*; **-fişara xwînê** (Wkt/ZF3) blood pressure: •***Fişara* wê *ya xwînê* ya bilind e** (Wkt) Her *blood pressure* is high. {also: wuşar (SS)} {syn: ç'ews; p'est; pêk'utî; zext I} < P fišār فشار; Sor guşar گوشار [Wkt/ZF3//SS]

fişk فِشك (MG) = first milk. See **firşik II**.

fitar فِتار *f*. **(-a;-ê).** iftar, breaking the fast of Ramadan: •**Şivan *fitara* xwe jî paşîva xwe jî li çol û mexelan *dixwin*** (aa.com.tr 3.vi.2018) The shepherds both *break their fast* and eat their early morning meal in the wilderness and by the sheepfolds; **-bangê fitarê** (Wkt) call to prayer which brings the daily fast to an end during Ramadan; **-fitar kirin** (Wkt)/**fitara xwe vekirin** (FD) to break the fast (of Ramadan): •**Bi banga mele ra *fitara xwe vedikin*** (aa.com.tr 3.vi.2018) With the mullah's call to prayer they *break their fast*. {also: fitare (FS/BF)} [Wkt/ZF3/FD//FS/BF]

fitare فِتارە (FS/BF) = iftar. See **fitar**.

fitil فِتِل *f*. **(;-ê).** turn(ing), rotation, circulation; walk, spin: •**Wexta me nanê xwe xwar, ez û Sûto řabûn, me *fitilek* dora pêz da, dît, wekî ew řeĥet mexel hatye** (Ba2-#2, 206) When we finished eating, Suto and I got up and took *a turn* around the sheep, and saw that they had returned to the pen without any trouble. {also: fetil (ZF3)} {syn: geř II} [Ba2/K/B//ZF3] <fetilîn>

fitilîn فِتِلين (K/B) = to rip; to turn around. See **fetilîn**.

fitîl فِتيل *f*. **(-a;-ê).** wick: •**Ave, ne ave, / Me'rê mirî di nave, / Teyrê zêřîn hindave / Ew çiye? [*P'ilta ç'irê, şemal*]** (Z-1796) It's water, it's not water / There's a dead snake in its middle / There's a golden bird above it / What is it? *[rdl.; ans.: wick and candle]*. {also: pilte (F/Z-1796); [pilté] پلته/[pilta qandili] پلتا قنديلى (JJ)} <Arc peṯīlā פתילא/peṯīltā פתילתא & Syr peṯīltā ܦܬܝܠܬܐ; NENA pṯilta *f.* (Krotkoff) & ptiltâ *f.* (Maclean); Ar fatīl فتيل; P patīle پتيله/fatīle فتيله; Sor piłîte پلیتە; cf. also Arm p'ilt'a[y] փիլթայ; Rus fitil´ фитиль. The Sor, JJ, and Arm forms feature a metathesis of -tl- to -lt-: for another example of this, see **fetilîn** and **filitîn**. [K/A/IFb/B/ZF3//F/JJ/Z-1796] <find>

fitîr فِتير (IFb) = alms at end of Ramadan. See **fitre II**.

fitre I فِترە **().** unit of measure for grain, c. 12-13 kg.; According to FS, 4 fitres = 1 'elb. {also: <fiṯre> فطره (HH)} {syn: 'elb [2]} [IF/SK/Erh/FS//HH]

fiṯre II فطره/**fitre** فِترە [FS] *f*. **().** alms given at the end of Ramadan: •**Carekî melayekî xelkê Pawe bû ... li melatîê digeřya ko wî biken e melaê gundekî, pêş-niwêjî bo wan biket û bangî bidet û millet jî *fitran* bidene wî w sedeqe w xêran bi wî biken** (SK 32:281) Once there was a mullah from Pawa ... seeking a post as mullah, that they should make him mullah of a village, to lead them in prayer and give the calls to prayer, and the people give him *tithes* and alms. {also: fitîr (IFb-2); <fiṯre> فطره (HH)} < Ar fiṭr فطر = 'fast breaking' & ṣadaqat al-fiṭr صدقة الفطر = 'almsgiving at the end of Ramadan'; Sor serfitre سەرفِترە [IFb/Sk/HH/FJ/CS/FS]

fîkandin فيكاندِن *vi.(B)/vt.(K)* **(-fîkîn-).** 1) to whistle; 2) {syn: fîtik I} [*f.* ().] whistling *(with lips)*: •**Carna**

bi strandin an bi *fîkandin*, bê tirs û telaş, wek pez kuviya, ji tehteke me xwe davête tehteke din (SW: Erebê Şemo. Şivanê Kurd, 43-44) Sometimes with singing or *whistling*, without fear or worry, they would leap from one rock to another like mountain goats •**Keriyê me bi nîzam li dû şivan diçû û duşivan û zaro li herdu alî, vir da wê da, bazdidan, ne dihiştin ku nîzam xirab be û bi kopalên xwe an bi *fîkandineke* xas di nav kerî de ji her pezî re ciyê wî nîşan didan** (SW: Erebê Şemo. Şivanê Kurd, 42) Our flock would follow the shepherd in an orderly way, and the assistants and boys on both sides, here and there, would run, not letting the order be lost, and with their staffs or by *whistling* a signal they would show each sheep its place. Cf. Sor fîk فیك = 'whistling (with lips)' [SW/K/A/B/RZ] <fîtik I>

fîkî فيكى *m./f.(B)* **(-yê/ ; /-yê).** fruit: •***Fîkî* li ser darê gîhane** (AB) *The fruit* ripened on the tree. {also: fekî; fêkî (K/JB3/B/SC); fêqî (JB1-A/SK/Bw/Zx); [fiki] فيكى (JJ); <fêkî> فيكى (HH)} {syn: ber V; êmîş [1]; mêwe} < Ar fākihah فاكهة [AB/JJ//K/JB3/B/HH/SC//JB1-A/SK/Bw/Zx] <balete; p'incar>

fîl فيل *m.* **(-ê;).** 1) {syn: *devlok} elephant; 2) bishop (in chess). {also: [fil] فيل (JJ); <fîl> فيل (HH)} Cf. Ar/P fīl فيل [Z-1/F/K/A/JB3/IFb/B/JJ/HH/GF/OK] <fêris [2]; k'erkedan; k'işik; şetrenc>

fîncan فينجان *f.* **(-a;-ê).** cup, coffee cup, teacup: •***fîncana* qawê** (EP-7) *cup of* coffee; coffee cup. {also: fincan (A/JB3/IF-2); [fyndjan] فنجان (JJ)} {syn: k'asik; t'as} Cf. Ar finjān فنجان = 'cup' <P pengān پنگان <Arc pinkā פינכא = 'dish, plate' < Gr pinax πίναξ (*gen.* pinakos πίνακος) = 'board, plank, tablet, platter, register'. For a discussion of the etymology of this word cluster (in Heb), see E.Y. Kutscher. *Milim ve-toldotehen* [=Words and their history]. (Jerusalem : Kiryat-Sefer, 1974), p. 93-95. [EP-7/K/IF/B//A/JB3/JJ]

fîq فيق *adj.* 1) widely spaced *(of teeth)*: •**Dranên min ji zarokiyê ve *fîq* in** (Wkt) Ever since childhood my teeth have been *wide apart*; 2) incisor: **-diranê fîq** (Qzl) incisor, front tooth. {*also*: **fîrk III**} [Qzl/Wkt] <diranfîq; qîç>

fîstan فيستان *f./m.(ZF/ZZ)* **(/-ê;).** type of woman's dress; *with long sleeves, open in front, tied at the waist with a drawstring* (Kmc-11). {also: fistan (RZ)} {syn: dêre; *taqî} Cf. Ar fustān فستان; T fistan; Mod Gr foustani φουστάνι; Romanian fustă; *for illustration, see Kmc-11, p. 1* [Kmc-11/IFb/GF/OK/ZF//RZ]

fît فيت (A/IFb) = whistle. See **fîtik I.**

fîtik I فيتِك *f.* **(-a;-ê).** 1) whistle *(with the lips)*, whistling: **-fîtik kutan** (IFb)/~ **lêdan** (IFb)/~ **lêxistin** (Srk/Mzg/IFb)/**fîtî dan(e)** (SK) [+ dat. constr.]/**fîtî vedan** (Bw) to whistle (at) {syn: fîkandin}: •**Ji gundê Argoş, ji 'eşîreta Mizûrî Jorî, muroek hebo, digotin ê Silê Şemfata ... 'Emrê wî nêzîkî ṣed salan bo ... Biçûkêt gundî daimî tirane bi wî dikirin** [sic], ***fîtî* didan e wî, ew jî tûr̄e dibo, cûnêt kirêt didan e biçûkan** (SK 59:690) There was a man from the village of Argosh, of the Upper Mizuri tribe, whom they called Sile Shamfata ... He was nearly a hundred years old ... The children of the village were always playing jokes on him, *whistling* at him, and he used to get angry and abuse them foully; 2) whistle (single-note woodwind instrument), tin whistle, pennywhistle: •**Wî pif kir *fîtikê*** (FS) He blew [into] *the whistle*. {also: fît (A/IFb); fîtî (Bw/SK)} [Srk/Mzg/IFb/OK/FS/ZF3//A/IFb//Bw/SK]

fît•ik II فيتِك *f.* **(•ka;).** snapping *(with fingers, as to summon a servant)*. [Qzl/Frq/ZF3/FD]

fîtî فيتى (Bw/SK) = whistle. See **fîtik I.**

Flamanî فلامانى *adj.* Flemish. {also: Flemenî (Wkp)} [ZF3//Wkp]

Flemenî فلەمەنى (Wkp) = Flemish. See **Flamanî.**

folklor فۆلكلۆر *f.* **(-a;-ê).** folklore: •**Bi kurdî bêjeya *folklorê* tê wateya zanista gelêrî an jî lêkolîna li ser gel** (YPA, 11) In Kurdish the word '*folklore*' means folk science or research about the folk. {syn: zargotin} [K/B/ZF/BF] <kelep'ûr>

folklornas فۆلكلۆرناس *m.* **(-ê;).** folklorist: •**Her wiha *folklornasê* kurd Îzeddîn Mistefa Resûl jî li ser heman baweriyê ye** (YPA, 12) Likewise, the Kurdish *folklorist* I.M. Rasul is also of the same opinion. [YPA/Wkt] <folklor>

form فـۆرم *f.* **(-a;-ê).** form, shape; way, manner, fashion: -**[bi] vê formê** (Z-1)/**wê formê** (Z-1) in this way: •[Qeretajdin didn't come to the mir's court for four days, because of his guest, Mem. The mir sends a messenger to see why Qeretajdin has been absent] **Xulam çû mala Q., wexta ç'e'v Memê k'et, îdî xwe bîr kir. *Wê formê* mîr sê-çar merî şandin** (Z-1) The servant boy went to Q's house, [but] when he laid eyes on Mem, he forgot himself. *In that way* the mir sent three-four men. [Z-1/K/IF/B/ZF3]

forq فۆرق *m.&f.* (**/-a; /-ê).** libertine, profligate: **•Heře wê *forqê* bive cîkî dûr bikuje** (HCK-1, 202) Go take that *slut* to some remote place and kill her. [Z-1/K/HCK/ZF3] <me'řis; p'ûşt; sebav>

fote فۆته (A/FD) = bedsheet. See **fûtik**[2].

frandin فراندِن (A) = to cause to fly. See **fiřandin**.

Fransî فرانسی (IFb/BF) = French. See **Firensî**.

freng فرەنگ, f. (Rh) = tomato. See **firingî**.

Frengsawî فرەنگساوی (ZF3) = French. See **Firensî**.

Frensî فرەنسی (Wkt/SS) = French. See **Firensî**.

frêqet فرێقەت (EH) = calm. See **firêqet**.

frêze فرێزە (IFb) = field of stubble. See **firêze.**

frnax فرناخ (HCK-2) = happy. See **fiřnax**.

frotin فرۆتِن = to sell. See **firotin**.

frtone فرتونه (HCK-2) = storm. See **firtone.**

frx̂ûn فرغوون (HCK) = horse-drawn cart. See **firx̂ûn**.

fulan فولان (SK) = so-and-so. See **filan**.

fûřîn فـووڕيـن *vi.* **(-fûř-).** 1) {syn: k'elîn} to boil *(vi.)*, rage (JB3/IF): **•Belê qehwa te *ne fûre*** (L) Your coffee *should not boil*; 2) {syn: k'el III çûyîn} to overflow, boil over; 3) to low, moo *(of cattle)*; to bellow, roar (IF/B). Cf. Ar fāwar III فاور = 'to boil' (vi.) [L/JB3/IFb/B/FJ/Qmş/ZF3/FD]

fûtik فـووتـِك *f.* **(;-ê).** 1){syn: çît I [3]} women's white headscarf; 2) {also: fote (A/FD)} {syn: çarşev; sipîç'al} bedsheet. {also: [fouti] فوتی (JJ); <fûtik> فوتك (HH)} [IFb/GF/HH/ZF3/Wkt/BF//JJ//A/FD]

G گ

ga گا *m.* **(gayê/gê; gê, vî gayî).** 1) {syn: boẍ} bull, ox: **•Jineke pîr hebûye ... *cote gaê* wê hebûye** (J) There was an old woman ... she had *a pair of oxen* **•Wekî em *gakî* şerjêkin** (J) If we slaughter *an ox* **•Van *gayan* bibe** (AB) Take these *bulls*; **-gaê k'ûvî** (B) = deer; wild ox. See **gak'ûvî**; 2) Taurus (astr.). {also: [ga] گا (JJ); <ga> گا (HH)} [Pok. g^{u}ou- 482.] 'ox, bull, cow': Skt gav- [gauḥ] *m./f.*; O Ir *gaw- [gāuš] (Ras p.216)/*gawa- (A&L p.87 [VIII, 1]): Av gāuš (*gen.* gōuš) *m./f.*; Mid P gāw (M3); Southern Tati dialects (all *f.*): Chali & Takestani māgāva = 'cow' & gāv = 'bull'; Ebrahim-abadi & Sagz-abadi gowa; Xiaraji magowa = 'cow'; Eshtehardi göw = 'bull' & gowa/gāwa = 'cow' (Yar-Shater); P gāv گاو; Sor ga گا; Za ga *m.* (Todd); Hau gawe *f.* = 'ox, bull' (M4); cf. also Arm kov (W: gov) կով; Germ Kuh [F/K/A/JB3/IFb/B/JJ/HH/JB1-A/SK/GF/TF/OK] <çêlek/mange = cow; ciwange/golik = calf; çavrî/dewar/gar̄eş = livestock; gamêş = buffalo; gar̄an = cattle; gavan = cowherd; ḧeywan = bovine; naxir = herd of cattle>

gac گاج (K) = alabaster; plaster. See **gec**.

gadoş گادۆش *f.* **().** 1) small wooden milk pail [satila piçûk a ji bo şîr] (Kmc/K/Tsab); 2) large clay jar with handles through which strings are laced for carrying (HH/IFb): *see photograph in Kmc#30, p. 1.* {also: gadoşk (Kmc#30-2); gadûş (FJ); <gadûş> گادوش (HH)} < ga = 'cow' + doş- = 'to milk' [Kmc#30/K/IFb/Kmc/Tsab//FJ/HH] <dewl I; satil>

gadoşk گادۆشك (Kmc#30) = milk pail; large portable clay jar. See **gadoş**.

gadûş گادووش (FJ/HH) = milk pail; large portable clay jar. See **gadoş**.

gakovî گاکۆڤی (A/IF/ZF3) = deer; wild ox. See **gak'ûvî**.

gak'ûvî گاکووڤی *m.* **(-yê;).** 1) {syn: ask; mambiz; xezal I} deer: **-çêlekeke gak'ûvî** (EP-4) doe, female deer; 2) {syn: gamêş} wild ox (B/A/IF); buffalo (IF); mountain ox (A). {also: gaê k'ûvî (B); gakovî (A/IF/ZF3); [ga kouwi] گاکوڤی (JJ)} Cf. P gāv-i kūhī گاو کوهی; Sor gakêwî گاکێوی = 'moose'? [EP-4/K/B/JJ//A/IF/ZF3] <ask; ga; gamêş>

gale-gal گاله گال (K)/galegal گالەگال (JB3/IF/B/ZF3) = chatter; bleating. See **galigal**.

galegurt گالەگورت (K[s]/IF) = noise; gossip. See **galegûrt**.

galegûrt گالەگوورت *f.* **().** 1) {syn: galigal[4]; hêwirze; hose; k'im-k'imî; qajeqaj; qalmeqal; qareqar; qerebalix; qîr̄eqîr̄; şerqîn; t'eqer̄eq} noise, commotion, tumult: **•Wê rojê, Beglî dibîne ku di nav bajarê Mixribiyan, *galegûrteke* giran e** (L) On that day, Begli sees that there is a great *tumult* in the city of Mighribiyan; 2) {syn: galigal; gotgotk; kurt û pist; paşgotinî; pitepit} gossip, idle talk. {also: galegurt (K[s]/IF)} [L//K(s)/IF] <galigal>

galgal گالگال (A/JJ) = chatter; bleating. See **galigal**.

galigal گالِگال *f.* **(-a;-ê).** 1) {syn: galegûrt [2]; gotgotk; kurt û pist; paşgotinî; pitepit} talk, chatter, gossip (K/A); conversation (JB3/IF): **•Ev *galigal* ji devê te derkeve** (L) This *talk* comes out of your mouth; 2) {syn: bar̄în II[1]} bleating *(of sheep)* (B/HH): **•*galegala* berxa** (B) *bleating of* lambs; 3) bitter crying, bawling (B): **-galegal kirin** (B): a) to bleat; b) to cry bitterly; 4) {syn: galegûrt; hêwirze; hose; k'im-k'imî; qajeqaj; qerebalix; şerqîn; t'eqer̄eq} din, noise made by a crowd (JJ); crowd, mob (JJ). {also: gale-gal (K); galegal (JB3/IF/B/ZF3); galgal (A); [galgal] غالغال/ گالگال (JJ); <kalkal> کالکال (HH)} Cf. Ar qīl wa-qāl قيل وقال = 'gossip' [L/K/A/JB3/IF/B/JJ/ZF3//HH]

gam گام (IFb/OK/Hej) = threshing sledge. See **kam**.

gamêş گامێش *m.* **(-ê;).** buffalo: **•Rûnê *gamêşan* ji yê bizinan pirtire** (AB) *Buffalo* butter is more plentiful than goat butter; **-mêş kirine gamêş** (Zeb/Dh) to make a mountain out of a molehill, exaggerate, overreact [lit. 'to make a fly into a buffalo' + rhyme]; **-mêgamêş** (JB3) female buffalo, cow-buffalo {syn: medek}; **-nêregamêş** (JB3/IF) (male) buffalo. {also: camûs (IF-2); [gaoumich گاوميش/gamēsh گاميش] (JJ); <gamêş> گاميش (HH)} {syn: kel IV} P gāvmīš گاوميش; Sor gamêş گامێش; cf. Ar jāmūs جاموس [AB/K/A/JB3/IF/B/JJ/HH/ZF3] <gedek/sak = buffalo-calf; medek = female buffalo; r̄evo/qevle = herd>

gan I گان *vt.* **(-gê-).** to copulate, make love, screw, fuck: **•Ne qelûna ber baî, ne *gana* ser gîhaî** (L) No [smoking of] pipes in the wind, no *copulating* on the grass *[prv.]*.{also: gayîn (K); [gan گـان/gàin گاين] (JJ); <gan> گان (HH)} {syn: k'utan; nayîn} Cf. O P gādan; P gāyīdan گـايـيـدان/gādan گـادن; Sor gan گـــان = 'copulation'; Hau ganî *f.* = 'copulation' & gay (ge-) *vt.* = 'to copulate with' (M4) [BX/A/IF/JJ/HH/ZF3//K]

gan II گان (IFb) = udder. See **guhan**.

gandîl گانديل (IFb) = udder. See **guhandîr**.

gar̄an گاڕان/**garan** گاران [B] *f.* **(-a;-ê).** herd of cattle: **•Dêla box̆ girt, box̆ k'uta, nav *gar̄anê* ger̄and** (J) He took hold of the ox's tail, beat the ox, caused him to run among *the cattle*. {also: [garan] گــاران (JJ); <garan> گاران (HH)} {syn: naxir} [K/A/IF/B//JJ/HH/ZF3] <çavrî; ga>

garanîk گــارانــيــك *f.* **(-a;).** 1) starling, zool. *Sturnus vulgaris* (a small black bird) (Bw); 2) cattle egret, zool. *Bubulcus ibis*. {syn: alik; r̄eşêlek; zerzûr} [Bw/Wkt/Wkp]

gar̄eş گــــاڕەش *f.* **().** livestock, cattle, bovines. {also: <gar̄eş> گــــاڕەش (Hej)} {syn: çavrî; t'ariş} = Sor r̄eşewułax ڕەشــەوولاخ [Zeb/OK/Hej/Wkt] <dewar; ga; gar̄an>

garis گــــارِس *m.* **(-ê; gêris, vî garisî).** 1) {syn: gilgil; herzin} millet, bot. *Panicum miliaceum*: **•Teyr got "Tê 'elbek *garis* bidî min, ezê bêm." Go, "Bi qirar ezê du 'elb bidim te"** (PS-I:13, p.32, ll.23-24) The bird said, "If you give me a measure of *millet*, I will come" [The other one] said, "I'll even give you two measures"; **-garisê sipî** (A/IFb) (white) millet [T ak darı]; **-garisê xabûrê** (A/IFb) type of millet which grows near the Habur River; **-garisê zer** (A/IFb) popcorn [T sarı darı/cin darısı]; 2) {syn: genimeşamî; genmok; gilgilê Stembolê (Haz); lazût; zuret I} corn, maize, bot. Zea mays (K): **-garisê stanbolî** (A) corn, maize [T mısır darısı]. {also: [gariz] گــــارس (JJ); <garis> گـارس (HH)} < O Ir *gawarsā (Morg3): ga = 'bull' + [Pok. 4. u̯el- 1139.] 'hair, wool, grass, ear (of corn)': {cf. Av varəsa-; Sgd wrs = 'hair'}: Khotanese Saka gausä; Mid P gāwars = 'sorghum, giant millet' (M3); Pamir dialects: Yidgha ɣavarso; Parachi gâš; Bajui ǰ^u wāxčʸ; Shughni ǰäwaus (Morg); Pashto ɣošt; P gāvars گــاورس; Sor garis گــارِس/gar̄is گــاڕِس [J/F/K/A/JB3/IFb/B/JJ/HH/GF/TF/OK] <genim; lazût; t̲ale>

garît•e گاريته *m.* **(•ê;).** thick wooden beams *(in ceiling of traditional Kurdish house, as opposed to **nîre**, thin wooden beams (Bw))*: **•Xanî bê *karîte* ava na be** (BF) A house without *beams* cannot stand. {also: karîte (Bw-2); k'arîte (K[s]); [karitá قــريــتــا (G)/ kārīta & gārīta گاريتا (Rh)] (JJ)} {syn: k'êran; max} <Syr qārītā ܩܪܝܬܐ = 'beam, plank' [Bw/IFb/OK/ZF3//K(s)//JJ] <nîre I; r̄ot>

gasin گاسِن (M-Ak/JJ-Rh) = ploughshare. See **gîsin**.

gav گــــاڤ *f.* **(-a;-ê).** 1) instant, moment; time: **-gava** = when *(conj.)*: **•*Gava* qundir wilo ji bavê xwe re got** ... (L) *When* the gourd said that [lit. 'thus'] to its father ...; **-gavek din** (L) in a minute, soon: **•Ezê *gavek din* bixwim** (L) I'll eat *in a minute*; **-gavekê** = once, one time; **-gavina/gavgavina** = sometimes, from time to time; **-vê gavê** = now; **-wê gavê** = then; 2) {syn: pêngav} step, pace: **•Em weke çarsid-pênsid *gava* ji pêz dûr k'etin** (Ba2:2, 205) We went about 400-500 *paces* away from the sheep; **-gav avêtin** (IFb) to take steps, take measures: **•Divê li welêt û Tirkiyeyê jî di vî warî de hinek *gav bêne avêtin*** (AW71D1) Both in the homeland and in Turkey some *measures should be taken* in this matter. {also: [gaw] گــــاڤ (JJ); <gav> گــــاڤ (HH)} <O Ir *gāman- (A&L p. 87 [VIII, 1]): Av gāman- = 'pace' M, v.1, p.220); Za gam f. = 'step' (Todd); also P hangām هــنــگــام = 'time, season'; Sor hengaw هــەنــگــاو = 'step, pace; time, season' [K/A/JB3/IFb/B/JJ/HH/GF/TF/OK] <car; dem; wext>

gavan گــــاڤــان *m.* **(-ê; gavên** [BK/B]/**gêvên** [B]/**gavîn** [B]/**gêvîn** [B], **vî gavanî).** cowherd, "cowboy," cattle herdsman. {also: [ga-van] گــــــــاوان (JJ); <gavan> گــــاڤــان (HH)} Cf. P gāvbān گــاوبــان = herdsman; Sor gawan گــــاوان {gavan[t]î} [L/K/A/JB3/IFb/B/JJ/HH/GF/TF/OK/BK/ZF3] <ga; golikvan; naxirvan; şivan>

gavanî گــــاڤــانــــى (TF/ZF3/Wkt) = cowherding. See **gavantî**.

gavantî گاڤانتى *f.* **(-ya;-yê).** profession of cowherd or cowboy; cattle herding: **•Nikare *gavantîya* dewarên gund bike** (lotikxane.com 9.xi.2011) He isn't [even] good at *herding* the village's cattle. {also: gavanî (TF/ZF3/Wkt)} [K/B//TF/ZF3/Wkt] <gavan; golikvanî>

gavzinde گاڤزِنده (M-Ak) = complaint. See **gazin**.

gayîn گايين (K) = to copulate. See **gan I**.

gaz I گاز (K/B/JJ/GF/TF) = ell. See **gez I**.

gazin گــــازِن *f.* **().** complaint (F/K/B); reproach (A/GF/OK): **-gazin kirin** (F/B)/**gazinde kirin** (SK) to complain: **•Eve ez çûmeve, *gavzinda neke*** (M-

Ak #657, p.296) Now I'm going, so *don't complain* •***Gazinda*** **ji min** ***neket*** (Bw) *Lest* he *complain* about me. {also: gavzinde (M-Ak); gazinde (SK/Bw); gazvinde (Ak/AA); [gazin] گازین (JJ); <gazind> گازند (HH)} {syn: gilî I [2]; şikyat} Sor gazinde گازِنده [F/K/A/JJ/B/JB1-S/GF/TF/OK//HH//SK/Bw//Ak//M-Ak]

gazinde گازِنده (SK/Bw) = complaint. See **gazin**.

gazî گـازی *f.* **(;-yê).** call, shout, yell: **-gazî kirin** (RZ): a) to shout, yell, call {syn: bang kirin; lê deng kirin}: •***Gazî*** **jina xo** ***kir*****, "Zû be, doşek û balgan da-nê û zadekî xoş ḧazir ke, ko mêwanekî zor ʻezîz bo me hatîye"** (SK 8:82) He *called* to his wife, "Hurry, set out mattresses and cushions and prepare some good food, for a very dear guest has come to us"; b) to summon, invite {syn: dawet kirin; ʻezimandin; vexwendin}: •**Em** ***gazî*** **wana gişka** ***kin*** (Ba) *Let's call* (*=summon*) them all {also: [gazi] گازی (JJ); <gazî> گازی (HH)} {syn: bang; hawar} Sor gaz گـاز = 'cry, call' [K/A/JB3/IFb/B/JJ/HH/JB1-A&S/SK/GF/TF/OK/RZ]

gaz û bêlan گـاز و بـێـلان *pl.?* mountaintops, summits, peaks; high mountains: •**Rabe,** ***gaz u belanê*** **bilind k'eve** (EP-4, #32) Get up, climb to *the* highest *peaks*. {syn: ḧeç'; kop I; k'umik; kumt} [EP-4/XF/SS] <çîya>

gazvinde گازڤنده (Ak/AA) = complaint. See **gazin**.

gebar گـەبـار *adj.* mixed up, confused. {syn: gildî (Wn)} [Wn/Wkt]

geboz گـەبـۆز *f.* **().** gully, ravine: **-gelî-geboz** (Ba2) do. {syn: dergelî; derteng; gelî II; zang; zer II} Cf. T boğaz = 'throat; mountain pass, gorge' [Ba2/K/CS/FS]

gec گـەج *f.* **(;-ê).** lime; alabaster, gypsum; plaster. {also: gac (K); geç (IF[s]); gêç (IF[s]-2/Wkt); [ghetch] گـچ (JJ); [ghiéz] گـز (JJ-G)} {syn: ces; k'ils} Cf. P gač گچ; Sor geç گەچ = 'gypsum' [F/B/JJ/ZF3//K//IF//Wkt]

geç گەچ (IF[s]) = alabaster; plaster. See **gec**.

gede گـەدە *m.* **().**1) tramp, vagrant, hobo; street urchin (K); beggar (JJ): **-gede-gûde** (K)/**gede-gûda** (Z-1) do.; 2) {syn: kuȓ II; law} boy, male child: •**Teyr** ***gede*** **bir çû adeke be'rêda danî** (EH) The bird picked up *the boy* and took him to an island in the sea. {also: [gheda] گدا (JJ); <geda> گدا (HH)} < P gadā گـدا = 'beggar' [Z-1/K/IF/B/JJ/HH/ZF3/FS] <p'arsek; xwazok>

gedek گـەدەک *f.* **(;-ê).** buffalo-calf. {also: gedeng (FS); [ghedek] گدك (JJ); <gedek> گدك (HH)} {syn: sak (Haz/IF)} [K(s)/A/JB3/IF/JJ/B/ZF3//FS] <gamêş; medek>

gedeng گەدەنگ (FS) = buffalo-calf. See **gedek**.

gef گـەف *m.(K)/f.(B/JB3/IF/FS)* **(/-a; /-ê).** threat, menace: **-gef [lê] xwarin** (K)/~ **kirin** (ZF3) to threaten: •**Mehmûd xeydî, dilê xweda** ***gef xwerin*** (EP-8) M. got angry, in his heart he *threatened them*. {also: [ghéf] گـف (JJ); <gef> گـف (HH)} [EP-8/K/JB3/IF/B/JJ/HH/ZF3/FS] <metirsî>

geh I گـەه *f.* **(-a;).** finger joint(s): **-geha destî** (Zeb) do. {also: gehe (GF/IFb-2); [gheh] گـه (JJ); <geh> گـه (HH)} [FK-1/A/IFb/HH/JJ/OK/Zeb/FS//GF] <hence; movik>

geh II گـەه *adv.* sometimes, at times: **-geh ... geh (jî)** (Cxn-KE/K) do.: •***Geh*** **ew li cem axê ye,/** ***Geh*** **jî li cem çelebî** (Cxn-KE: Rencberê Bi rûmet) *At times* he is with the agha, / *At times* he is with the gentleman. {also: [gheh-gheh] گهگه (JJ); <geh> گه (HH)} {syn: car[i]na; gavina} < P gāh گاه = 'time; place'; Sor ga ... ga گـا...گـا = 'at one time ... at another time' [Cxn-KE/K/A/IFb/JJ/HH/GF/TF] <car>

gehan گەهان = to arrive; to ripen. See **gihan I**.

geheştin گـەهـەشـتـِن (-gehej- [JB1-A]/-gehêj- [JB1-S]/-gihe- [SK]) (JB1-A&S/SK) = to arrive; to ripen, mature. See **gihîştin**.

gehiştin گـەهِـشـتـِن (-gehij-[IF]/-geh- [M-Zx]) (IF-2/M-Zx) = to arrive; to ripen, mature. See **gihîştin**.

gehîn گـەهـیـن (M) = to arrive; to ripen, mature. See **gihîştin**.

gehl گەهل (RC2) = crowd; people. See **gel**.

gel گـەل *m.* **(-ê;).** 1) multitude, crowd, pack: ***-gele*** **gur** (Ba) *a pack of* wolves; 2) {syn: net'ewe; xelq} people, folk, nation: •**Hêzên kolonyalîst dixwazin** ***gelê*** **me zêndî bikine gorê** (Ber) The colonialist forces want to bury our *people* alive: **-gelê K'urd** (ZF) the Kurdish people: •**Ev erdê han ê** ***gelê Kurd*** **e û bê wan kes tê de rûnane** (BX) This land belongs to *the Kurdish people*, and besides them nobody lives on it. {also: gehl (RC2); gele I (Ba)} <O Ir *garda-/*gṛda- (A&L p. 87 [VIII, 1] + 97 [XXI, 9]): Sor gel گـەل = 'assemblage, crowd' & 'people (K2)' [Ba/K(s)/A/JB3/IFb/Haz/ZF/Tsab/RZ//RC2]

gelac گـەلاج *adj. & m.* impostor, phony, charlatan, quack; corrupt, unjust. {also: gelaç (GF-2); [gheladj] گلاج (JJ); <kelaj> كلاج (HH)} [Zeb/A/JJ/GF/TF/OK/ZF3//HH] <ʻewan II; qumsî>

gelaç گەلاچ (GF) = charlatan; corrupt. See **gelac**.

gelale گەلالە *f.* **().** tonsil. {also: <gelale> گەلالە (Hej)} {syn: behîvok} =Sor ałû ئـاڵـوو [Ak/IFb/OK/Hej/Kmc-3/ZF3] <argûşk>

gelavêj گـەلاڤـێـژ *f.* **(;-ê).** Sirius, Canicula, Dog Star, *star in constellation Canis Major*. {also: gelawêj I (IFb/GF); gulavêj (FS); [ghill-aweizh] گلاڤيژ (JJ)} Sor gelawêj گـەلاوێـژ = 'Sirius; month in July-August' [Zeb/K(s)/JJ//IFb/GF//FS] <karwankuj; qurix; stêr>

gelawêj I گـەلاوێـژ (IFb/GF) = Sirius, Dog Star. See **gelavêj**.

Gelawêj II گەلاوێژ. A Sorani name for Persian month of *Murdād* مـــرداد [Leo] (July 23-Aug. 22). See chart of Kurdish months in this volume. <Tîrmeh; T'ebax I>

gelaz گەلاز (A) = plum. See **gêlaz** [2].

gelbaze گـەلـبـازە (IFb) = string of dried fruits. See **gelwaz**.

gelc گەلج (FS/JJ) = quarrel. See **gelş**.

gele I گەلە (Ba) = crowd; people. See **gel**.

gele II گەلە (B) = very; much. See **gelek**.

gelek گەلەك *adv.* 1) {syn: p'iř II; qewî; ze'f} very, very much: **•Ew gavan *gelikî* tirsîya** (L) That cowherd was *very much* afraid **•M. *gelekî* şaş û ȟeyrî ma** (EP-7) M. was *very* surprised and bewildered (=didn't know what to do) **•Ewê bihîst bû, wekî mêvanekî *gele* 'ezîz hatye mala Qeret'ajdîn** (EP-7) She heard that a *very* dear guest had come to Qeretajdin's house; 2) *[adj., pr. mod.]* {syn: p'iř II; ze'f; zor II} much, many: **•*Gelek* rêwîngê mîna te ji rê dadigeřîne** (EP-7) She leads *many* travelers like you off the road (=astray) **•*Gelekî* ewana xeber dan** (EP-7) They spoke *for a long time* [lit. 'much'] **•Bi taybetî Celadet Bedirxan û *gelek* ronakbîrên Kurd ...** (Ber) Especially C.B. and *several* Kurdish intellectuals **•di nav *gelek* salan da** (Ber) in *several* years; **-gelek gelek** (Zeb/ZF3) at [the very] most, maximum: **•Lewma *gelek gelek* şeş heyv bo avakirina qutabxanê divên** (Rêveberiya Perwerda Dihok Roj-ava 24.vii.2015) Therefore it will take 6 months *at the most* to build the school. {also: gele II (B-2); gelekî (Ba2); gelikî (L); gelle I; gellek; [ghelek] گلك (JJ); <gelek> گلك (HH)} = Sor zor زۆر [K/A/JB3/IF/JJ/B/ZF3//L]

gelekî گەلەکی (Ba2) = very; much. See **gelek**.

gelemperî گـەلـەمـپـەری *f.* **(-ya;-yê).** most, the majority of: **•*Gelemperîya* xelkên vî bajarî bi tirkî dizanin** (BX) *Most of* the people of this city know Turkish. {syn: bêt'ir [2]; p'iranî} [BX/ZF3/Wkt]

gelemş•e گـەلـەمـشـە *f.* **(•a;•ê).** (noisy) quarrel, dispute, conflict, difference (of opinion), disagreement; brawl, scene; uproar, tumult: **•*Gelemşa* wan çareser bû** (FS) Their *dispute* has been solved **•*Gelemşeyên* ku di nav salan de, li ser hev kom bûne hene** (Wlt 1:49, 16) There are *quarrels* which have accumulated over the years. {syn: cerenîx; cuře; de'w II; doz [1]; gelş; hengame; k'eft û left; k'eşmek'eş; k'êşe; mişt û miř; p'evçûn} [Wlt/A/IFb/OK/ZF3/FS/Wkt]

gelerî گـەلـەری (IF) = folksy, popular; national. See **gelêrî**.

***gelêr I** گەلێر *f.* **().** throng, multitude, crowd. [SW/JB3]

gelêr II گـەلـێـر (IF) = folksy, popular; national. See **gelerî**.

gelêrî گەلێری *adj.* 1) popular, folksy, folk: **•"Musikiya Geleriya Kurdistan"** = Folk Music of Kurdistan *(name of a series of cassette tapes produced by the Institut Kurde de Paris)*; 2) national (IF). {also: gelerî (IF-2); gelêr II (IF-2)} [IF/ZF3/Wkt/BF/TF/FD/SS]

gelgel•e گـەلـگـەلـە *m.* **(•ê;•eyî).** "carpet" of autumn leaves on the ground: **•Bayî li *gilgileyî* da û bir** (FS) The wind blew *the autumn leaves* away. {also: gelgelok (Zeb-2); gilgile (FS)} [Zeb//FS] <xezal II>

gelgelok گەلگەلۆك (Zeb) = autumn leaves. See **gelgele**.

gelikî گەلکی (L) = very; much. See **gelek**.

gelî I گـەلـی *vocative particle* O, hey *(used with plural nouns, corresponding to* **lo** *used with masc. singular nouns &* **lê** *with fem.; the accompanying noun is in the oblique case)*: **•*Gelî* hevala!** (B) *O* friends! **•*Gelî* mirovan** = *O/hey* men! **•*Gelî* şagirta!** (B) *O* students! **•*Gelle* bira** (IS-#142) *O* brothers! {also: gelle II (IS)} [K/A/IF/B/ZF3/FS] <lê III; lo; ya>

gelî II گەلی *m.* **(-yê ; gêlî, vî gelî[yî]).** 1) {syn: dergelî; derteng; geboz; zang; zer II} ravine, gorge, canyon, gully; mountain pass (JB3): **•Li derdorên *gelîyan* zinar wek dîwaran bilind dibin** (erdnigari.blogspot.com:Çîyayên Dêrsimê) Around *the ravines*, cliffs rise like walls: **-gelî-geboz** (Ba2) do.; 2) river valley, wadi (Haz). [Ba2/K/A/JB3/IF/B/Haz/ZF3/FS] <aran; kendal; newal; zuxir>

gelle I گەڵە = very; much. See **gelek**.

gelle II گەڵە (IS) = vocative particle. See **gelî I**.

gellek گەڵەك = very; much. See **gelek**.

gelmî گەلمی (MC-1) = ship. See **gemî**.

gelo گەلۆ *intrg.* 1) *intrg. particle (signals questions)*: •***Gelo* nave, wekî em evê qîza nazik bigihînine ewî xortê tu bêjî?** (Z-1) Shouldn't we bring this fine girl to that young man [who] you spoke of? [lit. 'you say'] [cf. P āyā آيـا; Ar hal هـل /a- أ]; 2) {syn: bê II; çika; ka; qe} whether *(introduces indirect questions)*: •**"Bizanin çav bidêrin û binêrin *gelo* xelk çi dibêjin (H.)"** (BX) Know how to wait and see what people say •**Bîne em êvarê p'eȓe k'axaza cigarê bikne bin doşeka Ûsib, lê ya her yanzde dinê herekê qoȓe bizmal bikne bin doşekê wan, çika k'î ji wana tê derdixe, *gelo* me tişt kirîye bin doşekê wana yanê na** (Ba) In the evening we will put a cigarette paper under Joseph's mattress, but under the mattresses of the others let's put a handful of nails, to see who guesses *whether* or not we put something under their mattresses •**Ḧeta ku em pê neḧesin, *gelo* ew çi dûye** (Ba2:2, 205) Until we find out what the smoke is. {also: [ghelo] گلو (JJ); <g[u]lo> گلو (HH)} [K/A/JB3/IFb/JJ/GF/TF//HH]

gelş گەلش *f.* **(-a;-ê).** quarrel, divergence, difference of opinion, dispute; conflict, disagreement; confusion: •***Gelşek* ketiye nav beyna me** (JB3) We can't reach an understanding [lit. '*A quarrel* has fallen between us'] •**Tu jî ji xweȓa binêȓe li vê t'emaşê, li vê *gelşê*** (Z-2) You also look at this sight, at this *conflict* •**Zelamê şûm: yê ku şeȓê xelkî dikit û *gelşa bo* wan *çê dikit*** (FS) a bellicose man: one who fights with people and *conflicts with* them. {also: gelc (FS); [gheldj گلج/ gheltch گلچ] (JJ); <geleş> گلش (HH)} {syn: cerenîx; cuȓe; de'w II [û doz]; gelemşe; k'eşmek'eş; k'êşe; mişt û miȓ; p'evçûn} [Z-2/IF/JB3/ZF3//HH//JJ/FS]

gelt گەلت *m./f.(ZF3)* **(-ê/;).** type of kilim, flat-weave pileless carpet. {also: [gildīke] گلديك (JJ/PS)} {syn: beȓ IV; cacim; cil II; k'ilîm; merş; tejik} [HB/A/Krs//PS/JJ/ZF3]

gelte گەلتە *f.* **().** 1) harmless tussle or scuffle, joking with one another (A); a game (HH); 2) {syn: de'w II; doz [1]} violent quarrel, dispute, argument (A/JJ). {also: [ghilté] گلتە (JJ); <gelte> گلتە (HH)} Sor gałte گاڵتە = 'joke, jesting' [A/HH/ZF3/BF//JJ]

gelveşîn گەلڤەشین *f.* **().** rag used for wiping the sweat off a horse: **-hesp gelveşîn kirin** (K) to tend to, care for (horse); to rub down: •**[Hespê xwe meḧes û *gelveşîn kir*]** (PS) He combed and *rubbed down* his horse. {also: gelweşîn (FS); [gäl-väšīn] گلوشين (JJ)} [PS/K/JJ//FS] <meḧes>

gelwaz گەلواز *f.(Hk/K/B/ZF3)/m.(Elk/Frq)* **(-a/ ;-ê/).** 1) {syn: şaran; xarûz} wreath or string of dried fruits or vegetables for winter use: in Dêrsim [Tunceli] often dried pears and apples (IFb), in Farqîn [Silvan] often garlic, onions, and the like; 2) garland, wreath *(of flowers)* (K). See **gulwaz**. {also: gelbaze (IFb-2); gewlaz (Frq/K/B); gilwaz (Elk); [gälvāz] گلواز (JJ-PS); <gelwaz> گلواز (HH)} [Elk//Frq/K/B//Hk/A/IFb/JJ-PS/HH/GF/ZF3] <benî II; meşlûr>

gelweşîn گەلوەشین (FS) = rag for rubbing down horse. See **gelveşîn**.

gem گەم *f.* **(-a;-ê).** bridle; bit, snaffle *(of horse's bridle)*: •***Gêm* û qentirmên hespa çawan in?** (Wlt 1:42, p.4) How are the horses' *bit* and bridles? {also: gêm (Wlt/OK); [ghem] گم (JJ); <gem> گم (HH)} {syn: bizmîk; celew I} <T gem = 'bit (of a bridle)' [F/K/A/IFb/B/JJ/HH/GF//Wlt/OK] <dizgîn; lixab; qet'irme II>

gemar گەمار (JB3/IF[1]/JJ) = dirty. See **gemarî**.

gemarî گەماری *adj.* 1) {also: gemar (JB3/IF[1]); [ghemar] گمار (JJ)} {syn: bi'ok; ç'epel; dijûn II; p'îs; qilêr; qirêj} dirty; filthy *(more intense than just dirty [**qilêr**])*; 2) *[f.]* dirt, filth, dirtiness, filthiness. [Ad/A/JB3/IF/B/Kş/ZF3]

gemirandin گەمِراندِن *vt.* **(-gemirîn-).** 1) to deface, distort; 2) daub *(with mud)*, [be]smear: •**gelifandin: bi *gemirandinê* hûr kirina tişteka hişk ya bi tişteka nerm ve mayîye** (MG) gelifandin (to dust off): when *something is smeared* [with mud], to crumble the dry thing [=mud] which is stuck to something soft [e.g., cloth]; 3) {syn: firikandin; miz I: miz dan} to rub: **-bêvila yekî gemirandin/firikandin/mizdan** (Kmc) to put s.o. in his place, to teach s.o. a lesson. {also: <gemirandin گمراندن (digemirîne) (دگمرينه)> (HH)} Cf. gemarî = 'dirty' [MG/K/IFb/GF/TF/HH/CS]

gemî گەمی *f.* **(-ya;-yê).** 1) {syn: k'eştî} ship, vessel (K/F/JJ); steamer, steamship (K); rowboat (K); 2) fleet (K). {also: gelmî (MC-1); [ghemi] گمی (JJ); <gemî> گمی (HH)} < T gemi = 'ship'; =Sor nawe ناوه [Z-2/F/K/IFb/B/JJ/HH/ZF/FS//MC-1] <beḧr; belem; cengk'eştî= 'battleship'; fergêt = 'frigate'>

gemnok گەمنۆك (Bw) = corn. See **genmok**.

*gen گەن (A) = tick. See **gene**.

genav گەناڤ *f.* **(;-ê).** fen, swamp, marsh; stagnant water. {syn: cimcime II; çirav} Sor genaw گەناو = 'evil-smelling pool (often sulphureous)' [Zeb/OK/Wkt]

gencîne گەنجینە *f.* **(-ya;).** treasure: **•Lê xwedê meke, ko tu seb talankirina *gencîneya* marî marî bikujî** (KH, p.34) God forbid that you kill the snake in order to pillage its *treasure*. {syn: defîne; xizne} cf. P ganjīne گنجينه; Sor genc گەنج = 'treasure' & gencîne گەنجینە = 'closet, store-room'; cf. also Ar kanz كنز = 'treasure' [KH/K/JB3/IFb/GF/OK/ZF3]

gendelî گەندەلی *f.* **(-ya;-yê).** corruption: **•Digel ku tu 'eleqa beşa me û cenabê mamosta Qedrî bi mesela *gendelî* û karên ne li rê tuneye jî, navê wî xistine** [sic] **nav vê dosyê** (VoA 20.xi.2014) Even though there is no connection between our division and Professor Q. in the matter of *corruption* and improper activities, they still added his name to the file. Sor gendeł گەندەڵ = 'mouldy, decaying' [(neol)VoA/Wkt/BF]

gen•e گەنە *f.(B/K)/m.(F)* **(•a/;•ê/).** tick *(parasite)*, zool. *Trichodectes*: **-gena texte** (K) bug [Rus klop клоп]. {also: *gen (A); [ghené] گنه (JJ)} {syn: qijnik; qirnî} Cf. P kane کنه --> T kene; Sor gene گەنە; Cf. Heb kinah כנה (*pl.* kinim כנים) = 'louse' (*pl.* 'lice') [F/K/IF/B/JJ//A] <kêç'; spî II; zûrî>

gengaz گەنگاز *adj.* 1) {syn: mumkin; pêkan} possible: **•Bo kesê zîrek her tişt *gengaz* e** (Wkt) For a smart person everything is *possible* **•*Gengaz* e ku Behrem îro bêt** (FS) It is *possible* that B. will come today **•Lê bi dest xistina Kela Dimdimê ji bo eceman *negengaz* bû** (Zend 2, iii [1997], 56) But getting hold of the Fortress of Dimdim was *impossible* for the Persians; 2) {syn: asan} easy, simple. [Zend/K/IFb/GF/TF/OK/RZ/ZF3/Wkt/FS]

gengazî گەنگازی *f.* **(-ya;-yê).** 1) possibility: **•*gengazîya* peyda kirina şolê** (arbetsformedlingen .se ii.2017) *the possibility of* finding work; 2) {syn: asanî} ease, simplicity. [IFb/GF/ZF3/Wkt]

gengeş•e گەنگەشە *f.* **(•a/•eya;).** debate, dispute, controversy, argument, disagreement, heated discussion: **•Bû *gengeşa* wan li ser navî** (FS) They had *a heated discussion* about the name **•Ez dixwazim bizanim *gengeşeya* hewe li ser çiye?** (BF) I want to know what your *dispute* is about **•Qanatê Kurdo di gramera xwe de dengên ku li ser wan di navbera zimannasên Kurdî de *gengeşî* hene yekoyek nîqaş kirîye** (Çandname: Dengên Kurdî yên ku bê nasname mane-3) In his grammar book, Q.K. discussed one by one the sounds about which there are *debates* among Kurdish linguists. {also: gengeşî (IFb/TF/FD/CS/ZF3-2/Wkt-2)} {syn: nîqaş; mişt û mir̄; micadele} [Çandname/IFb/TF/FD/CS//ZF3/FS/BF/Wkt] <k'êşe>

gengeşî گەنگەشی (IFb/TF/FD/CS/ZF3/Wkt) = debate, controversy. See **gengeşe**.

genim گەنم *m.* **(-ê; gênim, vî genimî).** wheat: **•Kur̄ derê** [=devê?] **t'êr̄a vedikin, *gênim* r̄o dikine 'erdê** (Ba-1, #37) The boys open the sacks [lit. 'the doors (or: mouths) of the sacks'], and pour out *the wheat* onto the ground **•T'êr̄a vekin, *genim* r̄axin, bira zuhyabe, xirab nebe** (Ba-1, #36) Open the sacks, scatter *the wheat*, let it dry out, lest it go bad; **-genimê şamî** (A/IFb)/~ **şam** (GF) = corn. See **genimeşamî**. {also: [ghenym] گنم (JJ); <genim> گنم (HH)} Cf. Skt godhūma- m.; O Ir *gantuma- (Ras p.216): Av gantuma-; P gandom گندم; Sor genim گەنِم; Za genim/genem *m.* (Mal); Hau genme *f.* (M4) [F/K/A/JB3/IFb/B/JJ/HH/SK/GF/TF/OK] <bijî III; garis; gilgil; herzin; korik; lazût; xirovî; types of wheat: bijîreş; gewre; qendarî; sorgul I>

genimeşam گەنِمەشام, f. (OK) = corn. See **genimeşamî**.

genimeşamî گەنِمەشامی *m.* **(-yê;).** corn, maize, bot. *Zea mays*. {also: genimeşam, f. (OK); genimê şamî (A/IFb); genimê şam (GF); genmeşam, f. (OK-2); [genim-ē shāmē] (JJ-Rh)} {syn: garis[ê stanbolî]; genmok; gilgilê Stembolê (Haz); lazût; zuret I} [K(s)/SK//OK//A/IFb//GF//JJ-Rh]

genimok گەنِمۆك (A/OK/ZF3) = corn. See **genmok**.

genî گەنی *adj.* 1) stinking, putrid, foul smelling: **•Bîna *genî* tê** (B) Something stinks [lit. '*putrid* smell comes'] **•Dijmin...zindanên xwe yên *genî*, ji keç û xortên me yên ciwan tijî kirin** (Wlt 2:59, p.7) The enemy...has filled its *stinking* prisons with our young people [lit. 'young/beautiful girls and youths'] **•Keftarê *genî*, em te nas dikin** (Wlt 2:100, p.13) *Stinking* hyena, we know who you are [or, we recognize you] **•Sosik ava *genî* xwer bû, nikarbû ji ç'êm derbaz bibûya** (FK-kk-13:129) Sosik [the horse] drank *putrid* water, [and] couldn't cross the river; 2) rotten, bad; 3) {syn: k'irêt} ugly (Çnr). {also: genû (IFb-2); [gheni] گنی (JJ); <genî> گنی (HH)} [Pok. g^{u}edh- 466.] 'to push, injure, destroy': Skt gandhá- *m.* = 'smell, odor'; O Ir *gandaka- (A&L p. 87 [VIII, 1]

+ 96 [XX, 3]): Av gaiñti- = 'stink'; Mid P gand = 'stench' & gandag 'stinking' (M3); Manich. Mid P gannagī; Sor genîw گـهنـیـو = 'rotten' [K/A/JB3/IFb/B/JJ/HH/JB1-A&S/GF/TF/OK/Çnr] <kuředer; řizîn>

genmeşam گەنمەشام, f. (OK) = corn. See **genimeşamî**.

genmok گـەنـمـۆك *f.* **(-a;).** corn, maize. {also: gemnok (Bw-2); genimok (A/OK/ZF3)} {syn: garis[ê stanbolî]; genimê şamî; gilgilê Stembolê (Haz); lazût; zuret I} <*dim. of* genim = 'wheat'; folk etymology: genim + nok = 'chick peas' (Bw) [Bw/A/OK/ZF3]

genû گەنوو(IFb) = stinking; ugly. See **genî**.

gep I گەپ (IFb/OK/JJ/Kş) = cheek. See **gup**.

gep II گەپ (Bşk) = nose. See **k[']epî**.

gep III گەپ *f./m.(FS)* **(/-ê;).** small piece, morsel, bite *(often with indefinite suffix -ek)*: •**Herekê me *gepeke*** (L) Each one of us is [only] *a bite* (=hardly worth eating) •**Wî *gepê* nanî kir di devê xwe da** (FS) He put *the piece of* bread in his mouth; -**gepek nan** (ZF3) a small piece of bread, a morsel of bread. [K/A/IF/ZF3/FS] <fiř I; parî; p'erçe>

gepir گەپر (ZF3/Wkt/FS) = throat, neck. See **qeper**.

ger I گەر (GF) = if. See **eger I**.

geř II گـەڕ *f.* **(-a;-ê).** 1) {syn: fitil} a walk, stroll, turn, spin; 2) {syn: govek} orbit, circle: •**Teyr *geřekê* serda zivirî** (EP-5, #17) The bird circled above her [lit. 'turned [in] *a circle* above']; 3) {syn: dor; nobet; sirê} one's turn (Bw): •**Ew zû nehat, lewra *geřa* wî şot** (FS) He didn't come early, so he lost his turn [lit. 'His *turn* (was) burned'] •**Îcar *gera* min e** (IFb) It's my *turn* now. {also: <ger> گـــر (HH)} Cf. Sor geř گـــەڕ = 'turn, bend, false claim, gulf, circle, circular motion, functioning' [EP-5/F/K/A/IFb/B/HH/OK/Bw]

geř III گـــــەڕ *f.* **(-a;).** 1) {syn: gol} lake (Hk/IFb); 2) pool (M-Am/IFb): •***Geř* êt heyn, pîçek biçûk in. Her şev dê avê berdenê, masî dê hên, dê tijî masî bin. Piştî hingî dê ber den, li wa *geřa* masî dê mînin têda** (M-Am #724, p.334) They have *pools*, which are rather small. Every night they let the water into them and the fish will come and they become full of fish. Afterward they let (the water) off and the fish stay in *the pools*. {also: <ger> گر (HH)} [Hk/M-Am/IFb/HH] <geřik II>

geran I گەران (A) = to wander; to look for. See **geřîn**.

geřan II گـــەڕان *m.* **().** mallet, sledgehammer. {also: giřan II (IFb); karan; kerane (TF/OK/IFb-2); <keřan> كـــران (HH)} {syn: mirc} [Haz/IFb//HH//TF/OK] <ç'akûç; mêk'ut; zomp>

geřandin گـەڕانـدِن**/gerandin** گـەرانـدِن *vt.* **(-geřîn-).** 1) to let wander, let roam (IF/A/BK): •**Dêla boẍ girt, boẍ k'uta, nav gařanê *geřand*** (J) He took hold of the ox's tail, beat the ox, *let him run* among the cattle •**Min zozana *bigerîne*** (J) *Let* me *wander* in the summer pastures; -**li ser zmanê xwe gerandin** (JB3) to gossip; 2) {syn: belav kirin} to pass out/ around, distribute (IFb/JB3): •**Çiřa M. îro derengî k'et? Nehat qawa dîwanê *negeřand*?** (EP-7) Why is M. late today? [Why] hasn't he come *pass out* coffee [to the members] of the court; 3) to wrap, envelop (JB3/BK): •**Destê xwe *li stoyê* min *gerand*** (JB3) He *embraced* me •**Ji xwe re terîş anî, li serê xwe *gerand*, xwe kir wek hecîkî** (RN 30/7/45) He took a bandage, *wrapped* it around his head, and made himself into a hadj [=Muslim pilgrim] •**Wî *belakê li ser* wî *gerand*** (JB3) He *caused* him *an unpleasant moment*; 4) to guide, direct, lead, drive: •[**Kulik mir, ew ḧukum *digeřîne*, Ferḧat Aẍa**] (PS-I) Kulik died, and that one *is in charge* [lit. 'leads the rule'], [i.e.,] Ferhat Agha; 5) {syn: xapandin} to deceive, fool: -**hevû-du gerandin** (JB3) to deceive one another. {also: **gêřan**; [gherandin] گراندين (JJ); <gerandin گراندن (digerîne) (دگرينه)> (HH)} [J/K/A/JB3/IFb/B/JJ/HH/ GF/TF/OK/BK] <geřîn>

geřandî گـەڕانـدى *adj./pp.* transitive *(gram.)*: -**lêkera (ne)gerandî** (IF) (in)transitive verb. {syn: derbazbûyî; gerguhêz} =Sor têpeř تێپەڕ [(neol)IF/ZF3] <lêker>

gerane گـــەرانـــە *adj.* subjunctive, optative *(gram.)*: -**řaweya gerane** (IF) subjunctive mood. {syn: bilanî II} [(neol)IF/ZF3] <řawe>

gerdan گەردان (JJ) = neck; collar. See **gerden**.

gerdek گـــــــــەردەك *f.* **(-a;-ê).** bridal chamber: -**çûn gerdekê** (IS-#268) to go to the bridal chamber, i.e., to get married. {also: [gherdek] گـــردك (JJ)} < P gerdak گـــردك = 'round tent; nuptial chamber' --> T gerdek; Sor gerdek گەردەك [IS/IF/JJ/ZF3]

gerden گـــەردەن *f.* **(-a;-ê).** 1) {also: [gherdan] گـــردان (JJ); <gerden> گـردن (HH)} neck; throat; 2) {also: [gherdan] گـــــردان (JJ)} collar: -**gerdena xwe pê aza kirin** (Dh/Zeb) to renounce one's claim to stg. *said by s.o. departing to those remaining behind* [=if I owe you stg. due to a wrongdoing, renounce your claim to it] [cf. T hakkını helal etmek]: •**Ez te bi xudê didem e sûndê ko ji şolêt min bi te**

kirî *gerdena min aza ke* (SK 9:89) I conjure you by God *to pardon me* for everything I have done to you •**Ȟakimî got, "Bismilla, ew kîye?" Gotê, "Huşşş, ez melayketê r̄uȟ-kêşanê me." Ȟakimî gotê, "Muhleta min bide ȟeta subey da ez r̄uxseta xo ‘eyalê xo bixazim, *gerdena xo pê aza bikem*."** (M-Ak #541) The governor said, "By God, who is that?" He said, "Hush, I am the angel who carries off souls." The governor said, "Give me a respite until tomorrow so that I may take leave of my family and *free myself of any obligation to them*"; 3) {also: gerdenî (IF/B); [gherdani/ gherdeni] گردنی (JJ); <gerdenî> گردنی (HH)} {syn: benî II; berdilk[3]; r̄istik; t’oq} necklace: •**Ew zêr̄ê *gerdena* xwe û guharê xwe jî datîne ser t’aê mêzînê** (Ba) She puts the gold of her *necklace* and earrings onto the pan of the scales. Cf. P kardan كردن --> T gerdan; Sor gerdin گەردِن = 'neck'; Hau gerden m. (M4) [Ba/K/A/JB3/IF/B/HH//JJ] <gewrî; p'êsîr [2]; stû>

gerdenî گەردەنی (IF/B/HH) = necklace. See **gerden**[3].

gerdenzer گەردەنزەر *adj.* having a beautiful throat or neck: •**Qeret’ajdînê minî *gerden zere*** (Z-2) You are my Qeretajdîn *of the beautiful neck*. < gerden = 'throat' + zer = 'yellow' [Z-2/K]

gerdom گەردۆم (SK) = oxcart. See **gerdûm**.

gerdûm گەردووم *f.* (;-ê). oxcart, cart, wagon: •**To neşêy parê dewletê zewt bikey. Ewe ȟukomet e, ‘esker heye, top o cebilxane heye. Kêrûşkê bi *gerdomê* digirît, merȟemetê digel te diket, egerne dişêt bi deqîqeyekî te xirab ket** (SK 14:138) You can't possess yourself of state monies. It's the government, it has soldiers, guns and ammunition. (It may) catch a hare with *a cart* and be merciful to you, otherwise it can destroy you in a minute. {also: gerdom (SK); gerdûn (GF); [gerdun] گردون (JJ-Rh)} {syn: ‘erebe} Cf. P gardūne گردونه = ‘chariot, cart, vehicle’; NENA girdûn ܓܪܕܘܢ = ‘a cart of very rough sort, for bringing home the harvest’ (Maclean) [Kmc/ZF/Wkt//SK//GF/JJ-Rh] <fayton; firxûn>

gerdûn گەردوون (GF/JJ-Rh) = oxcart. See **gerdûm**.

gere گەرە = it is necessary. See **gerek**.

gerek گەرەك. [it is] necessary, must: •**R̄astya xwedê jî eve, *gere* du serê çê neçine ser be’lgîkî** (Dz) This is God's truth, two good heads *must* not go on one pillow •**Her lîstikekê *gere* we cîyê xwe biguhasta, lê we usa nekir** (Z-1) You *should* have changed places for every game, but you didn't •**Evê lîstikê *gere* tu û Memêva cîyê xwe biguhêzin** (Z-1) For this game, you and M. *must* change places •***Gerekê* hûn r̄ind miqatî wî bin** (Ba) You *must* take good care of him. {also: gere; gerekê; [gherek] گرك (JJ)} {syn: divê(t) [viyan]; lazim; pêdivî; p’êwîst} < T gerek = 'necessary': Old T **keräk** & **kergäk I** (Nadeliaev, p. 300) & **kergek** 'necessity, necessary' became **kerek** by elision of the -g- at an unusually early date ... S[outh]W[est] Osm[anli] **gerek** (Clauson p. 742): Sor gerek گەرەك *(dialect of Sinneh [Sanandaj])* [Dz/Ba/K/JB3/IF/JJ/B]

gerekê گەرەکێ = it is necessary. See **gerek**.

gereksitêr گەرەکسِتێر (FJ) = planet. See **gerestêr**.

geremol گەرەمۆل *f.* (). disorder, chaos, mess: •**Welat bi her awayî tev lihev bûbû, alozî û *geremolên* siyasî û aborî li pey hev dihatin û her roj gelek meriv dihatin kuştin** (MUm, 51) The homeland was confused in every possible way, incidents of political and economic distress and *disorder* came one after the other and every day many people were killed. {syn: hêwirze; k’eft û left; k’af-k’ûn} [MUm/Frq/IFb/OK/ZF3]

gerestêr گەرەستێر *f.* (-a;). planet: •**Di Sîstema Rojê da *gerestêra* herî mezin Jupîter e** (RR 20.1.17) In the Solar System the largest *planet* is Jupiter. {also: gereksitêr (FJ); gerestêrk (FD/ZF-2); gerokestêr (RZ); stêra gerok (SS)} Cf. Sor estêrey ger̄ok ئەستێرەی گەڕۆك; *Other proposed term: rojgêran.* [RR/ZF//FD//FJ//RZ//SS] <stêr I>

gerestêrk گەرەستێرك (FD/ZF) = planet. See **gerestêr**.

gerguhêz گەرگوهێز *adj.* transitive *(verb)*: -**lêkera gerguhêz** (TaRK/Wkt) transitive verb. {syn: derbazbûyî; ger̄andî; *têper} = Sor têper̄ تێپەڕ [TaRK/Wkt/ZF3] <lêker; negerguhêz>

ger•ik I گەرك *f.* (•ka;). 1) {syn: tirabêlk; t’oz; xubar} fine powder or dust; 2) pollen (GF/OK/Hej); 3) sawdust; 4) bran dust: -**gerka sivîyê** (Zeb) do. {also: [ghirik] گرك (JJ); <girik> گرك (HH); <gerk> گەرك (Hej)} P garde گرده = 'fine powder, pouncing powder, pollen' [Bw/Zeb/GF/OK/Hej//JJ/HH/ZF3]

ger̄•ik II گەڕك *f.* (•ka;). puddle, little pool: -**ger̄ka avê** (Bw) do. {also: gerrek (IFb)} [Bw//IFb] <ger̄ III>

gerinende گەرنەندە (Rnh) = director. See **ger̄înende**.

geriyan گەریان (JB3/IF) = to wander; to look for. See **ger̄în.**

gerîh گەریه (IFb) = unripe almond. See **gêrih**.

gef̄în گـەڕيـن *vi.* **(-gef̄-).** 1) to wander, roam: **•Ezê *bigerim* heyanî sola min biqete** (L) I *will wander* until my shoes crack; 2) [+ **li**] to look or search for: **•Ez *li* te *digef̄im*** = I *look for* you **•Îsal heft salê min e ez li dinyaê *li* te *digerim*** (L) This year is the seventh year I *have been roaming* the world *in search of* you **•Keçelok ji xwe re *li* seyda teyra *digerîya*** (L) Kechelok was a bird hunter [lit. '*searched for* the hunt of birds']. {also: geran I (A); geriyan (JB3/IF); gerîyan (BX-2); [gheriian] گريان (JJ); <geran گران (digere) (دگره)> (HH)} [Pok. 3. u̯er- 1152.] 'to turn, bend': O Ir *vart- (Tsb 37/Tsb2 31) [or *gart- (A&L p. 84 [IV, 3] + note 9 [p. 101]): Av vart- (pres. varəta-); P gaštan گشتن (-gard-) (گـرد); Sor gef̄an گـەڕان (-gef̄ê-); Za geyrenã [geyrayiş] (Todd/Mal); Hau gêłay (gêł-) *vi.* = 'to go about, wander' (M4) [BX/K/B//JB3/IF/JJ//A/HH] <gef̄andin>

gef̄înek گەڕينەك/**gerînek** گەرينەك [IFb/GF/ZF3] *f.* **().** whirlpool, eddy. {also: [gherinek] گـريـنـك (JJ)} {syn: *gêjik (IFb); zivif̄ok} [Dy/IFb/JJ/GF/ZF3]

gef̄înende گەڕينەندە/**gerînende** گەرينەندە [IF/ZF3] *m.* **(-yê;).** director, manager, person in charge: **•Xwedî û *gerinendeyê* berpirsyar, Mîr Celadet Alî Bedir-Xan bû** (Rnh - intro) The owner and *director* in charge was Mîr Djeladet Ali Bedir Khan. {also: gerinende (Rnh)} [(neol)Rnh//K//IF/ZF3]

gerînî گەرينى *adj.* conditional *(gram.)*: **-f̄aweya gerînî** (K/IF/GF) conditional mood. {syn: hekînî} <eger = 'if' + -înî = adjectival ending [(neol)K/IF/GF/ZF3] <eger; gerane>

gerîyan گـەريـان (BX) = to wander; to look for. See **gef̄în.**

germ گـەرم *adj.* 1) warm, hot: **-ç'avêt xwe germ kirin** (Bw) to take a nap; **-germ kirin** (K/OK) to warm up, heat up; 2) [*f.* **(-a;-ê)**] warmth: **•Ez dareka mazinim: havînê wextê *germê* mirovek dê hêtin li f̄êkê, dê hête bin sêbera min, dê f̄û nêt** (M-Ak, #548) I am a big tree: in summer when it is hot [lit. 'the time *of warmth*'] a man will come along the road, he will come under my shade and sit down **•K'îjan ji wana zû xwe digihîne *germa* deşta** (Ba2:1, p.202) Which one of them will reach *the warmth of* the plains first [lit. 'early'] **•R̄ojekê, *germa* nîvro ber sîya kon Sîabend serê xwe danî ser çoka Xecê** (IS-#362) One day, in the noontime *heat*, in the shade of the tent, Siyabend lay his head down on Khej's knee. {also: [gherm] گرم (JJ); <germ> گرم (HH)} [Pok. g̯ʰer- 493.] 'warm': Av garəma-; P garm گـرم; Sor germ گـەرم; Za germ (Todd/Mal); Hau germ (M4); cf. also Gr thermos θερμός = 'hot, warm'; Arm ǰerm ջերմ = 'fever; warm'; Eng warm {germahî; germayetî; germayî; germî} [F/K/A/JB3/IFb/B/JJ/HH/GF/TF] <şarandin>

germahî گەرماهى (K/GF/OK) = warmth. See **germî.**

germav گـەرمـاڤ *f.* **(;-ê).** 1) hot springs, thermal springs; 2) {syn: ȟemam} bath (Bw/OK): **-Germav xoş bît** (Bw) *greeting said to s.o. who has just had a bath or shower* [cf. Ar na'īman نعيماً & T saatler olsun]; **-germavê k'etin** (OK) to bathe, take a bath. {also: [gherm-aw] گرماڤ (JJ); <germav> گرماڤ (HH)} Cf. P germābe گرمابه = 'bathhouse'; Sor germaw[an] گـەرمـاو[ان] = 'hot bath' [Bw/K/A/IFb/JJ/HH/GF/TF/OK]

germayetî گەرمايەتى (A) = warmth. See **germî.**

germayî گـەرمـايـى (K/A/IFb/B/GF/OK) = warmth. See **germî.**

germegerm گەرمەگەرم/**germe-germ** [K] *f.* **(-a;).** the high point, the acme, the heat of *(a battle, etc.)*. {syn: bin deqa germê (Zeb)} [Zeb/K/ZF3]

germixîn گـەرمِـخـيـن *vi.* **(-germix-).** 1) to stay a long time in the heat [di germê da pirr mayîn]: **•Pez *germixî* di gomê da** (Slm) The sheep "*languished*" in the sheepfold; 2) to ferment *(vi.)*: **•Genim *digermixe*** (Slm) The wheat *is fermenting*. {also: [ghermikhi] گـرمـخـى (JJ) = 'fermentation, puanteur'} [Slm/JJ/GF/FJ/ZF3] <mehîn II>

germî گـەرمـى *f.* **(-ya;-yê).** warmth; heat. {also: germahî (K-2/GF-2/OK-2); germayetî (A-2); germayî (K-2/A-2/IFb-2/B/GF-2/OK-2); [germātī گـرمـاتـى (JJ-Rh)/ghermaia گـرماى (JJ-G)/ghermi گـرمـى (JJ)]; <germî> گـرمـى (HH)} {syn: germ [2]} Sor germayî گەرمايى; Za germey (Mal) [K/JB3/IFb/JJ/HH/GF/TF/OK//A/B] <germ>

gernas گـەرنـاس *m.* **(-ê;).** hero. {also: girnas (GF)} {syn: 'efat; 'egît; fêris[1]; leheng; mêrxas; p'elewan} [K/IFb/TF/ZF3//GF]

geroh گەرۆه (ZF3) = unripe almond. See **gêrih.**

gef̄ok گـەڕۆك *m.* **(-ê;).** 1) playboy, epicurean, bon-vivant (K/B); person of loose morals (EP-5): **•Ew Leylê rinde,/ Bejinêda bilinde,/ Hema 'esil-'esasa/ *Gef̄oka* nava gundde** (EP-5, #13) That Leyla is fine,/ She is tall of stature,/ But her origins/ Stem from *the harlots* of the village; 2) vagabond, tramp (K/B); wandering beggar (A); 3) *[adj.]* traveling, itinerant; portable: -**kînoa gefok** (B) portable movie projector. [EP-5/K/A/IF/B/GF/ZF3] <gede; tolaz>

gerokestêr گەرۆكەستێر (RZ) = planet. See **gerestêr**.

gerrek گەرڕەك/گەڕەك (IFb) = puddle. See **gefik**.

gers گەرس (TF/RF) = tamarisk. See **gez II**.

ges kirin گەس کِرِن (BK) = to bite. See **gestin**.

gesik گەسِك (OK) = broom. See **gêzî**.

gestin گەستِن *vt.* **(-gez-).** to bite: •**Marê milê wê *gestime*** (FT, 159) The snake [growing from] her arm bit me •**Sedîmov ew ki dîtin, şabûna lêva xwe *gest*** (Ĥ.Cindî. Hewarî, 241) When S. saw them, he *bit* his lip for joy •**Zafokî destê wî *gest*** (FS) The child *bit* his hand. {also: ges kirin (BK); geztin (A/JB3/IF-2); gez kirin (JB3/IF/BK); [gheztin گزتین/ghezandin گزاندین] (JJ); <geztin گەزتن (digeze) (دگەزە)> (HH)} {syn: gevizandin [3]; leq dan [see leq I]} [Pok. geiĝ- 356.] 'to stab, bite': Mid P gazīdan (gaz-) = 'to bite' (M3); P gazīdan گزیدن; Sor gestin گەستِن (-gez-)/geztin گەزتِن/gezîn گەزین; Za gaz kenã [gaz kerdiş] (Srk); Hau gestey (gez-) *vt.* (M4); cf. Oss änγezun = 'to ferment'; W Oss γizun = 'to freeze' [K/IF/Wkt/ZF3/Tsab/FS//A/JB3/B/JJ/HH//BK]

geş گەش *adj.* 1) {syn: biriqok; fewşen; fohnî I} bright, brilliant, shining, radiant *(lit. & fig.)*: •**çirayeke *geş*** = a *bright* lamp; 2) joyous, gay, merry: -**geş bûn** (ZF) to come [back] to life, perk up, become energetic: •**Govend *geş* bû** (AB) The folkdance was *joyous*. {also: [guech] گش (JJ); <geş> گش (HH)} Skt ghṛṣuh/ ghṣvi = 'quick, gay'; O Ir *garš- (A&L p. 87 [VIII, 1] + 92 [XIV, 3]): Sgd wγaš = 'to be happy'; Parth gaš = 'to be happy'; Sor geş گەش = 'fresh, blooming, flourishing, beaming' {geşî} [K/A/JB3/IF/B/JJ/HH/ZF]

geşbîn گەشبین *m.&f.* **().** 1) optimist; 2) *[adj.]* optimistic. Sor geşbîn گەشبین {geşbînî} [TF/OK/RZ/ZF3] <≠feşbîn>

geşbînî گەشبینی *f.* **(-ya;-yê).** optimism: •**Rewşa niha di navbera reşbînî û *geşbînîyê* da** (WAAR TV 18.x.2017) The present state of affairs between pessimism and *optimism*. [TF/OK/ZF3] <geşbîn>

geşî گەشی *f.* **(-ya;-yê).** brightness, brilliance, radiance: •**şînîtî û *geşiya* biharê** (Alkan, 71) the verdure and *brilliance* of springtime. [K/ZF] <geş; şewq>

geşt گەشت *f.* **(-a;-ê).** 1) {syn: deroze; p'ars} alms, charity, stg. given to a beggar or a Roma (Gypsy) in response to begging (Krç); door-to-door begging of beggars, Roma, and Turkmens (IF): •**Serê salê, binê salê/ Xwedê bihêlê/ Xortê malê/ Ka *geşta* vê malê** (Ah) The start of the year, the end of the year/ May God protect/ The young man of the house/ Where are *the alms of* this house? [A chant recited by children going from house to house on New Year's, similar to our "Trick or treat"]; -**çûn geştê** (IF) to go begging; 2) portion given to a guest (A); 3) journey, trip. {also: [ghecht] گشت (JJ); <geşt> گشت (HH)} [Krç/K/A/JB3/IFb/JJ/HH/ZF3]

geştin گەشتِن (-ge-) (SK/M) = to arrive; to ripen, mature. See **gihîştin**.

gevestî گەڤەستی (EP-7) = gossip. See **geveztî**.

gevez گەڤەز *adj.* deep shade of red, blood red. {also: gewez (FJ-2); [ghevez/guvez] گوز (JJ); <gevez> گڤز (HH)} [Qzl/K/IFb/B/JJ/HH/GF/FJ/ZF3] <sor>

geveze گەڤەزە *m.* **().** 1) trouble-maker (F/K); 2) someone who talks too much (IF/JJ). {also: [ghewezé گڤزه/ ghevezé گوزه] (JJ); <geveze> گڤزه (HH)} {gevestî; gevezetî; geveztî} < T geveze = 'talkative; indiscreet' [Z-1/F/K/IF/B/JJ/HH/ZF3] <altax; 'ewan II; nemam; qumsî>

gevezetî گەڤەزەتی (B/ZF3) = gossip. See **geveztî**.

geveztî گەڤەزتی *f.* **(;-[y]ê).** gossip; slander, backbiting, talebearing (K) {also: gevestî (EP-7); gevezetî (B/ZF3)} {syn: altaxî; 'ewanî; qumsîtî; şef II[2]} [EP-7//K//B/ZF3] <geveze; nemam>

gevil گەڤِل (FJ/GF) = desire; morale. See **gêwil**.

gevizandin گەڤِزاندِن *vt.* **(-gevizîn-).** 1) to tear to pieces (K); 2) to cause to paw the ground *(horse)* (A/IF); 3) to roll stg. *(in the dust)* (HH): -**xwe gevizandin** (RN/IF) to roll around, wallow *(e.g., in the mud or dust)* {syn: gevizîn}: •**Wextê tu *xwe digevizînî*, tu miqateyê li hêlîna min bikî, ji bona ko tu çêlîkên min ne kujî** (RN) When you *roll around* [in the dirt], be careful of my nest, so that you don't kill (=crush) my babies [*said by a mother bird to an elephant in a folktale*]; 4) {syn: gestin} to bite (B). {also: <gevizandin گڤزاندن (digevizîne) (دگڤزینه)>} [K/A/IF/B/HH/ZF3] <[2] gevizîn; gevizk>

gevizîn گەڤِزین *vi.* **(-geviz-).** to roll around, wallow (e.g., in the dust). {also: [gheoŭzin] گوزین (JJ); <gevizîn گڤزین (digevizî) (دگڤزی)>} {syn: xwe gevizandin} [A/IF/HH/ZF3//JJ] <gevizandin [2]; gevizk; p'irpitîn>

gevizk گەڤِزك *f.* **(-a;-ê).** romping ground, scratching ground, place where animals wallow in the dirt to scratch themselves: **•Rabû têtî hêlîna xwe li tenişta *gevizka* fîl çêkir** (RN) The lark built her nest next to the elephant's *scratching ground.* {also: gevzek (A/IF)} [RN//A/IF]

gevzek گەڤزەك (A/IF) = scratching ground. See **gevizk**.

gewd•e گەودە *m.* **(•ê;).** 1) {syn: beden II; can I[2]; laş} body (Z-2): **•Ezê ... serê te ji *gewdê* te biqetînim** (Z-2) I will remove your head from your *body*; 2) fully grown adult (K); big fellow, hefty chap (K). <T gövde = 'body' [Z-2/K/ZF3]

gewende گەوەندە *m&f.* **().** *unflattering term for* Roma, Gypsy; musician, entertainer: **•Nêçîra keftaran karê *gewendan* e. Heke bê *gewendan* jî hinekên din hebin, teqez ew jî ji *gewendan* ne e dûr in** (O.Sebrî. Ronahî 17 [1943], 14) Hunting hyenas is the work of *Gypsies*. If there are others besides *Gypsies*, they are certainly not far from *Gypsies*. {syn: begzade; boşe; dome; mirt'ib; qereçî} [Rnh/A/IFb/FJ/GF/Kmc/ZF]

gewez گەوەز (FJ) = blood red. See **gevez**.

gewî گەوی *adj.* 1) {syn: bitiṟ I} spoiled, self-indulgent (from being rich); 2) {syn: bitiṟ I; quṟe} proud, haughty, arrogant, cocksure: **•Li Qamişloyê, rejîma Baesê ya ku hêz ji hebûna Rûsyayê ya li ser erda xwe girtî, *gewî* bû û xwe li serekî dagirkeriya erdên kantona Cizîrê ceriband** (Yeni Özgür Politika 25.iv.2016) In Qamishli, the Baath regime having felt empowered by the presence of Russia on their land, became *cocksure* and tried to occupy the canton of Jezirah **•Me xwest bang li wijdanan bikin û li dijî kesên ku xwe wekî xweda û *gewî* dibînin helwesta xwe nîşan bidin û bêjin bese** (ANFNews:Girtiyên ji doza PAJK'ê 28.xi.2012) We want to appeal to people's conscience and show our attitude towards people who see themselves as masters and are *haughty*, and to say enough is enough. [Qzl/Qmş/ZF3/Wkt/G]

gewlaz گەولاز (Frq/K/B) = string of dried fruits. See **gelwaz**.

gewr گەور *adj.* 1) {syn: bor I; boz; cûn I; kew II; xwelîreng} grayish, whitish {(J-PS): *said of a beard, a donkey, a white ox*}; white (Kş/FJ/TF); gray (Mzg/TF): **-dinya gewrik** (JB1-S) 'the white world' (the earth's surface, as opposed to underground, 'the black world': cf. South Slavic *beli svet* = 'the whole world' [lit. 'the white world']); 2) [*f.* **().**] a beautiful woman, a beauty: **•Singa *gewr* beyaz e** (RN) The *beauty*'s breast is white [line from a folksong]. {also: gewrik (JB1-S); [gheoûr/ġhaver (G)/gaur (PS)] گور (JJ); <gewr> گور (HH)} [RN/F/K/A/IF/B/JJ/HH/SK/Mzg/Kş/FJ/TF//JB1-S] <belek; bor I; cûn I; spî I>

gewre گەورە *m.* **().** *type of wheat*: each grain is round and light colored, makes a nice, white bread [liba wî girover e, rengê wî vekirî ye, nanê wî xweş e, sipî]. {syn: *beyazî} < gewr = 'white, gray' [Qzl/A] <genim>

gewrî گەوری *f.* **(-ya;-yê).** 1) {syn: ḧefik; qeper; qiṟik I} throat; pharynx, larynx: **•[Zanî ku mar kûvîyek dabeland lê strûyên** [sterène] **wî neçûne xwarê û mane li *gewrîya* wî da û jê aciz bû]** (BG, p.25) He understood that the snake had swallowed a wild animal, but its horns had not gone down and had stayed in his *throat* and he was suffering from this; 2) {syn: kovik; mastêrk} funnel (HD/RZ). {also: gewrû (K); [gheoûrou گورو/ gheoûri گوری] (JJ); <gewrî> گوری (HH)} Skt gala- *m.*; Av garah- = 'throat'; Pahl garūk; Pashto γāṛa *f.* & γarai = 'neck, windpipe' (Hübsch #928); P galū گلو (Horn #928); Sor gerû گەروو = 'throat, gorge, defile, pass' & gelî گەلی/gełû گەڵوو = 'gully, gorge'; Hau giłûe *f.* = 'throat' & giłûé *m.* = 'gorge, gully' (M4) [Z-922/K//F/A/JB3/IF/B/JJ/HH/RZ/HD] <gerden>

gewrû گەورو (K) = throat. See **gewrî**.

gez I گەز *f.* **(;-ê).** ell, cubit, yard, unit of measure, appr. 70 cm. (28 inches) [Tu arşın & endaze; Ar ḏirā' ذراع]: **•*gezeka* qumaşî** (Bw) *an ell of* cloth **•...Lixawekî asin dû *gez* dirêj, *gezek* pan, bi qeder zenda destî stûr bide çêkirin** (SK 33:297) Go and get an iron bridle made, two *yards* long, a *yard* wide and as thick as a man's wrist **•Qelata wî li-ser çya bû li hindawê ṟûbarê, sê-hizar *gez* bilind e** (SK 51:556) His fort was on a mountain above the river, three thousand *ells* high. {also: gaz I (K/B/GF-2/TF); [ghez گز/gaz گاز] (JJ) = 'aune, archine, mesure'} [Bw/IFb/JJ/SK/GF/TF/OK//K/B/TF] <erîn>

gez II گەز *f.* **(;-ê).** tamarisk, bot. *Tamarix*. {also: gers (TF/RF-2); <gez> گز (HH)} {syn: kifir II} Cf. Mid P gaz (M3); P gaz گز; Sor [dar]gez دارگەز [A/IFb/B/HH/GF/OK/RF/ZF3//TF]

gezek گەزەك (ZF) = nettle. See **gezgezok**.

gezende (IFb) گەزەندە = nettle. See **gezgezok**.

gezgezek گەزگەزەك (ZF) = nettle. See **gezgezok**.

gezgezik گـــەزگـــەزك (IFb/CS/ZF) = nettle. See **gezgezok**.

gezgezing گەزگەزنگ (Kmc) = nettle. See **gezgezok**.

gezgezok گـــەزگـــەزۆك *f.* **(-a;-ê).** stinging nettle, bot. *Urtica urens*. {also: gezek (ZF-2); gezende (IFb-2); gezgezek (ZF-2); gezgezik (IFb-2/CS/ZF-2); gezgezing (Kmc); gezgezk (K/A/B/RZ); gezing (GF-2); gezok (IFb-2/CS-2); [ghezghez گـزگـز/ghezghezk گـزگـزك] (JJ); perhaps also <geznik> گـزنـك (HH)} {syn: k'ergezk} < gez- = 'to bite': Cf. P gazneh گـزنـه; Sor gezne گـەزنـە/ giyagezne گـیـاگـەزنـە [QtrE/IFb/GF/TF/RZ/AD/ZF//K/A/B/JJ//CS//Kmc]

gezgezk گەزگەزك (K/A/B/RZ) = nettle. See **gezgezok**.

gezik گەزك (A/OK/Frq) = broom. See **gêzî**.

gezing گەزنگ (GF) = nettle. See **gezgezok**.

gezî گەزى (A) = broom. See **gêzî**.

gez kirin گەز كِرن (JB3/IF/BK) = to bite. See **gestin**.

gezo گـــــــەزۆ *m./f.(FS/Wkt)* **(/-a;/-yê).** sweet dew, "manna" {T kudret helvası}: "Another extraordinary appearance...is the manna which here, in the form of grain, descends with the dew. It has now been ascertained by travelers in the east,...that the manna is a distillation from trees which falls on the ground every morning. It is collected in vases at the break of day, and placed in the sun, in the warmth of which it melts and becomes a cheesy kind of substance, in which state it is eaten with bread at breakfast. I found it sweet like honey and of an agreeable smell...At Kirkuk all the fields and meadows are covered with it." (from Benjamin II. p. 136, quoted in YSFL, p.xxx); 'Ghezo', "Manna [called in Turkish kudret helvası, or the divine sweetmeat; in Arabic musee; in Persian ghezungabeen] is found on the dwarf oak, though several other plants are said to produce it, but not so abundantly, or of such good quality. It is collected by gathering the leaves of the tree, letting them dry, and then gently threshing them on a cloth. It is thus brought to market in lumps, mixed with an immense quantity of fragments of leaves, from which it is afterward cleared by boiling. There is another kind of manna found on rocks and stones, which is quite pure, of a white colour, and it is much more esteemed than the tree manna. The manna season begins in the latter end of June, at which period, when a night is more than usually cool, the Koords say it rains manna, and maintain that the greatest quantity is always found in the morning after such a night." [from: C.J. Rich. *Narrative of a Residence in Koordistan* ... (London: James Duncan, 1836), v. 1, pp. 142-43]. {also: gezû (GF/OK); [ghezou] گزو (JJ); <gezzo> گزّو (HH)} Cf. P gaz گـــــــز = 'a type of candy'; NENA ‘ar‘ūra (Zakho) = gezo. For a scientific explanation of **gezo** as a secretion of aphids, see: Marston Bates. *Gluttons and Libertines: Human Problems of Being Natural* (New York : Vintage Books, c1958, 1967), pp. 55 ff., & F. S. Bodenheimer. *Insects as Human Food* (The Hague : W. Junk, 1951) [K/A/IFb/JJ/TF//HH/ZF3/FS//GF/OK] <mazî>

gezok گەزۆك (IFb/CS) = nettle. See **gezgezok**.

geztin گەزتِن (A/JB3/IF-2) = to bite. See **gestin**.

gezû گەزوو (GF/OK) = manna. See **gezo**.

gêç گێچ (IF[s]/Wkt) = alabaster; plaster. See **gec**.

gêj گـــێـــژ *adj.* 1) stunned, dumbstruck; bewildered, confused, perplexed: **-gêj kirin** (JB1-A/Wlt): a) to stun, tranquilize: **•Nêçîrvan û nijdevanên jêhatî, zivistanan didin pey şopa guran, di berfê de diwestînin û di pozên wan de lê didin, *gêj dikin*, bi guhên wan digirin qîlên wan hildikin û wan ji cenewariya wan dixînin, bê zerar dikin** (Wlt 2:71, p.13) Skilled hunters and horsemen track down the wolves in the winters, tire them out in the snow and strike them on their snouts, *stun them*, grab them by their ears, pull out their fangs and remove their fierceness from them, make them harmless; b) to make dizzy; 2) dizzy, giddy *(lit. & fig.)*: **•Serê min dêşe, ez ji ber gêj bûm** (AB) I have a headache, and that's why I'm dizzy. {also: <gêj> گـــيـــژ (HH)} Cf. Geo giži გიჟი = 'crazy'; Sor gêj گـــێـــژ = 'giddy, silly, turning movement' {gêjayî; gêjî; gêjtî} [AB/K/A/JB3/IFb/B/HH/JB1-A/GF/TF/OK] <dîn II; neh̄iş; şêt>

gêjahî گێژاهى (ZF3) = dizziness. See **gêjtî**.

gêjatî گێژاتى (FS) = dizziness. See **gêjtî**.

gêjayî گێژایى (A/ZF3) = dizziness. See **gêjtî**.

gêjî گێژى (K/JB3/TF/OK/FS) = dizziness. See **gêjtî**.

gêjlok گێژلۆك (IFb) = hail[stones]. See **gijlok**.

gêjtî گـــێـــژتـــى *f.* **(-ya;-yê).** being stunned; dizziness, vertigo; giddiness; intoxication, drunkenness: **•Ji ber piçek *gêjayîya* şerabê Cafer ferq nekir ku ew keçika ciwan ... ew pîreka wî Ebbasa bû**

(Hezar efsaneyên M û P 8.ii.2009) Due to a little *giddiness* from the wine, J. did not notice that that pretty girl ... was his wife A. **•Wî *gêjatî* heye** (FS) He has *vertigo*. {also: gêjahî (ZF3-2); gêjatî (FS); gêjayî (A/ZF3); gêjî (K-2/JB3/TF/OK/FS-2)} [K/B//FS//A/ ZF3//JB3/TF/OK] <dînayî; gêj; neĥişî; şêtî>

gêlas گێلاس (OK/AA) = cherry. See **gêlaz**.

gêlaz گـــێــلاز *f.* **(-a;-ê).** 1) {syn: qeresî} cherry, bot. *Prunus* [ghilas] (JJ); sour cherry (K/F/JJ) [ghelás] (JJ): **•Ne dixum *gêlaza*, ne didim hevraza** (Dz #1208, 226) I won't eat your *cherries* or climb to the heights (=I won't leave your side) [*prv.*]; 2) cherry tree. {also: gêlas (OK/AA); gêraz (IFb); gilyas (IFb-2/GF/OK-2/FS); gilyaz (GF-2); gîlaz (F); [ghilas/ghelás] گيلاس (JJ)} Cf. P gīlās گيلاس; Ar karaz كرز; T kiraz; Sor gêlas گێلاس; Za gilyaz *f.* (Todd); Hau gêlas *m.* (M4). cf. also Lat cerasus = 'cherry tree' <Gr kerasos κερασος [K/B/RZ/Kmc-2// IFb//GF/FS//F//JJ/OK/AA] <alûçe; belalûk; hêrûg [1]>

gêl•e گـــێـــلـــه *f.* **(•a;).** ant. {also: gêre II (Srk); gêrik (IFb-2/FS/Wkt-2); gêring (FS-2)} {syn: mûrî I; kurmorî[2]; mûristan[2]} [Mzg/IFb/ZF3/Wkt//Srk//FS]

gêlm•e گێلمه *f.* **(•a;).** mixture, combination of foods: **-gêlma gavanî** (Zeb/BF/Wkt/AId) potpourri, hodgepodge, olio, odd mixture (originally, foods given to a cowherd, who puts them all in the same bowl) {syn: girara gavana}: •...**destûrekê ji corê "*gêlma gavanî* wek yê Îraqê" danin** (WAAR Media: Fazil 'Umer) That they should set up a constitution of the type of *hodgepodge* à la Iraq **•Eve ezmanê *gêlma gavanî* ye** (Diyarname: Ebd.Bamerrnî) This language is *a hodgepodge* **•Vê çendê kartêkirina xwe di zarokê me de kiriye ku ew di nav vê *gêlma gavanî* de berze bibe** (Kulturname: Newzad Hirorî) This has had an affect on our child such that he gets lost amid this *odd mixture*. = Sor çêştî micêwir چێشتی مِجێوِر [Zeb/BF/Wkt/AId]

gêm گێم (Wlt/OK) = bridle; bit. See **gem**.

gêr گـێـر: **-gêr bûn** (A/IFb/JJ/TF) to roll *(vi.)*, tumble, overturn *(vi.)* {also: [ghir bouin] گــر بــويــن (JJ)} {syn: gindirîn; girêl bûn; gulol bûn}: **•Xilolîkên hêsirên çavên mêrik di ser riwê wî yê nekurkirî de *gêr dibûn* ser çena wî û paşê dinuqutîn erdê** (KS, p.10) The tiny hailstones of the man's tears *rolled down* his unshaven face onto his chin and then dripped onto the ground; **-gêr kirin** (A/IFb/ JJ/HH/TF/OK) to roll *(downhill) (vt.)* {also: [ghir kirin] گر كرين (JJ); <gêr kirin گير كرن (gêr dike) (گـير دكـه)> (HH)} {syn: gildî kirin; gindirandin; gulol kirin}: **•"Cil ji xwe diqetin," Alfons dibêje. Bi taybetî ... dema mirov *xwe* di mêrgê de *gêr dike*** (BM, 15) "Clothes get torn on their own," Alfons says. Especially ... when one *rolls about* in the meadow. Cf. Sor gêr̄ گێڕ = 'curved, crooked, leaning, lame' [BM/A/IFb/HH/ GF/TF/OK//JJ] <gevizîn; gildî; gulol>

gêr̄an گـــێـــڕان *vt.* **(-gêr̄[în]-).** *Southern variant of* ***ger̄andin:*** 1) to cause s.o. to go around, give s.o. a tour (of a place): **•Çavan *digêrînit* = temaşa dike** (BF) He *moves* his eyes *around* = He watches **•Wî Azad li nav bajêrî *gêr̄a*** (FS) He *gave* A. *a tour* of the town; 2) to distribute, pass out or around: **•Çayê *digêrînit*, ang[o] didet xelkî, mêvanan** (BF) He *passes out* tea, i.e., gives it to the people, to guests; 3) to roll (a mud roof) flat: **•Wî serban bi loxî *gêr̄a*** (FS) He *rolled* the roof *flat* with a roller; 4) to run (a machine), operate: **•Wî aş *gêr̄a*** (FS) He *ran* the mill; 5) to tell, narrate, relate: **•Wî serhatiyek bo me *gêr̄a*** (FS) He *told* us an anecdote; 6) to hold, organize (a celebration, etc.): **•Wan şahiyanek *gêr̄a*** (FS) They *held* a celebration. {also: **ger̄andin**} Causative of **ger̄în** [M/FS/Wkt/BF] <ger̄în>

gêr̄anewe گـــێـــڕانـــەوە (SK) = to tell *(a story)*. See **vegêr̄an**.

gêraz گێراز (IFb) = cherry. See **gêlaz**.

gêr•e I گـــێـــره *f.* **(•a;•ê).** threshing of grain by leading oxen around in a circle to tread over it, to separate seeds (of wheat, barley, etc.) from the stalks: **•*Gêre* bi golka nabit** (Drş #270, 85) *Threshing* with calves won't do *[prv]*; **-gêre kirin** (IFb/FJ/ TF/ZF) to thresh corn, wheat, etc.: **Wî qesela genimê xwe *gêre kir*** (FS) He *threshed* the stalks of his wheat. {also: gêrî (FJ-2); [ghihré] گهره (JJ); <gêre> گـــيـــره (HH)} {syn: hol III} Cf. Sor gêre گـێـره = 'threshing with oxen' [CCG/K(s)/A/IFb/FJ/GF/TF/ HH/Kmc/ZF/SS/BF/FS//JJ] <bêder; coxîn>

gêre II گێره (Srk) = ant. See **gêle**.

gêrih گـێـرِه *f.* **(-a;).** unripe or green almond [T çağla]. {also: gerîh (IFb); geroh (ZF3)} {syn: behîvter̄; çil'în (Haz); nîv'în (Mtk)} [Frq//IFb//ZF3] <behîv>

gêrik گێرك (IFb/FSWkt) = ant. See **gêle**.

gêring گێرنگ (FS) = ant. See **gêle**.

gêrî گێری (FJ) = threshing with oxen. See **gêre I**.

gêsik گێسك (Bar/RZ) = broom. See **gêzî**.

gêsin گێسِن (A/JB1-A/HH) = ploughshare. See **gîsin**.

gêvil گێڤل (FJ/GF) = desire; morale. See **gêwil**.

gêwel گێوەل (ZF3) = desire; morale. See **gêwil**.

gêwil گـێـوِل *m.* **(-ê;).** 1) appetite, desire, feeling like doing stg.: **•*Te gêwil heye* em piçek derkevin?** (BF) *Do you feel like* going up a little [lit. 'that we go out']?; 2) morale: **•Çima *gêwelê* te ne xweş e?** (ZF3) Why are you in a bad mood?/Why is your *morale* not good? {also: gevil (FJ-2/GF-2); gêvil (FJ/GF); gêwel (ZF3)} [Kmc/BF/FD//FJ/GF//ZF3] <*gewz>

gêzbelî گێزبەلی (Zeb) = goatsbeard. See **gêzbelok**.

gêzbelok گێزبەلۆك *f.* **().** goatsbeard, bot. *Tragopogon pratensis; it grows in cold and mountainous habitats.* {also: gêzbelî (Zeb); <gêzbelok> گـێـزبـەلـۆك (Hej)} [Zeb//IFb/GF/OK/Hej/AA/ZF3/FS] <siping>

gêzer گێزەر (A/IF/HH/GF/FS) = carrot. See **gizêr**.

gêzik گێزك (IFb) = broom. See **gêzî**.

gêzî گێزی *f.* **(-ya;-yê).** 1) {syn: avlêk; bermalk; cerîvk (Bw); k'inoşe; melk'es; sirge (Ad); siqavêl; sivnik; sizik; şicing (Krs); şirt I} broom : **•Ew ot'axê pê *gêzîyê* paqiş dike** (B) He sweeps [lit. 'cleans'] the room with *a broom*; **-gêzî kirin** = to sweep {syn: maliştin; r̄êç kirin [r̄êç I]}: **•Bûk sibe rabû, nava malê *gêzîkir*** (J) The bride got up in the morning, and *swept* the (interior of the) house; 2) broom plant (K). {also: gesik (OK); gezî (A); gezik (A-2/IFb-2/OK-2/Frq); gêsik (Bar/RZ-2); gêzik (IFb-2); gêzîk (GF/OK-2); [ghizi گـيـزی/ ghizik گيزك] (JJ)} Sor gesik گەسِك/gis[i]k گِسِك; Za gezi; Hau gizî [F/K/IFb/JJ/B/TF/RZ//OK//A//Frq//Bar] <maliştin>

gêzîk گێزیك (GF/OK) = broom. See **gêzî**.

gi گِ (Ad) = all. See **gişk**.

gidark گِدارك *f.* **().** mushroom. {also: kidark (Twn); <kidarik> كـدارك (HH)} {syn: karî I; karkevîk (Mş-Malazgirt); kiyark; kufkarik; k'umik (A)} [Prw//Twn//HH]

gidîş گِـدیـش *f.* **(-a;-ê).** shock, stook, haycock, neat stack of wheat (barley, etc.) *sometimes 6-8 meters long, arranged in such a way as to prevent animals from eating the contents, and to protect against rain, sometimes kept for a month or more in the field before being transported to the threshing floor* [di nav zevîyê de piştî dirûnê, ew zadê ku didin hev (didrûn)]. {also: girîş (GF-2/ TF); **gîşe** (Zeb); [ghidich] گـديـش (JJ); <gidîş> گديش (Hej)} < Arc gadīš גדיש/gdīšā גדישא = 'heap, pile mound, esp. of sheaves, shock or stack of grain' (M. Jastrow); NENA gadîshâ ܓܕܝܫܐ = 'stack, heap, stook, shock, haycock' (Maclean); Turoyo gdīšo = 'stack of crops, about 30 quflo [see **qefil**]' (HR2); cf. also Ar kuds كـدس = 'heap, pile, stack (of grain, hay, etc.)'; Sor gîşe گـیـشـە = 'haycock, stook, conical mound of hay in a field, stack, rick' [Qzl/A/IFb/JJ/GF/Hej/AA//TF/FS//Zeb] <destî; qefil> See also **gîşe**.

giha گِها (GF) = grass. See **gîya**.

gihan I گِهان *vi.* **(-gihê-/-gih- [JB3]/-geh-).** 1) to arrive, reach, attain: **•*Digihên* ber avekê** (L) *They reach* a stream **•Şêrek û gurek û r̄ovîk *gihane hev* û bi hevr̄a çûn** (Dz) A lion, a wolf, and a fox *met up* [lit. '*reached each other*'] and traveled together **•B. *giha* bajarê Mîrê Sêrê** (L) B. *reached* the city of the Prince of Magic; 2) to ripen, reach maturity, grow up: **•Fîkî li ser darê *gîhane*** (AB) The fruits *have ripened* on the tree. {also: gehan; gihaştin; **gihîştin**; gîhan (AB); [ghehan] گـهـان (JJ)} *See etymology under **gihîştin**.* Sor geyîn گەیین/geyiştin گـەیـشـتـن (-ge-: 3rd p.s. -ga-) [K/A/JB3/IFb/JJ/ZF3] See also **gihîştin**.

gihan II گِهان (J) = udder. See **guhan**.

gihandin گِـهـانـدن *vt.* **(-gihîn-/-gîn-/-gîhîn-/-gehîn- [JB3]).** 1) to bring, take, cause to arrive [faire arriver]; to convey *(news, etc.)*: **•Gelo nave, wekî em evê qîza nazik *bigihînine* ewî xortê tu bêjî?** (Z-1) Shouldn't we *bring* this fine girl to that young man [who] you spoke of? [lit. 'you say'] **•Lazime go hûn van zilama *bigihêjînin* welatê wan** (L) You must *accompany/take* these men to their country **•Wana cab *gîhandine* dîwana Al-p'aşa** (Z-1) They *brought* the news to the court of A.p. **•Xwedê ga *negîhand*** (J) God *didn't bring* us an ox [lit. 'God did not cause an ox to come']; **-xwe gihandin** = to arrive, reach, betake o.s., come: **•K'îjan ji wana zû *xwe digihîne* germa deşta** (Ba2:1, 202) Which one of them will *reach* the warmth of the plains first [lit. 'early'];

2) to bring *(misfortune)*, visit, send, cause to befall, wreak: **•Fikra min heye ku ez *xirabiyekê bigehînimê*** (ZZ-10, 157) I have the idea to *do something bad to him* **•...Kur̄ê wî jî bêma'rîfet bûn, şeherê bavê xwe *gihyandine* [sic] xelayê** (Ba3) ...His sons were rude, they *brought* a famine *on* their father's city; 3) to cause *(damage)* (Zeb). {also: gihêjandin (L/K-2); gihyandin (Ba3);

gîhandin (K/BK); [ghehandin] گـهـانـديـن (JJ)} [K/A/JB3/IFb/JJ/GF/TF/OK/BK] <gihan I; gihîştin>

gihanek گـهـانـهك *f.* **(-a;).** conjunction *(grammatical category)*: •***Gihanek*** **bi serê xwe ne xwediyê tu wateyê ne, lê du hevokan, an du gotin an jî du bêjeyan bi hev ve girê didin** (M.Aykoç. Rêziman'a destî, 51) *Conjunctions* have no meaning of their own, but they connect two sentences, or two utterances or two words. {syn: p'evgirêdan} [M.Aykoç/S.Tan/K/IFb/Kmc/ZF3/Wkt/CS]

gihar گهار (GF) = earring. See **guhar**.

gihaştin گهاشتِن (-gihêj-/-gihê-/-gihîj-) (Z-1/BX/JB3) = to arrive; to ripen, mature. See **gihîştin**.

giheştin گـهـهشـتِـن (-gihe-) (M) = to arrive; to ripen, mature. See **gihîştin**.

gihêjandin گهێژاندِن (L/K) = to cause to arrive; to lead, take, accompany s.o. See **gihandin**.

gihêştin گـهێشـتِـن (A) = to arrive; to ripen, mature. See **gihîştin**.

gihîştin گهیشتِن *vi.* **(-gihîj-/-gîhij-).** 1) to arrive, reach, catch up with, attain: •**Ew** ***digîhijine*** **k'ewşanê gund** (Dz) They *reach* the village's plowed fields; **-gihîştin hev** (XF)/**geheştine êk** (Zeb): a) to come together, unite, meet (vi.): •**Dibêjin rojekê du perî** ***gehiştine êk*** (XF) They say that one day two fairies *met*; b) to [be] combine[d] (vi.): •**"Sîn" û "Şîn"** ***geheştine êk*** (Zeb) [The Arabic letters] sīn (س) and shīn (ش) *got combined* (i.e., got confused or mixed up); 2) to join (an organization): **-Ji bo ç[i] tu** ***gihîştî*** **PKK'ê?** ***-Gihîştina min a*** **PKK'ê ne tenê ji bo azadî û xelasiya gelê Kurd, lê ji ber ku min xelasiya mirovahiyê jî tê de dît, ez** ***gihîştimê*** (Wlt 1:35, 16) -Why did you *join* the PKK? -*My joining* the PKK was not only for freeing and rescuing the Kurdish people, but because I also saw the saving of humanity in it, I *joined it*; 3) to grow; to ripen (fruit and the like) (IF/JJ); to mature, reach puberty: •**Z. îdî** ***gihîştî bû*** (Z-1) Z. *had* [by] now *matured* (grown up); 4) to live (long enough) to see stg.: •**Memê mirîye danê sibê,** ***ez negihîjime*** **danê êvara** (Z-1) M. died in the morning, *may I not live to see* the evening; 5) to have enough time *(to do stg.)*: •**Paşa tê-geşt, siwik ȓa-bo,** ***negeşt*** **sola xo di pê ket, bi goran der-kewt** (SK 24:224) The Pasha understood, got up quietly and, *not managing to* [=not having time to] put on his shoes, escaped in his stockings. {also: geheştin (-gehej- [JB1-A]/-gehêj- [JB1-S]/-gihe- [SK]) (JB1-A&S/SK); gehiştin (-gehij-[IF]/-geh- [M-Zx]) (IF-2/M-Zx); gehîn (M-2); geştin (-ge-) (SK-2/M-2); **gihan I**; gihaştin (-gihêj-/-gihê-/-gihîj-) (Z-1/BX/JB3); giheştin (-gihe-) (M); gihêştin (A); gîhiştin; [ghehichtin] گـهـشـتـيـن (JJ); <gihîştin گـهیشـتـن (dighîje) (دگـهـیـژه)> (HH)} <O Ir *vi- (Tsb 72) + *hak- (Tsb 47): Sor geyîn گـهيين/geyiştin گـهيشـتـن (-ge-: 3rd p.s. -ga-); ***hak-**: [Pok. 1. seku̯- 896.] 'to follow': Skt sácate = 'accompanies, follows'; Av hak- (*pres.* hak-/hača-/hačaya-) = do.; cf. also Lat sequor, sequi = 'to follow' [Z-1/BX/JB3//JB1-A&S/ SK/M-Zx//A//M//F/Dz/K/IF/B/HH//JJ] See also **gihan I**.

gihîya گهييا (K) = grass; hay. See **gîya**.

gihûr گهوور (Wkt) = garbage; dung. See **guhûr**.

gihya گهيا (B) = hay. See **gîya** [2].

gihyandin گـهـيـانـدِن (Ba3) = to cause to arrive. See **gihandin**.

gij گِژ (K/A/IFb/HH/GF/TF) = erect; tense. See **girj**.

gijik گـِـــــــــــــژك *f.* **(-a;-ê).** tousled, unkempt hair *(of women)*: •***Gijika*** **xwe dikêşîne û di ber giriyê xwe re jî dibêje ...** (Ardû, 116) She pulls her *tousled hair* and says through her tears .... Cf. gijgijî (GF/AD) = 'unkempt (hair)' & [ghijikin] گژكين (JJ) = 'to stand on end (hair)' [Ardû/IFb/TF/Frq] <p'oȓ III>

gijlok گِژلۆك *f.* **(-a;-ê).** hail[stones] *(type of precipitation)*: •**Zîpika ku libên wê hûr in, jê re dibêjin** ***gijlok*** **an jî xilorîk** (Wkp) Hailstones that are tiny are called *gijlok* or xilorîk. {also: gêjlok (IFb-2); gişk II (Bw)} {syn: teyrok; xilolîk I; zîpik I} Note the form **tergijok** (Zeb) [Zx/IFb/FS/BF//Bw]

gijnik گژنك (RZ) = tick (insect). See **qijnik**.

gijnî گژنى (RZ) = tick (insect). See **qijnik**.

gijnîj گـِـژنـيـژ *f.* **(-a;-ê).** coriander, bot. *Coriandrum sativum*. {also: gijnîje (OK); gijnîş (CB); kişnîş (TF); [ksnís (G)/kišniš (Lx)] كـشـنـش (JJ)} Mid P gišnīz/kišnīz (M3); P gašnīz گـشـنـيـز --> T kişniş; Sor gijnîje گژنيژە [Am/Zeb/Kmc-3/IFb/(GF)/FS//OK/ZF3///CB//JJ/TF]

gijnîje گژنيژە (OK) = coriander. See **gijnîj**.

gijnîş گژنيش (CB) = coriander. See **gijnîj**.

gilar•e گـِــــــــــــلارە *m.* **(•ê;).** 1) {syn: gonc; qurm} tree stump: •**Wî** ***gilarekê dara*** **bi destê xwe girtibû** (FS) He had grabbed *a tree stump* with his hand; 2) short, thick piece of wood (HH/GF). {also: <gilare> گلارە (HH)} [IFb/HH/GF/FS/ZF3]

gilas گـِــــــــــــلاس *m./f.(ZF3)* **(-ê/;-î/).** drinking glass, tumbler. {also: <giłas> گــــــــلاس (Hej)} {syn: avxork; p'erdax; p'eyale[2]} <Eng glass --> P gelās گلاس [Bw/GF/ZF3//Hej]

gilç گِــلــچ (Şnx/FS) = sharp stick for uprooting plants. See **xilç**.

gildî گِــــــــلــــــدی *adj.* 1) {syn: gebar (Wn)} mixed up, confused (Wn); 2) {syn: gilol I; giroveř} round, circular (IF). [Wn/IF/ZF3]

gilêj گلێژ (IFb) = saliva. See **girêz**.

gilêş گِـلـێـش *m.* **(-ê;).** trash, garbage, rubbish, refuse: **•Wî *gilêşê* malê avêt** (FS) He threw out *the garbage of* the house. [Bw/RZ/FS/ZF]

gilêz گلێز (GF) = saliva. See **girêz**.

gilgil گِـلـگِـل *m.* **(-ê;).** millet, bot. *Panicum miliaceum* [T akdarı]; *because is grows well under dry conditions, in periods of drought it is used for making bread, particularly in Tunceli [Dersim], Elazığ, Bingöl, Muş, and Bitlis* (IFb/JJ) {syn: garis; herzin}: **-gilgilê Stembolê** (Haz) corn, maize {syn: garis[ê stanbolî]; genimeşamî; genmok; lazût; zuret I}. {also: [ghylghyl] گـلـگـل (JJ)} [Krç/Haz/A/IFb/JJ/GF/TF/ZF3/FS] <ṯale>

gilgile گلگله (FS) = autumn leaves. See **gelgele**.

gilih گِله (TF) = complaint. See **gilî I**[2].

gilik گِلِك *f.* **(-a;-ê).** clitoris. {also: <gilik> گلك (HH)} {syn: tîtilk; zîlik} Cf. Sor gulink گـولـنك = 'vagina'; = Sor mîtke مـيـتـكـه/qîtke قيتكه [Qzl/A/IFb/HH/GF/TF/ZF3/FS] <quz>

gilî I گِـلـی *m.* **(-yê;).** 1) {syn: xeber} talking, speech, word[s] (K/B): **•Wexta dîya min *gilîyêd xwe* k'uta kirin, min ew ȟemêz kir** (Ba2:2, 207) When my mother finished *her words*, I embraced her; **-gilî kirin** (Ba2) to tell, relate, recount (a story) {syn: kat kirin; neqil kirin; řiwayet kirin; vegotin; vegêřan}: ***•Gilî dikirin*** [sic]**, wekî navê Mistê Kalo dane ser gund bona wê yekê, ku...** (Ba2) *They used to recount* that they gave the name M.K. to the village because...; **-Gilîyê teye** = You are right {syn: Xebera teye}: **•Bek'o, welle, *gilîyê teye*** (Z-1) Beko, by God, *you are right*; **-gilî û gotin** (Z-1) talking; **-gilîyê xwe kirin yek** (K/EP-7) to come to an agreement or understanding; 2) {syn: gazin; şikyat} complaint: **-li *fk-ê* gilî kirin** (PS) to lodge a complaint against, to complain about s.o. {also: gilih (TF); gilîh (A); [ghili] گـلـی (JJ); <gilî> گـلـی (HH)} Skt √garh-, garhatē = 'to chide'; Av gerezā- = 'complaint' & √garz-, gerezaiti = 'to complain, lament'; Pahl garz(i)šn = 'complaint' & garzītan = 'to complain' (Horn, #930); Oss d. γärzun/t. gärẓin = 'to groan'; P gele گـلـه = 'complaint'; Sor glêyî گـلـێـيـی = 'complaint' [Ba/K/JB3/IFb/B/JJ/HH/GF//A//TF] <p'eyiv>

gilî II گِلی (SK/JJ-Lx) = branch. See **gulî II**.

gilîh گِلیه (A) = talk; complaint. See **gilî I**.

gilîzank گِلیزانك *f.* **(-a;-ê).** tickle, tickling: **•Ew hest bi *gilîzankê* dikit, gava ku êkî destda binê piyê wî** (FS) He feels *a tickle* whenever someone touches the bottom of his foot; **-gilîzank vebûn** (FS) to feel ticklish: **•Gava ku êkî destê xwe kir ṯenişta wî, *gilîzanka* wî *vedibit*** (FS) Whenever someone touches his side, *it tickles him*; **-gilîzankêt *fk-ê* vekirin** (Bw) to tickle s.o.: **•Ez gilîzankêt wê vedikem** (Bw) I tickle her. cf. qilî kirin (IFb/RZ) {also: girîzank (FS-2)} [Bw/FS]

gilok گِـلـۆك (A/IFb/GF/Mzg/Krş) = ball of thread. See **gulok**.

gilol I گِلۆل *adj.* round, circular: **-gulol bûn** (B) to roll *(vi.)* {syn: gêr bûn; gindirîn; girêl bûn}; **-gulol kirin** (B) to roll *(vt.)*. {also: gilor (IF-2); gulol (K/B)} {syn: gildî (IF); giroveř} cf. Skt glau- *m.* = 'round lump, wen-like excrescence'; P golūle گـلـولـه = 'ball, sphere'. [K/IF/B/JJ/HH/ZF3/Wkt] <gêr; gildî; gindirîn>

gilol II گِلۆل *f.* **().** pea, a legume, bot. *Pisum sativum*; small, black beans eaten by cattle (Wn). {also: gilûl (Wn); [ghiloul] گـلـول (JJ); <gilol> گـلـول (HH)} {syn: kelî I; polik II} [Wn/JJ//IFb/HH] <lowûk>

gilolîk گِلۆلیك (Qmş/Btm) = dish of ground meat and bulgur wheat. See **kilorîk**.

gilor گِلۆر (IF) = round. See **gilol I**.

giloverî گِلۆڤەری (ZF3) = roundness. See **guloveřî**.

gilpgilp گِـلـپـگِـلـپ (CS) = throbbing, beating. See **gurpegurp**.

gilûl گِلوول (Wn) = pea. See **gilol II**.

gilûz گِلووز (Bşk) = saliva. See **girêz**.

gilwaz گِلواز (Elk) = string of dried fruits. See **gelwaz**.

gilyas گِلیاس (IFb/GF/OK/FS) = cherry. See **gêlaz**.

gilyaz گِلیاز (GF) = cherry. See **gêlaz**.

gimgimok گِمگِمۆك (FJ) = lizard. See **qumqumok**.

gimîn گِـمـیـن *f.* **(-a;).** crashing, rumbling, thundering sound (K); skirl, shrill cry *(of musical instruments such as zurna or bagpipe)* (EP-4); buzzing sound made by beehives in the hive (IF): ***•gimîna* ȟeft def-zurnane** (EP-4) *the cry of* seven drums and zurnas. [EP-4/K/IF] <girmîn>

gimt گِمت (ZF3) = peak, summit. See **kumt**.

gince گنجه (FS) = dried dung. See **gincî**.

gincî گـنـجـی *f.(B/Qzl/Qtr-E/Elk)/m.(Bw/ZF3)* **(-ya/ ;-yê/).** dried dung that gets caught on sheep's wool: **•*gincîya* hirîya miha Mam Reşîd** (Elk) *the dried dung on* the wool of Mam Reshid's sheep. {also: gince (FS); <gincî> گـنـجـی (HH)} {syn: kemêl} [Qzl/QtrE/Elk/Bw/K/IFb/B/HH/GF/FJ/ZF3//FS]

gindir گـنـدِر *f.* **(-a;).** tarantula spider: **•*Gindire* ji mar û dûbişka xirabtire** (Msr) *The gindir* is worse than snakes and scorpions [*prv.*]. [Msr/QtrE/ZF3]

gindiřandin گندِراندِن *vt.* **(-gindirîn-).** to roll stg. *(vt.)*. {also: gundiřandin (FS-2)} {syn: gêr kirin; gildî kirin; gulol kirin} [A/JB3/IF/ZF3/FS] <gindiřîn>

gindiřîn گـنـدِریـن *vi.* **(-gindir-).** to roll *(vi.)*, tumble, overturn *(vi.)*. {also: gundiřîn (FS-2)} {syn: gêr bûn; girêl bûn; gulol bûn} Arc gandar גנדר = 'to roll (vt.) ' & igandar איגנדר = 'to roll (vi.) ' & Syr itgandar ܐܬܓܢܕܪ = 'to roll (vi.)' [L/A/JB3/IF/ZF3/FS] <gindiřandin>

gindol گِندۆل, f. (Wn) = watermelon. See **gindor I[2]**.

gindor I گِـنـدۆر *f.* **(-a;).** 1) {syn: kulind; kundir} pumpkin, gourd (K); squash, zucchini (IFb) [gundor/gindore]; 2) {syn: petêx; qawin} melon (A/JJ/Bw/IFb/AA) [IFb:gindor; AA:gundor]; watermelon (Wn): **•Werzekê *gundura* yê hey, *gundurêt* xo hemî bi bera ve dan, ev êt hindeyêt mezin perçiqandin, ev êt biçûk'oke yê didanîte ser** (JB1-A #189) He has a *melon* patch, he has thrown all his *melons* against the rocks, those that were this big he smashed, and those that were small he put on top. {also: gindol, f. (Wn); gindore (IFb-2); gundor I, m. (K-2/IFb-2/GF/OK/AA/Kmc-2); gundur (JB1-A); **kulind**; **kundir**; qundir (L); [goundour] گـنـدور (JJ)} [K/A/IFb/Bw//Wn//GF/OK/AA/Kmc-2//JJ/JB1-A] See also **kulind** & **kundir**.

gindor II گِندۆر (A/IFb/JJ/CS) = stone roof-roller. See **gundor II.**

gindor III گِـنـدۆر *f.* **(-a;).** bear's lair or den: **•Hirç zivistanê dikeve *gindora* xwe, radikeve û heta biharê dernakeve** (Ansîklopediya Zarokan, 70) In winter, the bear enters his *lair*, goes to sleep and does not come out until spring. {syn: lan; qûn [4]} [Ansîklopediya Zarokan]

gindore گِـنـدۆره (IFb) = squash, zucchini. See **gindor I**[1].

ginginok گِنگِنۆك *adj.* speaking with a nasal quality, through one's nose; someone who speaks through his nose (K/A/IF); nasal (B). {also: ginginokî (K)} [K/A/IF/B]

ginginokî گِنگِنۆکی (K) = speaking with a nasal quality. See **ginginok**.

gir I گِر *adj.* 1) {syn: mezin} large, big; tall, strapping; heavy; 2) {syn: zivir} coarse, rough, thick (HH/Bw). {also: gur III (Ba2); guř III (FK-eb-1); [ghir] گر (JJ); <gir> گر (HH)} Cf. Sor gewre گەورە; Za gird [Bw/F/K/JB3/IF/B/JJ/HH/GF/TF/OK] See also **gir II**. <girs>

gir II گِـر *m.* **(-ê;).** hill, mound: **•Hakim jî çûye serê *gir* rûniştîye** (L) As for the king, he went and sat on *a hill*. {also: [ghir] گـر (JJ); <gir> گـر (HH)} {syn: banî II; dîyar II; kuç'[3]; t'op III; zûr} <O Ir *gari- (A&L p. 87 [VIII, 1]) [L/K/A/JB3/IF/B/HH/JB1-A/SK/GF/TF/OK] <çîya; girik>

gir III گِـر *prep.* despite, in spite of, notwithstanding: **•Ew *gir* nexweşiya xwe derket** (JB3) He went out *in spite of* his illness; **-ji girê...ve** (BX) do.: **•*ji girê* min *ve*** (BX) *in spite of* me. {syn: digel [2]; dijî [2]; řexme} [BX/JB3/OK]

giř IV گِـــر *m.* **(-ê;).** 1) itch, itching (K/A/JJ): **•Filankesî *giř* ê girtî** (Zeb) So-and-so has been beset by *itching* **•Filankesî *giř* hatê** (Zeb) So-and-so became hysterical; 2) scab, mange, rash (K/A/IF/JJ/B/HH); 3) allergy (Qzl/Bw); 4) sexual urge or desire: **•*Giřê* wê jinê** (Zeb) That woman's *urges*. {also: [ghir] گر (JJ); <gir> گر (HH)} [K/A/IF/B/JJ/HH/GF/TF/Zeb]

giram گِـرام *f.* **(-a;).** respect, honor, esteem: **-giram girtin** (IFb/RF) to respect. {syn: hurmet [3]; me'rîfet; qedir I; řêz II; řûmet} [(neol)IFb/RF] <şeref>

giramgîr گِرامگیر *adj.* respectful: **•Gebranê Baço *bi awakî giramgîr* û dengekî bajariyane bi mêvanê wan î karmend dide zanîn ku ew jî ji vî gundî ye** (Lab, 42) G.B. *respectfully* and in a civilized voice informs their employee-guest that he too is from this village. [Lab/RF]

giran I گِـران *adj.* 1) heavy: **•Dibîne k'aşa zêřa ji ya Ûsib *girantire*** (Ba) He sees that the weight of the gold is more [lit. '*heavier*'] than Joseph['s weight]; 2) {syn: biha [2]; giranbiha; ≠erzan} expensive, costly; 3) [euph.] pregnant (Mzg); 4) {syn: řeş; tarî} dark (of tea, color, etc.) (Bw); 5) clumsy, awkward; slow; 6) hard (of hearing): **•Ji ber ku *guhên wî hinekî giran* bûn, carina deng baş nedibihîst û baş fêm nedikir** (Alkan, 72) Because he was a *little hard of hearing*, sometimes he didn't hear voices well and didn't understand well. {also: [ghiran] گـــران (JJ); <giran> گـــران (HH)} Cf. P garān گـران = 'expensive, heavy'; Sor giran گـران; Za giran {giranî} [K/A/JB3/IFb/B/JJ/ HH/SK/JB1-S/GF/TF/ Mzg/Bw]

gir̄an II گِران (IFb) = mallet. See **ger̄an II**.

giranbiha گـِرانـبـِها *adj.* expensive, costly, dear. {also: [ghiran beha] گـران بـهـا (JJ)} {syn: biha [2]; giran [2]; ≠erzan} [K/IF/JJ] <biha; erzan; nerx; qedir I; qîmet>

giranî گِرانى *f.* **(-ya;-yê).** 1) weight; heaviness: **•Ḧetta bi-qeder *giranîya* wî berey pare-y zêr̄ yan zîw neînim nahêmewe** (SK 12:117) I shall not return until I bring *the weight of* this stone in gold or silver; 2) being expensive; 3) {syn: lenger I[1]} anchor (F); 4) drought (HH). {also: <giranî> گـــرانـــى (HH)} [F/K/A/JB3/IFb/B/HH/SK/JB1-S/GF/TF] <giran>

girar گِــــــرار *f.* **(-a;-ê).** porridge made of buttermilk [Rus paxta пахта] and cooked barley groats seasoned with mint (Dz); pilav made with rice or barley groats (=bulgur) (IF/HH/Bw): **•Bê serwêrî *girara* p'ir̄a nak'ele** (Dz -#67) Without an instructor, *soup* for many won't boil *[prv.]* **•Derxwînê beroşê, dermanê *girarê* [Dûv]** (L[1937]) Cover of the pot, seasoning of *the soup [rdl.; ans.: sheep's fattail]*; **-girara gavana** (Şnx) potpourri, hodgepodge, olio, odd mixture (originally, foods given as payment to a cowherd, who puts them all in the same bowl) {syn: gêlma gavanî}. {also: [ghirar] گـــرار (JJ); <girar> گـرار (HH)} {syn: mehîr} [L (1937)/Dz/K/A/ IF/B/JJ/HH] <pişrûng>

girav I گِراڤ (B) = deposit, pledge. See **girêv**.

girav II گِراڤ/**gir-av** گِرئاڤ *f.* **(-a;-ê).** island (JB3/IF/ A): **•dûrxistin li *Girava* Madagaskar** (OS-intro) exile on *the island of* Madagascar **•Penaberên ku di ser behra Egeyê re bi belemê derbasî *giravên* Yewnenîstanê dibûn ketin nav behrê** (basnews 7.iii.2016) Refugees who were crossing *the islands of* Greece on the Aegean Sea by boat fell into the sea. {also: girdav (A)} {syn: ada; cizîr; dûrgeh} = Sor dûrge دوورگه [JB3/IFb/GF/TF/OK/RZ//A]

girdav گِرداڤ (A) = island. See **girav II.**

girde گِرده *f.* **().** thick, round bread roll with small hole in the center. Cf. P gerde گـــــــرده = 'round cake, loaf'; NENA girdéyâ ܓܪܕܝܐ = 'round cake, small loaf' (Maclean-Urmi) & girda = 'roll' (Garbell) & gar-day-ya = 'loaf of bread, especially flat loaf' (Oraham) [Bşk/ZF3] <loş; nan>

girdek گِــردەك *f.* **(;-ê).** capital letter, upper case letter: **•Navên deştan navdêrên taybetî ne, loma her bêjeya wan navan bi *girdekê* dest pê dike** (RR, 20.1.14.) The names of plains are proper nouns, therefore every word of their names begins with *a capital letter*. {also: girek (Wkt-2)} [RR/IFb/ZF/Wkt/ BF] <hûrdek>

girdik گـِـردِك *f.* **(-a;-ê).** thumb: **-tiliya girdikê** (ZF)/~ **gir[(d)ik]** (RZ) thumb; **-girdika pê** (SBx) big toe: **•Xelîl Beg li şofêrmehelî rûniştibû, di ser *girdika piyê* xwe re** (SBx, 12) Kh.B. had sat in the driver's seat [T], over his *big toe* …. {syn: beranek; tilîya beranî; t'ilîya mezin} [SBx//RZ//ZF]

gire گِره (JB3) = tumor. See **girê** [2].

giregir I گِـــــــرەگِـــــــر *pl.* the nobility, nobles; elders; grandees, potentates: **•Memê k'etîye, r̄eng lê nemaye, xûn ber bîye gol. Al-p'aşa û *giregirava* gelekî hev birin-anîn, yek go--sat'irceme, yek go--sermaye, yek go--tirsaye** (Z-1, 48) Mem was laid low, he was pale, his blood was boiling. Al-pasha and his *entourage* debated a great deal among themselves, one said it was the flu, one said it was a cold, one said it was out of fear. {syn: cindî [3]; 'eyan [3]; k'ubar} [Z-1/K/IFb/B/GF]

gire-gir II گِره گِر (F) = thunder. See **gur̄e-gur̄**.

girek گِرەك (Wkt) = capital letter. See **girdek**.

girev گِرەڤ (A/IFb) = strike. See **grev**.

girê گـِـرێ *f.* **().** 1) {syn: bend I[3]} knot: **-girê dan** (B) to tie. See **girêdan**; 2) {also: gire (JB3)} tumor. {also: girêh (JB1-S-2); girêk (K/A/JB3/IFb-2/ GF-2/TF); [ghiri] گـــرى/گـــره (JJ); <girê> گـــرى (HH)} Cf. Skt granth- = 'to tie, tie together, compose (a literary work)'; O Ir *graθya- (A&L p.85 [VI, 3]): OP gray- = 'to compose' (Kent); P gere گـره = 'knot'; Sor girê گـرێ = 'knot, phrase' [K/ A/JB3/TF//IFb/B/JJ/HH/JB1-A&S/SK/GF/OK] <[1] xilf; [2] tulḧ>

girê•dan گـِرێدان *vt.* **(girê-d-).** 1) {syn: bestin} to bind, tie: **•Daê, sibe bihare, ga tune, ezê te *girêdim*?** (J) Mom, spring is around the corner [lit. 'tomorrow'], there is no ox, *shall I tie* you [to the plough]? **•Wekî em gakî şerjêkin, sibe bihare, xelqê cot *girêde*, îja emê çi bikin?** (J) If we slaughter an ox, tomorrow is springtime, [other] people *will tie* [their bulls to] the plow, what will we do then?; 2) to conclude, establish *(a pact)*, enter into *(a bargain)*; 3) to gather up, summon, muster *(troops)*: **•Al-p'aşa r̄abû eskerê xwe *girêda*** (Z-1) A.p. got up and *gathered* his troops. {also: girê dan (B); [ghiri-dan] گريدان (JJ)} Cf. Za girêdanã [girêdayiş] (Srk) [K/JB3/IF/JJ/B]

girêday گـرێـداى (SK/JJ) = tied, bound; connected to; dependent upon. See **girêdayî**.

girêdayî گِـرێـدايـى *adj./pp.* 1) tied, bound: **•Dewê sey bi parîyekî *girê-day* bît çêtir e** (SK 54:626) It is better for the dog's mouth to be *tied* with a morsel [from Sa'di's Gulistan]; 2) connected (to/with), related (to): **-bi yekî/tiştekî ve girêdayî bûn** (CS) to be connected with s.o./stg.: ***•girêdayî* 60 [şêst] salîya bûyîna wî *va*** (B) *related to* his 60th birthday [the 60th anniversary of his birth]; 3) dependent (upon): -[**bi**] **hevra girêdayî bûn** (K) to be dependent on *or* connected/related to one another: **•Lê piraniya çîrokên wî, bi teknîka modêrn, monolog û dalog** [sic], **paş û pêşxistina demî û zincîra rûdanan, ȟeta dawiyê *bi hev re girêdayîye*** (X.Duhokî. Qefteka gulan, 129) But most of his stories *are connected to* each other in a modern technique, monologue & dialogue, transposing the time and order of events; -[**bi**] **hevra girêdayî kirin** (K) to make dependent on one another. {also: girêday (SK); [ghiri-daï] گرى داى (JJ)} Cf. Sor girêdiraw گـرێـدراو = 'tied in a knot, knotted' [K/A/B/IFb/FJ/TF/ZF/CS//JJ/SK] <têkildar>

girêh گرێه (JB1-S) = knot. See **girê**.

girêk گرێك (K/A/JB3/GF/TF) = knot; tumor. See **girê**.

girêl گِـرێـل : **-girêl bûn** (Urm/Slm): 1) {syn: gêr bûn; gindirîn; gulol bûn} to roll *(vi.)* (Slm/Dh); 2) to die *(used by Muslims in speaking of Christians)* (Urm/Slm). [Urm/Slm/Dh] <gort I>

girêv گِـرێـڤ *f.* **(;-ê).** deposit, pledge; token. {also: girav I (B)} Cf. Sor grêw گرێو [K//B] <r̄ehîn>

girêz گِـرێـز *f.* **(-a;-ê).** saliva, spittle, slobber, drool: **•Her ku wî digot fîl mest dibûn, av bi devê wan diket û *girêza* wan diherikî** (SF 19) The more he spoke the elephants became giddy, their mouths started watering and their *drool* began to flow **•Lê çavên wan têr nebûn. Bênder jî erd in. Erd jî tim *girêzê* bi devên wan dixîne** (HYma, 30) But they [lit.'their eyes'] were not satisfied. Threshing floors are land too, and land always makes them salivate [lit. 'puts *saliva* in their mouths']. {also: gilêj (IFb); gilêz (GF-2); gilûz (Bşk); [ghiliz] گليز (JJ)} {syn: ava dev; t'if; t'ûk II} [Bşk//SF/A/GF/ZF3//JJ//IFb]

girik I گِـرِك *f.* **(-a;-ê).** 1) small hill [*dim. of* **gir II**] (K/A/IF/JJ); 2) shoulder, shoulder blade(s) (B/JJ/Bw); clavicle, collar bone (IS): **-girka mil** (K)/[ghirk-i milan] گركى ملان (JJ) shoulder. {also: girk (IS); [ghirik] گرك (JJ)} [IS//K/A/IF/B/JJ/Bw] <gir II; mil>

girik II گِـرِك/**gir̄ik** گِـرِك [Zeb/FS] *f./m.(Zeb/FS)* **(;/-î).** hand mill used for removing rice husks; bottom circle is of stone, top one is of wood. {also: <girik> گـرك (HH)} {syn: destar̄} [Bw/IFb/HH/GF/OK//Zeb/FS] <aş>

giring گِـرِنـگ *adj.* important, significant. {syn: berkeftî} {also: girîng (Wlt/ZF3)} Cf. Sor giring گِرِنگ < giran = 'heavy' {giringî; girîngî} [K(s)/A/IFb/GF/TF/OK//Wlt/ZF3] <watedar>

giringî گِـرِنـگـى *f.* **(-ya;-yê).** importance, weight, significance: ***•Girîngiya* vê şadetiyê ji ya dîroknasan bêhtir e** (Rwş #3, 24) *The importance of* this testimony is greater than that of the historians **•Ji aliyê *girîngiyê* ve di dereca yekemîn de bû** (Wlt 1:39, 11) With regard to *significance*, it was of the first degree. {also: girîngî (Wlt/Rwş)} [(neol)Wlt/Rwş/ZF3//K(s)/GF/TF/OK] <giring>

giriyan گِريان (-giriy-) (JB1-S) = to cry. See **girîn**.

girî گِـرى *m.* **(-yê;-yî).** crying, weeping: **•Bi dengê îskilokên *girîyî* de** (MG. Jiyaneka Pêguhork) With the sound of sobbing [lit. 'sobs of *crying*'] ***•Girîyê* min tê** (B) I feel like *crying* **•Hêrsa mêran û *giriyê* pîrekan û zarokan tev de bidû xwe de hiştibû** (HYma 35) He left the rage of the men and *the weeping of* the women and children behind him. {syn: ah û zar} Cf. P geryeh گـريـه; Sor giryan گِـريـان [HYma/MG/K/B/IFb/GF/SK/JB1-A&S/CS] <girîn>

girîn گِرين *vi.* **(-girî-).** to cry, weep: **•Hersê r̄ûniştin li halê xwe û li ber r̄ebbê xwe *girîyane*** (Z-2, 66) The three of them sat and *cried* of their plight to their Lord **•Jina Osê biçûkekî sawa hebo, di landikêda bo. Berî spêdê biçûk *girî*** (SK 40:357) Oso's wife had a suckling infant which was in a cradle. Before dawn the baby *cried.* {also: giriyan (-giriy-) (JB1-S-2); gîran (IFb); [ghirin] گرين (JJ); <girîn گـريـن (digrî) (دگـرى)> (HH)} <Perhaps [Pok. 2. ger- 383.] 'to cry hoarsely': Mid P griyistan (griy-) (M3); P ger̄īstan گـريـستن/ gerye kardan گريه كردن = 'to cry'; Sor girîn گِرين/giryan گِـريـان; Hau gireway (girew-) *vi.* (M4); = Za

bermenä [F/K/A/JB3/B/JJ/HH/SK/GF/JB1-A&S//IFb]

giring گرینگ (Wlt/ZF3) = important. See **giring**.

giringî گرینگی (Wlt/Rwş) = importance. See **giringî**.

giriş گریش (GF/TF) = shock, stack, stook. See **gidîş**.

girîvan گریڤان *m.* **(-ê;).** collar: •**Emma r̄îwî serê xo bi *girîwanê* xoda şor kiribû, çawêt xo miçandibûn** (SK 4:35) But the fox hung his head down out of his *collar* and shut his eyes •**Were, vî kur̄ey *girîvanê* xo helkêşe da bîte kur̄ê te** (M-Ak #651, 294) Come and pull this boy up through your *collar* so that he may become your son (qv. **p'êsîr**). {also: girîwan (SK)} {syn: berstû; bestik; p'êsîr [2]; pisto; yax} Cf. gewrî = 'throat' [M-Ak//SK] <p'êsîr>

girîwan گریوان (SK) = collar. See **girîvan**.

girîzank گریزانك (FS) = tickle. See **gilîzank**.

girîze گریزه (IFb/GF) = shudder, quiver. See **girîzok**.

girîzok گریزۆك *m.* **().** shudder, quiver, trembling; goose bumps, gooseflesh: •***Girîzok* bi laşê min ve tê** (Nsb) I get *goose bumps* •**Mirin; çi gotineke ne xweş e, sar û tahl e. *Grûzî* bi canê meriv digre** (LC, 8) Death, what an unpleasant word, cold and bitter. It sends *a shudder* through one's soul. {also: girîze (IFb/GF); girîzonek (TF); grûzî (LC)} {syn: firk I[2]} [Nsb//TF//IFb/GF//LC]

girîzonek گریزۆنەك (TF) = shudder, quiver. See **girîzok**.

girj گرژ *adj.* 1) wrinkled, puckered (OK); 2) surly, morose, sullen (OK/K[s]); 3) {syn: bel; qişt; qund; r̄ep} erect, bristling, standing on end (SK): •**Gurgî got, "Mûyêt min *girj bûne*?"** (SK 6:69) The wolf said, "Have my hairs *stood up*?"; 4) puffed up, inflated: **-xwe gij kirin** (K) to puff o.s. up: •**Gava gur rivîna geş dît, xwe ji miyê bi dûr xist, *xwe gij kir* û diranên xwe qîc kirin** (EŞ 16) When the wolf saw the bright flame, it distanced itself from the sheep, *puffed itself up* and bared its teeth; 5) tense, taut. {also: gij (K-2/A/IFb/GF/TF); <gij> گژ (HH)} Sor girj گرژ/kirj کرژ = 'wrinkled, shriveled, puckered, sullen' [SK/K(s)/OK//K/A/IFb/HH/GF/TF]

girk گرك (IS) = small hill; shoulder. See **girik**.

girme گرمه (A) = thunder; crash. See **girmîn**.

girme-girm گرمەگرم, f. (K) = thunder; crash. See **girmîn** & **gur̄e-gur̄**.

girmîn گرمین *f.* **(-a;-ê).** 1) {syn: gur̄e-gur̄; r̄eqer̄eq} thunder: **-girmîna ewran** (IF) thundering of the clouds; 2) crash, din, loud noise. {also: girme-girm, f. (K); girme (A); xirmîn (IF-2)} [EP-8/K/A/IF/B] <birûsk; gimîn; gur̄în>

girnas گرناس (GF) = hero. See **gernas**.

girnijîn گرنژین *vi.* **(-girnij-).** to smile, grin. {also: <girnijîn> گرنژین (Hej)} {syn: beşişîn; bişkurîn; mizicîn} [Bw/IFb/(OK)/Hej/RZ] <k'enîn>

girofik گرۆفك (DBgb) = ball of yarn. See **girov**.

girov گرۆڤ *f.* **(-a;).** skein, ball *(of yarn)*: •**Ku hiriya li ser destê wê qeda, teşî vekir, rîsê xwe yê badayî kir *girofik*. Ev *girofik* têra cotek gore ji bo kalo heye** (DBgb 13) When the wool on her hands was used up, she opened the spindle, [and] made her twisted yarn into *a ball*. This *ball of yarn* is enough for a pair of socks for grandpa. {also: girofik (DBgb); [gouloufank/gouloufink] گلوفنك (JJ); <girûv> گروڤ (HH)} {syn: gulok; peng I} [DBgb//IFb/GF/FS//HH//JJ]

girover̄ گرۆڤەر *adj.* round, circular. {also: gulover̄ (K/F/BK/B); gurover (BK); [ghrover گراور/ ghelouver گلور] (JJ); <kirover> کروڤر (HH)} {syn: gilol I (IF); gildî (IF)} {gulover̄î; gulover̄tî} [A/JB3/IF/JJ//K/F/BK/B//HH]

girs گرس *adj.* big, huge, horsey, large and clumsy; plump: •**Berxên ȟilî berîya zivistanê çêdibin, zivistanê di koza da derbaz dikin, xurt û *girs* in** (Qzl) "Hilî" [early-born] lambs are born before the winter, and spend the winter in the sheepfold--they are fat and *plump*. [Qzl/K(s)/A/IFb/GF/FJ] <qerase I; zivir>

girsik گرسك (Hk/Hej/Kmc) = wild pear. See **kirosik**.

girtin گرتن *vt.* **(-gir-/-gr-).** 1) to take, take hold of, hold: •***Bi* destê wî *girt*** (L) He *took hold of* his (=s.o. else's) hand •**R̄ovî, te ev aqil ji k'u *girtye*?** (Dz) Fox, where did you *get* your sense from?; **-bi ser *ft-î* de girtin** (BX)/**ser *ft-î* girtin** (YZ-1) to prefer: •**Min honikahiya zozanan *bi ser* havîna deştê de *digirt*** (BX) I *used to prefer* the coolness of the summer pastures to the summer of the plain •**Tu çima Ûsib t'enê *ser* ȟemyar̄a *digirî*?** (YZ-1) Why *do you prefer* Joseph over all the others?; **-çi bigre** (Frq) almost: •***Çi bigre* her millet xwedî mîzaheke nivîskî ye jî** (LC, 3) *Almost* every nation also possesses [a tradition of] written humor; **-hev[din] girtin** (Wlt) to be consistent: •**Gotinêd te *hev din nagrin* = Tiştêd tu dibêjî *hev din nagrin*** (Wlt) Your words *don't bear each other out*; **-jê girtin**. See **jêgirtin**; **-nezer ji *fk-ê* girtin** (EP-7) to cast the evil eye on s.o.: •**Wekî**

nezer ji* te *negire (EP-7) Lest *the evil eye be cast on* you; **-serê hespê girtin** (Z-3) to rein in, ride *(a horse)* slowly {≠serê hespê berdan}: **•Ûn *serê hespê xo negrin* ḧeya devê derê dîwanê** (Z-3) Don't *let your horses slow down* until [you reach] the door of the diwan; **-xwe li *fk-ê* girtin** (XF): a) to depend, rely upon: **•Mîrî xweşbe, eme ji Kilḧanyênê, welatê meda nangiranîye, *me xwe li* te *girtîye*** (Ba-1, #31) Long live the emir, we are from Canaan, in our country food is scarce, *we are depending on* you; b) to head for, make for; 2) a) {syn: qefaltin} to seize, catch, capture: **•Dengek ji serê sûrehê seh kir, got, *bigire*** (Rnh 2:17, 307) He heard a voice from the top of the city wall, it said, '*Catch*!'; b) to catch, fall ill with, come down with (an illness) [*rev. con.*]: **•Nekisê ew *girtiye*** (FS) *He's been suffering from* shortness of breath [lit. 'sh.o.b. has seized him'] **•Vê şovê ew *girtiye*** (FS) This contagion *has spread to him/her* [lit. 'has seized'] **•Zikçûnê ew *girtiye*** (FS) He *has come down with* diarrhea [lit. 'D. has seized him']; 3) {syn: daxistin; ≠vekirin} to close, shut: **•Dergivan d[ê]rî *digire*** (L) The gatekeeper *closes* the gate **•S̱armayê li min daye û ximximkên min *hatine girtin*** (FS) The cold has hit me [or, I've caught a cold] and my nostrils *have gotten closed up*. {also: [ghirtin] گرتین (JJ); <girtin گرتن (digre) (دگره)> (HH)} [Pok. 1. ghrebh-/gherbh- 455.] 'to seize, reach': Skt √gr̥bh [IX. grbhṇāti]; Av gərəβiia-; O P garbāya-= 'to seize' (Kent); Mid P griftan (-gīr- < gr̥bya-) = 'to take, hold' (M3); P gereftan گرفتن (-gīr-) (گیر); Sor girtin گرتن (-gir-); Za genã [girotiş] = 'to get; to close' (Todd); Hau girtey (gêr-) *vt.* = 'to take, seize' (M4); cf. also Germ greifen; Eng grab/grasp/grip/grapple [F/K/A/JB3/IFb/B/JJ/HH/SK/JB1-A&S/GF/TF/OK]

girtin û berdan گرتن و بەردان *f.* **(-a;-ê).** commerce, business; comings and going, give and take: **•*Girtin û berdana* welatê Cizîrê destê wanda bû** (Z-1) *The comings and goings of* the state of Jizîra were in their hands. [Z-1/GF] <dan û standin>

girtina heyvê گرتنا هەیڤێ (ZF) = lunar eclipse. See **heyvgirtin.**

girtina řojê گرتنا ڕۆژێ (Zeb/RF) = solar eclipse. See **řojgirtin.**

girtî گرتی *adj./pp.* 1) {≠vekirî} closed, shut (K/B); enclosed (JJ); 2) *[m.&f.]* {syn: dîl; hêsîr I} prisoner, captive: **•Ḧevsa teda *girtîk* heye** (Ba3-3, #32) In your jail there is *a prisoner* **•Li girtîgehên Çanakkale ... yê zêdeyî 100 *girtiyên* siyasî bi mebesta protest[o]kirina şert û pestên îdareyê ketin greva birçîbûnê** (Wlt 2:59, 5) In the prisons of Çanakkale [et al.] more than 100 political *prisoners* held a hunger strike with the aim of protesting the [bad] conditions and oppression of [=at the hands of] the authorities. {also: [ghertía] گرتی (JJ); <girtî> گرتی (HH)} [K/IFb/B/JJ/HH/TF/ZF3]

girtîgeh گرتیگەه *f.* **(-a;-ê).** 1) {syn: ḧebs; zindan} prison, jail [British: gaol]: **•Du girtiyên tirk her êvar [m]ifteyên *girtîgehê* didizin, derî vedikin, û bi şev diçin ji xwe re digerin** (AW74B7) Two Turkish prisoners steal *the prison* keys every night, open the door, and go out at night and wander around; 2) concentration camp (K). [K/JB3/IFb/OK/Wlt/ZF3]

girvank•e گرڤانکه *f.* **(;•ê).** pound *(unit of weight)*; unit of weight equivalent to 410 grams (Hej): **•Deh *girvanke* ceh** (EP-5, #10) Ten *pounds of* barley. <Geo girvanka გირვანქა = 'pound': P girvānke گروانکه/gīrvānke گیروانکه; Az T girvənkə; T kırvanka [Çayağzı *Şavşat -Artvin] = 'scale, balance' (DS, v.8, p. 2839); Sor girwanke گروانکه (Hej)/ gerwanke گەروانکە (Hej/W&E) = 'packet' (W&E) [EP-5/K/B]

gistîl گستیل (K) = (finger) ring. See **gustîl.**

gistîlk گستیلک = (finger) ring. See **gustîl.**

giş گش (IFb/JB3/DM) = all. See **gişk.**

gişk I گشك *adj.* 1) {syn: her; ḧemû} all *[generally follows the word it modifies]*: **•Ezê *we gişka* qiřkim** (Ba) I'll kill *you all* **•*Gur gişk* berev bûn** (Ba) *All the wolves* assembled/gathered round **•*Gura gişka* sond xwar** (Ba) *All the wolves* took an oath; 2) *[prn.]* all, everyone, everybody: **•*Gişk* tên li Ûsib dinihêrin** (Ba) *All* come [and] look at Joseph **•*Gişke* birçîbûn** (Ba) They were *all* hungry; **-ji gişka ...-tir** = the ...-est of all (*expresses the superlative degree of adjectives*; cf. P az hameh behtar از همه بهتر = 'the best'): **•Ûsibî *ji gişka aqiltire*** (Ba) Joseph is *smarter than everyone* (=the smartest) **•Ev goharto *ji gişan tekûztir* e** (DM) This version is *the most complete/ perfect of all*; 3) everything: **•Ûsib çi ku ot'axêda dike, Zelîxe *gişkî* divîne** (Ba) Whatever Joseph does in the room, Zelikha sees *everything*. {also: gi (Ad); giş (IFb/JB3/DM); gişt (IFb/B-2); giştî [3] (IF-2); [gish گش/gi گی/gishk گشك/gisk (گسك)]

(JJ)} Cf. Sor gişt گِـشـت. M. Schwartz: The most plausible etymon for **gişk** is O Ir *visva- --> Av vispa-, Old P visa- = 'all,' cf. Skt viśva- & Rus ves′ весь, but **-ş-** is problematic, unless it is a second, less common reflex for O Ir -sw-; another possible source is P gaš گـــش = 'galore' <gašna <*gaźna- = 'treasure' (according to W.B. Henning in "Coriander," *Asia Major*, 10, ii (1963), 195-99); K gişk has been posited as the source of Mandaic guš = 'all' (see Macuch) [Ba/F/K/JB3/IFb/JJ/B]

gişk II گِشك (Bw) = hail[stones]. See **gijlok**.

gişt گِشت (IFb/B) = all. See **gişk**.

giştik گِشتِك *f.* **(-a;).** rolled-up ball of dough *(before it is flattened out and kneaded to make bread)*: **-giştika hevîrî** (FS) do. [Zeb/Şx/OK/FS] <hevîr>

giştî گِـشـتـی *adj.* 1) public: **-ȓaya giştî** (Wlt) public opinion; 2) general. < Sor giştî گـشـتـی [Hv/K/A/JB3/GF/TF/OK/RF/RZ]

giv گِـــڤ *m.* **(-ê;).** curd(s), unfiltered milk before it becomes cheese: **-givê penêr** (Şnx) do. {also: givî (IFb/FJ/GF/FD); givtî (FJ-2/GF-2); guvî (FJ-2/GF-2); [gouwi] گڤی (JJ); <givî> گڤی (HH)} {syn: şîrêj} [Şnx/ZF3//IFb/FJ/GF/HH/FD//JJ] <ç'ortan; keşk; lorik>

givaştin گِـڤـاشـتِـن (Ag/JB3/IFb/B) = to squeeze, press. See **guvaştin**.

givêrandin گِڤێراندِن *vt.* **(-givêrîn-).** 1) to digest: **•'Ûr xwarinê *digivêrînit*** (FS) The intestines *digest* food; 2) [*f.* **(;-ê).**] digestion. {also: givêrtin (ZF3-2); givirandin (ZF3-2); guvirandin (GF-2)} {syn: dehandin} [IFb/GF/ZF3/FD/FS/Wkt]

givêrtin گِڤێرتِن (ZF3) = to digest. See **givêrandin**.

givgiv گِـڤـگِـڤ (GF[Beh]) = whistling (of wind). See **guveguv**.

givir گِڤِر (IFb/OK/Hej/ZF3/FS) = wild cat. See **gîvir**.

givirandin گِڤِراندِن (ZF3) = to digest. See **givêrandin**.

givirdar گِڤِردار *adj.* dead, lifeless (K). {also: giv û dar (EP-7)} {syn: mirî} Cf. T gebermek = 'to die (of animals)' [EP-7//K] <gever bûn (JB3); mirin>

givî گِڤی (IFb/FJ/GF/HH/FD) = curd(s). See **giv**.

givîj گِڤیژ (Haz/Kmc-2) = hawthorn. See **gîjok**.

givtî گِڤتی (FJ/GF) = curd(s). See **giv**.

giv û dar گِڤ و دار (EP-7) = dead. See **givirdar**.

givzonek گِـڤـزۆنـەك (GF/ZF3) = milk thistle. See **givzonik**.

givzong گِڤزۆنگ (ZF3) = milk thistle. See **givzonik**.

givzonik گِـڤـزۆنِـك *f.* **(;-ê).** milk thistle, bot. *Silybum marianum*: **•Gotin kerê: "Were, em te bibin cenetê." Got: "Ma *givzonik* li wê derê heye?"** (L-#69) They said to the donkey, "Come, let us take you to paradise." He said, "Do they have *thistles* there?" [*prv.*] **•Li bijişkiya siruştî şîrê *givzonikê* tê bikaranîn** (Wkp) In natural medicine, the milk of *the milk thistle* is used. {also: givzonek (GF/ZF3); givzong (ZF3-2)} [L/K//GF/ZF3] <dirî; k'erbeş>

giwişîn گوشین (SK) = to squeeze, press. See **guvaştin**.

giwûr گووور (Wkt) = garbage; dung. See **guhûr**.

giya گِیا (JB3/IFb/GF) = grass. See **gîya** [1].

giyaben گِـیـابـەن (GF/Hej) = plant root used as folk remedy. See **giyabend**.

giyabend گِـیـابـەنـد *m./f.(FS)* **(-ê/;-î/).** fragrant plant (wormwood, bot. *Artemisia campestris*) [called farmūt فرموت in Arabic (GF)] or root of the **rêvaz** [rhubarb (Bw) = ribês] given as a folk remedy to people with stomach aches, diabetes, etc., {also: giyaben (GF-2); <giyaben[d]> گـیـابـەن(د) (Hej)} [Bw/GF/Hej] <ȓibês>

giyan گِیان (GShA) = soul; body; self. See **can I**.

gizêr گِـــزێـــر *m.(Xrs)/f.(K/B/ZF3)* **(/-a; /-ê).** carrot. {also: gêzer (A/IF-2/GF-2/FS); gîzer (GF); zirgêzer (IF-2); [ghizir] گزر (JJ); <gêzer> گـیـزر (HH)} Cf. Ar jazar جـــزر, Heb gezer גזר; P gazar گزر; Sor gêzer گێزەر [Xrs/K/IF/B/ZF3//A/HH/FS//JJ//GF]

gizêz گِزێز (Wkt) = clothes moth. See **bizûz**.

gizîz گِزیز (Wkt) = clothes moth. See **bizûz**.

gizûz گِزووز (Wkt) = clothes moth. See **bizûz**.

gîfik گیفِك (Bw/JJ) = tassel. See **gûfik**.

gîha گیها (F/K/L) = grass; hay. See **gîya**.

gîhan گیهان (AB) = to arrive; to ripen. See **gihan I**.

gîhandin گـیـهـانـدِن (K/BK) = to cause to arrive. See **gihandin**.

gîhiştin گـیـهِـشـتِـن = to arrive; to ripen, mature. See **gihîştin**.

gîjok گــــــیــــــژۆك *f.* **(;-ê).** hawthorn, azarole, Mediterranean medlar, bot. *Crataegus azarolus*: small orange-yellow fruit sold in the fall in large quantities strung together in wreaths [T alıç, Ar zuʿrūr زعرور, P zālzālak زالزالك, R boiaryšnik боярышник] (Mzg/Haz/Srk/K[s]); buckthorn, bot. *Rhamnus cathartica* [T akdiken] (IFb); wild cherry, (bot.) *Cerasus padus & Cerasus avium* [T yabani kiraz] (IFb). {also: givîj (Haz/Kmc-2); goyîj (K[s]/IFb-2); guhîj (GF/TF/OK/AA); guvîj (Srk); gûhûşk (Hk/Zeb/IFb); gûşk (OK-2/AA-2); <givîşk گڤیشك/guhîj گوهیژ/guhûşk گوهوسك>

(Hej)} Sor goyij گـــێــوژ/gêwij گـــۆيــژ [K3] = 'hawthorn' [Mzg/IFb/ZF3//K(s)//Haz/Kmc-2//GF/TF/OK/AA/Hej//Srk] <şîlan I>

gîlaz گيلاز (F) = cherry. See **gêlaz**.

gîlofîtik گيلۆفيتك (M.Dicle) = snowball. See **gulîfîtk**.

gînîk گينيك (Bw) = sack. See **gûnîk**.

gîran گيران (IFb) = to cry. See **girîn**.

gîro گيرۆ *adj.* late, delayed, behind: **-gîro bûn** (Bw) to be late, delayed {syn: awiqîn; egle bûn}: •[**Em jî *gîro nabîn***] (JJ) We *won't be late* either; **-gîro kirin** (SK/OK) to delay, restrain, make (s.o.) late {syn: awiqandin; egle kirin}. {also: [ghirou] / گيرو گرو (JJ)} {syn: dereng; egle} <T geri (older gerü) = 'behind, back' [Bw/JJ/SK/OK] <dereng>

gîsik گيسِك = one-year-old kid (goat). See **gîsk**.

gîsin گـــــيـــسِــن *m.* (**-ê;).** plowshare, the part of a moldboard plow that cuts the furrow: •**Ewî dît hindek masî der keftin digel *gasinî* bin axê** (M-Ak) He saw that a number of fish came out of the earth with the *ploughshare* •**Wekî *gîsnê* cot; çiqas bê şixulandin ewqas wê bibiriqe** (WM 1:2, 10) Like *a plowshare*, the more it is used, the more it shines; **-gîsinê seqa kirî** (Qzl) strong and clever man [lit. 'tempered plowshare']. {also: gasin (M-Ak); gêsin (A/JB1-A/Btm); [gisson گـسـان/gāsin گاسن (Rh)] (JJ); <gêsin> گيسن (HH)} < ga = 'ox' + ḧesin = 'iron': cf. P gāv'āhan گـاوآهـن; Sor gasin گـاسِـن/gaasin گـائـاسِـن; Hau gawesin *m.* (M4) [Ad/K/JB3/IF/B//A/JB1-A/HH/Btm//M-Ak/JJ] <cot [2]; halet; hincar; k'otan II; şûrik I>

gîsk گيسك *m.&f.* (**-ê/-a; /-ê).** one- to two-year-old goat; 3 to 6-month old kid (FS). {also: gîsik; [ghisk] گيسك (JJ); <gîsk> گيسك (HH)} {syn: hevûrî} Cf. Pahl vēsak = 'kid (young goat)'; Sor gîsk گـيـسـك = 'kid of 3 to 6 months'. See **183. gīsa** = 'two-year-old goat' (& **181. gīgī** = 'kid') in: D. Monchi-Zadeh. *Wörter aus Xurāsān und ihre Herkunft* (Leiden: E.J. Brill, 1990), p.61 [M/K/A/IFb/B/JJ/HH/GF/TF/OK/Bsk/ZF3] <bizin; kar I; kavir; kûr I = sayis; nêrî I; tuştîr>

gîş•e گـيـشـه *f.* (**•a;).** shock, stook, large sheaf, bale (of hay, etc.): **-gîşa genimî** (Zeb) sheaf of wheat. {also: **gidîş**; gûşe, m. (OK); <gîşe> گـيـشـه (Hej)} Sor gîşe گيشه = 'haycock, stook, conical mound of hay in a field, stack, rick' [Zeb/Hej//OK] <gurz II; xorim> See also **gidîş**.

gîvir گـيـڤِر *m.&f.* (**-ê/-a;).** wild cat, cougar, lynx; male cat. {also: givir (IFb/OK/ZF3); <givir گـڤـر/gîvir گيڤر> (Hej)} [Bw//IFb/OK/Hej/ZF3/FS] <k'itik II; p'isîk; weşeq>

gîya گـيـيا *m.* (**giyayê/giyê;).** 1) {syn: ç'ayîr[2]} grass: •**Ev çola hana *gîha* lê nema** (L) There's no more *grass* on this mountain; 2) plant; herb; 3) hay (F/K/B). {also: giha (GF-2); gihîya (K-2); gihya (B); giya (JB3/IFb/GF); gîha (F/K/L); gya (SK); [ghiia گـيـا/ ghiiah گـيـاه] (JJ); <giya> گـيـا (HH)} Cf. Av gaodāyu- = 'cattle-nourisher, *hence* grass' (per Gershevitch); P giyāh گـياه; Sor giya گـيـا; Hau gîwaw *m.* (M4). See **Grass** in: I. Gershevitch. "Outdoor Terms in Iranian," *A Locust's Leg : Studies in Honour of S.H. Taqizadeh* (London, 1962), pp.80-81; reprinted in his *Philologia Iranica*, ed. by N. Sims-Williams (Wiesbaden : Dr. Ludwig Reichert Verlag, 1985), pp. 174-75. [L/F/K//A/JJ/OK//JB3/IFb/HH/GF//B//SK] <ade I; heşînatî>

gîzan گيزان (IF/FS) = razor. See **gûzan**.

gîzer گيزەر (GF) = carrot. See **gizêr**.

gîzik گيزِك (IF) = ankle. See **gûzek**.

glok گلۆك (GF) = ball of thread. See **gulok**.

go I گۆ (L) = that *(conj.)*. See **ko I**.

go II گـــۆ (L) (I, you, he, etc.) said *[abbreviated past tense of the verb* **gotin** *= to say]*. {also: got}. See under **gotin**.

goc گـــۆج *adj.* crippled or paralyzed in one hand: **-destê goc** (FS) crippled hand; **-goc kirin** (Zeb) to cripple or paralyze in one hand. {syn: qop; şeht; şil II} Sor goc گـــۆج = 'maimed in the hand'; Hau goc (M4) [Zeb/IFb/OK/ZF3/FS] <nivîşkan I>

gog گـــۆگ *f.* (**-a;-ê).** 1) {syn: hol I; t'op II} ball: •**Li Hoskan ciwanên gund derketibûn rasta bêndera û ji xwe re bi *gogê* dilîstin** (AW69B4) In Hoskan [village] the young men of the village had gone to the threshing floor and were playing *ball*; 2) {syn: hol I[2]} *anything in a game which is hit with a* ***t'ûs*** [stick], such as tennis ball, hockey puck, etc. (Bw) {also: gok (K-2/A/TF)} [K/IFb/GF/Bw/Qzl//A/TF] <hol I; k'aşo; t'ûs>

gogerîn گۆگەرین (A/IFb) = dung beetle. See **gûgilêrk**.

gogird گۆگرد (K[s]/A) = sulphur. See **k'irgûd**.

goharto گۆهارتۆ (DM) = version. See **guharto**.

gohastin گۆهاستِن (-gohêz-) (JB1-S) = to (ex)change; to marry off. See **guhastin**.

gok گۆك (K/A/TF) = ball. See **gog**.

gol گۆل *f.* (**-a;-ê).** 1) lake, pond: **-Gola Wanê** (SB, 50) Lake Van {syn: Beḧra Wanê}; 2) pool, puddle (B). {also: [gol] گـول (JJ); <gol> گـول (HH)} < T göl = 'lake' [Ba2/K/A/JB3/IFb/B/JJ/HH/GF/TF/OK] <av; beȟr; bêrm; geř III; gom II>

golik گۆلِك *m./f.(B)* **(-ê/;-î/-ê).** calf, young bovine (Ad/ K/A/JB3); newborn calf, *as opposed to* ***k'endik*** = *one-year-old calf* (Ag); calf up to one year old (B/ HH): **-goştê golikan** = veal, calves' meat. {also: [golk/ golik] گولك (JJ); <golik> گولك (HH)} Sor gwêlik [gölik] گوێلك/gwêreke [göreke] گوێرەکە = 'sucking calf'; Hau goreke *m.* (M4) [Ad/Ag/K/A/JB3/ IFb/B/JJ/HH/GF/OK/ZF3/FS] <çêlek; ga; k'endik; malok; mozik I; parone>

golikvan گۆلِكڤان *m.* (; golikvên). calfherd: **•Êdî tu ji min re nebêjî Keçelokê *Golikvan*, ha!** (ZZ-4, 245) Don't call me Bald Boy *the Calfherd* anymore! {also: [golik-van] گولكوان (JJ)} [ZZ/K/B/ IFb/FJ/GF/JJ/ZF3] <gavan>

golikvanî گۆلِكڤانی *f.* **(-ya;-yê).** calfherding, profession of a calfherd: **•Keçelok sal-dozdeh mehan, *golikvaniya* gundê xwe dikir** (ZZ-4, 244) Bald Boy did *calfherding* for his village 12 months a year. [ZZ/IFb/GF/ZF3] <gavantî>

gom I گۆم *f.* **(-a;-ê).** 1) {syn: axil; axur; k'ox [1]} sty, fold, pen *(for small farm animals, e.g., sheep)*; {syn: bêrî I} sheepfold (JJ/B): **•Du řêwî řex *gomekê* derbaz dibûn** (Dz) Two travelers pass by *an animal pen* **•Herdu rêwîyê birçî çûne *gomê*** (Dz) Both of the hungry travelers went *to the pen*; **-goma pêz** (F) sheepfold; 2) summer hut or cabin (IFb): "Kom is more of a seasonal settlement … it refers to the seasonal, high, and distant settlements of houses (usually one room) inhabited by shepherds and animals together, more as a shelter for both in late spring." [from: Lale Yalçın-Heckmann. *Tribe and Kinship among the Kurds* (Frankfurt a.M. et al. : Peter Lang, 1991), p. 78]. {also: gov (A/TF/OK); kom I (Yalçın-Heckmann); [gom گوم/ gouw گوف] (JJ); <gov> گوف (HH)} Cf. Arm kom (W)/gom (E) գոմ {See: G. S. Asatrian. "O rannyx armenizmax v kurdskom" [=On early Armenianisms in Kurdish], *Patma-banasirakan Handes* = *Историко-филологический Журнал*, 113, (1986), 171-72} For anthropological discussions of *gom* [kom], see N. Tunçdilek. *Türkiye İskan Coğrafyası : Kır iskanı* (İstanbul : İstanbul Matbaası, 1967), pp. 129-32 & İ. Beşikçi. *Doğuda Değişim ve Yapısal Sorunlar: Göçebe Alikan Aşireti* (Ankara : Sevinç Matbaası, 1969), pp. 42-44. In: W.D. Hütteroth. *Die Türkei* (Darmstadt: Wissenschaftliche Länderkunden, 1982), p. 291, *kom* is referred to as a Kurdish name for animal fold. [Dz/F/K/IFb/JJ/B/Wn//A/HH/TF/OK] <afiř; dolge; guhêř; lêf; kotan I; mexel; mî I>

gom II گۆم *f.* **(-a;-ê).** small lake, pond: **•Çûn ȟetta geştine *gomekê*. Dîtin** [sic] **şoneyek di *gomê* da melewanî diket** (SK 4:39) They went until they came to *a pond*. They saw a drake swimming in *the pond*. {also: <gom> گۆم (Hej)} [Dh/IFb/SK/TF/OK/ Hej/FS] <bêrm; gol>

gomik گۆمِك (SS) = fingertip. See **gumik**.

gomink گۆمِنك *m.* **(-ê;).** clump *(of grass)*: **-gominkê şafir[î]** (Bw) a clump of *shafir*, green plant eaten by animals. [Bw] <gumtil>

gomirk گۆمِرك (Wkt) = customs (tax and office). See **gumrik**.

gomrik گۆمرك (Wkt) = customs (tax and office). See **gumrik**.

gon I گۆن *m.(K/ZF3)/f.(JB3/IFb)* **().** 1) {syn: řeng} color *[poetic]*; 2) form, shape; aspect. Cf. P gūn گون = 'color'--> Heb gaven גון, NA gawna (Krotkoff) & gônâ ܓܘܢܐ (Maclean), W Arm kuyn/ E Arm guyn գույն [K/JB3/IFb/ZF3]

gon II گۆن *m.* **(-ê;).** being in heat, rut, mating season *(for animals)*: **•Çaxa *gonê* pez *tê*, nêrî û berana berdidin nav** (GF) When the sheep *are rutting*, they let the billy goats and rams in ***•wextê gonê*** **pisîkan** (Frq) *mating season* for cats; **-gon xwarina pisîka** (Qzl/Qmş) mating time of cats. {also: guhn (GF-2); **guhnêr**} [Frq/Qzl/Qmş/A/GF/FJ]

gonc گۆنج *m.* **().** 1) tree stump; 2) root (OK/JB3). {syn: gilare; qurm} [JB3/IFb/OK/ZF3]

goncal گۆنجال *f.* **(-a;-ê).** pit, ditch, hole: **•Çel keleş agir kirîye, di *goncalekê* de** (L) 40 brigands made a fire in *a ditch* **•Di *goncala* xwe de xwe vedişêre** (SW1, 55) He hides in his *ditch*. {also: gonçal (K); koncal (RZ/CS)} {syn: cew; çal II; k'olge; k'ort II} [L/IFb/ZF/FS//K//RZ/CS] <k'olge>

gonçal گۆنچال (K) = pit, ditch. See **goncal**.

gopal گۆپال *m.* **(-ê;).** stick, club, cudgel, staff: **•Çonko xudanê kerî jî weto xiyal dikir ko her do hewalêt wî dê harî wî ken, nedizanî ko řezewanî her do lêbandine, dest da *gopalê* xo, hat e řezewanî** (SK 8:80) Since the owner of the donkey thought that his two companions would help him, not knowing that the gardener had deceived them, he reached for his *staff* and came at the gardener. {also: kopal (K-2); [koupal کوپال/ gopāl گوپال] (JJ); <gopal> گوپال (HH)} {syn: ço; çogan; çomax̂; kevezan; metreq; şiv[ik]} [K/A/IFb/B/JJ/HH/SK/GF]

gopk گـــۆپـــك *m./f.(RZ)* **(-ê/-a;).** 1) treetop; 2) mountaintop, summit, peak: **-gupika çiyê** (RZ) do. {also: gupik II (GF/RZ); gupk (Dh-2); **kop**; <gopik> گۆپك (Hej)} {syn: gaz û bêlan; ĥeç'; kop I; k'umik; kumt} [Dh//Hej//GF/RZ] See also **kop I**.

gor̄ I گـــــۆڕ *f./m.(JB1-A/Hk/Zeb)* **(-a/;-ê/).** 1) {syn: mex̂ber; mezel [3]; qebr; t'irb} grave, tomb; *derisive term for a grave* (B): **•Wellah, ezê di *gora* bavê çwîk nim!** (L) By God, I'll defile the *grave of* the sparrow's father *[curse]* **•Hêzên kolonyalîst dixwazin gelê me zêndî *bikine gorê*** (Ber) The colonialist forces want *to bury* our people alive; 2) stone placed under neck of corpse in grave (Msr). {also: gorn (Epl/IFb-2/GF-2); [gour] گور (JJ); <gor> گور (HH)} Cf. P gūr گور; Sor gor̄ گـۆڕ ; Za gor/gorn/gorr *m.* (Mal); Hau gûr [L/F/K/A/JB3/IFb/B/JJ/HH/JB1-A/GF/TF/OK/Msr//Epl] <gorbigor; gor̄istan>

gor̄ II گـــۆڕ *prep.* according to: **•*Gora* 'edetê berê** (K) *according to* custom; **-bi gor** (K)/**li gora** (DM/BX/K/JB3) do.: **•*li gora* vê kitêbê** (BX) *according to* this book **•*li gora* min** = *according to* me **•*li goreyî* xwe** (BX) *according to* one's own point of view; **-gor̄a *fk-ê* kirin** (K) to obey, heed s.o. {syn: lê guh dan (BX)}: **•Darbir̄ *gur̄a* wî *nekir*** (Dz) The woodcutter *paid no attention to* him/*did not heed* him. {also: gora... ; goreyî... ; gur̄ IV (Dz); [goura] گورا (JJ)} < T göre [BX/K/JB3/IFb/JJ]

gora گۆرا = according to. See **gor̄ II**.

gorange گـــۆرانـــگـــه *f.* **(-ya;).** 1) {syn: daristan; dehl; mêşe; r̄êl} grove of trees, woods: **•Lewra Elî, şevan ji malê derdiket û xwe dihavête *gorangeyên* xurmeyan** (GL, 14) Therefore Ali would leave the house at night and leap into the date *groves* **•Min dan e te spîndar o çinar o gûz o her darekî bilind o ĥelû di-naw *gorange* w r̄ezanda heye** (SK 1:4) I have given you the poplars and planes and walnut trees and every high and smooth tree there is in *woods* and orchards; 2) reed bed, rocky ground in which reeds [qeram] grow (GF). {also: gorangeh (GF/FS)} [GL/SK//GF/FS]

gorangeh گـــۆرانـــگـــه‌ه (GF/FS) = grove; reed bed. See **gorange**.

Goranî گـــۆرانـــی *adj. & f.* Gorani or Gurani, one of the Iranian languages of Eastern Kurdistan: "The term 'Gurani' or 'Gorani' is used to denote a number of different phenomena. It is used as a collective term for a group of dialects spoken in the Hawrāmān and Gurān regions; it is in this sense that Joyce [Blau] used the term in her publication 'Gourani et Zaza' [in R. Schmitt (ed.) *Compendium Linguarum Iranicarum.* (Wiesbaden: Reichert Verlag, 1989)]. When used in this way, however, 'Gurani' comprises two groups of living dialects *viz.* those of Hawrāmān and Gurān, which show marked differences from one another. ... Besides those 'natural', spoken forms of 'Gurani', the term is also used for another form of speech, which is used for literary purposes, and which is often described as a *koinè*. ... It is the contention of the present authors that a fundamental difference between *koinès* and literary Gurani is that the latter never functioned as a spoken language ..., but was exclusively a literary idiom intended to be intelligible to speakers of a range of 'Zagrosian' languages." [from: Philip G. Kreyenbroek & Behrooz Chamanara. "Literary Gurāni: Koinè or Continuum" in: *Joyce Blau: L'éternelle chez les kurdes* (Paris: Institut Kurde de Paris, 2013), p. 151-152]. Gorani songs are so beloved among the Kurds that the Sorani word for 'song' is ***goranî***. [IFb/Wkt/FD] <Hewramî>

gor̄bigor̄ گـــۆڕبـــگـــۆڕ/**gor̄ bi gor̄** گـــۆڕ بـ گـــۆڕ [K] *adj.* damned, cursed, accursed: **•Di dema Şahê *gorbigor* da** (Ber) During the time of the *accursed* Shah. < gor̄ bi gor̄ = 'grave in grave' [Ber/K]

gord گۆرد (Slm) = Christian graveyard. See **gort I**.

gor•e گـــــۆره *f.* **(•a/goreya; •ê).** sock(s), stocking(s): **•Paşa tê-geşt, siwik r̄a-bo, negeşt sola xo di pê ket, *bi goran* der-kewt** (SK 24:224) The Pasha understood, got up quietly and, not managing to put on his shoes, escaped *in his stockings*. {also: [gouré] گوره (JJ); <gore> گوره (HH)} {syn: kurik (IF)} Cf. P jūrāb جـــوراب -->T çorap --> Egyptian Ar šarāb شـــراب, Syrian Ar jōrab جـــورب; Sor gorewî گـــۆره‌وی/gorwa گـــۆروا [Sinneh]; Hau gorewe *m.* (M4) [F/K/A/JB3/IFb/B/JJ/HH/SK/GF/TF]

goreyî گۆره‌یی = according to. See **gor̄ II**.

gor̄istan گـــۆڕســـتـــان/**goristan** گـــۆرســـتـــان [A/IFb/GF] *f.* **(-a;-ê).** graveyard, cemetery: **•Li *goristana* Mehmeqiya defin bûye** (Nbh 132:12) He was buried in the Mehmeqiya *cemetery*. {also: gornistan (IFb-2/GF-2); [gouristan] گـــورســـتـــان (JJ)} {syn: qebristan} Cf. P gūrestān گـــورســـتـــان;

Sor gořistan گۆڕستان [Epl/A/IFb/GF//K//JJ] <goř I; gort I; meẍber>

gorî گۆری *f.* **(-ya;-yê).** sacrifice: •[**Ez dê agirî berdime keprê da bibit *gorî***] (PS-II) I will set the hut on fire, so that it may be *a sacrifice*]; **-Ez gorî** (IFb)/**Ez gorî te me** (GF) May I be sacrificed in your stead; **-gorî bûn** (B/K/IFb) to be sacrificed; **-gorî kirin** (B/K/IFb) to sacrifice. {also: [gouri] گوری (JJ)} {syn: cangorî; ḧeyran; qurban} <gorîn, variant of guhartin = 'to (ex)change', the idea being that a sacrifice is stg. taken in place of, or in exchange for, stg. else, cf. NA xlapa ܚܠܦܐ = 'sacrifice' < √x-l-p = 'to (ex)change' [PS-II/K/A/IFb/B/JJ/GF]

gorîn گۆرین (IF) = to (ex)change. See **guhartin**.

gorn گۆرن (Epl/IFb/GF) = grave. See **gor̄ I**.

gořnebaş گۆڕنەباش *m.* **().** 1) an animal resembling a hyena which allegedly enters graves and eats the corpses' bodies (HH); creature in Kurdish folklore which eats the flesh of corpses: *one hand is a claw [T pençe], the other a hammer, one foot is a pickaxe [T kazma], the other a shovel [T kürek]* (Wn); graverobber (IF): •**Bes e Seddam / ma qey hûn *gornebaşin*? / Tîyê xûnêne / birçîyê tarm û laşin** (Wn) Enough Saddam [Hussein] / are you *corpse-eating monsters*? / Thirsty for blood / hungry for cadavers and carrion? [poem learned in Van in 1988, after chemical bombs were dropped on Halabja in Iraq]; 2) {syn: k'eftař} hyena. {also: <gurnebaş> گرنباش (HH)} <gor̄ = 'grave' + Ar nabbāš نبّاش = 'excavator; grave robber'; Cf. Sor gořhełkene گۆڕهەڵکەنە = 'hyena, badger' < gořhełken گۆڕهەڵکەن = 'gravedigger' [Wn/K/IF/ZF3//HH] <k'eftař>

gořnepişk گۆڕنەپشك (FS) = mythical creature. See **gořnep[']işîk**.

gořnep[']işîk گۆڕنەپشیك *f.* **(;-ê).** vampire; terrifying creature resembling a cat, appearing in legends and folktales, whose existence is believed in by the folk (DS, v. 6: Erciş, Van) [gornapişik or goreşen]: •**Eva *gořnep'iştek* bûye, ku ew şehera gişk xarîye** (HCK-5, #8, 55) This was a *gornepisht*, which ate up that entire city. {also: gořnepişk (FS); gořnep'işt (HCK)} [K/B//FS//DS//HCK]

gořnep'işt گۆڕنەپشت (HCK) = mythical creature. See **gořnep[']işîk**.

gornistan گـۆڕنـسـتـان (IFb/GF) = graveyard. See **gořistan**.

gort I گـۆرت *m./f.(FS)* **(-ê/-a;).** graveyard, cemetery (term used by Muslims in speaking of Christians): **-gorta fela** (FS) Christian grave[yard]. {also: gord (Slm)} [QtrE/Urm/FS//Slm] <girêl; goristan>

gort II گـۆرت *adj.* unplowed, virgin (land): •**Di dema ajotina cot de, li erdê *kort*/beyar heşt ga bi kotan ve têne girê dan** (Nbh 124:32) When driving plowing teams, for unplowed land eight oxen are tied to the plow •***Gort*: Erdê tew nehatî cot kirin, yan jî cîhê cara yekemîn tê cot kirin. Ji bo vê têgînê gelek navên din jî tên bikaranîn, wek: "Bûr, bor, qiramî, xam"** (CCG, 17) *Gort*: Earth which has not yet been plowed, is being plowed for the first time. For this concept many other names are also used, such as "*Bûr, bor, qiramî, xam*". {also: kort I (Nbh/FS)} [CCG//Nbh/FS] <beyar; xozan>

gosartme گـۆسـارتـمـە (IFb) = marvel; tragedy; scandal. See **gosirmet**.

gosirmat گۆسِرمـات (K/CS) = marvel; tragedy; scandal. See **gosirmet**.

gosirmet گـۆسِـرمـەت *f.* **(;-ê).** 1) {syn: 'ecêb} strange thing, marvel: •**De hela ji xwe re li *gosirmetan* binêre, lo!** (E.Karahan: Çargurçik, nefel.com, 5/2007) Take a look at these *marvels*! [=Will wonders never cease?] •**Li vê *gosirmetê* binêre law!** (SBx, 18) Take a look at this *marvel*, boy!; 2) {syn: bela; boblat; qeda; siqûmat; şetele; t'ifaq} tragedy, disaster, catastrophe, calamity; 3) {syn: fehêt; sosret; şermezarî} scandal, shameful incident: •**Kanê bizina kol? Te îro li kuderê çêrandine? De qeyê ne *gosirmet* e ku gur ketibin nava pêz?** (Ardû, 115) Where is the hornless goat? Where did you take them to pasture today? Isn't it *scandalous* that the wolves attack the sheep?; 4) [*adj.*] strange, amazing (K/CS); funny (K/CS); stupid (K); scandalous, disgraceful [rısva, gülünç duruma düşmüş, soytarı (IFb)] (K/CS/IFb). {also: gosartme (IFb); gosirmat (K/CS)} Cf. T görsetme = gösterme = to show, showing [Ardû/Karahan/SBx/Wkt//K/CS//IFb]

goş•e گـۆشـە *m.(K/B)/f.(JB3/IF)* **(•ê/•eya;).** corner, angle: •**Sîabend bi *goşê* dezmalê girt** (IS-#88) Siyabend grabbed hold of *the corner of* the handkerchief. {also: [gouché گـوشـه/ gouj گـوژ/ kouché كـوشـه] (JJ); <goşe> گـۆشـه (HH)} {syn: k'unc; kujî; qorzî; qilçik; qulç} Cf. P gūše گـوشـه --> T köşe [EP-7/K/A/JB3/IF/B/JJ/HH]

goşt گـۆشـت *m.* **(-ê;-î).** meat, flesh: **•Tu *goştê* me p'ar bike** (Dz) You divide up our *meat*!; **-goştê beraz/ ~ xinzîr** (B) pork; **-goştê braştî** (JB3) roast meat; **-goştê ĥeywan** (Bw) beef; **-goştê kelandî** (JB3) boiled meat; **-goştê kizirandî/sorkirî** (JB3) grilled meat; **-goştê nerm** (Dz) soft meat; **-goştê qelî** (JB3) fried meat. {also: [goucht] گـوشـت (JJ); <goşt> گـوشـت (HH)} Cf. P gušt گـوشـت; Sor goşt گوشت; Za goşt *m.* (Todd); Hau goşt *m.* (M4) [F/K/A/JB3/IFb/B/JJ/HH/JB1-S/SK/GF/TF/OK]

goştberxik گـۆشـتـبـەرخـك (GF/FS) = edible plant. See **goştberxk**.

goştberxk گۆشتبەرخك *m./f.(FS)* **(-ê/;).** an edible plant, which is boiled and eaten (Bw); agaric, bot. *Agaricus campestris* (FS); sheep's sorrel (?) [Sor gwê berxołe گـوێ بـەرخـۆڵـە] (Hej). {also: goştberxik (GF/FS); <goştberxok> گۆشتبەرخۆك (Hej)} [Bw//GF//Hej]

goştfiroş گـۆشـتـفـرۆش *m.* **().** butcher, meat seller: **•Baasîyê me li serê kuçê sekinî û bi desta dikaneke *goştfiroş* nîşanî me da** (LC, 47) Our Baathist stood at the end of the street and with his hand pointed out a *butcher*[shop] to us. Sor goştfiroş گۆشتفرۆش [LC/K/IFb/B/GF]

gotar گـۆتـار *f.* **(-a;-ê).** 1) lecture, speech; sermon; 2) {syn: bend I[2]; nivîs[[ar]} {also: gûtar (A)} article; report (K/A): **•Rojnama "Rîya Teze" bi *gotara* rojnamevanê xwe Prîskê [M]hoyî li ser helbestvan Casimê Celîl deng kir. Em li jêr wê *gotarê* bi tîpên Latînî raberê xwendevanên xwe dikin** (Ber) The newspaper R.T. (New Path), in *a report* by its journalist P.[M]. spoke of the poet Jasim Jelil. Below we offer to our readers that *report* in Latin script. Sor wutar ووتـــــــــار = 'statement, speech; article' [Ber/K/A/JB3/IF/GF/OK] <[2] we'z>

gotegot گۆتەگۆت (IFb/GF) = rumor. See **gotgotk**.

gotgot گۆتگۆت (IFb) = rumor. See **gotgotk**.

gotgotk گـۆتـگـۆتـك *f.* **(-a;).** rumor, gossip: **•*Gotegot* mala merîya xirab dike** (GF) *Gossip* ruins people [lit. 'ruin people's home']. {also: gotegot (IFb/GF); gotgot (IFb-2)} {syn: galegûrt; galigal; kurt û pist; paşgotinî} [Zeb/Dh/BH//IFb/GF]

gotin گـۆتِـن *vt.* **(-bêj-/-bê-/-vêj-[Ba]/-vê-/-wê-[Ad]/ -wegî-** [JB1-S]/**[d]êj-** [MK2]; *subj.* **[bi]bêjim, [bi]bêjî,** etc.). 1) to say, tell: **•Min *got* ê** = I *told* him/her **•*Dibê*** (Ba/L)/***Divê* = *Dibêje*** = He/she *says* **•*Dibên*** (Ba)/***Divên* = *Dibêjin*** = They *say* **•Qurba, ez teȓa *divêm* dara mebiȓ** (Dz) My dear fellow, I'*m telling* you not to cut down the trees [lit. 'I tell you, don't cut the trees']; **-teyê bigota** (Z-1) nearly, almost, virtually [lit. 'you would have said']: **•Bor, *teyê bigota*, difiȓe** (Z-1) The horse *almost* flew; 2) [*f.* **(-a;-ê).**] word; speech, words: **•*Gotina* "Ez nizanim" li cem tine bû** (DBgb, 13) *The words* "I don't know" didn't exist for her **•*Gotinêd* te hev din nagrin** (Wlt) *Your words* don't bear each other out **•Ji pêncî carî bêhtir *gotina* "mist" di şûna *gotina* "mizdanê " de, bi çewtî hatiye bikaranîn** (AW73C2) More than 50 times *the word* "mist" was incorrectly used instead of *the word* "mizdan" **•Mirin; çi *gotineke* ne xweş e, sar û tahl e** (LC, 8) Death, what *an* unpleasant *word*, cold and bitter; **-gotina pêşîyan** (K) proverb {syn: met'elok}. {also: [goutin] گــوتــيــن (JJ); <gotin گـوتـن (dibêje) (دبــيــژه)> (HH)} **gotin**: perhaps < [Pok. 2. u̯ap-/ŭp- 1112.] 'to call, cry out' {*the following from Pok. have no Indo-Iranian examples:* [Pok. u̯āb- 1109.] 'to call, cry out, scream' & [Pok. 1. u̯ap- 1112.] 'to chatter, prattle'}: O P pres. stem gauba- = 'to say' (Kent); Sgd γwβ & Khwarezmian γwβ/γw = 'to praise'; Sassanid Pahl gōwēt = 'he says' (Kent); P goftan گفتن (-gū-) (گو); Sor gutin گوتِن/gotin گۆتِن (Arb)/ wutin ووتِـن/kutin كـوتِـن (Muk) (*suppletive present stems:* -łê-/eyj- [Sinne]); **bêj-**: [Pok. u̯ek[u̯]- 1135.] 'to speak': Skt √vac [III. vívakti] = 'to speak, say, tell'; O Ir *vak- (Tsb 41): Av vak- (*pres.* *vāčya-) = 'to say'; Sgd *pres. stem* w'β [wāv] *past stem* w'γt [wāγd] = 'to say'; Parthian *pres. stem* w'c [wāž] *past stem* w'xt [wāxt] (Boyce); Sor *present stem* **eyj-** [Sinneh] of **wutin** (elsewhere:-łê-); SoK üš-, uš-, üj-, iš-, ij-, ıš-/wıt-, vıt- (Fat 368); Za vanã [vatiş] (Todd)/vajenã; Hau watey (waç-) *vt.* (M4); cf. also Lat vox, vocis *f.* = 'voice' & vocare = 'to call' [F/K/A/JB3/IFb/B/JJ/HH/SK/JB1-A&S/GF/TF/OK] <p'eyiv>

gotî گۆتی *pp.* 1) said, told; **-rastî gotî** (K)/**ya rastî gotî** (K)/**bi rastî gotî** (AX) if truth be told, to tell you the truth; 2) supposed to, obliged to (B): **•*Gotî* em we'dêda xebata xwe biqedînin** (B) *We are supposed to* finished our work on time. [AX/K/B]

gov گۆڤ (A/HH/TF/OK) = sty, pen. See **gom I**.

govar گۆڤار (FS) = journal. See **kovar**.

govek گـۆڤـەك *f.* **(;-ê).** 1) {syn: geȓ II} circle, sphere, ball; orbit; **-govekêd 'ezmîne** (EP-7) heavenly vault, the heavens, the firmament [Cf. P čarx-i gerdān چـــرخ گـــردان]; 2) arena *(lit. & fig.)*; 3) radius; 4) volume, bulk, size; 5) generation. [EP-7/K/B]

govend گۆڤەند *f.* **(-a;-ê).** 1) folkdance, line dance {Cf. T halay}; •There is great variety in Kurdish dances, some of which are designated by the name of the region from which they come (Botanî, Derikî, Amûdî, etc.), while others may be called by the form of movements to be danced. The most widespread dance is *govend*, a round in which men and women, arms interlaced, perform quite complicated short steps, with very rhythmical balancing and changin of partners. There are dozens of variants, which include the Sêgavî or Sêpê[y]î (3 steps), the Çarpê[y]î (4 steps), the Giranî (slow round), the Xirfanî (langorous round), the Tesyok also called Milane, in which the partners dance shoulder to shoulder (www.institutkurde.org): **•Qora *govendê* tê û diçe** (AB) The *dance* line comes and goes (=goes forward and back); **-k'etin govendê** (JB3/IF) to join the dance. {also: [gouwend] گوڤند (JJ)} Cf. Arm gund գունդ /gunt գունտ = 'orb, sphere, globe; regiment' (<Av gunda & Pahl gund); = Sor hełpeřkê هـەڵـپـەڕکـێ [AB/F/K/A/JB3/IF/B/JJ/JB1-S] <govendgêr; řeqisîn; sema; sergovend; *names of dances*: Bablekan; Sêgavî; Şêxanî; Yarxişte>

govendgêr گـۆڤـەنـدگـێـر *m.&f.* **().** dancer, skilled folkdancer: **•Gelek dengbêj, stranvan, *govengêr*** [sic]**, çîrokbêj, mitrib, sazbend, bilûrvan û hunermend** (M.Uzun. Roja Evd. Zeyn., 147) Many bards, singers, *dancers*, storytellers, performers, musicians, flute players and artists. {also: govendker (A); govendvan (GF)} [Uzun/IFb//A//GF] <govend>

govendker گـــۆڤـــەنــــدكـــەر (A) = folkdancer. See **govendgêr**.

govendvan گـــۆڤـــەنـــدڤـــان (GF) = folkdancer. See **govendgêr**.

goyîj گۆییژ (K[s]/IFb) = hawthorn. See **gîjok**.

gozane گـۆزانـە *f.* **().** largest type of grape, lackluster in appearance (Msr); type of grape with large, round pits (HH). {also: gozene (ZF3); kozane (IF); <kozane> كوزانه (HH)} [Msr//ZF3//IF/HH] <tirî>

gozene گۆزەنە (ZF3) = type of grape. See **gozane**.

gozing گۆزِنگ (A) = ankle. See **gûzek**.

grev گـــــــــــرەڤ *f.* **(-a;-ê).** (workers') strike; **-greva birçîbûnê** (Wlt) hunger strike: **•Li girtîgehên Çanakkale ... yê zêdeyî 100 girtiyên siyasî bi mebesta protest[o]kirina şert û pestên îdareyê ketin *greva birçîbûnê*** (Wlt 2:59, 5) In the prisons of Çanakkale [et al.] more than 100 political prisoners held *a hunger strike* with the aim of protesting the [bad] conditions and oppression of [=at the hands of] the authorities. {also: girev (A/IFb-2); grêv (GF/IFb)} T g[ı]rev <Fr grève [(neol)Wlt//A//GF/IFb]

grêv گرێڤ (GF/IFb) = strike. See **grev**.

grûb گرووب *f.* **(-a;-ê).** group: **•Hûn ji kerema xwe re dikarin ji me re bibêjin, ka ev *grûb* kengê û çima hat damezrandin?** (Wlt 1:37, 16) Would you be so good as to tell us, when and why was this *group* established? {syn: biř I[3]; cêrge; k'om II} < T grup <Eng group & Fr groupe (m.) [(neol)Wlt/IFb] <cima'et; civat>

grûzî گرووزی (LC) = shudder, quiver. See **girîzok**.

gudrêj گودرێژ = donkey. See **guhdirêj**.

guh گـــوه *m.* **(-ê;-î).** ear: **•Vî *guhî* dixe, *guhê* dinêřa derdixe** (XF) In one *ear* and out the other; **-guh lê dan/~ kirin** = to listen to: **•Tu *li* min *guh nadî*/*nakî*** = You're *not listening to* me **•Min *guh dikir*** = I *was listening*; **-guh lê bûn** (Bw) to hear {syn: bihîstin; seh kirin}: **•Mi şnîka [=ji nû⁺ka] *guh lê bû*** (Bw) I'm hearing it for the first time/I'*ve* never *heard (of) it* before [lit. 'I have heard it as new']; **-lê guh dan** (BX) to obey {syn: gořa ... kirin}: **•Heke tu *li* min *guh nadî*, ezê li te xim** (BX) If you *don't obey* me, I'll beat you. {also: [gouh] گـوه (JJ); <guh> گه (HH)} {syn: keřik I[2] (Bg)} [Pok. ghous- 454.] 'to sound; to hear, listen' *(only Indo-Iranian)*: Skt ghoṣa- *m.* = 'noise, sound'; O Ir *gauša- (Ras, p.134): Av gaoša-/gāuš.a- *m.* = 'ear' & √gaoš [gūša- (*pres.* gūš-)] = 'to hear'; O P gauša- *m.* (Kent); Mid P gōš (M3); P gūš گـــوش = 'ear' & niyōšīdan نـیـۆشـیـدن (< ni-goš-īdan) = 'to listen'; Sor gwê [gö] گـوێ; Za goş *m.* (Todd); Hau goş *m.* (M4); cf. also [Pok. 1. keu- 587.] 'to pay attention, watch, observe, see, hear': Germanic *hausyan --> Old Eng hieran --> Eng hear [BX/F/K/A/JB3/IFb/B/JJ/ HH/SK/JB1-A&S/GF/TF/OK] <bihîstin; guhdarî; keřik II; seh>

guhan گـوهـان *m.(B/FS)/f.(K)* **(-ê/; guhên, vî guhanî/).** udder *(of cow)*; teat *(of animal)*: **•Şîr k'ete *gihana*** (J) Milk flows [lit. 'fell'] to *the udders* **•Pêz** [sic] **hat bêrîyê, bi *guhanên* tijî** (AB) The sheep came to the sheepfold, with full *udders*. {also: gan II (IFb-2); gihan II (J); [gouhan] گـــــــو هـــــــان (JJ); <guhan> گـــهـــان (HH)} {syn: çiçik[3]; guhandîr} < O Ir *gau-dāna- (<gau- = 'bovine product' + dāna- = 'container') (also A&L p.85 [V, 4]): Av gaodan- = 'bucket'; Sgd γoδn = 'bucket'; Baluchi gōdān ='udder'; Luri gūn; Laki gön; Pashto γulanja; Sor guwan گـــــووان ='udder'; Za *m.* guwan = 'udder' (Todd) [F/K/A/JB3/IFb/B/JJ/HH/GF/TF/OK] <çêlek = mange; şîr>

guhandîn گوهاندين (FS) = udder. See **guhandîr**.

guhandîr گـوهـانـديـر *f.* **(-a;).** udder *(of cow)*. {also: guhandîn (FS-2); gandîl (IFb)} {syn: çiçik[3]; guhan} Sor guwandên گووانديَن [K/FS//IFb] <çêlek = mange; şîr I>

guhar گوهار *m.(Mtk/Qzl)/f.(B)* **(-ê/ ; /-ê).** earring: **•Ew zêřê gerdena xwe û *guharê* xwe jî datîne ser t'aê mêzînê** (Ba) She puts the gold of her necklace and *earrings* onto the pan of the scales; **-guharê guh** = do.: **•*Guharê guhê* te me / xizêma pozê te me** (Mtk) I am *the earring in* your ear / I am the nose ring in your nose. {also: gihar (GF-2); guhark' (JB1-A); guher II (TF); [gouhar] گـوهـار (JJ); <guhar> گـهـار (HH)} Cf. P gūšvāre گوشواره; Sor gware گواره ; ?<fusion of a) P gōhar گـوهـر = 'jewel' + b) guh = 'ear' [Ba/F/K/A/JB3/IFb/B/JJ/HH/SK/GF/OK/Mtk/Qzl//JB1-A//TF] <guh>

guhark' گوهارك (JB1-A) = earring. See **guhar**.

guhartin گـــوهـــارتِـــن *vt.* **(-guhêr-).** to change *(vt.)*, exchange, switch: **•Ê ku ez anîme, wê min jî bivin, were em morê xwe li hev *biguhêrin*** (EP-7) Those who brought me will also take me away; come, let us *exchange* signet rings with each other. {also: gorîn (IF-2); guhastin (B); guherandin (A); guherîn (GF); guhêrîn (EP-7); guhorîn (-guhor-) (SK); [gouhourin] گـهـورين (JJ); <guherîn گهرين (diguherî) (دگهرى)> (HH)} <O Ir *vī-vart-: **vart-** < [Pok 3. u̯er- 1152.] 'to turn, bend': Av vĭ- + varət- (Tsb 72); Sor goȓîn گۆڕين = 'to change (vt.)' & goȓan گـــۆڕان = 'to change (vi.)' [BX/K/JB3/IF//B//EP-7//HH/GF//A//JJ/SK] See also **guhastin**.

guharto گوهارتو *f.* **(-ya;-yê).** 1) {syn: şax [6]; şov [6]} version (DM): **•Çend Ermenîyên kurdîzan jî 3 *gohartoyên* Memê Alan bi kurdî çap kirine** (DM) Some Kurdish-speaking Armenians printed three *versions* of Memê Alan in Kurdish; 2) variation; variant (JB3); 3) variety (JB3/IF). {also: goharto (DM)} [(neol)SW/JB3/IF/ZF3]

guhastin گـوهـاسـتِـن *vt.* **(-guhêz-).** 1) to change *(vt.)*, exchange, switch: **-berê xwe [jê] guhastin** (XF) to turn away from; to turn one's back on; to break or discontinue a relationship; to renounce, disavow, give up; to stop paying attention to, to express indifference toward; to stop loving or respecting; **-cî guhastin** (K) to change or switch places: **•Evê lîstikê gere tu û Memêva *cîyê xwe biguhêzin*** (Z-1) For this game, you and M. must *change places* **•Her lîstikekê gere we *cîyê xwe biguhasta*, lê we usa nekir** (Z-1) You should *have changed places* for every game, but you didn't; **-k'incê xwe guhastin** = to change one's clothes; to disguise o.s.; 2) to transfer, transport (IF/HH/SK). See **veguhastin**; 3) to bring the bride from her father's house to the groom's home, to marry off *(a girl)*: **•Sibeha *guhastina bûkê* xelkê gund û hemî xwendî li mala dawetê digehine yek** (Dilbirîn. "Kar û barên jin anînê li cem Êzidîyên Şingalê," Laliş 12:4) On the morning of *bringing the bride* the people of the village and all those invited meet at the home of the wedding party. {also: gohastin (-gohêz-) (JB1-S); guhaztin (JB3/IF); guhêstin (A/IF-2); [gouhastin] گهاستين (JJ); <guhastin گهاستن (diguhêze) (دگـهـيـزه)> (HH)} Sor gwastin•ewe گواستنەوە = 'to transfer' [Z-1/J/F/K/JJ/B/M-Zx//JB1-S//JB3/IF//A] <veguhastin> See also **guhartin**.

guhaztin گوهازتن (JB3/IF) = to change. See **guhastin**.

guhdar گـــوهـــدار *m.&f.* 1) listener, one who listens, auditor (K/A/JB3/IF); *[pl.]* audience: **•Ez *guhdarim*** (K) I'*m listening*; 2) *[adj.]* obedient (K). {also: [gouh-dir گـوهـدر/ghohe-dar گـوهـدار] (JJ)} {guhdarî; guhdartî} [K/A/JB3/IF/JJ/B/JB1-A/GF/TF/OK]

guhdarî گـــوهـــدارى *f.* **(-ya;-yê).** 1) (act of) listening: **-guhdarî kirin** = to listen to; to pay attention {syn: guh kirin/dan; seh kirin}; 2) attention (JJ). {also: guhdartî (B-2); gûdarî (Bg); [gouhdari] گـوهـدارى (JJ)} [K/A/JB3/IFb/B/JJ/OK] <bihîstin; goȓ II; guh>

guhdartî گـــوهـــدارتـــى (B) = listening; attention. See **guhdarî**.

guhdirêj گـوهـدرێـژ *m.* **(-ê;).** donkey, ass; *polite word for donkey used in the presence of elders and superiors* (B). {also: gudrêj; guhdrêj; [gouh-dirij] گـوهـدريژ (JJ)} {syn: k'er I} < guh = 'ear' + dirêj = 'long' [J/K/JJ/B]

guhdrêj گوهدرێژ = donkey. See **guhdirêj**.

guher I گوهەر (A/IF/JJ/HH) = open-air pen for sheep. See **guhêr̄** II.

guher II گوهەر (TF) = earring. See **guhar**.

guherandin گـوهـەرانـدِن (A) = to (ex)change. See **guhartin**.

guherîn گـوهـەریـن (HH/GF) = to (ex)change. See **guhartin**.

guhêr I گوهێر (FS) = mating season. See **guhnêr**[1].

guhêr̄ II گـوهـێـڕ *f.* **(-a;-ê).** open-air pen or enclosure *for sheep and goats*; stopping place or resting place for sheep and the like: **-guhêr̄ kirin** (K) to round up *(sheep and goats, to put them in a* ***guhêr̄*** *to rest)*: **•Lazekî şûnda me pez av da, *guhêr̄ kir*, em gişk berevî ser hev bûn, me çend mî dotin, dest bi xwarinê kir** (Ba2-2, 206) A moment later we watered the sheep, we *rounded them up*, we all gathered together, milked a few ewes, [and] began to eat. {also: guher I (A/IF); [gouher] گـوهـر (JJ); <guher> گـهـر (HH)} {syn: kotan I; k'oz; mexel} K>T güher [Ahlat -Bitlis] (DS, v.6, p.2216) = 'place in the mountains for sheep to rest, pen' [Ba2/K/B/GF//A/IF/JJ/HH] <afir̄; axil; axur; bêrî I; dolge; gom I; k'ox; lêf; mexel>

guhêrîn گـوهـێـریـن (EP-7) = to (ex)change. See **guhartin**.

guhêstin گوهێستِن (A/IF) = to change. See **guhastin**.

guhê şeyṯanan گـوهـێ شـەیـطـانـان (FS) = snail. See **guhşeytan**.

guhgiran گـوهـگِـران *adj.* deaf, hard of hearing. {syn: ker̄ II} [K/ZF3/BF]

guhişandin گـوهـِشـانـدِن *vt.* **(-guhişîn-).** to surprise, amaze, astound, astonish: **•Xemsariya wan *ez guhişandim*** (Hk) Their indifference *surprised me.* {also: guhoşandin (SS-2)} {syn: hingaftin [3]} [Hk/SS/BF/FS/ZF3]

guhişîn گـوهـِشـیـن *vi.* **(-guhiş-).** to be surprised, amazed, astounded, astonished; to be bewildered, confused (CS): **•Min bawer nedikir ku Kurd li himberî zimanê xwe hind xemsar bin. Ez bi xemsariya wan *guhişîm*** (Hk) I didn't believe that the kurds were so indifferent to their own language. I *was shocked* by their indifference. {syn: 'ecêbmayî man; hicmetî bûn; ḧeyrîn; met'elmayî bûn} [Hk/CS/BF/ZF3/FS]

guhîj گـوهـیـژ (GF/TF/OK/AA/Hej) = hawthorn. See **gîjok**.

guhkişîn گوهکِشین = children's game. See **guhkişînk**.

guhkişînk گـوهـکِـشـیـنـك *f.* **( ).** a game played with knucklebones [**k'ap II**] [lit. 'pulling each other's ears']. {also: guhkişîn (ZF3)} [Qzl//ZF3] <k'ap II>

guhn گوهن (GF) = being in heat. See **gon II**.

guhnelî (BF) = mating season. See **guhnêr**[1].

guhnevîl گـوهـنـەڤـیـل (FS) = mating season. See **guhnêr**[1].

guhnêl گـوهـنـێـل (HH/Bw/Zx) = mating season; dense flock. See **guhnêr**.

guhnêr گـوهـنـێـر *f.* **(-a;).** 1) mating season of various animals; rut, heat, estrus: a) of sheep (FJ/GF/A) and mountain goats (IFb/HH); b) {syn: qels II} of fish: **•Dema dibû *guhnêra* masiyan, yên nêr, li pêş, hêkên xwe berdidan, yên mê diketin dû wan** (DBgb, 53) When it was fish *mating season*, the males, in front, dropped their eggs, the females then followed behind them; 2) sex, sexual intercourse, mating; 3) dense flocks (of wolves, etc.) which come out in February (Bw/Zx): ***-guhnêla* gurgî/guhnêla ḧeywanê kûvî** (Bw/Zx) *flocks of* wolves/flocks of wild animals. {also: **gon II**; guhêr I (FS-2); guhnelî (BF); guhnevîl (FS-1); guhnêl (Bw/Zx/FS); guhnêrî (BF-2); gulên (FS-2); gunhêl (Zx-2); gunhîl (Şnx); [ghunéla] گـونلا (JJ-G); <guhnêr گـهـنـیـر/guhnêl گـهنـیل> (HH)} {syn: gon II} [DBgb/A/IFb/FJ/GF/HH//Bw/Zx/FS//JJ-G//BF] <pezk'ûvî; perîn>

guhnêrî (BF) = mating season. See **guhnêr**[1].

guhnîr گـوهـنـیـر *m.* **().** oxbow, the rods tied around the draft animal's neck on a yoke. {also: guhnîrk (GF)} {syn: k'ulabe; samî} [CCG/Flk/AD//GF]

guhnîrk گوهنیرك (GF) = oxbow. See **guhnîr**.

guhorîn گوهۆرین (-guhor-) (SK) = to (ex)change. See **guhartin**.

guhoşandin گوهۆشاندِن (SS) = to surprise, amaze. See **guhişandin**.

guhşeytan گـوهـشـەیـتـان *f./m.(Wkt)* **(/-ê;).** snail, zool. *Helix*: **•Spî ye, ne kesk e, guh bele, ne mişk e; buhara ter e, havîna hişk e [*guhşeytan*]** (L) It's white, not green, it pricks up its ears, but isn't a mouse; in the spring it's wet, in the summer it's dry *[rdl.; ans.:* snail*]*. {also: guhê şeyṯanan (FS)} {syn: hiseynok; şeytanok} [L/K/ZF3/Wkt//FS]

guhûr گوهوور *m.* **(-ê;).** 1) {syn: zibil} garbage, refuse (IF); 2) {syn: sergîn} dung, manure (IF). {also: gihûr (Wkt); giwûr (Wkt-2)} [IF/ZF3//Wkt]

gujeguj گوژەگوژ**/guje-guj** گوژە گوژ [K] *f.* **(-a;-ê).** 1) sound of wind or water during a storm : **•Baranê *gujeguje*** (K) The rain is *pitter-pattering* ***•guje-***

***guja* avê** (GF) *purling, murmuring of* water; **-gujeguj kirin** (K/B) to rage, storm; 2) rumble or humming sound of a motor (B). [EP-4/K/B/GF/ZF3] <ba; baran; şiřîn II>

gul گــــــــول *f.* **(-a;-ê).** 1) {syn: çîçek; kulîlk; mom I} flower: **•Memo, mi du baq *gul* kiřîne, yek sor e, yek zeř e, ĥeyran, ezê wan ĥerdu *gulan* ya sor destê min ê řastîye, ya zeř min ê çepî ye** (MC-1, #153) Memo, I have bought two bouquets of *flowers*, one is red, one is yellow; the red ones are in my right hand, the yellow ones in my left hand; 2) rose: **•Memê gihîşt ser kanîkê, dora kanîyê bi sosin, beybûn, *gul* u riĥana xemilandî bû, Memê peya bû** (FK-eb-1, 268) Mem reached a spring adorned with lilies, camomile, *roses*, and basil. He dismounted. {also: gol (JB1-A); [goul] گــــل (JJ); <gul> گــــل (HH)} < [*wṛd] *root of unknown origin*: Av vareδā- = 'a plant' (Hübsch #927); Pahl vartā/vardā (Horn #927) = 'rose' (>Arm vard վարդ = 'rose'); Southern Tati dialects (all *f.*): Chali, Takestani, Eshtehardi, Xiaraji & Sagz-abadi vela = 'flower' (Yar-Shater); P gol گــل--> T gül; Sor guł گــوڵ; Za vil *f.* (Todd); Hau wilî *f.* (M4); cf. also [*wrod-o-] Gr rhodon ῥόδον/ Sapphic brodon βρόδον [F/K/A/JB3/IFb/B/JJ/HH/SK/GF/TF/OK//JB1-A] <bişkoj [2]; solîn II>

gula berbiroj گــولا بــەربــڕۆژ (IFb) = sunflower. See **gulberroj**.

Gulan گــــــــــولان *f.* **(-a;-ê).** May (month): •**[Heyva *Gulanê*, xweyî řeza bi kul û kovanê]** (BG) The month *of May*, the vintner [vineyard owner] is worried and uneasy *{fearing hailstorms which could ruin the grape harvest} [prv.]* **-meha Gulanê** = do. {also: [goulan] گــلان (JJ); <gulan> گــلان (HH); [goulane] (BG)} *Perhaps originally* ***meha gulan*** *= 'the month of flowers'; corresponds to last part of* Gułan گوڵان/Banemeř بـانــەمــەڕ (P ordī behešt اردی بــهــشــت) [Taurus] *& 1st part of* Cozerdan جــۆزەردان or Cehzeran جــەهــزەران/ Codirew جــۆدِرەو/Baranbiřan بــارانــبِــڕان [/ Bextebaran بەختەباران] (P xurdād خرداد) [Gemini] [K/A/JB3/IFb/B/JJ/HH/GF/TF/OK//BG]

gulaş گــولاش *f.* **(;-ê).** wrestling: **-gulaş girtin** (K/IFb/ B/GF/OK) to wrestle: **•Gundê me da kesekî dil nedikir wîřa *gulaş bigirta*** (Ba2:1, 204) In our village no one would dare *to wrestle* with him. {also: <gulaş> گــــلاش (HH); cf. also [goulech-ghir] گــولــشــگــیــر (JJ) = 'athlete, fighter'} {syn: bimbarekîya desta; pijan I} < T güreş [Ba2/K/IFb/B/ HH/GF/OK/ZF3]

gulavêj گولاڤێژ (FS) = Sirius, Dog Star. See **gelavêj**.

gulbend گــولــبــەنــد *f.* **().** garland, wreath (K): **-gulk û gulbend** (Z-2) do. {syn: gulwaz} [Z-2/K/Wkt]

gulberoj گــــولــــبــــەرۆژ (Bw/ZF3) = sunflower. See **gulberroj**.

gulberroj گولبەڕۆژ/گولبەررۆژ *f.* **(-a;-ê).** sunflower, bot. *Helianthus annuus*: **-tovkêt gulberojê** (Bw) sunflower seeds. {also: gula berbiroj (IFb); gulberoj (Bw/ZF3); gulbiřoj (K); <gulaber-berojkê> گــولابــەربــەرۆژکێ (Hej)} Sor gułebeřoje گوڵەبەڕۆژە [Bw/ZF3//OK//K//IFb//Hej]

gulbiřoj گولبِڕۆژ (K) = sunflower. See **gulberroj**.

gulçîsk گولچیسك (Bw) = kidney. See **gurçik**.

guldan گولدان (K/A/B/GF/OK) = vase. See **guldank**.

guldang گولدانگ (B/TF) = vase. See **guldank**.

guldank گــولــدانــك *f.* **(-a;-ê).** vase: •...**kengî Doktor Sertaç firsend dîtibû û ew *guldanka* tijî gulên hişkkirî kişandibû ber wî wêneyî** (KS, 40) ...when had Dr. Sertaç found the chance to put [lit. pull] that *vase* full of dried roses in front of that picture? {also: guldan (K/A/B/GF/OK-2); guldang (B-2/TF)} {syn: gulwaz[2]} [KS/IFb/OK//K/A/ B/GF//TF]

gulderxûn گــولــدەرخــوون (Wkp) = crown imperial, Fritillaria imperialis. See **gulexîn**.

guldexîn گـولـدەخـیـن (Hk) = crown imperial, Fritillaria imperialis. See **gulexîn**.

gul•e گــولــە *f.* **(•a;•ê).** bullet: **•*Gulleyên* sor û çirsavêj li hewa dilîstin** (Nofa, 94) Red and sparkling *bullets* danced in the air **•Ĥeco pîçek enîya xo ji pişta *binegûzê îna der. Osê der-ĥal celeboka qutebotanîyê kêşa, *gulle* li nîweka her do biroyan kewt, ji patika ser ço der. Ĥeco der-ĥal bê-řoĥ bo** (SK 40:363) Hajo brought his forehead out a little from behind the trunk of the walnut tree. Oso immediately pulled the trigger of his Short Botani and *the bullet* hit him right between the eyebrows and went out at the back of his neck. Hajo immediately dropped lifeless; **-gule kirin** (B) to shoot to death, execute by shooting. {also: gulle (K/SK/GF/FS); gûle (JB1-S); [goulé] گــولــە (JJ)} {syn: berik II} Cf. P golūle گــلــولــە = 'ball, sphere, bullet'--> T gülle = 'cannon ball, shell'; Sor gule گولە [F/IFb/B/JJ/Ba2//K/SK/GF/FS//JB1-S] <ç'ek; sîleĥ; t'ifing; zirêç>

gulebaran گــولــەبــاران *f.* **(-a;-ê).** torrent of bullets, shelling: **-gulebaran kirin** (Wlt/ZF3) to rain down bullets on, shower with bullets, rake, shell {also: gullebarandin (K)}: **•Piştî êrîşa gerîlayan leşkerên qereqolê jî êrîş birin** [sic] **ser gund û xaniyên gund *gulebaran kirin*** [sic] (Wlt 1:41, 3) After the guerrilla attack, the police forces launched an attack on the village, and *showered* the village houses *with bullets*. [Wlt/IFb/ZF3/Wkt//K] <derb; gule; şêlik>

gulexîn گـــولـــەخـــيـــن *f.* **().** crown imperial, imperial fritillary or Kaiser's crown, bot. *Fritillaria imperialis*, a flowering plant of the lily family, native to Anatolia, Iraq, Iran and continuing to the Himalayan foothills (= T ters lale): **•Min *gulexînek* jêkir** (Ç. Özel. Kürtçe dil ve eğitim hakları, 50) I picked *a crown imperial*. {also: gulderxûn (Wkp/ZF3); guldexîn (Hk-2); gulnexûn (Wkp-2)} [Ç. Özel/Hk//Wkp/ZF3]

gulên گولێن (FS) = mating season. See **guhnêr**[1].

gulik گـــولـــك *f.* **(-a;-ê).** 1) little flower (K) [gulik]; ornamental/rose-colored flowers (IF): **-gulk û gulbend** (Z-2) garland, wreath; 2) {also: gulîvank (FS)}{syn: gûfik; r̄îşî I} *[pl.]* fringes, pompons, tassels (K) [gulk]. {also: gulk (K-2/Z-2)} [Z-2/K/IF/ZF3] <gul>

gulî I گـــولـــى *f./m.(JB3)* **(-ya/ ;-yê/).** 1) lock *(of hair)*, curl, ringlet (F/K/JB3/JJ); plait, tress, braid (F/K/A/IF); the hair that hangs at the back of the head (HH): **•*Gulîyê* Zînê yek-yek diqişirîne** (Z-1) He could see each one of Zin's *braids*; 2) {syn: bijî I} mane (of horse): **-gulîya hespî** (Zeb/Dh) do. {also: [gouli] گولى (JJ); <[g]ulî> گلى (HH)} [Z-1/F/K/A/JB3/IF/B/JJ/HH/Mzg] <bisk; kezî; mû; p'or̄ III; t'ûncik>

gulî II گـــولـــى *f./m.(SF)* **(-[y]a/-yê;).** branch: **•Min dan e te spîndar o çinar o gûz o her darekî bilind o ḧelû ... hêlîna xo li-ser *gilîya* wan çê-ke** (SK-I:4) I have given you the poplars and planes and walnut trees and every high and smooth tree ... Build your nest in their *branches* **•Pelên *guliyê* dara çinarê yê ku ew li ser bû, kil bûn** (SF 17) The leaves of the plane tree *branch* he was on trembled. {also: gilî II (SK); [gíli] (JJ-Lx)} {syn: ç'iq[il]; çirpî; şax [1]; ta VI} Za gıl *m.* = 'branch' (Mal) [SK/JJ-Lx//IFb/GF/TF/OK/Mzg] <dar I>

gulî III گولى (GF/FS) = snowflake. See **kulî II**.

gulîfît گوليفيت (Rûdaw) = snowball. See **gulîfîtk**.

gulîfîtk گـوليفيتك *f.* **(-a;).** snowball: **•Pisîkeke piçûk. Spî. *Gulîfîtka* berfê... *Gilofîtika* berfê, wekî ku bikeve nav tasa dimsê** (M.Dicle. Nara, 82) A little kitten. White. *A ball of snow ... A snowball,* as if it had fallen into a bowl of *dims* [grape molasses] **•Zarokan mirovê berfê (peykerê mirov ji berfê) çêkirin û têra xwe bi şadî û kameranî *gulîfît* avêtin hevdû** (Rûdaw 8.1.2015) The children made a snowman and joyfully and successfully threw *snowballs* at each other. {also: gîlofîtik (M.Dicle-2); gulîfît (Rûdaw)} [M.Dicle//Rûdaw] <kulî II>

gulîvank (FS) = tassles, fringes. See **gulik**[2].

gulk گولك (K/Z-2) = little flower. See **gulik**.

gulle گولله (K/SK/GF/FS) = bullet. See **gule**.

gullebarandin گولله‌باراندِن (K) = to shower with bullets. See **gulebaran kirin** under **gulebaran**.

gulm گولم (K/MUm) = steam; breath. See **hilm**.

gulnexûn گـــولـــنـــەخـــوون (Wkp) = crown imperial, Fritillaria imperialis. See **gulexîn**.

gulok گـــولـــۆك *f.* **(-a;-ê).** skein, ball *(of yarn, thread, etc.)*: **•Pîreke k'esîve ku serî binî sê *gulok* dezîê wê hebûne, ew jî dive mişterîê Ûsiv** (Ba3-3, #26) A poor old woman who possessed nothing but three *balls of* thread, she too wanted to buy Joseph; **-guloka t'êla** (F) ball of thread. {also: gilok (A/IFb/GF/Mzg/Krş); glok (GF-2); [ghilouk] گـــلـــوك (JJ)} {syn: girov; peng I} Sor giłołe گلۆلە = 'ball (string, thread, wool, etc.)' [Ba3/F/K/B//A/IFb/GF/Mzg/Krş//JJ] <dezî; masûr>

gulol گولۆل (K/B) = round. See **gilol I**.

gulor گولۆر = round. See **gilol I**.

gulover̄ گولۆڤەڕ (K/F/BK/B) = round. See **girover̄**.

gulover̄î گـــولـــۆڤـــەڕى *f.* **(-ya;-yê).** roundness. {also: gilover̄î (ZF3); gulover̄tî (B)} [K//ZF3//B] <girover̄>

gulover̄tî گولۆڤەڕتى (B) = roundness. See **gulover̄î**.

gulpe-gulp گـولـپـەگـولـپ (K) = throbbing, beating. See **gurpegurp**.

gulpîn گولپين (K) = throbbing, beating. See **gurpîn**.

gulwaz گـــــولـــــواز *m.(Dh)/f.(ZF3)* **(/-a;).** 1) {syn: gulbend} wreath of flowers, garland; 2) {syn: guldank} vase. {also: **gelwaz**} [Dh/OK/ZF3/Wkt/BF]

guman گومان *f.* **(-a;-ê).** 1) {syn: şik} suspicion, doubt: **•*Bi gumana min* tiştek di binda heye** (Z-2) *I suspect* that there is something under it; 2) {syn: r̄aman} thought, idea; 3) {syn: hêvî} hope: **•Darbir̄o, dara mebir̄, *gumana* xwe ji xwedê mebir̄** (Dz) Woodcutter, don't cut down trees, don't cut off your *hope* from God [*prv.*];

-guman[a xwe] ***fk-î/ft-î* anîn** (B) to hope: **•Me jî řazedilîa xwe dida û *gumana xwe danî* wekî ew jî wê řoja dawetê meřa t'evayî şa bin** (Ba2:2, 208) We also agreed and *hoped* that they would celebrate the wedding day with us; **-bê guman**, see **bêguman**. {also: gûman; [gouman] گمان (JJ)} <prefix vi- = 'away, apart' + √mān- = 'to think' ('of disparate minds'): Av vīmanah- = 'doubt' (Horn #932); O P vimāna- (Hübsch #932); Pahl gumān; P gomān گمان; Sor guman گومان = 'doubt, thought' [F/Dz/K/A/JB3/IF/JJ/B]

gumgum گومگوم *m.(K)/f.(B)* **(-ê/ ; /-ê).** 1) carafe, decanter (K); flask, water bottle (K); clay water jug (B); vessel for holding rosewater (IF); water vessel (JJ): **•Leylê rabû, *gumgum* hilda hat ser kanîê, avê, bive** (EP-5, #14) Leyla took her *water jug* and went to the spring, to fetch water; 2) coffee pot (HR-1/JJ). {also: [ghimghim/ goumgoum] گمگم (JJ)} Cf. Ar qumqum قمقم = 'long-necked bottle'; Heb qumqum קומקום = 'tea kettle, coffee pot' [HR-1/K/IF/B/JJ] <cer; kûp>

gumgumatik گومگوماتِك (GShA) = lizard. See **qumqumok**.

gumgumok گومگومۆك (IFb/GF/TF) = lizard. See **qumqumok**.

gum•ik گومِك *f.* **(•ka;).** fingertip: **•Herdu jî, ji sermayê direcifîn, diranên wan direkrikîn, *gûmikên* Zîzê qerisî bûn** (H v. 1, 83 [1932 1:4]) Both of them were shivering from cold, their teeth were chattering, Z.'s *fingertips* had frozen **•Stirîyek çû di *gumka tila wî* řa** (FS) A thorn went into *the tip of his finger*. {also: gomik (SS); gûmik (H/IFb); <gumk گومك/ gûmk گوٗمك> (Hej)} {syn: serê tipla} [H/IFb//K/GF/FS/ZF/Wkt//Hej//SS] <bêç'î II; tilî I>

gumirk گومِرك (Wkt) = customs (tax and office). See **gumrik**.

gumre گومره (B/IFb) = huge. See **gumreh**.

gumreh گومرەه *adj.* 1) {syn: gir I; mezin; qerase I} big, huge, enormous, great; well-fed, well-watered (JJ); 2) powerful, mighty, great *(lit. & fig.)* (K/B): **•Îlahî zivistanê, çaxê ba û suř *gumreh* dibûn** (Ba2) Especially in the wintertime, when the wind and cold were *strong* **•Vira şik û şayîşîêd min *daha gumreh* bûn** (Ba2:2, 205) At this point my worries became [even] *greater*; **-baê gumreh** (B) strong wind. {also: gumre (B-2/IFb-2); [goumreh] گمره (JJ); <gumreh> گمره (HH)} [Ba2/K/IFb/B/JJ/HH/GF/TF]

gumrig گومرگ (Rûdaw) = customs (tax and office). See **gumrik**.

gumrik گومرك *f.* **(-a;-ê).** customs (tax and office) [Fr douane]; customs house: **•Wî *gumrika* pertalên xwe da** (FS) He paid *the customs duty* on his merchandise **•Wî pertalên xwe birin *gumrikê*** (FS) He took his merchandise to *customs*; **-baca gumrigê** (Rûdaw) tariff, tax on imports, customs duty or tax: **•Ev 3 salin Wezareta Çandinî ya Herêma Kurdistanê, ji bo qedexekirina hawirdeya berhemên biyanî, *baca gumrigê* dixe ser fêkiyan jî** (Rûdaw 30.vii.2016) For 3 years, to ban the import of foreign produce, the Ministry of Agriculture of the Kurdistan Region has been imposing *a tariff* [lit. '*customs tax*'] on fruit. {also: gomirk (Wkt-2); gomrik (Wkt-2); gumirk (Wkt); gumrig (Rûdaw); gumrî (K); gumruk (Wkt-2); gumurk (Wkt-2); [goumrouk/ghumrók (G)] گمرك (JJ); <gumrik> گمرك (HH)} < Gr kommerkion κομμέρκιον = 'commerce, business' <Lat commercium: T gümrük; Ar jumruk جمرك [Rûdaw//IFb/HH/ZF3/FS/FD//Wkt//JJ//K]

gumrî گومری (K) = customs (tax and office). See **gumrik**.

gumruk گومروك (Wkt) = customs (tax and office). See **gumrik**.

gumtil گومتِل *m.* **(-ê;-î).** 1) clump, clod, cluster, ball: **•Hirç řa-westa ĥetta mêş li ser-o-çawêt wî bon e *gumtil*** (SK 10:99) The bear waited until there was *a cluster of* flies on his face **•Ra-bon, her yêkî zewîyek kir e xê. Muroek ji wan řojekî ço, sera zewîya kirî e xê bidet, da bizanît ka şîn bîye, şîn nebîye, çizika xê daye, nedaye. Wextê ço, di-naw zewîyê geřya, ji wî serey ço wî serî, çu nedît. Got, "Da *gumtilekî* axê řa-kemewe, belko di-bin *gumtilî*da çizika xo dabît." Wextê *gumtilê* axê řa-kir duroşûşika dûpişkî der-kewt** (SK 19:178) They went away and each one put a field to salt. One of them went one day to visit his field put to salt, to see whether it had sprouted or not. When he went he wandered about the field from this side to that, but saw nothing. He said, "Let me lift *a clod of* earth, perhaps it has sprouted under *the clod*." When he lifted *the clod of* earth the sting of a scorpion appeared; **-gumtilê axê** (Bw) a clod of earth; 2) lump, swelling, tumor (IFb/OK). {also: gutil (TF); <gumtil> گومتل (Hej)} Cf. Sor gundik گوندِك/gunk گونك [=kiło

كلۆ] = 'lump, clod' [Bw/IFb/JB1-A/SK/OK/Hej//TF]

gumurk گومورك (Wkt) = customs (tax and office). See **gumrik**.

gun گـــون *m.* **(-ê;).** testicle(s), 'balls', 'nuts': **•Eger tu qewî sil î, here, awa şar pawêje *gunêt* xo** (SK 36:324) If you are very upset, go and throw cold water on your *testicles* **•Em ne 'erş û kursîyan dibînîn û ne ga û masîyan. Em noke pişta *gunê* xo jî nabînîn** (SK 39:349) We see neither the Dais nor the Throne, nor the Ox and the Fish. We cannot even see behind our own *testicles* now. {also: gundik; gurn (IFb-2); [goun] گن (JJ); <gun گن/gunik گنك> (HH)} {syn: batî; hêlik [1]} Cf. P gond گـنـد = 'testicle'; Sor gun گـون; Hau gun *m.* (M4) [K(s)/A/IFb/JJ/HH/SK/GF/TF] <kîr; ȓitil II>

gunahkar گـونـاهـكـار (JJ/SK) = sinner; guilty. See **gunehk'ar**.

guncandin گـونـجـانـدِن *vt.* **(-guncîn-).** to adapt stg. to, adjust stg. to: **-xwe guncandin** (ZF3) to abide by, comply with, agree with (grammar): **•Divê *xwe* li gorî qanûnê nû *biguncîne*** (ZF3) You must *adjust* according to [i.e., comply with/abide by] the new law. **•Lêkera transitîv ya dema borî, ne wek adetî, *xwe* li gel objekta hevokê *diguncîne*** (nefel.com: N.Hirorî 10.vi.2005) The past tense transitive verb, unusually, *agrees with* the object of the sentence. Sor guncandin گـونـجـانـدِن = 'to make feasible/workable; adapt, adjust to a specified use/ situation' [(neol)ZF3/Wkt/BF]

guncêşk گـونـجـێـشـك *m.* **().** sparrow, zool. *Passer domesticus*. {also: guncîşk (K[s])} {syn: beytik; çûk I} Cf. P gunjišk گنجشك [F/Wkt//K(s)]

guncik گـــونـــجِـك *f.* **().** pepper, sweet pepper, bot. *Capsicum*. {syn: back; bîber; ȟiçȟar; îsot} [HR-I/RZ/ZF3/Wkt] <dermanê germ; îsot>

guncîşk گونجيشك (K[s]) = sparrow. See **guncêşk.**

gund گــونــد *m.* **(-ê;-î).** village: **•Navê *gund* namûsa *gund* e** (BGpk #2184, 223) The name [i.e., reputation] *of the village* is the honor *of the village [prv.]*. {also: [gound] گـنـد (JJ)} Cf. Mid P gund = 'army, troop; group, gathering'; = Sor dê دێ [F/K/A/JB3/IF/JJ/B/ZF3/FS]

gundik گوندِك = testicles. See **gun**.

gundiȓandin گـــونـــدِڕانـــدِن (FS) = to roll (vt.). See **gindiȓandin**.

gundiȓîn گوندِڕين (FS) = to roll (vi.). See **gindiȓîn**.

gundî گــــونـــدى *m.* **(-yê;).** villager, peasant. {also: [goundi] گندى (JJ)} {gundîtî} [F/K/A/JB3/IF/JJ/B/ZF3/FS]

gundîtî گـونـديـتـى *f.* **(-ya;-yê).** 1) peasantry, being a peasant: **•*Gundiyatîya* berê bizeȟmet bû** (FS) It was hard *to be a peasant* in the old days; 2) agricultural work: **•xebata *gundîtîê*** (HCK-5) work *of peasants*, i.e., farm work. {also: gundiyatî (FS)} [K/A/B/IF/ZF3//FS] <gundî>

gundor I گـــونـــدۆر, m. (K/IFb/GF/OK/AA/Kmc-2) = pumpkin, gourd; melon. See **gindor I**.

gundor II گـــونـــدۆر *m.* **(-ê;).** stone roof-roller, long stone cylinder for rolling down mud roofs. {also: gindor II (A/IFb/CS); [gindōr] گـنـدور (JJ)} {syn: bagirdan; lox} [Qzl/FJ/GF/TF/ZF/Kmc//A/IFb/JJ/CS]

gundur گوندور (JB1-A) = melon. See **gindor I**.

gune I گـونـه *adj.* 1) {syn: bêsûc} innocent, guiltless: **•Em *gunene*** (Z-922) We are *innocent* **•Tuyê evî xelqê bêsûc û *gune* qiȓ nekî** (Z-1) Don't destroy this guiltless and *innocent* people; **-Guneye** = It's a pity to waste it {syn: nestêlê}: **•Eva merîkî am û t'ame, *guneye*** (Z-922) This is a perfectly innocent man, *it would be a shame [to kill him]* **•Ȟeywanê bin meda *gunene*** (Z-1) *It's a shame [to waste]* the animals under us (=on which we are riding) **•Ez îslehê wan ji wan bidizim, wê namûsa wan bişkê, *guneh e*** (L) If I stole their weapons from them, it would ruin their honor, *it would be a sin (or, a shame)*. {also: guneh (L)} [Z-1/Z-922]

gun•e II گـونـه *m.* **(•ê;).** 1) {syn: sûc; t'awan I} guilt, sin; responsibility [for ending s.o.'s life]: **•Me *gunê* vî k'esîvî, zaȓê wî kire stuyê xwe** (Z-922) We have taken *the responsibility [for the lives of]* this man and his children on ourselves [lit. 'on our own necks']; **-gunê *fk-ê* hilanîn** = to take on the responsibility [for having killed s.o.] **•Ez *gunehê* we *hilneynim*** (L) I *don't want to be responsible for* you (=for your death) **•Ez ber mirazim, ez te nakujim, *gunê* te *hilnaynim*** (Z-1) I've gotten what I want, I won't kill you, I *won't take on the responsibility* [for killing you]; 2) {syn: ȟeyf [2]} pity: **•*Gunê min li* we *hatye*** (EP-7) *I felt sorry for* you **•Te qey digot *gunê wî li* Sûsîkê *tê*, naxwaze, ku ew t'enê bimîne** (Ba2:2, 206) It was as if *he felt sorry for* Susik, and didn't want her to be alone; **-gunê xwe li *fk-ê* anîn** (XF)/**gunehê xwe lê anîn** (K) to pity, take pity on, feel sorry for: **•Wî ȟeyamî êmîşî bol bû, em dizîva dik'etne baẍa, me êmîş didizya, carna jî xweyêd hine baẍa *gunê xwe li me danîn*, îzna me didan, wekî**

em êmîşêd ji dara k'etî ... xweřa berevkin (Ba2-4, 224) At that time [of year] fruit was abundant, we would sneak into orchards and steal fruit, and sometimes the owners of some orchards *would take pity on us* and allow us to pick fruit which had fallen from the tree. {also: guneh (IF); [gounah گناه/gouné گنه] (JJ)} Cf. P gunāh گناه --> T günah; *See etymology at* ***binas***. [Z-922/B/JJ//IF] <binas; sûc>

guneh گونه‌ه (IF/L) = innocent; (It's) a pity. See **gune I**: guilt, sin; responsibility. See **gune II**.

gunehbar گونه‌هبار *adj.* accused, suspected. {also: gunehber (GF)} {syn: t'awanbar} [Dh/K(s)/OK/ZF3//GF] <gune II>

gunehber گونه‌هبه‌ر (GF) = suspected. See **gunehbar**.

gunehk'ar گونه‌هكار *m.&f.* **().** 1) sinner: **•Ewřo wezîfa min ew e, bo dujminan o *gunahkaran* jî çakîyê bikem** (SK 4:47) Today my duty is this, to do good to enemies and *sinners* alike; 2) criminal; 3) culprit; 4) *[adj.]* guilty; criminal *(adj.)*: **•Way bo ȟalê me. Em dê çito cewaba xudê deyn? Em gelek *gunahkar* o řû-řeş boyn li-ber dergahê xudê** (SK 9:89) Alas for us. How shall we answer to God? We have become most *guilty* and shamed before the court of God; **-gunehk'ar kirin** (RZ) to accuse s.o. of stg.: **•...we *em* bi hevalbendîya Înglîz *gunehkar dikirin*** (Bkp, 7) ... you *used to accuse us* of having an alliance with the English. {also: gunahkar (SK); gunehker (A); gunek'ar (EP-7/B); [gounah-kar] گناهكار (JJ)} {gunehk'arî; gunek'arî} [EP-7/B//F/K/JB3/IFb/GF/RZ/ZF//JJ/SK//A]

gunehk'arî گونه‌هكارى *f.* **(-ya;-yê).** sin, crime; sinfulness: **•Mîna ku ez bi van gotinên xwe *gunehkariyekê dikim*, birayê min zûzûka peyvê li min dibire** (Epl, 22-23) As if in saying these words I *was committing a sin*, my brother quickly interrupted me. {also: gunek'arî (B)} [F/K/IFb/ZF//B]

gunehker گونه‌هكه‌ر (A) = sinner; criminal. See **gunehk'ar**.

gunek'ar گونه‌كار (EP-7/B) = sinner; criminal. See **gunehk'ar**.

gunek'arî گونه‌كارى (B) = sinfulness. See **gunehk'arî**.

gunhêl گونهێل (Zx) = mating season; sex. See **guhnêr**.

gunhîl گونهيل (Şnx) = mating season; sex. See **guhnêr**.

gunî گونى (RZ) = sack. See **gûnîk**.

gup گوپ *f.* **(-a;).** cheek; inside of cheek (IFb). {also: gep (IFb-2/OK/Kş); gupik I (K); gûp (IFb); [ghep] گپ (JJ)} {syn: alek; hinarik; lame; řû[3]} Cf. P kab كب = 'inside of cheek' & (Afghani) P gap گپ = 'talk; mouth'; Sor gûp گووپ = 'inside of cheek, cheek when inflated'; Hau gip *m.* = 'cheek' (M4) [Msr/ZF3//K//IFb//JJ/OK/Kş]

gupik I گوپك (K) = cheek. See **gup**.

gupik II گوپك (GF/RZ) = top, summit. See **gopk**.

gupik III گوپك *f.* **(-a;).** 1) {syn: aj; bişkoj; terh; zîl} bud, blossom, shoot, sprout: **•Bûkmezave ... *Gupikên* wê pir caran dernexûnî ne. Hundir *gupikên* wê li destpêkê spî ne. Qert bibe, sor dibin** (FE) The poppy ... its *buds* are often pointing downward (upside down). The interior of its *buds* are [!] white in the beginning. When it matures, they turn red; 2) glans, head of penis. {also: gopik (BF); [goupik] گوپك (JJ)} [FE/K/B/IFb/FJ/GF/JJ/FS/ZF3//BF]

gupk گوپك (Dh) = top, summit. See **gopk**.

gur I گور/**guř I** گوڕ [K] *m.* **(-ê;).** wolf: **•*Gurno, gurê* keřî-lalo** (Ba) *O wolves*, deaf and dumb *wolves* **•Kire gazî, ku ȟemû *gurê* wan dera berevî cem wî bin. *Gur* gişk berev bûn** (Ba) He called all the *wolves* of those parts (=of that area) to gather before him. All *the wolves* gathered; **-gele gur** (Ba) pack of wolves. {also: gurg (M-Ak/SK/GF-2/OK-2/Bw); [gour] گور (JJ); <gur> گر (HH)} {gurtî (K)} [Pok. u̯ḷkᵘ̯os 1178.] 'wolf': Skt vṛka-m.; O Ir *wṛka-: Av vəhrka-; Khwarezmian 'wrk [ŭřk] *m.*; Sgd wyrk [wirk-]; Southern Tati dialects: Chali varg *m.* = 'wolf' & varga *f.* = 'she-wolf' (Yar-Shater); Shughni group: Shughni/Roshani/Bartangi/Oroshori u̯ŭřǰ *m.* & Shughni/Roshani wirjin *f.*; Yazghulami u̯ařǧ (Morg2); P gorg گرگ; Sor gurg گورگ; Za verg *m.* (Todd); Hau werg *m.* (M4); cf. also Gr lykos λύκος *m.*; Lat lupus; Rus volk волк [F/B/A/JB3/IF/JJ/HH/GF/TF/OK//K//M-Ak/SK/Bw] <dêlegur; p'eřanî; řovî I; torî I>

guř II گوڕ/**gur II** گور [GF/TF/OK] *adj.* gushing, strongly flowing, pouring *(rain)*: **•Zargotina me piř dewlemend e. Miletê me ew zargotin afirandiye, niha jî diafirîne. Ew kaniyeke *guř* e** (Wlt 2:59, 16) Our folklore is very rich. Our people has created this folklore, and is still creating it. It is a *gushing* source; **-barana guř** (B) driving or pouring rain. Cf. T gür = 'abundant, dense, thick; gushing' [Wlt/K/IFb/B//GF/TF/OK] See also **gir I**.

guř III گوڕ (FK-eb-1)/gur III گور (Ba2) = large. See **gir I**.

guȓ IV گوڕ = according to. See **goȓ II**.

gur V گــــــــور (Bw/IFb/FS/ZF3) = *weaving term*. see **gurd**.

gurandin گــــورانــــدِن *vt.* **(-gurîn-).** 1) to skin, flay; 2) {syn: şerjêkirin} to slaughter: **•Lê ji bo dawetê dîk û mirîşk *digurandin*** (Rnh 3:22, 426) For the wedding they *were slaughtering* roosters and chickens. {also: guron (-guro-) (M); [gurāndin] گـورانـديـن (JJ)} [Rnh/K/A/IFb/B/JJ/GF/TF/OK//M] <ç'erm; kuştin>

Gurc I گورج *m.&f.* **().** 1) Georgian *(native of Georgia in the Caucasus)*: **-jina ~** (K)/**k'ulfeta ~** (B) Georgian woman; **-zimanê gurca[n]** (K) Georgian language, Kartuli; 2) *[f.]* beautiful woman; fairy; "The Gurj live in a special land at the end of the world, beyond India ... the people run around naked and eat and drink all day long. Their women are of extraordinary beauty ... a fairy-like being" (PN II, 381, note 62,5): **•Maymûn rabû, çermê xwe ji xwe jêkir, biderket *gurc*** (PS I:11, 25) The ape threw off her pelt, and it turned out that she was a *gurj* [fairy]. {also: [gurj] گــورج (JJ-PS); <g[u]rç> گرچ (HH); <gurc> گورج (Hej)} [PS/K/A/B/JJ/GF/Hej//HH]

gurc II گــــورج *adj.* (too) short *(of a rope, skirt, etc.)*: **•Ev werîse yê *gurc* e** (Zeb) This rope is *too short*. {also: <gurc> گــــورج (Hej)} {syn: kurt I} [Zeb/Hej] <kin>

Gurcî گــــورجــــى *adj.* 1) [Gurcî] Georgian (from the Georgian Republic, in the South Caucasus); 2) {syn: bedew; cindî; spehî} beautiful, sexy, gorgeous *(of a woman)*. Sor gurcî گــورجــى = 'sexy' [Zeb/IFb/ZF3/Wkp/Wkt] <gurc I>

gurcik گورجِك (B) = kidney. See **gurçik**.

gurçik گورچِك *f.* **(-a;-ê).** kidney. {also: gulçîsk (Bw); gurcik (B-2); gurç'î (S&E-Turkmenistan); gureçik (HB-2); [gourtchik] گرچك (JJ); <gurçik> گرچك (HH)} Av vərəδkā f.; Mid P gurdag (M3); P gorde گرده; Sor gurçik گورچك/gurçîle گورچيله; Za velke *f.* (Mal); Hau wiłk *m.* (M4) [F/K/A/JB3/IF/B/JJ/HH/ZF3//Bw]

gurç'î گــــورچــــى (S&E-Turkmenistan) = kidney. See **gurçik**.

gurd گـــــورد *f.* **(-a;).** *system of threads involving the warp and woof/weft in weaving on a loom* [T gücü ipliği]; **-gurda tevnê** (ZF3)/**gura tevnî** (FS) do. {also: gur V (Bw/IFb-2/FS/ZF3-2); <gurd> گــورد (Hej)} [Kmc-13/IFb/Hej/ZF3//FS] <firêt; hevo>

gureçik گورەچِك (HB) = kidney. See **gurçik**.

guȓed گوڕەد (FS) = leek. See **kurad**.

guȓe-guȓ گوڕەگوڕ/**guȓeguȓ** گوڕەگوڕ [B] *f./pl.(Rnh)* **(-a/ ;-ê/).** 1) {syn: girmîn; ȓeqeȓeq} thunder(ing): **•Ev ne *guregurên* Hîtler, lê yên Xwedê ne** (Rnh) Those are not *the rumblings of* Hitler [=Nazi bomber planes], but rather those of God; **-guȓe-guȓ kirin** (K/B) to thunder, rumble: **•'Ewr *dikine guȓeguȓ*** (B) It is thundering [lit. 'The clouds *are making thunder*']; **-gurgura ezmên** (IF/JB3) thunder; 2) grumble, grumbling; rumble, rumbling; boom(ing). {also: gire-gir II (F); girme-girm (K-2); gurgur (IF/JB3)} Cf. Sor girmey hewr گرمەی هەور = 'thunder' & guȓeşey hewr گوڕەشەی هــەور = 'mutterings of distant thunder'; Za gurme-gurm = 'rumble, boom' [Rnh/K/B/ZF3//F//IF/JB3] <birûsk>

gurêx گورێخ (IFb/GF) = fierce. See **gurêẍ**.

gurêẍ گــــورێــــغ *adj.* fierce, ferocious, ill-tempered, vicious: **-dêlika gurêx** (GF) fierce female dog; **-seêd gurêẍ** (Ba2) fierce sheepdogs {syn: sepandî}: **•Ḧer kerîkî pêz ȓa sê-çar *seêd gurêẍ* derdik'etne çolê, ewe usa diȓ bûn, ku kesekî dil nedikir nêzîkî pêz be** (Ba2:1, 203) With every flock of sheep, 3-4 *sheepdogs* would go out to the wilderness: they were so fierce that no one dared approach the sheep. {also: gurêx (IFb/GF); kurîx (HoK2); [gourikh] گـوريـخ (JJ)} [Ba2//IFb/GF//JJ//Hok2] <diȓ; diȓende; hov>

gurg گورگ (M-Ak/SK/GF/OK/Bw) = wolf. See **guȓ I**.

gurgur گورگور (IF/JB3) = thunder. See **guȓe-guȓ**.

guȓî گـوڕى *adj.* 1) mangy, scabby, covered with scabs: **•Devê *guȓî* bêwane** (B) *Mangy* (or *bald*) camels are unlucky [=bring bad luck]; 2) bald, balding, hairless (IF/A/B): **-guȓî bûn** (A/IF) to go bald; **-guȓî kirin** (A/IF) to make bald, cause to lose one's hair; 3) barren, devoid of vegetation *(land)* (IF). {also: [giri گـرى/gouri گــورى] (JJ)} Cf. Sor giȓwê گــــــــــــڕوێ = 'mangy, attacked by dry rot, honeycombed' [F/K/A/IF/B/GF//JJ] <K'eçelok>

guȓîn گـوڕين *vi.* **(-guȓ-).** 1) to thunder, roar; to make a loud noise; 2) [*f.* **().**] loud noise, crash, din, uproar, rumbling. [MC-1/K/B/IF] <girmîn>

gurm! گـــــورم *interj.* plop! bang!: **•Beyrim li ser devê çalê şemitî, ew jî li çalê ket û go: "*Gurm*!"** (L) B. slipped at the mouth of the pit, he too fell into the pit and went [lit. 'said'] '*Plop!*' [L/K]

gurn گورن (IFb) = testicles. See **gun**.

guron گورۆن (-guro-) (M) = to skin. See **gurandin**.

gur̄oş گوڕۆش (EP-7) = small coin, penny. See **qurûş**.

gurover گورۆڤەر (BK) = round. See **girover̄**.

gurpegurp گـــورپـــەگـــورپ *f.* **(-a;).** palpitation, throbbing, violent beating *(of heart)*; gurgling: **•Min dêna xwe da ser laşê xwe û min jê zanî ko ew *gurpegurp* û heydedan ji dilê min dihat** (MG. Tavê ew dît) I took a look at my body and I knew from it that that *palpitation* and excitement was coming from my own heart **•Xwîdaneke sar li eniya wî dide der û dilê wî wek aşekî xirabe *dike gurpegurp*** (Ardû, 148-149) A cold sweat appears on his forehead and his heart *is beating* like a broken mill. {also: gilpgilp (CS); gulpegulp (K)} {syn: p'irtep'irt I} Sor gurpegurp گوروپەگورپ = 'continued palpitation, throbbing' [Ardû/MG//K//CS]

gurpîn گورپین *f.* **(-a;).** palpitation, throbbing, violent beating *(of heart)*: **•*Gurpîna* dilê mêrik sist dibe û kêfa guhên wî direve** (Ardû, 19) *The throbbing of* the man's heart weakens and he no longers enjoys what he hears. {also: gulpîn (K)} Sor gurpe گـورپـە = 'palpitation, rapid beating (of the heart)' [Ardû/FJ/CS//K] <k'utan>

gurtî گورتی *f.* **(-ya;).** 1) wolf-like habits, wolfishness: **•Vî di bin çerma berx de *gurtîya* xwe nîşan dayibû** (kurmesliler.de: I.Banguş. CHP û Baykal) He had shown his *wolfishness* under the lambskin; 2) ferocity. [K/ZF3] <gur I>

gurz I گـــورز *m.* **(-ê;).** club, mace *(weapon)*; **-gurzê at'aşî** (EP-7) torch: **•Nav Cizîrê *gurzêd at'aşî* ba kirin** (EP-7) They waved *torches* [lit. 'clubs of fire'] throughout Jizîr. {also: [gourz] گــــرز (JJ); <gurz> گــــرز (HH)} {syn: ciniḧ; hiwêzî} Calvert Watkins. "The Name of Meleager," in: *O-o-pe-ro-si: Festschrift für Ernst Risch zum 75. Geburtstag*, hrgb. von Annemarie Etter (Berlin & N.Y.: Walter de Gruyter, 1986), pp. [320]-328: Skt vajra- *m./n.* = 'Indra's thunderbolt, mace'; O Ir *vazra-: Av vazra-; Old P *vaδra-; Mid P wazr/warz = 'club, mace' (M3); (wazr-->*wizr-->*wurz -->) P gorz گـرز -->T gürz; Sor gurz گـــورز = 'club with pliant handle'; Za gurz m. = 'mace' (Mal). [K/A/JB3/IFb/B/JJ/HH/GF]

gurz II گـــــورز *f.(K/Elk)/m.(B/ZF3)* **(-a/-ê;).** bundle, bale, bouquet: **•*Gurza* mezin xorim e** (Elk) *A large bundle* is a 'xorim'. {also: gurze (FJ); [gourz/gurs (Rh)] گـرز (JJ); <gurz> گـرز (HH)} Cf. Arm xowrc խուրձ = 'bouquet'; Sor gurze گـــــورزە = 'bundle' [Elk/K/A/IFb/B/JJ/HH/ZF3//FJ] <gîşe; xorim>

gurze گورزە (FJ) = bale. See **gurz II**.

gustêr گوستێر (A) = (finger)ring. See **gustîl**.

gustîl گــوســتــیــل *f.* **(-a;-ê).** (finger)ring: **•Ax çawa *gustîlka* Memê ji Zîna qîza mîr nedizî, minê îro pê wê *gustîlkê* Memê bistenda** (FK-eb-1, 271) Oh! Had I only stolen Mem's *ring* from Zîn, the mîr's daughter, I could have gotten Mem today with it **•Va diyariyek baş, *hingulîskek* min ji te re anîye!** (SW1, 54) Here is a good present, I have brought you *a ring*!; **-gustîlka nîşanê** (B) engagement ring; **-t'ilîya gustilê** (B/Msr)/~ **gustilkê** (B/IF)/~ **gustîlkirinê** (K)/~ **hinglîskê** (IF) ring finger {syn: tilîya bênav (K)}. {also: gistîl (K); gistîlk; gustêr (A); gustîlk (A/JB3/IF-2/B); gustîr (Ad/SK/FS); gustîrk' (JB1-A); gustrîk (Frq); hinglîsk (IF-2); hingulîsk (SW1); hingustîl (SW/JB3-2); hûngilîsk (Btm/Mzg); [goustir گستر/ goustil گـسـتـل] (JJ); <gustîl گـسـتـيـل/hungustîl هـنـگـسـتـيـل> (HH)} {syn: mor II[1]; p'îlat} Cf. P angoštar انگشتر; Sor emust[ew]île ئەموستەویلە; Za engiştane *m.* (Todd); Hau engusewêłe *m.* (M4) [F/K/IFb/JJ/HH//A/JB3/B//Ad/SK/FS//JB1-A//Frq//SW//SW1//Btm/Mzg]

gustîlk گــوســتــیــلــك (A/JB3/IF/B) = (finger)ring. See **gustîl**.

gustîr گوستیر (Ad/SK/FS) = (finger)ring. See **gustîl**.

gustîrk' گوستیرك (JB1-A) = (finger)ring. See **gustîl**.

gustrîk گوستریك (Frq) = (finger)ring. See **gustîl**.

guşpan گوشپان (IFb) = thimble. See **gûzvan**.

gutil گوتِل (TF) = clump, lump. See **gumtil**.

guvaştin گـوڤـاشـتـِن *vt.* **(-guvêş-).** to squeeze, press, wring *(the water/juice/life out of)*: **•Rîwî ji xefletwe dew hawêt e stukira marî, girt o çak *giwişî* ḧetta mar temam bê-r̄oḧ kir o kuşt** (SK 2:16) The fox suddenly snapped at the snake's neck, seized it and *squeezed* it hard until he completely throttled the snake and killed it **•Şerbikê awî xalî îna, tizbî *giwişî*, aw jê hat** (SK 12:121) They brought an empty water pot, he *squeezed* his rosary and water came out of it. {also: givaştin (Ag/JB3/IFb-2/B); giwişîn (SK); guvişandin (IFb-2/GF-2); guvşandin (S&E/K/A); [ghewachtin] گـڤـاشـتـيـن (JJ); <guvaştin گـڤـاشـتـن (diguvêşe) (دگـڤـيـشـه)> (HH)} Cf. P gavīstan گویستن/ kavīstan کویستن = 'to beat, pound' [S&E/K/A//IFb/JJ/HH/GF/TF/BK//JB3/B/Ag//SK]

guveguv گوڤەگوڤ *f.* **(-a;).** whistling, sighing *(of the wind)*: **-guvguva ba** (GF) whistling or sighing of the wind: **•Di ber camên nîv daxistî re *guve guva bayê* payîza paşîn bû** (SBx, 12) In front of the half shut window panes, there was *the whistling of the wind of* late autumn. {also: givgiv (GF-2[Beh]); guvguv (IFb/GF)} Sor givegiv گـڤـەگـڤ = 'sustained and prolonged rustling sound' [SBx/FJ//IFb/GF]

guvguv گـوڤـگـوڤ (IFb/GF) = whistling (of wind). See **guveguv**.

guvirandin گوڤِراندِن (GF) = to digest. See **givêrandin**.

guvişandin گوڤِشاندِن (IFb/GF) = to squeeze, press. See **guvaştin**.

guvî گوڤى (FJ/GF/JJ) = curd(s). See **giv**.

guvîj گوڤيژ (Srk) = hawthorn. See **gîjok**.

guvşandin گـوڤـشـانـدِن *vt.* (-guvşîn-) (S&E/K/A) = to squeeze, press. See **guvaştin**.

guwîzan گوويزان (A) = razor. See **gûzan**.

guzêz گوزێز (Wkt) = clothes moth. See **bizûz**.

guzîz گوزيز (Wkt) = clothes moth. See **bizûz**.

guzûz گوزووز (Wkt) = clothes moth. See **bizûz**.

guzvan گوزڤان (IFb) = thimble. See **gûzvan**.

gû گـوو *m.* **(-yê/giwê;).** excrement, feces, shit: **•Bêna *gû* tejî xanî bû** (SK 28:257) The stench of *excrement* filled the house **•Sofî 'Ebdullah Şikak û muroêt wî gelek li Wanê [r̄ûniştin]... pîwazek bo wan ḧasil nebû. Gelek peşîman bûn, gotin** [sic], **"Ewe çi *gû* bû me xarî!"** (SK 48:511) Sofi Abdullah Shikak and his men sat in Van for a long time ... but not an onion did they get. They were most regretful, saying, "What *dung* we have eaten!" {also: [gou/gaou] گـو (JJ); <gû> گـو (HH)} {syn: destava stûr} [Pok. gᵘ̯ōu-/gᵘ̯ū- 483.] '(cow) dung; disgust, annoyance': Skt gūtha- *m.*; O Ir *gū̆θa- (A&L p.85 [VI, 3]): Av gūθa- *n.*; Mid P gūh (M3); P goh گـه; Sor gû گـوو; Za gî *m.* (Todd); Hau gû *m.* (M4); cf. Arm ku (W: gu) կու/ko[y] կոյ; Rus govno говно. *Possibly related to the etymon for 'cow, ox'--see* ***ga***. [M/K/A/IFb/JJ/HH/SK/GF/TF] <destav; r̄itin; sergo>

gûbir̄ گووبِڕ (Msr/Wkt)= noxious insect. See **gûbir̄k**.

gûbir̄k گـووبِـڕك *f.* **().** insect that damages tomatoes in kitchen gardens (le'tik). {also: gûbir̄ (Msr-2/Wkt-2)} [Msr/Wkt] <gûgilêrk>

gûdarî گوودارى (Bg) = listening. See **guhdarî**.

gûf•ik گـووفِـك *f.* **(•ka;).** (small) tassel, fringe: **-gûfika dersokê** (FS) the tassel of the headdress; **-gîfk û qutas** (Bw) tassels large and small. {also: gîfik (Bw); [ghifik گيفك/ghiwik گيوك] (JJ)} {syn: gulik [2]; r̄îşî I} [Bw/JJ/FS//IFb/OK] <qutas>

gûgerîn گووگەرين (IFb) = dung beetle. See **gûgilêrk**.

gûgêr̄ik گووگێڕك (SK) = dung beetle. See **gûgilêrk**.

gûgilêrk گـووگِـلـێـرك *f.* **().** dung beetle, scarab, zool. *Scarabaeus*: **•Wextê wan temaşa kir *gûgêr̄ik* di-naw mewîjanda biziwtin** (SK 20:186) When they looked *the beetles* were moving among the raisins. {also: gogerîn (A/IFb-2); gûgerîn (IFb-2); gûgêr̄ik (SK); gûgirêfk (IFb/OK)} [Zeb//IFb/OK//SK//A] <gûbir̄k; k'êzik>

gûgirêfk گـووگـرێـفـك (IFb/OK) = dung beetle. See **gûgilêrk**.

gûhûşk گووهووشك (Hk/Zeb/IFb/Hej) = hawthorn. See **gîjok**.

gûle گووله (JB1-S) = bullet. See **gule**.

gûlik گـــــووڵِـــــك *f.* **(-a;-ê).** 1) asphodel (bot.); 2) shoemaker's and bookbinder's paste or glue made of powdered asphodel root {T çiriş} (Wn/Bt/GF). {also: gûlîk (Wn-2/Bt-2)} [Wn/Bt/IFb/GF/ZF3] <soryas; şîrêz>

gûlîk گووليك (Wn/Bt) = shoemaker's paste. See **gûlik**.

gûman گوومان = suspicion; thought. See **guman**.

gûmik گوومِك (H/IFb) = fingertip. See **gumik**.

gûnî گوونى (FS) = sack. see **gûnîk**.

gûnîk گوينيك/گوونيك [Bw] *m.* **(•ê;).** (factory made) sack. {also: gînîk (Bw-2); gunî (RZ); gûnî (FS)} {syn: ç'ewal; ferde; t'elîs} [Bw/RZ//A/TF//FS] <mêşok; t'êr̄ III>

gûp گووپ (IF) = cheek. See **gup**.

gûsinc گووسِنج *f.* **().** oleaster, wild olive tree, Russian olive, bot. *Elaeagnus angustifolia* [T iğde ağacı]. {syn: sinc} [IFb/RF/ZF3]

gûşe گووشه, m. (OK) = sheaf. See **gîşe**.

gûşî گـــووشـــى *m.* **(-yê;).** bunch, cluster *(of grapes)*: **•*Wîşîyê* tirî li hindawê r̄êkan ḧetta nêzîkî zistanê dima. Kes nediwêra dest biket ê** (SK 51:554) *Bunches of* grapes would remain (hanging) above the roads until nearly winter. Nobody dared to touch them. {also: gwêşî (IFb-2); gwîşî (IFb-2); hûşî (GF-2); ûşî (JB3/IFb-2/GF-2/Bw); wîşî (SK); [ouchi اوشـــى/kouchi كوشى/khouchi خوشى] (JJ)} Cf. P xoše خوشه; Sor hêşû هـێـشـوو; Hau hoşe *m.* (M4) [F/K/IFb/B/GF//JB3/JJ/Bw//SK] <mêw; tirî>

gûşk گووشك (OK/AA) = hawthorn. See **gîjok**.

gûtar گووتار (A) = article, report. See **gotar** [3].

gûz گويز/گووز [Bw] *f.* **(-a;-ê).** walnut, bot. *Juglans*: **•Diya min çend nan, du çeng mewîj, bîst-sih lib *gwîz* dixistin tûrikê Gulîstanê** (Alkan, 71) My mother would put some bread, two handfuls of raisins, 20-30 *walnuts* into Gulistan's bag; **-dara gûzê** (SK) walnut tree: **•R̄îwî çû bin *dara gûzê*, berê xo daê, hêlîna destexîşka kotirê li ser gilîya *gûzê* ye** (SK 3:23) The fox went beneath *a walnut tree*, looked up at it and saw that the nest of the pigeon's dear friend was on a branch of the *walnut tree*. {also: gwîz; [gouz] گـوز (JJ); <gûz> گـوز (HH)} < Ar jawz جـوز --> T ceviz, cf. Heb egoz אגוז; Mid P gōz = 'walnut' (M3); Sor gwêz [göz] گوێز; Za goz *f.* (Todd); Hau wezî *f.* (M4) [K/JB3/IFb/B/JJ/HH/JB1-A/SK/GF/OK] <ç'erez; kakil>

gûzan گـووزان *m.* **(-ê; gûzên, vî gûzanî).** razor, razor blade: **•Hef̄e şeê wî, *dûzanê* wî, k'ûpikê ava wî, hersîya hilde û hespê qer syar be** (HCK-3, #16, 177) Go get his comb, his *razor*, his water jug, all 3 of them, and mount the black horse **•Ji van pêve hêsîrên elemanî *cûzanên jîlet* jî kiri bûn nav kartolan** (Rnh 1:11, 195) In addition, the German prisoners put [=hid] *razor blades* in potatoes **•S̱ofî hêdî hate nik Ḧafiz, *gûzanek* di destîda, hawêt e kîrê Ḧafiz, di binîr̄a bir̄î** (SK :684) Sofi slowly approached the hafiz with *a razor* in his hand, which he struck at the hafiz' penis, cutting it off at the base. {also: cûzan (Rnh); dûzan (K-2/B-2/FJ); gîzan (IF-2/FS-2); g[u]wîzan (A); gwîzan (KS); [gouzan گوزان/djuzan جزان] (JJ)} Cf. Sor gwêzan [gözan] گـوێـزان [F/K/JB3/IFb/B/JJ/JB1-A/SK/GF/OK/FS//A//Rnh//FJ]

gûzek گـــــــووزهك *f.* **(-a;-ê).** ankle; anklebone. {also: gîzik (IF); gozing (A); gûzik (Bşk); [gouzek-a link] گوزكا لنك (JJ); <gozek> گوزك (HH)} Cf. P qūzak قــــوزك = 'ankle' < qūz قــــوز = 'lump, protuberance'; Sor gwêzîng [gözîng, etc.] گوێزینگ /gwêzing گوێزِنگ/gwêzilik گوێزِلِك; Za gozeke *f.* (Mal) [F/K/B/JJ/Ks//IF//A//HH//Bşk]

gûzik گووزك (Bşk) = ankle. See **gûzek**.

gûzvan گـووزڤـان *f.* **().** thimble. {also: guşpan (IFb-2); guzvan (IFb/ZF3)} Cf. P angoštāne انـگـشـتـانـه/ angoštvāne انـگـشـتـوانـه --> Ar kuštubān كـشـتـبـان; =Sor emustîley dirûman ئەموستیلەی دِروومان [Msr/Wkt//IFb/ZF3]

gwêşî گوێشی (IFb) = bunch of grapes. See **gûşî**.

gwîşî گویشی (IFb) = bunch of grapes. See **gûşî**.

gwîz گویز = walnut. See **gûz**.

gwîzan گویزان (A/KS) = razor. See **gûzan**.

gya گیا (SK) = grass. See **gîya**.

gyan گیان (SK) = soul; body; self. See **can I**.

H ه

ha I هـــــــــا *part.* 1) here *(presentative)*: **-ha...ha** = now...now; whether...or: •**Ûsib *ha* hevraz nihêrî *ha* berjêr** (Ba) Joseph looked *now* up, *now* down; 2) so, such: •**Eva gişk fenê tene, wekî *ha* hate serê M.** (Z-1) It is all your doing [lit. 'your tricks'], that *such a thing* has happened to M. [lit. 'has come to M.'s head']. [K/(A)/ZF3] <wiha>

ha II ها (BX) = this; that. See **han**.

hac هاج (A/IF) = pilgrimage (to Mecca). See **ĥec**.

hacet هـــاجـــهت *m.(BK)/f.(K/B/F)* **(-ê/; hêcet** [BK]/-ê [B]**).** 1) {syn: ĥewce} necessity, need, requirement; 2) tool, instrument, equipment: •**Ewî îcar *hacetê* xwe frêqet derxist serê Îskender kuř kir** (EH) Then he calmly took out his *equipment* and shaved Iskender's head. {also: [hadjet حـاجـت/ haïdjet حـايـجـت] (JJ)} < Ar ḥājah حـاجـة = 'necessity; thing' [BK/F/K/IF/JJ/B/ZF3] <gerek; lazim; pêwist>

hacî هاجى (A/IF/GF) = pilgrim to Mecca. See **ĥecî**.

hacîreşk هاجيرهشك (JB3/IF/TF/OK) = stork; swallow. See **ĥacîřeşk**.

haf هاف (IFb/FJ/ZF/Tsab) = side, edge. See **ĥaf**.

hafa هافا, see **ĥaf**.

hafiř هافِر, m. (Bw) = trough. See **afiř**.

hafiz هافِز = Koran reciter; blind. See **ĥafiz**.

haftyê هافتيێ (JB1-S) = seventh. See **ĥefta**.

haga هــاگــا (M-Ak/SK) = awareness; information. See **hay I**.

haj هــاژ, m. (K/B/JJ/JB1-A) = awareness; information. See **hay I**.

hajotin هــاژۆتِــن (M/Bw) = to drive *(a horse or car)*. See **ajotin**.

hal هال (IFb/TF/OK) = condition, state. See **ĥal**.

halan هــالان *m./f.(ZF3)* **().** encouragement; incitement: •***Halan* di hev dan** (BX) They gave each other *encouragement*. [BX/K/IF/ZF3] <p'aldan [3]>

halet هـــالـــهت *m./f.(OK)* **().** plough/plow: •***Halet* û gîsinan li pey xwe xweş dikêşin** (AB) They pull *the plow* and plowshares behind themselves *(said of oxen)*. {syn: cot [2]; hevcař; k'otan} < T alet = 'instrument' < Ar ālah آلـة; cf. Turoyo āle = 'plow; instrument'; Za ĥaletî *f.* (Todd). *According to IFb, this word is used in the Tur 'Abdîn (Torî) region of Mardin* [DS/AB/A/JB3/IFb/GF/TF/OK] <gîsin; hincar; kêlan; mijane; nîr I; sermijank; şûrik I; xenîke; xep>

Halkuşta هالكوشتا = men's folk dance. See **Yarxişte**.

hambal هامبال (Tsab) = porter. See **ĥemal**.

han هــان *adj.* 1) this, that *(indeclinable emphatic dem. which follows the ezafeh form of the noun. In certain regions, such as Ad, Krç, Bg, ha[n] contracts with preceding noun, e.g., ev mir-á (BX) this man; ev jinik-á (BX) this woman, cf. Sor em pyaw-é = this man)*: •**(Ev) çiyayên *ha[n]*** (BX) *These* mountains *here* •**(Ew) jinika *ha[n]*** (BX) *That* woman *there* •**(Ew) mirovê *ha[n]*** (BX) *That* man *there* •***Ev* erdê *han* ê gelê Kurd e û bê wan kes tê de rûnane** (BX) *This* land belongs to the Kurdish people, and besides them nobody lives on it •***Ev* pîra *hana* dîya wî hûtê go ... ye** (L) *This* old lady *here* is the mother of the monster who... •**Ewê k'itêbê neyîne, *k'itêba han* bîne** (Ks) Don't bring that book, bring *that book* over there •**[Ne] ew xort hat, *xortê han* hat** (K2) It's not that young man who came, *that one over there* came •**Tuê wê *çola hana* dibînî?** (L) Do you see *that desert there*? •**Ya Beyrim, *ev zilamê hana* bavê min e!** (L) Hey B., *this man here* is my father!: **-yê han** = this one: •***Ya han* hat malê** (K2) *That one* (f.) came home •***Yê han* çû gund** (K2) *This one* went to the village •***Yêd han* řind dilîzin** (K2) *These (ones)* play well. {also: ha II (BX); hana (L); hanê (IF/B-2); he (BX); [han هــان/hani هانى] (JJ)} {syn: ev; ew} [L//BX/K/B/JJ/ZF3//IF]

hana هانا (L) = this; that. See **han**.

hanê هانێ (IF/B) = this; that. See **han**.

hanîn هانين (Ba3) = to bring. See **anîn**.

haqa هاقا (B) = so much. See **haqas**.

haqas هــاقــاس *adv.* so much: •**Çima ez nagihim te, ez *haqas* dibezim?** (Dz) Why don't (=can't) I catch up with you? I'm running *so* fast [lit. '*so much*'] •***Heqas wext* tu li k'u bûyî?** (B) Where have you been *all this time*? {also: aqas; **ewqas**; ewqeys[e]; haqa (B-2); heqa[s] (B); hewqas} {syn: hinde (MK); ewqedr (JB3)} [Dz/F/K/B] <qas>

har هـــــار *adj.* rabid, mad; furious: **-har û dîn** (HM) totally mad. {also: [har] هــار (JJ)} [Pok. 3. al- 27] 'to wander/roam about aimlessly; also, to be emotionally lost'; Gr ēleós ἠλεός = 'bewildered, dumbfounded'; Latv ãl'a = 'half-crazed person'. Also Ir words for madness, e.g., Sgd "r'k [ārē] = 'crazy, mad'; Mid P halag = 'foolish, imprudent' (M3); Oss ærræ (Abaev); P hār هـــــــــار = 'wild, rabid'; Sor har هار = 'mad, rabid'; Za har (Todd) -- see **alîn**; Hau har (M4) {harayî; harbûn; harî; hartî} [HM/K/A/IF/B/JJ/ZF3] <ḧêç'>

haran هـــــاران (GF) = to ache; to be upset or irritated. See **arîn**.

harayî هارايى (B) = fury; rabies. See **harî**.

harbûn هاربوون (B) = fury; rabies. See **harî**.

harî هـــــارى *f.* **(-ya;-yê).** 1) madness; fury; 2) rabies. {also: harayî (B-2); harbûn (B-2); harîtî (Wkt-2); hartî (K-2/B/Wkt-2)} [K/JB3/JJ/ZF3/FS/Wkt//B] <har>

harîk'arî هاريكارى (JB1-A) = help. See **arîk'arî**.

harîtî هاريتى (Wkt) = fury; rabies. See **harî**.

Harkoşte هاركۆشته = men's folk dance. See **Yarxişte**.

Harkuşta هاركوشتا = men's folk dance. See **Yarxişte**.

harsem هارسه‌م (K) = unripe grapes; grape cluster. See **harsim**.

harsim هـــارسِم *m.* **(-ê;).** 1) {syn: besîre; cûr I; *şilûr (IF)} unripe and sour grapes [T koruk, Ar ḥiṣrim حــصــرم, P γūre غــوره]: **•Bav *harsim* dixwê, dranên kur disekihin** (BX) The father eats *sour grapes*, and the son's teeth are set on edge *[prv.]* **•Garis hîna kal e, tirî *hersime* e, nîsk û nok hîn şîr e!** (Ardû, 148) The corn is still unripe, the grapes are still *sour*, the lentils and chickpeas are still not ripe; 2) {syn: gûşî} cluster, bunch *(of grapes)* (K). {also: harsem (K); hersim (Ardû); [ḥárṣem] حرصم (JJ)} < Ar ḥiṣrim حصرم = 'unripe & sour grapes' [BX/IF/ZF3//JJ/K] <kerik I; sekihîn; tirî>

hartî هارتى (K/B/Wkt) = fury; rabies. See **harî**.

hasê هـــاســێ = caught, stuck; inaccessible; rebellious. See **asê**.

hasil هاسِل *f.* **(-a;-ê).** 1) product; result: **-hasil bûn** = a) to be produced, to result (SK); b) to work out (vi.), turn out all right (Bw): **•Ew pareyêt te divîyan *ḧasil bûn?*** (Bw) Did you get the money you wanted (i.e., *did it come through*)?; **-hasil kirin** = a) to get, procure, obtain, acquire (JJ/Bw); to succeed in getting (Bw): **•Min telefona Zaxo *ḧasil kir*** (Bw) I *succeeded in getting through to* Zakho by phone; b) to produce (SK/JJ); 2) {syn: deramet I; dexl û dan; zad} produce; harvest, crop; 3) income; 4) (mathematical) difference, remainder (B): **•*hasila* du r̄eqema** (B) *a difference of* two (numbers). {also: ḧasil (JB1-S/SK/OK); [hasil] حـاصـل (JJ)} <Ar ḥāṣil حـاصـل = 'result, income, crop, storehouse, main content' < √ ḥ-ṣ-l حـصـل = 'to arise, come about; to result, happen, occur; to be produced' [Bw/K/IFb/B//JJ/JB1-S/SK/OK] <encam>

hatin هـاتِن *vi.* **([t]ê-/-hê-** [Bw]**;** *neg.* **na[y]ê-/nê-** [Ad]/ **nahê-** [Bw]**;** *subj.* **bê-/bihê-** [Bw]/**wer-;** *imp.* **were).** 1) {syn: werîn} to come: **-hatin dinyaê** (K) to be born; **-hatin pê** (ZF): a) to happen, occur: **•Civatê dît ku tiştekî ne bixêr *hatibû pê*** (M.Uzun. R.Evd.Zeyn, 148) The group saw that something unwholesome *had happened* **•Çi *bi* te *hatîye?*** (L) What *has happened to* you?/What has come over you?; b) to come about, come into existence: **•Pêşî ji pingav û çiravan *têne pê*** (IFb) Mosquitoes *come into existence* from stagnant water; **-hatin xwarê** (K/ZF): a) to go down, descend; b) {syn: dest/dev jê berdan} [+ **ji**] to back down from, give up on: **•*Ji ser* ya xwe *newer xwar*** (Nsb) *Don't give up on* your idea **•Merikê reben çi dike nake, jinik qet *ji* gotina xwe *nayê xwarê*** (Sadînî. Ji kelepora Kurdî pêkenok, 122) No matter what the poor fellow does, the woman absolutely *will not back down*; **-ji** [**destê**] ***fk-ê* hatin** (K) to succeed: **•Ew şixul *ji destê min nayê*** (K) This [matter] *is not in my power* **•T'u tişt *ji destê min ne dihat*** (K) I *couldn't do anything about* it **•Û *ḧeta ji we tê*, xwe bi mi gihîne** (Z-2) And *to the best of your ability*, catch up with me; **-li hev hatin** = to agree [se mettre d'accord]; **-pey hatin** = to follow: **•*Pey* wî *hatin*** (BX) *They followed* him; **-ser hatin** = to befall, happen to s.o.: **•Bira sond xar, ku tiştek *serê* Ûsib *naê*** (Ba) The brothers swore that *nothing would happen to* Joseph **•Çi zirar *hatye serê* Ûsib ji destê biraye** (Ba) Any harm *that has befallen* Joseph is from his brothers' hands (=is his brothers' fault/doing) **•Wekî tiştek *bê serê wî*, zanibin, ezê we gişka qir̄ kim** (Ba) If *anything happens to him*, know that I will kill you all; 2) to blow *(of wind)*: **•Ba *tê*** (AB) The wind *is blowing*; 3) + inf. *[direct or oblique case]* expresses the passive voice: **•Bi tonan erzaqên ku bi alîkariya xêrxwazan *hatin berhevkirin* [j]i Mislimanên Arakanî re *tên belavkirin*** (cinarinsesi.com 13.x.2017) Tons of supplies which *have been collected* by volunteers *are* *being distributed* to the Muslims of Arakani [Rohingyas] **•Îro em di zivarîyê de ne, malên me ji destên me *hatin[e] standin*** (H v. 1, 83-84 [1932, 1:4]) Today we are in poverty, our homes *have been taken* from us [lit. 'from our hands'] **•Lê bêjeyên ku ji navên kesan *hatine çêkirin*, bi hûrdekê dest pê dikin** (RR, 20.2.2.) But words which *have been made* from the names of people begin with a small letter **•Li nîvgirava Sînayê 16 milîtan *hatin kuştinê*** (rojname.com 11.ii.2018) In the Sinai Peninsula 16 militants *were killed* **•Li pey genim û ka ji hev *hatin qetandin*, genim wek qûrçek li ser palasan *tê civandin*, ji vê komrişka genim re "têx" *tê gotin*** (CCG, 72) After the wheat and straw *have been separated* from each other, the wheat *is gathered* in [lit. 'like'] a pile on mats [or rugs], this stack of wheat *is called* a têx. {also: [hatin] هاتن (JJ); <hatin هاتن (tê) (تێ)> (HH)} Sor hatin هـاتِـن ([d]-ê-); SoK hâtın: hât-, hat-, yât-, yat- (Fat 361, 542); Za yenã (past : ame) (Todd) [BX/F/K/A/JB3/B/IFb/JJ/HH/GF/M/ZF] <anîn; çûn>

hatin-çûyîn هاتِن چوويين (K) = traffic; relations. See **hatin û çûn**.

hatin û çûn هـاتِـن و چـوون *f.* **(-a;-ê).** traffic; contact, intercourse, relations: **•Dibêjin di nihalekîda řîwîyek hebû. ... bazeberek hebû, řîwî lê derbaz dibû her wextê ĥez kiriba. ... Marek jî di wê nihalêda hebû. Nedişya li bazeberî derbaz bibît. Zor ĥez dikir ew jî wekî řîwî *hat-u-çonê biket*, çu çare nedît** (SK 2:9) They say that there was a fox (living) in a ravine. ... There were stepping-stones and the fox crossed over whenever he liked. ... There was also a snake in that ravine. He could not cross over the stepping-stones. He very much wanted *to come and go* like the fox, but could see no solution **•Ez qebûl nakem muroêt te *hat-u-çona* wan gundane biken** (SK 41:389) I will not permit your men to *come and go among* these villages **•*Hatin û çûyîn* ort'a wan gundada t'une** (B) There is no *contact* between those villages. {also: hatin-çûyîn (K); hatin û çûyîn (B); hat-u-çon (SK); hatûçûn (A)} Sor hat-û-ço هـات و چـۆ = 'coming and going, social intercourse' [GF/SS//B//K//A//SK] <peywendî; t'êkilî>

hatin û çûyîn هـاتـن و چـوويـيـن (B) = traffic; relations. See **hatin û çûn**.

hat-u-çon هـات و چـۆن (SK) = traffic; relations. See **hatin û çûn**.

hatûçûn هـاتـووچـوون (A) = traffic; relations. See **hatin û çûn**.

haveyn هـاڤـەيـن (IFb/GF/TF/OK) = leaven, yeast. See **hêvên**.

havên هاڤێن (K/GF) = leaven, yeast. See **hêvên**.

havêtin هاڤێتِن (M/Bw) = to throw. See **avêtin**.

havil هـاڤِـل *f./m.* **().** benefit, use, advantage: ***•Bê havil e*** (HH) It's *of no use*/to no avail; **-havil jê dîtin** (ZF3) to benefit from; **-havil kirin** (GF/SS): to benefit, be of use: **•Mêrik qudûmşkestî dibe û di dilê xwe de dibê, "Bi navê Xwedê, van bîst û yek mehên min jî tiştek *havil ne kir*"** (Ardû, 19) The man becomes upset and says in his heart, "By God's name, these 21 months of mine *have produced nothing* [lit. '*did not benefit* a thing']. {also: <havil> هـاڤـل (HH)} {syn: feyde; menfa'et & mifa} [Ardû/K/IFb/FJ/GF/SS]

havin هـاڤِـن (; hêvin/havên) (B) = leaven, yeast. See **hêvên**.

havî هـاڤـی**: -havîbûn** هـاڤـيـبـوون *vi.* 1) to detach o.s., stray *(of a sheep from the flock)*; to dissociate o.s., isolate o.s., withdraw, retire, secede: **•Heke pezek xo ji kerê pezî bidete paş, dê bêjin 'Ev peze yan ev mîhe *ya havî bûy'*--ya xo ji kerê pezî hemî daye paş** (editor of Havîbûn) If a sheep detaches itself from the flock, they will say 'This sheep or this ewe *has strayed*' --it has dissociated itself from the whole flock; 2) [*f.* **(-a;-ê).**] detachment, isolation, separation [Germ Entfremdung]: **•Şelel êk e ji şêwêt serekî yêt *havîbûnê*** (Peyv 3[1996], 38) Paralysis is one of the main types of *isolation*; 3) *name of a journal published in Berlin* (1997- . [Havîbûn/Peyv/IFb/FS] <xwe dane paş>

havîn هاڤين *f.* **(-a;-ê).** summer.: ***•Havîna* par germ bû** (FS) Last year's *summer* was hot. {also: hawîn (SK); [hawin] هـاڤـيـن (JJ); <havîn> هـاڤـيـن (HH)} [Pok. 3 sem- (gen. s_{e}m-ós) 905.] 'summer': Skt sámā *f.* = '[half]year, season'; Av ham-/hãmina- (M, v.1, p. 220); Sgd "myny /āmeinē/ (A&L p. 94 [XVII]); Mid P hāmīn (M3); Pashto manai; P hāmen هـامـن; Sor hawîn هـاويـن; Za amnan *m.* (Mal); Hau hamin *m.* (M4) [F/K/A/JB3/IFb/B/JJ/HH/GF/TF/OK/FS//SK]

havîtin هاڤيتِن = to throw. See **avêtin**.

havlek هاڤلەك (Mzg) = broom. See **avlêk**.

havlêk هاڤلێك (IF/IFb) = broom. See **avlêk**.

havlik هاڤلِك (Krç) = broom. See **avlêk**.

havo هاڤو (Qzl) = weft, woof. See **hevo**.

hawa هاوا (L) = manner, style. See **awa**.

hawamte هاوامته (Wkt) = useless, worthless. See **hewante**.

hawante هاوانته (Hej/Wkt) = useless, worthless. See **hewante**.

hawar هاوار *f.* **(-a;-ê).** 1) call or cry for help, SOS: **-bi hawara *fkî* çûn** (IF) to come to the rescue; **-hawar kirin** = to call or cry for help: **•Ez niha *bikim hawar*, wê bavê min bê te bikuje** (L) [If] I *cry for help* now, my father will come kill you; 2) name of a Kurdish journal published in Syria during the 1930s & 1940s . {also: hewar (K/A-2/B); hewarî (B-2); [hevar] هوار (JJ)} Sor hawar هاوار; Hau hawar *m.* (M4) [L/K/A/JB3/IF/B/JJ]

hawente هاوەنته (JB1-A) = useless, worthless. See **hewante**.

hawêrdor هاوێردۆر (K/IFb) = surroundings. See **hawirdor**.

hawirde هاوِرده *f.* **(-ya;-yê).** import(s): **•Ev 3 salin Wezareta Çandinî ya Herêma Kurdistanê, ji bo qedexekirina *hawirdeya* berhemên biyanî, baca gumrigê dixe ser fêkiyan jî** (Rûdaw 30.vii.2016) For 3 years, to ban *the import of* foreign produce, the Ministry of Agriculture of the Kurdistan Region has been imposing a tariff [lit. 'customs tax'] on fruit; **-hawirde kirin** (Rûdaw) to import: **•Kurdistan her sal 50 hezar ton gulberojk *hawirde dike*** (Rûdaw 18.viii.2017) Every year Kurdistan *imports* 50,000 tons of sunflower seeds. Sor hawurde هاووورده = 'import(s)' < hawurdin هاووورڕدِن = hênan هێنان = 'to bring' (Cf. P āvordan آوردن) [(neol)ZF3/Wkt]

hawirdor هاوِردۆر *f./m.(ZF3)* **(-a/-ê;).** surroundings; all around [*n. & adv.*]: **•*Hawirdor* geremol e, li alîyekî nûr e, li alîyekî tarî ye** (M.Uzun. Roja Evd. Zeyn., 149) *All around* is chaos, on one side there is light, on the other side is darkness; **-hawirdora** *[prep.]* (HR/K)/**hawirdorê** (ZF3) around, about, surrounding: **•Dimêzênê kû *hawirdora* bexçe sûni [sûrih?] e** (HR 3:87) He sees that *around* the garden is a wall **•Ez *li hawirdorê* xanî geriyam** (ZF3) I circled *around* the house **•*Hawirdora* me** (K) *[all] around* us. {also: hawêrdor (K/IFb); hawîrdor (K-2/FJ/TF/GF)} {syn: dorhêl; dorpêç} [HR/Uzun//K/IFb//FJ/TF/GF/ZF3]

hawîd هاویـد (IFb/GF/[FJ]) = camel's hump or saddle. See **ḧawid**.

hawîn هاوین (SK) = summer. See **havîn**.

hawîrdor هاویردۆر (K/FJ/TF/GF) = surroundings. See **hawirdor**.

Hawramanî هاورامانی (Wkt) = Hawrami (Gorani dialect). See **Hewramî**.

Hawramî هاورامی (Wkt) = Hawrami (Gorani dialect). See **Hewramî**.

hay I های *f./m.(JB1-A/K-2)* **(-a/;).** 1) {syn: agah} awareness; consciousness (JB3); news, tidings (JB1-A); knowledge, (possession of) information: **-haj [pê] hebûn** (B)/**hay [jê] bûn** (JB3/IF)/**hay jê hebûn** (Msr)/**haga lê bûn** (M-Ak): a) to be informed, be in the know, find out about; to be conscious, aware (of) {syn: pê ḧesîn}: **•Bi hevr̄a dileyîzin û *haya wan ji* tiştekî t'inîne** (Z-2) They play together and *are unaware of* anything else **•Bû se'et ne, hind *haga lê bû* teqênek hat** (M-Ak #663, 300) It turned nine o'clock, then *he became aware of* a knocking **•Gava rismê min kişand, *haya min jê tunebû*** (Msr) When they took my picture, *I was not aware of it* **•Lê Qeret'ajdîn *haj* ḧunurê Memê *heye*** (Z-1) But Q. *finds out (knows) about* M.'s skill (or bravery) **•Zikê t'êr *haj* zikê birçî *t'une*** (K)/**Zikê t'êr haj ê birçî t'ineye** (Dz-#1632) A full stomach *doesn't understand a* hungry one *[prv.]* **•Zînê hema roja 'ewlinda *haj* hatina Memê delal *hebû*** (Z-1) Zin *found out* immediately on the first day *about* dandy Mem's arrival; b) to look after, take care of, be attentive to (Msr/B): **•Tu *hay ji* malê *hebî*** (Msr) You t*ake good care of* the house (in my absence); **-haj xwe hebûn** (K) [=**hay ji xwe hebûn**] do.: **•*Haj* ḧişê *xwe nînbû*** (Z-1) He *had lost sight of himself* **•Mîr sê cara Memê bir, çimkî ḧuba Zînê usa Memê biribû, Memê delal *haj xwe t'unebû*** (Z-1) The prince beat Mem three times [at chess], because love of Zin had made Mem *lose sight of himself* (=forget himself) **•R̄o hatye, nîvro, ew hê *haj xwe t'uneye*** (Dz) Day has dawned, noon has passed, she still *hasn't budged/woken up*; 2) *[adj.]* conscious, aware, informed (JB1-A). {also: haga (M-Ak/SK); haj, m. (K-2/JB1-A); [haj هاژ/ haij هایژ] (JJ)} *The form **haga** (M-Ak & SK) may be a metathesis of **agah**, and **hay** may be a shortened form of **haga**.* haj = hay + ji; Hau hay *m.* (M4) [Z-1/B/JJ/JB1-A//Msr/K/JB3/IF//M-Am/SK] hay II هـاى: hay kirin هـاى كـرن (RZ) = to expel. See **hey: -hey kirin**.

haydar هــايــدار *adj.* informed (about), aware (of), conscious (of): **•Belkî hemî xwendevan bi wan nizanibin û *di heqê* wan *da haydar nebin*** (Bkp, 2) Perhaps all the readers won't know about them and *are not informed about* them; **-haydar kirin** (ZF) to inform, let s.o. know: **•Jibo ku em ... di heqê wan bûyer û kesan da hemî xwendevanan *haydar bikin*, me li ser wan ferhengokek amade kir** (Bkp, 2) In order *to inform* all the readers about those events and people, we have prepared a glossary about them. {syn: agahdar; serwext} < hay I + -dar. [Bkp/IFb/FJ/TF/ZF/CS] <hay I>

haydarî هــايــدارى *f.* **(-ya;-yê).** information, knowledge, consciousness: **•Jibo ku xwendevan bikarin maneyên wan peyv û peyvikan û *haydarîyên* li ser wan bûyer û kesan di ferhengokê da bi hêsanî bibînin ...** (Bkp, 2) In order that the readers be able to easily find the meanings of those words, and *the information* about those events and people. {syn: agahdarî} [Bkp/IFb/ZF/CS/ZF3]

hazir هازِر (K/IFb/B/GF) = ready. See **ḧazir**.

hazirayî هــازِرايــى (B) = readiness; attendance. See **ḧazirî**.

hazirî هــازِرى (K/B/IFb/ZF/CS) = readiness; attendance. See **ḧazirî**.

he هه (BX) = this; that. See **han**.

heban هەبان *f.* **(-a;-ê).** sack made of treated sheepskin, used for provisions, haversack, leather container: **•Derwîş dizane li *hebana* derwîş çi heye** (L) The dervish knows what is in the dervish's *sack [prv.]*. {also: hevan (B/EP-4/EP-8); [heban هـبـان/ enban/ ombán/umbán انــبــان]} < *ham-pāna-: Baluchi aphān = 'leather bag for flour'; P anbān انــبــان/ hanbān هنبان; Sor hem[b]ane هەمبانە = 'bleached skin bag (used for storing grain)'. See **5. aphān** in: G. Morgenstierne. "Notes on Balochi Etymology," *Norsk Tidsskrift for Sprogvidenskap*, 5 (1932), 40, reprinted in: *Irano-Dardica* (Wiesbaden : Dr. Ludwig Reichert Verlag, 1973), p. 151. [K/A/IF/JJ//B/EP-4] <'eyarşîrk; k'unk; meşk>

hebandin هەباندِن (JB3/IF) = to love. See **ḧebandin**.

hebon هەبۆن (M/SK) = to exist. See **hebûn.**

hebs هەبس (JB3/IFb) = prison. See **ḧebs**.

hebûn هـەبـوون *vi.* **(heye,** *pl.* **hene).** 1) to be, to exist: **•heye** = there is **•hene** = there are **•hebû** = there was; **-Hebûye t'u nebûye/Hebû nebû** = Once upon a time [lit. 'There was, there wasn't']: ***•Hebûye t'u nebûye*, xêncî xwedê kes t'u nebûye** (Ks) do. [lit. '*There was, there wasn't*, besides God there was no one']; 2) [+ *oblique case for logical subject* (in Southern dialects); + *ezafeh construction added to thing possessed* (in Northern dialects)] to have: **•*Min* xûşkek *heye*** (or, ***ya hey***) (Southern = M/SK/Bw/Zeb/Dh/Hk/ Elk) = **Xûşkeke *min heye*** (Northern) *I have* a sister. {also: hebon (M/SK); [he-būn هـبـون /hein هين] (JJ)} [BX/K/JB3/IFb/JJ/B/GF/TF//M/SK] <bûn>

hebûrî هــەبــوورى (ZF3) = billy goat, male goat. See **hevûrî**.

hec I هەج (IF) = pilgrimage (to Mecca). See **ḧec**.

hec II هەج (Kmc) = branches, twigs. See **hej I**.

hecac هــەجــاج *f.* **().** cloud (of dust); stormcloud; duststorm: **•Nerî go toz û *hecac* ji berîyê hiltê** (L) He saw dust and *clouds* (=a cloud of dust) come up from the plain. {also: ecac (GF/ZF); êcac = ecac (GF); icac (TF/ZF-2); [ajāg] اجــاك (JJ)} {syn: 'ewr; p'elte; t'elp} <Ar 'ajāj عــجــاج = 'swirling dust; smoke' [L/K/Tsab//ZF//TF] <babelîsk; talaz>

hecer هەجەر (Wkt) = new. See **'ecer**.

hecet هەجەت (SK) = grounds, excuse. See **hêncet**.

hechecik هـەجـهـەجِـك (IF) = swallow *(bird)*. See **ḧacḧacik**.

hechecîk هـەجـهـەجـيـك (A) = swallow *(bird)*. See **ḧacḧacik**.

hecheçoq هەجهەچۆق (JB3/OK) = swallow *(bird)*. See **ḧacḧacik**.

hecî هەجى (IF) = pilgrim to Mecca. See **ḧecî**.

hecr هــەجــر (K) = separation; reason; insult. See **hecran**.

***hecran** هەجران *f.* **(-a;).** 1) separation, parting (K); 2) agent, factor, reason, cause (IF): ***•Hecrana* xewna min çiye?** (Z-2) What is *the reason for* my dream?; 3) insult, offense (K); 4) calamity, disaster (IF). {also: hecr (K); hicran (K/IF); ḧecran (Z-2); <hicran هــجــران [=cause, reason]/ ḧicran حــجــران [=disaster]> (HH)} < Ar hijrān هجران = 'separation, abandonment' [Z-2//K/IF/HH]

heçik هەچِك (Qzl) = ring, hook. See **heçî I**.

heçî I هــەچــى *f./m.(Qzl/ZF3)* **(/-yê;).** wooden ring or hook through which a rope passes in fastening a load onto a pack saddle or the like: **-Heçîyê wî qelişîye** (Qzl/ZF3) "His hook is cracked," i.e., he has such a bad reputation that whatever he does will be seen in a bad light. {also: eçî (Srk); heçik (Qzl-2); heçû (Wkt-2); [hetchik هـچـك/hetchou هـچـو] (JJ)} {syn: werqîl} [Mzg/A/IFb/GF/Qzl/ZF3/Wkt//JJ//Srk] <k'urtan; olk I>

heçî II هەچی (IF) = each; as for. See **herçî**.

heçû هـەچـوو (Wkt) = ring or hook for fastening rope. See **heçî I**.

hed هەد (JB3/IF) = border. See **ḧed**.

hedad هەداد (ZF3) = blacksmith. See **ḧedad**.

hedan هەدان *f.* **(-a;-ê).** 1) patience, endurance, composure (K); 2) rest, calm (Msr/HH): ***•Hedana* min nayê** (Msr) I can't sit still; **-sekin û hedan** (Msr) do. See under **sekin**. {also: hêdan (K); <hedar> هـدار (HH)} Cf. Ar hādi' هـادئ = 'calm (adj.)' [Msr/ZF3/Wkt//K//HH]

hedar هەدار (HH) = patience; rest, calm. See **hedan**.

hefdehem هـەفـدەهـەم (ZF) = seventeenth. See **hevdehem**.

hefdemîn هـەفـدەمـيـن (IFb) = seventeenth. See **hevdehem**.

hefik هەفِك (IFb/BF) = throat; pharynx. See **ḧefik**.

hefsar هەفسار (JB1-A&S) = halter; reins. See **hevsar**.

hefsed هەفسەد (IFb) = seven hundred. See **heftsed**.

heft هەفت (A/IFb/OK) = seven. See **ḧeft**.

heftan هەفتان (IF) = seventh. See **ḧefta**.

heftcan هـەفـتـجـان (ZF3) = with seven lives. See **heftcanî**.

heftcanî هەفتجانی *adj.* with seven lives *(of cats, etc.)*: **•Bi serê şêx, ev pisîkek *heftcanî* ye** (HYma, 24) By the sheikh's head [=By Jove], she's a cat *with seven lives* (said of s.o. who lives to be very old). {also: heftcan (ZF3)} {syn: ḧeftriḧ} <heft/ḧeft = '7' + can = 'soul, spirit' [HYma//ZF3]

heftdeh هەفتدە (IF) = seventeen. See **hevdeh**.

heftdehem هـەفـتـدەهـەم (GF) = seventeenth. See **hevdehem**.

heftdehemîn هـەفـتـدەهـەمـيـن (GF) = seventeenth. See **hevdehem**.

hefte هەفتە (A/JB3/IFb/TF/OK) = week. See **ḧeftê I**.

heftem هـەفـتـەم *adj.* seventh, 7th. {also: heftemîn (TF/IFb-2/CT-2/ZF-2/Wkt-2); hevtem (Wkt-2); **ḧefta**} Cf. P haftom هفتم; Sor ḧewtem[în] حەوتەم[ين] [A/IFb/CT/ZF/Wkt//TF] <ḧeft>

heftemîn هـەفـتـەمـيـن (TF/IFb/CT/ZF/Wkt) = seventh. See **heftem**.

heftê هەفتێ (A/IFb/TF/OK) = seventy. See **ḧeftê II**.

heftêmîn هەفتێمین (IFb) = seventieth. See **heftêyem**.

heftêyem هـەفـتـێـيـەم *adj.* seventieth, 70th. {also: heftêmîn (IFb-2); heftêyemîn (IFb-2/Wkt-2); heftiyemîn (GF)} Cf. P haftādom هـفـتـادم; Sor ḧeftahem حەفتاهەم/ḧeftamîn حەفتامین [IFb/Wkt//GF] <ḧeftê II>

heftêyemîn هـەفـتـێـيـەمـيـن (IFb/Wkt) = seventieth. See **heftêyem**.

heftik هەفتِك (GF) = a children's game. See **heftok**.

heftiyemîn هەفتِیەمین (GF) = seventieth. See **heftêyem**.

heftî I هەفتی (JB3/IFb) = seventy. See **ḧeftê II**.

heftî II هەفتی (IF/JJ) = seventh. See **ḧefta**.

heftok هـەفـتـۆك *pl.* **().** *children's game played with stones or tiles* [cf. T beştaş]: **•Me bi *heftoka* dilîst** (Alkan, 71) We played *heftok*. {also: heftik (GF-2); <heftok> هـەفـتـۆك (Hej)} [Alkan/A/GF/Hej] <nehberk>

heftsed هـەفـتـسـەد *num.* seven hundred, 700. {also: hefsed (IFb-2); ḧevsid (B); ḧevtsed (K); ḧewt-s̱ed (SK)} Av hapta sata; P haft sad هـفـت صـد; Sor ḧewtsed حەوتسەد [IFb//K//SK//B]

heger هەگەر (JB1-S) = if. See **eger I**.

hej I هـەژ *m./f.(ZF3)* **(-ê/ ;).** 1) small dry branches, twigs, sprigs, used for lighting fires: ***•Hejên daran* bi nermahî li ber bayê direqisîn** (Nofa, 29) *The tree branches* were gently dancing in the wind; 2) twigs that have fallen off the tree (FS): **•Wî *hejê darî* ji ser rêkê rakir** (FS) He removed *the dry tree branches* from the road. {also: hec II (Kmc-2); [hej هـژ/hezink هـزنـك] (JJ), cf. êzing} [Nofa/A/IFb/JJ/Kmc/ZF3/FS/BF/FD/CS] <hejik>

hej II هەژ (A) = movement. See **ḧej I**.

hejan هەژان (GF) = to tremble. See **ḧejîn**.

hejandin هەژاندِن (A/JB3/IFb/JJ/HH/GF/TF/OK/FS) = to shake. See **ḧejandin**.

hejde هەژدە (SK) = eighteen. See **ḧîjdeh**.

hejdeh هەژدە (A/IFb/JJ) = eighteen. See **ḧîjdeh**.

hejdehem هـەژدەهـەم *adj.* eighteenth, 18th. {also: hejdehemîn (IFb-2/ZF-2/Wkt-2); hejdeyem (Wkt-2); hejdeyemîn (Wkt-2); heştdehem (GF); heştdehemîn (GF-2); heştdemîn (IFb-2); hijdehem (CT/Wkt-2); hijdehemîn (Wkt-2); hijdeyem (Wkt-2); hijdeyemîn (Wkt-2)} Cf. P hijdahom هـجـدهـم; Sor hejdehem هـەژدەهـەم/hejdemîn هەژدەمین [IFb/ZF/Wkt//GF//CT] <ḧîjdeh>

hejdehemîn هـەژدەهـەمـيـن (IFb/ZF/Wkt) = eighteenth. See **hejdehem**.

hejdeyem هـەژدەيـەم (Wkt) = eighteenth. See **hejdehem**.

hejdeyemîn هـەژدەیـەمـیـن (Wkt) = eighteenth. See **hejdehem**.

hejihan هەژهان (HR) = to tremble. See **ĥejîn**.

hejik هـەژك *m.* (). 1) small twigs used as firewood: **-hejik û pejik** (GF-Cigerxwîn) small branches, twigs; 2) sharp, pointy twigs used for making wooden fences (Zeb). {also: hejik (JB1-A/GF/TF); <hejik> هـەژك (HH)} [Haz//HH/JB1-A/GF/TF/Zeb] <êzing; hej I; qoçik>

hejiyan هەژیان (FS) = to tremble. See **ĥejîn**.

hejîn هەژین (A/IFb/TF/AD) = to tremble. See **ĥejîn**.

hejîr هـەژیر *f.* **(-a;-ê).** 1) fig, bot. *Ficus*: **•Adetên bav û bapîran, kerik xweştir in ji *hêjîran*** (BX) [If] the customs of the ancestors [will it], unripe figs are better than *ripe ones [prv.]*; 2) fig tree. {also: hêjîr (HB/BX/IFb-2/B/Kmc-2); hijîr (Bw/SK); hijîrk' (JB1-A); hujîr (AA); [hejir] هـەژیـر (JJ); <hejîr> هەژیر (HH)} <O Ir *anačiθra- *in reference to erroneous view that the fig did not flower* (Laufer 411): Southern Tati dialects: Ebrahim-abadi anjila-dāra *f.* = 'fig tree' (Yar-Shater); P anjīr انـجـیـر -->T incir --> Rus inžir инжир; Sor hencîr هـەنـجـیـر; Za encil *m.*/incılı *f.* (Mal); Hau henjîr [HB/BX/B/Kmc-2//F/K/A/JB3/IFb/JJ/HH/GF/OK//Bw/SK//JB1-A//AA] <kerik I; kitik I>

hejmar هـەژمـار *f.* **(-a;-ê).** 1) number; numeral: **•Meşa Pridea Stockholmê ya roja şemiyê bi *hejmara* beşdar û temaşevanên xwe gihîşte rekorê** (sverigesradio.se 4.viii.2014) On Saturday, Stockholm's [Gay] Pride Parade broke a record with *the number of* participants and observers; 2) issue *(of a journal)*: **•Ev berhevoka destê we, ji hemû *hejmarên* kovara "Ronahî" pêk hatiye** (Ronahî-intro) This collection that [you are holding] in your hands consists of all *the issues of* the journal "Ronahî." {also: hêjmar (Ber); ĥej[i]mar (B); jimar (F/K-2/B); jimare (IF-2); jmar (IF-2); [ejmar اژمـار/ jimar ژمـار/ hijmar هژمـار] (JJ)} Cf. Mid P ōšmārag = 'calculation, reckoning' (M3); P šomāre شـمـاره = 'number'; Sor jimare ژمـاره/hejmar هـەژمـار [Ber//K/A/JB3/IFb/JJ/GF/TF/OK/ZF3//F/B] <hejmartin>

hejmarin هەژمارِن (SK) = to count. See **hejmartin**.

hejmartin هـەژمـارتـن *vt.* **(-hejmêr-/-jmêr-[IF]).** 1) to count, reckon: **•*Jimirîn* yek-yek minarane** (Z-1) They counted the minarets one by one **•Wî perên xwe *jimartin*** (FS) He counted his money **•Wî pezê xwe *hijmart*** (FS) He *counted* his sheep; 2) to consider, deem, regard (as): **•Ez te *dihejmêrim ... wekî* birayê xwe** (Wkt) I *regard* you *as* a brother. {also: hejmarin (SK); hemjartin (Mzg); hêjmartin (IF-2); hijmartin (M/OK-2/FS); jimartin (-jimir-) (F/K-2/B/IF-2/FS); jmartin; jimirîn (K-2); [ejmartin اژمـارتـیـن/ jimartin ژمارتین/hejmartin هژمارتین] (JJ)} O Ir *uz/uš- + *hmar- (Tsb 42): ***hmar-**: [Pok. (s)mer- 969.] 'to remember, recall, care for': Skt smar- = 'to remember' Av [hiš]maraiti = 'he notices'; Mid P ōšmurdan (ōšmār-) = 'to count, reckon; consider' (M3); P šomordan شـمـردن (-šomār-) (شـمـار) = 'to count'; Sor jimardin ژمـاردِن (-jimêr-); Za omorenã [omordiş (Todd)/omarıtış & homarıtış & ûmardış/ ûmarıtış (Mal)] & amorenã [amordiş] (Srk) [BX/K/A/JB3/IFb/TF/OK/Wkt//F/B/JJ//M/FS] <hejmar>

hek هەك = if. See **eger I**.

heke هەکە (OK)/hek'e (JB1-A&S) = if. See **eger I**.

hek'er هەکەر (JB1-S) = if. See **eger I**.

hekîm هەکیم (IFb) = doctor. See **ĥekîm**.

hekînî هـەکـیـنـی *adj.* conditional *(gram.)*: **-řaweya hekînî** (IF/GF) conditional mood. {syn: gerînî} <hek (=eger) = 'if' + -înî = adjectival ending [(neol)IF/GF/ZF3] <eger I>

hek'o هەکۆ (JB1-A) = if. See **eger I**.

hela I هـەلا *interj.* Come on!, C'mon! *(particle used with imperatives)*: **•*Hela* řave** (Z-1)/***Hela* řave were** (Z-1) [*Come on and*] get up! **•*Hela* binhêře** (Z-1)/***Hela* heře binhêře** (Z-1) *Come*/go look. {also: hila I} Cf. T hele [Z-1/K/IF/B] <de I>

hela II هەلا (F/K/B) = (not) yet. See **hila II**.

helaftin هەلافتِن (CCG-Rh/Mzg) = to throw up (high); to kick with both hind legs; to winnow. See **hilavêtin**.

helal هەلال (IF) = religiously permissible. See **ĥelal**.

helalok هـەلالـۆك (Dh/OK) = cornelian cherry. See **helhelok**.

helalûk هـەلالـووك (IFb) = cornelian cherry. See **helhelok**.

helan هەلان (IFb) = boulder. See **ĥelan**.

helanîn هـەلانـیـن (L/JB1-A) = to remove, pick up; to save. See **hilanîn**.

helatin هەلاتِن (IFb) = to rise (sun). See **hilhatin**.

helavêtin هـەلاڤێتِـن (IFb) = to throw up (high); to kick with both hind legs; to winnow. See **hilavêtin**.

helaw هەلاو (IFb/ZF3) = halvah. See **helva**.

helawîstin هـەلاویـسـتِـن (SK) = to hang up. See **hilawîstin**.

helbest هەلبەست *f.* **(-a;-ê).** poem [cf. Ar qaṣīdah قصيدة]: •***Helbestên*** **Cegerxwîn ji bilî yên ku nehatine çapkirin, di 8 dîwanan de, hatine berhevkirin** (Wlt 1:36, 16) Jegerkhwin's *poems*, excepting those that have not been printed, have been collected in eight diwans. {syn: hozan I; şêr II} Sor hełbest هەڵبەست = 'verse' [K(s)/A/JB3/IF/ZF3/Wkt/BF/FS]

helbestkar هەلبەستكار (ZF) = poet. See **helbestvan.**

helbestvan هەلبەستڤان *m.* **(-ê;).** poet: •***Helbestvan*** **şa'irekê navdar bûye** (I.Badî. Remezanê Cizîrî di dwîvçûn û twêjandineka dîtir da, 12) *The poet* was a prominent poet. {also: helbestkar (ZF)} {syn: biwêj I; hozanvan; şayîr} [Ber/IFb/Wkt/ZF3//ZF]

helbet هەلبەت *adv.* 1) certainly, of course (K/F/JJ); **-qey elbet** (K) undoubtedly, doubtless; 2) {syn: 'ese; mitleq; t'eqez} absolutely, without fail (A/IFb/JJ). {also: elbet (K-2/IFb-2); ḧelbet (B-2); ḧilbet (EP-7); [albetté البتة /helbét هلبت] (JJ)} < Ar al-battah (al-battata) البتّة [EP-7//F/K/A/IFb/JJ/B]

helbijartin هەلبژارتن (IFb/TF) = to elect. See **hilbijartin.**

helbirîn هەلبرين (IFb) = to lift. See **hilbir̄în.**

heldan هەلدان (Bar/IFb) = to raise, lift. See **hildan.**

helemor هەلەمۆر *f.* **(-a;-ê).** ashes with embers in them, glowing ash(es): •**Şivanî çaydankê xwe kir di nav *felemorê* r̄a ku çaya wî germ bibit** (FS) The shepherd put his tea kettle into *the glowing ashes* so that his tea would warm up. {also: felemor (MG/FS); xelamûr, m. (GF/FJ); <hełemur> هەڵەمور (Hej)} {syn: fehm II} = Sor jîlemo ژيلەمۆ = 'glowing ash' [Zeb/Hej/Wkt//GF/FJ//MG/FS] <ant'êx̌; bizot; xwelî>

helengiftin هەلەنگفتن (hel-engiv-) (M) = to stumble. See **hilîngiftin.**

helez هەلەز (GF) = alfalfa. See **heliz.**

helfirîn هەلفرين (IFb) = to jump or fly up. See **hilfir̄în.**

helgirtin هەلگرتن (IFb) = to lift; to load. See **hilgirtin.**

helgîn هەلگين *m.* **().** bucket, pail. {syn: dewl I; 'elb; sîtil} Cf. T helgin [Haruniye *Bahçe-Adana] & helke, halke, etc. = 'type of pail, generally made of copper, larger than a bakraç [copper bucket], used for holding water, milk, and the like' [su, süt vb. şeyleri koymaya yarayan, çoğunlukla bakırdan yapılan, bakraçtan büyük bir çeşit kova] (DS, v. 7, p. 2334-35) [Krş/Wkt]

helhelok هەلهەلۆك *f.* **(-a;-ê).** cornelian cherry, bot. *Cornus mas* [T kızılcık]: •**Te lêv al wek *helhelokê*** (pen-kurd.org:Ş.Berwarî. Dilê min borî êvar) Your lips are red like *cornelian cherries*. {also: helalok (Dh-2/OK); helalûk (IFb); <hilhilok> هلهلوك (HH)} [Dh/Kmc-7/TF/CB//OK//IFb//HH]

helisandin هەلساندن (IFb/GF) = to scratch; to crush. See **her̄işandin.**

helisîn هەلسين *vi.* **(-helis-).** to rot, go bad *(of fruit)*: •**Ji kerema xwe re destê xwe pirr nede tirîyan *wê bihellisin*!** (LM, 30) Please don't touch the grapes, they*'ll rot*. {also: hellisîn (LM)} {syn: r̄izîn} [LM//IFb/TF/ZF3]

heliyan هەليان (JB3/IFb) = to melt; to thaw. See **ḧelîn.**

heliz هەلز *f.* **(-a;).** *plant that grows in cold places such as mountainsides, fed to livestock*; lucerne, alfalfa? {also: helez (GF-2); helîz (TF); [heliz] هليز (JJ); <heliz> هلز (HH)} Sor hełîs هەڵيس = 'hay' (WE/K2); hełiz هەڵز = 'lucerne' (Hej: wênce) [Bw/A/IFb/HH/GF/ZF3//JJ/TF] <r̄izyane>

helî I هەلى (Bg) = mirror. See **hêlî.**

-helî II هەلى (GF) = step-, pseudo-. See **-ḧilî I.**

helîn هەلين (IFb) = to melt; to thaw. See **ḧelîn.**

hel înan هەلينان\هەل ئينان (SK) = to remove, pick up; to save. See **hilanîn.**

helîr هەلير (IFb) = confection of boiled grape juice. See **ḧelîl.**

helîz هەليز (TF/JJ) = alfalfa. See **heliz.**

helkehelk هەلكەهەلك (IFb/FJ/CS) = gasping, panting. See **hilkehilk.**

helkelk هەلكەلك (GF/SS) = gasping, panting. See **hilkehilk.**

helkirin هەلكرن (IFb/JB1-A/M) = to lift; to ignite. See **hilkirin.**

helkişandin هەلكشاندن (IFb) = to pull up; to pull out. See **hilk'işandin.**

helkişiyan هەلكشيان (IFb) = to climb. See **hilk'işîn.**

helkişîn هەلكشين (IFb) = to climb. See **hilk'işîn.**

hellisîn هەللسين (LM) = to rot. See **helisîn.**

helm هەلم (IFb) = steam; breath. See **hilm.**

helpekîn هەلپەكين (IFb) = to stumble. See **hilpekîn.**

helpisarin هەلپسارن (SK) = to lean, support. See **hilp'esartin.**

helpisartin هەلپسارتن (M) = to lean, support. See **hilp'esartin.**

helşîn هەلشين (IFb) = to be destroyed. See **hilweşîn.**

helva هەلڤا *f.* **().** halvah *(sweet made of ground sesame and caramel)*: •***Helva*** **ji şîrêzê çênabe** (BX) *Halvah* is not made of resin [*prv.*]. {also: helaw (IFb/ZF3); helwa (IFb-2/ZF3-2); helwe (K-2); ḧelaw, f. (K/GF); ḧelwe, f. (B); ḧewle (K-2);

[heoûla حـولا/ helaoû حـلاو] (JJ); <ȟelaw> حـلاو (HH)} [BX//K/JJ/HH/GF//B//IFb/ZF3] <xebûs>

helwa هەلوا (IFb/ZF3) = halvah. See **helva**.

helwe هەلوە (K) = halvah. See **helva**.

helwest هـەلـوەسـت *f.* **(-a;-ê).** attitude, approach: **•Di beşdarî û perwendehiya jinan de *helwesta* PKK'ê çawa ye?** (Wlt 1:36, 16) What is the PKK's *attitude* about the participation and training of women? **•Ev *helwest* nahêle ku HEP bibe xwedî şexsiyet** (Wlt 1:43) This *attitude* does not allow HEP to have a personality of its own **•Her wiha *helwesta* Tirkiyeyê ya nijadperest derkete ber çavê gelê cîhanê** (AW69C1) Likewise, Turkey's racist *attitude* has been noticed by the peoples of the world. {syn: şêl} Sor hełwêst هەڵوێست [(neol)Wlt/AW/Hej/ZF3]

hema هـەمـا *adv.* 1) immediately, soon: **•*Hema* zaro şûrê xwe avêt ser dûvê marî, dûvê marî peritand** (KH, 34) The child *immediately* swung his sword at the snake's tail, and severed the snake's tail **•Şêr ji vê p'arkirinê p'iř xeyîdî *hema* řabû ser xwe û lepek li nav ç'avê gur da** (Dz) The lion was furious at this division [of the spoils]; he *immediately* jumped up and struck the wolf between the eyes with his paw **•Zînê *hema* roja 'ewlinda haj hatina Memê delal hebû** (Z-1) Zin found out *immediately* on the first day about dandy Mem's arrival; 2) [*conj.*] but rather: **•Qet meçe nav Cizîrê, *hema* min hilde û ji vir bive** (EP-7) Don't go to Jazirah, *but rather* take me away from here; 3) the very one (B): **•Eva *hema* ew k'itêbe, ya ku ez lê digerim** (B) That is the *very* book that I am looking for. {also: heman II; [hema هـمـا/ heman هـمـان] (JJ)} Cf. P hamān هـمـان; T hemen. *See AKR (p. 68-71) for detailed discussion of **hema**.* [Dz/BX/K/JB3/IF/B/AKR]

hemal هەمال (IFb/Tsab) = porter. See **ȟemal**.

hemalî هـەمـالـی (IFb) = profession of porter. See **ȟemalî**.

hemam هەمام (JB3/IFb/OK) = bathhouse. See **ȟemam**.

hemamçî هـەمـامـچـی (OK) = bathhouse attendant. See **ȟemamçî**.

hemamiş هەمامِش (L) = bathing. See **ȟemamîş**.

heman I هـەمـان *adj./ pr. mod.* same, identical: **•di *heman* demê de** (YPA, 32) at *the same* time **•Her wiha folklornasê kurd Îzeddîn Mistefa Resûl jî li ser *heman* baweriyê ye** (YPA, 12) Likewise, the Kurdish folklorist I.M. Rasul is also of *the same* opinion **•Libasê xo temam guhorî, řast ço *heman* qehwe-xane ya şurê wî lê çoy** (SK 28:258) He changed his clothes completely and went straight to that *same* coffee-house where he had lost his goods. {also: [hema هما/heman همان] (JJ)} {syn: 'eynî} Cf. P hamān هـمـان; Sor heman هەمان [YPA/GF/JJ/SK/ZF/Wkt/SS]

heman II هەمان = immediately; rather. See **hema**.

hemandin هـەمـانـدِن (K/IFb/FJ) = to protect from. See **ȟemandin**.

hembal هەمبال (Tsab) = porter. See **ȟemal**.

hemberê هـەمـبـەرێ (K) = vis-à-vis; compared to. See **himberî**.

hemberî هـەمـبـەری (JB3/IF) = vis-à-vis; compared to. See **himberî**.

hembêz هەمبێز (IFb/ZF/FS) = embrace. See **ȟemêz**.

hembiz هـەمـبِـز *adj.* 1) {syn: hûr} tight *(of stitches)* (Zeb): **-dirwara hembiz** (Zeb) tight stitch; 2) dense, thick (of hair or vegetation) (HH/GF): **•porê wî yê reş û xweşik û *himbiz*** (SH 6) his black, beautiful, *thick* hair **•Wî gul *himbiz* çandin** (FS) He planted the flowers *very close together/ on top of each other.* {also: himbiz (GF); <himbiz> همبز (HH); <himbiz> همبز (Hej)} [Zeb//HH/GF/Hej/FS]

hemcinsî هـەمـجِـنـسـی (ZF3/Wkt) = homosexuality. See **hevcinsî**.

hemdem هـەمـدەم *adj.* modern, contemporary: **•Herçiqas av ji bo hemû jîndaran çavkaniyeke bingehîn be jî, îro di destê mirovên "*hemdem*" de wek pergaleke ji holê rakirina berhemên dîrokê tê bi kar anîn** (Wlt 1:21, 16) Although water is a basic resource for all living things, today it is being used by "*modern*" man as an instrument for destroying historical artifacts. {also: hevdem (GF/TF)} {syn: hevç'erx; nûjen} <P ham هم = 'same' + dem = 'time' [(neol)Wlt/K(s)/IFb/ZF3//GF/TF]

hemêz هەمێز (KS/IFb) = embrace. See **ȟemêz**.

hemin هەمِن (ZF3) (ZF3) = indeed, insofar as, etc. See **hemîn**.

hemis هـەمِـس (FS/ZF3) = black with white face (of goats). See **ȟemis**.

hemî هـەمـی (A/JB3/IFb/HH/JB1-A&S/SK/OK) = all. See **ȟemû**.

hemîn هـەمـیـن *adj.* 1) (It's) all the same, (makes) no difference; 2) *[adv.]* just now; from now on (IF); 3) already; yet (IF); 4) indeed, as a matter of fact, you know: **•Qîza qenc, *hemînî* ez kuřê p'adşê me, tu jî qîza p'adşêyî** (EH) Fair maiden, *just as* I am the son of a king, so are you the daughter of a king **•Wekî M. k'ê nestîne, *hemîn* wê min bistîne** (EP-7) If M. marries anyone, it must be me; 5) insofar as, since, as long as (K/B): ***•Hemîn* tu diçî, kuřê min jî xweřa bibe** (B) *Since* you're going anyway, take my son along with you. {also: hemin (ZF3); hemînî (EH)} [EP-7/K/JB3/IF/B//ZF3]

hemjartin هەمژارتِن (Mzg) = to count. See **hejmartin**.

hempar هەمپار (K) = companion; partner. See **hevp'ar**.

hemşîr•e هەمشیره *f.* **(•eya;•ê).** nurse, medical nurse: **•Di demeke kurt de pizîşkek ligel *hemşîreyekê* derbasî hundir bûbûn** (S.Birûsk. Xwezî, 101) In a short time a doctor had gone inside together with *a nurse*. P hamšīre همشيره = '(foster) sister' (nursed by the same woman) --> T hemşire = 'nurse' [S.Birûsk/ZF3/Wkt/RZ]

hemû هەموو (IFb/JB1-S/GF/OK) = all. See **ĥemû**.

hemwelat هەموەلات (K) = compatriot. See **hemwelatî**.

hemwelatî هەموەلاتی *m.* **().** compatriot, fellow countryman: **•Ez bi *hemwelatiyên* xwe re li ser vê axivîm** (Wlt 1:37, 16) I discussed this matter with my *compatriots*. {also: hemwelat (K)} [(neol)Wlt/ZF3/Wkt//K]

hencandin هەنجاندِن (IFb) = to cut into small pieces. See **hincinîn**.

***hence** هەنجه **().** joint *(anat.)*: **-Li ser *hencekî* maye** (IFb) It was about to come apart/It reached a point of change (a joint or node): **•Tu car *li ser hencekî nemîne*, tim xurtbe** (M.Çobanoğlu. Jiyana min neşelife) *Don't* ever *come apart*, always be strong. {syn: movik [1]} [IFb] <geh I>

hendeko هەندەكۆ (FJ) = clover. See **'endeko**.

hendekû هەندەكوو (GF) = clover. See **'endeko**.

hendeqû هەندەقوو (GF) = clover. See **'endeko**.

hene I هەنە (OK) = henna. See **ĥene**.

hene II هەنە = there are. See **hebûn**.

henek هەنەك (A/JB3/IF/JJ) = joke. See **ĥenek**.

henekoyî هەنەكۆیی (TF) = comedian. See **henekvan**.

henekvan هەنەكڤان *m.* **(-ê;).** comedian, jokester, joke teller: **•Kesên ku di nav civatên me Kurdan de henekan dikin an jî pêkenokan dibêjin, ew 'henekvan' in** (CP, 6) People who crack jokes or tell humorous anecdotes at the gatherings of us Kurds are 'comedians'. {also: henekoyî (TF); ĥenekbaz (K-2); ĥenekçî (K/B/GF/FS); ĥenekdar (B-2); ĥenekok (K); [hanakchi] هنكچی (JJ)} [CP/IFb/AD/ZF3/Wkt//K/B/GF/FS] <qeşmer>

hengam•e هەنگامە *f.* **(•eya;•ê).** commotion, tumult: **•Lê di vê *hengamê* da marî jî pê veda** (Dz #22, 390) But in this *commotion* the snake bit him. {also: hengeme (FJ); hingime (A)} {syn: gelemşe; hoqeboq; k'eft û left; qerebalix} Sor hengame هەنگامە [Dz/IFb/TF/ZF3//FJ//A]

hengeme هەنگەمە (FJ) = commotion, tumult. See **hengame**.

hengil هەنگِل (RZ/SS) = hip, haunch. See **hingul**.

heniz هەنِز (K[s]) = at that very moment. See **ĥeniz**.

henî هەنی (Krç) = forehead. See **'enî**.

hepik هەپِك *m./f.(ZF3)* **(;-î/-ê).** metal comb *for tightening the threads and beating down the woven fabric on a loom*: **•Wî bi *hepikî* tevn quta** (FS) He struck the loom with *the metal comb*. {also: hepo (FS-2); <hepik> هپك (HH); <hepik> هەپِك (Hej)} [Bw/Zx/IFb/HH/GF/OK/Hej/ZF3/FS] <befş; hevo; pîjik I; t'evn>

hepo هەپۆ (FS) = metal comb. See **hepik**.

heps هەپس (HYma) = prison. See **ĥebs**.

heq هەق *m.* **(-ê;).** 1) {syn: destûr [2]; ĥed [2]; maf} right (as in 'inalienable rights') ; 2) truth; 3) law; 4) reward: **-heqê *fk-î* da hatin** (B) to punish s.o. according to his deserts, to pay s.o. back, get even with s.o. [Cf. T hakkından gelmek]; **-heqê xwe standin** (Z-2): a) to earn, merit, deserve: **•Min *heqê* zehmetê xwe *stand*** (K) I *received payment* for my labor/I was paid for my trouble; b) ?to charge s.o. (money) for stg.; 5) wages, earnings, salary: **•Emê *heqê* wî bidinê** (EP-5, #9) We will give [=pay] him his *due* **•Nîvekî *heqê* xwe da** (EP-5, #10) He paid half of his *wages* **•Şuxulê şivana zaf çetin bû, lê *heqê* xebata wana gelekî kêm bû** (Ba2:1, 204) The shepherds' job was very hard, but their *earnings* were very small [lit. 'few']; 6) price (HH); 7) [*adj.*] true, right: **•Gotina wan *heq* bû** (IF) What they said was *right*. {also: ĥeq (FS); [haq] حق (JJ); <ĥeq> حق (HH)} <Ar ḥaqq حقّ = 'truth, correctness, duty' [Z-1/K/JB3/IF/B//JJ/HH/FS]

heqa هەقا (B) = so much. See **haqas**.

heqas هەقاس (B) = so much. See **haqas**.

heqîat هەقیئات (B) = remuneration. See **heqyat**.

heqîb هەقیب *f.* **(-a;-ê).** saddlebag: **•Şûr, mertal û kincên Memê Alan di *heqîbê* de bûn** (roniwar47.

wordpress.com: Bozê Rewan 30.ii.2015) M.A.'s sword, shield and clothes were in *the saddlebag*. {also: heqîv (IFb-2)} {syn: xurc; xurcezîn} < Ar ḥaqībah حقيبة = 'suitcase; handbag' [CCG/K/IFb/FJ/GF/Tsab/ZF/Wkt]

heqîv (IFb) = saddlebag. See **heqîb**.

heqyat هەقیات *f.* **(-a;).** payment, recompensation, remuneration *(for services rendered)*: **•Ĥeta r̄oja *heqyata* te bê, ez te bimalêva bidim xweykirinê, nehêlim kêmasîêd te hebin** (EH) Until the day of your *recompense* comes [i.e., for the rest of your life], I will see that you are well looked after, I won't let you lack anything. {also: heqîat (B)} [EH/K//B] <heq [4]>

her هەر *pr. mod.* 1) {syn: gişk; ĥemû; t'emam} [+ -ek] each, every; all: **•Ĥer kitêb*ek* hêjaye çar maneta** (B) *Every* book costs four rubles; **-her car**, See **hercar**; **-her çûye** = more and more, increasingly [cf. T gittikçe] **•Şovenîzm li Kurdistanê *her çûye* tûjtir bûye** (Ber) Chauvinism in Kurdistan has become *increasingly more* severe; **-her du** (IFb) = both. See **herdu**; **-her gav**, see **hergav**; **-her ro** (IFb/GF)/**her roj** (CS/GF/RZ), See **her̄o**; **-her û her** = continually; -**heryekî** = each one: **•heryekî ji me** (Bz) each (one) of us; 2) {syn: hergav; hert'im; t'im} always. {also: ĥer (B); [her] هـــر (JJ); <her> هـر (HH)} [Pok. solo- 979.] 'whole' & *sol(e)u̯o- (Ras, p.132): Skt sárva- = 'whole, entire, all, every'; O Ir *haru̯a- (Ras, p.132): Av haurva-; O P haruva- = 'all' (Kent); Mid P har(w) (M3); P har هـر (Horn #1090) --> T her; Sor her هەر = 'each, every, any; just, exactly, only, etc.' [K/A/JB3/IFb/JJ/HH/JB1-A&S/SK/GF/TF/OK//B] <herçî; herdu; hersê>

herac هەراج *f.* **().** auction: **-herac kirin** (OK) to auction off. {also: ĥerac II (GF); <ĥerac> حـراج (HH); <ĥerac حەراج/her̄ac هەڕاج> (Hej)} {syn: mezad} <Egyptian Ar ḥarāg حـراج = 'auction' [IFb/OK/ZF3//HH/GF/Hej]

heraftin هەرافتِن (SK) = to demolish. See **hêrivandin**.

heram هەرام (IF) = forbidden. See **ĥeram**.

heramî هەرامی (Wkt) = religious prohibition. See **ĥeramî**.

herboqe هەربۆقە (FS) = slipknot. See **xerboqe**.

hercar هەرجار *adv.* all the time, constantly, always. [K/IF/ZF3]

herçend هەرچەند/**her çend** هەر چەند *conj.* 1) although, even though, though: **•*Herçend* e ew neyê jî, ez dê bêm** (Wkt) *Even though* he may not come, I will come **•*Herçend* hê biçûk e jî lê dîsan jî pirr biaqil e** (Wkt) *Although* he is still small, he is very smart **•*Herçend* r̄îwî biraê kiçke ye, emma ji me têgeştîtir e, çêtir şolan dizanît** (SK 6:62) *Although* the fox is the younger brother he is nevertheless more intelligent than us and understands affairs better; 2) no matter how much, however much {syn: çendî}: **•*Herçend* kore xo newî kir o xo bi 'erdîwe nûsand emma fayde nekir** (SK 13:132) *However much* the blind man crouched and clung to the earth it was pointless **•*Herçendî* min anîbû bîra wî jî, ew nehat** (RZ) *No matter* how much I reminded him, he did not come **•*Herçend* min pêkol kir ko bihêm cem te, ez neşiyam** (BF) *No matter how hard* I tried to come to you, I was unable to **•*Her çend* veqetîna ji Gulê ji bo wî zehmet bû jî mêr bû û li xwe danetanî bide der** (R. Sorgul. Gurxenêq, 60) *No matter how* difficult it was for him to be parted from G., he was a man and he did not let himself show it; **-herçend ... ewçend** (BX) as ... as, the (more) ... the (more): **•*Herçend* mirov nezan e, xwe *ewçend* zana dihesibîne** (BX) *The* more foolish one is, *the* wiser one thinks one is. {also: herçendî (K-2/RZ)} Cf. Sor herçend هەرچەند = 'no matter how much, regardless of how many, whenever' [R.Sorgul/BX/K/IFb/FJ/GF/TF/Wkt/ZF3/BF/FD/SK/SS//RZ]

herçendî هەرچەندی (K/RZ) = although; however much. See **herçend**.

herçî هەرچی *adj./prn.* 1) each, every; all; everything: **•Ĥerçê ku ez derheqa çandina kûkûrûzda zanim, ezê wer̄a gilîkim** (B) I'll tell you *all* I know about sowing corn **•R̄ovî r̄abû *herçî* goştê nerm û bez li ber şêr danîn û *herçî* ûr û r̄ovî li ber xwe danîn** (Dz) The fox [got up and] put *all* the soft meat and fat before the lion, and *all* the entrails he put before himself ; **-herçî ko** (IF) whichever, whatever; whoever: **•*Herçî ko* gire bibijêre** (IF) Choose *whichever* is biggest **•*Herçî ko* birçîne werin** (IF) Come *whoever* is hungry **•Heçî ko mar e dijminê mirov e** (IF) All snakes are man's enemies/*Whatever* is a snake is man's enemy; 2) the one(s) who; 3) as for... [Fr quant à] (BX): **•*heçî* ez** (IF) *as for* me **•Û *ĥeç'iyê* xwarina rehne, bi kevç'îyê darî dixun, deqene devê wa neşewitê** (HR-I 1:38) And *as for* liquid foods [=soup], they eat them with wooden spoons, lest they burn their mouths. {also: heçî II (IF-2);

ȟeç'î[yê] (HR-I); ȟerçê (B); ȟerçî (B); [her-tchi] هرچی (JJ); <herçî> هرچی (HH)} < her = 'each' + çî = 'what' [BX/Dz/IF/JJ/HH//B] <her>

herd هەرد (Z-1) = both. See **herdu**.

herdu هەردو/**her du** هەر دو (JB3/IFb) *prn.* both: •***Herdu* rêwîyê birçî** (Dz) *Both* hungry travelers •***Herdu* ga li paş in** (AB) *Both* oxen are in the back •**Ew *herd jî* nazik û bedewin** (Z-1) *Both of them* are fine and beautiful. {also: herd (Z-1); ȟerd[u] (B); [her-douan هردوان/ her-doukan هردوکان] (JJ)} < her = 'each' + du = 'two' [Z-1/Dz/AB/K/JB3/IFb//JJ//B] <her; hersê>

here I هەرە *adv.* 1) {syn: ji hemû -tir; t'ewrî; -tirîn} *superlative degree of adjectives:* (the) most, -est: •**çiyaê *herê* bilind** (IF) *the* high*est* mountain •**desmala *here* r̄ind** (B) *the* fin*est* handkerchief •**şeherê *here* mezin** (K) *the* larg*est* city; 2) {syn: gelek; p'ir̄ II; ze'f} very, extremely. {also: herî II (IFb)} Cf. Sor here هەرە = 'the most' [K-dş/K/B//IFb]

herem هەرەم *f.* **(-a;-ê).** harem, separate area of house for the womenfolk: •**Rave her̄e *herema* qîza p'adşê** (HCK-5, #41, 226) Get up and go to *the harem of* the princess [king's daughter]; **-ehlê ȟeremê** (SK) womenfolk: •**Belko dilê paşa di malda ji biçûkan o ji *ehlê ȟeremê* 'aciz bobît** (SK 22:198) Perhaps the Pasha's heart has been grieved at home by the children or the *womenfolk*. {also: heremxane (K-2); ȟeramxane (B); ȟerem (SK)} {syn: heremodesî (EH)} < Ar ḥarām حرام = '(ritually) forbidden' [K/IFb/Tsab//JR/SK//B]

heremodesî هەرەمۆدەسی *f.* **(-ya;).** harem, special quarters for the womenfolk: •**Dê îda t'erka wê xeberê da, çû *heremodesîya* xwe** (EH) His mother dropped the subject, and went to her *room*. {syn: herem} < herem (qv.) + T odası = 'its room' [EH]

heremxane هەرەمخانە (K) = harem. See **herem**.

herêm هەرێم *f.* **(-a;-ê).** province, region, district: •**Şova jimare (13) bi destê Oskar Mann li *herêma* Sawcbilaxê (Mehabada niha) hatîye nivîsandinê** (K-dş) Version number 13 was recorded by Oskar Mann in *the district of* Soujbulaq (now Mehabad) •**Weke tê zanîn tirba Ehmedê Xanî li Bazîdê ye û weke ziyaretgeha xelkê *herêmê* ye** (Wlt 1:37, 3) As is known, the tomb of Ahmed-i Khani is in [Doğu]bayazit, and is like a shrine for the people *of the region*. {syn: navçe; neȟî} Cf. Sor herêm هەرێم = 'district, region' [K-dş/Wlt/K(s)/JB3/IFb/TF/OK/ZF3] <dever I[2]>

her̄fî هەرفی *adj.* old, senile, decrepit, doddering *(can be used as a substantive)*: •**Ewe cahil bû, pîrê hemîn *her̄fî* bû** (EH) She was young, but her mother was *very old* •***Her̄fîye* p'or̄spî bû** (EH) She was a white-haired *old woman* •**Te ȟevtê sal 'emr kirye, tu pîreke *her̄fî*** (EH) You have lived seventy years, you are a *doddering* old woman. {also: herifî (ZF3)} [EH//ZF3] <pîr; xerifîn>

hergav هەرگاڤ *adv.* all the time, constantly, always: •***Her gav* diya mirov kur nayne carinan qîz jî tîne** (ZF3) One doesn't always get what one hopes for/Life is full of little surprises [*idiom*] [lit. 'The mother of men doesn't always bear sons, sometimes she bears daughters as well']. {syn: her [2]; hert'im; t'im} [F/K/ZF3]

hergê هەرگێ (F) = if. See **eger I**.

her hosa هەر هۆسا (GShA) = likewise. See **her wiha**.

herifandin هەرِفاندِن (GF/Frq) = to demolish. See **hêrivandin**.

herifî هەرفی (ZF3) = old, decrepit. See **her̄fî**.

herikandin هەرِکاندِن/**her̄ikandin** هەرِکاندِن (K) *vt.* **(-herikîn-/-her̄ikîn- [K]).** to cause to flow, move (of water): •**Nûçeyên şehîdbûna wan hêstirên me *diherikînin*** (Wlt 1:32, 2) News of their martyrdom *causes* our tears *to flow*. [Msr/A/IFb/GF/TF/ZF3//K] <herikîn>

herikîn هەرِکین/**her̄ikîn** هەرِکین [K] *vi.* **(-herik-/-her̄ik- [K]).** to flow, move *(of water)*: **-Av *diherike*** (IF) The water *flows*. {also: [herekin] حرکین (JJ)} {syn: k'işîn} <Ar ḥarakah حركة = 'movement' [Msr/Haz/A/IFb/GF/TF/ZF3//K//JJ] <herikandin>

herimîn هەرمین (IFb/OK) = to be defiled; to go bad. See **ȟer̄imîn**.

herin هەرِن (IF) = to go. See **her̄în**.

heristandin هەرِستاندِن (IFb) = to crush. See **her̄işandin**.

her̄işandin I هەرِشاندِن *vt.* **(-her̄işîn-).** to crush, smash, mash; to thrash, shatter; to tear apart: •**Ez o to li-naw Herkîyan cotê kela yne. Digel spêdê şaxêt xo deyn e-ber yêk ka kî *dê* kê *her̄işînît*** (SK 40:361) Among the Herkis, you and I are a pair of buffaloes. At dawn, let's lock horns to see who *will tear* whom *apart*. {also: helisandin (IFb-2/GF); heristandin (IFb-2); [herichandin هرشاندین/ arešând(in) ارشاندین (G/Lx)] (JJ)} {syn: dan ber lingan; dewisandin; 'eciqandin; p'ekandin; p'elaxtin; p'erçiqandin; pêpes kirin; t'episandin}

<Ar √hrs هرس = 'to crush, mash' [JJ/SK/IFb/FJ/ZF3//GF]

heřîşandin II هەرِشاندن (K)/he'řîşandin هەعرِشاندن (HCK) = to scratch. See ĥeřîşandin.

heřîşîn هەرِشین *vi.* **(-heřîş-).** 1) to be crushed, smashed, mashed: •**Ev gundor *heřîşîye*** (FS) This melon *got crushed* •**Kabra p [=bi] her do pîya ser cendikê keft ĥeta mar têda *heřîşî*, îna mareke kuşt** (M-Ak, #555) The fellow fell upon the bag with both feet until the snake *was crushed* inside it, and so killed the snake; 2) to be crushed (by s.o.'s words or actions): •**Ew bi axaftina Zoroyî *heřîşî*** (FS) He *was crushed* by Z.'s words. {also: [herichin] هرشين (JJ)} <Ar √hrs هرس = 'to crush, mash' [FT/M/JJ/ZF3/FS] (K/B: ĥeřîşîn = to be scratched)

herî I هەری (IFb/HH) = wool. See **hirî**.

herî II هەری (IFb) = the most; very. See **here I**.

heřî III هەرِی (IFb/JJ) = mud. See **ĥeřî**.

heřîn هەرِین *vi.* **([di]heř-/[t]eř-;** *neg.* **naheřim/na rim** [JB3]; *subj.* **heřim;** imp. **here!).** to go *(most commonly used in the present tense and its derivatives)*: •**Lazime tu *herî*** (L) You must *go* •***Ezê heřim* be'rê bişewtînim** (Dz) I *will go* set the sea on fire. {also: herin (IF); [herin] هرين (JJ)} {syn: ç'ûn} [Pok. 1. ser- 909] 'to flow': Skt √sar [sarati] = 'to flow': *See note under* ***ç'ûn***. [BX/JB3/B/JJ/IF] <hatin; werîn>

herîr هەریر *m.* **().** silk. {also: [ḥarīr حرير/ḥalīl حليل] (JJ); <ĥelîl> حليل (HH)} {syn: hevirmiş} < Ar ḥarīr حرير = 'silk' [K/IF/JB1-S/JJ/ZF3//HH]

herke هەرکە (Z-3) = if. See **eger I**.

herkê هەرکێ (EP-1) = if. See **eger I**.

hermet هەرمەت = woman; respect. See **hurmet**.

hermê هەرمێ *f.* **().** 1) {syn: karçîn} pear; 2) pear tree, bot. *Pyrus communis* (IFb). {also: hermî (IFb-2/ZF3); hirmê (Kmc-2/RZ); hirmî (A/IFb-2/TF/OK-2/AA/RZ-2); hurmê (K/F/Ba2/B); [hirmi] هرمى (JJ)} Cf. Mid P urmōd = 'pear' (M3); P amrūt امروت/ amrūd امرود /Clq. armūd ارمود --> T armut & clq. Iraqi Ar. 'armūṭ عرموط; Sor hermê هەرمێ; Za mıroy *f.* (Mal); Hau hemrû [Ad/IFb/OK//K/F/Ba2/B//ZF3//Kmc-2/RZ//A/JJ/TF/AA] <alîsork; ĥezîranî; karçîn; kirosik; şekok; şitû>

hermiş هەرمِش = silk. See **hevirmiş**.

hermî هەرمی (IFb/ZF3) = pear. See **hermê**.

hermûş هەرمووش (F) = silk. See **hevirmiş**.

heřo هەرِۆ/**hero** هەرۆ [IFb/FJ/RZ/CS] *adv.* every day, daily: •**Eydî *heřo*, serê sibehê lawik dihat cihê mêr û li bilûra xwe dixist** (Dz, #22, 389) So *every day*, in the morning the boy came to the snake's place and played on his flute •***Heřo* kuřî dayka xo nesîĥet dikir, dayka wî jî digot, "Ĥewale-y xudê bike"** (SK 15:147) *Every day* the boy would admonish his mother, but all she would say was, `Leave him to God.' •**Xezaleke bi şîr *hero* sê cara dihate ser Birahîm û şeş meha şîrê xo didayê** (GShA, 227) A gazelle that had milk came to Ibrahim 3 times *a day* and fed him milk for six months. {also: her ro (IFb-2/GF); her roj (CS-2/GF-2/RZ-2); herro (K-2); herřo (B-2); herroj (K/FJ-2/CS-2); ĥero (B-2); ĥeřo (B); ĥerřo (B-2); [her rouj/ehro/her-ro] هرروژ (JJ)} Sor her řojê[k] هەر رِۆژێ[ك] [Dz/JB1-A/SK//IFb/FJ/RZ/CS//GF//K//B]

herro هەررۆ (K)/herřo هەررِۆ (B) = every day. See **heřo**.

herroj هەررۆژ (K/FJ/CS) = every day. See **heřo**.

herset هەرسەت (L) = sorrow. See **hesret**.

hersê هەرسێ *prn.* all three: •***Evana hersêk* bira bûn** (Z-1) *The three of them* were brothers •***Me ĥersêka* eva xebata kirye** (B) *The three of us* did that work. {also: hersêk (Z-1); hersêka; ĥersê[k] (B); [her si] هرسى (JJ)} < her = 'each' + sê = 'three' [Z-1/K/JJ//B] <her; herdu>

hersêk هەرسێك (Z-1) = all three. See **hersê**.

hersêka هەرسێکا = all three. See **hersê**.

hersim هەرسِم (Ardû) = unripe grapes; grape cluster. See **harsim**.

hert'im هەرتِم *adv.* always, constantly: •**Ew *ĥert'im* te bîr tîne** (B) He *constantly* mentions you •***Ĥert'im* ewê ez jî xweřa dibirim wê derê** (Ba2-#2, 206) She *always* used to take me there with her. {also: ĥert'im (B/Ba2)} {syn: her [2]; hergav; t'im} [Ba2/B//F/K]

hervaz هەرڤاز (FK-eb-1) = slope; up. See **hevraz**.

hervêz هەرڤێز (FK-eb-1) = slope; up. See **hevraz**.

herweha هەروەها (BF) = likewise. See **her wiha**.

herwanî هەروانی (Qzl/Kmc-#3507) = type of coat. See **hewran I**.

herwekî هەروەکی *adv./conj.* 1) as: •**Ji xwe *herwekî* nas e** (SW) *As* is known •***Herwekî* me got** (SW) *As* we said •***Herwekî* em nikarin biçin welatê xwe** (IF) *As* we cannot go to our homeland; **-herwekî ko** (JB3) do.; 2) [*conj.*] as if: •***Herwekî* here ber mirinê** (BX) *As if* he were going to [his] death. [SW/BX/K/JB3/IF] herwesa هەروەسا (BF) = likewise. See **her wiha**.

herwiha/her wiha هـــەر وهـــا *adv.* likewise: •**Ev serokatî ne bi tenê Serokatiya Neteweyî ye; *her wiha* serokatiya her kesê ku azadiyê dixwaze, pêst û kotekiyê dibîne, ye** (AW78A3) This leadership is not only national leadership; it is *likewise* the leadership of every person who desires freedom, who has experienced oppression and beatings •***Her hosa* çîroka here mezin ku Êzidî behs diken, çîroka Birahîm û Nemrûde** (GShA, 226) *Likewise* the greatest story that the Yezidis speak of is the story of Ibrahim and Nemrud •***Her wiha* ew balê dikişînin ser piştevaniya dewletên Ewrûpayê jî** (AW71A3) *Likewise* they draw attention to the support of the European states as well. {also: her hosa (GShA); herweha (BF); herwesa (BF-2); her wisa (GF); herwîsa (AD)} Sor her wa هـــەر وا [AW//GF//AD//GShA//BF]

her wisa هەر وسا (GF) = likewise. See **her wiha**.

herwîsa هەرویسا (AD) = likewise. See **her wiha**.

herzal هـــەرزال *f./m.(SK)* **(;-ê/-î).** raised platform on which people sit while on the roof, balcony, or in a vineyard; summer shelter of reeds erected on the roof (SK); raised platform on which beds and the like are placed (IFb); throne-like structure on four poles on which one sits while watching over vineyards and the like (IFb): •**Havîna diderk'evî-ye serê bana, û ji dêla texta *'enzêla* çêdikin, û li ser r̄azihin** (HR-I 1:35) In the summer they go out onto the roof, and instead of beds they make *platforms* ('enzêla) and sleep on them •**Memê, Ç'ekan, 'Efan, Qeret'ajdînva der tên ser banê *zêrhelê*** (FK-eb-2) Mem, Chekan, 'Efan, and Qeretajdîn go out onto the (roof or top of the) *platform* •**Wextê hawînê bû. Mala Osê hemî di keprê da bû. *Herzalekî* bilind jî çêkirî bû, Oso û jina xo li ser *herzalî* diniwistin, kur̄êt wî û mala wî jî di kepra binî da bûn** (SK 40:357) It was summertime. All of Oso's family was in a bough-hut. A high *superstructure* had also been made, and Oso and his wife were sleeping on *the superstructure* while his sons and household were in the hut beneath. {also: erzêl (RF/IFb-2);'enzêl (HR-I); 'erzêl (GF); herzalik (IFb/OK); herzêl (FS); hezêlk (Bw); zêrhel (FK-eb-2); <'erzêl> عـرزیـل (HH)} <Arc arzelā ארזלא (urzīlā אורזילא)/ arzīlā ארזילא/'arsal ערסל/'arselā ערסלא = 'cradle, hammock for watchmen in gardens' (< 'eres ערס/ 'arsā ערסא = 'bedstead') & Syr 'arzālā ܥܪܙܠܐ = 'a booth or hut of interwoven branches; a lodge in a cucumber-garden or vineyard'; Sor herzałe هـەرزاڵە = 'low platform, stand (for bed, furniture, etc.)' [FK-2//SK//GF//IFb/OK//FS//Bw] <kepir; kol II>

herzalik هـــەرزالِـــك (IFb/OK) = raised platform. See **herzal**.

herzan هەرزان (K[s]) = cheap. See **erzan**.

herzêl هەرزێل (FS) = raised platform. See **herzal**.

herzin هـــــــــــەرزن *m.* **(;-î).** millet, bot. *Panicum miliaceum*: •**Elbette dişêt du'ayekî wato biket her r̄oj hembanekî *herzinî* bo te ji xudê bixazît** (SK 4:34) He can certainly pray and ask God for a sack *of millet* for you every day. {also: herzîn (IFb)} {syn: garis; gilgil} < Proto-Ir *(h)ārzana-: Pamir dialects: Yidgha yurzʊn; Ormuri ažan; Parachi ârzən; Sanglechi wuẓdän; Wakhi yīrz^n (Morg); Pashto ẓdan & Wanetsi ēždən; Mid P arzan (M3); P arzan ارزن; Sor herzin هـــــەرزن/ herzîn هـــەرزیـــن = 'giant millet' [K(s)/SK/SS//IFb] <genim; xirovî>

herzîn هەرزین (IFb) = millet. See **herzin**.

hesab هەساب (IFb/GF/OK) = [ac]count; consideration. See **ḧesab**.

hesan I هەسان (A) = quiet; easy. See **asan** & **hêsa**.

hesan II هـــــەســـــان *m.* **(-ê; ḧesên** [B]**).** whetstone, sharpening stone: -**hesan kirin** (GF)/**ḧesan kirin** (K/B) to hone, sharpen, whet: •**Min dasa xwe *hesankir*** (GF) I *sharpened* my sickle. {also: hisan [2] (Bw); ḧesan (K/B); [hesan/husān (Rh)] هـــسان (JJ); <hesan> هسان (HH)} Cf. P fesān فسان; Sor hesan هـــەسان; Hau hesan; = Za kerra seqênayîşî [Bw/BF//A/IFb/JJ/HH/GF/TF/OK/SS//K/B] <hesûn; sûtin>

hesandin هـــەســـانـــدِن (IFb/OK) = to cause to feel; to inform. See **ḧesandin**.

hesawil هەساوِل (Tsab) = guard, soldier. See **ersewil**.

hesedî هەسەدی (MG) = envy, jealousy. See **ḧevsûdî**.

hesêb هـــەســـێـــب (IFb) = [ac]count; consideration. See **ḧesab**.

hesibandin هـــەسِـــبـــانـــدِن (JB2/Rnh/IFb/TF/OK) = to consider. See **ḧesibandin**.

hesin هەسِن *m.* **(-ê;).** 1) iron *(metal)*: •***Ḧesinê* bê'esas ne dibe k'êrendî, ne dibe de's** (Dz-#698) Unsmelted *iron* becomes neither scythe nor sickle *[prv.]*; 2) anchor (JJ). {also: asên (JB1-A); asin (A-2/SK/Bw); ḧesin (K/B); [hesin هـــســـن/hasin

هـــاسـن] (JJ); <hesin> هــــســـن (HH)} <O Ir *ans(u)wan-, cf. Tokharian eñcuwo; Old P aθwanya-; ?Av haosafna-?; Sgd 'spyn [aspēn]; Mid P āhan/āhen (M3); P āhan آهن; Sor asin ئاسِن; Za asin *m.* (Todd); Hau asin *m.* (M4). See: M. Schwartz. "Irano-Tocharica," in: *Mémorial Jean de Menasce*, ed. Ph. Gignoux & A. Tafazzoli (Louvain : Imprimerie Orientaliste : Fondation Culturelle Iranienne, 1974), p. 409, note 33 [K/B//F/A/JB3/IF/JJ/HH//SK/Bw//JB1-A] <p'ola>

hesinger هەسِنگەر *m.* **(-ê;).** blacksmith: •**Mem kuřê *hesinger* bû** (K-dş, 88) Mem was the son of *a blacksmith*; -**Kawayê hesinkar** (PÇ) Kawa the blacksmith, *protagonist of the story of Newroz (Iranian New Year)*. {also: asinger (SK); hesingêr (IF); hesinkar (PÇ); hesinker (IF-2); [hasin-gher] هاسنگر (JJ)} {syn: ĥedad} Cf. P āhangar آهنگر; Sor asinger ئـاسِـنـگـەر [K-dş/GF/ZF3//JJ//SK//IF//PÇ] <hesin>

hesingêr هەسِنگێر (IF) = blacksmith. See **hesinger**.

hesinî هـەسِـنـی *adj.* made of iron, iron *(adj.)*: •**Ew jî dibê kevç'îyê *hesinî*, di nav girara germ da disincirê; ji wê yekê kevç'îyê darî qîmetlitir e** (HR-I, 1:40) They also say that *iron* spoons [lit. 'the iron spoon'] melt [or, heat up] in hot porridge; for this reason wooden spoons are [lit. 'the wooden spoon is'] more valuable •**Solek *hesinî* ji xwe re çêkir** (L) She had shoes *of iron* made [for herself]. {also: ĥesinî (K); [hasini] هاسنی (JJ)} Cf. P āhanī آهنی & āhanīn آهنين; Sor asinîn ئاسِنين; Za asınin/asınên (Mal) [L/A/IF/GF/HR-I//JJ//K] <hesin>

hesinkar هەسِنكار (PÇ) = blacksmith. See **hesinger**.

hesinker هەسِنكەر (IF) = blacksmith. See **hesinger**.

hesiyan هـەسِـيـان (JB3/IFb/OK) = to feel, sense. See **ĥesîn**.

hesîn هەسين (IFb/OK) = to feel, sense. See **ĥesîn**.

hesîl هەسيل (A) = mat. See **ĥesîr**.

hesîr هەسير (IFb/GF/TF) = mat. See **ĥesîr**.

hesk هـەسـك *f.* **(-a;-ê).** 1) {syn: çemçik; k'efgîr[1]} wooden ladle: •***Heskek* serê çawîş xist, serê çawîş şikest** (Z-1) She took *a ladle* to the servant's head, and broke his skull; 2) scoop (B). {also: heskû (FS); huskîk (Bw); ĥesik (B); [hesk هسك/heské هسكی/heskou هسكو] (JJ); <hesko> هسكو (HH)} Sor eskwê [eskö] ئەسكوێ [Z-1/K/A/JB3/IF/JJ//B//HH//FS//Bw] <çoçik; kefçî; k'efgîr>

heskû هەسكوو (FS/JJ) = ladle. See **hesk**.

hesp هـەسـپ *m./f.* **(-ê/-a; hêsp, vî hespî/-ê).** 1) horse *(m.)*; mare *(f.)* *(in Adiyaman, **hesp** refers to a young horse: **bergîr** is the more general word for horse there)*: •**Ez li *hêsp* suwar bûm** (BK) I mounted *the horse* •**Ez *li hespê* suwar bûm** (BK) I mounted (=got on the back of) *the mare*; -**ĥespê nêr** (B) colt, foal; -**ĥespa mê** (B) mare {syn: mehîn I}; 2) *used in names of several insects*: -**ĥespa bûkê/ĥespa gihîyê** (B) dragonfly {syn: teşîrok}; -**hespê fatma nebî** (ZF3/FS/Kmc)/**hespê nebî** (FJ/GF/Wkt)/**hespikê nebiya** (Kmc)/ **hesp[ik]ê pêxember** (IFb/Wkt) praying mantis {syn: balbalok}. {also: ĥesp (B); ĥesp' (JB1-A); [hesp] هسپ (JJ); <hesp> هسپ (HH)} {syn: bergîr; bor; *nijda} [Pok. eḱu̯o-s 301.] 'horse': Skt aśva- *m.*; O Ir *aswa-: Av aspa- m.; O P asa-; Mid P asp (M3); P asp اسـپ; Sor esp ئـەسـپ; Za istor *f.* (Todd)/estor/istor *m.* (Mal); Hau esp *m.* (M4); cf. also Lat equus; Gr hippos ἵππος; *perhaps* Arm ēš էշ = 'donkey' [and T eşek?] [Ad/BX/F/K/A/JB3/IF/JJ/ HH/ BK/SK//B/JB1-A] <bijî I/gulî I[2] = 'mane'; canî/kuřik = 'colt, foal'; êrdek = 'spare/extra horse'; hêstir II = 'mule'; k'er III = 'donkey'; k'iĥêl = 'bay horse'; mehîn I = 'mare'; me'negî = 'pedigreed horse'; řevo = 'herd of horses'; t̲ewle = 'stable'>

hesret هـەســرەت *f.* **(-a;-ê).** 1) {syn: derd; xemgînî} sorrow, grief: •**Tirsa min ... ez bimirim û *herseta* wan teresê birê min di dilê min de bimîne** (L) I'm afraid that I'll die, while *sorrow over* my good-for-nothing brothers remains in my heart; 2) longing, yearning; desire: •**Dîtina hilatina tavê *hesreta* min e** (M.Uzun Roja Evd. Zeyn., 93) Seeing the sun rise is my *desire* •**Ez *bi hisreta* wan çavên te yên reşî belek *mame*** (ZZ-6, 122) I *have been longing for* those black eyes of yours. {also: herset (L); hisret (ZZ); ĥesret (B); [hasret] حسرت (JJ); <ĥesret> حسرت (HH)} < Ar ḥasrah حسرة --> P ḥasrat حـسـرت --> T hasret [L//K/IFb/ZF//B/HH//JJ/ /ZZ]

hest هەست *f./m.(ZF3)* **(;-ê/).** sense, feeling: •**Piştî ku min pêşgotina pirtûkê xwend, *hîs* û baweriyeke wusa li min peyda bû ku ez binivisînim** (Epl 11) After I read the introduction to the book, *a feeling* and belief overcame me that I should write; -**hest kirin** = to feel, sense: •**Gava ez bi kurdî dipeyivim ez rehet dibim, ez *xwe* rehet *hîs dikim*** (Nûdem 30 [1999], 10) When I speak Kurdish, I relax, I *feel* comfortable •**Wî *hest dikir* ev jîngehe ya dibîte hêzeka rêgir beramber viyanêt wî yêt hunerî û viyana wî bo serbestîyê** (Peyv 3[1996], 38)

He *felt* that this environment was getting in the way of [lit. 'becoming a preven-tive force against'] his artistic desires and his desire for freedom. {also: hîs (Epl); [hys] حس (JJ)} < Ar ḥiss حسّ = 'feeling'; Sor hest هەست [Peyv/K(s)/A/IFb/GF/TF//JJ/Epl/ Nûdem]

hest•e هەستە *m.* **(•ê;).** 1) {syn: arbeşk; berheste} flint; 2) steel *(used for striking fire from a flint)*: **-heste lêxistin** (IF) to strike a light; 3) cigarette lighter. {also: ḧeste (B); [hesté] هسته (JJ); <heste> هسطه (HH)} Sor estê ئەستێ = 'steel (for use with flint to produce fire)' [Wr/K(s)/A/IF/JJ//HH//B] <cigare; çeqandin>

hesterik هەستەرك (MK) = star. See **stêr I**.

hestir هەستِر (K) = camel. See **ḧêştir**.

hestirvan هەستِرڤان = camelherd. See **heştirvan**.

hestiyarî هەستِيارى *f.* **(-ya;-yê).** 1) sensitivity; sensibility: **•Heya salên du hezarî nivîs û helbest bêtir berên *hestiyariyê* bûn** (Nbh 135:52) Until [i.e., before] the year 2000 writing and poetry were more products *of sensibility*; 2) allergy. {also: hestîyarî (TF); hestyarî (ZF/Wkt)} [Nbh//TF/ /ZF/Wkt]

hestî هەستى *m.* **(-yê;).** bone: **•*Hestûê* min navêje, *hestûê* min têke torbekî** (J) Don't throw my *bones* out, gather my *bones* in a sack **•Û *hestî* ji şêrr̄a danîn** (Dz) and he left [lit. 'put'] *the bones* for the lion; **-hestîyê fîla** (L) ivory: **•qesefek ji *hestîyê fîla*** (L) a cage of *ivory* [lit. 'of bones of elephants']; **-ḧestuyê çokê** (B) kneecap. {also: hestû (J/F); hêstik (SK/Zeb); ḧestu (B); ḧestû (B-2); [hesti] هستى (JJ); <hestî> هستى (HH)} [Pok. ost(h)- 783.] 'bone' --> *OestE/r/n: Skt ásthi *n.* (*gen.* asthnas); O Ir *ast- *n.*; Av ast- *n.*; Sgd stk- [stak] --> Yaghnobi sətak; Mid P ast/ astag/astuxān (M3); P ostoxān استخان; Sor êsk ئێسك/êskan ئێسكان/êsqan ئێسقان; Za iste *m.* (Todd)/heste (Mal); cf. also Hittite ḫastāi; Gr osteon ὀστέον; Lat os, ossis *n.*; Arm oskr ոսկր (-k- < *-tw-). M. Schwartz: For the early Iranian peoples, bone represented essence, that which gives shape, e.g., Av astuuaṇt-, *fem.* astuuaitī- = 'material (world)' [L/K/A/JB3/IF/JJ/HH//J/F//B//SK/Zeb]

hestîf هەستيف *f.* **(-a;-ê).** 1) baker's peel, *a long-handled, spade-shaped instrument used by bakers for getting bread in and out of the oven*; 2) scraper, spatula *for scraping dough from trough* (B). {also: hestîv (K/GF-2/FS-2); hestîvk (FS); ḧestîf (B); ḧestîv (B-2); [hestiw] هستيف (JJ); <hestîf> هستيف (HH)} [A/IF/HH/GF/ZF3//K/JJ//FS//B] <hevîr; nan>

hestîv هەستيڤ (K/GF/JJ/FS) = baker's peel. See **hestîf**.

hestîvk هەستيڤك (FS) = baker's peel. See **hestîf**.

hestîyarî هەستييارى (TF) = sensitivity; allergy. See **hestiyarî**.

hestû هەستوو (J/F) = bone. See **hestî**.

hestyarî هەستيارى (ZF/Wkt) = sensitivity; allergy. See **hestiyarî**.

hesûd هەسوود (IF) = envious, jealous. See **ḧevsûd**.

hesûdî هەسوودى (IF) = envy, jealousy. See **ḧevsûdî**.

hesûn هەسوون *vt.* **(-hes-/-husû-** [SK]**/-ḧusû-** [JB1-A]**).** 1) to rub; to polish (K); to wipe: **•Hingo 'adet kirîye, kesê destê merḧemetê bi serê hingoda bînît dê leqekî li wî destî den, we kesê pîyê bi-gû di serê hingo *bihusût* mirç-mirç dê wî pê maç ken** (SK 57:661) If anyone lays a compassionate hand upon your head you have been accustomed to bite that hand, and if anyone *wipes* a dung-covered foot on your face then you kiss that foot noisily; 2) to whet, sharpen (JJ). {also: husûn (M/SK); ḧûsûn (JB1-A); **sûtin**; [hesoun] هسون (JJ)} [Pok. ḱē(i)-: ḱō(i)-: ḱə(i)- 541-2.] 'to sharpen, whet'--probably extension of afi- = 'sharp': Skt śi-śā-ti/śy-áti = 'sharpens, whets'; O Ir *su-/*sav-: Av saēni- = 'tip, point'; P sūdan سودن (-sāy-) (ساى) & sōhān سوهان = 'file (tool)'; Sor s[u]wan سووان = 'file; to be rubbed' & sûn سوون = 'to rub'; Za sawenã [sawitiş] = 'to rub, sharpen' (Mal/Srk) [S&E/K/JJ//M/SK//JB1-A] See also **sûtin**. <êge; hesan II; k'artik; r̄endin>

heş هەش *f.* **(-a;).** indigo, dark blue, bot. *Indigofera tinctoria* [Ar nīl نيل, nīlaj نيلج]: **•*Heşa* Mûşê ye, li min venabe** (in a song of Miḧemed Arif Cizîrî) It is *the indigo of* Mush, it won't open up for me. {also: [hech] هش (JJ); <heş> هش (HH)} {syn: çivît} Sor heş هەش; *back formation from **heşîn***. [Zeb/JJ/ HH/GF/Wkt] <heşîn>

heşaftin هەشافتِن (FJ) = to distort; to obliterate. See **heşifandin**.

heşandin هەشاندِن *vt.* **(-heşîn-).** to prepare with stuffing, to stuff *(meat)*: **•Herin jê re berxekî *biheşînin* û bînin** (L) Go *stuff* a lamb for him and bring it. {also: hêşandin (K); ḧeşandin (FS)} < Ar ḥašá حشى = 'to stuff' [L/ZF3//K//FS]

heşfandin هەشفاندِن (FJ) = to distort; to obliterate. See

heşifandin.

heşifandin هەشِفاندِن *vt.* **(-heşifîn-).** 1) to blur, distort, render indistinct or unclear: •**Lê divê bête gotin ku ev hewcedarî, rengên destnîşankirinên li jor *diheşifîne*** (R. Alan. Bendname, 108) But it must be said that this necessity *blurs* the aforementioned designations; 2) to blot out, obliterate, wipe out, destroy (FJ/GF/HH). {also: heşaftin (FJ); heşfandin (FJ-2); ḧeşifandin (K[s]); <ḧeşifandin حشفاندن (diḧeşifîne) (دحشفينه)> (HH)} [Alan/ZF//K(s)/HH//FJ//GF]

heşifîn هەشِفین *vi.* **(-heşif-).** to become blurred, indistinct, unclear; to be distorted: •**Kaxidekî ku *biheşife*, êdî ji nivîsînê re nabe** (Wkt) Paper which *has become ruined* [by spilt ink, etc.], is no longer of use for writing •**Rêgeza ku nivîskar ji xwe re kiriye rêber *heşifiye*** (R. Alan. Bendname, 107) The principle which the writer made his guide *has been distorted*. [Alan/ZF]

heşîn هەشین *adj.* 1) {syn: sût II} blue; 2) {syn: k'esk} green (K/B/HH); **-heşîn bûn** = a) to grow green; b) to grow, bloom, blossom: •**Ser wî kulîlkêd ḧemû řenga û cûřa *hêşîn dibûn*** (Ba2:1, 202) On it [=Mount Dumanlu] flowers of all colors and types *would grow*. {also: hêşîn (Z-1/K/B/IFb-2/ZF3-2); hêşin (A); şîn II (ZF3); [hichin هشين/chin شين] (JJ); <heşîn> هشين (HH) - cf. also [hech] هش (JJ) = 'indigo'} "The words for 'black', 'blue', and (dark) 'green' are frequently interchangeable in Ir. and Ind. languages" [Georg Morgenstierne. "Notes on Balochi Etymology," *Norsk Tidsskrift for Sprogvidenskap* 5, (1932), 50, ¶81, reprinted in: *Irano-Dardica* (Wiesbaden : Dr. Ludwig Reichert Verlag, 1973), p. 161.] Cf. Av axšaina- = 'color of blue vitriol'; Mid P xašēn/axšēn (Scythian); Pamir dialects: Yidgha axšīn = 'blue'; Ormuri ṣ̌īn = 'blue; green' (Morg); Pashto šīn = 'blue; green'; Sor şîn شین = 'blue, green (of nature)'; K heşîn --> T heşin [Şenoba, Uludere-Hakkâri] = 'green, blue' (DS, v. 7, p. 2349); cf. P xašīnsār خشینسار [lit. 'blue head'], type of bird. Etymology of Euxine (Greek name for Black Sea < Euxeinos < Axeinos < Scythian *axšaina- challenged by François de Blois in: 'The Name of the Black Sea,' in: Macuch, Maria and Maggi, Mauro and Sundermann, Werner, (eds.), *Iranian languages and texts from Iran and Turan : Ronald E. Emmerick memorial volume*. (Wiesbaden: Harrassowitz, 2007) pp. 1-8. {heşînahî; heşînatî; hêşînatî; hêş[î]nayî; şînkatî; [hichinàï هشناى/ shīnātī شیناتی] (JJ)} [K/B//A//JB3/IFb/HH//JJ//ZF3] <heş; tebesî>

heşînahî هەشیناهی (Rnh 2:17) = greenness; vegetation. See **heşînatî**.

heşînatî هەشیناتی *f.* **(-ya;-yê).** 1) greenness, verdure; 2) vegetation; greenery; 3) {syn: deramet I; dikak; êmîş [2]; p'incar} vegetable(s). {also: heşînahî (Rnh 2:17, 308); hêşînatî (K); hêşînayî (B); hêşnaî (F); hêşnayî (K); şînkatî (Bw); [hichinàï هشناى/ shīnātī شیناتی] (JJ)} [K/F//JB3/IF//JJ/B//Bw] <gîya; heşîn>

heşîya هەشییا (IS) = thing, object. See **eşya**.

heşt هەشت (A/JB3/IFb/JB1-A&S/SK/GF/TF/OK) = eight. See **ḧeyşt**.

heştan هەشتان (IF) = eighth. See **ḧeyşta**.

heştdeh هەشتدەه (IFb) = eighteen. See **ḧîjdeh**.

heştdehem هەشتدەهەم (GF) = eighteenth. See **hejdehem**.

heştdehemîn هەشتدەهەمین (GF) = eighteenth. See **hejdehem**.

heştdemîn هەشتدەمین (IFb) = eighteenth. See **hejdehem**.

heştek هەشتەك (GF) = an eighth. See **heştêk**.

heştem هەشتەم *adj.* eighth, 8th. {also: heştemîn I (GF/TF/RZ/IFb-2/Wkt-2); heyştem (A/Wkt-2); heyştemîn I (Wkt-2); **ḧeyşta**} Cf. P haštom هشتم; Sor heştem[în] هەشتەم[ین] [CT/IFb/ZF/Wkt//A//GF/TF/RZ] <ḧeyşt>

heştemîn I هەشتەمین (GF/TF/RZ/IFb/Wkt) = eighth. See **heştem**.

heştemîn II هەشتەمین (IFb) = eightieth. See **heştêyem**.

heşteyemîn هەشتەیەمین (IFb) = eightieth. See **heştêyem**.

heştê I هەشتێ (A/IFb/HH/TF/OK) = eighty. See **ḧeyştê**.

heşt'ê II هەشتێ (JB1-A) = eighth. See **ḧeyşta**.

heştêk هەشتێك *f.* **(-a;).** an eighth, 1/8: •***Heştêka* (*heşt yeka*) řezî min kiřî** (AR, 288) I bought *an eighth of* the vineyard. {also: heştek (GF); ḧeyştyek (K)} Sor heşt-yek هەشتیەك (Sulaimania & Kerkuk)/ heşt-yêk هەشتێك (Arbil) [Zeb/AR//GF//K]

heştêmîn هەشتێمین (IFb) = eightieth. See **heştêyem**.

heştêyem هەشتێیەم *adj.* eightieth, 80th. {also: heştemîn II (IFb-2); heşteyemîn (IFb-2); heştêmîn (IFb-2); heştêyemîn (Wkt-2); heştiyemîn (GF-2); heştîyem (GF); heyştemîn II (IFb); heyştêyem (Wkt-2); heyştêyemîn (Wkt-2)} Cf. P haštādom

هشتادم; Sor heşta[he]mîn هه‌شتاهه‌مین [Wkt//GF//IFb] <ḧeyştê>

heştêyemîn هـه‌شـتـێـیـه‌مـیـن (Wkt) = eightieth. See **heştêyem**.

heştir هه‌شتِر (JB3/IFb) = camel. See **ḧêştir**.

heştirme هـه‌شـتِـرمـه (IFb/Wkt/FD) = ostrich. See **hêştirme**.

heştirvan هـه‌شـتِـرڤـان *m.* **(;-î).** camelherd, cameleer: •***Ḧêştirvanî* ḧêştir birin çerê** (FS) *The camelherd* took the camels to pasture. {also: hestirvan; hêstirvan (K); hêştirvan (GF/OK/ZF3); ḧêştirvan (FS); [huchtur-van] هشـتـروان (JJ)} {syn: selwan} Cf. P ušturbān اشـتـربـان/ šotorbān شـتـربـان; Sor ḧuştirewan حوشترەوان/wuştirwan ووشتروان [JB3/ IFb//K//GF/OK/ZF3//JJ//FS] <ḧêştir>

heştiyemîn هـه‌شـتِـیـه‌مـیـن (GF) = eightieth. See **heştêyem**.

heştî I هه‌شتی (JB3/GF/OK) = eighty. See **ḧeyştê**.

heştî II هه‌شتی (IF/JJ) = eighth. See **ḧeyşta**.

heştîyem هه‌شتییه‌م (GF) = eightieth. See **heştêyem**.

heştpê هه‌شتپێ *f./m.(FS)* **(-ya/-yê;-yê/).** octopus *(lit. & fig.)*: •***Heştpê* yan axtepot hov e û bi piyên xwe nêçîra xwe digire** (Wkp: Heştpê) *The octopus* is wild and it catches it prey with its arms [lit. 'legs'] •**Piştî tev welatiyê van bajar û navçeyan bi xorti koçber kir dê *heştpêyê* (ahtapotê) xwe li van wargehan cih bike** (S. Feqiyanî. Xendan 9.ii.2016) After it has exiled all the citizens of these cities and districts it will install its *octopus* in these regions. {also: ḧeyştp'ê (K)} [Wkp/IFb/ZF3/Wkt/FD/FS/ /K]

heşt-ṣed هـه‌شـت صـه‌د num. eight hundred, 800. Av ašta sata; P hašt ṣad هـشـت صـد; Sor heştsed هه‌شتسه‌د [SK]

heştyê هه‌شتیێ (JB1-S) = eighth. See **ḧeyşta**.

heta هه‌تا = until. See **ḧeta** & **t'a IV**.

hetahetayî هـه‌تـاهـه‌تـایـی (JB3/IF) = eternity. See **ḧetaḧetayî**.

hetanî هه‌تانی = until. See **ḧeta** & **t'a IV**.

hetaw هه‌تاو (SK) = sun. See **tav I**.

hetik هه‌تِك (A/IFb) = honor, decency. See **hetk**.

hetikber هـه‌تِـكـبـه‌ر *adj.* slandering, gossiping about others. [Dh/Zeb/ZF3] <hetk>

hetk هـه‌تـك *f.* **(-a;-ê).** honor, decency, good reputation; **-hetka *fk-ê* birin** (SK/Zeb) to disgrace, ruin s.o.'s reputation; to dishonor, insult: •**Dengê xwe bilind neke, te *hetka me bir*** (Zeb) Don't raise your voice, you'*ve disgraced us* [=the neighbors will hear] •**Eger te kêmatîyek di mêvandarîya me da dît, *hetka me nebe*--ango nebêje xelqî** (Zeb) If you find a defect in our hospitality, *don't ruin our reputation*--i.e., don't tell anyone •**Mamê Ṝezgo gazî kirê, "Ho mamê kal, were, digel me kebaba bixo." Got, "Ez digel sa naçime ser keleşê mirar." Dîsa xulaman gotin** [sic], **"Aẍa, da biçînê, *ewî hetika me bir*"** (SK 37:331) Mam Razgo called to him, "Ho, old fellow, come and eat kebabs with us." He said, "I don't go to a carcass of carrion with dogs." Again the henchmen said, "Agha, let us go for him, *he has insulted us*" •***Te ḧetka me bir*** = **Te em şermezar/ rûreş kirîn** = *You humilitated/disgraced us*. {also: hetik (A); ḧetk (K/XF); <hetk> هه‌تك (Hej)} cf. Ar hatk هـتـك = 'tearing; exposure, exposé; dishonoring, disgracing, debasement' [Zeb/JJ/SK/GF/Hej//A//K/XF] <bêhetik; hetikber; şerm>

hetta هه‌تتا (IS) = until. See **ḧeta** & **t'a IV**.

hev هـه‌ڤ *prn.* each other, one another (*Western dialects* -BX); together: •**Me *hev* dît** = We saw *each other* •**Me *hevûdû* nas kir** = We knew [or, met] *one another* •**Didine *hevdin*** (Ad) They are arguing [lit. 'They are giving [it] to *each other*'] •**Em brayên *hev* in** = We are brothers [lit. 'We are *each other's* brothers']; **-ber hev kirin** = to collect, gather. See **berhev**. {also: hevdi; hevdin (Ad); hevdu (K); hevdû; hevûdin; hevûdî; hevûdu (JB3); hevûdû; ḧev I (JB1-S); [hew] هـڤ (JJ)} {syn: yek[3]} [Pok. 2. sem- 902.] 'one, in unison, with': Cf. Mid P ham = 'also; same' (M3); P ham هـم; Sor haw هـاو [BX/K/JB3/IF/JJ/B//JB1-S] <jev; lev; p'ev; t'ev>

heval هـه‌ڤـال *m.&f.* **(-ê/-a; hevêl [B], vî hevalî/).** 1) friend, companion, pal, buddy, chum: •**Kuṝ ṝabû cotê xwe û nîrê xwe derxist, gaê xwe girêda, dya xwe kire *hevalê* gê** (J) The boy got up and took out his plough and yoke, tied up his ox, and made his mother *the companion of* the ox (=tied her up to the other side of the yoke); **-heval û hogir** (Z-1) do.; 2) comrade *(in socialist parlance, equivalent of Russian tovarishch товарищ)*: •***Hevala* Semîre tu di nava komê de ya herî ciwan î** (AW73A3) *Comrade* Semira, you are the youngest member of the group •**Pîvanên eşîriyê ne mane, pîvanên piçûk û meziniyê ne mane, lawê min î naşî radibe ji min re dibêje: *heval*** (Epl, 99-100) The standards of tribalism are gone, respect for age [lit. 'standards of smallness and largeness'] is gone, my teenage son calls me '*heval*'. {also: hewal (SK); [heval هـــــوال/hewal هڤال] (JJ); <heval هڤال/haval هاڤال>(HH)} {syn: dost; hogir; yar [1]} <ham- = 'with' + ahl = 'goal' (Tsb2, 10) <Av *arθa- = 'intention, goal' [someone with a shared goal], cf. Skt sam•artha- = 'suitable or fit for, having proper aim or object'; Mid P hamāl/hamahl = 'equal, peer, comrade' (M3); P hamāl هـمـال; Sor aweł ئـاوەڵ/hawał هـاوەڵ/*also* heval هەڤال *(recent borrowing)* = hawřê هاوڕێ & birader بــــــــرادەر; =Za embaz {hevalî; hevaltî; hevalîtî; hewalînî} [F/K/A/JB3/IFb/B/JJ/HH/JB1-A&S//SK]

hevalbend هــەڤــالــبــەنــد *m.&f.* **(-ê/ ;).** 1) {syn: sondxwarî} ally: **•Ji K.P. ra têlgraf şandîye û daye zanîn ku ew *hevalbendê* wî ... ye** (Bkp, 29) He sent a telegram to K.P. and let him know that he is ... his *ally* **•Qerargeha *Hevalbendan* a mezin** (RN) The main *Allied* headquarters; 2) {syn: endam [2]} member *(of an organization, etc.)*. {hevalbendî} [RN/K/JB3/IFb/B/GF/TF/OK/ZF]

hevalbendî هــەڤــالــبــەنــدی *f.* **(-ya;-yê).** 1) alliance; coalition: **•Di salên 1920'an da hun hevalbendên Rûsyayê bûn..., hingê we em bi *hevalbendîya* Înglîz gunehkar dikirin** (Bkp, 7) In the 1920's you were Russia's allies..., so you accused us of having *an alliance* with the English; 2) membership *(in an organization, etc.)*. [JB3/IFb/B/GF/TF/ZF] <hevalbend>

heval biçûk هەڤال بِچویك/هەڤال بِچووك (JH) = placenta. See **hevalçûk**.

hevalcêmk هەڤالجێمك (Bw) = twin. See **cêwî**.

heval cêwî هەڤال جێوی (Dyd/Wn) = twin. See **cêwî**.

hevalçûk هــەڤــالــچــووك *f./m.(JH)* **(/-ê;-ê/).** placenta, afterbirth: **•Heke jinikekê biçûk nebin ... dê zêrevanîyê li jinikeka zayî ket, da ku *heval biçûkê* wê bidizît** (JH, 17) If a woman has no children [=cannot get pregnant] ... she will keep watch over [or, spy on] a woman in childbed, in order to steal her *placenta*. {also: heval biçûk (JH); hevalok (IFb); heval piçûk (GF); [avál-a piciuk] (JJ-G)} {syn: pizdan} [B//JJ-G//GF//JH//IFb]

hevalî هەڤالی (K) = friendship. See **hevaltî**.

hevalînî هەڤالینی (Bw) = friendship. See **hevaltî**.

hevalîtî هەڤالیتی (KH) = friendship. See **hevaltî**.

hevalok هەڤالۆك (IFb) = placenta. See **hevalçûk**.

heval piçûk هــەڤــال پــچــووك (GF) = placenta. See **hevalçûk**.

hevaltî هــەڤــالــتــی *f.* **(-ya;-yê).** 1) friendship: **•Êdî navbêna me de *hevalîtî* nemaye** (KH, 35) *The friendship* between us is no more **•*Hevaltiya* bi herkesî re, ne *hevaltiyeke* jidil e** (Ardû, 38) *Friendship* with everyone is not a sincere *friendship*; 2) companionship. {also: hevalî (K-2); hevalînî (Bw); hevalîtî (KH); hewalînî (SK)} {syn: dostî; yarî I[1]} [K/A/JB3/IFb/B/GF/TF/OK/F//Bw//KH//SK] <heval>

hevan هــەڤــان (B/EP-4/EP-8) = sheepskin sack. See **heban**.

hevastin هەڤاستِن (CCG) = to repair, darn (clothing). See **hîvastin**.

hevbeş هەڤبەش *m.* **().** 1) {syn: hevp'ar} partner (K[s]/A/IF); companion (K[s]); peer, equal (IF); 2) *[adj.]* common, shared (VoA). [AX/K(s)/IF/A]

***hevbûk** هــەڤــبــووك *m.* **().** brother-in-law [pl. brothers-in-law], specifically the relationship between the husbands of two sisters. {syn: bacinax (Haz); hevling (IF/A/Hk)} [IF/ZF3/Wkt]

hevcar̄ هــەڤــجــاڕ *m.* **(-ê;-î).** plow: **•Wî zeviya xwe bi *hevcar̄î* kêla** (FS) He plowed his field with *the plow*. {syn: cot; halet; k'otan II} Sor hewcar̄ هـەوجـاڕ = 'beam of the plough to which the share is attached' [CCG/FS/FJ/GF/Kmc/SS/AD] <hincar>

hevcins هەڤجِنس *adj & m.&f.* 1) homogeneous, of the same species, genre, or sex; same-sex: **•Li Îranê, li gor lêkolîneke ku di 2009an de hatiye kirin, ji sedî 24 ji jinan û ji sedî 16 ji mêran, seks bi *hevcinsên* xwe re kirine** [sic] (Rûdaw 22.vi.2016) In Iran, according to research done in 2009, 24% of women and 16% of men have had sex with *members of their same sex*; 2) homosexual, gay: **•Biryara zewicandina *hevcinsan* ji aliyê komîsyona dêrê, metranan û civîna dêrê ve hatiye dayîn** (Nûçe LGBT:RadioSweden 27.ix.2011) The decision to marry *gays* was made/taken by the church commission, the bishops and the church gathering **•Cîhan û Karwan, ku *hevcins* in û li kampên penaberan diman behsa tahde û zordariya ku pêrgî hatine dikin** (player.fm/series/radio-sweden-kurdish 3.iii.2016) J. and K., who are *gay* and were staying in refugee camps, speak of the abuse and oppression that they have encountered **•Çalakî bo wekheviya *hevcins*** (nefel.com 22.xii.2010) Action for *gay* equality **•Mafê jinên *hevcins* yên wek her jineke din heye ku alîkariyê bistîne ji bo ku zarokan bîne, bi rêya aviskirina sunî**

(sverigesradio.se 31.vii.2015) *Homosexual* women [i.e., lesbians] have the same right as other women to receive help in giving birth, through artificial impregnation. {syn: hevcinsxwaz; hevzayend} [Rûdaw/Nûçe LGBT/radio-sweden/sverigesradio.se/nefel]

hevcinsî هەڤجِنسى *f.* **(;-yê).** 1) homosexuality, gayness, being gay: **•*Hevcinşezî* li Almanyayê tiştekî normal e (wezîrê kar û barê derve yê kevin bi şêweyekî vekirî *hevcinşez* bû)** (refugeeguide.de/ku) In Germany homosexuality is a normal thing (the former minister of foreign affairs was openly gay); 2) [*adj.*] related to homosexuality or gayness: **•Zewaca *hevcinsî* lêgal e û dikare weke zewaca klasîk bi awayekî fermî were tomarkirin** (refugeeguide.de/ku) *Gay* marriage is legal and can officially be registered as a classical marriage. {also: hemcinsî (ZF3/Wkt); hevcinşezî (refugeeguide.de-2)} {syn: hevzayendî} [refugeeguide.de]

hevcinsxwaz هەڤجِنسخواز *m.&f.* **().** homosexual, gay: **•Ji duşemê ve festîvala Stockholm Pride dest pê kirîye, festîvala *hevcinsxwazan* ango homoseksuel, bisseksuel û transseksuelan** (sverigesradio.se 2.viii.2011) The Stockholm Pride Festival began on Monday, the festival of gays, i.e., homosexuals, bisexuals and transsexuals. [sverigesradio.se]

hevcinşezî هەڤجِنشەزى (refugeeguide.de-2) = homosexuality. See **hevcinsî**.

hevç'erx هەڤچەرخ *adj.* 1) {syn: hemdem; nûjen} modern, contemporary; 2) [*m.* **(-ê;).**] one's contemporary, someone living in the same era: **•Hizir bo hindê diçin ku *hevçerxê* Melayê Cizîrî bûye yan jî bi çendekê piştî wî jiyaye** (I.Badî. Remezanê Cizîrî di dwîvçûn û twêjandineka dîtir da, 12) It is thought that he was *a contemporary of* Melayê Jizîrî or that he lived a little bit after him. [Zeb/Wkt/BF/Badî] <ç'erx[2]>

hevde I هەڤدە (A) = seventeen. See **hevdeh**.

hevde II هەڤدە (Qzl) = weft, woof. See **hevo**.

hevdeh هەڤدەه *num.* seventeen, 17. {also: heftdeh (IF-2); hevde I (A); hêvde (GF); hîvdeh (K); ḧifdeh (F); ḧivde (Z-3); ḧivdeh (B); [hefdeh هفده/hewdeh هڤده] (JJ); <hevdeh> هڤده (HH)} Skt saptádaśa; Av haptadasa = seventeenth; Mid P haftdah (M3); P hefdah هفده; Sor hevde هەڤدە/hevve هەڤڤە; Za ḧewtes/desuḧewt; Hau ḧewd̲e (M4) [Z-3//BX/IFb/HH/JJ//K//A//F//B//GF] <ḧeft>

hevdehem هەڤدەهەم *adj.* seventeenth, 17th. {also: hefdehem (ZF); hefdemîn (IFb); heftdehem (GF); heftdehemîn (GF-2); hevdehemîn (Wkt-2); hevdemîn (A); hevdeyem (Wkt-2); hevdeyemîn (Wkt-2); hivdehem (Wkt-2); hivdehemîn (Wkt-2); hivdeyem (Wkt-2); hivdeyemîn (Wkt-2); huvdehem (CT)} Cf. P hafdahom هفدهم; Sor ḧevdehem حەڤدەهەم/ḧevdemîn حەڤدەمین [Wkt//CT//ZF//IFb//GF//A] <hevdeh>

hevdehemîn هەڤدەهەمین (Wkt) = seventeenth. See **hevdehem**.

hevdem هەڤدەم (GF/TF) = modern, contemporary. See **hemdem**.

hevdemîn هەڤدەمین (A) = seventeenth. See **hevdehem**.

hevdeyem هەڤدەیەم (Wkt) = seventeenth. See **hevdehem**.

hevdeyemîn هەڤدەیەمین (Wkt) = seventeenth. See **hevdehem**.

hevdi هەڤدِ = each other. See **hev**.

hevdin هەڤدِن (Ad) = each other. See **hev**.

hevdu هەڤدو (K) = each other. See **hev**.

hevdû هەڤدوو = each other. See **hev**.

hevedudanî هەڤەدودانى *adj.* compound, composite: **-lêkera hevedudanî** (IF) compound verb; **-navê hevedudanî** (JB3) compound noun. [(neol)K/JB3/IF/ZF3]

hevêr هەڤێر, m. (FS) = nighttime sheepfold. See **hevêz**.

hevêz هەڤێز *f.* **(-a;).** nighttime sheepfold: **-hevêza pezî** (Zeb) do. {also: hevêr, m. (FS); <hevêz هەڤێز/hewêz هەوێز> (Hej)} {syn: hevşî} Cf. NENA hâ-wîzâ ܗܘܝܙܐ = 'a place for sheep in summer' (Maclean) [Zeb/IFb/OK/Hej/AA/ZF3//FS] <bêrî I; palîn I; şevîn>

hevgirtî هەڤگِرتى *adj./pp.* consistent; coherent, cohesive: **•pêkanîna rastnivîs û rêzimaneke rast û *hevgirtî*** (Wlt 2:100, 2) the creation of a correct and *consistent* orthography and grammar. [(neol)Wlt/GF/ZF3]

hevirmiş هەڤِرمِش *m.* **(-ê;).** 1) {syn: herîr} silk; 2) [*adj.*] silken: **•dezmala *hevirmiş*** (B) *silk[en]* handkerchief **•kirasê *hevirmiş*** (K) *silk[en]* shirt. {also: armîş, f. (SK); armûş; ebreşûm (F-2); erimûş (IS); ermûş; hermiş; hermûş (F); hevirmîş (ZF3); hevirmûş; hevrîşim (IF); hevrûşim, f. (JB3); [hewirmouch هڤرموش/armouch ارموش/hevirmouch هڤیرموش/ebrichim ابرشیم] (JJ); <hevrîşim> هڤریشم (HH)} <*upa-rēšma (<rēs- =

'to spin (wool)') --> Mid P abrēšom (M3) --> P abrīšam ابریشم; Shughni dialects: Yazghulami vrīx̌əm; Sarikoli varax̌īm/valax̌ūm; Shughni virēx̌um (Morg2); Sor hewrêşm هەورێشم; cf. Ar ibrīsam/ibrīsim ابريسم; T ibrişim; W Arm abršum աբրշում; NA awrúšum (Garbell); **rēs-**: [Pok I. rei- 857ff.] 'to scratch, tear, cut' --> [reik(h)- --> reiḱ-]: Skt reś- = 'to pluck, tear out'; O Ir *rais- (Tsb 40): Av raēš-/iriš- = 'to wound, damage'; P ristan رستن/rištan رشتن = 'to spin (wool)' & abrīšam ابریشم = 'silk'. See **2. "Silk"** in: H.W. Bailey. "Three Pahlavi Notes," *Journal of the Royal Asiatic Society* (1931), 425-26. [K/B//F//IF/HH//JJ//JB3/SK//ZF3] <rêstin>

hevirmîş هەڤرمیش (ZF3) = silk. See **hevirmiş**.

hevirmûş هەڤرمووش = silk. See **hevirmiş**.

hevîn هەڤین = love. See **evîn**.

hevîr هەڤیر *m.* **(-ê; hêvîr, vî hevîrî).** dough: **•Şirînê *hevîr* li ser xwanikê pehn kir** (FS) Sh. flattened *the dough* on the little table; **-hevîr kirin** (Zeb/Dh) to knead {syn: stiran II; şêlan [1]}. {also: [hewir] هڤير (JJ); <hevîr> هڤير (HH)} Cf. Ar/P xamīr خمير = 'leavened dough' --> T hamur; Sor hewîr هەویر; Za mîr, *m.* [AB/K/A/(JB3)/IFb/B/JJ/HH/GF/TF/OK] <ard; giştik; hestîf; stiran II>

hevîrtirş هەڤیرترش *m.* **(-ê;).** 1) {syn: hêvên} yeast, leaven; 2) leavened dough (IF); piece of dough *(for leavening)* (B). {also: hevîrtirşk (B); [hewir tyrch] هڤيرترش (JJ); <hevîr ṯirş> هڤيرطرش (HH)} < hevîr = 'dough' + tirş = 'sour'; Sor hewîrtirş هەویرترش [EP-7/K/A/IFb/JJ/GF/TF/OK/Zeb//HH//B] <stiran II>

hevîrtirşk هەڤیرترشك (B) = yeast; piece of dough. See **hevîrtirş**.

hevk'ar هەڤکار *m.&f.* **().** colleague, co-worker, partner. {syn: hevp'ar[2]; şirîk} Cf. P hamkār همکار = 'fellow worker, competitor'; Sor hawkar هاوکار = 'confederate, colleague, cooperator' [VoA/K/IFb/GF/TF/OK/ZF3]

hevk'arî هەڤکاری *f.* **(-ya;-yê).** cooperation, partnership. Cf. P hamkārī همکاری = 'competition'; Sor hawkarî هاوکاری = 'cooperation' [VoA/K/(A)/IFb/GF/OK/ZF3]

hevling هەڤلِنگ *m.* **(-ê;).** brother-in-law [*pl.* brothers-in-law], specifically the relationship between the husbands of two sisters; husband of a man's *baltûz (qv.)* [cf. Ar ʻadīl عديل; Clq (Palestinian) Ar šaqqit-xurj شقّة خرج; P bājināγ باجناغ; T bacanak]. {also: hevlink (Haz--> Hk)} {syn: bacinax; hevbûk} [IF/A/Hk/Bozarslan/ZF3]

hevlink هەڤلِنك (Haz-->Hk) = brother-in-law. See **hevling**.

hevnasî هەڤناسی *f.* **(-ya;-yê).** familiarity (with stg.), (mutual) acquaintance(ship): **•*Hevnasiya* min û Kurdan bi karekî rojname-geriyê dest pê kir** (Nbh 135:47) My *familiarity* with the Kurds began with a work of journalism. {also: hevnasîn (K/A/IFb)} < hev + nas- [Nbh/TF/Wkt/ZF/CS//K/A/IFb]

hevnasîn هەڤناسین (K/A/IFb) = acquaintance, familiarity. See **hevnasî**.

hevo هەڤۆ *m.* **(-yê;).** weft, woof *(of a fabric)* [=T atkı; Ar laḥmah لحمة; P pūd پود]: **•*hevo*: Benê ku di tevnê de berwarkî tê avêtin** (Nbh 124:32) *weft/woof*: The thread in a loom which is threaded [lit. 'thrown'] sideways. {also: havo (Qzl); hevde II (Qzl-2)} = Sor po پۆ; P pūd [CCG/Hej//Qzl//Nbh] <firêt; gurd; hepik; hîvastin>

hevok هەڤۆك *f.* **(-a;-ê).** sentence (*grammatical term*): **•Bi vî awayî di *hevokê* de kirde û bireser ji hev cuda dibin** (TaRK, 90) In this way, the subject and object are kept separate in *the sentence* **•Ez te dibînim. Min tu dîtî. Di *hevoka* yekemîn de lêker li gorî kirdeyê (ez), di ya duyem de jî li gorî bireserê (tu) hatiye kişandin** (Wkp) I see you. I saw you. In the first *sentence* the verb agrees with (lit. is conjugated according to) the subject (ez=I), and in the second one, it agrees with the object (tu=you). = Sor rîste ڕستە [K/A/FJ/GF/TF/Kmc/RZ/ZF/CS]

hevoksazî هەڤۆکسازی *f.* **(-ya;-yê).** syntax: **•*Hevoksazî*, bi me dide zanîn bê cureyê peyvan di kîjan devera hevokê de cih digirin û çawa bi hev ve têne girêdan** (Wkp) *Syntax* tells us in what part of the sentence the parts of speech are located and how they relate to one another. [FJ/GF/Kmc/ZF/CS/Wkt] <peyivsazî>

hevor هەڤۆر (IFb/OK) = billy goat, male goat. See **hevûrî**.

hevorî هەڤۆری (FS) = billy goat, male goat. See **hevûrî**.

hevp'ar هەڤپار *m.* **().** 1) {syn: hevbeş} companion (K); 2) {syn: hevbeş; şirîk} partner (K/IF); 3) {syn: beşdar; pişkdar} shareholder, s.o. having a part/share (of stg.). {also: hempar (K)} [AX/IF//K] <beşdar>

hevpeyivîn هەڤپەیڤین (Wkt) = interview. See

hevpeyvîn.

hevpeyîvîn هـەڤـپـەیـیـڤـیـن (IFb) = interview. See **hevpeyvîn**.

hevpeyvîn هـەڤـپـەیـڤـیـن *f.* **(-a;-ê).** interview: **•Ji bo *hevpeyvînê* em spasdariya we dikin** (Wlt 1:37, 16) We are grateful to you for *the interview.* {also: hevpeyivîn (Wkt); hevpeyîvîn (IFb)} = Sor çaw-pê-kewtin چاو پێ کەوتِن [(neol)Wlt/ZF3//Wkt//IFb]

hevran هەڤران (IFb) = poplar tree. See **evran**.

hevraz هەڤراز *m.(K/B/Bw)/f.(F/OK)* **(-ê/; hevrêz/).** 1) {syn: berwar; jihelî; p'al; pesar; p'êş II[2]; qunt'ar; sîng; teřazin} uphill slope; 2) [*adv.*] {syn: bala/banî; jor; berbijor/serbijor} up, upward (Ba/JJ): ***•Hevraz* t'ûkim - simêle, berjêr t'ûkim - řûye** (Dz - #665) If I spit *upward*, there's my moustache, if I spit downward, there's my beard *[prv.]* (i.e., Damned if I do, damned if I don't: cf. T Aşağı tükürsem sakal, yukarı tükürsem bıyık) **•Ûsib ha *hevraz* nihêřî ha berjêr nihêřî** (Ba) Joseph look now *up*, now down; **-hevraz kirin** (FK-eb-1) to raise, lift, pick up: **•Serê xwe *hervaz*** [sic] ***kir* û got** (FK-eb-1) He *raised* his head and said. {also: evraz (Bw/IFb-2/GF-2/OK-2); ewrazî (SK); hervaz (FK-eb-1); hervêz (FK-eb-1); hewraz, f. (F/IFb-2); ḧevraz, m. (B); [awraz اڤراز/ hewraz هڤراز] (JJ); <ervaz> ارڤاز (HH)} [F//Ba/K/IFb/JJ//B/GF/TF/OK//Bw//SK//HH] <berwar; fêz>

hevrêstin هەڤرێستِن (Kmc) = to repair, darn (clothing). See **hîvastin**.

hevrik هـەڤـرِك *m.&f.* **().** opponent; rival, competitor: **•Di vê nivîsarê de ez dê yek bi yek li ser argûmentên parêzkar û *hevrikên* van du herfên kurdiyê rawestim** (A Zêrevan: Nûdem 22:114) In this article I will investigate--one by one--the arguments of the proponents and *opponents* of these two Kurdish letters [of the alphabet]. {also: <hevrik> هـــــەڤـــــرك (Hej)} {syn: 'edû; neyar [2]} {hevrikî} [Zêrevan-Nûdem/Zeb/GF/Hej] <lec; řik'>

hevrikî هەڤرِکی *f.* **().** competition, rivalry; opposition, resistance: **•Em bi şanazî û serbilindî dibêjîn di çu ciře û *hevrrikîyêt* navxoyê da heta kêmtirîn behr jî têda nebûye** (R 15 [4/12/96] 2) We can proudly say that we had not even the slightest part in any internal arguments or *rivalries* **•Holendîya deverên kendavê li rexê Îranê girtin û li dûmahîka çerxê hevdê rikatî û *hevrikîyeka* dijwar ya peyda bû di navbera Holendîya û Ingilîza û Ferensîya** (Metîn 62[1997]:26) The Dutch took the gulf regions on the Iranian side and by the end of the eighteenth century, a fierce *rivalry* had developed between the Dutch, the English, and the French. [Zeb/Metîn/GF/OK] <berêkanê; hevrik; lec; pêşbazî>

hevring هـەڤـرِنـگ *f.* **(-a;-ê).** scissors or shears for shaving wool off sheep, sheep shears. {also: abring; abrîng; hevrîng (K/F/B); [hebrink] هـبـرنـك (JJ); <hevring> هڤرنگ (HH)} {syn: qilix II} [S&E/Kg/A/IF/HH//F/K/B//JJ] <cawbiř; meqes>

hevris هەڤرِس *m./f.(ZF3/Wkt)* **(/-a;-î/-ê).** juniper tree, bot. *Juniperus*; tree with small spiked leaves that ignites quickly and remains green after being cut (HH). {also: evrist (IFb); êvist (MG); hevrist (IFb-2/TF/Kmc/ZF3); hevrîs (K/Tsab); hêvrist (Kmc-2); [avrést] اورست (JJ); <êrvist ايـرڤـسـت/ hêvrist هـيـڤـرسـت> (HH)} {syn: merx} <O Ir *hampṛsā- (Morg3): Av *hapṛsi- ~ *hapṛsā *f.*; Baluchi apurs; P āris آرس = 'juniper tree'/avirs اورس = 'mountain cypress'; Sor hewrîs هەوریس = 'juniper tree'. See: M. Schwartz. "Viiāmburas and Kafirs," *Bulletin of the Asia Institute* 4, 1990 [1992], p. 251-252. [K/Tsab//A//IFb/JJ//HH//TF/Kmc/ZF3//MG]

hevrist هەڤرِست (IFb/TF/Kmc/ZF3) = juniper tree. See **hevris**.

hevrişk هەڤرِشك (IF) = dish consisting of bread toasted in butter. See **hevrîşk**.

hevrîng هەڤرینگ (K/B) = shears for shaving wool off sheep. See **hevring**.

hevrîs هەڤریس (K/Tsab) = juniper tree. See **hevris**.

hevrîşim هەڤریشِم (IF/HH) = silk. See **hevirmiş**.

hevrîşk هەڤریشك *m.(B/Msr)/f.(K/ZF3)* **(-ê-a;/-ê).** *dish consisting of bread toasted in butter* (K/B/IF); crushed bread fried in oil {T bulamaç} (Msr); slice of warm bread with butter, [tartine] (JJ). {also: hevrişk (IF); hevroşk (Msr); [hewroujk] هـڤـروژك (JJ)} {syn: biçrik} Cf. P afrose افـروسـه/ afroše افـروشـه = 'dish made of butter, honey, and flour; dish made of egg yolk, milk, and syrup' [K/JB3/B/ZF3//IF//JJ]

hevroşk هـەڤـرۆشـك (Msr) = dish consisting of bread toasted in butter or oil. See **hevrîşk**[2].

hevrûşim هەڤرووشِم, f. (JB3) = silk. See **hevirmiş**.

hevs هەڤس (Ba3-3) = prison. See **ḧebs**.

hevsar هـەڤـسـار *m.* **(-ê; hevsêr, vî hevsarî).** 1) {syn: bûsat; řext [3]; řişme} halter, head-harness *(for horse)* (JJ/IF); 2) {syn: dizgîn; gem; lixab; lîwan; qet'irme} reins (K/B/JB1-A); reins placed on an unsaddled horse (JB1-S); bridle (K/JB3/B). {also: hefsar (JB1-A&S); ĥevsar (B); [hewsar] هـفـسـار (JJ); <hefsar> هـفـسـار (HH)} Cf. Av aiwisāra- (Horn #97); Pahl afsār; P afsār افسار; Sor hewsar هـەوسـار = 'bridle'; Za wesar *m.* (Todd/Mal); cf. *also of Iranian origin* Arc afsārā אפסרא/afsīrā אפסירא = '(horse's) bit' [Z-2/K/JB3/IF/JJ//JB1-A&S /HH//B] <dizgîn; hesp; zîn>

hevser هـەڤـسـەر *m.&f.* **(-ê/-a;).** spouse, better half, mate, life partner; [f.] wife; [m.] husband: **•*hevsera* min** (Wkt) my *wife* **•*Hevserê* min ne li malê ye** (ZF3) My *husband* isn't at home **•Hibriya diya xwe ya ku xwîna xwîşk û *hevserê* w[ê] li ser zuha bûye** (Nofa, 95) Her mother's headscarf, on which the blood of her sister and her *husband* had dried. Cf. P hamsar هـمـسـر; Sor hawser هاوسەر [Nofa/GF/Wkt/ZF3/G/FD/FS] <jin; mêr I>

hevsû هەڤسوو = envious, jealous. See **ĥevsûd**.

hevsûd هەڤسوود (B) = envious, jealous. See **ĥevsûd**.

hevsûdî هـەڤـسـوودی (B/YZ-1) = envy, jealousy. See **ĥevsûdî**.

hevş هەڤش (GF/Hej) = sheep resting area. See **hevşî**.

hevşî هەڤشی *m.(Kmc-8/FS)/f.(K)* **(-yê/-ya;).** nocturnal resting area *for a flock of sheep*: **-hevşîyê berêspêdê** (Kmc-8) sheep resting at daybreak; **-hevşîyê hingorî** (Kmc-8) sheep resting at night. {also: hevş (GF); <hefşî> هـفـشـی (HH); <hevş[î]> هەڤش[ی] (Hej)} {syn: hevêz} [Kmc-8/K/Hej/FS//HH//GF] <bêrî I; palîn I; şevîn>

hevtem هەڤتەم (Wkt) = seventh. See **heftem**.

hevterîb هـەڤـتـەریـب *adj.* parallel: **•Dem û dezgeh û kesayetên ku li Tirkîyeyê di warê wêjeya bi Kurdî dixebitin, *hevterîbî* bar û doxa şerî ya 30 salên dawî, her tim tûşî astengkirinan hatine** (J. Bahoz. KurdîLit 17.ix.2016) Institutions and personalities who work in the field of literature in Kurdish in Turkey, *parallel to* the war conditions of the last 30 years, have always encountered obstacles **•*Hevterîb li gel* vê armanca xwe, berhemê ji têbînî û fikrên çend pisporên din ên zimanê kurdî jî istifade kiriye** (E. Öpengin. "Pirsên Rênivîsa Kurmancî," *Derwaze* 1 [2017], 181) *Parallel to* this purpose, the work has benefited from comments and thoughts of other Kurdish language experts. Cf. Sor terîb تـەریـب = 'parallel; ornamental stitching' [Derwaze/Wkt]

hevûdin هەڤوودِن/هەڤ و دِن = each other. See **hev**.

hevûdî هەڤوودی/هەڤ و دی = each other. See **hev**.

hevûdu هـەڤـوودو/هـەڤ و دو (JB3) = each other. See **hev**.

hevûdû هەڤوودوو/هەڤ و دوو = each other. See **hev**.

hevûrî هـەڤـووری *m.* **().** billy goat, male goat (IFb); one-year-old male goat (JJ/TF); 1 1/2 - 2-year-old male goat (GF); two-year-old male goat (HH); three-year-old male goat (A/IFb). {also: evor (GF); hebûrî (ZF3); hevor (IFb-2/OK); hevorî (FS); [hewour] هڤور (JJ); <hefûrî> هفوری (HH)} [A/IFb/GF/TF//HH//JJ//FS//OK//GF//ZF3] <gîsk; nêrî I; kûr I = sayis>

hevzayend هـەڤزایـەند *adj.* & *m.&f.* homosexual, gay: **•Li Amerîkayê di sala 2011an de astengiyên li hember leşkeriya jin û mêrên *hevzayend* hatibûn rakirin û niha heman xebat bo LGBTyiyan jî tê kirin** (lgbtnuce.blogspot.com/2016/:Sputnik) In America in 2011 the obstacles to military service of *gay* men and women were lifted and now the same thing is being done for LGBT folks **•Li bajarê Silêmaniyê yê Başûrê Kurdistanê derhênerekî gênc fîlmek liser jiyana *hevzayendan* çêkir ... *Hevzayend* jî beşek in ji civakê. Di fîlm de rûyê wan dixuyê** (lgbtnuce.blogspot.com/2016/:Rûdaw) In the city of Sulaimania of Southern Kurdistan a young producer has made a film on the life of *gays* ... *Gays* are also part of society. In the movie they are presented [lit. 'their faces are shown'] **•Obama bo piştevaniya *hevzayendan* dê li New Yorkê peykerekî biçikîne** (lgbtnuce.blogspot.com/2016/:Sputnik) Obama will erect a statue in New York in support of *gays*. {syn: hevcins[xwaz]} [lgbtnuce/Rûdaw/Sputnik]

hevzayendî هـەڤـزایـەنـدی *f.* **().** 1) homosexuality, gayness, being gay {syn: hevcinsî}: **•Wekî hunermend karê min nîşandana mijarên tebû ye. Wekî mînak, *hevzayendî*. Ez bi hunera xwe dixwazim nîşan bidim ku ew jî beşek ji komelgeha me ne** (lgbtnuce.blogspot.com/2016/:Rûdaw) As an artist my job is to portray taboo subjects. For example, *homosexuality*. With my art I want to show that they are also part of our society; 2) [*adj.*] related to homosexuality or gayness: **•Tarhan, dema li girtîgeha leşkerî rastî kiryar û pêkanînên xerab hatibû, her wiha ji ber nasnameya wî ya *hevzayendî* xwestibûn bi darê zorê wî muayene bikin** (lgbtnuce.blogspot.com/2015/:BestaNûçe) When T. was in military prison he was subjected to bad treatment, and likewise because of his *gay* identity they wanted to examine him by force. [lgbtnuce/Rûdaw/BestaNûçe]

hew هـــــــەو *adv.* 1) *polite, gentle negative*: hardly, scarcely, barely: •**Kevir dileqe *hew* cî digire** (L) Once a rock starts moving, it cannot stand still [lit.'it *scarcely* stands still'] *[prv.]* •**Mîr dibêje: "Ko em yekê ji xo bidinê, ji me bizewice, *hew* ji ba me diçe, wê bimîne li ba me"** (ZK-3) The emir says, "If we marry him off to one of our womenfolk, then *instead of* leaving us, he would stay with us [lit. 'he would *hardly* leave us, [but rather] stay with us']; -**hew** [**me**] **dît** (XF) [We] scarcely saw (*him, etc.*); He vanished in a flash *(used when s.o. seems to vanish into thin air)*; -**hew mabû** (XF) almost, nearly; hardly, scarcely, barely; -**hew nihêȓî** (XF) suddenly, unexpectedly [lit. '[We] hardly looked']; -**hew zanibû** (XF) as if; it would seem: •***Min hew zanibû*, ku tuê herî** (B) *I thought* (=it is as if I knew) that you would go •**Leylê ç'e'v pê k'et usa ḧuba wê çû cem, *hew* zanibû, 'Eynê dya Mecrûme** (EP) As soon as Leyla laid eyes on her, she loved her, *as if she knew* that Ayna was Mejrum's mother; 2) no longer, not at all, never (BX): -**hew piştir** (ZK-3) from now on: •***Hew piştir*, ti neçî ser devê bîrê** (Z-3) *From now on* you are not to go to (the mouth of) the well. *See AKR (p. 59-61) for detailed discussion of **hew**.* [Z-3/K/IF/B/XF/L/BX/AKR] <t'ew II>

hew•a هـــەوا *f.* (**•a;•ê/•aê**). 1) air; atmosphere: •***Hewa* ot'axê giran e** (B) *The air in* the room is close •**Şivan xweȓa nava kulîlkada digeȓin, bîna *hewa* ç'îyaye t'emiz dik'işînin** (Ba2:1, 203) Shepherds roam among the flowers, breathing in pure mountain *air*; 2) weather; climate: •**Îro *hewa* xweş e** (B) *The weather* is nice today; 3) passion (SK/JJ). {also: [heva] هوا (JJ); <hewa> هوا (HH)} < Ar hawā' هـــــواء = 'air'; Sor hewa هـــەوا = 'air, weather, climate; tune' [F/K/JB3/IF/JJ/HH]

hewal هەوال (SK) = friend, companion. See **heval**.

hewalînî هەوالینی (SK) = friendship. See **hevaltî**.

hewan I هەوان (A/IF) = to seek shelter. See **ḧewîn**.

hewan II هەوان (TF) = to calm down. See **ḧewhan**.

hewandin هـــەوانـــدِن (A/IF/JB1-A) = to lodge; to calm. See **ḧewandin**.

hewante هـــەوانـــتـه *adj.* 1) worthless, good-for-nothing, useless, wasted, silly, baseless; in vain: •**Ez dema van tespîtan dikim, mebesta min ne ew e ku ez bibêjim, tiştên heta niha hatine kirin tewş in û *hewante çûne*, berevajî ez dibêjim, xwîn û xwêdana ewqasî salî hêjayî vê encamê nîne** (R. Sorgul. Bi tevahî boykot. PUKmedia 14.ix.2013) When I make these charges, I do not mean that what has been done up till now is worthless and *has been wasted*, on the contrary, I am saying that the blood and sweat of so many years does not deserve this result •**Ji demekê û vir de ye ku minaqaşeyeke *hewante* tê kirin** (E. Karahan. Bang ji Qeşmerok… amude.com 30.xi.2004) For some time a *silly* debate has been being waged •**Lê gumana min ji hinêr û hunera vegotin û nivîsîna Karahanî *hewante* bû û ne tenê *hewante* jî** (nefel.com: H. Muhammed. "Ferheng" 9.ix.2011) But my doubt about the art and skill of Karahan's descriptions and writing were *baseless*, and not only *baseless*; 2) for free, gratis: •**Ma *hewante* ye ku tu van gundora dê bo xwe bî?** (FS) Do you think they are *free*, that you are taking these melons for yourself? {also: awamte (Wkt-2); awante (Wkt-2); ewante (Wkt-2); hawamte (Wkt-2); hawante (Hej-2/Wkt-2); hawente (JB1-A)} T avanta & M Gr avanda = 'something for free'; Sor hewante هـــەوانـــتـه = 'freeloading, cadger' [IFb/CS/Hej/Wkt/FS//JB1-A]

hewar هـــەوار (K/A/JJ/B) = call for help; funeral. See **hawar** & **hewarî**.

hewarî هـــەواری *f.* (**-ya;-yê**). 1) funeral, rites of burial; coming to the aid of the bereaved or those in mourning: •**Gava ku mir, tu dibêjî ji bo çi ne Tirk, ne jî Kurd ne hatine *hewarîya* wî?** (Hêvî 12-18.xii.98:9) When he died, why do you think that neither Turks nor Kurds came to his *funeral*?; 2) call for help. See **hawar**. {also: hewar (B-2)} [Frq/Xrz/B/Hêvî] <behî>

hewas هەواس = desire, interest. See **ḧewas**.

hewask'ar هەواسکار = amateur; interested; interesting. See **ḧewask'ar**.

hewayî هـــــەوایـــی *adj.* aerial, atmospheric: •**Çekê emerîkanî ê *hewayî* 30 ton bombe berdane hêjagehên Japona** (RN) American *aerial* forces dropped 30 tons of bombs on Japanese targets. Cf. Sor hewayî هـەوایـی = 'aerial, pertaining to the air' [RN/K/IF] <hewa>

hewce هەوجە (IFb/GF) = need. See **ḧewce**.

hewdel هـــەودەل (A/IFb/GF/TF) = dish made of boiled grape syrup. See **ḧewdel**.

hewe هەوە (Bohtan/Bw/OK/FS) = you *(pl.)*. See **hûn** & **we**.

hewes هەوەس (IF) = desire, interest. See **ḧewas**.

heweskar هەوەسكار (IF/GF) = amateur; interested; interesting. See **ḧewask'ar**.

heweskarî هەوەسكارى (IF) = interest. See **ḧewask'arî**.

hewê هەوێ (IF) = co-wife. See **hêwî**.

hewî هەوى (A/IF) = co-wife. See **hêwî**.

hewîc هەويج (AA) = scrotum. See **'ewîc**[2].

hewl هەول *f.* **(-a;-ê).** attempt, try, effort, endeavor: **•Bi hêviya û *hewla* avêtina gavên mezintir, em 101 saliya rojnamegeriya Kurdistanê li hemû hempîşeyên û gelê xwe pîroz dikin** (AW69D1) In hopes and *attempts* to take bigger steps, we congratulate all our colleagues and our people on the 101st anniversary of Kurdistani journalism **•Ev *hewl* ji aliyê polîsan ve hatiye berbendkirin** (AW71A6) This *attempt* has been banned by the police; **-hewl dan** (IFb/GF/TF): a) to try, attempt, make an effort: **•Di vê semînerê de Haşim *hewl da* ku bersiva vê daxwazê bide** (AW69D3) In this seminar, Hashim *tried* to respond to this request **•Divê ku kurd bi xwe *hewl bidin* da ku bibin xwediyê welatê xwe** (AW71D5) The Kurds themselves must *try* to take possession of their own country **•Ez *dê hewl bidim*, ku ji vir bi şûn ve alîkariya wê bikim** (AW69A3) I *will try* to help her from now on; b) [*f.* **(-a;-ê).**] attempt, try, effort: **•Lewre divê ji bo pêşveçûna rojnamegerên kurd, em bikevin nava *hewldaneke* mezin** (AW70A2) Therefore for the advancement of Kurdish journalists, we must make a great *effort*. < Ar ḥāwala III حاول = 'to try' [IFb/GF/TF/SS/ZF3]

hewq هەوق *m.* **(-ê;).** rung *(of a ladder)*: **-ḧewqê pêstirkê** (FS) do. {also: hewqa (?Haz); ḧewq (GF); <ḧewq> حەوق (HH)} Cf. Syr ḥūq ܚܘܩ /ḥawqā ܚܘܩܐ = 'stairs' & NENA hôqâ ܗܘܩܐ (Maclean) & ḥuqqa (Sabar: Dict) = 'rung of a ladder' [?Haz//IFb/Wkt//HH/GF/FS] <p'êstirk>

hewqa هەوقا (?Haz) = rung (of a ladder) . See **hewq**.

hewqas هەوقاس = so much. See **ewqas** & **haqas**.

hewr I هەور (K[s]) = cloud. See **'ewr**.

hewr II هەور (ZF/Kmc) = poplar tree. See **evran**.

Hewramanî هەورامانى (Wkt) = Hawrami (Gorani dialect). See **Hewramî**.

Hewramî هەورامى *adj. & f.* Hawrami, Avromani, *a dialect of Gorani* (qv.): "Avromani, the dialect of Avroman properly Hawrāmi, is the most archaic of the Gōrāni group. All Gōrāni dialects exhibit a number of phonological features which link them with the dialects of central Iran and distinguish them from Kurdish. While the main Gōrāni language area, to the west of Kermānshāh, is an island in a sea of chiefly Kurdish dialects, the Hawrāmān now forms a separate islet to the north." [from: D.N. MacKenzie, "Avromani," in: *Encyclopaedia Iranica* (New York: Bibliotheca Persica, 2001-), v. 3, p. 111]. {also: Hawram[an]î (Wkt-2); Hewramanî (Wkt-2)} [Wkp/Wkt] <Goranî>

hewran I هەوران *m.* **(-ê;).** coat, overcoat, short coat with broad, short sleeves: **•Di kurk û *hewranê* xwe de razan** (L) They went to sleep in their furs and *coats*. {also: herwanî (Qzl/Kmc-#3507); hewranî (GF)} {syn: qap'ût} [L/K(s)/Wkt//Qzl/Kmc//GF]

hewran II هەوران (IFb) = poplar tree. See **evran**.

hewranî هەورانى (GF) = type of coat. See **hewran I**.

hewraz هەوراز, f. (F/IFb) = slope; up. See **hevraz**.

hewş هەوش (JB3/IF/A) = courtyard. See **ḧewş**.

hewtehewt هەوتەهەوت (CS) = barking. See **'ewte'ewt**.

hewthewt هەوتهەوت (DBgb) = barking. See **'ewte'ewt**.

hewtîn هەوتين (AW) = to bark. See **'ewtîn**.

hewy هەوى (SK) = moon. See **hîv**.

hewz هەوز (A/IFb/ZF) = pool. See **ḧewz**.

hey I هەى *conj.* since, because, as long as: ***•Hey* ez hatime heyanî vê derê, ezê daxil bibim nav bajêr** (L-5, 146, l. 14-15) *Since* I've come this far, I'll enter the city. {syn: madam} [L/ZF3]

hey II هەى**: -hey kirin** (Bw) to kick out, expel. {also: hay II: hay kirin (RZ)} [Bw//RZ]

heya هەيا = until. See **ḧeta** & **t'a IV**.

heyam هەيام *m.* **(-ê;).** period of time, a while: **•Carekê *ḧeyamê* zivistanê em çûne nêç'îrê** (B) Once *during* the winter we went hunting ***•heyamek* bû**... (Bw) [It was] *not too long ago* **•Îna *be'de heyamekî* mela helsta da çite mala kiçekê** (M-Ak: 686) *After a while* the mullah got up to go to the girl's house **•Xwezîka li gel kompitura xwe ez ji xwe re di *heyamê* însanên şikevtan de bijîyama. Qe nebe di heyamê wan de derdê cilşuştina wek îro tunebû** (LC, 13) I wish that I lived in *the time of* the cavemen, together with my computer. At least in their time they didn't have the problems with laundry that we have today. {also: ḧeyam, f.[B] (K/B/JB1-A)} {syn: bîstek; kêlî [2]} <Ar ayyām أيّـــام = days (*pl. of* yawm يــــوم) [Bw/M-Ak/IFb/JB1-S/GF/TF/OK//K/B/JB1-A] <dem I>

heyanî هەيانى = until. See **ĥeta & t'a IV**.

heybetî هــەيــبــەتــى (AId) = surprised, bewildered. See **ĥêbetî**.

heye هەيە = there is. See **hebûn**.

heyf هەيف (JB3/IF) = revenge; pity. See **ĥeyf**.

heyirî هەيرى (JB3) = amazed; astray. See **ĥeyrî**.

heyirîn هــەيــريــن (L/JB3/IF) = to be astonished; to get lost. See **ĥeyrîn**.

heyî هــەيــى *adj.* 1) existing, extant, current, present, prevailing: **•Di Newrozê de gel bêdengiya *heyî* ji holê rakir** (Şûjin Gazete 2017.05.09) On Nawroz the people lifted the *prevailing* silence **•Di rewşa *heyî* de divê tu kes hesabên şaş nekin** (ANHA 2017.02.03) In the *current* state [of affairs] no one should make wrong calculations **•Êdî gelên Îranê nikarin di bin zilma *heyî* de bijîn** (Roj News 2017.04.23) The peoples of Iran can no longer live under the *current* oppression; 2) {syn: maldar; dewlemend} rich, wealthy: **•*Heyî* be û kuřê kerî be** (FS/BF) Be *wealthy* and be the son of an ass *[prv.]*. {also: [heïi] هــيــى (JJ)} [IFb/GF/FJ/ZF/FS/BF/JJ/Wkt/SS]

***heyîn** هەيين**: -navê heyînê** (K/B) substantive (noun). [(neol)K/B] <nav I[3]>

heyk'el/heykel [B] هەيكەل *m./f.(F/B)* **(; /-ê).** 1) {syn: p'eyker} statue; sculpture; monument; 2) cabalistic writing (JJ). {also: heykel (B); hêkel; ĥeîkel (F); <ĥêkel> حـيـكـل (AX); [heïkal] هـيـكـل (JJ)} < Ar haykal هيكل; Sor heykel هەيكەل [AX/K/IF/JB3/JJ//F/B]

heyneyse هــەيــنــەيــســە *interj.* at any rate, in any case: **•*Heyneyse*, bi wî ĥesabî, ewana seknîn** (EH) *At any rate*, with that understanding, they stood... <T her neyse = 'whatever' [EH]

heyran هــەيــران (IFb/Kmc/CS) = sacrifice; admirer; my dear. See **ĥeyran**.

heyşet هــەيــشــەت *f.* **(-a;-ê).** densely populated settlement, population center, town, city: **•Hûn werin lêzim werin / Gund û çînarêt *hêşetê*** (GShA, 318) You come, you must come / Villages and neighbors [?] *of the town* **•[Qenc e ewe ku em evne bi ezmanê şirîn û lêp bînine nîva *heyşetê*]** (JR #40,124) It is best to lure them into *town* with sweet talk and guile. {also: hêşet (GShA); [heichet هـيـسـت/hech[i]t هـشـت] (JJ); <heyşet> هــەيــشــەت (Hej)} {syn: bajar} Cf. Sor ĥeşîmet حـەشـيـمـەت/ĥeşamat حـەشـامـات = 'dense crowd of people' (Hej) ?<Ar √ḥ-š-r حـشـر = 'to be crowded, packed, jammed together' [JR/K/JJ/Hej/BZ/FS//GShA] <avan; şênî>

heyşt هەيشت (A) = eight. See **ĥeyşt**.

heyşta هەيشتا (ZZ) = eighth. See **ĥeyşta**.

heyştem هەيشتەم (A/Wkt) = eighth. See **heştem**.

heyştemîn I هەيشتەمين (Wkt) = eighth. See **heştem**.

heyştemîn II هــەيــشــتــەمــيــن (IFb) = eightieth. See **heştêyem**.

heyştêyem هەيشتێيەم (Wkt) = eightieth. See **heştêyem**.

heyştêyemîn هــەيــشــتــێــيــەمــيــن (Wkt) = eightieth. See **heştêyem**.

heyştê هەيشتێ (A) = eighty. See **ĥeyştê**.

heyv هــــەيــــڤ (A/JB3/IF/BK/Zx/Czr/Bw) = moon; month. See **hîv**.

heyvan هەيڤان (A) = leaven, yeast. See **hêvên**.

heyveron هەيڤەڕۆن (IFb) = moonlight. See **hîveřon**.

heyvgirtin هەيڤگرتن *f.* **(-a;-ê).** lunar eclipse, eclipse of the moon [Ar xusūf خـسـوف; P mihtāb'giriftagī مـهـتـاب گـرفـتـگـى; T ay tutulması; Heb likui levanah ליקוי לבנה]: **•*Heyvgirtina* herî dirêj a sedsala 21an îşev e** (rudaw.net 27.vii.2018) The longest *lunar eclipse* of the 21st century is this evening. {also: girtina heyvê (ZF); heyvgîrî (AA); hîvgirtin (Wkp-2); hîvgirtî (GF)} {syn: *heyvẍeyrîn (Bw); *xirabûna heyvê (CS)} Sor manggîran مـانـگـگـيـران [rudaw/SS/Wkp//AA//GF//ZF] <řojgirtin>

heyvgîrî هــەيــڤــگــيــرى (AA) = lunar eclipse. See **heyvgirtin**.

heyw هەيو (SK) = moon. See **hîv**.

heywan I هــەيــوان *f.* **(-a;).** reception hall, parlor, well-ventilated room with three walls, looking onto the central court of the house, where one sits during the summer (JB1-S); lobby, foyer, vestibule; patio, veranda: **•Jinkê řabû, *heywana* qesra malî** (JB1-S #199, 160) The woman got up and swept the palace *vestibule* **•Li gorî hotêleke Rojhilata Navîn û bajarekî piçûk, ku em paqijîyê deynin alîyekî, *hêwana* wê jî ne xerab bû** (KS, 57) For a small-town Middle Eastern hotel, if we disregard cleanliness, its *lobby* was not bad. {also: eywan (IFb); hêwan (KS); [aivan ايــوان/haivan هــيــوان] (JJ); <eywan> ايــوان (HH)} Cf. Ar īwān إيــوان = ' hall with columns, portico'; Sor heywan هــەيــوان = 'veranda' [KS//A/JB1-S/GF/OK//IFb/HH//JJ] <berbanik; bersifk; dîwanxane; sivder>

heywan II هـــــــيـــوان (JB3/IFb/GF) = animal. See **ḧeywan**.

hez هەز: hez kirin (A/JB3/IFb/OK) = to love. See **ḧez**.

hezar هـەزار *num.* thousand, 1,000. {also: hizar (SK); ḧezar (K/B/F); [hezar] هـزار (JJ); <hezar> هـزار (HH)} [Pok. ĝhéslo- 446.] 'thousand': Skt sahásram (<sm̥-ĝhéslom = 'one thousand'); Av hazaŋrəm; Sgd z'r [zār]; Mid P hazār (M3); P hazār هـزار; Sor hezar هـەزار; Za hezar (Mal)/ ḧezar (Todd); Hau hezar (M4) [A/IFb/JJ/HH/JB1-A&S/GF/TF/OK//F/K/B//SK] <bi hezaran; hezarem>

hezarem هـــــەزارەم *adj.* thousandth, 1,000th. {also: hezaremîn (IFb/Wkt-2); hizarem (Wkt-2); hizaremîn (Wkt-2)} Cf. P hazārom هـــزارم; Sor hezarem[în] هەزارەم[ین] [GF/Wkt//IFb] <hezar>

hezaremîn هـــەزارەمـــیـن (IFb/Wkt) = thousandth. See **hezarem**.

hezaz هـــــــــــــەزاز *f.* **(-a;).** 1) landslide, collapse: **•Malbatên 16 karkerên ku di *hezaza* kanê de mabûn** (FB) The families of 16 workers (miners) who had gotten stuck in *the collapse of* the mine; 2) deep and wide pit (made by lightening bolt) (FS/Wkt): **-hezaza birûskî** (FS) do. <Ar √h-z-z هـــزّ = 'to shake, rock, tremble' [FB/IFb/ZF/CS/FS/Wkt] <aşît; r̄enî>

hezêlk هەزێلك (Bw) = raised platform. See **herzal**.

Hezîran هـــــەزیـــــران (A/IFb/GF/OK) = June. See **Ḧezîran**.

hezîranî هەزیرانی (IF) = type of pear. See **ḧezîranî**.

hê هـــێ (EP/BX/F/Dz/K/B/IFb/FJ/GF/CS/RZ/ZF/SS/Tsab) = still, yet. See **hêj**.

hêbetî هـێـبـەتـی (BF/Wkt) = surprised, bewildered. See **ḧêbetî**.

hêc هێج (TF) = furious, mad. See **ḧêç'**.

hêcet هـــێـــجـــەت (Bw/OK) = grounds, excuse. See **hêncet**.

hêç I هێچ (GF)/hêç' I (K) = furious, mad. See **ḧêç'**.

hêç' II هـــێـــچ (K/B) = not at all; not any; nothing. See **hîç**.

hêçandin هـێـچـانـدِن *vt.* **(-hêçîn-).** to test, try out: **•Ka were, em *bihêçînin* mirov çawa şer bike** (BM, 10) Come on, let's *test* how one fights. {syn: cer̄ibandin} <hêç' II/hîç = 'not at all', cf. T yoklamak = 'to examine, inspect' < yok = 'there is not; nonexistent' [(neol)BM/IFb/TF/OK] <hîç>

hêdan هێدان (K) = patience; rest, calm. See **hedan**.

hêdî هێدی *adj./adv.* 1) slow(ly): **-hêdî-hêdî** (K/A/JB3/IF) very slowly/quietly; 2) quiet(ly); soft(ly) (SK). {also: êdîka (L); hêdîka (L/IF-2/B-2); hidî; [heidi] هـیـدی (JJ); <hêdî> هـیـدی (HH)} <Ar hādi' هـادئ = 'calm' [F/K/A/JB3/IFb/B/JJ/HH/JB1-S/SK/GF/TF/OK]

hêdîka هێدیكا (L/IF/B) = slow(ly); quiet(ly). See **hêdî**.

hêj هێژ *adv.* still, yet: **•Ew sibe bû *hêjka* zûbû** (EP-8) It was morning, *still* early **•Hergê derbaz bû - *hê* jarim ez** (J) If it passes through, [then] I'm *still* thin **•*Hê* zûye** (B) It's *still* early **•*Hêj* qet nebû derya û ber̄, baxoy nivîsî xeyr û şer̄** (FT, 174) Neither sea nor land existed *yet*, God had already designated [lit. 'wrote'] good and bad **•Lê marîya bêbext a ku ew dan kuştin *hêj* jî dixwend** (AB, 52) But the treacherous female, which had gotten them killed, was *still* singing **•R̄o hatye, nîvro, ew *hê* haj xwe t'uneye** (Dz) Day has dawned, noon has passed, she *still* hasn't budged/woken up **•Şeher t'emam r̄azaye, hûn *hê* ḧişîyarin?** (Z-922) The entire city has gone to sleep, you (pl.) are *still* awake? **•Tu *hê* neçûyî?** (B) Haven't you gone *yet*?/Didn't you go *yet*? **•Wî tevrê** [sic] **xwe yê *hêj* heriya wê bi devê wê ve hişknebûyî pesart dîwarê** (MG. Jiyaneka pêguhork) He leaned his hoe, on whose blade the mud was not *yet* dry, against the wall. {also: hê (EP/BX/F/Dz/K-2/B/IFb-2/FJ-2/GF-2/CS-2/RZ-2/ZF-2/SS-2/Tsab); hêja II (B); hêjî (Wlt); hêjka (EP-8); hêjta (JB1-A); hêşka (EP-7); hêşta (JB1-A-2/SK-2/RZ-2/SS-2/Bw); [heij هیژ/ heija هیژا/ heijam هیژام] (JJ); <hêj> هیژ (HH)} {syn: hila II; hîna} Sor hêşta هێشتا [EP/BX/F/Dz/B/Tsab//K/IFb/FJ/TF/GF/SK/CS/RZ/ZF/SS//JJ/HH//Wlt//EP-8//EP-7//JB1-A//Bw]

hêja I هێژا *adj.* 1) worth, equal to *(the value of)*: **•*Hêja* *bûne* çar bra hevr̄a xeberda** (EP-7) *They were like (=equal to)* four brothers talking together **•Ḧer kitêbek *hêjaye* çar maneta** (B) Every book *is worth* four rubles **•Eva k'itêba *çi hêjaye*?** (B) What *does* this book *cost*?/What *is* this book *worth*? **•Ev t'embûr qîmetê wê çende, *hêjaye*? Go: Wella, ev t'embûr *hêjayê* panzde zêr̄e** (JB1-S, #216) How much *is* this tembur *worth*? He said, "By God, this tembur *is worth* fifteen gold pieces"; 2) {syn: layîq [2]; stêl} deserving, worthy: **•Tu mêrxasekî *hêjayî*** (Z-1) You are a *worthy* man; 3) {syn: 'ezîz; xweşdivî} dear, precious; costly, expensive: **•Xwendevanên *hêja*!** (Ber) *Dear* readers!; 4) of good quality. {hêjayî} [EP-7/K/A/JB3/IFb/B/JB1-S/ GF/TF]

hêja II هێژا (B/JJ) = still, yet. See **hêj**.

hêjageh هـێـژاگـەه *m./f.(ZF3)* **(-a;).** strategic place, important military position or target (K): **•Çekê emerîkanî ê hewayî 30 ton bombe berdane *hêjagehên* Japona** (RN) American aerial forces dropped 30 tons of bombs on Japanese *targets*. [RN/K/ZF3]

hêjahî هێژاهی (ZF3) = value; merit. See **hêjayî**.

hêjayî هێژایی *f.* **(-ya;-yê).** 1) value, worth: **•Ez bawer im bona tesbîtkirina *hêjahîya* her tiştî, ... pîvanek peyda dibe** (zazaki.net:Derbarê pêşbazîya çîrokan a Nûbiharê de) I believe that to determine *the value of* everything, …a measurement [criterion] emerges ; 2) merit, virtue. {also: hêjahî (ZF3-2)} [Z-1/K/A/JB3/IF/ZF3] <hêja I>

hêjde هێژده (GF) = eighteen. See **ĥîjdeh**.

hêjî هێژی (Wlt) = still, yet. See **hêj**.

hêjîr هێژیر (HB/BX/IFb/B/Kmc-2) = fig. See **hejîr**.

hêjka هێژکا (EP-8) = still, yet. See **hêj**.

hêjmar هـێـژمـار (Ber) = number; issue *(of a journal)*. See **hejmar**.

hêjmartin هێژمارتِن (IF) = to count. See **hejmartin**.

hêjta هێژتا (JB1-A) = still, yet. See **hêj**.

hêk هـێـک *f.*/**hêk’** *m.* [JB1-A] **(-a/;-ê/).** egg. {also: hêlik[3] (SK); [heik هیك/ hi هی (JJ); <hêk> هیك (HH)} [Pok. au̯ei- 86.] 'bird' --> [*ōwyo-/* əyo-/*ōwo-] 'egg': Av *āvaya-; P xāye خـایـه = 'testicle(s)'; Sor hêlke هـێـلـکـه; Za hak *m.* = 'egg; testicle' (Todd/Mal); Hau hêłe *m.* = 'egg' (M4) [F/K/A/JB3/IFb/B/JJ/HH/JB1-A/GF/TF/OK//SK] <hêlik; mirîşk; spîlik I; zerik II>

hêkel هێکەل = statue. See **heyk’el**.

hêkerûn هێکەروون/**hêkeřûn** هێکەڕوون [B] *f.* **(-a;-ê).** fried eggs, omelette. {also: hêkrûn (AD)} {syn: sewikê hêka} Sor hêlke-w-řon هێلکە و ڕۆن [K/IFb/B/GF/TF/ZF3//AD]

hêkesor هـێـکـەسـۆر *f.* **(-a;-ê).** Easter: **-cejna hêkesorê** (RZ-2) do.: **•Bihar bû; nêzîkî ceşna *hêkesorê* bû** (Nûdem 29 [1999], "Keçika Misilman," 15) It was springtime, it was almost *Easter* time. {also: hêkesork (ZF3); [heik-a sor] هیکاسور (JJ)} [Nûdem/RZ//JJ//ZF3]

hêkesork هێکەسۆرك (ZF3) = Easter. See **hêkesor**.

hêkrûn هێکروون (AD) = fried eggs. See **hêkerûn**.

hêl I هێل (BK/ZF3/Wkt) = strength. See **ĥêl**.

hêl II هـێـل *m.(Ad/Wr)/f.(K/ZF3)* **(-ê/-a;/-ê).** 1) {syn: alî; k’êlek; tenişt; teref} side, direction; 2) country; province; district; surroundings (K/IFb/JB3). [Ad/Wr/K/JB3/IFb/TF/ZF3/FS]

hêlan I هێلان (K[s]/JB1-A&S/M/Bw) = to leave, let; to allow. See **hiştin**.

hêlan II هێلان (A) = swing. See **hêlekan**.

hêlanek هێلانەك (IF) = swing. See **hêlekan**.

hêlecan هێلەجان (K) = swing. See **hêlekan**.

hêleç’an هێلەچان (B) = swing. See **hêlekan**.

hêlekan هـێـلـەکـان *f.* **(-a;-ê).** 1) {syn: colan; deydik; dolîdang I; hêzok} swing (playground ride): **•Ji *hêlekanê* ket û serê xwe şikand** (Wkt) S/he fell off *the swing* and broke his/her head; 2) catapult (HH). {also: hêlan II (A); hêlanek; hêlecan (K); hêleç’an (B-2); <hêlikan> هیلکان (HH)} [IF/B//HH/ZF3/Wkt//A]

hêlik هـێـلِـك *f./m.(Msr/ZF3)* **(/-ê;).** 1) {syn: batî; gun; řitil II} testicles, scrotum; 2) {syn: çûçik I[3] (Msr) = baby boy's; ‘ewîc; kîr; teřik [2]; xir (Msr)} penis (Msr): **•hêlk û gunik** (Msr) penis and testicles, cock and balls; 3) egg (SK). See **hêk**. {also: [hilik] هیلك (JJ); <hêlik> هیلك (HH)} Cf. Sor hêlke هێلکە = 'egg' [K/A/IFb/B/JJ/HH/TF/Msr/ZF3] <hêk; kîr; řitil II>

hêliştin هـێـلِـشـتِـن (Czr) = to leave, let; to allow. See **hiştin**.

hêlî هـێـلـی *f.* **(-ya;-yê).** mirror: **•Tîmurê Leng ... ruyê xwe nedîtibu, dema Tîmur sêrî *hêlîyê* kir û rûyê xwe yê kiret dît, berxwe ket** (newroz.com: Bêdengî û kuştina Ferît Uzun 1, 30.xi.2010) Tamerlane … had never seen his own face, when T. looked into *the mirror* and saw his ugly face, he was very upset . {also: helî I (Bg); hîlî (IFb)} {syn: ‘eynik; mirêk; nênik I; qotî I} < Arm hayeli հայելի = 'mirror' [Krç/ZF3//Bg//IFb]

hêlîn هـێـلـیـن *f.* **(-a;-ê).** (bird’s) nest: **•Çwîk di ser hêlîna xwe de ye** (L) The sparrow is in [lit. 'on'] its nest. {also: hêlîng; hêlûn (F); [hiloun هـلـون/ hilin هیلین] (JJ)} Cf. P lāne لانه; Sor hêlane هێلانە; Za halên/halîn *m.* (Mal); Hau hêlane *m.* (M4) [Ad/L/K/JB3/IFb/B/SK/GF/TF/OK//F//JJ] <landik>

hêlîng هێلینگ = nest. See **hêlîn**.

hêlk هێلك = penis. See **hêlik**[2].

hêlm هێلم (F) = steam; breath. See **hilm**.

hêlûn هێلوون (F) = nest. See **hêlîn**.

hêman هـێـمـان *f.* **(-a;-ê).** element, factor, constituent: **•Di kurdî de hevok, li ser sê *hêmanên* bingehîn, kirde, bireser û lêkerê, tên sazkirin** (Amîda Kurd) In Kurdish, the sentence is founded on 3 *elements*, subject, object, and verb. [Amîda Kurd/IFb/GF/Kmc/CS/ZF3]

hêncet هـێـنـجـەت *f.* **(-a;).** 1) occasion, cause, grounds (for); 2) pretext, excuse: **-bi hênceta ...** (K) on the pretext of, on a plea of: **•Doz *bi hinceta ku* bi riya çapemenîyê propagandeya parvekarîyê li dijî Tirkiyeyê hatiye kirin vebûye** (Wlt 2:103, 8) The trial was opened *on the pretext that* separatist propaganda against Turkey was being made through the press **•Her r̄oj Mela 'Ebbas *bi heceta* dest-niwêjê ji medresê diçû mala ḧacî** (SK 15:146) Every day Mullah Abbas would go from the school to the Haji's home *on the pretext of* performing his ritual ablutions. {also: hecet (SK); hêcet (Bw/OK-2); hicet (OK); hincet (Wlt); [heidjet] حيجت (JJ); <ḧêcet> حيجت (HH)} <Ar ḥujjah حجّة = 'argument, pretext, plea'; = Sor biyanû بيانوو [SW/K/JB3/IFb/GF/TF// OK//SK//Wlt//Bw//JJ/HH]

hênijîn هێنژين *vi.* **(-hênij-).** 1) {syn: p'onijîn[1]} to doze, slumber (K/A/B/IF/OK): **•Nobeçî li ber devê derî sekinî ye û *dihênije*** (L) The guard on duty was stationed by the door, *dozing*; 2) {also: honijîn (OK)} {syn: bawişkîn; bêhnijîn [2]} to yawn (JJ); 3) {syn: bêhnijîn; pêkijîn} to sneeze (K/F). {also: [henijin هنژين/ hounijin هونژين] (JJ)} [L/F/K/A/IFb/B/JJ/OK]

hênik هێنك *adj.* cool, fresh: **•Derva *hênike*** (B) It's *cool* outside **•Du tas dewê *hênik* dianî datanî ber me** (Alkan, 71) She would bring two glasses of *cool* yoghurt drink and place them before us. {also: hîn III (Bw/OK-2); hînik (IFb-2/GF/TF/SK); honik (K[s]/IFb/JB3); [hounek هونك {*note: incorrectly glossed as **fraîcheur** = 'coolness, freshness'} /henik/hīnik هينك] (JJ); <hênik> هينك (HH)} Cf. P xonak خنك; Sor fênik فێنك = 'cool'; Za honik {hênikahî; hênikaî; hênikayî; hênikî; honikahî; honikayî; [hounekàï] هونكاى (JJ)} [F/K/A/ IFb/B/HH/OK//JJ//K(s)/JB3/IFb// SK/GF/TF//Bw]

hênikahî هێنكاهى (IF) = coolness. See **hênikayî**.

hênikaî هێنكائى (F) = coolness. See **hênikayî**.

hênika•yî هێنكايى *f.* **(;•yê).** coolness, freshness. {also: hênikahî (IF); hênikaî (F); hênikî (IF); honikahî (BX/IFb); honikayî (K[s]); [hounekàï] هونكاى (JJ)} Sor fênikayî فێنكايى = 'cool, cool place' & fênikî فێنكى = 'cool[ness]' [K/B//IFb//B//BX//K(s)/JJ] <hênik>

hênikî هێنكى (IF) = coolness. See **hênikayî**

hêran هێران/**hêr̄an** هێڕان [JB1-A] *vt.* **(-hêr-/-hêr̄- [JB1-A]).** to grind, crush: **•Hişên qazê ... "Gelo ev zalim ê min çito bixwe, çawa daqultîne; ê min bi carekê ve di hindir devê xwe yê mezin de, bi diranê xwe yên tûj *bihêre*"** (ŞBS-W,9) The goose's thoughts ... "I wonder how this tyrant will eat me, how he will swallow me; will he *grind* me *up* all at once inside his huge mouth, with his sharp teeth?" {also: hêrandin (JB3/GF-2/ OK); hêrîn (OK-2/GF-2); hêr̄în (IFb); hêr̄t'in (JB1-A-2); [hiran] هيران (JJ); <hêran> هيران (HH)} Sor har̄în[ewe] هاڕين[ەوە]/hêr̄în هێڕين (Pijdar); Hau har̄ay (har̄-) *vt.* (M4) [F/K/A/B/HH/ JB1-A/GF/TF/BK//JB3/OK//IFb/JJ] <dan II; danhêrk; destar̄>

hêrandin هێراندن (JB3/GF/OK) = to grind. See **hêran**.

hêratî هێراتى *f.* **(-ya;-yê).** women's brightly colored headscarf: **•*Hêratîya* serê wê şiqitî bû** (Zerîn Tek:RN2 56[1998] 6) Her *headscarf* had fallen off **•Paş kuştina Sêvdîn, Zezê ... *hêratîya* reş da serê xwe** (Zerîn Tek:RN2 56[1998] 6) After Sevdin was killed, Zazeh ... put a black *headscarf* on her head. {also: êrat'î (K-2)} [Zerîn Tek/K/B/ZF3] <ḧibrî; k'itan; k'ofî; laç'ik; p'oşî; t'emezî; xavik>

hêrifandin هێرفاندن (-hêrifîn-) (IFb/OK) = to demolish. See **hêrivandin**.

hêriş هێرش (Bw) = attack. See **êrîş**.

hêrivandin هێرڤاندن *vt.* **(-hêrivîn-).** to demolish, knock down, destroy, tear down; to do away with: **•Ew lata te xwest ji binî de *bihêrivîne*** [sic] ***wê bê hêrivandin*** (Wlt 2:59, 7) That boulder which you wanted *to demolish* from the bottom up *will be demolished.* {also: heraftin (SK); herifandin (GF/Frq); hêrifandin (-hêrifîn-) (IFb/OK)} {syn: hilweşandin} [Wlt/TF//IFb/OK//GF/Frq//SK]

hêr̄în هێڕين (IFb)/hêrîn هێرين (OK/GF) = to grind. See **hêran**.

hêro هێرۆ *f.* **(-ya;-ê).** hollyhock, rose mallow, bot. *Althea rosea*; marshmallow, bot. *Althea officinalis*: **-gula hêroê** (Bw) do. {also: hêrû (A/ TF); hîro (IFb-2); [hirou/ehru (G)/hīrő (PS)] هيرو (JJ); <hêrû> هيرو (HH)} Sor hêro هێرۆ = 'hollyhock' [Bw/K(s)/IFb/OK/ZF3/FS/Wkt//A/HH/TF//JJ]

hêrs هێرس *f.* **(-a;-ê).** anger, wrath, fury, ire: **-hêrsa *fk-ê* hatin** (Ks) to get angry at s.o., rage, become furious *(rev. constr.)*: **•*Hêrsa* Memê *gelekî hat*** (FK-eb-1) M. *flew into a rage*; **-lê hêrs bûn** = a) to be or get angry at: **•Hûn çima *li* Memê birê me *hêrs dibin*?** (Z-1) Why *are you getting angry at* our brother Mem?; b) to get excited, nervous, upset. {also: hêrsî (F-2); hêrz (A/OK-2); [hyrs/ ḥirs] حرص (JJ)} {syn: 'ern; k'erb [2]} <Ar ḥirṣ حرص = 'zeal' [Z-1/Ks/F/K/JB3/IFb/B/GF/TF/OK//A//JJ]

<k'eribîn; xeyidîn; ẍezibîn>

hêrsî هێرسی (F) = anger; grudge. See **hêrs**.

hêr̄t'in هێڕتن (JB1-A) = to grind. See **hêran**.

hêrû هێروو (A/TF/HH)= hollyhock. See **hêro**.

hêrûg هـێـرووگ *f.* **(-a;).** 1) {syn: ħilû I; încas} plum; 2) {also: arûng (Kmc-2); hîrog (IFb)} {syn: mişmiş; qeysî; zerdelî} apricot. {also: arûng (Kmc-2); erûk(GF); hêrûng (ZF3-2); hîrog (IFb); [erūk] اروك (JJ-Lx)} <T erik = 'plum' [DZK//JJ//IFb] <alûçe; dembûl; şilor>

hêrûng هێرروونگ (ZF3) = plum; apricot. See **hêrûg**.

hêrve هـێـرڤـه *adv.* on or to this side, this direction, hither: •***Hirve* dar û wêve dar / yê di navê da seyê har [xencer e]** (AZ #3, 73) Wood *on this side* and wood on that / what's in the middle is a rabid dog *[rdl.: ans.: it's a dagger]*; **-ji *ft-î* û hêrve** (Bw) this side of [T -den beri; clq Ar min ... u-la-jāy مـن ... ولـجـاى]: **•*ji* cisrî *û hêrve*** (Bw) *this side of* the bridge **•*ji êrwe* wêwe** (SK) *from here* to there. {also: êrwe (SK); hêve (Dh); hirve (Bw-2); <hirve هرڤه/hire هره> (HH)} [Bw//HH/AZ//SK] <wêve>

hêrz هێرز (A/OK) = anger; grudge. See **hêrs**.

hêsa هێسا *adj.* 1) quiet, peaceful, calm (K): **-hêsa bûn** (B): a) to rest, relax {syn: vês girtin (Ad)}: **•Îzna carîya jî da, wekî ew jî her̄in xwer̄a *hêsa bin*** (Z-1) She also gave the maidservants permission to go *take a rest*; b) to be or become easy; **-hêsa kirin** (K) to make easier, facilitate: **•Van ħemû tişta şuxulê wanî çetin *hêsa nedikir*** (Ba2:1, 204) All these things *did not make* their hard work *easier*; 2) {syn: bi sanahî; sivik} easy, simple (F/K/B/IF). See **asan**. {also: hesan I; hêsan (IFb/GF/TF/OK); [asan] اسان (JJ)} Cf. P āsān آسان = 'easy' [Z-1/F/K/B//IFb/GF/TF/OK]

hêsan هـێـسان (IFb/GF/TF/OK) = quiet; easy. See **asan** & **hêsa**.

hêsanî I هێسانی (JB3/HH) = easy. See **asan**.

hêsanî II هێسانی (IFb/GF/TF/OK) = ease. See **asanî**.

hêsir هێسِر (Z-1/Dyd/Çnr/Kp/Srk) = tears. See **hêstir I**.

hêsîr I هـێـسیر *m.* **(-ê;).** 1) {syn: dîl; girtî [2]} prisoner *(of war)*, captive: **•Ez *hêsîrê* çavên te me** (Muşlu Ihsan: name of his song) I am *a captive of* your eyes; 2) slave (K/B); 3) *[adj.]* {syn: r̄eben} poor, wretched, miserable: **•Zînê tûyî, *hêsîr*, p'or̄kur̄ Memo ezim** (Z-3) You are Zîn, *miserable*, headshaven, [and] I am Mem. {also: exsîr (JB1-S); êxsîr (SK); [hisir] هسیر (JJ); <hêsîr> هـێـسیر (HH)} < Ar asīr أسـيـر = 'prisoner'; Sor yexsîr یەخسیر [Z-3/K/IF/B/HH//JJ//JB1-S//SK]

hêsîr II هێسیر (Wn) = tears. See **hêstir I**.

hêsk هێسك (FS/BF) = swing. See **hêzok**.

hêstik هێستِك (SK/Zeb) = bone. See **hestî**.

hêstir I هێستِر *pl./f.(JB1-S)* teardrops: **•*Hêstîr* ji çavên min dihatin** (Xecê's twitter acct) *Tears* were flowing from my eyes. {also: êsir (L); hêsir (Z-1/Dyd/Çnr/Kp/Srk); hêsîr II (Wn); histêrik (Klk); ħestir (Grc/Btm); ħêsir (Erg); stêrik (Haz); stêrk II (Msr)} {syn: r̄onî II[2]; sirişk} Cf. O Ir *asru(ka)--> Mid P ars (M3) --> P āšk آشك; Sor esrîn ئـەسـریـن = firmêsk فـرمـێـسـك; Za ħers *f.* (Todd)/hesri/hesir *f.* (Mal) [F/K/A/JB3/JB1-S/Czr//L//Z-1/Dyd/Çnr/Kp/Srk//Wn//Klk//Grc/Btm//Erg//Haz//Msr]

hêstir II هـێـستِر *m.(K)/f.(JB3/IF/SK)* **().** mule: **•Hêştir radibin hev, *hêstir* û ker bin lingên wan de diçin** (BX) When camels fight, *mules* and donkeys perish under their feet *[prv.]*. {also: histêr (IF-2); histir (IF-2)} {syn: exte; qant'ir} Cf. P astar اسـتـر = 'mule' < *asp-tar: asp = 'horse' + -tar = -er *(suffix for comparative degree)*: 'more like a horse'; Sor êstir ئێستِر/hêstir هێستِر; cf. also Za istor *f.* = 'horse, mare' (Todd); Hau hesere *f.* (M4) = 'mule' [K/A/JB3/IF/SK/Hk/Czr/Grc/Kp/Btm/Msr/Haz/Zx] <hesp; k'er III; k'ur̄ik; mak'er; zir̄în>

hêstir III هێستِر = camel. See **ħêştir**.

hêstirvan هێستِرڤان (K) = camelherd. See **heştirvan**.

hêsû هێسو (FK-kk-2&3) = tent flap. See **hêşî**.

hêş هێش, m. (K) = tent flap. See **hêşî**.

hêşandin هێشاندِن (K) = to stuff or prepare (meat) . See **heşandin**.

hêşet هێشەت (GShA) = town, settlement. See **heyşet**.

hêşin هێشِن (A) = green; blue. See **heşîn**.

hêşî هـێـشـی *f.* **(-ya;-yê).** 1) outer flap of tent (K/A/IF/JJ); back part of a tent which touches the ground (B): **•Beyrim *hêşîya* kon hilgaft** (L) Beyrim lifted up the *outer side/flap of* the tent; 2) fringe, ornamental border made of threads (IF). {also: hêsû (FK-kk-2&3); hêş, m. (K); hîşî (IF-2); [heïchi] حـیـشـی (JJ)} Cf. Ar ḥāšiyah حـاشـيـة = 'border, edge' [L/A/IFb/JJ/B//K//FK-kk-2&3] <[1] kon; xêvet; [2] gûfik; r̄îşî>

hêşîn هێشین (Z-1/K/B/ZF3) = green; blue. See **heşîn**.

hêşînatî هـێـشـیـنـاتـی (K) = greenness; vegetation. See **heşînatî**.

hêşînayî هـێـشـیـنـایـی (B) = greenness; vegetation. See **heşînatî**.

hêşka هێشكا (EP-7) = still, yet. See **hêj**.

hêşnaî هـێـشـنـائـی (F) = greenness; vegetation. See **heşînatî**.

hêşnayî هـێـسـنـایـی (K) = greenness; vegetation. See **heşînatî**.

hêşta هـێـشـتـا (JB1-A/SK/RZ/SS/Bw) = still, yet. See **hêj**.

hêştir هێشتِر (JB3/IFb/GF/OK) = camel. See **ḧêştir**.

hêştirme هـێـشـتِـرمـه *f.* (). ostrich [Ar na'ām نـعـام; T devekuşu; P šotormory شـتـرمـرغ]: •***Heştirme* û kerkûvî gelek caran bi hev re dijîn, daku xwe ji talûkeyan biparêzin** (deskgram.org:rasteqîn vi.2018) *Ostriches* and zebras often live together, to protect themselves from dangers. {also: heştirme (IFb/Wkt/FD)} Sor ḧuştirmirẍ حـوشـتِـرمِـرغ/ḧuştirmel حوشتِرمەل/wuştirmirx ووشتِرمِرخ [deskgram/IFb/Wkt/FD//ZF3]

hêştirvan هـێـشـتِـرڤـان (GF/OK/ZF3) = camelherd. See **heştirvan**.

hêt هـێـت *f.* **(-a;-ê).** thigh, haunch; thigh *of animal (cf. r̄an/rehn = thigh of humans)* (Bw); leg of mutton (JJ): •**Gule *hêta* wîda hasê bûye** (B) The bullet got stuck [or, was lodged] in his *thigh*. {also: [hit] حـيـت (JJ)} {syn: kulîmek; r̄an; tilor I} <O Ir *haxti- (A&L p. 88 [X, 6] + note 4 (p. 100); cf. Skt sákthi- *n.* (Tsb2, 15); Av haxti-; Sgd 'γt [aγd]; Oss aγd; Mid P haxt (M3); Za hêt-ı *f.* (Mal) [F/K/IFb/B/GF/Bw/Zx//JJ] <hingul; k'elef I; k'emax>

hêtîm هێتیم (M-Ak) = orphan. See **êt'îm**.

hêton هێتۆن (K) = limekiln. See **hêtûn**.

hêtûn هـێـتـوون *f.* (;-ê). 1) {syn: k'ûre} limekiln: •***Hêtûn* jî halo tê şewitandin: Havînê, wextê ç'ilo qewîn dibê, xurdê xwe ḧazir dikin. Piştr̄a, dest bi *hêtûnê* dikin. Kû *hêtûn* temam bû, wê xurdê xwe ḧemûî kşênine ber *hêtûnê*** (HR-I, 1:23-26) This is how *the limekiln* is used [lit. 'burnt']: In summer, when the shrubbery is dense, they prepare their kindling wood. Then, they start *the limekiln*. When *the limekiln* is ready, they drag all their kindling wood to *the limekiln*; 2) *(fig.)* a very hot place, hell (OK) [hêtûn]; intense heat (JJ) [heītoun]: •**Sor im wek *êtûn*** (IFb) I'm as red as *an oven*/I'm as hot as hell. {also: atûn (A/IFb/GF); etûn (IFb-2/GF-2); êtûn (Bw/IFb-2/TF/OK-2); hêton (K-2); veytûn (GF-2); [heītoun هيتون/ētūn اتون <sic>] (JJ); <atûn> آتـون (HH)} <Arc atūnā אתונא = 'fireplace, stove' --> Ar at(t)ūn أتـــون = 'kiln, furnace, oven'. *K gives meanings 'coal, brand; ashes'* [HR-I/K/OK/RF//Bw/JJ/TF//A/IFb/HH/GF] <k'ils>

hêvarî هێڤاری (M-Ak) = evening. See **êvar**.

hêvde هێڤده (GF) = seventeen. See **hevdeh**.

hêve هێڤه (Dh) = on this side. See **hêrve**.

hêvên هـێـڤـێـن *m.* **(-ê;).** ferment, leaven; yeast: **-havin girtin** (B) to ferment *(vi.) (of milk products)*: •**Şîr *havin girtye*** (B) The milk *has fermented*; **-hêvênê mastî** (Bw) yoghurt "starter." {also: haveyn (IFb-2/GF-2/TF/OK); havên (K-2/GF); havin (; hêvin/havên) (B); heyvan (A); [hawin/hewin] هـڤـيـن (JJ)} {syn: hevîrtirş} Sor hewên هـەوێـن = 'leaven'; Za amîn (Todd/Mal)/amên (Mal), *m.* = 'starter (for making yoghurt) ' [Bw//IFb/TF/OK//K/GF//B//A//JJ] <hevîr; mast>

hêvirze هێڤِرزه (FS) = noise; havoc. See **hêwirze**.

hêvişandin هێڤِشاندِن(F/IF) = to spare. See **hêvşandin**.

hêvî هـێـڤـی *f.* **(-ya;-yê).** 1) {syn: çare; guman; îman; îtbar; omîd} hope: **-hêvî kirin** = to hope (see also [3] below): •**Ez hêvî dikim** = I hope; 2) waiting; expectation: **-hîvîyê bûn/man/sekinîn** (K)/**li hêvîya fk-ê/ft-î man** to wait for, await, expect {syn: ç'avnihêrî li r̄îya... kirin; li bendî ...man; p'an I; sekinîn}: •***Li hêvîya* hev *man*** (BX) They *waited for* each other •**T'emam *hîvîya* Memê delal *bûn*** (Z-1) They *were all waiting for* darling Mem; 3) {syn: lavahî; limêj; t'eweqe} prayer; request: **-jê hêvî kirin** = to request, beg: •***Ji te hêvî dikim*** = I *beg* you; please; 4) *name of a Kurdish journal published in Paris*. {also: hîvî (F/K/B/JB1-A); hîwî (SK); [hiwi] هـڤـی (JJ); <hê[f]î> هيفی (HH)} Cf. P omīd اميد --> T ümit; Sor hîwa هـيـوا [A/JB3/IFb/JB1-S/GF/TF/OK//F/K/B/JB1-A//JJ//SK//HH] <guman>

hêvîdar هـێـڤـیـدار *adj.* 1) hopeful: •**Em *hêvîdarin ku* xwendawarên me ...** (DM) We *hope that* our readers ... •**Ez *hîvîdarim*** (K) I *hope*; 2) expectant; waiting for. {also: hîvîdar (K)} Sor hîwadar هیوادار [DM/K/A/IF]

hêvîsandin هـێـڤـیـسـانـدِن (FJ/CCG) = to repair, darn (clothing). See **hîvastin**.

hêvîsîn هێڤیسین (FJ/CCG) = to repair, darn (clothing). See **hîvastin**.

hêvrist هێڤرست (Kmc/HH) = juniper tree. See **hevris**.

hêvşandin هـێـڤـشـانـدِن *vt.* **(-hêvşîn-).** to spare, use sparingly, (be)grudge *often used in the negative*: •**Qet gilya *nehêvşîne*** (Ba3-3, #21) *Don't mince* words •**Tê gilîê r̄ast *nehêvşînî*/** (Ba3-3, #21)

Don't spare true words [=don't refrain from speaking the truth]; **-qeweta xwe nehêvişandin** (F) not to spare one's strength: **•Gerek e em ji bo xebatê *qewata xwe nehêvşînin*** (FS: S.Semend. Xezal) We must *spare nothing* for work. {also: hêvişandin (F/IF); hêwşandin (K); [heoŭchandin هوشاندين/hevichin هوشين] (JJ)} [Ba3/Rwn//F/IF//K/JJ] <t'exsîr kirin>

hêwan هـــێـــوان (KS) = reception hall; foyer. See **heywan I**.

hêwerze هێوەرزە (B) = noise; havoc. See **hêwirze**.

hêwirandin هـــێـــورانـــدِن *vt.* **(-hêwirîn-).** 1) {syn: ȟewandin} to place, accomodate, put up *(guests)*; to [cause to] stop: **•Memê navda *dihêwrîne*** (EP-7) She *placed* Mem among [the mattresses]; 2) to calm, soothe, silence (a crying child) (Zeb/Hej). {also: [everandin] اوراندين (JJ)} [EP-7/K/JB3/IFb/GF/Zeb/Hej//JJ] <hêwirîn>

hêwirg•e هـــێـــورگـــە *f.* **(•a;•ê).** abode, residence; accommodation, place to stay (for the night). {also: êwirge; hêwirgeh (B-2/ZF)} {syn: mek'an[2]} [EP-8/K/B//ZF]

hêwirgeh هێورگەه (B/ZF) = abode. See **hêwirge**.

hêwirîn هـــێـــوِريـــن *vi.* **(-hêwir-).** 1) to make a halt, stopover *(on a trip)*, stop to rest, alight (K/IFb/JJ/B): **•Çol û basta digeȓîya, / Li cî-wara ne *hêwirîya*** (EP-8) He roamed over desert and plain, /he *stopped* at no campsite **•Teyr li darê *dihêwirin*** (IF) The birds *alight* on the tree; 2) to stay, live, dwell (JB3). {also: [everin] اورين (JJ)} [EP-8/K/JB3/IFb/JJ/B] <hêwirandin; ȟewîn; qonax>

hêwirz•e هـــێـــوِرزە *f.* **(•eya; •ê).** 1) {syn: biȓbiȓ; galegûrt; galigal; guȓîn; hose; k'im-k'imî; qajeqaj; qalmeqal; qareqar; qerebalix; qîȓeqîȓ; ȓeqeȓeq; şerqîn; t'eqeȓeq} noise, din: **•Her û her kaos û *hêwirzeya* dengan e ku li ber guhê me dikeve** (Nbh 135:26) We keep on hearing the chaotic *din of* voices [lit. 'it is continually the chaos and din of voices which falls before our ear']; 2) {syn: geremol; k'af-k'ûn; k'eft û left; t'evdan} havoc, chaos, disorder. {also: hêvirze (FS-2); hêwerze (B-2)} [Nbh/K/B/ZF/FS/Wkt/CS]

hêwî هـــێـــوی *f.* **(-ya;-yê).** co-wife *(in a polygynous household); term of address between co-wives* [cf. Ar ḍirrah ضـرّة; T kuma; P havū هـوو]. {also: hewê (IF-2); hewî (A/IF); [hewou هڤو/ hewi هڤی/ hevi هـوی] (JJ); <hewî> هـوی (HH)} {syn: berbû [3]} Skt sapatnī *f.*; O Ir *hapaθnī- < ha- = 'with' + paθni- = 'wife': Av hapaθnī-; Sgd pn'nc (-'nc is suffixal); Southern Tati dialects: Chali hōva = 'co-wife' (Yar-Shater); Shughni dbīn; Pashto bən; Baluchi awox/(h)afōx; P havū هـــوو; Sor hewê هـــەوی; Za wesni *f.* (Mal). See **#50. hapōk** in: G. Morgenstierne. "Notes on Balochi Etymology," *Norsk Tidsskrift for Sprogvidenskap*, 5 (1932), 47, reprinted in: *Irano-Dardica* (Wiesbaden : Dr. Ludwig Reichert Verlag, 1973), p.158. [Kg/MK/K/JJ/B//A/IF/HH] <jinbav>

hêwşandin هێوشاندِن (K) = to spare. See **hêvşandin**.

hêz هـــێـــز *f.* **(-a;-ê).** 1) {syn: birî I; ȟêl; qedûm [2]; qewat; t'aqet; zexm I [2]; zor I} power, force (K/IF/JJ): **•Têkoşîna rizgariyê *hêz* divê** (Ber) Striving for freedom requires *force*; **-hêz û têhn** (Zeb) energy, power; 2) brigade (JB3/IF). {also: [heĭz] هيز (JJ)} [Ber/K/JB3/IF/JJ] <bihêz>

hêzar هـــێـــزار *f.* **(-a;-ê).** bridal veil. {also: hîzar (Z-3/ZF3)} {syn: xêlî I} Sor hîzar هـــيـــزار = 'headband tied around a woman's headdress' [Z-3/ZF3//K(s)/IF] <ç'adir[1]; ç'arik[2]; ç'arşev[1]; doẍe>

hêzing I هێزنگ = firewood. See **êzing**.

hêzing II هێزنگ (K) = sigh. See **ȟezing**.

hêzok هـــێـــزۆك *f.* **(;-ê).** swing, children's playground accoutrement: **•Zaȓo li *hêzokê* siyar bû** (FS) The child climbed on *the swing*. {also: hêsk (FS/BF)} {syn: colan [2]; deydik; dolîdang I; hêlekan} [Zeb/Bar/Dh/GF/OK/ZF3//FS/BF]

hibrî هِبری (Ceylanpınar) = girl's headscarf. See **ȟibrî**.

hicet هِجەت (OK) = grounds, excuse. See **hêncet**.

hicmetî هِجمەتی *adj.* shocked, surprised: **-hicmetî bûn** (Zeb/BF) to be shocked, surprised {syn: guhişîn}: **•Te çiye tu hosa *hicmetî bûy*?** (BF) What is wrong with you that you *are* so *shocked*? {syn: 'ecêbmayî; ȟêbetî; met'elmayî} [Zeb/BF]

hicran هِـجـران (K/IF) = separation; reason; insult. See **hecran**.

hiçhar هِچهار (JB3/IFb/OK) = red pepper. See **ȟiçȟar**.

hidî هِدی = slow(ly); quiet(ly). See **hêdî**.

hifare هِفارە (GF) = chaff; unpicked fruit. See **'efare**.

hijandin هِـــژانـــدِن (M/SK) = to shake, rock (vt.) ; to brandish. See **ȟejandin**.

hijdehem هِـــژدەهـــەم (CT/Wkt) = eighteenth. See **hejdehem**.

hijdehemîn هِـــژدەهـــەمـــيـــن (Wkt) = eighteenth. See **hejdehem**.

hijdeyem هِژدەیەم (Wkt) = eighteenth. See **hejdehem**.

hijdeyemîn هِـــژدەيـــەمـــيـــن (Wkt) = eighteenth. See

hejdehem.

hijîr هژير (Bw/SK) = fig. See **hejîr**.

hijîrk' هژيرك (JB1-A) = fig. See **hejîr**.

hijmartin هژمارتِن (M/FS) = to count. See **hejmartin.**

hik'ayet هِكايەت = tale. See **ḧekyat.**

hikûmat هِـــكـــوومـــات (IFb) = government. See **ḧuk'umet**.

hikûmet هِـــكـــوومـــەت (IFb/TF) = government. See **ḧuk'umet**.

hik'yat هِكيات = tale. See **ḧekyat.**

hikyatbêj هِكياتبێژ (ZF3) = storyteller. See **ḧik'îyatdar.**

hila I هِلا = Come on! See **hela I**.

hila II هِـــلا *adv.* 1) {syn: hêj; hîna} still, yet: •**Fêrîk lawo, miqatî Sûsîkê be, ewe *hela* biç'ûke, dibe biweste, paşda bimîne, bixalife, tu jê dûr nek'eve, alî wê bike** (Ba2:2, 206) Ferik my son, take care of Susik, she is *still* small, perhaps she will get tired, fall behind, [or] get lost; you stay close to her [lit. 'don't fall far from her'], help her; 2) [+ neg.] not yet, still not: •***Hela* tavê nedabû ḧeç'êd ç'îya** (Ba2:1, 204) The sunlight had not *yet* touched the mountain peaks •**Ûsibî xame, *hila* t'u cîyada neçûye** (Ba) Joseph is inexperienced, he hasn't gone anywhere *yet* [on a trip]. {also: hela II (F/K/B)} Cf. T hâlâ [Ba/F/K/B]

hilandin هِلاندِن (Qzl) = to melt. See **ḧelandin**.

hil•anîn [هِل ئـانـيـن] هِـلانـيـن *vt.* **(hil[t]în-).** 1) {syn: hildan} to pick up, lift; to remove, take away [Fr soulever, ôter, brandir] (BX/K/A/JB3/IF): •**Aqilê xwe ji dûwê řep *hilîna*** (Dz) She *got* her "brains" (=took her cue/learned her lesson) from the [wolf's] protruding tail *[proverbial saying, cf. "the lion's share"]* •**Çel keleş bi xwe re *helanîne*** (L) They *took* forty brigands with them •**Ewa tê kûz dibe, t'eşîê *hiltîne*** (J) She comes [and] stoops over, [and] *picks up* the distaff •**Konaẍek *helanî* û yek danî** (L) He completed one day's traveling, and started out again the next morning [lit. 'He *picked up* one stage of the trip and put one down'] [Au bout de deux étapes] •**Memê serê xwe ji xewa şîrin *hiltîne*, / Husul-cemalekê p'aşla xweda divîne** (EP-7) Mem awakes [lit. '*lifts* his head'] from sweet sleep / He sees a beauty in his arms; **-gunehê *fk-ê* hilanîn** = to take on responsibility [for causing s.o.'s death]: •**Ez ber mirazim, ez te nakujim, *gunê* te *hilnaynim*** (Z-1) I've gotten what I want, I won't kill you, I won't *take on the responsibility* [for killing you] •**Welatê me dûr e ez *gunehê* we *hilneynim*** (L) Our country is far, I *don't want to be responsible for* you (=for your life); **-jê ḧeyf hilanîn** = to avenge, take revenge on: •**Ezê te bikujim, *heyfa* bavê xwe *ji te hilînim*!** (L) I'll kill you, *I'll take revenge on you for* my father['s death]; **-mirî hilanîn** (IF) to bury the dead {syn: binax kirin; veşartin [2]}; **-sifre hilanîn** (IF) to clear the table; 2) to keep, save, preserve (IF): •**Min pare yê xwe *hilanî*** (IF) I *saved* my money; **-hilanîn zivistanê** (IF) to save for the winter; 3) to brandish *(a sword)* (JJ): •**Emê soranîa *hilînin*** (FK-eb-2) We *will brandish* swords. {also: helanîn (L/JB1-A); hel înan (SK); hilînan (Dz); [hil-anin] هلانين (JJ); <hilanîn هلانين (hiltîne) (هلتينه)> (HH)} [BX/K/A/JB3/IF/JJ/HH/JB1-S/GF/TF/OK//L/JB1-A//SK//Dz]

hilatin هِـلاتِـن (IF/B/OK) = to rise (the sun, etc.) . See **hilhatin**.

hil•avêtin هِـلاڤـێـتِـن *vt.* **(hil-d-avêj-).** 1) to throw high up *into the air*: **-xwe hilavîtin** (K) to jump up, leap up: •**Zarokê *xwe* ji keyfan *dihilavêt*, ango xwe bilind kir** (BF) The child *leapt up* out of joy, i.e., he raised himself up; 2) {syn: tîzik lê dan} to kick with both hind legs *(of animals)* (IFb/Mzg); 3) {syn: dêrandin} to winnow *(grain)*: •**Wî coxîn *hilavêt*, da bayî ku dan û ka jêk cuda bibin** (FS) He *winnowed* the threshing [floor], threw (lit. gave) it to the wind, so that the seeds and straw would separate; 4) {syn: veřeşîn} to throw up, vomit. {also: helaftin (CCG-Rh/Mzg); helavêtin (IFb-2); hilavîtin (K); [al-awetin] هـلاڤـيـتـن (JJ); <hilavêtin هلاڤيتن (hiltavêje) (هلتاڤيژه)> (HH)} [CCG/Mzg//IFb/HH/FJ/GF/TF/ZF/FS/BF/JJ//K]

hilavistin هِلاڤِستِن (GF) = to hang up. See **hilawîstin.**

hilavîtin هِلاڤيتِن (K) = to throw up (high); to kick with both hind legs; to winnow. See **hilavêtin.**

hilawistin هِـــلاوِســـتِـــن (OK) = to hang up. See **hilawîstin.**

hil•awîstin [هِل ئـاويـستِـن] هِـلاويـستِـن *vt.* **(hil-awîs-/-hilawîs-[Bw]).** to hang (up): •**Şîşek li wî milê wî da, yê řastê da, yê çepê derêxist, *hilawîst* bi xanî ve** (M-Zx #750) He stuck a spit through his right shoulder, bringing it out at the left, and *hung* him *up* in the house. {also: helawîstin (SK); hilavistin (GF); hilawistin (OK); [hil-awistin] هلاوستن (JJ); <hilawîstin> هلاويستن (HH)} {syn: daliqandin; darda kirin; řaxistin} Sor heławasîn هەڵاواسين = 'to hang up' [Bw/IFb/HH//JJ/OK//SK//GF//TF]

hil•bijartin هِلبِژارتِن *vt.* **(hil-bijêr-).** 1) to elect, vote into office; 2) {syn: bijartin; jêgirtin; neqandin I} to choose, select; 3) [*f.* **(-a;-ê).**] election: **•Di vî babetî de *hilbijartina* serokatiya Ame[r]îka gelekî balkêş e. *Hilbijartinê* hinek Kurd û dewleta Tirk kire du şeq** (Wlt 1:37=38, 2) In this respect the American presidential *election* is very interesting. *The election* split the Kurds and the Turkish state into two factions. {also: helbijartin (IFb-2/TF)} Cf. Sor hełbijardin هـەڵـبـژاردِن = 'select, elect; election (EM)' [Wlt/IFb/GF/ZF//TF]

hilbiřandin هِلبِراندِن (K[s]/F/B) = to lift. See **hilbiřîn**.

hil•biřîn هـِـلـبِـرِيـن *vt.* **(hil-biř-).** to lift, pick up *(a person)*; to raise, cause to rise *(lamp wick, etc.)* (IFb); to remove (GF): **•Gundê me da kesekî dil nedikir wîřa gulaş bigirta, lê wekî nişkêva yekî dil bikira, ewî ew *hildibiřî* jorê û, wekî zirarê nedê, fesal dadanî ser piştê** (Ba2:1, 204) In our village no one would dare to wrestle with him, but if suddenly someone were to dare, he *would pick* that person *up* and, so as not to harm him, carefully put him on his back **•Zînê û carîa hevřa *hilbiřîn*** [sic] (EP-7) Z. and her maidservants *lifted* [M. out of the dungeon by pulling on a rope tied around his waist]. {also: helbirîn (IFb); hilbiřandin (K[s]/F/B)} {syn: bilind kirin; hilanîn; hildan} [EP-7/K/GF//IFb///F/K(s)/B]

hil•bûn هِـلـبـوون *vi.* **(hil-b-).** 1) to ascend, rise *(e.g., of dust, smoke)*: **•Min *hilbûye* t'oz û xubara van kerîyaye** (Z-1) The dust of these flocks [of sheep] *rose up* [over] me; 2) to catch fire (JJ); to go on *(of a light)*, light up *(vi.)*, be ignited (Bw). {also: [hil-bouin] هلبوين (JJ); <hilbûn هلبون (hildibe) (هلدبه)> (HH)} [Z-1/K/IFb/HH/GF/Bw//JJ] <řabûn>

hilç'andin هِلچاندِن (K-dş/K) = to scoop up; to extract. See **hilçinîn**.

hilç'inandin هِلچِناندِن (K) = to scoop up; to extract. See **hilçinîn**.

hil•çinîn/hil•ç'inîn [B] هِلچِنين *vt.* **(hil-ç'in-; hil-çîn- [IF]).** 1) to scoop up, ladle up, draw up *(water from well)*; to bail out *(of a boat)*; 2) to extract, take out, pull out (K/JB3); to extract, derive, draw: **•Me eva şova ji wê kitêbê *hilçandîye*** (K-dş) We have *extracted* this version from that book; 3) to gather up *(from the ground)* (IF); 4) to envelop, cover: **•Tarîyê 'erd *hilç'inî*** (K/B) Darkness *covered* the earth. {also: hilç'andin (K-dş/K); hilç'inandin (K); [hil-tchinin] هلچنين (JJ) = ravauder} Cf. Sor hełçinîn هەڵچِنین = 'to pile up; to mop up' [Z-2/B//JB3/IF/JJ//K]

hil•dan هِـلـدان *vt.* **(hil-d-).** 1) to gather up *(countable items, e.g., pieces of gold, grains)*: **•Ev zêřa *hildide* xweřa** (Ba) He *takes* the gold [pieces] for himself **•Û toximê xwe *hilda*** (J) And he *picked up* his grain; 2) to gather (living beings): **•Rojekê wan çend giregir û cindîyê şeherê Cizîrê *hildan*, hatine dîwana mîr Sêvdîn** (Z-1) One day they *took (=assembled)* some elders and nobles of the city of Jizirah, and went to the court of the prince S. **•Û karê xwe *hildide* dibe ç'îê** (J) And she *picks up* her kids (=young goats) and takes them to the mountain; 3) to pick up, grab, take in one's hand: **•Keç'ik t'eşîyê û hrîê *hildide*** (J) The girl *picks up* the spindle and wool **•Melle řabû nanê xwe *hilda* hat** (Dz) The mullah got up, *took* his bread, and set out [lit. 'came'] **•Vira dewlçî dewlê *hildide*** (Ba) Here the bucket carrier *picks up* the bucket **•Xort k'ax̌eza xwe *hilda*** (J) The lad *took* the paper; 4) {syn: hilanîn} to lift, raise, hoist *(flag, etc.)*; *also fig.* to raise *(one's voice)*: **•Alaya Kurdistanê *helda*** (Bar) He *raised (hoisted)* the flag of Kurdistan **•Îşev serê mi têşihê. K'esek ji we dengê xo *nehildin*!** (HR 4:2-3) Tonight I have a headache. Nobody (from among you) *should raise* his voice!; 5) {syn: hilk'işandin; hilmiştin; şemirandin; vedan; vemaliştin} to roll up *(pants' leg, sleeve)*: **•Berîya bighêy avê, delingê xwe *hilnede*** (Z-1339) Before you reach the river, *don't roll up* the hem of your trousers *[prv.]*; 6) *various expressions*: **-hildan dilê xwe** (XF) to take stg. to heart, to perceive stg. with heightened sensibility, to feel or experience stg. strongly: **•Dê va gilîyana *hilda dilê xwe*** (Ba) The mother, these words *offended her* [lit. 'she took them to her heart']; **-salix hildan** (K) to find out about stg., get news or information: **•Wexta Al-p'aşa *salixê* kalê *hilda*, îdî xwexa řabû çû pey kalê** (Z-1) When A.p. *received news of* the old woman (=learned of the old woman's existence), he got up and went to the old woman. {also: heldan (Bar/IFb-2); <hildan هلدان (hildide) (هلدده)> (HH)} [K/A/JB3/IFb/B/HH/TF/ZF//Bar]

hilfiřiyan هِلفِريان (FJ) = to jump or fly up. See **hilfiřîn**.

hil•fiřîn هِلفِرين *vi.* **(hil-fiř-).** to jump up (with a start), fly up: **•Mussolînî hema *hilfirîye* û gotîye: "Ez dikarim bigirim!"** (Bkp, xxviii) Mussolini *jumped up* and said, "I can catch it!". {also: helfirîn (IFb); hilfiriyan (FJ); hilfiryan (GF); cf. also: [hil-perin هلپرين /hil-perkin هلپركين] (JJ)} Sor hełfiřîn هەڵفڕين = 'to fly up/away' & hełpeřîn هەڵپەڕين = 'to dance; to jump up and be restless (e.g., from pain)' [Bkp/K/TF/Kmc/CS//IFb//FJ/GF] <fiřîn>

hilfiryan هِلفِريان (GF) = to jump or fly up. See **hilfiřîn**.

hil•gaftin هِلگافتِن *vt.* **(hil-gêv-).** to pick up, raise, lift *(into the air)*: **•Beyrim hêşîya kon *hilgaft*** (L) Beyrim *lifted up* the outer flap of the tent **•Gelî bira, min *hilgêvin*, ezê herim ser sûrê bisekinim** (L-5, 144, l. 32) Brothers, *lift* me *up*; I want to go [lit. 'I will go'] stand on top of the city wall. {also: hilgavtin (JB3/IFb)} [L/K//JB3/IFb]

hilgavtin هِلگاڤتِن (JB3/IFb) = to raise, lift. See **hilgaftin**.

hil•girtin هِلگِرتِن *vt.* **(hil-g[i]r-).** 1) to pick up, lift (K/A/JB3/JJ); to take on, shoulder, load up (IF); to hoist, load onto one's shoulder, carry (burden) (B); 2) to hold, contain (of vases, etc.) (JJ); 3) to keep, preserve (Bw). {also: helgirtin (IFb); [hil-ghirtin] هلگرتين (JJ); <hilgirtin هلگرتن (hildigre) (هلدگره)> (HH)} Sor hełgirtin هەڵگرتِن = 'lift up, pick up, carry, support, put up with, acquiesce in, deserve, be worthy of, choose, take away, put aside, withdraw (hand), abduct, store, keep reserve, shut up (shop)' [K/A/JB3/B/JJ/HH//IFb]

hil•hatin هِلهاتِن *vi.* **(hil[t]ê-).** 1) to rise, come or go up, appear *(the sun, etc.)*; to rise *(of dough)*: **•Nerî go toz û hecac ji berîyê *hiltê*** (L) He saw a cloud of dust *rise* (rising) from the plain; 2) to escape, flee (OK/SK): **•'Eskerê Fazil Paşa li naw dolê şaş bûn, nezanîn kêwe *biḧelên*** (SK 48:488) Fazil Pasha's troops went astray in the middle of the canyon, not knowing whither *to flee*. {also: helatin (IFb-2); hilatin (IF-2/B/OK-2); ḧelatin (-ḧelê-) (SK); [hil-atin] هلاتين (JJ); <hilehtin هلهتن [sic] (hiltê) (هلتى)> (HH)} Sor hełhatin هەڵهاتِن = 'come up, swell up, ferment, rise (sun, moon, star), escape, change color' [L/K/IF[b]/OK//B/JJ//HH//SK] <řojhilat>

-hilî هِلى (TF) = step-, pseudo-. See **-ḧilî I**.

hilînan هِلينان (Dz) = to remove, pick up; to save. See **hilanîn**.

hil•îngiftin هِلينگِفتِن *vi.* **(hil-îngiv-).** to stumble, trip *(over stg., also of horses)*: **•Hesp *yê thilîngivît*** (Bw) The horse *is stumbling*. {also: helengiftin (hel-engiv-) (M); hilîngivîn (Bw-2)} {syn: alîn [2]; hilpekîn; lik'umîn; şelifîn; teḧisîn} Sor heł•engûtin هەڵ ئەنگووتِن [Bw//M]

hilîngivîn هِلينگِڤين (Bw) = to stumble. See **hilîngiftin**.

hilkehilk هِلكەهِلك *f.* **(-a;-ê).** gasping, panting, being out of breath: **•Bi vê ramanê rojekê *bi hilkehilk* dibeze hafa mîr û jê re dibêje** ... (Ardû, 48) With this thought, one day, he runs *panting* up to the emir and says to him ...; **-helkehelka *yekî* bûn** (CS) to pant: **•Kûçik *helke helka* xwe *ye*** (IFb) The dog *is panting* deeply; **-helkelkê kirin** (SS) to pant. {also: helkehelk (IFb/FJ/CS); helkelk (GF/SS); [houlqahoulq] حلقاحلق (JJ); <ḧileḧil> حلەحل (HH)} [Ardû/K/B/TF//IFb/FJ/CS//GF/SS//JJ//HH] <bêhntengî>

hil•kirin هِلكِرِن *vt.* **(hil-k-).** 1) {syn: hilanîn; hilk'işandin} to remove, lift, take off (K/JB1-A/OK); to uproot, extirpate, pull out by the roots (A/IF/JJ/HH/JB1-A/GF/TF/OK): **•Du mû ji laşê xwe *hilkirin*** (L) He *plucked* two hairs off his body; **-zevî hilkirin** (IF) to plow a field; 2) {syn: dadan; pêxistin; vêxistin} to light, ignite, kindle (JJ/JB1-A); to turn on (lights) (Bw): **•Me bo xo agir di wê dirkêve *helkir*** (M-Am 714) We *made* [or, *lit*] a fire for ourselves there. {also: helkirin (IFb/JB1-A/M); [hil-kirin] هلكرين (JJ); <hilkirin هلكرن (hildike) (هلدكه)> (HH)} [L/K/A/JB3/JJ/HH/GF/TF/OK/Bw//IFb/JB1-A/M]

hilkişan هِلكِشان (TF) = to climb. See **hilk'işîn**.

hil•k'işandin هِلكِشاندِن *vt.* **(hil-k'işîn-).** 1) to bring up, pull up, raise, lift, cause to ascend (K/IF/B/JJ): **•Wexta ku ew dewlê *hildik'işîne*** (Ba) When he *pulls* the bucket *up* [out of the well]; 2) {syn: hilkirin [1]} to uproot, pull out, extract (IFb): **•Piştî 35'an êdî yeko yeko mirov di nav porê xwe de rastî çend tayên sipî tê ... Di destpêkê de yek-du ta bûn, min bi destan *hildikişandin*, yanê min zora wan dibir** (LC, 5) After age 35, one by one one finds some white hairs amid the hair on one's head ... At first there were one or two hairs, I *pulled* them *out* by hand, i.e., I was victorious over them **•Sturî ji lingê xwe *hilkiş-and*** (IF) He *pulled* the thorn out of his foot; **-mix hilkişandin** (IF) to pull out a nail; 3) {syn: hildan; hilmiştin; şemirandin; vedan; vemaliştin} to roll up *(sleeves)* (B); **-milê xwe hilk'işandin** (B) to roll up one's sleeves. {also: helkişandin (IFb);

[hil-kichandin] هـلـكـشـانـديـن (JJ)} [K/JB3/B/JJ//IFb] <hilk'işîn>

hilkişiyan هلكشِيان (OK) = to climb. See **hilk'işîn**.

hil•k'işîn هِـلـكِـشـيـن *vi.* **(hil-k'iş-).** to climb, ascend, mount *(stairs, etc.)*: •**Beran** ***helkişiya ser*** **mîyê** (IFb) The ram *mounted* the ewe •**Hatin û [li] derenca re** ***hilkişîyan*** (L) They came and *climbed* up the stairs •***Hilkişiya*** **jorê** (IF) He *climbed* up •**Hirç** ***hilkişiya*** **darê** (IF) The bear *climbed up* the tree •**Lawê pîrê li dîwêr de** ***hilkişîya*** (L) The old woman's boy *climbed* up the wall. {also: helkişiyan (IFb-2); helkişîn (IFb); hilkişan (TF-2); hilkişiyan (OK-2); hilkişîyan (JB3/IF); [hil-kichian] هلكشيان (JJ)} {syn: r̄ap'elikîn} [K/B/GF/TF/OK//JB3/IF/JJ//IFb] <hilk'işandin>

hilkişîyan هِلكِشييان (JB3/IF) = to climb. See **hilk'işîn**.

hilm هِـلـم *f.* **(-a;-ê).** 1) steam, vapo[u]r: •**Di şevên sayî de,** ***hilma*** **erdê di navbera erd û ezmanan de wek perdeke zîvîn disekine** (BX/Hawar) On clear nights, the *steam* [rising] from the soil hovered between earth and sky like a silver curtain; 2) {syn: bîn I [2]} breath (IF); 3) {syn: qulap} puff, drag, draw *(on a cigarette or pipe)*: •**Gebranê Baço** ***hilma*** **dawîn li cixara xwe dixe** (Lab, 55) G.B. takes the last *drag* [*puff*] on his cigarette •**Piştî çend** ***gulmên*** **cixarê tu dîsan hatî ser xwe** (MUm, 16) After a few *puffs on* your cigarette, you revived. {also: gulm (K); helm (IFb-2); hêlm (F); hulm (K); ħulm (B); hulmgulm (B-2)} Sor hełm هـهڵـم = 'vapour' [BX/A/JB3/IFb/GF/ TF//F//K/MUm//B] <dû IV; mij>

hilmaştin هِـلـمـاشـتِـن (hil-maş-) (IFb) = to roll up (sleeves). See **hilmiştin**.

hil•miştin هِـلـمِـشـتِـن *vt.* **(hil-mal-).** to roll up *(one's sleeves)*. {also: hilmaştin (hil-maş-) (IFb); [häl-myştin] هلمشتن (JJ)} {syn: hildan; hilk'işandin; şemirandin; vedan; vemaliştin} [JJ/PS//IFb] <maliştin>

hilmî هِـلـمـی *adj.* aspirated *(phonetics)*: •**Bo nimûne, peyva ka eger bi k'yeke** ***hilmî*** **be bi maneya pirtika pirsê (wek "li ku?") ye, lê eger k** ***nehilmî*** **be bi maneya "giyayê hişk yê dibe alifê dewaran" e** (E.Öpengin. "Pirsên Rênivîsa Kurmancî", Derwaze 1, 186) For example, if the word ka is with an *aspirated* k, it means an interrogative particle (like "where?"), but if it is an *unaspirated* k it means "straw, dry grass, animal fodder" •**Di Kurdî de tîpên (ç, k, p, t) du dengên cuda nîşan didin, beşek ji wan** ***hilmî*** **(aspirative) ne, beşa din jî** ***nehilmî*** **(unaspirative) ne** (Navenda Ciwanan ji bo Zimanan, FB) In Kurdish the letters (ç, k, p, t) each indicate two separate sounds, one in each pair is *aspirated*, and one is *unaspirated*. [Öpengin/Navenda Ciwanan/Tan/Wkt] <nehilmî>

hilpe•kirin هِـلـپـەكِـرِن *vt.* **(hilpe-k-).** to jump, leap, spring: •**Çima kurik berbijor** ***hilpedike*?** (Gz) Why does the boy *jump up*? [To retrieve his balloon from high in a tree] •**Çima kûçik** ***hilpedike*** **pêş?** (Gz) Why does the dog *leap* forward? [In pursuit of a mouse]. {syn: bazdan[2]; çeng III bûn; firqas kirin; lotik dan; pengizîn; (xe) qevaztin; qevz dan} [Gz/Efr/AD]

hilpekiyan هِلپەكِيان (FJ) = to stumble. See **hilpekîn**.

hilpekyan هِلپەكيان (GF) = to stumble. See **hilpekîn**.

hil•pekîn هِلپەكين *vi.* **(hil-pek-).** to stumble, trip: •**Li ber deriyê hewşê ji nişka ve** ***hilpekiya.*** **Tiliya mezin ya lingê rastê li kevirekî ket. Kir qîrîn** (HYma, 18) At the door to the yard she suddenly *tripped*. Her right big toe hit on a stone. She screamed. {also: helpekîn (IFb-2); hilpekiyan (FJ); hilpekyan (GF)} {syn: alîn [2]; hilîngiftin; lik'umîn; teħisîn} Cf. Sor pekkewtin پـەككەوتِن = 'be disabled, be handicapped' [HYma]

hilperastin هِـلـپـەراسـتِـن (FJ) = to lean, support. See **hilp'esartin**.

hil•p'esartin هِـلـپـەسـارتِـن *vt.* **(hil-p'esêr-).** to lean, support *(vt.) (stg. against a wall, etc.)* (BK): •**Rîwîyek fêr bûbû her sal di wî wextîda dihat, kilka xo** ***di-hel-pisar*** **e çyay, gazî dikir e kotirê, `Hey kotirê!'** (SK 3:18) Every year at that time a fox had learnt to come along, to *prop* its tail *up* against the mountain and call to the pigeon, `Hi, pigeon!'. {also: helpisarin (SK); helpisartin (M); hilperastin (FJ)} {syn: p'esartin} Sor hel•pesardin هەڵپەساردِن [SK//M//TF/GF//FJ]

hilqeys هِـلـقـەيـس *adv.* so much, so many: •**Û ji bona wan** ***hilqeysê*** **teb û sêfilî min dît** (L) and (=after) I experienced [lit. 'saw'] *so much* torment and humiliation for their sake. {syn: ewqas/haqas; hinde} [L/K]

hilşandin هِـلـشـانـدِن (F/K/IFb/GF) = to destroy. See **hilweşandin**.

hilşiyan هِلشِيان (IFb) = to be destroyed. See **hilweşîn**.

hilşîn هِـلـشـيـن (RN/K/IFb/GF) = to be destroyed. See **hilweşîn**.

hilşîyan هِلشييان (F) = to be destroyed. See **hilweşîn**.

hilû I هِـلـوو *adj.* smooth. {also: hulû II (FS-2); ḧelû (SK); ḧilî II (Bw); ḧilû III (F/FS); ḧulî II (SK-Ak); [hilou/hulu (Rh)/ellu (G)] حـلـو (JJ); <hillû> هلو (HH)} [Bw//IFb/GF/OK//F/FS//SK//JJ//HH]

hilû II هِلوو (GF/TF) = plum. See **ḧilû I**.

hilûreşk هِلوورەشك (IFb) = black plum. See **ḧûlîr̄eşk**.

hilûtirşk هِلووترشك f. (-a;-ê) (Msr) = plum. See **ḧilû I**.

hilûyêreş هِلوويێرەش (GF) = black plum. See **ḧûlîr̄eşk**.

hil•weşandin هِـلـوەشـانـدِن *vt.* **(hil-weşîn-).** to destroy, tear down, ruin, raze, annihilate: **•Lê her ku roj bilind dibû ... zelaliya wê tîna xwe bi ser siyê ve *hildiweşand*** (Alkan, 70) But as the sun rose higher ... the purity of its warmth *annihilated* the shade **•Paşê dev ji *hilşandina* koşkê berdan** [sic] (RN) Then they left off *tearing down* the palace. {also: hilşandin (RN/F/K/IFb/GF-2); [houlou-chandin] هلوشاندن (JJ)} [RN/F/IFb//Wlt/K/GF/Frq//JJ] <hilweşîn>

hil•weşîn هِـلـوەشـيـن *vi.* **(hil-weş-).** 1) to be destroyed, torn down, ruined, razed: **•Ev qelîştekên ji bingeh hetanî banî dirêjbûyî didan xuya kirin ku koşk *ewê* ji nişkave *hilşe*** (RN) These cracks made their appearance from the foundations and extended to the roof, so that the palace *could* suddenly *collapse*; 2) {syn: şihitîn} to be dissolved, disintegrate (SK): **•Dostînîya wan *helweşyawa*** (SK 31:280) Their friendship *was dissolved*. {also: helşîn (IFb-2); helweşyanewe (SK); hilşiyan (IFb); hilşîn (RN/K-2/IFb/GF-2); hilşîyan (F); [houlouchin] هـلـوشـيـن (JJ)} [RN/IFb//K/GF/Wlt/Frq//SK//F//JJ] <hilweşandin>

himal هِمال (ZZ-10) = porter. See **ḧemal**.

himalî هِـمـالـى (ZZ-10) = profession of porter. See **ḧemalî**.

himandin هِـمـانـدِن (CS) = to protect from. See **ḧemandin**.

himberî هِـمـبـەرى *prep.* 1) toward *(fig., e.g., one's feelings toward s.o.)*, vis-à-vis: **•ḧizkirina wana *himberî* Memê delal** (Z-1) their love *for* [lit. '*toward*'] Mem; 2) compared to *or* with (B): **•*himberî* sala par** (B) *compared with* last year **•*himberî* qeweta xwe** (B) *compared with* or *according to* his strength; 3) across, opposite, on the other side of (IFb): **•*hemberî* newalê** (IFb) *on the far side of* the gulley; 4) *literal translation of Turkish* ***karşı***: *against* = **dijî**. {also: hemberê (K); hemberî (JB3/IFb)} [Z-1/B//K//JB3/IFb]

himbêz هِمبێز (GF/HH/FS) = embrace. See **ḧemêz**.

himbiz هِمبِز (GF/HH/Hej) = dense. See **hembiz**.

himehim هِـمـەهِـم *f.* **(-a;).** booming sound; humming, buzzing, droning; grunting: **•*himhima* berazan** (GF) *grunting of* pigs **•Ma niha ev çi *hime hima* vê televizyonê ye bi ser me de ji bona Xwedê?** (SBx, 17) Now what is this *booming of* this television over our heads, for heaven's sake?; **-himhim kirin** (K) to buzz, drone, hum. {also: himhim (K/IFb/FJ/GF)} {syn: xumxum I} Cf. Ar hamhamah هـمـهـمـة = 'hum, buzz, drone; inarticulate utterance ("hmm, hmm")' [SBx/ZF//K/IFb/FJ/GF]

himet هِـــمـــەت (K/JB1-A) = magnanimity, helpful intervention. See **himmet**.

himêz هِمێز (GF) = embrace. See **ḧemêz**.

himhim هِمهِم (K/IFb/FJ/GF) = booming, buzzing. See **himehim**.

himmet هِـمـمـەت *f.* **(-a;).** *used in extremely formal and polite language to superiors*: generosity, magnanimity; help, intercession, helpful intervention; solution, remedy: **•Em hatîne mala te, bo xatira xudê tedbîrekî li ḧalê me bike. Çi bi du'a, çi bi niwîştî, bi her terzê dibît bo me *himmetekî*** [sic] ***bifermû*** (SK 33:295) We have come to your house that, for God's sake, you may do something for us. Either by prayer or by charms, however it may be, please *arrange something* for us **•Ḧetta noke eger te gayek xaribît, paşî *himmeta* munasibî, to dê duyan xoy** (SK 34:311) If up to now you have eaten one ox, after *the intervention of* the shrine you will eat two **•Quwet û *hummet* ş-xudê [=ji xudê] xwest** (HR 3:144) He requested strength and *help* from God **•Xudanê malê ji wî pirsî, 'Tu dê kêwe çî?' Got, 'Dê çime ser munasibê Elenya, belkû *himmetekî*** [sic] **bo min biket, pîçek me'da min xoş bît'** (SK 34:309) The owner of the house asked, 'Where are you going?' He said, 'I am going to the shrine of Alanya in the hope that it will be of *some benefit* to me and my stomach will be a bit better'; **-himmet kirin** = to be so kind as to do stg., to deign to do stg.: **•'Eynî deqê dane, zamanê ko epey *himmet kir*, birîna Bor qenc bû, tûka sipî lê hat** (MC-1 #83) At that very moment, when [God] *showed* a good deal of *magnanimity* Bor's wound healed, and white hair grew over it **•Marî got, 'Me'lûmî cenabê hingo ye ez bêpê me. Neşêm li bazeberî derbaz bim. Dibît cenabê mam r̄iwî *himmet biket*, bende derbaz ket'** (SK 2:11) The snake said, 'As your honour knows, I have no feet. I cannot cross over the stepping-stones. Your honour Uncle Fox must *help* me to cross' •**Wellahî, ew ji wextê te sefer beṯal kirîn û ḧeta nûhû em faydekî yê li me qet'e bî. Çu fayde negehîte destê me û em r̄ica' tkeyn tu careka dî *himet ke*.** (JB1-A #4,98) By God ... ever since you stopped making business trips, our profit has ceased. No profit has reached us, and we beg you *to be magnanimous* once again. {also: himet (K/JB1-A); hummet (HR); [hemet] هـمـت (JJ); <himmet> هـمّـت (HH)} < Ar himmah هـمّة = 'endeavor, intention; high-minded ambition, zeal' --> P hemmat هـمّـت = 'ambition; high mindedness; effort' & T himmet = 'help, favor, protection'; Sor hîmet هیمـەت = 'zeal' [MC-1/IFb/HH/SK//K/JB1-A//JJ//HR]

hin هِـن *pr. mod.* some *(pl. indef. article)*: •**hin hesp** = *some* horses; **-hin ... hin jî** (Ba2/B) both ... and; **-hin bi hin** (IF) little by little, bit by bit; **-hin caran** (IF) sometimes. Sor hend هەند [BX/K/A/JB3/IF/B]

hinar هِنار *f.* **(-a;-ê).** pomegranate (tree and fruit), bot. *Punica granatum*: **-hinarê r̄ûyan** (K - poet.) cheeks; **-ḧinara sûr[e]t** (B) round part of the cheek. {also: ḧenar (F); ḧinar (B); [hinar] هـنـار (JJ); <hinar> هنار (HH)} Mid P anār (M3); P anār انـار --> T nâr; Sor henar هەنار; Za henar/henari/hinari *f.* (Mal) [K/IFb/JJ/HH/GF/TF/OK/Kmc-2/AA//F//B]

hinarde هِـنـارده *f.* **(-ya;-yê).** export(s): •**Rêjeya *hinardeya* bajarê Amedê bilind bûye** (Rûdaw 4.iv.2018) The rate of *exports from* the city of Diyarbakir (Amed) has risen. Sor henarde هەنارده = 'export(s)' < [he]nardin هەناردِن = 'to send' (Cf. hinartin) [(neol)ZF3/Wkt]

hinarik هِـنـارِك *f.* **(-a;-ê).** cheek; cheekbone. {also: hinarok (FS); ḧinarik (K)} {syn: alek; gup; lame; r̄û [3]} <hinar = 'pomegranate', because of the red color of the cheeks. [IFb/GF/TF/OK//K//FS] <dêm II>

hinarin هِنارِن (SK) = to send. See **hinartin**.

hinarok هِنارۆك (FS) = cheekbone. See **hinarik**.

hinartin هِـنـارتِـن *vt.* **(-hinêr-).** to send, dispatch: •**Wî namek bo dayka xwe *hinart*** (FS) He *sent* a letter to his mother. {also: hinarin (SK); [hinartin] هـنـارتـيـن (JJ); <hinartin> هـنـارتـن (HH)} {syn: şandin; [ve]r̄êkirin} Cf. Manichaean Mid P han(n)ār- = 'to direct (the eyes)' < ham + √dar (M2, p.79 & Henning Verbum, p.193): Sor nardin (-nêr-) ناردِن & henardin هەناردِن; SoK hanārdın = kıl kırdın (Fat 406) [M/Zx/K(s)/JB3/IFb/JJ/HH/GF/OK/FS//SK]

hinav هِـنـاڤ *m.* **(-ê; ḧinêv** [B]**).** organs of the chest cavity (heart, lungs) : **-dil û hinav/dil-hinav** = do.; used fig. for the heart: •**Wexta Memê Ala eva gilîya digotin, agir û alavê *dil û hinavê* qîz û bûka disotin** (Z-1) When M.A. said these words, *the hearts and spleens of* the girls and brides burned with fire and flame (=they were disappointed). {also: ḧinav (B); [henaw] هـنـاڤ (JJ); <hinav> هناڤ (HH)} [Z-1/K/A/IFb/JJ/HH//B] <dil; fater̄eşk; k'ezeb; p'işik; pizûr; sîh; zirav II>

hincan هِـنـجـان *m./f.(ZF3)* **(;/-ê).** clay pot *(the size of a tub/basin, with a wide lip)*. {also: <hincan> هنجان (HH)--corrected from *<hicnan> هـجـنـان} {syn: dîz} [HB/A/HH/ZF3] <cer; lîn; sewîl>

hincar هِـنـجـار *m.* **(;-î).** plow-beam: •**Çû 'eynî wê zevîyê, cotê xo girêda, des havête *hincarî*** (M-Ak #612, 278) He went ... to that very field, harnessed his team and put his hand to *the plough* •**Ev ṯaê hanê yê başe bo *hincar*** (M-Ak, #548) This bough here is a good one for *a plough-beam*. Cf. Sor hewcar هـەوجـار = 'vertical steering haft of plough' [M-Ak/AA/OK/Wkt] <cot [2]; destedû; gîsin; halet; hevcar̄; k'otan II; şûrik I; xenîke; xep>

hincet هِنجەت (Wlt) = grounds, excuse. See **hêncet**.

hincinandin هِنجِناندِن (GF) = to cut into small pieces. See **hincinîn**.

hincinîn هِنجِنين *vt.* **(-hincin-).** to chop up fine, mince, dice, cut into small pieces *(tobacco, etc.)*: •**Kurd bi çeqoka min *dihincinin*** (Bw) The Kurds *chop* me *up* with their knives. {also: hencandin (IFb); hincinandin (GF); <hincinîn> هـنـجـنـيـن (Hej)} Sor encinîn ئەنجِنین [Bw/Zeb/TF/Hej//IFb//GF]

hind هِـنـد *f.* **(;-ê).** so, that much, so much *(declined like a f. noun)*: a) [*prn.*]: •**"...Eger te *hind* musa'ede kiriba, pîçek stukira xo kêşaba pêş çawêt min û carekî dî di pêş mirina xo da min çawêt te dîtibana, paşî bila ez miribam, da di dilê min da nebîte keser." Marî got, "Ser çawan, ser seran, *ew hinde* çu nîye."** (SK 2:15) "...If you would be so kind as to stretch your neck a little in front of my eyes so that I could see your eyes once again before my death, then let me die, there would be no regret in my heart." The snake said, "On my head and eyes (be it), *that much* is nothing" •**Wextê r̄iwî yeqîn kir ko êdî dirêj kirin fayde nîye *hinde* got e kotirê** (SK 3:22)

When the fox realized that there was no point in carrying on, he said *this much* to the pigeon; b) [*adv.*]: •**Ez jî ji şukra wê iħsana *hinde* mezin diçime ħeccê** (SK 4:41) I am going on the pilgrimage in thanksgiving for this great bounty [for this bounty *so* great] •**Şerm e bo te muroê *hinde* mezin û maqûl li çawrê te li ser pîyan r̄awestît** (SK 4:38) It is a shame for you that *such* a great and respected person should stand and wait for you; **-hinde ... ko** (A/JB3) so much that..; c) [*adj., pr. mod.*]: •**Ez dê çi li *hinde* genimey kem?** (M-Ak #597) What shall I do with *so much* wheat? •**Madam ew gunde ho muħtac e hêşta barê min negeştîye 'erdî *hind* kir̄yar dê cema bin. Do sa'et nakêşît hemî tiştê min dê kir̄in bi qîmeta ko ez ħez dikem** (SK 16:157) Since this village is so needy *so many* customers will gather before my load reaches the ground [that] it won't take two hours for them to buy all my things at whatever price I like •**Te bo çî *hinde* sal e bo min negot?** (SK 3:20) Why haven't you told me in all these [=*so many*] years?; **-hinde car** (JB3/IF) so often, so many times; sometimes; d) [*f.*]: **-digel vê hindê** (K) nevertheless; **-ew hind** (SK) that much, that many: •**Xetaêt hingo bûn *ew hinde* 'eskere hate naw me** (SK 18:167) It was your fault that *this many* soldiers came among us; **-ji ber hindê** (JB1-A) that's why, therefore; since, as; **-ser wê hindêr̄a jî** (SK) moreover, what's more. {also: hinde (SK-2/JB1-A); [hind هند/hindé هنده] (JJ); <hinde> هنده (HH)} {syn: ewqas} Sor ewende ئەوەندە [JJ/SK/JB1-A/OK///MK/K/A/JB3/IFb/JJ/HH] <ewqas/haqas; ewqedr; hilqeyse>

hinda I هندا *prep.* near, by, at the house of, over s.o.'s house [Fr chez]: •**Ez çûm *hindê wî*** (IFb) I went *to where he was*. {also: hindê (IFb); [hínda] هندا (JJ)} {syn: bal I; cem; ħafa [*see* ħaf]; lalê; li def (Bw); nik I; r̄ex I} cf. Ar 'inda عند [BX/Ad/K/JJ/B//IFb]

hinda II هندا (Z-2/Msr/Snd) = lost. See **winda**.

hindam هندام (Ber) = side, direction. See **hindav**.

hindav هنداڤ *f./m.(SK)* **(-a/-ê;-ê/).** 1) {syn: alî} side, direction: •**Bi hevalekî me ... re cihetnimayek hebû. Me *hindava* xwe pê rast dikir** (Rnh 1:11, 196) One of our friends had a compass. We kept checking our *direction* with it; 2) {syn: hol II} midst, one's immediate surroundings, the area around one: •**Dûrî *hindava we* pê k'etîye** (B) God forbid!/Present company excepted/Apart from you •***Ji hindavda* r̄abû** (JJ) He got *up* •**Serê xwe *hindavda* hilde mêzeke bi t'ûşe** (EP-7) Raise your head *up* and look ahead; **-hindava xweda** (B) for his part, as far as he is concerned; 3) {syn: fêz} position above or over (Zeb/SK/Hej/JJ): •**Ave, ne ave, / Me'rê mirî di nave, / Teyrê zêr̄în *hindave* / Ew çiye? [P'ilta ç'irê, şemal]** (Z-1796) It's water, it's not water / There's a dead snake in its middle / There's a golden bird *above* it / What is it? *[rdl.; ans.: wick and candle]* •**Çû serê kopikî, pariste *hindawê* lata çyay, bizanît pezê kîwî li wê derê heye yan ne. Wextê çû *hindawê* latê dît hirçek liser dara keskanêye** (SK 10:95) He went on top of the crest and crept *above* a patch of mountain pasture to see whether there were wild sheep there or not. When he went *above* the stretch of meadow he saw that there was a bear in the top of a terebinth tree •**Li *hindawê* cer̄ikêt ximî qaydeye kulek bo r̄onaîyê dibît** (SK 4:28) It is customary for there to be a skylight *above* the dye vats for the light to get in •**Qelata wî li-ser çya bû *li hindawê* r̄ûbarê, sê-hizar gez bilind e** (SK 51:556) His fort was on a mountain *above* the river, three thousand ells high; **-hindav serê** (Zeb/JJ) above, over: •**Marek li kuna dîwar têtе der û diçite *hindav serê* mîr û 'Îsa şîrê xo li kawlan dîînite der da marî bikujît** (letter from VoA listener) A snake comes out of the hole in the wall and goes to a place *above* the emir's head and Isa takes his sword out of its sheath in order to kill the snake. {also: hindam (Ber); hindaw (SK); [hindāv] هنداڤ (JJ); <hindav> هنداڤ (Hej)} [EP-7/K/JB3/IFb/JJ/B/JB1-A/Hej/Zeb/Dh//SK]

hindaw هنداو (SK) = above. See **hindav**[3]

hinde هنده (MK/K/A/JB3/IFb/JJ/HH) = so much, so many. See **hind**.

hindek هندەك (SK) = a little; some. See **hindik** & **hinek**.

hindê هندێ (IFb) = near, by. See **hinda I**.

hindik هندك *adv.* a little, a little bit, a small amount: •**P'ir̄ diçin, *hindik* diçin** (Dz) They keep on going and going [lit. 'They go much, they go *little*'--Cf. T 'Az gitmiş, uz gitmiş'] •**Şîrê çêlek û bizinên diya min *hindik* bû** (Alkan, 70) The milk of my mother's cows and goats was [only] *a small amount*; **-hindik maye** = soon; almost: •***Hindik maye* maşîne bê** (B) The train will arrive *soon* [lit. 'little has remained [until] the train will come']; **-kêm-hindik** (Ber) a little bit, hardly at all; more or less. {also: hindek; **hine I**; hinek; [hindik] هندك (JJ); <hindik> هندك (HH)} {syn: çîçik II; ȟebek(î); *ȟekekî (Ad); kêm I; piçek; ≠gelek; ≠p'iȓ II; ≠ze'f} [K/A/IF/B/JJ/HH] See also **hinek**.

hindir هِندِر = inside. See **hunduȓ**.

hindiȓu هِندِرو (HR) = inside. See **hunduȓ**.

Hindî I هندى *adj.* Indian (from India); Hindi. {also: Hindustanî (Wkt-2/BF-2)} Sor Hîndî هيندى [Wkt/BF/Wkp/SS]

hindî II هِندى (BX/K/JB3) = then; afterward. See **hingê**.

hunduȓ هِندور *m.* **(-ê;).** 1) {syn: daxil; nav II[1]; zik} interior: **-hundurê dest** (LM) palm of the hand; 2) [*adv./prep.*] {syn: zik} inside: **•*Di hindurê* wê qesrê *de*** (L) *Inside* that palace **•Diz *k'etin hunduȓê* malê** (K) Thieves *broke into* the house; **-çûn/hatin/k'etin hunduȓ** (K) to enter, get into; **-hunduȓda** (B)/**hunduȓva** (B) inside; **-ji hunduȓ derxistin** (K) to lead out, expel; to exclude; **-ji hunduȓ va** (K) from inside; **-kirin hunduȓ** (K) to introduce, bring in; to put in, insert; **-li hunduȓ** (K) inward, inside (motion to which). {also: hindir; hindiȓu (HR); hundir; hunduȓ (K/IF-2/B); [hindourou] هندورو (JJ); <hindirû> هندرو (HH)} Cf. P andar اندر [L/K/B/Ba2/F//JB3/IFb//HH//HR//JJ/JR]

Hindustanî هِندوستانى (Wkt/BF) = Indian (from India). See **Hindî I**.

hine I هِنه *adv.* a little, some: **•*hine* nan yane *hine* goşt** (Ba) *a little* bread or *a little* meat **•*Hine* ȓûnê min hebû min anî teȓa kire p'êxûn** (Dz) [If] I had *a little* butter, I would have brought [it and] made you some *pêxûn (qv.)*. [K/B] See also **hin & hindik**.

hine II هِنه (F/TF) = henna. See **ȟene**.

hinek هِنەك *adv.* 1) a little. **-hinekî** (Ks/Ba/GF) a little: **•Doşeka wî *hinekî* bilind bûye** (Ba) His mattress had risen *a little bit* **•*Hinek* nan û *hinek* pîvaz** (IFb) *a little [bit of]* bread and *a little bit of* onion; 2) {syn: bejnek} someone, somebody; some people: **•*Hinek* pê dimirin, *hinek* jê re dimirin** (IFb) *Some* die of it, *some* die for it *[prv.]* **•Tirsa min *hinek* hespê min bidizin** (L) I'm afraid that *someone* might steal my horse(s); **-Hineka go ... hineka go ...** (L) Some said ... and some said ... ; 3) *[pr. mod.]* some: **•*Hinek* nivîskar diyar dikin ku MHP xwe ji nû ve saz dike û ber bi demokratîkbûnê ve diçe** (AW69A1) *Some* writers declare that the MHP [Nationalist People's Party] is re-making itself and becoming more democratic; **-hindek caran** (SK) sometimes. {also: hindek (SK); [hinek] هنك (JJ)} [AW/K/A/IFb/JJ/TF] See also **hindik**.

hiner هِنەر *m./f.(IF/B/SK/OK)* **(-ê/-a; /-ê).** 1) art; 2) {syn: fereset [2]; sen'et [1]} talent, skill (JB3); resourcefulness, inventiveness (B); means, remedy, way out *(of a difficult situation)*: **•Ka behs bike, behsa *hunerên* wan mexlûqên piçûk bike** (SF 18) Speak, speak of *the skills of* those tiny creatures **•Lê Qeret'ajdîn haj *ȟunurê* Memê heye** (Z-1) But Q. finds out (knows) about M.'s *skill* [or *bravery*] **•Li ber defa sîngê xwe erbaneyekê bi eşq û *hunereke* welê diricifîne** (Tof, 7) He shakes a tambourine in front of his chest with such passion and *skill*; **-ȟunar dîtin/kirin** (B) to find a way out *(of a difficult situation)*; 3) courage, bravery; virtue. {also: huner (IFb-2/SK/GF-2/TF); ȟunar (B/Ba2); ȟunur (Z-1); [houner] هنر (JJ); <hiner> هنر (HH)} Cf. Skt sundara- (?<sūnára-) = 'beautiful, handsome, lovely'; Av hunara- = 'highness, loftiness, skill, ability'; O P ūvnara- 'skill, accomplishment' (Kent); Pahl hunar; P hunar هنر = 'virtue, skill, art, ability' (Horn #1108) --> T hüner; Sor huner هونەر = 'skill, art'; cf. also Arm hnark' հնարք = 'means, way, resource, invention' [Z-1//K/A/JB3/IFb/HH/SK/GF/OK//JJ/TF//B/Ba2] <îlac>

hinermend هِنەرمەند (K[s]) = artist. See **hunermend**.

hingaft هِنگافت (BX/JB3) = then; afterward. See **hingê**.

hingaftin هِنگافتِن *vt.* **(-hingêv-).** 1) to attain, reach; to touch; 2) to hit *(a target)*; to strike (M): **•[Dibêjin ku hespê mîr *hatîye hingavtin*]** (JJ) They say that the emir's horse *has been hit* [by bullets]; **-namûs hingavtin** (Wlt) to say or do stg. which touches s.o.'s honor; to dishonor, humiliate {syn: hetik birin}: **•Dijmin ... zarokên li ser pêçekê kuştin, *namûs hingavtin*, pîsî bi me dan xwarin** (Wlt 2:59, 7) The enemy...killed infants in swaddling clothes, *humiliated* [=raped], made us eat filth; 3) to amaze, stun, sting to the quick: **•Bedewya Zelîxê îsan *dihingavt*** (Ba) Zelikha's beauty *stunned* people. {also: hingavtin (K/IFb-2/TF/OK-2); hingawtin (-hingêw-) (SK); hingiftin

(GF); hingivandin (A/OK-2); hingivîn II (A-2); [hingawtin هنگاوتین/hinghiwtin هنگفتین] (JJ); <hingaftin هنگافتن (dihingêve) (دهنگیڤه)> (HH)} [Ba/Wlt/K/JJ/TF//IFb/HH/OK/M/Bw//SK//GF//A]

hinganî هنگانی (BX) = then; afterward. See **hingê**.

Hingarî هنگاری (BF) = Hungarian. See **Hungarî**.

hingavî هنگاڤی (BX/JB3) = then; afterward. See **hingê**.

hingavtin هنگاڤتن (K/IFb/TF/OK/JJ) = to touch, reach; to stun. See **hingaftin**.

hingawtin هنگاوتن (-hingêw-) (SK) = to touch, reach; to stun. See **hingaftin**.

hingê هنگێ *adv.* 1) then, at that time: **•Guh biden, cewabê bidem. Eger çak bû qebûl biken, eger xirab bû ez *hingî* řazî me bi 'eyba xo** (SK 22:202) Listen and I'll give you an answer. If it is good--accept it, if it is bad *then* I am prepared to accept the shame **•Lê wextê M. derda çû, mîr ji ber wî rabû, Qeret'ajdîn *hingê* dezmala xwe avîte bin doşeka wî** (EP-7) But when M. entered, the prince stood up before him [out of respect], Qeretajdin *then* placed [lit. 'threw'] his handkerchief beneath his (=the prince's) mattress (=seat) **•Me'lûm *hingî* dê gelek çêtir bît** (SK 19:179) Certainly it will be much better *then*; 2) {syn: dûřa; paşê; şûnda; (di) pişt re} afterward, later. {also: hindî II (BX/K/JB3); hingaft (BX/JB3); hinganî (BX); hingavî (BX/JB3); hingî (A/JB3); [hinghi] هنگی (JJ)} *See AKR (p. 65-68) for detailed discussion of* ***hingê***. [EP-7/BX/K/A/JB3/IFb/JJ/JB1-A/SK/TF/OK/AKR//B/JB1-S]

hingiftin هنگفتن (GF) = to touch, reach; to stun. See **hingaftin**.

hingil هنگل (BF) = hip, haunch. See **hingul**.

hingime هنگمه (A) = commotion, tumult. See **hengame**.

hingiv هنگڤ *m.* **(-ê;).** honey. {also: hingivîn I (Bw); hinguv (GF-2); hingûn (SK); hungiv (F); [hingouw هنگوف/ hinghiw هنگیف/ hinghiwin هنگڤین] (JJ); <hingivîn هنگڤین/hingiv هنگڤ> (HH)} Cf. Mid P angubēn; P angabīn انگبین/ angom انگم; Sor heng هەنگ = 'bee' & hengwîn هەنگوین = 'honey'; Za hing = 'bee' (Todd) & engimyê (Lx)/hingemîn m. (Todd) = 'honey' [K/A/IFb/B/JJ/HH/GF/TF/OK//F//Bw//SK]

hingivandin هنگڤاندن (A/OK) = to touch, reach; to stun. See **hingaftin**.

hingivîn I هنگڤین (Bw/HH) = honey. See **hingiv**.

hingivîn II هنگڤین (A) = to touch, reach; to stun. See **hingaftin**.

hingî هنگی (K/A/JB3/B/JB1-S) = then; afterward. See **hingê**.

hinglîsk هنگلیسك (IF) = (finger)ring. See **gustîl**.

hingo هنگۆ (SK) = you (pl. obl.). See **hûn** & **we**.

hingor هنگۆر (K/IFb) = dawn; dusk. See **hingûr**.

hingorî هنگۆری (Hk/HH) = dawn; dusk. See **hingûr**.

hingul هنگول *m.* **().** hip, haunch: **•Mêrik di bin çavan re li cîrana xwe dinêre, ruyekî gulover, dev û pozekî lihevhatî, tilor û *hingulên* qelew dilê wî jî xirab dike** (Ardû, 12) The man sneaks a peek at his neighbor's wife: a round face, an agreeable mouth and nose, chubby thighs and *hips* make him think unseemly thoughts [lit. 'ruins his heart']. {also: hengil (RZ/SS); hingil (BF)} {syn: k'emax; qořik [2]} Sor hengił هەنگڵ [Ardû//BF//RZ/SS] <hêt>

hingulîsk هنگولیسك (SW1) = (finger)ring. See **gustîl**.

hingur هنگور (MUm) = dawn; dusk. See **hingûr**.

hingustîl هنگوستیل (SW/JB3) = (finger)ring. See **gustîl**.

hinguv هنگوڤ (GF) = honey. See **hingiv**.

hingû هنگوو (BX-Behdinan) = you. See **hûn.**

hingûn هنگوون (SK) = honey. See **hingiv**.

hingûr هنگوور *f.* **(-a;).** 1) {syn: berbang; elind; ferec; segur; serê sibê; siȟar; spêde; şebeq} dawn, daybreak, sunrise; 2) {syn: segur [2]} dusk, twilight: **•*Hingura* wê êvarê tê bîra te?** (MUm, 14) Do you remember that evening's *twilight*? {also: hingor (K/IFb); hingorî (Hk); hingur (MUm); [hingour] هنگور (JJ); <hingorî> هنگوری (HH)} [Wn/JJ/GF/TF//MUm//K/IFb//HH/Hek] <berbang; berêvar; êvar; moẍrib>

hingûv هنگووڤ (FJ) = suitable. See **hink'ûf**.

hinkov هنكۆڤ (SS) = suitable. See **hink'ûf**.

hinkuf هنكوف (IFb/GF) = suitable. See **hink'ûf**.

hink'ûf هنكووف *adj.* suitable, appropriate: **•Ḧesenî Xudêdayî qîzê dewletîya qayîl nave, go, wê çawa bê bive *hink'ûfê* me, te bixweze** (HCK-4, #19, 105) Hasan won't even accept the daughters of the wealthy, how will he come be *suitable for* us, and ask for your hand [lit. 'request you'] **•Hinkufê hev** (GF) compatible, an appropriate match. {also: hingûv (FJ); hinkov (SS); hinkuf (IFb/GF)} {syn: babet II[1]; layîq [1]} [SW/A//IFb/GF//FJ//SS]

hirbî هربی (Qzl) = girl's headscarf. See **ḧibrî**.

hirç هِرچ (A/JB3/IF/JJ/HH/SK/JB1-A) = bear *(animal)*. See **ḧirç**.

hirî هِری *f.* **(-ya;-yê).** wool: **•Keç'ik t'eşîyê û *hrîê* hildide** (J) The girl picks up the spindle and *wool* **•Te îro qe *hrî* r̄ist?** (J) Have you spun any *wool* today? {also: herî I (IFb-2); hrî (J); xurî I (SK); [hirí] هری (JJ); <herî> هری (HH)} Sor xurî خوری [J//Z-1/K/A/JB3/IFb/B/JJ/HH/JB1-A/GF/TF//SK] <kej II; kulk; liva; livajen; merez II; r̄êstin; r̄îs; t'eşî>

hirmê هرمێ (Kmc-2/RZ) = pear. See **hermê**.

hirmî هِرمی (A/IFb/TF/OK/AA/RZ) = pear. See **hermê**.

hirve هرڤە (Bw/HH) = on this side. See **hêrve**.

hisan هِسان *m.* **(-ê;).** 1) knife *(for cutting meat)*; 2) whetstone. See **hesan II**. [Bw] <k'êr III; sat'or; şefir>

hisandin هِساندِن (TF) = to cause to feel; to inform. See **ḧesandin**.

hiseynok هِسەینۆك *f.* **().** snail; *"The snail is called ... **şeytanok** (little devil) [or **guhşeytan** (devil's ear)]. The Yezidis, who must not pronounce the devil's name [şeytan], replace **şeytanok** with **hiseynok** (little Husayn, irreverent reference to Husayn, son of Ali)."* [L, vol. 1, p.236, apud #48 *(my translation)*] {also: hisênok (ZF3)} {syn: guhşeytan; şeytanok} [L/Qzl//ZF3]

hisênok هسێنۆك (ZF3) = snail. See **hiseynok**.

hisret هسرەت (ZZ) = sorrow. See **hesret**.

histêr هستێر (IF) = mule. See **hêstir II**.

histêrik هستێرك (Klk) = tears. See **hêstir I**.

histir هستِر (IF) = mule. See **hêstir II**.

histiran هِستِران (BK) = to knead *(dough)*. See **stiran II**.

histukur هِستوكور (IFb) = nape of neck. See **stukur**.

hiş هِش (A/JB3) = mind; sense. See **ḧiş**.

hişk هِشك (A/JB3/IFb/JB1-A&S/JJ/SK/GF/TF/OK) = dry. See **ḧişk**.

hişkatî هِشكاتی (FS) = dryness. See **ḧişkî**.

hişkayî هِشكایی (TF) = dryness. See **ḧişkî**.

hişketî هِشكەتی (A) = dryness; frost. See **ḧişkî**.

hişkî هِشكی (IFb/JJ/GF/OK) = dryness. See **ḧişkî**.

hiştin هِشتِن *vt.* **(-hêl-/-hîl-).** 1) {syn: berdan} to leave *(vt.)*, abandon: **•Bira, *te* tiştek ji min re *ne hişt?*** (L) Brother, *didn't you leave* anything for me? **•Lê çaxê cerdê xwe davîte ser kerîyê pêz, diqewimî, wekî dest-p'îyê şivana girê didan ... *ew* jî li çolê bê xwarin û vexwarin *dihiştin*** (Ba2:1, 205) But when the brigands pounced on the sheep flock, it happened that they would tie up the shepherds' hands and feet ... and *leave them* in the wilderness without any food or drink; 2) {syn: berdan; dev jê berdan; qeran; t'erkandin} to abandon (JJ); to leave off, quit, stop (doing stg.): **-dilê *fk-ê* hiştin** (K)/**hîştin** (XF) to offend, hurt s.o.'s feelings; to grieve, distress, pain: **•Qeret'ajdîn naxwaze *dilê* wînakê *bihêle*** (Z-3) Q. does not want *to offend* him; 3) {syn: îzin dan; r̄êdan} to allow, permit: **•Ev helwest *nahêle* ku HEP bibe xwedî şexsiyet** (Wlt 1:43) This attitude *does not allow HEP* to have a personality of its own **•Nezer *nahêle* Memê Zînê bivîne** (EP-7) Destiny won't *let* Mem see Zin; 4) to spare s.o.'s life, keep alive, save: **•Seva xatirê te, ezê pênca bikujim, duda *bihêlim*** (FK-kk-13: 129) For your sake, I will kill five and *spare* two **•Xwedê bo te *bihêlit*** (Bw) May God *leave [them alive]* for you [said when speaking of s.o.'s family] **•Xwedê te *bihêle*** (L) May God *spare* you; **-kitek jê nehîştin** (XF) not to leave a single person alive, to kill off down to the last person: **•Erke ko vêga mîr pê biḧese, em *kitkê ji hev û dinê nahêlin*** (Z-3) If the emir finds out, we *won't leave a single person alive.* {also: hêlan I (K[s]/JB1-A&S/M/Bw); hêliştin (Czr); hîştin (XF); [hichtin هشتین/hilan هلان] (JJ)} [Pok. selĝ- 900.] 'to release, let loose': Skt sṛjati/sárjati = 'he lets loose, shoots, pours': O Ir *hṛd-/z-: Av harəz- (*pres.* harəza-/hərəza-/hərəz(a)ya-); P heštan هشتن (-hel-) (هل); Sor hêştin هێشتن (-hêł-); SoK (h)il-/hišt-, hıšt-, išt- (Fat 362); Hau astey (az-) *vt.* = 'to let, allow' (M4) [K/JB3/IFb/B/JJ/GF//Czr//JB1-A&S/ M/Bw] <man; nehiştin>

hişyar I هِشیار (A/JB3/IFb/JB1-A&S/GF/TF/OK) = awake; aware. See **ḧişyar**.

hişyar II هِشیار (CB) = red pepper. See **ḧiçḧar**.

hişyarî هِشیاری (IFb/GF/TF/FS) = awakeness; awareness. See **ḧişyarî**.

hivdehem هِڤدەهەم (Wkt) = seventeenth. See **hevdehem**.

hivdehemîn هِڤدەهەمین (Wkt) = seventeenth. See **hevdehem**.

hivdeyem هِڤدەیەم (Wkt) = seventeenth. See **hevdehem**.

hivdeyemîn هِڤدەیەمین (Wkt) = seventeenth. See **hevdehem**.

hivêzî هِڤێزی (ZF3) = club, mace. See **hiwêzî**.

hiwêzî هوێزی *m.* **(-yê;).** club, mace *(weapon)*. {also:

hivêzî (ZF3); huwêzî (FS)} {syn: ciniĥ; gurz} [BX/K/IFb//ZF3]

hizar هزار (SK) = thousand. See **hezar**.

hizarem هزارەم (Wkt) = thousandth. See **hezarem**.

hizaremîn هِـــزارەمــــيـــن (Wkt) = thousandth. See **hezarem**.

Hizeyran هزەیران (JB3) = June. See **Ĥezîran**.

hizir هزِر *f.* **(-a;).** thought, idea: **•*Hizir* bo hindê *diçin* ku hevçerxê Melayê Cizîrî bûye** (I. Badî. Remezanê Cizîrî di dwîvçûn û twêjandineka dîtir da, 12) *It is thought* that [lit. 'thoughts go for such that'] he was a contemporary of Melayê Jizîrî; **-ĥizir kirin** (Z-3/HH)/**hizra xû [xwe] kirin** (XF) to think, ponder, reflect: **•Mîr jî *ĥizir nake*, ew jî ji berva ȓadibe** (Z-3) The emir also stands up *without thinking* **•Wî *hizra xû kir*, kû eve xewne** (XF) He *thought* that this was a dream. {also: ĥizir (Z-3); <ĥizirkirin حزرکرن (ĥizirdike) (حزردکە)> (HH)} {syn: fikar; fikir; mitale; ȓaman I; xiyal} <Ar √ḥ-z-r حـــــــزر = 'to guess' [Z-3/HH//K/XF] <fikirîn I; p'onijîn [2]; ȓaman I>

hîc هیچ (FJ) = type of sandwich. See **ĥoç**.

hîç هـيـچ *adv.* 1) [+ neg.] {syn: qet I} not at all, never: **•Êdî paşî hingî ehlê Pawe li wan etrafane *hîç* xo aşkera naken** (SK 12:122) Moreover, people from Pawa *never* show themselves in these parts since then **•Keşkele zor fasiq e, *hîç* tobe naket, daimî fikra wî zerera xelkî ye** (SK 4:42) The magpie is very villainous and does not repent *at all*. He is always thinking of how to harm people **•Welehîn min *hîç* nizanibû ku ew mara delalok bûka te ye** (ZZ-7, 241) By God, I had no idea [lit. 'did not know *at all*'] that that lovely snake was your daughter-in-law *(from folktale)*; 2) [*adj.*] {syn: t'u II} not any, no, none: **•Eger muroekî çak li-naw qebrêt cûan difn biken *hîç* zerer nîye, we eger cû li-naw qebrê Imam Ĥuseyn difn biken *hîç* fayde nîye** (SK 60:724) If they bury a good man among the graves of the Jews there is *no* harm, and if they bury a Jew in the grave of Imam Husayn it is to *no* avail **•Ya Ellah, ya ȓebbî, to ȓidînekî direĵ o pan o 'ezmanekî lûs bideye kuȓê min, êdî *hîç* ȓizqî nede wî, bila ȓizqê wî li-ser wî bît** (SK 12:116) O God, my Lord, (if) Thou givest my son a long and broad beard and a smooth tongue, give him *no further* sustenance, let his sustenance be on his own head; 3) [*prn.*] {syn: t'utişt} nothing: **•Wextê kalûme hebît delîlêt dî hemî duro ne w *hîç* in** (SK 43:418) When there is a sword, other proofs are lies and *nothing*. {also: hêç' II (K/B)} Cf. P hīč هيچ; Sor hîç هیچ; cf. also Arm [v]oč' ոչ = 'no' [ZZ/IFb/TF/FJ/GF/SK/ZF/CS//K/B]

hîjdeh هیژدەه (K) = eighteen. See **ĥîjdeh**.

hîle هیلە (IFb) = trick, ruse. See **ĥîle**.

hîlebaz هیلەباز (IFb) = trickster. See **ĥîlebaz**.

hîlî هیلی (IFb) = mirror. See **hêlî**.

hîm هـيـم (SW/JB3/IFb/JJ/GF/TF/OK) = basis. See **ĥîm**.

hîmî هیمی (GF/CS) = basic. See **ĥîmlî**.

hîmlî هیملی (K) = basic. See **ĥîmlî**.

hîn I هـيـن: **-hîn[î *ft-î*] bûn** (IFb): a) to learn {syn: 'elimîn; fêr bûn; hû kirin (Kg)}: **•Mem li pêşîyê te'lîm û terbîyeta xwe li cem dayê distand, paşê li cem lele cure-cure 'ulim *hîn bûye*...** (K-dş, 88) Mem received his first education and training from his mother, then he *learned* various sciences from his pedagogue...; b) to get used to, grow accustomed to {syn: 'elimîn; ȓahatin}: **•Memo *hîn dibe*, her ȓo ji ber xova ȓadibe diçe odê** (Z-3) Mem *gets into the habit of* getting up and going to the room every day; ***-fk-ê* hîn[î *ft-î*] kirin** (IFb/ZF3): a) to teach {syn: 'elimandin; fêr kirin; hel dan/kirin}: **•... Ew *hînî* suwarîyê, tîravêjîyê *dikirin*** (K-dş, 88) ...They *taught* him horse-back riding [and] archery **•*hînkirina* zimanê kurdî** (Ber) *the teaching of* the Kurdish language; b) to accustom to, make s.o. get used to {syn: lê banandin: **•Sînor, ew hêdî hêdî *hînî* êş û mirinê *dikirin*, ango li mirinê dibanandin** (Nofa, 89) The border slowly *got* them *used to* grief and dying, i.e. it accustomed them to death. {also: hû (Kg); [hin] هین (JJ)} = Sor fêr فێر [F/K/A/JB3/IFb/B/JJ/ZF3]

hîn II هین (K/A/IF) = still, even. See **hîna**.

hîn III هین (Bw/OK) = cool. See **hênik**.

hîna هـيـنـا *adv.* [+ comparative adj.] still, even {+ ...-er}: **•Dîya wî nerî go jina Mhemmed Xan ji wî *hîna* bedewtir e** (L) His mother saw that M. Khan's wife was [lit. 'is'] *even more* beautiful than he **•Ev jina te ji te *hîna* ne bedewtir be, ezê ismê sêrê li we bixwînim** (L) If this wife of yours isn't *even more* beautiful than you, I will cast a spell on you [both]. {also: hîn II (K/A/IF)} {syn: hêj} [L/BX/K/A/IF] <hila II>

hîndarî هـيـنـدارى *f.* **(-ya;-yê).** exercise, drill:

•**Amerîka, Japonya û Koreya Başûr *hîndarîyên* hevbeş pêk anîn** (rojname.com 18.ix.2017) Ameri-ca, Japan and South Korea carried out joint *exercises* •**pirtûka *hîndarîyê*** (E.Dirêj. Kurdî Kurmancî) *exercise* book. <hîn I = 'used to/accustomed to, learned' + dar + î [(neol)IFb/TF/Wkt/FD/CS]

hînik هينك (IFb/GF/TF/SK) = cool. See **hênik**.

hîro هيرۆ (IFb/JJ) = hollyhock. See **hêro**.

hîrog هيرۆگ (IFb) = apricot. See **hêrûg** [2].

hîs هيس (Epl/Nûdem) = feeling. See **hest**.

hîşî هيشى (IF) = tent flap. See **hêşî**.

hîştin هيشتن (XF) = to leave, let, abandon, allow. See **hiştin**.

hît هيت (IFb) = angora goat. See **ḧîtik**.

hîtik هيتك (FJ) = angora goat. See **ḧîtik**.

hîv هيڤ *f.* **(-a;-ê).** 1) moon: •**Îşev *hîv* pir rohnî ye** (AB) Tonight *the moon* is very bright; **-Civata Heyva Sor** (BK) The Red Crescent Association *(Muslim equivalent of the Red Cross)*; **-heyva çarde şevê** (K/JB3) full moon [lit. 'moon of the 14th night [of the lunar month]'] •**Riwê te ji *heyva çardehê* rewşentir e** (BX) Your face is brighter than *the moon on the 14th* [of the month] (=than the full moon); **-heyva yekşevî** (Zeb/Hk/Am) moon on the first night of the lunar month; **-tava heyvê** (JB3)/~ **hîvê** (Ag) moonlight; full moon; 2) {syn: meh} month (Zx/Czr/Bw). {also: hewy (SK); heyv (A/JB3/IF-2/BK/Zx/Czr/Bw); heyw (SK-2); [hiw] هيڤ (JJ); <hîv> هيڤ (HH)} =Sor mang مانگ = 'moon, month'; Za aşme/aşmî/aşmi *f.* = 'moon' (Mal/Todd) & meng(i) *f.* = 'month' (Mal/Todd) [F/BX/AB/Kg/ Ag/K/IF/B/JJ/HH/Rh//A/JB3/BK/Zx/ Czr/Bw//SK] <řoj; stêr; tav>

hîvastin هيڤاستن *vt.* **(-hîvêz-).** to darn, mend, repair damaged cloth; to weave; to crochet: •**Wê kuna şelwalî *hîvast*** (FS) She *mended* the hole in the trousers •**Xalîçeyên xwe yên efsûnî şuştin, cihên wan ên qetiyayî *hîvrêz kirin*** (EN) They washed their magic carpets, *mended* their torn places. {also: hevastin (CCG-2); hevrêstin (Kmc-2); hêvîsandin (FJ/CCG-2); hêvîsîn (FJ-2/CCG-2); hîvaştin (GF-2/FS-2); hîvaxtin (-hîvêx-) (IFb-2/ RZ); hîvaztin (IFb/TF); hîvrêz kirin (EN)} {syn: *arastin; *şirt kirin} [CCG/GF/Kmc/FS//IFb/TF//RZ//EN] <hevo; hûnan>

hîvaştin هيڤاشتن (GF/FS) = to repair, darn (clothing). See **hîvastin**.

hîvaxtin هيڤاختن (-hîvêx-) (IFb/RZ) = to repair, darn (clothing). See **hîvastin**.

hîvaztin هيڤازتن (IFb/TF) = to repair, darn (clothing). See **hîvastin**.

hîvdeh هيڤدەه (K) = seventeen. See **hevdeh**.

hîveřon هيڤەرۆن *f.* **(;-ê).** 1) {syn: tavehîv} moonlight, moonshine (IFb); brightness of the moon (JJ); 2) full moon (K/B). {also: heyveron (IFb); [hiwé rohen] هيڤه روهن (JJ)} [K/B//IFb//JJ]

hîvgirtin هيڤگرتن (Wkp) = lunar eclipse. See **heyvgirtin**.

hîvgirtî هيڤگرتى (GF) = lunar eclipse. See **heyvgirtin**.

hîvî هيڤى (F/K/B) = hope. See **hêvî**.

hîvîdar هيڤيدار (K) = hopeful; expectant. See **hêvîdar**.

hîvrêz kirin هيڤريز كرن (EN) = to repair, darn (clothing). See **hîvastin**.

hîz هيز (IF/A) = wineskin. See **ḧîz**.

hîzar هيزار (Z-3/ZF3) = veil. See **hêzar**.

hoc هۆج (FJ) = type of sandwich. See **ḧoç**.

hoç'ik هۆچك (K[s]) = sleeve. See **huçik**.

hodax هۆداخ *m.* **(; hodêẍ** [B]**).** 1) farm hand, laborer, worker (K); 2) cowherd (B); 3) *man's name* (K). {also: hodaẍ (B)} <W Arm hōdał հօտաղ = '(young) shepherd' < hōd հօտ = 'herd'; T hodah [Iğdır -Kars] = 'cowherd' & [Erciş -Van] = 'drover' & hodak [Gümüşhane; Artvin; Kars; Erzurum; Tercan -Erzincan; Kiğı (-Bingöl); Doğubayazıt -Ağrı; Ahlat -Bitlis; Harput -Elâzığ] = 'farm hand, male servant' & hotak [Erzincan; Van] = 'cowboy, one who looks after animals' (DS, v.7, p. 2391) {hodax[t]î} [K/ZF3//B] <gavan; p'ale; şivan>

hodaxî هۆداخى (K) = farm work; servanthood. See **hodaxtî**.

hodaxtî هۆداختى *f.* **().** farm work, being a farm hand. {also: hodaxî (K-2)} *For etymology, see* ***hodax***. [K/Wkt] <hodax; p'aleyî>

hodaẍ هۆداغ (B) = farm hand; cowherd. See **hodax**.

hogec هۆگەج (FS) = young ram. See **hogiç**.

hogeç هۆگەچ (Wn/K) = young ram. See **hogiç**.

hogic هۆگج (FS) = young ram. See **hogiç**.

hogiç/hogiç' هۆگچ *m.* **().** three-year-old male sheep, pre-adult ram (Wn/Bşk/RJ); two-year-old ram (K/ B); three-year-old ewe (JJ). {also: hogec (FS-2); hogeç (Wn/K); hogic (FS); hogij (FS-2); hogoç (FS-2); ogeç (K-2); [(pez-i) hoghetch] پز هوگچ (JJ); hōgich (RJ)} {syn: xirt} Cf. T oveç [Çepni, Gemerek-Sivas] = 'castrated ram' (DS, v. 9, p. 3299) [Bşk/A/B/RJ//Wn/K/JJ//FS] <beran; berx; kavir; mî I; pez>

hogij هۆگِژ (FS) = young ram. See **hogiç**.

hogir هـــۆگِــر *m.* **().** friend, companion (K/JB3/IF): **-heval-hogir** = do.: **•*Heval-hogirê* Memê gelekî jê ḧiz dikirin** (Z-1) Mem's *friends and companions* were very fond of him. {also: [hogher] هـوگـر (JJ)} {syn: dost; heval; yar [1]} [Z-1/K/JB3/IF/JJ]

hogoç هۆگۆچ (FS) = young ram. See **hogiç**.

hoker هـــۆكــەر *f.* **(-a;).** adverb: **-hokerên awakî** (IF) adverbs of manner; **-~ên cihkî** (IF) adverbs of place; **-~ên çiqasî** (IF) adverbs of quantity; **-~ên demkî** (IF) adverbs of time; **-~ên gumanî** (IF) adverbs of doubt (?); **-~ên neyînî** (IF) adverbs of negation. {syn: *nîr I[2] (IF); r̄engpîşe; zerf} [(neol)K/IF/ZF3]

hol I هۆل *f.* **(;-ê).** 1) {syn: gog [1]; t'op II} large ball *[as opposed to* **gog**, *small ball]*; sphere: **-hol bûn** (K) to roll *(vi.)*; **-hol kirin** (K) to roll *(vt.)*; 2) {syn: gog [2]} (hockey) puck, round wooden disk *which is hit with a stick in a game*; 3) a game, played outdoors in summer, in which a ball (or puck) is driven along with a stick [cf. hockey & polo]. {also: [hol] هـول (JJ); <hol> هـول (HH)} [K/IFb/B/JJ/HH/GF/FS/Wkt] <gog; k'aşo>

hol II هـۆل *f.* **(;-ê).** one's immediate surroundings, the area around one, midst: **-anîn holê** (IFb) to bring forth, produce: **•Karên baş *anîn holê*** (IFb) [They] *produced* good work; **-derk'etin holê** (Wlt) to become evident, be clear, turn out *(e.g., that stg. is true)*: **•Li gor lêgerîn û lêkolînên hatine kirin, *derketiye holê* ku** ... (Wlt) According to examinations and research that has been done, *it has come out* [or, it is clear] that ...; **-ji holê r̄abûn** (Wlt) to disappear; to be eliminated; **-ji holê r̄akirin** (Wlt) to do away with, eliminate: **•Herçiqas av ji bo hemû jîndaran çavkaniyeke bingehîn be jî, îro di destê mirovên "hemdem" de wek pergaleke *ji holê rakirina* berhemên dîrokê tê bi kar anîn** (Wlt 1:21, 16) Although water is a basic resource for all living things, today it is being used by "modern" man as an instrument for *destroying* historical artifacts **•*Ji holê rakirina* hebûna Kurdistan a leşkerî, aborî, siyasî û civakî** (Wlt) *Doing away with* the military, economic, political, and social existence [or entity] of Kurdistan. {syn: hindav [2]} Cf. T hol = 'marketplace' <Fr halle [(neol)Wlt/IFb/GF/TF/FS] <ort'e>

hol III هـــــۆل **().** threshing of grain by having horses tread over it: **•Li devera Wêranşarê jî çend hesp** [sic] **bi he**[v] **ve girêdin** [sic] **û liser bêdera çeltîkan didin gerandin, ji vê re "*hol*" dibêjin** (CCG, 71) In the region of Viranşehir they tie a few horses together and have them go around the rice threshing floor, this is called '*hol*'; **-hol kirin** (Kmc) to thresh. {also: hor (Kmc-2)} {syn: gêre I} Sor hole هۆله = 'threshing (of harvest') [CCG/Kmc]

Holandî هـۆلانـدى (ZF3/CS) = Dutch; Dutchman. See **Holendî**.

Holendî هـــۆلـــەنـــدى *adj.* 1) Dutch; 2) [*m.&f.* **().**] Dutchman; Dutch woman. {also: Holandî (ZF3/CS)} Sor Hołendî هۆڵەندى [Wkt/IFb/BF/SS//ZF3/CS]

holik هۆلِك (IFb/JJ/GF/TF/FS) = hut. See **ḧolik**.

holîdang هۆليدانگ. See **dolîdang II**.

hon هۆن (IF/JB3/OK) = you. See **hûn.**

honan هـۆنـان (-hon-) (IFb) = to twist; to smooth. See **hûnan.**

honandin هۆنـانـدِن(IFb/OK/Wlt) = to twist; to smooth. See **hûnan.**

honijîn هۆنِژين (OK/JJ) = to yawn. See **hênijîn**[2].

honik هۆنِك (K[s]/IF/JB3) = cool. See **hênik**.

honikahî هۆنِكاهى (BX/IFb) = coolness. See **hênikayî.**

honikayî هۆنِكايى (K[s]) = coolness. See **hênikayî.**

honîn هـــۆنـــيـــن (-hon-) (K[s]/JB3/IF) = to twist; to smooth. See **hûnan.**

hongo هۆنگۆ = you. See **hûn.**

hoqboq هۆقبۆق (Qzl) = clamor; chaos. See **hoqeboq**.

hoqe هۆقە (K/IFb/B) = oka (unit of weight). See **ḧuqe**.

hoqeboq هـۆقـەبـۆق *f.* **(-a;-ê).** clamor, uproar; chaos, confusion: **•...Piştî kêlikekê wê pîrka min veşêrin... Laş di nav paçê spî de dilebitî ... *Hoqe boq* bi gund ketibû** (HYma 22) In a moment they will bury my grandmother ... The corpse was stirring in its white cloth ... *Confusion* broke out in the village. {also: hoqboq (Qzl)} {syn: bir̄bir̄; hengame; hêwirze; qareqar; qerebalix; qîr̄eqîr̄} [HYma//Qzl]

hor هۆر (Kmc) = threshing. See **hol III**.

horî هـــــــۆرى *f.* **(-ya;-yê).** houri, beautiful maiden inhabiting paradise (according to Islam) : **•Zînê ji *horîya* bedewtir bû** (Z-1) Zin was more beautiful than *the houris* **•Zînê ... mîna *horîke* bik'ur li bihiştê bû** (EP-7) Zin was like a virgin *houri* in paradise. {also: hûrî I (IF-2/GF); ḧorî (SK); [houri حـورى/hour حـور] (JJ); <ḧûrî> حـورى (HH)} < Ar ḥūrīyah حورية; Sor ḧorî حۆرى [Z-1/F/K/IF/B//GF//SK//JJ/

HH]

horîstan هـۆریـسـتـان *f.* **(;-ê).** land of the houris: **•Ew bajarê horîaye, ew *horîstane*** (Ba3-3, #11) It's the city of the houris, it's "*houri-land*" **•Hewzê minî meṙmeṙ heye, înî-înî ji *horîstanê* sê qîz tên, dik'evne avê û paşê fiṙ didin diçin** (Ba3-3, #4) I have a marble pool, every Friday three maidens come from "*houri-land*," they get in the water and later fly away. [Ba3] <horî>

hosa هۆسا (GShA) = thus, so. See **wisa**.

hos•e هـۆسـه *f.* **(•a;•ê).** 1) {syn: galegûrt; galigal[4]; hêwirze; k'im-k'imî; qajeqaj; qalmeqal; qareqar; qerebalix; qîṙeqîṙ; şerqîn; t'eqeṙeq} noise, commotion (Bw): **•Biçûk zêde *hosê* çê dikin** (Bw) [The] children make too much *noise* **•*Hosa* biçûkan nexoş e** (Bw) *The noise of* children is not pleasant; 2) anarchy, chaos, uproar (OK). [Bw/OK] <bi hose; galigal; k'eft û left>

hosta هۆستا = (B) master. See **osta**.

hostatî هـۆسـتـاتـی (K) = masterliness, expertise. See **ostatî.**

hostayî هـۆسـتـایـی (BF) = masterliness, expertise. See **ostatî.**

hov هـۆڤ *adj.* wild, savage, primitive, uncouth, cruel: *{of uncultured people: for wild animals,* ***k'ûvî*** *(qv.) is used (Haz)}.* {syn: ç'olî I; k'ûvî; wahş: ≠kedî} {hovî; hovîtî} [Ber/K/JB3/IFb/GF/TF/OK/Haz]

hovî هۆڤی (K/GF) = savagery. See **hovîtî.**

hovîtî هۆڤیتی *f.* **(-ya;).** 1) wildness, savagery; 2) act of savagery, cruelty: **•*Hovîtyek* ji rejîma Îraqê** (Ber) *An act of savagery* from the Iraqi regime. {also: hovî (K-2)} {syn: wehşî} [Ber/K/IFb/TF/OK//GF] <hov>

hox هـۆخ *m.* **(-ê;).** plowed field: **•Bere hoxê we bajon / Hun sê sed û ew dido** (Cxn-2: Cotkar û Zevî) Let them plow your *fields* / You are 300, and they [are only] two. {syn: k'ewşan [1]} <Arm hoł հող = 'earth, land, soil' [Cxn-2/K/A/GF/Hej] <beyar; k'ewşan; k'irêbe; zevî>

hoz هۆز *f.* **(-a;).** tribe, clan: **•Melayê Cizîrî ... ji *hoza* kurdên Buxtî ye** (E.Zivingî. Gerdeniya Gewherî, v. 1, t.p. verso) Mela Jiziri ... is from *the clan of* the Bukhti [Bohti] Kurds. {syn: 'eşîret} Cf. Sor hoz هـۆز = 'households belonging to the same tîre/clan' [Zivingî/K(s)/IFb/FJ/GF/ZF/SS] <berek; binemal; îcax; obe; qebîle; tayfe>

hozan I هـۆزان *f.* **(-a;-ê).** poem, poetry: **•Me pêkol-kiriye, ku li dwîv şiyanan di şilovekirina *hozanên* wanda babetî bîn** (B.Y. 'Ebdulla. Hozana afretan di edebê Kurdîda, 6) We have strived as much as possible to be objective in interpreting their *poems*. {syn: helbest; şêr II} [Ber/Hej/Bw/Zeb/FS]

hozan II هۆزان (A/IFb/GF) = poet. See **hozanvan.**

hozanvan هـۆزانـڤـان *m.* **(-ê;).** 1) {syn: biwêj I; helbestvan; şayîr} poet: **•*Hozanvanê* jêhatî û şehreza di vehandina hozan û helbestan da, desthel û pisporê lêkînana peyivan, evîndarê ciwanîya siruştê Kurdistanê bi çiya û gelî û dol û rûbarên xo ve** (N.Hacî. "Feqê Teyran û Çîrokên Binavkirina Wî," Peyam 5-6 [1996], 2) *The poet* skilled and expert at composing poems and verses, handy and clever at putting words together, enamored of the Kurdistan's natural beauty with its mountains, valleys, ravines, and rivers **•*Hozanvanêt* Kurd** (HoK) Kurdish *poets [name of an important book by Sadiq Baha' al-Din Amêdî]*; 2) littérateur, writer, man of letters, scholar, intellectual [cf. Ar adīb أديـب]. {also: hozan II (A/IFb/GF-2); <hozanvan> هـۆزانـڤان (Hej)} Cf. T ozan = 'bard'; *now incorrectly used for 'poet', an overzealous puristic attempt to replace the Arabic word* ***şair***. [Ber/HoK/Bw/Zeb/GF/Hej/FS//A/IFb] <hozan I>

hrî هری (J) = wool. See **hirî.**

hubir هوبر (EP-8) = ink. See **ḧubir.**

hucum هوجوم (IF) = attack. See **ḧucûm.**

huç•ik هوچك *f.(PS/K[s])/m.(SK)* **(•ka/•ikê;).** 1) {syn: mil [3]; zendik} sleeve: **•[Memê Ala herdu kezîyêd Xatûn Zînê ji *huçka* kevilî nîşa Qeretajdîn kirîye]** (PS-II) Memê Alan showed Qeretajdîn both of Lady Zîn's braids [sticking out] from [under] *the sleeve of* the cloak; 2) cuff *(of sleeve)*. {also: desthûçik (IFb); hoç'ik (K[s]); hûçik (GF); [húck-] (PS); [hüčk-] هـچـك (JJ)} Cf. NA húčke = 'long, open sleeve' (Turoyo: Ritter); = Sor feqyane فەقیانە [PS-II/JJ/SK//K(s)//GF] <lewendî>

hufehuf هـوفـەهـوف *m.(L)/f.(K/FS)* **(-ê/-a;).** raging or crashing *(of sea, waves)*, blustering *(of wind)*: **•Bû *hufehufê* pêlan** (L) There was *a crashing of* waves. {also: hufe-hûf, f. (K)} [L/FS//K]

hufe-hûf هـەفـەهـەووف, f. (K) = raging, blustering. See **hufehuf.**

hujîr هوژیر (AA) = fig. See **hejîr.**

hukm هوکم (IFb) = power; command. See **ḧuk'um.**

hukumat هـوکـومـات (IFb) = government. See **ḧuk'umet.**

hukûmet هـوکـوومـەت (OK) = government. See **ḧuk'umet.**

hulî هولی (OK/AA) = plum. See **ĥilû I**.

hulîreşk هولیرەشك (IFb) = black plum. See **ĥûlîr̄eşk**.

hulm هولم (K) = steam; breath. See **hilm**.

hulû I هولوو (GF) = plum. See **ĥilû I**.

hulû II هولوو (FS) = smooth. See **hilû I**.

hummet هـومـمـەت (HR) = magnanimity, helpful intervention. See **himmet**.

hun هون (IFb/OK) = you. See **hûn.**

hunandin هـونـانـدِن (TF) = to twist; to smoothe. See **hûnan.**

hundir هوندِر = inside. See **hindur̄**.

hundur̄ هوندور (K/IF/B) = inside. See **hindur̄**.

hune هونه (IFb) = henna. See **ĥene**.

huner هونەر (IFb/SK/GF/TF/JJ) = art, skill. See **hiner**.

hunermend هـونـەرمـەنـد *m.&f.* **(-ê/ ;) artist: •Heke Şivan xwe bi *hunermendê* gel, *hunermendekî* şoreşgêr binase**, ... (Roj 1[1996]:52) If Shivan considers himself *an artist of* the people, a revolutionary *artist*, ... {also: hinermend (K[s])} Cf. P honarmand هـنـرمـنـد = 'artist, artisan'; Sor hunermend هونەرمەند = 'skillful' [Roj/IFb/GF/TF/ZF3/FS//K(s)] <hiner>

hung هونگ (SK) = you. See **hûn**.

Hungarî هـونـگـارى *adj.* Hungarian. {also: Hingarî (BF)} {syn: Macarî} Sor Hengarî هەنگاری [Wkt/SS//BF]

hungiv هونگِڤ (F) = honey. See **hingiv**.

hunîn هونین (M) = to twist; to smoothe. See **hûnan.**

huqe هوقه (A) = oka (unit of weight). See **ĥuqe**.

hur̄a bayî هورا بایی (FS) = storm. See **hureba**.

hureba هورەبا *m./f.* **(;-yî/). storm, windstorm: •Ji ber *hurûbayî* em nikarin ji mal derkevin** (BF) Because of *the windstorm* we cannot leave the house. {also: hur̄a bayî (FS); hurûba (BF)} {syn: bager; bahoz; bap'eşk; barove; tofan} [Bw//BF//FS] <firtone; ĥabûr>

hurmet هورمەت *f.* **(-a;-ê).** 1) {syn: k'ulfet; jin; pîrek} woman: **•Wî xwexwa dest bi serhatîya vê *hurmetê*, neynesîya dînbûna wê kir** (X. Çaçan. Benê min qetiya, 22) Of his own accord he began the story of this *woman*, the reason for her insanity; 2) wife; 3) {syn: 'erz; giram; me'rîfet [1]; qedir I; r̄êz II; r̄ûmet} respect, honor, esteem: **-hurmet girtin** (Ba2) to respect: **•Dasinî mezhebek e, Êzedî jî dibêjinê ... mezinekî wan zemanekî hebû, nawê wî 'Elî Beg bû ... zêdetir *ĥurmeta* melan û qeşan *digirt* ji koçekan. Ew dibêjine 'ulemaêt xo koçek** (SK 39:344) The Dasinis are a sect, also called Yezidis ... once they had a leader whose name was Ali Beg ... He *respected* the mullahs and Christian priests more than the kochaks. They call their own religious authorities 'kochak' **•Ewî** [sic] **gelekî dilşewat bû û t'u cara merîya r̄a xirabî nedikir, lema jî gund da gişka *hurmeta wî digirt*** (Ba2:1, 204) He was very sympathetic and never harmed anyone, so in the village everyone *respected him*; **-hurmet kirin** (JJ) to receive (a guest) favorably; 4) authority (K/B). {also: hermet; ĥermet (Z-2); ĥurmet (SK); [hurmet kirin] حرمت كرين (JJ); <ĥirmet> حرمت (HH)} < Ar ḥurmah حـــرمــــة = 'sacredness, reverence; woman'--> T hürmet [Z-2//F/K/IF/B/JJ//HH//SK]

hurmê هورمێ (K/F/Ba2/B) = pear. See **hermê**.

hurûba هورووبا (BF) = storm. See **hureba**.

huskîk هوسكیك (Bw) = ladle. See **hesk**.

husnûcemal هوسنووجەمال (ZF3) = beautiful woman. See **husulcemal**.

husta هوستا = (M-Zx) master. See **osta**.

husulcemal هوسولجەمال/**husul-cemal** هوسول جەمال [EP-7] *f.* **(). a beauty, a beautiful woman: •Memê serê xwe ji xewa şîrin hiltîne, / *Husul-cemalekê* p'aşla xweda divîne** (EP-7) Mem awakes [lit. 'lifts his head'] from sweet sleep / He sees *a beauty* in his arms. {also: husnûcemal (ZF3); ĥusilcemal (K)} {syn: p'erî [2]} < Ar ḥusn wa-jamāl حـسـن وجـمـال = 'handsomeness and beauty' [EP-7/Z-1//K//ZF3]

husûn هوسوون (M/SK) = to rub. See **hesûn.**

huşyar هوشیار (L) = awake; aware. See **ĥişyar**.

huvdehem هـوڤـدەهـەم (CT) = seventeenth. See **hevdehem**.

huwêzî هووێزی (FS) = club, mace. See **hiwêzî**.

hû هوو: hû kirin (Kg) = to teach. See **hîn I**.

hûçik هووچك (GF) = sleeve. See **huçik**.

hûlî هوولی (Mzg) = eagle; falcon. See **elîh**.

hûn هــــوون *prn.* (*obl.* **we**/**hewe** [Botan/Bw/OK-2]/ **hingo** [SK]). you *(pl.)*. {also: hingû (BX-Behdinan); hon (IFb/JB3/OK-2); hongo; hun (IFb-2/OK-2); hung (SK); hûng (JB1-A/GF-2/OK-2); ûn (Z-2/F); [houn] هـون (JJ); <hûn> هـون (HH)} Cf. P šomā شما; Sor êwe ئێوە (Sulaimania/ Kerkûk/ Warmawa)/engo ئـەنگۆ (Mukriyan/Arbil/ Rawanduz/ Xoşnaw); Za şima [F/K/A/IFb/BK/JJ/HH/GF/OK//BX//JB3//SK//JB1-A] <tu I> See also **we**.

hûnan هوونان *vt.* **(-hûn-).** 1) {syn: vehûnan} to twist, wind; to braid, plait; to [inter]weave: •**Berhem li ser heqîqetê *hatiye honandin*** (Wlt 2:59, 12) The [literary] work *is based* on [lit. 'woven around'] the truth •**Çîroka fîlm *li ser* mirovekî ku naxwaze here leşkeriya dewleta Tirk û li ser kekê wî, *hatiye honandin*** (Wlt 2:59, 11) The plot [lit. 'story'] of the film *has been woven around* a man who doesn't want to serve in the Turkish army, and around his brother; 2) to smooth (M). {also: honan (-hon-) (IFb); honandin (IFb-2/Wlt/OK); honîn (-hon-) (K[s]/JB3/IF-2); hunandin (TF); hunîn (M); hûnandin (-hûn[în]-) (K-2/B-2/GF); [hounan] هـونـان (JJ)} Sor honîn[ewe] هۆنینەوە (-hon-) = 'to plait, string (beads)' [K/B/JJ//JB3/IF//M] <hîvastin>

hûnandin هووناندِن(-hûn[în]-) (K/B/GF) = to twist; to smoothe. See **hûnan.**

hûng هوونگ (JB1-A/GF/OK) = you. See **hûn.**

hûngilîsk هوونگِلیسك (Btm/Mzg) = (finger) ring. See **gustîl.**

hûr I هـوور *adj.* 1) small, petty *(change)*; 2) tiny; 3) fine, minute: **-hûr kirin** = a) to mince, chop up, cut finely {syn: hincinîn}: •**Çûn ji B. re berxek şerjêkirin** [sic] **û ji birîncî, ji sinûbera û ji dûvê wî *hûr kirin* li nav hev du û heşandin** (L, #5, 166, l. 9-11) They went and slaughtered a lamb for B. and stuffed it with rice and pine nuts, and *chopped up* its tail; b) to make change *(of money)*: •**Ev zêřê hana ji miřa *hûr bike*, t'emam bike mecidîne, quruş û çerxîne** (Z-2) *Make change* for these gold pieces, give me silver coins, twenty piasters and five piasters; **-hûr nihêrin** (K) to examine carefully, go over with a fine-tooth comb; **-lê hûr bûn** (IFb/RZ/CS) to examine, investigate, look into (closely); to analyze: •**Ji bo ku ev çîroka ha were nivisandin, ... bi dehsalan li ser ne sekinî û *lê hûr ne bû*** (Epl, 7) In order for this story to be written ... it was not the subject of research for decades *nor was it investigated*; 4) short *(of stature)* (Bw). {also: [hour] هـور (JJ); <hûr> هـور (HH)} Cf. P xurd خـرد; Sor wurd وورد/hûrd هوورد (K2-2) = 'small (esp. of children under ten years old), precise, attentive' {hûranî; hûrayî; hûrî II} [L/K/A/JB3/IF/B/JJ/HH/GF]

hûr II هوور (A/JJ) = bowels, intestines. See **ûr.**

hûranî هوورانی (K) = smallness. See **hûrayî.**

hûrayî هوورایی *f.* (). tininess, minuteness; smallness, pettiness. {also: hûranî (K); hûrî II (K)} [K/Wkt] <hûr I>

hûrdek هـووردەك *f.* **(;-ê).** small letter, lower case letter: •**Lê bêjeyên ku ji navên kesan hatine çêkirin, bi *hûrdekê* dest pê dikin** (RR, 20.2.2.) But words which have been made from the names of people begin with *a small letter.* {also: hûrek (Wkt-2)} [RR/IFb/ZF/Wkt] <girdek>

hûrdem هووردەم *f.* **().** minute, unit of time consisting of sixty seconds. {syn: deqe} [(neol)IFb/OK/ZF3]

hûrek هوورەك (Wkt) = capital letter. See **girdek.**

hûrgilî 1 هـوورگِـلی *adj./adv.* 1) detailed, in detail: •**Řojtira dinê êvarê met'a Zozan hate mala me û derheqa wê yekêda *hûrgilî* meřa gilî kir** (Ba2-#2, 208) The next day in the evening, Aunt Zozan came to our house and told us *in detail* about it; **-bi hûrgilî** (Wkt) do. 2) [*f.* **().**] detail. [Ba2/K/B/ZF3/Wkt]

hûrhûrik' هـوورهـوورك *adj.* 1) fine *(in small particles)*; 2) ?unripe, immature. {also: hûrhûrî (K/B)} [JB1-A//K/B] <hûr I>

hûrhûrî هـوورهـووری (K/B) = fine. See **hûrhûrik'** & **hûrik.**

hûrik هـوورك *adj.* 1) fine *(in small particles)* (K); tiny (B/A/IF): **-hûrik-hûrik**: a) [en peu] (JJ); b) gently, easily, slowly (HR-1); **-hûrik-mûrik** (IF) itsy-bitsy, teeny-weeny; 2) [*m.* **(-ê;).**] crumb, tiny bit (K/B); particle, atom (JJ): **-hûrikê nan** (ZF3) bread crumb; 3) small change, petty cash (K/JB3). {also: [hourik] هـورك (JJ)} [HR-1/K/A/JB3/IF/B/JJ] <hûrhûrik'>

Hûrisî هوورِسی (Wkt) = Russian. See **Řûsî.**

hûrî I هووری (IF/GF) = houri. See **horî.**

hûrî II هووری (K) = smallness. See **hûrayî.**

hûşî هووشی (GF) = bunch of grapes. See **gûşî.**

hût هووت *m.* **(-ê;-î).** 1) {syn: k'afir [2]} monster, ogre (K/JB3/IF/B): **-ȟûtê binê be'rê** (B) underwater monster; 2) whale (IF/JJ). {also: ȟût (K/B); [hout] حـوت (JJ)} < Ar ḥūt حـوت = 'whale, leviathan, large fish' [L/JB3/IF/JJ//K/B] <dêw>

hwd. هـود *abbr.* (=her wekî din) et cetera, etc. =Sor htd. هتد (heta duwayî هەتا دوایی) [Wlt/IFb]

Ḧ ح

*__ḧabûr__ حـــابـــوور *f.* **(-a;).** snowstorm, blizzard: **-ḧabûra berfê** (Şng) do. {syn: bager; bakuzîrk; bamişt} [Şng] <hureba>

ḧac حاج (K) = pilgrimage (to Mecca). See **ḧec.**

ḧacḧacik حـاجـحـاجِـك *f.* **(-a;-ê).** swallow *(bird)*, zool. *Hirundo.* {also: hechecik (IF); hechecîk (A); hecheçoq (JB3/OK); ḧecḧeck (K/B/FS); ḧecḧeçoq, m. (OK-2); ḧejḧejîk (Srk); ḧicḧicok (Haz); [hadj-hadjk] حـاج حـاجـك (JJ)} {syn: dûmeqesk; ḧacîreşk [2]; meqesork; qerneqûçik} [Ad//K/B/FS//A//JB3/OK//IF//JJ//Srk//Haz]

ḧacî حـــاجـــی (K/F/JJ/HH) = pilgrim (to Mecca). See **ḧecî.**

ḧacîr̄eş حاجیرەش (HH) = swallow. See **ḧacîr̄eşk.**

ḧacîr̄eşk حاجیرەشك *f.* **(-a;-ê).** 1) {syn: legleg} stork, zool. *Ciconiidae* (K/B); 2) {syn: dûmeqesk (F); ḧacḧacik; meqesork (F); qerneqûçik (IF)} swallow, zool. *Hirundo* (JB3/IF/JJ/TF/GF); swift, a variety of swallow (HH) [Ar xuṭṭāf خـطّـاف]. {also: hacîreşk (JB3/IF/TF/OK); ḧacîr̄eş; [ahhgi resc] (JJ-G); [h'āji r̲ešk] (JJ-Lx); <ḧacîr̄eş>حـاجـی رەش (HH)} [JB3/IF/TF/OK/FS//K/GF//JJ//HH]

ḧaf حــــاف *f.* **(-a;-ê).** side, edge: **•*ḧafa* gund** (B) *the edge of* the village **•Xecê gelekî ger̄iya, hate *ḧafa* gêlî, lê nihêr̄î -- Siyabend binê gêlî dane** (Ereb Şamilov. Berbang, 99) Khej searched a great deal, came to *the edge of* the ravine, she saw -- Siyabend was at the bottom of the ravine; **-ḧafa** (K) near, beside, at, at or to the presence of {syn: bal I; cem; hinda I; lalê; li def (Bw); nik I; r̄ex I}: **•Zilamek çû ew hekîm anî *hafa* bûka Paşê** (ZZ-7, 225) A man went and brought that wise man *into the presence of* the Pasha's bride. {also: haf (IFb/FJ/ZF/Tsab-2); [haf] حــــاف (JJ); <ḧaf> حـــاف (HH)} < Ar ḥāffah حـــافّـة = 'border, hem, fringe, edge, bank (of river)' [ZZ/IFb/FJ/ZF//K/B/GF/JJ/HH/Tsab]

ḧafa حافا, see **ḧaf.**

ḧafiz حافِز *m.* **(-ê;).** 1) Quran (Koran) reciter; 2) {syn: kor} blind, blind man: **•Nav û dengê wê bihîstiye go çavê *hafiza* çêdike** (L-1 #3,74, ll.25-26) He had heard of her fame, that she healed the eyes *of the blind*; 3) keeper, tender (JJ). {also: hafiz; [hafiz] حـافـظ (JJ)} < Ar ḥāfiẓ حـافـظ; ***hafiz** means "Quran reciter" [récitateur du Qoran]. Since blind men often filled this office, the word Hafiz came to be synonymous with* **kor** *(blind)* (L) [p. 250] [L/K/IF/JJ]

ḧakim حــاكِـم *m.* **(-ê;-î).** 1) {syn: p'adşa; qiral} ruler, magistrate, king; governor of a province (JJ): **-qîza hakim** (L) princess, magistrate's daughter; 2) {syn: dadger; dadpirs; qazî} judge. {also: hakim (L); [hakim] حاكم (JJ)} < Ar ḥākim حاكم [L/K/JB3/IF/M/JJ]

ḧal حــال *m.* **(-ê;-î).** 1) {syn: dest û dar; ḧewal; kawdan; r̄ewş} condition, state: **•Bavê me di çi *ḧalî* da e** (HR 3:177) What *state* is our father in?/What has happened to our father?; **-bi ḧal** (Bw) pregnant; **-ḧalê *fk-ê* /ḧal [di] *fk-ê* da neman/nebûn** = to be in bad shape {syn: r̄uḧ ... neman}: **•*Halê* min *t'une*** (Z-1) I'*m in bad shape* **•*Ḧal* Memêda *nemaye*, du-sê r̄oja şûnda Memê wê çetinayêda nadebire** (Z-1) M. *is in bad shape*; in two or three days he will no [longer] be alive from the hardship of it **•Hespekî bavê M. hebû, ... pişta wî bûbû bir̄în, *ḧal têda nemabû*** (Z-1) M.'s father had a horse ... its back was wounded, *it was in bad shape*; **-ḧal û ḧewal** (B)/**ḧalḧewal** (K) circumstance, condition, state (of affairs): **•Mirovî banî kur̄ê xwe kir û *hal û ḧewalê* xwe û marî jêr̄a da zanîn** (Dz #22, 389) The man summoned his son and explained to him his *circumstances* regarding the snake; **-ji halê xwe razî bûn** (IF) to be happy with one's lot; **-mal û ḧal** (Z-1) household responsibilities: •[After the death of Mem & Zin] **Destê P'erî-xatûnê ji *mal û ḧala* sar bûbû** (Z-1) Peri Khatun lost interest [lit. 'her hand got cold from'] her *household duties* **•Min *mal û ḧalê* xwe, bavê xwe t'erkandye** (EP-7) I have left my *home* and father (=family); **-xwe xistin vî halî** = to be in a bad way [lit. 'to drop o.s. into this state']: **•Qîza min, çima te *xwe xistîye vî halî?*** (L) My daughter, why *are you in such bad spirits*?; 2) health; state of health; 3) [*f.* **(-a;).**] fever, typhus. {also: hal (IFb/TF/OK-2); [hal] حــال (JJ); <ḧal> حــال (HH)} < Ar ḥāl حــال [Z-1/K/JB3/B/JJ/HH/JB1-A&S/SK/GF/OK//IFb/TF/ZF3] <ḧewal>

ḧalû حالوو (K) = being on edge *(of teeth)*. See **alû I.**

ḧamam حامام (JB1-S) = bath. See **ḧemam.**

ȟambal حامبال (HCK-4) = porter. See **ȟemal**.

ȟasil حـــــــــاسِــــل (JB1-S/SK/OK/JJ) = product; crop; income. See **hasil**.

ȟawid حـــــــاوِد *m.* **(-ê;).** 1) {syn: milik} camel's hump (Qzl/IFb): **•Devê (= deveyê) ji *hawidê* xwe bixwe** (Qzl) Said of s.o. who is dipping into his own savings, living at his own expense [lit. 'Camel which eats from its own hump']; 2) camel's packsaddle (GF/FJ). {also: hawîd (IFb/GF/[FJ])} [Qzl//IFb/GF/(FJ)] <ȟêştir>

ȟazir حـــــــازِر *adj.* 1) {syn: amade} ready, prepared: **•Wacib me ya ȟel kirî, belê hemî me neȟel-kirîye. Vê care k'eyfa te ye, k'anê dê tu çi li me key, em t *ȟazir* în** (M-Am #717) We ... did our homework, but we haven't done all of it. Now it's as you please. We are *ready* for whatever you will do to us; **-ȟazir kirin** (JJ/HH/JB1-A/SK): a) to prepare, make ready: **•Mêrî got ê, "Dibêjim do derwêş mêwanêt me ne. Zadekî *ȟazir ke*." Jinê got, "Ma tu nizanî çu di kawilemala teda nîye? Ez ji kê-derê *ȟazir bikem*?"** (SK 23:212) The husband said, "I say that we have two dervishes as guests. *Prepare* a meal." The wife said, "Why, don't you know that in this ruin of yours there isn't anything? Where am I *to prepare it* from?"; b) to summon, have s.o. brought: **•Paşî 'Îso *ȟazir kir*, got e 'Îso, "Here, bizane ew çi qafile ye."** (SK 22:204) Then he *had* Iso *brought* and said to him, "Go and find out what caravan this is" **•Rojekî** [sic] **dî qafileyek hat e Amêdîyê. Paşa hemî xulamêt xo *ȟazir kirin*** (SK 22:203) Another day a caravan came to Amadiya. The Pasha *summoned* all his henchmen; c) to bring: **•Paşa kasikekî çînî bo aw-xarinewa xo hebo, gelek çak bo. Li meclisê *ȟazir kir*. Hemî xulamêt xo gazî kirin** (SK 22:198) The Pasha had a very fine china cup from which to drink water. He *brought it* to the assembly and summoned all his henchmen; 2) present, in attendance: **•S̱adiq Beg izna xo xast, ço mala xo. Şewê hemî xulamêt xo digel aẍaêt *ȟazir* bon gazî kirin** (SK 26:240) Sadiq Beg took his leave and went home. At night he summoned all his henchmen and the aghas who were *present* **•Wê berxê gelek cûn dane min. Se w şwan *ȟazir* bon, neşyam tola xo we-kem** (SK 5:57) That lamb abused me greatly. The shepherd and his dog were *present* so I could not take my revenge. {also: hazir (K/IFb/B/GF); [hazir] حـــاضـــر (JJ); <ȟazir> حاضر (HH)} < Ar ḥāḍir حاضر = 'ready, present'; Sor ȟazir حازِر [JB1-A/SK//JJ/HH//K/IFb/B/GF]

ȟazirî حـــازرى *f.* **(-ya;-yê).** 1) preparedness, readiness: **-hazirîya *ft-î* kirin** (ZF) to prepare stg., make preparations for: **•Elî jî *haziriya* daweta xwe û Fedîlayê *kir*** (ZZ-10, 143) And Ali *made preparations* for his and F.'s wedding; 2) attendance, being present. {also: hazirayî (B); hazirî (K/B/IFb/ZF/CS); [haziri] حاضرى (JJ)} [ZZ/JB1-A/JJ//K/B/IFb/ZF/CS//B]

ȟeb حـــب *f.(K/B/JB1-S/OK [2])/m.(OK [1&4])* **(;-ê/).** 1) {syn: lib} seed, kernel, grain; 2) small quantity, small amount: **-ȟebek[î]** = a little bit {syn: hinekî; ȟekekî (Ad); piçek}: **•Lawo, xewa min tê, ez dikim *hebekî* razêm** (L) Son, I'm sleepy, I'm going to lie down *for a bit*; 3) *general counting word (for things and people)*: **•dû ȟeb** = two (=didû) [in answer to a question such as 'How many would you like?'] **•Sivê lêxin, serê neh-deh *ȟeva* jî bişkênin** (FK-kk-1) Tomorrow beat up [more children], crack the skulls of nine or ten; 4) pill, tablet *(medicine)* (K/IF). {also: ȟev II (FK-kk-1); [heb] حـــب (JJ); <ȟeb> حـــب (HH)} < Ar ḥabb[ah] حبّ[ة] = 'grain(s), seed(s)' [L/K/JB3/B/JJ/JB1-S/GF/ OK//FK-kk-1] <[3] kit>

ȟebandin حەباندِن *vt.* **(-ȟebîn-).** to love: **•Ȟemû xortê yêrê bûbûn maşoqê wê, lê wê t'u kes *nediȟeb-and*** (Ba) All the local youths were in love with her, but she *didn't love* anyone. {also: hebandin (JB3/IF); [hebandin] حـــبـــانـــديـــن (JJ)} {syn: jê ȟez kirin} < Ar ḥubb حـــــبّ = 'love' [Ba/F/K/JB3/IF/JJ/M/B] See also **evandin**. <ȟub>

ȟebs حـەبـس *f.* **(-a;-ê).** prison, jail [gaol]: **•Aqûb Sixir aza dike *ji hevsê*** (Ba3-3, #3) Jacob frees Sikhir *from prison* **•Heger şerdê wî nanîn, wan digire, dixe *hebsê*** (L) If they don't complete his [assigned] tasks, he arrests them, and throws them *into prison* **•Yekî din sûnd xwar ku hevalekî wî berî rojekê Benîşto *di hepsê de* dîtibû** (HYma, 29) Another one swore that a day ago a friend of his had seen B. *in jail*; **-ȟebs kirin** (SK)/**avêtin ȟebsê** = to imprison, throw in jail: **•'Usmanîyan zanî, hatin, hindek ji wan kuştin, hindek girtin, birine Mûsilê, *ȟebs kirin*** (SK 48:511) The Ottomans found out and came, they killed some of them, captured some of them, took them to Mosul and *imprisoned them*. {also: hebs (JB3/

IFb); heps (HYma); hevs (Ba3-3); ḧevs (Ba3-3); [habis] حـبـس (JJ); <ḧebs> حـبـس (HH)} {syn: girtîgeh; zindan} < Ar ḥabs حـبـس [L/K/B/HH/SK//JB3/IFb//JJ//HYma]

ḧec حـهـج *f.* **(-a;-ê).** pilgrimage to Mecca, hadj, *one of the five pillars of Islam*: **•Dotr̄a r̄oja, ko mêrik berê xwe da *ḧecê*** (Dz-anecdote #22) The day after the man left for *the hadj*, ...; **-çûne ḧacê** (K) to go on the hadj. {also: hac (A/IF); hec I (IF-2); ḧac (K); ḧecc (SK); [höǰǰ] حـجّ (JJ)} <Ar ḥajj حـجّ [cf. Heb ḥag חג = '(Jewish) holiday']--> T hac; Sor ḧec حـهـج [Dz//SK//A/IF//K//JJ] <ḧecî>

ḧecc حهجج (SK) = pilgrimage (to Mecca). See **ḧec**.

ḧecḧeck حـهجـحـهجـك (K/B/FS) = swallow *(bird)*. See **ḧacḧacik**.

ḧecḧeçoq حـهجـحـهچـۆق, m. (OK) = swallow *(bird)*. See **ḧacḧacik**.

ḧecî حـهـجـى *m.* **(-yê;).** one who has completed the pilgrimage to Mecca, hadji: **•Roja veger̄a *ḧeciyan* hatî bû** (Dz-anecdote #22) The day of the *hadjis' [=pilgrims']* return had arrived. {also: hacî (A/IF/GF-2); hecî (IF-2); ḧacî (K/F); [hadj حاج/hadji حـاجـى] (JJ); <ḧacî> حـاجـى (HH)} <Ar ḥājj حـاجّ --> T hacı; Sor ḧacî حـاجـى [Dz/B/SK/GF//F/K/JJ/HH//A] <ḧec>

ḧecran حـهجـران (Z-2) = separation; reason; insult. See **hecran**.

ḧeç' حـهـچ *m.* **(-ê;).** summit, peak, top *(of mountain)*: **•Çaxê mêriv jêla li *ḧeç'ê ç'îyê* dinihêr̄î, mêriv t'irê wê derê kela çê kirine** (Ba2:1, 203) When one looked at *the mountaintop*, one would think they had built a fortress there. {also: ḧeç'ik f. (B)} {syn: gaz û bêlan; gopk; kop I; k'umik; kumt} [Ba2//B]

ḧeç'ik حهچِك f. (B) = mountain peak. See **ḧeç'**.

ḧeç'î[yê] حهچی[يێ] (HR-I) = as for. See **herçî** [3].

ḧed حـهد *m.* **(-ê;).** 1) {syn: sînor; t'ixûb} border, limit, frontier, boundary: **•Çîrokên din jî hene. Li ser kesên ku *hedê* xwe nizanin** (K.Burkay. Aso, 65) There are other stories as well. About people who don't know their *limits*; **-ḧed û sed** (EP-7) obstacles and barriers (lit. Ar 'border and dam/ barricade'): **•Dinyaêda heye *ḧed û sed*** (EP-7) In the world there are *obstacles and barriers*; 2) {syn: destûr [2]; heq [1]; maf} (legal) right: ***•Ḧedê* bavê k'ê heye ...** (Z-1) Whose father has *the right to* [or dares to] ***•Ḧedê* min t'une ez ewê bikim** (Z-1) I don't have *the right to* do that ***•Hedê* wî çiye ko navê min kar tîne?** (IFb) What *right* does he have to [=How dare he] use my name? **•Kê *ḧedd hebû* ji qirşekî ḧetta pûşekî tiştekî bêjite wî?** (SK 36:323) Who *would have dared to* say anything [lit. 'from shavings to dry grass'] to him? {also: hed (JB3/IF); ḧedd (SK); [hed] حد (JJ)} < Ar ḥadd حدّ; Sor ḧed حـهد = 'limit, authority, right' [Z-1/K/JJ/B/OK//JB3/IFb//SK]

ḧedad حـهداد *m.* **(-ê; ḧedêd, vî ḧedadî).** blacksmith. {also: hedad (ZF3); ḧedadçî; [hedad] حـداد (JJ)} {syn: hesinger; nalbend; solbend} < Ar ḥaddād حدّاد [K/B/JJ//ZF3]

ḧedadçî حهدادچى = blacksmith. See **ḧedad**.

ḧedd حهدد (SK) = limit, authority, right. See **ḧed**.

ḧef•ik حـهفِك *f.* **(•[i]ka;•[i]kê).** 1) {syn: gewrî; qeper} throat, front of neck (Ak/Bw/Zx/IF/JJ): **•Kur̄ê wî bire ber selbê, şirît îna ku dê *ḧefika* wî têda înin** (M-Ak #677, 306) His son was taken to the gallows and a rope brought to put his *neck* in **•Sîkar vi *ḧefka* wî dikevît û r̄iha *ḧefkê* lê diqetînît** (X. Saliḧ. Hindek serhatiyên Kurdî, 89) The knife enters his *throat* and cuts his jugular vein; 2) pharynx (IFb/ZF3). {also: hefik (IFb/BF); ḧewik (SK); [afk(a) افك/havk هوك] (JJ)} Sor ewik ئـهوِك = 'throat' [Ak/Bw/Zx//IFb/BF//JJ//SK]

ḧeft حـهفت *num.* seven, 7: **•her *heft* jî** (Dz) all *seven* of them. {also: heft (A/IFb/OK-2); ḧevt (B); ḧewt (SK-2); [heft] هفت (JJ); <ḧeft> حفت (HH)} [Pok. septṃ 909.] 'seven': Skt saptá; O Ir *hafta (<haftṃ): Av hapta; Mid P haft (M3); P haft هفت; Sor ḧewt حـهوت/ḧeft حـهفت (Arbil [M])/'eft عـهفت (Arbil [M]); Za ḧewt; Hau ḧewt (M4) [A/JB3/IFb/JJ/GF/TF//K/HH/SK/JB1-A/OK//B] <hevdeh; ḧeftê II; ḧeftêk>

ḧefta حـهفـتـا *adj.* seventh, 7th. {also: haftyê (JB1-S); heftan (IF); **heftem**; heftî II (IF-2); ḧeftan (K-2); ḧeft'ê III (JB1-A); ḧevta (B); [hefti/haftē (Rh)] هـفـتـى (JJ)} Cf. P haftom هـفـتـم; Sor ḧewtem[în] حـهوتـهم[ين]; Za ḧewtin (Todd) [F/K//JB1-S//IF//JB1-A//B//JJ] <ḧeft>

ḧeftan حهفتان (K) = seventh. See **ḧefta**.

ḧefte حهفته (Rh) = week. See **ḧeftê I**.

ḧeft•ê I حـهفـتـێ *f.* **(•îya;•îyê:** *indefinite*: **ḧeftîyek).** week: **-heftiya borî** (WM 1:2, 14) last week. {also: hefte (A/JB3/IFb/TF/OK); ḧefte (Rh); ḧeftî; ḧevtê I m. (B); ḧewtî (SK); [heftê] هـفـتـه (JJ); <ḧeftî> حفتى (HH)} {syn: înî [2]} Cf. P hafte هفته --> T hafta; Sor ḧefte حـهفته; Za ḧefte *m.* (Todd) [K//A/JB3/IFb/JJ/TF/OK//B//HH//Rh//SK]

ḧeftê II حـهفـتـى *num.* seventy, 70. {also: heftê (A/IFb/TF/OK-2); heftî I (JB3/IFb-2); ḧevtê II (B); [hefti] هـفـتـى (JJ); <ḧeftê> حـفـتـى (HH)} Skt saptatí-; Av haptāiti-; P haftād هـفـتـاد; Sor ḧefta حـهفـتـا; Za ḧewtay (Todd); Hau ḧefta (M4) [K/HH/OK//A/IFb/TF//JB3/JJ//B] <heftêyem; ḧeft>

ḧeft'ê III حهفتى (JB1-A) = seventh. See **ḧefta**.

ḧeftêk حهفتێك *f.* **(-a;).** a seventh, 1/7. {also: <hevtêk> هەڤتێك (AR)} Sor ḧewt-yek حەوتيەك (Sulaimania & Kerkuk)/ḧeft-yêk حەفتيێك (Arbil) [Zeb//AR]

ḧeftî حهفتى = week. See **ḧeftê I**.

ḧeftriḧ حـهفـتـرِح *adj.* with seven lives *(of cats, etc.)*: **-kitka ḧeftriḧ** (Zeb/Bar) cat with 7 lives, i.e., resilient. {syn: heftcanî} < ḧeft = '7' + r̄iḧ/r̄uh = 'soul, spirit' [Zeb/Bar]

ḧeftûzk حهفتووزك *f.* **(-a;-ê).** sore or boil in the armpit. {also: ḧevtûzk (K/B)} [Qzl//K/B]

ḧeîkel حهئيكهل (F) = statue. See **heyk'el**.

ḧeîşta حهئيشتا (F) = eighth. See **ḧeyşta**.

ḧeîwan حهئيوان (F) = animal. See **ḧeywan**.

ḧej I حـهژ *f.* **(-a;).** motion, movement (in its various meanings) . {also: hej II (A); [hej] هژ (JJ)} [F/Dz//A/JJ] <bizav>

ḧej II حهژ: ḧej kirin (BX) = to love. See **ḧez**.

ḧejan حهژان (K) = to tremble. See **ḧejîn**.

ḧejandin حـهژانـدِن *vt.* **(-ḧejîn-).** 1) {syn: veweşandin} to rock *(vt.)*, shake, cause to sway: **•Serê wî *dihejîne*** (L) She *rocks* his head; 2) to brandish, wave *(a weapon)* in a menacing fashion (M): **•Min şivdara xwe bilind kir û ser wî da *ḧejand*** (Ba2:2, 206) I raised my staff and *waved* it at him **•Şûr bi ser mîr Zêydînva *diḧejîne*** (Z-2) He *brandished* his sword at Mîr Zêydîn. {also: hejandin (A/JB3/IFb/GF/TF/OK/FS); hijandin (M/SK); [hejandin] هـژانـديـن (JJ); <hezandin هـزانـدن (dihezîne) (دهـزيـنـه)/hejandin هـژانـدن (dihejîne) (دهـژيـنـه)> (HH)} Cf. Ar √ h-z-z هزّ = 'to shake' [L/K/B//A/JB3/IFb/JJ/HH/GF/TF/OK/FS//M/SK] <daweşandin; ḧejîn; kil II kirin; lorandin>

ḧejde حهژده (HH) = eighteen. See **ḧîjdeh**.

ḧejdeh حهژدهه (HH) = eighteen. See **ḧîjdeh**.

ḧejḧejîk حـهژحـهژيـك (Srk) = swallow *(bird)*. See **ḧacḧacik**.

ḧejik حهژك (Haz) = twigs. See **hejik**.

ḧejimar حـهژمـار (B) = number; issue *(of a journal)*. See **hejmar**.

ḧejîn حهژين *vi.* **(-ḧej-).** to shake, tremble, quiver *(vi.)*; to sway, rock *(vi.)*: **•Banê gewr çû hat *hejiha* ji giranîya teyra Sîmir̄** (HR 3:258) The roof *rocked* to and fro from the weight of the Simurgh; **-ji cî ḧejîn** (B)/**ji cîyê xwe ḧejîn** (K) to stir, budge, move from its place. {also: hejan (GF/FS); hejihan (HR); hejiyan (FS-2); hejîn (A/IFb/TF/AD); ḧejan (K-2); [hejiian] هـژيـان (JJ); <hezîn هـزيـن (dihezî) (دهـزى)/hejîn هـژيـن (dihejî) (دهـژى)> (HH)} {syn: kil II bûn; lerzîn; r̄e'ilîn; r̄icifîn; r̄ikr̄ikîn} [K/B//A/IFb/HH/TF/AD//JJ//HR//GF/FS] <ḧejandin>

ḧejkirî حهژكِرى = beloved. See **ḧezkirî.**

ḧejmar حهژمار (B) = number; issue *(of a journal)*. See **hejmar**.

ḧekaêt حهكائێت (SK) = story. See **ḧekyat**.

ḧekayet حهكايهت (SK) = story. See **ḧekyat**.

ḧekete حهكهته (JB1-A/OK) = story. See **ḧekyat**.

ḧekîm/ḧek'îm [B-2] حـهكـيـم *m.* **(-ê;).** doctor, physician: **•Eger sa'etekê pêştir hung nexoşîya xo bi *ḧakîmêt* ḧaziq û xêrxaz derman neken, mikrobê cehaletê û şefrayê sefahetê ... pîçek maye hingo bikujît** (SK 57:660) If you do not have skilled and well-meaning *physicians* treat your disease within the hour, then the microbe of ignorance and the bile of stupidity ... will kill you within a short while. {also: hekîm (IFb); [hekim] حـكـيـم (JJ); <ḧekîm> حـكـيـم (HH)} {syn: bijîşk; duxtor; nojdar} < Ar ḥakīm حكيم [Z-1/K/B/JJ/HH/SK/GF/OK//IFb]

ḧekyat حـهكـيـات *f.* **(-a;-ê).** story, tale: **•*Ḧik'yatêd* Cima'eta Kurdîê** (J) Tales of the Kurdish Community *(title of a book of Kurdish folktales compiled by Cindî)* **•*Ḧikyeta* me vira xilas dibe** (Ks) Our *tale* ends here. {also: hik'ayet; hik'yat; ḧekaêt (SK); ḧekayet (SK-2); ḧekete (JB1-A/OK); ḧik'îyat (B); ḧikyat (J); ḧik'yat (B); ḧikyet (Ks); [hikat] حكات (JJ); <ḧikayet> حكايت (HH)} {syn: çîr̄ok; mesel; qise} < Ar ḥikāyah حـكـايـة --> P ḥikāyat حـكـايـت; --> T hikâye; --> Arm hēk'eat' հէքեաթ; Hau ḧekayete *f.* = 'story' (M4) [Ks//F/K//B//J//JJ/HH//SK//JB1-A/OK]

ḧekyatçî حـهكـيـاتـچـى *m.* **().** storyteller. {also: ḧik'î[y]atçî (B)} {syn: biwêj I[2]; çîr̄okbêj; ḧik'î[y]atdar (B)} [F/K//B]

ḧel حـهل *m.* **().** 1) {syn: çareserî} solution *(to a problem)*: **-ḧel kirin** (Ba3): a) to solve *(mystery)*, interpret *(dream)* {syn: şîrove kirin}: **•Hûn evê xewna min *ḧel bikin*, ji minr̄a bêjin** (Ba3) *Interpret* this dream of mine, tell me [what it means]; b) to do (one's homework): **•Me wacib gelek hebûn, me wacibêt xo hemî *ħel nekirin*** (M-Am #716) We had a lot of homework and we *haven't done* all our homework; 2) interpretation *(of a dream)* (Ba3). {also: [hel] حل (JJ)} <Ar ḥall حل (√ḥ-l-l) = 'solution' [Ba3/K//JJ] <çareser>

ħelal حه‌لال *adj.* 1) {≠ħeram} permitted, allowed (according to Islam), lawful, legitimate, right: **•Mamê Rezgo çend tiştêt ji lawê namerd standibon hemî dane wî [=mamê kal] û ji-nik xoȓa jî xencerek xelat da mamê kal, got ê, "Here, bi xêr biçî, to li-ser çawêt me hatî. *Te ħelal bin* ew tiştane, bo te laîq in, te pîroz bin** (SK 37:333) Mam Razgo gave him [=the old man] all the things which had been taken from the cowardly youth and added a dagger as a present from himself, saying, "Go, farewell, and welcome. *It is right for you* to take these things, and they befit you, may they be fortunate for you" **•*We ħelal be* berx û karo** (Ba) May your lambs and kids *be blessed* [=they are legitimately yours]; **-ħelal kirin** (L): a) to ask forgiveness before departing or dying; "Mutually to ... forgive all that has been ... unjustly taken or done (usually performed on death beds, before battles, or long separations)" [RTI, p. 471]; "to forgive each other any outstanding obligations (before a long separation, upon concluding an agreement)" [RC, p. 163]; b) to slaughter ritually (SK): **•Herin, ȓonaîyekê bibene helê, da bihêm, çê-kem, ser-o-ber kem. Min bi zor *ħelal kir*** (SK 30:272) Go and take a light into the stall so that I can come and prepare it. I had difficulty *slaughtering it*; 2) pure, clean; 3) honest, sincere: **•Ew [=Qanatê Nadir] merivekî *ħelal* e, em pê amin dibin, bira wî bînin** (Cindî. Hewarî, 299) He [Q.N.] is an *honest* person, we trust him [or, feel safe with him], let them bring him. {also: helal (IF); [helal] حلال (JJ); <ħelal> حلال (HH)} < Ar ḥalāl حلال --> T helâl {ħelalî} [K/B/JJ/HH/SK//IF]

ħelalî حه‌لالی *f.* **(-ya;).** being permitted or licit *(religious; according to Islam)*. {also: [ḥalālí حلالی/ḥalāltia حلالتی] (JJ)} [B/JJ] <ħelal>

ħelan حه‌لان *m.* **(-ê;).** boulder; large, flat rock. {also: helan (IFb); <ħelan> حه‌لان (Hej)} [Zeb/Hej/FS//IFb] <kevir; tat>

ħelandin حه‌لاندِن *vt.* **(-ħelîn-).** to melt, smelt, dissolve: **•Te cemeda ser dilê xwe *hiland*** (Qzl) You *melted* the ice in your heart. {also: hilandin (Qzl); [helandin] حلاندين (JJ)} {syn: bihoştin} [K/B/JJ/(GF)//IFb/TF/RZ//Qzl] <ħelîn>

ħelatin حه‌لاتِن (-ħelê-) (SK) = to flee. See **hilhatin** [2].

ħelaw حه‌لاو f. (K/GF/JJ/HH) = halvah. See **helva**.

ħelbet حه‌لبه‌ت (B) = of course; absolutely. See **helbet**.

ħelhan حه‌لهان (M-Zx/Bw) = to melt; to thaw. See **ħelîn**.

-ħelî حه‌لی (GF) = step-, pseudo-. See **-ħilî I**.

ħelîl حه‌لیل *f.* **(;-ê).** confection made of boiled grape juice and flour, which is dried, cut into chunks and eaten [T kesme]. {also: helîr (IFb); ħerîl (FS-2); <ħerîr حریر/ħelîl حلیل> (HH)} [Krb/Mdt/HH/FS//IFb] <bastîq; dims>

ħelîn حه‌لین *vi.* **(-ħel-).** 1) to melt *(vi., also fig.)*: **•Wexta Memê dihat dîwana mîr ... [Zînê] t'imê Memê didît û bi ħizkirinê *diħelîya*** (Z-1) When Mem would come to the prince's court ... [Zin] would always see Mem and *would be melting* with love **•Çiqas Memê zîndanêda *diħelîya* usa jî Zîna delal diha ze'f bona Memê xwe *diħelîya* û dip'eȓitî** (Z-1) ... The more Mem rotted [lit. '*melted*'] in prison, the more Zin *melted* and pined for him; 2) to thaw, melt (of snow): **•Yêrê wî gundî aran bû, zivistana wî gundî qe t'unebû, her carna berf dik'et ew jî zû *diħeliya*** (JB2-Şamilov) That village was situated in a warm plain, it had no winter at all, [and] every time snow fell it quickly *melted*; 3) to dissolve (also fig.). {also: heliyan (JB3/IFb); helîn (IFb-2); ħelhan (M-Zx/Bw); ħelyan (M); [heliian] حليان (JJ); <ħelan حلان (diħele) (دحله)> (HH)} <Ar ḥalla حل √ḥ-l-l = 'to dissolve, fade' [Z-1/K/GF//JB3/IFb/JJ/B//M//M-Zx/Bw//HH] <bihoştin; ħelandin>

ħelû حه‌لو (SK) = smooth. See **hilû I**.

ħelwe حه‌لوه f. (B) = halvah. See **helva**.

ħelyan حه‌لیان (M) = to melt; to thaw. See **ħelîn**.

ħemal حه‌مال *m.* **(-ê;).** porter, carrier: **•Ez jî dixwezim xweȓa heȓim, bivime *ħembal*, xweȓa bixevitim** (HCK-5, #41, 224) I want to go become *a porter*, to work for myself **•Mela Me'som hat, lixaw dît, got, 'Sindoqekî çê-ke, da-ne têda, bide pişta *ħemmalekî*, digel min were, biçîn e Wanê lalî Teħsîn Paşaê walî'** (SK 33:298) Mullah Ma'sum came and saw the bridle and said, "Make a box, put it in it, put it on *a porter*'s back and come with me to Van, to the Governor, Tahsin

Pasha". {also: hambal (Tsab-2); hemal (IFb/Tsab-2); hembal (Tsab-2); himal (ZZ-10); ĥambal (HCK-4); ĥembel (B); ĥemmal (SK); [hemal] حمال (JJ); <ĥemmal> حمّال (HH)} {syn: bargir} {ĥemalî} < Ar ḥammāl حمّال; Sor ĥemał حەماڵ [HCK/K/JB1-A&S/Tsab/JJ//SK/HH//B] <k'olber>

ĥemalî حەمالی *f.* **(;-yê).** profession of porter or carrier; lugging: **-ĥembel[t]î kirin** (B) to work as a porter: **•Ezê heřime şeherê Rewanê, xweřa heřim *ĥembalyê bikim*** (HCK-5, #41, 224) I will go to the city of Erevan, go *work as a porter*. {also: hemalî (IFb); himalî (ZZ-10); ĥembalî (HCK); ĥembelî (B); ĥembeltî (B-2); [hemali] حمالی (JJ); <ĥemmalî> حەمّالی (HH)} [HCK/JJ//HH//IFb//B] <ĥemal>

ĥemam حەمام *f.* **(-a;-ê).** bath(house): **•Rojekê Ehmed Çelebî çû *hemamê*. Ji *hemamê* derket, zêrek da hemamçî** (Rnh 2:17, 307) One day Ahmed Chelebi went to *the bathhouse*. [When] he came out of *the bathhouse*, he gave the bathhouse owner a gold piece. {also: hemam (JB3/IFb/OK-2); ĥamam (JB1-S); ĥimam (HR); [hemam] حمام (JJ); <ĥemam> حمام (HH)} {syn: germav [2]} < Ar ḥammām حمّام <√ḥ-m-m حمّ = 'to be hot' [K/B/JJ/HH/JB1-A/OK//JB3/IFb//JB1-S//HR] <ĥemamîş; şûştin>

ĥemamçî حەمامچی *m.* **().** 1) bathhouse owner, keeper of a bathhouse: **•*Ĥemamçî* deriyê hemama xwe girt, çû mala xwe. Jina wî got-ê, tu çire hatî ji hemama xwe? Got, tucar min wek îro kar ne kiriye; yek hatiye zêrek daye min** (Rnh 2:17, 307) *The bathhouse owner* closed the door of his bathhouse, and went home. His wife asked him, "Why have you come from your bathhouse?" He said, "I've never made a profit like today; someone came and gave me a gold piece!"; 2) bathhouse attendant (F/K/B/HH). {also: hemamçî (OK); [hemamdji] حمامجی (JJ); <ĥemamçî> حمامچی (HH)} <ĥemam + -çî = T suffix denoting profession [Rnh/F/K/B/HH//OK//JJ] <delak; ĥemam; serşo>

ĥemamîş حەمامیش**: -ĥemamîş bûn** (K/B) to bathe *(vi.)*, take a bath; **-ĥemamîş kirin** (K/B) to bathe (vt.), give s.o. a bath: **•Da pey bire ĥimam *ĥimamîş kir*** (HR 3:168) He followed him, took him to the bathhouse, *bathed* him **•Tê mi bibî ĥemamê, *ĥemamîş bikî*** (Z-4) You will take me to the bathhouse [and] *bathe* me. {also: hemamiş (L); ĥimamîş (HR)} <ĥemam + -miş T verbal suffix [Z-4/K/B//L//HR] <ĥemam>

ĥemandin حەماندِن *vt.* **(-ĥemîn-/-ĥemên-** [HR]**).** to protect or shield s.o. from stg.: **•Paşaêm ezê di xebera ştexilim, lê belê mêşê min *biĥemêne*! ... dirajê [=dirahêjê] dismala xwe diderexê û mêşê k'eçel *diĥemênê*** (HR 3:226) My pasha, I will say 2 words, but *shield* me from the fly! ... He reaches for his handkerchief, takes it out and *shields* the bald one from the fly. {also: hemandin (K/IFb/FJ); himandin (CS); <ĥemandin حماندن (diĥemîne) (دحمینه)> (HH)} {syn: p'arastin} < Ar √ḥ-m-y حمی = 'to defend, protect, guard against' [HR/GF/HH//K/IFb/FJ//CS] <qorix>

ĥembalî حەمبالی (HCK) = profession of porter. See **ĥemalî**.

ĥembel حەمبەل (B) = porter. See **ĥemal**.

ĥembelî حەمبەلی (B) = profession of porter. See **ĥemalî**.

ĥembeltî حەمبەلتی (B) = profession of porter. See **ĥemalî**.

ĥembêz حەمبێز = embrace. See **ĥemêz**.

ĥemêz حەمێز *f.* **(-a;-ê).** embrace, hug: **•Wî zařo *da ber himbêza xwe*** (FS) He *embraced* the child; **-ĥemêz kirin** (K/B)/**himbêz kirin** (GF) to hug, embrace *(vt.)*: **•Bênams dibeze cem bavê, wî *ĥemêz dike* û destê wî paç' dike** (Ba #35, 319) B. runs to his father, *embraces* him and kisses his hand; **-hev ĥemêz kirin** (B) to hug *(vi.)*, embrace each other. {also: hembêz (IFb-2/ZF/FS-2); hemêz (KS/IFb); himbêz (GF/FS); himêz (GF-2); ĥembêz; [hemiz] همیز (JJ); <himbêz> همبیز (HH)} {syn: p'aşil [2]} Sor amêz ئامێز/ambaz ئامباز [Z-1/K/B//JJ//KS/IFb//ZF//HH/GF/FS]

ĥemilandin حەمِلاندِن *vt.* **(-ĥemilîn-).** 1) to allow s.o. to mount *(a horse)*: **•Merivê xerîb wekî heře nava hespê wî, hesp *naĥemlînin*** (HCK-3, #16, 176) If a strange man goes in among his horses, the horses *won't let* him *ride* them **•Mîrze Me'mûd lêda hat. Hespê wî meriv *nediĥemilandin* pêştirî p'adşê ... Hespê hindik mabû avayî ser xweda bavîta** (HCK-1, 75) Mirza M. came. His horses *didn't let* anyone except the king *ride* them ... The horse almost turned the building upside down; 2) to allow to step on or enter: **•Ay 'ardê Xudê Şahsenamê *naĥemilîne*** (JB1-S, #263, 180) O land of God, which *doesn't allow* Sh. *to tread* on it.< Ar √ḥ-m-l حمل = 'to carry, bear' [HCK/JB1-S]

ḧemis حەمِس *adj.* 1) black *(of dogs)* (Rwn/K); 2) with white face and black body *(of goats)* (Frq): **•bizina *ḧemis*** (Frq) nanny goat *with white face and black body*. {also: hemis (FS/ZF3)} [Rwn/K/Frq] <qer II; reş>

ḧemî حەمی (OK/HH) = all. See **ḧemû**.

ḧemle حەملە *adj.* pregnant *(only of human females)*, expecting, in the family way, with child: **•Hespa teyê avis derk'eve, jina teyê *ḧemle* derk'eve** (Z-922) Your mare will become pregnant [avis], and your wife will become *with child* [ḧemle] **•Qîz *ḧemle* derk'et** (EP-7) The girl became *pregnant*. {also: [hamilé] حاملە (JJ)} {syn: avis; bihemil (L); bi ḧal (Bw); duhala; giran [3]} <Ar ḥāmil حامل = 'pregnant' < √ḥ-m-l حمل = 'to carry' [EP-7/K/B//JJ]

ḧemmal حەممال (SK/HH) = porter. See **ḧemal**.

ḧemû حەموو *pr. mod.* all; every [generally precedes the word it modifies]: ***•Ḧemû* gurê wan dera** (Ba) *All* the wolves of those parts ***•Ḧemû* xortê yêrê bûbûn maşoqê wê** (Ba) *All* the local youths fell in love with her **•Ser Dûmanlûê t'u mêşe t'unebûn, vira dar jî hêşîn nedibûn, lê wexta bahar dihat, ew ji xewa giran ḧişyar dibû û bi *ḧemû* r̄engava dixemilî** (Ba2:1, 202) On [Mount] Dumanlu there were no forests, trees did not even grow here, but when springtime came, it awoke from a great sleep and became colorfully [lit. 'with *all* colors'] adorned **•Tu çima Ûsib ji *ḧemû* kur̄a ze'ftir ḧizdikî?** (Ba) Why do you love Joseph more than *all* [the other] sons? {also: hemî (A/JB3/IFb/JB1-A&S/SK/OK-2); hemû (IFb-2/JB1-S-2/GF/OK); ḧemî (OK-2); ḧemûşk (B-2); [hemou] همو (JJ); <ḧemî حمی/hemî همی> (HH)} {syn: gişk; her; t'emam} [Pok. s$_e$mo- 903.] 'someone, anyone': Skt sama- = 'any, every'; O P & Av hama- = 'all, whole'; Pahl hamāk & Pāzand hamā; early Mid P hamak/late Mid P hamag (<*hama-ka- Ras, p.133); P hame همه (Hübsch #1103); Sor hemû هەموو; Za heme (Mal) [Ba/K/B//A/JB3/IFb/HH/JB1-A&S/SK//JJ/GF/OK]

ḧemûşk حەمووشك (B) = all. See **ḧemû**.

ḧena حەنا = henna. See **ḧene**.

ḧenar حەنار (F) = pomegranate. See **hinar**.

ḧen•e حەنە *f.* **(;•ê).** henna, bot. *Lawsonia inermis*: **-ḧene kirin** (B) to daub with henna. {also: hene I (OK); hine II (F/TF); hune (IFb); ḧena; ḧina; ḧine (K); xena (FS); xene (OK-2); xenha (Bw); [hené حنە/khené خنە] (JJ); <ḧene> حنە (HH)} <Ar ḥinnā' حنّاء; T kına; Sor xene خەنە [B/JJ/HH//OK//F/TF//IFb//K//FS//Bw]

ḧenek حەنەك *f.* **(-a;-ê).** joke; humor: **•Birê şivan, min *ḧenekê xwe kir*, xwest te bicêr̄bînim** (Dz) Brother shepherd, I *was joking*, I wanted to test you **•Ew tiştekî *ḧenek* nîne** (B) This is no *laughing matter* **•Wê rojê, li mal ma, ewî û dergistîya xwe *kêf û heneka xwe kirin*** (L) On that day he stayed home [and] he and his fiancée *had fun and fooled around* **•Ya hakimê min, ev *ne îşê henekê* ye, ev îşekî giran e** (L-2, 24) O my king, this is *no joke*, this is a serious matter. {also: henek (A/JB3/IF); [henek] هنك (JJ); <ḧenek> حنك (HH)} {syn: meselok; pêk'enok; qerf; tewz; tinaz; t'ir̄ane; yarî II} Cf. Arm hanak' հանաք [Krç/L/Dz/K/B/HH/FS//A/JB3/IF//JJ]

ḧenekbaz حەنەکباز (K) = comedian. See **henekvan**.

ḧenekçî حەنەکچی (K/B/GF/FS) = comedian. See **henekvan**.

ḧenekdar حەنەکدار (B) = comedian. See **henekvan**.

ḧenekok حەنەکۆك (K) = comedian. See **henekvan**.

ḧeniz حەنِز *adv.* just then, at that very moment: **•Xort fkirî, go, --Ez xwe ber̄dim, ezê bik'evim avê, bixenqim. *Ḧeniz*, teyr xort bir û baẍê dya wîda peya kir** (EH) The young man [being carried by a giant bird] thought to himself, "I'll let go, and fall into the water and drown." *Just then*, the bird brought the boy to his mother's garden and let him off. {also: heniz (K[s])} Cf. P hanūz هنوز = '(not) yet'--> T henüz [EH//K(s)]

ḧeq حەق (JJ/HH/FS) = right; truth; law. See **heq**.

ḧer حەر (B) = every; always. See **her**.

ḧerac I حەراج (F) = tax; expense. See **xerac**.

ḧerac II حەراج (GF/HH/Hej) = auction. See **herac**.

ḧeram حەرام *adj.* forbidden, prohibited *(religious, according to Islam)*. {also: heram (IF); [ahhram] حرام (JJ)} {syn: qedexe; ≠ḧelal} < Ar ḥarām حرام {ḧeramî} [K/B//IF//JJ]

ḧeramî حەرامی *f.* **(-ya;-yê).** (religious) prohibition. {also: heramî (Wkt)} [K/B//Wkt]

ḧeramxane حەرامخانە (B) = harem. See **herem**.

ḧerebaşî حەرەباشی *m.* **(-yê;).** brigand, bandit: **•Ew ç'ya ç'yaê *ḧerebaşyane* – çil yek ḧev bûn** (HCK-3, #2, 23) This mountain belongs to the *brigands* – there were 41 of them. {syn: k'eleş II; nijdevan; r̄êbir̄} < ḧeram + T başı ? [HCK/B]

ḧerçê حەرچێ (B) = each; as for. See **herçî**.

ḧerçî حەرچی (B) = each; as for. See **herçî**.

ḧerd[u] [و]حەرد (B) = both. See **herdu**.

ḧerem حەرەم (SK) = harem. See **herem.**

ḧeřimîn حەڕمین [K/B]/**ḧerimîn** حەرمیك [OK/M] *vi.* **(-ḧeřim-** [K/B]/**-ḧerim-** [OK/M]**).** 1) to become sullied, dirty *(of hands, clothing)* (B); to be defiled, become ritually impure; 2) {syn: fesidîn (Bw)} to be ruined, go bad, spoil *(vi.)*, be spoiled *(of food, water)* (B/Srk); 3) ?to be forbidden (OK). {also: herimîn (IFb/OK-2); [heremin] حرمين (JJ)} <Ar √ḥ-r-m حرم = 'to be ritually forbidden or unclean' [Srk/K/B/OK/M//JJ//IFb] <ḧeram; řizîn>

ḧeřişandin حەڕشاندِن *vt.* **(-ḧeřişîn-).** to scratch: **•Sîrikê serê min qîza p'adşê ç'e'v pê k'evin, wê serê min *bihe'řişînin*** (HCK-3, #16, 180) If the princess [lit. 'king's daughter'] notices the dandruff on my head, they *will scratch* my head. {also: arêşandin (K-2); heřişandin II (K-2)/he'řişandin (HCK); ḧeřiştin (-ḧeřêş-) (K-2)} <Ar √ḥ-r-š حرش = 'to scratch' [K/B//HCK]

ḧeřişîn حەڕشین *vi.* **(-heřiş-).** to be scratched. <Ar √ḥ-r-š حرش = 'to scratch' [K/B]

ḧeřiştin حەڕشتِن (-ḧeřêş-) (K) = to scratch. See **ḧeřişandin**.

ḧeřî حەڕی *f.* **(-ya;-yê).** mud, mire; clay: **•Baran hat û 'erd bû *ḧeřî*** (FS) The rain came and the earth turned to *mud*; **-teqn û ḧeřî** (Zx) mud. {also: heřî III (IFb); [heri هری/kheri خری] (JJ); <ḧerî> حری (HH)} {syn: quř; řiṯam; t'eqin} M. Schwartz: cf. O Ir √xard = ' to make feces, refuse, filth, garbage'; Cf. P xar[r]a خره = 'mud sticking to the bottom of a tank or cistern'; Luri xarra/hara; Sor heř هەڕ = 'clay, mud' (Kurdoev) & Sanandaji heřig هەڕگ = 'mud' (Wahby & Edmonds); Za ḧerr *f.* = 'soil, dirt, earth' (Todd) & [hařa] = 'dust, mud; earth'; Hau heře *f.* (M4); See: Vahman & Asatrian. "Gleanings from Zāzā Vocabulary," in: *Iranica Varia: Papers in Honor of Professor Ehsan Yarshater, Acta Iranica,* 3ème série: Textes et mémoires, vol. 16 (Leiden : E.J. Brill, 1990) p. 272. [Ag/F/K/B/HH/JB1-S/FS//IFb//JJ] <qilêr; qiřêj>

ḧeřîl حەڕیل (FS) = confection of boiled grape juice. See **ḧelîl**.

ḧerkê حەرکێ (B) = if. See **eger I**.

ḧermet حەرمەت (Z-2) = woman; respect. See **hurmet.**

ḧero حەرۆ (B)/ḧeřo حەڕۆ (B) = every day. See **heřo**.

ḧeřřo حەڕڕۆ (B) = every day. See **heřo**.

ḧersê[k] [ك]حەرسێ (B) = all three. See **hersê**.

ḧert'im حەرتم (B/Ba2) = always. See **hert'im**.

ḧesab حەساب *m.* **(-ê; hesêb** [B]/**-î).** 1) count, calculation, reckoning; account; bill: **•Dîtin** [sic], **wekî *ḧesabê* tav û teyrê çolê û steyrkê 'ezmana *hene*, *ḧesabê* minara *t'une*** (EP-7) They saw that it was *possible to count* the beasts and birds of the wilderness and the stars in the sky, but it *wasn't possible to count* the minarets; 2) consideration, regard: **-ḧesabê** (IS) as, like, in the capacity of: **•Dar li pişta pîlê wî k'et. *Ḧesabê* rimekî defa sîngê wîřa avît** (IS-#386) The tree pierced the back of his shoulder. It came through his chest *like* a spear; **-ḧesab bûn** = to be considered, be counted, be regarded: **•Babê min û Xal Eḧmed qewî dost bûn, wekî biraêt daybabî bûn, malek *ḧisab bûn*** (SK 8:81) My father and Uncle Ahmad were great friends,they were like blood brothers, they *were counted as* one family **•*Hesab e* go hûn bi me re hatin heya welatê me** (L) *I consider you* to have come with us as far as our country; **-ḧesab kirin** = to consider, regard, deem: **•Çi serê wîřa şev derbaz bûbû, ewî *ḧesab dikir* xewn** (Z-1) What had happened to him during the night *he considered* a dream. {also: hesab (IFb/GF/OK-2); hesêb (IFb-2); ḧesav; ḧisab (SK/OK); ḧisêb (SK-2); [hisab] حساب (JJ); <ḧesab> حساب (HH)} < Ar ḥasāb حساب --> T hesap; Sor ḧisêb حِسێب = 'account' [K/B/HH//JJ/SK//IFb/GF/OK]

ḧesa-ḧes حەسا حەس (EP-4) = suspicion. See **ḧeseḧes**.

ḧesan حەسان (K/B) = whetstone. See **hesan II**.

ḧesand حەساند (K) = easy. See **asan**.

ḧesandin حەساندِن *vt.* **(-ḧesîn-).** 1) to cause s.o. to feel, give s.o. the feeling (that…); 2) to inform, let s.o. know (that…); to apprise s.o. of: **-pê ḧesandin** = do. {also: hesandin (IFb/OK); hisandin (TF); [hesandin] حساندين (JJ); <ḧesandin حساندن (diḧesîne) (دحسينه)> (HH)} [Rnh/IFb/OK//K/B/JJ/HH//TF] <ḧesîn>

ḧesav حەساڤ = [ac]count; consideration. See **ḧesab**.

ḧeseḧes حەسەحەس *f.* **(;-ê).** suspicion: **-k'etin [ser] ḧeseḧesa** (B) to suspect: **•Birê Xecê *ser ḧesa-ḧesa k'etin*, dilê Xecê k'etîye Sîabend** (EP-4, #7) Khej's brothers *suspected* that she was in love with Siyabend. {also: ḧesa-ḧes (EP-4)} [EP-4//B] <şik>

ḧesibandin حەسِباندِن *vt.* **(-ḧesibîn-).** to consider *stg. to be so*, think *that stg. is so*, mistake *stg./s.o. for* *stg./s.o.*: •**Di wê navberê da mêrikê koçer çîroka xwe û dirende ji yekî dikançî ra dibêje û texmîna xwe ko seyê mîr *hesibandiye* jêra bi ser va zêde dike** (JB2-O.Sebrî/Rnh 14[1943] 8-9) In the meantime, the nomadic man tells the story about himself and the wild animal to a shopkeeper, and adds his assumption that he *thought* it was the emir's hound •**Herçend mirov nezan e, xwe ewçend zana *dihesibîne*** (BX) The more foolish one is, the wiser one *thinks* one is. {also: hesibandin (JB2/Rnh/IFb/TF/OK-2); [hesibandin] حسباندين (JJ)} <Ar √ḥ-s-b حسب = 'to reckon, figure' [JB2/Rnh/IFb/TF//K(s)/JJ/OK]

ħesik حەسِك (B) = ladle. See **hesk**.

ħesin حەسِن (K/B) = iron. See **hesin**.

ħesinî حەسِنی (K) = made of iron. See **hesinî**.

ħesiyan حەسِيان (-ħesiy-) (JB1-A) = to feel. See **ħesîn**.

ħesîn حەسین *vi.* **(-ħes-).** 1) to feel, sense, perceive: **-pê ħesîn** (K/JB3) to find out about, learn of, be aware of {syn: hay jê hebûn; seh kirin}: •**Rojekê ew di nav kulîlk û giyanda *bi* xişexişekê *hesiya*** (Dz #22, 389) One day he *noticed* a rustling amid the flowers and grass •**Şivan û gavana pirsîn, *pê ħesîyan*, wekî Memê û Zînêva wefat bûne** (Z-1) They asked shepherds and cowherds, and *found out* that Mem and Zin were dead •**Zelîxe xatûn jî *pê dihese* derheqa hatina Ûsibda** (Ba) Zelikha also *learns of* Joseph's arrival; 2) {syn: bihîstin} to hear: •**Ȓojekê gur gilîê wana *diħese*** (J) One day a wolf *hears* their talk. {also: hesiyan (JB3/IFb/OK); hesîn (IFb-2/OK-2); ħesiyan (-ħesiy-) (JB1-A); [hesiian] حسيان (JJ); <ħesan حسان (diħese) (دحسه)> (HH)} < Ar aḥassa IV أحسّ = 'to feel' < √ḥ-s-s حسّ [Ba/K/B//JB3/IFb/OK//JJ/JB1-A//HH] <ħesandin>

ħesîr حەسیر *f.* **(-a;-ê).** mat: •**Me do liħêf û do *ħesîr* hene. Bila ew şewe liħêfek û *ħesîrek* bo her do derwêşan bin, liħêfek û *ħesîrek* jî bo min û te bin** (SK 23:213) We have two quilts and two *reed mats*. Tonight let one quilt and one *mat* be for the two dervishes, and one quilt and one *mat* be for you and me. {also: hesîl (A); hesîr (IFb/GF/TF); ħêsîl (Dh); [hasir حصير/hasīl (Rh)] (JJ); <ħeṣîr> حصير (HH)} {syn: qisîl} < Ar ḥaṣīr حصير; Sor ħesîr حەسیر [Dh//A//IFb/GF/TF//SK//JJ/HH]

ħesod حەسۆد (SK) = envious, jealous. See **ħevsûd**.

ħesodî حەسۆدی (SK) = envy, jealousy. See **ħevsûdî**.

ħesp حەسپ (B)/ħesp' (JB1-A) = horse. See **hesp**.

ħesret حەسرەت (B/HH) = sorrow. See **hesret**.

ħeste حەستە (B) = flint; steel; cigarette lighter. See **heste**.

ħestir حەستِر (Grc/Btm) = tears. See **hêstir I**.

ħestîf حەستیف (B) = baker's peel. See **hestîf**.

ħestîv حەستیڤ (B) = baker's peel. See **hestîf**.

ħestu حەستو (B) = bone. See **hestî**.

ħestû حەستوو (B) = bone. See **hestî**.

ħesûd حەسوود (F/K) = envious, jealous. See **ħevsûd**.

ħesûdî حەسوودی (K/F) = envy, jealousy. See **ħevsûdî**.

ħeş حەش: ħeş kirin (JB1-A) = to love. See **ħez**.

ħeşandin حەشاندِن (FS) = to stuff or prepare (meat). See **heşandin**.

ħeşifandin حەشِفاندِن (K[s]/HH) = to distort; to obliterate. See **heşifandin**.

*__ħeşikandin__ حەشِكاندِن *vt.* **(-ħeşikîn-).** to stuff, cram, stick, insert (into) : •... **Rabe, serê me jêke, di jina Bako Awan *biħeşikîne*** (HM) Get up, cut off my [lit. 'our'] head, *stuff it up* the wife of B.A. {syn: ç'ikandin; dewisandin} [HM]

ħeşîya حەشییا (F) = thing; goods. See **eşya**.

ħeşt حەشت (HH) = eight. See **ħeyşt**.

ħeştê حەشتێ (HH) = eighty. See **ħeyştê**.

ħeta حەتا *prep.* 1) until, till, up to, as far as: •**Em çûne *heta* gund** (BX) We went *as far as* the village •***Heta* li mirinê, çav li kirinê** (BX) *Until* death, think of action [lit. 'eyes on doing'] *[prv.]* •***Heyanî* nîv saetê îşê wan heye** (L) They have *up to (=no more than)* a half hour's work •***Heyanî* vê rojê** (BX) *Until* this day; **-heta dawiyê** (BX) et cetera [lit. 'until the end']; 2) *[conj.]* until [+ **ko** + *neg. subj.*]: •**Ez te 'afw nakem, *ħeta* tu pişta min *ne*vemalî (*ne*perxînî)** (Bw) I won't forgive you, *until* you rub my back •***Ħeta ku* em pê *ne*ħesin, gelo ew çi dûye** (Ba2:2, 205) *Until* we find out what the smoke is •***Heta ku* wî li filan kesî *ne*şidand, parên wî nedanê** (FS) *Until* he pressed /squeezed so-and-so, he wouldn't give him his money; 3) as soon as, when: •***Heyanî* hakim ji xew rabû** (L) *As soon as* the king awoke; 4) as long as, so long as: •***Ħeta* Zînê mala tedaye, ew namûsa teye** (EP-7) *As long as* Z. is in your house, she is your honor; 5) {syn: bila; bona [2]; da II; deqene; wekî [2]} [+ **ko** + *subj.*] in order to, so that: •**Wî mirovî xweş p'if dikir bilûrê û *ħeta ko* wextê xwe *bi*borîne li bilûra xwe dida** (Dz-anec #22) That man [a shepherd] played the flute well, and *in order to* pass time he would play his flute. {also: heta (JB3/IF); hetanî; hetta (IS-2); heya; heyanî; ĥetanî (B-2); ĥetta (IS); ĥeya (B-2); ĥeyanî (B-2); **t'a IV**; [hata] حـتـى (JJ); <ĥetta حتّا/heyya حيّا> (HH)} < Ar ḥattá حتّى; Sor heta [ku] [كـو] هـهتـا [K/B//BX/JB3/IF//JJ//HH] See also **t'a IV**.

ĥeta-ĥetaîyê حەتاحەتائییێ (F) = forever. See **ĥetaĥetayî.**

ĥetaĥetayî حـەتـاحـەتـايـى *f.* **().** 1) eternity (K/JB3); 2) *[adj. & adv.]* everlasting, eternal(ly) (K/F/IF); forever: •**Em şer bikin *hetahetayî* ko me azadiya xwe girt** (IF) We will fight *forever* until we attain our liberation. {also: hetahetayî (JB3/IF); ĥeta-ĥetê (B/EP-7); [2] ĥeta-ĥetaîyê (F); ĥetanî ĥetê (B-2)} [B/EP-7//F/K/JB3/IF]

ĥeta-ĥetê حـەتـاحـەتـێ (B/EP-7) = eternity. See **ĥetaĥetayî.**

ĥetanî حەتانى (B) = until. See **ĥeta** & **t'a IV**.

ĥetanî ĥetê حەتانى حەتێ (B) = forever. See **ĥetaĥetayî**.

ĥetk حەتك (K/XF) = honor, decency. See **hetk**.

ĥetta حەتتا (IS) = until. See **ĥeta** & **t'a IV**.

ĥev I حەڤ (JB1-S) = each other. See **hev**.

ĥev II حـەڤ (FK-kk-1) = seed; counting word. See **ĥeb**.

ĥevraz حەڤراز, m. (B) = slope. See **hevraz**.

ĥevs حەڤس (Ba3-3) = prison. See **ĥebs**.

ĥevsar حەڤسار (B) = halter; reins. See **hevsar**.

ĥevsid هەڤسِد (B) = seven hundred. See **heftsed**.

ĥevsûd حـەڤـسـوود *m.* **().** 1) envious or jealous person; 2) slanderer; 3) *[adj.]* {syn: dexes; k'umřeş} envious, jealous; 4) slandersome, gossiping. {also: hesûd (IF); hevsû; hevsûd (B-2); ĥesod (SK); ĥesûd (F/K); [housoud] حـسـود (JJ)} <Ar ḥasūd حـسـود = 'jealous, envious'; Sor ĥesûd حـەسـوود = 'envious' {hesûdî; hevsûdî; ĥesodî; ĥesûdî; ĥevsûdî} [B//IF//SK//F/K//JJ] <'ewan; qumsî>

ĥevsûdî حـەڤـسـوودى *f.* **(-ya;-yê).** 1) {syn: ç'avnebarî; ç'avřeşî; dexesî; k'umřeşî} envy, jealousy: •***Hesedîyê* dilê wan girt** (M.Gundikî. Tavê ew dît) *Jealousy* took hold of their hearts; **-ĥevsûdî kirin** (B/XF): a) to envy, be jealous of: •**Dêmařîya Ûsib *hevsûdîya ji* Ûsib *kir*** (YZ-1) Joseph's stepmother *was jealous of* him; b) to badmouth, gossip about, slander (XF); 2) slander(ing). {also: hesedî (MG); hesûdî (IF); hevsûdî (B-2/YZ-1); ĥesodî (SK); ĥesûdî (K/F); [ahhsúdía] (JJ/G)} <Ar ḥasūd حـسـود = 'jealous, envious'; Sor ĥesûdî حـەسـوودى = 'envy' [YZ-1//B/XF//IF//SK//K/F//JJ/G//MG] <ĥevsûd>

ĥevt حەڤت (B) = seven. See **ĥeft**.

ĥevta حەڤتا (B) = seventh. See **ĥefta**.

ĥevtê I حەڤتێ, m. (B) = week. See **ĥeftê I**.

ĥevtê II حەڤتێ (B) = seventy. See **ĥeftê II**.

ĥevtsed حەڤتسەد (K) = seven hundred. See **heftsed**.

ĥevtûzk حـەڤـتـووزك (K/B) = sore in the armpit. See **ĥeftûzk**.

ĥewal حـەوال *m.* **().** 1) {syn: dest û dar; ĥal; kawdan; řewş} condition, state, situation (JJ/B): •**Go *hewalek* li mala wan diqewime** (L) If *something* [lit. '*a situation*'] happens at their house •**Îro *hewalek* Mhemmed Xan *heye*, loma ne hatîye bi me re** (L) Today *something is up with* M. Khan, since he hasn't come with us; 2) thing, occurrence, event: •**Go *hewalek* li mala wan *diqewime*** (L) If *something happens* at their house. {also: [havāl] حـوال (JJ)} < Ar aḥwāl أحـوال, pl. of ḥāl حـال = 'state, condition'; Sor hewał هـەواڵ = 'condition, events, news' [K/B//JJ] <ĥal>

ĥewandin حـەوانـدِن *vt.* **(-ĥewîn-).** 1) {syn: cî kirin; hêwirandin} to shelter, give refuge (to); to lodge, accommodate, put up, house; to receive *(guests)*: •**Tu îşev mêvana *biĥewîne*** (Z-4) Tonight you *take in* the guests; 2) to calm, soothe, pacify. {also: hewandin (A/IF/JB1-A); [hevandin] حـوانـديـن (JJ); <ĥewandin حـوانـدن (diĥewîne) (دحـوينـه)> (HH)} <Ar awá أوى = 'to seek refuge' & awwá II أوّى = 'to shelter'; Sor ĥewandinewe حـەوانـدِنـەوە = 'to lodge, give asylum to, help to prosper'. For the two meanings of this verb, cf. Ar سـكـن √S-K-N = 1) to dwell; 2) to become calm. [Z-4/K/B/JJ/HH/GF//A/IF/JB1-A] <ĥewîn>

ĥewas حـەواس *f.* **(-a;-ê).** 1) {syn: 'elaqe; meraq; pûte} desire *(for)*; inclination, predilection, partiality, passion *(for)*, enthusiasm; interest *(in)*, curiosity *(about)*: •**Gava Memê li hespê dinhêře, *ĥewasa* meřîa pêřa tê** (FK-eb-2) When/the way Mem looks at the horse arouses one's *desire* [perhaps to ride the horse or to own a horse]; 2) *mood, temper, humor (B); 3) *feeling, sensation (K); 4) *gladness, joy; gaiety, merriment (B). {also: hewas; hewes (IF); ĥewes; [heves] هـوس (JJ); <hewes> هـوس (HH)} < Ar hawas هـوس = 'foolishness, craze, frenzy, infatuation'--> P havas هوس = '(capricious) desire, whim, passing fancy'; --> T heves = 'strong desire, inclination; zeal, mania'; Sor hewes هەوەس = 'desire, liking' [K-dş/FK-eb-2/K/B//IF/JJ/HH] <'elaqe>

ḧewasdar حـــەواســــــدار (B) = amateur; interested; interesting. See **ḧewask'ar**.

ḧewasdarî حـــــەواســــــداری (K/B) = interest. See **ḧewask'arî**.

ḧewask'ar حەواسكار *m.* **(-ê;).** 1) amateur, s.o. with an inclination, predilection, passion (for), interest (in); s.o. with a hobby; 2) *[adj.]* {syn: eleqedar} interested, curious; 3) {syn: balk'êş} interesting (K-dş): **•Dastana "Mem û Zînê" dastana here *hewaskar* e** (K-dş) The story of Mem û Zîn is the most *interesting* story. {also: hewask'ar; heweskar (IF/GF); ḧewasdar (B-2); ḧewesk'ar} Cf. P havaskār هـوسـكـار--> T heveskâr = 'desirous, inclined; amateur, having a hobby'; Sor heweskar هـەوەسـكـار = 'amateur' {heweskarî; ḧewasdarî; ḧewask'arî} [K-dş/K/B//IF/GF] <ḧewas>

ḧewask'arî حەواسكاری *f.* **(-ya;-yê).** curiosity, interest: **•ḧewasdarî (*ḧewask'arî*) berbi têxnîkaê** (B) *interest* in technique **•T'emamîa cime'tê *bi ḧewask'arî* Meyanê dinihêře** (Ba3-3, #9) The entire group looks at Meyaneh *with interest.* {also: heweskarî (IF); ḧewasdarî (K/B)} [Ba3/K/B//IF] <ḧewask'ar>

ḧewc حەوج (B) = need. See **ḧewce**.

ḧewc•e حـــەوجـە *m.* **(•ê;).** need; necessity: **-ḧewcê *f-tî* bûn** (K/B) to need stg., be in need of stg.: **•Ez *ne ḧewcê* arîkarîya te*me*** (K) I *don't need* your help. {also: hewce (IFb); ḧewc (B); [haoŭdjé حـوجـه/ haoŭdjeï حوجهى] (JJ); <ḧewcehî> حوجهى (HH)} {syn: divêt [see at **vîn**]; pêdivî} <Ar ḥājah حـاجـة/ ḥawj حـــــوج = 'need' {ḥājah also = 'thing'}; Sor ḧewece حـــەوەجـە = 'need, necessity' [K/SK//B//IFb/GF] <divêt [see at **viyan**]; gerek; hacet; kêr I; lazim; muhtac; p'êwîst>

ḧewdel حـــــەودەل *f.* **(-a;-ê).** dish consisting of boiled grape syrup [**dims**], to which flour, egg, and water are added. {also: hewdel (A/IFb/GF/TF); <ḧewdel> حـــودل (HH)} {syn: pelor} [Krb/HH/FS//A/IFb/GF/TF] <dims>

ḧewes حەوەس = desire, interest. See **ḧewas**.

ḧewesk'ar حەوەسكار = amateur; interested; interesting. See **ḧewask'ar**.

ḧewês حەوێس *adj.* bald. {syn: k'eçel} [Bw/FS]

ḧewhan حـــەوهـان *vi.* **(-ḧewh-).** to stand still, be calm, be soothed, calm down *(of children)*: **•Biḧewhe!** (Bw) *Settle down!/Stand still*; **•Naḧewhît** (Bw) *He doesn't stand still.* {also: hewan II (TF); ḧewîn [2] (-ḧew-) (K/B); ḧewyan (-ḧewyê-) حـــەويـان (Bw-2/ Dh/Zeb); [heviian] حـــويـــان (JJ); <ḧewan حـــوان (diḧewe) (دحـــــــوه)> (HH)} {syn: řeḧet sekinîn; t'ebitîn} [Bw//Dh/Zeb/JJ//K/B//HH//TF] See also **ḧewîn**.

ḧewik حەوك (SK) = throat. See **ḧefik**.

ḧewî حـــــەوى *f.* **(-ya;).** ease, comfort, solace: **-ḧewî hatin** (AId) to be at one's ease, enjoy life, be comforted (*often used in the neg.*): **•Rîwîyek hat e serbanê oda ximî, serê xo di kulekêda şor kir, bêna mirîşkan li difna wî da. Êdî *ḧewîya* wî li *çu cîyan *nehat*** (SK 4:28) A fox came onto the roof of the dye-house and hung his head down through the skylight, when the smell of chickens assailed his nose. Thenceforth he *could not contain himself* at all **•Wextê ko nijda Cindî Aẍa bi wî ḧalê kirêt û perîşan geřyawe Cindî Aẍa nihayet 'aciz bû. *Ḧewîya* wî li cîyekî *nehat*** (SK 40:364) When Jindi Agha's raiding party returned in this sorry and distressed state Jindi Agha was extremely angry. *Nothing* would *console* him. {also: <ḧewî hatin> حـــەوى هـــاتـن (AId)} {syn: dilmînî; řeḧetî; t'eselî} [SK/AId]

ḧewîn حـــەويـــن *vi.* **(-ḧew-).** 1) {syn: hêwirîn} to seek shelter or refuge; to settle, take up (temporary) residence, stop for the night, dwell, lodge *(vi.)*; to be received *(of guests)*; 2) to calm down *(vi.)*, be soothed (K/B). See **ḧewhan**. {also: hewan I (A/IF); ḧewyan (-ḧewyê) (M); [heviian] حـــويـــان (JJ); <ḧewan حـــوان (diḧewe) (دحـــوه)> (HH)} <Ar awá أوى = 'to seek refuge' & awwá II أوّى = 'to shelter'; Sor ḧewanewe حـــەوانـــەوە = 'to lodge in comfort, prosper after adversity'. For the two meanings of this verb, cf. Ar سكن √S-K-N = 1) to dwell; 2) to become calm. [Z-4/K/B/JJ/HH/GF//A/IF/JB1-A] <ḧewandin> See also **ḧewhan**.

ḧewle حەولە (K) = halvah. See **helva**.

ḧewq حەوق (GF/HH) = ladder rung. See **hewq**.

ḧewş حـــــــەوش *f.* **(-a;-ê).** 1) yard, courtyard (K/JB1-[A&S]/JJ/JB3/IF/A); enclosed or fenced-in area (K): **•Vî dûvê mi bibe di *ḧewşa* xwe da biçîne** (HR-7, #11, 2) Take this tail of mine and plant it in your *yard* **•zikê *ḧewşê*** (K) inside *the courtyard*: **-ḧewş kirin** (K) to enclose, fence in; 2) porch, patio (Çnr); 3) open-air sheep and goat pen bounded on all sides by trees and the like (IF); 4) {syn: malbat} *family (A). {also: hewş (A/JB3/IFb/GF/TF/OK-2); ḧewşe (F); [haoŭch] حـــــوش (JJ); <ḧewş> حـــوش (HH)} < Ar ḥawš حـــوش; Sor ḧewşe حەوشە/ḧewşê حەوشێ [L/K/B/JJ/HH/JB1-A&S/SK/

OK//F//A/JB3/IFb/GF/TF]

ḧewşe حەوشە (F) = yard. See **ḧewş**.

ḧewt حەوت (SK) = seven. See **ḧeft**.

ḧewtî حەوتی (SK) = week. See **ḧeftê I**.

ḧewt-sed حـــەوت صـــەد (SK) = seven hundred. See **heftsed**.

ḧewyan حـــەويـــان (-ḧewyê-) = to calm down (Bw/Dh/Zeb); to dwell, lodge (M). See **ḧewhan** & **ḧewîn**.

ḧewz حـــەوز *m./f.(ZZ-7/ZF)* **(-ê/; /-ê).** pool; reservoir: **•Ev car qewraşa Axê rabû çû ser *hewzê* da av bibe malê** (ZZ-7, 222) This time the Agha's maidservant arose and went to *the reservoir* to bring water home. {also: hewz (A/IFb/ZF); [haouz] حـــوض (JJ)} < Ar ḥawḍ حـــوض --> T havuz; Sor ḧewz حـــەوز = 'tank, cistern' [EP-7/K/B/JJ//A/IFb/ZF]

ḧeya حەيا (B) = until. See **ḧeta** & **t'a IV**.

ḧeyam حـــەيـــام, f.[B] (K/B/JB1-A) = while, period. See **heyam**.

ḧeyanî حەيانی (B) = until. See **ḧeta** & **t'a IV**.

ḧeyf حـــەيف *f.* **(-a;-ê).** 1) {syn: 'evdîn; t'ol II} revenge, vengeance: **-ḧeyf hildan/standin/~a xwe vekirin/jê hilanîn** = to avenge, take revenge: **•Ezê te bikujim, *heyfa* bavê xwe *ji* te *hilînim*!** (L) I'll kill you, I'*ll take revenge on* you for my father's death; 2) {syn: gune II[2]} pity: **-ḧeyfa *fk-î* [li] *fk-î* hatin** = to feel pity for [lit. 'for the pity of [the one feeling pity] to come to [the one who is the object of that pity]'] **•*Ḧeyfa* wî min *naê*** (K) He *doesn't pity/feel sorry for* me **•*Ḧeyfa* min te û kiḧêla te *hat*** (Z-1) I *felt sorry for* you and your horse **•Mêrik *ḧeyfa* wî *li* me *hatye*** (EP-7) The man *felt sorry for* us. {also: heyf (JB3/IF); [heïf] حـــيـــف (JJ)} [L/JB3/IF//K/B/JJ] <mixabin>

ḧeyran حـــەيـــران *f.* **(-a;-ê).** 1) {syn: gorî; qurban} sacrifice, victim; 2) admirer, fan: **•Ez *heyrana* wan çavên reş bim** (IFb) I am *crazy about* [lit. 'may I be a sacrifice for'] those black eyes **•*Ḧeyrana* te *me*** (B): a) I *admire* you; b) I *beg* you: **•*Ḧeyrana* teme, tiştekî nebêje kur̄ê min** (B) *I beg you*, don't say anything to my son; 3) my dear *(form of address)*: **•*Ḧeyran*, ji boy xwedê be, nekin nemerdî, min navêne be'rê** (HCK-2, 182) *My dear man*, for God's sake, don't act dishonorably, don't throw me into the sea **•*Ḧeyran*, tu çi ji min dixwazî?** (B) *My dear boy*, what do you want from me? {also: heyran (IFb/Kmc/CS); <ḧeyran> حـــيـــران (HH)} < Ar ḥayrān حـــيـــران = 'confused, perplexed, at a loss'; Sor ḧeyran حـــەيـــران = 'captivated, enthralled' [HCK/K/B/GF/HH/JB1-S/Tsab//IFb/Kmc/CS]

ḧeyrî حـــەيری *adj.* 1) {syn: 'ecêbmayî; hicmetî; ḧêbetî; mendehoş; met'elmayî; şaşmayî} amazed, astonished, surprised: **-ḧeyrî man** = to be amazed, astonished at; **-şaş û ḧeyrî** (EP-7) do.: **•M. gelekî *şaş û ḧeyrî* ma** (EP-7) M. was *surprised and bewildered* (=didn't know what to do); 2) astray, lost. {also: heyirî (JB3)} [EP-7/K/JB3]

ḧeyrîn حـــەيـــرين *vi.* **(-ḧeyr-).** 1) {syn: 'ecêbmayî man; guhişîn; met'elmayî bûn} to be astonished, amazed (K/JB3); 2) to get lost, lose one's way (K); 3) [+ **bi ... re**] to be worried or concerned about (L/K): **•Ya rebbî, ez *bi* van birê xwe *re heyirîm*** (L) By God, I'*m worried about* these brothers of mine. {also: heyirîn (L/JB3/IF); [heïrin] حيرين (JJ)} <Ar ḥā'ir حائر = 'bewildered' <√ḥ-y-r حير = 'to be confused, helpless' [L/K/JJ//JB3/IF]

ḧeyşt حـــەيـــشـــت *num.* eight, 8. {also: heşt (A/JB3/IFb/JB1-A&S/SK/GF/TF/OK); heyşt (A-2); ḧeşt (SK-2); [hecht] هشت (JJ); <heşt هشت/ḧeşt حشت> (HH)} [Pok. oḱtō(u) 75.] 'eight': Skt aṣṭā́[u]; O Ir *aštā *(a dual form)*: M. Schwartz: Av (h)ašti/a = 'group of four fingers' + *dual ending* -ō (cf. Lat duō = 2, octō = 8), since 2 groups of 4 fingers = 8 (very early form of counting): Av aštā = 'eight' ; Mid P hašt (M3); P hašt هشت; Sor heşt هەشت; Za ḧeşt (Todd); Hau heşt (M4) [K/B//A/JB3/IFb/JJ/HH/SK/JB1-A&S/GF/TF] <heştem; heştêk; ḧeyştê; ḧîjdeh>

ḧeyşta حـــەيـــشـــتـــا *adj.* eighth, 8th: **•Heft kurên min hene, tu jî kurê *heyşta*** (ZZ-7, 148) I have 7 sons, and you are the *eighth* son. {also: heştan (IF); **heştem**; heşt'ê II (JB1-A); heştî II (IF-2); heştyê (JB1-S); heyşta (ZZ); ḧeîşta (F); ḧeyştan (K-2); [hechti/hashtē (Rh)] هـــشـــتـــی (JJ)} Cf. P haštom هشتم; Sor heştem[în] [هەشتەم[ین; Za ḧeştin (Todd) [K/B//ZZ//IF//JB1-A//JB1-S//F//JJ] <ḧeyşt>

ḧeyştan حەيشتان (K-2) = eighth. See **ḧeyşta**.

ḧeyştê حـەيشتـی *num.* eighty, 80. {also: heştê I (A/IFb/TF/OK); heştî I (JB3/GF/OK-2); heyştê (A-2); ḧeştê; [hechti] هـــشـــتـــی (JJ); <heştê هـــشـــتـــی/ḧeştê حشتی> (HH)} Skt aśītáy-; Av aštā[i]tīm *[acc.]*; Mid P haštād (M3); P haštād هـــشـــتـــاد; Sor heşta هەشتا; Za ḧeştay (Todd); Hau heşta (M4) [K/B//A/IFb/HH/TF/OK//JB3/JJ/GF] <heştêyem>

ḧeyştp'ê حەيشتپی (K) = octopus. See **heştpê**.

ḧeyştyek حەیشتیەك (K) = an eighth. See **heştêk**.

ḧeywan حـــەیـــوان *f./m.(F)* **(;-ê/ḧeywên** [B-2]**).** 1) animal: **-heywanên kedî** (JB3) tame, domestic animals; **-heywanên kovî** (JB3) wild animals: **•Me gelek *ḧeywanêt k'îvî* bi r̄êve dîtin, şibetî gurg û r̄îvî û wa tişta, em gelek jê tirsyayn** (M-Am #714) On the way we saw many *wild animals*, such as wolves and foxes and those things, and we were very afraid of them; 2) {syn: ga} cow, bovine: **-goştê ḧeywan** (Bw) beef. {also: heywan II (JB3/IFb/GF); ḧeîwan (F); [heĭvan] حیوان (JJ)} < Ar ḥayawān حیوان [K/JJ/B/Bw//F//JB3/IFb/GF] <canewar; dir̄ende; ga; ḧeywanet; r̄awir; sewal I; tabe; terawil>

ḧeywanet حەیوانەت *m.* **(-ê;).** animals; cattle, livestock (B): **•...û çiqa *ḧeywanetê* Xudê ti'ala di wî ç'iyayîda hene, ḧemûçik wê êne te** (HR 3:137) And however many of God's *animals* are on this mountain, they will all come to you. < Ar ḥayawānāt حـیـوانـات = 'animals' [Ba2/K/B] <dewar; gar̄an; ḧeywan; pez>

ḧez حەز *f.* **().** desire, wish; love; pleasure (JJ): **-jê ḧez kirin** = to love, like {syn: ḧebandin}: **•Tu çima Ûsib *ji* ḧemû kur̄a ze'ftir *ḧizdikî*?** (Ba) Why do you *love* Joseph more than all [the other] sons? **•*Hejî* [=hez ji] te *dikim*** (BX) I *love* you. {also: hez (A/JB3/IFb/OK-2); ḧej II (BX); ḧeş (JB1-A); ḧiz (B); [haz] حظ (JJ)} <Ar ḥaẓẓ حظ ='portion, luck'--> P ḥaẓẓ kardan حظ کردن; Sor ḧez حەز = 'wish, liking, love, desire' [F/K/OK//A/JB3/IFb//BX//B//JJ] <evîn; ḧub>

ḧezar حەزار (K/B/F) = thousand. See **hezar**.

ḧezing حـــەزنـــگ *f.* **(;-ê).** deep, sad sigh: **-ḧezing k'işandin** (B) to heave a sigh: **•Paşê hêdîka destê xwe danî ser milê Fêrîk, *ḧezing k'işand*, got...** (Ba2-#2, 210) Then slowly he put his hand on Ferik's shoulder, *heaved a sigh*, [and] said... {also: hêzing II (K)} {syn: axîn [2]; k'eser} [Ba2/B/FS//K]

Ḧezîran حـــەزیـــران *f.* **(-a;-ê).** June: **•[Yazde bi *Hezîranê*, serê havînê, berê xwe bide zivistanê]** (BG) The eleventh of *June* (Julian calendar - BG), the start of summer, look toward the winter *[proverbial expression]*. {also: Hezîran (A/IFb/GF/OK-2); Hizeyran (JB3); [kheziran] خـزیـران (JJ); <ḧezîran> حـزیـران (HH); [hezirane] (BG)} Syr Ḥazīrān ܚܙܝܪܢ --> Ar ḥazīrān حـــزیـــران; *corresponds to last part of* Cozerdan جۆزەردان or Cehzeran جەحزەران/Codirew جۆدِرەو/Baranbir̄an بارانبِران[/Bextebaran بەختەباران] (P xurdād خـــــرداد) [Gemini] & *1st part of* Germaciman گەرماجمان/Pûşper̄ پووشپەڕ (P tīr تیر) [Cancer] [K/B/HH/OK//A/IFb/GF//JB3//JJ]

ḧezîranî حەزیرانی *f.* **().** *a type of* pear *which ripens in June.* {also: hezîranî (IF); ḧizranî (Msr); <ḧezîranî> حـزیـرانـی (HH)} [Msr//HH//IF] <alîsork; hermê; încas [1]; karçîn>

ḧezkirî حـــەزکِـری *adj./m.&f.* **(-yê/-ya ;).** beloved: **•Ewê nedixast r̄ûyê kesekî bibîne, xêncî *ḧizkirîyê* xwe** (Ba) She didn't want to see the face of anyone except for her *beloved*. {also: ḧejkirî; ḧizkirî (B)} {syn: meḧbûb} [K//B]

ḧêbetî حێـبـەتـی *adj.* surprised, bewildered, perplexed, confused; amazed, astonished, shocked: **•Ew *ḧêbetî ma* û nizanî ka çi bêjit** (FS) He *was bewildered* and did not know what to say **•Xelk *mane ḧêbetî*** (X. Saliḧ. Hindek serhatiyên Kurdî, 42) People *were perplexed*; **-hêbetî bûn** (BF/Wkt)/**ḧêbetî bûn** (FS)/**heybetî bûn** (AId) to be surprised, bewildered, etc. {also: heybetî (AId); hêbetî (BF/Wkt)} {syn: 'ecêbmayî; hicmetî; ḧeyrî; mende-hoş; met'elmayî; şaşmayî} [X.Saliḧ/FS//BF/Wkt//AId]

ḧêc حێج (SK) = furious, mad. See **ḧêç'**.

ḧêç' حـــێـــچ *adj.* fierce, furious, frenzied; mad, raving; rowdy, boisterous, unrestrained, wild: **•Ez îro hinek *ḧêç'* bûme** (Frq) Today I have been a little *rowdy*; **-har û hêç** (GF) do. {also: hêc (TF); hêç I (GF); hêç' I (K); ḧêc (SK); <ḧêç> حیج (HH)} <Ar hā'ij هـائـج = 'agitated, excited' [Frq/HH//TF//GF//K//SK] <har>

ḧêkel حێکەل (AX) = statue. See **heyk'el**.

ḧêl حـــێـــل *f.* **(-a;).** 1) strength, force, might; 2) [*adj.*] strong, mighty: **•Wî kulmeka *ḧêl* li Zoroyî da** (FS) He gave Z. a *mighty* punch; 3) fast, quick, swift: **•Ew *ḧêl* çû** (FS) He went quickly. {also: hêl I (BK/ZF3/Wkt)} {syn: birî I; hêz; qedûm [2]; qewat; t'aqet; zexm I [2]; zor I} [BK/ZF3/Wkt//JB1-S/FS]

ḧêsir حێسِر (Erg) = tears. See **hêstir I**.

ḧêsîl حێسیل (Dh) = mat. See **ḧesîr**.

ḧêştir حـێـشـتِـر *m./f.* **(-ê/-a; /-ê).** camel: **•*Hêştir* radibin hev, hêstir û ker bin lingê wan de diçin** (L) When *camels* fight with one another, mules and donkeys perish under their feet *[prv.]* **•*Hêştira* yekmilik û *hêştira* dumilik heye** (A. Incekan. Compact Kurdish-Kurmanji 52) There is a one-humped *camel* and a two-humped *camel*. {also: hestir (K); hêstir III;

heştir (JB3-2/IFb-2); hêştir (JB3/IFb/GF/OK); [huchtur هشتر/ chutur شتر] (JJ); <ḧêştir> حيشتر (HH)} {syn: deve I} Cf. Skt úṣṭra- *m.* = 'buffalo, camel'; Av uštra- *m.*/uštrā *f.*; P šotor شتر; Sor ḧuştir حوشتِر/wuştir ووشتِر [HH/FS//JB3/IFb/GF/OK//K//JJ] <arwane; cencilok; dundil; heştirvan; ḧawid; lok' II; mencî; qent'er; torim; xiya bûn & kirin>

ḧêştirvan حێشتِرڤان (FS) = camelherd. See **heştirvan**.

ḧibrî حِبرى *f.* **(-ya;-yê).** silk kerchief, head scarf worn by girls, *which distinguishes them from married women (who wear a* ***k'itan****)*: **•Cotê hirbîyan pev ve ye** (Qzl) *Head scarves* are made in pairs **•*Ḧibrî* bi ser xo werkir ji kulîlkên hinarê /** (Dilawerê Zengî [Syrian Kurdish poet] Pêdarî, 1985) She covered her head with *a kerchief* of pomegranate blossoms. {also: 'eborî (Xrz); ebrî (GF); eprî (Nsb); evrî (GF-2/OK); 'evrî (Zeb); hibrî (Ceylanpınar); hirbî (Qzl-2); [abri] ابرى (JJ); <'ebûrî> عبورى (HH)} [Qzl/Elk//Xrz//HH// GF/JJ//Nsb//OK//Zeb] <hêratî; k'itan [2]; laç'ik; t'emezî; terḧî; xavik>

ḧicḧicok حِجحِجۆك (Haz) = swallow (bird). See **ḧacḧacik**.

ḧicûm حِجووم (B) = attack. See **ḧucûm.**

ḧicûmkirin حِجوومكِرِن (B) = attack. See **ḧucûmkirin.**

ḧiçḧar حِچحار *m.(Czr)/f.(OK)* **(-ê/;).** pepper; red pepper (IFb); allspice, Jamaica pepper, bot. *Pimenta dioica* (OK): **-ḧiçḧarê şîrîn** (Czr) sweet pepper; **-ḧiçḧarê tûj** (Czr) hot pepper. {also: hiçhar (JB3/IFb/OK); hişyar II (CB)} {syn: back; bîber; guncik; îsot} [Czr//JB3/IFb/OK//CB] <dermanê germ>

ḧiddet حِددەت *f.* **(-a;-ê).** vehemence, fury, passion. < Ar ḥiddah حدّة --> T hiddet [MC-1/SK] <tundî>

ḧifdeh حِفدەه (F) = seventeen. See **hevdeh**.

ḧik'îatçî حِكيئاتچى (B) = storyteller. See **ḧekyatçî.**

ḧik'îatdar حِكيئاتدار (B) = storyteller. See **ḧik'îyatdar.**

ḧik'îyat حِكييات (B) = story, tale. See **ḧekyat**.

ḧik'îyatçî حِكيياتچى (B) = storyteller. See **ḧekyatçî.**

ḧik'îyatdar حِكيياتدار *m.* **().** storyteller. {also: hikyatbêj (ZF3); **ḧekyatçî**; ḧik'îatdar (B-2); ḧik'yatdar (B-2)} {syn: biwêj I[2]; çîrokbêj; ḧekyatçî} [B//ZF3] <ḧekyat>

ḧikûmet حِكوومەت (OK) = government. See **ḧuk'umet**.

ḧikyat حِكيات (J)/ḧik'yat (B) = story, tale. See **ḧekyat.**

ḧik'yatdar حِكياتدار (B) = storyteller. See **ḧik'îyatdar.**

ḧikyet حِكيەت (Ks) = story, tale. See **ḧekyat**.

ḧilbet حِلبەت (EP-7) = of course; absolutely. See **helbet**.

ḧilî I حِلى *adj.* 1) born early *(of animals, who are fat and plump as a result, cf.* ***virnî*** *= born late)*: **•Berxên *ḧilî* berîya zivistanê çêdibin, zivistanê di koza de derbaz dikin, xurt û girs in** (Qzl) *Early-born* lambs are born before the winter, and spend the winter in the sheepfold--they are fat and plump; 2) sown or planted early *(fig.)*: **•Min *ḧilî* çand, lê virnî ket** (Qzl) I planted *early*, but [the crop] came up late, i.e., I married early, but my children didn't come until (much) later [Min zû jin anî, lê zarokên min dereng çêbûn]; 3) {also: -helî (GF-2); -hilî (TF); -ḧelî (GF)} {syn: ziř- زِر} *suffix* step-, foster-, pseudo-: **-kuřḧilî** (Frq) stepson; **-qîzḧilî** (Frq) stepdaughter. [Qzl/Frq//GF//TF] <nevisî; virnî; ziřdayîk>

ḧilî II حِلى (Bw) = smooth. See **hilû I**.

ḧilû I حِلو *f.* **().** plum, bot. genus *Prunus*. {also: alû II (K); hilû II (GF/TF); hilûtirşk f. (-a;-ê) (Msr); hulî (OK-2/AA); hulû I (GF-2); ḧulî III (OK); [alou] الو (JJ); <hillû> هلّو (HH)} {syn: hêrûg [1]; încas [2]} Cf. P ālū آلو ; Sor hełûje هەڵووژە/hełûçe هەڵووچە [Sinneh]; Hau hełû *m.* (M4) [Haz//K/JJ//GF/TF//IFb//Msr//HH//OK/AA] <alûçe; dembûl; şilor>

ḧilû II حِلو (F) = being on edge *(of teeth)*. See **alû I**.

ḧilû III حِلو (F/FS) = smooth. See **hilû I**.

ḧimam حِمام (HR) = bath. See **ḧemam**.

ḧimamîş حِماميش (HR) = bathing. See **ḧemamîş**.

ḧina حِنا = henna. See **ḧene**.

ḧinar حِنار (B) = pomegranate. See **hinar**.

ḧinarik حِنارِك (K) = cheek. See **hinarik**.

ḧinav حِناڤ (B) = internal organs. See **hinav**.

ḧine حِنە (K) = henna. See **ḧene**.

ḧirç حِرچ *f./m.(F)* **(-a/-ê; -ê/).** bear (animal), zool. *Ursida*: **-ḧirçê nêr** = male bear {syn: nêreḧirç}; **-ḧirça mê** = female bear. {also: hirç (A/JB3/IF/SK/JB1-A); [hirtch] هرچ (JJ); <hirç> هرچ (HH)} [Pok ṛ́kþo-s (*or* ṛ́k-s-os & ṛ́k-to-s?) 875.] 'bear': Skt ṛ́kṣa-; Av arəša-/Young Av arša-; Mid P xirs (M3); Oss ars; P xers خرس; Sor wirç ورچ/wurç وورچ; Za ḧeş *f.* (Todd); Hau heşşe *f.* (M4); cf. also Lat ursus; Gr arktos ἄρκτος *f.*; W Arm arč/E Arm arǰ արջ [F/K/B//A/JB3/IF/JJ/HH/SK/JB1-A]

ḧisab حِساب (SK/OK) = [ac]count; consideration. See **ḧesab**.

ḧisêb حِسێب (SK) = [ac]count; consideration. See **ḧesab**.

ḧiş حِش *m.* **(-ê;).** mind, "brains," thoughts, attention, (sense of) reason, intelligence; reason, consciousness: •***Hişê* wê çû** (L): a) Her *mind* wandered; b) She lost her *mind*, went crazy •***Hiş* lê çûbû** (Ba) *Her reason* left her •***Ḧişê* gur hate serî** (J) The wolf's *reason* came to his head (=he regained consciousness): **-dan ḧişê xwe** (K) to think, reflect: •**Ewê qîzê gelekî *da ḧişê xwe*, çika çawa bike** (EP-7) That girl *gave a lot of thought to* (or, *spent much time thinking about*) what she should do. {also: hiş (A/JB3); [hich] هش (JJ); <hiş> هش (HH)} {syn: aqil II} Cf. P hūš هوش = 'sense, intelligence, understanding'; Sor hoş هۆش = 'feeling, sense, sentiment, consciousness, awareness' [K/B//A/JB3/IF/JJ/HH]

ḧişîyar حِشييار (Z-922) = awake; aware. See **ḧişyar**.

ḧişk حِشك *adj.* 1) {syn: dêm I [2]; ziwa} dry, arid *(of inanimate things, e.g., trees, plants, earth; whereas **ziwa** [qv.] is dry of living things and clothing)* {≠teř}; lifeless, lacking in life-sustaining fluids (Mş): •**Dar *ḧişk dibe*** (Qzl) The tree *dries up* •**Giya *ḧişk dibe*** (Qzl) The grass *dries up*; 2) {syn: meḧkem; qalin [2]} tight, firm; hard: •**Şivan nêzîkî wî bû, girt avîte 'erdê, dest-p'ê wî *ḧişk* girêda** (Dz) The shepherd approached him, grabbed him and threw him to the ground, and bound his hands and feet *tightly* •**Lawê pîrê, Keçelok *hişk* bi nigê Teyrê Sêmir girt** (L) The son of the old woman, Kechelok [Bald Boy] *tightly* held the foot of the Simurgh Bird •**Malatê wî yê *hişk*** (JB1-A) his *movable* goods/property; 3) {syn: zîz I[3]} shrill *(sound)*: •**Bi dengekî *ḧişk* dileîînin** (HM) They shout in a *shrill* voice. {also: hişk (A/JB3/IFb/JB1-A&S/SK/GF/TF/OK); 'işk (GF-2/Mş); [hychk] هشك (JJ); <ḧişk حشك/hişk هشك> (HH)} [Pok. saus-/sus- 880. & sus-ko- 881.] 'dry, arid': Skt śúṣka-; O Ir *huška- (Ras, p.133): Av huška-; OP uška- (Kent); Mid P hušk; P xošk خشك = 'dry'; Sor wuşk ووشك; Za wişk ='dry, hard, dead (of plants)' (Todd); Hau wuşk (M4); also Lat sūdus = 'dry'; Rus sukhoĭ сухой = 'dry' {hişkayî; hişkî; hişketî; ḧişkayî; ḧişkî} [K/B/HH//A/JB3/IFb/JB1-A&S/JJ/SK/GF/TF/OK//Mş] <çik I>

ḧişkayî حِشكايى (K/B) = dryness; frost. See **ḧişkî**.

ḧişkî حِشكى *f.* **(-ya;-yê).** 1) dryness (K/A/JJ); drought (B): •***Hişkatîya* wê şalê bû egera hişkbûna gelek dar û bara** (FS) *The drought of* that year caused the drying up of many trees and bushes; 2) frost (B); 3) stability, durability; strength; hardness. {also: hişkatî (FS); hişkayî (TF); hişkî (IFb/GF/OK); hişketî (A); ḧiskayî (K/B-2); [hychki] هشكى (JJ)} [Ber/K/B//A//IFb/JJ/GF/OK//TF//FS] <ḧişk>

ḧişyar حِشيار *adj.* 1) awake: **-ḧişyar bûn** = to wake up, awake *(vi.)* {also: şiyar bûn}: •**Belê niha, bavê min *şiyar bûye*** (L) By now, my father *must have woken up* •**Ser Dûmanlûê t'u mêşe t'une-bûn, vira dar jî hêşîn nedibûn, lê wexta bahar dihat, ew ji xewa giran *ḧişyar dibû* û bi ḧemû řengava dixemilî** (Ba2:1, 202) On [Mount] Dumanlu there were no forests, trees did not even grow here, but when springtime came, it *awoke* from a great sleep and became colorfully adorned; **-ḧişyar kirin** (K) to wake s.o. up *(vt.)*: •**Gavan jî li nik wî rûnişt; *hişyar ne kir*** (Rnh 2:17, 307) The cowherd sat down beside him, [but] *didn't wake him up*; 2) aware; intelligent. {also: hişyar I (A/JB3/IFb/JB1-A&S); huşyar (L-2); ḧişîyar (Z-922); şiyar; şîyar (L); [hichiar] هشيار (JJ); <hişyar> هشيار (HH)} Cf. P hūšyār هوشيار; Sor hoşyar هۆشيار = 'conscious, alert' {ḧişyarî; ḧişyaretî} [L//K/B//A/JB3/IFb/JJ/HH/JB1-A&S/GF/TF/OK]

ḧişyaretî حِشيارەتى (B) = awakeness; awareness. See **ḧişyarî**.

ḧişyarî حِشيارى *f.* **(-ya;-yê).** 1) state of being awake, awakeness; 2) awareness. {also: hişyarî (IFb/GF/TF/FS); ḧişyaretî (B-2)} [K/B//IFb/GF/TF/FS] <ḧişyar>

ḧivde حِڤده (Z-3) = seventeen. See **hevdeh**.

ḧivdeh حِڤدەه (B) = seventeen. See **hevdeh**.

ḧiz حِز: -ḧiz kirin (B) = to love. See **ḧez**.

ḧizir حِزِر (Z-3/HH) = thought, idea. See **hizir**.

ḧizkirî حِزكِرى (B) = beloved. See **ḧezkirî**.

ḧizranî حِزرانى (Msr) = type of pear. See **ḧezîranî**.

ḧîç حيچ (GF) = type of sandwich. See **ḧoç**.

ḧîjde حيژده (B) = eighteen. See **ḧîjdeh**.

ḧîjdeh حيژدەه *num.* eighteen, 18. {also: hejde (SK); hejdeh (A/IFb); heştdeh (IFb-2); hêjde (GF); hîjdeh (K); ḧejde; ḧejdeh; ḧîjde (B-2); [hej-deh] هژده (JJ); <ḧejde[h]> حژده (HH)} Skt aṣṭādaśa; Av aštadasa = eighteenth; Mid P haštdah (M3); P heždah هژده; Sor hejde هەژدە; Za ḧeştês/desuḧeşt (Todd); Hau hejde (M4) [B/F/SC//SK//A/IFb/JJ//K//GF//HH] <hejdehem; ḧeyşt>

ḧîl•e حيله *f.* **(•a;•ê).** trick, ruse, stratagem: •[118] **Dibêjin carekê muroekî [=miroveki] Paweî hate laê Somaê û Biradost û Kuresinîyan, xo kiribû şêx ... her gundê diçûê, li pêş çawêt xelkî**

tizbîyêt xo li bin huçikê 'ebay li hindawê şerbikê aw-xarinewê digiwişî, aw bi suruk jê dihate xar, xelk hemî muteȟeyyir dibûn … [121] **'Elî Xan şêx gazî kire mala xo li qelata Çarîyê, gote wî, "Ȟez dikem awa ȟeyatê bideye min jî." Şêx got, "Baş e." Şerbikê awî xalî îna, tizbî giwişî, aw jê hat. 'Elî Xan muteȟeyyir bû, nezanî ewe çawan e, gote xulaman, "Şêxî r̄ûs ken." Şêx tengaw bû, emma çare nebû, xulase şêx r̄ûs kirin** [sic], **dîtin** [sic] **r̄iwîekî gay, tejî aw, serek li bin şûtikê girêday, serê dî li naw paxilê li naw huçikê kirasî înaye nik zenda destî, girêday, wextê tizbî digiwişît, serê r̄iwîe dîinîte hindawê şerbikî, aw ji r̄iwîyê tête xar. Bi wê *ȟîlê* cahilêt ker hemî lêbandibûn** (SK 12:118,121) [118] They say that a Pawai man came to Somay and Biradost and the Kurasinis and made himself out to be a Shaikh … in every village that he visited he would, in full view of the people, squeeze his rosary, under the sleeve of his cloak, over a water pot. Water would flow in a stream out of it. The people were all amazed … [121] Ali Khan summoned the Shaikh to his home in the fortress of Chari. He said to him, "I would like you to give me some of the Water of Life too." The Shaikh said, "Very well." They brought an empty water pot, he squeezed his rosary and water came out of it. Ali Khan was amazed and did not know how it was. He said to his servants, "Strip the Shaikh." The Shaikh was desperate but there was no escape. In the end they stripped the Shaikh. They saw that he had the gut of an ox, full of water, with one end tied under his cummerbund and the other end coming under his armpit, inside his shirt-sleeve, being brought down and tied near his wrist. When he squeezed his rosary he would bring the end of the gut over the water pot and water would come down out of the gut. By means of this *trick* he had deceived all the stupid asses. {also: hîle (IFb); [hilé] حيله (JJ); <ȟîle> حـيـلـه (HH)} {syn: delk'; fêl I; lêp} < Ar ḥīlah حيلة = 'artifice, ruse, stratagem, trick, means to accomplish an end, expedient'; Sor ȟîle حـيـلـه [SK/H/JJ/HH/JB1-A/GF//IFb]

ȟîlebaz حـيـلـه‌بـاز *m.* **(-ê;).** trickster, cheat: •**Muroêt** [=mirovêt] **qehwexanê qewî şeytan û *ȟîlebaz* bûn, gotine** [sic] **yek û do "Werin, tedbîrekî weto bikeyn ku pertala wî muroê** [=mirovê] **Kurd bibeyn û ew bizanît û hîç deng neket û r̄azî bît, û r̄azî nebît bo wî cîyê axiwtinê nabît"** (SK 28:253) The men of the coffee house were great *tricksters*, they said to one another, "Come, let us devise a plan to take this Kurdish fellow's goods, and when he discovers it he will acquiesce and say nothing, and even if he doesn't acquiesce he won't have anything to say." {also: hîlebaz (IFb); [hilebaz/heilebáz (Lx)] حـيـلـه‌بـاز (JJ); <ȟîlebaz> حـيـلـه‌بـاز (HH)} {syn: dek'baz} Cf. P ḥīle'bāz حيله‌باز = 'cunning person, tricky fellow, cheat'; Sor ȟîlebaz حـيـلـه‌بـاز {ȟîlebazî} [Zeb/K/JJ/HH/SK/GF//IFb]

ȟîlebazî حيله‌بازى *f.* **(-ya;-yê).** trickery. Cf. P ḥīle'bāzī حيله‌بازى = 'trickery' [K/GF] <ȟîlebaz>

ȟîm حـيـم *m.* **(-ê;).** 1) {syn: binat'ar [2]; bingeh; binî; esas; şengiste} base, basis, foundation *(e.g., of a house)*: •**Hila mek't'eb nehatibû vekirinê, çi kêmasîyê wê hebûn û herçê wî çaxî mimkûn bûn qedandin û mek't'eb anî ser *ȟîmê* p'ak** ('E. Şamîlov. Jîyîna bextewar, 232) The school had not opened yet, whatever was lacking and whatever was possible at that time, he set right and established the school on a firm *basis*; 2) large stone or rock: •**Jina Azir ji ber tirsa Nemrûd ço ber zinarekî (yan ber hîmekî) serê bajêrê Rûhayê. Piçûk bû. Navê wî kirine** [sic] **Berhîm, çûnke li ber berî bû, anku bi ber *hîmî* ew piçûk hate dinyayê (*Hîm* zinar e)** (GShA, 227) Because of her fear of Nemrud, Azir's wife climbed up on a rock about the city of Urfa. The baby was born. They named him Berhîm [Ibrahim] because he was born on a rock, i.e. that baby came into the world on *a stone* (*Hîm* is a stone). {also: hîm (SW/JB3/IFb/GF/TF/OK/Kmc/Tsab-2/RZ/SS/CS); xîm (Msr/Hk/A/FJ-2/GF-2/Kmc-2/Tsab-2); [him هيم/khym خيم] (JJ); <xîm> خـيـم (HH)} Cf. Arm himn հիմն = 'foundation' [SW/JB3/IFb/JJ/GF/TF/OK/Kmc/RZ/SS/CS//F/K/B/Tsab//A/HH/Msr/Hk]

ȟîmî حيمى (K) = basic. See **ȟîmlî.**

ȟîmlî حيملى *adj.* basic, fundamental, principal: •**Ew mesele û met'eloka *ȟîmlî* Ȟesen Ȟebeş … gotine** (Dz, 41) These proverbs and sayings were told *principally* by H.H. {also: hîmî (GF/CS); hîmlî (K); ȟîmî (K-2)} {syn: bingehîn} See ȟîm + T -li [Dz/B//K//GF/CS] <ȟîm>

ȟît حـيـت (HH/FS) = angora goat (with mohair). See **ȟîtik.**

ḧîtik حيتِك *f. & adj.* angora goat, *variety of goat with long, silky hair (mohair)*: **-bizna ḧît** (FS) do. {also: hît (IFb); hîtik (FJ); <ḧît> حيت (HH)} {syn: ç'ûr I} [Qzl//FJ//IFb//HH/FS] <bizin>

ḧîz حيز *m.* **(-ê;).** 1) wineskin, water skin (K/B/JJ); untreated animal skin in which oil is stored (IF); 2) large jug (K); 3) {syn: qûnde} catamite, passive homosexual (HH/IFb). {also: hîz (IF/A); [hiz] حيز (JJ); <ḧîz> حيز (HH)} [Pok. aiĝ- 13.] 'goat': O Ir *izya-ka- = 'goat'; Av izaēna- = 'made of (goat) leather'; O P iðya-ka-; Sgd 'zyh = 'leather bag'; Pamir dialect: Sanglechi xēčē = 'inflated skin' (Morg); Pashto žai; Ormuri īz; Baluchi hīz; Oss xyzäg; Khotanese Saka häysä; P xīk خيك = 'leather bottle'; Sor ḧîz حيز = 'catamite, coward' & hîze هيزه = 'black skin used as receptacle for [clarified butter], syrup, etc.' & xîge خيگه = 'skin bottle for liquids'. See **Appendix II** to: M. Schwartz. "Proto-Indo-European √ĝem" *Monumentum H.S. Nyberg*, Acta Iranica, Series 2: Hommages et Opera Minora, 5 (Leiden : E.J. Brill, 1975), vol. 2, p. 210 + note p. 207 (misprint). [F/K/B/JJ/HH//A/IFb] <meşk; pêst; sirsûm; xinûsî>

ḧoç حوّچ *m./f.(FS)* **( ).** type of sandwich, "wrap" [T dürüm]: **•Totik ji hev kir, hêk danî ser, kire *hoç* û xwar** (GF) He took the biscuit apart, put an egg on it, made it into *a sandwich*, and ate it. {also: hîc (FJ-2); hoc (FJ); ḧîç (GF-2)} {syn: balolk} [Rwn/K/GF/FS//FJ]

ḧol حوّل *f.* **(;-ê).** hut, shack; mud cottage. {syn: kol II; k'ox [2]} [K/JB3]

ḧolik حوّلِك *f.* **(-a;-ê).** hut, shack {dim. of **ḧol**}: **•K'eç'ik jî ṙadive dik'eve *holka* qaza** (HCK-3, #16, 181) The girl enters the geese *shack*. {also: holik (IFb/GF/TF/FS); [holik] هولك (JJ)} [K/B//IFb/JJ/GF/TF/FS] <kepir>

ḧorî حوّرى (SK) = houri. See **horî**.

ḧub حوب *f.* **(-a;-ê).** love: **•Mîr sê cara Memê bir, çimkî *ḧuba* Zînê usa Memê biribû, Memê delal haj xwe t'unebû** (Z-1) The prince beat Mem three times [at chess], because *love of* Zin had made Mem lose sight of himself (=forget himself); **-ḧuba dilane** (EP-7) do. [lit. 'the love of hearts']; **-ḧuba wet'ên** (B) patriotism, love of the fatherland. {syn: dildarî; eşq; evîn[darî]} < Ar ḥubb حبّ [Z-1/K/B] <ḧebandin; ḧez kirin>

ḧubir حوبِر *f.* **(;-ê).** ink. {also: hubir (EP-8); [houbr] حبر (JJ); <ḧibr> حبر (HH)} < Ar ḥibr حبر [EP-8//F/K/B/JJ//HH]

ḧucim حوجم (B)= attack. See **ḧucûm.**

ḧucum حوجوم (B) = attack. See **ḧucûm.**

ḧucûm حوجووم *f.* **(;-ê).** attack. {also: hucum (IF); ḧicûm (B); ḧucim (B-2); ḧucum (B-2)} {syn: êrîş; ḧucûmkirin} <Ar hujūm هجوم; Sor hurujm هوروژم = hêriş هێرش = pelamar پەلامار [K//B]

ḧucûmkirin حوجوومكِرِن *f.* **(;-ê).** attack. {also: ḧicûmkirin (B)} {syn: êrîş; ḧucûm} [F/K//B]

ḧuçḧuçe حوچحوچه (FS) = chubby. See **ḧut.**

ḧuk'met' حوكمەت (JB1-A) = government. See **ḧuk'umet**.

ḧukomet حوكۆمەت (SK) = government. See **ḧuk'umet**.

ḧuk'•um حوكوم *m.* **(•mê;).** 1) {syn: emir I} power, authority, reign; order, command; 2) influence, effect (B): **-ḧuk'um kirin** (B) to influence, effect; 3) verdict, sentence (K); 4) {syn: dan III} *used in time expressions*: ***•Di ḧukmê* sê roja*da* ewan gihan malê** (K) *In the space of* three days they reached home ***•Di ḧukmê* 'esrê ezê bêm** (K) I'll come *toward* evening/in the [late] afternoon ***•ḧukmê* nîvro** (K) *at* noon. {also: hukm (IFb); [houkm] حكم (JJ)} < Ar ḥukm حكم [K/A/JB3/IFb] <desthilat; ḧakim>

ḧukumat حوكومات (F) = government. See **ḧuk'umet.**

ḧuk'umet حوكومەت [B]/**ḧukumet** [K]/**ḧuk'umet'** [JB1-A] *f.* **(-a;-ê).** government. {also: hikûmat (IFb-2); hikûmet (IFb/TF); hukumat (IFb-2); hukûmet (OK-2); ḧikûmet (OK); ḧuk'met' (JB1-A-2); ḧukomet (SK); ḧukumat (F); ḧuk'ûmet' (JB1-S); [houkoumet] حكومت (JJ); <ḧukûmat> حكومات (HH)} <Ar ḥukūmah حكومة; T hükümet; Sor ḧukûmet [K/B/JB1-A//IFb/TF//OK//SK//F//JB1-S/JJ//HH] <fermandarî>

ḧuk'ûmet' حوكوومەت (JB1-S) = government. See **ḧuk'umet**.

ḧulî I حولى (B) = being on edge *(of teeth)*. See **alû.**

ḧulî II حولى (SK-Ak) = smooth. See **hilû I**.

ḧulî III حولى (OK) = plum. See **ḧilû I**.

ḧulm حولم (B) = steam; breath. See **hilm**.

ḧulmgulm حولمگولم (B) = steam; breath. See **hilm**.

ḧunar حونار (B/Ba2) = art, skill. See **hiner**.

ḧunur حونور (Z-1) = art, skill. See **hiner**.

ḧuq•e حوقه *f.* **(;•ê).** oka, ounce, unit of weight, 400 dirhems or 2.8 lb (1282 grams): **•[Mirovek ji du *ḧuqan* kêmtirî gule barîdî hilnagrin** (sic)] (BN

136) One never takes less than two *okas* of bullets and gunpowder. {also: hoqe (K/IFb/B); huqe (A); <ḧuq[e]/ḧoq[e]> [ە]حـوق (BN); <ḧuqqe> حـقّـه (HH)} {syn: weqî} Cf. Ar uqqah أقّة/ḥuqqah حـقّة & T okka & NENA ḥuqqa (Sabar: Dict); Sor ḧoqe حۆقە [BN//HH//A//K/IFb/B]

ḧur̄ حـور *adj.* 1) unbridled, unruly: **•Min pirsa xwe ji teyrê *ḧur̄* kirê** (EP-5, #17) I asked my question of the *unruly* eagle; 2) impertinent, insolent, cheeky, smart-alecky: -**ḧur̄ bûn** (K/B) to act in an insolent manner: **•Ez qîza p'adşê bûm, eze *ḧur̄* bûm, min k'apêd geda avîtin, bela kirin** (EH) I was the king's daughter, I became *insolent*, [and] threw the guys' knucklebones all over the place. <Ar ḥurr حرّ = 'free' [EH/K/B] <p'arsûstûr; zimandirêj>

ḧurmet حورمەت (SK) = woman; respect. See **hurmet.**

Ḧuseynî حـوسـەيـنـى *m.* (). Muslim *(term used by Yezidis)*: **•Dasinî mezhebek e, Êzedî jî dibêjinê … Ew dibêjine 'ulemaêt xo koçek û dibêjine musulmanan *Ḧuseynî.* Daimî mabeyna Dasinî û *Ḧuseynîyan* dujminatî ye** (SK 39:344) The Dasinis are a sect, also called Yezidis … They call their own religious authorities 'kochak' and Muslims they call *'Husaini'*. There is always enmity between the Dasinis and the *'Husainis'*. {syn: misilman} [SK]

ḧusilcemal حوسِلجەمال (K) = beautiful woman. See **husulcemal**.

ḧut حـوت *adj.* chubby, fat and round: -**ḧut û pit** (Hk) do. {also: ḧuçḧuçe (FS)} [HK//FS]

ḧûlîr̄eşk حووليرەشك *m.* (). black plum. {also: hilûreşk (IFb); hilûyêreş (GF); hulîreşk (IFb-2)} {syn: încas [2]} [JB1-A//IFb/GF] <ḧilû I>

ḧûr حوور (B) = bowels. See **ûr**.

ḧûsûn حووسوون (JB1-A) = to rub. See **hesûn** & **sûtin**.

ḧût حووت (K/B) = monster; whale. See **hût**.

I ئِ

Ibranî ئبرانی (YPA) = Hebrew. See **Îbranî**.

icac ئِجاج (TF/ZF) = cloud of dust. See **hecac**.

iddi'a ئِددِعا (SK) = claim. See **îdî'a**.

idî ئدی (EP-7) = more; still; now. See **êdî** & **îdî**.

'ifare عِفاره (GF)/ifare ئِفاره (Kmc) = chaff; unpicked fruit. See **'efare**.

ilho ئِلهۆ (Bw) = eagle. See **elîh**.

illa ئِللا (JB1-A/OK) = unless; absolutely. See **îlla**.

illac ئِللاج (JB1-S) = cure, remedy. See **îlac**.

ille ئِلله (K/L) = unless; absolutely. See **îlla**.

'ilm عِلم (SK/HH) = knowledge; science. See **ulm**.

imbar ئِمبار (Ba3-3) = storehouse. See **'embar**.

imkan ئِمکان (CS/JJ)/imk'an (K/Tsab) = possibility. See **îmk'an**.

in ئِن (K) = mommy. See **inik**.

incûr ئِنجوور (ZF3) = type of cucumber. See **'ecûr**.

incûz ئِنجووز/**'incûz** عِنجووز [EP-5] *f.* **(-a;-ê).** wild plant whose leaves are dried and smoked: •**Nav herdada ew niqitka xûnê bû *dir̄ike uncûz*, şîn bû** (EP-7) This drop of blood between the two of them became *a thorn bush*, and grew; -**incûza dewra berê** (XF) senile old gossiping woman; -**bûye pîra incûz** (XF) = a) to be a stay-at-home; b) to be cunning. {also: uncûz (EP-7)} [EP-7//B] <dir̄dir̄k; dir̄î>

'indeko عِندەکۆ (HR) = clover. See **'endeko**.

inê ئِنێ (B) = mommy. See **inik**.

Ingilîz ئِنگِلیز (JB3) = Englishman. See **Înglîz**.

'ingirîn عِنگِرین (FS) = to be angry. See **erinîn**.

inik ئِنِك *f.* **().** mother, mommy: •***Inê*, bavo, ez xulamê weme** (Ba2:2, 207) *Mommy*, Dad, I'm your servant [i.e., I'll do as you say]. {also: in (K-2); inê (B)} {syn: dê I; mak} [F/K//B]

'inir̄în عِنِرین (FS) = to be angry. See **erinîn**.

inkar ئِنکار (SK/JJ/HH) = denial; refusal. See **înk'ar**.

insiyatîf ئِنسِیاتیف *f.* **(-a;-ê).** initiative: •**Divê dewleta Norwecê di NY'ê de ji bo munaqeşe kirina pirsgirêka Kurd, bibe xwediyê *insiyatîfê*** (Wlt 1:37, 16) Norway should take *the initiative* in discussing the Kurdish problem in the UN. {also: înîsiyatîf (ZF3)} <Fr initiative-->T inisiyatif; =Sor destpêşxerî دەستپێشخەری [(neol)Wlt//ZF3]

int ئِنت (ZF) = stubbornness; hatred. See **'eynat**.

int'ham ئِنتهام (OrK) = test, exam. See **îmt'îhan**.

int'în ئِنتین *vi.* **(-int'-).** 1) to groan, moan (K/B); 2) to wheeze, grunt, breathe heavily (K); 3) to sigh deeply (K); 4) [*f.* **(-a;-ê).**] {also: int'înî f. (;-yê). (K-2/B-2)} {syn: axîn; nalenal; nalîn} groaning, moaning (K/B): •**Bû *int'îna* Bek'oê 'Ewane** (FK-eb-1) *A groan* came from Beko Awan [villain of the Mem û Zîn story]. [FK-1/K/B/ZF3]

int'înî ئِنتینی, f. (;-yê). (K/B) = groaning, moaning. See **int'în** [4].

iqna kirin ئِقنا کِرِن (K) = to convince. See **îqna'**.

Iraq ئِراق (JB3) = Iraq. See **Îraq**.

ir̄in ئِڕِن, f. (K) = anger, rage. See **'ern**.

irn ئِرن (J2)/ir̄n ئِڕن (K) = anger, rage. See **'ern**.

iro ئِرۆ (Ad) = today. See **îro**.

isbat ئِسبات (SK) = proof. See **îspat**.

islah ئِسلاه = weapon. See **sîleh I**.

isleh ئِسلەه = weapon. See **sîleh I**.

ism ئِسم = name. See **îsm**.

Ispanî ئِسپانی (Wkt) = Spanish. See **Spanî**.

Ispanyayî ئِسپانیایی (Wkt) = Spanish. See **Spanî**.

istrî ئِستری (HM) = thorn. See **stirî I**.

'işk عِشك (GF/Mş) = dry. See **ḧişk**.

işkene ئِشکەنە (lezzetler.com) = dish of chicken legs in broth. See **eşkene**.

***işqir** ئِشقِر **().** type of grape. [Msr] <tirî>

ixt'îyar ئِختییار (K) = old man. See **îxt'iyar**.

iyar ئِیار (RN) = goatskin sack. See **'eyar I**.

izin ئِزِن (JB3) = permission. See **îzin**.

Î ئـ

Îbranî ئیبرانی *adj.* Hebrew: **•Di sedsala XIIan de ji erebî hat wergerandin bo *ibranî*** (YPA, 43) In the 12th century it was translated from Arabic to *Hebrew*. {also Ibranî (YPA)} < Ar 'ibrānī عبراني [YPA//IFb/ZF]

îca ئیجا (B/IF) = this time; then. See **îcar**.

îcar ئیـجار *adv.* 1) this time; 2) {syn: hingê} then: **•Îja emê çi bikin?** (J) What will (=should) we do *then*? {also: îca (B-2/IF-2); îja (BX/J/B-2); înca (JB3); încar} Sor inca ئـنـجـا. *See AKR (p. 65-69) for detailed discussion of* **îcar**. [BX/B/IF//K/A//BX/J/AKR//JB3] <car>

îcax ئـیـجـاخ *f.* **(-a;-ê).** 1) origin, ancestors; 2) {syn: berek; binemal} clan, tribe; family, lineage: **•Tu ji kîjan *îcaxê* yî?** (BF) Which *clan* are you from? [Zx/Bw/BF] <azbat; 'eşîret; hoz; qebîle; tayfe> See also **ocax**.

îda ئیدا (K/B) = more; still; now. See **êdî** & **îdî**.

îddia ئیددیا (IFb) = claim. See **îdî'a**.

îddîa ئیددیئا (CTV) = claim. See **îdî'a**.

îdî ئـیـدی *adv.* 1) now; already [Cf. T artık]: **•Box̄, wextê xarina teye *îdî*** (J) Ox, it's time for you to eat *now* (or, It's time to eat you *now*!) **•Daê, *îdî* xelq t'oxim dir̄eşîne!** (J) Mom, *now* people are sowing seed! **•De r̄abe nan bîne *îdî*!** (J) Get up and bring bread *already*! **•*Îdî* merî nema şeherda, Al-p'aşa gazî nekirê, nanî: îdî k'oçek, îdi ḧekîm û kal û pîrê zemanî** (Z-1) *By now* there wasn't a man left in the city whom A.p. hadn't called: neither hermit, nor doctor, nor old man **•Wexta Al-p'aşa salixê kalê hilda, *îdî* xwexa r̄abû çû pey kalê** (Z-1) When A.p. received news of the old woman (=learned of the old woman's existence), *at that point* he got up and went to the old woman; **-îdî sibê** (Z-1) any minute now [lit. 'now, tomorrow']: **•Q. birava vegerîyane, wê *îdî sibê* bigihîjine Cizîrê** (Z-1) Q. [and his] brothers have returned, they will reach Jizirah *any minute now*; 2) more; still. See **êdî**; 3) the …-est (superlative degree of adjs) (Msr): **•Ez *îdî mezin*im** (Msr) I am *the biggest/oldest one*. {also: **êdî** (IF); idî; îda (K/B); [eïdi] ایدی (JJ)} Sor îtir ئـیـتـر = 'then, in future, any more' [J/A//K/B//IF/JJ] See also **êdî**. <niha>

îdî'a ئـیـدیـعـا *f.* **(-ya;-ê).** claim, assertion, maintaining *(that stg. is true)*: **•Leşkerê Tirkîyê, hukumeta sivîl, *bi îddîaya ku* "ji rîya Kemal Paşa avarê bûye", wergerand** (Bkp, 35) The army of Turkey overturned the civil government *with the claim that* it "had departed from the path of Kemal Pasha [=Ataturk]" **•Li gorî *hin îdîayan* Atîna ji bo xwe ji daxwazên Kohen rizgar bike, wê soz bide Amerîka ku di der barê PKKê de ji bo hevkariyê amade ye** (CTV107) According to *some claims*, in order to free itself of [William] Cohen's demands, Athens will promise America that it is ready to cooperate regarding the PKK; **-îdî'a kirin** (OK)/**iddi'a kirin** (SK) to claim, maintain, allege: **•Barzanî *îddîa kir* ku planên Emerîka ji bo hilweşandina desthilatiya Saddam Huseyin hene** (CTV57) Barzani *claimed* that America has plans to destroy Saddam Hussein's power **•Delîla her dînekî ḧeqq bît çar tişt in. Eger yêk nuqsan bît ḧeqq nîye. Ewwel, *dibît* r̄e'îsê wî dînî *iddi'a biket* ko, "Ez ji laê xudê hatime hinarin bo te'lîma insanan"** (SK 39:348) The proof of every true religion lies in four things. If one is lacking it is not true. First, the leader of the religion *must claim that*, "I have been sent from God to instruct mankind." {also: iddi'a (SK); îddia (IFb); îddîa (CTV-2)} {syn: angaşt} < Ar iddi'ā' إدّعـــــــاء = 'claim' < VIII of √d-'-w دعو; Sor îdî'a ئیدیعا [CTV//OK//IFb//SK]

îdqat ئیدقات (K) = faith. See **îtîqad.**

îfade ئیفاده *f.* **().** statement, assertion: **-îfade kirin** (K/IFb/JJ) to state, assert, express {syn: dan der; diyar kirin}: **•Ez dikarim bi rehetî *îfade bikim* ku em tev di vê dibistana Nûbiharê de bi pêş ketine** (Nbh 125:4) I can confidently *state* that all of us in this Nûbihar school have progressed. {also: [ifadé] افـــــاده (JJ)} < Ar ifādah إفـــادة = 'notification, message' < afāda IV أفــــاد (√f-y-d) [Nbh/K/IFb/ZF/Tsab/ZF3//JJ]

îfrît ئیفریت (IF) = jinn. See **ferḧît.**

îfşa ئـیـفـشـا *m.(ZF3)/f.(Wkt)* **().** revealing, exposing, uncovering, divulging (of something secret): **-îfşa kirin** (IFb/Wkt) to reveal, expose, uncover, divulge: **•Kî oldarekî ji dil e û kî minafiq e bê**

tirs û xof wan *îfşa dike.* Rûpoşa wan dadixîne û li ser wan dinivisîne (A.Taş. Kevirê Namûsê, 42) Whether one is genuinely religious or one is a hypocrite, he *exposes* them without any fear. He removes their mask and writes about them. <Ar ifšā' إفشاء, verbal noun of afšá IV أفشى = 'to reveal, expose, divulge' (√f-š-w فشو) [A.Taş/IFb/ZF3/Wkt]

îḧsan ئيحسان *f.* **(;-ê).** bounty, benevolence, beneficence, charity: •[**Eger mirofek ji t̲ayifa xwendîyan *îḧsan* û sedeqeyekê weyaxû t̲e'am û zadekî bidine feqîrekî ez dê çomaẍekî li vê deholê bidim**] (JR-2) If someone from the class of the learnèd should give *charity* or food to a poor person, I will strike a blow on this drum. {also: [ehsan] احسان (JJ); <iḧsan> احسان (HH)} < Ar iḥsān إحسان [verbal noun of √ḥ-s-n IV أحسن] = 'beneficence, charity, alms giving' [JR/JJ/HH/SK//OK] <s̲edeqe>

îja ئيژا (BX/J/B) = this time; then. See **îcar**.

îkbal ئيكبال = good luck; fate. See **îqbal**.

îlac ئيلاج *f.* **(-a;-ê).** 1) {syn: ç'are; derman} cure, remedy *(lit. & fig.)*; 2) {syn: hiner} way out *(of a situation)* (B): •**Bav dinihêre *îlac* nabe** (Ba) The father sees there is no *use* [lit. '*remedy*'] •**Ê go em çi *'elacê* jê bikin? – Go: Emê wî kujin** (HR 3:186) Well, what should we do to him? [lit. 'what *solution* should we do from him'] – We'll kill him •**T'u *îlac* t'une** (B) There is no *solution*; **-îlac bir̄în** (B) to cut out any possibility, miss the chance: •**Lê çaxê *îlaca* dê û bavêd wana *dihate bir̄înê*, wana parî nanê ḧişkolekî dida zar̄a, ew ker̄ dibûn** (Ba2-3, 216) When all else failed [lit., 'when their parents' *remedy or solution was cut*'], they would give the children a piece of dried bread, and they [=the children] would quiet down; **-îlac dîtin/kirin** (B) to find one's way out (of a situation) . {also: 'elac (HR); illac (JB1-S); [iláj] علاج (JJ); <'ilac> علاج (HH)} < Ar 'ilāj علاج = 'remedy, cure' [K/IFb/B//JJ/HH//JB1-S/HR]

îlahî ئيلاهى *adv.* especially, particularly: •[**Ç'îyayê] Dûmanlû Zer̄îbxane û gundêd dine nêzîk ji baêd şimalêne sar xwey dikir, *îlahî* zivistanê** (Ba2:1, 202) [Mount] Dumanlu protected Zeribkhaneh and other nearby villages from the cold northern winds, *especially* in the winter •**Gurêd birçî ji nava xilxilê kevira derdik'etin û r̄adihiştne ser pêz, *îlahî* çaxê baran dibarî** (Ba2:1, 203) Hungry wolves came out from the rock heaps and pounced on the sheep, *especially* when it was raining. {syn: bi taybetî; nemaze; nexasme} [Ba2/K/B]

îlam ئيلام (MUm) = unless; absolutely. See **îlla**.

îlla ئيللا *conj.* 1) [+ *subj.*] unless: •**Ez te 'afw nakem, *îlla* tu pişta min vemalî (biperxînî)** (Bw) I won't forgive you, *unless* you rub my back •**Nexoş sax (çê/baş) nabît, *îlla* biçite nexoşxanê** (Bw) A sick person doesn't (won't) get well *unless* he goes to the hospital; 2) {syn: 'ese; helbet [2]; teqez} [often +*subj.*] absolutely, without fail: •**Ev hût *ille* lawê wî hene, ev ne bi tenê ye** (L-1 #3, 46, l.17) This monster *must* have sons, he is not alone •***Îlla* ez cigar[ek]ê bikêşim piştî zadî/xarinê** (Bw) I *absolutely must* have a cigarette after eating •***Îlla* tu înîyê biçî?** (Bw) Do you *absolutely have to* go on Friday? •[**T̲ayfeyêd Ekrad we bê 'aql in, dûmahîya şolê milaḧeze nakin. Herçî bête 'aqlê wan, *îla* dê kin**] (JR 6: 30) The Kurdish tribes are so stupid, they do not think about the end [or consequences] of an affair. Whatever comes to their mind, they *absolutely must* do •**We dît çi qewimî? Cizdana min ne li ser min e! Min ew *îlam* li derekî** [sic] **xist--yan jî li derekî ji bîr kir** (MUm, 29) Do you see what has happened? I don't have my wallet on me! I *must have* dropped it somewhere--or forgotten it somewhere. {also: illa (JB1-A/OK); ille (K/L); îlam (MUm); [ila] الا (JJ)} <Ar illā إلّا (< in lā إن لا) = 'except; unless' --> T illa/ille = 'or else; come what may' [Bw/JR/IFb//JB1-A/OK//K/L//JJ//MUm]

Îlon ئيلۆن *f.* **(-a;-ê).** September: •**Di 19'ê *Îlona* 1992 an de komcivîna awarte ya duyemîn a HEP'ê li Enqerê li dar ket** (Wlt 1:43, 9) On the 19th of *September* 1992 HEP's second irregular congress took place in Ankara •[***Îlonê* zik t'êrê ye, û dunya xêrê ye**] (BG) In *September* the stomach is full, and the world is [full of] goodness. {also: Êlûn (GF/TF); Îlûn (B); [iloulايلول/ilún/īlun/ailun] (JJ); <îlûn> ايلون (HH); [ilône] (BG)} < Syr elūl ܐܝܠܘܠ [ēlūl ܐܝܠܘܠ; Heb elul אלול] --> Ar aylūl أيلول --> T Eylûl/Eylül; *corresponds to last part of* Gelawêj گەلاوێژ/Berewpayîz بەرەوپاییز (P šahrīvar شهريور) [Virgo] *& 1st part of* Mîran ميران/R̄ezber رێزبەر (P mehr مهر) [Libra] [F/K/A/JB3/IFb/OK//GF/TF/BG//B/HH//JJ]

Îlûn ئيلون (B/HH) = September. See **Îlon**.

îlxî ئیلخی, f. (B) = herd of horses. See **îrxî**.

îman ئـیـمـان *f.* **(-a;-ê).** 1) {syn: bawer[î]} faith, belief: **•*Îmana* we pêgirtî ye betale / *Îmana* we pêgirtî xirabe** (GShA, 228-229) *The beliefs* you hold are void / *The beliefs* you hold are wrong **•*Îmana* xo der-ĥeqq zatê 'alî wekî *îmana* ĥewarîyan der-ĥeqq ĥezreti Mesîĥ o *îmana* çar yaran der-ĥeqq ĥezreti Muĥemmed dizanîn** (SK 4:44) Our *faith* in your excellency is like *the faith of* the apostles in the Lord Jesus and *the faith of* the four Companions in the Lord Muhammad; **-îman kirin** [+ **bi**] (SK) to believe in: **•Her kesê şirîkan bo xudê çê-ket o sicde bo seneman biket, wî bikujin, bila *îmanê bi* min *biket*** (SK 48:513) Every person who makes partners for god and bows down before idols, kill him, he *should believe in* me; 2) {syn: ît'bar} trust, confidence; 3) [*adj.*] conscientious (B): **•Ew merîkî *îmane*** (B) He is a *conscientious* man. {also: [aímán] ایمان (JJ) ; <îman> ایمان (HH)} <Ar īmān إيمان = 'faith' [F/K/B/IFb/JJ/HH/FJ/SK]

îmk'an ئـیـمـكـان *f.* **(-a;).** 1) {syn: derfet; k'ês; mecal; mefer} possibility, ability; 2) resource, wherewithal: **•Û hindik be jî bi *îmkanên* dewletê, di du-sê waran de pêşî li zimanê Kurdî vekir** (Nbh 125:5) And as little as the state's *resources* would allow, in 2 or 3 areas it paved the way forward for the Kurdish language. {also: imkan (CS-2)/imk'an (K-2/Tsab-2); mik'an I (B); [imkan] امـكـان (JJ)} < Ar imkān إمـكـان = 'possibility, ability' < amkana IV أمكن [Nbh/K/IFb/ZF/Tsab/CS//JJ//B] <mumkin>

îmtĥan ئیمتحان (B) = test, exam. See **îmt'îhan**.

îmtihan ئیمتِهان (IFb/RZ) = test, exam. See **îmt'îhan**.

îmt'îhan ئـیـمـتـیـهـان *f.* **(-a;-ê).** test, examination: **•Emerîkê Serdar *întama* dewletêye pêşin zef baş daye** ('E.Serdar. Mukuřî, 4th plate after p. 202) E. Serdar did very well on the first national *exam*; **-îmt'îhan bûn/k'etin îmt'îhanê** (K) to take an exam/test. {also: int'ham (OrK); îmtĥan (B); îmtihan (IFb/RZ); înt'ab (B-2); înt'am (K-2); înt'ĥab (B-2); întĥam (B-2); [imtihan] امتحان (JJ)} {syn: ezmûn [1]} < Ar imtiḥān إمتحان [E.Serdar//K/F/ZF//IFb/RZ//JJ//B//OrK]

În ئین (A/JB3/IF/HH/Msr) = Friday; week. See **Înî**.

înad ئیناد (IFb) = stubbornness; hatred. See **'eynat**.

înan ئینان (M/MK) = to bring. See **anîn** & **înandin**.

înandin ئیناندِن *vt.* **(-înîn-).** 1) to bring in; to transport, transfer (JJ): **•Qursê zêřa ji mala *înandibû*** (EP-8) He *brought in* bars of gold from the houses; 2) to take or capture booty, to plunder: **•Pêncî extirme *înandibû*** (EP-8) He *brought in* (=captured) 50 horses. {also: [inandin] ایـنـانـدیـن (JJ)} [EP-8/K/JJ/Bw] See also **anîn**.

înca ئینجا (JB3) = this time; then. See **îcar**.

incar ئینجار = this time; then. See **îcar**.

încas ئـیـنـجـاس *f.* **(-a;-ê).** plum (AB/TG2); black plum (IF). {also: încaz (K/JB3/TG2); [anjas/injāz] انجاز (JJ)} {syn: hêrûg [1]} < Ar injāṣ إنـجـاص = 'pear', cf. Heb agas אגס = 'pear' [AB//K/JB3/IF/TG2/Frq/ Qzl/Czr//JJ] <alûçe; dembûl; şilor>

încaz ئینجاز (K/JB3/TG2) = pear; plum. See **încas**.

Îndonezî ئـیـنـدۆنـەزی *adj.* Indonesian. {also: Îndonîsî (BF)} Sor Îndonîzî ئیندۆنیزی [IFb/Wkp/SS//BF]

Îndonîsî ئیندۆنیسی (BF) = Indonesian. See **Îndonezî**.

Înê ئینێ (F) = Friday; week. See **Înî**.

Îngilîz ئینگلیز (IF) = Englishman. See **Înglîz**.

Înglîs ئینگلیس (B) = Englishman. See **Înglîz**.

Înglîsî ئینگلیسی (F) = English. See **Înglîz**.

Înglîz ئـیـنـگـلـیـز *m.* **().** Englishman: **-jina înglîz** (K) Englishwoman; **-zimanê înglîza[n]** (K) English language. {also: ingilîz (JB3); îngilîz (IF); înglîs (B-2)} [F/K/B//JB3//IF]

Înglîzî ئیننگلیزی *adj.* English: **-zimanê înglîsî** (F) the English language. {also: înglîsî (F)} [F/K]

Înî ئینی *f.* **(-ya;-yê).** 1) {syn: Cume} Friday; 2) {syn: ĥeftê I} week. {also: Eynî II (SK); În (A/JB3/IF/Msr); Înê (F); [ein این/īni اینی] (JJ); <în> این (HH)} Cf. Manichean Sgd ''dyng /āðēnē/; P ādīne آدینه; Sor heynî هەینی = 'Friday'; Za îne (Todd)/ êne (Mal) *m.* = 'Friday' [K/B/JJ/Rh//A/JB3/IF/HH/Msr//SK//F]

înîsiyatîf ئینیسیاتیف (ZF3) = initiative. See **insiyatîf**.

înk'ar ئـیـنـكـار *f.* **(-a;-ê).** 1) denial: **-înk'ar kirin**: a) to deny: **•Hêstirek ji ç'a'vê Xecê k'ete ser suretê Sîabend. Sîabend rabû, got: "Xecê, tu çima girîyay?" Xecê *înk'ar kir*** (IS-#369) A tear fell from Khej's eye and fell on Siyabend's face. He asked, "Khej, why were you crying?" [But] Khej *denied* [that she had been] **•Siyaseta ku heta niha *înkara* Kurdan *dikir*** (Nbh 125:5) The policy that until now *has been denying [the existence of]* the Kurds; b) to refuse; 2) refusal: **•Hinek xan û mîrêd K'urda qirar kir komekê bidin xanê Ç'engzerîn, hineka jî jêřa nivîsîn *înk'ar*** (EP-8-#78) Some khans and princes of the Kurds promised to help Khan Chengzerin, while others wrote him their *refusal*. {also: inkar (SK); înk'arî (B/K-2); [inkar kirin] انكار كرين (JJ); <inkar kirin انكار كرن (inkar dike) (انكار دكه)> (HH)} <Ar inkār إنكار, verbal noun of ankara IV أنكر = 'to deny' -->T inkâr [EP-8/IS/F/K/IFb/B//JJ/HH/SK]

înk'arî ئینکاری (B/K) = denial; refusal. See **înk'ar**.

însan ئینسان *m.* **(-ê; însên/îsên** [Ba]). 1) {syn: bende; benîadem; 'evd I; kabra; mêr; meriv} person, human being: **•Mala xwe kir wek *a îsana*** (L) He made his house like *everyone else's* [lit. 'like that *of the people*']; **-'evd û însan** (EP-7) human beings **•Me îro di *însan* weke hevdu dîtine** (HR 4:5) Today we have seen two *people* who are alike [=of equal beauty]; 2) {syn: meriv [4]} one, they, people (*for general or impersonal statements*): **•Bedewya Zelîxê *îsan* dihingavt** (Ba #17, 315) Z.'s beauty stunned *people* **•Ne axir ç'evê *îsên* tek ji xalîyê t'êr dibe** (Ba #16, 315) After all, it is only from earth/dirt/soil that *one* has one's full. {also: îsan (Ba/L); [insan] انسان (JJ)} <Ar insān إنسان [Ba/L//HR/K/IF/B/JJ]

înt'ab ئینتاب (B) = test, exam. See **îmt'îhan**.

înt'am ئینتام (K) = test, exam. See **îmt'îhan**.

înt'ĥab ئینتحاب (B) = test, exam. See **îmt'îhan**.

întĥam ئینتحام (B) = test, exam. See **îmt'îhan**.

îprax ئیپراخ *f.* **().** stuffed grape leaves: **•Xarina bajerîya, ko şirînî, pilaw, goşt, *êprax*, şorbawa bi dermanêt bênxoş û tiştê wekî wane bo wî didanane ser sifrê** (SK 31:274) He would set on the tablecloth townsmen's food, which is sweetmeats, pilaf, meat, *stuffed vine-leaves*, soup with fragrant spices and other such things. {also: aprax (Wkt); êprax (SK)} {syn: dolme} <T yaprak = 'leaf' [Dh/OK/FS//SK//Wkt]

îqbal ئیقبال *m./f.(ZF3)* **(-ê/-a; /-ê).** 1) {syn: siûd [2]} good fortune, good luck (K/JJ): **•*Êx̂balê* we şixulî** (K) You are in *luck*! [lit. 'Your luck worked']; **-siĥûd û îqbal** (Z-2) good fortune; 2) fate, destiny (K). {also: êxbal; êx̂bal (K); îkbal; [eqbal] اقبال (JJ)} <Ar iqbāl إقبال = 'welfare, good fortune, prosperity' [Z-2/IF/ZF3/Wkt//K//JJ]

îqna' ئیقناع**: -îqna' kirin** ئیقناع کِرِن *vt.* 1) {syn: êqîn kirin; qani' kirin} to convince, persuade: **•Fehmî Yezdan *iqna* dike ku Ew rê bide Fehmî daku vebigere welatê xwe** (Gulistan 1:4 [2002], 98) F. *convinces* God to allow him to return to his homeland; 2) to satisfy (SK). {also: iqna kirin (K); îqna kirin (IFb/ZF3/Wkt/RZ)} < Ar iqnā' إقناع, verbal noun of aqna'a IV أقنع = 'to convince' (√q-n-' قنع) [IFb/ZF3/Wkt/RZ//K]

Îran ئیران *f.* **(;-ê).** Iran: **-K'urdistana Îranê** (K) Kurdistan of Iran, Iranian Kurdistan. {also: [iran] ایران (JJ)} Cf. P īrān ایران [Ba2/K/A/JB3/JJ] <Faris>

Îraq ئیراق *f.* **(;-ê).** Iraq: **-Ĥuk'umeta Îraqê** (Ba2) The Republic of Iraq; **-K'urdistana Îraqê** (K) Kurdistan of Iraq, Iraqi Kurdistan. {also: Iraq (JB3)} Cf. Ar al-'irāq العراق [K/A/JB3/IF]

îrixçî ئیرِخچی (F) = horse herder. See **îrxîçî**.

Îrî ئیری (Wkt) = Irish. See **Îrlandî**.

Îrlandayî ئیرلاندایی (ZF3) = Irish. See **Îrlandî**.

Îrlandî ئیرلاندی *adj.* 1) Irish; Gaelic; 2) [*m.&f.* ().] Irishman; Irish woman. {also: Îrî (Wkt); Îrlandayî (ZF3-2); Îrlendî (SS)} Sor Êrlendî ئێرلەندی [IFb/BF/ZF3//SS//Wkt]

Îrlendî ئیرلەندی (SS) = Irish. See **Îrlandî**.

îro ئیرۆ/**îr̄o** ئیرۆ [JB1-S] *adv.* 1) today: **•*Îro* ez nexweş im** (L) *Today* I'm sick **•30 sal berê seeta bavê min ketibû vê bîrê, min jî *îro* derxist** (LM, 12) 30 years ago my father's watch fell into this well, *today* I brought it out; **-îroda** (B) from today on; **-ji îro û pê de** (IF) from today on; 2) nowadays: **•Komara Tirkiyê ne weke berê ye. *Îro* pêşketin, wekhevî heye, dadmendî (edalet) heye** (Wlt 2:59, 13) The Turkish Republic is not like before. *Nowadays* there is progress [and] equality, there is justice. {also: evro (Zx); evr̄o (JB1-A); ewr̄o (SK); iro (Ad); îroro (BX-2); îrû; [irou] ایرو (JJ); <îro> ایرو (HH)} Cf. P emrūz امروز; Sor emr̄o ئەمڕۆ [imr̄o إمڕۆ]/emr̄oke ئەمڕۆکە/ewr̄o ئەوڕۆ; Za ewro (Todd); Hau aro (M4) [BX/F/K/A/JB3/IF/B/HH//JB1-S//Ad//JJ//Zx/JB1-A//SK] <dihî; r̄oj; sibê>

îroro ئیرۆرۆ (BX) = today. See **îro**.

îrû ئیروو = today. See **îro**.

îrxî ئیرخی *m.(K)/f.(B)* **(; /-yê).** herd *(of horses)*. {also: îlxî, f. (B)} {syn: qefle; r̄evo} Cf. T yılkı = 'herd of horses or asses turned loose to range at will' (RC) & ılgı/ilhi & ırhı [Erzurum] = 'herd of horses, donkeys, or goats' (DS, v.7, p. 2467) [K//B] <hesp; îrxîçî; r̄evo>

îrxîçî ئیرخیچی *m.* **().** horse herder. {also: îrixçî (F)} {syn: r̄evoçî} [K//F] <hesp; îrxî; r̄evo>

îsaf ئیساف *f.* **(-a;-ê).** 1) {syn: dad[mendî]} justice, fairness (K/B/JJ); 2) conscience (B). {also: [insaf] انصاف (JJ)} < Ar inṣāf إنصاف [Z-1/K/B//JJ]

<wicdan>

îsal ئـيـسـال *adv.* this year. {also: evsale (Zeb); [isal] ایسال (JJ)} Cf. P emsāl امسال; Sor emsał ئەمساڵ; Za emser (Todd) [BX/K/A/JB3/IF/JJ/B//Zeb] <par; sal>

îsan ئیسان (Ba/L) = person. See **însan**.

îsbat ئیسبات (IFb/B/RZ) = proof. See **îspat**.

îsk ئـيـسـك *pl.* 1) {syn: qilpik[1]} hiccup(s): **-îskêt xarinê** (Zeb) do.; 2) death rattle: **-îskêt mirinê** (Zeb) do. {also: <îsk> ایسك (HH)} = Sor nizgere نزگەره = 'hiccup' [Zeb/Dh/IFb/GF/HH/TF] <qilpik>

Îskoçî ئیسکۆچی (Wkt) = Scottish. See **Skotlendî**.

Îskoçyayî ئیسکۆچیایی (Wkt) = Scottish. See **Skotlendî**.

îslah ئیسلاه = weapon. See **sîleh I**.

îsleh ئیسلەه = weapon. See **sîleh I**.

Îslendî ئـيـسـلـەنـدى *adj.* Icelandic. {also: Ayslendî (SS/Wkt)} Sor Ayslandî ئایسلاندی [Wkp//SS]

îslêh ئسلێه (L) = weapon. See **sîleh I**.

îsm ئـيـسـم *m.* **(-ê;).** name: **-îsmê sêrê** (L) words of magic, incantation, spell; **-îsmê sêrê xwendin** (L) to cast a spell. {also: ism; îsme (B); [ism] اسم (JJ)} {syn: nav I} < Ar ism اسم = 'name' --> T isim [L/K/IFb//JJ//B] <sêr I; t'ilism>

îsme ئیسمه (B) = spell, incantation. See **îsm**.

îsot ئـيـسـۆت *f.* **(-a;-ê).** pepper *(plant, vegetable)*, bot. *Piper nigrum, Capsicum* {syn: back; bîber; guncik; ḧiçḧar}: **•*Îsotê* devê min şewitand** (AB) *The pepper* burnt my mouth; **-îsotê hûr** (Ad) black pepper (spice) {syn: dermanê germ (Msr/A/JJ-PS)}. ?< T ısı ot = 'hot herb'; cf. S-Cr isiot = 'ginger'; Za îsot *m.* = 'pepper' (Mal) [AB/A/JB3/IFb/GF/TF/Msr/Erh] <dermanê germ>

îspanax ئیسپاناخ (Kmc) = spinach. See **spînax**.

Îspanî ئیسپانی (IFb/SS) = Spanish. See **Spanî**.

îspat ئـيـسـپـات *f.* **(-a;).** proof: **•Bê *isbat* kes ḧeqq nîye Mîrza Ḧesen ḧebs biket** (SK 54:621) Without *proof* no one has the right to imprison M.H.; **-îspat kirin** (IFb/ZF)/**isbat ~** (SK)/**îsbat ~** (RZ)/**îzbat ~** (K/B) to prove, establish the truth of: **•Bi awayekî qutubirr ê ku ji çu gumanek ra cî nahêle *hatîye îspatkirin* ku ev zilam dijminê dewletê û komarê ye** (Bkp, 8) It *has been proven* in a decisive manner which leaves no room for doubt that this man is an enemy of the state and of the republic **•Eger wan *isbat kir* ko teslîmi me yan feqîran boye çak e, egerne şer'en o qenûnen dikewîte ser wan** (SK 54:605) If they *prove* that it has been handed over to us or to the poor that's fine, otherwise according to Islamic and civil law it falls to them. {also: isbat (SK); îsbat (IFb/B-2/RZ); îzbat (K/B); [sebit ثبت/isbat اثبات/sabit kirin ثابت كرين/ispāt kirin (Rh)] (JJ)} {syn: *delîl} < Ar iṯbāt إثبات = 'assertion; proof, evidence' < aṯbata IV أثبت = 'to prove'; = Sor selmandin سەلماندِن & saẍ kirdinewe ساغ کِردِنەوە [Bkp/IFb/ZF/OrK//RZ//SK//K/B]

îspatî ئیسپاتی *m.* **().** clubs *(suit of playing cards)*. {syn: sînek} [Elk/Qzl/Wn]

îspenax ئـيـسـپـەنـاخ (K/ZF/G/CS/Wkt) = spinach. See **spînax**.

îspînax ئیسپیناخ (Wkt) = spinach. See **spînax**.

Îsraîlî ئیسرائیلی *adj.* Israeli. {also: Îsrayîlî (BF)} Sor Îsraîlî ئیسرائیلی [IFb/ZF3/SS/Wkt/CS//BF]

Îsrayîlî ئیسرایلی (BF) = Israeli. See **Îsraîlî**.

îstekan ئیستەکان *f.* **(-a;-ê).** small glass for tea. {also: îstkan (IFb); stekan (B-2/GF)} {syn: p'eyale; şûşe [3]} < Rus stakan стакан --> P estekān استکان; Sor îstîkan ئـيـسـتـيـكـان [K/B/TF//IFb//GF] <avxork; p'erdax>

îstgah ئیستگاه (K[s]) = station. See **îstgeh**.

îstgeh ئـيـسـتـگـەه *f./m.(Wkt)* **(-a/-ê;).** station; radio station: **-îstgeha radyoyê** (ZF3) radio station. {also: îstgah (K[s]); îzgeh (IF-2)} Cf. P īstgāh ایستگاه; Sor îstge ئیستگه [(neol)JB3/ZF3/Wkt//K(s)//IF] <bihîstok (neol.); pêlweş (IF); ȓadyo>

îstkan ئیستكان (IFb) = tea glass. See **îstekan**.

îş ئـيـش *m.* **(-ê;).** work, job: **•*Îşê* te pê tune be** (L) There will be nothing more for you to do [lit. 'You won't have *work* on it']. {also: [īš] ایش (JJ)} {syn: şuxul; xebat} < T iş; Sor îş ئیش [L/K/JB3/IF/B/JJ]

'îşandin عیشاندِن *vt.* **(-'îşîn-).** to perceive; to notice, look at; to listen to: **•Memê çiqa bi herdu ç'e'va li ya p'êşî *di 'îşîne*, / Gustîla xwe di t'ilîya wêda dibîne** (Z-2) When Memê *notices* the [girl] in front with both of his eyes, / He sees his ring on her finger **•Memê dîsa li a p'êşî *di'îşîne*** (Z-2, 79) Memê once again *notices* the one in front **•Stîya Zîn derk'etîye p'acê li wan *di'îşîne*** (Z-2) Lady Zîn went out and *views* them through the skylight **•[Bek'o] Çû di ber oda Memêda, ç'e'vê xwe di p'acêda *di'îşîne*, / ko va stîya Zîn û Memê di odêda ȓûniştîne** (Z-2) [Beko] passed before Memê's room, *looks in* through the skylight, / that here are Lady Zîn and Memê sitting in the room **•Stîya Zîn ji xweȓa disekine, / Û li xeberdanê wî *di'îşîne*** (Z-2) Lady Zîn stands there, / And *listens* to what he says. [Z-2] <ĥiş>

îşev ئیشەڤ *adv.* tonight, this evening. {also: evşeve (Zeb); [ichewé] ایشڤە (JJ); <îşev> ایشڤ (HH)} Cf. P emšab امشب; Sor emşew ئەمشەو = 'tonight'; Za emşo = 'tonight' (Todd); Hau êşew (M4) [BX/K/A/IFb/B/HH/JB1-S/GF//JJ] <şev>

îşik ئیشِك (IFb) = stick for tightening ropes. See **îşk I**.

îşk I ئیشك *f.* ( ). turn of the loop *(in tightening a rope tied around a load on a horse's back)*; small stick used for this purpose (HH): **-îşk lê dan** (Qzl/Ag/Qtr-E) to tighten a load, *by looping the rope--each turn of the loop is an "îşk."* {also: îşik (IFb); <îşk> ئیشك (HH)} [Qzl/Ag/QtrE/K(s)/HH//IFb] <darşixre>

îşkenc•e ئیشکەنجە *f.* (;•ê). torture: **-îşkence dan** (OK/GF)/**îşkence kirin** (K[s]/OK) to torture, torment: **•Di meha Mijdarê de hinek hevalên min hatin binçavkirin û li wan *îşkence hatibû kirin*** (Wlt 2:66, p.2) In November some of my friends *were* arrested and *tortured*; **-îşkence dîtin** (OK)/**k'etin şkencê** (K[s]) to be tortured. {also: şkenc (GF-2); şkence (K[s]/GF); [skengia] شکنجە (JJ-G)} <T işkence <P šekanje شکنجه [Wlt/IFb/OK//K(s)/JJ-G/GF]

îşlik ئیشلِك *m.* (**-ê;).** shirt. {also: <îşlik> ایشلك (HH)} {syn: kiras [1]; qemîs; qutik I} < T işlik = 'shirt' (DS, v.7, pp. 2564-65) [Plt/Dy/K/A/HH/GF/TF/RZ]

Îtalî ئیتالی *adj.* Italian. {also: Îtalyanî (Wkt-2); Îtalyayî (Wkt-2)} Sor Îtałî ئیتاڵی [IFb/Wkt/BF/ZF3]

Îtalyanî ئیتالیانی (Wkt) = Italian. See **Îtalî**.

Îtalyayî ئیتالیایی (Wkt) = Italian. See **Îtalî**.

ît'bar ئیتبار *f.* (;**-ê).** 1) trust, confidence; faith; 2) value, worth (IF); 3) *[adj.]* {syn: emîn [2]; ewlekar; saxlem [2]} reliable, dependable, trustworthy (K/B/Bw): **•mirovekî gelek *extûbar*** (Bw) an extremely *reliable* person. {also: extûbar (Bw); îtibar (IF); ît'par (Z-3); [îtibar] اعتبار (JJ)} < Ar i'tibār اعتبار = 'consideration, respect', *verbal noun of* i'tabara VIII اعتبر [√'-b-r عبر] = 'to consider, regard'; Sor îtîbar ئیتیبار = 'reputation, credit' [EP-7/K/B//IF/JJ//Bw]

îtibar ئیتِبار (IF) = trust; value. See **ît'bar**.

îtiqat ئیتِقات = faith. See **îtîqad.**

îtîqad ئیتیقاد *f.* (). faith, belief: **-îtîqad bûn** = to believe, hope: **•Paşê M. *îtqat bû*, wekî ew Cizîre, ya ko ew dixaze** (Z-1) Then M. *believed* that this Jizirah was the one he was seeking [lit. 'that he wants']. {also: îdqat (K); îtiqat; îtqat (Z-1); [îtiqad] اعتقاد (JJ)} Cf. Ar i'tiqād اعتقاد = 'belief', verbal noun of i'taqada VIII اعتقد [√'-q-d عقد] = 'to believe' [Z-1/K/JJ] <bawer; ewle I; ol>

ît'par ئیتپار (Z-3) = trust; value. See **ît'bar**.

îtqat ئیتقات (Z-1) = faith. See **îtîqad.**

îxt'iyar ئیختِیار *m.* (). old man. {also: ixt'îyar (K); îxtîyar} {syn: kal I} < clq Ar ixtiyār اختیار & T ihtiyar [L/IF//K] <bapîr; navsera; sere I>

îxtîyar ئیختییار = old man. See **îxt'iyar**.

îza ئیزا *m.(Drş)/f.(K)* (**-yê/;**). 1) {syn: zeĥmet} trouble, annoyance: **•Hêdî hêdî pelepel kir, bi hizar *derdeserî w îza* ji ceřikê ximî hate der** (SK 4:28) Slowly he struggled and with a thousand *difficulties* he got out of the dye vat; **-îza dan** (K/SK)/~ **kirin** (K) to trouble, annoy: **•Hey meyşom, hey bê-yumn, ez texmîn dikem dîsa te mihe xarîewe w dayka xo *îza daye*** (SK 9:92) O luckless wretch, I suppose you've been drinking too much again and *hurting* your mother; 2) {syn: t'ab} suffering, grief: **•Qirê got: Ez babim û çêlîk çêlîkên min in, ezê li gel xwe bibim. Kevokê got ne çêlîkên min in û min *îzayê* xwe pêve bûrandîye û ji nave hinavên min derketine** (Drş #427, 121) The crow said, "I'm the father and the chicks are mine, I'll take them with me. The dove said, "No, they're my chicks and I bore *the suffering* with them, and they have emerged from my loins; **-îza kêşan** (Drş) to endure suffering: **•To ji kûyî û hûn bi kûve çûn, hewe gelek *îza kêşa*?** (Drş #427, 129) Where are you from and where did you all go, did you *endure* much *suffering*? {also: [iza] ایذا (JJ)} < Ar īdā' إیذاء = 'harm, offense, grievance' < ādá آذی IV (√'-d-y اذي) = 'to harm, hurt, wrong, cause pain' [SK/Drş/K/JJ/CS/Hej]<cefa; k'eder; kovan>

îzafe ئیزافە *f.* (**-ya;-yê).** *ezafeh*, a grammatical ending on nouns in Kurdish, Persian and other Iranian languages, which links a) a noun with another noun or pronoun in a genitive construction, or b) a noun with its adjective, or c) as a relative pronoun with a definite antecedent: **•Pirtika *îzafeyê*, ji bo navdêrên nêr yên yekhejmar her wekî ya navdêrên nêr yên binavkirî "-ê" ye** (RR 23.1.) The *ezafeh* ending for masculine singular nouns and likewise for masculine definite nouns is -ê. {also: îzafet, m. (K/IFb-2)} Ar iḍāfah إضافة --> P izāfah اضافه [RR/IFb/ZF/Wkt//K]

îzafet ئیزافەت, m. (K/IFb) = ezafeh. See **îzafe**.

îzah ئیزاه *f.* (). explanation, clarification: **-îzah kirin**

(IFb/ZF) to explain, clarify {syn: r̄ave kirin; şîrove kirin; têgihandin}: •**Li alîyê din jî seydayan kitêbên Erebî bi Kurdî *îzah kirine*** (Nbh 125:4) On the other hand, teachers have *explained* Arabic books in Kurdish. {syn: r̄ave; şîrove} < Ar īḍāḥ إيضاح = 'clarification, explanation' < awḍaḥa IV أوضح (√w-ḍ-ḥ وضح) [Nbh/IFb/ZF]

îzbat ئیزبات (K/B) = proof. See **îspat**.

îzgeh ئیزگەه (IF) = station. See **îstgeh**.

îz•in ئیزِن *f.* (**•na; îz[i]nê).** permission: **-îzna *fk-ê* dan** = to permit, allow s.o.: **•T'ewaqe[t] ji wî bikin, bira ew *îzna* Ûsib *bide*, ku ew ji wer̄a her̄e nêç'îrê** (Ba) Beg him *to allow* Joseph (=so that *he gives* Joseph *permission*) to come hunting with you (=that he come hunting with you) **•Emê *îzna* Memê *bidin*, bira her̄e ser kanîyê** (Z-1) We will *permit* Mem to go to the spring. {also: izin (JB3); îzn (IFb-2/B-2)} {syn: destûr; r̄êdan} < Ar iḏn إذن [Ba/K/IFb/B//JB3]

îzn ئیزن (IFb/B) = permission. See **îzin**.

J ژ

jahr ژاهر (A) = poison. See **jehr**.

jajî ژاژی *f./m.(FS)* **(-ya/-yê;-yê/).** type of creamy cheese, strained yoghurt [T çökelek, Rus tvorog творог] made of yoghurt or ***dew*** [*qv.*] {syn: je‘jî (K-2/B); [jaji] ژاژی (JJ); <jajî> ژاژی (HH)} {syn: toraq} Cf. T cacık = 'yoghurt with cucumber and garlic' [K/A/IFb/FJ/GF/TF/JJ/HH/ZF/FS//B]

jale ژاله *f.* **().** oleander. {syn: r̄ûl; ziqûm (IF)} Sor jałe ژاڵه [K(s)/IF/OK/ZF3/Wkt]

jan ژان *f.* **(-a;-ê).** 1) sorrow: **-jana dila** (IF) heartache: **•Ji *jana dil* laş diare** (O. Basî. Te dil bi xwe re bir, 64) The body smarts from *heartache*; 2) {syn: azar; çîk; derd; êş} (sharp) pain: **•*Jana* min pir giran e** (BF) My *pain* is very severe; **-jana drana** (IF) toothache; **-jana r̄eş** (IF/A) melancholia; **-jana seriya** (IF/A) headache; 3) {syn: çîk} labor pains: **•*Janên* biçûkî hatin wê** (FS) She is having labor pains [lit. '*Pains* of the little one came to her']; 4) {syn: nesaxî; nexweşî; pejî} disease; epidemic: **•*Jan* lê k'et** (K) He took ill; **-jan girtin** (K) to fall ill; **-jana zirav** (A) tuberculosis. {also: [jan] ژان (JJ); <jan> ژان (HH)} [K/A/IF/B/JJ/HH/ZF3/BF] <êşîn>

jandarm ژاندارم (F) = gendarme. See **cendirme**.

Japanî ژاپانی (BF/Wkt) = Japanese. See **Japonî**.

Japonî ژاپۆنی *adj.* Japanese. {also: Japanî (BF/Wkt-2); Japonyayî (Wkt-2); Yabanî (BF-2/Wkt-2)} Sor Yabanî یابانی [IFb/GF/ZF3/Wkt/SS/CS//BF]

Japonyayî ژاپۆنیایی (Wkt) = Japanese. See **Japonî**.

jar I ژار *adj.* 1) {syn: lawaz; leẍer; narîn; qels I; qor̄ III; zeyf; zirav I; ≠k'ok I; ≠qelew} thin (K/JB3/B/JJ/IF); lean (of meat) (B); 2) {syn: zeyf} weak (K/JB3); 3) poor, wretched, miserable (K/A/JJ/IF): **•[Tiştekî nadine *jaran*]** (JR) They don't give anything *to the poor*; 4) religious Muslim (JJ). {also: [jar] ژار (JJ); <jar> ژار (HH)} Cf. P zār زار = 'weak, thin'; Sor hejar هەژار {jarayî; jaretî; jarî; jartî} [K/A/JB3/IF/JR/B/JJ/HH/FS/ZF3]

jar II ژار (IF)/ja‘r II ژاعر (IS) = poison. See **jehr**.

jarayî ژارایی (B) = thinness. See **jarî**.

jaretî ژارەتی (A) = thinness. See **jarî**.

jarî ژاری *f.* **(-ya;-yê).** thinness, leanness. {also: jarayî (B-2); jaretî (A); jartî (B)} {syn: narînî (K)} [K/JB3/IF/ZF3/Wkt//B//A//B]

jartî ژارتی (B) = thinness. See **jarî**.

jebeş ژەبەش (Zx/HH) = watermelon. See **zebeş**.

jeh ژەه (GF) = bowstring. See **jîh**.

jehir ژەهِر = poison. See **jehr**.

jehr ژەهر *f.* **(-a;-ê).** poison; venom: **•Te cixarên xwe temam bi *jahrê* pêçane, te qehwa xwe giş bi *jahrê* çêkir** (ZZ-10, 138) You have rolled your cigarettes with *poison*, you made your coffee completely with *poison*. {also: jahr (A); jar II (IF-2); ja'r II (IS); jehir; jehre (JB1-S); jer (F); je'r (B/Z-2); je're (JB1-S); [jaîr ژائر /jar ژار] (JJ); <jeȟr ژحر/jeȟrî ژحری> (HH)} {syn: axû (HB/K/JB3)} [Pok. g^{u}hen-(ə)- 491.] 'to strike, hurt' --> [*g^{u}hṇ-tro-]: Skt hatru- [hiṁsra-] = 'injurious, harmful': O Ir jaθra- = 'means of causing death, poison' (Tsb2, p.11); P zahr زهر --> T zehir; Sor jar ژار/jehir ژەهِر; Za ja‘r/je‘r *m.* & ja‘ri/je‘ri *f.* (Mal) [AB/K/JB3//A//B//F//JB1-S//JJ//HH] <mergemûş>

jehre ژەهرە (JB1-S) = poison. See **jehr**.

je‘jî ژەعژی (K/B) = strained yoghurt. See **jajî**.

jenan ژەنان (TF) = to strike; to play (music); to card (wool). See **jendin**.

jendin ژەندِن *vt.* **(-jen-).** 1) {syn: k'utan; lêdan; lêxistin} to strike, beat, hit: **•Guleyê ew *jend*** (ZF) The bullet *struck* him; 2) {syn: lêdan[2]} to play *(a musical instrument)*: **•Çeng: sazeka têlkirî ya sêgoşe ye û bi tilîyan *tê jendin*** (BFK 1:501) Harp: it is a triangular string instrument and *is played* with the fingers; **-tembûr jenîn** (BF) to play the tambur; 3) {syn: şkinîn} to card, gin *(wool, cotton)*: **-herî jendin** (IFb) to card, gin wool; 4) to strike *(a match, lightening)*: **-birûsk jendin** (IFb) for lightening to strike; 5) [*vi.*] {syn: arîn; êşîn} to hurt, ache, smart: **•Birîna destê min gelek *a dijenît*** (Bw) The wound on my hand *hurts* a lot. {also: jenan (TF-2); jenîn (Bw/B/GF-2/BF/Kmc); jentin (K[s]-2/FJ/CS/GF-2); [jenin] ژنین (JJ); <jendin ژندن (dijene) (دژنه)> (HH)}[Pok. g^{u}hen-(ə)- 491.] 'to strike, hurt': Proto Ir *jan- = 'to kill, strike'; P zadan زدن (-zan-) = 'to hit, strike'; Sor jendin ژەندن (-jen-)/jenîn ژەنین = 'to churn (milk, yoghurt); to play (musical instrument); to rock, sway' [BFK/K(s)/A/IFb/TF/GF/HH/OrK//Bw/B/JJ/Kmc/BF//CS]

jene ژەنە *f.* **().** (bee)sting(er). {syn: dirêşûşk} [S&E/K/SS]

jeng ژەنگ *f.* **(;-ê).** rust: **-jeng girtin** (IFb)/**zingarê lê avêtin** (JB3) to rust. {also: **zeng** (K/A/IFb-2/B/Ba2); zengar (MK2); zingar (JB3); [jenk] ژنك (JJ); <zeng> ژنگ (HH)} Cf. P zang زنگ; Sor jeng ژەنگ; Za zincar (Todd); Hau jenge *f.* (M4) [Haz/Bw/IFb/K(s)/JJ//K/A/B/HH/Ba2//MK2//JB3] <jengarî> See also **zeng**.

jengar ژەنگار (IFb) = rusty. See **jengarî** & **zengarî**.

jengarî ژەنگارى *adj.* rusty. {also: jengar (IFb); jengdar (IF/K); jenggirtî (B-2); jengî (SK); jingar (IFb-2); **zengarî** (A); zeng[g]irtî (K/B); [jenk ghirtiié] ژنك گرتيه (JJ)} [Haz//A//IFb/K//B//JJ] <jeng> See also **zengarî**.

jengdar ژەنگدار (IF/K) = rusty. See **jengarî** & **zengarî**.

jenggirtî ژەنگگرتى (B) = rusty. See **jengarî** & **zengarî**.

jengî ژەنگى (SK) = rusty. See **jengarî** & **zengarî**.

jenîn ژەنين (Bw/B/GF/BF/Kmc) = to strike; to play (music); to card (wool). See **jendin**.

jentin ژەنتن (K[s]/FJ/CS/GF) = to strike; to play (music); to card (wool). See **jendin**

jenu ژەنو (GF) = knee. See **ejnû**.

jer ژەر (F)/je'r ژەعر (B/Z-2) = poison. See **jehr**.

je're ژەعرە (JB1-S) = poison. See **jehr**.

jev ژەڤ *prep.* + *prn.* 1) {syn: jêk} from each other, from one another, apart: **-jev qetîyan** (IF) to part, separate (vi.) {syn: jêk qutin (JB1-S)}; 2) *[adj.]* open, gaping (e.g., a wound) (B): **•birîna** ***jev*** (B) an *open* wound. < ji = 'from' + hev = 'each other' [BX/K/A/IF/B/ZF3]

jê I ژێ = from him/her/it. See **ji**.

jê II ژێ (M) = bowstring. See **jîh**.

jê•bûn ژێ بوون *vi.* **(ji** *ft-î* **-b-).** 1) {also: jêk bûn (JB1-S)} to come apart, become detached or severed: **•Bi destên jinekê serê mêrekî** ***jêdibe*** (HYma 32) A man's head *is severed* by a woman **•Tiliya min** ***jê bû*** (IFb) My finger *came off/got cut off*; 2) to be weaned off: **•Berxên me** ***ji*** **şîr** ***bûn*** (IFb) Our lambs *have been weaned off* milk. [HYma/A/IFb/GF/FJ/TF//JB1-S]

jêder ژێدەر *m.* **().** 1) {syn: ç'avkanî; kan} source, origins: **•Bi mebesta ku em ji** ***jêderên*** **saxlem xwe li ser rewşa êzîdiyan bikin xwedî zanîn me ji devê Mîrê êzîdiyên Duhokê pirsgirêkên wan guhdarîkirin** (Wlt 2:73, 16) With the purpose of informing ourselves about the situation of the Yezidis from reliable *sources*, we have listened to their problems straight from the mouth of the Mîr of the Yezidis of Dihok; 2) {syn: mesder; r̄ader} *infinitive *(gram.)* (OK). [(neol)Wlt/GF/OK/Hej]

jêderxistin ژێدەرخستن *f.* **(;-ê).** subtraction *(math.)* [Ar ṭarḥ طرح, T çıkarma, P tafrīq تفريق]: **•Ez ji kirariyên** [i.e., **kiryarên**] **hesêb pirtir ji jêderxistinê hez dikim** (Babylon-software.com) Of the arithmetic functions I like subtraction the most. = Sor lê derkirdin لێ دەركردن [endazyar. org/ZF3/Kmc]

jê•girtin ژێ گرتن *vt.* **(ji ... -g[i]r-).** 1) {syn: bijartin I; neqandin I} to pick, choose, select: **•[Go: "Babo, hespek bide min da'z lê suwar bim." Gotê: "Kurê min, de here tavilê, hezar û du me'negî wê li tavilê da, bo xwe êkî** ***jê bigre.*** **" Çû bo xwe êkî** ***ji*** **ȟemiya** ***girt*****, îna derê]** (PS-II #34, 104, ll.22-24) He said, "Papa, give me a horse so that I can ride." He told him, "My son, go to the stable, there are 1,002 horses in the stable, *choose* one for yourself." He went and *picked* one, and brought it out; 2) to effect s.o. *[negatively]*: **•Ewê xeberê gelekî** ***ji*** **min** ***girt*** (XF ж-#37) Those words *had* quite *an effect on* me; 3) to copy, photocopy (IFb/ZF/CS); 4) to quote, cite (ZF); 5) [*f.* **(-a;-ê).**] citation, quotation: **•Di vê** ***jêgirtinê*** **de ji bo edebiyatê du pêwîstî xwe didin dest** (R.Alan. Bendname, 109) In this *quotation* 2 require-ments for literature give themselves away. < ji + wî/wê = jê + girtin [Zeb/PS-II/OK/XF/AId/IFb/ZF/CS]

jêhatî ژێهاتى *adj./pp.* 1) quick-witted, sharp, clever (K); 2) able, capable (A/JB3/IF/JB1-S); skilled (JJ/IF); one who knows his profession well (JJ/JB1-S). {also: [ji-hati] ژيهاتى (JJ)} [AB/K/A/JB3/IF/JJ/JB1-S]

jêhelî ژێهەلى (Bw) = incline. See **jihelî**.

jêk ژێك *prep. & prn.* from each other, from one another, apart: **-jêk anîn** (JB3) to disunite, separate; **-jêk bûn** (JB1-S/ZF3) to be beheaded or decapitated; **-jêk kirin** (JB1-S) to behead, decapitate, slice off {syn: serjêkirin}; **-jêk qutin** (JB1-S) to part, separate (vi.) {syn: jev qutîyan}; **-jêk ve kirin** (JB1-A) to open. {syn: jev} < ji = 'from' + êk = 'one' [BX/JB3/JB1-A&S/ZF3]

jêk bûn ژێك بوون (JB1-S) = to come apart, be severed. See **jêbûn**.

jêhilî ژێهلى (FS) = incline. See **jihelî**.

jê•kirin ژێكرن *vt.* **(jê-k-).** to cut or chop off, to snap off, amputate, remove: Cf. **-serjêkirin/şerjêkirin** = to behead, decapitate, chop s.o.'s head off. {also: [ji-kirin] ژیکرین (JJ)} [Z-1/K/A/IF/B/JJ/JB1-S]

jêkirî ژێکِری *pp./adj.* severed, cut off, detached: **•Ji banan endamên cinsî, qalind, qehwe, tarî û *jêkirî* dibarin** (HYma 32) From the roofs thick, brown, dark and *severed* sexual organs are raining. [HYma/A/FJ/GF/ZF3]

jêla ژێلا *adv.* upward, from below: **•Çaxê mêriv *jêla* li ĥeç'ê ç'îê diniheřî** (Ba2) When people look *upward* to the mountain peak [from below] **•Ew bi *jêlilî* ve çû** (FS) He went upwards/up hill **•Qjikê *jêla* nukulê xwe li cêř xist, cêř qul bû** (EH) The bird thrust its beak into the clay jug *from below*, and poked a hole in it [lit. 'the jug became pierced']. {also: jêlilî (FS); jêlî II (IF)} [Ba2/K/B//IF//FS] <jihelî>

jêlilahî ژێلِلاهی (Hk) = incline. See **jihelî**.

jêlilî ژێلِلی (FS) = upward, from below. See **jêla**

jêlî I ژێلی *prep.* since (time). {syn: ewey; ji ... û vir de; jîrkî} [BX/JB3/IF/ZF3]

jêlî II ژێلی (IF) = upward, from below. See **jêla**.

jê qarihan ژێ قارِهان (HR) = to stop, quit, abandon, leave off. See **qeran**.

jê qeran ژێ قەران = to stop, quit, abandon, leave off. See **qeran**.

jê qeriyan ژێ قەرِیان (HYma) = to stop, quit, abandon, leave off. See **qeran**.

jêr ژێر *f.* **(-a;-ê).** 1) lower part, underside, bottom: **•*Jêra* bîrê tarî ye** (FS) *The bottom of* the well is dark; 2) *[adv.]* {syn: xwar; ≠jor} downward, down, downstairs: **-berbijêr/serbijêr** = do.; **-jêrê** (B) down, downward *(motion toward)*: **•Ewana ji ser k'oşkê hatine *jêrê*** (EP-7) They went *down* from the roof of the palace; 3) {syn: başûr; cenûb; nişîv (Bw)} south (IF): **•Welatên *jêr*** (IF) The *southern* countries. {also: [jir] ژیر (JJ)} <O Ir *hača = 'from' + *adari = 'below': Mid P azēr = 'below, under' (M3); Sgd c'dr [čadir]; P zīr زیر = 'beneath'; Sor jêr ژێر = 'under side, bottom; under, below, down'; Za cêr = 'down(ward)' (Todd); Hau çêr-û = 'under' (M4) [F/K/A/JB3/IF/JJ/B/ZF3] <jêrîn; nişîv>

jêrenot ژێرەنۆت *f.* **(-a;-ê).** footnote: **•Di *jêrenota* xwe de diyar dike ku wî ev agadarî ji Mêjûyî Edebî Kurdî ya Alaeddîn Seccadî wergirtiye** (warbotan.com 21.ix.2015) In his *footnote* he states that he got this information from A.S.'s "History of Kurdish Literature" **•Dîsa di vê *jêrenotê* de ji bo çêlekan/dewaran dibêje pezê reş** (DiyarName.com 30.xi.2010) Again in this *footnote* he calls cows/cattle "black pez [sheep]" **•Em vê yekê ji *jêrenota* di bin helbesta wî ya bi navê Wuslet fêr dibin** (RiaTaza 1.v.2017) We learn this from the *footnote* under his poem called "Wuslet". {syn: têbînî} < jêr = 'under, beneath' + -e- + not = 'note' [ZF3/Wkt/CS] <têbînî>

jêrin ژێرِن (B) = lower. See **jêrîn**.

jêrî ژێری (SK) = lower. See **jêrîn**.

jêrîn ژێرین *adj.* lower, inferior. {also: jêrin (B-2); jêrî (SK); [jirin ژیرین/jiri ژیری] (JJ)} Cf. P zērīn زیرین = 'lower, under' [K/IFb/B/GF/TF/ZF3//SK] <bin I & II; jorîn; xwar>

jêrzemîn ژێرزەمین (ZF3/Wkt) = basement. See **zêřzemîn**.

jêve•bûn ژێڤەبوون *vi.* **(jêve-b-).** to let alone, leave alone, let stg. be; to drop, change *(the subject)*; to detach o.s., separate o.s. from: **•Ez *jêve bûm*** (Bw) I *left it alone* [=Min hêla]. [Bw/GF/OK] <hiştin>

ji I ژِ *prep.* 1) from [Cf. Germ. von, Rus. ot от]: **•Mala min *ji* bajêr dûr e** (BX) My house is far *from* town **•Koçer *ji* deştê hatine** (BX) The nomads came *from* the plain; **-ji xwe** = a) naturally [lit. 'from itself'] (BX); b) already (Hk). *See AKR (p. 62-63) for detailed discussion of **jixwe***; 2) from, out of, of *[often with pl.]* [Cf. Germ. aus, Rus. iz из]: {also: ji ... re}: **•Ewê *ji* qehrê guldank şikest** (BX) She broke the vase *out of* anger **•*Ji* nêza mir** (BX) He died *of* hunger **•Mîz kir *ji* tirsa *re*** (L) He pissed *out of* fear **•*Ji* kêfa *re* bezîya, hat malê** (L) *Out of* joy (=full of joy) he ran home **•M. wê *ji* k'erba bit'eqe** (EP-7) M. is about to burst *with/out of* grief **•Lêvên min *ji* tînan ziwa bûn** (AB) My lips became dry *from* thirst; 3) of, from among: **•Yekî *ji* wan** = One *of* them; 4) made of or from: **•Helva *ji* şîrêzê çênabe** (BX) Halvah is not made *of* resin *[prv.]*; 5) since *(time)*; 6) than [+ comparative adjs.]: **•*Ji* pêncî carî bêh*tir* gotina "mist" di şûna gotina "mizdanê" de, bi çewtî hatiye bikaranîn** (AW73C2) More *than* 50 times the word "mist" was incorrectly used instead of the word "mizdan" **•Riwê te *ji* heyva çardehê rewşen*tir* e** (BX) Your face is brighter *than* the moon on the 14th [of the month]; 7) *indicates manner*: **•*ji* piya** (BX) standing, *on* foot [cf. Sp de pie]; 8) *used together* *with postpositions*:

-ji ... de = ever since *(time)*, starting from: •***Ji* jor *de* hate xwar** (BX) He came down [lit. '*from* on high he came down'] •**Lê pirçemekê xwe ruçikand dibû [=ruçikandi bû]: *ji* wê rojê *de* şerm dike ko bi ro derkeve** (SW) But the bat had already plucked out its feathers: *ever since* that day [or, *from* that day *on*] it was ashamed to come out during the day •**Roja xweş *ji* sibehê *de* xweş e** (BX) A good day is good *from* the morning *on* [*prv.*];

-ji ... der = a) outside of *(physical location)*; beyond: •**Ew *ji* şeher *der* dijî** (K) He lives *outside of* the city •**Ewa tu dibêjî *ji* qewata min *dere*** (FK-eb-1) What you're asking is *beyond* my power •***ji* reya me *der*** (BX) *outside of* our path; b) besides, except for: •***jê der*** (K) *except for him* •***Ji* koma me *der* kesekî xebat nekirîye** (K) *Except for* our group, nobody did any work;

-ji ... pê ve = outside of, except for {syn: bê (I[2]); ji bilî; pêştir [+ji]; xêncî}:•***Ji* te *pê ve*** = *except for* you •***jû pê ve*** (=**ji wî û pê ve**) = moreover •**Me Kurdan edebiyateke nivîskî, *ji* çend klasikên *pê ve*, hesêb nîne** (SW) *Except for* a few classics, we Kurds cannot be considered to have a written literature;

-ji ... re [or: **r̄a**] a) to *[in Serhedan region often shortened to simply -re/-r̄a]*: •**Ez *ji* te *re* hertiştî dibêjim** (BX) I tell *you* everything •***jê ra*** = *to him/her/it* •***ji* te *ra*** = *to* you [thee] •**Min *ji xwe re* digot** (BX) I told *myself* •***Ji* Hono *re* bêbextî kirin** [sic] (BX) They betrayed Hono •**Xwedê teala qundirek *jê re* şand** (L) God sent *him* a gourd; **-k'êfa *fk-ê* ji *behvan* re hatin** = to like, to be pleasing to s.o.: •**Kêfa min *jê re* tê** (BX) I like it/It pleases me; b) {See [2] above};

-ji ... û vir de = since (time) {syn: ewey; jêlî I; jîrkî}: •***Ji* wê rojê *û vir de*** (BX) *Ever since* that day;

-ji ... ve = according to: •***ji* te *ve*** = *according to* you; •***ji* mêj *ve*** = for a long time *(up to and including the present moment)* •***ji* nêzîk *ve*** = soon; *from* nearby, *from* up close •***ji* dûr *ve*** = *from* afar •***ji* nişkêva** = suddenly. See **nişkêva** •***ji* piya *ve*** [or, **ji piya**, (see above)] = standing [cf. Sp de pie]. {also: [ji] ژ (JJ)} Note: ji + wî/wê = jê; ji + hev = jev. [Pok I. sek'- 896.] 'to follow' --> *(instrumental case of thematic root-noun* *sek^{u}o-s = 'one following'): Skt sácā = 'with'; Av hačā = 'with'; OP hačā = 'from'; Mid P az = 'from, than' (M3); P az از; = Sor le ... -ewe لـه ...ەوە; = Za -r̄a; Hau je/çene = 'from, in' & je/çene ... -ewe = 'from, to' (M4) [BX/K/A/JB3/IF/JJ/B/ZF3/Wkt]

ji II ژ (Şnx/Slv/Zx) = also. See **jî I**.

ji aş û baş ژ ئـــاش و بـــاش (ZF3/Wkt) = trivial. See under **aş I**.

ji ber ژ بەر = because of, for. See under **ber II**.

ji ber kirin ژ بـەر کِـرِن *vt.* **(ji ber -k[e]-).** 1) to learn by heart, memorize {syn: *rewa kirin}; 2) to take off, remove *(eyeglasses)*: •**Ez berçavkêt xo *ji ber dikem*** (Bw) *I take off* my glasses [lit. 'I take them from in front of me']. Cf. P az bar از بر = 'by heart' --> T ezber [Bw/K/A/IFb/GF]

ji ber ko ژ بـەر کۆ *conj.* because, since (reason): •**Bes, çaxê kû baran aw berf tê, her k'es banê xwe digerênê û dimalê, *ji ber kû* avaîyê wa ȟemû bi kevir û k'ilsê ne** (HR-I 1:18) But, when it rains or snows, everyone rolls and sweeps his roof, *because* their houses are all of stone and lime •***Jiberko* Hêja qutabîyekê zîreke, mamostay xelat kir** (BF) *Because* H. is a clever student, the teacher rewarded him •***Ji ber ku* Alexandre Jaba di sala 1857an de destnîşan kiriye ku Mela 60 sal[î] bûye, sala 1797an wek ya rojbûna wî tê pejirandin** (Nbh 129:5) *Because* A. Jaba indicated that Mela [Mahmûd Bayazîdî] was 60 years old in 1857, 1797 has been accepted as his birth year •***Ji ber ku* êdî nikare li ber heqaret û lêxistinê tab bike, rojekê dîsa direve** (Nbh 132:12) *Because* he can't stand the insults and beatings anymore, one day he runs away again •**Lê *ji ber ku* min xelasiya mirovahiyê jî tê de dît, ez gihîştimê** (Wlt 1:35, 16) But *because* I also saw the saving of humanity in it, I joined it. {also: ji ber ku (ZF3/RZ/FD); ji ber kû (HR)} {syn: ç'iku ko; ç'imkî} [BX/IFb/BF//ZF3/RZ/FD//HR]

ji ber ku ژ بـەر کـو (ZF3/RZ/FD) = because. See **ji ber ko**.

ji ber kû ژ بەر کوو (HR) = because. See **ji ber ko**.

ji bilî ژ بِـلـی *prep.* apart from, besides, other than, except for (mostly **ji bilî**): •**[ji] bilî wî** = apart from him, other than him; **-ji bil ... ve** (BX) do.:

•Ji bil min ve kes ne ma bû (BX) Other than me, nobody was left. {also: bijlî (Zeb); [sbel] زبـــــل (JJ)} {syn: bê I[2]; ji ... pê ve; pêştir [+ji]; xêncî} [BX/K//JJ//Zeb]

jidandin ژدانـــــدِن (HR) = to tighten, bind tightly. See **şidandin**.

jidil ژدِل *adj.* 1) sincere, frank, heartfelt: **•Hevaltiya bi herkesî re, ne hevaltiyeke *jidil* e** (Ardû, 38) Friendship with everyone is not a *sincere* friendship **•Şerîfo Teker erd û ezman bi sûndên qelew û *jidil* direşandin** (HYma 48) S.T. sprayed earth and heaven with thick and *heartfelt* oaths; 2) [*adv.*] sincerely, frankly, from the heart, with all one's heart: **•Go, "Ti ĥenekê xwe bi mi dikê, kengî wilo didê min?", go, "Wele ez *ji dil* dibêjim"** (HR 3;173) [One] said, "You're joking with me, when do you give me such a thing?" [the other] said, "Really, I'm saying it *with all my heart*". < ji + dil [HR/HYma/CS] <dil>

jih ژه (IFb/GF/TF/Wkt/FS) = bowstring. See **jîh**.

jihelî ژهـهـلـی *m.* **(-yê;).** uphill slope, ascent, incline: **•Çu *jihelî* bê jordanî nîne** (Bw) What goes up must come down [lit. 'there is no *uphill slope* without a downhill slope'] *[prv.]*. {also: jêhelî (Bw-2); jêhilî (FS); jêlilahî (Hk)} {syn: berwar; hevraz; p'al; pesar; p'êş II[2]; qunt'ar; sîng; teřazin} [Bw//FS//Hk] <berwar; ≠jordanî>

jijo ژژۆ (A/IF) = hedgehog. See **jûjî**.

jijû ژژوو (B) = hedgehog. See **jûjî**.

jimar ژمار (F/K/B) = number; issue *(of a journal)*. See **hejmar**.

jimardin ژماردِن = to count. See **hejmartin**.

jimare ژمـاره (IF) = number; issue *(of a journal)*. See **hejmar**.

jimartin ژمارتِن (-jimir-) (F/K/B/IF/FS) = to count. See **hejmartin**.

ji me ç'êtir ژ مـه چـێـتـر *pl.* jinns, genies, demons, devils: **•*Ji me çêtir* newêrin xo nizîkî wî cihî biken yê ku asin lê bît** (JH, 17) *Jinns* don't dare to approach a place where there is iron **•*Jime çêtira*, her tim li zarûkên xweşik, bi gan û goşt dinitirin** (MB, 23) *Jinns* always keep an eye out for beautiful, plump children. {syn: cin} lit. = 'those better than us'; cf. NENA an bištof minnan = 'demons, ghosts (lit. those who are better than us)' (Sabar:Dict) [MB/JH/XF/ZF3] <ç'êtir; dêw; ferĥît; şeytan>

jimirîn ژمِرین (K) = to count. See **hejmartin**.

jin ژن *f.* **(-a;-ê).** 1) {syn: afret; pîrek} woman; 2) {syn: hevser [f.]; kevanî; k'ulfet; pîrek; zêç} wife, married woman: **-jin anîn/~standin** = to take a wife, be married *(said of a man)*; **-jina bî** (B/F) widow. See **jinebî**. {also: [jin] ژن (JJ)} [Pok. g^{u}ĕnā-/g^{u}enə-/g^{u}enī-, *gen.* g^{u}n-ās/*g^{u}en-ās 473.] 'woman' [*g^{u}énH$_2$-, *originally paradigmatically linked to* *g^{u}néH$_2$- (Mayrhofer)]: Skt jáni- *f.* = 'woman'; Young Av ǰaini- *f.*; Mid P zan (M3); Parthian jn; P zan زن; Sor jin ژن; Za cenî *f.* (Todd); Hau jenî *f.* (M4); cf. also Arm kin կին; Gr gynē γυνή (*gen.* gynaikos γυναικός); Rus žená жена = 'wife'; Eng queen (originally = 'woman') [F/K/A/JB3/IFb/B/JJ/JB1-A&S/ SK/GF/TF/OK] <bûk I>

jinabî ژنابی = widow. See **jinebî**.

jinap ژنـــــــاپ *f.* **(-a;-ê).** aunt, wife of paternal uncle *(ap, qv.)*: **•Înca hingê apê wî, *jinapa* wî ze'f ji wî ĥiz dikin** (Z-4) Then his uncle (=father's brother) and his *aunt* (=*uncle's wife*) loved him very much. [cf. clq Ar mart 'amm مرة عمّ]. {also: [jin ap] ژن عاپ (JJ)} {syn: amojin; jinmam} [Z-1/K/A/IF/JJ/B/ZF3] <ap; mam; jinxal>

jinbab ژنباب (Bw) = stepmother. See **jinbav**.

jinbav ژنـــــبـــــاڤ *f.* **(-a;-ê).** stepmother; mother of children engendered by a previous union. {also: jinbab (Bw); [jin-bab] ژن بـــــاب (JJ); <jinbab> ژنـبـاب (HH)} {syn: dêmarî; zirdayîk} [K/A/JB3/IF/B/ /JJ/HH/ZF3//Bw] <bavmarî; hêwî; nevisî; zirbav>

jinbir ژنبر (A/ZF3) = sister-in-law, brother's wife. See **jinbira**.

jinbir•a ژنـبِـرا *f.* **(•a;•ê).** sister-in-law, brother's wife. {also: jinbir (A/ZF3)} [L/K/IF/B//A/ZF3] <baltûz; bûk I; cayî; diş; jint'î II>

jinebî ژنـهبی *f.* **(-ya;-yê).** widow. {also: jinabî; jina bî (B/F); jinûbî; [jin-a bi] ژنا بی (JJ); <jinebî> ژنبی (HH)} {syn: bêjin; bî I} Cf. P bīve بـیـوه; Sor bêwejin بێوهژن; Za [cenîya] vîya (Todd) [K/A/IF/HH/ FS/ZF3//F/B/JJ] <bî I; jinmirî>

jingar ژنگار (IFb) = rusty. See **jengarî**.

jinik ژنِك = dim. of **jin**.

ji nişka ve ژ نـشـکـا ڤـه (JB3/GF/OK) = suddenly. See **nişkêva**.

ji nişke ve ژ نشکه ڤه (IFb) = suddenly. See **nişkêva**.

jinînî ژنینی (Kmc/ZF3) = womanhood. See **jintî I**.

jinîtî ژنیتی (GF/TF/ZF) = womanhood. See **jintî I**.

jinmam ژنـمـام *f.* **(-a;-ê).** aunt, wife of one's paternal uncle (**mam**, qv.) [cf. clq Ar mart 'amm مـــــرة عمّ]. {also: jirmam (JB1-A/Bw); [jin mam] ژن مام

(JJ)} {syn: amojin; jinap} [Msr/IF/JJ/FS/ZF3//JB1-A/Bw] <ap; mam; jinxal>

jinmirî ژنـمِـرى *m.* **().** widower, man whose wife is dead: **•Ga bidin gamirîyan, keç bidin *jinmirîyan*!** (Wkt) Give a bull to those whose bulls have died, [and] a girl to *the widowers [prv.].* {syn: mêrê bî} [Bw/K/FS/ZF3/Wkt] <bî I; jinebî>

jinmîr ژنـميـر *f.* **(-a;-ê).** wife of an emir, emir's wife; queen, princess: **•Wextê mîr di keviya çemê mezin de hate kuştin Heyzebûn ewçend giriya bû ko *jinmîr* bi xwe hêstirên xwe dimaliştin û li ber dilê cêriyê dida** (Rnh 3:23, 5) When the emir was killed on the banks of the big river, Heyzebûn cried so much that *the emir's wife* herself wiped away her own tears and consoled the servant girl. [Rnh/GF/OK/ZF3/FS/Wkt] <dotmîr; mîr I; pismîr>

jintî I ژنـتـى *f.* **(-ya;-yê).** womanhood; womanliness, femininity. {also: jinînî (Kmc/ZF3-2); jinîtî (GF/TF/ZF)} {syn: pîrekî} Sor jinêtî ژنێتى [K/B//GF/TF/ZF//Kmc]

jint'î II ژنـتـى *f.* **(-ya;-yê).** sister-in-law, wife of husband's brother: **•Navbera min û *jintîya* min Gulben pirr baş e** (Qado Şêrîn 5.ix.2007) I get along well with my *sister-in-law* G. {syn: cayî; hêwerjin (K[s]); jinbir} [Czr/Wn/Hk/Bw/GF/TF/OK/ZF3] <birajin; bûrî; diş; t'î II>

jinû I ژنوو (K) = knee. See **ejnû**.

ji nû II ژ نوو (SK) = anew. See **ji nû ve**.

jinûbî ژنووبى = widow. See **jinebî**.

jinûva ژنووڤا (K) = anew. See **ji nû ve**.

ji nû ve/jinûve [OK] ژنـووڤـه *adv.* anew, once again; *used in northern dialects to express 're-' (e.g., reopen, redo, reestablish, etc.), expressed in southern dialects with suffix -eve, qv.*: **•Gundek *ji nû awa kir* li ma-beyna 'eşîreta Balikan û 'eşîreta Xoşnawan. nawê wî gundî da-na Xaneqa** (SK 45:435) He *reestablished* a village between the Balik and Khoshnaw tribes. He called the village Khanaqa **•Hinek nivîskar diyar dikin ku MHP *xwe ji nû ve saz dike* û ber bi demokratîkbûnê ve diçe** (AW69A1) Some writers declare that the MHP [Nationalist People's Party] *is remaking itself* and becoming more democratic; **-ji nû ve kiřîn** (JJ) to rebuy, repurchase. {also: ji nû II (SK); jinûva (K); [ji-nouwé] ژنـوڤـه (JJ)} = Sor ser le nwê [nö] سـەر لـه نـوێ [IFb/JJ/OK//K] <dîsa; -eve>

jinxal ژنـخـال *f.* **(-a;-ê).** aunt, wife of maternal uncle (**xal**, qv.) [cf. clq Ar mart xāl مـرة خـال]. {syn: pîlik (A/IF); xalojn} [F/K/A/IFb/B/ZF] <amojin; jinap; xal>

ji řêve ژرێڤه *adv.* first, at first: **•Dibêjin bestekî** [sic] **beran li-t̲enişt gundê wan heye. Wextê diçin e seferê *ji řêwe* diçine naw besta beran, çawêt xo dimiçînin, pêş paş diçin, panîya pîyê wan geheşt e kîşk berî dê înin, bi t̲erazîyê kêşin çend der-kewt dê sûndekî mezin û kirêt xot ko, "Ḧetta bi-qeder giranîya wî berey pare-y zêř yan zîw neînim nahêmewe"** (SK 12:117) They say that there is a stony vale next to their village. When they go on a journey they go *first of all* to the vale of stones, shut their eyes, go back and forth and, whichever stone the heel of their foot touches, they will bring it and weigh it in a balance and, however much it turns out, they will swear a mighty and ugly oath that, "I shall not return until I bring the weight of this stone in gold or silver." {also: ji řêwe (SK)} {syn: berêda} [Zeb/Wkt//SK]

ji řêwe ژرێوه (SK) = at first. See **ji řêve**.

jirmam ژرمـام (JB1-A/Bw) = aunt, wife of paternal uncle. See **jinmam**.

jivan ژڤـان *m./f.(Wkt)* **(-ê/-a;-î/).** rendezvous, date, appointment: **•Min û sêpêkê *jivan* e/Min û sêdarê *jivan* e** (from poem by Muayyid Tayyib of Dihok) I have *a rendezvous* with the gallows, /I have *a rendezvous* with the gibbet. {also: civan (Mdt/A/TF/FS-2); covan (FS-2); jîvan (IFb)} Sor juwan ژووان = 'tryst, appointment, rendezvous' [Bw/MuayyidTayyib/FS//IFb//Mdt/A/TF]

jivjî ژڤژى (Zeb) = hedgehog. See **jûjî**.

jixwe ژخوه. See under **ji I**.

jiyan ژيان (Lab) = life. See **jîn**[3].

ji zûde ژ زووده (GF) = for a long time. See **zûda**.

jî I ژى *adv.* 1) also, too: **•Agir xweş e, lê xwelî *jî* jê çêdibe** = Fire is good, but ashes are *also* produced from it *[prv.]* **•Merîyêd ku *qe* tiştek *jî* jê ne lazim bûya** (Ba) People who wouldn't need anything *at all*; **-... jî ... jî** = both ... and: **•Ezê darê cahil *jî* bibiřim, yê pîr *jî*** (Dz) I will cut down *both* young trees *and* old ones; 2) as for: **•Bêrîvanan *jî* pez dotin** (AB) *As for* the milkmaids, they milked the sheep **•Lê her dehê dinê *jî* ji dêkê bûn** (Ba) But *as for* the other ten, they were from one mother **•Qîza te *jî*, di nabên

çît û perda de ye (L) *As for* your daughter, she is in the women's quarters [lit. 'among the drapes and curtains']; 3) even [+ *subj.*]: •**Perên ku didane me ne pir bin *jî*, *dîsa jî* ji meaşên hemû karmend û karkerên wan zêdetir bûn** (AW72B3) *Even* if the money they gave us was not a lot, it was *still* more than the wages of all their workers •**Wele, wekî ezê bimirim *jî*, ezê xweȓa rabim, li Memê t'emaşe- kim** (EP-7) By God, *even* if I were dying, I'd get up to have a look at Mem; **-ne jî** = nor, not even. {also: ji II (Şnx/Slv/Zx); jîk I (Bw); [ji] ژى (JJ)} [Pok. I. kᵘ̯e 635.] 'and' (enclitic): O Ir ca; Av ča; O P čā; *also* Lat -que; Cf. Mid P -iz = 'also, even' (M3); -z in P nīz نيز; Sor -[î]ş يش; Za zî (Todd). *See AKR (p. 54-57) for detailed discussion of **jî**.* [F/K/JB3/IF/B/JJ/JB1-A&S/SK/GF/TF/OK/AKR]

jî II ژى (IFb/GF/OK/ZF3) = bowstring. See **jîh**.

jî III ژى *m.* **(-yê;).** age, years of one's life: •***Jîyê* te çende?** (BF) How old are you? [lit. 'How much is your *age*?'] •**Xudê *jîyê* te gelek dirêj ke** (BF) Long may you live [lit. 'May God make your *age* long']. {also: [ji] ژى (JJ); <jî> ژى (HH)} {syn: 'emir II; t'emen} [Dh/JJ/HH/ZF] <salî>

jîh ژيه *m./f.(B/FS)* **(/-a;).** bowstring; string made from animal guts; (violin) string: •**jiha kivanî** (FS) bowstring. {also: jeh (GF-2); jê II (M); jih (IFb-2/GF/TF/Wkt/FS); jî II (IFb-2/GF-2/OK); jîk II (K/B/F); [jih] ژه (JJ); <jih> ژه (HH)} Skt jyā́ *f.*; Av jyā-; Mid P zīh = 'bow-string' (M3); P zih زه; Sor jê ژێ = 'line, cord, string (of bow, musical instruments, pyjamas, etc.)' [A/IFb//JJ/HH//F/K/B//M//GF/TF/Wkt/FS//OK/ZF3] <kevan; tîr>

jîîn ژيئين (F/B) = to live. See **jîn**.

jîjo ژيژۆ (A/IF/Msr) = hedgehog. See **jûjî**.

jîjok ژيژۆك f. (-a;) (Msr) = hedgehog. See **jûjî**.

jîk I ژيك (Bw) = also. See **jî I**.

jîk II ژيك (K/B/F) = bowstring. See **jîh**.

jîn ژين *vi.* **(-jî-).** 1) to live, be alive: **-Bijî ... !** = Long live ... ! Bravo!; 2) to dwell, reside; 3) [*f.* **(-a;-ê).**] life: **-ava jînê** (AB) the water of life. {also: jiyan (Lab); jiyîn (JB3); jîîn (F/B-2); jîyan; jîyîn (K/B/TF); [jin] ژين (JJ)} [Pok. 3. gᵘ̯ei̯-/gᵘ̯ei̯ə- 467.] 'to live': Skt jīvātu-ḥ = 'life'; O Ir ǰyati/ǰyatu (Schwartz) & *gay- (Tsb 43) [Pok. gᵘ̯ī-(u̯-) 468.]: Av gay- (*pres.* ǰiva-); O P jiv-; P zīstan زيستن = 'to live'; Sor jiyan ژيان; Hau jîway (jîw-) *vi.* (M4); cf. also Lat vivo, -ere; Gr zō ζῶ; Rus žit' жить (živu) (живу) [BX/A/IFb/JJ/SK/GF/OK/M//F//K/B/TF//JB3]

jîndar ژيندار *adj.* 1) {syn: zêndî} alive, living; 2) [*m.&f.* **().**] living creature, animal: •**Herçiqas av ji bo hemû *jîndaran* çavkaniyeke bingehîn be jî, îro di destê mirovên "hemdem" de wek pergaleke ji holê rakirina berhemên dîrokê tê bi kar anîn** (Wlt 1:21, 16) Although water is a basic resource for all *living things*, today it is being used by "modern" man as an instrument for destroying historical artifacts. = Sor giyan•leber گيان لەبەر [(neol)Wlt/K/IFb/GF/TF/ZF3] <ȟeywan; saẍ>

jînenigarî ژينەنِگارى (IFb) = biography. See **jînenîgarî**.

jînenîgarî ژینەنیگاری *f.* **(-ya;-yê).** biography: •**Digel *jînenîgariya* Ö. dîroka PKK'ê jî di nava rûpelên pirtûkê de cih digire** (AW75B6) In addition to O's *biography*, the history of the PKK also occupies part of the book [lit. 'takes a place amid the pages of the book']. {also: jînenigarî (IFb); jînenîgerî (Wkt)} [AW/ZF3/BF//IFb//Wkt] <serhatî>

jînenîgerî ژينەنيگەرى (Wkt) = biography. See **jînenîgarî**.

jîngeh ژینگەه *f.* **(-a;-ê).** environment: •**Wî hest dikir ev *jîngehe* ya dibîte hêzeka rêgir beramber viyanêt wî yêt hunerî û viyana wî bo serbestîyê** (Peyv 3[1996], 38) He felt that this *environment* was getting in the way of [lit. 'becoming a preventive force'] his artistic desires and his desire for freedom. Sor jînge ژينگە [(neol)Peyv/VoA/ZF3]

jîr ژير *adj.* 1) {syn: aqil I; aqiljîr; aqilmend; aqiltîj (Bw); bi fêm; bi zihn} smart, intelligent, clever (K/A/IF): •**Azad kurekî *jîr* e** (AB) Azad is a *smart* boy; 2) skillful, adroit (A); 3) alive, dynamic, energetic, lively (B/K); 4) zealous, striving (B). {also: jîrek (IF-2); zîrek (IFb-2); [jér] ژير (JJ)} Cf. P āžīr آژير & zīrak زيرك = 'intelligent, clever' {jîrahî; jîrayî; jîrî; jîrtî} [K/A/JB3/IFb/ZF3/FS] <jêhatî>

jîrahî ژيراهى (K) = zeal; liveliness. See **jîrayî**.

jîrayî ژيرايى *f.* **(-ya;-yê).** 1) {syn: aqil; ȟiş} "brains", intelligence; 2) zeal; 3) liveliness. {also: jîrahî (K-2); jîrî (K-2); jîrtî (B-2)} [K/B/ZF3/Wkt] <jîr>

jîrek ژيرەك (IF) = smart; skillful; dynamic. See **jîr**.

jîrî ژيرى (K) = zeal; liveliness. See **jîrayî**.

jîrkî ژيركى *prep.* since *(time)*: •***Jîrkî* ez hatim vî bajarî, min tu polîsek nedît** (Wkt:Azad Ekkaş di koma "Zimanê Kurdî" ya li ser Rûnameyê de, i.2012) *Ever since* I came to this city, I have not seen a single policeman; **-jîrkî ko...** (BX) ever since. {syn: ewey; jêlî I; ji ... û vir de} [BX/K/Wkt]

jîrtî ژیرتی (B) = zeal; liveliness. See **jîrayî**.

jîvan ژیڤان (IFb) = rendezvous. See **jivan**.

jîyîn ژییین (K/B/TF) = to live. See **jîn**.

jmar ژمـــار (IF) = number; issue *(of a journal)*. See **hejmar**.

jmartin ژمارتِن = to count. See **hejmartin**.

jojî ژۆژی (IF) = hedgehog. See **jûjî**.

jor ژۆر *f.* **(;-ê).** 1) upper part, top (K/B/JJ); 2) *[adv.]* {syn: bala; hevraz [2]; ≠jêr; ≠xwar} up, upward, upstairs; above, over: **•Dewle ze'f girane, ew ancax-ancax dik'işîne *jorê*** (Ba) The bucket is very heavy, he can scarcely pull it *up*; -[**ji**] **jor de/ jorda** = from above, downward: **•*Ji jor de* hate xwar** (BX) He went down, descended [lit. '*from above* he went down'] **•Ser sîngê Dûmanlûê cîcîna xulexula cewikêd avê bû, êd ku mînanî mara *jorda* dişûlikîn** (Ba2:1, 202) On the slope of {Mount] Dumanlu here and there was the babbling of brooks (of water), those which crept *from above* like snakes **•Zîna Bek'ir *jorda* 'erdê k'et** (EP-7) Z.B. fell *down* [lit. 'fell to earth *from above*']; **-berbijor/serbijor** = up, upward; 3) inside, in: **•Çon *bo jorve*, ... çon *di jorve*, r̄ûnişt'in** (M-Zx, #760, 352) They went *inside*, ... they went *inside* and sat down **•Dê, r̄abe, here *jor*, bo xo larîya digel bike** (M-Ak, #671, 302) Get up and go *inside* and play with her **•Wextê ço *jor* dît jinek meşkê dihijînît, ya r̄ûs bo, tiştek di berda nebo** (SK 16:156) When he went *inside* he saw a woman shaking a goatskin churn, naked, without a thing on. {also: [jori ژوری/jorin ژورین] (JJ); <jor> ژور (HH)} <O Ir *hača = 'from' + *upari = 'below': Mid P azabar = 'above' (M3); Sgd cwpr [čupar]; P zabr زبر; Sor jûr ژوور = 'upper part, top, inside, room'; Za cor = 'up[ward]' (Todd); Hau çûer = 'inside' (M4) [K/A/JB3/IFb/B/HH/GF/TF/OK/SK//JJ]

jordanî ژۆردانی *m.* **(-yê;).** downhill slope, incline, descent: **•Çu jihelî bê *jordanî* nîne** (Bw) What goes up must come down/Every cloud has a silver lining [lit. 'there is no uphill slope without *a downhill slope*'] *[prv.]*. {syn: nişîv} [Bw/Hk/FS] <berwar; ≠jihelî>

jorîn ژۆرین *adj.* upper, highest; superior: **•Li rewqa *jorîn*** (EP-7) In the *upper* pavilion. [EP-7/K/JB3/IFb/GF/TF/OK] <jêrîn; jor>

junî ژونی (IFb) = knee. See **ejnû**.

jûjî ژووژی *m./f.(Msr)* **(-yê/ ; /-yê).** hedgehog, zool. *Erinaceus europaeus*: **•*Jûjî* dibêje ji pirça têjikên min nermtir qet tune ye** (ZF3) *The hedgehog* says there is nothing softer than the fur of my little ones *[prv.]* **•Porê wê mîna *jûjîyê* bû** (Bîrnebûn 39, payîz 2008, 27) Her hair was like *a hedgehog's*; **-jûjûyê berezî** (F) porcupine, zool. *Hystricidae*. {also: jijo (A/IF-2); jivjî (Zeb); jijû (B); jîjo (A/IF-2/Msr); jîjok f. (-a;) (Msr-2); jojî (IF-2); jûjû (F/K); jûşik (K[s]); [jouji/jevji] ژوژی (JJ)} Cf. Av dužaka-; Mid P zūzag (M3); P žūž ژوژ/žūže ژوژه; Sor jîşik ژیشِك/jîjî ژیژی/jîjû ژیژوو/jûjik ژووژِك/jûjî ژووژی/jûjû ژووژوو/jûşik ژووشِك; Za dije *m.* (Todd) [AB/IF/JJ//F/K//A/Msr//B//Zeb] <sîxur>

jûjû ژووژوو (F/K) = hedgehog. See **jûjî**.

jûr ژوور (Haz/HH/GF) = unripe grapes. See **cûr I**.

jûşik ژووشِك (K[s]) = hedgehog. See **jûjî**.

K/K' ك

ka I كا *f.* **(-ya;-[y]ê).** straw *(grain)*: **•Afir tijî *ka* ye** (AB) The trough is full of *straw* **•Di destpêkê de min ew bi ceh û *kayê* xwedî dikir** (HYma, 11) At first I fed him barley and *straw*; **-ava bin kaê** (XF/Dz) insidious, crafty, sly, cunning; untrustworthy, unreliable [lit. 'the water under the straw']. {also: kah (F); [ka كا/ kah كاه] (JJ); <ka> كا (HH)} Cf. P kāh كاه; Sor ka كا [AB/K/A/JB3/IF/JJ/B/HH/Msr//F] <kadîn; p'ûş I>

k'a II كا *intrg.* 1) {syn: k'u II; k'u derê} where? *used particularly when one does not see something that one expected to see* [Cf. T hani]: **•Serê salê, binê salê/ Xwedê bihêlê/ Xortê malê/ *Ka* geşta vê malê** (Ah) The start of the year, the end of the year/ May God protect/ The young man of the house/ *Where* are the alms of this house? [A chant recited by children going from house to house on New Year's, similar to our "Trick or treat"]; 2) {syn: bê II (L); çika (J/Z); qe (Z)} *introduces indirect questions*; Let's see, whether, if: **•Binêre *ka* ê were an na** (Msr) See *if* he's coming or not **•Kur̄o, ca her̄in binhêr̄in *k'a* çira Memê îro derengî k'et?** (EP-7) Boys, go see why Mem is late today **•Wî cewdikê avê şilqand *ka* av têda heye *yan ne*** (FS) He shook the flask *to see whether or not* there was water in it. {also: **k'anî II**; [kani] كانى (JJ); <ka كا / kanê كانى> (HH)} Cf. T hani [EP-7/K/A/B//JJ/HH] See also **k'anî II**.

kab I كاب (GF) = knucklebone. See **k'ap II**.

k'ab II كاب (A) = knee. See **kabok**.

k'abira كابِرا (K[s]/ZF3) = fellow, person. See **k'abra**.

k'abok كابۆك *f.* **(-a;-ê).** knee: **•Pa wextê dawisand, qerpe qerpe wî, weke yek ra[hê]jê darekî hişk ti bidê *kaboka* xwe û bişkênê, hewqa deng jê hat** (HR-I 2:79) And when he pressed on it [=broken arm], it made a cracking sound, like when you pick up a dry twig and break it on your *knee*, such a sound did it make. {also: k'ab II (A); [kābe] كابه (JJ)} {syn: çok; ejnû} cf. Ar ka'b كعب = 'heel' [HR-I/GF/TF/RZ/ZF3//JJ//A]

k'abra كابرا *m.* **(;-y).** man, fellow, chap; person: **•Marî çi kir, r̄a bo ser kilka xo, ço bereka *kabray*** (M-Ak, #545) What did the snake do but raise itself up on its tail and go in front of *the fellow*. {also: k'abira (K[s]/ZF3)} {syn: însan; meriv} <kak = 'older brother' + bira = 'brother'?; Sor kabra كابرا = 'person, fellow (known but not named)' [M-Ak/Bw/IFb/OK//K(s)]

kac كاج *f.* **(-a;-ê).** 1) pine tree, bot. *Pinus (of the family Pinaceae)* (K[s]/IF[s]); 2) {syn: darûk (F)} spruce or fir tree (F): **-dara kac** (F) spruce or fir tree. {also: kaj (K[s]/IF[s]-2/Wkt/FS); qac (IFb); qaj (IFb-2)} Sor kac كاج/kaj كاژ/qac قاج/qaj قاژ [F/ZF3//IFb//K(s)/Wkt/FS] <dar I; k'ajûk (JB1-A)>

***kaçkaçk** كاچكاچك *f.* **(;-ê).** dried (and sliced) fruit: **•Wekî *kaçkaçkê* lêhatî** (Bw) He's old and shriveled (i.e., like *a piece of dried fruit*). [Bw] <çîr; kitik I>

kadan كادان (K) = hayloft. See **kadîn**.

k'ad•e/kade [A] كاده *f.(Bw)/m.(K/B/ZF3)* **(•a/•ê;).** pastry filled with crushed walnuts (**gûz**). {also: k'ate (K/B); [kadé كاده/kadik كادك] (JJ); <kadeh> كاده (HH)} Cf. Arm kat'a[y] կաթայ; Geo k'ada კადა; cf. also Fr gâteau [Bw/A/IFb/JJ/SK/GF/OK/CB/ZF3//K/B//HH] <kuloç; sode I>

kadiz كادِز *m./f.* **(;/-ê).** 1) straw thief; 2) the Milky Way: **-R̄îya Kadiz** (K/B)/**R̄îya Kadizan** (JJ/GF/OK) do.: **•Gelo berê jî ezmanê welêt bi ewçend stêrik bû? … Min çavên xwe li *riya Kadizê* gerand** [sic], **min ew jî dît** (KS, 48) Did the heavens above [my] homeland have so many stars in the past? … I sought out *the Milky* Way with my eyes, and I found it too. {also: kehdiz (Wîkîpediya-2); [rē-a kadizān] ريا كادزان (JJ); <kadiz> كادز (HH)} [KS/K/A/IFb/B/JJ/HH/GF/OK/ZF3] <stêr>

kadî كادى (RZ) = smoke. See **kadû**.

kadîn كادين *f.* **(-a;-ê).** hayloft; barn, granary: **•Belkî ar keti be *kadîna* wane** (LT-Mîşo) Perhaps fire has broken out in their *hayloft* **•Fira mirîşkê heta *kadînê* ye** (RN2, 51 [1998], 27) The flight of a chicken is [only] as far as *the hayloft [prv.]*. {also: kadan (K); kadîng (ZF3-2); [kadin] كادين (JJ); <kadîn> كادين (HH)} {syn: merek} Cf. P kāhdān كاهدان [AB/A/JB3/IF/B/JJ/HH/ZF3//K] <'embar; ka I; pange>

kadîng كادينگ (ZF3) = hayloft. See **kadîn**.

kadû كادوو *f./m.(Wkt)* **(-ya/;).** (cigarette) smoke. {also: kadî (RZ-2)} {syn: dû IV; dûk'el} [Zeb/K(s)/

OK/RZ/Wkt]

k'afir كـــافِـــر *m.&f.* **(-ê/ ;).** 1) {syn: xwedênenas} unbeliever, infidel, non-Muslim: •**Wey li *kafirê* pir çêra / Ewan mehdera Birahîm Xelîl bi xirabî digêra** (GShA, 230) Oh the blasphemous *heathen* / They vilified Ibrahim the Friend; 2) {syn: hût} monster: •**Wextê k'etîye ser enîşk'a xo bera xo daê, eve *k'afirekî* têtin, çil o êk destêt pêve, serî li 'esmanî, pê li 'erdî** (M-Am, #742, 342) When he leant back on his elbow he noticed *a monster* coming, with 41 hands, his head in the sky and his feet on the earth. {also: [kafer/kafar] كـافـر (JJ); <kafir> كـافـر (HH)} < Ar kāfir كـافـر = 'unbeliever, infidel, atheist'; cf. Heb kofer ba-'iqar כופר בעיקר = 'denier of the basis [of Judaism]; unbeliever, atheist'; Sor kafir كـــافِـــر [GShA/M-Am/K/A/B/IFb/FJ/JJ/HH/SK/CS] <bêol; k'ifir I>

kafkulîlk كـافـكـولـيـلـك (Qtr-E) = mushroom. See **kufkarik**.

k'af-k'ûf كـاف كـووف (K) = disorder; ruin. See **k'af-k'ûn**.

k'af-k'ûn كاف كوون *f.* **().** 1) {syn: geremol; hêwirze; k'eft û left} disorder, chaos: •**Çi dinyake *k'af-k'ûne*** (EP-7) What a *chaotic* world; **-kaf û yekûn bûn** (Wkt) to be chaotic, be turned upside down: •**Piştî qezayê ew malbat *kaf û yekûn bû*** (Wkt) After the accident that family *was turned upside down*; 2) destruction, ravage, ruin. {also: k'af-k'ûf (K); k'af û k'ûf; k'af û k'ûn} [EP-7/K//Wkt/ZF3]

k'af û k'ûf كـــاف و كـــووف = disorder; ruin. See **k'af-k'ûn**.

k'af û k'ûn كـــاف و كـــوون = disorder; ruin. See **k'af-k'ûn**.

kaf û yekûn bûn كاف و يەكوون بوون (Wkt). See **k'af-k'ûn**.

kah كاه (F/JJ) = straw. See **ka I**.

kahraba كاهرابا (CS) = electricity. See **kehreb**.

kahreba كاهربا (IFb) = electricity. See **kehreb**.

kaj كاژ (K[s]/IF[s]/Wkt/FS) = pine tree. See **kac**.

kajêrî كاژێری, f. (Zeb) = jaw muscle. See **karêj**.

k'ajûk كاژووك **().** pine branch. [JB1-A] <kac>

kak كاك (K/IF) = older brother. See **kek**.

kakil كـاكِـل *m./f.(B)* **(-ê/ ; /-ê).** 1) kernel, core; nucleus (K/JJ/F); nut meat, 'meat' contained within nutshell (Tkm/IF/JJ/JB1-S/F); core of walnut or almond (A): **-kakilê gûzê** (Tkm/K/F/B) nut meat; 2) snack or hors d'oeuvres consisting of [pistachio, walnut, almond, etc.] nut meats (IF). {also: [kakil] كـاكـل (JJ); <kakil> كـاكـل (HH)} Sor kakił كـــاكِـــڵ ; cf. also Geo k'ak'ali კაკალი = 'walnut' [Tkm/F/K/A/IFb/B/JJ/HH/JB1-S/GF/TF] <gûz>

kal I كـــــــال *adj.* 1) {syn: îxtîyar; kal I; kokim [3]; mezin[2]; navsera; pîr; sere I; ≠xort} old *(of persons)*: **-kal bûn** (B) to grow old; **-kal kirin** (B) to make old; **-kal û bav** (B) ancestors; 2) *[m.]* {syn: îxtîyar; kalik I; kokim [1]} old man: •***Kalê*** [sic] **jê dipirse, divê ...** (Dz) *The old man* asks him, says ... •**R̄êva r̄astî *kalekî* tê** (Dz) On the way he comes across *an old man*. {[kal] كـال (JJ); <kal> كـال (HH)} cf. Ar kahl كـهـل = 'middle-aged, man of mature age' {kalî I; kalîtî; kaltî I} [K/A/JB3/IFb/B/JJ/HH/SK/GF/TF/FS] <kevn>

k'al II كـــــال *adj.* unripe, green *(of melons; of corn)*: •**Garis hîna *kal* e, tirî hersime e, nîsk û nok hîn şîr e!** (Ardû, 148) The corn is still *unripe*, the grapes are still sour, the lentils and chickpeas are still not ripe •**gundorê kal** (FS) unripe melon. {also: [kal] كـال (JJ)} {syn: xam; xang II} {k'altî II} [K/A/JJ/B/GF/TF/FS] <talik>

k'al III كال *m.* **().** 1) {syn: şiftî; zebeş} watermelon; 2) melon (B). {also: k'alik III (A); [kalak] كـالـك (JJ)} [K/B/Wkt//JJ//A]

kalan كـــــالان *m.* **(-ê; kalên** [EP-7]**).** (sword) sheath, scabbard: •**Şilfa dar çêdike dike *kalanê* şûr** (Z-922) He makes the wooden sword blade and puts [it] in the sword *sheath*; **-kavlanê xencerê** (Bw) dagger sheath. {also: kalwan (SK); kavlan (Bw/FS-2); kevlan (FS-2); <kalan> كــالان (HH)} {syn: qab I} M. Schwartz: < O Ir *kārta-dāna --> kārtdān --> kārdān (not ancient -rd- --> -l-) --> kālān; Sor kalan كـالان/kêlan كـێـلان; Za kalenî *f.* (Mal); Hau kêlane *f.* (M4) [Z-922/K/A/IFb/HH/OK//FS/SK//Bw] <qebd; şûr>

kalik I كـالِـك *m.* **(-ê; kêlik, vî kalikî).** 1) {syn: îxtîyar} {also: kal I[2]} old man; 2) {syn: bapîr} grandfather (Tkm/Wn/JJ): **-kalik û pîrik** (B) grandparents; ancestors; 3) great-grandfather (Msr); 4) forefather, ancestor (IF). {also: [kalik] كـالـك (JJ); <kalik> كـالـك (HH)} [F/K/A/IF/JJ/B/HH/Rh/ZF3] <bapîr; dapîr>

k'al•ik II كالِك *f.* **(•ka;).** peasant shoe or sandal made of leather. {also: [kalek (G)/kālik (Rh)] كـالـك (JJ); <kalik> كـالـك (HH)} Sor kałe كـاڵـە = 'shoe of soft leather laced over instep'; cf. Lat caliga = 'soldier's leather shoes'. See T.F. Aristova. *Material'naia kul'tura Kurdov XIX-pervoĭ* poloviny XX v.* (Moskva : Nauka, 1990), photos #42, 46, 47 (following p. 128), & drawing p. 140. [Bw/A/IFb/JJ/HH/SK/TF/ZF3] <p'êlav; ȓeşik II; sol>

k'alik III كالِك (A) = watermelon. See **k'al III**.

kalî I کالی *f.* **(-ya;-yê)**. old age; being or growing old: **•Îro ez du caran gelkî xemgîn bûm û bi *kalîya* xwe hesiyam** (hindik-rindik 17.iii.2010) Today I was sad twice and I felt my *old age* **•Tu *bi kaltîya xwe* hatî şerê min?** (RiaTaza 25.iii.2018) You've come to fight me *in your old age*? {also: kalîtî (K/ZF3-2); kaltî I (B)} [K/ZF3/Wkt//B] <kal I>

kalî II كالى (ZF3) = immaturity. See **k'altî II**.

k'alîn کالین *vi.* **(-k'al-)**. to bleat *(sheep)*: **•Mî û berxa *k'alîya bûn*** (Z-2) The sheep and lambs *had bleated* **•Xecê, tu bi wê k'eserê ku *pê dik'alî u dinalî*, niha nêzîke, ne dûre** (IS-#271) Khej, you and your grieving! The one you *are 'pissing and moaning' about* is nearby, he is not far off. {also: [kalin كالين/ kaliian كاليان] (JJ)} {syn: mikîn} [AB/K/A/JB3/IF/B/JJ/ZF3] <baȓîn II; bizin; mî I>

kalîtî كاليتى (K/ZF3) = old age. See **kalî I**.

kalome كالۆمه (ZF3) = old (of knives). See **kalûme**.

kaltî I كالتى (B) = old age. See **kalî I**.

k'altî II کالتی *f.* **()**. immaturity, unripeness *(of fruits)* {also: kalî II (ZF3)}. [A//ZF3] <k'al II>

kalûme کالووومه *m.&f. {according to the accompanying noun}* **( )**. 1) {syn: kevlû [3]} old, rusty sword, knife, axe, etc.: **•kalûmeke dasan** = old, rusty sickle *[**das**, f.]* **•kalûmeke k'êran** = old, rusty knife *[**k'êr III**, f.]* **•kalûmekî biviran** = old, rusty axe *[**bivir**, m.]* **•kalûmekî şûran** = old, rusty sword *[**şûr I**, m.]* **•Ma tu nizanî delîla ji hemî delîlan qahîmtir *kalûme* ye? Her kesê *kalûme* heye, mulk bo wî ye ... Ew delîlêt şer' û qanûnan hemî piȓ-û-pûç in, bê-fayde ne. Ew hingî bi kar tên ku *kalûme* nebît. Wextê *kalûme* hebît delîlêt dî hemî duro ne û hîç in** (SK 43:418) Why, do you not know that *the sword* is a stronger proof than any other? Whoever has *the sword*, possession is for him ... Those proofs of the religious and civil law are all rubbish and quite useless. They are only of any use when there is no *sword*. When there is *a sword* all other proofs are lies and void; 2) *[m.]* sheathed sword (Qzl); 3) old, senile, feeble *(of people)*: **•kalûmeke jinan** = old, feeble woman **•kalûmekî mêran** = old, senile man. {also: kalome (ZF3); [kắlma/kắlme] کالمه (JJ) ; <kalûme> كالومه (HH); <kalûme> كالوومه (Hej)} *For another example of special words for old things see **şekal**.* [SK/A/IFb/HH/GF/Hej/FS//JJ] <bivir; das; k'êr III; şûr I>

kalvêj کالفێژ *f.* **()**. girl or young ewe who is sexually active before the proper time. [Qzl]

kalvêjî کالفێژی *f.* **()**. being sexually active before the proper time *(of sheep or women)*; precociousness, precocity: **•Ne min bi berxî têr şîr xwar, û ne *bi kalvêjî* têr kîr xwar** (Qzl) I neither drank my fill of milk as a lamb, nor had my fill of penis *as an all-too-young ewe [prv.]*. {also: kavêjî (ZF3); kavijkî (FJ); kavişkî (GF); kawêşkî (Trg)} [Qzl//FJ//GF//Trg//ZF3]

kalwan كالوان (SK) = sheath. See **kalan**.

kam I کام *f.* **(;-ê)**. (wooden) threshing sledge, threshing board *(with flint blades set in the bottom)* [T döven]: **•Du serîye / ȟeyşt ling / ser dare / binî kevire / ew çiye? [*kam*] varîant: Ser dar, bin kevir / sê serî, deh ling / ew çiye? [*kam*]** (Z-1805) It's two heads, eight legs / wood on top / stone on bottom / what is it? *[rdl.: ans.: threshing sledge]* variant: Top wood, bottom stone / three heads, ten legs / what is it? *[rdl.; ans.: threshing sledge]*. {also: gam (IFb-2/OK); [kam] کام (JJ); <gam> گام (Hej)} {syn: moşene} *For picture, see Kmc-16, " Alavên çandiniyê"-G [p. 4]* [Z-1805/Kmc-16/K/A/IFb/B/JJ/ZF3//OK/Hej] <cencer>

kam II کام *f.* **()**. disease of horses and donkeys: *blood blisters appear in animal's mouth, and it won't graze or drink water*. {also: <kam> کام (Hej)} Sor kam کام (Hej) [Elk/K(s)/Hej/FS] <tebeq I>

kamaş/k'amaş [A] کاماش *f.* **(-a;-ê)**. low-quality tobacco *which is picked while green*: **-tûtina kamaş** (Qzl/Wn) do. {also: <kamaş> کاماش (HH)} [Qzl/Xrz/Wn/A/IFb/HH/GF/FJ/ZF3] <t'itûn>

k'ambax کامباخ *adj.* 1) {syn: xirab} in ruins, ruined, destroyed, razed to the ground, laid waste; in bad condition: **-Mala te k'ambax be** (B) May your house be destroyed *[curse]* **•Piştî ku çete di doza xwe ya 'tolhildanê' de bi ser bikevin, dê rewş ji îro gelekî *kambaxtir* bibe** (AW73D3) After the gangs succeed in their cause for "revenge," the situation will be much *worse* than it is today; 2) *[f.]* ruins (K). {also: k'embax (BF/FS); <kembax> كمباخ (HH)} [FK-1/K/A/IF/B/ZF3//HH/BF/FS]

kan I کان *f.* **(-a;)**. 1) {syn: ç'avkanî; jêder} source, origin: **•Dibistan *kana* zanînê ye** (AB) School is *the source of* knowledge; 2) (mineral) mine (JB3/

JJ/IF). {also: [kan] کـــان (JJ)} Cf. P kān کـــان = 'mine, quarry' [AB/K(s)/JB3/IF/JJ/ZF3] See also **kanî I**.

kan II کان (FS) = to churn. See **k'ilan**.

Kanadayî کانادایی (Wkp) = Canadian. See **K'enedayî**.

Kanadî کانادی (Wkp) = Canadian. See **K'enedayî**.

k'anê کـــانـێ (B/IF) = Come on!; where? See **k'a II** & **k'anî II**.

kanin کانِن (K) = to be able, can. See **karîn**.

kanî I کــانــی *f.* **(-ya;-yê).** 1) {syn: ç'avkanî; selef; serê avê} spring, source, origin: •**Keçik çû ser *kanîyê*** (AB) The girl went *to the spring* •**Řokê k'ete pêşya bizinê xwe, bir ser *kanyê* avde** (Dz) One day he led his goats to *a spring* to water them; 2) fountain: •**Belediya Agirî, berî demekê çend *kaniyan* dide çêkirin** (Wlt 1:37, 3) A while ago, the city of Ağrı had some *fountains* built. {also: kanîng; kehnî (HR-I); [kani] کـانـی (JJ); <kanî کانی /kehnî کـهـنـی> (HH)} Cf. Skt khan- [khanī] *f.*; Av xan- [xā] *f.* = 'well, fountain'; Mid P xān = 'spring, source' (M3); P xānī خــانــی = 'fountain' & kandan کـنـدن = 'to dig'; Sor kanî کـانـی/kanî-w-aw کـانـی و ئاو/kanîyaw کانییاو = 'spring'; Hau hane *m.* (M4) [F/K/A/JB3/IF/JJ/B/HH/GF//HR-I] See also **kan I**.

k'anî II کـــانـــی *interj.* 1) Come on!: •***Kanî* destê xwe bidin min** (L) *Come on*, give me your hands! •***Kanî*, emê B. di binê vê bîrê bihêlin** (L) *Come on*, let's leave B. at the bottom of this well; 2) well?!; 3) Let's see!; 4) where?: •**Birayê mino *kanî* xortaniya te?** (KS, 9) My brother, *what happened to* your youth? {also: k'anê (B/IF); **k'a II**; [kani] کانی (JJ)} Sor kwanê کوانێ [L/K/JJ//B/IF//A]

kanîn کـــانـــیـن (IFb/GF/ZF/CS) = to be able, can. See **karîn**.

kanîng کانینگ = spring, fountain. See **kanî I**.

K'anûn کـــانـــوون *f.* **(-a;-ê).** *name of two winter months*: 1) December: -**K'anûna pêşin** (K)/~ **pêşî** (OK)/ **ewil**/[kanoun beri کـــانـــون بـــری/-evel اول] (JJ)/ [kanuna awell] (BG) December {syn: Çileya pêşîn}: •[***K'anûnê* û *K'anûnê*, berf tête ji ezmanê** [j'ouzmané]**, qiřa 'ebd û însanê**] (BG) In *December* and *January*, snow falls from the sky, the ruin of all humanity *[proverbial saying]*; *corresponds to last part of* Agirdan ئـــاگِـــردان/ Sermawez سـەرمـاوەز (P āẕer آذر) [Sagittarius] & *1st part of* Sehołbendan سـەهـۆڵـبـەنـدان/Befranbar بـەفـرانـبـار (P dey دی) [Capricorn]; 2) January: -**K'anûna paşin** (K)/[kanoun pachi کـانـون پـاشـی/-sani ثـانـی] (JJ)/[kanuna pâchy] (BG) January {syn: Çileya paşîn} *corresponds to last part of* Sehołbendan سـەهـۆڵـبـەنـدان/Befranbar بـەفـرانـبـار (P dey دی) [Capricorn] & *1st part of* Nawzistan نـاوزسـتـان/Řêbendan ڕێـبـەنـدان (P bahman بـهـمـن) [Aquarius]. <Syr kānūn حمم --> Ar kānūn (al-awwal & al-ṯānī) (الأول والثاني) كانون [Zx/K/IFb/B/JJ/HH/GF/OK] <Çile I; Çirî>

kap I کاپ *m./f.(ZF3)* **(-ê/;).** rope: •**Ev *kapê* qirka min te dîtîye?** (J) Have you seen *the rope for* my neck? [lit. 'this rope of my neck'] •**Serê xwe ber *kapra* derbazke** (J) Pass your head through *the rope*['s loop]. {syn: k'indir [2]; qirnap; werîs} [J/K/IFb/ZF3] <kapik>

k'ap II کـــــــــاپ *f.* **(-a;-ê).** knucklebone, anklebone; *metacarpal or metatarsal bone of a sheep used in games and divination*: -**k'apa lîstinê** (F) do. {also: kab I (GF); kaw; [kap] کـــعـــب (JJ); <kap> کـاپ (HH)} Cf. Ar ka'b کـعـب = 'ankle(bone), heel' [F/K/IFb/B/JJ/HH/Wkt//GF] <cûg; çik II; çit; deq II; diz II; doq; guhkişînk; ker IV; mîr II; pik; sofî II; zar III>

kapêk کـــاپـێـك *f./m.(B)* **().** kopeck (USSR). [Z-922/K/B] <manat; şeyî>

kapik کاپك *m.* **().** 1) diminutive of **kap I** = rope; piece of rope (HH); 2) foot ropes for binding animals (A); binding a horse's legs with a stake while pasturing (IFb). {also: kapok (IFb); <kapik> کـاپـك (HH)} [HB/A/HH/GF/ZF3//IFb] <şerît; werîs>

kapok کاپۆك (IFb) = type of rope. See **kapik**.

kar I کار *f.* **(-a;-ê).** kid, goat's young: •**Sê *kara* tîne** (J) She brings forth (=gives birth to) three *kids*; -**karê xezala[n]** (K)/**kara xezal** (B) fawn, young of deer. {also: kehr (GF-2/M-Zx); [kar کــار/karik کــارك] (JJ); <karik> کــارك (HH)} Sor kar کــار; SoK kâr/kârila/kyar (Fat 227) [J/F/K/A/JB3/IFb/JJ/B/ SK/GF//HH] <bizin; gîsk; nêrî I>

k'ar II کار *m./f.(B)* **(-ê/-a; /-ê).** affair, business (JB3/B) {(JB3): *[m.]* = action, work, job; *[f.]* = profit, benefit, business}; -**k'ar bûn** = to be prepared, get ready: •**Gerekê tu meřa *k'arbî*** (EP-7) You must *be ready* for us (=to come with us); -**k'arê *fk-ê* [ji] *bk-ê*, *bt-î* nek'etîye** (XF): a) for stg. to have nothing to do with stg. else; b) s.o. need not worry or concern o.s. with stg.: •***K'arê* te *ji* Ûsiv *nek'etîye*** (Ba3-1) *Don't worry about* Joseph •***K'arê* te wî ne *k'etîye*** (XF) Don't *have anything to do with* him; -**k'ar kirin** (IFb) to work {syn: şixulîn; xebitîn}; -**k'arê xwe kirin/xwe k'ar kirin** (K) to prepare o.s., get ready for: •**Hakim rabû,**

qîza xwe *kar kir* û rihel û cihazê wê çêkir (L) The king got up, *prepared* his daughter, got her dress clothes and trousseau together •**Min *xwe kar kir*** (JB3) I am ready [lit. 'I have *made myself ready*']; **-k'ara zivistanê kirin** (JB3) to get ready for winter, to get in supplies. {also: [kar] كـار (JJ); <kar> كار (HH)} Cf. P kār كار [L/K/A/JB3/IFb/JJ/B/HH/SK/GF/TF]

karaba كارابا (GF) = electricity. See **kehreb**.

karan كاران = mallet, sledgehammer. See **gef̄an II**.

k'arbidest كـاربِـدهسـت *m.(often pl.)* **().** official, civil servant. {syn: f̄ayedar} Sor karbedes كـاربـهدهس [Voa/K(s)/IFb/GF/ZF3]

karçik I كارچك (JB3/IFb/GF/OK/Msr/Czr/ZF3) = pear. See **karçîn**.

karçin كارچِن (K) = pear. See **karçîn**.

karçîn كـارچـيـن *f.* **(-a;).** type of pear; wild pear (JJ); a small, round wild pear that grows in deserts and arid places (Msr); *in Şnx this is the simple word for pear [=hermê].* {also: karçik (Msr/JB3/IFb-2/GF/OK/ZF3-2); karçin (K); [kartchin كـارچـيـن/ kakhtchin كاخچين] (JJ); <karçîn> كارچين (HH)} {syn: hermê} [A/IFb/JJ/HH//JB3/GF/OK/Msr/Czr/ZF3//K] <alîsork; ḧezîranî; kirosik; şekok; şitû>

kardî كاردى (Qzl) = arum. See **karî II**.

kareb كارهب (FS) = electricity. See **kehreb**.

kareba كارهبا (IFb/BF/Wkt) = electricity. See **kehreb**.

k'arêc كـارێـج *f.* **(;-ê).** wooden pitchfork. {also: karêç (ZF3); k'arêj II (B/GF); <karêc> كـاريـج (HH)} {syn: milêb; tebûr} [IFb/HH//ZF3//B/GF]

karêç كارێچ (ZF3) = pitchfork. See **k'arêc**.

karêj I كارێژ *m.* **().** jaw muscle. {also: kajêrî, f. (Zeb); <kajêr كـاژێـر/karêj كـارێـژ> (Hej)} [Zeb//IFb/OK/Hej/Wkt] <çene; çeng II; lame>

k'arêj II كارێژ (B/GF) = pitchfork. See **k'arêc**.

kar̄êt كـارێـت *f.* **(;-ê).** carriage, coach. {syn: fayton} < Rus kareta карета [EP-7]

k'ar̄êz كـارێـز/**k'arêz** كـاريـز [B] *f.* **(;-ê).** 1) {syn: serdab; tûn} subterranean canal (K/IF); ditch for bringing subterranean water to the surface (B); 'kahreez' "a subterraneous channel for conducting a spring from the hills to the cultivation in the plain; with shafts or wells sunk at intervals, which mark its line" [C.J. Rich. *Narrative of a Residence in Koordistan* (London: James Duncan, 1836), vol. 1, p. 36]: •**Hîmê kelê hîmkirin, / Bin kelêr̄a *kar̄êz* birin** (EP-8) They made the foundations of the fortress,/Under the fortress they put in [lit. 'took'] *subterranean canals* •**P'ala *k'ar̄êz* anî bûn nav kelê** (EP-8) The workers had put in [lit. 'brought'] *subterranean canals* beneath the fortress; 2) water conduit (K); 3) cold land, mountain pasture *(used in the summer)* (HH); 4) {syn: kanî I} spring of water (HH). {also: <karêz> كـاريـز (HH)} < P kārīz كـاريـز = 'subterranean canal, sewer'; Sor karêz كارێز [EP-8/K/IFb/B/HH/TF/Rich] <şolîn I>

k'arguzarî كـارگـوزارى *f.* **(-ya;-yê).** service, providing service: •**Îro hacetên ku em bi kar tînin, tirampêlên ku em pêdigerin, ... telefonên ku di navbera şeş kîşweran da karê ragihandinê dike** [sic] **... mirovên van derdu kîşweran kirine *karguzarîya* mirovên cîhan** (RC2. Ku heye Xwedê hiş bide gelê Kurd) The instruments which we use today, the cars that we go around in, ... the phones that communicate between 6 continents ... people of these 2 continents have put them at *the service of* the people of the world; **-karguzarî kirin** (RC2) to serve: •**Dewlet, mewlet jibo me Kurdan ne pêwîst e, bila Tirk, Ereb, Faris bimînin xudan dewlet, ji me ra *karguzarî bikin*, baştir e** (RC2. Ku heye Xwedê hiş bide gelê Kurd) No state is necessary for us Kurds, it's better for the Turks, Arabs and Persians to keep their states, and *serve* us. {syn: xizmet} <Sor karguzarî كـارگـوزارى = 'serviceablity, usability; attendance, help'; cf. P kārguzārī كـارگـذارى = 'agency of ministry of foreign affairs' [RC2/IFb/SS/ZF3]

karik كـارِك *m.* **().** 1) dim. of **kar I**; 2) Capricorn (astr.). {also: kehrik (Bw/TF)} [Bw/TF//Wlt/Ro/IFb/OK/ZF3]

karin كارِن (F/K/B/M) = to be able, can. See **karîn**.

karî I كـارى *f.* **(-ya;-yê).** mushroom (F/K/JJ/Wn). {also: karok (Wn); [kari] كـارى (JJ)} {syn: gidark (Prw); karkevîk (Mş-Malazgirt); kiyark (Bt)/ kîvark (Prw); kufkarik; k'umik (A)} Sor karg كـارگ/qarçik قـارچِـك = 'mushroom. See: Georg Morgenstierne. "'Mushroom' and 'Toadstool' in Indo-Iranian," *BSOAS*, 20 (1957), 451-57, reprinted in: *Irano-Dardica* (Wiesbaden : Dr. Ludwig Reichert Verlag, 1973), pp.17-23. [F/K/A/IFb/B/JJ/GF//Wn/Bt]

karî II كـارى *f.* **(-ya;).** dragon arum, cuckoopint, bot. *Arum maculatum* [T dana ayağı] (A/IF/Bt); arum, edible plant similar to calla lily (Bw): **-karî çûçik** (Zeb) *a tiny variety of arum*; **-karî kel** (Zeb) *a* *large variety of arum.* {also: kardî (Qzl)} Sor karî کـــــاری = 'black arum lily, cuckoo-pint' & kardû کاردوو = 'dock' [Bw/A/IFb/OK/AA/Zeb//Qzl]

karîn/k'arîn [JB1-S] کـاریـن *vt.* **(-kar-/-k'ar-**[JB1-S]/**-kan-**[K-2/Bg]/**-ka-**[Ad]; *pres.* **[di]karim;** *neg.* **nikarim;** *subj. & past tenses formed with* **karibûn:** *subj.* **bikaribim;** *past* **min karibû).** 1) [+ *subj.*] {syn: pê ç'êbûn; şe kirin [şe II]; şiyan} to be able to, can: **•Go ne ew be, *kes nikare*** (L) If he can't, *no one can* **•Lê eva gilî-gotinê Al-p'aşa û giregira, heval û hogira dilê Memêyî evînîyê *nikarbûn* vegeřandana** (Z-1) But the things that A.p. and his councellors, and all his friends said *couldn't* turn Mem's heart back from love **•Tu *nikarî*** = You *can't* **•Vira zinarê usa mezin hebûn, ku weke panzdeh-bîst soyara *dikaribû* piş wana veşarta** (Ba2) Here there were such great boulders that fifteen or twenty bandits *could* hide behind them; 2) to be strong enough for, to be able to withstand or bear; to be a match for, be able to beat: **•Gur dike-nake bizina kûvî *nikare*** (J) No matter what the wolf does, he's *no match for* the wild goat; **-bi xwe karîn** (Qmş) to control o.s.: **•Min da xuya kirin ku ez *dikarim bi* xwe** (Qmş) I showed that I *could control* myself. {also: kanin (K-2); kanîn (IFb-2/GF-2/ZF-2/CS-2); karin (F/K/B/M); qarin (M-Sheikhan); [karin کـاریـن/ kāniyān کـانـیـان] (JJ); <karîn کـاریـن (dikarî) (دکـاری)> (HH)} Cf. W Arm garenal կարենալ = 'to be able' & E Arm karoł կարող = 'able' [A/JB3/IFb/GF/JJ/HH/ZF/CS//JB1-S//F/K/B]

karîte کاریته (Bw)/k'arîte (K[s]) = wooden beams. See **garîte**.

k'arker کـــــارکـــــەر *m.* (). 1) {syn: p'ale; řêncber; xebatkar} worker, workman, toiler, proletarian: **•Perên ku didane me ne pir bin jî, dîsa jî ji meaşên hemû karmend û *karkerên* wan zêdetir bûn** (AW72B3) Even if they didn't pay us much, it was still more than the salaries of all the other employees and *workers*; 2) employee (JB3). {also: k'arkir (Haz)} {karkerî (IF)} [K/A/JB3/IFb/GF/TF/Haz] <p'ale>

k'arkerî کارکەری *f.* **(-ya;-yê).** being a worker. [IFb/GF/TF/ZF3]

***karkevîk** کـارکـەڤـیـك **().** mushroom {syn: gidark (Prw); karî I; kiyark (Bt)/kîvark (Prw); kufkarik; k'umik (A)} [Mş-Malazgirt]

karkinî کـارکِـنـی *pl.* **( ).** trouble, grief: **•Kurd ji wî demî heyanî evro jî dilsojêt vî olî û ayînî bûne, wê dilsojîyê gelek cara *karkinî* înayne serê wan** (Hok, 90 [Hok2 66]) From that time until today the Kurds have been devotees of this religion, and this devotion has often brought them *trouble*. {syn: cezaret} [Zeb/Hok]

k'arkir کارکِر (Haz) = worker. See **k'arker**.

k'armend کـــارمـــەنـــد *m.&f.* **(-ê/-a;).** employee: **•Di nava kesên girtî de herwiya gelek *karmendên* dewletê jî hene** (CTV43) Among the people arrested there were also many government *employees*. [(neol)CTV/IFb/TF/OK/ZF3]

karo کـــارۆ *f.* **( ).** diamonds *(suit of playing cards)*. {syn: dînar} <Fr carreau --> T karo [Wn/IFb/ZF3]

karok کارۆك (Wn) = mushroom. See **karî I**.

kartik کـارتِـك**/k'artik** کـارتِـك [FS] *f.* **(;-ê).** file (tool), rasp: **•Wê kêrik bi *kartîxê* xweş kir** (FS) She sharpened the knife with *the file*. {also: kartîx (IFb-2/OK-2/FS); <kartîk> کـارتـیـك (HH)} {syn: êge; *qewre (A/IF)} [A//IFb/OK/ZF3//HH//FS] <hesûn; řendin; sûtin>

kartîx کارتیخ (IFb/OK/FS) = file (tool). See **k'artik**.

k'artol کـارتـۆل**/kartol** کـارتـۆل [K/A/B] *f.* **(-a;-ê).** potato: **-êxnîya k'artola** (Msr) potato purée, mashed potatoes. {also: kertol (JB3/IFb-2/TF)} {syn: bin'erdk [2]} < Germ Kartoffel --> Rus kartofel' картофель--> K; --> T kartol [Gümüşhane; Kağızman, Posof, Çıldır-Kars; Kurtelek, Cimin, Haşhaşı-Erzincan; Doğubeyazit-Ağrı; Van; Bitlis; Varto-Muş; Malatya; etc.] & [Sarıkamış-Kars] = 'potato' [patates] (DS, v. 8, p. 2671; v. 12, p. 4536) & ķartol (Gemalmaz, v. 3, p. 192) [Msr/F/K/A/IFb/B/GF/ZF3//JB3/TF]

k'ar u bar کـــــار و بـــــار (JB1-A)/karubar (OK) = preparations; matters. See **k'ar û bar**.

k'ar û bar کار و بار**/k'arûbar** کاروبار *m.* **(-ê;).** 1) preparations: **-karûbarê şerî** (IFb/OK) war preparations, war tactics; **-k'ar û bar dîtin/~ kirin** (B) to make all sorts of preparations; 2) affairs, matters: **•Pîra diya min Xamê sibehê zû radibû û çêlekên xwe, bizinên xwe didotin û şîrê xwe dikeland, *kar û barên* malê yên dîtir dikirin** (Alkan, 70) My old mother Khameh would get up early in the morning, milk her cows and goats, and boil her milk, [and] she would tend to other household *matters*. {also: k'ar u bar (JB1-A); karubar (OK); <karbar> کاربار (HH)} Sor kar-u-bar کار و بار = 'affairs' [Voa/K/A/IFb/B/GF//JB1-A/OK/

/HH]

k'arvan (K)/karvan (A/IFb/OK) كارڤان = caravan. See **karwan**.

karvankuj كارڤانكوژ (A/RF) = Venus. See **karwankuj**.

karwan/k'arwan [JB1-S] كاروان *m.* **(-ê; k'erwên [B]).** caravan, convoy *which moves merchandise for business purposes*, cf. **řevend**, nomadic migration: **•Ȟetta em bi *karwanê* keran diçîne Ormîyê yan Mûsilê û tênewe pişka pitir ji kerêt me di bin barî da seket dibin** (SK 19:176) By the time we go to Urmiya and Mosul with a donkey *caravan* and return the greater part of our donkeys die under the loads **•*Karwanê* wan ber bi Merîwanê ket rê** (FS) Their *caravan* set out for Meriwan. {also: k'arvan (K)/karvan (A/IFb-2/ OK-2); kervan (F); k'erwan (B); kewran; [karvan كاروان/kavran كاوران] (JJ); <karwan> كاروان (HH)} {syn: bazirgan [2]} Cf. P kārvān كاروان --> T kervan [K//JB3/IFb/SK/GF/TF/HH/OK/ZF3/BF/FS//JB1-S//F//B] <bazirganbaşî; řevend>

karwankuj كاروانكوژ *f.* **().** the morning star, Venus. {also: karvankuj (A/RF); <karwankuj> كاروانكوژ (Hej)} lit. 'caravan-killer'; Sor karwankuj كاروانكوژ [Zeb/IFb/GF/OK/Hej/ZF3//A/RF] <Qurix>

karwanvan كاروانڤان *m.* **().** caravaneer, caravan leader. {syn: bazirganbaşî} [ZF3/Wkt]

k'asik كاسِك *f.* **(-a;-ê).** cup, drinking bowl: **•Paşa *kasikekî* [sic] çînî bo aw-xarinewa xo hebû, gelek çak bû. Li meclisê ȟazir kir. Hemî xulamêt xo gazî kirin. ... Got e xulaman, "Ȟez dikem yêk ji hingo wê *kasikê* bişkînît." Hemîyan gotin [sic], "{Esteẍfiru-llah,} ji me zêde ye em *kasika* paşa bişkînîn"** (SK 22:198) The Pasha had a very fine china *cup* from which to drink water. He brought it to the assembly and summoned all his henchmen. ... He said to the henchmen, "I want one of you to break this *cup*." They all said, "God forbid! It is beyond us to break the Pasha's *cup*." {also: [kasik كاسك/kasé كاسه] (JJ); <kasik> كاسك (HH)} {syn: fincan; t'as} Cf. Ar ka's كأس = 'cup, drinking glass'; Sor kase كاسه = 'bowl'. *According to HH, the **kasik** is used by the poor.* [A/IFb/B/JJ/HH/SK/GF/TF] <peyale>

kastekast كاستەكاست *f.* **(-a;-ê).** barking *(of dogs)*; prolonged howling, wailing *(of dogs)* (B): **-kastekast kirin** (B) to bark, howl, wail, yelp. {also: kazkaz (WT)} {syn: bile-bil (F); 'ewte-'ewt; kute-kut (F); řeyîn I} [Ba/K/B/Wkt] <řeyîn I>

k'aş I كاش *f.* **(-a;-ê).** 1) (person's) weight: **•Dibîne *k'aşa* zêřa ji ya Ûsib girantire** (Ba) He sees that *the weight of* the gold is more [lit. 'heavier'] than [that of] Joseph **•Qîmetê wî tuyê beranberî *k'aşa* wî zêřa bavêjî mêzînê** (Ba) [To reckon] his worth, you will put gold coins on the scale according to his *weight*; 2) {syn: bar I} burden, load: **-k'aş kirin** (K/IFb/HH/GF/OK) to drag, pull: **•Dûre jî bi alîkariya gundiyan, me bavê te *kaşî* malê *kir*** (Ardû, 117) After that, with the help of some villagers, we *dragged* your father home **•Segmanên qesirê bêjî û peyayên wî tev de kuşti bûn û cendekê mîrê bêjî *kaş kiri bûn* [sic] heta ber deriyê qesirê** (Rnh 3:23, 7) The palace guards killed the bastard together with his men, and *dragged* the corpse of the bastard emir up to the gates of the palace. {also: k'êş II (F)} [Ba/K/IFb/B/HH/OK//F] <k'işandin>

k'aş II كاش *f.* **().** 1) slope *(of hill)*; angle (JJ); steep slope (JJ); side *(of mountain)* (A/IF): **•Rovî ji ser teht daket û li du sê *kaşan* qulipî** (SW) The fox got down from the steep precipice and crossed two or three *slopes*; 2) >*mountain road, caravan route through the mountains (K); 3) >*hollow, depression (geog.); ravine, gully (K). {also: [kach] كاش (JJ); <kaş> كاش (HH)} [SW/K/A/IF/JJ/HH/GF/TF/ZF3] <berwar; jihelî; nişîv>

k'aşholo كاشهۆلۆ (EP-7) = game resembling polo. See **k'aşo**.

k'aşo كاشۆ *m.* **().** 1) a Kurdish game that resembles polo or pall-mall, i.e., a game in which a wooden ball is driven with a mallet; 2) mallet used in the game of Kasho (K/IF). {also: k'aşholo- (EP-7); [kachou] كاشو (JJ)} [EP-7//K/A/IF/ZF3//JJ] <cerîd; gog; hol I>

kaşûl كاشوول (IFb) = melon rinds. See **qaşil**.

kaşxank كاشخانك (SS) = ceiling. See **kuşxank**.

kat I كات**: -kat kirin**: a) {syn: gilî kirin; neqil kirin; řiwayet kirin; vegotin; vegêřan} to tell, recount (Lab): **•Lê divê ez jê re *kat bikim*--hemû tiştên ku ez dizanim** (Lab, 9) I must *tell* her–everything that I know; b) {syn: ç'êl kirin: see ç'êl III} to mention (F). *Hesenê Metê (author of Lab) took **kat kirin** from the Kurds of Konya to fill a gap in the vocabulary: a word for 'to tell, recount' [T anlatmak]* [Lab/MUm/RZ/RF/ZF3]

kat II كات *f.* **(-a;-ê).** a ploughed and sown field which has not been harvested: it will yield a crop the following year without being reploughed. Cf. Arc katā כתא = 'after-crop' & Syr kāṯā ܟܬܐ/kā'ṯā ܟܐܬܐ = 'an uncultivated crop which grows of itself, a crop growing after a former harvest' [Qzl/Kmc-8/ IFb/ ZF3] <beyar; bor III; k'ewşan; k'irêbe; zevî>

Katalanî کاتالانی *adj.* Catalan. [Wkt/ZF3]

k'ate کاته (K/B) = type of walnut-filled pastry. See **k'ade**.

ka û dan کا و دان (Latîf Nerweyî-VoA) = condition, state. See **kawdan**.

kavêjî کاڤێژی (ZF3) = premature sexual activity. See **kalvêjî**.

kavijkî کاڤژکی (FJ) = premature sexual activity. See **kalvêjî**.

kavil کاڤِل *m.* **(-ê;).** ruins *(of a building)*: •**Herkî çûne mala xo. Şemdînan jî man li ser *kawilêt* sotî** (SK 40:381) The Herki went to their homes. The Shemdinan were left among their burnt *ruins*; 2) {syn: wêran I; xirab [2]} *[adj.]* ruined, destroyed. {also: kawil (SK); [kawil] کاڤل (JJ); <kavil> کاڤل (HH)} Sor kawul کاوول = 'ruined, devastated'; Hau kawil = 'ruined, destroyed' (M4) [Zeb/K/A/IFb/B/ JJ/HH/GF/TF/OK//SK]

kavir کاڤِر/**kaviř** کاڤِر [K/B] *m./f.(B)* **(-ê/ ; /-ê).** 1) one-year-old male sheep (Bşk/Ag/JJ); two-year-old male sheep, ram (K/A/B/Haz); *term used for male sheep between one and three years old*: •**Wî *kaviřê* ku kiřî bû, vegeřand** (FS) He returned *the ram* that he had bought; 2) young ewe *(up to first lambing)* (B). {also: [kawir] کاڤر (JJ); <kavir> کاڤر (HH)} [Pok. kapro- 529.] 'he-goat, buck': proto Ir *kău-ra/*kăwa-ra- (A&L, p.86 [VII]); Sor kawuř کاووڕ = 'lamb three to six months old'; Za kaviř *m./f.* = 'lamb' (Todd/Mal); Hau kawiř *m.* = 'gelded sheep'; cf. also P čapuš چپش = 'one-year-old male goat'; Lat caper *m.* = 'goat' [K/B//J/F/A/JJ/HH/ Haz/Bşk/Ag] <beran; berx; hevûrî; mî I>

kavişkî کاڤشکی (GF) = premature sexual activity. See **kalvêjî**.

kavlan کاڤلان (Bw/FS) = sheath. See **kalan**.

kaw کاو = knucklebone. See **k'ap II**.

kawdan کاودان *pl.* condition, state, circumstances, situation: •***Kawdanên* deverê dijwartir û aloztir lê hatîne** (Metîn 62[1997]:25) *The situation of* the region has become harder and more complex •**Kesanên van çîroka bi timamî ageh ji *kawdanêt* xo yêt nexoş heye** (Peyv 3[1996], 39) The characters in those stories are completely aware of their awful *state*. {also: ka û dan (Latîf Nerweyî-VoA)} {syn: dest û dar; ḧal; ḧewal; řewş} [Metîn/Peyv/Bw/ /Latîf Nerweyî-VoA/FS]

kawêşkî کاوێشکی (Trg) = premature sexual activity. See **kalvêjî**.

kawil کاول (SK) = ruins. See **kavil**.

k'axaz کاخاز (Ba) = paper. See **k'aẍez**.

k'axet کاخەت = paper. See **k'aẍez**.

kaxez کاخەز (JB3/IF) = paper. See **k'aẍez**.

k'axit کاخِت (K) = paper. See **k'aẍez**.

k'axiz کاخِز (A) = paper. See **k'aẍez**.

kaẍet کاغەت (L) = paper. See **k'aẍez**.

k'aẍez کاغەز *f./m.(Msr)* **(-a/-ê;-ê/).** 1) paper {(B): k'aẍet = thin, fine paper; k'aẍez = paper}; **-p'eře k'axaza cigarê** (Ba) a sheet of cigarette paper; 2) {syn: mek't'ûb; name} letter, epistle: •**Ewî řabû zar dya gede *k'aẍezek* nivîsî, go: "Lawo, tu çawa çûyî, jina te qav derk'et." *K'aẍez* çêkir, û şand şeher** (HCK-3, #2, 20) He wrote *a letter* in the voice of the fellow's mother, saying "Son, as soon as you went away, your wife turned into a slut." He finished *the letter* and send it to town •**Ezê *k'aẍeteke*ê bidim te** (FK-eb-1) I will give you *a letter* [to deliver] •**Xeber gehîşte Nebî Ken'an ku êk li Misrê bi navê Nemrûd wê bûye xûndkar. ... *kaẍezek* jêre virêkir. Nemrûdî cewaba *kaẍeza* wî da, gotê: Emê li meydana şerî yek û du bînîn** (GShA, 226) Word reached the ruler of Canaan that someone by the name of Nemrud had become ruler in Egypt ... He wrote him *a letter*. Nemrud answered his *letter* saying, "We shall meet on the battlefield". {also: k'axaz (Ba); k'axet; kaxez (JB3/IF); k'axit (K); k'axiz (A); kaẍet (L); kaẍiz, m. (Msr); [kaghiz] کاغذ (JJ); <kaẍez> کاغەز (HH)} Cf. P kāγaẕ کاغذ; T kâğıt; Sor kaẍez کاغەز/qaqez قاقەز = 'paper, letter, playing card' [Ba//HH/Bw/HCK/GShA//K/B// A//JB3/IF//JJ] <belg [2]; p'eř [3]; řûp'el>

kaẍiz کاغِز, m. (Msr) = paper. See **k'aẍez**.

k'ayin کاین (Btm) = (to chew one's) cud. See **k'ayîn**.

k'ayîn کایین *vi.* **(-k'ayê).** 1) to ruminate, chew one's cud *(of cows & sheep)*; 2) *[f.]* cud. {also: k'ayin (Btm); [kàin] کاین (JJ); <kaîn> کائین (HH)} [Pok. note on p. 634.]: Numerous Indic words of non-Indo-Germanic origin with initial kh- are treated in F.B.M. Kuiper. *Proto-Munda Words in Sanskrit* (Amsterdam, 1948), pp. 634ff.; Skt khādati = 'he bites, chews'; O Ir *xad- (Tsb 46): Av xad- (*pres.*

xa∂/*xādaya-) = 'to knead'; P xāyīdan خـايـيـدن (-xāy-) (خــــاى) = 'to chew, gnaw'; = Sor kawêj kirdin کاويژ کِردِن [Btm//K/IF/ZF3//HH] <cûtin>

Kazaxî کازاخی (BF/Wkt) = Kazakh. See **Qazaxî**.

kazkaz کازکاز (WT) = barking. See **kastekast**.

k'ebab کـەبـاب *m.(F)/f.(K/B/ZF3)* **(/-a; /-ê).** shish-kebab, meat on skewers. {also: k'ivav (Dz); [kebab] كباب (JJ)} cf. Ar kabāb كباب; T kebap [Dz//F/K/B/ZF3//IF/JJ]

kebanî کەبانی (Bw/IFb/HH/GF/TF/OK) = (house)wife. See **kevanî**.

kebrît کەبریت (F) = match(es). See **k'irpît**.

keç کـەچ *f.* **(-a;-ê).** girl; daughter; *term for an unmarried girl* (HH): **•Mi *kiça* xo ya daê, ya me<u>z</u>in** (M-Gul) I have given him my eldest *daughter.* {also: kiç (M-Ak/Bw/JB1-A/OK-2/RZ-2)/kiç' (JB1-S-2); kîj (OK-2/Bar); [kitch] كچ (JJ); <keç> كچ (HH)} {syn: dot; pit; qîz} Sor kiç کچ; = Za keyna [Ad/Ks/K/A/JB3/IFb/B/HH/JB1-S/GF/TF/OK/RZ//JJ/JB1-A/SK/M-Ak/Bw//Bar]

keçebav کـەچـەبـاڤ *f.* **().** brave, strong or "manly" woman *(meant as a compliment)*: **•Dêya wan jinikeke jêhatî, *keçebavek* zarowên xwe dabûn hev û guhastibû** [sic] **bajarekî kiçik** (H v. 1, 83 [1932 1:4]) Their mother was a clever little woman, a *manly woman* [who] got her children together and moved them to a small town. <keç + bav [H/K/CS/ZF3]

k'eçel کـەچـەل *adj.* bald; scurfy. {also: [ketchel] كچل (JJ); <keçel> كچل (HH)} {syn: ħewês} Cf. P kačal كـچـل; Az T keçəl = 'bald'; Sor keçeł کـەچـەڵ {k'eçel[t]î} [K/A/IFb/B/JJ/HH/GF/TF]

k'eçelî کـەچـەلـی *f.* **(-ya;-yê).** baldness; scurf: **•Vî kenî bi *keçelîya* xwe re girê dide** (Rohat.Serdestiyeke jinan, 79) He connects this laugh [of hers] with his *baldness.* {also: k'eçeltî (B-2/ZF3-2); <keçelî> كچلى (HH)} Cf. P kačalī كـچـلـی [A/IFb/B/HH/GF/TF/ZF3] <k'eçel; keletor>

K'eçelok کـەچـەڵۆك *m.* **(-ê;).** 1) Bald-Boy, 'Baldpate'; *a character in Kurdish, Turkish, and Iranian folklore, a trickster figure; also known as **Lawê Pîrê** or **Kur̄ê Pîrê** (=The Old Woman's Son)*; 2) vulture (IF); 3) a dish made of cracked wheat germ (bulgur) and lentils: **•*Keçelok*: savar û nîsk, pîvaz diqelînin û dikene ber** (Dh/Zeb) *Kechelok*: [a dish of] bulgur and lentils, they fry onions and add them. Cf. P kačal كچل; Az T keçəl = 'bald'; cf. also T Keloğlan = 'Bald-Boy' character in folktales [K/A/IF/B/HCK/ZF3/Dh/Zeb] <gur̄î>

k'eçeltî کەچەلتی (B/ZF3) = baldness. See **k'eçelî**.

keçhilî کەچهلی (TF/ZF3) = stepdaughter. See **keçĥelî**.

keçĥelî کـەچـحـەلـی *f.* **(-ya;-yê).** stepdaughter. {also: keçhilî (TF/ZF3)} {syn: nevisî; qîzĥilî (Frq)} [GF//TF/ZF3] <-ĥilî I; zir̄dayîk>

keçik کەچك = dim. of **keç**.

k'ed/ked [JB1-S] کـەد *f.* **(-a;-ê).** 1) work, labor, toil; effort: **•Bi *keda* mejî û milan, bi *keda* çavan em dikarin gelek tişt bînin cem hev** (Wlt 1:35, 4) With *the labor of* the brain and the arms, with *the labor of* the eyes, we can accomplish many things: **-k'eda *fk-ê* xarin** (XF)/**k'eda xelqê xwarin** (B) to harvest the fruit of s.o. else's labor, to exploit: **•Rewşa jinên Kurd di civakê de çawa bû? ... ji aliyê serdestan ve dihatin perçiqandin û *keda wan dihate xwarin*** (Wlt 1:35, 16) What was the situation of Kurdish women in society? ... they were crushed and *exploited* by the authorities **•Wî, hewl dida xwedî li keda xwe derkeve, *bi* kesekî *nede xwarin*** (AW77B1) He tried to be his own master, *not to be exploited* by anyone; 2) earnings, profit: **•Îsal *ked* pir e** (AB) This year there is much *profit.* {also: <ked> كد (HH)} [AB/K/IFb/B/HH/JB1-S/GF/TF/OK/ZF3]

k'eder کـەدەر *f.* **(-a;-ê).** care, worry, concern; grief, sorrow: **•*Kedera* min çende ciwan e** (M.Şêxo - song) How lovely is my *sorrow*; **-k'eder k'işandin** (FK-eb-1) to worry, fret: **•Ewî *k'işand* gelek *k'ederê*** (FK-eb-1) He *was* greatly *worried.* {also: [keder] كدر (JJ); <keder> كدر (HH)} {syn: cefa; fikar; k'erb; k'eser; kovan; kul I; qilqal; şayîş; t'alaş; tatêl; xem; xiyal [2]} < Ar kadar كدر = 'worry' --> T keder [FK-eb-1/K/B/IF/JJ/HH/ZF3] <meraq; xax>

kedî کـەدی *adj.* tame, domesticated: **-ħeywanên kedî** (JB3) tame, domesticated animals; **-kedî kirin** = to tame, domesticate. {also: kehî (Bw/OK/M-Ak); keyî (SK); [kedi كدى/keï كـيـى/kyahī (Rh)] (JJ); <kedî> كدى (HH)} {≠hov;≠k'ûvî;≠t'or̄ II;≠wahş} {kedîbûn; kedîtî} [HB/K/A/JB3/B/JJ/HH//Bw/OK//SK] <sernerm>

kedîbûn کەدیبوون (K) = tameness. See **kedîtî**.

kedîn کەدین (FS) = water jug. See **k'edûn**.

kedîtî کـەدیـتـی *f.* **().** tameness *(of animals)*. {also: kedîbûn (K)} [A/ZF3//K] <kedî>

k'edûn کـەدوون *m.* **(-ê; -î).** medium-sized water jug (Btm); small water jug (IF/HH): **•Wî ava *kedînî* vexwar** (FS) He drank the *jug* water. {also: kedîn

(FS); <kedûn> کـدون (HH)} {syn: lûlik (IF)} [Btm/IF/HH/ZF3//FS] <cer; k'ûz[ik]; şerbik>

k'edxur کەدخور (K/B) = exploiter. See **k'edxwar**.

k'edxurî کەدخوری (K/B) = exploitation. See **k'edxwarî**.

k'edxurtî کەدخورتی (B) = exploitation. See **k'edxwarî**.

k'edxwar کەدخوار *m.* **(-ê;).** 1) exploiter; colonizer; parasite, sponge; 2) *[adj.]* exploit[at]ive; colonizing, imperialist(ic); parasitic, sponging: **•Heta roja mirinê jî, ew bi xwe li hember dijminê *kedxwar* çek dananiye** (Wlt 2:73, 11) Until his dying day, he never let down his guard concerning the *imperialist* enemy. {also: k'edxur (K/B); kedxwer (TF/Wkt)} <k'ed = 'labor' + xwar- = 'eat(er)' {k'edxur[t]î; kedxwarî; kedxwerî} [Wlt/IFb/OK/ZF//TF/Wkt//K/B] <k'urtêlxur>

k'edxwarî کەدخواری *f.* **(-ya;-yê).** exploitation; colonization, imperialism. {also: k'edxurî (K/B); k'edxurtî (B-2); kedxwerî (TF/ZF3)} [IFb/OK/ZF//TF/ZF3//K/B] <k'edxwar>

kedxwer کەدخوەر (TF/Wkt) = exploiter. See **k'edxwar**.

kedxwerî کەدخوەری (TF/ZF3) = exploitation. See **k'edxwarî**.

k'ef I کەف *f.* **(-a;-ê).** 1) {also: [kef] کف (JJ); <kef> کف (HH)} foam, froth, lather, scum: **-k'efa be'rê** (EP-7) sea foam; 2) {also: **k'efik** (B); kefik (F); [kifik] کفك (JJ)} mold, fungus. Skt kapha- *m.* = 'slime'; Av kafa- *m.* = 'foam, froth'; Khotanese Saka khavā- = 'foam'; Oss xæf = 'slime'; P kaf کف = 'foam, froth, scum, lather'; Sor kef کەف = 'foam, froth, lather'; Za kef *m.* (Mal); Hau kef *m.* (M4). See I. Gershevitch. "Iranian Words Containing -ān-," *Iran and Islam: in Memory of the Late Vladimir Minorsky*, ed. C. E. Bosworth (Edinburgh, 1971), p.287, note 24; reprinted in his *Philologia Iranica*, ed. N. Sims-Williams (Wiesbaden : Dr. Ludwig Reichert Verlag, 1985), p. 257, note 24. [EP-7/K/A/IFb/B/JJ/HH/GF/TF] <dewjin>

k'ef II کەف *f.* **(-a;-ê).** 1) {syn: çeng I; ç'epil; hundurê dest; pank I [panka destî]} palm of the hand: **-k'efa dest** (RZ/CS) do.; 2) small span (Ar fitr فتر). {also: [kef] کف (JJ); <kef> کف (HH)} <Ar kaff کفّ [Bw/K/A/B/JJ/HH/ZF3/BF/Wkt/FD/G]

kefçik کەفچك (HB) = spoon. See **kefçî**.

kefçî کەفچی *m.* **(-yê; kêvç'î [B]).** 1) spoon: **•Carekê gundîyek diçe li malekê dibe mêvan. Kebanîya malê jê re şorbê tîne datîne ber, lê *kevçî* ji bîr ve dike** (LM, 7) Once a villager is a guest at a house. The lady of the house brings him soup and sets it down before him, but she forgets [to bring] *a spoon* **•Ew jî dibê *kevç'îyê* hesinî, di nav girara germ da disincirê; ji wê yekê *kevç'îyê* darî qîmetlitir e** (HR-I, 1:40) They also say that iron *spoons* [lit. 'the iron *spoon*'] melt [or, heat up] in hot porridge; for this reason wooden *spoons* are [lit. 'the wooden *spoon* is'] more valuable **•Lê her ku *kevçiyê* şerbetê yan jî liba derman nêzîkî devê xwe dikir, dikir ku vereşe** (HYma, 34) But whenever he brought a *spoonful* of syrup or pill near his mouth, he almost threw up; 2) perforated spoon, straining spoon (K). {also: kefçik (HB-2); kevçing (A-2); k'evçî (F); kevçî (A); kevç'î (B/HR-I); [kewtchi] کڤچی (JJ); <kevçî کڤچی/kevçik کڤچك> (HH)} Cf. Southern Tati dialects (all *f.*): Takestani kemcia; Eshtehardi kömcia; Xiaraji kancia = 'spoon' (Yar-Shater); cf. P čamče چمچه/kafče کفچه & T kepçe = 'ladle' [K/JB3/IFb/GF//A/JJ//F/HH//B/HR-I//HB] <çemçik; hesk; k'efgîr>

k'efen کەفەن *m.* **(-ê;).** shroud, cerement: **•Wextê te maye bîst deqîqe. *Kifinê* xo ḧazir ke, wesyetêt xo bike û destûrîyê ji mal û 'eyalê xo bixaze. Nawê xudê bîne, êdî dûmaîya 'emrê te ye** (SK 40:361) You have twenty minutes left. Get your *shroud* ready, make your testament and take leave of your wife and family. Invoke the name of God, for the end of your life has come; **-k'efen kirin** (B) to enshroud. {also: kifin (SK); [kifin] کفن (JJ); <kefen> کفن (HH)} {syn: ç'arşev[4]} < Ar kafan کفن [L/F/K/A/JB3/IFb/B/HH//JJ/SK]

k'efgir کەفگر = ladle; strainer. See **k'efgîr**.

k'efgîr کەفگیر *f.* **(-a;-ê).** 1) {syn: çemçik; hesk} ladle, scoop; 2) strainer (IFb). {also: k'efgir; k'evgîr (EP-7/K/B); [kef-ghir] کفگیر (JJ); <kefgîr> کفگیر (HH)} Cf. P kaf gīr کف گیر = 'skimmer, that which takes the foam off' --> clq Ar. kafkīr کفکیر = 'ladle'; Hau kewgîr *m.* = 'perforated ladle (for straining boiled rice)' (M4) [EP-7/K/B//A//JB3/IFb/JJ/HH] <kefçî>

k'efik کەفِك *f.* **(;-ê).** mold, mildew. {also: k'ef I[2] (K); kuffik (GF); kufik (IFb/ZF3); [kifik] کفك (JJ)} [B/F//JJ//IFb/ZF3//GF//K] <jeng; zeng>

k'efikî کەفِكی *adj.* moldy: **•Çend 'embarê dinêda di binîda *k'efikî* bûbû** (EP-8) Some storage bins were *mouldy* at the bottom. {also: kufikî (IFb);

kûfikî (Zeb)} [EP-8/K/B//IFb//Zeb]

k'efî كەفى *f.* **(-ya;-yê).** kerchief, cloth: •**B. digirî û *kefî* di destê wî de ye** (L) B. cries, and he has *a handkerchief* in his hand •**B. poz û guhê çel keleşê** [sic] **ji cêba xwe derxist, di nav *kefîkê* de bûn** (L) B. took the noses and ears of the 40 brigands out of his pocket; they were [wrapped] in *a cloth.* {also: [kefi] كفى (JJ); <kefî> كفى (HH)} Cf. Ar kaffīyah [kūfīyah] كوفية [L/K/JJ/HH] <destmal; kevnik; k'ofî; laç'ik>

k'efş I كەفش *m.* **(-ê;).** armpit: •**Ĥemmalî des da centê, *bin kefşê* xo na, bo xo birineve** (M-Ak #622) The porter picked up the satchel, put it *under his arm* and took it away for himself. {syn: binç'eng} Mid P kaš = 'armpit' (M3); P kaš كش = 'groin, armpit, bosom' [M-Ak/IFb/OK/ZF3]

k'efş II كەفش (IF) = evident, obvious. See **k'ifş.**

k'eftar̄ كەفتار *f.(F/K)/m.(B)* **(/-ê; / k'eftêr̄, k'evtêr̄** [B]**).** 1) {syn: gornebaş (K)} hyena, zool. genera *Hyaena & Crocuta*; 2) old fogey, crotchety old man (B). {also: k'evtar̄, m. (k'evtêr̄) (B); [ķeftár] كفتار (JJ); <keftar كفتار/ĥeftar حفتار> (HH)} Cf. Sgd 'βt'r; Mid P haftār (M3); Baluchi haptār; P kaftār كفتار; Sor kemt[i]yar كەمتیار. See I. Gershevitch. "Iranian Words Containing -ān-," *Iran and Islam: In Memory of the Late Vladimir Minorsky*, ed. C. E. Bosworth (Edinburgh, 1971), p.287, note 24; reprinted in his *Philologia Iranica*, ed. N. Sims-Williams (Wiesbaden : Dr. Ludwig Reichert Verlag, 1985), p.257, note 24. [F/K/A/IF/JJ/HH//B] <gornebaş>

k'efteleft كەفتەلەفت (K[s]/IFb/GF/TF)/kefte left كەفتە لەفت (HYma/Hej) = effort; commotion. See **k'eft û left.**

keftin كەفتِن (M)/k'eftin (M-Am) = to fall. See **k'etin.**

k'eft û left كەفت و لەفت *f.* **(-a;-ê).** 1) {syn: bizav; p'êk'ol; xebat} struggle, effort, hard work: •**Tu gelek *keft û leftê dikey* bo jiyana xo** (Dh) You are *working* very hard; 2) {syn: cerenîx; gelemşe; hengame; hêwirze; qerebalix} argument, quarrel, fight; commotion, chaos, stir: •**Wê rojê *kefte left* bi gund ketibû** (HYma, 30) That day there was quite *a stir* in the village. {also: k'efteleft (K[s]/IFb/GF/TF)/kefte left (HYma); <kefteleft> كەفتە لەفت (Hej)} [Dh/A//HYma/K(s)/IFb/GF/TF/Hej] <geremol; k'af-k'ûn>

kefxwê كەفخوێ (GF) = village chief. See **k'ewxwe.**

k'efzer كەفزەر (IFb) = moss. See **k'evz.**

kehdiz كەهدِز (Wkp) = The Milky Way. See **kadiz.**

k'ehêl كەهێل (K/A/IF) = bay horse. See **k'iĥêl.**

kehî كەهى (Bw/OK/SK-Ak) = tame. See **kedî.**

kehnî كەهنى (HR-I/HH) = spring, fountain. See **kanî I.**

kehr كەهر (GF/M-Zx) = kid, young goat. See **kar I**

kehreb كەهرەب *f.* **(-a;-ê).** electricity: **-soba karebê** (FS) electric stove. {also: kahraba (CS); kahreba (IFb-2); karaba (GF-2); kareb (FS-2); kareba (IFb/BF/Wkt); kehreba (ZF3); kehrebe (SS-2); kehruba (GF)} {syn: ceryan} <Ar kahrabā' كهرباء = 'amber; electricity' [FS/FD/SS//ZF3//IFb/BF/Wkt//GF]

kehreba كەهرەبا (ZF3) = electricity. See **kehreb.**

kehrebe كەهرەبە (SS) = electricity. See **kehreb.**

kehruba كەهروبا (GF) = electricity. See **kehreb.**

kehrik كەهرِك (Bw/TF) = kid, young goat. See **kar I & karik.**

keĥêl كەحێل (FS) = bay horse. See **k'iĥêl.**

kej I كەژ *adj. a term for the color of hair*: 1) redhead; 2) blond): •**Porê dîya te jî *kej* e. Tu li dîya xwe çûyî** (DZK) Your mother's hair is *blond* also; you take after your mother; 3) sandy, light brown. [DZK/K/A/IFb/B/GF/TF] <ç'ûr̄ II>

kej II كەژ *f./m.(FS)* **(-a/-ê;).** goat's wool [hirîya bizinan]: •***kejê* bizina çûr** (FS) angora goat's *wool.* [Mdt/GF/TF/FS] <ç'ûr I; hirî; kulk; liva; merez II>

kejî كەژى *f.* **(-ya;).** 1) saddle-girth, bellyband; strap or band for a saddle or packsaddle; a strap tied under the belly of a beast of burden (Ag); 2) woven silk string which women tie around their backs and heads (Qzl). {also: kejû (IFb); [keji] كژى (JJ)} {syn: kolan I; navteng; qoş [1]; teng II} Sor kejû كەژوو/kejî كەژى [Ag/JJ/Qzl//IFb] <zîn I>

kejû كەژوو (IFb) = saddle-girth. See **kejî.**

kek كەك *m.* **(-ê;).** 1) {syn: kokim [2]} older brother [cf. T ağabey]; 2) *term of address for a man.* {also: kak (K/IF-2); kekê (A); [kek] كك (JJ)} Sor kak كاك [K//A//JB3/IF/JJ/ZF3] <bira I; etik>

kekarik كەكارِك (Elb) = mushroom. See **kufkarik.**

kekê كەكێ (A) = older brother. See **kek.**

kel I كەل *m.* **().** 1) hornless goat (BK); type of sheep (A); ram or billy goat with short horns (IF); female sheep (=ewe) with horns (IF); female sheep with horns, or male sheep with short horns (HH/GF); **-beranê kel** (K) ram with twisted horns; 2) two-year-old calf (IF); 3) rut, heat, mating instinct of animals: •**Çêl *li kel* e = Çêl hat *kel*** (FS) The cow is *in heat*; 4) *[adj.]* horned (of animals) (B); 5) maturing *(of plants and animals)* (IF); 6) fertile, productive; powerful, strong (IF). {also: <kel> كـــل (HH)} Sor keł کەڵ = 'male, strong, powerful, high, buck, ram (esp. moufflon, ibex), bull'; Hau keł *m.* = 'ibex, mountain goat' (M4) [BK/K/A/IFb/B/HH/GF] <[1] bizin; mî I; k'ol IV; qoç'; [2] golik>

kel II کەل (Bw) = fortress. See **kela**.

k'el III کـــەل *f.* **(-a;-ê).** 1) {syn: coş} boiling: **•*K'ela* avê danî** (K) The water has stopped *boiling* **•sîtile ava *k'el*** (EP-7) a bucket of *boiling* water; **-k'el çûyîn** (B/JJ) to boil over {syn: fûřîn[2]}; 2) heat; hot object (HH): **•*K'ela* tavê danî** (K) The sun has stopped burning/*The heat of* the sun has cooled down; **-k'el û şewat** (Z-1) passion: **•bi k'el û şewat** (Z-1) passionately; 3) *[adj.]* hot *(to the touch)*, boiling hot: **-ava k'el** (Bw) (boiling) hot water (e.g., water for tea). {also: [kel] كـــل (JJ); <kel> كـــل (HH)} [Z-1/F/K/A/IF/BK/JJ/B/HH/Bw/FS] <k'elandin; k'elîn>

kel IV كـــەل *m.* **(-ê;-î).** buffalo; bullock: **•'Aqlê muroekî yek dawa mû e, ze'îf e, belê wextê gelek mû geheştine yêk-u-do dibîte werîs, *kelan* pê girê diden** (SK 41:393) A man's mind is but a single thread of hair, and weak, but when many hairs come together it becomes a rope fit to tie *buffaloes* **•Ez o to li-naw Herkîyan cotê *kela* yne. Digel spêdê şaxêt xo deyn e-ber yêk ka kî dê kê heřişînît** (SK 40:361) Among the Herkis, you and I are a pair *of buffaloes*. At dawn, we'll point our horns at each other to see who will smash whom; **-çûne kelî** (SK) to be put to the bull: **•Jinikê got, "Noke di 'uzreyda me. Bila *biçim e kelî*, paşî dê keyfa xo keyn"** (SK 58:682) The woman said, "I am now a virgin. Let me *be put to the bull*, afterwards we will enjoy ourselves". {also: [kel] كل (JJ-Rh)} {syn: gamêş} Cf. P kal كـل = 'male buffalo'; Sor keł کەڵ = 'male (esp. of large animals), buck, ram (esp. moufflon, ibex), bull' [SK/K(s)/JJ-Rh/Kmc/CS/FS]

kel•a كـــەلا *f.* **(;-ê/kela[y]ê).** 1) {syn: birc [2]} fort, fortress; castle: **•Lap zûva ew *kelêda* rûniştîye** (Ba3) For quite some time (=since quite early on) he had sat in *the castle* (=dungeon) **•Li hindav û nêzî Wanê û Gola Wanê *kelehên* mezin û dîrokî hene, du *keleh* ji van *kelehan* li raserî lêva golê ne** (SB, 50) Above and beside Van and Lake Van there are large and historic *fortresses*, [and] two of those *fortresses* overlook the shore of the lake **•*Qelata* wî li-ser çya bû li hindawê řûbarê, sê-hizar gez bilind e** (SK 51:556) His *fort* was on a mountain above the river, three thousand ells high; **-Kela Dimdim** (EP-8) The fortress of Dimdim, south of Urmiyah/Reza'iyeh in Kurdistan of Iran; a Kurdish rebellion against Shah Abbas which took place there in 1608-1610 is the subject of a famous Kurdish romance by the same name; 2) prison, jail (B). {also: kel II (Bw); kelat (JB3/IFb-2/TF/OK); kele I (A/IFb/GF); keleh (SB/JB1-S/OK-2); kelha; qela I (HB/GF-2/OK-2); qelat (A-2/SK); qele I (IFb-2); [qelé] قـــلـعـه (JJ); <kelh> كله (HH)} Cf. Ar qal'ah قلعة (loan word from Ir?)--> T kale; P kalāt كــــلات; Cf. also Arm k'ałak' քաղաք = 'town'; Sor qeła قـــــەڵا = 'fort, castle, rook (chess)' & kełat کەڵات /qełat قەڵات = 'hill fort' [Z-1/K/B//A/IFb/GF//JB3/TF/OK//HH//JJ//HB] <asêgeh>

k'elan کەلان (JB3) = to boil (vi.) . See **k'elîn**.

k'elandin كـــەلانـدن *vt.* **(-k'elîn-).** to boil *(vt.)*, bring to the boil; to cook: **•Çar çewal birinc anîn û timam di diştekî mezin de *kelandin*** (L) They brought four sacks of rice and *boiled* them all in a large cauldron **•Lazime tu qehwakê ji mi re *bikelînî*** (L) You must *boil* some [lit. 'a'] coffee for me; **-av k'elandin** (IF) to boil water. {also: <kelandin كلاندن (dikelîne) (دكلينه)> (HH)} {syn: k'emitandin; k'ewitandin} [F/K/A/JB3/IF/B/HH/SK] <k'el III; k'elîn; pe'tin>

kelaş كـــەلاش (JB3/ZF3) = sandal(s); peasant shoe(s). See **kelêj I**.

k'elaşe کەلاشە (K[s]) = rag slipper(s). See **kelêj I**.

kelat کەلات (JB3/IFb/TF/OK) = fortress. See **kela**.

k'elb کەلب *m.* **().** dog. {syn: kûçik; se} <Ar kalb كلب [K/B]

kelbeş كـــەلـــبـــەش (GW) = thistle, camel thorn. See **k'erbeş**.

kele I کەلە (A/IFb/GF) = fortress. See **kela**.

k'ele II کەلە (B) = head. See **k'elle II**.

kele III کەلە (FS) = snow shoe. See **kelle I**.

kelebest كـــەلـەبـەست *f.* **().** dry riverbed, wadi: **•Çend zelam ên bi gopal, das, bivir û çelte bi milve wê li nav *kelebestan* de … digerin û tên û diçin** (H 56:5) Some men with clubs, sickles, axes and satchels [slung] over their shoulders are roaming, coming and going amid *the dry riverbeds*. [H/TF/ZF3/FS]

k'elecan کەلەجان *f.* **(-a;-ê).** excitement, enthusiasm: **•Êdî ew *kelecan* û meraq vemiribû** (N.Mîro. Gava mirî biaxife, 34) That *excitement* and interest had died down **•Li Kurdistana Rojava *kelecana* hilbijartinê** (Nerinaazad 22.ix.2017) In Western [=Syrian] Kurdistan *the excitement of* the elections **•Sekerat û *kelecanê* bi hevdû re dijîm** (Ç.Lodî. Rê û rê: "Tevlîhev", 17) I experience death throes and *enthusiasm* all together. {also: k'elecanî (FS)} {syn: coş} < k'el III = 'boiling, heat' + can = 'soul, spirit' (cf. Ar hayajān هيجان --> T heyecan = 'excitement') [N.Mîro/Ç.Lodî/ZF3/Wkt//FS]

k'elecanî کەلەجانی (FS) = excitement. See **k'elecan**.

k'eledoş کەلەدۆش *f.* **(-a;-ê).** keledosh, *name of a traditional Kurdish dish, prepared differently according to region; conversely, a name for several completely different dishes, such as*: 1) a dish made of sheep trotters [serûpê] (Wkt); 2) dish made of raisins and beaten wheat (A/IFb); 3) type of stew [kasha] made of bread, lentils, dried curds with butter (OrK); 4) cooked grain stew [kasha] with meat, mixed with yoghurt [pakhtan'e] (B); 5) famous Kurdish dish made of meat, dried curds, *heliz* [lucern?], oil and lentils (ZF3): **•Ew jî weke pîrika xw ji şekirê tirş, pîvaz, *keledoş* û siwarbûna hespan hez dike** (M.Şarman. Pirça winda, *title page verso*) Like his wife he loves sour sugar, onions, *keledosh* and horse riding **•*Keledoşa* herî xweş a xelkê ye** (Wkp) The best *keledosh* is that of the folk. [Wkp/A/B/IFb/Wkt/ZF3/OrK/FD]

k'elef I کەلەف *m.* **(-ê;).** *woman's* thigh: **•Li gor encama vê lêkolîna ku neh (9) salan ajotiye, derketiye holê ku Omega 3 *kelefên* jinan mezin dike û jinên kelefmezin jî pir zîrek, şareza û biaqil in** (Lotikxane 10.ii.2016) According to this research which lasted 9 years, it has come out that Omega 3 enlarges women's *thighs* and that large-thighed women are very clever, focused and intelligent. [Lotikxane/A/Frq/ZF3/Wkt] <ḧêt; r̄an>

kelegîrî کەلەگیری (IFb) = bursting into tears. See **k'ewgirî**.

kelegîrînî کەلەگیرینی (Msr) = bursting into tears. See **k'ewgirî**.

keleh کەلەه (SB/JB1-S/OK) = fortress. See **kela**.

kelek I کەلەک *f.* **(-a;-ê).** raft, *particularly one held up by inflated animal skins*; "...rafts called keleks (branches piled atop inflated goat skins)" in: *The New Yorker*, Jan. 5, 2015, p. 46: **•Erebistana Siûdî û Îsraîl êdî di heman *kelekê* de ne** (rewanbej.net 2.iv.2015) Saudi Arabia and Israel are in the same boat [lit. '*raft*']. {also: [kelek] كلك (JJ); <kelek> كلك (HH)} {syn: 'ebrik; k'erx} Akk kalakku > Syr kalkā ܟܠܟܐ; NENA kâlâk ܟܠܟ = 'a raft, supported by inflated sheepskins' (Maclean) & kalak = 'type of raft (made of bound logs only)' (Sabar: Dict2); Sor kełek کەڵەک [Zeb/K/A/IFb/JJ/HH/GF/TF/OK/ZF] <kelekvan; meşk>

k'elek II کەلەک *f.* **(-a;).** fence or hedge made of a pile of stones, *for defining the end of one's property in a field*: **-keleka bera** (FS) do. Sor kełek کەڵەک = 'pile, stack, heap' [Zx/BF/FS/Wkt/ZK3] <şkêr>

kelekvan کەلەکڤان *m.* **(-ê;-î).** raftsman, one who steers a raft. {also: [kelek-van] كلكوان (JJ)} [Zeb/K/A/IFb/JJ/GF/TF/ZF3] <kelek I>

kelem I/k'elem [K/B] کەلەم *f.(K/JB3)/m.(B)* **(-a/ ;).** 1) cabbage; 2) cauliflower (HH): **-k'elema gul** = do. {also: kelemî (BF/FS); [kelem] كلم (JJ); <kelem> كلم (HH)} Cf. P kalam كلم; Sor kelerm کەلەرم; cf. also Egyptian Ar kurumb كرمب = 'cabbage'; W Arm gałamp կաղամբ [F/K/A/JB3/IF/B/JJ/HH]

kelem II/k'elem [JB1-A] کەلەم *m.(K/JB1-A)/f.(B)* **(-ê/; kelêm** [BK]/**-ê** [B]/**-î** [FS]**).** thorn; thornbush (Z-2): **•Şîn tê dibe *kelemeke* mezin** (Z-2) A large *thorn[bush]* grows there. {syn: dir̄î; stirî I; şewk[3]} [K/BK/B/Z-2//JB1-A]

kelemêş کەلەمێش (IFb) = mosquito. See **k'ermêş**.

kelemî کەلەمی (BF/FS) = cabbage. See **kelem I**.

keleng کەلەنگ (B/IF) = wild artichoke. See **kereng**.

kelepaçe کەلەپاچە (FS) = sheep's head and trotters. See **k'elle paçe**.

k'elep'arçe کەلەپارچە (B) = sheep's head and trotters. See **k'elle paçe**.

kelep'ûr کەلەپوور *m.* **(-ê;).** 1) inheritance *(lit. & fig.)*; heritage, legacy: **•Bi vê çapkirinêva Ḧacîyê Cindî xwestibû cime'ta Ermenîyan bike nasê *kelepûrê* miletê Kurd** (K-dş) By printing [them], Hadji Jndi wanted to acquaint Armenian society with *the heritage of* the Kurdish nation; 2) anything acquired at no cost (e.g., as inheritance); anything acquired dishonestly at no cost; 3) {syn: folklor; zargotin} folklore [neol.]. {also: <kelepûr كلپور/kerepûl كرپول> (HH)} Cf. T kelepir = 'chance bargain, golden opportunity; very cheap'; T kelepir [Çankırı; Malatya] = 'unclaimed property' & kelepür [Merzifon-Amasya; Bayadı-

Ordu; Gürün-Sivas]/kelepur [Rize] = 'something gotten for cheap or by trickery' (DS, v. 8, p. 2729); T kelepir [Afşar *Pınarbaşı-Kayseri] = 'booty, loot' (DS, v. 12, p. 4543) < Gr kelepúri κελεποῦρι = 'a find, bargain, windfall'; Sor kełepûr کەڵەپوور = 'things left for relatives after the death of a relation; cheap, free (of charge)' [K-dş/IF/HH//DS/ZF3]

k'eleş I کەلەش *m.(SK/Zeb)/f.(OK)* **(-ê/ ;).** corpse, dead body, cadaver; carcass, carrion: **•R̄abî, *kelexê* wî bi kêrikê hemî şeqşeq kir** (M-Zx #755, 350) He got up and cut his *carcass* into pieces with a knife **•Romî xertel in, xoşîya wan ew e *keleş* mişe bin** (SK 61:740) Turks are vultures, their pleasure is that *carrion* be abundant. {also: kelex (Bw/Zeb-2/OK-2/M-Zx); <keleş کەلەش/kelex کەلەخ> (Hej)} {syn: berat'e; cendek; cinyaz; leş; meyt'; t̪erm} Sor kelak کەلاک [Zeb/SK/OK/Hej]

k'eleş II کەلەش *m.* **(-ê;).** brigand, robber: **•Çel *keleş* bi xwe re helanîne** (L) They took 40 *brigands* with them; **-keleşên deryayê** (lemonde-kurdî #22 ix.2011) pirates; **-k'eleşê hewayê** (glosbe.com) hijacker. {also: [kelé̄š] قلش (JJ)} {syn: ḧerebaşî; nijdevan; r̄êbir̄} {keleş[t]î} [L/K/A/IFb/GF/ZF3/FS//JJ]

k'eleş III کەلەش *adj.* 1) {syn: bedew; cindî; spehî} beautiful, handsome *(B: of men; IF/HH: of people or animals)*; 2) nice, charming; 3) [*m.*] man's name. {also: [kelech] کلش (JJ); <keleş> کلش (HH)} [Z-1/K/B/IFb/JJ/HH/ZF3/FS]

k'eleşî کەلەشی *f.* **(;-yê).** brigandage, highway robbery; piracy. {also: keleştî (IFb-2)} {syn: nijdevanî; r̄êbirî} [IFb/ZF3/Wkt] <k'eleş II>

keleştî کەلەشتی (IFb) = brigandage. See **k'eleşî**.

keletor کەلەتۆر *f.* **(-a;).** dandruff, scurf: **-keletora serî** (Zeb) do. {also: <keletor> کەلەتۆر (Hej)} {syn: nemes; sîrik II} = Sor kir̄êj کِرێژ/kir̄êş کِرێش [Zeb/OK/AA/Hej/Wkt/FS] <k'eçelî>

k'elex کەلەخ (Bw/Zeb/OK/M-Zx) = carcass. See **k'eleş I**.

kelê کەلێ (A/IFb/GF/FJ/Nsb/FS) = saltless. See **kelî II**.

kelêj I کەلێژ *f.* **().** sandal(s); peasant shoe(s); rag slipper(s) (K[s]). {also: kelaş (JB3/ZF3); k'elaşe (K[s])} Sor kełaş کەڵاش = 'rag sole, shoe with such sole and woven upper'; cf. also 'galosh' [A/IFb/K(s)//JB3/ZF3] <sol; şekal>

kelêj II کەلێژ (Bw) = tailbone. See **kilêjî**.

kelêjî کەلێژی (ZF3/FS) = tailbone. See **kilêjî**.

kelha کەلها = fortress. See **kela**.

kelik کەلِک *f.* **(-a;-ê).** basket: **•Nêçîrvanî jî ... *kelika* di destê wî de raberî bermaliya xwe kir** (MG. Jiyaneka Pêguhork) And N. ... presented *the basket* in his hand to his spouse. {also: kelîk I (FJ); <kelik> کلك (HH)} {syn: 'edil; sebet; selik} [MG/IFb/HH/RZ/ZF3//FJ] <qûfik; sewî>

kelişandin کەلِشاندِن (Bw/Zx) = to tear, crack *(vt.)*. See **qelişandin**.

kelişîn کەلِشین (JR/Bw/Zx) = to tear, crack *(vi.)*. See **qelişîn**.

kelîştek کەلِشتەک (JB3) = hole; crack. See **qelîştek**.

kelî I کەلی *f.* **(-ya;).** pea(s), bot. *Pisum sativum*: **-kelî kizin** (Zeb) small type of pea; **-kelî xatûn** (Zeb) sweetpea?. {also: kelîk II (FS-2) <kelu> کەلو (Hej)} {syn: gilol II; polik II} [Zeb/OK/AA/FS//Hej] <lowûk>

kelî II کەلی *adj.* saltless, without salt (of food), bland, unseasoned. {syn: bê xwê} {also: kelê (A/IFb-2/GF/FJ/Nsb/FS-2); <kelî> کلی (HH)} [Wn/IFb/B/HH/FS//A/GF/FJ/Nsb] <şor̄ III; xwê>

kelîk I کەلیك (FJ) = basket. See **kelik**.

kelîk II کەلیك (FS) = pea(s). See **kelî I**.

k'elîn کەلین *vi.* **(-k'el-).** to boil *(vi.)*, come to the boil. {also: k'elan (JB3); [keliian کلیان/kelin کلین] (JJ); <keliyan> کلیان (HH)} {syn: fûrîn} Za keleyenã [kelayiş] (Srk) [Z-922/K/B/A/IF//JB3//JJ/HH] <k'el III; k'elandin>

kelkele کەلکەلە *m.* **().** 1) long, tube-like, hollow reed that grows in marshy areas, proverbial for its dryness (Wn): **•Usa ḧişk bû, bû fenanî *kelkele*** (Wn) It was as dry as the *kelkele* plant; 2) baby's breath, bot. *Gypsophila paniculata* [Rus perekati-pole перекати-поле] (Dz): **•*Kelkele*, misk'enê te li k'uye? Go, Ba dizane** (Dz) "*Baby's breath*, where do you live?" It said, "The wind knows" [*prv.*]. [Wn/Dz/FS]

kell•e I کەللە *f.* **(•a;).** type of snow shoe consisting of an animal skin held taut over a round frame: **•Wî *kele* kirin pîyên xwe û liser befrê çû** (FS) He put *kelles* on his feet and went out into the snow. {also: kele III (FS)} {syn: lîyan II (Bw)} For a photograph, see Aristova, photo #41 (after p. 128) [Bw//FS]

k'elle II کەللە *m.* **( ).** head; crown (of head); skull. {also: k'ele II (B); [kelé] کله (JJ)} Cf. P kalleh کله = 'head; top, upper part'; Sor kele کەلە [K/IFb/GF] <k'ilox; qehf; ser I>

k'elle paçe کەللە پاچە *f.* **().** sheep's head and trotters:

•**Wan *kelepaçeka* germ li spêdê xwar** (FS) They ate warm *kelle paçe* in the morning. {also: kelepaçe (FS); k'elep'arçe (B); <kelepaçe> کلپاچه (HH)} {syn: ser û p'ê} Cf. P kalleh pāčeh کـلـه پاچه; Sor kelepaçe کەلەپاچە [IFb//GF//HH/FS//B]

k'elmel کەلمەل (B/GF) = equipment. See **k'el û p'el**.

kelmêş کەلمێش (IFb/GF) = mosquito. See **k'ermêş**.

k'elogrî کـەلۆگری (FK-eb-2) = bursting into tears. See **k'ewgirî**.

keloştin کەلۆشتِن = to crack nuts. See **kelotin**.

kelotin کەلۆتِن *vt.* **(-keloj-).** to crack (nuts, seeds, etc.) with the teeth: •**Tovka *dikelojî*** (Bw) You *crack* sunflower seeds. {also: keloştin; <kelotin کـەلـۆتِـن/ kelojtin کـەلـۆژتِـن> (Hej)} Sor [da]kiro[j]tin داکِرۆژتِن [Bw/Zeb/Msl/Hej/FS]

k'elpîç کەلپیچ *m.* (). brick. {also: k'erpîç' (K/GF/ZF3); k'erpînc (B); kerpûç (OK-2/ZF3-2); [kerpitch] کرپچ (JJ); <kelpîç> کلپیچ (HH)} {syn: tabûq; xişt II} cf. T kerpiç; Rus kirpič кирпич [Zeb/Dh/A/IFb/HH/OK/FS//K/JJ/GF/ZF3//B] <xişt II>

kelş کەلش *f.* **(-a;).** crack, fissure: •**Kezîyêt wê kiçikê şor bibîn di *kelşa* p'irê r̄a** (M-Zx #776) The girl's braids were hanging down through *a crack* in the bridge. {also: qelş (K/A/IFb/GF/TF); [qelch/ qalch] قلش (JJ)} {syn: derz; *devlo[k] II; qelîştek; terk; tîş I} [Bw/Zx/M-Zx//K/A/IFb/JJ/GF/TF]

kelumel کەلومەل (OK) = equipment. See **k'el û p'el**.

kelupel کەلوپەل (OK) = equipment. See **k'el û p'el**.

kelûmel کـەلـوومـەل (IFb/GF) = equipment. See **k'el û p'el**.

k'el û p'el کـەل و پـەل/**k'elûp'el** کـەلـووپـەل *m.(B)/ f.(OK)/often pl.* (). effects, objects, equipment: -**kelûpelên cengê** (GF) war materiel. {also: k'elmel (B/GF-2); kelumel (OK-2); kelupel (OK); kelûmel (IFb/GF-2)} Sor kel-u-pel کـەل و پـەل= 'bits and pieces, effects, movable property' & kel-u-pelî nawmałî کەل و پەلی ناوماڵی = 'chattels' [Voa/ K(s)/IFB/GF/TF//OK//B] <amîr; tişt>

kem کـەم *f.* **(-a;-ê).** bush, shrub *(2 meters high)*: •**Evê kor hema xwe jê dûr dixe û diçe dikeve paş *kemeke dirriyê* ditele** (ZZ-4, 170) The blind man distances himself from him and goes and hides behind *a thornbush*. {syn: devî; k'ol III; t'er̄aş II; t'ûm} [Frq/IFb/ZZ/ZF3]

k'emax کـەمـاخ *f.* **(-a;-ê).** hip *(of people)*, haunch *(of animals)*; rear, backside, posterior (OK/GF): •**Yê tex̌me kirîye *kumax̌a* wî** (JB1-A #91) He has been branded on his *hip*. {also: kumax (IFb-2/ OK); kumax̌ (JB1-A); <kemax> کماخ (HH)} {syn: qor̄ik [2]} [A/IFb/HH/GF//OK//JB1-A] <hêt; r̄an>

k'embax کـەمـبـاخ (BF/FS/HH) = ruined, destroyed. See **k'ambax**.

kembel کەمبەل (GF) = dried sheep dung. See **kemêl**.

k'ember کەمبەر *f.* **(-a;-ê).** 1) waist; 2) belt, waistband; wide silver or golden belt (B): •**Çû ba şahê 'ecemo/ Jê xwest k'êr û *k'embero*** (EP-8) He went to the king of the Persians,/ asked him for a knife and *a belt*. {also: k'emer (B/IF-2); [kamar] کمر (JJ); <kember> کمبر (HH)} Cf. P kamar کمر --> T kemer [EP-8/K/A/IF/JJ/HH/BF/FS//B]

kembêl کەمبێل (Qtr-E) = dried sheep dung. See **kemêl**.

kemçik کـەمـچِـك (Wn) = ladle, wooden spoon. See **çemçik**.

k'emer کەمەر (B/IF) = waist; belt. See **k'ember**.

kemêl کـەمـێـل *f.* **(-a;-ê).** 1) {syn: gincî} dried sheep dung stuck to the sheep's tail; 2) dirty [kembêlgirtî]. {also: kembel (GF); kembêl (Qtr-E)} Sor kemêl کەمێل = 'sheep's wool matted with dung' [Qzl/A/IFb/FJ/FS/ZF3//GF//Qtr-E]

k'emilîn کـەمِـلـیـن *vi.* **(-k'emil-).** 1) to ripen, mature; 2) be perfected, completed, finished: •**Ew yekîtiya tov, ked, xwêdan û hêviyê bi evîna vejînek nû hêşîn dibe, *dikemile* û bi daxwaz û hêviya pêşerojeke baş tê çinîn** (CCG, 73) This unity of seeds, labor, sweat and hope blossoms and *is completed* with the love of new rebirth, and planting is done with desire and hope for a good future. {also: [kemilin] کـمـلـیـن (JJ)} <Ar kamala/ kamila كمل = 'to be whole or complete(d)' [CCG/K/JJ/ ZF/Wkt/CS]

k'emitandin کـەمِـتـانـدِن *vt.* **(-k'emitîn-).** to boil, scald, scorch, pour boiling water over: •**Bamyê di nav avê da *dikemitînin*** (Kurdî1-Cooking Show) They *scald* the okra in water. {syn: k'elandin; k'ewitandin} Cf. NA q-m-y = 'to scorch (by iron)' [Kurdî1/B/IFb/ZF]

kemn کەمن (Kg) = old *(of things)*. See **kevn**.

k'en کـەن *m.* **(-ê;-î).** smile, laugh[ter]: •**Paşê bi carekê ve *kenê* xwe birî** (KS, 8) Then at once he interrupted his *laughter* (or, stopped laughing). {also: [ken] کن (JJ); <ken> کن (HH)} [Z-1/K/A/JB3/IF/B/JJ/HH] <k'enîn>

k'enandin کەناندِن *vt.* **(-k'enîn-).** to make s.o. laugh or smile; to amuse, entertain: •**Hinekan *dikenînim*, hinekan jî bi girî vedikim** (D.Kelogirî. Doxînsist-îzm, 5) I *make* some people *laugh*, and I bring some people to tears •**Wî yariyek bo me got, *em* hemî *pê***

kenandin (Wkt) He told us a joke, and *made us* all *laugh*. {also: [kenandin] كنانديـن (JJ); <kenandin كنانـدن (dikenîne) (دكنينه)> (HH)} [D.Kelogirî/K/A/B/IFb/FJ/GF/TF/JJ/HH/ZF3/Wkt/BF/FD/G/FS/CS] <k'enîn>

kenar کەنار (F) = crossbeam. See **k'êran**.

kendal کەندال *m.* **(-ê; kendêl, vî kendalî).** 1) ditch, gully, ravine; two sides of deep cliff (IFb); cliff, crag, precipice (K): **•Rojekê ez çûme nik p'ira Se'donî, wêrê *kendalek* ê hey. Kuřikekî hevalê min di wêrê řa hat, gote min, "Tu dişêy xo bi vî *kendalî* da bavêjî?"** (M-Zx #778) One day I went by the Saadun bridge, where there is *a cliff*. A boy friend of mine came by there and said to me, "Can you throw yourself off this *cliff*?"; 2) slope, slight rise (IFb/HH); 3) man's name. {also: [kendal] كندال (JJ); <kendal> كندال (HH)} [K/A/IFb/B/JJ/HH/GF/TF] <gelî; newal>

kendav کەنداڤ *f./m.(Metîn)* **(-a/-ê;-ê/-î).** gulf; bay, inlet; canal: **-Şerê Kendavê Farisî** (Metîn) the Gulf War. {also: kendaw (TF)} Sor kendaw کەنداو = 'canal, bay, gulf' (K2) [Metîn/VoA/OK/ZF3/FS//TF]

kendaw کەنداو (TF) = gulf, bay. See **kendav**.

k'endik کەندِك *m.* **().** one-year-old calf, as opposed to **golik** = newborn calf (Ag). {also: k'indik (K)} {syn: malok; mozik I} [Ag/K/ZF3/FD] <ç'êlek/mange; ga; golik>

K'enedayî کەنەدایی *adj.* Canadian. {also: Kanadayî (Wkp-2); Kanadî (Wkp); Kenedî (BF)} Sor Kened[ay]î کەنەدایی [Wkt//BF]

Kenedî کەنەدی (BF) = Canadian. See **K'enedayî**.

kenêr کەنێر (A/IFb/GF) = mahaleb cherry. See **kinêr**.

k'enga کەنگا = when. See **k'engî**.

kenger کەنگەر (Dy/Srk/TG2/Mzr) = wild artichoke. See **kereng**.

k'engê کەنگێ (K/B/F/IFb/GF/Msr) = when. See **k'engî**.

k'engir کەنگِر (K[s]/OK/FS) = wild artichoke. See **kereng**.

k'engî کەنگی *intrg.* 1) {syn: çiçaxî; çiwext (Bg)} when?: **•Dijmin *kengî* bûye dost, heta ku tu li dostaniya mar digerî?** (CP, 15) Since *when* have enemies become friends, that you are seeking the friendship of the snake? **•Ĥetta *kengî* dê hutuwe bê-şol di xanîda řû-nêy, linga dirêj key?** (SK 9:91) *How long* are you going to sit idle like this in the house, (simply) stretching your legs? **•Ma *kengî* sultanê Istembolê nanek daye te, kêm yan zor çakîyek digel te kirîye?** (SK 17:161) *When* has the Sultan of Istanbul ever given you a loaf, or done you any good, great or small?; 2) [*conj.*] when: **•*Kengê* ez hatim, min got** (J) *When* I came, I said ... {also: k'enga; k'engê (K/B/F/IFb/GF/Msr); kinga (Ad/GF-2); kingî (Ag); [qenghi/kenghi/kangi/kinga] قنغى (JJ); <kengê> كنگى (HH)} Sor key کەی/kengê کەنگێ/kengî کەنگی; Za kinga/key (Todd) [A/JB3/SK/TF//F/K/IFb/B/HH/GF//Ad//Ag//JJ]

kenişt کەنِشت (K[s]) = synagogue. See **kinîşt I**.

kenişte کەنِشتە (IFb)/k'enişte (A) = synagogue. See **kinîşt I**.

k'enîn کەنین *vi.* **(-k'en-).** to laugh; to smile: **•Em ne 'erş o kursîyan dibînîn o ne ga w masîyan. Em noke pişta gunê xo jî nabînîn.' 350. 'Elî beg bi wî xeberî *kenî* w ehlê dîwanê jî hemî *kenîn*** (SK 39:349-350) We see neither the Dais and the Throne, nor the Ox and the Fish. We cannot even see behind our own testicles now.' 350. Ali Beg *laughed* at that and everybody present *laughed*. {also: [kenin] كنين (JJ); <kenîn كنين (dikenî) (دكنى)> (HH)} O Ir *xan- (Tsb 38): P xandīdan خنديدن; Sor pê kenîn پێ کەنین; SoK xanin (Fat 566); Za huwenã [watiş/huwayiş] (Todd/Srk); Hau xûay (xû-) *vi.* (M4) [K/A/JB3/IFb/B/JJ/HH/JB1-A&S/SK/GF/TF] <bişkurîn; devlik'en; k'enandin; mizicîn>

kepen کەپەن (Zx/IFb) = shepherd's cloak. See **k'epenek**.

kepene کەپەنە (FS) = shepherd's cloak. See **k'epenek**.

k'epenek کەپەنەك *m.* **(-ê;).** shepherd's felt cloak or vest: **-kepenê şivan** (Zx) do. {also: kepen (Zx/IFb-2); kepene (FS); [kapán کپان/kapanek کپنك] (JJ); <kepenek> كپنك (HH)} Cf. P kapanak كپنك & T kepenek [Zx/IFb//FS//K(s)/A/HH/GF//JJ] <kulav>

kep•ir/k'ep'•ir [M-Am] کەپِر *f.* **(•ra;•rê).** bower, temporary hut made of branches, *similar to the Jewish sukkah*; summer hut: **•[Ez dê agirî berdime *keprê* da bibit gorî]** (PS-II) I will set *the hut* on fire, so that it may be a sacrifice] **•*Kepir* çerm / pêpelîsk asin [zînê hespî]** (AZ #9, 74) *Bower* of hide / ladder of iron *[rdl.: ans.: horse's saddle]* **•Wextê hawînê bû. Mala Osê hemî di *keprê* da bû. Herzalekî bilind jî çêkirî bû, Oso û jina xo li ser herzalî diniwistin, kuřêt wî û mala wî jî di *kepra* binî da bûn** (SK 40:357) It was summertime. All of Oso's family was in *a bough-hut*. A high superstructure had also been made, and Oso and his wife were sleeping on the superstructure while his sons and household were in *the hut* beneath **•Xelkê wê dirkê hemî dijîn di *k'ep'ra* ve. [Di]çine çiyay, tiştekî tînin--dibênê çulî--dihavêne ser *k'ep'ra*, dibîte sîber û gelek xoş dibin** (M-Am #721, 332) The people there all live in *bough shelters*. They go to the mountains and bring something called 'chuli' [young, leafy branches of oak] and put them on top of *the shelters* and it makes a shade and they are very pleasant; **-kepra tirî** (Slv) grape bower; **-kol û kepir** (PS-II) do.: **•[Agir berda *kol û keprêd* rengîne]** (PS-II) He set fire to the many-colored *huts*. {also: kepr (SK/GF-2); [kepir] كـــپـــر (JJ); <kepir> كپر (HH)} Cf. P kapar كپر = 'hut, shanty'; Sor kepr کەپر; Hau kepre *f.* (M4); cf. also NENA qüprânâ ܩܘܦܪܢܐ = 'a booth, esp. in a vineyard' (Maclean). *According to GF, this word occurs in Hekkari and Behdinan.* [M-Am/PS-II/K(s)/IFb/JJ/HH/GF/OK/BF/FS//SK] <herzal; ḧol[ik]; kol II>

kepirşîn کەپرشین (FS) = Sukkot, autumn festival. See **kepreşîne**.

kepî/k'epî [A] کـــەپـــی *f./m.(ZF3/FS/BF)* **(/-yê;-yê/).** 1) {syn: difn [2]; poz I} nose; 2) {syn: bêvil[1]; firn[ik]; kulfik I (Wn); ximximk} nostril(s). {also: gep II (Bşk); kepû (IFb-2/GF-2/OK-2/FS)/k'epû (K); [kep كپ/kepou كپو] (JJ); <kepû> كپو (HH)} Cf. Sor kepû کـەپـوو = 'nose, snout' [A//K//IFb/B/ZF3//JJ/HH/GF/OK/FS//K/RZ//Bşk]

kepr کەپر (SK/GF) = hut. See **kepir**.

kepre şîn کەپرە شین (GF) = Sukkot. See **kepreşîne**.

kepreşîne کـــەپـــرەشـــیـــنـــە *f.* **( ).** Sukkot, Feast of Tabernacles, Jewish holiday in autumn (early October). {also: kepirşîn (FS); kepre şîn (GF-2); <kepreşîne> کـەپـرشـیـنـە (Hej)} "Kapra shīne" = 'blue hut' (Sukkot) [Brauer, p.315]; Sor kepreşîne کەپرەشینە/kepresewze کەپرەسەوزە [Brauer//GF/Hej//FS] <kepir>

kepû کـــەپـــوو (IFb/JJ/HH/GF/OK/RZ/FS)/k'epû (K) = nose; nostril. See **kepî**.

ker I/keř [A] کـــەر *m.* **(-ê; kêrî [B]).** piece, part: ***•kerê* nanî** (FS) *piece of* bread; **-ker kirin** = to cut or divide into parts or pieces **•Evê sêvê *ker ke*** (Z-921) *Divide* this apple. {also: **kerî I** (B/IF); [ker] كر (JJ); <ker> كر (HH)} {syn: p'ar II; qet II} [Z-921/K/JB3/JJ/HH/FS//A//B/IFb/GF/TF] See also **kerî I**. <beş I>

keř II کـــەڕ *adj.* 1) {syn: guhgiran} deaf: **•Ez ne j[î] t'opalim, ji p'îya / ne *kerr*im, ji guha / ne şilim, ji desta** (FK-kk-13:124) I am neither lame in the feet / nor *deaf* in the ears / nor limp in the hands; **-keř û lal** (IF) deaf and dumb: **•gurê *keřî-lalo*** (Ba) *deaf-mute* wolves; 2) silent, quiet: **-keř bûn/xwe keř kirin/cîyê xweda keř bûn** (K) to be quiet, shut up; to fall silent: **•Mîr li wan venegerand û *xwe ker kir*** (SW) The emir didn't answer them, and *kept quiet*. {also: kher (JB3); qar I; [ker] كـــر (JJ); <ker> كـــر (HH)} Cf. Av karəna- (Morg3, p.340): Mid P karr (M3); P kar كر; Sor keř کـەڕ; Za kerr (Todd) {keřayî I; keřbûn; keřî III; keřtî I} [F/K/A/IFb/B/JJ/HH/GF/TF/Msr//JB3]

k'er III کـــەر *m.&f.* **(-ê/-a; /-ê).** donkey, ass: **•Siwarê *kerê* ne tu siwar e** (BX) He who rides *a she-ass* is no rider *[prv.]*; **-k'era mê/mak'er** = she-ass, female donkey; **-k'erê nêr/nêrek'er** = male donkey; **-k'erê kûvî** (SS) = zebra. See **k'erk'ûvî**. {also: [ker] كـــــر (JJ); <ker> كـــــر (HH)} {syn: guhd[i]rêj} <O Ir *xara- (A&L, p.87 [X,1]): Baluchi kar; Paratchi khör; P xar خر; Sor ker کەر; Za her *m./f.* (Todd); Hau her *m.* (M4) {k'erayî II; k'eretî} [K/A/JB3/IFb/B/JJ/HH/SK/JB1-A/GF/TF/Msr] <cehş/dehş; exte; hesp; hêstir II; k'uřik; mak'er; qantir; ziřîn>

***ker IV** کـــەر *adj.* flat side up (of knucklebones **k'ap II**): **-ker û çik** (Qzl) a losing combination of knucklebones; **-ker û pik** (Qzl) a winning combination of knucklebones; **-du ker** (Qzl) double win {syn: çit}. {syn: mîr II (Wn)} [Qzl] <k'ap II>

k'eramet کەرامەت *m.* **(;-î).** miracle, wonder, marvel, wondrous deed: **•Keşkele zor fasiq e, hîç tobe naket, daimî fikra wî zerera xelkî ye, i'tiqada wî ne bi mu'cizatêt pêxemberan e û ne bi *kerametêt* ewliya'u-llan e** (SK 4:42) The magpie is very villainous and does not repent. He is always thinking of how to harm people and he believes neither in the miracles of the prophets nor in *the wondrous deeds* of holy men **•Li vir em wan conegan dixapînin û navê vî *kerametî* jî bi zimanê me gundiyan zorgayî ye** (Epl, 12) Here we fool those young bulls, and the name of this *miracle* in the language of us villagers is 'zorgayî' **•Nê tu nizanî, ev zilam şêx e, *kerametên* wî hene! Dema bixwaze bireve, dikare wek çivîkek bifire û here hey here!** (Bkp, 36) Don't you know, this man is a sheikh, he has *wondrous* *powers*! When he wants to escape, he can fly like a bird and he's gone for good! {also: k'eremet (K-2)} {syn: 'ecêb; gosirmet} < Ar karāmah كرامة = 'nobility; miracle that God effects through a saint (Islamic popular belief)' [Epl/K/IFb/SK]

keran کەران (F) = crossbeam. See **k'êran**.

kerane کەرانە (TF/OK/IFb) = hammer. See **gefan II**.

***keřanî** کەرانی *adj. pattern of* **bergûz** *material:* alternating long white stripe and stripe consisting of series of black lines on white. [Bw] <bergûz>

keraş کەراش *m.* **(; qerêş** [FS]**/-î** [FS]**).** 1) {syn: aşvan} miller; mill-hand [aide-meunier] (JB3): **•Mĥemmed Xan xwe kirîye *keraş* û jina xwe jî kirîye dorçî** (L) M. Khan turned himself into *a miller*, and his wife into a customer **•*Qeraşî* arê wî hûr hêra** (FS) *The miller* finely ground his flour; 2) {syn: aş I} mill (K[s]). {also: qeraş (K[s]/A/JB3/IFb/GF/TF/FS); [karráš] كراش (JJ)} [L/K(s)/A/JB3/IFb/GF/TF/FS//JJ]

keřayî I کەرایی *f.* **().** deafness. {also: keřbûn (B); keřî III (K/IFb); keřtî (B/K)} [B/K/ZF3/Wkt//IF] <keř II>

k'erayî II کەرایی (B) = stupidity; stubbornness. See **k'eretî**.

k'erb/kerb [JB1-A] کەرب *f.* **(-a;).** 1) {syn: cefa; fikar; k'eder; k'eser; kovan; kul I; qilqal; şayîş; t'alaş; tatêl; xem; xiyal [2]} sorrow, grief, distress; worry, care: **-[ji] k'erba** (B) out of excitement; out of sorrow or grief: **•Bor dîna xwe daê, M. wê *ji k'erba* bit'eqe** (EP-7) Bor saw that M. was about to burst *with/from/out of grief* **•Ew *k'erba* kuřê xwe nexweş k'et** (B) She fell ill *out of sorrow for* her son; 2) [*m./pl.* **().**] anger (JB1-A/SK): **-kerbêt *fk-î* bûnewe = vebûn** (SK) to become angry, fly into a rage: **•*Kerbêt wî dê binewe*, dê cûna det, şeřî dê ket.** (SK 52:561) *He will lose his temper* and become abusive and start fighting. {also: [kerb] كرب (JJ); <kerb> كرب (HH)} < Ar karb كرب [Z-1/K/A/JB3/IFb/JJ/HH/JB1-S/SK/GF/TF/OK//JB1-A] <k'eribîn>

k'erbeş کەربەش *f.* **(-a;-ê).** a thistle eaten by donkeys; camel thorn, bot. *Alhagi maurorum* (IF); holly, bot. *Ilex* (OK): **-Bihar e û *kerbeş* çêbûye** (GW) It's springtime and *thistles* have sprouted *(said of people who will eat anything, whether it is helal or not)*. {also: kelbeş (GW-2); <kerbeş> كربش (HH)} [Msr/A/IFb/HH/TF/OK/GW/ZF3/Wkt] <givzonik>

keřbûn کەربوون (B) = deafness. See **keřayî**.

kerebalix کەرەبالغ (L) = noise; crowd. See **qerebalix**.

keřekeř کەرەکەر**/kereker** کەرەکەر [FJ/GF/CS] *adv.* silently, secretly: **•Seyra Dinê lê nihêřî melle diçe tewlê tê. Seyra Dinê *keře-keř* pey çû** (HCK-5, #8, 58) S.D. saw the mullah going to and coming from the stable. S.D. *secretly* followed behind him. {syn: teletel} [HCK/K/B/Kmc//FJ/GF/CS]

kerekewî کەرەکەوی (CS) = zebra. See **k'erk'ûvî**.

k'erem کەرەم *f.* **(-a;-ê).** goodness; generosity: **-Ji k'erema xwe [ra]** = Please! *(when asking s.o. to do stg.)*; **-k'erem kirin** = *(in polite speech)* to be so kind as to, to deign, to condescend to do stg.: **•K'erem [bi]kin** = Please!; Come in!; Sit down!; Help yourself! *(said by host when serving something)* [cf. Ar tafaḍḍal تفضّل; T buyrun; P befarmā'īd بفرمائيد; Sor fermû فەرموو; Arm hrammec'ēk' Հրամմեցէք]: **•*Kerem bikin*, gelî mêvana, peye bin** (L) *Please*, O guests, dismount! {also: [kerem] كرم (JJ); <kerem> كرم (HH)} < Ar karam كرم [K/JB3/IFb/B/JJ/HH/GF]

k'eremet کەرەمەت (K) = miracle. See **k'eramet**.

kereng کەرەنگ *m./f.(B/ZF3)* **(/-a; kerêng** [BK]**/-ê** [B]**).** tumble thistle, Bot. *Gundelia tournefortii* [Ar 'akkūb عكّوب], with edible leaves, stems, roots, and undeveloped flower buds; wild artichoke (B); edible wild plant, cardoon, bot. *Cynara cardunculus*; "large perennial plant related to the artichoke and cultivated for its edible root and leafstalks" (Webster): **•*Keleng* hê hişk nebûye, qîvarê** [sic] **wê tê xwarin** (IFb) *The cardoon* isn't dry yet, and its stamen is [already] being eaten *[prv.]*. {also: keleng (B/IFb-2); kenger (Dy/Srk/TG2/Mzr); k'engir (K[s]/OK/FS-2); [käräng] كرنك (JJ) = 'arbuste épineux'; <kerenk> كرنك (HH)} P kangar كنگر = 'prickly artichoke, cardoon'; Sor kengir کەنگر = 'artichoke'; Za kenger *m.* (Mal); cf. also W Arm gangaṙ կանկառ/gankaṙ կանգառ = 'artichoke'; T enginar = 'artichoke'; Gr kinara κινάρα/kynara κυνάρα [Dy/Srk/TG2/Mzr//K(s)/OK//K/A/IFb/BK/JJ/GF/TF/Qmş/Hk/Kmc-#40/FS//H//B] <qîvar>

kereste کەرەستە *m.* **(-yê;).** material: **-keresteyê xav** (GF) raw materials; **-keristeyê avayî** (OK) construction materials. {also: keriste (OK/VoA-Barzan)} Cf. T kereste = 'lumber, timber'; Sor keres[t]e کەرەستە = 'material, equipment' [VoA/OK//K(s)/IFb/GF/TF]

k'eretî کەرەتی *f.* **(-ya;-yê).** 1) stupidity; 2) donkey-like stubbornness, being or acting like a donkey, asininity. {also: k'erayî II (B); k'ertî II (K/ZF3)} [A//B//K/ZF3] <k'er III>

k'ergah کـــەرگـــاه *f.* **(;-ê).** embroidery frame, lace-frame: **•Eva bû çil şev û çil roj ez ji boy te serê vê p'irê rûniştime ser nexişê *k'erge*** (EP-7) I have sat on this bridge for 40 days and nights for you, [working] on an *embroidery* frame. {also: k'erge (EP-7)} Cf. P kārgāh کـــارگـــاه, T gergef [EP-7//B]

k'erge کـــەرگـــە (EP-7) = embroidery frame. See **k'ergah**.

k'ergedan کـــەرگـــەدان = rhinoceros; chesspiece. See **k'erkedan**.

k'ergeden کەرگەدەن (K/GF) = rhinoceros; chesspiece. See **k'erkedan**.

k'ergedor کەرگەدۆر (B) = rhinoceros; chesspiece. See **k'erkedan**.

k'ergezk کەرگەزك *f.* **(;-ê).** stinging nettle, bot. *Urtica urens*: **•Hinek li Çiyayê Kurmênc, heger *kergezk* teze be, dikin sermûsak û duxin ... Hinek jî pê bawer in, ku ew qelewbûnê datîne. *Kergezkê* dikelînin, û ava wê hiltînin û diparzinînin** (FE) In Çiyayê Kurmênc (Efrin), if *the nettle* is fresh, some people make it into a sermûsak [fried between bread slices] and eat it ... Some believe that it reduces obesity. They boil *the nettle*, remove its water and strain it. {also: kergezok (FE-2); k'evgez (K/B); kevgezk (Wkt); kevzer (AD)} {syn: gezgezok} [Efr/FE//Wkt//K/B//AD]

kergezok کەرگەزۆك (FE) = nettle. See **k'ergezk**.

k'ergu کەرگو = rabbit. See **k'erguh**.

k'erguh کـــەرگـــوه *m./f.(K/FS)* **(-ê/;/-ê).** rabbit, hare. {also: k'ergu; k'ergû (K[s]); k'ergûşk (K); keroşk (GF-2); kevroşk (JB3/IFb-2/GF-2); k'eworşk (A); kêrgo (RZ-2); k'êrgu[h] (B); k'êrgûşk (Ag); k'êroşk (A/RZ-2); k'êrûşik (A); kêrûşk (SK); kêrwîşk (RZ-2); k'êvrîşk (FS/BF); k'êvroşk; k'êwrîşk, f. (;-ê) (FK-eb-1); k'êwrûşk (K/F); k'iwîşk (Bşk); k'îroşk (IFb-2); [kiwroujk] كڤروژك (JJ); <kêvroşk> كيڤروشك (HH)} < k'er = 'donkey' + guh = 'ear[s]', cf. Mid P xar-gōš (M3); P xargūš خرگوش; Sor kerwêşk کەروێشك/kewrêşk کەورێشك [Sinneh]; Za arwêş (Todd/Mal)/hargûş (Mal) *m.*; Hau hewrêşe *m.* (M4). See **1. The "Hare" in Pahlavi** in: H.W. Bailey. "Three Pahlavi Notes," *Journal of the Royal Asiatic Society* (1931), 424-25. [IFb/GF/RZ/FS//K/F//A//SK//JB3//HH//FS/BF//B//JJ//Ag//Bşk] <xirnaq>

k'ergû کەرگوو (K[s]) = rabbit. See **k'erguh**.

k'ergûşk کەرگووشك (K) = rabbit. See **k'erguh**.

k'eribîn کـــەرِبـيـن *vi.* **(-k'erib-).** 1) {syn: xem xwarin} to feel sad (A/TF/CS); to feel worried (TF/ZF); 2) {syn: erinîn; hêrs bûn; xeyidîn; ẍezibîn} to be or get angry (JJ/CS): **•Nava Jêhat dişewitî, ji esker diqeherî, ji xwe diqeherî, *dikeribî* û nizanîbû wê çi bike** (SBx, 11) J's insides were boiling, he was fed up with the soldier, he was fed up with himself, he *was angry* and didn't know what he should do. {also: [kerebin] كربين (JJ)} [SBx/A/TF/ZF/CS//JJ] <k'erb>

keȓ•ik I کـــەڕك [IFb/GF/TF/Qzl/Bw]/**kerik I** کـــەرك [BX/HH/OK/TF-2/Bw-2] *f.* **(•ka;).** *name for various unripe fruits:* 1) unripe fig(s) (BX/TF): **•Adetên bav û bapîran, *kerik* xweştir in ji hêjîran** (BX) [If] the customs of the ancestors [will it], *unripe figs* are better than ripe ones *[prv.]*; 2) unripe grapes (Qzl). {also: <kerik> كرك (HH)} [IFb/GF/TF/Qzl/Bw//BX/HH/OK] <harsim; hejîr>

keȓik II کەڕك *m./f.(K/B)* **(-ê/-a; /-ê).** 1) earlobe (F/IF); 2) {syn: guh} ear (Bg/IFb); inner ear (B): **-keȓika guh** (B) inner ear. [Bg/F/K/B/IFb]

keriste کەریستە (OK/VoA) = material. See **kereste**.

keritandin کـــەرِتـانـدِن *vt.* **(-keritîn-).** to devour, gobble up, eat bite by bite: **•Ew merivê tu dibêjî kanê, nîşanî min bide ez *bikeritînim*** (J2, 24) Where is that man you're talking about, show me so that I can *gobble him up*. {also: kiritandin (A)} Cf. Sor kirtandin کِرتاندِن/qirtandin قِرتاندِن = 'to clip, trim, gnaw, nibble' [J2//A] <vegevizandin; xwarin>

k'erixîn کـــەرِخـيـن *vi.* **(-k'erix-).** to be or get sick and tired of, be fed up with; to have an aversion to stg., be disgusted by stg.; to have an aversion to a dish from eating it too much: **•*Dilê wî ji* îpraxa *kerixîye*** (FS) He *is sick and tired of eating* 'îprax' (stuffed grape leaves) **•Ez *kerixîm*** (Msr) I*'ve had it*! {also: *k'erxin (A); [kerikhin] كـــرخـــيـــن (JJ); <kerixîn كرخين (dikerixî) (دكرخى)> (HH)} {syn: zivêr bûn} Cf. Ar kariha كـــره = 'to hate' [Msr/IFb/JJ/HH/GF/FS//A]

kerî I کـــەری *m.* **(; kêrî).** piece, part: **-kerî kirin** = to cut or divide into parts or pieces. {also: ker I; <kerî> كـــــری (HH)} {syn: p'ar II; parî; qet II} [Z-921/K/B/HH] See also **ker I**. <beş I>

kerî II کـــەری *m.* **(-yê; kêrî).** large flock or herd *(of sheep or goats)* (K); small flock or herd *(of sheep or goats)* (B): **•Ḧer kerîkî pêz ȓa sê-çar seêd**

gurêx̂ derdik'etne çolê (Ba2:1, 203) With *every flock of* sheep, 3-4 sheepdogs would go out to the wilderness •**Min hil bûye t'oz û xubara van *kerîyaye*** (Z-1) The dust of these *flocks* [of sheep] rose up (over) me: **-kerîêd pêz** (Ba2) flocks of sheep; **-kerîkî mî** (Haz) a flock of sheep (ewes) ; **-kerîkî berx** (Haz) a flock of lambs; **-kerî-sûrî** (F) flock, herd: •**Awqa mal, zêr, zîvê te heye, *kerî sûrîyê* te heye** (FK-kk-1) You have so much wealth--gold and silver, so many *herds*. {also: <kerî> کـرى (HH)} {syn: col; sûrî I; x̂ar II} [Z-1/K/JB3/IFb/B/HH/TF/OK/Haz/BK] <bir̄ I[4]; celeb II; mî I; pez; r̄af; r̄evo = qefle I>

ker̄î III کەڕی (K/IFb) = deafness. See **ker̄ayî**.

k'erkedan/kerkedan کەرکەدان *m.* **().** 1) rhinoceros; 2) a chess piece: knight: •**R̄êya ku fîl û *kerkedan* ku hatin** (MC-1) The way the bishop and [*knight*?] were going (in a chess game). {also: k'ergedan; k'ergeden (K/GF); k'ergedor (B); <kerkedan> کـرکـدان (HH)} Skt khaḍgá.dhenu *f.* < 'sword' + 'milch cow' --> P kargedan کـرگدن/karg کـرگ --> Ar karkaddan/karkadann کـرکـدن & T gergedan; Sor kerkeden کـەرکـەدەن = 'rhinoceros; unicorn' [MC-1/A/IFb/HH//K/GF//B] <fêris [2]; fîl [2]; k'işik; r̄ex II; şetrenc>

kerkon کـەرکـۆن *m.* **(-ê;).** rag, piece of felt (JJ): •**kerkonê r̄eş** (MC-1) black cloth. {also: [kerkoun] کرکون (JJ)} {syn: kevnik [2]; p'aç' II & p'aç[']ik; p'ate II; p'er̄ok; pîne; p'ot; qerpal} [MC-1//JJ] <kulav>

kerkovî کەرکۆڤی (FD) = zebra. See **k'erk'ûvî**.

k'erk'ûvî کەرکووڤی *m.* **().** zebra: •**Heştirme û *kerkûvî* gelek caran bi hev re dijîn, daku xwe ji talûkeyan biparêzin** (deskgram.org:rasteqîn vi.2018) Ostriches and *zebras* often live together, to protect themselves from dangers. {also: kerekewî (CS); k'erê kûvî (SS); kerkovî (FD)} Sor kerekêwî کەرەکێوی [deskgram/GF/FS/BF/Wkt//SS//FD//CS]

k'erm•e کـەرمـە *m./f.(B)* **(; /•ê).** dried cow dung (IF); cake or lump of pressed dung used as fuel (K/IF); manure of large domestic animals such as cows and bulls {cf. r̄îx} (Ag). {also: <kerme> کـرمـه (HH)} [Ag/K/A/IFb/B/HH/GF/ZF3] <bişkul/pişkul ; ç'êrt; deve II; dirg; guhûr; keşkûr; peyîn; qelax; r̄îx; sergîn; sergo; sêklot; t'epik II; t'ers; t'ert[ik]; zibil; zirîç>

k'ermêş کـەرمێش *f.* **(-a;-ê).** *several types of insect:* 1) {syn: p'êşî II} mosquito; midge, large mosquito; 2) gadfly, horse-fly: •**Jê tê bîhna pîs tev av û dûlop / Tev mêş û *kelmêş* pêşî û dûpişk** (Cxn-2:412) A bad smell comes from it, with dripping water / With flies and *gadflies*, mosquitoes and scorpions; 3) wasp, hornet (K/A). {also: kelemêş (IFb-2); kelmêş (IFb-2/GF-2); [ker-mich] کـرمـش (JJ); <kermêş> کرميش (HH)} < k'er = 'donkey' + mêş = 'fly'; cf. P xarmagas خـرمـگس [Msr/K/A/IFb/B/JJ/HH/GF/ZF3/FS] <axûrk; mêş; moz>

ker̄obî کەڕۆبی (SK) = cherub. See **kerûbî**.

keroşk کەرۆشك (GF) = rabbit. See **k'erguh**.

k'erpîç' کەرپیچ (K/GF/ZF3) = brick. See **k'elpîç**.

k'erpînc کەرپینج (B) = brick. See **k'elpîç**.

kerpûç کەرپووچ (OK/ZF3) = brick. See **k'elpîç**.

kersil کەرسِل (Bw/JJ/FS) = donkey dung. See **serkul**.

ker̄tî I کەڕتی (B/K) = deafness. See **ker̄ayî**.

k'ertî II کـەرتـی (K/ZF3) = stupidity; stubbornness. See **k'eretî**.

kertol کەرتۆل (JB3/IFb/TF) = potato. See **k'artol**.

kerûbî کـەرووبـی *m.* **().** cherub (pl.: cherubim): •**Bi deng û hîseke efsûnî re hew dîtiye ko *kerûbiyek* li pêş wî sekinîye. Bi erdekî kej û spî, bi dirûvên zarokekî bûye, çep û rastê wê bi bask bûne** (Tof, 12) He scarcely noticed that *a cherub* was standing before him, with a magical voice and feeling. Blond and fair in one place, with the looks of a child, she had wings on her left and right sides •**We *ker̄obî* ne, ko melekêt 'ezabê ne, we r̄oḧanî ne, ko melekêt r̄eḧmetê ne** (SK C5) And there are *the cherubim*, who are the angels of punishment, and the spiritual ones, who are the angels of mercy. {also: ker̄obî (SK)} < Ar karūbī كروبى = 'cherub, archangel' < Heb keruv כרוב [Tof//SK] <melek>

kervan کەرڤان (F) = caravan. See **karwan**.

k'erwan کەروان (B) = caravan. See **karwan**.

k'erx کـەرخ *f.* **(;-ê).** raft, *particularly for transporting logs*: •***K'erxa* çê tkin [=dikin], *her k'erxê* sih ta yê têdanin** (M-Zx #783, 362) They make *rafts*, *each raft* having 30 stems in it •**Wî dar bi *kerxê* tînan** (FS) He brought logs (lit., pieces of wood) by *raft*. {syn: 'ebrik; kelek I} NENA karxa (Sabar: Dict2) [M-Zx/SS/FS/ZF3]

*k'erxin کـەرخـِن (A) = to be sick and tired of. See **k'erixîn**.

kes/k'es [K/A/JB1-A&S] کـەس *m.* **(-ê;-î).** 1) {syn: nefer; zat} person; 2) {syn: bejnek; hinek} someone; anyone; 3) [+ *neg.*] nobody, no one; not anyone: **•Ewê *ne*dixast r̄ûyê *kesekî* bibîne** (Ba) She did*n't* want to see *anyone's* face **•Go ne ew be, *kes ni*kare** (L) If he can't, *no one* can **•*Kesek* li wan dera *tune*** (L) There is *no one* there **•*Kesî* dey *ne* kir** (L) *No one* responded **•Ne ew û ne *keskî din*** (L) Neither he nor *anyone else* **•Wîşîê tirî li hindawê r̄êkan ḧetta nêzîkî zistanê dima. *Kes ne*diwêra dest biket ê** (SK 51:554) Bunches of grapes would remain (hanging) above the roads until nearly winter. *Nobody* dared to touch them. {also: [kes كس/kes-ek كسك] (JJ); <kes> كس (HH)} Cf. P kas كس; Sor kes کەس = 'person; anybody'; Za kes = 'person; someone; no one' (Mal) [K/A/JB1-A&S//B/JB3/IFb/JJ/HH/SK/GF/TF] <filan; t'akekes>

kesanetî کەسانەتی *f.* **(-ya;-yê).** personality; character, strength of character: **•Divê ku hunermend xwedî *kesanetîyeke* pir̄ zelal be** (Wlt 2:73, 11) An artist must possess a pure *character* **•Em dixwazin *kesanetiyê* di jinan de biafirînin** (Wlt 1:35, 16) We want to instill *character* in women. {also: kesayetî (VoA); kesîtî (IFb/GF)} [(neol)Wlt//VoA//IFb/GF/ZF3] <şexsîyet>

kesax کەساخ (FJ/TF/ZF/FS)/k'esax (A) = pruning, trimming. See **k'ezax**.

kesaxtin کەساختِن (ZF) = to prune. See **k'ezaxtin**.

kesayetî کەسایەتی (VoA) = personality. See **kesanetî**.

k'ese کەسە *adj.* short, direct: **-r̄îya k'ese** (K/B) shortcut: **•--Gelo *r̄ya k'ese* k'îjan heye, wekî em îşev derêne malê? – Ê, go, *r̄ya k'ese* nav mêşeda heye, lê herçê çûye, nehatîye** (HCK-2, 91) "Which is *the shortcut*, so that we can get home this evening?" "There is *a shortcut* through the forest, but whoever goes there, has not come [back]". {syn: kurt I} <T kısa = 'short' [HCK/K/B/Tsab]

k'eser کەسەر *f.* **(-a;-ê).** 1) {syn: axîn; ḧezing} sigh; 2) {syn: cefa; fikar; k'eder; k'erb; kovan; kul I; şayîş; t'alaş; tatêl; xem; xiyal [2]} grief, distress; regret; sadness (JB3): **•Rîwî got, "Wextê ko ez û to wêkr̄a diger̄yayn gelek meḧebbeta min hebû der-ḧeqq çawêt te. Eger te hind musa'ede kiriba, pîçek stukira xo kêşaba pêş çawêt min û carekî dî di-pêş mirina xoda min çawêt te dîtibana, paşî bila ez miribam, da di dilê minda nebît e *keser*"** (SK 2:15) The fox said, "When you and I used to go about together I had a great affection for your eyes. If you would be so kind as to stretch your neck a little in front of my eyes so that I could see your eyes once again before my death, then let me die, there would be no *regret* in my heart" **•Xecê, tu bi wê *k'eserê* ku pê dik'alî u dinalî, niha nêzîke, ne dûre** (IS-#271) Khej, you and your *grieving*! The one you are 'moaning and groaning' about is nearby, he is not far off. < Ar kasr كسر = 'fraction, breaking' [BX/K/A/JB3/IFb/B/GF/TF]

k'esidandin کەسِداندِن *vt.* **(-k'esidîn-).** 1) to pickle, preserve in brine: **-îsotên kesidandî** (WM 1:[25], 6) pickled peppers; 2) to preserve meat for the winter (HH/GF/IFb). {also: <kesidandin کسداندن (dikesidîne) (دکسدینه)> (HH)} [WM/A/IFb/HH/GF/TF/ZF3] <qelî>

kesixandin کەسِخاندِن (CCG) = to prune. See **k'ezaxtin**.

k'esîb کەسیب *adj.* 1) {syn: feqîr; xizan} poor, destitute; 2) [*m.* ().] pauper. {also: k'esîv (Z-921)} cf. Az T kasyb = 'poor' <Ar kāsib كاسب = 'winner; earner, provider'; Sor kasib کاسِب = 'tradesman' {k'esîbayî; k'esîb[t]î; k'esîvayî; k'esîv[t]î} [F/K/B//Z-921]

k'esîbayî کەسیبایی (B) = poverty. See **k'esîbtî**.

k'esîbî کەسیبی (B/K/ZF3/Wkt) = poverty. See **k'esîbtî**.

k'esîbtî کەسیبتی *f.* **(-ya;-yê).** poverty. {also: k'esîbayî (B-2); k'esîbî (B-2/K-2/ZF3/Wkt); k'esîvayî (B-2); k'esîv[t]î (B-2)} {syn: feqîrî; sêfîlî; xizanî; zivarî} [K/B//ZF3/Wkt] <k'esîb>

kesîtî کەسیتی (IFb/GF) = personality; character. See **kesanetî**.

k'esîv کەسیڤ (Z-921) = poor. See **k'esîb**.

k'esîvayî کەسیڤایی (B) = poverty. See **k'esîbtî**.

k'esîvî کەسیڤی (B) = poverty. See **k'esîbtî**.

k'esîvtî کەسیڤتی (B) = poverty. See **k'esîbtî**.

k'esk کەسک *adj.* green; dark green (B). {also: [kesk] كسك (JJ); <kesk> كسك (HH)} {syn: heşîn [1]} Cf. Mid P kāskēnēn = 'blue-green; of lapis lazuli' (M3); Sor kesk کەسک = sewz سەوز {keskanî; k'eskayî; [keski] كسكى (JJ)} [Ad/K/A/JB3/IFb/B/JJ/HH/GF/TF]

keskan کەسکان (SK/OK/Zeb) = terebinth. See **kezan**.

keskanî کەسکانی (JB3/IFb) = greenness. See **k'eskayî**.

k'eskayî کەسکایی *f.* **(-ya;-yê)**. greenness; verdure: **•Ji *keskayîya* çavên te bû** (Xemgînê Remo in Helbestname, 224) It was from *the greenness of* your eyes. {also: keskanî (JB3/IFb); [keski] كسكى (JJ)} {syn: heşînatî} [K/A/GF/TF/ZF3//JB3/IFb//JJ] <k'esk>

k'eskesor کەسکەسۆر *f.* **(-a;-ê).** rainbow. {also: k'eskûsor (A/BF)/kesk û sor (FS); [keske-sor] کسکه سور (JJ); <keskesor> کسکصور (HH)} {syn: kêrestûn} < k'esk = 'green' [+ û = 'and'] + sor = 'red'; = Sor kołke•zêrîne کۆڵکەزێرینە [F/K/JB3/IFb/B/JJ/HH/GF/Wkt//A/BF//FS]

k'eskûsor کەسکووسۆر (A/BF)/kesk û sor کەسك وصۆر (FS) = rainbow. See **k'eskesor**.

keskûyî کەسکوویی *adj. pattern of* **bergûz** *material:* purple with green undertones. [Bw] <bergûz>

kesnedîtî I کەسنەدیتی *adj. pattern of* **bergûz** *material:* monochrome (êkreng) violet/purple (worn by Christians [Fileh]). [Bw] <bergûz>

k'esper کەسپەر *adj.* blue-eyed, having grayish-blue eyes: **-çavkesper** (Xrz) do. {syn: çavşîn} [Xrz/A/IFb/ZF3]

kesrevan کەسرەڤان (M. Top. Hakkari) = women's headdress. See **k'esrewan**.

k'esrewan کەسرەوان *f.* **().** traditional Kurdish women's headdress: •**Ji wê demê ve êdî li Botanê jin *kesrewanan* bê kesk, sor û zer çênakin û wekî tac nadin serê xwe** (Azadiya Welat, 23 Kanûn 2015) Ever since then, women don't make *headdresses* without green, red and yellow colors, and they don't wear them on their heads like crowns. {also: kesrevan (M. Top. Hakkari)} [Hakkari//A/IFb/FJ/GF/ZF3]

k'eşe کەشە (A/FJ/TF/CS) = priest. See **k'eşîş**.

k'eşe-k'eş کەشە کەش (K[s]) = fight; scandal. See **keşmekeş**.

k'eşîş کەشیش *m.* **(-ê; k'êşîş).** priest; monk: •**Ya *keşîşo*, ya tu dibêjî we nabê** (GShA, 228) *Priest,* may what you say not come true. {also: k'eşe (A/FJ-2/TF-2/CS-2); [kechich] کشیش (JJ)} {syn: qeşe} < Syr qaššīš ܩܫܝܫ; Sor keşîş کەشیش [GShA/K/B/IFb/FJ/TF/GF/JJ//A] <êris; r̄eben II>

keşk/k'eşk [A] کەشك *m./f.(B)* **(-ê/-a; /-ê).** dried cheese made of curds or skimmed milk, rolled into balls: •**Hawînê *keşkêt* wan li serbanêt r̄eş-malan û keprokan û xanîyan direwêm, dixom** (SK-I:3) In summer I snatch their *buttermilk*, (drying) on the roofs of tents and bough-huts and houses, and eat it. {also: [kechk] کشك (JJ); <keşk> کشك (HH)} {syn: çortan} Mid P kašk = 'dried buttermilk' (M3); P kašk کشک = 'dried, condensed whey'; Sor keşk کەشك = 'dried curds'; Hau keşkî *f.* = 'dried buttermilk' (M4) [SK/Bw/K/A/IFb/B/JJ/HH/JB1-S/GF/OK] <giv; şîrêj>

keşkel•e کەشکەلە *f.* **(•a;•ê).** magpie, zool. *Pica pica*: •...**Eger *keşkele* bît şarezakarê qewmî, dê r̄êberîya wan ket bo r̄êkêt helakî** (SK 4:43) If the *magpie* becomes the guide of a people, he will lead them along the roads of destruction; **-Wek keşkele ye** (Zeb) [He] is very skinny (cf. 'as thin as a rail'). {also: keşkêlenê (IFb)} {syn: qijik [4]} Sor qişqer̄e قشقەڕە = 'magpie' [SK/Zeb//IFb]

keşkêlenê کەشکێلەنێ (IFb) = magpie. See **keşkele**.

keşkûr کەشکوور *f.* **().** dried cow dung *(as a fuel)*: **-lodê keşkûran** (IF) {syn: qelax; sergo} pile of dried manure cakes. {syn: k'erme; sergîn} Cf. W Arm kšgur կշկուր [IFb/Wkt/ZF3] <dirg; k'erme; qelax; sergîn; t'epik II>

k'eşmek'eş کەشمەکەش *f.* **(-a;-ê).** fight, brawl: •[**Miqdarê penc û şeş deqîqan bi vî terzî *keşmekeşa* wan dibe**] (JR) For five or six minutes their *fight* is like this (=they fight like this). {also: k'eşe-k'eş (K[s])} {syn: cerenîx; cur̄e; de'w II; doz; gelemşe; k'êşe} Cf. P kešmekeš کشمکش --> T keşmekeş = 'great confusion, disorder' [JR/K(s)]

keşt کەشت (IFb) = ship. See **k'eştî**.

k'eştî کەشتی *f.* **(-ya;-yê).** ship, boat: •**Di encama binavbûna *keştîyê* de 46 penaber jiyana xwe ji dest dan** [sic] (ilkha.com 7.vi.2018) As a result of the sinking of *the ship*, 46 refugees lost their lives. {also: keşt (IFb); [kišti] کشتی (JJ)} {syn: gemî} Mid P kaštīg (M3); P kaštī کشتی; Sor keştî کەشتی [K(s)/JB3/JJ/GF/TF//IFb] <belem>

k'eşxe کەشخە *adj.* 1) {syn: law [4]} fine, nice, pretty; neat, smart, chic, fancy (Bw/OK/Hej); 2) [*f.* **().**] elegance. {also: <keşxe> کەشخە (Hej)} <Clq. Iraqi Ar kašxa کشخە = 'fine, impressive, sharp; bragging' <√k-š-x کشخ [kišax] = 'to show off, boast; (with b-) to waste, squander' [Bw/JB1-S/GF/OK/Hej/FS]

ket کەت *m./f.(K/B)* **(-ê/-a; /-ê).** type of clover [T yonca], bot. *Trifolium*. {also: <ket> کت (HH)} [Wn/K/IFb/B/HH/GF/ZF3/Wkt] <nefel>

ketav کەتاڤ (Slm) = farcy. See **ketew**.

k'etew کەتەو *f.* **(;-ê).** respiratory ailment of horses and donkeys, farcy: •***Ketewê* hêstir girtiye** (FS) *Farcy* infected the mule/The mule came down with *farcy*. {also: ketav (Slm); [ketevi] کتوی (JJ); <ketew> کتو (HH); <ketew کەتەو/kedew کەدەو> (Hej)} [Elk/IFb/B/HH/Hej/ZF3/FS//JJ//Slm]

k'etewî کەتەوی *m.* **().** horse or donkey afflicted with farcy. {also: [ketevi] کتوی (JJ)} [Elk/IFb/JJ/FS]

ketik کەتك (GF/OK/Zeb/FS) = dried figs. See **kitik I**.

k'etin كەتِن *vi.* **(-k'ev-/-k'ew-[Dz]).** 1) {syn: weşîn} to fall: **-agir k'etin** = to catch fire: **•Çiqas xirabyê bikî,** ***agir*** **be'rê** ***nak'ewe*** (Dz) No matter how much evil you do, the sea *won't catch on fire [prv.]*; **-ber** ***fk-ê, ft-î*** **k'etin** (XF): a) to think, experience, be excited about; b) to be sick *(at heart)* over, to worry, feel sorrow, be concerned about: **•Ez** ***ber te nak'evim,*** **ez** ***ber*** **wê yekê** ***dik'evim,*** **ko t'ext û t'acê bavê te bêxuyî ... mano** (Z-2) I *don't grieve for you, I grieve* because your father's crown and throne have become ownerless (i.e., he has no heir); **-ber pîrka ketin** (L) to give birth, be in childbed [lit. 'to fall before the midwives']; **-ber xwe k'etin** = to be depressed or sad: **•'Eyan û k'ubarê şeherê M.-ê û Al-p'aşava gelekî** ***berxwe k'etin*** **bona Memê** (Z-1) The nobles of the city M. and Al-Pasha *were* very *sad about* [what happened to] Mem; **-bi dû** ***fk-ê*** **k'etin** = to go after, go in search of, set out after: **•*Bi dû*** **wan** ***k'et*** = *She set out after* them; **-bîn pozê** ***fk-ê*** **k'etin** (Dz) to catch the scent or smell of, to smell stg.: **•Nişkêva** ***bîna*** **k'ivava** ***k'ete pozê*** **wan** (Dz) Suddenly *they smelled* kebabs [lit. 'the smell of kebabs fell to their noses']; **-k'etin nava hev** (IFb) to be scrambled, get all mixed up: **•Rabirdû û niha** ***ketine nav hev*** (MUs, 8) The past and present *have gotten all mixed up*; **-k'etin serê** ***fk-ê*** = to make sense to s.o.; to convince: **•Boẍ ew gilî got,** ***k'ete serê*** **gur** (L) The ox said these words, they *made sense to* the wolf (=convinced or persuaded him) **•Xeberên te** ***nak'evin serê*** **min** (K) Your words *make no sense to* me; **-ya xwe k'etin** (XF) to grow old *(of people)*: **•Ez û dîya teva îdî** ***ya xwe k'etine*** (Z-1) Your mother and I *have grown old*; 2) {syn: têk'etin} to enter, get in: **•Ewî ...** ***kete hindurê*** **tatê** (L) He *entered* the rock: **•Êvarê kuř** ***k'etne nava*** **cîya** (Ba) In the evening the boys *got in* bed **•*Kete*** **qulê** (L) It *entered* its hole; 3) to undertake *(task)*, hold *(a strike)*: **•Li girtîgehên Çanakkale ... yê zêdeyî 100 girtiyên siyasî bi mebesta protest[o]kirina şert û pestên îdareyê** ***ketin greva*** **birçîbûnê** (Wlt 2:59, 5) In the prisons of Çanakkale [et al.] more than 100 political prisoners *held a* hunger *strike* with the aim of protesting the [bad] conditions and oppression of [=at the hands of] the authorities. {also: keftin (M); k'eftin (M-Am); [ketin كتين/kewtin كڤتين] (JJ); <ketin كتن (dikeve) (دكڤه)> (HH)} [Pok. kob- 610.] 'to suit, fit, succeed': O Ir *kap- (Tsb 38): Mid P kaftan (kaf-) = 'to fall' (M3); Sor kewtin كەوتِن (-kew-); SoK kaftın (561); Za kewnã [kewtiş] (Todd); Hau kewtey (gin-) *vi.* (M4); cf. also Eng **hap** in: mishap, happy, happen. See M. Schwartz' review of H.W. Bailey. "Indo-Scythian Studies," in: *JAOS*, 89, ii (1969), 445-46; also, H.W. Bailey "Miṣṣa Suppletum," *BSOAS* 21 (1958), 43 ff. [K/A/JB3/IFb/B/JJ/HH/GF/TF//M] <avêtin; xistin>

k'etin pêş كەتِن پێش (IFb) = to advance; advancement. See **pêşk'etin**.

keval كەڤال *m./f.(ZF3)* **(-ê;).** 1) {syn: dep[edar]} wooden board: **•...û karê roja xo bi dilxoşî û bistehî li ser rûyê vî** ***kevalê*** **delal dikirin** (Serferaz Alî Neqşebendî. Dilînî, 9) ... and happily and confidently he would do his daily work on this lovely *board*; 2) {syn: řesim; şikil; wêne} picture, painting: **•Ew şaswarên swarî bayê felekê bûyn bûyne** ***keval*** **û serhatîyên van gotar û serhatîyan** (A.Xalid. Perlemanê mişkan, 7) Those riders who have ridden the wind of fortune have become *the pictures* and stories of those articles and memoirs. [S.A.Neqşebendî/Zeb/RZ/ZF/BF/SS/ZF3/Wkt]

kevan كەڤان *m./f.(B)* **(-ê/ ; /-ê).** 1) bow, arch; violin bow: **-tîr û kevan** (BX) bow and arrow; 2) Sagittarius (astr.). {also: kuvan I (BK); [kiwan] كڤان (JJ); <kevan> كڤان (HH)} [Pok. kam-er- 524.] 'to bend; a vault': Skt kmárati = 'is crooked'; Av kamarā *f.* = 'belt; *vault, arch'; Mid P kamān = 'bow' (M3); P/Ar kamān كمان = 'bow' & kamar كمر = 'waist, girdle, stg. arched'; Sor kewan كەوان = '(archer's) bow, carder's bow, Sagittarius'; Za kemane *m.* = 'bow'; Hau keman *m.* = 'bow' (M4) cf. also Lat camur(us) = 'bent inward, concave'; Gr kamara καμάρα = 'vault' [K/A/JB3/IFb/JJ/B/HH/GF/TF/OK//BK] <jîh; tîr I>

kevanî كەڤانی *f.* **(-ya;-yê).** 1) {syn: bermalî} housewife: **•Jin** ***kevanîya*** **malê ye** (AB) Woman is *the manager of* the house; 2) {syn: jin; pîrek; k'ulfet; zêç} wife; a polite way to refer to s.o.'s wife (Bw): **•*Kewaniya*** **xwe ya ciwan dide kêleka xwe û ji bajarê D'ê hêdî hêdî ber bi bakur dajo** (Lab, 6) He puts his pretty *wife* at his side and slowly drives north from the city D. {also: kebanî (Bw/IFb/GF/TF/OK); kewanî (IFb-2); <kebanî> كبانى (HH)} cf. P kadbānū كدبانو = 'matron, mistress of house, housewife'; Sor kaban کابان/ keybanû کەیبانوو = 'head wife in polygamous establishment, housewife' [AB/K/A/B//IFb/HH/GF/TF/OK/ Bw] <jin; pîrek>

kevçing کەڤچِنگ (A) = spoon. See **kefçî**.

kevçî کەڤچی (A)/kevç'î (B/HR-I)/k'evçî (F) = spoon. See **kefçî**.

kevel کەڤەل (IFb/GF) = animal skin or hide. See **kevil**.

kever کەڤەر *adj.* piebald, spotted or blotched with black & white *(of goats and sheep)*: **•Ey, nêryê *kevero*, tu qelew bûyî** (HCK-5, #8, 57) Hey, *piebald* billy goat, you've grown fat **•Nêrîyê minî *keverî*, hustu zengilo, tu jî were heře** (HCK-5, #8, 56) My *piebald* billy goat, bell-necked, you come and go too! {also: <kever> کڤر (HH)} {syn: belek I} [HCK/K/B/A/IFb/FJ/GF/HH/FS/BF] <bel; k'ol IV; qer II; taq; xez>

kevezan کەڤەزان *m.* **(-ê;).** stick: **•Wextekê ĥişyar bû bala xwe daê *kevezanê* destê wî t'une, virdda *kevezan*, wêda *kevezan*, xêr, *kevezan* nedît** (Abbasian #4:143) When he awoke he noticed that his *stick* was missing; he began to look for the stick [lit. 'here *stick*, there *stick*'], but no, he could not find *the stick*. {syn: cinih̃; çomax̃; gopal; metreq; şiv[dar]} < W Arm kavazan (gavazan) գաւազան = 'stick' [Rwn/Abbasian]

k'evgez کەڤگەز (K/B) = nettle. See **k'ergezk**.

kevgezk کەڤگەزك (Wkt) = nettle. See **k'ergezk**.

k'evgîr کەڤگیر (EP-7/K/B) = ladle; strainer. See **k'efgîr**.

kevil کەڤِل *f./m.(Rnh)* **(/-ê;).** (animal) skin, hide, pelt; sheepskin); hair (of animal): **•kevilekê merez** (M-Ak) goat's pelt. {also: kevel (IFb/GF-2); kewl (K[s]); [kewil] کفل (JJ); <kevel> کفل (HH)} Cf. Sor kewł کەوڵ [M/JB3/JJ/GF/Bw//IFb/HH//K] <k'unk; meşk; p'ost>

kevin کەڤِن (JB3/TF) = old *(of things)*. See **kevn**.

kevir کەڤِر *m.* **(-ê; kêvir, vî kevirî).** 1) {syn: ber II; kuç'} rock, stone; large rock {*as opposed to **ber II** = small stone, rock*} (Bw/Zeb): **•Hemi neqişandi ye bi *kevirê* mermer** (L) It was all inlaid with marble [*stones*]; **-dan ber keviran**. See under **dan I**; **-kevir kirin** (IFb/JJ) to stone to death {syn: dan ber beran/keviran}; **-Nigê *fk-ê* kevira nek'eve** (XF) May s.o. not encounter obstacles [lit. 'May s.o.'s foot not hit against a rock'] {also: **Nigê *fk-ê* kevir-kuç'ika nek'eve!**}: **•Lingê hespê wî *kevir dik'eve*** (Z-2) His horse's foot *hit against rocks* [or came across obstacles]; 2) checker, disk used in the game of checkers or backgammon [cf. T taş]: **•Çiqas Memê *kevir* datîne, Bek'o *kevirê* wî hiltîne** (Z-2) Beko picked up every *checker* that Memê put down. {also: [kewir] کفر (JJ); <kevir> کڤر (HH)} [Pok. 2. ak- 18.] 'sharp; stone': Skt áśman- *m.* = 'rock, cliff; heaven'; Av asman- = 'stone; heaven'; O P asman- = 'sky, heaven'; [*more under* **'ezman I**]; Za kemer *m.* = 'rock, stone' & kemere *f.* = 'rock, cliff' (Mal); Hau kemer *m.* = 'rock' (M4); cf. also Gr akmōn ἄκμων = 'anvil'; Lith ašmuõ, -eñs = 'sharpness' & akmuõ, -eñs = 'stone'; OCS kamy, -ene & Rus kamen´ камень = 'stone'; Old Norse hamarr = 'cliff, crag; hammer (originally stone implement)'; Eng & Germ Hammer. See: M. Schwartz. "The Old Eastern Iranian World View according to the Avesta," in: *The Cambridge History of Iran* (Cambridge, Eng. : Cambridge Univ. Press, 1985), v. 2, p. 642; J. Peter Maher. "*H₃eḱmon: '(Stone) Axe' and 'Sky' in I-E/Battle-Axe Culture," *Journal of Indo-European Studies*, 1, iv (1973), 441-62; reprinted in his *Papers on Language Theory and History*, I (Amsterdam : John Benjamins, 1977), pp.85-106. [K/A/JB3/IFb/B/JJ/HH/GF/TF] <bixûr; dame; 'ezman I; ĥelan; sel; tat; xîç'ik>

kevirî کەڤِری *adj.* made of rock or stone. {also: kevirîn (CS); kevrî (GF)} [FJ/AD//GF//CS]

kevirîn کەڤِرین (CS) = made of rock. See **kevirî**.

kevirkan کەڤِرکان *m.* **().** sling for throwing stones. {also: kevirkanî, f.(K/GF/ZF3)/m.(AD); kevkanî, f. (Tof); kewkanî, m. (; kewkênî) (B)} {syn: berkanî} [Efr//K/GF/AD/ZF3//Tof//B]

kevirkanî کاڤِرکانی, f.(K/GF/ZF3)/m.(AD) = sling. See **kevirkan**.

kevî I کەڤی *f.* **(-ya;-yê).** 1) {syn: k'êlek; p'eř [4]} edge, rim; lip or edge of jug; 2) {syn: bar II; perav} shore, bank *(of river)*: **•Wextê mîr di *keviya* çemê mezin de hate kuştin Heyzebûn ewçend giriya bû ko jinmîr bi xwe hêstirên xwe dimaliştin û li ber dilê cêriyê dida** (Rnh 3:23, 5) When the emir was killed on *the banks of* the big river, Heyzebûn cried so much that the emir's wife herself wiped away her own tears and consoled the servant girl. {also: <kevî> کڤی (HH)} [SW/K/A/JB3/IFb/B/HH/GF/TF] <tî I>

kevî II/k'evî [A] کەڤی *f./m.(ZF3)* **(-ya/-yê;).** patches of unmelted snow left after the thaw: **-kevîya**

befrê (Bw/OK)/**keviyê berfê** (ZF3) do. {also: kevîreş (GF); kêwî II (TF); [kävi] کـــــــوى (JJ); <kevî> کەڤی (HH)} [Bw/Zeb/A/IFb/JJ/HH/OK//GF/ZF3/BF//TF] <berf; zivistan>

kevîng کـەڤـینـگ *f.* **(-a;-ê).** kerchief or kaffiyeh which Kurdish men wrap around their head: **•*Kevînka* wî nû ye** (FS) His *kaffiyeh* is new. {also: kevînk (FS/Wkt)} {syn: cemedanî; dersok; p'oşî; şemil} [Zx//FS/Wkt]

kevînk کەڤینك (FS) = man's kerchief. See **kevîng**.

kevîreş کـەڤـیـرەش (GF) = snow left after the thaw. See **kevî II**.

kevjal کـەڤـژال *f.* **(-a;-ê).** 1) crab, zool. *Brachyura*; 2) Cancer (astr.). {also: kevjinik (B); kevjnîk (OK); kêfşing (IFb-2); kêvjal (TF); kêvjale (FS/BF); [kiwjal کـڤـژال/kevzník کـڤـزنـك] (JJ)} Pahl klčng [karčang/karzang]; Mid P kyrzng; P xarčang خرچنگ/kalčang کلچنگ; Sor qirjał قرژاڵ/qirjang قِـرژانـگ; Hau qirjangî *f.* (M4). K and JJ give incorrect meanings: K '*duck'; JJ '*turtle; *shrimp; crab' [K/IFb/GF/ZF3//JJ//TF//FS/BF//B//OK]

kevjinik کەڤژِنك (B) = crab. See **kevjal**.

kevjnîk کەڤژنیك (OK) = crab. See **kevjal**.

kevkanî کەڤکانی, f. (Tof) = sling. See **kevirkan**.

kevlan کەڤلان (FS) = sheath. See **kalan**.

kevlû کـەڤـلـوو/کـەڤـلـوی *f.* **(-ya;).** 1) lull or break in the rain (Zeb): **•Eger *kevlûyek* bikevîte baranê, em dê çîn** (Zeb) If there is *a break* in the rain, we will go; 2) {syn: delîve; derfet; fesal; firset; k'ês} opportunity, chance (SK/Zeb): **•Hişyar bin, çak bizanin, fersetê fewt neken. Taze *kewlîya* hingo hatîye** (SK 57:678) Awake, therefore, and be sure not to miss the opportunity. Your *chance* has come at last **•Suto zanî *kewlî* heye ko Teto bilêbînît** (SK 61:768) Suto knew that there was *a chance* to fool Teto; 3) {syn: kalûme} old, rusty knife (Zeb/Hej). {also: kewlî (SK); <kevlo> کـەڤـلـۆ (Hej)} [Zeb//Hej//SK]

kevn کەڤن *adj.* old *(of things)*: **•hevalê kevn** (B) an old friend *(as opposed to a new friend; an aged or elderly friend would be* ***hevalê kal****)* **•k'incê *kevn*** (B) *old* clothes; **-kevnek jina** (L/Z-2) some woman: **•Ji bona xatirê *kevnek* jina te xwe xistîye vî halî** (L) Because of *some* woman you are in this [bad] state **•ji bona *kevneke jinêye*** (Z-2) for *some woman*'s sake; **-kevn bûn** (B) to grow old *(of things)*; **-kevn kirin** (B) to make old *(of things)*. {≠nû} {also: kemn (Kg); kevin (JB3/TF); kewn (IF-2/SK); [kewin] کـڤـن (JJ); <kevin> کـڤـن (HH)} O Ir *kafna-: Mid P kahwan (M3); Parthian kfwn; P kohne کـهـنـه & kohan کـهـن; Sor kon کـۆن; Za kehen (Mal); Hau kone (M4). O Ir *kafna- related to *kap- = 'to fall' (Tsb 38) [old = falling apart] See M. Schwartz' review of H. W. Bailey. "Indo-Scythian Studies," in: *JAOS*, 89, ii (1969), 445-46. {kevnahî; kevnayî} [K/A/IFb/B/HH/GF//JB3/JJ/TF//Kg] <îxtîyar; kal I; pîr>

kevnahî کەڤناهی (K) = oldness. See **kevnayî**.

kevnar کـەڤـنـار (K[s]/A/JJ) = decrepit, worn out. See **kevnare**.

kevnare کـەڤـنـاره *adj.* 1) decrepit, broken down, worn out; antique, old; 2) dried up *(of plants)* (K[s]). {also: kevnar (K[s]/A); [kewnar] کـڤـنـار (JJ)} [Z-2/JB3/IF//K(s)/A/JJ] <kevn>

kevnatî کەڤناتی (GF/FS) = oldness. See **kevnayî**.

kevnayî کـەڤـنـایـی *f.* **(-ya;-yê).** oldness, antiquity, old age (of things). {also: kevnahî (K-2); kevnatî (GF/FS)} [K/A/IFb/TF/ZF3//GF/FS] <kevn>

kevneşop کـەڤـنـەشـۆپ *f.* **().** tradition; custom: **•Gelo di *kevneşopiyên* we de ev tiştekî normal e ku di meclîsa we de qomîteyên wiha tên lidarxistin?** (Wlt 1:37, 16) According to your *traditions*, is it normal in your national assembly for such committees to be formed? {also: kevneşopî (IFb/Wlt-2)} {syn: 'adet; řewişt; tîtal; t'oře} [(neol)Wlt/IFb/TF/ZF]

kevneşopî کـەڤـنـەشـۆپـی *adj.* 1) traditional; customary: **•Siyaseta pirraniya îslamvanên *kevneşopî*, xelet e** (Wlt 1:49, 16) The policy of the majority of *traditional* Islamists is misguided; 2) [*f.* **().**] (IFb/Wlt) = tradition. See **kevneşop**. [(neol)Wlt/IFb/TF/ZF]

kevnik کـەڤـنِـك *f.(Z-3)/m.(B/IF)* **(-a/-ê;).** 1) {syn: destmal} handkerchief (Z-3/Z-1366); 2) {syn: kerkon; p'aç' II & p'aç[']ik; p'ate II; p'eřok; pîne; p'ot} rag; old things, old clothes (K/B). [Z-3/K/A/IFb/B/GF] <k'efî>

kevodk کەڤۆدك = pigeon, dove. See **kevok**.

kevok کـەڤـۆك *f.* **(-a;-ê).** pigeon, dove, zool. *Columba livia*: **-kevotka 'edilayê** (B) the dove of peace; **-pirepirê kevoka** (L) the fluttering of doves. {also: kevodk; kevot II (Ad); kevotk (K/B); kewotk (Z-1); [kewouk] کڤوك (JJ); <kevok> کڤوك (HH)} < O Ir *kapauta-: Mid P kabōd (M3); P kabūd کبود/kabūtar کبوتر; Sor kotir کۆتِر [Z-1//K/B//JB3/IFb/HH/GF/TF/Msr] <kew I>

kevot I کـەڤـۆت *f.* **(;-ê).** maple tree, bot. *Acer aceae*,

Acer campestre (IFb/GF); boxwood, bot. *Buxus sempervirens* (TF); tree from which wooden spoons are made (IFb/HH/GF). {also: <kevot> کـڤـوت (HH)} Sor kewt کـەوت = 'maple (tree)' [Bw/IFb/HH/GF/TF/Hej]

kevot II کەڤۆت (Ad) = pigeon, dove. See **kevok**.

kevotk کەڤۆتك (K/B) = pigeon, dove. See **kevok**.

kevrî کەڤری (GF) = made of rock. See **kevirî**.

kevroşk کەڤرۆشك (JB3/IFb) = rabbit. See **k'erguh**.

k'evtar̄ کەڤتار, m. (k'evtêr̄) (B) = hyena. See **k'eftar̄**.

k'evz کـەڤـز *f.* **(-a;-ê).** moss, bot. *Musci*; water moss: **-k'evz girtin** (B) to be[come] overgrown with moss (of rocks). {also: k'efzer (IFb-2); kevze (IF); kevzê (Btm [Ḧatḧatkê]); [keoüz کـوز/kefz کـفـز] (JJ); <kefz کفز/kez کز> (HH)} [Btm (Ḧatḧatkê)//IFb//K/A/B/GF/TF//JJ/HH]

kevze کەڤزە (IF) = moss. See **k'evz**.

kevzer کەڤزەر (AD) = nettle. See **k'ergezk**.

kevzê کەڤزێ (Btm [Ḧatḧatkê]) = moss. See **k'evz**.

kew I کـــــــو *m./f.(B)* **(-ê/ ; kêw/-ê).** partridge, zool. *Perdix perdix*: **-kewê nêr/nêrekew** = male partridge; **-kewa mê/mêkew** = female partridge. {also: kewşîng, f. (B-2); [keoŭ] کو (JJ); <kew> کو (HH)} Cf. Mid P kabk; Sor kew کــــــەو = 'hill-partridge' [BX/K/A/IFb/B/JJ/HH/SK/GF/TF/OK] <'ebdal; kevok; k'êr̄asû; por I; qebîn; r̄ibat>

kew II کـــەو *adj.* 1) {syn: bor I; boz; cûn I; gewr[1]; xwelîreng} grey/gray *(color of sheep's coat)*: **-mîya kew** (B) grey ewe; 2) {syn: heşîn} blue (IFb/JJ). {also: [kew] کــــو (JJ)} Sor kew کـــەو = 'blue' [S&E/K/IFb/JJ/B]

kewal کـــەوال *f.(FS)/pl.(Bw)* **(-a;-ê).** small number or small flock of sheep and goats *(as opposed to* ***pez*** *= a large flock)*: •**Me çend *kewalek* yêt heyn** (Bw) We have a few *sheep*. {also: <keval> کـەڤـال (Hej)} [Bw/OK/Dh/FS//Hej] <pez>

kewan کەوان (TF/FS) = to be healed. See **k'ewîn**.

k'ewandin کـەوانـدِن *vt.* **(-k'ewîn-).** 1) to cauterize; 2) {syn: dax̆ kirin} to brand *(cattle)*. {also: [kevandin] کـوانـدیـن (JJ); <kewandin کـوانـدن (dikewîne) (دکوینـه)> (HH)} <Ar √k-w-y كوى = 'to burn, cauterize' [Qzl/K/A/IFb/JJ/HH/GF] <k'ewîn>

kewanî کەوانی (IFb) = (house)wife. See **kevanî**.

kewaq کەواق (L) = potter. See **qewaq**.

kewar کـــــەوار *f./m.(L)* **(-a/-ê;-ê/).** 1) {syn: s̲elmêşk} beehive. **-kewara mêşa** (IFb-2)/**kewara mêşan** (JB3-2)/**kewarê mêşan** (L)/**kewarê hingivî** (L) {also: kewarmêş (Haz-2)} do.; 2) bin *(of clay, filled from the top with opening at bottom)*; small silo for storing animal fodder, corn-bin: •**Paşî mişk hate pêş, got "... cuhal û hemban û *kuwaran* jî didir̄înim û bi kun dikem"** (SK 1:7) Then the mouse came forward and said, "... I tear and make holes in sacks and bags and *corn-bins*". {also: kuwar (SK); [kouvar] کـــوار (JJ); <kuwar> کــــــوار (HH)} <Arc kvartā (kortā) כורתא & Syr kortā ܟܘܪܬܐ: P kavāre کـــواره/ gavāre گـــواره; Ar kuwārah کـــوارة = 'beehive'; Sor kuwar کـــووار = kendû کـــەنـــدوو = 'bin (of earthenware, gen. filled from top with opening at bottom; Za kuwarı = 'honeycomb' (Mal) [Haz/K/JB3/IFb/GF/OK/L//JJ/HH] <hingiv; mêş; xilêfe>

kewarmêş کـــەوارمـــێـش *f.* **().** beehive. {also: **kewar**; kewara mêşa (IFb); kewara mêşan (JB3-2)} {syn: s̲elmêşk} [Haz//IFb//JB3]

kewax̆ کەواغ (FS) = potter. See **qewaq**.

Kewçêr کـــەوچـــێـر. A Sorani name [Kewçerîn کەوچەرین] for Persian month of *Mehr* مهر [Libra] (Sept. 23-Oct. 22). See chart of Kurdish months in this volume. <Îlon; Çirîya Pêşîn>

kewde کەودە (GF) = troops, forces. See **kewte**.

kewer کـــەوەر *f.* **().** leek, bot. *Allium porrum*. {syn: kurad} Sor kewer کەوەر [K(s)/IFb/GF/OK/AF/AA]

kewgir کەوگِر (A/ZF3) = partridge hunter. See **kewgîr**.

k'ewgirî کەوگِری *adj.* having burst into tears; about to burst into tears (B): •***Kelegirî* k'efte hinava** (Zeb) He held back tears; **-k'ewgirî bûn** (B) to be about to burst into tears. {also: kelegirî (Zeb); kelegîrî (IFb); kelegîrînî (Msr); k'elogrî (FK-eb-2)} [Z-1/K/JB3/B//IFb//Zeb] <girîn>

kewgîr کـەوگـیـر *m.* **().** partridge hunter. {also: kewgir (A/ZF3); kewgîrvan (Bw); <kewgîr> کوگیر (HH)} [Bw//A/ZF3//HH/FS] <kew I>

kewgîrvan کـەوگـیـرڤـان (Bw) = partridge hunter. See **kewgîr**.

k'ewhan کـەوهـان (-k'ewh-) (Bw) = to be healed. See **k'ewîn**.

kewihan کەوِهان (FS) = to be healed. See **k'ewîn**.

kewitandin کـەوِتـانـدِن *vt.* **(-kewitîn-).** to cook the outside surface only, roast, sear (Zeb/Ak); to bring to the boil, boil slightly *(e.g., of beans [fasûlye])* (Krb/Mdt). {syn: *zer vekirin (Frq)} [Zeb/Ak/Krb/Mdt] <k'elandin; k'emitandin>

k'ewîn کەوین *vi.* **(-k'ew-).** 1) {syn: qenc bûn; sax bûn} to heal (vi.), be healed *(wound)*; {syn: cebirîn} to knit *(bones)*: •**Birînêt dilê min *nak'ewhin*** (Bw)

The wounds of my heart *can't be healed* •**Piştê şeş heyvan birînên Efo *dikewin*** (H.Akyol. Zava ker in, 9) After 6 months, Efo's wounds *heal*; 2) to be cauterized *(wound)*: •**Birîna wî *kewya*** (BF)/~ ***kewa*** (FS) His wound *was cauterized* (i.e., stopped bleeding). {also: kewan (TF/FS); k'ewhan (-k'ewh-) (Bw); kewihan (FS-2); kewyan (G)} <Ar √k-w-y كــــــوى = 'to burn, cauterize' [Bw//K/B/IFb/ZF3/Wkt/FD/BF//G//TF/FS] <k'ewandin>

kewkanî كــەوكــانــى, m. (; kewkênî) (B) = sling. See **kevirkan**.

kewkurd كەوكورد (IFb) = sulphur. See **k'irgûd**.

kewkurt كەوكورت, m. (JB3) = sulphur. See **k'irgûd**.

kewl كەول (K[s]) = animal skin or hide. See **kevil**.

kewlî كەولى (SK) = opportunity. See **kevlû**[2].

kewn كەون (IF/SK) = old *(of things)*. See **kevn**.

k'eworşk كەوۆرشك (A) = rabbit. See **k'erguh**.

kewotk كەوۆتك (Z-1) = pigeon, dove. See **kevok**.

kewran كەوران = caravan. See **karwan**.

k'ewşan كــەوشــان *m.* **(-ê; k'ewşên).** 1) {syn: hox} ploughed field; sown area, area under crops: •**Ew digîhijine *k'ewşanê* gund** (Dz) They reach the village's *ploughed fields*; 2) countryside, rural area, outskirts (JJ). {also: k'ewşen (K/B-2); [keoûchen] كوشن (JJ)} [Dz/B//K/JJ] <beyar; bor III; kat II; k'irêbe; zevî>

k'ewşen كــەوشــەن (K/B/JJ) = ploughed or sown field; countryside. See **k'ewşan**.

kewşîng كەوشينگ f. (B) = partridge. See **kew I**.

k'ewt كەوت (K) = troops, forces. See **kewte**.

kewt•e كــەوتــە *f.* **(•a;).** troops, forces, army: •**Duhî tevdana *kewte* û sedmêran dom kiriye** (RN) Yesterday the movements *of troops* and companies continued. {also: kewde (GF-2); k'ewt (K)} [RN/GF/ZF3/FS//K]

kewte-kewt كەوتەكەوت (K/B/IFb/Wkt) = barking. See **kute-kut**.

kewtkewt كەوتكەوت (FJ/GF) = barking. See **kute-kut**.

k'ewxw•e كــەوخــوە *m.* **(•ê;).** village chief or head. {also: kefxwê (GF); k'uxa; kûxe (FS) [keoû-khi] كــوخــى (JJ)} {syn: k'eya; muxtar } Cf. P katxodā كــتــخــدا; Sor kwêxa [köxa] كــوێــخــا [S&E/K//JJ//FS//GF] <gund>

kewyan كەويان (G) = to be healed. See **k'ewîn**.

kewzan كەوزان (Hk) = terebinth. See **kezan**.

k'exbe كــەخــبــە (FK-eb-1) = woman's garment. See **k'ex̌be**.

k'ex̌b•e كــەغــبــە *m.* **(•ê;).** type of woman's overcoat or garment (ZF3: cepken = embroidered jacket with full sleeves): •**Xweyê *k'ex̌bê* hêşînim** (Z-1)/ **[Xweya] *k'exbê* hêşînim** (FK-eb-1) I own a green (or blue) *garment*. {also: k'exbe (FK-eb-1); k'ixme, f. (K/ZF3)} [Z-1//FK-eb-1//K/ZF3]

k'eya كەيا *m.* **(-yê;).** village chief or head: •**Bin konê *k'eya* digihîne** (Z-2) He brings [them] to below the tent of *the village chief*. {also: k'îya (Z-4); [kiia] كيا (JJ); <keya> كيا (HH)} {syn: k'ewxwe; muxtar} Cf. T kâhya < P katxodā كــتــخــدا [Z-2/A/IFb/HH/ZF3//JJ] <gund>

keyandin كەياندِن (IFb/HH) = to churn. See **k'ilan**.

keyf كــەيــف (JB3/IFb/HH) = pleasure, fun; condition, state. See **k'êf**.

keyfxwaşî كەيفخواشى (IF) = happiness. See **k'êfxweşî**.

keyfxweşî كــەيــفــخــوەشــى (JB3) = happiness. See **k'êfxweşî**.

keyî كەيى (SK) = tame. See **kedî**.

keys كــەيــس (IF/ZF3/FS)/k'eys (A) = opportunity, chance. See **k'ês**.

kezan كــەزان *f.* **().** terebinth, bot. *Pistacia terebinthus*, the seeds of which are large and with hard shells {as opposed to **bêmk/bêwk**, which are small and with softer shells} {cf. Ar ḥabb al-xaḍrā' حــبّ الــخــضــراء, buṭm بــطــم}; nettle tree berry, honey berry, bot. *Celtis australis* {T çitlembik, menengiç} (CB). {also: keskan (SK/OK-2/Zeb); kewzan (Hk); kezwan (IFb/OK/CB/Kmc-2/FS); kizwan (CB-2); qizban (IFb-2); [kizvan/kezvān (PS)/kazuván (G)] كــزوان (JJ); <kezwan> كــزوان (HH)} {syn: şengêl} Sor qezwan قەزوان. *Possibly from **kesk** = 'green', parallel with Ar* ḥabb al-xaḍrā' حبّ الخضراء (xaḍrā' = green) [Bw//IFb/HH/OK/CB/FS//JJ//Hk//SK/Zeb] <bêmk>

k'ezax كــەزاخ *f.* **(-a;).** pruning, trimming, clipping, lopping off (of trees, vines, etc.): •**Çandiniya nîskan xilas kiribû, diçû *kezaxa* rez** (DBgb, 51) When he had finished planting lentils, he would go *trim* the vineyard. {also: kesax (FJ/TF/ZF/FS-2); k'esax (A)} <Arc ksaḥ כסח = 'to cut down, clear (of thorns, bushes, etc.), to trim' (see **k'ezaxtin**); Sor kezaxe كەزاخە = 'vine trimming' [DBgb/GF/FS//FJ/TF/ZF/A]

k'ezaxtin كەزاختِن *vt.* **(-k'ezêx-).** to prune, trim, clip, lop off (of trees, vines, etc.). {also: kesaxtin (ZF); kesixandin (CCG); kezixandin (GF); <kezaxtin كــزاخــتــن/kezixandin كــزخــانــدن (dikezixîne)

(دكزخينه)> (HH)} {syn: çipilandin; pejikandin; t'eřişandin} <Arc ksaḥ כסח = 'to cut down, clear (of thorns, bushes, etc.), to trim' & Syr kesaḥ ܟܣܚ = 'to prune, esp. a vine, to lop'; NENA kâsikh (Old Syr) = 'to prune, esp. vines ; to cut off the head of' & kâsükhtâ = 'pruning-knife, mason's chisel' & kasâkhâ (Old Syr) = 'a pruner' (Maclean); =Sor heł•perdawtin هەڵپەرداوتن [Bw/K(s)/IFb/HH/OK//GF//CCG//ZF]

k'ezeb/kezeb [K/B] کەزەب *f.* **(-a;-ê).** *designates several internal organs*: 1) {syn: ceger[a reş]/cerg; mêlak; p'işa řeş} liver: **-k'ezeba řeş** (IF/JB3/B) liver; 2) {syn: cegera spî; mêlak[a sor]; p'işa spî; sîh I; =Sor sêpelak} lungs: **-kezeba sipî** (B) lungs; 3) {syn: hinav} internal organs (K); 4) *idioms*: **-k'ezeb *fkî* reş kirin** (ZF3/tirsik.net): a) to make s.o. sick, give s.o. tuberculosis; b) to irritate, infuriate, drive s.o. crazy: **•Te *kezeba* min *reş kir*** (tirsik.net) You *make* me *sick/infuriate* me/*turn* my *stomach/drive* me *crazy*. {also: kezev (B-2); [gezeb] گزب (JJ); <kezeb> کزب (HH)} Cf. Arc kavda כבדא & Syr kavdā ܟܒܕܐ = 'heaviness; liver [seat of anger and melancholy]': NENA kôdâ (Maclean: listed as Old Syr) = 'liver, bowels, entrails, heart'; Ar kibdah كبدة = 'liver'; Heb kaved כבד. [K/JB3/IF/B/HH//JJ] <ceger; fateřeşk; hinav; zirav II>

k'ezebreşî کەزەبرەشی *adj.* 1) agitated, frustrated, irritated, upset: **-kezebreşî bûn** (ZF3/Kmc) to be fed up, disgusted, sick and tired: **•Hawara Xwedê, welle û bille û tille, ji kerbê van xwelîserên me ez *kezebreşî bûme*, hayhoooo!** (Lotikxane: Pişo Mihemed [2006]) For crying out loud, by God, I *have become extremely agitated* out of concern for these unfortunate people of ours **•Hevoka ku ez pê *kezebreşî dibim*** (tirsik.net, 01.xi.2013) The sentence [in the text] about which I *get upset/frustrated/irritated*; 2) *f.* **().** suffering; agitation, irritation, frustration: **•Gilgamêş ji devereke dûr hatiye, gelek azar û *kezebreşî* dîtiye** (Dastana Gilgamêş, 8?) G. has come from a distant region, he has experienced [lit. 'seen'] much torment and *suffering*. < k'ezeb + řeş + -î [ZF3/Wkt/Kmc] <kulecergî; kulzikî>

k'ezelik کەزەلِك *adv.* immediately, on the spot: **-bi wê k'ezelkê** (EH) thus, in that manner: ***•Bi wê k'ezelkê* gede ȟeyştê şevî ma cem qîzikê** (EH) *In this fashion* the fellow stayed with the girl for eighty nights. <Ar kaḏālik كذلك = 'thus, like that' [EH//K]

kezev کەزەڤ (B) = liver. See **k'ezeb**.

kezixandin کەزخاندِن (GF/HH) = to prune. See **k'ezaxtin**.

kezî کەزی *f.* **(-ya;-yê).** braid, plait, tress *(of a girl's hair)*; curl, lock, ringlet: **•*Kezîyêt* wê kiçikê şor bibîn di kelşa p'irê řa** (M-Zx #776) The girl's *braids* were hanging down through a crack in the bridge. {also: [kezi] كزى (JJ); <kezî> كزى (HH)} [Haz/K/A/IFb/B/JB3/JJ/HH/GF/TF/ZF3/FS] <bisk; gulî I; mû; p'oř III; t'ûncik>

kezîk•e کەزیکە *f.* **(•a;).** large vein in sheep's leg: **-kezîka pezî** (Trg) do. {also: <kezîge> کەزیگە (Hej)} [Trg//Hej]

kezîkure کەزیکورە (GF) = miserable (woman). See **kezîkurê**.

kezîkurê کەزیکوری *f.* **().** wretched, miserable, unfortunate *(woman)*: **•Dema jinan bixwestan gotinek pir bi êş ji xwe re, an ji yek din re bigotan, digotin "Hey *kezîkurê*" an "Wey li min *kezîkurê*." Li gor vê baweriyê ji kurkirina porê mezintir ti felaket bi ser jinan de nayên** (DBgb, 9) When women wanted to say something very painful to themselves or to someone else, they would say "Oh *kezîkurê* [cut-braids]" or "Woe is me *kezîkurê*". According to this belief, by cutting the longer hair, no disaster would befall the women. {also: kezîkure (GF)} {syn: p'epûk I[2]} < kezî = 'braid, plait' + kuř IV = 'shaved' [DBgb/FJ//GF] <belengaz; řeben I>

kezwan کەزوان (IFb/OK/HH/CB/Kmc-2/FS) = terebinth. See **kezan**.

kêç' کێچ *f.* **(-a;-ê).** flea, zool. *Siphonaptera*: **-kêç' k'etine çerm** (IF) to become impatient, to be itching to do stg., to have ants in one's pants. {also: [ketch] كيچ (JJ); <kêç> كيچ (HH)} Mid P kayk (M3); P keik كيك/kak كك; Sor kêç کێچ; Za keke/keki *f.* (Mal) [Msr/F/K/A/IF/B/JJ/HH/FS] <gene; spî II>

kêderê کێدەرێ (M-Ak) = where? See under **ku II**.

k'êf کێف *f.* **(-a;-ê).** 1) pleasure, fun, recreation: **•*Ji kêfa re* bezîya, hat malê** (L) Full of joy [lit. '*out of joy*'] he ran home [lit. 'ran, came home'] **•Her êvar tu *kêfa* me jî dişkenînî** (L) Every evening you upset us too [lit. 'break our *pleasure*']; **-K'êfa te ye** = It's up to you: **•Wacib me ya ȟel kirî, belê hemî me neȟelkirîye. Vê care *k'eyfa te***

ye, **k'anê dê tu çi li me key, em t ḧazir în** (M-Am #717) We ... did our homework, but we haven't done all of it. Now it's *as you please*. We are ready for whatever you will do to us; **-k'etin k'êfa dunîayê** (FK-eb-1) to indulge in the pleasures of this world; **-k'êf [û] ḧenek** (EP) "fun and games"; *euphemism for lovemaking*: **•Şev û ro Memê bire herema xwe, xwer̄a *k'êf, ḧenek*, xwerin û daîn *dikirin*** (EP-1) Night and day she brought Mem to her private quarters, where they *had fun*, joked and feasted; **-kêfa *fk-ê* ji *bk-î* r̄a hatin** (BX)/ **kêfa *fk-ê* bi *bk-î* hatin** (Bw/Zeb) to please s.o.; to like *(rev. constr.)* {syn: lê xweş hatin}: **•*Kêfa* gavan *hat*** (L) The cowherd *was pleased* **•*Kêfa* min *jê re tê*** (BX) I *like* it/It *pleases me*; 2) condition, state; disposition, inclination: **•Di çi *kêfê* de ne** (L) What *state* are they in? How are they doing? {also: keyf (JB3/IFb-2); [keif] كيف (JJ); <keyf> كيف (HH)} < Ar kayf كيف [K/A/IFb/B/GF//JB3/JJ/HH]

k'êfnexweşî كێفنەخوەشی *f.* **(-ya;).** displeasure, unhappiness: **•Hemû *kêfnexweşîya* xwe di rûyê xwe de dabû der** (ŞWWM, 12) He expressed all his *displeasure* through his facial expression. <kêf + ne + xweş + î [ŞWWM/ZF3]

kêfşing كێفشنگ (IFb) = crab. See **kevjal**.

k'êfxweş كێفخوەش *adj.* happy, merry; elated, in good spirits: **-k'êfxweş bûn** (B) to rejoice; **-k'êfxweş kirin** (B) to make happy: **•Cilên nû zarûkan *kêfxweş dikin*** (AB) New clothes *make* the children *happy*. {syn: dilxweş} {k'êfxweşî; keyfxwaşî; keyfxweşî; [keif khochi] كيف خوشى (JJ)} [AB/K/A/B/ZF3]

k'êfxweşî كێفخوەشی *f.* **(-ya;-yê).** happiness, mirth, gaiety. {also: keyfxwaşî (IF); keyfxweşî (JB3); [keif khochi] كيف خوشى (JJ)} {syn: dilxweşî} [K/A/ZF3//IF//JB3//JJ] <k'efxweş>

kêl I كێل *f.* **(-a;-ê).** tombstone. {also: kêlik I (IFb-2); <kêl> كيل (HH)} [K/A/IFb/HH/GF/ZF3/FS]

kêl II كێل *f.* **(-a;-ê).** a stitch *(in sewing or surgery)*: **-kêl dan** (A/HH)/~**lêxistin** (Qzl) to sew a stitch: **•*Kêlekê* lêre *bide*** (Ak) *Stitch* it for me here. {also: kêlek (GF) = kêl + ek; <kêldan كيلدان (kêldide) (كيلدده)> (HH)} =Sor teqeł تەقەڵ [Qzl/Zeb/Ak/A/IFb/B/HH/(GF)/TF/ZF3] <dirûtin; dirwar>

kêl III كێل *f.* **(-a;).** unit of weight, dry measure: 8 *tilms* = 640 or 800 kg. (CCG); 8 or 16 *olçeks* (IFb/Wkp); 12 *ṣā's* or 72 kg. (GF). {also: [kil كيل/keilé كيله/kilik كيلك] (JJ)} Cf. Ar kayl كيل = 'a dry measure' [CCG/IFb/GF/Wkp/ZF3//JJ] <kod[2]; olçek; tilm>

kêlan كێلان *vt.* **(-k'êl-).** to plow: **•Ezê zeviya mi rifsê kirî ezê *bikêlim*** (MD-Byt, 161) I *will plough* the field that I irrigated. {also: <kêlan كيلان (dikêle) (دكيله)> (HH)} {syn: cot ajotin/kirin} Sor kêłan كێڵان (-kêł-) [MD-Byt/Hk/K(s)/IFb/HH/OK] <cot; halet; k'otan>

kêlb كێلب (SK/OK) = fang. See **kilb**.

k'êlek كێلەك *f.* **(-a;-ê).** 1) {syn: kevî I; p'er̄ [4]} edge, flank, outskirts: **•Ew *li kêleka* gund dimîne** (K) He lives *on the edge of* the village **•Zyaretek ... *li k'êleka* şeherê Mixurzemîne** (EP-7) [There is] a shrine *on the outskirts of* the city of M; 2) {syn: alî; hêl II; tenişt} side; side of a human being, from the armpit to the waist (HH): **•Kewaniya xwe ya ciwan dide *kêleka xwe* û ji bajarê D'ê hêdî hêdî ber bi bakur dajo** (Lab, 6) He puts his pretty wife *at his side* and slowly drives north from the city D. {also: [keïlik] كيلك (JJ); <kêlik> كيلك (HH)} [EP-7/K/A/JB3/IFb/B/ JB1-S/TF//JJ/HH/Haz]

k'êlendî كێلەندی *f.* **(;-yê).** scythe, pruning hook: **•Di nava erdên xwe de bi qalûç û *kêlendûran* paliyên xwe dikin** (Ardû, 149) They do their harvesting on their land with sickles and *scythes* **•Ḧesinê bê'esas ne dibe *k'êrendî*, ne dibe de's** (Dz-#698) Unsmelted iron becomes neither *scythe* nor sickle *[prv.]*; **-k'êrendî k'utan** (B) to whet or sharpen a scythe. {also: kêlendûr (Ardû); kêlimtî (Folklora Kurdan: Erxanî); kêlindî (Kmc-6); k'êrendî (B); [kirendou كرندو/kirendi كرندی] (JJ); <kêlendî> كيلندی (HH)} {syn: diryas; melexan; qirim; şalok} < W Arm keranti գերանդի [EP-8/F/K/IFb/HH/GF/ZF3/FS//Kmc-6//B/JJ//Ardû//Folklora Kurdan] <das; diryas; şalok>

kêlendûr كێلەندوور (Ardû) = scythe. See **k'êlendî**.

kêlestûn كێلەستوون (AF/FS) = rainbow. See **kêrestûn**.

kêlik I كێلك (IFb) = tombstone. See **kêl I**.

kêlik II كێلك (IFb) = moment. See **kêlî**.

k'êlimîn كێلمین *vi.* **(-k'êlim-).** to speak *(of animals, in folktales and the like)* [Cf. T dile gelmek]: **•Bor ... bi Memêr̄a *k'êlimî*** (Z-1) Bor [the horse] ... *spoke* to Mem **•Ç'êlek pêr̄a *dik'êlime*** (J) The cow *speaks* to her. {syn: deng çûn; ştex̄ilîn} < Ar kallama II كلّم = 'to speak' [Z-1/J/K/B]

kêlimtî كێلمتی (Folklora Kurdan: Erxanî) = scythe. See **k'êlendî**.

kêlindî كێلندی (Kmc-6) = scythe. See **k'êlendî**.

kêlî كێلی *f.* **(-ya;-yê).** 1) {syn: çirik I} instant, second: **•Îro tiştek li kudera dinyayê bibe bila bibe, mirov di eynî rojê, heta eynî saetê *di kêliyekê de* pê dihise** (Wlt 1:37=38, 2) Today wherever in the world a thing may happen, one finds out about it on the same day, even in the same hour, *in an instant*; 2) a moment; a while: **•*Kêlîkê* li cem me be** (GF) Stay with us *for a little while*. {also: kêlik II (IFb); kêlîk (GF)} [Wlt/TF/ZF3/FS//IFb//GF] <kêl II>

kêlîk كێليك (GF) = moment. See **kêlî**.

kêlok كێلۆك (Bw) = Nestorian girl. See **kîlo I**.

kêm I کێم *adj.* 1) {syn: çîçik II; hindik; piçek} few, small in number; little, a little bit, a small amount: **-kêm-hindik** (Ber) a little bit, hardly at all; **-kêmtir** = less; 2) rare(ly): **•Nava wan kevir û kuç'ikada hêşînayî, kulîlk zaf *kêm*in** (Ba2) Among those rocks, greenery and flowers are very *sparse*; 3) deficient, lacking, missing; 4) minus (-), *used in telling time*: **•Saet deh *kêm* bîst û pênc e** (memrise Kurdisch für Anfänger) It is 9:35 [lit. '10:00 *minus* 25'] **•Saet pênc *kêm* yek bû min cixareyek vêxist** (dehabertr.blogspot.com xii.2012) It was 4:59 [lit. '5:00 *minus* 1'], I lit a cigarette. {also: [kim] کيم (JJ); <kêm> کيم (HH)} <O Ir *kambyah- (A&L p. 86 [VII] + p. 96 [XIX, 4]): Av & OP kamna- = 'little, few' (Brand); Sgd kβn (Gersh); Mid P kam = 'little, small, few' & kem = 'less, fewer' (M3); P kam کم; Sor kem کەم {kêmasî; [kimasi] کيماسی (JJ); kêmanî; kêmayî; kêmî} [Ba2/K/A/JB3/IF/B/HH//JJ]

k'êm II کێم *f.* **(-a;-ê).** pus, matter: **•*kêma* birînê** (FS) *the pus of* the wound; **-k'êm girtin** (K/B)/~ **jê hatin** (K) to suppurate, discharge pus. {also: [kim] کيم (JJ); <kêm> کيم (HH)} {syn: 'edab; nêm} Sor kêm کێم [F/K/B/HH/ZF3/FS//JJ] <pizik>

kêmahî کێماهی (FS) = minority; lack, deficit. See **kêmanî**[1], **kêmasî** & **kêmayî**.

kêmanî کێمانی *f.* **().** 1) {also: kêmatî (RZ/FS); kêmayetî (RF/TF); kêmayî (OK)} {syn: *hindikahî} minority (VoA); 2) deficit, shortage (IFb/JB3). See **kêmasî** & **kêmayî**; 3) *[adv.]* usually with **bi** = at least: **•Daku di rojên pêş de bikaribim bi mêjîyekî paqij û nîv-vala kevneçîrok û çîrvanokan ji bebika xwe re bibêjim. An jî *bi kêmanî* jê re qala bebiktîya wê bikim** (LC, 151) So that in days to come I might with a clean and half-empty brain be able to tell my baby daughter old stories and anecdotes. Or *at least* speak to her of her infancy. *The VoA coined **kêmanî** for 'minority' to parallel **p'iranî** = majority.* [VoA/IFb/JB3//RZ/FS//RF/TF//OK]

kêmasî کێماسی *f.* **(-ya;-yê).** 1) {syn: qusûr} deficit, dearth, scarcity, want, lack, shortage, paucity, deficiency: **•*Kêmasîya* te çîye?** (IS-#105) What is it you lack?/What are you missing?/What is wrong?; 2) {syn: qusûr} defect, flaw, imperfection, shortcoming (JB3). {also: kêmanî (IFb/JB3); **kêmayî**; kêmî (K/A); [kimasi] کيماسی (JJ)} [B/IFb/JB3/JJ/HH/SK/GF/ZF3/FS//K/A] <kêm I>

kêmatî کێماتی (RZ/FS) = minority; lack, deficit. See **kêmanî** [1], **kêmasî** & **kêmayî**.

kêmayetî کێمايەتی (RF/TF) = minority; lack, deficit. See **kêmanî** [1], **kêmasî** & **kêmayî**.

kêmayî کێمايی *f.* **(-ya;-yê).** 1) {also: kêmahî (FS); kêmanî (IFb/JB3); **kêmasî**; kêmî (K/A)} deficit, dearth, scarcity, lack, shortage; 2) minority (OK). See **kêmanî**[1]. [B//K/A//FS//JB3/IFb//HH/JJ] <kêm I>

kêmdiravî کێمدِراڤی *f.* **(-ya;-yê).** shortage of funds, lack of funds. [Zeb/VoA]

kêmî کێمی (K/A/SK) = deficit, shortage. See **kêmasî** & **kêmayî**.

kêm îĥsan کێم ئیحسان *adj.* not very generous, of little benevolence or bounty, stingy, ungenerous: **•[Xwendîyêd ĥemû milletan ekserî *kêm îĥsan* û kêm îkram dibin]** (JR-2) For the most part the learnèd of all nations are *wanting in benevolence* and generosity. {also: [<kim ehsan>] کيم احسان (JR)} [JR]

kêmr̄ûn کێمڕوون *adj.* containing or cooked with only a small amount of oil or butter. {syn: r̄ij} [Qzl/ZF3] <bêr̄ûn; r̄ûn>

kêndere کێندەرێ (M-Ak) = where? See **ku II**.

kêr I کێر *adj.* necessary, needed; essential, vital; useful: **-kêrî *fk-ê* hatin** (K/B/HH)/**bi kêrî yekî hatin** (IF) to be needed, necessary, be of use or help to: **•Em nikarin bi p'akî *kêrî* we *bên*** (Ba2:2, 206) We can't really *be of help to* you **•Ew k'itêb *kêrî* me *naê*** (B) That book *is of no use to* us; We don't need that book **•*Kêrî* çi *tê*?** (XF) Who needs it?/*Of* what *use is it*? **•Xorto, han van xişrê min xwer̄a hilde, eze pîrim, *kêrî* min *naên*** (Ba-1, #24) Lad, take these jewels of mine, I'm old, they *are of no use to* me. {also: [kir] کير (JJ); <kêr-> کير (HH)} [Ba-1/K/A/IF/B/HH/JB1-A&S/GF//JJ] <bêkêr; kêrhatî>

kêr̄ II کێڕ *adj.* crookèd: **•Dît ku dareke mezine**

***kêr̄bûyî*, va çiqekî t'eze pêve şînbûye** (Abbasian #4:143) He saw a big, *crooked* tree, and behold a green branch was growing on it. {also: kêr̄bûyî (Abbasian)} {syn: ç'ewt; xwaro-maro} < Arm keṛ կեռ = 'crooked' [Abbasian//K/B/SC]

k'êr III کێر *f.* **(-a;-ê).** knife: **•kalûmeke *k'êran*** = old, rusty *knife* **•Xuşkê xuşkê, ca ji kerema xwe tu dikarî ji min re *kêrê* bînî!** (LM, 7) Sister, sister! Please can you bring me *the knife*!; **-k'êr dan** (L) to sever, cut *(with a knife)*: **•*Kêr dan* şerîtî** (L) *They cut* the rope; **-k'êra pola** = steel knife. {also: k'êrik (Msr/HH); [kir] کـــيـــر (JJ)} [Pok. (s)ker-/(s)kerə-/(s)krē- 938.] 'to cut' (p. 941 b: (s)ker-t-/(s)kre-t-): Av karəti-; Mid P kārd (M3); P kārd کارد; Sor kêr[d] کێرد/kard کارد [Sinneh]; Za kardî *f.* (Todd); Hau kar<u>d</u>î *f.* (M4) [K/A/JB3/IF/B/JJ/Msr] <hisan; kahûr; kalûme; kefçî; k'êrik; sat'or I; sîkar; şefir>

K'êrakî کێراکی *f.* **().** Sunday. {also: <kêrakî> کيراکی (HH)} {syn: Le'd; R̄oja bazarê (F)} < Gr Kyriakē Κυριακη = 'the lord's [day]' < kyrios κυριος = 'lord' -->Arm Kiraki (W: Giragi) կիրակի [A/HH/ZF3]

k'êran کـــێـــران *m.* **(-ê; k'êrên).** crossbeam, made of poplar wood, *used to brace the ceiling in traditional houses, placed at intervals of several meters* (Haz); long beam applied to ceiling (IFb); log, beam, girder, post (K/HH): **•Ji dûê tendûra *k'êranêd* xanîya r̄eş bûbûn** (Ba2-3, 213) From the smoke of the ovens, *the beams of* the houses had turned black. {also: kenar (F-2); keran (F); [kiran] کــران (JJ); <kêran> کـــيـــران (HH)} {syn: beşt; garîte; max} [Haz/K/IFb/B/HH/GF//JJ//F] <kûtek; mertak; nîre I; r̄ot>

kêrasî کێراسی (ZF3) = quail. See **k'êr̄asû**.

k'êr̄asû کـــێـــڕاســوو *f.* **(;-yê).** quail, zool. *Coturnix coturnix*. {also: kêrasî (ZF3-2); k'êr̄esî (Z-904-2); k'êr̄esû (Z-904-2/ZF3); [kirasou] کـيـراسـو (JJ)} {syn: 'ebdal; kutefir} [Z-904//JJ/ZF3] <kew I; lorî I; por I>

kêr̄bûyî کێربوویی (Abbasian) = crooked. See **kêr̄ II**.

k'êrendî کێرەندی (B) = scythe. See **k'êlendî**.

k'êr̄esî کێڕەسی (Z-904) = quail. See **k'êr̄asû**.

kêrestûn کێرەستوون/کێرەستوین *f.* **(-a;-ê).** rainbow: **•[Ji dengê re'dê biharî / wî hilat *kêrestûne*]** (HoK, 251: Mela Men<u>s</u>ûrê Gêrgaşî) From the sound of the thunder of springtime / there sprang up for him *a rainbow*. {also: kêlestûn (AF/FS-2); kêrstûn (Zeb-2); <kêrestûn> کێرەستوون (HoK); <kêrstûn> کــێــرســتــون (Hej)} {syn: k'eskesor} = Sor kołke•zêr̄îne کۆڵکەزێڕینە [Zeb/HoK/FS//Hej//AF]

k'êr̄esû کێڕەسوو (Z-904/ZF3) = quail. See **k'êr̄asû**.

kêrê کێرێ (M-Ak) = where? See under **ku II**.

kêrgo کێرگۆ (RZ) = rabbit. See **k'erguh**.

k'êrgu[h] کێرگو[ه] (B) = rabbit. See **k'erguh**.

k'êrgûşk کێرگووشك (Ag) = rabbit. See **k'erguh**.

kêrhatî کـــێـــرهـــاتـــی *adj./pp.* useful, helpful. {also: <kêrhatî> کيرهاتی (HH)} [IF/HH/JB1-A/ZF3] <kêr I>

k'êrik کـــێـــرِك *f.* **(-a;-ê).** 1) knife [dim. of **k'êr III**]; 2) pocketknife, penknife: **•Wî bi *kêrikê* gundor spî kir** (FS) He peeled the melon with the *pocketknife*. {also: <kêrik> کـــيـــرك (HH)} [Msr/HH/ZF3/FS] <k'êr III>

k'êroşk کێرۆشك (A/RZ) = rabbit. See **k'erguh**.

kêrstûn کێرستوون (Zeb) = rainbow. See **kêrestûn**.

k'êr̄ûşik کێڕووشِك (A) = rabbit. See **k'erguh**.

kêrûşk کێرووشك (SK) = rabbit. See **k'erguh**.

kêrwîşk کێرویشك (RZ) = rabbit. See **k'erguh**.

k'ês کـــێـــس *f.* **(-a;).** opportunity, chance; possibility: **-k'ês lê anîn** (A) to cause an opportunity to arise, to make stg. happen; **-k'ês lê hatin** (A/JB3/IF) to have an opportunity or chance, find the right time or conditions to do stg.: **•Gur kir nekir *kêsa* wî *lê ne hat* ko bigire** (SW) No matter what the wolf did, *he couldn't manage to* catch it **•*Kês li* min *hat*** (JB3) I *had the opportunity* **•*Keysa* min *lê hat*** (IF) I *found the opportunity*; **-k'êsa *fk-ê* bûn** = to have an opportunity, etc.: **•*Keysa* wî *nabe*** (IF) He *doesn't get a chance to ...* **•*K'êsa* me *tune* kitêbê destxin** (K) We *have no chance of* acquiring the book. {also: k'eys (A); keys (IF/ZF3/FS); [keïs] کيس (JJ); <keys> کيس (HH)} {syn: delîve; derfet; fesal [1]; firset; kevlû [2]} Cf. T kez = 'time' [SW/K(s)/JB3/JJ//A/IF/HH/ZF3/FS] <mecal>

k'êş II کێش (F) = weight. See **k'aş I**.

k'êşan کـــێـــشـــان (A/IF/JB1-S/M) = to pull. See **k'işandin**.

k'êş•e کێشە *f.* **(•a;).** argument, disagreement, dispute, controversy: **•*Kêşa* wan dirêj bû** (FS) Their *argument* was long. {also: <kêşe> کـــێـــشـــە (Hej)} {syn: bêt'ifaqî; cerenîx; cur̄e; de'w II; doz; dubendî; gelemşe; gelş; k'eşmek'eş; nakokî} Cf. P kašākaš کـشـاکـش = 'contest, struggle' [Zeb/OK/Hej/FS/ZF3] <mişt û mir̄>

k'êşîn کـــێـــشـــیـــن *vi.* **(-k'êş-).** 1) to be pulled, dragged, drawn; to move along *(vi.)*; to move one after the other *(of masses of people, troops, cattle, etc.)* (B): **•Wê r̄ojê sibê ĥeta êvarê ‘esk’er *k’işya* berbi frontê** (B) That day troops were continually *moving* toward the front from morning till evening; 2) {syn: herikîn} to flow, stream *(vi.)* (B). See **k’işîn**; 3) to creep, crawl *(of snakes, lizards, etc.)* (B); 4) *[vt.]* to weigh *(vt.)* (IF/JB1-S/HH/JJ). {also: k’işîn (K/B); [kichan] كـشـان (JJ); <kêşan كـيـشـان (dikêşe) دكـيـشـه> (HH)} Cf. P kašīdan كشيدان = 'to pull'; Sor kêşan كێشان (-kêş-) = 'to pull, drag, attract; smoke; suffer'; Hau kêşay (kêş-) *vt.* (M4) [AB/JB1-A/ZF3//K/B//JJ] See also **k’işîn**. <k’işandin>

kêşwer كـيّـشـوەر (CS) = continent; kingdom. See **k’îşwer**.

k’êtik كێتِك (Bw/FS) = cat. See **k’itik II**.

kêve كێڤە (M-Ak) = whither? where to? See **ku II**.

kêvjal كێڤژال (TF) = crab. See **kevjal**.

kêvjale كێڤژاله (FS/BF) = crab. See **kevjal**.

k’êvrîşk كێڤریشك (FS/BF) = rabbit. See **k’erguh**.

k’êvroşk كێڤرۆشك (HH) = rabbit. See **k’erguh**.

kêwî I كێوی (Bw) = wild. See **k’ûvî**.

kêwî II كێوی (TF) = snow left after the thaw. See **kevî II**.

k’êwrîşk كـێـوريـشـك, f. (;-ê) (FK-eb-1) = rabbit. See **k’erguh**.

k’êwrûşk كێورووشك (K/F) = rabbit. See **k’erguh**.

Kêẍî كـيّـغـى **().** Kiğı, town in province (il/vilayet) of Bingöl (Çapaxçûr/Çewlîg), Kurdistan of Turkey. [Kg]

k’êz كێز (Zeb) = beetle. See **k’êzik**[2].

k’êzik كێزِك *f.* **(-a;-ê).** 1) (small) insect, bug; 2) beetle, scarab (JJ/HH/GF); black or dark green beetle (Zeb) [k’êz]. {also: k’êz (Zeb); [kizik] كـزك (JJ); <kêzik> كـيزك (HH)} [Msr/Frq/F/K/A/IFb/B/HH/GF/TF//Zeb//JJ] <gûgilêrk>

k’ibrît كِبريت (K/B) = match(es). See **k’irpît**.

kiç كِچ (JJ/JB1-A/SK/M-Ak/Bw) = girl. See **keç**.

kidark كِدارك (Twn) = mushroom. See **gidark**.

kiferî كِفێرى (IFb/ZF3/Wkt) = tamarisk. See **kifir II**.

kifin كِفِن (SK/JJ) = shroud. See **k’efen**.

k’ifir I كِفِر *f.* **(;-ê).** 1) atheism, unbelief; lack of faith: **•Hingî Birahîm Xudêyê xo bi Heq naskir û giyanê xo ji *kifriyê* xilas kir** (GShA, 227) So Ibrahim recognized God as the Truth and freed himself from *unbelief*; 2) cursing, blasphemy (B/JJ). {also: kifr (IFb/ZF3); kifrî (GShA); [koufr/kufr (Rh)] كـفـر (JJ); <kufr> كـفـر (HH)} < Ar kufr كفر = ‘unbelief; blasphemy’; Sor kifr كِفر [GShA//K/B//IFb/ZF3//JJ/HH] <k’afir>

kifir II كِـفِـر *f.* **(;-ê).** tamarisk, tree with small fragrant violet flowers, bot. *Tamarix*. {also: kiferî (IFb/ZF3/Wkt); kuferî (IFb-2)} {syn: gez II} Sor kifr كِفر [Dh/OK/RF//IFb/ZF3/Wkt]

kifkarek كِفكارەك (Wkt) = mushroom. See **kufkarik**.

kifkarik كِفكارِك (Wkt) = mushroom. See **kufkarik**.

kifr كِفر (IFb/ZF3) = atheism; curse. See **k’ifir I**.

kifrî كِفرى (GShA) = atheism; curse. See **k’ifir I**.

kifrît كِـفـريـت (JB3/IFb/HH) = match(es); sulphur. See **k’irpît**.

k’ifş كِـفـش *adj.* 1) {syn: aşkere; berç’av II; diyar; xanê; xuya} evident, obvious, apparent, clear, showing; visible; known: **•Qeret’ajdîn dezmala destê xwe, wekî *k’ivş* bû, avîte bin mîr** (Z-1) Qeretajdin threw his handkerchief, which was *showing* (=sticking out), under the prince; **-k’ifş kirin** = a) to define; to determine, set, fix: **•Memê ... çil rojî we‘de *k’ifş kir*** (EP-7) Mem *set* a term of 40 days ...; b) to mark, designate; 2) prominent, well known: **•Lakin eger ew meyt begzade weyaxû aẍa û mirovekî *kivş* bûya, elbette paşî panzdeh rojan ĥakimê wî welatî xelatek ĥazir dikirin** ... (BN, 183) But if the dead man were the son of a beg or an agha, or if he were a *prominent* individual, after two weeks the ruler of that land would prepare gifts ...; 3) *[n.]* investigation (JJ/IF). {also: k’efş II (IF-2); k’ivş (K/B/Z-1); [kiwch] كـفـش (JJ); <kifş> كـفـش (HH)} ?< Ar kašf كـشـف = 'discovery, uncovering' {k’ifşî; k’ivşayî; k’ivşî; kiwşî} [Z-1/K/B/JJ//A/IF/HH] <r̄ep>

k’ifşî كِـفـشـى *f.* **(;-yê).** clarity, obviousness, palpability: **-K’ivşayî heye** (B) It is obvious that... : **•*K’ivşî* heye gura ew xwarîye** (Ba3-1) *It is obvious that* the wolves have eaten him. {also: k’ivşayî (B); k’ivşî (Ba3-1); kiwşî (SK)} [Ba3-1//B//SK//Wkt] <k’ifş>

k’ihêl كِهێل = bay horse. See **k’iĥêl**.

k’iĥêl كِـحـێـل *adj.* 1) bay, reddish-brown *(color of horses)*; 2) *[f./m.* **(-a/ ;).]** bay (colored) horse: **•Nîşanî min kin *k’iĥêlekî* usa, wekî ewê min bigihîne mirazê min** (Z-1) Show me a *bay horse* which will take me where I want to go. {also: k’ehêl (K/A/IF); keĥêl (FS); k’ihêl} < Ar kaḥīl كـحـيـل/ kuḥaylī كـحـيـلي = 'horse of noblest breed' [Z-1//K/A/IF//FS] <hesp>

kil I كِـل *m.(ZF3)/f.(B)* **(-ê/ ; /-ê).** collyrium, kohl, eye shadow: •**Gulê ez *kilê* çavê te me** (KHT, 242) Gulê, I am *the kohl* of your eyes; -**kil dan** (K) to dye, darken *(hair, eyebrows, etc.)* by applying kohl: •**Zîna delal ... xwe r̄ind xemiland, ç'e'vê xwe *kilda*** (Z-1) Darling Zin ... adorned herself, *darkened* her eyes. {also: [kil كل/kohol كحل] (JJ); <kil> كل (HH)} <Ar kuḥl كحل [Z-1/K/IF/B/JJ/HH/ZF3]

kil II كِل: -**kil bûn** (Qzl) to shake, tremble *(vi.)* {syn: ḧejîn; lerzîn; r̄e'ilîn; r̄icifîn; r̄ikr̄ikîn}: •**Pelên guliyê dara çinarê yê ku ew li ser bû, *kil bûn*** (SF 17) The leaves of the plane tree branch he was on *trembled*; -**kil kirin** (Qzl/GF): a) to shake *(vt.)*, cause to tremble {syn: ḧejandin}; b) to wave stg. *(vt.)*: •**Siltanê Fîlan rawestiya, hilma xwe stend, piştî ku xortima xwe bi vir de û wê de *kil kir*, got** ... (SF 29) The Elephant Sultan stopped, drew a breath, and after *waving* his trunk this way and that, said .... [SF/Qzl/GF/TF/ZF3]

k'il III كِل *m./f.(B)* **(/-a; /-ê).** 1) {syn: meşk; sirsûm} churn *(for making butter)* (BK); 2) lump or ball of butter obtained when churning sour milk (K/B); shaking of butter in a butter-churner (K/B). [BK/K/B/FS] <k'ilan; meşk>

kilab كِلاب (DBgb) = soil plowed one time. See **k'irêbe**.

kilabe كِلابه (IFb/FS) = shaft, pole; rods on draft animal's neck. See **k'ulabe**.

k'ilam/kilam [K] كِلام *f.* **(-a;-ê).** song; "The dengbêjs divide the kilams into *kilamên şer* (war songs) and *kilamên evîn* (love songs)" (Hamelink, p. 60): •**Al-p'aşa ḧukum kir, ku asiq *k'ilameke* evînîyê bêje seva Memê wî** (Z-1) A.p. ordered the ashik to sing a love *song* for his [son] Mem; -**kilam avêtin ser fk-ê** (EP-7) to sing to s.o.: •**Ewana bi sirê *k'ilam avîtne ser* M.** (EP-7) They took turns *singing to* M.; -**k'ilam gotin/k'ilam stiran** (B) to sing {syn: stiran I}; -**k'ilama bêşîkê** (B) lullaby, cradle song; -**k'ilamêd daweta** (B) wedding songs; -**k'ilamêd dilk'etinê** (B) lyrical love songs; -**kilamên govendê** (IFb) dance songs; -**k'ilamêd mêranîyê** (B) heroic songs. {also: k'ulam (FK-eb-1/FK-eb-2); [kelam] كلام (JJ)} [=Sor goranî گۆرانی] < Ar kalām كلام = 'words, speech, talking' [Ks/K/IFb/JJ/ZF3//B/Z-1] <dengbêj; dîlan; dûrik; lawuk; lewẍet [4]; leylan; lorî II; stiran I; şer̄ I[3]>

k'ilan كِلان *vt.* **(-k'il-).** to churn *(butter and the like)*: •**Çiqa kevanya malê dew *dik'ila* r̄ûn dikire k'ûpekî** (Dz-anec #32) Whenever the lady of the house *churned* 'dew' (=yoghurt and water), she would put it in a clay jar •**Meşka cara *dê kêyeve*** (song by Teḧsîn Taha) You *will rechurn* the skin-bag [i.e., butter-churn] of yore •[**Nêrgisa koçer**] ... **lolep di dest de dew *kîyaye* bêyî ku meşka wê çilkan bireşîne** (Lab, 8) [Nergis the nomad girl] ... with a wooden handle bar in her hand, *churned* the buttermilk without her skin sack spilling a drop •**Piştî ku diya min dewê xwe *dikila*, meşka xwe ya reş ji darê dadixist** (Alkan, 71) After my mother *churned* her buttermilk, she removed her black skin butter churner from the wooden frame. {also: kan II (FS); keyandin (IFb-2); k'ilandin (IFb/B-2/GF); kiyan (-kê-) (Bw); kîyan (-kê-) (Zeb); [kilan] كلان (JJ); <keyandin كيياندن (dikeyîne) (دكيينه)> (HH); <kiyan> كيان (Hej)} =Sor jandin ژاندِن/jendin ژەندِن [Dz/F/K/JJ//IFb/B/GF//HH///Bw/Hej//Zeb//FS] <k'il III; meşk; r̄ûn; sirsûm>

k'ilandin كِلاندِن (IFb/B/GF) = to churn. See **k'ilan**.

kilaw كِلاو (SK) = hat. See **kulav**[4].

kilb كِلب *m.* **(-ê;).** fang, canine tooth: •**Gurgî ji xeflet xo hawête ser pişta gaê sor, leqek da-na pişta stukira gay. *Kilbêt* wî tê çon, ga birîndar kir** (SK 6:69) The wolf suddenly flung himself onto the back of the red ox and bit into the back of the ox's neck. His *fangs* went in and wounded the ox •**R̄îwî çû, got, "...ḧîleyekî li qelê bikem, belkû tola xo jê wekem" ... R̄îwî çû bin dara gûzê ... xo li bin gûzê dirêj kir, xo mirand. Çavêt xo ber spî kirin, dewê xo beş kir, *kêlbêt* xo gir kirin, mêş hatine dewê wî** (SK 3:23) The fox went away, saying, "I had better go and play a trick on the crow. Perhaps I can have my revenge on her." ... The fox went beneath a walnut tree ... he stretched himself out at the foot of the walnut tree and made out to be dead. He turned up the whites of his eyes, hung his mouth open and bared his *teeth*. Flies came into his mouth. {also: kêlb (SK-2/OK); <kilb> كلب (HH)} {syn: qîl} cf. Ar kalb كلب = 'dog'; Sor kełbe کەڵبە = 'fang, canine tooth' [SK/IFb/HH/GF//OK]

kilêb كِلێب (IFb) = soil plowed one time. See **k'irêbe**.

kilêjî كِلێژی *m./f.(ZF3/FS)* **().** coccyx, tailbone; base of the spine. {also: kelêj II (Bw); kelêjî (ZF3-2/FS)} {syn: qarç'ik} Sor kilênçke كِلێنچکە [Kmc-6/IFb/OK/ZF3//Bw] <mezmezk>

kilîd كِليد (GF/Wkt) = key. See **kilît**[2].

kilîfe كِليفه *m.* **().** small gecko lizard [Ar abū brayṣ أبو بريص]. [Zeb/Wkt] <marmaroşk>

kilîl كِليل (Bw/JJ/FS) = key. See **kilît**[2].

k'ilîm كِليم *f.* **(-a;-ê).** kilim, flat-weave pileless carpet: **•Remziye bi kedek mezin mahfûr ango *kilîmê* bi destê xwe dihûne** (jinha.com.tr 14.v.2015) With great effort, R. weaves a rug, i.e. a *kilim*, by hand. {also: kîlîm (IFb)} {syn: beř IV; cacim; cil II; gelt; merş tejik} Cf. T kilim; Ar kilīm كليم; P galīm گليم; Sor kilîm كِليم = 'pileless carpet' [K/GF/ZF3/Wkt//IFb]

kilîs كِليس (IFb) = lime, chalk. See **k'ils**.

kilît/k'ilît [K/B/JB1-S] كِليت *f.* **(-a;-ê).** 1) lock: **-k'ilît û mifte** (Z-1) lock and key; 2) {syn: mifte} key [kilîl]. {also: kilîd (GF-2/Wkt); kilîl (Bw/FS); kilîtk (JB1-A); [kilid كـلـيـد (=lock)/klíl كـلـيـل (=key)](JJ); <kilît> كليت (HH)} Mid P kilēl (M3); P kalīd كـلـيـد = 'key', T kilit = 'lock', Gr kleídhi κλειδι = 'key'; Sor kilîl كِليل = 'key'; Hau kirêł *m.* (M4) [Z-1/K/B/JB1-S//JB3/IFb/HH/GF//JB1-A//JJ/Wkt//Bw/FS]

kilîtk كِليتك (JB1-A) = key. See **kilît**[2].

k'ilk كِـلـك *f./m.(OK)* **(-a/;).** tail; short or docked tail *(e.g., tail of rabbit, goat, etc.)* (IFb): **•Marî çi kir, řa bo ser *kilka* xo, ço bereka kabray** (M-Ak, #545) What did the snake do but raise itself up on its *tail* and go in front of the fellow. {also: kilik (IFb/OK)} {syn: boç'[ik]; dêl II; dû II; kurî I (Bw); qemç[ik]; teřî I[1]} Sor kilk كِـلـك = 'finger, pen, handle, haft, tail' [M-Ak/K(s)/SK//IFb/OK]

kilmiş كِلمِش (OK/RJ) = mucus. See **k'ilmîş**.

kilmîç كِلميچ (OK) = mucus. See **k'ilmîş**.

k'ilmîş كِلميش *m.(Bw/FS)/f.(OK)* **(-ê/ ;).** mucus, snot: **•Wî *kilmîşê* xwe paqij kir** (FS) He cleaned up (or wiped up) his *mucus*. {also: kilmiş (OK); kilmîç (OK-2); kilmûç (IFb-2/OK-2/ZF3); [kilmish] (RJ)} {syn: çilka poz; çilm; fiş; lîk} [Bw/IFb/FS//OK/RJ//ZF3]

kilmûç كِلمووچ (IFb/OK/ZF3) = mucus. See **k'ilmîş**.

kiloc كِلۆج (B) = round bread or cake. See **kuloç**.

kiloç كِلۆچ (B) = round bread or cake. See **kuloç**.

kilor كِـلـۆر *m./f.(ZF3)* **(/-a;).** type of pastry eaten on Lesser Bayram ('Id al-Fitr): pirog (K); börek, çörek (round, ring-shaped or braided cake) (IF/HH); small oven-baked bread [tandır ekmeği] with holes in it (A/IF); cake (JB3). {also: kulor (K-2); <kilor كلور/kiloç كلوچ>(HH)} {syn: kuloç; sewik (IF)} [K/A/JB3/IFb/GF/ZF3] See also **kuloç**.

kilorîk كِـلـۆريك *f.* **().** dish made of ground meat and bulgur wheat [savara nîv hûr, goştê hêrayî; T ekşili köfte]. {also: gilolîk (Qmş/Btm); kulorîk (QtrE); xilolîk II (CB); xilorîk I (Qzl/Qrj)} [Wn//QtrE/ZF3//CB//Qzl/Qrj//Qmş/Btm]

k'ilox كِلۆخ *m.* **(-ê;).** skull. {also: k'ulox (Dh/FS/BF); [kelōx (PS)] كلوخ (JJ); <kilox> كلۆخ (Hej)} {syn: k'elle II; qehf} [Dh/FS/BF//IFb/HH/GF/OK/RZ/Hej/Kmc-6/ZF3//JJ-PS] <qerqode>

k'ils كِلس *f.* **(-a;-ê).** lime[stone], chalk; gypsum: **•Bes, çaxê kû baran aw berf tê, her k'es banê xwe digeřênê û dimalê, ji ber kû avaîyê wa ħemû bi kevir û *k'ilsê* ne** (HR-I 1:18) But, when it rains or snows, everyone rolls and sweeps his roof, because their houses are all of stone and *lime*. {also: kilîs (IFb-2); kisil (IFb-2/Zeb-2); [kils كلس/ kisil كسل] (JJ); <kils> كلس (HH)} {syn: ces; gec} Ar kils كـلـس = 'lime' [HR-I/K/A/IFb/B/JJ/ HH/TF/OK/Zeb] <hêtûn>

kim كِم (IF) = hat. See **k'um**.

kimekim كِمەكِم (B) = noise. See **k'im-k'imî**.

k'im-k'imî كِم كِمی *f.* **(;-[y]ê).** noise: **•Dîwan *k'im-k'imî* bû bi 'eyan û k'ubarê şeherê M.-va** (Z-1) The court was [astir with] *the noise of* the nobles and notables of the city of M.; **-bi k'im-k'imî** (EP-7) noisily. {also: kimekim (B)} {syn: galegûrt; galigal[4]; hêwirze; hose; qajeqaj; qalmeqal; qareqar; qerebalix; qîřeqîř; şerqîn; t'eqeřeq} Cf. [kemkemou] كمكمو (JJ) = 'talkative, chatterbox' [EP-7//B]

kimt كِمت (GF/Hej) = mountaintop. See **kumt**.

kin كِـن *adj.* short *(of stature)*. {also: <kin> كـن (HH)} {syn: kurt I; qut I[2]} O Ir *kanya- = 'small' (Tsb2, p.11) {kinayî; kinnî; kinî} [HB/K/A/JB3/IFb/B/HH/GF/TF/Haz] <gurc II>

kinahî كِناهی (ZF3) = shortness. See **kinayî**.

kinatî كِناتی (ZF3) = shortness. See **kinayî**.

kinayî كِـنـايـی *f.* **(-ya;).** shortness. {also: kinahî (ZF3-2); kinatî (ZF3-2); kinî (IFb); *kinnî (A)} {syn: kurtayî} [B/ZF3//A//IFb] <kin>

k'inc كِـنـج *m.* **(-ê;).** clothing, clothes; dress; linens: **-k'incê xwe danîn** (Ad) to get undressed, take off one's clothes; **-k'incê xwe guhastin** = to disguise o.s.: **•Padşa û wezîr *k'incguhastî* hatin mala pîrê** (J) The king and his vizier went to the old woman's house *in disguise*; **-k'incê xwe li xwe kirin** (JB3) to get dressed, put one's clothes on. {also: [kindj] كنج (JJ); <kinc> كـنـج (HH)} {syn: bûsat [1]; cil I; ç'ek; libs} M. Schwartz: < O Ir *kanzu- --> *kanju-; unless a metathesis of *kazn- [cf. *ganza- (<*gazna-) --> *ganja-]; *or* √*kanz- < [Pok. 1. kenk- 565.] 'to gird, bind': Lat cingo = 'to gird': Skt kañcuka- *m./f./n.* = 'dress fitting close to upper part of body; armor, mail' (possibly borrowed from Ir); Khotanese Saka kangā = 'skin, hide'; Khwarezmian knc(y)k = 'skin (of snake); shirt, garment'; Parthian qnjwg = 'coat (?)' (Boyce); cf. also Gr kandys κάνδυς *m.* = 'Median cloak with sleeves' (< Iranian form *kanə/zu- ?). See M. Schwartz' review of H. W. Bailey. "Indo-Scythian Studies," in: *JAOS*, 89, ii (1969), 447; H. W. Bailey. "Saka Miscellany," in: *Indo-Iranica : Mélanges présentés à Georg Morgenstierne à l'occasion de son soixante-dixième anniversaire* (Wiesbaden : Otto Harrassowitz, 1964), pp.10-11. [Ad/Ag/F/K/A/JB3/IF/B/JJ/HH] <dilqe>

k'incdirû كِـنـجـدِروو *m.* **().** tailor: **•Ewî xwe bi *k'incdrûr̄a* gihîand, k'incê xas ji xwer̄a da drûtinê** (FK-eb-1) He betook himself to *the tailor*, had a special garb made for himself. {also: k'incdrû (FK-eb-1)} {syn: cildirû; xeyat; t'erzî} [FK-eb-1//K/B] <dirûtin>

k'incdrû كِنجدروو (FK-eb-1) = tailor. See **k'incdirû**.

k'indik كِندِك (K) = one-year-old calf. See **k'endik**.

k'indir كِـنـدِر *m./f.(Z-2)* **(-ê/ ; /-ê).** 1) hemp (K/B/JJ/IF/A); 2) rope (K/IF/A): **•Dîsa Şêx, avêtibûn** [sic] ***kindirê* sêpê da** (Ah) Once again they hanged [lit. 'threw'] the sheikh on the gallows *rope* **•Min *kindir* li nava wî girêda û ew bera binê bîrê da** (ZZ-10, 149) I tied *the rope* around his waist and let him down into the well; **-şirît û k'indîr** (Z-2) rope and twine. {also: k'indîr, f. (Z-2); [kändīr] كـنـديـر (JJ)} Sor kindir كِـنـدِر; Za kendir = 'rope' (Todd); Cf. T kendir = 'hemp'--> Rus kendyr' кендырь [Z-2/JJ//K/A/IFb/B/ZF] <kap I; qirnap; şerît; werîs>

k'indîr كِنديرِ, f. (Z-2) = hemp; rope. See **k'indir**.

kinêr كِـنـێـر *f.* **(;-ê).** mahaleb cherry tree, St. Lucie cherry, bot. *Prunus mahaleb: sticks and cigarette mouthpieces are made from its wood, and fences are made from its thorns* (Bw); **-dara kinêrê** (Zeb) do. {also: kenêr (A/IFb-2/GF-2); [k̲enír] كنر (JJ); <kinêr> كنير (HH); <kinêr> كنێر (Hej)} Sor kinêr كِنێر/kenêre کەنێرە = 'melilot' [Zeb/Bw/IFb/HH/GF/TF/OK/AA/Wkt//A//JJ] <çilak>

kinêre كِنێرە (IFb) = bird's foot trefoil. See **kinêrok**.

kinêrok كِـنـێـرۆك *f.* **().** bird's foot trefoil, babies'-slippers, bot. *Lotus corniculatus* [Ar qarn al-γazāl قرن الـغـزال]. {also: kinêre (IFb-2)} [Zeb/IFb/GF/OK/AA/FS]

kinga كِنگا (Ad/GF) = when. See **k'engî**.

kingî كِنگى (Ag) = when. See **k'engî**.

kinî كِنى (IFb) = shortness. See **kinayî**.

kinîşt I كِنيشت *f.* **(-a;-ê).** synagogue: **•Cuhî li şembîya diçin *kinîştê*** (FS) Jews go to *synagogue* on Saturday **•*Kinîşta* Amêdiyê yek ji kevintirîn *kinîştên* Kurdistanê bû** (Wkp:Cihûtî) The *synagogue* of Amadiah was one of the oldest *synagogues* in Kurdistan **•S̲ubey zû S̲adiq Beg deh pez̲êt qelew înan, do xulam bê çek digel xo birin, çû ber derê *kinîştê*, r̄awesta** (SK 26:238) Early next morning Sadiq Beg brought ten fat sheep, took two unarmed followers with him and went to the door of *the synagogue* and stopped. {also: kenişt (K[s]); kenişte (IFb)/k'enişte (A);*kenîst (GF); kinîşte (FS)} < Arc knīštā כנישתא & Syr knūštā ܟܢܘܫܬܐ = 'congregation, synagogue' & Jewish NENA kništa (Sabar: Dict/Garbell/Brauer); Cf. Ar kanīs كـنـيـس; Sor kenişt کـەنِـشـت/kenişte کـەنِـشـتـە [SK//K(s)//A/IFb//FS//*GF] <malim>

kinîşte كِنيشته (FS) = synagogue. See **kinîşt I**.

*kinnî كِنّى (A) = shortness. See **kinayî**.

k'inoşe كِنۆشە *f.* **().** broom. {also: kinûşe (Bt); kinûşik (JB3/Twn); <kinoşe> كـنـوشـه (HH)} {syn: avlêk; cerîvk (Bw); gêzî; melk'es; sirge (Ad); siqavêl; sivnik; şicing (Krs); sizik; şirt I} <NENA kânüshtâ ܟܢܘܫܬܐ = 'broom' (Maclean): cf. Arc knaš כנש & Syr √k-n-š ܟܢܫ = 'to gather, to sweep', also knāštā ܟܢܫܬܐ = 'sweepings, rubbish'; cf. also Ar kannasa II كنّس = 'to sweep' & miknasah مكنسة = 'broom' [A/IFb/HH/ZF3//Bt//JB3/Twn] <gêzî; maliştin>

kinûşe كِنووشە (Bt) = broom. See **k'inoşe**.

kinûşik كِنووشِك (JB3/Twn) = broom. See **k'inoşe**.

kir I كِـر *f.* **(-a;).** grudge, rancor: **-kira *fk-ê* lê danîn** (Msr) to vent one's spleen, get one's revenge: **•*Kira* min *lê danî*** (Msr) I *had* my *fill* [of beating s.o. up] **•*Kira* min *lê dananî*** [=***daneanî***] (Msr) I *didn't have* my *fill* of it **•Wî *kira* xwe *lê danî*** (Msr) He *got enough* [to drink]/He quenched his thirst. [Msr/ZF3] <t'êr I>

k'ir̄ II كِـر *m.* **(-ê;).** 1) excitement: **-k'ir̄ê kesekî anîn/r̄akirin** (K) to excite s.o.; **•*K'ir̄ê* min *hat*** (K) = a) I *was excited*; b) I was irritated; 2) irritation: **-k'etin k'ir̄ê kesekî** (K/B) to pester, tease, irritate s.o.; 3) predilection, weakness (for). [K/B]

k'ira کِرا, f. (;-ê/k'irê) (B) = rent. See **k'irê**.

k'irab کِـــراب (HB/HH) = land plowed once. See **k'irêbe**.

kiras کِـــراس *m.* **(-ê; kirês, vî kirasî).** 1) {syn: îşlik; qemîs; qutik I} shirt: **•Aqû p'êxember *wî kirasî* nêzîkî ç'avê xwe dike** (Ba-1, #37) Jacob the prophet brings *this shirt* close to his eyes; **-Kirasê Ûsib** (Ba) Joseph's shirt (of many colors): **•Wî çaxî ji t'êřekê *kirasê* Ûsib derdik'eve, Bênams *kirês* hildide, dide bavê** (Ba-1, #37) Then Joseph's *shirt* comes out of the sack, and Benams [=Benjamin] takes *the shirt* and gives it to [his] father; 2) dress, woman's garment, *with long sleeves [lewendî] tied in back*; 3 {syn: cil [3]} menstruation, woman's period (K/B): **-kirashatin** = do. {also: [kiras] کـــــراس (JJ); <kiras> کـراس (HH)} < *kirwas <Proto Ir *kṛpa-pāθra- (A&L, p. 82 [I.2] &86 [VII]); *for illustration of 2) dress, see Kmc-11, page 1, #19* [Ba/F/K/A/JB3/IFb/B/JJ/HH/JB1-S/SK/GF/TF/OK/RZ/Kmc-11/Frq/Hk]

kirde کِـــرده *f.* **(-ya;-yê).** grammatical subject: **•Bi vî awayî di hevokê de *kirde* û bireser ji hev cuda dibin** (TaRK, 90) In this way, *the subject* and object are kept separate in the sentence **•Di hevoka "Ew nanî dixwe" de "ew" *kirde* ye, "nanî" bireser e û "dixwe" lêker e** (Wkt) In the sentence "He eats the bread", "he" is *the subject*, "the bread" is the object and "eats" is the verb. Sor kirde کِـــرده = 'work, performance; doing' [TaRK/Wkt/ZF3] <bireser>

kiret کِرەت (F) = ugly. See **k'irêt**.

k'irê کِـرێ *f.* **(-ya;).** rent, lease, hire: **•Mal ji wan řa gelek teng e, lê çi bikin, *kirêya* malên fireh p'iř buha ye** (DZK) The house is too small [lit. 'narrow'] for them, but what can they do? *The rent* on bigger [lit. 'wide'] houses is very expensive; **-bi k'irê girtin** (SK) to hire, rent; **-k'irê dan** (K)/ **k'ira dayîn** (B) to rent out (said of the landlord) ; **-k'irê kirin** (K/IF)/**k'ira kirin/ hildan** (B) to rent, lease (said of the tenant). {also: k'ira, f. (;-ê/k'irê) (B); [kiri] کری (JJ); <kirê> کری (HH)} <Ar kirā' کـراء = 'rent, hire, lease'--> T kira; Sor kirê کِرێ; also from Ar is P kerāye کرایه [DZK/F/K/A/IF/HH/SK//B//JJ]

k'irêb کِرێب (A/OK) = fallow land. See **k'irêbe**.

k'irêbe کِرێبه *f.* **().** 1) land plowed once (Qzl/Kmc-8); field, plowable land (HB); land that has been tilled once (HH): **-erdê kirêb** (Kmc-#2923) field plowed once; **-kilab/kilêb kirin** (IFb) to turn soil over with a spade or fork: **•Hinek ji cotyaran nîsk û nok diçandin, hinan gindor û zebeş, hinan jê şovên *kilabkirî* dugêsin dikirin** (DBgb, 7) Some farmers planted lentils and chickpeas, some planted melons & watermelons, some of them plowed for a second time *once-plowed* furrows; 2) fallow land (A/IFb/OK/ZF3). {also: kilêb (IFb); k'irab (HB/HH); k'irêb (A/OK/Kmc-#2923); <kirab> کـراب (HH)} <Arc √k-r-b: krav כרב = 'to plow' & krāvā כרבא = 'plowing' & karviṯā כרביתא = 'like a plowed field'; Syr krābā ܟܪܒܐ = 'plowing, tilling, fallow ground, furrow'; NENA krîwâ ܟܪܒܐ = 'furrow, fallow ground' (Maclean); Ar √ k-r-b کـــرب = 'to plow (the ground) before (sowing)' & Iraqi clq Ar kirab کرب = 'to plow, till' [Qzl//HB/HH//A/OK/Kmc-#2923/ZF3//IFb//DBgb] <beyar; bor III; kat II; k'ewşan; zevî>

k'irêt کِرێت *adj.* 1) {syn: bi'ok; genî (Çnr); sêfîl [4]; sik I} ugly; repulsive, disgusting; hateful, horrible, bad: **•Lalî Xan qewî zêde *kirête*** (JR) Lali Khan [a young girl] is extremely *ugly*; 2) dirty, filthy (IF). {also: kiret (F); [kirit] کـريـت (JJ); <kirêt> کـريـت (HH)} {k'irêtî} [JR/K/IFb/JB3/JJ/HH/SK/GF/TF/Bw/FS]

k'irêtî کِرێتی *f.* **(-ya;-yê).** 1) ugliness; repulsiveness: **•Ji ber ku *kirêtiya* şer nayê zanîn** (SF 25) Because *the ugliness of* war is not known; 2) ugly or unjust action or deed: **•Bi dû vê *kirêtiyê* jî, dijminê Kurdan navê Kurd û Kurdistanê ji defteran derxistin û welat kirin wêran** (M.Uzun. Roja Evd.Zeyn., 10) After this *unjust deed*, the enemy of the Kurds removed the name of the Kurds and Kurdistan from the registers and turned the country into a shambles. [K/IFb/JB3/SK/GF/TF/ZF] <k'irêt>

Kirgîzî کِرگیزی (BF) = Kirghiz. See **Qirgizî**.

k'irgûd کِـرگـوود *f.(B/ZF3)/m.(JB3)* **(;-ê/).** sulphur/ sulfur. {also: gogird (K[s]/A); kewkurd (IFb-2); kewkurt, m. (JB3); k'irgût (B); k'irk'ût (K)/ k'irkût (EP-7); kukurd (IFb); [koughir کــوگــر/ kigourt کــيــگــورت] (JJ)} O Ir *gaukṛta-: Mid P gōgird (M3); Sgd γōkt; P gūgerd گــوگـــرد --> T kükürt; ; Sor gogird گۆگرد/gogirt گۆگرت; cf. also Ar kibrīt کـبـريـت [for which see **k'irpît**]. See: M. Schwartz. "Pers. *Saugand Xurdan*, etc. 'to Take an

Oath' (Not *'to Drink Sulphur')," in: *Études Irano-Aryennes offertes à Gilbert Lazard* (Paris : Association pour l'avancement des études iraniennes, 1989), pp. 293-95. [F/ZF3//K//A//JB3//IF//JJ//BB] <k'irpît>

k'irgût کِرگووت (B) = sulphur. See **k'irgûd**.

kirim کِرم (BF) = worm. See **kurm**.

kirin I کـرن *vt.* **(-k-/-ke-** [Bw/M/SK/Hk]**).** 1) to make, do; *{used in conjunction with a noun, adjective, adverb, or preposition to form compound verbs, e.g.,* ***ber hev [berev] kirin*** *= to collect, gather}*: **-xwe kirin** = to turn into: **•Mḧemmed Xan** ***xwe kirîye*** **keraş û jina xwe jî kirîye dorçî** (L) M. Khan *turned himself into* a miller, and his wife into a customer; 2) {syn: danîn} to put, place: **•Bavê xwe li pişta xwe** ***kir*** (L) He *put* his father on his back [to carry him across a stream] **•Çiqa kevanya malê dew dik'ila r̄ûn** ***dikire*** **k'ûpekî** (Dz-anec #32) Whenever the lady of the house churned dew (=yoghurt and water), she *would put it in* a clay jar **•Ewî mirovî çi kir, dest da marî,** ***kire*** **di cendikê da** (M-Ak, #544) What did the man do but lay hold of the snake and *put it* in his bag; **-jê kirin** = to remove, take off: **•Çel kevok hatine û perîyê xwe** ***ji*** **xwe** ***kirin*** (L) 40 doves came and *took off* their feathers (plumage); **-lê kirin** = to put on *(clothes)*: **•Libsê xwe** ***li*** **xwe** ***kir*** (L) [They] *put* [their] clothes *on*/[They] got dressed; 3) [+ *subj.*] to intend to, be about to: **•R̄ojekê gundîk r̄adibe** ***dike*** **her̄e cem xwedê** (Dz) One day a villager decided to go see God [lit. 'gets up and *is about to* go to God'] **•Qîzê** ***dikir*** **wî kur̄î bikuje** (EP-7) The girl *was going to* kill this child **•Bek'o go: Mîr, Memoyî kur̄îne,/** ***Dike*** **mîr û cindîyava bixapîne** (Z-1) Beko said, Prince, Memo the boy/ *intends to* trick the prince and [his] nobles. {also: [kirin] کـریـن (JJ); <kirin کرن (dike) (دکه)> (HH)} [Pok. 1. k$^{\underline{u}}$er- 641.] 'to make, form': Skt kṛ-, pres. kṛṇōti = 'he makes'; O Ir *kar- (Tsb 38): Av kərənaoiti = 'he makes'; OP kar- = 'to do, make, build' (Kent); P kardan کردن (-kon-) (کن); Sor kirdin کِردِن (-ke-; *3rd pers. sing.* -ka-); SoK kirdin: ka-/kird- (Fat 357, 539); Za kenã [kerdiş] (Todd/Srk); Hau kerdey (ker-) *vt.* (M4) [F/K/A/JB3/IF/B/JJ/HH/ZF3/FS]

k'irin II کِرن (Bw) = tick. See **qirnî**.

kiritandin کِرتاندِن (A) = to gobble up. See **keritandin**.

k'irîb کِریب = godfather; Yezidi; Christian. See **kirîv**.

k'irîbtî کِریبتی (K) = godfatherhood. See **kirîvtî**.

kirîfok کِریفۆک (AA) = type of wild bee. See **kur̄îfok**.

k'ir̄în کـریـن *vt.* **(-k'ir̄-).** to buy, purchase: **•Emê pê ji xwe re tişkî** [=**tiştekî**] ***bikirin*** (L) We *will buy* something for ourselves with it. {also: [kerin] کرین (JJ)} {syn: standin [3]} [Pok. k$^{\underline{u}}$rei- 648.] 'to buy': Skt krīṇāti = 'he buys': O Ir *xrīn- (Tsb 44 & M2, p.71): OP *xrīn-, *xṛ-na-tiy; P xarīdan خریدن; Sor kir̄în کِرین; Za (h)erînenã [(h)erînayiş] (Todd/Srk) [F/K/A/JB3/IFb/B/JJ/JB1-A&S/GF/OK] <bik'ir̄çî>

kirîsk کِریسک (IFb/OK/ZF3/FS) = cricket. See **kirîstik**.

kirîst•ik کِـریـسـتِـک *f.* **(•ka;).** cricket, zool. *Gryllidae*. {also: kirîsk (IFb/OK)} [Zeb//IFb/OK/ZF3/FS] <kulî I; sîsirk>

kirîv/k'irîv [K/A/B] کِـریـڤ *m.* **(-ê;).** 1) godfather, the man who holds a male child who is being circumcised (a fictive kinship relationship); *according to Sedat Veyis Örnek, this phenomenon is known in Turkey south of an imaginary line drawn between Kars and Sivas, and east of one drawn between Sivas and Mersin [roughly the area of Kurdistan]: it is virtually unknown to the west and north of this area* [see his *Türk Halkbilimi* (Ankara : Ajans-Türk Matbaası, 1977), p. 183]: **•*Kirîv*** **di şîn û şahiyan de bi ser hev de diçin û tên, di siqûmat û serpêhatîyên xirab de alîkarîya hev dikin** (Wkp: Kirîvatî) *Kirîvs* [fictive kin/ godparents, etc.] come and go in times of sorrow and joy, they help one another in disasters and bad episodes **•Li devera me Sêmêlê her kesê mirov zaroyê xwe di danga wî de sunet bikit dibite** ***kirîvê*** **mala wî zarokî û viyan di navbera wan de peyda dibit** (Sêmêl-Ertoşî) In our region of Sêmêl, anyone in whose lap a [male] child is circumcised becomes the *kirîv* [± godfather] of that child's household, and good will reigns between them; **-kirîv û sanik** (ZF3) (*approximately*) godfather and godson; 2) *nickname for various religious minorities*: a) Yezidi (Zx); b) Christian [=Armenian or Assyrian/Chaldean] (HH). {also: k'irîb; [qiriw] قـریـڤ (JJ); <kirîv کـریـڤ/kirîva کـریـڤـا> (HH)} <Arc ḳarev קריב = 'near, related': NENA qūrîwâ ܩܘܪܒܐ = 'godfather, sponsor' (Maclean) --> T kirve/kivre; [cf. Ar 'arrāb عـرّاب] A curious thing about **kirîv** is the initial **k-** rather than the expected **q-**: of the Kurdish sources, only JJ gives a form with [q]. For another example of initial **k-** substituting for **q-**, see **qirnî/k'irnî**. {k'irîbtî; k'irîvatî; k'irîvî; k'irîvtî} [BX/K/A/IF/B//HH/

/JJ] <sanîk>

kirîvatî [FS]/k'irîvatî [K] کِـــریـــڤـــاتـــی (K/FS) = godfatherhood. See **kirîvtî**.

k'irîvî کِریڤی (A) = godfatherhood. See **kirîvtî**.

kirîvtî کِـــریـــڤـــتـــی *f.* **(-ya;-yê).** relationship of fictive kinship, analogous to Spanish *compadrazgo* ('godfather-hood'), between a boy and the man who holds him while he is being circumcised: •***Kirîvatîya* wan ji mêje ye** (FS) Their *kirîv[a]tî* is of long standing. {also: k'irîbtî (K-2); kirîvatî (FS)/k'irîvatî (K-2); k'irîvî (A)} [K/IF/ZF3//FS//A] <kirîv>

kiȓkiȓk کِـــرکِـــرك *f.(B/F)/m.(K)* **(-a/;-ê/).** cartilage, gristle. {also: kirkirîtk, f. (F); kirtik (IF); *kirtirte [=kirkirte?] (A)} Cf. P karkarānak کـــرکـــرانـــك (Steingass); Sor kirkiroçke کِرکِرۆچکە [K/B/FS//F//IF//A] <hestî>

kirkirîtk کِرکِریتك, f. (F) = cartilage. See **kiȓkiȓk**.

*kirkirte کِرکِرتە (A) = cartilage. See **kiȓkiȓk**.

k'irk'ût کِـــرکـــووت (K)/k'irkût (EP-7) = sulphur. See **k'irgûd**.

kirm کِرم (FS/Wkt) = worm. See **kurm**.

Kirmanc کِـــرمـــانـــج (K[s]) = Kurd; peasant. See **Kurmanc**.

kirmî کِرمی (Wkt/HH) = wormy; rotten. See **kurmî**.

kirnî کِرنـی (HH)/k'irnî (Bw)/kiȓnî کِرنـی (FS) = tick. See **qirnî**.

kirosik کِرۆسِك *m./f.(ZK3/FS)* **(-ê/;).** type of wild pear [T ahlat]. {also: girsik (Hk/Kmc); kirosk (IFb/FJ/AA/FS); kirostik (ZF3-2); klostik (Urm); <girsik گـرسـك/girosik گـرۆسـك/kirosik كـرۆسـك> (Hej)} {syn: şekok} Sor kirosk کِـرۆسـك = 'wild pear' [Urm//Slm/Hej//IFb/FJ/AA/FS//ZF3//Hk/Kmc] <alîsork; hermê; karçîn; şitû>

kirosk کِـــرۆســـك (IFb/FJ/AA/FS) = wild pear. See **kirosik**.

kirostik کِرۆستِك (ZF3) = wild pear. See **kirosik**.

kirov•e کِرۆڤە/**kiȓov•e** کِرۆڤە [FS] *f.* **(•a;•ê).** 1) {syn: dûman; mij; moran} mist, fog: **-mij û kirove** (Zeb) mist, fog: •***Mij û kirovê* qubêt bilind nixaftin** (Zeb) *Mist and fog* covered the high peaks; 2) blizzard, snowstorm with wind (Bw->Barzanî, Dolemerî, Surçî/FS). {also: <kiruve کروڤە/kirêve کریڤە> (Hej)} Sor kiȓêwe کِرێوە = 'blizzard' [Zeb/Bw//FS//Hej]

k'irpît کِـــرپـــیـــت *f.* **(-a;-ê).** 1) {syn: neft[ik]; pitik I} match(es) *(for lighting fire)*; 2) {syn: k'irgûd} sulphur: •**Vêga ezê vî bajarî ezê bi *k'ufritê* şewitênim** (HR 3:216) Then I will burn up this city with *sulphur*. {also: kebrît (F); k'ibrît (K/B); kifrît (JB3/IFb); k'ufrît (HR); [kirbit] کـربـت (JJ); <kifrît> کـفـریـت (HH)} < Ar kibrīt کـبـریـت or Arc kabrīṯā/kovrīṯā כבריתא & Syr kevrītā/kavrītā ܟܒܪܝܬܐ: Sor kibrît کِبریت/kifrît کِفریت = 'sulphur match'; Za kirbît *m.* (Mal) [Ag//JJ//F//K/B//JB3/IFb/HH//HR] <agir; cigare; k'irgûd; qelûn>

kirsî کِرسی (BX) = chair. See **k'ursî**.

kirtik کِرتِك (IF) = cartilage. See **kiȓkiȓk**.

kirûng کِروونگ *f.* **().** 1) Armenian woman (Mzg); 2) prostitute (Wkt). {syn: kîlo I} [Mzg/Wkt]

K'irwatî کِرواتی *adj.* Croatian. {also: Kroatî (Wkp-2); Xirvatkî (ZF3); Xirwatî (Wkt/Wkp)} Sor Kirwatî کِرواتی [BF//Wkt/Wkp//ZF3]

kiryar کِـــریـــار *f.* **(-a;-ê).** act, action, deed; operation; process: •**Hizar gotin gorî *kiryarekê* bin** (BF) 1,000 words are a sacrifice to *one deed*, i.e., Actions speak louder than words. {also: [keriára] کـریـار (JJ-G); <kiryar> کـریـار (Hej)} P kardār کـردار = 'action, deed'; Sor kirdar کِـردار [VoA/K(s)/IFb/JJ-G/GF/Hej/ZF3/BF]

kirzin کِرزِن (Bw) = vetch. See **kizin**.

kisil کِسِل (IFb/JJ/Zeb) = lime, chalk. See **k'ils**.

kisix کِسِخ (FJ) = shallot. See **k'ixs**.

kisk کِسك (Dh) = crackling, bits of sheep fat. See **kizik**.

k'iş کِـش *f.* **(-a;).** 1) chessboard and chessmen (EP-7): **-k'iş û berk'iş** (ZF3) attack and counter-attack (in chess); **-k'iş û berk'iş kirin** (XF) to assiduously attack s.o.; 2) word used by chess player when defending his bishop {ilá tanḥiyat fīlih إلـى تـنـحـيـة فـيـلـه} (HH); warning when the king (or another piece) is in check (in the game of chess). {also: <kiş> کـــش (HH)} [EP-7/A/IF/HH/ZF3/FS] <k'işik; t'exte>

k'işandin کِـشـانـدِن *vt.* **(-k'işîn-).** 1) {also: k'êşan} to pull, drag, draw: •**B. şwîrê xwe *kişand*** (L) B. *drew* his sword •**Halet û gîsinan li pey xwe xweş *dikêşin*** (AB) They (=the oxen) *drag* the plow and plowshares along behind them •**Şivek *kişand* namila dê** (J) He *pulled* a stick [=*held* a stick] over his mother's shoulder ; **-dest ji *ft-î* kişandin** = to leave, abandon, give up, renounce {syn: dev jê berdan; qeran; hiştin; t'erkandin}: •**...Şîret li Memê dikirin, wekî Memê destê xwe *ji* vê yekê *bik'şîne*** (Z-1) They advised Mem *to renounce* this [his plan]; 2) to take *(photographs with a camera)*: **-wêne k'işandin** (ZF3) do.; 3) {syn:

vexwarin} to smoke *(cigarettes)*: •***Nak'işînim*** = I *don't smoke*; 4) to breathe, inhale: •**Şivan xweȓa nava kulîlkada digeȓin, bîna hewa ç'îyaye t'emiz *dik'işînin*** (Ba2:1, 203) Shepherds roam among the flowers, *breathing in* pure mountain air; 5) to weigh *(vt.)*: •**Dikandarî mêwîj bi şehînê *kêşan*** (FS) The shopkeeper *weighed* the raisins on the scales •**Wî sêv bi teraziyê *kêşan*** (FS) He *weighed* the apples on the scale; 6) {syn: ajotin; dirêj kirin[c]; domîn; k'udandin; vek'işîn[2]} to take time, last: •**Xeberdana me gele wext *k'işand*, lê t'u deng û bas ji lawika nedihat** (Ba2-#2, 205) Our conversation *lasted* a long time, but there was not a sound to be heard from the boys; 7) to endure, bear, stand, suffer: •**De xwedê hebînî yanê ne ez bim kî kane vî derdî *bikşîne*?** (LC, 12) For God's sake, if not for me, who can *stand* this trouble? •**Quretîya wî nema *tê kêşan*** (glosbe.com) His arrogance *can* no longer *be endured*; 8) to conjugate *(verbs)*: •***Kişandina* lêkeran** (Kmc) verb *conjugation*. {also: k'êşan (A/IF/JB1-S/M); [kichandin] كشاندين (JJ); <kişandin كشاندن (dikişîne) (دكشينه)>(HH)} [Pok. I. k^{u}el-/k^{u}elə- 639.] 'to revolve, move around, sojourn, dwell' (+ -s- amplification): Skt kṛṣáti/ kárṣati = 'he pulls, plows' & karṣ´ū *f.* = 'furrow'; O Ir *karš- (Tsb 39): Av karš- (pres. karəša-/karšaya-) = 'he drags, plows' & karša- *m./n.* = 'furrow'; Mid P kešīdan (M3); P kašīdan كشيدن = 'to pull'; Sor kêşan كيشان (-kêş-) = 'to pull, drag, attract; smoke; suffer'; Hau kêşay (kêş-) *vt.* (M4) [K/A/JB3/IF/JJ/B/HH] <k'êşîn; k'işîn>

k'işik كِشِك *pl./f.(B/FS)* **(; /-ê).** 1) {syn: şetrenc; şaxmat} chess: •**Wan du destên *kişikê* kirin** (FS) They played two rounds *of chess*; **-k'işik lîstin** = to play chess or checkers; 2) {syn: dame} checkers (K). {also: [kichik] كشك (JJ)} [Z-1/K/JJ/B/FJ/ZK3/FS] <ferzîn = 'queen'; fêris = 'knight' (Z-1); fîl = 'bishop'; k'erkedan = ?'knight'; peyak = 'pawn'; ȓex II = 'castle, rook'>

k'işîn كشين *vi.* **(-k'iş-).** 1) to be pulled, dragged; to pull; 2) {syn: herikîn} to flow *(water)*: •**Ji wan cewika hinek ... hêdîka nava çayîra ȓa *dik'işyan*** (Ba2:1, 202) Some of those brooks ... slowly *meandered* through the meadows •**Li kanîyê av *dikişe*** (BX) Water *flows* from the spring; 3) to rise, pour out (smoke): •**Daqul bû, nerî go devê miẍarakê xwîya ye; ew dixan ji miẍarê *dikişe*** (L-1 #3, l.14-15, 46) He bent down, and saw that the cave's mouth was visible; the smoke *was coming from* the cave; 4) to creep, crawl: •**Xar e, ne dar e / Dimike, ne kar e / *Dik'şe*, ne me'r e / Ew çiye?** [Av] (Z-1702) It's crooked, it's not a tree / It bleats, it's not a kid / It *creeps*, it's not a snake / What is it? *[rdl.; ans.: water]*. Cf. P kašīdan كشيدن = 'to pull' [BX/K/B/IFb] See also **k'êşîn**. <k'işandin>

kişmiş كِشمِش (IFb/GF/TF/OK/FS) = currant(s); raisin(s). See **k'işmîş**.

k'işmîş كِشميش *m.(F/K)/f.(B)* **(;-î/-ê).** 1) {syn: mewîj} raisin(s); seedless raisins, *as opposed to* ***mewîj*** *[raisins with seeds]* (Ag/GF): •**Cêva xwe t'ijî çerez dikir, *k'şmîş*, noqit** (HCK-2, 181) He filled his pockets with snacks, *raisins*, chick peas; 2) currant(s) (IFb); 3) sultanas, type of tiny, black seedless grape. {also: kişmiş (IFb/GF/OK/FS); k'îşmîş (Tkm); k'şmîş (HCK)} Cf. P kešmeš كشمش = 'raisins, currants'; Sor kişmîş كِشميش = 'sultana raisin' [K/B/F/ZF3/Wkt//Tkm//IFb/GF/TF/OK/FS//HCK] <mewîj; tirî>

kişnîş كِشنيش (TF) = coriander. See **gijnîj**.

k'işwer كِشوەر, m. (K)/kişwer (FJ/GF/CS/ZF3) = continent; kingdom. See **k'îşwer**.

kit/k'it [A] كِت *f.* **(-a;).** one *(of a pair)*, *counting word for paired things (e.g., shoes)* (K/B): •***kita* pêlavê** (FS) *a single* shoe •***Kita* sêva bi darê ve nemane** (FS) *A single* apple was not left on the tree •[***kitek* tepançe**] (JR) *one* pistol. {also: <kit> كت (HH)} {syn: fer I; t'ek[1]} cf. P tak تك = 'sole, single' --> T tek [JR/K/Ba4/PS/B/HH/ZF3/FS//A] <cot; ȟeb [3]; lib>

k'itan كِتان *f./m.(ZF3)* **(;-ê/).** 1) flax; 2) {syn: caw} linen; 3) married women's head covering made of flax, *as opposed to the silk* ***ȟibrî*** *worn by unmarried girls*: •***Kitan*, jin pê porê xwe vedişêrin. Şarê jî li ser *kitanê* girêdidin û didin ber enîya xwe** (xalko.ezkime.com 30.i.2017) *Kitan*, women hide their hair under it. They tie a shar [scarf] over *the kitan* and apply it to their foreheads. {also: [kitan] كتان (JJ)} < Ar kattān/ kittān كتّان = 'flax, linen'--> T keten [Qzl/Elk/Krş/K/A/IFb/B/JJ/GF/TF/OK/ZF3/Wkt] <hêratî; ȟibrî; laç'ik; t'emezî; terȟî>

kite كته (Wkt/FJ/GF/FS) = syllable. See **k'îte**.

k'itêb كِتيب *f.* **(-a;-ê).** book. {also: k'itêv; k'têb; k'têv; [kitib] كتب (JJ); <kitêb> كتيب (HH)} {syn: nivîsk;

p'irtûk} < Ar kitāb كـتـاب --> P ketāb كـتـاب & T kitap; Sor kitêb كِـتـێـب; Hau kitêb *m.* (M4) [K/JB3/IFb/B/HH/SK/GF/ZF3]

k'itêbxan•e كِـتـێـبـخـانـه *f.* **(•eya;•ê).** library. {also: [koutoub-khané] كتبخانه (JJ)} {syn: p'irtûkxane} Cf. P kitābxāne كتابخانه; Sor kitêbxane كِتێبخانه [K/B/IFb/GF/JJ/FJ/CS/ZF3/Wkt]

k'itêbxanevan كِتێبخانەڤان *m.&f.* **().** librarian. [ZF3/Wkt/SS]

k'itêv كِتێڤ = book. See **k'itêb**.

kit•ik I كِـتِـك *f.* **(•ka;).** dried fruit, esply. dried figs: **-kitka helîkê** (Bw) dried plums; **-kitka hêjîrê** (Bw/FS) dried figs. {also: ketik (GF/OK/Zeb/FS-2)} [Bw/FS//GF/OK/Zeb] <çîr; hejîr; kaçkaçk>

k'it•ik II كِـتِـك *f./m&f.(OK)* **(•ka/•kê;).** cat; small cat (HH): **•*Kitik* ne li mal e navê mişk Evdirehman e** (ZF3) = When *the cat*'s away the mice will play *[prv.]*; **-k'itka mê** (OK) female cat; **-k'itkê nêr** (OK) male cat, tomcat. {also: k'êtik (Bw/FS-2); kittik (GF); [qitik/kiték (G)/kitték (PS)] قطك (JJ); <kitik> كتك (HH)} {syn: p'isîk} cf. Ar qiṭṭ قِط; Sor kitik كِتِك; Hau kite f. (M4) [JR/K(s)/A/IFb/HH/SK/OK/Czr/Prw/ZF3/FS//Bw//GF//JJ]

kitle كتله (Wkt) = the masses. See **kîtle**.

kitm كِـتـم *adj.* unregistered, lacking identification papers: **•Li gelek bajarên Tirkiyeyê yên mezin û yên Kurdistanê, kesên wek hilbijêrên DEP'ê tên qebûlkirin bêqeydin. Navên wan di lîsteya hilbijêran de nîn in, *kitm* in** (Wlt 2:101, 8) In many large cities in Turkey and Kurdistan, people who are identified as [potentially] voting for DEP [=Democratic Worker's Party] are unregistered. Their names do not appear in the voter roster, they are *unregistered.* {also: <kitm> كتم (Hej)} [Wlt/Hej/ZF3]

kittik كِتِك (GF) = cat. See **k'itik II**.

kivark كِڤارك (OK) = mushroom. See **kiyark**.

k'ivav كِڤاڤ (Dz) = shish-kebab. See **k'ebab**.

kivî *m.(FS)/f.(ZF3)* كِـڤـى **(-yê/;).** earthenware jar with narrow mouth: **•Rûn û toraq, di *kivîyan* de tên parastin** (Wkt) Oil and toraq [strained yoghurt] are kept in *jars*; **-kivîyê rûnî** (FS) oil pitcher. {also: <kivî> كڤى (HH)} [Kmc#30/A/IFb/FJ/GF/HH/FS/Wkt] <kûp; k'ûz II>

k'ivş كِڤش (K/B/Z-1) = evident, obvious. See **k'ifş**.

k'ivşayî كِڤشايى (B) = obviousness. See **k'ifşî**.

k'ivşî كِڤشى (Ba3-1) = obviousness. See **k'ifşî**.

k'iwîşk كِويشك (Bşk) = rabbit. See **k'erguh**.

kiwşî كِوشى (SK) = obviousness. See **k'ifşî**.

k'ixme كِـخـمـه, f. (K/ZF3) = woman's garment. See **k'eẍbe**.

k'ixs كِـخـس *f./m.* **(-a;).** shallot, bot. *Allium ascalonicum*. {also: kisix (FJ); kixse (IFb/Kmc-2); kixsik (Kmc-2); <kixs> كخس (HH)} [Hk/Mzr/HH/RF/Kmc-4330/ZF/FS//IFb//FJ] <pîvaz>

kixse كِخسه (IFb/Kmc) = shallot. See **k'ixs**.

kixsik كِخسِك (Kmc) = shallot. See **k'ixs**.

kiyan كِيان (-kê-) (Bw/Hej) = to churn. See **k'ilan**.

kiyark كِـيـارك *f.* **().** mushroom. {also: kivark (OK); kîvark (Prw); [kiiark كـيـارك/kivar كـوار] (JJ); <kiyarik> كيارك (HH)} {syn: gidark (Prw); karî I; karkevîk (Mş-Malazgirt); kufkarik; k'umik (A)} [Bt/JJ//HH//Prw//OK]

k'izek'iz كِزەكِز *f.* **(-a;).** sizzling, hissing, sputtering *(sound of boiling liquids)*: **•Dema ko miqilk û dohn danî ser agirî dengê qiçeqiça dohnî bi *kizekiza* kerengan re derket** (MGJiyaneka pêguhork) When she put the saucepan and the fat on the fire, the sound of the sputtering of the fat coincided with *the sizzling of* the cardoons. {also: kizkiz (FJ-2/GF-2)} {syn: k'izîn} Cf. Sor kizekiz كِزەكِز = 'sustained smarting/sharp pain' [MG/K/FJ/GF/ZF3]

kizên كِزێن (FS) = sizzling. See **k'izîn**.

kizik كِـزِك *f.(B/Ag/Dh/Qrj)/pl.(K/Qmş)* **(;-ê).** crackling, crisp bits of fat left over from sheep's fattail after it is melted down or rendered. {also: çizirik (Qrj); kisk (Dh); k'izirk (Qzl/K/A/B); kizrik (Ag); [kizik] كزك (JJ); <kizik> كزك (HH)} Sor çizlîk چِزلیك = 'dish made of fattail of sheep after most of fat has been melted down' [Ag//Qzl/K/A/B//Qmş/IFb/JJ/HH/GF/TF/ZF3/FS//Dh//Qrj]

kizin كِزِن *f.* **().** *type of vetch*, ers, kersenneh, bot. *Vicia ervilia* (IFb); black pea, black vetchling; grain similar to lentils but larger, used as animal fodder, particularly for goats. {also: kirzin (Bw); kuşne (IFb-2); kûşnê (Mzg); [kezīn] كـزيـن (JJ); <kizin كزن/kuşnî كـشـنـى> (HH)} Cf. T küşne = burçak = 'vetch, Vicia or Lathyrus' [Haz/Srk/Qzl/A/IFb/HH/ GF/TF/ZF3/Wkt//JJ/OK//Mzg//Bw] <maş; şolik>

k'izirandin (K/A/B)/kizirandin (IFb/HH/GF/TF) كِزِراندِن = to singe. See **kuzirandin**.

k'izirîn (K/B)/kizirîn (IFb/TF/HH) كِـزِريـن = to be singed. See **kuziryan**.

k'izirk كِـزِرك (Qzl/K/A/B) = crackling, bits of sheep fat. See **kizik**.

k'izîn كِـزيـن *f.* **(-a;-ê).** hissing, sizzling, sputtering (*when singeing wool, or grilling meat*): **•*K'izîna* goştê mîêye** (EH) *The sizzling of* mutton [lit. 'of the meat of the ewe']; **-k'izîn dil hatin/k'etin** (B) to feel strong pressure on the heart: **•*K'izîn* k'ete nav dilê min** (K) I felt *a strong pain* in my heart. {also: kizên (FS); kizînî (ZF3)} [EH/K/B//ZF3//FS] <k'izek'iz>

kizînî كِزینی (ZF3) = sizzling. See **k'izîn**.

kizkiz كِزكِز (FJ/GF) = sizzling sound. See **k'izek'iz**.

kizrik كِزرك (Ag) = crackling, bits of sheep fat. See **kizik**.

kizwan كِزوان (CB) = terebinth; nettle tree berry. See **kezan**.

kî/k'î [K/A/B/JB1-A&S/M-Am] کی *intrg. prn.* **(kê/k'ê** [K/B/JB1-A&S/M-Am]**).** 1) who?: **•*Kî* hat?** (FS) *Who* came? **•Te *kî* dît?** (FS) *Whom* did you see?; 2) *[rel. prn.]* he who: **•*K'î* zane -- zane, *k'î* nizane -- baqê nîskane** (Dz #18, 385) *He who* knows, knows; *he who* doesn't know [thinks it's] a handful of lentils [i.e., 'It's not as innocent as it looks'] [*prv.*]. {also: [ki] کی (JJ); <kî> کی (HH)} [Pok k^{u}o-/k^{u}e- 644.] *(relative & interrogative pronouns)*: Av kō (*gen.* ka-hyā/ča-hyā), *fem.* kā = 'who?; which?'; O P ka- (Kent); Mid P kē (M3); P kī کی; Sor kê کێ; Za kê (Todd); cf. also Lat quis (*m./f.*)-quid (*n.*) = 'who, what', qui (*m.*)-quae (*f.*)-quod (*n.*) = 'who, which, that' [K/A/JB3/IF/B/JJ/HH/ZF3/FS/Dz/JB1-A&S]

k'î derê کی دەرێ = where? See under **ku II**.

k'î dirkê کی دِرکێ (M-Am) = where? See under **ku II**.

k'îjan کیژان *intrg.* which?: **•Tu *kîjan* hespî dixwazî?** (BX) *Which* horse do you want? **•Wextê diçin e seferê ji r̄êwe diçin e-naw besta beran, çawêt xo dimiçînin, pêş paş diçin, panîya pîyê wan geheşt e *kîşk* berî dê înin, bi terazîyê kêşin çend der-kewt dê sûndekî mezin û kirêt xot ko, "Ḧetta bi-qeder giranîya wî berey pare-y zêr̄ yan zîw neînim nahêmewe"** (SK 12:117) When they go on a journey they go first of all to the vale of stones, shut their eyes, go back and forth and, *whichever* stone the heel of their foot touches, they will bring it and weigh it in a balance and, however much it turns out, they will swear a mighty and ugly oath that, "I shall not return until I bring the weight of this stone in gold or silver." {also: kîjik (OK-2); kîjk (OK-2); kîş (OK)/k'îş (JB1-A); kîşk (SK/OK-2/Bw)/k'îşk' (JB1-A-2/M-Am); [kijan كژان/kijk كژك/kij كیژ] (JJ); <kîjan> کیژان (HH)} <k'î ji wan = 'who from them/which of them' [BX/K/JB3/IF/JJ/B/HH//SK/Bw//OK//JB1-A//M-Am]

kîj کیژ (OK/Bar) = girl. See **keç**.

kîjik کیژك (OK) = which. See **k'îjan**.

kîjk کیژك (OK) = which. See **k'îjan**.

k'îler کیلەر *f.* **(-a;-ê).** pantry, larder; store room: **•Embar û *kîlerên* ku di nav zinaran de yan jî li bin erdê hatine vedan, hîn jî tên xuyakirin** (Wkt:R.Lezgîn. Cihê Rastîn Yê Eshabê Kehf vii.2008) Pantries and *larders* which were etched into the cliffs or [dug] underground, are still visible. {also: [kiler] كلر (JJ); <kîler> کیلەر (Hej)} Cf. T kiler = 'pantry, larder' < Gr kellari κελλάρι [Hk/K/B/JJ/Hej/ZF3/Wkt]

kîlîm کیلیم (IFb) = kilim, flat-weave carpet. See **k'ilîm**.

kîlo I کیلۆ *f.* **().** Assyrian or Armenian (i.e., Christian) girl {according to JJ, kaló = female calf, a nickname given to Christian and Jewish girls by Muslims}: **•[Nêzûkî kela Xoşabê dû gundêd Mexînan hen navê yekî Qesir û navê yekî Pagan. Di gundê Paganêda *kîloyeke* qewî zêde rind navê Barnîk hebûye]** (JR) Near the fortress of Hoşap there are two Nestorian villages, one named Qesir, and one named Pagan. In the village of Pagan there was a very beautiful *Assyrian girl* named Barnîk. {also: kêlok (Bw); [kilo] كلو (JJ); [...kîloyekê] کی لویکی (JR)} {syn: kirûng (Mzg)} <NENA kâlû/kilû ܟܠܘ (=kaltâ ܟܠܬܐ) = 'bride; daughter-in-law; wife of any near relation' (Maclean) [JJ/JR//Bw] <file(h); mexîn>

k'îlo II کیلۆ *f.* **(-ya;-yê).** kilo, kilogram: **•*Kîloya* vî hingivî bi 10 hezar lîreyî ye** (TRTNûçe 10.x.2015) *A kilo of* this honey is for 10,000 liras. [IFb/ZF3/Wkt/FS]

k'în کین *f.* **(-a;-ê).** malice, spite; hatred: **-bêk'în** (Z-1) without malice or hatred. {also: [kin] کین (JJ); <kîn> کین (HH)} Cf. Mid P kēn (M3); P kīn کین, T kin [Z-1/K/A/JB3/IF/JJ/B/HH/ZF3]

K'îprî کیپری (Wkp) = Cypriot. See **Qibrisî**.

kîr کیر *m.* **(-ê;).** penis: **•*Kîrê* te radibe?** (Msr) Do you have a 'hard-on' [=erection]? **•Ne min bi berxî têr şîr xwar, û ne bi kalvêjî têr *kîr* xwar** (Qzl) I neither drank my fill of milk as a lamb, nor had my fill of *penis* as an all-too-young ewe *[prv.]* **•Sofî hêdî hat e-nik ḧafiz, gûzanek di destîda, hawêt e *kîrê* ḧafiz, di binîr̄a bir̄î** (SK :684) Sofi slowly approached the hafiz with a razor in his hand, which he struck at the hafiz' *penis*, cutting it off at the base. {also: [kir] کیر

(JJ); <kîr> کـیـر (HH)} {syn: çûçik I[3] (Msr) = baby boy's; 'ewîc; hêlik [2], m. (Msr); teřik [2] (Msr); xir (Msr)} Mid P kēr (M3); P kīr کیر; Sor kêr کێر; Za kir *m.* (Mal) [A/IFb/JJ/HH/SK/GF/TF/OK] <gun; hêlik; quz; řitil II>

k'îrê کیرێ (M-Am) = where? See under **ku II**.

kîrhar کـیـرهـار *adj.* wild in sexual matters (of men). < kîr = 'penis' + har = 'rabid' [Msr] <quzhar>

k'îroşk کیرۆشك (IFb) = rabbit. See **k'erguh**.

k'îs کـیـس *m.* **(-ê;).** 1) pouch, purse; 2) {also: k'îsikê t'itûnê} tobacco pouch; 3) *[fig.]* account, expense: **•Mihleta çil rojan bide min, ezê biçim ji te re bînim. Mesrefa min û mala min ji *kîsê* hemamçî** (Rnh 2:17, 308) Give me a respite of 40 days, and I'll go bring [them] for you. The expenses for me and my family from *the pocket of* the bathhouse owner; **-ji k'îsê *fk-ê* jîyîn** (K) to sponge off s.o., to live off s.o. else's earnings. {also: kîse (SK); <kîs> کـیـس (HH)} Cf. Ar/P kīs کـیـس = 'bag, purse', also Arc kis כיס = 'receptacle, pouch, bag'; Sor kîs کـیـس = 'blister; bag' & kîse کـیـسه = 'bag'; Za kise *m.* = '(money) purse' (Mal); Hau kîse *m.* = 'pocket' (M4) [K/A/IF/HH//SK] <mesref>

kîse کیسه (SK) = pouch, purse. See **k'îs**.

k'îsik کیسِك *m.* **(-ê;).** *diminutive of* ***k'îs***: 1) purse, bag, money pouch: **•Rahişte *kîsikê* zêran xist berîka xwe** (ZZ-7, 243) He picked up *the purse of* gold and put it in his breast pocket; 2) tobacco pouch: **-k'îsikê t'itûnê** (JJ/Ba2) do.: **•Vira apê Kotê *k'îsikê t'it'ûnê* ji cêba xwe derxist** (Ba2-#2, 210) Here Uncle Koteh took his *tobacco pouch* out of his pocket. {also: [kisik] کیسك (JJ); <kîsik> کیسك (HH)} *for etymology see **k'îs**.* [Ba2/F/A/IF/B/JJ/HH/SK] <k'îs>

k'îsilfis کیسِلفِس (Zx) = tortoise. See **k'ûsî I**.

k'îso کـیـسـۆ (IFb/HH/TF/Çnr/Grc/Btm) = tortoise. See **k'ûsî I**.

k'îsofis کیسۆفِس (Czr) = tortoise. See **k'ûsî I**.

k'îsok کیسۆك, f. (-a;-ê) (Msr) = tortoise. See **k'ûsî I**.

kîş کیش (OK)/k'îş (JB1-A) = which. See **k'îjan**.

kîşk کـیـشـك (SK/OK/Bw)/k'îşk' (JB1-A/M-Am) = which. See **k'îjan**.

k'îşmîş کـیـشـمـیـش (Tkm)= currant(s); raisin(s); grapes. See **k'işmîş**.

k'îşwer کیشوەر *f.* **(-a;-ê).** 1) {syn: *parzemîn; *qita} continent, land mass: **•Welatên ser *kîşwera* Awrûpa** (RC2. Ku heye Xwedê hiş bide gelê Kurd) Countries of *the continent of* Europe; 2) kingdom. {also: kêşwer (CS-2); k'işwer, m. (K)/kişwer (FJ/GF/CS/ZF3)} < Sor kîşwer کـیـشـوەر = 'continent'; cf. P kišvar کـشـور = 'country, land' [RC2/IFb//K/FJ/GF/CS/ZF3]

k'ît کیت (K/FS/TF/Wkt) = syllable. See **k'îte**.

k'îte کـیـتـه *f.* **(-ya;-yê).** syllable: **•Di vê hevokê da, guvaşa ku bi lêkerê va eleqedar e, li ser *kîteya* yekem e** (RR 27.8.2) In this sentence, the stress related to the verb, is on the first *syllable* **•Wek mînak peyva "av" ji yek *kîteyê* pêk tê** (Wkp:kîte) For example the word "*av*" [water] consists of one syllable. {also: kite (Wkt/FJ-2/GF-2/FS-2); kît (K/FS-2/TF/Wkt-2)} = Sor biřge بڕگه/kerte کەرتە [RR/IFb/GF/FJ/RZ/ZF//K/TF/FS//Wkt] <duk'îteyî; p'iřk'îteyî; yekk'îteyî>

kîtle کـیـتـلـه *pl.* the masses, mobs of people: **•rik û hêrsa *kîtleyan*** (Ber) anger and fury *of the masses*. {also: kitle (Wkt)} < Ar kutlah کـتـلـة = 'lump, mass'--> T kitle = 'lump, mass; crowd of people' [Ber//Wkt]

kîvark کیڤارك (Prw) = mushroom. See **kiyark**.

k'îvî کیڤی (M-Am) = wild. See **k'ûvî**.

k'îya کیا (Z-4) = village chief. See **k'eya**.

kîyan کیان (-kê-) (Zeb) = to churn. See **k'ilan**.

kîzmas کـیـزمـاس *m.* **(-ê;).** watercress, bot. *Nasturtium officinale*. {also: kûzî, f. (IFb/OK)} {syn: pîz; t'ûzik} [Bw//IFb/OK] <řeşad>

kloç کلۆچ (HCK) = round bread or cake. See **kuloç**.

klostik کلۆستِك (Urm) = wild pear. See **kirosik**.

ko I کـــــــۆ *rel.prn./conj.* 1) [*rel. prn.*] that, which {preceded by noun in ezafeh [=construct]; **ko** can also be omitted in such cases, e.g., Ew rîya [ko] tu li ser = This road [which] you are on}: **•Hevoka *ku* ez pê kezebreşî dibim** (tirsik.net, 01.xi.2013) The sentence [in the text] about *which* I get upset/frustrated/irritated; **•Pelên guliyê dara çinarê *yê ku* ew *li ser* bû, kil bûn** (SF 17) The leaves of the plane tree branch *which* he was *on* trembled **•Serokatiya her kesê *ku* azadiyê dixwaze** (AW78A3) The leadership of every person *who* desires freedom; 2) *[conj.]* that: **•Bifikirin *ku* min hevala xwe Sêvê ji porê wê yê kurişkî naskir** (VOA) Imagine *that* I recognized my friend S. by her curly hair **•Min da xuya kirin *ku* ez dikarim bi xwe** (Qmş) I showed *that* I could control myself; 3) if: **•*Go* ne ew be, kes nikare ...** (L) *If* he can't, no one can ... **•*Ko* tu hatî, emê pev**

re şîvê bixwin (BX) *If* you come, we will have dinner together •***Ku* we pere ji min bixwesta, min ê biçûya deyn bikira** (Epl, 22) *If* you had asked me for money, I would have gone and borrowed some.{also: go I (L); ku I (J/Ba/IF-2/B/F); [kou] كو (JJ)} Cf. P ke كه; Sor ke كه [K/JB3/IF/JJ/BX//J/Ba/B/F//L]

ko II كۆ (GF) = dull. See **kuh**.

koç I كۆچ (Dh) = knee. See **çok**.

k'oç II کۆچ *f./m.(IS)* **(-a/-ê;-ê/).** 1) nomad encampment: •**K'oçer--şev deng pê k'et, bar kirin. Pîrê çû dewsa *k'oçê* wana. Dewsa *k'oçê* wana zaȓeke t'ezebûy dît** (IS-#4-6) A voice came to the nomads at night, and they packed up their things [and left]. The old woman went to the site of their *encampment*. She found a newborn infant there; 2) nomadic existence, wandering; migration: •**Bi dû payiza jiyanê re *koça* dawîn** (MUs, 7) The final *migration* after the autumn of life; **-k'oç kirin** (K/B/JJ) to pack up and move on (of nomads), to migrate; 3) nomadic caravan (EP-5): •**Rojekê, golik xweȓa diç'êrîyan lê nihêȓî *k'oç* tên, diçin, hildik'işin ç'îya, zozana** (EP-5, #10) One day, [while] the calves were grazing, he saw *caravans* [of nomads] coming and going, climbing the mountains, to the summer pastures. {also: [kotch] كوچ (JJ)} Cf. P kūč كوچ = 'decamping'-->T göç = 'migration'; Sor koç کۆچ; Za koç/kûç *m.* (Mal) [IS/K/A/IF/B/JJ] <bar; k'oçer; war; zozan>

k'oçber كۆچبەر *m.&f.* **().** an exile, person in exile; immigrant: •**Bavê min li Elmaniya bû *koçber*** (Wkt) My father became *an immigrant* in Germany. [(neol)Wlt/ZF3/Wkt/BF] <derbeder; mişext; p'enaber>

k'oçberî كۆچبەری *f.* **(-ya;-yê).** exile, banishment; immigration: •**Gelê Şirnexê niha bi tevayî *di koçberiyê de* ye** (Wlt 1:37, 16) The people of Şırnak are now completely *in exile*. {syn: sirgûn; ẍurbet} [(neol)Wlt/ZF3/Wkt]

k'oçek كۆچەك *m.* **().** 1) hermit, recluse (K/B); 2) spiritual leader among the Yezidis, to whom is ascribed the power to predict the future (RK/B): •**Dasinî mezhebek e, Êzedî jî dibêjinê ... mezinekî wan zemanekî hebû, nawê wî 'Elî Beg bû ... zêdetir Ḧurmeta melan û qeşan digirt ji *koçekan*. Ew dibêjine 'ulemaêt xo *koçek*** (SK 39:344) The Dasinis are a sect, also called Yezidis ... once they had a leader whose name was Ali Beg ... He respected the mullahs and Christian priests more than the *kochaks*. They call their own religious authorities '*kochak*'; 3) {syn: [moïdé] مويده (JJ) = jeunes garçons employés à la danse, travestis en femme [see: Heinrich Karl Brugsch. *Reise der K. preussischen Gesandtschaft nach Persien 1860 und 1861* (Leipzig: J. C. Hinrichs, 1862-63) vol. 1, p. 387]} (formerly) youth who performed erotic dances in woman's garb [T köçek] (JJ/HH); 4) {syn: kûdik [3]} camel foal (JJ). {also: [k(i)otchek] كوچك (JJ); <koçek> كوچك (HH)} Cf. T köçek = 'foal of a camel; youth who performed erotic dances in woman's garb; frivolous person' [Z-1/K/B/IFb/JJ/HH/SK/ZF3]

k'oçer كۆچەر *m.&f.* **(/-a;).** 1) nomad: •**konekî *k'oçeran*** = a nomad tent [lit. 'a tent *of the nomads*'] •**Muroekî Arṯûşî *koçer* digel tacirekî Mûsilî dost bû** (SK 31:274) A man of the Artushi *nomads* was friendly with a merchant of Mosul; 2) bungler, vagrant worker (JJ). {also: k'oçervan (B-2); kuçer (J); [kotcher كوچر/kotchergi كوچرگی] (JJ); <koçer> كوچر (HH)} Cf. P kūč كوچ, T göçebe {k'oçerî} [K/A/IFb/B/JJ/HH/SK/TF//J]

k'oçerî كۆچەری *f.* **(;-yê).** 1) nomadic way of life: •**Dûre jî bi zarekî xweş dûrûdirêj ji min re çêlî jiyana *koçeriyê* kir** (Lab, 11) Afterward he articulately described *the nomadic way of life* to me in detail; 2) type of circle dance. {also: koçertî (ZF3-2)} [IFb/B/GF/TF/ZF3] <k'oçer>

koçertî كۆچەرتی (ZF3) = nomadic way of life. See **k'oçerî**.

k'oçervan كۆچەرڤان (B) = nomad. See **k'oçer**.

koçik كۆچك (EH/JB3/IF)/k'oçik (B) = palace; reception hall. See **k'oçk**.

koçk/k'oçk [K/A] كۆچك *f.* **(-a;-ê).** 1) quarters, rooms; elevated house (HH): •**Tînine *k'oçka* Zelîxê** (Ba) They take [him] to Zelikha's *quarters*; 2) palace: **-k'oçk û rewaq** (EP-7) do.; **-k'oçk û seray**, m. (Z-1)/**k'oçk-sera** (Z-1)/**koşk û seray** (IF) do.; 3) reception hall (JB3/IF); among Kurdish nobility, quarters made ready for guests (HH). {also: koçik (EH/JB3/IF)/k'oçik (B-2); k'oşk (K/B/IF-2); [kochk] كوشك (JJ); <koçk> كۆچك (HH)} Mid P kōšk = 'pavilion, palace, kiosk' (M3); P kūšk كوشك --> T köşk--> Eng kiosk [Ba/A/HH//K/B/JJ//JB3/IF]

k'oçk-sera كۆچك سەرا (Z-1) = palace. See **k'oçk** [2].

kod كۆد *f.* **(-a;-ê).** 1) *various types of vessel or* *container*: bowl, basin, bucket, tub (K); cask, barrel (JB3); vessel carved out of wood (A); wooden container used in milking sheep (IFb/HH); dipper or jug-shaped metal cup (IFb); clay cup used for drinking water (HH): **•Gava ku *kod* bir gîhande aşvan, aşvan *kod* dest girt** (J) When he took *the tub* and reached the miller, the miller took hold of *the tub* **•Ħurmet, r̄abe, *koda* mezin bibe bin mihîya r̄eş, bidoşe, tejî şîr bike** (SK 31:277) Wife, go and take the big *wooden bowl* to the black ewe, milk her and fill it with milk **•P'adşê me gotîye, "Bira *koda* zêr̄a ji minr̄a bişîne"** (J) Our king said, "Let him send me a *basin* [full] of gold [pieces]" ; 2) unit of measure equal to 2 kilograms (IFb); dry measure, *ranging from 8-12 pounds in different regions* (B/K). {also: kot II; [kod] كـود (JJ); <kod> كـود (HH)} [J/K/A/JB3/IFb/B/HH/JJ/SK/ZF3] <devo; kêl III; olçek; somer>

kodandin كـۆدانـدِن (TF) = to set out on horseback. See **k'udandin**.

kod•e كـــــــــــــــۆده *f.* **(•a;).** 1) grazing fee, fee paid to landowner in exchange for use of pastureland: **•Bedela bi-kar-înana zozanê, mirov dê *kode* bidete ax̄ayî [xudanê zozanê]** (Hk) In exchange for using the summer pasture, one will give (or, pay) *kode* [= *grazing fee*] to the agha [owner of the summer pasture]; 2) taxes, animal tax (Zeb/FS). {also: <kode> كـــوده (HH); <kode> كـــۆده (Hej)} = Sor pûşane پووشانه = 'grazing fee' [Zeb/Hk/IFb/HH/GF/OK/Hej/ZF3/FS] <qamçûr̄; xûk>

k'ofî كـــۆفــی *f.* **(-ya;-yê).** Kurdish women's cylinder-shaped headdress, covered with motley-colored tasseled silk scarves; *with knots above the forehead for adornment* (IFb): **•*Kofî* şewqeya jinan ya kevneşopî ye** (tirsik.net:perxudres 26.ii.2014) *The kofî* is the women's traditional hat. {also: [koufi] كــوفــی (JJ); <kofî> كـــوفـــی (HH)} *for illustration, see Kmc-11, page 1, #14* [K/A/IFb/B/JJ/HH/GF/TF/OK/Haz/Krç/Kmc-11/ZF3] <hêratî; k'efî; k'um; laç'ik; p'oşî; t'emezî; terĥî; xavik>

koflet كۆفلەت (JB2) = wife; family. See **k'ulfet**.

kojandin كـۆژانـدِن *vt.* **(-kojîn-).** to nibble *(at meat left on a bone)*. [Haz/ZF3] <kotin>

k'ok I كـۆك *adj.* 1) {syn: qelew; ≠jar} fat, stout (K/B): **•Ezê *k'ok'*bim** (J) I'll grow *fat*; 2) pretty, adorned (IF/JJ); 3) perfect (JJ/HH). {also: [kok] كـوك (JJ); <kok> كـوك (HH)} Cf. Az T kök = 'fat' {k'okayî; k'okî; k'oktî} [J/K/B/JJ/HH]

k'ok II كـۆك *f.* **(-a;-ê).** root *(lit. & fig.)* (F/K/IF/JJ/B): **-k'ok anîn** (XF)**/birin/birîn/rakirin/qelandin** (K) to pull out by the roots; to extirpate, annihilate, uproot, destroy: **•Wekî Q. Memo wî ħalîda dît, wê şeher xirab ke û *k'ok'a* me *biqelîne*** (Z-1) If Q. sees Memo in this condition, he'll sack the city and *annihilate* us **•*Wê* sibê *k'ok'a* te û cindîa t'ev *bîne*** (EP-7) Tomorrow he *will annihilate* you and the nobles together; **-k'ok girtin/dayîn** (B) to take root; **-k'okêva derxistin/r̄akirin** (B) to extirpate, uproot, pull out by the roots. {also: k'ok' (Z-1); [kok] كـــوك (JJ)} < T kök = 'root' [Z-1/F/K/IF/JJ/B/ZF3/Wkt]

k'okayî كـۆكـايـی *f.* **().** fatness, stoutness, plumpness. {also: k'okî (K); k'oktî (B)} {syn: qelewî} [K//B] <k'ok I>

kokim كـۆكِـم *m.* **().** 1) {syn: kal I[2]; kalik I} old man (K): **•her du *kokimê* apane** (L) both old uncles [lit. 'all two *old men* of uncles']; 2) {syn: kek} older brother (K); 3) *[adj.]* {syn: îxtîyar; kal I; pîr; sere I} elderly, old, advanced in years (of human beings) (IF): **•Bavê kal û dîya *kokim*** (IF) old father and *elderly* mother [L/K/IF]

k'okî كۆكی (K) = fatness. See **k'okayî**.

k'oktî كۆكتی (B) = fatness. See **k'okayî**.

kol I كۆل (K) = slave. See **kole**.

k'ol II كـــۆل *f.* **().** hut, cabin: **-kol û kepir** (PS-II) do.: **•[Agir berda *kol û keprêd* rengîne]** (PS-II) He set fire to the many-colored *huts*; **-kol[ik]ê mirîşka** (Slv) chicken coop. {also: k'olik (ZF3); kolît (IF); kulît, m. (SK); [kōl] كـــول (JJ)} Cf. Sor kołît كۆڵیت/kałît كـاڵیـت = 'hut, shelter' [PS-II/JJ/GF//ZF3//IF//SK] <herzal; ĥol; kepir>

k'ol III كـۆل *f.* **(;-ê).** bush, shrub: **•Nava wan kevir û kuç'ikada hêşînayî, kulîlk zaf kêmin, lê ĥer dera *k'olêd* şîlanê hêşîn dibin** (Ba2:1, 203) Among those rocks and boulders, plants and flowers are very scarce, but everywhere dogrose *bushes* blossom. {syn: devî; kem; t'er̄aş II; t'ûm} [Ba2/K/B]

k'ol IV كـۆل *adj.* having no horns, hornless, polled *(of sheep and goats)*: **•Kanê bizina *kol*?** (Ardû, 115) Where is the *hornless* goat?; **-beranê kol** (Kmc-8) hornless ram. {also: [kol] كـــول (JJ); <kol> كـــول (HH)} Cf. P kol كـل = 'docked, cut short, bobbed'; Sor kuł كـــوڵ = 'docked, cut (tail)' [Ardû/K/A/IFb/B/JJ/HH/GF/Kmc-8] <bel; kel I[1]; kever; qoç'; qer II; strû;

taq; xez>

kol V كۆل (Bar) = dull, blunt. See **kuh**.

kolan I كـۆلان *f.* **(-a;).** saddle-girth, bellyband. {syn: kejî; navteng; qoş [1]; teng II} T kolan [IFb]

kolan II كـۆلان *f.(JJ/SK/JB1-A/Elk/Czr)/m.(K)* **(-a/;-ê/).** street, alley, lane: **•Dengê tifing û mitralyozan ewçend nîzing bû bûn ko mirov digot qey şer gihaştiye *kûçe û kolanên* bajêr** (H2 9:31, 775) The sound of rifles and machine guns was so close that people were saying that the war had reached *the streets of* the city. {also: k'olane (A); [kolan] كـولان (JJ)} {syn: ca'de; k'ûç[']e; zaboq; zikak} Cf. Sor kołan كـۆلان = 'street, lane' [K/IF/JJ/JB1-A/SK/OK/Elk/Czr//A] <dirb; ewcan; r̄ê>

k'olan III كـۆلان *vt.* **(-k'ol-).** 1) {syn: vedan [2]} to dig: **•Rabî, her do biraêt xwe qebr bo *k'olan*, veşartin** (M-Zx #755) He rose and *dug* graves for both his brothers and buried them; 2) to carve (M). {also: kolîn (IF-2/M-2); [kolan] كـولان (JJ); <kolan كـولان (dikole) (دكـولـه)> (HH)} Cf. Sor kołîn كـۆلـيـن (-koł-) = 'to dig out' [K/A/JB3/IF/B/JJ/HH/OK/M/FS] <vek'olîn>

k'olane كۆلانه (A) = street. See **kolan II**.

kolar•e كـۆلاره *f.* **(;•ê).** kite (bird), zool. *Milvus*: **•Ji r̄êwe *kolare* hate pêş, got, "Zerera min eweye, wextê mirîşkêt wan cûcikan dîinin e der ez ħetta bişêm dibem, dixom. We hawînê keşkêt wan li serbanêt r̄eş-malan û keprokan û xanîyan direwêm, dixom"** (SK-I:3) First *the kite* came forward and said, "This is my injury. When their hens hatch chicks I carry off as many as I can and eat them. And in summer I snatch their buttermilk, (drying) on the roofs of tents and bough-huts and houses, and eat it." {also: kulelemar (OK); kulemar (IFb-2)} Sor kur̄kur̄e كورکوره = 'kite (bird)' [SK/K/IFb//OK] <başoke>

k'olber كـۆلـبـەر *m.* **().** *kolbar*, porter, *particularly Kurdish porters on the Iran-Iraq border*: **•Serbazên Îranê 2 *kolberên* kurd kuştin û gel rabû ser piyan** (Rûdaw 4.ix.2017) Iranian soldiers killed two Kurdish *kolbars* and the people stood up and protested **•Pîranşar...Hêzên ewlehiya Îranê dîsa li *kolberan* gule barand!** (basnews 22.vi.2017) Pîranşar ... Iranian security forces again strafed (rained down bullets on) *kolbars*. {syn: bargir; ħemal} < Sor koł كـۆڵ = 'load (carried by person on the back)' + -ber بـەر < birdin بِردِن = 'to bear, take' [Rûdaw/basnews/Wkt]

k'ole كـۆلـه *m.* **().** slave. {also: kol I (K); [kolé] كـولـه (JJ); <kole> كوله (HH)} {syn: bende; benî I; 'evd I; qûl} <T köle [L/A/IF/JJ/HH/GF/FS//K] <xulam>

k'oledar كـۆلـەدار *m.* **().** slave owner, slave trader; enslaver: **•Teto û Seto û ħeya îro dijminatiya Kurd bi Kurd her dibû û *kolîdarên* Kurdistanê pê bi hêztir dibûn** (ST-I, 19) Tato and Suto, and even up to today, have felt enmity toward one another as Kurds, and *those who enslave* Kurdistan have been made stronger by this. {also: kolîdar (ST-I)} [ST-I//K/GF/FS/ZF3] <k'ole>

k'olg•e كـۆلـگـه *f.* **(;•ê).** ditch, gully: **•Tu serê qamîşekî *k'olgekî* [sic] xwer̄a çêkî, bik'evî bin *k'olgê* xwe veşêrî ... Mîrze Me'mûd r̄abû çû xwer̄a *k'olge* çêkir, k'etê** (HCK-3, #16, 182) You make yourself *a ditch* among the reeds, go hide under *the ditch* ... M.M. went and made himself *a ditch*, [and] got into it. {also: k'olgeh (K[s])} {syn: cew; çal II; goncal; k'ort II} < k'olan III = 'to dig' + geh [HCK//K(s)/Wkt]

k'olgeh كۆلگەه (K[s]/Wkt) = ditch. See **k'olge**.

k'olik كۆلِك (ZF3) = hut, cabin. See **k'ol II**.

kolîdar كۆليدار (ST-I) = slave trader. See **koledar**.

kolîn كۆلين (IF/M) = to dig, carve. See **k'olan III**.

kolît كۆليت (IF) = hut, cabin. See **k'ol II**.

k'olos كـۆلـۆس (K/IFb/FJ/GF/Tsab/JJ) = cone-shaped hat. See **k'oloz**.

k'oloz كـۆلـۆز *m.* **(-ê;).** cone-shaped man's felt hat: **•Xwedê zane, go, *k'oloz* çi r̄inde; germe, go, serê min germ xwey dike** (HCK-4, #1, 31) God knows how nice the *koloz* is; it's warm, it'll keep my head warm. {also: k'olos (K-2/IFb-2/FJ/GF-2/Tsab-2); [kolos] كلوس (JJ); <koloz> كولوز (HH)} Cf. Ar qalansuwwah قـلـنـسـوة = 'conical hat'. *For illustration, see Kmc p. 98, #34 (Kmc-11, p. 2, #34)* [HCK/K/A/B/IFb/GF/HH/Kmc/Tsab//FJ/JJ] <k'um>

kom I كۆم (Yalçın-Heckmann) = summer hut. See **gom I**.

k'om II كـۆم *f.* **(-a;-ê).** 1) {syn: t'op I} crowd, mob; 2) {syn: bir̄ I; cêrge; grûb} group; society; collective: **•Zîna delal bi *k'oma* carîyava** (Z-1) Lovely Zîn with *a group of* maidservants; **-k'om bûn** (Zeb/Dh) to meet *(vi.)*, come together {syn: berhev bûn; civîn; t'op bûn; xir̄ ve bûn}; **-k'om kirin** (K/A/IFb/B/HH/JB1-S/GF/TF): a) to gather, collect, assemble {syn: berhev kirin; civandin; t'op kirin; xir̄ ve kirin}: **•Govar dixebite ewan ro[ş]enbîr û lêgeroka ewên [ş]arezayî li ser Êzidiyan heyî li**

dora xwe ***kom bike*** (Roj 1[1996-:4) The journal tries *to assemble* those scholars and researchers who are experts on the Yezidis; b) to add *(math)*: 3) {syn: kuç' [2]; lod; londer} pile, heap (A/Bw). {also: <kom> كـــوم (HH)} Hau koma *f.* = 'heap, pile' (M4) [Z-1/K/A/IFb/B/HH/GF/Bw]

k'omar كــــۆمـــــار *f.* **(-a;-ê).** republic: **-Komara Mehabadê** (Ber) the Republic of Mahabad; **-Komara Tirkiyeyê** (WM 1:2, 15) the Republic of Turkey. [Ber/JB3/IFb/ZF]

kombar كۆمبار *m.* **(-ê;).** wall-to-wall carpet *{factory made, as opposed to* ***mehfûr*** *= woven carpet or rug}*. {also: kumbar (Wkt)} [Bw//Wkt] <mehfûr; xalîçe>

k'omek كــــۆمــــەك *f.* **(;-ê).** 1) {syn: arîk'arî} help, assistance, aid: **•Lê bi** ***k'omekîa*** **min, bi cefakî mezin ew qayîl bûn ji nava kevira derk'evin** (Ba2-#2, 206) But with my *help* [and] with a great deal of effort they agreed to come out from among the rocks; **-k'omek dan/kirin** = to help, aid, assist: **•Nava wan salada min hin** ***k'omekî dida*** **dîa xwe** (Ba2-#2, 207) In those years I *used to help* my mother [lit. 'give my mother some help(s)'] **•Xwest** ***k'omekê bide*** **nêç'îrvan** (Z-1) He wanted *to help* the hunter; 2) *sentence *(grammar)* (JB3). {also: k'omekî (Ba2); k'omektî (K-2)} Cf. P komak كـمـك; Sor komek كۆمەك = 'help' [Z-1/K/JB3/B]

k'omekî كۆمەكی (Ba2) = help. See **k'omek**.

k'omektî كۆمەكتی (K) = help. See **k'omek**.

komel كـۆمـەل, f. (JB3/IFb/GF) = group, organization; political party. See **k'omele**.

k'omelayî كـــۆمـــەلايـی (A) = group, organization; political party. See **k'omele**.

k'omel•e كـۆمـەلـە *f.* **(•eya;).** 1) group; organization, association: **-Komeleya Mafên Mirovan** (Wlt) Human Rights Association; 2) (political) party (K[s]): **-Komeleya Şoreşger û Zehmetkêşên Kurdistana Îranê** (Wkp) Komala Party of Iranian Kurdistan. {also: komel, f. (JB3/IFb/GF); k'omelayî (A)} [K(s)//A//JB3/IFb/GF]

k'omkirin كـــۆمـــكـــرن *f.* **(-a;-ê).** addition *(math.)* [Ar jam' جَـمـع, T toplama, P jam' zadan جـمـع زدن]: **-nîşana komkirinê** (buyerpress.com) plus sign (+). = Sor kokirdinewe كۆكردنەوە [Kmc/RZ/ZF3/SS]

k'omkujî كـــۆمـــكـــوژی *f.* **(-ya;-yê).** massacre: **•Eger DAIŞ û El-Nusra têkevin gundên Êzîdîyan, bi rastî dibe ku** ***Komkujîya*** **Şingalê dubare bibe** (VoA 25.i.2018) If ISIS and al-Nusrah enter the Yezidi villages, it is truly possible that the Shingal [Sinjar] *massacre* will be repeated. [ZF/SS/Wkt] <qiř kirin>

kon كـــۆن *m.* **(-ê;).** tent: "The *kons* of wealthy Kurds were large, divided into several sections adorned with carpets and felt cloths (koşme); there was a separate compartment for visitors and a larder for the products of milking [sheep]: butter, cheese and curds. Among the less well-to-do, the kon was considerably smaller and consisted of a living compartment and a larder. The tents were pitched in isolation or in small groups on the mountain slope or in the ravines ... From afar one could mistake the groups of kon for a military encampment." {B. Nikitine. *Les Kurdes : étude sociologique et historique* (Paris : Imprimerie Nationale : Librairie C. Klincksieck, 1956), p. 47}: **-kon vegirtin/lê xistin** (B) to pitch a tent. {also: kûn II (Bw/FS); [kon] كون (JJ); <kon> كون (HH)} {syn: ç'adir; řeşmal; xêvet} [L/K/A/JB3/IFb/B/JJ/HH/GF/TF//Bw/fS] <sing I>

konax̱ كۆناغ = day's journey. See **qonax**.

koncal كۆنجال (RZ/CS) = pit, ditch. See **goncal**.

kondere كۆندەرە (F) = shoe. See **qondere**.

kontax كۆنتاخ = hillside. See **qunt'ar**.

kop I كـــۆپ *f.(Bw/GF)/m.(OK)* **(-a/ ;).** crest, peak, summit *(of mountain, tree, etc.)*: **•Evca rabît ew kirasê ji serê** ***kupa*** **ji davêt rojê min bo înay/** (verse from poem by Muayyid Tayyib) That blouse from the *mountaintops*, sunbright, which I brought her. {also: kup (Bw)} {syn: gaz û bêlan; ȟeç'; k'umik; kumt} [Bw//IFb/GF/TF/OK] See also **gopk**.

kop II كــۆپ (Nbh 124:32) = front & rear cart boards. See **kopî**.

kopal كۆپال (K) = stick. See **gopal**.

kope كۆپە (Elk) = hearts (in card games). See **kupe**.

kopî كـــۆپـی *m.* **(-yê;).** 1) {also: kop II (Nbh 124:32)} wooden front and rear boards of a cart (Kmc/Nbh 124:32): **-kopîyê paşî** (Kmc) back board; **-kopîyê pêşî** (Kmc) fore/front board; 2) cross beams of a sled[ge] (Kmc). [Kmc//Nbh] <gerdûm; parxêl; taxok>

kor كـــۆر *adj.* 1) {syn: ȟafiz [2]} blind: **•Ma hun** ***kor*** **in, hun mi nas nakin?** (HR 3:175) Are you *blind*, don't you recognize me?; **-ç'avekî kor bûn** = to be blind in one eye: **•Dewlçî** ***ç'evekî kor*** **bû** (Ba) The bucket carrier was *blind in one eye*; **-herdu ç'ava kor bûn** (EP-7) to be blind in both eyes; 2) childless, lacking an heir, extinct (of a family line) : **-ocax kor bûn** (K)/**war kor man** (SW) to be wiped out, extinct: **•Belê diviya bû jin bikira da ko *warê* wî *kor nemînit*** (SW) Yes, he should get married, so that his *family line doesn't die out*; **-ocax kor kirin** (K) to wipe out s.o.'s family line, cut off the continuation of a race, render extinct. {also: kore (SK); kûr II (BK); kwêr (JB1-S-2); kwîr (Tof); [kōr] كور (JJ); <kor> كور (HH)} Cf. P kūr كـور --> T kör; Sor kwêr [kör] كـوێر; Za kor (Mal); Hau kor (M4); cf. also W Arm guyr/E Arm kuyr կույր {koraî; koranî; korayî; [kōrahī] كـوراهـى (JJ)} [K/A/JB3/IFb/B/JJ/HH/JB1-S/GF/TF/ZF//BK//SK//Tof]

koraî كۆرائى (SK) = blindness. See **korayî**.

koranî كۆرانى (K) = blindness. See **korayî**.

korayî كـۆرايـى *f.* **(-ya;-yê).** blindness: **•Sed *korayî* ji bona wî** (K2-Fêrîk) May he be blind 100 times [curse]. {also: koraî (SK); koranî (K-2); [kōrahī] كوراهى (JJ)} [K/A/IF/B//JJ//SK] <kor>

kore كۆره (SK) = blind. See **kor**.

korefam كۆرەفام (IFb) = stupid. See **korfe'm**.

korewar كۆرەوار (BF) = childless. See **warkor**.

K'oreyî كـۆرەيـى *adj.* Korean. {also: Korî (BF-2); Koryayî (BF)} Sor Korî كۆرى [Wkt/ZF3//BF]

kor fehm كۆرفهم (GF) = stupid. See **korfe'm**.

korfe'm كـۆرفـەعم *adj.* stupid, thick-skulled. {also: fe'mkor (Mzg/Haz); korefam (IFb); kor fehm (GF)} {syn: bêaqil} [Srk//GF//IFb//Mzg/Haz]

korik كـۆرك *f./m.(FS)* **(;-ê/).** disease of wheat plants that turns the wheat black, wheat smut. {also: kûrik II (Zx); kwîrik (Qzl)} [Frq/Xrz/TF/GF/FJ/ZF3/FS//Zx//Qzl] <genim>

Korî كۆرى (BF) = Korean. See **K'oreyî**.

kořîfok كـۆريـفـۆك (Zeb) = type of wild bee. See **kuřîfok**.

korna كۆرنا (ZF3) = horn. See **qorne**.

korne كۆرنه (RZ) = horn. See **qorne**.

kort I كۆرت (Nbh/FS) = unplowed. See **gort II**.

k'ort II كـۆرت *f.* **(-a;-ê).** pit, hole; cavity, hollow; crater: **•Çûme Bedlîsê, xopanê di *kortê* da/ Hatim Bedlîsê, xopanê di *kortê* da** (Ah) I went to Bitlis, ruins in *a pit*/ I came to Bitlis, ruins in *a pit [from a famous elegy]*. {also: k'ortal (K/JB3/IF-2); <kort> كـورت (HH)} {syn: cew; çal II; goncal; k'olge} [Srk/Mzg/A/IF/B/HH/Wkt//K/JB3] <bîr II>

k'ortal كۆرتال (K/JB3/I) = pit, hole. See **k'ort**.

Koryayî كۆريايى (BF) = Korean. See **K'oreyî**.

k'ose I كـۆسه *adj.*1) beardless; 2) [*m.* **(;-yî).**] {syn: xapînok} swindler: **•Got xadima xwe rabe bibe sûkê bifroşe belê hişyar bî nedî *mirovên kose*** (Drş #427, 126) She told her servant, "Get up and take it to the market and sell it, but be careful not to give it to *swindlers*" **•Sê bira hebûn le bajêrê *kose* bûn** (M-Surçî #509, 228) There were 3 brothers in the market who were *swindlers*. {also: [kosé] كوسه (JJ); <kose> كوسه (HH)} Cf. P kūsah كوسه = 'thin-bearded' > T köse [Drş/M-Surçî/IFb/FJ/GF/JJ/HH/ZF/BF/CS]

k'ose II كۆسه: **-k'ose misirî** = Egyptian saber, type of sword: **•Emê destê daynin ser qevdê *k'ose misirîya*** (Z-2) Once we touch the hilt of our *Egyptian saber*, ... {also: [kosé mysri] كـوسـه مـصـرى (JJ)} Cf. P kūsah كـوسـه & Ar kawsaj كوسج = 'swordfish' (of Mid P origin) [Z-2/JJ/LC-1]

kosî كۆسى (Dyd/Erg/Kp/Rh) = tortoise. See **k'ûsî I**.

k'oş كـۆش *f.* **(-a;-ê).** lap; bosom: **•Yê di *koşa* mi da rûnîtin xarê** (Bw) He's sitting on my *lap*. {also: [koch] كوش (JJ); <koş> كوش (HH)} {syn: damen; dang} Sor koş كۆش = 'lap (of a person)' [Bw/K/A/IFb/B/JJ/HH/GF/OK]

k'oşk كـۆشـك (K/B/IF) = palace; reception hall. See **k'oçk**.

k'oşk'ar كۆشـكـار *m.* **(-ê;-î).** cobbler, one who repairs shoes: ***•Koşkarî* pêlav pinî kir** (FS) The cobbler patched the shoe. {also: <koşkar> كوشكار (HH)} {syn: solbend; soldirû} <Arm koškakar կոշկակար = 'shoemaker' < košik կոշիկ = 'shoe' {k'oşk'arî} [DZK/A/HH/ZF3/FS/Wkt] <sol>

k'oşk'arî كۆشـكـارى *f.* **(;-yê).** profession of cobblers, shoe repair(ing). [DZK/ZF3/Wkt] <k'oşk'ar>

koşk û seray كۆشك و سەراى (IF) = palace. See **k'oçk** [2].

kot I كـۆت *adj.* naked, bare (particularly of head), bareheaded: **•Dê řûnêt, dê şûtika xo veketeve, dê serê xo *kot ket*** (M-Ak ¶548) He will sit down, undo his sash and *bare* his head. {also: qot (GF/RZ)} {syn: serqot} [M-Ak/JB3/SS//GF/RZ] <řût; tazî I; zelût>

kot II كۆت = vessel, container. See **kod**.

kotan I كۆتان *f.* **(-a;-ê).** roofless corral, pen, stockade for sheep: **•Şivanî pez dakir di *kotanê* ve** (FS) The shepherd herded the sheep into *the corral*. {syn: guhêř; k'oz; mexel} [Bw/FS/ZF3/BF/Wkt] <k'ox>

k'otan II كـۆتـان *f.* **(;-ê).** plough/plow; heavy plow (made of iron or steel) (IF/B); plow to which are harnessed 6-12 pairs of oxen (JJ); all-metal wheel plow (Kmc-6): •**weke xeta *kotanê*** (L) like a *plow* furrow (=straight as an arrow). {also: [kotan] كـوتـان (JJ); <kotan> كـوتـان (HH)} {syn: cot [2]; halet; hevcar̄} Cf. W Arm kut'an/E Arm gut'an գութան: *A pan-Caucasian word (JJ)*: Az T kotan, Geo k'utani კუთანი, Oss gut'on, Avare kutan, Udian k'ot'an, Thusch gutan, Abkhaz kotan, Tchetchen gotan, Kurinian küṭén, Ingush gotanger, Kizilbash & Kazakh kotan [L/F/K/A/IFb/B/JJ/HH/GF/Kmc-6/ZF3/Wkt] <gîsin; hincar; kêlan; mijane; nîr I; sermijank; şûrik I>

kotefir كۆتەفِر (FJ/GF/FS) = quail. See **kutefir**.

k'otek كـۆتـەك *f.* **(;-ê).** 1) a beating, thrashing, blows: •**Ev serokatî ne bi tenê Serokatiya Neteweyî ye; her wiha serokatiya her kesê ku azadiyê dixwaze, pêst û *kotekiyê* dibîne, ye** (AW78A3) This leadership is not only national leadership; it is likewise the leadership of every person who desires freedom, who has experienced oppression and *beatings*; 2) violence, force (K/JJ/HH); seizure by force, usurpation (A/IF); oppression (K): **-bi k'otek** (K)/**bi k'otekî** (IF/FS) by force: •**Wî kerê xwe *bi kotekî* ji Zoroyî stend** (FS) He took his donkey [back] from Z. *by force*. {also: kotekî (AW); k'utik II (Z-3); [koutek] كـوتـك (JJ); <kotek> كـــوتـــك (HH)} [Z-2/K/A/IF/JJ/B/HH/FS//AW] <k'utan; t'undûtîjî>

kotekî كۆتەكى (AW) = beating; violence. See **k'otek**.

k'otel كـۆتـەل *f.* **(;-ê).** 1) funeral procession: •***Bi k'otel bir[i]n*** [sic] **ç'e'lk[i]rin** [sic] **û vegerîan malêd xwe** (FK-eb-1) They *made* her a *funeral*, buried her, and returned home; **-k'otel girêdan** (K/JB2) to carry out a funeral *(including procession)*; 2) funeral banner made of a woman's red dress (B); 3) horse dressed up for funerals (JB2). [FK-eb-1/K/B/JB2]

kotin كـۆتِـن *vt.* **(-koj-).** to gnaw, nibble; to chew: •**Agir p'arxanê min yeko-yeko *dikoje*** (Z-1) Fire is *gnawing* my ribs one by one. {also: [kotin] كوتين (JJ); <kotin كـوتـن (dikoje) (دكـوژه)> (HH)} {syn: kurisandin I} Za koçenã [kotiş] (Srk) [Z-1/K/JB3/IF/B/JJ/HH] <cûtin; kojandin>

k'otî كـۆتـى *adj.* 1) infectious; contagious; 2) mangy, scabby; 3) suffering from any of a number of skin diseases: mange or scabs (B); leprosy (HH/IF); syphilis (B); 4) rotten, putrefied; 5) lice-ridden, lousy. {also: <kûtî> كوتى (HH)} [K/A/B/IF//HH]

k'otîbûn كـۆتـيـبـوون *f.* **().** 1) infection (K); 2) leprosy (BR/A/IF). {also: k'otîtî (B); <kûtîbûn> كـوتـيـبـون (HH)} [BR/K/A/IF//HH//B]

k'otîtî كۆتيتى (B) = infection; leprosy. See **k'otîbûn**.

kovan كـۆڤـان *f.* **().** 1) {syn: cefa; fikar; k'eder; k'erb; k'eser; kul I; şayîş; t'alaş; tatêl; xem; xiyal [2]} sadness, sorrow, grief; worry; 2) *[adj.]* ravaged, devastated, ruined (B); 3) sad, sorrowful (B); uneasy, apprehensive, worried, anxious: •[**Heyva Gulanê, xweyî r̄eza *bi kul û kovanê***] (BG) The month of May, the vintner [vineyard owner] is *worried and uneasy {fearing hailstorms which could ruin the grape harvest} [prv.]*. {also: kuvan II (BK); <kûvan> كـوڤـان (HH)} [K/JB3/IF/B//BK//HH] <meraq; zeh̄metk'êş>

kovar كـۆڤـار *f.* **(-a;-ê).** journal, periodical, magazine. {also: govar (FS)} Sor govar گۆڤار [(neol)Hv/K/JB3/IF//FS] <ç'apemenî; r̄ojname>

kovik كـــۆڤِـك *f.* **(;-ê).** 1) {syn: gewrî [2]; mastêrk} funnel *(for pouring liquids)*; 2) anus (IFb). {also: <kûvik> كوڤك (HH)} [HB/K/A/IFb/B//HH]

k'ovî كۆڤى (A/JB3/IF) = wild. See **k'ûvî**.

k'ox كۆخ *m./f.(HYma)* **(; /-ê).** 1) {syn: axil; axur; gom I; mexel} stable, pen, coop *(for animals)*: •**li ber deriyê *koxê*** (HYma, 49) at the door *of the animal pen*; 2) {syn: h̄ol[ik]} hut, shack, hovel (K/JB3/IF/B); 3) larder, storage shed (B). {also: koxî (JB3/IF-2); k'oẍ (B/HB-2)} Cf. < Ar kūx كـوخ; Sor kox كـۆخ & koxte كـۆخـتـه = 'hut, hovel' [HB/K/A/IFb/ZF//JB3//B] <afir̄; axil; axur; guhêr̄; gom I; k'oz; lîs; mexel>

koxî كۆخى (JB3/IF) = animal pen; shack. See **k'ox**.

k'oẍ كۆغ (B/HB) = animal pen; shack. See **k'ox**.

k'oz كـــــۆز *f.* **(-a;-ê).** 1) {syn: guhêr̄; kotan I; mexel} open-air sheep pen: **-k'oz kirin** (K/B) to chase into the pen *(of sheep)*; **-k'oza berxa[n]** (K) do. ; 2) place with brown, dry grass where sheep graze in winter and fall {as opposed to **çerwan**, which has green grass} (Bw): **-k'oz û çerwan** (Bw) [all manner of] pastureland (both dry and lush). {also: [kouz] كـــوز (JJ); <koz> كـــوز (HH)} Cf. T koz [Erzincan; Ahlat -Bitlis; Elâzığ] = 'animal stable beneath the house' [evlerin altında bulunan davar ağılı] & [Gümüşhane; Sarıkamış -Kars; Hasankale -Erzurum] = 'pen in a stable where animals give birth' [ahırda yavruların konmasına yarayan bölme, yer] (DS, v. 8, p. 2944); Sor koz كـۆز = 'sheep pen (in open air)' [Wlt/K/IFb/B/HH/GF/OK/Bw//JJ] <axil; çerwan; dolge; gom I; k'ox; lêf>

kozane كۆزانه (IF/HH) = type of grape. See **gozane**.

k'ozel كۆزەل (B) = chaff. See **k'ozer I**.

k'ozer I کـــۆزەر *f.* **(;-ê).** coarse chaff, waste product from threshing and winnowing: **•Min çi xêr dît ji bênderê, çi bibînim ji *kozerê*** (FS) What good have I seen from the threshing floor, what shall I see from *the chaff*? *[prv.]* {also: k'ozel (B); kozere (IFb/FJ/GF/Kmc-2); kûzir (Kmc); [kozer] کـــوزر (JJ); <kûzer> کـــوزر (HH)} {also: 'efare; *xiz} Sor kozere کـــۆزەره = 'separated chaff/grain husks' [CCG/K/A/JJ/FS//B//IFb/FJ/GF//HH//Kmc] <belim>

k'ozer II كۆزەر (K) = embers. See **k'ozir**.

kozere كۆزەره (IFb/FJ/GF/Kmc) = chaff. See **k'ozer I**.

k'ozik I کـۆزِك *f.* **(-a;-ê).** 1) {syn: çeper; p'ercan; sênc; tan} enclosure; hedge, fence; 2) {syn: çeper I; senger} trench, entrenchment, foxhole, dug-out, ditch: **•Frensîzên ko berî nîvro ji / Şamê rabû bûn, vegeriyan *kozik* û asêgehên xwe** (H2 9:31, 775-6) The French, who had left Damascus before noon, returned to their *trenches* and strongholds **•Kewa marî danî ser zinarê hemberê *kozikê*, li dorê jî lext reşand û xwe di kozikê da veşart** (AB, 52) He put the female partridge on the rock opposite *the ditch*, sprinkled birdseed around and hid in the ditch; **-çeper û k'ozik** (GF/IFb)/**k'ozik û çeper** (Bw) trenches and foxholes. [Bw/K/IFb/GF/TF/FJ/Kmc/CS]

kozik II كۆزِك (FS) = small clay jug. See **k'ûzik**.

k'ozir کـــــۆزِر *f.* **(;-ê).** embers, ashes with glowing coals. {also: k'ozer II (K)} {syn: bizot; tiraf} [HB/IFb/ZF3//K]

Kroatî كرۆئاتى (Wkp) = Croatian. See **K'irwatî**.

k'şmîş كشميش (HCK) = raisins. See **k'işmîş**.

k'têb كتێب = book. See **k'itêb**.

k'têv كتێڤ = book. See **k'itêb**.

ku I كو (J/Ba/IF/B/F) = that *[rel. prn.]*. See **ko I**.

ku II/k'u [K/B] کـو *intrg.* where? what place?: **-di k'u re** = by what route: **•Tu *di ku re* hatîye?** (L) *How (=by what route)* did you come?; **-ji ku** = from where, whence: ***•Ji ku* kare here hestîyê fîla bîne?** (L) *Where* can he bring ivory *from*? ***•Ji ku* tê, wê here *ku*** (L) *Where* he is coming *from*, *where* he is going; **-k'ûve** (M-Zx)/**kêve** (M-Ak) whither? where to?; **-ku derê?** (Bg/Ad) where? {also: kê[n]derê (M-Ak); kêrê (M-Ak-2); k'î derê; k'î dirkê (M-Am-2); k'îrê (M-Am)}; **-li ku [de]** = do.: **•Tuê *li ku de* bî, ezê bêm cem te** (L) *Wherever* you are, I'll come to you. {also: kû (BX/JB3); [kou] کـو (JJ)} Cf. P kojā کـجـا/ kū کـو; Sor kwê [kö] کوێ [BX/JB3/L//K/IF/B//JJ] <k'a II>

k'ubar کـــوبـــار *f.* **().** 1) {syn: keşxe} elegance, grace, refinement; pride: **•K'îjan şerê wana berê xwe bidayê, bi altindarî û *k'ubar* vedigeřîyan** (Z-1) Whatever battle they went to, they would return in splendor and *pride*; 2) *[adj.]* elegant, graceful, refined; noble, grand; 3) proud, haughty (B/HH). {also: [koubar] كبار (JJ); <kubar> كبار (HH)} Cf. T kibar = 'well-bred' <Ar kabura كبر = 'to be large, old, or great' [Z-1/K/B/JJ/HH/ZF3]

kuç' کـوچ *m.* **(-ê;).** 1) {syn: ber III; kevir} rock, stone; large rock, rock that can be lifted: ***•Kuçek* li lingê wî ket** (FS) *A rock* fell on his leg; 2) {also: qûç' [1]} {syn: k'om II [3]; lod; londer} heap, pile (K/Z-2 [note]); 3) {syn: banî II; dîyar II; gir II; t'op III; zûr} hill (Z-2 [note]). {also: kuç'[i]k I (B); **qûç'**; [kotch] کـوچ (JJ); <kuç> کـوچ (HH)} [Z-2/Ba2/K/A/IF/HH/ZF3/FS//JJ//B] See also **qûç'**.

kuçe کوچه (TF/LC) = street. See **kûçe**.

kuçer کوچەر (J) = nomad. See **k'oçer**.

kuç'ik I کـوچِك (B)= 1) dim. of **kuç'** [1]; 2) rock (B). See **kuç'**.

kuçik II کـوچِك/**kuçik'** [JB1-A] *f.(Frq/JB1-A)/m.(K/B)* **(-a/-ê;-ê/).** 1) {syn: t'ifik} oven, furnace; hearth, fireplace: **•Navbir êxist'inê: eve bo *kuçk'ê* u eve bo ĥazirîyê u eve bo nivist'inê** (JB1-A #63) She put partitions in it [=her tent]: this one for *the hearth* and this one for receiving [guests], and this one for sleeping **-kuç'ik dadan/danîn** (B) to light or kindle a fire in the oven; 2) {syn: dûstan; sêp'î [1]} stone supporting a cooking pot near the fire, tripod, trivet (IFb/GF): **•Min beroşa malê girt û anî danî ser *kuçik* û agir da binî** (LC, 24) I took the household cauldron and put it on *the hearthstone* and lit a fire underneath it. {also: kuç'k II (B); [koutchik] کوچك (JJ)} [Haz/Frq/K/IFb/B/JJ/JB1-A/GF/OK] <firne; tendûr>

kuçik III کوچِك (TF) = dog. See **kûçik**.

kuç'k I کوچك (B) = rock. See **kuç'**.

kuç'k II کوچك (B) = oven. See **kuç'ik II**.

k'udandin کودانْدِن *vt.* **(-k'udîn-).** 1) to urge (a horse) on, set out (on horseback), take to the road: **•...derbas bû li riya xwe *kudand* çû** (ZZ-4, 203) ...He passed by and *urged* [his horse] *on* and rode off; 2) {syn: ajotin[2]; dirêj kirin[c]; domîn[2]; k'işandin[6]; vek'işîn[2]} to last, continue, take (time), drag on: **•Serketina zalima zêde**

nakudîne (IFb) The victory of the oppressors *won't last* long. {also: kodandin (TF); <kudandin كداندن (dikudîne) (دكدينه)> (HH)} [ZZ/A/IFb/FJ/GF/HH/ZF/RZ//TF]

kudik كـودِك (IFb/B/K/GF) = piglet; cub, whelp; camel foal. See **kûdik**.

kudî كـودى (IFb/OK) = piglet; cub, whelp; camel foal. See **kûdik**.

kudîk I كوديك (Bw) = cub, whelp. See **kûdik**.

kudîk II كوديك (JB1-A) = box. See **qut'î**.

kuferî كوفێرى (IFb) = tamarisk. See **kifir II**.

kuffik كوففِك (GF) = mold, mildew. See **k'efik**.

kuffin كوففين (GF) = to hiss. See **k'ufîn**.

kufik كوفِك (IFb/ZF3) = mold, mildew. See **k'efik**.

kufikî كوفكى (IFb) = moldy. See **k'efikî**.

k'ufîn كوفين *vi.* **(-k'uf-).** 1) to hiss *(of snakes, etc.)*; 2) [*f.* **(-a;)**] hissing *(of snakes, etc.)*: **•Ev bûyinan gişt wisa bi lez qewimîbû ku, Meyro bi '*kufîn'a* mar, ancax tê gîhîşt çi hat serê wê** (MB-Meyro) All these things happened so quickly, that Meyro only understood by *the hissing of* the snake what had happened to her. {also: kuffin (GF); kûfên (-kûfê-) (OK)} [MB//GF//OK] <mar I>

kufkarik كـوفـكـارِك *f.* **().** mushroom. {also: kafkulîlk (Qtr-E); kekarik (Elb); kifkarek (Wkt); kifkarik (Wkt-2)} {syn: gidark (Prw); karî I; karkevîk (Mş-Malazgirt); kiyark; k'umik [4]} [Krç/IFb/OK/ZF3//Wkt//Elb//Qtr-E]

kuflet كوفلەت (JB2/FS) = wife; family. See **k'ulfet**.

k'ufrît كوفريت (HR) = match(es); sulphur. See **k'irpît**.

kuh كـــوه *adj.* 1) dull, blunt, obtuse *(of knives, etc.)*: **•Kêra min *kûhî* bûye min divêt wê bisûm** (IFb) My knife has gone *dull*, I need to sharpen it; 2) blunt, on edge (of teeth) (Bw/JJ): **•Diran *kuh* dibin** (Bw) The teeth are *on edge*; 3) dazzled *(of eyes)* (JJ): **•[Çavê min *kûh* bûye]** (JJ) My eyes are *dazzled* [lit. '...eye is']; 4) unaccomplished, dull, obtuse, having incomplete mastery of a subject, being neither beginner nor expert in a subject (Bw). {also: ko II (GF-2); kol V (Bar); kûh (IFb); [kouh] كوه (JJ)} Cf. Sor kuçke كوچكه = 'blunt point' [Bw/GF/TF//IFb/JJ//Bar] <alû I>

kuj كوژ (K/B/RZ) = corner. See **kujî**.

kuje كوژه, m. (F) = marten. See **kûze**.

kujî كـوژى *m./f.(OK)* **(-yê/-ya;).** corner; angle. {also: kuj (K/B/RZ); kûjî (IFb)} {syn: goşe; k'unc; qorzî; qilçik; qulç} [Bw/OK/K/B/RZ/ZF3//IFb]

kukurd كوكورد (IFb) = sulphur. See **k'irgûd**.

kul I كـــول *m.(L)/f.(B/JB1-S/Bw)* **(-ê/-a; /-ê).** 1) {syn: cefa; fikar; k'eder; k'erb; k'eser; kovan; şayîş; t'alaş; tatêl; xem; xiyal [2]} grief, distress, emotional pain: **-bikul** = grieved, in distress: **•[Heyva Gulanê, xweyî ȓeza *bi kul û kovanê*]** (BG) The month of May, the vintner [vineyard owner] is *worried and uneasy* {fearing hailstorms which could ruin the grape harvest} *[prv.]*; 2) infectious disease; wound, sore (JB1-S): **-kula Ĥelebê** (Bw) freckle; 3) *[adj.]* sore, infected: **•Çavêt wî *t kul* in** (Bw) His eyes are *sore* **•Go t'êr xwê mi kirîye tilya xwede, kû xwê dik'evê dereka *kul*da dişewitê dipeȓitêê** (HR 3:281) He said, I put a fair amount of salt on my finger, when salt enters a *sore* place it burns and smarts. {also: qul II (L/K/A/JB3); [koul] كـــل (JJ); <kul> كـــل (HH)} [L/K/A/JB3//IFb/B/JJ/HH/JB1-S/GF/TF/OK/Bw/ZF] <bikul; meraq; xem>

kul II كول (AB/L) = hole. See **qul I**.

kulab II كولاب (B) = felt *(material)*. See **kulav**.

k'ulabe كـــولابـــه *f.(B)/m.(K)* **().** 1) shaft, pole, beam *(attached to front axle of cart)*; 2) {syn: guhnîr; samî} oxbow, the rods tied around the draft animal's neck on a yoke; rod or staff of draft animal yoke: **•Li her seriyê nîr du qul hene, di van qulan re du dar tên derbaz kirin, stoyê ga dikeve nava van daran, ji van daran re *kulabe* tê gotin** (CCG, 16) In every yoke there are two holes, 2 pieces of wood are passed through those holes, the ox's neck goes between those pieces of wood, which are called *kulabe*. {also: kilabe (IFb/FS); kulave (GF/CCG-2); k'ulave (B); [koulabé] كلابه (JJ); <kulabe> كلابه (HH)} [K/A/JJ/HH/FJ/TF/Kmc//IFb/FS//B/GF] <xenîke>

k'ulam كولام (FK-eb-1/FK-eb-2) = song. See **kilam**.

kulav كـــــــولاڤ *m./f.(EP-8)* **(-ê/ ; kulêv/-ê).** 1) felt *(material)*; 2) felt coat: **•Beyrim ... di *kûlavekî* de razaye** (L) Beyrim ... was sleeping [wrapped] in *a felt coat* **•Şivan bin sîya *kulavê* k'etîye xewa k'ûr** (EP-8) The shepherd fell fast asleep in the shade of [his] *felt coat*; 3) {syn: taṯî} felt carpet (JJ): **•Bi rewşa mîrekî mezin rûmeteke bilind da min, li ser *kulavê* xwe î nexşîn ciyek da min** (Lab, 11) He treated me like a great emir, and made a place for me on his embroidered *felt carpet* **•Di tenişta diwaran de *kulavên* raxistî û li ser *kulavan* jî mînderin** (MUm, 18) Beside the wall are *carpets* spread out and on *the felt carpets* there are mattresses •**Were li ser *kulêv* rûne** (ZZ-10, 154) Come sit on *the carpet*; 4) {also: kilaw (SK)} {syn: k'um; şewqe} hat, cap (Bw/SK): •***Kilawê* dezî û cemedanîya sor bo paşa baş e** (SK 47:461) A cotton *cap* with a red kerchief is good for the Pasha. {also: kilaw (SK); kulab II (B-2); kûlav (L); [koulaw] كـــــلاڤ (JJ); <kulav> كـــلاڤ (HH)} Mid P kulāf = 'cap, bonnet' (M3); P kulāh كـــلاه = 'hat'; Sor kiław كِـلاو = 'head-dress, hat'; Hau kiławe *f.* = 'skull-cap, bonnet' (M4) [F/K/A/IFb/Wn/B/JJ/HH/Bw//L//SK] <k'epenek>

kulave كـــولاڤــه (GF/CCG)/k'ulave (B) = shaft, pole; rods on draft animal's neck. See **k'ulabe**.

kulbe كولبه *f./m.(ZF3)* **().** hoe: **-kulbe kirin** (IFb/ZF) to hoe. {syn: tevir} Cf. T kulbik [Yukarıkale, Koyulhisar -Sivas] = 'hoe' [çapa] (DS, v. 8, p. 2995) & külbe [Kemaliye -Erzincan; Arapkir -Malatya; Kesme, Divriği, Gürün -Sivas; Keskin -Ankara] = 'small pickaxe, hoe' [küçük kazma, çapa] (DS, v. 8, p. 3027) & [Beyelması, Ağın -Elâzığ] = 'single-blade hoe' [tek ağızlı çapa] (DS, v. 12, p. 4576); cf. Syr kúlbā ܟܘܠܒܐ/ kalbā ܟܠܒܐ = 'axe, hatchet pickaxe'; = Sor paçekołe پاچەکۆڵە [CCG/IFb/ZF/CS/ZF3]

kulecergî كولەجەرگی *adj.* sick with grief, with a hole in one's liver: •**Te ez *kulecergî kirim*** (Hk) You've made me sick with grief [lit. 'You've *put a hole in my liver*']. [Hk/Kmc/ZF3/FS] <k'ezebreşî; kulzikî>

kulek I كولەك *adj.* 1) {syn: goc; kût I; qop; şeht; şil II} lame, limping: •**Çima du bizinên te yên sax hene, tu *ya kulek* didî min?** (Nivîs: Bajarê Keran [2001]) Why, when you have two healthy goats, do you give me *the lame one*?; 2) [*f.* **(;-ê).**] lame sheep or goat: •**Herkê tu camêr î û r̄astî jî şivan î, hine goştî me r̄a biqelîne, axê te dengê xwe te r̄a nake seva *kulekekê*, heqê wê *kulekê* çi hêja ye, emê bidin** (Erebê Şemo. Berbang/Tsab) If you are a man and a true shepherd, roast some meat for us; your agha won't yell at you over *a lame goat*, and whatever that *lame goat* is worth, we will pay for it. {also: kullek (TF/GF); [koulek] كـــولـــك (JJ); <kullek> كلّك (HH)} [Nivîs/K/B/A/IFb/FJ/ZF/Tsab/CS/JJ/FS//TF/GF/HH]

k'ulek II كـــولـــەك *f.* **(-a;-ê).** 1) {syn: p'ace; r̄ojin} skylight, opening in ceiling to let in sunlight; dormer-window, window set vertically in a structure projecting through a sloping roof: •**[Îcarî Behram tifinga xwe beraberî bejna xwe digire û xwe li *kuleka* aşxaneyê hêdî bi jêrda berdide]** (JR) Then Behram takes his rifle together with his belt and quietly lowers himself in through the *sunlight opening* <kulek> of the kitchen; 2) fortochka (K), small hinged pane for ventilation: •**Dû ji *kulekê* bilind dibe** (AB) Smoke rises from the *vent window*. {also: [koulek] كـــولـــك (JJ); <kullek> كـلـك (HH)} [JR/K/IF/Ba2/F/B/JJ//HH] <kulêr; pixêrîk>

kulelemar كولەلەمار (OK) = kite (bird). See **kolare**.

kulemar كولەمار (IFb) = kite (bird). See **kolare**.

kulêmek كولێمەك (Qzl/LM) = thigh. See **kulîmek**.

kulêr كـــولـــێـر *f.* **(-a;-ê).** small window: •**Banê holê *kulêr* û pîpokên kulekên wê şikestibûn** (H v. 1, 83-84 [1932 1:4]) The roof of the hut, *the small windows* in its skylight were broken •**Wî di *kulêrê* r̄a berê xwe da jiderve** (FS) He went [or looked] outside through *the window*. {also: qulêr (FJ-2/GF-2/FS-2)} [H/FJ/GF/FS] <k'ulek II; p'ace; p'encere>

k'ulfet كـــولـــفـــەت *f.* **(-a;-ê).** 1) {syn: afret; hurmet; jin; kevanî; pîrek; zêç} wife; woman: •**Lawo, ya hatîye serê vê *kulfetê*, bira neyê serê gurê çiyan** (X. Çaçan. Benê min qetiya, 22) Son, what has happened to this *woman*, shouldn't even befall a wolf in the mountains; 2) {syn: malbat} family, children. {also: koflet (JB2-2); kuflet (JB2/FS); [koulfet كلفت/kuflet كفلت] (JJ)} Cf. T külfet = 'trouble, inconvenience' <Ar kulfah كـــلـــفـــة = 'trouble, inconvenience; lady's maid'; NENA kilpat ܟܠܦܬ (Maclean) & kilpet (Urmi: Polotsky) = 'family; wife' [Ba2/K/IF/B/JJ/ZF3//JB2/FS]

kulfik I كولفِك *f.* **(;-ê).** nostril(s). {syn: bêvil [1]; difn [2]; firn[ik]; k[']epî [2]; ximximk} [Wn/Wkt]

kulind كـــولـــنـــد *m.* **(-ê;).** pumpkin; squash, zucchini. {also: **gindor I**; kundik (Am); **kundir**; [kolend كلند/kouloundyr كولندر/كلندر] (JJ); <kulindir> كـولـنـدر (HH)} Sor kûleke كووولەكە = 'pumpkin, vegetable marrow' [Bw/IFb/GF/TF/OK//JJ//HH//Am] See also **gindor I** & **kundir**.

k'uling كـــولِـــنـــگ *m.* **(-ê;).** pick[axe], mattock. {also: kulîng (OK); kulling (Kmc-6)} Cf. P kolang كلنگ; Sor kułing كوڵنگ [Kmc-13/K/IFb/B/GF/TF/ZF3/Wkt//OK//Kmc-6] <tevir>

kulî I كـــولـــی *f.* **(-ya;-yê).** 1) {syn: kirîstik; sîsirk} cricket; 2) grasshopper; 3) locust, cicada. {also: kûlî (Srk/Kş/Mzg); [kouli] كـلـی (JJ); <kulî كـلـی/kule كله> (HH)} Mid P kullag = 'locust' (M3); Sor kule كـولـه = 'locust, grasshopper' [Srk/Kş/Mzg//A/IF/B/

HH/JJ]

kulî II كـولـى *f.* **(-ya;-yê).** snowflake: -**gulîya berfê** (GF)/**kulîya befrê** (SK) do.: •**R̄idîna wî wekî *kulîya befrê* spî bû** (SK 59:690) His beard was white like *a snowflake.* {also: gulî III (GF/FS); [kouli] كـولـى (JJ)} [K/A/B/IFb/JJ/SK/ZF/Wkt/FD/CS//GF/FS] <gulîfîtk>

kulîlk كـولـيـلـك *f.* **(-a;-ê).** flower; little flower: •**Ser wî *kulîlkêd* ħemû r̄enga û cûr̄a hêşîn dibûn** (Ba2:1, 202) On it [=Mount Dumanlu) *flowers of* all colors and types would grow. {also: <kulîlk> كليلك (HH)} {syn: çîçek; gul; mom I} [Ba2/K/JB3/IFb/B/HH/GF/TF/OK] <bilbiz = iris; gul = rose; pîvok = crocus/tulip/snowdrop; sosin, f. = lily>

kulîmek كـولـيـمـهك *f.* **(-a;-ê).** thigh: •**Jinikê vê sibê darek welê li *kulêmeka* min xistîye ku ji êşa wê ez nikarim rabim ser xwe!** (LM, 20) This morning the wife gave me such a whallop on *the thigh* that I can't stand up from the pain of it. {also: kulêmek (Qzl); kulîmik (GF); [koulimek] كـولمك (JJ); <kulîm[i]k> كليمك (HH)} {syn: hêt; r̄an; tilor I} Cf. Arm kołm կողմ = 'side' [Qzl/LM//IFb/JJ/TF/Kmc-4484/FS//HH/GF] <t'eşk>

kulîmik كوليمِك (GF/HH) = thigh. See **kulîmek**.

kulîn I كـولـيـن *vi.* **(-kul-).** to limp, be lame: •**Ew di rê ve çûnê da *dikulit*** (FS) He walks with a limp [lit. 'He *limps* in walking']. {also: kullîn; [kouliian] كـولـيـان (JJ)} {syn: lengirîn; licimîn} [K/JB3/IF/B/FS/ZF3//JJ] <t'opal>

kulîn II كـولـيـن *f.* **(-a;-ê).** pantry, larder, storeroom: a) for storing milk products, *in a nomadic tent* (K/B/Kmc); b) place for storing bedding *during the daytime* (JJ/FJ/CS/IFb/GF). {also: kulûn (Kmc-2); [koulin] كـولـين (JJ)} [K/B/JJ/Kmc/FJ/CS/IFb/GF/ZF3] <stêr̄ II>

kulîng كولينگ (OK) = pickaxe. See **k'uling**.

kulît كوليت, m. (SK) = hut, cabin. See **k'ol II**.

kulk كـولـك *f.* **(-a;-ê).** layer of goat's hair that becomes more prominent the fatter the goat gets (Qzl); high quality goat's hair used in making socks and gloves (GF): •[**Te**] ***kulka* xwe weşand** (Qzl) [You] are doing quite well, coming along nicely [=Kêmasîya te nema], i.e., You have let your *layer of goat's hair* grow out *[idiom]*. {also: [koulk] كلك (JJ)} Sor kułk كـولْـك/kurk كـورك = 'soft kinds of wool and hair, fleecy, flossy, foaming' [Qzl/JJ/GF/FJ/FS] <hirî; kej II; liva; r̄îs>

kullek كوللهك (TF/GF/HH) = lame. See **kulek I**.

kulling كولِلنگ (Kmc-6) = pickaxe. See **k'uling**.

kullîn كوللين = to limp. See **kulîn I**.

k'ulm كـولـم *f.* **(-a;-ê).** 1) {syn: baq; mist; qor̄e} handful, *also as a unit of measure*: •**Du *kulm*, ribek e** (Frq) 2 *handfuls* are a rib (dry measure) •**Ewê nêzîkaya k'ûpê r̄ûn *k'ulme dudu* ar ser 'erdê r̄eşand** (Dz-anec #32) Near the butter jug she sprinkled on the ground *a handful or two* of flour •***K'ulme* xwelî bavêje t'aê zêr̄a** (Ba) Throw *a handful of* dirt onto the scale with the gold •**Qîzê sê cara *k'ulma* xwe avêda kir û xar** (EP-7) The girl took three *handfuls of* water and drank •**Zelîxe *k'ulme* xalî davêje t'aê zêr̄a** (Ba) Zelikha throws *a handful of* dirt onto the scale with the gold; 2) {syn: mist} fist (IFb/TF). {also: [kouloum كـلـم /koulmek كلمك] (JJ); <kulm> كلم (HH)} [Ba/F/K/JB3/IFb/B/HH/GF/TF/OK//JJ]

kulmêrû كولميَروو (FS) = anthill. See **kurmorî**[1].

kulmîro كولميرۆ (FJ/GF) = anthill. See **kurmorî**[1].

kulmorî كولمۆرى (RZ-) = ant. See **kurmorî**[2].

kuloç كـولـۆچ *m./f.(FS/ZF3)* **(-ê/-a;).** unleavened cake (JJ); round bread (K). {also: kiloc; kiloç (B); kloç (HCK); [kouloutch] كـلـوچ (JJ); <kiloç> كـلـوچ (HH)} {syn: kilor} Cf. Rus kalač калач = 'white wheatmeal loaf' & kulič кулич = 'Easter cake', Yiddish koyletsh קוילעטש = 'braided challah (bread)' [K/B/JJ/FS//HH] <k'ade> See also **kilor**.

kulor كـولـۆر (K) = type of round bread or cake. See **kilor**.

kulorîk كـولـۆريـك (QtrE) = dish of ground meat and bulgur wheat. See **kilorîk**.

k'ulox كولۆخ (Dh/FS/BF) = skull. See **k'ilox**.

kulûn كـولـوون (Kmc) = pantry, storeroom. See **kulîn II**.

kulzikî كـولـزكـى *adj.* upset, bent out of shape, fed up, sick and tired, frustrated; resentful, holding a grudge: •**Te ez kirim *kulzikî*** (F.Mihemed. Ferhengoka Sêwregê) You've *upset* me very much/You're gonna make me old before my time/I've had it with you; -**bi kulzikî** (E.Serdar/RiaTaze) half-heartedly, resentfully, spitefully, against one's will:•-**Reşîd çira gazî te kir? --Min gotê, wekî perê goştê ç'êlekê dixweze. Hêrs ket, nifirî min û Mîrzoev kir. Min *bi kulzikî* pere hildan, çûme nivîsxana kolxozê** (E. Serdar. Mekteba Me û Dersdarê Minî Pêşin) "Why did Rashid call you?" -- "I told him that he wants the money for beef [the meat of a cow]. He flew into a rage, and cursed me and Mirzoev. I *resentfully/half-heartedly* took the money and went to the main office of the *kolkhoz*" **•[rêfêrêndûma Kurdistanê]...hinek ji wan piştgirîya Kurdan dikin û bi dil şadibin, hinek ji wana jî *bi kulzikî* dij derdikevin** (RiaTaze 13.viii.2017) [regarding the Kurdish referendum (Sept. 2017)] … some of them support the Kurds and are genuinely rejoicing, while some of them are *resentfully* opposing it. < kul = 'hole' + zik = 'belly, stomach' + -î [E.Serdar/RiaTaze/Frq/Kmc] <k'ezebreşî; kulecergî>

k'um كــوم *m./f.(K)* **(-ê/ ;).** hat; skullcap. {also: kim (IF-2); [koum] كــوم (JJ); <kum> كـم (HH)} {syn: kulav [4]; şewqe} [K/A/JB3/IF/B/HH/JJ/ZF3/FS/Wkt] <k'ofî; k'oloz>

kumax كوماخ (IFb/OK) = hip. See **k'emax**.

kumaẍ كوماغ (JB1-A) = hip. See **k'emax**.

kumbar كومبار (Wkt) = carpet. See **kombar**.

k'umeyd كومەيد (B) = bay colored. See **k'umeyt**.

k'umeyt كــومــەيــت *adj.* bay, reddish-brown, chestnut colored *(of horses)*: **•hespekî qer, hespekî boz, hespekî *k'umeyt*** (HCK-3, #16, 177) a black horse, a gray horse, a *bay* horse. {also: k'umeyd (B); kumêt (IFb/GF/FJ-2); [koumeït] كميت (JJ)} {syn: k'iḧêl} < Ar kumayt كــمــيــت = 'reddish-brown, chestnut, bay, maroon' [HCK/K/FJ/TF/JJ//IFb/GF//B]

kumêt كــومــێــت (IFb/GF/FJ) = bay colored. See **k'umeyt**.

k'umik كومِك *m.* **(-ê;).** 1) little hat, cap; 2) {syn: gaz û bêlan; gopk; ḧeç'; kop I; kumt} top, summit, crest *(of mountain)* (B); 3) circumflex (^); 4) {syn: gidark (Prw); karî I; karkevîk (Mş-Malazgirt); kiyark; kufkarik} mushroom (A). {also: [koumyk] كومك (JJ)} [Ber/K/A/B/JJ]

kumorî كومۆرى (Wkt[Dyr]) = ant. See **kurmorî**[2].

k'umr̄eş كــومــــــــڕەش *adj.* 1) {syn: dexes; ḧevsûd} jealous: **•Ew zelamekê *kumr̄eş* e** (FS) He is a *jealous* man; 2) suspicious, untrusting (JJ). {also: [koumrechi] كــومــرشــى (JJ)} < k'um = 'hat' + r̄eş = 'black' {k'umr̄eşî; k'umr̄eştî} [F/K/B/JJ/ZF3/FS]

k'umr̄eşî كــومــڕەشــى *f.* **(-ya;-yê).** jealousy; **-k'umr̄eşî kirin** (K/B) to be jealous of: **•Zîna r̄emildar *k'umr̄eşî dikir*** (FK-eb-1) Zîn the geomancer *was jealous*. {also: k'umr̄eştî (B-2)} {syn: dexesî; ḧevsûdî} [K/B/ZF3/FS] <k'umr̄eş>

k'umr̄eştî كومڕەشتى (B) = jealousy. See **k'umr̄eşî**.

kumt كــومــت *m.* **(-ê;).** mountaintop, peak, summit: **-kumtê çîyay** (Bw) do. {also: gimt (ZF3); kimt (GF); qimt (GF-2); <kimt> كـمـت (Hej)} {syn: gaz û bêlan; gopk; ḧeç'; kop I; k'umik} <Ar qimmah قمّة [Bw/FS//GF/Hej//ZF3]

kun I كــــــــــون (M-Ak/KH)/k'un I (K[s]/IFb/JJ/HH) = buttocks; anus; hole; lair. See **qûn**.

k'un II كون (A/FS) = goatskin. See **k'unk**.

k'unc كونج *m.* **(-ê;).** angle, corner: **-k'uncê be'rê** (B) inlet, bay. {also: kuncik (IF-2/GF); qunc, f. (IFb-2); quncik (IFb-2/GF-2); qurcik (GF-2); qurçik (A); [kounj كنج/koundjik كنجك] (JJ); <kunc كنج/quncik قنجك> (HH)} {syn: goşe; kujî; qorzî; qilçik; qulç} Cf. P konj كـنـج [S&E/K/IFb/B/JJ/HH/ZF3//A//GF]

kuncik كونجِك (IF/GF) = angle, corner. See **k'unc**.

kuncir̄ كونجِڕ (Bw) = cockle bur. See **quncir̄k**.

kuncî كــونــجــى *m./f.(FS/ZF3)* **(; /-yê).** sesame, bot. *Indicum*. {also: [kondji] كنجى (JJ); <kuncî> كنجى (HH)} Mid P kunjid (M3); P konjed كـنـجـد --> Rus kunžut кунжут; Sor kuncî كونجى [K/A/JB3/IF/JJ/B/HH/FS/Wkt]

kund كــونــد *m.* **(-ê;).** 1) {syn: bûm} owl, zool. order *Strigiformes*; screech-owl, barn-owl [Fr chouette] (JJ): **-kundê kor** (K) eagle owl; 2) [adj.] dull, blunt, stupid (B); 3) miser (JB3). {also: [quṅd] قــونــد (JJ-Lx); <kund> كــنــد (HH)} [F/A/K/JB3/IF/B/HH/ZF3//JJ]

kundik كوندِك (Am) = pumpkin, squash. See **kulind**.

kundir كوندِر *f./m.(K/GF)* **(-a/-ê;-ê/).** pumpkin, gourd, squash, zucchini, bot. *Cucurbita*: **•Çîroka qundirê** (L) The tale of the pumpkin. {also: **gindor I**; **kulind**; kundr (B-2); kundur (A); qundir (L); [koundyr] كــنــدر (JJ); <kundir كــنــدر/kundik كنــدك> (HH)} [L//K/IFb/B/HH/GF//A] <xirtik I> See also **gindor I** & **kulind**.

kunêr كونێر (OK) = boil, abscess. See **qunêr**.

kunik كونك (ZF3) = goatskin bag. See **k'unk**.

k'unk كونك *m.* **(-ê;).** goatskin in which water is stored in summer; "Water could also be carried in a goatskin bag. This was a whole skin, of which the neck and limbs protruded from the filled body when the woman carried it away. The barrel-shaped skin bag was not carried on the shoulder but lay across the woman's loins, and she held it with both arms" (from: Henny Harald Hansen. *Daughters of Allah: Among Moslem Women in Kurdistan* (London : George Allen & Unwin, 1960), p. 66); **-k'unkê avê** (Bw) do. {also: k'un II (A/FS); kunik (ZF3); k'unnik (A-2)} {syn:

cewdik} [Bw//A/FS//ZF3] <meşk>

kunmêrî کونمێری (SS/FS) = anthill. See **kurmorî**[1].

kunmîro کونمیرۆ (FJ/GF) = anthill. See **kurmorî**[1].

kunor•e کـــونـــۆرە *m.* **(•ê;).** two-pronged pitchfork. {also: <kinoře> کنۆڕە (Hej)} [Bw/FS//Hej] <milêb>

kup کوپ (Bw) = peak. See **kop**.

kup•e کـــوپـــە *f.* **(;•ê).** hearts *(suit of playing cards)*. {also: kope (Elk); kuppe (Bw); <kûpe> کـــوپـــە (Hej)} {syn: dilik} cf. T kupa [Bw//Qzl//Elk//Hej]

kuppe کوپپە (Bw) = hearts *(in card games)*. See **kupe**.

kur I کور (IF) = short. See **kurt I**.

kuř II کـوڕ *m.* **(-ê;).** son; child, boy: **•Azad *kurekî* jîr e** (AB) Azad is *a* smart *boy*. {also: [kour] کـــور (JJ); <kur> کر (HH)} {syn: gede [5]; law; mindal; t'ifal; zaro} <O Ir *kura-: Sgd wkwr /wi-kūr/ = 'of the (same) lineage'; Oss igurun = 'to be born'; Sor kuř کـوڕ; Za kurri *m.* = 'colt, foal' (Mal); Hau kuř *m.* = 'boy, son' (M4) {kuřtî II} [K/IFb/B/JJ/HH/JB1-A&S/SK/GF/TF/OK/BK] <kuřĥilî>

kuř III کوڕ *m.* **(-ê;).** head. {syn: ser[î]} [Mzg/IFb/ZF3]

kuř IV کـوڕ/**kur** کـــور [A/IFb/HH] *adj.* 1) shaved, shorn: **-kuř kirin** (F/K/A/IFb/B/JJ/Mzg) to shave, cut *(hair)*: **-gulîyê/p'ořê xwe kuř kirin** (K) to trim one's hair *(said of a woman recently bereft of loved ones)*; **-řûyê xwe kuř kirin** (K) to shave one's beard **-serê xwe kur kirin** (IF) to have one's head shaved: **•Berberê serê te *kuř dikin*, tu çima serê wana didî potkirin** (EH) The barbers *shave* your head, why do you have their heads chopped off?; 2) crop-eared *(of sheep)* (B/HH): **-mîya kuř** (B) crop-eared sheep. {also: [kour kirin] کور کرین (JJ); <kur> کر (HH)} [F/K/A/IFb/B/JJ/HH/Mzg] <berber I; delak; gûzan>

kuř V کوڕ (FS) = mud. See **quř**.

k'ur VI کـــــــور (BK) = young donkey; colt, foal. See **k'uřik**.

kurad کـوراد *f.* **(;-ê).** leek, bot. *Allium porrum*. {also: guřed (FS-2); qurad (Wkt); quřad (FS); [kourad] کـــراد (JJ)} {syn: kewer} Cf. Arc krātayā כרתיא & Syr karṯā ܟܪܬܐ & NENA kîrâthâ/chîrâthâ ܟܪܬܐ (Maclean); Ar kurrāṯ کـــرّاث = 'leek'; = Sor kewer کەوەر [JJ/GF/TF/OK//Wkt//FS]

kuřader کورادەر (Qmş) = stench, stink. See **kuředer**.

kuřap کـــوراپ/**kurap** کـــوراپ [F/A/IFb] *m.* **(-ê;-ê/kuřêp).** first cousin, son of one's father's brother. {also: [kour-i api] کـــوری عـــاپـــی (JJ)} {syn: kuřmam; lawê ap; pismam} < kuř II + ap = 'paternal uncle'; = Sor amoza ئـامـۆزا [FK-kk-1/F/ K/A/IFb/B/GF//JJ] <pismam>

kurbeşik کـــوربـــەشـیـك (IFb) = badger; mole. See **kuřebeşk**.

kurbeşk کـــوربـــەشـك (IFb/ZF3) = badger; mole. See **kuřebeşk**.

K'urd کـــــورد *m.* **().** Kurd: **-jina K'urd** (K)/**k'ulfeta K'urd** (B) Kurdish woman. {also: Ek'rad; [kourd] کـرد (JJ); <kurd> کـرد (HH)} {K'urdayetî (K[s]); K'urdanî (K); K'urdîtî (K/A)} *For a discussion of the possible etymologies of this word, see:* **Chap. 1** "Les Kurdes, leur origine et leurs caractéristiques linguistiques et anthropologiques," in B. Nikitine. *Les Kurdes: étude sociologique et historique* (Paris: Imprimerie Nationale : Librairie C. Klincksieck, 1956), pp. [1]-22. [K/A/JB3/IF/B/JJ/HH] <Kurmanc>

k'urdane کـــوردانـــە *adv.* à la kurde, in the Kurdish fashion or manner. [BX/ZF3]

K'urdanî کوردانی (K) = Kurdishness. See **K'urdayetî**.

K'urdayetî کوردایەتی *f.* **(;-yê).** Kurdishness, Kurdish identity; "**Kurdayetî** is a Kurdish concept which expresses the transferral of the Kurds' awareness of themselves as a people into cultural and political activity..." (translated from: Erhard Franz. *Kurden und Kurdentum: Zeitgeschichte eines Volkes und seiner Nationalbewegungen* [Hamburg: Deutsches Orient-Institut, 1986], p. 19) {also: K'urdanî (K); K'urdîtî (K/A)} See also: Amir Hassanpour-Aghdam. *The Language Factor in National Development: The Standardization of the Kurdish Language, 1918-1985*. Doctoral dissertation (Urbana, Ill.: University of Illinois, 1989), p. 60, note #8 p.64. [K(s)//K/A]

k'urdewarî کـــــوردەواری *adj.* (typically, peculiarly, traditionally) Kurdish: **•Şêx, çûnkû hêşta di umûrêt siyasî da puxte nebibû, û di meşrebê 'eşîretî û *kurdewarî* da bû, û ecela wî jî hatibû, nesîĥetê qunsol nekewte 'aqlê wî, xiyalekî dî kir** (SK 48:505) The Shaikh, as he was not yet versed in political affairs, and was fixed in his tribal, *Kurdish* nature, and also because it was his fate, did not accept the Consul's advice, but thought otherwise **•Wextê geheşte naw leşkirê mirîdan dît hemî tifengêt *kurdewarî* xirab, bê kar e** (SK 47:459) When he came among the army of the disciples, he saw that they all had bad, useless, *locally made* guns. {also: <kurdewarî> کوردەواری (Hej)} Sor kurdewarî کـوردەواری = 'the

Kurdish world, stg. typically Kurdish' [Bw/IFb/SK/Hej]

K'urdistan کوردِستان *f.* **(-a;-ê).** Kurdistan, homeland of the Kurdish people: **-K'urdistana Îraqê** (K) Kurdistan of Iraq, Iraqi Kurdistan [Başûr]; **-K'urdistana Îranê** (K) Kurdistan of Iran, Iranian Kurdistan [Rojhilat]; **-K'urdistana Romê** (K)/ **K'urdistana Tirkî** (K) Kurdistan of Turkey, Turkish Kurdistan [Bakur]; **-Kurdistana Sûriyê** = **Rojavaya Kurdistanê** (Google) Kurdistan of Syria, Western Kurdistan [Rojava]. {also: [kurdistán] كردستان (JJ)} [K/A/JB3/IF/JJ]

K'urdî کوردی *adj.* Kurdish. {also: [kurdi] كردى (JJ)} {syn: Kurmancî} [K/A/JB3/IF/B/JJ] <Kurmanc>

Kurdîaxêf کوردی ئاخێف (Wkt) = Kurdish-speaking. See **K'urdîaxêv**.

K'urdîaxêv کوردی ئاخێڤ *m.&f.* **().** 1) Kurdish speaker; 2) [*adj.*] Kurdish-speaking {syn: K'urdîzan[1]}: **•Nêrîna wî xortî ya li wê qîza *kurdîaxêv* ne nerîneke evîndar e; ew xort bi çavê dêyekê, bi çavê xwişkekê li wê qîza *kurdîaxêv* dinêre** (Twitter: Metowski) The young man's glance at that *Kurdish-speaking* girl was not an amorous glance; he looks at her with the eyes of a mother, the eyes of a sister. {also: K'urdîaxêf (Wkt-2); K'urdîaxif (Wkt-2); K'urdîaxiv (Wkt)} [ZF//Wkt]

K'urdîaxif کوردی ئاخِف (Wkt) = Kurdish-speaking. See **K'urdîaxêv**.

K'urdîaxiv کوردی ئاخِڤ (Wkt) = Kurdish-speaking. See **K'urdîaxêv**.

K'urdîtî کوردیتی (K/A) = Kurdishness. See **K'urdayetî**.

K'urdîzan کوردیزان *adj.* Kurdish-speaking, who knows or speaks Kurdish: **•Çend Ermenîyên *kurdîzan*** (DM) Some *Kurdish-speaking* Armenians. {syn: K'urdîaxêv[2]} < Kurdî = 'Kurdish' + zan- = 'know' [DM/K]

Kurdmanc کوردمانج = Kurd; peasant. See **Kurmanc**.

K'urdnas کوردناس (FS/FD) = Kurdologist. See **K'urdolog**.

K'urdnasî کوردناسی (FS) = Kurdology. See **K'urdolojî**.

K'urdolog کوردۆلۆگ *m.&f.* **(-ê/-a;).** Kurdologist, scholar who specializes in studying the Kurds and their language, customs, folklore and history: **•*Kurdologa* hêja M.B.Rudenkoyê, Mem û Zîna Ahmedê Xanî jî bi herfên Erebî û bi tercumeya wê ya Rûsî amade kir** (PDK-Xoybûn) The respected *Kurdologist* M.B. Rudenko prepared Ahmedî Khanî's Mem û Zîn in Arabic letters and with her Russian translation **•Profesor û *kurdologê* navbilind Mîkayîl Lazarêv çû ser dilovaniya xwedê** (Radyo Dengê Rûsya 17.iii.2010) The professor and prominent *Kurdologist* Mikhail Lazarev passed away. {also: Kurdnas (FS-2/FD-2); K'urdzan (K)/ Kurdzan (FS/FD)} < K'urd + -olog [R.DengêRûsya/ Wkt/ZF3//K/FS/FD]

K'urdolojî کوردۆلۆژی *f.* **(-ya;-yê).** Kurdology, scholarly study of the Kurds and their language, customs, folklore and history: **•Piştî Abovyan, Peter J.A. Lerc (1828-1884) yek ji hîmdar û sazkerên *kurdolojîya* Sovyetê tête qebûlkirin** (Ziman û Dîyalekt 17.v.2014 10) After Abovian, Peter J.A. Lerch is considered one of the founders of Soviet *Kurdology*. {also: Kurdnasî (FS-2); K'urdzanî (K)/Kurdzanî (FS)} [Ziman û Dîyalekt/ZF3/Wkt]

K'urdzan کوردزان (K)/Kurdzan کوردزان (FS/FD) = Kurdologist. See **K'urdolog**.

K'urdzanî کوردزانی (K)/Kurdzanî کوردزانی (FS) = Kurdology. See **K'urdolojî**.

kurebeş کورەبەش (A) = badger; mole. See **kuřebeşk**.

kuřebeşk کورەبەشك *f./m.(FS)* **(;-ê/).** 1) badger, zool. *Meles*; 2) mole, zool. *Talpidae* (HH). {also: kurbeş[i]k (IFb); kurebeş (A); kuribeşk (GF-2); qurbeşe (M-Ak); quřbeşk (FS); [kouré-bechk] كوره بشك (JJ); <korebeşk> كوربشك (HH)} [K/F/JJ/ B/GF//IFb/ZF3//HH//A//M//FS]

kuředer کورەدەر *f.* **(;-ê).** stench, stink, putrid smell, foul smell: **•Bila *quředer* bit li ser te** (Dh) May it turn into *poison* for you *[curse]* **•Keçik gava dinêře serê wê, bîna *kuře derê* jê tê** (J) When the girl looked at her (=the old woman's) head, [she noticed that] *a bad smell* came from it. {also: kuřader (Qmş); quředer (Frq/Dh)} [J/B//Qmş//Frq/Dh] <genî>

kuřefêng کورەفێنگ (Zeb) = type of wild bee. See **kuřîfok**.

kurhelî کورهەلی (GF) = stepson. See **kuřĥilî**.

kurhilî کورهِلی (TF/ZF3) = stepson. See **kuřĥilî**.

kuřĥilî کورحِلی *m.* **().** stepson. {also: kurhelî (GF); kurhilî (TF/ZF3)} {syn: nevisî} [Frq//TF/ZF3//GF] <- ĥilî I; zirdayîk>

kuribeşk کوربەشك (GF) = badger; mole. See **kuřebeşk**.

k'uřik کورِك *m.* **().** 1) {syn: cehş; dehş} young donkey; 2) {syn: canî} colt, foal. {also: k'ur VI

(BK); kur̄î II (IF); k'urîk (K); kurîn (JB3)} Cf. Clq. Ar kurr كـرّ = 'young donkey'; Za kurri *m.* = 'colt, foal' (Mal) [ZF3/Wkt//K//JB3//IF//BK] <hesp; k'er III>

kurinc كورِنج (ZF3) = wool-carder. See **kûrinc**.

kurisandin I كورِساندِن *vt.* **(-kurisîn-).** to gnaw, nibble at: **•Rovî, duhêlê li şêr gerandî bû, *kurisandin* û şêr vekir** (RN 16.vii.1945, 3) The fox *gnawed at* the threads tied around the lion, and freed the lion. {syn: kotin} [RN/TF/OK]

kurişkî كورشكى (VoA) = curly. See **kurîşk**.

kurî I كورى *f.* **(-ya;).** tail. {syn: boç'[ik]; dêl II; dû II; k'ilk; qemç[ik]; ter̄î I[1]} [Bw/FS]

kur̄î II كـــــــوڕى (IF) = young donkey; colt, foal. See **k'ur̄ik**.

kur̄îfok كوڕيفۆك *f.* **(-a;).** species of wild bee, *smaller than **zilketk** [qv.], resembling a small gray flying ant with stripes [**r̄av II**] on its back--it makes a delicious, light (white) honey which tastes like **gezo** [qv.]* (Zeb). {also: kirîfok (AA); kor̄îfok (Zeb-2); kur̄efêng (Zeb-2); kur̄îvok (FS); <kurîfok> كوريفوك (Hej)} = Sor bedreme بەدرەمە [Zeb/Hej//FS//AA] <mêş [2]; moz I; zilketk>

k'urîk كـــوريـــك (K) = young donkey; colt, foal. See **k'ur̄ik**.

kurîn كورين (JB3) = colt, foal. See **k'ur̄ik**.

kurîşk كـوريـشـك *adj.* 1) curly {also: kurişkî (VoA); kurîşkî (A/B)}: **•Bifikirin ku min hevala xwe Sêvê ji porê wê yê *kurişkî* naskir** (VoA) Imagine that I recognized my friend S. by her *curly* hair **•Porê min reş û *kurîşk* e** (Hînker) My hair is black and *curly*; **-p'or̄ê kurîşkî** (B) curly hair; 2) *f.* **(;-ê).** curl. [Hînker/K/FJ/GF/ZF/RZ/Wkt/G/CS//A/B]

kurîşkî كوريشكى (A/B) = curly. See **kurîşk**.

kur̄îvok كوڕيڤۆك (FS) = type of wild bee. See **kur̄îfok**.

kurîx كوريخ (HoK2) = fierce. See **gurêx̌**.

kurk I كـــــورك *f.* **(;-ê).** brooding hen. {also: [kourk] كـورك (JJ)} Cf. Clq. Palestinian Ar qruqqah قـرقّـة [S&E/K/A//B/FS/ZF3/Wkt//JJ] <mamir; mirîşk>

k'urk II كــــورك *m.* **(-ê;).** 1) fur; 2) garment made of fur; long fur-lined cloak or coat, pelisse: **•Wî *kurkê* xwe bi xwe werkir** (FS) He put on his *fur coat*. {also: kûrk I (IF-2); [kourk] كـورك (JJ)} <T kürk [K//B//IFb/GF/FS/ZF3//JJ]

kurm كـــــــورم *m.* **(-ê;).** worm: **-kurmê hevirmiş** (B) silkworm. {also: kirim (BF); kirm (FS/Wkt); [kouroum] كـــرم (JJ); <kurm> كـــرم (HH)} [Pok. k^{u}rmi- 649.] 'mite, worm': Skt kṛmi-; Mid P kirm = 'worm, serpent' (M3); Southern Tati dialects (all *f.*): Chali/Takestani/Sagz-abadi kelma; Eshtehardi/ Xiaraji kerma (Yar-Shater); P kerm كـرم; Sor kirm كـرم; Za kerm *m.* = 'larva' (Mal)/*f.* = 'worm [larva]' (Todd) [F/K/A/JB3/IFb/B/HH/GF//JJ//FS/Wkt//BF] <maşot>

kur̄mam كوڕمام [K(s)/B]/**kurmam** كـورمام [OK] *m.* **(-ê;-ê [B]).** male first cousin on one's paternal side, son of paternal uncle. {syn: kur̄ap; pismam} < kur̄ II + mam = 'paternal uncle'; = Sor amoza ئامۆزا [Rnh/A/IFb/OK//K(s)/B]

Kurmanc كــورمـــانــج *m.* **().** 1) Kurd, *specifically, the name by which the speakers of the northern dialects call themselves*: **-jina kurmanc** (K)/ **k'ulfeta kurmanc** (B) Kurdish woman; 2) non-tribal peasant (K[s]); "Kurmanj," the term used for non-tribal peasants in northern Kurdistan, was used in southern Kurdistan for a segment of the tribal élite [M. van Bruinessen. "Kurdish Society, Ethnicity, Nationalism and Refugee Problems," in: *The Kurds: A Contemporary Overview*, ed. Philip G. Kreyenbroek & Stefan Sperl (London & New York : Routledge, 1992), note #9, p. 220]. {also: Kirmanc (K[s]); Kurdmanc; <k[u]rmanc> كرمانج (HH)} *Minorsky's etymology:* Kur(d) + Manneans/Mantianoi, seeing the Kurdish nation as an amalgam of two tribes, the Kyrtioï and the Mardoï (p. 12); *Marr's etymology:* Armenian: har-men < *kar-mentch, kar-mendj/kurmandj (p. 15). See: **Chapter 1**,"Les Kurdes, leur origine et leurs caractéristiques linguistiques et anthropologiques," in B. Nikitine. *Les Kurdes: étude sociologique et historique* (Paris : Imprimerie Nationale : Librairie C. Klincksieck, 1956), pp. 12-15. [K/A/IF/B/HH] <K'urd>

Kurmancî كــورمـــانـــجـــى *adj.* Kurdish *(language), specifically, the northern dialects.* {also: [kourmandji] كـــرمـــانـــجـــى (JJ); <k[u]rmancî> كرمانجى (HH)} [K/A/IF/B/JJ/HH] <K'urdî>

Kurmancîaxêf كورمانجى ئاخێف (Wkt) = Kurmanji-speaking. See **Kurmancîaxêv**.

Kurmancîaxêv كــورمــانــجــى ئــاخــێــڤ *m.&f.* **().** 1) Kurmanji speaker: **•Ew ji deverên *kurmancîaxêvan* jî dûr bû** (Kulturname: Emîr Hesenpûr) He was also far from the regions *of the Kurmanji speakers*; 2) [*adj.*] Kurmanji-speaking: **•Hêrkî *kurmancîaxêv* û misilman in** (Wkp) The Herkis are *Kurmanji-speaking* and Muslim **•Li Sûriyeyê, wek li Yekîtiya Sovyetê bi timamî *kurmancîaxêv***

in (Kulturname: Emîr Hesenpûr) In Syria, as in the Soviet Union, [Kurds] are entirely *Kurmanji-speaking.* {also: Kurmancîaxêf (Wkt-2); Kurmancîaxif (Wkt-2); Kurmancîaxiv (Wkt)} [ZF//Wkt]

Kurmancîaxif کورمانجی ئاخِف (Wkt) = Kurmanji-speaking. See **Kurmancîaxêv**.

Kurmancîaxiv کورمانجی ئاخِڤ (Wkt) = Kurmanji-speaking. See **Kurmancîaxêv**.

kur̄met/kur̄met' [B] کورمەت *m.* **(;-ê** [B]**).** first cousin, son of paternal aunt: **•Du muro hebûn ji 'eşîreta Mizûrî Jorî ... her du ji ocax̄ek[ê] bûn ... her du xizmêt yêk jî bûn. 'Ebdî** ***kur̄ê meta*** **'Ezîz bû, 'Ezîz kur̄ê xalê 'Ebdî bû** (SK 18:166) There were two men of the Upper Mizuri tribe ... they were both of one clan ... Moreover they were related to each other. Abdi was *the son of* Aziz's *paternal aunt,* Aziz was the son of Abdi's maternal uncle. {also: kur̄metî (K)} <kur̄ = 'son' + met = 'aunt, father's sister' [Bw/B/OK/RZ//K]

kur̄metî کورمەتی (K) = son of paternal aunt. See **kur̄met**.

kurmî کورمی *adj.* 1) wormy; worm-eaten: **-kurmî bûn** (IFb/TF/JJ) to have worms (of animal): **•Cewrikê din** ***kirmî bû*****, mîna bi nexweşiya firengiyê lê be** (Wt, 87) The other puppy *had worms* [lit. 'was wormy'], as if it was afflicted with syphilis; 2) rotten, decayed, rancid. {also: kirmî (Wkt-2); [kourmi bouin] کرمی بوین (JJ); <kirmî کرمی /kirmbûyî کرمبویی> (HH)} < kurm/ kirm = 'worm' [WT/K/A/IFb/B/FJ/GF/TF/JJ/ZF//Wkt/HH]

kurmorî کورمۆری *f.* **(-ya;-yê).** 1) {syn: mûristan[1]} anthill {also: kulmêrû (FS); kulmîro (FJ/GF); kunmêrî (SS/FS-2); kunmîro (FJ-2/GF-2)}: **•Wî** ***kunmêriya*** **li ber dîwarî xirab kir** (FS) He destroyed *the anthill* near the wall; 2) {syn: mûristan[2]; mûrî I; gêle} ant, zool. *Formicidae* {also: kulmorî (RZ-2); kumorî (Wkt[Dyr]-2); kurmûrî (IFb/RZ/CS-2); kurmwîrî (G)}: **•Şêr li ser devê qula** ***kurmoriyan*** **radikeve** (H.Akyol. Tajiya Qazûxa, 54) The lion sleeps at the opening to *the ants'* den. < kur/kul/qul/kun = 'hole; den, lair' + morî/ mûrî/mêrî, etc. = 'ant'; Sor: mêrûle مێرووله = 'ant'; şare mêrûle شاره مێرووله = 'anthill' [H.Akyol/ ZF3/Wkt(Dyr)/CS//IFb/RZ//G//FJ/GF//FS//SS] <mûrî I>

kurmûrî کورمووری (IFb/RZ/CS) = ant. See **kurmorî**[2].

kurmwîrî کورمویری (G) = ant. See **kurmorî**[2].

k'ursî/kursî [JB1-A] کورسی *f./m.(E/Z-3)* **(-ya/-yê; -yê/).** 1) chair: **•Divê maseya ku we dît bi kêmanî çar** ***kursî*** **li dorê hebin ... di pê re hûnê ji çar** ***kursîyan kursîyekê*** **hinekî bi paş de bikşînin** (LC, 33) There must be at least four *chairs* around the table you found ... then you will pull back one of the four *chairs* a little; 2) throne: **•Sê** ***kursî*** **hebûn ...** ***kursîyek*** **li layê jorê, yêk li layê r̄astê, yêk li layê çepê bû.** ***Kursîya*** **layê jorê Ĥezretê Imam Ĥuseyn li ser r̄ûniştî bû,** ***kursîya*** **layê r̄astê cenabê Muctahid,** ***kursîya*** **layê çepê mu'ezzin li ser r̄ûniştî bûn** (SK 11:108) There were three *thrones* ... one *throne* was above, one on the right and one on the left. The great Imam Husain was seated on the upper *throne*, his honor the Mujtahid was seated on the right-hand *throne* and the muezzin on the left-hand *throne*; 3) low four-cornered stool, covered with a blanket, under which is placed a brazier with coals to warm the feet of those seated; 4) {syn: azû} molar tooth, grinder (HH/GF): **-diranên kursî** (K/IFb) molars, back teeth. {also: kirsî (BX); [koursi] کرسی (JJ); <kursî> کرسی (HH)} < Ar kursī كرسي [BX//K/JB3/IFb/B/JJ/HH/SK/JB1-A&S/GF/TF]

kurşe کورشه *f.(ZF3)/m.(FS)* **(;/-yî).** crisp, frozen snow (good for sliding on): **•Ew di ser** ***kurşeyî*** **ra çû** (FS) He walked on the *frozen snow*. {also: <kurşe> کورشه (Hej)} < Arc qrēš/qraš קריש = 'to congeal, become solid' & Syr qraš ܩܪܫ = 'to become chilled, frozen', cf. also NENA qârish ܩܪܫ = 'to be crisp, as snow' (Maclean) [Zeb/GF/Hej/FS/ ZF3] <berf>

kurt I کورت *adj.* short *(of inanimate objects, rather than people)*. {also: kur I (IF-2); [kourt] کورت (JJ); <kurt> کرت (HH)} {syn: gurc II; k'ese} {kurtayî; kurtî I} [K/A/JB3/IF/B/JJ/HH] <kin>

kurt II کورت *m.* **(-ê;).** vulture, zool. *Accipitridae*. {also: <kurt> کرت (HH)} {syn: sîsalk} [IFb/HH/GF/ OK] <başok; baz I; elîh; keçel; xertel>

kurtan/k'urtan [K/A] کورتان *m.* **(-ê;).** donkey saddle, pack-saddle for mules or donkeys. {also: <kurtan> کرتان (HH)} {syn: p'alik} [Btm/IFb/HH/GF/ TF/OK/Bw//K/A] <heçî I; teng II>

kurtayî کورتایی *f.* **(-ya;-yê).** shortness, brevity: **-bi kurtayî** (Ber)/**bi kurtî** (IF) briefly, in summary: **•Tu dikarî** ***bi kurtayî*** **xwe bidî naskirin?** (Ber) Can you *briefly* introduce yourself? {also: kurtî I (K/IF-2); [kourti] کورتی (JJ)} {syn: kinayî} [Ber/A/

IF//K/JJ] <kurt I>

kurteçîrok کورتەچیرۆك/**kurteçîrok** کورتەچیرۆك *f.* **(-a;-ê).** short story: •**Bi navê "Tayek porê sipî" *kurteçîrokeke* Qedrî Can heye** (LC, 5) Qedri Jan has *a short story* called "A single white hair" •**Pişt ra dest bi nîvisandina *kurteçîrokan* kirîye** (Torî. Qolinc - back cover) Afterward he began to write *short stories*. Sor kurte çîrok کورتەچیرۆك (Gizîng) [(neol)Ardû/Qolinc/TF/LC/ZF3]

kurtek کورتەك (MG/IFb) = shirt. See **qutik I**.

kurtepist کورتەپست (TF) = gossip. See **kurt û p'ist**.

k'urtêl کورتێل *f.* **(-a;-ê).** crumbs, orts, scraps of food: •**Li kolana ma bê cî, tazî û birçî. Hindebo rabû ji xwe re *kurtêlê* ji ber devê xelkê diman didan hev û dixwar. Carna gepek peyda dikir û carna birçî dima** (FB: Z. Osman. Mafê çêrê parastî ye) Hindebo was left on the streets, homeless, naked and hungry. He gathered together *scraps of* other people's food and ate them. Sometimes he found a bite to eat, sometimes he went hungry. [Qzl/A/IFb/FJ/GF/ZF/Wkt/FS]

k'urtêlxur کورتێلخور *m.&f.* **().** freeloader, parasite, scrounger, sponger: •**Ji roja ku dinya afirîye û heta niha *kurtêlxwer* û berjewendperest hene û wê ji îro û pêve jî hebin** (Lotikxane) From the day the world was created until now there have always been *freeloaders* and people looking out for their own interests, and from today onward there will always be [such people]. {also: kurtêlxwer (FJ/GF)} <k'urtêl = 'food scraps' + xur/xwer = 'eater(s)' [Qzl/ZF//FJ/GF] <k'edxwar>

kurtêlxwer کورتێلخوەر (FJ/GF) = freeloader, parasite. See **k' urtêlxur**.

kurtik کورتِك (RZ/ZF) = shirt. See **qutik I**.

kurtî I کورتی (K/IF) = shortness. See **kurtayî**.

kur̄tî II کوڕتی *f.* **(-ya;-[y]ê).** 1) sonhood, state of being the son of s.o.: •**Îdî *kur̄tîya* min ter̄a boşe** (Z-1) I am no longer your son [lit. 'Now my *sonhood* to you is void'] •**Yanê tuê wê Leylê min̄ra bixwezî, yan ez ter̄a t'u *kur̄tîê* nakim** (EP-5, #12) Either you request that [girl] Leyla for me [in marriage], or I am no longer your son [lit. 'or I will do no *sonhood* for you']; 2) filial piety [Cf. Ar birr بِرّ]. [Z-1/K] <kur̄ II>

kurtpist کورتپست (GF) = gossip. See **kurt û p'ist**.

kurtupist کورتوپست (GF/OK) = gossip. See **kurt û p'ist**.

kurt û p'ist کورت و پست/**kurtûpist** [IFb] کورتووپست *f.* **(-a;-ê).** 1) {syn: galegûrt; galigal; gotgotk; paşgotinî} gossip(ing), rumor; idle chatter, empty talk (OK): •**...bi fikira ku ji Diyarbekiriyan re nebe mijara *kurt û pistê*, wê mala Doktor Sertaç çêtir dîtibû** (KS, 38) ...thinking that she should not be a topic *of gossip* for people in Diyarbakir, she chose Dr. Sertaç's house instead •**Lê gava *kurtûpista* ku wî di bin tesîra apê xwe de xweha xwe kuştiye li bajêr belav bûbû, pir kesan bawer nekiribûn** (KS, 11) But when *the rumor* spread across the city that he had killed his sister under his uncle's influence, many people could not believe it; 2) whisper(ing) (GF). {also: kurtepist (TF); kurtpist (GF-2); kurtupist (GF/OK)} [KS/IFb//GF/OK//TF] <p'isep'is>

k'urumk' کورومك, m. (JB1-S) = bonfire. See **k'ûrme**.

kur̄xal کوڕخال/**kurxal** کورخال *m.* **(;-ê [B]).** first cousin, son of one's mother's brother: •**Her heft *kurxalên* wan li hev kom bûn** (ZZ-7, 167) All seven of their *maternal first cousins* gathered together.{also: [kour-i khali] کوری خالی (JJ)} {syn: *lawxal (RZ); *pisxal (RZ/Kmc)} [ZZ/A/RZ/ZF/CS/Kmc//K/B//JJ]

***kuş I** کوش *adj.* hollow, *quality of a rock or stone: if its interior is full of holes like a sponge (i.e., if the wind blows through it), it is called* **kuş**. {syn: fisfisok (Wn); ≠qesp (Qzl)} [Qzl/GF]

k'uş II کوش *f.* **(-a;).** silent fart, noiseless flatulence, "SBD" (=silent but deadly), *as opposed to* **tir̄** = *audible fart*: •***Kuşa* wî hat** (FS) He farted/He broke wind [lit. 'his fart came'] •**Wî *kuşek* berda/kir** (FS) He cut *a silent fart*/He passed gas silently. {syn: fis} Cf. P čos چس [Wkt/BF/ZF3/FS] <tir̄>

kuşne کوشنە (IFb) = vetch. See **kizin**.

k'uşpil کوشپل (FS) = sheep or goat manure. See **bişkul & pişkul**.

kuştin کوشتِن *vt.* **(-kuj-).** to kill: •**Wana teyrek *kuşt*** (Ba) They *killed* a bird •**Teyrê Sêmir hat go çwîkê beytik *bikuje*** (L) The Simurgh came *to kill* the sparrow; **-hatin kuştinê** (B) to be killed. {also: [kouchtin] کشتين (JJ); <kuştin کشتن (dikuje) (دکژه)> (HH)} {syn: mirandin [1]} O Ir *kauš- (Tsb 37): Av kaoš- (*pres.* kuša-); P koštan کشتن (-koš-) (کش); Sor kuştin کوشتِن (-kuj-); SoK kwıštın (Fat 561); Za kişenã [kiştiş] (Srk/Mal); Hau kuştey (k^{W}ş-) *vt.* (M4) [K/A/JB3/IF/JJ/B/HH] <gurandin; mirin; şerjêkirin>

kuşxank کوشخانك *pl.* ceiling: •***kuşxankêt* xanîyê me** (Bw) *the ceiling of* our house. {also: kaşxank (SS)} {syn: ar̄îk; asraq; *binban (Kmc); *qarçik (Kmc/RZ); s̲apîtke} [Bw//SS]

k'uta کـوتـا *f.* (). end, result: **-k'uta bûn** = a) to be relieved, rescued, rid of: •**Wele, ezê xwe bavêjim be're, bra *ji* 'ezebê dinê *k'uta bim*** (EP-7) By God, I'll throw myself into the sea, so that I *am done with* the pain of the world; b) to be finished, completed, done, over; **-k'uta kirin** (IFb/GF/TF) to finish, complete {syn: qedandin; xilas kirin}: •**Wexta dîya min gilîyêd xwe *k'uta kirin*, min ew ḧemêz kir** (Ba2:2, 207) When my mother *finished* her words, I embraced her. {also: [koutahi] کـوتـاهـی (JJ)} {syn: axirî; dawî; encam} Sor kota کـۆتـا = 'ended' [EP-7/K/JB3/IFb/ B/GF/TF/OK//JJ] See also **k'utasî**.

k'utan کـوتـان *vt.* **(-k'ut-).** 1) {syn: jendin; lêdan; lêxistin; r̄epandin} to strike, hit, beat: •**Xort da pey boẍ, dêla boẍ girt, boẍ *k'uta*** (J) The young man ran after the ox, caught hold of the ox's tail, *beat* the ox •**Bi dîwêr ve *kutta*** (BK) He *drove* [it, i.e., a nail] into the wall; 2) to pound, pulverize: •**[Û di ekserêd malan da cuhnî û mêkut heye bi xwe dermanî *diqut̲in* û çê dikin]** (BN 135) And in most households there is a mortar and pestle [which they use to] *pound* and make medicines; 3) to thrust, insert, stick into (BK); 4) [+ **di**] to screw, copulate with, fornicate with, fuck {syn: gan I; nayîn}: •***Ezê di te bikutim*** (Msr) I *will screw* you! *[insult]* {also: kuttan (BK); qutan (M); [koutan] کوتان (JJ); <kuttan کتان (dikutte) (دکته)> (HH)} O Ir *kup-(Tsb p.37): Mid P kōftan (kōb) = 'to beat, pound, crush' (M3); P kōbīdan کـوبـیـدن = 'to pound, smash, beat, thresh'; Sor kutan کـوتـان (-kutê-); Za kwenã [kwatiş] (Srk); Hau kûay (kû-) *vt.* (M4) [BX/F/J/K/A/JB3/IF/B/Msr//BK/HH//M]

k'utasî کـوتـاسـی *f.* **(-ya;-yê).** 1) {syn: axirî; dawî; encam} ending, end: •***K'utasîya* civatêda** (B) At *the end of* the meeting; **-bê k'utasî** (B) endless, interminable; **-bi k'utasî** (B) finally; **-ḧeta k'utasîyê** (B) until the end, to the end; **-[di] k'utasîyêda** (B) in the end; 2) to make a long story short, in short. {also: <kutasî> کتاسی (HH)} Cf. P kūtāh کـوتـاه = 'short' [Z-1/K/B/HH] See also **k'uta**.

kutefir کوتەفِر *f.* **(;-ê).** quail, zool. *Coturnix coturnix.* {also: kotefir (FJ/GF-2/FS)} {syn: 'ebdal; k'êr̄asû} [Kmc/GF/ZF3//FJ/FS] <kew I; lorî I; por I>

kutek کوتەك (IFb) = mallet. See **k'utik I**.

kute-kut کـوتـەکـوت *f.* **().** barking, howling, yelping: •**Le'zek sekinî, du sa hatin, *kirne* [sic] *kewte-kewt*** (HCK-5, #8, 58) He waited a minute, 2 dogs came, they *barked.* {also: kewte-kewt (K/B/IFb/ Wkt); kewtkewt (FJ/GF); <kûtekût> کـوتـکـوت (HH)} {syn: bile-bil; 'ewte'ewt; kastekast; r̄eyîn I} [F//HH//K/B/IFb/Wkt//FJ/GF]

k'ut•ik I کـوتِـك *m.* **(•kê;).** mallet used for beating burghul or wheat: **-k'utkê genmî** (Zeb) do.. {also: kutek (IFb)} [Zeb/K(s)//IFb] <çakûç>

k'utik II کوتِك (Z-3) = beating, blow. See **k'otek**.

k'ut'ilik' کـوتِـلِـك (M-Zx) = typed of stuffed patty (food). See **k'utilk**.

k'utilk/kutilk' [JB1-A]/**k'ut'ilk'** [JB1-S/M-Zx] کوتِلك *f.(JB1-A&S/OK)/m.(Bw)* **(-a/-ê;).** type of food made with **danhêrk** (type of wheat flour) consisting of patties stuffed with ground meat and minced onions: •**Dayê, bo çî *k'ut'ilik'a* xalê min şîn e?** (M-Zx, #767, 354) Mother, why is my uncle's *kutilk* blue? **-tirşika kutilka** (CB) do. {also: k'ut'ilik' (M-Zx); kutlik (IFb-2); kuttilk (GF); [kotélk] کتلك (JJ); <kutlik> کتلك (HH)} Cf. the pan-Middle Eastern kuftah کفتة (T köfte) [Bw/IFb/JJ/ JB1-A&S/OK/CB//M-Zx//GF//HH] <doẍeba; tirşik>

kutkut کـوتـکـوت *f.* **(-a;-ê).** woodpecker, zool. *Picus*: **-kutkuta sor** (Dy[EW]) red woodpecker [cf. T kırmızı ağaçkakan]. {also: kutkutik (DZK/ZF3); kutkutok (IF)} {syn: darnekol (Dy)} [Dyr(EW)//DZK/ ZF3//IF]

kutkutik کـوتـکـوتِـك (DZK/ZF3) = woodpecker. See **kutkut**.

kutkutok کوتکوتۆك (IF) = woodpecker. See **kutkut**.

kutlik کوتلِك (IFb) = typed of stuffed patty (food). See **k'utilk**.

kuttan کوتتان (BK/HH) = to hit, beat. See **k'utan**.

kuttilk کـوتـتِـلـك (GF) = typed of stuffed patty (food). See **k'utilk**.

kuvan I کوڤان (BK) = bow, arch. See **kevan**.

kuvan II کوڤان (BK) = sadness. See **kovan**.

kuwar کووار (SK) = corn-bin. See **kewar**[2].

K'uweytî کوویتی *adj.* Kuwaiti. {also: Kuwêtî (Wkt)} [BF/Wkp//Wkt]

Kuwêtî کووێتی (Wkt) = Kuwaiti. See **K'uweytî**.

k'uxa کوخا = village chief. See **k'ewxwe**.

k'uxîn کـوخـین *vi.* **(-k'ux-).** to cough. {also: [koukhin] کوخین (JJ); <kuxîn کخین (dikuxî) (دکخی)> (HH)}

[M/F/K/A/JB3/IF/B/JJ/HH] <xendxendok>

kuzirandin کـوزراندِن *vt.* **(-kuzirîn).** to singe, scorch, sear, burn on the surface: **•Ger bavê te di wê deqê de ne gihiştiba min, ez *ê* bi saxî *bihatama kuzirandin*** (ÎBS-W, 7-8) If your father hadn't reached me at that minute, I *would have been scorched* alive. {also: k'izirandin (K/A/B); kizirandin (IFb/GF/TF); <kizirandin کــزرانـــدن (dikizirîne) (دكزرينـه)> (HH)} {syn: qemandin} [Zeb//K/A/B//IFb/HH/GF/TF] <kuziryan; sotin>

kuziryan کــوزريــان *vi.* **(-kuzirê-).** 1) to be singed, scorched, seared, burnt on the surface; 2) to be dry enough to catch fire *(skin, hair, etc.)*; to be on the verge of catching fire, due to proximity or prolonged contact with heat source (Zeb). {also: k'izirîn (K/B); kizirîn (IFb/TF); kuzurîn (GF); <kizirîn كزرين (dik[i]zirî) (دكزرى)> (HH)} [Zeb/M//GF//K/[A]/B//IFb/HH/TF]

kuzîn کــوزيــن (FJ/TF/GF) = to howl; howling. See **kûzîn**.

kuzurîn کوزورين (GF) = to be singed. See **kuziryan**.

kû كوو (BX/JB3) = where. See **ku II**.

kûç•e/k'ûç•e [K/A/B] کــــووچـــه *f.* **(•a;•ê/•eyê).** (narrow) street, lane: **•Baasîyê me li serê *kuçê* sekinî û bi desta dikaneke goştfiroş nîşanî me da** (LC, 47) Our Baathist stood at the end *of the street* and with his hand pointed out a butchershop to us **•Dengê tifing û mitralyozan ewçend nîzing bû bûn ko mirov digot qey şer gihaştiye *kûçe û kolanên* bajêr** (H2 9:31,775) The sound of rifles and machine guns was so close that people were saying that the war had reached *the streets of* the city. {also: kuçe (TF/LC); [kūčah] کـــوچـــه (JJ-Khorasan)} {syn: ca'de; kolan II; zaboq; zikak} Mid P kōy = 'street, lane' (M3); P kūče کـــوچـــه = 'street, lane'; T küçe [Diyarbakır] = 'street' (DS, v. 12, p. 4575); Az T küçə; Sor kûçe کـــووچـــه = 'street, lane'; Za kuçe *m.* (Todd) = 'street'; cf. also Geo kuča ქუჩა [F/K/A/IFb/B/JJ/GF//TF/LC] <dirb I; 'ewc; r̄ê>

kûç•ik کـووچِـك *m.* **(•kê; vî kûçikî).** 1) {syn: k'elb; se} dog: **-kûçikê avê** (F) beaver; 2) puppy (Bw). {also: kuçik III (TF); kûtî (Krç/IFb-2); [koutchik] کـوچـك (JJ); <koçik> کـوچـك (HH)} < O Ir *kauti-(ka)-: <*koč-ik; Sgd 'kwty [θkuti]; Oss kui/kuj; Cf. S-Cr kuče/Bulg kuče куче [K/A/IFb/B/JJ/GF/OK/Ag//HH//TF//Krç] <bocî; gur̄ I; ḧemis; r̄ovî I; tajî; torî I>

kûdik کـــوودِك *f./m.(K/OK)* **(-a/;-ê/).** *term denoting the young of several animals:* 1) piglet, young of pigs (Haz/IFb/OK) [kudî] {syn: çêlkê beraz}: **-kûdika weḧşê** (Haz) do.; 2) young of lion, tiger, bear, etc.; cub, whelp (IFb/Bw) [kudik]: **•*kodîka* hirçê ya min** (Bw) my bear *cub*; 3) {syn: k'oçek [4]; torim} young of camels (B). {also: kudik (IFb/B/K/GF); kudî (IFb/OK); kudîk I (Bw)} [Haz//IFb/OK//Bw//B/K/GF] <beraz; cewr; ç'elîk; çêje; mahû; xifş>

kûfên کووفێن (-kûfê-) (OK) = to hiss. See **k'ufîn**.

kûfikî كوفِكى/كووفِكى (Zeb) = moldy. See **k'efikî**.

kûh كووه (IFb) = dull, blunt. See **kuh**.

kûje كووژه (B) = marten. See **kûze**.

kûjî كووژى (IFb) = corner. See **kujî**.

kûlav كوولاڤ (L) = felt *(material)*. See **kulav**.

kûlî کـوولـى (Srk/Kş/Mzg) = cricket; grasshopper. See **kulî** I.

kûn I كوون (K/IFb) = buttocks; hole. See **qûn**.

kûn II كوون (Bw/FS) = tent. See **kon**.

kûp/k'ûp [K/B] کــــــووپ *m.* **(-ê;).** 1) wide-mouthed pitcher, large clay jug or jar: **•Çiqa kevanya malê dew dik'ila r̄ûn dikire *k'ûpekî*** (Dz-anec #32) Whenever the lady of the house churned dew (=yoghurt and water), she would put it in *a clay jar* **•Mîna mêşa ku bikeve *kûpê* dimsê û pêve bimîne** (Lab, 74) Like the fly that falls into *a jug of* grape molasses and gets stuck; 2) {syn: sarinc} cistern (B). {also: [koup] کـوپ (JJ); <kûp> کـوپ (HH)} [IFb/JJ/HH/GF//K/B] <cer; kivî; k'ûz II; qom>

kûpik کـووپِك *m.* **(-ê;).** clay jug {dim. of **kûp**}. {also: [koupik] كوپك (JJ)} [Btm/JJ/GF]

kûr I کـــوور *m.* **().** young male goat, kid 2-3 years old: **•Wextê ko Smail Paşa zanî dîharîya maqûlêt Mizûrîyan *kûr* in, pîçek di dilê xo da sil bû. Gote pêşxizmetêt xo, "Têşta wan ṣewar bît. Sênîyan tejî biken, serê wan qubbeyî biken, pişkêt qelîya goştê *kûran* bi r̄exêt ṣewarê we-nên. Her sênîyekî kilkekî *kûr̄ī* di nawa serî biçeqînin weto ko qund r̄awestît"--Wextê wan temaşe kir ko têşta wan ṣewar--û li nik wan ṣewar gelek 'eybekî mezin e bo mêwanêt mu'teber--we ser wê hindê r̄a jî kilkêt *kûran* li ser sênîyan çeqandine, di yêk-û-do fikirîn, destêt xo kêşane paş. Pêkwe gotin, "Paşa, me têr xar. Xudê zêde ket ..."** (SK 24:222,224) When Ismail Pasha learnt that the present of the Mizuri elders was *kids*, he became a little annoyed in his heart. He said to his attendants, "Let their morning meal be of crushed wheat. Fill the trays, pile them up like a dome and put the pieces of fried *kid*-meat round the boiled what. On each tray stick a *kid*'s tail in the middle of the pile so that it stands erect." ... When they saw that their meal was of crushed wheat--and with them crushed wheat [instead of rice] was a most shameful thing for respectable guests--and that in addition the tails *of kids* had been stuck on top of the trays, they looked at each other and withdrew their hands. They all said together, "Pasha, we have eaten our fill. May God increase it for you." {also: [kour] کـور (JJ); <kûr> کـوور (Hej)} {syn: hevûrî; sayis} Cf. Sor kûr کـوور = 'angora kid' [Kmc-8/JJ/SK/Hej] <bizin; gîsk; nêrî I>

kûr II کوور (BK) = blind. See **kor**.

k'ûr III کـــوور *adj.* deep, profound: •**Avîtne bîreke *k'ûr*** (Ba) They threw [him] into a *deep* well. {also: [kour] کور (JJ); <kûr> کور (HH)} {≠tenik} {Pok. 2 (s)keu- 951.] 'to cover, conceal': O Ir *kaura- < *kor < *kau (A&L p.101, note 15); Sor qûł قـووڵ {k'ûrahî; k'ûranî; k'ûrayî; k'ûrî} [Ad/K/A/(JB3)/IFb/B/JJ/HH/SK/GF/TF/OK]

k'ûrahî کـــووراهـی (K/IFb/GF/OK) = depth. See **k'ûrayî**.

k'ûranî کوورانی (K/B) = depth. See **k'ûrayî**.

k'ûrayî کـوورایـی *f.* **(-ya;-yê).** depth, profundity. {also: k'ûrahî (K-2/IFb/GF/OK-2); k'ûranî (K-2/B-2); k'ûrî (K-2)} [K/B/OK//IFb/GF] <k'ûr III>

k'ûr•e/kûr•e کـــووره *f.* **(•eya/•a;•ê).** forge, forger's oven; limekiln, potter's kiln; furnace: •**Paşî me dît 'ewrekî r̄eş tarî li-bin r̄onaîyê peyda dibo, zincîrekî asin, gelek stûr, wekî taze ji *kûrê* înaye der sor bo, peroşk didan, li-naw wê 'ewrê hebo** (SK 11:108) Then we saw a dark, black cloud appearing beneath the light. In that cloud there was a very thick iron chain, red and sparking as if it had just been brought out of *the furnace*; **-k'ûra êgir** (B)/~ **agir** (K) forge; stoke-hole; **-k'ûra navê** (K) noon, midday: •**Ro hilhat *k'ûra navê*** (K) It is high *noon*. {also: kûrih (FJ-2/GF-2); <kûre[h]> کـوره (HH)} {syn: hêtûn} Cf. P kūre کـــــوره = 'furnace, forge, kiln'; Sor kûre کــــــووره = 'fireplace, hearth; furnace, kiln' [SK/Kmc#30/K/A/B/IFb/FJ/GF/HH/SK/ZF/Tsab]

kûrih کـوورِه (FJ/GF) = forge, kiln, furnace, oven. See **k'ûre**.

kûrik I کـوورك *f.* **(-a;-ê).** pocket. {also: kûrk II (OK); k'ûrk' II (JB1-S); [kour(i)k] کـــــورك (JJ)} {syn: berîk; cêb} [JR/IFb/JJ/GF/TF//JB1-S/OK]

kûrik II کوورك (Zx) = disease of wheat. See **korik**.

kûrinc کــــوورنـــج *m.&f.* **(-ê/;).** wool-beater, wool-comber, wool-carder, wool-fluffer: •***Kûrinc* livayî dijenî bo çêkirina çoxa, kulava, teĥtîya, kepena** (Bw) *A wool-carder* beats virgin wool for making [Kurdish traditional garments]. {also: kurinc (ZF3)} {syn: livajen} [Bw//ZF3] <liva>

k'ûrî کووری (K) = depth. See **k'ûrayî**.

kûr̄în کـــوورِیـــن *vi.* **(-kûr̄-).** to cry loudly, screech, shriek: •**Wek pepûkek birîndar *dikûre* û digirî** (Ardû, 116) Like a wounded cuckoo she *shrieks* and cries. {also: [korīn] کـریـن (JJ)} [Ardû/K/IFb/B//JJ] <qîr̄în; qûr̄în>

kûrk I کوورك (IF) = fur coat. See **k'urk II**.

kûrk II کـــوورك (OK)/k'ûrk' II (JB1-S) = pocket. See **kûrik I**.

kûr̄kûr̄ کــوورِکـــوورِ *m.(F)/f.(B)* **(-ê/-a; /-ê).** turkey (fowl): **-kûrkûrê nêr** (F) male turkey; **-kûrkûra mê** (F) female turkey. {syn: bûqelemûn; coqcoq; culûx̂; 'elok; şamî)} [F/B]

k'ûrm•e کـوورمـه *f.* **(•a;•ê).** bonfire; camp-fire; fire *for heating and cooking while camping out*: •**Dora *k'ûrma* êgir r̄ûniştine** (Ba2:2, 206) They sat down around *the camp-fire*. {also: k'urumk', m. (JB1-S)} [Ba2/F/K/B//JB1-S]

kûsel کووسەل, m. (JB3/QtrE) = tortoise. See **k'ûsî I**.

kûsele کووسەله, f. (Hk/Bw/JJ) = tortoise. See **k'ûsî I**.

k'ûsî I کـــووســی *m.* **(-yê;).** tortoise, land turtle, zool. order *Testudinata*; **-bi r̄êvaçûna k'ûsî r̄ê çûn** (XF) to go at a snail's pace, to move very slowly. {also: k'îsilfis (Zx); k'îso (IFb-2/TF/Çnr/Grc/Btm); k'îsofis (Czr); k'îsok, f. (-a;-ê) (Msr); kosî (Dyd/Erg/Kp/Rh-2); kûsel, m. (JB3/QtrE); kûsele, f. (Hk/Bw); [kuselá کـوسـلـه/kessal کـسـال] (JJ); <kewsel کـوسـل/kîso کـیـسـو> (HH)} {syn: r̄eq I; şkevlatok (JB3)} Skt kaśyápa- *m.*; Av kasyapa- *m.*; Mid P kašawag (M3); P kašav کـشـو/ kašaf کـشـف = 'tortoise'; Southern Tati dialects (all *f.*): Takestani kasu(y)a; Xiaraji kasawa = 'turtle' (Yar-Shater); Sor kîsał کـیـسـاڵ; Za kesa *f.* (Todd); cf. also Oss xæfs = 'toad, frog'. See I. Gershevitch. "Iranian Words Containing -ān-," *Iran and Islam: In Memory of the Late Vladimir Minorsky*, ed. C. E. Bosworth (Edinburgh, 1971), p.287, note 24; reprinted in his *Philologia Iranica*, ed. N. Sims-Williams (Wiesbaden : Dr. Ludwig Reichert Verlag, 1985), p. 257, note 24. [F/K/IFb/B/GF//JB3/QtrE//JJ/Hk/Bw//HH/TF/Çnr/Grc/Btm//Czr//Msr//Dyd/Erg/

Kp]

kûşik کویشِك/کووشِك (Zeb) = marten. See **kûşk**.

kûşk کویشك/کووشك *m.* **().** marten, stone-marten, zool. Martes. {also: kûşik (Zeb-2); **kûze**; qujî (FS); <kuşk> کـوشـك (Hej)} = Sor dełek دەڵـەك [Zeb/OK//Hej] See also **kûze**.

kûşnê کووشنێ (Mzg) = vetch. See **kizin**.

kût I کووت *adj.* lame (of foot), disabled: **•Çi heqê te li bizina min bû ku te lingê wê *kût* kir?** (Nivîs: Bajarê Keran [2001]) What share in did you have in my goat that you made her foot *lame*? = What right did you have to make my goat's foot lame? {syn: kulek I; qop; şeht; şil II} [Qzl/CS/Wkt]

k'ût II کـــــووت *m.* **().** 1) bread that has "fallen" while baking (and is ruined): **-k'ût kirin** (K) to ruin (bread) while baking; 2) pellet, small sphere or ball (K). {also: <kût> کوت (HH)} [K/IFb/B/HH]

kûte کووته (IFb) = type of cucumber. See **qitik**.

***kûtek** کووتەك *m.* **().** *in village houses,* a pillar used to prop up a **kêran** [=crossbeam] that would otherwise fall. [Haz] <kêran; mertak>

kût•ik کـویـتِـك/کـووتِـك *f.* **(;•kê).** unripe cucumber: **•Xiyara li *kûtkê* diyar e** (Bar) The cucumber is [already] apparent at its unripe stage *[prv.]*. {also: qîtik I (Wn)} {syn: tûtik II; xirtik I} [Bar/OK//Wn] <xiyar>

kûtî کووتی (Krç/IFb) = dog. See **kûçik**.

k'ûve کووڤه (M-Zx) = whither? where to? See **ku II**.

k'ûvî کـــووڤـــی *adj.* 1) {syn: ç'olî I; hov; t'oř II; weȟş [3]; ≠kedî} wild, untame(d) {*of animals: for 'wild' in the sense of 'savage, primitive, uncultured', see* ***hov*** (Haz)}: **•Me gelek ȟeywanêt *k'îvî* bi řêve dîtin, şibetî gurg û řîvî û wa tişta, em gelek jê tirsyayn** (M-Am #714) On the way we saw many *wild* animals, such as wolves and foxes and those things, and we were very afraid of them; **-bizina k'ûvî** (J) wild she-goat; 2) of mountains. {also: kêwî I (Bw); k'îvî (M-Am); k'ovî (A/JB3/IF); [kouwi] کوڤی (JJ); <kûvî> کوڤی (HH)} Cf. P kūhī کوهی = 'of mountains' < kūh کوه = 'mountain' (cf. Ar ṭūrī طـــوری = 'wild' < ṭūr طـــور = 'mountain'); Sor kûwî کـــووی/kêwî کـــێـــوی [J/K/HH/JJ//A/JB3/IF] <dirende>

kûxe کووخه (FS) = village chief. See **k'ewxwe**.

kûz I کــــــووز *adj.* hunchbacked, humpbacked: **-kûz bûn** = to stoop, bend over: **•Ewa tê *kûz dibe*** (J) She comes [and] *stoops over*. {also: piştkûz (F); qilûz (Qrj); qûz (B); [kouz] کــــــوز (JJ)} {kûzayî; qûzayî} [K/JJ//F//B//Qrj] <qopik; xûz>

k'ûz II کووز *m.* **(-ê;).** clay jug: **•Tavilê têdigêhîje ku wan ji bo vî *kwîzê* zêran şer dikir. Mêrik radihêje *kwîz* û xençerê, zûzûka ji wir dûrdikeve** (Ardû, 20) He immediately grasps that they were fighting over this *jug of* gold pieces. The man picks up *the jug* and the dagger, and quickly distances himself from there. {also: kwîz (Ardû/CS-2); [kouz] کــــوز (JJ)} {syn: kûp; qom} < Ar kūz كوز [Ardû//K/B/IFb/FJ/TF/GF/JJ/Kmc/CS] <kivî>

kûzayî کـــــووزایـــــی *f.* **().** hunchbackedness, hump-backedness. {also: qûzayî (B-2)} [B] <kûz I>

kûz•e کـــــــــــــووزه *f.(B)/m.(F)* **(;•ê/).** marten, zool. *Martes foina*: **•Di çîya û daristanan da heywanên kûvî wekî hirç, gur, beraz, pezkûvî, řovî, kewroşk, *kûze* û kew p'iř in** (DZK) In the mountains and forests, there are many wild animals, such as the bear, wolf, boar, wild ram, fox, rabbit, *marten*, and partridge. {also: kuje, m. (F); kûje (B); **kûşk**; qujî (FS); [koujé کـوژه/{kousi کوسی <hérisson=hedgehog>}] (JJ); <kûze> کوزه (HH)} Cf. Za kuza = 'marten'; W Arm guz կուզ & gznak'is կզնաքիս = 'marten'; T kuze [Bitlis] = 'marten' [sansar] (DS, v. 8, p. 3021); =Sor dełek دەڵـەك [DZK/IF/HH//B/JJ//F] See also **kûşk**.

kûze-kûz کووزەکووز (K)/kûzekûz کووزەکووز (B/GF) = whimpering. See **kûzkûz**.

k'ûzik کـــووزك *m.* **(-ê;-î).** small clay jug. {also: kozik II (FS); [kouzik] کـــوزك (JJ)} {syn: kûpik} < Ar kūz كوز [IFb/TF/Kmc/GF//FS] <k'edûn; k'ûz II>

kûzir کووزِر (Kmc) = chaff. See **k'ozer I**.

kûzî کووزی, f. (IFb/OK) = watercress. See **kîzmas**.

kûzîn کـــووزیـــن *vi.* **(-kûz-).** 1) {syn: 'ewtîn; kastekast kirin; řeyîn I} to wail, whimper, yelp, howl *(of dogs)*; to sob *(of people)*; 2) [*f.* **(;-ê).**] doleful whimpering, wailing, yelping, howling *(of dogs)*; sobbing *(of people)*: **•T'ûlê *kir kûzîn*, serê xwe hevraz kir** (HCK-4, #17, 98) The pup *howled*, he raised his head up. {also: kuzîn (FJ/TF/GF)} [HCK/K/B/IFb/OrK//FJ/TF/GF] <kûzkûz>

kûzkûz کـــووزکـــووز *f.* **(-a;-ê).** whimpering, yelping *(of dogs)*: **•...lê heywanê kûvî bi awakî welê diranên xwe xistibûn qiri[k]a Çavreş ku *kûzkûzên* seyê reben ji yên gur bilin[d]tir bûn** (EŞ, 15) ...but the wild animal dug its teeth into [the dog] Chavresh's throat in such a way that *the yelps of* the poor dog were louder than those of the wolf. {also: kûze-kûz (K); kûzekûz (B/GF)} [EŞ/

IFb//K/B/GF] <'ewte-'ewt; r̄eyîn I>

kwêr كوێر (JB1-S) = blind. See **kor**.

kwîner كوينەر (K) = boil, abscess. See **qunêr**.

kwîr كوير (Tof) = blind. See **kor**.

kwîrik كويرِك (Qzl) = disease of wheat. See **korik**.

kwîz كويز (Ardû/CS) = clay jug. See **k'ûz II**.

L ل

la لا (SK/Bw/Zeb) = side, direction. See **alî**.

laban لابان (FS) = to be fooled. See **lêbyan**.

labandin لاباندِن (FS) = to deceive. See **lêbandin**.

labût لابـووت *f.* **(-a;-ê).** a piece of flat metal mounted on a stick used to clean the mud off a plow: **•Misasa cot, alîyekî wî bizmarek e ku dibêjnê 'zixt,' alîyê din hesinekî serî pan--'*labût*'** (Qzl) An oxgoad has a nail on one end, called 'zixt', and the other end has a flat piece of metal--'*labût*' **•Bi *labûta* wê jî ax ji gîsinan tê paqij kirin** (de.glosbe.com:misas) And with its *labût* dirt is cleaned from the plowshare. {also: labûte (IFb); lawûte (IFb-2)} [Qzl/A/GF/FJ//IFb] <misas; zixt>

labûte لابـووتـه (IFb) = flat metal tip for cleaning mud off a plow. See **labût**.

laç'ik لاچِـك *f.* **(-a;-ê).** white muslin woman's head kerchief: **•*Laç'ka* jina serê te be!** (XF) Shame on you!/May you be disgraced! [lit. 'May a woman's *kerchief* be on your head'] **•Sifetê wî mîna *laç'ikê* ye** (B) He is as white as a ghost [from fear or illness] •[**Weku jin bî û *laçika* xwe raxîne nîva wan elbette ew du tayife ji yek û du dibin**] (BN, 181) If it is a woman and she spreads out her *kerchief* between them, the two parties will surely cease their fighting. {also: [latchik] لاچِك (JJ)} {syn: ç'arik; terĥî} [BN/K/IFb/B/JJ/GF/TF] <destmal; hêratî; ĥibrî; k'efî; k'itan; k'ofî; p'oşî; t'emezî; xavik>

laêf لائێف (L) = quilt. See **liĥêf**.

Lahd لاهد (IF) = Sunday. See **Le'd**.

lahor لاهـۆر *f.* **().** sword of Lahore steel, type of high-quality sword from India: **-şûrê lahor** (Z-2) do. {also: lahûr (K); <lahor> لاهـــور (HH)} [Z-2/IF/HH/ZF3//K] <şûr>

lahûr لاهوور (K) = type of sword. See **lahor**.

laîq لائيق (B/F/SK) = suitable; worthy. See **layîq**.

laîqî لائيقى (F) = suitability; worthiness. See **layîqî**.

lakan لاكـــان, m. (F)/lak'an, f. (B) = snow shoe. See **lîyan II**.

lal I لال *adj.* mute, dumb: **•gurê keřî-lalo** (Ba) deaf-mute wolves. {also: [lal] لال (JJ); <lal> لال (HH)} Cf. P lāl لال; Sor lał ڵال = 'dumb' {lalayî; lalbûn; laletî; lalî I; laltî} [K/A/JB3/IF/JJ/HH/B] <keř II>

lal II لال *m./f.(B)* **(; /-ê).** ruby, garnet: **-lal [û] dur** (Z-1) rubies and pearls: **•Zînekî usa hespê minřa çê ke, wekî t'emam *lal û duř* be** (Z-1) Make a saddle for my horse, so that it's full of *rubies and pearls*. {also: lel, f. (B); [laal] لـــعـــل (JJ)} {syn: yaqût} Cf. P/Ar la'l لـــعـــل; Sor lal لال = 'ruby, crimson' [Z-1/K/A/IF//JJ//B] <duř; mircan; xişir>

lalangî لالانگى (CB) = mandarin orange. See **lalengî**.

lalayî لالايى (B) = muteness. See **lalî I**.

lalbûn لالبوون (B) = muteness. See **lalî I**.

lalengî لالـەنـگـى *f.* **().** mandarin orange, bot. *Citrus reticulata*. {also: lalangî (CB); lalîngî (Bw); naringî (OK-2/AA); <lalengî> لالـەنـگـى (Hej)} Cf. P nārangī نـارنـگـى = 'mandarine, tangerine'; Sor lalengî لالەنگى [Bw///IFb/TF/OK/Hej/ZF3/Wkt//CB//AA] <narinc; p'irteqal>

laletî لالەتى (A) = muteness. See **lalî I**.

lalê لالـێ *prep.* 1) {syn: bal I; cem; hinda I; ĥafa [*see* ĥaf]; li def (Bw); nik I; řex I} by, near, at, at the house of [Fr chez]: **•Ew *lalê* me bû** (FS) He was *with* us/*at* our *house* **•Hung xencerêt xo û debancêt xo û elbîsê xo *lalî* min da nên, paşî herine lalî ĥakimî** (M-Ak, #537) Put your daggers and your pistols and your clothes down *with* me and then go before the governor; 2) against, opposite (JJ). {also: lalî III (M-Ak); [lālē] لالـێ (JJ)} < li = 'at, to' + alîyê = 'the side of' [MK/K/JJ/FS//M-Ak]

lalî I لالـــــــــى *f.* **(-ya;-yê).** muteness, dumbness: **•20 helbestên kurt ên ku bi *lalî*ya xwe dipeyivin** (kulturname.com 16.xi.2011) 20 short poems that speak with their *muteness*. {also: lalayî (B-2); lalbûn (B-2); laletî (A); laltî (B-2)} [K/IF/B/BF/ZF3/Wkt//A] <lal I>

lalî II لالـــــى *f.* **(-ya:).** large, flat dish, platter (Msr); medium-sized plate (Bşk/Erh); wide bowl for rice (A); long, shallow copper vessel in which such foodstuffs as rice and bulghur are served (HH). {also: lalîk II (BF); lalû (Bşk); lalûk (Erh); <lalî> لالى (HH)} [Msr/A/IFb/HH/ZF3//Bşk//Erh//BF] <firaq>

lalî III لالى (M-Ak) = by, near, at. See **lalê**.

lalîk I لاليك (Wkt) = mattress. See **nehlîk**.

lalîk II لاليك (BF) = type of plate. See **lalî II**.

lalîngî لالينگى (Bw) = mandarin orange. See **lalengî**.

lalînk لالينك (Wkt) = mattress. See **nehlîk**.

laltî لالتى (B) = muteness. See **lalî I**.

lalû لالو (Bşk) = type of plate. See **lalî II**.

lalûk لالوك (Erh) = type of plate. See **lalî II**.

lam لام (JB3/IFb/HH/GF/TF/OK/Erh) = cheek. See **lame**.

lam•e لامه *f.* **(•a;).** 1) {syn: gup} pouch of the cheek [T avurt]; 2) {syn: alek; gup; hinarik; r̄û [3]} cheek; 3) {syn: çeng II} jaw (JJ/JB3/IFb/GF/OK). {also: lam (JB3/IFb-2/GF/TF/OK/Erh); [lamé] لامه (JJ); <lame لامه/lam لام> (HH)} <Arc lugmā לוגמא = 'puffed-up cheek': NENA lāmā ܠܡܐ/ܠܓܡܐ = 'bridle, jaw' (Maclean) [HB/A/IFb/JJ/HH//JB3/GF/TF/OK/Erh] <dêm II; karêj I>

lan لان *f.* **(-a;).** den, lair, nest *(of wild animal)*: **•Dibêjin şêrek û gurgek û r̄îvîyek bûne şirîk. Çûne çiyayekî, gayekî kîwî û bizinekî kîwî û kêrûşkek girtin, înane** ***lana*** **xo** (SK 7:71) They say that a lion, a wolf, and a fox became companions. They went to a mountain, caught a wild ox, a wild goat, and a hare and brought them to their *lair*; **-landana kêvrîşkê** (Bw) rabbit's lair **-lenda şêra** (Zeb) lion's den. {also: landan (Bw); lehn (GF-2); lend (Zeb/IFB-2); lewd (Zeb-2); [lan لان/lané لانه] (JJ); <lehn> لهن (HH)} {syn: gindor III; qûn [4]} P lane لانه = 'nest'; Sor lan لان/lane لانه = 'nest, lair' [Bw//K(s)/A/IFb/JJ/SK/GF/OK//HH//Zeb] <hêlîn>

landan لاندان (Bw) = animal lair. See **lan**.

landek لاندەك (K/JJ) = cradle. See **landik**.

landik لاندِك *f.* **(-a;-ê).** cradle, crib: **•*Landika* nevyê wêderê bû, ber te'ldê *landikê* rûnişt** (Dz) The grandchild's *cradle* was there, he sat down under the concealment of (=hidden by) *the cradle*. {also: landek (K); lanik (IF-2); lehandik (Bw); lendik (IF-2); [làndek] لاندك (JJ); <lendik> لندك (HH)} {syn: bêşîk, f. (F); colan; dara dergûşê; dergûş [2]} Sor lanik لانِك; *according to Nöldeke 123, dim. of* ***lane*** *= 'nest'* [Dz/F/JB3/IF//K/JJ// HH//Bw]

lanet لانەت (IFb/GF/CS) = curse. See **ne'let**.

lanik لانِك (IF) = cradle. See **landik**.

lap لاپ *adv.* 1) completely, totally, quite; wholly, entirely, utterly, fully: **•Bîrêda merîk heye, ewî ew qederî bedewe, ku ji şewqa wî hundur̄ê bîrê *lap* r̄onayîye** (Ba3-1) There is a man in the well, he is so beautiful that from his radiance the interior of the well is *completely* light **•Nevyê te hela zarûnin, serê neh-deh ȟeva şkênandine, sive mezin bivin, lêxin, wê rojê yek-dudu bikujin, ezê *lap* batmîş bivim** (FK-kk-1) Your grandchildren are still children [and] they have smashed in the heads of nine or ten, tomorrow they will grow up, and then they will kill one or two, [and] I will be *completely* disgraced; 2) very (much), highly, extremely: **•*Lap* zûva ew kelêda rûniştîye** (Ba3) For quite some time (=since *very* early on) he had sat in the castle (=dungeon) **•Wî gundîda ew merîê *lapî* dewletî û hurmetlî bûye** (Ba2) He was the richest and *most* respected man in that village. {also: lapde (B-2)} Az T lap = 'very, completely, exactly' [Ba2/K/B/ZF3]

lapde لاپده (B) = completely, totally. See **lap**.

laqa لاقا (K) = encounter, meeting. See **leqa**.

laqirdî لاقِردى *m./f.(B)* **(-yê/ ; /-yê).** 1) words, conversation (JJ): **•K'etne k'êf û ȟeneka û *laqirdîyane*** (Z-2) They fell to amusement, jokes and *talk*; 2) {syn: ȟenek} joke, amusement (K/B): **•Eva tiştekî *laqirdî* nîne** (B) It's not *a joke*; **-laqirdî kirin** (B) to joke: **•Ew *laqirdîyê* xwe te dike** (B) He'*s joking* with you. {also: [laqyrdi] لاقردى (JJ)} < T lâkırdı = '(idle) talk'; cf. Gr loghodiarroia λογοδιάρροια = 'garrulity, non-stop talking' [Z-2/K/JJ/B/ZF3]

laqum لاقوم (B) = sewer; mine. See **leqem**.

laqumçî لاقومچى (B) = sewerman. See **leqemçî**.

laqûm لاقووم (B) = sewer; mine. See **leqem**.

laqûmçî لاقوومچى (B) = sewerman. See **leqemçî**.

larî kirin لارى كِرِن (M-Ak) = to play. See **yarî II**.

lasik لاسِك (FJ/GF) = plant stalk. See **lask**.

lask لاسك *m.* **().** stem *or* stalk *of plant*. {also: lasik (FJ/GF)} Sor lask لاسك [CCG/IFb/TF/ZF/FD//FJ/GF] <sap>

laş لاش *m.* **(-ê;).** 1) {also: leş (JB1-A&S/GF/OK-2)} {syn: beden II; can I[2]; gewde} body: **•Du mû ji *laşê* xwe hilkirin** (L) He plucked two hairs off his [own] *body*) **•Ji jana dil *laş* diare** (O. Basî. Te dil bi xwe re bir, 64) *The body* smarts from heartache; 2) {syn: berat'e[2]; cendek; cinyaz; k'eleş I; meyt'; term} corpse, cadaver, dead body (K/JJ). See **leş**[1]; 3) carrion, body of dead animal (Wn/JJ/TF). See **leş**[2]. {also: **leş**; [lach/lāš (PS)/lash (Rh) لاش/lech/leš (Lx/G) لش] (JJ); <leş> لش(HH)} Cf. P lāš لاش = 'corpse' --> T leş; Sor laşe لاشه = 'corpse, carcass' & leş لهش = 'body' [Wn/K/IFb/JJ/TF/OK//M-Zx/B/HH/JB1-A&S/GF]

laşe لاشه (GF/OK) = corpse. See **leş**.

lat لات *f.* **(-a;-ê).** 1) {syn: ferş} flat, level crag; huge (flat) rock: **•Çû serê kopikî, pariste hindawê *lata***

çyay, bizanît pezê kîwî li wê derê heye yan ne. Wextê çû hindawê *latê* dît hirçek liser dara keskanêye (SK 10:95) He went on top of the crest and crept above a patch of *flat rock* to see whether there were wild sheep there or not. When he went above the stretch of *flat rock* he saw that there was a bear in the top of a terebinth tree **•Ew *lata* te xwest ji binî de bihêrivîne** [sic] **wê bê hêrivandin** (Wlt 2:59, 7) That *boulder* which you wanted to demolish from the bottom up will be demolished **•Mirovê tirsonek weke bayê reviya û çû xwe di pişt *latekî*** [sic] **de veşart** (AW69B8) The cowardly man ran like the wind and went and hid behind *a rock*; 2) {syn: *gûrî (IF); tej} unit of measure equal to one fourth (1/4) of a dönüm, or 250 square meters (IFb) [Cf. T evlek]; plot of land, terrace (SK); acre, parcel of land (OK). [BX/K/A/JB3/IFb/SK/GF/TF/OK] <ferş; le'tik; zinar>

lauk لائوك (Lx) = song. See **lawij**.

lava لاڤـــا (K/IF/B/Ba2/BF/FS) = request, prayer. See **lavahî**.

lavahî لاڤـاهـى *f.* **().** request, prayer: **-lavahî kirin** (K)/ **lava[yî] kirin** (B)/**lave kirin** (Msr) to request, ask for; to beg, implore, entreat {syn: jê hêvî kirin; limêj kirin; t'eweqe kirin} **•[Her çend jin û xweh *lavahî dikin*...Meḧmed beg dibêje ku: "Nabe!"]** (JR) No matter how much [his] wife and sister *implore* [him]...Mehmed beg says, "No way!" {also: lava (K-2/IF/B/Ba2-2/BF/FS); lavayî (Ba2/B-2); [lavahi kirin لاوهـى/labehi لابـهـى] (JJ); <lavekirin> لاڤكرن (HH)} [JR/K/JJ/ZF3//IF/B/Ba2/BF/FS//HH]

lavayî لاڤايى (Ba2/B) = request, prayer. See **lavahî**.

lave kirin لاڤه كِرِن (Msr/HH) = to request; to beg. See **lavahî: -lavahî kirin**.

lavij لاڤژ (GF/ZF/FS) = hymn. See **lawij**.

lavîlavî لاڤيلاڤى (Zeb) = ivy. See **lavlav**.

lavje لاڤژه (FS) = hymn. See **lawij**.

lavlafk لاڤلافك (A) = ivy. See **lavlav**.

lavlav لاڤـــلاڤ *f.* **(-a;-ê).** ivy, bot. *Hedera*. {also: lavîlavî (Zeb); lavlafk (A); lavlavik (GF); lavlavk (ZF3/FS); <lavlavik> لاڤـلاڤـك (HH)} Cf. Ar lablāb لـبـلاب = 'English ivy'; Sor lawlaw لاولاو = 'convolvulus' [Zeb//IFb/OK/AA//HH/GF//ZF3/FS//A] <daralînk>

lavlavik لاڤلاڤك (GF/HH) = ivy. See **lavlav**.

lavlavk لاڤلاڤك (ZF3/FS) = ivy. See **lavlav**.

lavz لاڤـز *m./f.(ZF3)* **().** 1) {syn: bêje; peyiv; pirs [2]; xeber; zar I} word (Msr/K/JJ); 2) speech, talk; dialect (K); language (B). {also: lefz (ZF3/Wkt); lewz (K/B); [lefz] لـفـظ (JJ)} < Ar lafẓ لـفـظ = 'accent; pronunciation' [Msr//K/B//JJ/ZF3/Wkt]

law لاو *m./m.&f.(B)* **(-ê;).** 1) {syn: gede [5]; kur̄ II; mindal; t'ifal; zaro} boy, son; child *(male or female)* (B): **•*Lawa* min** (B) My *daughter* **•*Lawê* min** (B) My *son* **•Lawo!** = Boy! Son! (voc.) **•Mamoste, gava ku ez dihatim mektebê *lawikek* li pey min bû, hema bela xwe di min dida** (LM, 16) Teacher, when I was coming to school *a boy* was behind me, he was bothering me; 2) young man (JJ/HH/TF); 3) beloved, lover (Bw): **•Da yara min nebêjîtin "*lawê* min mir"** (Sube dayê by Muayyid Tayyib) Lest my beloved say "My *lover* is dead"; 4) *[adj.]* {syn: keşxe} nice, pretty (Bw); youthful, handsome (SK). {also: [laoŭ] لاو (JJ); <law> لاو (HH)} Cf. Arm law լաւ = 'good'; Sor law لاو = 'youth, young person' [K/A/JB3/IFb/B/JJ/HH/JB1-S/SK/GF/TF/OK/Bw]

lawanta لاوانتا (TF) = lavender water. See **lewante**.

lawante لاوانـــتـــه (IFb/CS) = lavender water. See **lewante**.

lawaz لاواز *adj.* 1) {syn: jar I; leẍer; narîn; qels I; qor̄ III; zeyf; zirav I} thin, slim, slender, lean; puny, undersized; emaciated *(from hunger or disease)*, skin and bones: **-birçî û lawaz** (Z-4) emaciated, skin and bones: **•Gur̄î *birçîye û lawaze*** (Z-4) 'Baldhead' is *skin and bones*; 2) {syn: qels I[1]; sist; zeyf [2]} weak: **-lawaz kirin** (IFb): a) to make s.o. lose weight; b) to weaken: **•Her wesa Ingilîzan bizav kir ji bo *lawazkirina* rolê welatên biyanî li wê deverê** (Metîn 62[1997]:26) Likewise, the English strove *to weaken* the role of foreign countries in that region; 3) lean *(of meat)* (K[s]). {also: [lāvāz] لاواز (JJ-Rh)} Cf. Sor lawaz لاواز = 'weak' [Z-4/K(s)/A/IFb/JJ]

lawij لاوژ *f.* **(-a;).** religious hymn or chant; song: **•*Lavja* ku wî gotî, xoş bû** (FS) *The hymn* which he chanted was nice **•Muṯirb geştine bederê qesra aẍa gotin** [sic]... **em jî ewe heşt neh r̄oj e ji laê Silêmanî û Kerkûkê li dû nawbangê Eḧmed Aẍaê Berwarî têyn da bo wî def û kemança lê deyn û *lawjan* bêjîn, belkû keremekî çak digel me biket** (SK 27:243) The minstrels arrived before the gate of the agha's mansion and said ... for 8 or 9 days now we have come from the direction of Sulaimaniya and Kerkuk following the fame of Ahmad Agha

Barwari, in order to play the drum and viol for him and to sing him *songs*, hoping that he will reward us well. {also: lavij (GF/ZF-2/FS); lavje (FS-2); lawîj (Lwj); lawjan (K[s]-2); lawje (Prw-2); lawuj (K[s]); lewij (K[s]-2); [lavouj لاوژ/lavyjk لاوژك] (JJ)} [Lwj//IFb/ZF//GF/FS//Lx/K(s)] <beyt; lawuk>

lawik I لاوِك = dim. of **law**.

lawik II لاوِك (A/IF/JB3/Wkt) = song; lament; epic; melody. See **lawuk**.

lawir لاوِر (Kmc-10/Hej)/lawiȓ لاوِر (Zeb/BF/FS) = small animal. See **ȓawir**.

lawîj لاویژ (Lwj) = hymn. See **lawij**.

lawjan لاوژان (K[s]) = sad song. See **lawij**.

lawje لاوژه (Prw) = love song. See **lawij**.

lawuj لاووژ (K[s]/JJ) = heroic song. See **lawij**.

lawuk لاووك *f.* (). 1) {syn: kilam; stiran I} song, folk song; love song; lament, sad song: ; 2) epic, épopée, saga [lawik]; 3) melody (A) [lawik]. {also: lauk (Lx); lawik II (A/IF/JB3/Wkt)} Sor lawuk لاووك = 'short lyrical poem (a genre of Kurdish folk song)' [Tkm/Prw//A/IF/JB3/Wkt] <kilam; lawij; stiran I>

lawûte لاووته (IFb) = flat metal tip for cleaning mud off a plow. See **labût**.

laxer (ZF3) = thin and weak (of animals), decrepit; lean. See **leẍer**.

layeq لایەق (JB1-S) = suitable; worthy. See **layîq**.

layiq لایِق (ŞBS/ZF3) = suitable; worthy. See **layîq**.

layiqî لایِقی (Wkt) = suitability. See **layîqî**.

layîq لایـیـق *adj.* 1) {syn: babet II[1]; hink'ûf} fitting, suitable, proper, appropriate, decent: •***Layîq* e** (K) It is *fitting/proper* •***Layîq* nîne** (K/JJ)/**Ne *layîq* e** (K) It is not *fitting/proper*; -**layîq dîtin** (K) to consider proper; 2) {syn: hêja I[2]; stêl} [+ -**î**] worthy, deserving (of): -**laîq bûn** (B) = a) to be awarded: •**Ew *laîqî* p'êşk'êşîya dewletê *bû*** (B) He *was bestowed with* a government award; b) to earn, deserve, merit: •**Gelo qîzeke çewa wê ȓastî Memê wîyî ȟizkirî bê, wekî *layîqî* Memê *be*?** (Z-1) How will a girl meet his beloved Mem, who *is worthy of* him? •**Hemû *layiqî* eynî mafa *ne*** (ŞBS, 61) Everyone *deserves* the same rights •**Tu *laîqî* wê keç'ikê *nînî*** (B) You *do not deserve* (=*are not worthy of*) that girl; -**laîq kirin** (B) = a) to make worthy; b) to favor with, vouchsafe, condescend to grant, deign to give (sarcastic) : •**Ewî *laîq nekir* bê me bibîne** (B) He *considered it beneath his dignity* to come to see us. {also: laîq (B/F/SK); layeq (JB1-S); layiq (ŞBS/IFb/ZF3); [làiq] لایــق (JJ); <layiq> لایــق (HH)} <Ar lā'iq لائـق active participle of √l-y-q لیـق = 'to be proper, suitable'--> T lâyık; Za layiq (Mal) {laîqî; layîqî; [làiqi] لایقی (JJ)} [Z-1/K//B/F/SK//JB1-S//JJ//IFb/HH/ZF3/ŞBS]

layîqî لایـیـقـی *f.* **(-ya;-yê).** 1) suitability, propriety, properness, decency; 2) worthiness, merit. {also: laîqî (F); layiqî (Wkt); [làiqi] لایقی (JJ)} [K//Wkt//F/JJ] <layîq>

laze لازه, m. (B) = moment. See **le'z II**.

lazek لازەك, m. (B) = moment. See **le'z II**.

lazim لازم *adj.* necessary: •**Merîyêd ku qe tiştek jî jê *nelazimbûya*** (Ba) People who *didn't need* anything at all; -**lazim e** [+ *subj.*] = it is necessary that..., [you] must ... [cf. Fr il faut que ...] •***Lazim* e tu herî** (L) You *must* go •***Lazime*, ku em wextêda k'arê zivistanê bibînin** (B) We *must* make ready for winter on time. {also: [lazim] لازم (JJ); <lazim> لازم (HH)} {syn: divêt [see at **viyan**]; gerek; ȟewce; pêdivî; p'êwîst} <Ar lāzim لازم--> P lāzim لازم --> T lâzım {lazimatî; lazimayî; lazim[t]î} [L/K/IFb/B/HH/JJ/SK]

lazimatî لازِماتی (K/B) = necessity. See **lazimayî**.

lazimayî لازِمایـی *f.* **(-ya;).** necessity. {also: lazimatî (K-2/B-2); lazimî (K-2/B-2/Wkt); lazimîtî (Wkt); lazimtî (K-2/B-2/Wkt-2); lazmatî (ZF3)} [K/B//Wkt//ZF3] <lazim>

lazimî لازِمی (K/B/Wkt) = necessity. See **lazimayî**.

lazimîtî لازِمیتی (K/B/Wkt) = necessity. See **lazimayî**.

lazimtî لازِمتی (K/B/Wkt) = necessity. See **lazimayî**.

lazmatî لازماتی (ZF3) = necessity. See **lazimayî**.

lazût لازووت *m./f.(ZF3)* **(-ê/-a;-î/-ê).** corn [British: maize], bot. *Zea mays*: •***Lazûtê* min piȓ xurt bûye** (Krç) My *corn* has grown very well. {also: zalût (ZF3-2); [lazout] لازوت (JJ)} {syn: garis[ê stanbolî]; genimeşamî; genmok; gilgilê Stembolê (Haz); zuret I} [Krç/Haz/Mzg/IFb/JJ/Wkt/ZF3] <genim; xirovî>

leban لەبان (FS) = to be fooled. See **lêbyan**.

lebandin لەباندِن (FS) = to deceive. See **lêbandin**.

lebat I لـەبـات *f.* **(-a;).** 1) motion, movement; 2) {syn: çalakî; livbazî} action, activity: •**Program û livbaziyên (*lebatên*) HEP'ê dikarin bibin mijarên rexneyê** (Wlt 1:43, 9) The programs and *activities* of HEP can be the subject (or, object) of criticism; -**lebat kirin** (ZF3/Wkt) to move about, thrash about: •**Rûvî gelek *lebat kir* ku xwe ji telhê bînit der** (FS) The fox *thrashed about* a lot to get itself out of the trap. {also: libat (IFb-2); [lipat] لـــــــپـــات (JJ)} [Wlt/K/A/IFb/GF/ZF3/BF/FS//JJ] <t'evgeř> See also **lipat**.

lebat II لەبات *m.* **(-ê;).** limb, member, organ (of the body): •**Çav *lebatekê* leşî yê piř giring e** (FS) The eye is an important organ of the body. {syn: endam} [FS/ZF3]

lebê لەبێ *interj.* 1) Here I am; At your service: •**Cêrî jî wextê ku derk'et ç'e'v bi dewarekî k'et, di nav bexçe de go, "Xanima-m!" Go, "Hay *libê* cêryê"** (HR 3:54) And when the maidservant went out, she noticed a horse in the garden, she called, "My lady!" The lady replied "Here I am, maidservant"; 2) Come again?; What did you say? {also: libê (TF/IFb-2); <lebê> لـــبـــی (HH)} < Ar labbayka لَبَّيك = 'At your service' [HR/K/B/IFb/FJ/GF/HH/Tsab//TF]

lebitandin لەبتاندن (HH) = to (cause to) move *(vt.)*. See **lipitandin**.

lebitîn لەبتين (HH) = to move, budge *(vi.)*. See **lipitîn**.

lec لەج *f.* **(-a;-ê).** 1) {syn: berêkanê; pêşbazî} competition, contest, race; **-hevra k'etin lecê** (K) to compete with each other, enter a competition: •**Ew usa lez dik'etin, mêriv qey digot ew *hevřa k'etibûne lecê*, çika k'îjan ji wana zû xwe digihîne germa deşta** (Ba2:1, 202) They [=the brooks] fell so quickly, that people said (=it seemed as if) they *were racing each other*, to see which one of them will reach the warmth of the plains first [lit. 'early']; 2) argument, fight, quarrel: •**Di *leca* navbera du malbatan derketî de xwîn rijiya** (trtnûçe.com 4.vii.2014) In *an argument* that broke out between 2 families, blood was spilt. {also: [ledj] لـج (JJ)} < Ar lajj لَجّ = 'quarreling'; Za lej *m.* = 'war, fight' (Todd) [Ba2/K/JB3/IFb/B/JJ/OK/ZF3/Wkt]

Le'd لەعد *f.* **(;-ê).** Sunday: **-Le'dê** (Msr) on Sunday. {also: Lahd (IF-2); Lehd (IF); Leȟt (Czr/Btm); [lad لاد/rouj-a ladi روژا لادی] (JJ); <leȟd> لـحـد (HH)} {syn: Bazar [3]; Yekşem} < Ar (yawm) al-aȟad يوم الأحد ; cf. Judeo-Spanish alxád [Msr/K/B/SC//IF//JJ//HH//Czr/Btm]

lefz لەفز (JJ/ZF3/Wkt) = word; speech. See **lavz**.

legan لەگان *f.* **(-a;-ê).** basin, tub, metal or brass vessel *(for washing clothes or dishes, or kneading dough)*: •**Jinekê *legeneka* nîskê digel sê çar naneka birin, li ber danan** (M-Ak 278, #613) The woman took *a basin of* lentils with 3 or 4 pieces of bread and placed them before him •**Va ez ê *legana* xwe bibim û herim** (ZZ-10, 154) I will take my *basin* and leave. {also: legen (FJ-2/GF-2/M-Ak); [leghen] لـگـن (JJ); <legen> لـگـن (HH)} {syn: şikev; t'eşt} Sor legen لەگەن = 'basin (for washing)'; Hau legan *m.* (M4); cf. Syr lgīnā لجىىا & Arc lgīnā לגינא = 'bottle, vessel', *also* lqīnā לקינא = 'bottle, flask'; Ar lakan لكن = 'brass or copper basin' & Iraqi Clq Ar ligan لـقـن = 'large metal wash basin'; T leğen; Gr & Mod Gr lekanē λεκάνη = 'basin, bowl' & Gr lagynos λάγυνος = 'flask, flagon'; *also* Rus lokhan' лохань = '(wash) tub'; Lat lagena = 'bottle' [ZZ/K/A/B/IFb/FJ/GF/JJ/HH/ZF/Kmc/CS]

legen لەگەن (FJ/GF/M-Ak) = basin. See **legan**.

legleg لەگلەگ *f.* **(-a;-ê).** stork, zool. *Ciconia ciconia*: •***Legleg* jî zû têt, wextê hatina wê hêşta befr û şilowe ye, serma ye, bihar nîye** (SK 29:263) *The stork* also comes early. When it comes there is still snow and slush and it is cold, it is not spring; **-ȟe'cî legleg** (B) do. {also: leglege, m. (FS/BF); [leqleq لقلق/leghlegh (G) لگلگ] (JJ); <legleg> لگلگ (HH)} {syn: ȟacîreşk} Cf. Ar laqlaq لقلق/laqlāq لقلاق; P laglag لگلگ; T leylek; Sor leqleq لەقلەق/ȟacî leqleq حاجی لەقلەق [SK/K/A/TFb/B/HH/GF/TF/OK/ZF3//JJ//FS/BF]

leglege لەگلەگە , m. (FS/BF) = stork. See **legleg**.

lehandik لەهاندِك (Bw) = cradle. See **landik**.

Lehd لەهد (IF) = Sunday. See **Le'd**.

leheng لەهەنگ *m.* **(-ê;).** hero, champion: •**Bê guman e Celadet Bedirxan, *lehengê* ziman, rojname û çanda Kurdî giştî bû** (1:42, 10) Without a double Jeladet Badirkhan was the general *champion of* Kurdish language, newspapers and culture. {syn: 'efat; 'egît; gernas; mêrxas; p'elewan} [Wlt/IFb/GF/TF/OK/ZF3/BF]

lehêf لەهێف (K) = quilt. See **liȟêf**.

lehî لەهی *f.* **(-ya;-yê).** flood, inundation, high water *(as result of springtime thaw)*: •**Dema buhar tê, hêdî hêdî berf ji erdê radibe, çiya û banî hêşîn dibin, berf dihele, ava çeman zêde dibin*, li gelek cihan ev şaxên çeman digihîjin hev û dibin *lehî*. *Lehî* carna gund û avahiyan dide ber xwe û dibe** (Wlt 1:42, 4) When spring comes, the snow slowly rises from the ground, the mountains and hillsides turn green, the snow melts, river waters increase, in many places these river branches come together and become *a flood*. Sometimes *the flood* pushes villages and structures before it and carries them off **•Semedê rabûna *leyîyê*, barana dijwar û gurr e** (BZ, v. 1:567) The cause of the rising *waters* is the heavy and abundant rain. {also: leyî (BZ/ZF-2); lêvî (QtrE); [leï] لـی (JJ); <leyî> لـیـی (HH)} [Wlt/K/A/IFb/GF/TF/OK/ZF//JJ/HH/BZ] <avřabûn; lêmişt; sêlav; t[']ofan>

lehîstik لەهیستِك (K) = game. See **lîstik**.

lehîstin لەهیستِن = to play; to dance. See **lîstin**.

lehîstok لەهیستۆك (K) = toy. See **lîstok**.

lehîzîn لەهیزین (K[s]) = to play; to dance. See **lîstin**.

lehîzvan لـەهـیـزڤـان (Kmc/FJ) = player; dancer. See **lîstikvan**.

lehn لەهن (GF/HH) = animal lair. See **lan**.

lehtik (ZF3) = plot of land. See **le'tik**[2].

Leḧt لەحت (Czr/Btm) = Sunday. See **Le'd**.

lek لەك *f.* **().** 1) ten thousand (10,000) *in Kurmanji*; one hundred thousand (100,000) *in Sorani*; 2) large division of soldiers; army corps consisting of 100,000 men (JJ). {also: [lek] لـك (JJ)} Cf. Skt lakṣa- = 100,000; P lak لك = 100,000; Sor lek لەك = 100,000 [BK/IFb/JJ/GF/Kmc/FJ/BX/CS/Tsab]

lekan لـەکـان (IFb/TF/JJ)/lek'an, m.(K)/f.(B) (K/B) = snow shoe. See **lîyan II**.

lekaş لەكاش (IF) = (old) shoe. See **şekal**.

lek•e لـەکـە *f.* **(•a;•ê).** 1) spot, blemish, stain; 2) (fig.) mark of disgrace, blemish *(on one's reputation)*: **•*Lek'a* 'Eynê çîye?** (EP-5, #6) What is wrong with Ayneh? [lit. 'What is Ayneh's *blemish*?']. {also: [leké] لـکـه (JJ); <leke> لـکـه (HH)} Cf. P lakke لكه --> T leke; Sor leke لەکە [EP-5/F/K/IF/B/JJ/HH/GF]

lekedar لەکەدار *adj.* stained, spotted. [SK/GF/ZF3] <leke>

lel لەل, f. (B) = ruby. See **lal II**.

lele لەلە *m.* **(-yê;).** manservant or tutor of the son of a sultan, king, etc.; pedagogue: **•Mem li pêşîyê te'lîm û terbîyeta xwe li cem dayê distand, paşê li cem *lele* cure-cure 'ulim hîn bûye, ew hînî suwarîyê, tîravêjîyê dikirin** (K-dş, 88) Mem received his first education and training from his mother, then he learned various sciences from his *pedagogue*; he learned horseback riding [and] archery. Cf. P lale لله --> T lala [EP-7/IF/ZF3/FS]

lem لـەم *m.* **(-ê;).** vine stock, long vines of squash, watermelon, cucumber plants, etc.: **-lemê 'encûra** (Qrj) Russian cucumber vine; **-lemê qundira** (Qrj) squash or zucchini vine; **-lemê zebeşa** (Qrj) watermelon vine. {also: <lem> لـم (HH)} [Qrj/A/IFb/HH/GF/TF/CB/ZF3] <mêw; p'arêz I>

lema لـەمـا *conj.* 1) {syn: çimk'î} because, for, since (reason): **•Îro hewalek Mhemmed Xan heye, *loma* ne hatîye bi me re** (L) Today something is up with M. Khan, *since* he hasn't come with us; 2) therefore, hence [often + **jî**]: **•Jinê jî zanibû, wekî Ûsibî ze'f aqile, *lema* jî ewê ç'e'vnebarî li wî dikir** (Ba) The woman also knew that Joseph was [lit. 'is'] very smart, *therefore* she despised him **•Lê birê te ji mala min tişt dizîne, *lema* jî min ew girtine** (Ba3) But your brothers stole things from my house, and *therefore* I arrested them •[Khan Chengzerin never cursed horses or their god-protectors ('Pîrê hespa')] ***Lema* p'îrê hespa xan hez kir** (EP-8) *Therefore* the god-protector of horses liked the khan **•Herê Zînê, *lema* divên: qismî jin heye p'arsû xare** (Z-1) Come Zin, *for* they say that some women are fickle •[***Lewranî* qesmi xwendî û mela di nîv ekradan bi tima û xestî(?) meşhûrin**] (JR) *Because of this*, learned people and mullahs have a reputation among the Kurds for being greedy. {also: lewma (K/JB3); lewma (ko) (IF); lewra (K[s]/IF/JB1-A); lewre (K[s]); lewranî (JR); loma (L/B-2); [lúma لوما/leoŭ لو /leoŭra لورا /leoŭrani لـورانـی (JJ); <lewre> لـوره (HH)} [Ba/K/F/B//F/JB3/IF//K(s)/HH//IF/JB1-A//JR//L]

lend لەند (Zeb/IFb) = den, lair. See **lan**.

lendik لەندِك (IF/HH) = cradle. See **landik**.

le'net لەعنەت (K) = curse. See **ne'let**.

leng I لـەنـگ *adj.* 1) {syn: t'opal} lame, limping; 2) awkward *(lit. & fig.)*: **•*Ya leng* e** (Zeb) It [=the sentence] is *awkward*. {also: [lenk] لـنـگ (JJ); <leng> لـنـگ (HH)} Cf. P lang لنگ; Sor leng لـەنـگ = 'lame, out of balance' [Zeb/IFb/JJ/HH/GF/RZ/ZF3]

leng II لەنگ (GShA) = foot, leg. See **ling**.

lenger I لـەنـگـەر *f./m.(ZF3/Wkt/FS)* **(/-ê;).** 1) {syn: giranî} anchor: **•Qesr û qonaxê Alan-p'aşa li ser çar *lengerane*** (Z-2) Alan pasha's palace is [held up] on four *anchors*; 2) in architecture, the 'camel foot' [deve ayağı] of a bridge (IF); 3) equilibrium, balance (IF); 4) [*adj.*] lame: **•bizina *lenger*** (FS) the *lame* goat. Cf. P langar لنگر; Sor lenger لەنگەر = 1) sofa cushion; 2) rhyme; 3) anchor [Z-2/F/K/A/IF/

(JJ)/ZF3/BF/Wkt/FS]

lenger II لەنگەر (IFb) = tray. See **lengerî**.

lengerî لەنگەری *f.* **(-ya;-yê).** wide tray, wide platter; flat copper tray on which food is served: **•Eva hersê zeveşa tîne dixe *negerîke* t'emiz, spîç'alekê davêje ser** (HCK-3, #16, 180) He brings those three watermelons, puts them on *a* clean *tray,* [and] throws a sheet over them **•Pîrê rabû, çû dik'anê, *lengerîk* t'ijî sêvê babetî Xecêr̄a k'ir̄î, anî** (IS-#263) The old woman went to the story and bought *a platter* full of fine apples for Khej [lit. 'apples worthy of Khej']. {also: lenger II (IF); lengerîk (JB1-A); negerî (HCK); [langheríe (G)/langarī (Rh)] لنگری (JJ); <lengerî> لنگری (HH)} {syn: mersef; sênî} [IS/B/JJ/HH//IFb/FS/ZF3//JB1-A//HCK] <berkeş; mecme‘; tiryan>

lengerîk لەنگەریك (JB1-A) = tray. See **lengerî**.

lengirîn لەنگِرین *vi.* **(-lengir-).** to limp, be lame. {also: <lingirîn> لنگرین (Hej); cf. also [langhin] لنگین (JJ)} {syn: kulîn; licimîn} [Frq/ZF3//Hej] <leng>

lep لەپ *f./m.(K/ZF)* **(-a/-ê;-ê/).** 1) {syn: çeng I} paw *(of an animal)*; 2) whole hand, including palm and fingers; 3) blow with the paw: **•Şêr *lepek* li hesp da kuşt** (Dz) The lion killed the horse with one *blow of his paw* [lit. 'gave a paw to/at the horse, killed [him]']. {also: [lep] لپ (JJ); <lep> لپ (HH)} Sor lep لەپ = 'palm of hand'; Za lep *m.* = 'hand, palm' (Mal); Cf. also Rus lapa лапа = 'paw' [F/Dz/K/A/IFb/B/JJ/HH/GF/ZF]

lepik لەپك *m.* **(-ê;).** 1) {syn: destgork (Bw); t'etik [2]} glove: **-lepikê herî** (IF) woolen gloves; 2) handle *(e.g., on a fan or knapsack)* (Bw); 3) string *(on an apron, or connecting the two arms of a pair of eyeglasses).* {also: [lepik] لپك (JJ); <lepik> لپك (HH)} [Ad/F/K/A/JB3/IFb/B/JJ/HH/GF/OK/Zeb]

lepitandin لەپِتاندِن (K) = to (cause to) move *(vt.)*. See **lipitandin**.

lepitîn لەپِتین (K) = to move, budge. See **lipitîn**.

leq I لەق *f.* **(-a;).** bite, biting: **•Cihê *leqa* wî li destê Behremî diyar bû** (FS) The site of his *bite* was visible on B.'s hand; **-leq dan [+li]** (Bw/SK) to bite {syn: gestin}: **•Hingo ‘adet kirîye, kesê destê merḧemetê bi serê hingoda bînît dê *leqekî* li wî destî *den*, we kesê pîyê bi-gû di serê hingo bihusût mirç-mirç dê wî pê maç ken** (SK 57:661) If anyone lays a compassionate hand upon your head you have been accustomed *to bite* that hand, and if anyone wipes a dung-covered foot on your face then you kiss that foot noisily. [Bw/IFb/SK/ZF3/BF]

leq II لەق *adj.* loose, slack, lax: **•Eger temenê wî pêncî be, weke devan *leq* e** (ZZ-7, 268) If his age if 50, he is as *loose* as camels; **-leq bûn** (IFb) to be or become loose: **•Diranê min *leq bûye*** (IFb) My tooth *has become loose.* [ZZ/K/IFb/ZF/FS]

leqa لەقا *f.* **().** encounter, meeting: **-leqayî *fk-î* bûn** (IFb) to meet, encounter, bump into: **•*Leqayî* yekî ixtîyar *dibin*** (Z-3) They *encounter* an old man. {also: laqa (K); [liqa bouin] لقا بوین (JJ)} <Ar liqā’ لقاء = 'meeting' [Z-3/IFb/ZF3//K//JJ] <r̄ast>

leqandin لەقاندِن *vt.* **(-leqîn-).** to (cause to) move, stir, budge *(vt.)*: **-ji cî leqandin** = to move stg. from its place, to dislodge: **•T'u qeweta nikaribû wana *ji cî bileqîne*** (Ba2:1, 203) No force could *budge* them. {also: [leqandin] لقاندین (JJ); <leqandin لقاندن (dileqîne) (دلقینه)/leqliqandin لقلقاندن (dileqliqîne) (دلقلقینه)> (HH)} {syn: bizaftin; lipitandin; livandin} [Ba2/K/A/IFb/B/JJ/HH/GF/TF/OK/ZF3] <leqîn>

leqat لەقات (ZF3) = corn left in field after harvest. See **liqat**.

leqatvan لەقاتڤان (ZF3) = gleaner. See **liqatvan**.

leqem لەقەم *f.* **(-a;-ê).** 1) underground passage, tunnel; sewer: **•Li mezelka min ḧeta li mezelka kur̄ê Eḧmed Ḧelwaçî bo min *leẍmeyekê* lê den, çendê bideme hungo?** (M-Ak #658, 298) If you make *a tunnel* from my room to the room of Ahmed Halwachi's son, how much must I give you?; 2) {syn: tepînk} land mine (hidden explosive). {also: laqum (B); laqûm (B-2); lexem (IFb/GF/ZF3); lexim (GF-2); leẍem; leẍme (M-Ak); [leqoum] لقم (JJ); <leẍm> لغم (HH)} <Ar laγam/luγm لغم = 'mine' & T lağım = 'sewer'; Sor leẍem لەغەم = 'mine, tunnel' [Z-1/K//B/JJ//HH//IFb/GF/ZF3] <k'ar̄êz>

leqemçî لەقەمچی *m.* **().** 1) someone who works in underground passages, tunneler, sewerman: **•*Leẍmeçîya* leẍme lê da ḧeta nîveka mezelka kur̄ekey der êxist** (M-Ak #658, 298) *The tunnelers* made a tunnel and brought it out in the middle of the boy's room; 2) sapper, land mine expert. {also: laqumçî (B); laqûmçî (B-2); leẍmec[î] (GF); leẍmeçî (M-Ak); <leẍmçî> لغمچی (HH)} <T lağımcı = 'sewerman' [Z-1/K//HH//M-Ak//GF//B]

leqîn لەقین *vi.* **(-leq-).** to move, stir, budge *(vi.)*: **-ji cî leqîn** (K) to move from its place, get going: **•Wekî ew nişkêva *ji cîêd xwe bileqyana*** (Ba2:1,

203) If they were suddenly *to move from their place*. {also: [leqiian] لـقـيـان (JJ); <leqan لـقـان (dileqe) (دلقه)> (HH)} {syn: biziftin; lipitîn; livîn I} [Ba2/K/A/JB3/IFb/B/GF/TF/OK//JJ] <leqandin>

lerizîn لـەرزيـن (K/B/IFb/TF) = to shake *(vi.)*. See **lerzîn**.

lerzeta لـەرزەتـا *f.* **(;-yê).** malaria: **•Bi saxbûna wan birînan re *lerzeta* jî diçû** (Wkp:Lerzeta) With the healing of those wounds *the malaria* also subsided. {also: lerzûta (GF)} {syn: ta û lerz [t'a III]} Sor lerz u ta لەرز و تا [Wkp/IFb/ZF3BF/FD/SS//GF]

lerzîn لـەرزيـن *vi.* **(-lerz-).** to tremble, shake *(vi.)*; to shiver: **•S̲one ji tirsan *lerzî*** (SK 4:51) The drake [=male duck] *shook* with fright. {also: lerizîn (K/B/IFb-2/TF); [lerzin] لـرزيـن (JJ); <lerizîn لـرزيـن (dilerizî) (دلـرزى)> (HH)} {syn: ĥejîn; kil II bûn; r̄e'ilîn; r̄icifîn; r̄ikr̄ikîn} Cf. P larzīdan لرزيدن; Sor lerzan لـەرزان (lerzê-)/lerzîn لـەرزيـن (lerz-) = 'to tremble, shiver, palpitate (heart)'; Za lerzenã [lerz(ıy)ayiş] (Todd/Mal); Hau lerzay (larz-) *vi.* (M4) [F/A/IFb/JJ/SK/GF/OK//K/B/HH/TF]

lerzûta لەرزووتا (GF) = malaria. See **lerzeta**.

leş لـەش *m.* **(-ê;).** 1) {also: laş (K/JJ-2); laşe (GF-2/OK-2)} {syn: berat'e[2]; cendek; cinyaz; k'eleş I; meyt'; term} corpse, cadaver, dead body: **•Bîne nanê genimî, duhn bide, bêxe *leşê* min, ezê sax bim** (M-Zx #757) Bring wheat bread, spread it with fat, put it on my *body* and I shall be cured [i.e., come to life again]; 2) {syn: qetirme I}{also: laş (Wn/JJ/TF)} carrion, carcass, body of dead animal; 3) {syn: beden II} body. See **laş**. {also: **laş**; laşe (GF-2/OK-2); [lach لاش/lech لـش] (JJ); <leş> لـش (HH)} Cf. P lāš لاش = 'corpse' --> T leş; Sor laşe لاشـە = 'corpse, carcass' & leş لـەش = 'body' [M-Zx/IFb/B/JJ/HH/JB1-A&S/GF/OK//Wn/K/TF]

leşker لـەشكـەر *m.* **(-e;).** 1) {syn: artêş; esker [2]; ordî} army: **•Digel nîwr̄o beraîya *leşkirê* Cindî Ax̱a geheşte nêzîkî gundî** (SK 40:365) At midday the vanguard of Jindi Agha's *army* came near the village **•To digel *leşkirî* here, dest bi şer̄î biken** (SK 40:365) You go with *the army* and start fighting; 2) {syn: serbaz} soldier (IFb/TF). {also: leşkir (SK); [lechkir] لـشـكـر (JJ)} Cf. P laškar لـشـكـر= 'army' (also Ar 'askar عـسـكـر = 'army' possibly al-'askar الـعـسـكـر with definite article **al-** <P laškar); Sor leşkir لەشكِر [Voa/K/A/IFb/GF/TF//JJ/SK]

leşkergeh لـەشكـەرگـەه *f.* **(-a;-ê).** army camp, military camp: **•Ji lewra qaymeqam birayê min da ber çend leşkeran û şande nav *leşkergeha* Midyadê** (Cxn, 47) Therefore the governor sent my brother to *the army camp* in Midyat, escorted by some soldiers. Cf. P laškargāh لـشـكـرگـاه; Sor leşkirga لەشكِرگا [Cxn/K(s)/IFb/GF/FJ/TF/Kmc/CS]

leşkir لەشكِر (SK/JJ) = army. See **leşker**.

le'tik لـەعـتِـك *f.* **(-a;-ê).** 1) vegetable garden where peppers, tomatoes, etc. are grown, kitchen garden (Msr); 2) small plot of land (HH/ZF3). {also: lehtik (ZF3); <leĥtik> لحتك (HH)} Cf. Sor let لـەت = 'piece, fragment' [Msr//ZF3//HH] <lat [2]; p'arêz I>

letilandin لـەتِـلانـدِن *vt.* **(-letilîn-).** to leave, abandon: **•Tu xema gişka *biletilîn*** (FK-eb-1) *Leave aside* all grief. [FK-1/K/ZF3]

lev لـەڤ *adv.* from each other; to each other. {also: lihev} {syn: lêk} < li = 'to' + hev = 'each other' [BX/K/B//ZF3]

levandin لەڤاندِن (OK/JJ) = to move *(vt.)*. See **livandin**.

leven لـەڤـەن *m.* **(-ê;).** reed, cane, bot. *Trichoon phragmites*: **-levenê şekir** (IFb) sugar cane, bot. *Saccharum officinarum*. {syn: qamîş[1]; qeram; zil} Sor lewan لـەوان = 'coarse kind of reed, bamboo' [Dh/Bar/K(s)/IFb/GF/OK/RZ/ZF3]

lewant•e لـەوانـتـە *f.* **(•a;).** lavender water: **•Zûzûka diçe ruyê xwe kur dike, kincên bajêr li xwe dike, hinek *lewante* jî di xwe dide** (Ardû, 11) He quickly goes and shaves his face, puts on city clothes, and sprays some *lavender water* on himself. {also: lawanta (TF); lawante (IFb-2/CS); lewende (FJ/GF)} < Lat lavandula; Sor lawante لاوانته [Ardû/IFb/AD//TF//CS//FJ/GF]

lewaş لەواش, m. (; lewêş) = lavash bread. See **loş**.

lewd لەود (Zeb) = den, lair. See **lan**.

lewende لـەوەنـدە (FJ/GF) = lavender water. See **lewante**.

lewendî لـەوەنـدى *f.* **(-ya;).** hanging sleeve, sleeve ending; "Although I had worn Kurdish dresses in Mawana and in Mr. Sheikhzadeh's village, I had not dressed myself before. Now I had to struggle to put the kiras over my head, wrap the sash of this underdress around my waist, and draw the long pointed sleeve endings out so that when I put on the fistan I could tie the kiras sleeve ends and throw them over my head, where they would ride on my back." [from: Margaret Kahn. *Children of the Jinn* (New York : Seaview Books, 1980), pp. 179-80]. {also: [lawandī] لـونـدى (JJ-Rh); <lewendî> لـەوەندى (Hej)} = Sor feqyane فـەقيانە

[Bw/Zx/JJ-Rh/OK/Hej/ZF3] <huçik>

lewij لەوژ (K[s]) = song. See **lawuk**.

lewitîn I لەوتین *vi.* **(-lewit-).** to be soiled, be defiled, be polluted, to get dirty: **•Ê ko keska pêxember dide serê xwe, nahêle tu carî *bilewite*, ê te, tu ê herî keska pêxember, di nav heriyê bidî û tu qîmeta wê nizanî** (RN 3:52, 2) He who puts the green [turban] of the prophet on his head, never lets it *get dirty*, and you, you will go put the prophets green [turban] in the mud, you don't know its worth. {also: [leoütin] لوتين (JJ)} <Ar lawwaṯa II لوّث = 'to pollute, sully'; Sor lewtan لەوتان (Hej) [RN/K/A/B/TF/BF]

lewleb لەولەب *f.(Zeb)/m.(Alkan)* **(-a/-ê;).** wooden handle bar inserted between forelegs and hind legs at each end of a skin sack used for churning: **•[Nêrgisa koçer] ...** ***lolep*** **di dest de dew kîyaye bêyî ku meşka wê çilkan bireşîne** (Lab, 8) [Nergis the nomad girl] ... with *a wooden handle bar* in her hand, churned the buttermilk without her skin sack spilling a drop **•Piştî ku diya min dewê xwe dikila, meşka xwe ya reş ji darê dadixist ... bi destê rastê bi *lewlebê* pêşî û bi yê çepê jî bi *lewlebê* paşî digirtin û dewê çîl-sipî vala dikir beroşê** (Alkan, 71) After my mother churned her buttermilk, she removed her black skin butter churner from the wooden frame ... and held the front *handle bar* with her right hand and the back *handle bar* with her left, and emptied the snow white buttermilk into the pail. {also: lole (IFb-2); lolep (Lab)} Sor lûrelep لوورەلەپ (W&E)/ lorelep لۆرەلەپ (Hej) [Alkan/A/IFb/TF//Lab] <meşk>

lewma لەوما (K/JB3)/lewma (ko) (IF) = because; therefore. See **lema**.

lewra لەورا (K[s]/IF/JB1-A/JJ) = because; therefore. See **lema**.

lewre لەورە (K[s]/HH) = because; therefore. See **lema**.

lewranî لەورانی (JR/JJ) = because; therefore. See **lema**.

lewẍet لەوغەت *f.* **(-a;).** 1) {syn: gilî [1]; peyiv; pirs [2]; xeber; zar I} word; 2) phrase; 3) {syn: ziman} language; 4) singing: **•Teyrê te xweş teyr e, *lewẍeta* wî xweş e** (L) Your bird is a fine bird, its *song* is fine. {also: loqet (JB1-S); [loughet] لغت (JJ); <lixet> لغت (HH)} <Ar luɣah لغة = 'language' --> P loɣat لغت = 'word'; --> T lûgat = 'dictionary'. For the meaning of 'singing', cf. **kilam** = 'song', from an Arabic word meaning 'speaking' [L/K//JB1-S//JJ//HH] <peyiv; ziman>

lewz لەوز (K/B) = word; speech. See **lavz**.

lexem لەخەم (IFb/GF/ZF3) = sewer; tunnel; mine. See **leqem**.

lexer لەخەر (MB/ZF3) = thin and weak (of animals), decrepit; lean. See **leẍer**.

lexim لەخِم (GF) = sewer; tunnel; mine. See **leqem**.

lext لەخت *f.* **().** birdseed: **•Kewa marî danî ser zinarê hemberê kozikê, li dorê jî *lext* reşand û xwe di kozikê da veşart** (AB, 52) He put the female partridge on the rock opposite the ditch, sprinkled *birdseed* around and hid in the ditch. {syn: qût} [AB/CS]

leẍem لەغەم = sewer; tunnel; mine. See **leqem**.

leẍer لەغەر *adj.* thin and weak (of animals), decrepit; lean *(of meat)*: **•Em sê-çar ritil titûn li kerê xwe ê *lexer* bar dikin** (MB) We load three or four rotls of tobacco onto our *decrepit* donkey. {also: laxer (ZF3); lexer (MB/ZF3-2); [lagher] لاغر (JJ); <leẍer> لغر (HH)} {syn: jar I; lawaz; narîn; qels I; qoṟ III; zeyf; zirav I} < P lāɣar لاغر --> T lağar; Sor leṟ لەڕ [MB//JJ//ZF3//HH/FS]

leẍlemîş لەغلەمیش: **-leẍlemîş bûn** (K) to crowd, gather around: **•Dîwana Al p'aşa t'ijî meriv bû, *leẍlemîş bû bûn*, gi li hîvîa Memê bûn** (FK-eb-1) Al pasha's diwan was full of people [who] had *gathered around*, waiting for Mem. Cf. T lehlemek [Sarıkamış, Selim-Kars; Erzurum; Ağrı; Erciş-Van] & lahlamak [Ahlat-Bitlis] = 'to pant with fatigue' (DS, v. 9, p. 3070) & leklemek [Kars] (AC-1, p. 265) = 'to be stopped up, to gasp for breath, to pant' & Az T lählämäk = 'to pant' [FK-1/K]

leẍme لەغمە (M-Ak) = sewer; tunnel; mine. See **leqem**.

leẍmecî لەغمەجی (GF) = sewerman; sapper, landmine expert. See **leqemçî**.

leẍmeçî لەغمەچی (M-Ak) = sewerman; sapper, landmine expert. See **leqemçî**.

leyistin لەیِستِن (JB1-S/JB3/HH/TF) = to play; to dance. See **lîstin**.

leyistok لەیِستوك (JB3) = toy. See **lîstok**.

leyî لەیی (HH/BZ/ZF) = flood. See **lehî**.

leyîstik لەییستِك (IFb) = game. See **lîstik**.

leyîstin لەییستِن (IFb) = to play; to dance. See **lîstin**.

leyîstok لەییستوك (IFb/TF) = toy. See **lîstok**.

leyîzvan لەییزڤان (FJ/GF) = player; dancer. See **lîstikvan**.

leylan لەیـلان *f.* **(-a;-ê).** 1) {syn: newa; nexme} tune, melody; 2) {syn: kilam} song: •**Stran û *leylanên* k'urdî** = Kurdish songs and *melodies*; 3) mirage: •**Wî *leylan* li ser cehdê dît** (FS) He saw *a mirage* on the highway. [K/A/JB3/IFb/B/ZF3/FS/Wkt] <lêlandin>

Leyla û Mecnûn لەیلا و مەجنوون (KS) = Gemini. See **leyl û mecnûn**.

leyl û mecnûn لەیل و مەجنوون *f.* **(;-ê).** Gemini *(star constellation)*: •**Bi şiyarbûnê re min dît ku ew stêrka li nêzîkî *Leyla û Mecnûn* rijiya erdê** (KS, 49) Upon awakening I saw that that star near *the Gemini constellation* had fallen to earth. {also: Leyla û Mecnûn (KS); leyl u mecrûm (GF-2/OK); <leylumecrum> لەیلومەجروم (Hej)} {syn: cêwî} <Ar Laylá wa-Majnūn ليلى و مجنون, the names of two lovers [KS//IFb/GF//OK/Hej]

leyl u mecrûm لەیل و مەجرووم(GF/OK) = Gemini. See **leyl û mecnûn**.

leymûn لەیموون (A/TF/RZ/CB) = lemon. See **lîmon**.

leystik لەیستِك (Msr) = game. See **lîstik**.

leystin لەیستِن (B/Msr) = to play; to dance. See **lîstin**.

lez I لەز *adj.* 1) fast, quick, rapid: **-lez bi lez** (IFb)/**lez û bez** (IFb) in a jiffy, lickity split; 2) urgent, hurried, hasty; 3) [*f.*] haste, rush (JJ/HH). {also: [lez لز/lezi لزى] (JJ); <lez> لز (HH)} {lezahî; lezanî; lezî; lez[a]tî} [K/A/JB3/IFb/B/JJ/HH/GF/TF] <bilez>

le'z II لەعز *f.* **().** moment: **-le'zekê** = for a moment: •**Em *le'zekê* vegeřin dîwana Al-p'aşa** (Z-1) Let's go back to A.p.'s court *for a moment*. {also: laze[k], m. (B); le'ze (B); [lehzé] لحظه (JJ)} < Ar laḥẓah لحظة [Z-1/K//B/JJ]

lezahî لەزاهی (IF) = speed. See **lezatî**.

lezandin لەزاندِن *vt. & vi.* **(-lezîn-).** 1) to hurry s.o. up *(vt.)*; to accelerate, speed stg. up: **-xwe lezandin** = to hurry, be in a hurry; 2) to hurry *(vi.)*. {also: [lezandin] لزاندين (JJ); <lezandin لزاندن (dilezîne) (دلزينه)> (HH)} [K/JB3/IF/B/HH/JJ/ZF3] <lez I>

lezanî لەزانی (K) = speed. See **lezatî**.

lezatî لەزاتی *f.* **(-ya;-yê)**. speed, rapidity, velocity: •**Bahoza Marîya bi *lezatîya* 280 kîlometran di satekê da gehiştîye nêzîkî sinorên girava Vêrcin** (rojname.com 20.ix.2017) Hurricane Maria at *the speed of* 280 km per hour has arrived near the bounda-ries of the Virgin Islands •**Di dîrokê da *bi vê lezatîyê* jinav neçûne** (waarmedia. com 27.x.2016) They have never disappeared *at this speed* in history. {also: lezahî (IF); lezanî (K); lezayî (ZF3-2); lezî (K-2/Wkt); lezîtî (ZF3-2); leztî (K/B); [lezi] لزى (JJ)} [K/B//IF//JJ/Wkt//ZF3] <lez I>

lezayî لەزایی (ZF3) = speed. See **lezatî**.

le'ze لەعزە (B) = moment. See **le'z II**.

lezet لەزەت *f.* **(-a;-ê).** 1) {syn: k'êf} delight, pleasure (K/IF/B): **-lezet dayîn** (B) to give pleasure; **-lezet dîtin** (K/JJ/B)/~ **stendin** (B)/~ **girtin** (ZF3) to take delight in, enjoy: •**Min *lezetek* ji vê pirtûkê *negirt*** (ZF3) I *did not enjoy* this book; 2) taste, flavor (JB3/IF/JJ). {also: [lezet] لذت (JJ); <lezet> لزت (HH)} < Ar laḏḏah لذّة [EP-7/F/K/JB3/IF/JJ/B/HH/ZF3]

lezî لەزی (K/JJ/Wkt) = speed. See **lezatî**.

lezîtî لەزیتی (ZF3) = speed. See **lezatî**.

leztî لەزتی (K/B) = speed. See **lezatî**.

lê I لێ *conj.* 1) {syn: bes I; lêbelê} but: •**Em dibêjin, *lê* ew guřa me nake** (B) We tell [him], *but* he doesn't listen to us; 2) but rather, rather: •**Ev ne guregurên Hîtler, *lê* yên Xwedê ne** (Rnh) Those are not the rumblings of Hitler [=Nazi bomber planes], *but* rather those of God •**Sibê na *lê* dusibê ezê bême cem we** (F) I will come to [visit] you not tomorrow, *but* rather the next day. {also: [lē] لى (JJ)} [F/K/JB3/IF/B/JJ/JB1-A&S]

lê II لێ *prn.* from him/her/it. < li = 'from; to' + ê/wê/wî = 'her, him' [BX/K/IF/B]

lê III لێ *voc. particle.* O, hey *(when calling one female: **lo** is used when calling one male; **gelî** is used in calling more than one person)*. {also: <lê> لى (HH)} [K/IFb/HH/GF/TF] <lo; gelî I>

lêb لێب (K[s]/GF/JJ-Rh) = trick, ruse. See **lêp**.

lê banandin لێ باناندِن *vt.* **(li... -banîn-).** to make s.o. used (to stg.), accustom (to), habituate (to), train: •**Sînor, ew hêdî hêdî hînî êş û mirinê dikirin, ango *li* mirinê *dibanandin*** (Nofa, 89) The border slowly *got them used to* grief and dying, i.e. it *accustomed them to* death. {syn: hîn kirin[b]} [Nofa/A/IFB/FJ/ZF3/WKT/G/FD/CS] <lê banîn>

lêbandin لێباندِن *vt.* **(-lêbîn-).** to fool, deceive, trick: •**'Usmanîyan teltîfa Kurdan o *lêbandina* wan faydetir o senayîtir zanîn** (SK 56:647) The Turks considered it more profitable and easier to placate the Kurds and *deceive* them •**Suto zanî kewlî heye ko Teto *bilêbînît*** (SK 61:768) Suto knew that there was a chance *to fool* Teto •**Xudanê kerî jî weto xiyal dikir ko her do hewalêt wî dê harî wî ken, nedizanî ko řezewanî her do *lêbandine*** (SK 8:80) The owner of the donkey thought that his two companions would help him, not knowing that the gardener *had deceived them*. {also: labandin (FS-2); lebandin (FS)}{syn: xapandin} *for etymology see* **lêbyan** [SK/RZ//FS] <lêp>

lê banîn لـى بـانـيـن *vi.* **(li ... -ban-).** to grow used to gradually, warm up to *(e.g., animals to a newcomer)*: **•Berx *li* mîyê *dibane*, lê mîh *li* berxê *nabane*** (Qzl) The lamb *warms up to* the ewe, but the ewe *doesn't warm up to* the lamb. {also: banîn (A/IFb); lê banyan (Qzl-2)} [Qrj/Qzl/ZF3//A/IFb//GF] <'elimîn; hîn I;lê banandin; r̄ahatin>

lê banyan لـى بـانـيـان (Qzl) = to grow used to. See **lê banîn**.

lêbelê لـى بـهـلـى *conj.* but, however. {syn: bes I; lê I} Za labelê; =Sor bełam بەڵام [BX/K/IFb/GF/TF]

lêborin لى بۆرن (IFb) = to pardon. See **lêborîn**.

lê•borîn لـى بـۆريـن *vt.* **(li… -bor-).** 1) to pardon, forgive: **•[Eger mirovek qebaĥetekî mezin bike û biçe xwe bavêje bextê yekî elbette *ji* qisûra wî *diborin*]** (BN, 197-98) If a person commits a great sin and goes and pleads for mercy [lit., throws himself at the luck of s.o.], they will certainly *forgive* him; 2) [*f.* ().] pardon, forgiveness. {also: bihurtin[4] (OK); lêborin (IFb); lêbûrin (OK-2); [borīn/burīn] بـوريـن (JJ-Rh) = 'to pardon (let stg. pass)'}{syn: bexşandin; 'efû kirin; lê xweş bûn} Sor lêburdin لى بوردِن = 'to pardon, dispense with, let go' [BN/JJ-Rh//RF/RZ//IFb//OK] See also **bihurtin**.

lêbûrin لى بوورِن (OK) = to pardon. See **lêborîn**.

lêbyan لێبيان *vi.* **(-lêbyê-).** to be fooled, deceived: **•Bi dewê her kesê *nelêbyêt*** (SK 2:17) *Let him not be deceived* by what each person says **•Zoro *bi* axiftinên wî *leba*** (FS) Z. *was fooled by* his words. {also: laban (FS-2); leban (FS)} {syn: xapîn} cf. Skt √rēp- = 'to deceive'; P firēftan فـريـفـتـن (firēb) (فـريـب) <pra- + √rēp-(or perhaps cf. Ar √l-'-b لعب = 'to play') [SK//FS] <lêp>

lê civîn لى جِڤين *vi.* **(li ... -civ-).** to gang up on: **•Do ew û çar birê xwe *li* min *civiyan*** (Qzl) Yesterday his four brothers and he *ganged up on* me **•Ez *li* we *civiyam*** (Qzl) I've *beaten* you guys (in cards) *[humorous usage]* [Qzl]

lêç لـێـچ *adj.* slanted, at an angle, sloping downward. {also: lêj (Slm/OK)} Sor lêj لـێـژ = 'sloping downward' [Qzl/IFb//Slm/OK] <vêl>

lêç'ûn لێچوون *f.* (). expenses, expenditures, outgoes: **•Hatina ji firotana silq, tevrik û kartolan ancax têrî *lêçûn û mesrefa* malê dikir** (ŞWWM, 11) The income from selling beets, radishes and potatoes was just barely enough [to cover] the household *expenses*; **-lêçûnên malbatê** (FD) household expenses. [ŞWWM/GF/FJ/FD/ZF3]

lê•dan لـــــــى دان *vt.* **(lê-d-).** 1) {syn: jendin; k'utan; lêxistin; r̄epandin} to strike, hit, beat: **-lêdan çûn** = to 'up and leave', depart {syn: lêxistin ç'ûn}: **•Ez lêdam çûm** (Z-922) I up and left **•Lêdidin diçin** (Z-922) They up and leave; **-xwe lêdan** (Zeb) to wrestle; 2) {syn: jendin[2]} to play *(musical instrument)*: **•Em jî ewe heşt neh r̄oj e ji laê Silêmanî û Kerkûkê li-dû nawbangê Eĥmed Axayê Berwarî têyn *da* bo wî def o kemança *lê-deyn* o lawjan bêjîn** (SK 27:243) For eight or nine days now we have come from the direction of Sulaimaniya and Kerkuk following the fame of Ahmad Agha Barwari, *in order to play* the drum and viol for him and to sing him songs. {also: [le-dan] لى دان (JJ); <lêdan ليدان (lêdide) (ليدده)> (HH)} [Z-922/K/A/IFb/B/JJ/HH/GF/SK]

lêf لێف *f.* **(-a;).** pen or enclosure in which ewes lamb, lambing pen: **•Kurd xwe pêk tînin, da bi keriyên xwe ve herin *lêfa*** (SW-#18 [Ereb Şemo]) The Kurds get ready to go to *the lambing pen* with their flocks. {syn: dolge} [SW-#18/K(s)/GF] <axil; gom I; guhêr̄; k'oz; mexel>

lê•hatin لـى هـاتِـن *vi.* **(lê-[h]ê-).** 1) {syn: bûn[2]} to become, get: **•Ez diçûm li def doktorî, ez xirabtir *lê hatim*** (Bw) I went to the doctor, and I *got* worse **•Kawdanên deverê dijwartir û aloztir *lê hatîne*** (Metîn 62[1997]:25) The situation of the region *has become* harder and more complex **•Ku min tu dîtî, ez çêtir *lê hatim*** (Bw) When I saw you, I *felt/became* better; 2) to happen to, become of, befall: **•Çi *lê hat*?** (Bw) What *happened to him*?/What *became of him*?; 3) to be fitting, suitable, appropriate: **-k'ês lê hatin** (A/JB3/IF) to have an opportunity or chance, find the right time or conditions to do stg.: **•Gur kir nekir *kêsa wî lê ne hat* ko bigire** (SW) No matter what the wolf did, he *couldn't manage to* catch it **•*Kês li min hat*** (JB3) *I had the opportunity* **•*Keysa min lê hat*** (IF) *I found the opportunity*; 4) to agree with s.o., suit (e.g., of food one has consumed): **•Çakêtê xalê min ê şîn bi rastî jî pir *lê tê*; lê xalojina min jê hez nake** (Xalbêhnok çi ye?) My uncle's blue jacket really *suits him*; but my aunt doesn't like it **•*Li* min *nehat*** (Bw) [X] *did not agree with* me/*gave* me *a stomach ache*. [Bw/Zeb/Dh/Metîn/K/A/IFb/GF/TF]

<*lêkînandin>

lêhmişt لێهمشت (Bw) = flood. See **lêmişt**.

lê hûr bûn لێ هوور بوون (IFb/RZ/CS) = to investigate. See under **hûr I**.

lêj لێژ (Slm/OK) = slanted. See **lêç**.

lêk لێك *adv.* from each other, from one another. < li = 'from; to' + êk = 'each other' {syn: lev} [BX/IF]

lêk•dan لێكدان *vt.* **(lêk-d-).** 1) {syn: berhev kirin; civandin} to bring together, gather (vt.), assemble (scattered things): •**Wî bi sêguhê qirş *lêkda*** (FS) He *gathered* the brushwood with the pitchfork •**Wî nokên li nîva mezelê *lêkdan*** (FS) He *assembled* the [spilt] beans in the middle of the room; **-xwe lêkdan** (M.Tayyib) to gather (vi.), assemble: •**Rojekê beqa hemiya *xo lêkda*** (Wkt:M.Tayyib. Kepir, 1:1, [2003-2004], 6) One day all the frogs *assembled*; 2) {syn: ser û ber kirin} to bring into order, tidy, straighten: •**Wan mala xwe *lêkda*** (FS) They *tidied* their house; 3) to clash, collide: •**Du tirimbêla *lêkda*** (FS) 2 cars *collided*; 4) {syn: carandin} to multiply: **-lêkdana hijmaran** (BF) multiplication (in arithmetic): •**Du *lêkdana* duwê** (FS) 2 x 2 [two *times* two]. [ZF3/FS/BF/Wkt]

lêker لێكەر *f.* **(-a;-ê).** verb: •**Di kurdî de hevok, li ser sê hêmanên bingehîn, kirde, bireser û *lêkerê*, tên sazkirin** (Amîda Kurd) In Kurdish, the sentence is founded on 3 elements, subject, object, and *verb*; **-lêkera arîkar** (IF) auxiliary verb; **-lêkera bêrêz** (IF) irregular verb; **-lêkera (ne)gerguhêz** (TaRK/Wkt)/~ **(ne)gerandî** (IF) (in)transitive verb; **-lêkera hevedudanî** (IF) compound verb; **-lêkera nekesîn** (IF) impersonal verb; **-lêkera rêzdar** (IF) regular verb. {syn: fêl II; other suggested words: *pêşing (IF); *pîşk (IF)} [(neol)K/JB3/IFb/GF/Kmc/RZ/TaRK]

lê•kirin لێ كِرن *vt.* **(lê-k-).** 1) {syn: bar kirin} to put on, load up; **-bar lêkirin** (IF) to load up; **-k'inc lêkirin** (K/IF) to dress s.o. *(vt.)*: •**Xulam xizmetk'ara k'incê wî *lêkirin*** (Z-1) The servants *dressed* him [lit. 'put his clothes on him']; **-k'inc li xwe kirin** (K) to dress *(vi.)*, get dressed; 2) to pour, spill *(liquids)* (HH); to load or pour stg. from above onto stg. (IF): **-av lêkirin** (IF/B) to give s.o. a shower, bathe s.o. *(by pouring warmed water over s.o. in a basin)*: •**Di van rojan da Şahan sibê dereng radibe. Dîya wî *avê lê dike* û kincên wî diguhure** (DZK, 81) On those days Shahan wakes up late in the morning. His mother *bathes him* and changes his clothes. {also: [le-kirin] لی کرین (JJ); <lêkirin لیکرین (lêdike) (لیدکه)> (HH)} [Z-1/K/A/IF/JJ/B/HH]

lêkolan لێ كۆلان (IFb/TF/OK) = to investigate. See **lêkolîn**.

lê•kolîn لێ كۆلین *vt.* **(lê-kol-).** 1) {syn: li ser ft-î r̄awestan/sekinîn} to study, investigate, examine, research, look into: •**Civat ne wek mahkemê ye. Heqê xweparastinê nade te, ... Bê taloq û bê ku *lêbikole*, di celsa pêşî de te mahkum dike** (LC, 15) Society is not like a court. It doesn't give you the right to defend yourself ... Without delay and without *doing any research*, it condemns you at the first session; 2) [*f.* **(-a;).**] a study, investigation, examination; research: •**Berî ku em werin ser *lêkolîna* Alaeddîn Seccadî ya berfireh** (CA, 67) Before we come to Alaeddin Sejjadi's wide-ranging *study* •***lêkolîn* li ser zimanê Kurdî** (IFb) *research* on the Kurdish language. {also: lêkolan (IFb-2/TF/OK-2)} Sor lê•kołînewe لێ كۆڵینەوە [(neol)CA/IFb/GF/OK/RF//TF] <hûr; vek'olîn>

lê•kuştin لێ كوشتِن *vt.* **(li ... -kuj-).** to deduct *(money)*: •**Wî bîst dînar *ji* qanê wî *kuştin* û yên dî danê** (FS) He *deducted* 20 dinars from his debt and gave him the rest of it. [Zeb//FS]

lêlandin لێلاندِن *vt.* **(-lêlîn-).** 1) {syn: stiran I} to sing; 2) to shout (HM/JJ): •[**Bi dengekî ḧişk *dilelînin***] (HM) They *shout* in a shrill voice. {also: lîlandin (K/KS); [līlāndin] لیلاندین (JJ)} [HM//K/JJ/KS] <leylan>

lêlav لێلاڤ *f.* **(-a;).** slush, melting snow: **-lêlava befrê** (Zeb) do. {also: <lêlav> لیلاڤ (HH)} [Zeb/IFb/HH/GF] <berf; şilop'e>

lêmişt لێمشت *f.* **(-a;-ê).** 1) {syn: sêlav [2]; t'ofan [1]} flood, deluge, inundation; 2) lava (Zeb). {also: lêhmişt (Bw); [li-micht] لیمشت (JJ); <lêmişt> لێمشت (Hej)} <lê + mişt- (-mal-) = 'to sweep'; =Sor lafaw لافاو = 'flood, torrent' [Zeb/K/IFb/B/GF/RZ/Hej//JJ//Bw] <avr̄abûn; lehî>

lê•nan لێ نان *vt.* **(lê-n-** [JB1-A]/**-lên-** [Bw]**).** to cook, prepare a meal, make *(a dish)*: •**Ew jirmama min t'êşt' *a lênay* û tu û mamê min dê vêkr̄a xon** (JB1-A #149) This aunt of mine *has made* breakfast, and you and my uncle will eat together •**Ez *dê* p'ilavekê *lênim*** (JB1-A #142) I *will make* [i.e., *cook/prepare*] rice. {also: lênandin (Bw-2)} Sor çêşt lênan چێشت لێنان = 'to cook (food)' [Bw/JB1-A/OK] <patin>

lênandin لێ ناندِن (Bw) = to cook. See **lênan**.

lêp لێپ *f.* (**;-ê).** trick, guile, ruse, deceit: •[**Kuştina wî li ûstûyê min, ez dê *lêpekê li wî bikim* û bê zeḧmet ewî bidime kuştin**] (JR #40,125) Killing him is my responsibility [lit. 'on my neck'], I will *play a trick on him* and with no trouble have him killed •[**Qenc e ewe ku em evne bi ezmanê şirîn û *lêp* bînine nîva heyşetê**] (JR #40,124) It is best to lure them into town with sweet talk and *guile*. {also: lêb (K[s]-2/GF-2); [lip/lēb (Rh)/laēbi (G)] لـيـپ (JJ); <lêp> لـيـپ (HH)} {syn: delk'; fêl I; ḧîle} *for etymologies see* **lêbyan** [JR/K/IFb/B/JJ/HH/GF] <lêbandin; lêbyan>

lêr لێر, m. (SK) = forest. See **r̄êl**.

lê sor kirin لـێ سـۆر کـِرِن *vt.* (*fk-î* **li** *fk-î* **sor -k-**). to incite, provoke: •**Ez hevala *li* hev *sor dikim*** (Qzl) I *incite* the friends *against* each other •**Ez te *li* Reşoyî *sor dikim*** (Qzl) I *incite* you *against* R. •**Tu jî wî *li* me sor *dikî*** (ZF3) And you *are inciting* him *against* us. {syn: nav tê dan; şarandin; têkdan} [Qzl/A/IFb/ZF3/CS/Wkt] <azirandin>

lêstik لێستِک = game. See **lîstik**.

lêv لێڤ *f.* (**-a;-ê).** 1) lip: •***Lêvên* min ji tînan ziwa bûn** (AB) My *lips* became dry from/with thirst; -**bi lêv kirin** (GF) to pronounce; -**lêva jêrîn** (OK) lower lip; -**lêva jorîn** (OK) upper lip; -**lêva xwe gestin** (B/FK-eb-2): a) to bite one's lips *(out of boredom)*; b) to keep one's mouth shut, be silent: •**Ew zane wekî Memêye, *lêvê xwe digeze*** (FK-eb-2) He knows it is [about] Mem, [but] *he keeps his mouth shut*; 2) shore, coast (B); side, bank (IFb/TF): •**Li hindav û nêzî Wanê û Gola Wanê kelehên mezin û dîrokî hene, du keleh ji van kelehan li raserî *lêva* golê ne** (SB, 50) Above and beside Van and Lake Van there are large and historic fortresses, [and] two of those fortresses overlook *the shore of* the lake; -**lêva be'rê** (B) seashore. {also: [liw] لڤ (JJ); <lêv> ليڤ (HH)} [Pok. lĕb-/lŏb-/lăb-/ləb- 655.] 'lip': Mid P lab (M3); P lab لب; Sor lêw لێو; Za lew *m.* (Todd); Hau liç *m.* (M4); cf. also Lat labium; Germ Lippe [K/A/JB3/IFb/B/HH/SK/GF/TF/OK//JJ]

lêve•bûn لێڤەبوون *vi.* (**lêve-b-**). to change one's mind, go back on one's word, renege: •**Ew bazar̄ê ku kiribû, *lê vebû*** (FS) He *reneged* on the deal that he had made •**Ew peymana xwe *lê vebû*** (FS) He *backed out of* his contract •[**Heke tiştek dibêjit paşî *lêve nabiteve***] (RJ) If he says something, afterwards he *will not go back on his word.* [Bw/RJ/FS] <hatin xwarê>

lêvî لێڤی (QtrE) = flood. See **lehî**.

lê•xistin لێ خِستِن *vt.* (**li... -x-**). 1) {syn: jendin; k'utan; lêdan; r̄epandin} to hit, strike, beat: -**lêxistin çûn** = to depart, leave, to "up and leave" {syn: lêdan ç'ûn}: •**Xort cotê xwe *berda û lêxist, çû* mala p'adşê** (J) The youth put aside his plow, *got up and went* to the king's house •***R̄abû, lêxist çû* mala xwe** (J) He *got up and went* home; 2) to play (musical instrument): •***Li* tembûra xwe *dixe*** (L) He *plays* his tambur (saz) . {also: [li-khystin] لـی خستین (JJ); <lêxistin ليخستن (lêdixe) (ليدخه)> (HH)} [K/A/IFb/B/HH/GF/TF//JJ]

lê•xur̄în لێ خوڕین [Dh/K]/**lê•xurîn** لێ خورین [JJ-Rh/ SK/GF] vi. (**li... -xur̄-**). to yell at s.o., to attack (verbally), abuse, revile: •**Her sê *li* wî *xurîn*, gotine** [sic] **wî, "kir̄ be, egerne dê zopan xoy!"** (SK 8:78) All three *abused* him, saying, "Shut up, or you'll take a cudgelling" •**Tu bo *li* min *dixur̄î*?** (Dh) Why are you *yelling at* me? {also: [lē-khorīn (Rh)] لـی خـوریـن (JJ)} cf. Sor lêxur̄în لـه خـوریـن = 'to drive forward, urge on (animal) with cries' [Dh/K//JJ-Rh/SK/GF]

lê xweş bûn لێ خوەش بوون *vi.* (**li** *fk-î* **xweş -b-**). 1) {syn: bexşandin; 'efû kirin; lêborîn} to forgive, pardon: •**Ya xudê, to *li* me *xoş bî*, qusûra me 'efw key** (SK 9:90) O God, *forgive* us and pardon our fault; 2) [**lêxweşbûn** *f.* ().] forgiveness, pardon. [SK/A/OK] <xweş>

li لِ *prep.* 1) in, at [*location; with or without motion*]: •**Gurgîn *li* mal e** (BX) G. is *at* home •***Li* avê xist** (BX) He threw himself *at* the water/ jumped *into* the water •**Ez duhî *li cem te* bûm** (BX) Yesterday I was *at your house* •***li* malê** (K) *at* home •***li* ku?** = where? {syn: k'u derê?} •***li* herçar beşên Kurdistanê jî** (Ber) *in* all four parts of Kurdistan; 2) for [*purpose*]: •***Li* şera xal û xwarzî; *li* xwarina, mam û brazî** (BX) *For* fighting, maternal uncles and sisters' sons; *for* eating, paternal uncles and brothers' sons *[prv.]*; 3) on, onto [*with or without motion*]: •**Çavê min *li* te ye** (BX) I have my eye *on* you •***Li* ç'îyê berf k'et** (K) *On* (or, *in*) the mountains snow fell •***Li* hespê swar bûn** (K) to get *on* (=mount) a horse; -**li 'erdê xistin** (K) to throw on[to] the floor; 4) about, regarding, concerning: •**Min ji Tacîn *li* te pirsî** (BX) I asked T. *about* you; 5) in, about, around: •**Ew *li* otaxê dihat-diçû** (K) He paced *about* the room •***Li* çolê gerîyan** (K) They wandered/roamed about *in* the desert; 6) with *[instrument, means]*: •**Tuê here ji mi re *li* van pera tişta bikire!** (L) Go buy me some things *with* this money; 7) from: •***Li* kanîyê av dikişe** (K) Water flows *from* the spring •***li* zevîyê nan berev kirin** (K) to gather or harvest bread *from* the field. {also: [li] لى/لِ (JJ)} [li + wê/wî = lê; li + hev = lev; li + êk = lêk] [BX/K/JB3/IF/B]

lib لِـب *f.* **(-a;-ê).** 1) {syn: ḧeb} a single grain or seed: **-yek lib** (Qzl) ace *(in card games)* {syn: *as; beg [2]; *bilî (Bw); yeklî (Wn)}; 2) *counting word for fruits, nuts, etc.*: •**Diya min çend nan, du çeng mewîj, bîst-sih *lib* gwîz dixistin tûrikê Gulîstanê** (Alkan, 71) My mother would put some bread, two handfuls of raisins, 20-30 walnuts into Gulistan's bag. {also: [lib لـب/lip لـپ] (JJ); <lib> لـب (HH)} < Ar lubb لُـبّ = 'kernels, core (of fruits)' [Alkan/K/A/IFb/B/JJ/HH/ GF/TF/Qzl] <dan II; ḧeb; kit>

libas لِـبـاس, m. (-ê; libês) (K/B/IF/JJ/HH) = clothing. See **libs**.

libat لِبات (IFb) = movement; activity. See **lebat I**.

li ber xwe dan لِ بـەر خـوە دان *vt.* **(li ber xwe -d-).** to resist, oppose, put up a fight: •**Frensîzan di wê qadê de gelek *li ber xwe dida* û bi xurtî şer dikir** (H2 9:31, 776) The French *resisted* a great deal on this front and fought fiercely. {also: ber xwe dan (IFb/ GF/Mzg/Krş)} [H2/TF/RZ//IFb/GF/Mzg/Krş]

libê لِبى (TF/IFb) = At your service. See **lebê**.

Libnanî لِـبـنـانـى (BF/Wkp/Wkt) = Lebanese. See **Lubnanî**.

libs لِبس *m.* **(-ê;).** clothing, dress, garb. {also: libas, m. (-ê; libês) (K/B-2/IF); [libas] لـبـاس (JJ); <libas> لباس (HH)} {syn: cil I; ç'ek; k'inc} < Ar libs لبس/ libās لباس [L/K/B//IF/JJ/HH]

libûcen لِبووجەن (Erciş) = wool-beater. See **livajen**.

libûjen لِبووژەن (Bw) = wool-beater. See **livajen**.

Libyayî لِبيايى (Wkt) = Libyan. See **Lîbî**.

licimîn لِـجِـمـيـن *vi.* **(-licim-).** to stagger, reel, totter, sway; to walk slowly like an ill person; to limp, be lame. {syn: kulîn; lengirîn} [Frq/GF/FJ/ZF3]

li dar k'etin لِ دار كـەتِـن *vi.* **(li dar -k'ev-).** to take place, occur; to be held *(meeting)*: •**Di 19'ê Îlona 1992 an de komcivîna awarte ya duyemîn a HEP'ê li Enqerê *li dar ket*** (Wlt 1:43, 9) On September 19, 1992, the second emergency meeting of the People's Labor Party (HEP) *took place*. [(neol)Wlt/ZF3/Wkt] <li dar xistin; pêkhatin; qewimîn>

li dar xistin لِ دار خِـسـتِـن/**lidar xistin** لِـدار خِـسـتِـن/**li darxistin** لِ دارخِـسـتِـن *vt.* **(lidar -x[în]-).** to organize, set up, hold *(a conference, etc.)*: •**...Ev tiştekî normal e ku di meclîsa we de qomîteyên wiha *tên li darxistin*?** (Wlt 1:37, 16) Is it normal [lit. 'a normal thing'] that committees such as this *are organized* in your assembly? {syn: pêkanîn [3]} [Wlt/IFb/ZF3/Wkt] <damezirandin; li dar k'etin>

li def لِ دەف (Bw) = at, over (someone's house). See **def II**.

ligel لِگەل (Bw) = with. See **digel**.

lihev لِهەڤ (ZF3) = to or from each other. See **lev**.

li hev anîn لِ هەڤ ئانين *vt.* **(li hev [t]în-).** 1) {syn: aşt kirin; fesil kirin} to reconcile, make peace between *(opposing parties)*: •**Dê û bavê xort jî hatine, peyre wan şiyandiye dûv melakî, wî jî fesla wan kiriye û ew *li hev anîne*** (Mdt) The parents of the young man came, then they sent for a mullah, and he settled the feud between them [=the two families] and *reconciled* them; 2) to cause to agree, bring into agreement, harmonize (lit. & fig.). {also: [li-hew anin] لـهـڤ انـيـن (JJ); <lêk anîn ليك ءانين (lêk tîne) (ليك تينه)> (HH)} [Mdt/K/IFb/JJ/GF/TF/AD/ZF3//HH] <li hev hatin>

li hev hatin لِ هـەڤ هـاتِـن [IFb/XF/AId]/**lihevhatin** لِـهـەڤـهـاتِـن *vi.* **(lihev[t]ê-).** 1) to be reconciled, make peace with one another, make up; 2) {syn: r̄êkk'etin} to meet, agree, come together; to coincide: •**Paşê me çend cara soz dida hev, ku cîkî talde r̄astî hev bên û ji gund bir̄evin, lê ew yek mer̄a *li hev nedihat*** (Ba2-#2, 209) Then we promised each other several times that we would meet in a secret place and run away from the village, but this *did not come together* for us [i.e., we couldn't get it together]. {also: [li-hew hatin] لهڤ هاتن (JJ)} [Ba2/K/A/IFb/JJ/GF/XF/AId/ZF3] <aştî>

lihêf لِهێف (IFb) = quilt. See **liḧêf**.

liḧêf لِحێف *f.* **(-a;-ê).** blanket, quilt: •**Me do *liḧêf* û do ḧesîr hene. Bila ew şewe *liḧêfek* û ḧesîrek bo her do derwêşan bin, *liḧêfek* û ḧesîrek jî bo min û te bin** (SK 23:213) We have two *quilts* and two reed mats. Tonight let *one quilt* and one mat be for the two dervishes, and *one quilt* and one mat be for you and me •**Wî *liḧêf* bi ser xwe da û nivist** (FS) He covered himself with *a blanket* and fell asleep. {also: laêf (L); lehêf (K); lihêf (IFb); [lehif لحيف/ lihaf لحاف] (JJ); <liḧêf> لحيف (HH)} {syn: mêzer} <Ar liḥāf لحاف [F/B/HH/SK/GF/FS//IFb//L//K//JJ] <doşek; orxan>

likimandin لِكِمانِدِن (FS) to cause s.o. to stumble. See **lik'umandin**.

likimîn لِكِمين (FS) = to stumble. See **lik'umîn**.

likmandin لِكمانِدِن (FJ) = to cause s.o. to stumble. See **lik'umandin**.

lik'umandin لِكومانِدِن *vt.* **(-lik'umîn-).** to trip s.o. up, cause s.o. to stumble: **•Ji ber *lukumandina* di dil de ji *lukumandina* zimên bi xêrtir e** (Qzl) Because *causing someone to stumble* in his heart is better than *causing someone to stumble* in speaking [lit. 'in the tongue']. {also: likimandin (FS); likmandin (FJ); lukumandin (Qzl)} {syn: şemitandin; teḧisandin} [Qzl//K/TF/GF//FS//FJ]

lik'umîn لِكومين *vi.* **(-lik'um-).** to stumble, trip [lingê te ji ber dihere (ji-ber-ç'ûn)]: **•Berf li erdê hebû, mehîn *likumî* û lawik di bîrekê werbû** (ZZ-10, 163) There was snow on the ground, the mare *stumbled* and the boy rolled down into a well **•Nan di destek** [sic] **wî dabû, xiyar jî di destê din. Dema nêzîkî li se kir, lingê wî li singekî dewara *likumî*. Xwe ra negirt û bi ser dev ket erdê** (MB, 11) He had bread in one hand, and a cucumber in the other. When he got near the dog, his foot *tripped* on a cattle post. He lost his balance and fell down, flat on his face. {also: likimîn (FS)} {syn: alîn[2]; hilîngiftin; hilpekîn; şelifîn; teḧisîn} [Nsb/MB/K/GF/TF//FS]

limêj لِمێژ *f.* **(-a;-ê).** 1) namaz, salah, Islamic prayer ritual: **-limêj kirin** (BX) to request, ask *(s.o. to do stg.)* {syn: jê hêvî kirin; lavahî kirin; t'eweqe kirin}; 2) {syn: destnimêj} ritual ablutions, performed prior to Islamic prayer (HH/PS): **•Misînê wî ê *limêjê*** (L) His *prayer* ewer or pitcher. {also: **nimêj**; [lämüž] لموژ (JJ); <lemêj> لميژ (HH)} Cf. P namāz نماز --> T namaz {See: Introd. to HH, p. 27 (in French) & p. 52 (in English)} [K/A/TF//HH//JJ] See also **nimêj**.

ling لِنگ *m.* **(-ê;).** foot, leg: **•*Lingê* berxa me şikest** (AB) Our lamb's *leg* broke **•*Lingê* xwe weke beř̄a xwe dirêjke** (B) Stretch out your *legs* according to the length of your carpet *[prv.]*; **-binê ling** (B) sole *(of foot)*. {also: leng II (GShA); nig (Ad/Bg/IF); ning; [link/lank] لنك (JJ); <ling> لنگ (HH)} {syn: p'ê II; qor I} Cf. P leng لنگ = 'leg (from the groin to the tip of the toe)'; Mazanderani ling; Za ling *f.* (Mal) [AB/F/K/JB3/IF/B/HH/JB1-S/SK/GF/OK//JJ//Ad/Bg//GShA] <belek II; boqil; ç'îm I; çîp; çok; p'ê II>

lipat لِپات *f.* **(;-ê).** movement, stirring, thrashing about: **•[Bi zûyî qemeyê hildigre û qemekê li serê Behram dide û yekî dinê û yekî dinê, xulase îdî Behram micala *lipatê* nebûyî]** (JR) He quickly takes the dagger and strikes Behram again and again, in short Behram is in no condition *to move*. {also: [lipat] لپات (JJ)} [JR/K/JJ/FS] <lipitîn> See also **lebat I**.

lipitandin لِپتانِدِن *vt.* **(-lipitîn-).** to budge, move *(vt.)*, cause to be displaced. {also: lepitandin (K-2); [lepytandin] لپتاندين (JJ); <lebitandin لبتاندن (dilebitîne) (دلبتينه)> (HH)} {syn: bizaftin; leqandin; livandin} [K/B/FS//JJ//HH]

lipitîn لِپِتين *vi.* **(-lipit-).** to move *(vi.)*, budge, stir *(vi.)*: **•Qet ji ciyê xwe jî *nelipitî*** (FS/Tosinê Reşîd) He *didn't budge* from his place. {also: lepitîn (K-2); [lepatin/lepytin] لپتين (JJ); <lebitîn لبتين (dilebitî) (دلبتى)> (HH)} {syn: biziftin; leqîn; livîn I} [EP-8/K/B/FS//HH//JJ] <lipat; lipitandin>

liqat لِقات *f.* **(-a;-ê).** ear of corn left in the field after a harvest, gleaning. {also: leqat (ZF3); <liqaṯ> لقاط (HH)} {syn: simbil I} < Ar luqāṭ لقاط = 'left ears of grain, gleanings' [F/K/B//HH//ZF3]

liqatvan لِقاتڤان *m.&f.* **().** gleaner, person who gathers leftover ears of corn (etc.) in the field. {also: leqatvan (ZF3)} <liqat + -van [Wkt/Kmc//ZF3] <liqat>

li ser لِ سەر = about. See **ser II**.

liv•a لِـڤـا *f.* **(•a;•ê/liva[y]ê).** fine wool; lamb's wool; wool of a lamb up to the age of six months (HH): **-liva berxî** (FS) do. {also: [liva] لوا (JJ); <liva> لڤا (HH)} [BX/K/A/JB3/IFb/B/HH/OK/Bw/ZF3/FS/BF//JJ] <ç'ûr I; hirî; kej II; kulk; livajen; merez; r̄êstin; r̄îs; t'eşî>

livajen لِـڤـاژەن *m.&f.* **().** wool-beater, wool-comber, wool-carder, wool-fluffer. {also: libûcen (Erciş); libûjen (Bw-2); livojen (K-2); livûjen (B-2)} {syn: kûrinc (Bw)} <liva + jen- = 'to beat.' *Perhaps in the forms libûcen/libûjen, **liva** is being confused with Ar labad* لبد = *'felt'* [=kulav] [Erciş//Bw/K/B/ZF3/FD] <liva>

livandin لِڤاندِن vt. **(-livîn-).** to (cause stg. to) move, put or set stg. in motion, shake stg. (vt.): **•Ba belgên daran *dilivînit*** (BF) The wind *makes* the tree leaves *move* **•Bayî belgên dara *livandin*** (FS) The wind *made* the tree leaves *move* **•Pisîkê tiriya xwe *livand*** (FS) The cat *moved* its tail. {also:

levandin (OK); [levandin] لـقـانـديـن (JJ)} {syn: bizaftin; leqandin; lipitandin} [K/A/IFb/B/GF/TF//JJ/OK/ZF3/BF/FS] <livîn I>

livbazî لِڤبازی *f.* **(-ya;-yê).** action, activity: **•Program û *livbaziyên* (lebatên) HEP'ê dikarin bibin mijarên rexneyê** (Wlt 1:43, 9) The programs and *activities* of HEP can be the subject (or, object) of criticism. {syn: çalakî; lebat} [(neol)Wlt/ZF3/Wkt]

livîn I لِڤين vi. **(-liv-).** 1) {syn: biziftin; leqîn; lipitîn} to move *(vi.)*, budge, stir *(vi.)*: **•Heft şev û heft rojan ji ciyê xwe *ne liviyaye*** (Tof, 12) For seven nights and seven days he *hasn't moved* from his spot **•Tiştek di nav pûşî da *livî*** (FS) Something *moved* amid the hay **•Ûsib, tu ji cîê xwe *nelive*** (Ba3) Joseph, *don't move* from your spot; 2) [*f.*] movement (JB3). {also: livyan (FS-2); [liwiian لِڤيان/ liwin لِڤين] (JJ)} [Ba3/K/JB3/IFb/B/JJ/GF/TF/ZF3/FS] <livandin>

livîn II لِڤين (Msr) = bed, bedding. See **nivîn**.

livojen لِڤۆژەن (K) = wool-beater. See **livajen**.

livûjen لِڤووژەن (B) = wool-beater. See **livajen**.

livyan لِڤيان (FS/JJ) = to move (vi.). See **livîn I**.

liwane لِوانه (Tsab) = bridle, rein, bit. See **lîwan**.

li wir لِ وِر (GF) = there. See **wir**.

lixab لِخاب (IFb/OK) = rein, bridle. See **lix̆ab**.

lixav لِخاڤ (GF/OK) = rein, bridle. See **lix̆ab**.

lix̆ab لـغـاب *m.(JB1-A/OK)/f.* **(-ê/ ;).** rein; bridle; bit: •...***Lix̆awekî* asin dû gez dirêj, gezek pan, bi qeder zenda destî stûr bide çêkirin** (SK 33:297) Have [them] make an iron *bridle* made, two yards long, a yard wide, and as thick as a man's wrist **•Wext'ê hat'in, hak'im û wezîr. her du b[i] cot *lix̆avê* hesp'ê ȟak'imî girt' û got'ê: Ȟak'im, p'eya bibe** (JB1-A #151) When they came, the prince and the minister, the two of them together, he took *the bridle of* the prince's horse {note: a sign of respect} and said, "Prince, get down." {also: lixab (IFb/OK); lixav (GF/OK-2); lix̆av (JB1-A); lix̆aw (SK); [ligab] لـغـاب (JJ); <lix̆ab> لـغـاب (HH)} {syn: bizmîk; celew I; dizgîn; gem; lîwan; qet'irme II} <Syr lúgmā ܠܘܓܡܐ/lgāmā ܠܓܡܐ= 'bridle, bit, curb' & NENA lâmâ ܠܓܡܐ/ܠܓܡܐ; Ar lijām لجام; Sor lix̆aw لِغاو; Hau lex̆am *m.* (M4) [K/JJ/HH//IFb/OK//GF//JB1-A//SK] <hevsar>

lix̆av لِغاڤ (JB1-A) = rein; bridle. See **lix̆ab**.

lix̆aw لِغاو (SK) = rein; bridle. See **lix̆ab**.

liyan لِيان (IFb) = snow shoe. See **lîyan II**.

Lîbî لـيـبـى *adj.* Libyan. {also: Libyayî (Wkt); Lîbyayî (Wkp-2/SS-2)} [Wkt/BF/Wkp/SS]

Lîbyayî ليبيايى (Wkp/SS) = Libyan. See **Lîbî**.

lîç ليچ *f.* **(-a;-ê).** 1) puddle, rainwater puddle (IF); pool, reservoir (JJ); pool of water in a dry riverbed (HH): **•Kî dikare wan masîyên di wê *lîçê* da mirî yan gîyanî bigire?** (Bkp, xxviii) Who can catch those fish in that *pool*, dead or alive? ***•Lîç* tijî av e** (AB) *The pool* is full of water; 2) puddle, rainwater puddle (IFb); 3) dirty mud (Msr); 4) mucus, snot. See **lîk**. {also: [litch] لـيـچ (JJ); <lêç> لـيـچ (HH)} < W Arm lič լիճ = 'lake' [AB/A/IFb/JJ/Msr//HH] <bêrm>

lîk ليك *f./m.(FS)* **(-a/-ê;).** 1) any of the body secretions such as phlegm, mucus, saliva; 2) {syn: çilka poz; çilm; fiş; k'ilmîş} mucus: ***•Lîka* min tê** (Msr) My nose is running [lit. 'My *mucus* comes']. {also: lîç [4]; lîkav (IFb-2)} Sor lîk لـيـك = 'spittle' [Msr/IFb/GF/ZF3/FS] <ava dev; belxem; tif; t'ûk II>

lîkav ليكاڤ (IFb) = mucus. See **lîk**.

lîlandin ليلاندِن (K/JJ/KS) = to sing. See **lêlandin**.

lîmo ليمۆ (K/JJ/GF/OK/AA) = lemon. See **lîmon**.

lîmon لـيـمـۆن *f.* **(-a;-ê).** lemon, bot. *Citrus limon*. {also: leymûn (A/TF/RZ-2/CB-2); lîmo (K-2/ GF/OK-2/AA); lîmû (GF-2); [limo] لـيـمـو (JJ)} Cf. P līmū ليمو & Ar laymūn ليمون; Sor lîmo ليمۆ [Kmc-2/K/IFb/B/OK/RZ/CB//JJ/GF/AA//A/TF]

lîmû ليموو (GF) = lemon. See **lîmon**.

lîn لـيـن *m.* **(-ê;).** large earthenware jar or vat *in which doşav [grape molasses] and the like is stored*:
-lînê avê (OK) clay water jug. {also: lîne (IFb); [lina] لـيـنـا (JJ)} cf. Arc lgina לגינא = 'bottle, medium-sized vessel'; Gr lagynos λάγυνος & Lat lagena = 'flask' [Bw/IFb/GF/OK] <cer; den I; hincan; sewîl>

lîne لينه (IFb) = large clay jar. See **lîn**.

lîrê ليرێ, m. (F) = forest. See **r̄êl**.

lîrîn ليرين (Wkt) = to howl. See **lûrîn**.

lîs لـيـس *m./f.(ZF)* **(;-î/).** perch, roost for birds to rest on: **•Kew çû *lîsî*** (Bw) The partridge went *to roost*;
-lîs bûn (SK) to roost: **•Dibêjin ximdarek hebû, şeş ȟevt mirîşkêt qelew hebûn. Şevê di oda ximî da *lîs dibûn*** (SK) They say there was one a dyer who had six or seven fat chickens. At night they *used to roost* in the dye-house. {also: lûs (A/ZF-2); <lîs> لـيـس (HH)} Sor lîs لـيـس = 'roosting place for wild birds' [Bw/K(s)/A/IFb/HH/SK/GF/TF/OK/ZF//A]

lîsîn ليسين (Kmc/Wkt) = to perch, roost. See **lûsîn**.

lîsk ليسك = game. See **lîstik**.

lîstik ليستِك *f.* **(-a;-ê).** 1) {syn: t'iṙane; yarî II} game; amusement (B); 2) {syn: govend} dance (B). {also: lehîstik (K); leyistik (TF); leyîstik (IFb); leystik (Msr); lêstik; lîsk} [K/A/JB3/IFb/B/RZ//Msr] <lîstok; yarî II>

lîstikçî ليستِكچى (FK-1/F/K/B) = player; dancer. See **lîstikvan**.

lîstikvan ليستِكڤان *m.* **().** 1) {syn: yarîker} player; 2) dancer. {also: lehîzevan (GF); lehîzvan (Kmc/FJ); leyîzvan (FJ-2/GF-2); lîstikçî (FK-1/F/K/B); lîzvan (GF-2)} [FK-1/F/K/B//Kmc/FJ//GF//Z-2/IFb/ZF/RZ/SS] <lîstik; lîstin; şanoger>

lîstin ليستِن *vt./vi.* **(-lîz-[B]/-lêz-[Wn]/-lehîs-/-leyiz-** [JB1-S]**).** 1) to play: •**Li Hoskan ciwanên gund derketibûn rasta bêndera û ji xwe re bi gogê *dilîstin* *[vi.]*** (AW69B4) In Hoskan [village] the young men of the village had gone to the threshing floor and *were playing* ball •**Me bi heftoka *dilîst* *[vt.]*** (Alkan, 71) We *played* heftok •**Zarûk bihevra veşartokê *dilîzin*** (AB) The children *are playing* hide-and-seek together; **-ṙolekê leyîstin** (ZF3) to play a part or rôle; 2) to dance [cf. T oynamak = to play & to dance]; 3) to jump (JB1-S). {also: lehîstin; lehîzîn (K[s]); leyistin (JB1-S/JB3/TF); leyîstin (IFb-2); leystin (B-2/Msr); [leïztin] ليزتين (JJ); <leyistin ليستن (dileyize) (دليزه)> (HH)} [Pok. 3. leig-/loig- 667.] 'to leap, tremble': Skt rejate = 'he leaps, jumps'; O Ir *rais- (Tsb 40): P ālēxtan آليختن/ālīzīdan آليزيدن (-ālēz-) = 'to spring, lash out, kick (of horses)' [K/A/IFb/B/GF/Ad/Çnr//K(s)//JB1-S/JB3/HH/TF//JJ//Msr] <lîstik; lîstok>

lîstok ليستۆك *f.* **(-a;-ê).** toy, plaything. {also: lehîstok (K); leyistok (JB3); leyîstok (IFb/TF)} [GF/RZ//K//JB3//IFb/TF] <lîstik; lîstin>

lîtik ليتِك (Bw) = kick. See **lotik**[2].

lîwa ليوا *f.* **(-ya;-yê).** administrative district. < Ar liwā' لواء [BX/IF]

lîwan ليوان *f.* **(-a;-ê).** bridle, rein, bit *(of horse)*: •**Zengû, zexme, rikêb û hesinê *lîwanê* hespê mîna tîrêjên tavê diçirûsîn** (M. Uzun. R. Evd. Zeyn., 108) The horse's stirrups, straps, spurs & iron *bit* sparkled like rays of the sun. {also: liwane (Tsab)} {syn: lixab} <Syr lúgmā ܠܘܓܡܐ/lgāmā ܠܓܡܐ= 'bridle, bit, curb' & NENA lâmâ ܠܓܡܐ/ܠܐܡܐ [Uzun/K/IFb/GF/FJ/TF/CS/AD//Tsab] <hevsar>

lîyan I ليیان *adj.* suffering, in pain (K): •**Dilê me *lîyane*** (Z-2) Our heart *is in pain*/We are distressed {also: [läyā̃n(e)] ليانه (LC-1)} [Z-2/FK-eb-1/K]

lîyan II ليیان *f.(Bw)/m.(OK)* **(-a/ ;).** type of snow shoe consisting of an animal skin held taut over a round frame. {also: lakan, m. (F); lak'an, f. (B); lekan (IFb-2/TF); lek'an, m.(K)/f.(B) (K/B-2); liyan (IFb-2); [lekan] لكان (JJ)} {syn: kelle I (Bw)} Sor liyan. *For a photograph, see Aristova, photo #41 (after p. 128)* [Bw/IFb/OK//F/B//K/TF/JJ] <berf; p'êlav>

lîzvan ليزڤان (GF) = player; dancer. See **lîstikvan**.

lo لۆ *voc. particle.* O, hey *(when calling one male: **lê** is used when calling one female; **gelî** is used in calling more than one person)*: •***Lo* mirovo!** = O man!/*Hey* man! {also: [lo] لو (JJ); <lo> لو (HH)} [K/A/IF/JJ/HH] <lê III; gelî I>

lobandin لۆباندِن (Wkt) = to mourn; to sob. See **lûbandin**.

lobik لۆبِك (CB) = pea(s). See **polik II**.

lod لۆد *f.(K/B)/m.(IF)* **(;-ê/).** 1) {syn: k'om II; kuç' [2]; londer} pile, heap (IF/A/JJ/HH); stack, rick (K); **-lodê keşkûran** (IF) pile of cow dung cakes {syn: qelax; sergo}; 2) shock, stook (of corn) (B). {also: lot (A); [lod(é)] لوده (JJ); <lod> لود (HH)} [K/IF/JJ/B/HH//A]

lodik لۆدِك = jump, leap. See **lotik**.

lok I لۆك (GF/JJ) = trot. See **loq**.

lok' II لۆك *m.* **(-ê;).** 1) male camel; camel of noble breed (HH); 2) brave, courageous man (HH). {also: [lok] لوك (JJ); <lok> لوك (HH)} Cf. Southern Tati dialects: Eshtehardi lök *m.* = 'male camel' (Yar-Shater) [Erg/A/IF/B/HH/JJ] <deve I; dundil; ḧêştir; qent'er>

lok•e لۆكە *m.* **(•ê;).** cotton (on plant, *as opposed to **pembû** = processed cotton*). {also: [loka] لوكه (JJ-Rich)} Sor loke لۆكە [Zeb/IFb/JJ/OK/BF/ZF3] <pembû>

lole لۆلە (IFb) = handle bar used in churning butter. See **lewleb**.

lolep لۆلەپ (Lab) = handle bar used in churning butter. See **lewleb**.

loma لۆما (L/B) = because; therefore. See **lema**.

lomandin لۆماندِن *vt.* **(-lomîn-).** to blame, denounce: •**Cindîye Cizîrê me *dikin dilomînin*** (Z-1) The nobles of Jizira *are denouncing* us. < Ar lawm لوم = 'blame' [Z-1/ZF3/Wkt]

londer لۆندەر **().** pile, heap, a lot of: •**Li ber derî *londerek* sol çêbûbû** (SBx, 7) Before the door *a pile of* shoes had formed. {syn: k'om II; kuç' [2]; lod} [SBx/Kmc/ZF3]

lop لـۆپ *f.* **(;-ê).** 1) thick overgarment, garment made of coarse wool or sackcloth; 2) carpet made of coarse wool (B/JJ). {also: [lop] لـوپ (JJ); <lop> لوپ (HH)} [HB/K/A/B/JJ/HH]

lopik لۆپك (GF/OK/AA) = pea(s). See **polik II**.

loq I لـۆق *m./f.(B)* **(-ê/; /-ê).** 1) large slice *(of bread)*: **•Nahêlî ez pê wî şîrî** ***loqê*** **nan bixum** (EH) You don't let me eat *a slice* of bread with that milk; 2) *counting word for slices of bread* (K); 3) big piece, chunk (A): **•Pêşî taştiya me hazir dikir û her yekê me** ***loqek*** **rûnê nîvişk li ser nên pahn dikir** (Alkan, 71) First she would make our breakfast and each of us would flatten out *a chunk of* butter on bread; 4) pinch (of salt) (B). {also: [loqek] لوقك (JJ)} [EH/K/A/B/GF//JJ]

loq II لـۆق *f.* **().** trot, moderately fast gait of a horse *in which the legs move in diagonal pairs*. {also: lok I (GF-2); loqe (Zeb); [lok] لـوك (JJ)} Sor loqe لـۆقە [Zeb//IFb/GF/OK/ZF3/FS//JJ] <çargav>

loqe لۆقە (Zeb) = trot. See **loq**.

loqet لـۆقـەت (JB1-S) = word; phrase; language. See **lewẍet**.

lor لۆر (B/Zeb) = curds. See **lorik**.

lorandin لـۆرانـدِن *vt.* **(-lorîn-).** 1) to rock, swing *(a cradle)*; 2) {also: lorîn [2]} to sing lullabies, to lull to sleep (IFb): **•Ku xudê kuřekî** [sic] **da te, ... / Gava tu wî têxî dergûşê, wî biḧejîne, wî bimijîne, / Ji xořa hêdî-hêdî li serê** ***bilorîne*** (Z-4) If God gives you a son, ... / When you put him in [his] crib, rock him, nurse him, / [Stand] at his head [and] softly *sing* him *to sleep*. [Z-4/K/IFb/OK/DZK] <ḧejandin>

lorik لـۆرك *f./m.(Zeb)* **(-a/-ê;-ê/).** 1) curds (and whey) [Fr caillebotte] which forms from the water that drips off cheese that is being made; 2) jajik *(yoghurt, garlic, and cucumbers)* [cf. T cacık; Gr dzadziki τζατζίκι] (A). {also: lor (B-2/Zeb); <lorik> لـورك (HH)} [K(s)/A/IF/B/HH//Zeb] <ç'olik II; ç'ortan; giv; toraq>

lorî I لـۆری *f.* **(;-yê).** predatory bird, gray with black wings (K/B); quail (JJ). {also: [lour] لور (JJ)} [AB/K/B//JJ] <'ebdal; k'êrasû; tewal[ê nêçîrvan]>

lorî II لـۆری *f.* **(-ya;-yê).** lullaby: **•Wê bo zařoyê xo** ***lorî*** **got, heta ku nivist** (FS) She sang her child *a lullaby*, until it fell asleep. {also: lûrî (K/SC)} cf. Sor lore لۆرە = 'type of song' [A/IFb/TF/ZF3/FS//K/SC]

lorîn لـۆرین *vi.* **(-lor-).** 1) {syn: lûbandin} to wail, lament for the dead: **•Mêr bêdeng bûn, jin diqîrîyan û** ***diloriyan*** (DZK, 135) The men were silent, the women screamed and *wailed*; 2) to sing a lullaby (TF). See **lorandin** [2]. [DZK/IFb/GF/TF] <zêmar>

loş لـۆش *m./f.(ZF3/FS)* **(/-a;).** lavash, type of long and flat bread. {also: lewaş m. (; lewêş); lûşe (Bşk); [levach] لـواش (JJ); <loş> لـوش (HH)} Cf. P lavāš لـواش; T loş [Malatya] = 'long flat bread [pide]' (DS, v. 9, p. 3088); Sor lewaşe لـەواشە = 'bread in long flaps baked in oven'; NENA lâ-wâshâ ܠܘܐܫܐ = 'a flap of thin bread, about 2 ft. long' (Maclean) & lwaša = 'flat thin cake of bread' (Garbell), cf. Arc √l-y-š ליש = 'to knead (dough)' [Bşk//K/HH//B/JJ] <nan>

lot لۆت (A) = pile, heap. See **lod**.

lotik لۆتِك *f.* **(-a;-ê).** 1) {syn: banz; ç'indik; firqas; qevz II} jump, leap: **-lotik dan xwe** (K) to jump, leap {syn: ba[n]zdan; çeng bûn [çeng III]; firqas kirin; hilpekirin; pengizîn}: **•Boẍ** ***da lodka*** (J) The ox *leaped*; 2) {syn: çivt; p'eĥîn; řefes; tîzik} kick: **-lîtik havê[ş]tin** (Bw) to kick *(of animals)*; 3) uncomfortable moving about (HH). {also: lîtik (Bw); lodik; <lotik> لـوتك (HH)} Cf. P lagad لـگد [K/A/JB3/IF/HH/Bw/ZF3/FS] <ba[n]z dan; p'eĥîn>

lovik لۆڤك (TF/OK/ZF3) = pea. See **lowûk**.

lowik لۆوك (IFb) = pea. See **lowûk**.

lowûk لـۆووك *f.* **().** pea; bean (OK). {also: lovik (TF/OK/ZF3); lowik (IFb)} *Perhaps a variant of* ***polik II/lopik*** [Mzg//IFb//TF/OK/ZF3] <gilol II; kelî I; nok; polik II>

lox لـۆخ *f./m.(FS/ZF3)* **(-a/-ê; /-î).** long stone cylinder for rolling down mud roofs, roof-roller: **•Heře ser xênî** ***lox bike*****, bira dilop bên biřîn** (FS) Go on top of the house and *tamp down [the roof]*, so that the dripping will be cut off **•Wî serban bi** ***loxî*** **gêřa** (FS) He rolled the roof flat with *a roller*. {also: luq (IFb)} {syn: bagirdan; gundor II} Cf. T loğ[taşı]; = Sor ba[n]girdên بـانـگِـردێن/bagirdan بـاگِـردان. *For an illustration, see Atılcan, p. 118.* [DZK/Dy(EW)//IFb/ZF3/FS] <t'apan>

Lubnanî لـوبـنـانی *adj.* Lebanese. {also: Libnanî (BF/Wkp/Wkt-2)} Sor Lubnanî لوبنانی [IFb/Wkt//BF/Wkp]

lukumandin لوكوماندن (Qzl) = to cause s.o. to stumble. See **lik'umandin**.

luq لوق (IFb) = stone cylinder roof-roller. See **lox**.

lûbandin لـووبـانـدِن *vt.* **(-lûbîn-).** 1) {syn: lorîn; şîn kirin; zêmar kirin} to mourn, lament (K); 2) {syn: girîn} to sob, cry (B). {also: lobandin (Wkt)} [Z-1/

K/B/ZF3/FS//Wkt] <şîn I; zêmar>

lûl•e لـوولـه *f.* (**•[ey]a;•ê**). 1) {syn: qelûn} pipe; tube; conduit; 2) muzzle, barrel (of gun) (B): **-lûla t'ivingê** (B) rifle barrel; **-lûla t'opê** (B) cannon barrel. {also: [loulik] لولك (JJ); <lûle> لوله (HH)} [K/JB3/IF/B/HH/ZF3//JJ]

lûlik لـوولِك *f.* (**-a; **). 1) {syn: k'edûn} small water jug (IF); 2) spout of a water jug, pipe, tea kettle. {also: [loulik] لولك (JJ)} [IF/JJ/OK/ZF3] <lûle>

lûr لـــــوور *f.* **()**. rash, inflammation on the arm (Qzl); hives, nettle rash, urticaria (IFb). [Qzl/IFb/AA/ZF3/Wkt]

lûrî لووری (K/SC) = lullaby. See **lorî II**.

lûrîn لوورین/**lûr̄în** لووڕین [SK] *vi.* (**-lûr-/-lûr̄-**[SK]). to howl: **•Hemî *lûr̄în* û r̄ewîn wekî s̱an** (SK 32:291) They all *howled* and barked like dogs. {also: lîrîn (Wkt); [lurin] لـــوريـــن (JJ-G)} Sor lûrandin لووراندِن = 'to howl (wolf, gale, etc.)' [JJ-G/SK/OK/FS//Wkt] <r̄eyîn I>

lûrk لوورك (IFb/A/KZ) = oleander. See **r̄ûl**.

lûs لووس (A/ZF) = perch, roost. See **lîs**.

lûsiyan لووسِيان (FJ) = to perch, roost. See **lûsîn**.

lûsîn لووسين *vi.* (**-lûs-**). to perch, roost *(of birds)*: **•Bû pirte pirta çûkên di nav de *lûsiyayî*** (SBx, 18) There was a fluttering of fledgelings *perched* in it [=the tree] **•Gelek fîrrinde li ser daran *dilîsin*** (Wkt) Many birds *roost* in the trees. {also: lîsîn (Kmc/Wkt); lûsiyan (FJ); lûsyan (GF)} [SBx/ZF3//FJ//GF//Kmc/Wkt] <lîs>

lûsyan لووسيان (GF) = to perch, roost. See **lûsîn**.

lûşe لووشه (Bşk) = lavash bread. See **loş**.

lût لووت (K[s]) = naked, nude. See **r̄ût**.

Made in United States
Orlando, FL
13 February 2023